Birds of
New York State

Coastal dunes and sea beach in autumn at Fire Island, Suffolk Co., Long Island. Hovering American Kestrel (*Falco sparverius*) and other raptors from left to right: Merlin (*Falco columbarius*); Northern Harrier or Marsh Hawk (*Circus cyaneus*); Peregrine Falcon (*Falco peregrinus*). These species are regular fall migrants along the outer beaches, the last-named now a rarity. Painting by Neil Ward.

Birds of
New York State

including the 1976 Supplement

John Bull

Department of Ornithology
The American Museum of Natural History

COMSTOCK PUBLISHING ASSOCIATES

A division of CORNELL UNIVERSITY PRESS

Ithaca and London

Reissued 1985 by Cornell University Press, with supplement and corrections. Comstock|Cornell Paperbacks edition first published 1985.

Birds of New York State first published in 1974 by Doubleday/Natural History Press. The *Supplement*, a Special Publication of the Federation of New York State Bird Clubs, Inc., 1976, is reprinted with their permission.

Printed in the United States of America

The paper in this book is acid-free and meets the guidelines for permanence and durability of the Committee on Production Guidelines for Book Longevity of the Council on Library Resources.

Library of Congress Cataloging-in-Publication Data

Bull, John L.
  Birds of New York State

  Bibliography: p.
  Includes index.
  1. Birds—New York (State) I. Title.
QL684.N7B833   1985   598.29747   85-17415
ISBN (cloth) 0-8014-1897-6 (alk. paper)
ISBN (paper) 0-8014-9314-5 (alk. paper)

To a patient and

understanding wife

PREFACE TO THE 1985 EDITION

First published in 1974, the *Birds of New York State* has been out of print for some time. There has been a great demand for a reissue of this book by those who never acquired the original volume. This 1985 reprint includes corrections. A supplement to the original book, published in 1976 by the Federation of New York State Bird Clubs, has also been added to at the end of this volume.

I am grateful to Cornell University Press for publishing this edition. My special thanks go to Robb Reavill, Science Editor of Cornell University Press, for her enthusiasm in starting this project. Thanks are also due the Federation of New York State Bird Clubs for permission to incorporate the 1976 *Supplement* into this reprint edition. I am also grateful to the Federation's current president, Charles R. Smith—Associate Director of the Cornell University Laboratory of Ornithology—for his interest in this project, as well as to Richard B. Fischer, also of the Cornell University faculty.

The decimation of the tropical rain forests by wholesale removal, and the despoiling of the boreal and temperate forests by acid rain and other pollutants, are of utmost concern. Not only are the wintering grounds of many bird species being affected, but the breeding areas as well. It is imperative to document the effect these changes in habitat have had on the avifauna of New York. By censusing both migrants and breeders, we will be able to report whether these changes have been for the better or worse. The highly important New York State breeding bird atlas, now in preparation, will tell us what has happened.

John Bull

New York City

ACKNOWLEDGMENTS

Many persons have contributed to the realization of this book, for it is, to a large extent, a cooperative project.

Foremost is the generosity of Dan Caulkins of New York, without whose financial assistance this undertaking would never have started, let alone have been completed. Additional grants were obtained from the Leonard Sanford Trust Fund of the American Museum of Natural History and from the James Savage Memorial Fund of the Buffalo Museum of Science, the latter through the efforts of Harold Mitchell of that museum, who was also very helpful in many other ways.

I am especially indebted to Dean Amadon, former Chairman of the Department of Ornithology of the American Museum, who took a keen interest in this project from the very beginning. He read and reviewed the entire manuscript and made many valuable suggestions.

My wife, Edith, spent many days and nights typing virtually the entire text, as well as proofreading and editing it to completion, for which I am eternally grateful. With much patience she encouraged me throughout this venture; without her help, this work would remain unfinished.

To my colleagues at the American Museum's Department of Ornithology, I am much indebted for help and advice in many ways, especially from the following: Eugene Eisenmann, Wesley Lanyon, Mary LeCroy, Charles O'Brien, and Lester Short. Others on the Ornithology Department staff whose suggestions and aid were invaluable were John Farrand, James Greenway, Helen Hays, Stuart Keith, the late Robert Cushman Murphy, Allan O'Connell, and Charles Vaurie, and also two departmental volunteers, Helen Lapham and Joan Meintjes, who were especially helpful in checking the bird-banding recovery data; the former also was of inestimable help in preparing much of the Index. Vincent Manson, Chairman of the Mineralogy Department, was of the greatest assistance in computerizing, programming, and decoding a vast amount of bird-banding recovery data from the printout sheets. Joseph Sedacca and his able draftsman, Juan Barberas, of the Graphic Arts Department rendered the many fine maps of both banding recoveries and of breeding distribution; Elwood Logan and his assistant, Arthur Singer, of the Photography Department, converted numerous color slides into black-and-white prints for reproduction. Ruth Chapin and Mary Wissler, formerly of the Museum's main library, were most helpful in locating certain items of literature.

The writer is grateful to the following curators and associates of other museums for permission to examine the collections in their care: Robert Andrle and Harold Axtell, Buffalo Museum of Science; Jerry Czech, Rochester Museum of Arts and Sciences; Ian Galbraith, Derek Goodwin, Patricia Hall, and Shane Parker, British Museum (Natural History); Ralph Palmer and Edgar Reilly, New York State Museum; Raymond Paynter, Museum of Comparative Zoology, Harvard University; George Watson, Alexander Wetmore, and Richard Zusi, United States National Museum; and in the same museum, John Aldrich and Richard Banks, U. S. Fish and Wildlife Service collection; Richard Weisbrod, Cornell University Museum. I also wish to thank William Vaughan for introducing me to that great birding spot, Grand Island in the Niagra River.

The following persons were of particular assistance in helping with special projects: Bird-banding—Earl Baysinger, Chandler Robbins, and William Russell, U. S. Fish and Wildlife Service, Laurel, Maryland, and Stephen Browne, New York State Conservation Department, Albany; nest record cards—Edith Edgerton, Cornell University Laboratory of Ornithology; breeding distribution maps—Gwendolyn Gillette, New York State Museum; preparation of gazetteer—Robert Wolk and his assistant, Dorothy Lauber, Nassau County Museum, Seaford, New York.

The author is especially indebted to the following field correspondents who supplied much valuable information from various portions of the state: Long Island—Tom Davis, William Post, Dennis Puleston, and the late Walter Terry; Staten Island—Howard Cleaves; downstate—Stanley Grierson and Otis Waterman; central New York—Margaret Rusk and Robert Yunick; Adirondacks and northern New York—John Belknap, Geoffrey Carleton, Greenleaf Chase, the late Harriet Delafield, David Gordon, Gordon Meade, and especially Walter Spofford; western New York—Lou Burton, Stephen Eaton (son of Elon Eaton), and Richard Rosche.

The following are also due thanks for their aid in many ways: Robert Arbib, Sid Bahrt, Allen Benton, Walter Bock, Richard Brownstein, Arthur Clark, Stephen Clark, Richard Cohen, Dorothy Crumb, Harry Darrow, Granger Davenport, Robert Dickerman, Aline Dove, David Duffy, Orville Dunning, Dave Ewert, Davis Finch, Richard Fischer, Darrel Ford, Robert Giffen, the late Thomas Gilliard, Michael Gochfeld, Clayton Hardy, the late Francis Harper, Joseph Hickey, Stephen Hopkins, Fred Hough, Ferdinand La France, Douglas Lancaster, Dorothy McIlroy, Laura Moon, Jack Orth, Kenneth Parkes, Allan Phillips, Eleanor Pink, Nate Potter, William Robertson, Charles Rogers, Walton Sabin, Fred Schaeffer, Albert Smiley, Chris Spies, Sally Spofford, Robert Sundell, Joe Taylor, and John Taylor.

Last, but not least, are the numerous members of the Federation of New York State Bird Clubs and of the affiliated member clubs, especially the Linnaean Society of New York, who made available their records in the *Kingbird*.

To Elizabeth Knappman, Maureen Mahon, and Ellen Rickman, editors for Doubleday, to Elfrieda Hueber, designer, and Diana Klemin, art director, my deep gratitude for seeing this work through press.

Finally, thanks to our daughter, Doris, who helped check a number of literature citations and assisted with some of the typing.

J.B.

CONTENTS

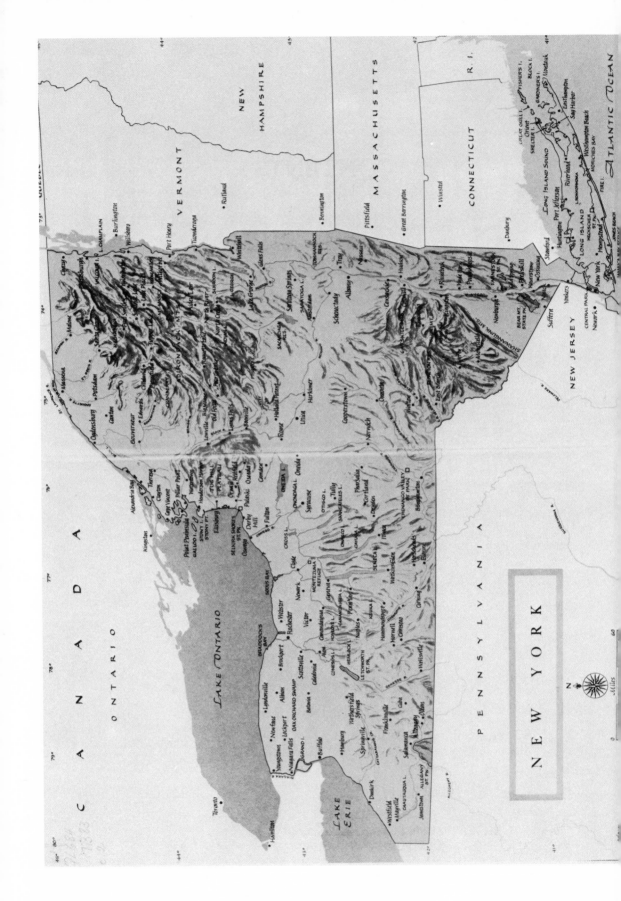

PART I

INTRODUCTION

COUNTIES OF NEW
YORK STATE

CLINTON

FRANKLIN

ESSEX

ST. LAWRENCE

WARREN

HAMILTON

WASHINGTON

SARATOGA

FULTON

MONTGOMERY

SCHDY

RENSSELAER

HERKIMER

LEWIS

ONEIDA

MADISON

SCHOHARIE

ALBANY

COLUMBIA

JEFFERSON

OSWEGO

ONONDAGA

CHENANGO

OTSEGO

DELAWARE

GREENE

DUTCHESS

PUTNAM

ULSTER

ORANGE

2

1

NIAGARA

ORLEANS

GENESEE

MONROE

WAYNE

ONTARIO

CAYUGA

SENECA

CORTLAND

TOMPKINS

SCHUYLER

TIOGA

BROOME

SULLIVAN

3

7

8

6

5

4

ERIE

WYOMING

LIVINGSTON

YATES

CHEMUNG

SUFFOLK

CHAUTAUQUA

CATTARAUGUS

ALLEGANY

STEUBEN

1—ROCKLAND   5—RICHMOND

2—WESTCHESTER   6—KINGS

3—BRONX   7—QUEENS

4—NEW YORK   8—NASSAU

SCALE IN MILES

10 0 10 20 30 40 50

44°   43°   42°   41°

72°   73°   74°   75°   76°   77°   78°   79°

RAND G GILLETTE 1956

During the latter half of the nineteenth century, when New York ornithology was in its infancy, and up to the first two or three decades of the twentieth century, the field ornithologist collected birds for identification and amassed nest and egg collections to establish breeding records. Illustrated field guides and prism binoculars were unheard of. To prove that a particular species was breeding, mere presence of a bird during the "nesting season" was insufficient, particularly for the rarer ones. In the case of a Great Horned Owl, for instance, one had to climb the tree to reach the nest and then collect the eggs or young to furnish actual proof of breeding. This might entail hours of tramping through mosquito-infested swamp just to reach the nest tree, to say nothing of being attacked and mauled by the adult owl while climbing to the nest, or of risking a possible fall from the tree. Then the weary trip back home, or to the museum, to preserve the eggs or skins.

Thanks to these early and intrepid collectors, the museum collections of today are here for us to examine and study and, most important, to establish beyond doubt the identity of difficult and questionable species—for the museum specimen is the ultimate proof and final evidence of correct identification. Many a question is answered and debate settled for both amateurs and professionals by critical analysis of the properly labeled museum specimen.

With modern optical and photographic equipment and a proliferation of field guides and regional bird books, the present-day field ornithologist records what is seen and heard, without the necessity of procuring specimens, save on rare occasions. Present-day techniques of capturing birds alive with traps and mist-nets for banding and for studying their distribution, relative abundance, longevity, and diseases, enable the observer to examine the bird in detail in the hand. Last, but not least, are the latest sound-recording techniques to place on tape permanently the voices of nocturnal species, as well as making possible "playback" experiments with closely related species difficult to identify by sight alone.

The present work is based on Eaton (1910, 1914), museum collections, the literature, nest record cards, banding data, unpublished notes, and the writer's field work of nearly 40 years covering portions of most areas in the state.

In 1914 the second of two volumes of Eaton's great work, *Birds of New York*, appeared. At that time 366 species were recorded from the state. Eaton's figure of 411 "species" included some that would be treated today merely as subspecies, plus a number of species reported on insufficient evidence, such as lack of specimens or photographs, and others based on old, vague reports. His list of breeding birds comprised 190 species.

During the succeeding 60 years the total state list, as of 1974, included 410 species—an increase of 44. The breeding species increased correspondingly to 228—a gain of 38 since 1914. These breeders represent nearly 56% of the total avifauna. For the most part these 38 additional breeders recorded since Eaton's time reflect range extensions from the north, south, and west. However, a few species found breeding in the Adirondack Mountains in recent years had probably been overlooked previously due to a lack of observers, but even today some of these birds are very rare and local. Others now nesting on Long Island were rarely reported, even as nonbreeders, during Eaton's time.

One aim of this book is to document these changes and trends and they are treated in detail in the species accounts. The species records are based on (1) specimens and (2) photographs.

(1) SPECIMENS: The vast majority (402) of 410 species recorded in the state are supported by specimens collected and deposited in museums and in the few remaining private collections. A few of these specimens are apparently no longer in existence but their occurrence was confirmed years ago by com-

petent ornithologists and accounts of them were published in the literature.

(2) PHOTOGRAPHS: Seven species are based on photographic evidence available for examination in the files of the American Museum of Natural History. These seven species are: Yellow-nosed Albatross, Cattle Egret (breeds, or has bred), Tufted Duck, Ash-throated Flycatcher, Boat-tailed Grackle, Black-headed Grosbeak, Harris' Sparrow. An eighth species —the Smew—appears in Beardslee and Mitchell's *Birds of the Niagara Frontier Region.*

All other species (22) reported from the state are relegated to hypothetical status. These 22 are included in phylogenetic sequence in the species accounts within brackets, rather than as a separate list. Reasons for their conjectural status are found under each species. They are: Western Grebe, Greater Flamingo, Trumpeter Swan, Red-crested Pochard, Crested Caracara, Willow Ptarmigan, Chukar Partridge, Whooping Crane, Greenshanks, Trudeau's Tern, Great Auk, Common Ground Dove, Carolina Parakeet, Lewis' Woodpecker, Fork-tailed Flycatcher, Carolina Chickadee, Redwing, Swainson's Warbler, Townsend's Warbler, Brambling, Brewer's Sparrow, Golden-crowned Sparrow.

The following 44 species are new to the state list since Eaton (1914):

1. Yellow-billed Loon	23. White-winged Dove
2. Eared Grebe	24. Monk Parakeet (breeds)
3. Yellow-nosed Albatross	25. Burrowing Owl
4. Northern Fulmar	26. Chuck-will's-widow
5. Manx Shearwater	27. Scissor-tailed Flycatcher
6. South Trinidad Petrel	28. Ash-throated Flycatcher
7. Red-billed Tropicbird	29. Willow Flycatcher (breeds)—"fitz-bew"
8. Cattle Egret (breeds)	30. Black-billed Magpie
9. Mute Swan (breeds)	31. Bewick's Wren
10. Fulvous Tree Duck	32. Sage Thrasher
11. Tufted Duck	33. Bell's Vireo
12. Smew	34. Black-throated Gray Warbler
13. Gray Partridge (breeds)	35. Western Meadowlark (breeds)
14. Bar-tailed Godwit	36. Brewer's Blackbird
15. Lesser Black-backed Gull	37. Boat-tailed Grackle
16. Thayer's Gull	38. Black-headed Grosbeak
17. Black-headed Gull	39. Painted Bunting
18. Franklin's Gull	40. House Finch (breeds)
19. Bridled Tern	41. Green-tailed Towhee
20. Sandwich Tern	42. Bachman's Sparrow
21. Thin-billed Murre	43. Clay-colored Sparrow (breeds)
22. Rock Pigeon (breeds)	44. Harris' Sparrow

Of these, numbers 9, 13, 22, 24, and 40 are introductions. The Rock or Domestic Pigeon was, of course, established long before Eaton's day, but was not included by him. A few of these, for example, numbers 11, 25, and 39, might be based in part on zoo or aviary escapes.

The following 38 species were not recorded as breeding by Eaton (1914). The year after the species name indicates time of first known breeding.

1. Double-crested Cormorant (1945)	5. Cattle Egret (1970)
2. Great Egret (1953)	6. Yellow-crowned Night Heron (1938)
3. Little Blue Heron (1958)	7. Glossy Ibis (1961)
4. Louisiana Heron (1955)	8. Mute Swan (?)

9. Canada Goose (?)
10. Gadwall (1947)
11. Pintail (1945)
12. Baldpate (1959)
13. Redhead (1952)
14. Ring-necked Duck (1946)
15. Lesser Scaup (1946)
16. Red-breasted Merganser (1912)
17. Turkey Vulture (1925)
18. Gray Partridge (1927)
19. Black Rail (1937)
20. Oystercatcher (1957)
21. Willet (1966)
22. Great Black-backed Gull (1942)
23. Ring-billed Gull (1936)
24. Black Skimmer (1934)
25. Rock Pigeon (?)
26. Monk Parakeet (1971)
27. Willow Flycatcher (1927)
28. Mockingbird (1956)
29. Ruby-crowned Kinglet (1942)
30. Philadelphia Vireo (1963)
31. Prothonotary Warbler (1931)
32. Tennessee Warbler (1926)
33. Cape May Warbler (1947)
34. Bay-breasted Warbler (1926)
35. Western Meadowlark (1957)
36. Evening Grosbeak (1947)
37. House Finch (1943)
38. Clay-colored Sparrow (1960)

Except for an old breeding record of the Snowy Egret in 1885, it was not until 1949—64 years later—that this species nested again. The Blue-gray Gnatcatcher was reported to have bred once in 1890, but not again until 1943—53 years later.

It should be stressed here that more observers are needed on pelagic trips off Long Island at various times of the year, and in the greater part of the state during the breeding season. Birdwatchers are out in full force during both the spring and fall migrations, the winter months—especially at the Christmas count period and the January waterfowl counts—and during late summer when the shorebirds return. With the notable exception of the *Kingbird*'s Regions 1 (Niagara Frontier) 2 (Rochester area), 3 (Ithaca region), 5 (Syracuse area), and 10 (Long Island), the remaining regions in the state are relatively neglected during the nesting season—notably from late May through July. Chief among these neglected areas are the montane districts—especially the Adirondacks (much of it admittedly a vast wilderness area) and the Catskills. It is certain that few people frequent the large tracts of boreal bogs and stands of montane forest during the breeding season. Without question the breeding distribution maps representing birds of the "North Woods" have notable gaps and the areas that are blank are woefully undermanned and probably unknown ornithologically speaking. It can be stated unequivocally that this is particularly applicable to large stretches of St. Lawrence, Clinton, and Lewis counties, and to portions of other Adirondack Mountain counties, as well. In the Catskills, the counties of Otsego, Schoharie, Delaware, Greene, and Sullivan are notably neglected in nesting time, as well as the relatively low altitude counties of Washington, Fulton, Montgomery, Wayne, and Steuben. The bird clubs and *Kingbird* regional editors should see to it that these counties have, at least, partial coverage of the breeding bird life. As for regions 6 and 7 (St. Lawrence valley and Adirondacks) with their dearth of observers, more visiting birders are sorely needed during the summer months. Some of the most exciting and rewarding birds are to be found there without too much difficulty.

The original deadline or cutoff date for nonbreeding reports was December 31, 1970, with the exception of several really outstanding records—most notably the first definite record for New York of a Fulmar (*Fulmarus glacialis*) during the fall of 1971. However, breeding data were accepted through 1972 and even a few noteworthy reports for the summer and fall of 1973 have been included. In no instance is there any record after December 31, 1973. All significant literature citations are included up through the end of 1972.

TEXT

The heart of this book lies in the Species Accounts. For each species both the common and the scientific names are given. Under each species appropriate subheadings are used. Each species supported by a specimen (i.e., which has been collected in the state at least once) has an asterisk (*) after its name. Species that have bred within the state have the letter "B" after the name.

Range: One or more of the world's six faunal regions are included here. Extralimital breeding and winter ranges for the species are mentioned when significant. Special emphasis is placed on distributional limits in eastern North America, particularly those areas adjacent to New York.

Status: A résumé is given of the bird's presence in New York during the migrations, winter, and breeding seasons; occurrence, frequency, and relative abundance are included.

Change in status: This is included only for those species for which there has been a drastic or marked change in status, for example, if a great increase or decrease has occurred since the appearance of Eaton's two volumes (1910–1914).

Occurrence is used only for those species which do *not* nest within New York, whereas **Nonbreeding** refers to the migration and winter seasons of all New York *breeding* species in contrast to their **Breeding** season. Where significant, distribution in various portions of the state is mentioned; *inland* and *coastal* occurrence and abundance are compared where necessary (=maxima). Extreme dates are used whenever a species is rare-to-absent in winter, i.e., spring arrival and fall departure; or conversely, if rare-to-absent in summer, spring departure and fall arrival. If the dates are significantly different at *inland* and *coastal* areas, these are specified; if, however, no breakdown as to area is indicated, it is understood that only one set of dates covers the entire state. Only in instances of great rarity, exceptional numbers, and unusual dates are observers' names mentioned.

Breeding: This is a most important category in the species write-ups. Great emphasis is placed on the breeding birds of the state, as it is mainly these species that are indicators of increase or decrease, or of range extension or range reduction. Nearly half (over 100) of the breeding species in the state are accompanied by distribution maps.

A general account of the breeding range within the state is followed by details (when known) of species ecology or habitat and placement of nests (or nest sites)—on the ground, in trees, on cliffs, in marshes, etc. If the nest is in an arboreal situation, height above ground is stated, as well as tree species, when known.

Range of clutch size is given and, in a few instances, the brood size, when known, in the absence of eggs.

Dates for eggs, nestlings, and fledglings are included; these dates represent the known extremes, earliest and latest. In a few instances incubation periods or nestling periods are specified when known.

In *all* cases only New York data are utilized. Every egg date, nest site, and remarks on habitat explicitly refer to this state and nowhere else—unless specifically stated to the contrary on a few occasions.

Maximum numbers are given for all colonial breeders, such as herons, larids, and swallows.

Banding: Significant banding returns and recoveries are mentioned whenever they occur. In many instances the banding recovery maps are self-explanatory, but for dates and localities of banding, as well as of recovery, the text must be consulted. The vast majority are of birds banded as nestlings and so stated when known. In a number of cases longevity is given.

Subspecies: In all instances where polytypic species are involved, if one or more geographic races or subspecies (other than the nominate form) occur in New York, brief descriptions or comparisons are given. Comparisons are usually made with the nominate subspecies or with the nearest geographical population. For example, *Accipiter gentilis atricapillus,* the race occurring in New York, is compared with *A. g. gentilis;* however *Sterna hirundo,* also a polytypic species occurring in New York, is not compared with its component races as only nominate *hirundo* is known to occur in New York, the other subspecies being of extralimital range only. If a subspecific population is *not* recognized, reasons for rejection will be found under the next category.

Remarks: Subspecies not considered valid in

the present work, and miscellaneous topics not covered in the species accounts are discussed here.

ILLUSTRATIONS

(1) Color. In addition to the end maps of the state showing both physiographic and political features, there are paintings depicting some of the outstanding areas in New York with representative birds. These color plates consist of the following: three of Long Island, two of the Adirondacks, and one each of Montezuma Marshes, Oak Orchard Swamp, and the Niagara Falls area. The selection was made mainly on the basis of breeding specialties of the areas. The Catskills are not represented because no breeding species occur there that are not found in the Adirondacks as well. There are also included a color plate of hybrid warblers, a tinted "wash" of migrating hawks and, on the book jacket, a photograph of the state bird. Credits for these appear with the illustrations.

(2) Black and white. More than 80 photographs, chiefly of breeding habitats, nests, and a few birds are shown. Again, credits for these accompany the photographs.

(3) Maps, other than the state map mentioned above, fall into two categories: (a) breeding, and (b) banding.

(a) There are 107 New York State breeding distribution maps of species deemed significant either because they are rare or local or because of range extensions or withdrawals. The captions and legends are self-explanatory. Another three of these New York State maps depict the 62 counties, some of the outstanding birding areas, and the main migration "routes" or flyways.

(b) There are 57 banding recovery maps— 54 North American and three South American; these maps concern species of special interest, banded in large numbers and subsequently recovered, illustrating interesting dispersal patterns.

It is important to stress here that the straight lines from point of banding to place of recovery indicate approximate and probable "routes" only and that time limits are ordinarily within a six-month period, usually much less. These represent the so-called "direct" recoveries. Those maps showing solid triangles and *not* connected by lines are the so-called "indirect" recoveries, usually of birds recovered in subsequent years.

The black dots signify final destination of banded birds (=recoveries).

To obtain maximum usefulness from these maps—both breeding and banding—the reader should consult the main text under the species concerned.

ORNITHOLOGICAL HISTORY

A. Pre-Eaton period (before 1914)—What may be described as the first comprehensive accounts of birds in New York State were those of DeKay and Giraud, both in 1844. The former wrote a zoology of the state with the second part devoted to birds. The latter restricted his work to the avifauna of Long Island. For the succeeding seventy years various important lists were published on the different sections of New York, the following being the most outstanding: 1878—Mearns on the Hudson Highlands and Merriam on the Adirondacks; 1882—Bicknell on the Catskills;

1887—Dutcher on Long Island; 1901—Eaton on western New York; 1906—Chapman on the New York City region; 1907—Braislin on Long Island; 1909—Reed and Wright on the Finger Lakes; 1910—Eaton on the entire state.

This was the era of skin and egg collecting. In addition to the aforementioned, the following collectors figured prominently in those early days: (1) Upstate—Bagg, Bowdish, Burtch, Davison, Embody, Fuertes, Guelf, Kibbe, Maxon, Parker, Pember, Posson, Ralph, the Reinecke brothers, Short, Stone, Tabor, Webster, and Woodruff. (2) Downstate—

Brownell, Cherrie, Fisher, Foster, Helme, Hendrickson, Howell, Latham, Lawrence, and Worthington. Roy Latham, who commenced his activities in the early 1900s, is still active in the 1970s!

B. Post-Eaton period (after 1914)—With the end of the professional collecting era, ornithologists turned their attention to the study of the living bird. At this time the very first of the field guides written by Chapman and Reed awakened interest in field work in which camera and binoculars largely replaced the gun. Also at this time protection was afforded most birds through various conservation laws. Colleges, most notably Cornell, were instrumental in training students for future work in conservation, wildlife management, ecology, behavior, population studies, sound recording, banding, bird painting, photography, and many other ornithological activities. Three men come

to mind as the pioneers of teaching or training people, and also as a result of their many publications: Arthur Allen at Cornell University, Frank Chapman at the American Museum of Natural History, and Aretas Saunders at the state-owned summer camps in the Adirondacks and especially at Allegany State Park. Many of their pupils ultimately became leading ornithologists, both at professional and at amateur levels.

Foremost of the detailed regional bird accounts of this latter period were: (1) Upstate—1923–1942, Saunders; 1923, Silloway; 1931 and 1935, Spiker; 1932, Stoner; 1939, Hyde; 1947, Axtell; 1949, Benton; 1953, S. W. Eaton; 1954, Parkes; 1965 and 1970, Beardslee and Mitchell, also Andrle; 1967, Rosche; (2) Downstate—1923 and 1933, Griscom; 1942, Cruickshank; 1964 and 1970, Bull.

All of these publications are listed in the Bibliography.

THE ENVIRONMENT

New York State, nearly 48,000 square miles in area, is twenty-fifth in size among the 50 states. Within this area exists varied terrain ranging from sea level, where the waters of the Atlantic Ocean bathe the south-shore sand beaches of Long Island, to the 5000-foot peaks of spruce and fir in the Adirondacks, some of which tower above tree line.

New York is bounded on the south by the Atlantic Ocean and the states of New Jersey and Pennsylvania; on the east by the states of Connecticut, Massachusetts, and Vermont; on the west by Lake Erie and a small portion of Ontario; and on the north by Lake Ontario and the Canadian provinces of Ontario and Quebec. Within the state are 62 counties, the easternmost—Suffolk Co.—extending as far as the Connecticut-Rhode Island state line at 72 degrees west longitude; the southernmost—Richmond Co.—encompassing all of Staten Island, its southern tip located just south of 40°30′ north latitude; the westernmost—Chautauqua Co.—nearly as far as 80° west

longitude; and the three northernmost counties —Clinton, Franklin, and St. Lawrence—extending to 45° north latitude.

These extremes in altitude, together with a north-south latitudinal range of nearly five degrees and an even greater east-west longitudinal distance of almost eight degrees, produce considerable diversity in climate, topography, and vegetation. This diversification is reflected in the correspondingly varied and large number of avian species within the temperate zone. Of the 410 species definitely recorded in New York State, more than half (228, or 56%) have bred within the state.

CLIMATE

Those areas nearest the sea do not have the extremes of heat and cold that occur in most of the state. The moderating effect of the ocean waters on the adjacent land areas tempers the climate both summer and winter. Consequently during the summer, the prevailing winds from a generally southerly direction are cooled by the sea. Conversely, in winter the prevailing winds are from a northerly or northwesterly quarter bringing subzero temperatures to much of upstate New York; at the same time the ocean and adjacent land areas may be twenty degrees higher and even slightly above freezing, due to the relatively warm sea-water temperatures. Temperature differences are striking at either season only twenty miles away from the ocean. New York City and nearby inland areas may undergo a severe heat wave with 90°-plus temperatures, while beachfront localities enjoy seventies or low eighties. Even more striking is the fact that during winter within five miles of the ocean it may be snowing, while on the barrier beaches with temperatures eight to ten degrees higher it may be raining. During snowstorms areas near the sea invariably receive less accumulation.

This great variance in winter temperatures has a profound effect on the birdlife, especially waterfowl and other aquatic species, which are driven out of icebound inland waters to relatively ice-free waters of the coastal bays and estuaries and to the ocean itself. The upland birds, especially those of open country, may find food more readily along the shore because of lesser amounts of snow there. Furthermore, the marine regions with their extensive areas of salt marsh, rarely freeze over except during prolonged and severe cold waves. Finally, tidal action keeps the immediate seacoast clear of ice and snow and provides a suitable feeding area.

At the other extreme, driving winds and bitter cold during a period of precipitation make the country directly to the east of Lake Ontario, especially the Tug Hill area and the western Adirondacks, an enormous snow depository—rightly called the "snow belt" of the state, although rivaled by some regions in the

Fig. 1 Little Galloo Island, eastern Lake Ontario, Jefferson Co., June 10, 1967. Black-crowned Night Herons breed in these trees; a Pintail nest with eggs was found under the bushes in the foreground, and a Red-breasted Merganser with downy young were observed in the lagoon. Photo by Robert G. Wolk

western parts of the state. Accumulations of many feet of snow are not unusual. Moreover, at times the winter season is prolonged well into April.

Generally speaking wind direction directly affects the weather. No matter what the season the prevailing westerlies bring clear weather whereas winds from an easterly quarter, especially if strong or of more than one day's duration, usually mean precipitation.

Within the state, factors of altitude, latitude, temperature, relative humidity, and exposure to sun and wind determine the types of vegetation to be found, and in turn the vegetation determines the breeding bird species.

TOPOGRAPHY

The vast majority of New York State was affected by the last glaciation, at least 10,000 years ago. The only sections that are essentially unglaciated are the narrow coastal plain south of the terminal moraine along the south shores of Long Island and Staten Island (although glacial outwash—gravel and sand—is present) and a relatively small portion of the Allegany Plateau in southwestern New York. The following is taken from Muller (in Wright and Frey, 1965: 100–103).

"The southern limit of glaciation enters New York in two areas. The one extends the length of Long Island and crosses Staten Island. The other borders the Salamanca re-entrant on the Pennsylvania State line in western New York.

"A semicircular area of the Appalachian Upland south of the Allegheny River in southwestern New York bears no evidence of glaciation. This area, otherwise continuous with and similar to the adjacent upland to the north, is the Salamanca re-entrant, the northernmost unglaciated area in the region between the Mississippi River and the Atlantic Ocean."

The dominant water areas of the southern portion of the state are the Atlantic Ocean and Long Island Sound, the latter separating Long Island from the mainland. In upstate New York, Lake Erie and especially Lake Ontario are the principal large bodies of water, the latter stretching from the Niagara peninsula for more than 200 miles east to where Lake Ontario narrows into the St. Lawrence River (Figs. 1, 2, and 3). Along these lake plains, agriculture is carried on extensively.

The principal mountains of the state are the Adirondacks, the Catskills, and the northern extension of the Appalachians—the Alleghenies. To the west of the Adirondacks, separated by the Black River valley, is the Tug Hill plateau (see Fig. 4), much less elevated than the Adirondacks according to Muller (*op. cit.*).

"The Tug Hill Upland is a plateau remnant isolated from the closely related Appalachian Upland by the Mohawk Lowlands, and from the adjacent Adirondack Highlands by the Black River Valley. With strata dipping regionally southeast from the Adirondack massif, Tug Hill owes its prominence primarily to erosional resistance of the Ordovician Oswego sandstone. Lacking significant through valleys, this upland contains some of the most extensive wilderness areas in New York."

In this connection, note that very few roads traverse this region, except the northern and eastern portions near the Black River. Because of the rugged terrain and poor soil, most of the farms were abandoned long ago.

The Adirondacks themselves are unique in the state in being isolated from other mountain ranges or highlands, as follows: To the north and west is the wide plain of the St. Lawrence River valley; to the east, separated from Vermont's Green Mountains, is the Lake Champlain-Hudson River lowland district; and to the south the narrow Mohawk River "effectively" isolates the Adirondacks from the Catskills. The highest mountains in the state are situated in the Adirondacks, with Mt. Marcy in Essex Co. the highest of all—over 5300 feet in elevation (see Fig. 5). There are a number of lesser peaks in the Adirondacks well over 4000 feet, most of them also in Essex Co. Numerous lakes dot the Adirondacks. Glacial drift blocked their drainage systems. The remaining present-day rivers of the northern Adirondacks have their outlets into the St. Lawrence River.

To the northeast the Catskills are connected with the Helderberg Plateau (see Fig. 6), the escarpment of the latter extending east nearly to Albany. To the south in Pennsylvania are the Poconos and still farther the Appalachians. The highest peaks in the Catskills are Slide Mtn. in Ulster Co., just over 4200 feet, and Hunter Mtn. in Greene Co., slightly over 4000 feet (see Fig. 7). Unlike a number of Adirondack peaks—the upper slopes of which are

Fig. 2 Gull Island, eastern Lake Ontario, Jefferson Co., June 10, 1967. Large elm at left, breeding site of Double-crested Cormorants and Black-crowned Night Herons; Herring and Ring-billed gulls nest on the ground. Photo by Robert G. Wolk

Fig. 3 Perch River Refuge, Jefferson Co., July 22, 1956. Breeding habitat of Green-winged Teal, Redhead, and Black Tern. Photo by David Gordon

Fig. 4 Southern edge of Tug Hill district, Redfield Township, Oswego Co., June 27, 1964. Mixed black spruce—white pine—alder swamp. An interesting admixture of northern and southern breeders found here, such as Hermit Thrush, Golden-winged, Nashville, Chestnut-sided, and Blackburnian warblers, and Rufous-sided Towhee and White-throated Sparrow. Photo by Margaret Rusk

Fig. 5 View of Mt. Marcy, Essex Co., highest peak in New York (5344 feet). Lake Tear of the Clouds in foreground, source of the Hudson River, Oct. 11, 1969. Photo by Wesley E. Lanyon

above tree line—even the highest Catskill peaks are wooded to their summits, being more than 1000 feet lower than their northern counterparts.

East of the Hudson River, close to the Massachusetts state line and running parallel to it, are the Taconics, an outlier of the Berkshires. In the southeastern portion of the state south of the Catskills are the Shawangunks which continue in a southwesterly direction into New Jersey along the east side of the Delaware River where they are known as the Kittatinnies. Farther south in New York the Ramapos likewise lie in a northeast-southwest direction and also continue into New Jersey. The Hudson Highlands (see Figs. 8 and 9), again running in the same direction, cross the Hudson River through the counties of Putnam,

Orange, and Rockland, where they are practically contiguous with the Ramapos at their southern extremity. Few of the above exceed 2000 feet. Finally the basalt escarpment on the west bank of the Hudson—the Palisades (see Fig. 10)—extends from Rockland Co. south into New Jersey.

In central New York to the west of the Catskills is a broad region of elevated uplands, increasing in elevation toward the south; the highest extends into Pennsylvania. These are the Allegheny Mountains, which in New York State run slightly over 2500 feet elevation at their highest. Altitude decreases northward and westward as the lake plains are reached, and in several spots cliff-like escarpments are a notable feature of the landscape. In the heart of this central upland region lie a series of

Fig. 6 View from Indian Ladder trail, Thacher State Park, Helderberg Plateau, Albany Co. Barns in middle distance have nesting Cliff Swallows, and the deciduous woodlands at the extreme left are the breeding grounds of Worm-eating Warblers. Photo by Allen Benton

Fig. 7 Base of Hunter Mountain, at Stony Clove, Greene Co., summit altitude 4025 feet. Mixed evergreen-deciduous forest supports such breeding species as Myrtle and Blackpoll warblers, Yellow-bellied Flycatcher, and near the summit, Gray-cheeked Thrush. Photo by Allen Benton

Fig. 8 Portion of Bear Mountain State Park, Orange and Rockland counties; altitude approximately 1000 feet. Most of the area is secondary deciduous forest with an admixture of pine and hemlock, resulting in such different zonal types of birds as Hooded Warbler on the lower slopes and Black-throated Blue Warbler higher up. July 8, 1970. Photo courtesy Palisades Interstate Park Commission

Fig. 9 Portion of Harriman State Park, Orange and Rockland counties, showing mixed maple-beech forest, second-growth stage. Red-eyed Vireo, Ovenbird, and Wood Thrush are among the common breeding birds. July 8, 1970. Photo courtesy Palisades Interstate Park Commission

north-south bodies of water known as the Finger Lakes. With the exception of Canandaigua Lake, glacial drift at the north end of these lakes effectively blocked drainage into Lake Ontario. However, at least one of the south-north flowing streams, the Genesee River, passing through the canyons of Letchworth State Park, penetrates the lake plain and empties into Lake Ontario at Rochester.

A glance at the large physiographic map shows how broad is the Lake Ontario plain, in some places as much as 30 to 40 miles in width. The largest fresh-water marshes and wooded swamps (see Fig. 11) in the state are found here, the best known and most spectacular from a wildlife point of view being Montezuma and Oak Orchard. At the western extremity of the Lake Ontario plain in New York State is the Niagara River on the Canadian border. Here at the extreme eastern end of Lake Erie at Buffalo the Niagara River flows northward through the world-famous cataract at Niagara Falls and then empties into Lake Ontario which is considerably lower than Lake Erie. In contrast to the Lake Ontario plain, the extremely narrow Lake Erie plain in Chautauqua Co., south of Dunkirk, is but a mile or so in width through much of its length. At its widest it is barely 15 miles across.

At the opposite end of the state is Long Island, well-named, projecting into the Atlantic for more than 120 miles. It is by far the largest island along any coast of the continental United States, excepting the islands off Alaska.

Fig. 10 Palisades near Sparkill, Rockland Co.; Hudson River in foreground. The cliffs formerly supported breeding Peregrine Falcons and still contain an occasional cliff-nesting pair of Great Horned Owls. The deciduous woodland on the lower slopes have breeding Hooded and Worm-eating warblers. Photo by H. Gilmore, Palisades Interstate Park Commission

Fig. 11 Mixed deciduous swamp forest, Reed Road Swamp, Monroe Co., interesting admixture of breeding northern and southern forms found here. Winter Wren, Northern Waterthrush, and Mourning Warbler; Red-bellied Woodpecker, Blue-gray Gnatcatcher, and Cerulean Warbler. Summer 1969. Photo by Joseph W. Taylor. See also Brown (*Kingbird*, 1970, 20: 68–69).

VEGETATION

The various plant associations which affect the breeding distribution of birds within the state are varied and somewhat complex, but may be broken down into two main categories: forest types and those of open country.

Forest Habitats: In pre-colonial times much of the state was covered with a vast and unbroken primary forest. Most of this forest was cut down during the eighteenth and early nineteenth centuries for lumber and to "open up" the land for agriculture. Today only remnants of this virgin forest may be found in small stands on the more precipitous mountain slopes, in the few remaining swampy areas, and where protected in forest preserves in the Adirondack and Catskill districts. After about 1870 most of the state, where not devoid of trees, was and is today secondary forest, that is chiefly without a canopy, allowing some sunlight to penetrate to the forest floor, thereby encouraging an understory of various shrubs, vines, and herbaceous plants. Little of this undergrowth occurs in the darkness of a primary forest with its "complete" canopy preventing sunlight from reaching the ground.

In recent years with the decline in agriculture and abandonment of farms, open areas have reverted to second-growth woodland. In other places reforestation has been practiced.

As with bird species, the distribution of the woodland trees is greatly affected by temperature, humidity, and soil conditions, the last not only influencing the vegetation but also limiting the breeding distribution of several local species of birds—Nighthawk and Pine Warbler on sandy soil, for example.

The two forest types in New York State, as in much of the northeast, are composed of evergreen or coniferous species and deciduous or broad-leaved species. However, it must again be emphasized that depending on altitude, latitude, moisture content, and edaphic conditions (soil types) there is often an intermingling of evergreen and deciduous trees—the "mixed" forest. The three most dominant and widespread forest tree associations in the state are (1) the southern hardwoods, oak-hickory (and formerly chestnut)—see Fig. 12; (2) the northern hardwoods, beech-birch-maple (also some hemlock); and (3) at higher altitudes, the northern conifers, spruce-fir, and more locally in bogs, larch (tamarack)-white cedar—see Figs. 13, 13a, 14, 15.

The state, situated as it is, has an interesting admixture of northern and southern tree species. For instance, in the Allegany Plateau region many of the hillside streams and gorges run in a generally east-west direction with their slopes facing to the north and south. Depending on altitude, the north side of the ravine (*facing south*), receiving the sun's warmth, has trees of southern affinities such as various oaks and hickories, while the opposite south bank (*facing north*), being in the shade and considerably cooler, has northern types such as hemlock, yellow birch, striped and mountain maples, and American mountain ash. The same temperature conditions along these slopes also contain an admixture of breeding birds with southern and northern affinities. In the former category are Tufted Titmouse, Carolina Wren, Louisiana Waterthrush, and Worm-eating and Hooded warblers; in the latter category are Winter Wren, Solitary Vireo, Magnolia and Canada warblers, Northern Waterthrush, and Slate-colored or Dark-eyed Junco.

In the Catskills, by climbing Slide Mtn. to the summit (slightly over 4000 feet) one can see or hear all five species of eastern "brown" thrush. First the Wood Thrush and Veery are found near the base of the mountain in oak-hickory woodland; then up through maple-beech-birch-hemlock forest where the Hermit and Swainson's thrushes reside, the latter species occurring also at higher elevations in the red spruce zone; and finally on and near the summit where the shy Gray-cheeked Thrush nests among the thick growth of stunted and windswept balsam fir.

As may be seen from the following list of the more prevalent tree and shrub species, nearly all of the conifers and some of the deciduous forms are of northern origin. The southern deciduous element is confined mainly to the north shore of Long Island, Staten Island, the lower Hudson valley, the Delaware, Susquehanna, and Allegheny valleys near the Pennsylvania state line, and along the plains of lakes Erie and Ontario. There are, in addition, a number of widespread species. The list includes those of (WD)—Widespread Distribution, (N)—chiefly Northern, (S)—chiefly Southern, (W)—chiefly Western.

Fig. 12 Edge of mixed primary-secondary oak-hickory-maple forest, with some 40-foot sassafras trees, Gardiner's Island, Suffolk Co., Apr. 6, 1912. Formerly the breeding haunts of Great Blue Herons, and Great Horned Owls. The violent September 1938 hurricane nearly completely demolished this splendid forest. Photo by Francis Harper

Fig. 13 Raquette Lake, Hamilton Co., Aug. 7, 1957. Spruce-sphagnum bog; breeding habitat of Rusty Blackbird and White-throated Sparrow. Photo by Richard Rosche

Fig. 13a Spruce-sphagnum bog near Woods Lake, Webb Township, Herkimer Co., July 7, 1968. Breeding habitat of Boreal Chickadee and Lincoln's Sparrow. Photo by Margaret Rusk

Fig. 14 Cranberry Lake, St. Lawrence Co., July 17, 1954. Breeding habitat of Black-backed Three-toed Woodpecker, Gray Jay, Bay-breasted Warbler, Rusty Blackbird, and Lincoln's Sparrow. Photo by David Gordon

Fig. 15 Ferd's Bog, near Eagle Bay, Hamilton-Herkimer Co. line. A "typical" boreal Adirondack bog containing sphagnum, cranberry, pitcher plant, leatherleaf, spruce, tamarack (larch), and other acid-loving plants. Most of the boreal type breeding birds of the Adirondacks are found at this locality. Among them are Spruce Grouse, Gray Jay, both three-toed woodpeckers, Boreal Chickadee, Yellow-bellied and Olive-sided flycatchers, Rusty Blackbird, Lincoln's Sparrow, and others. Photo by Marge Rusk, July 10, 1972

Botanical Associations

PART I—EVERGREENS OR CONIFERS

Pinus strobus—white pine (N), up to 2500′ in Adirondacks (see Fig. 16).

P. resinosa—red pine (N), in dry, sandy soil; local-inland only.

P. rigida—pitch pine (S), sandy soil, forming the pine barrens of Long Island; more local inland.

Picea alba—white spruce (N), south to the Adirondacks.

P. nigra—black spruce (N), also locally in lowland bogs.

P. rubra—red spruce (N), up to 4500′ in Adirondacks and over 3300′ in Catskills.

Larix laricina—American larch or tamarack (N), chiefly in swamps and bogs (leaves deciduous).

Tsuga canadensis—hemlock (N), up to 2000′ in Adirondacks.

Abies balsamea—balsam fir (N), up to 5000′ in Adirondacks.

Thuja occidentalis—arborvitae or northern white cedar (N), up to 3500′ in Adirondacks; in wet soil and along stream banks.

Chamaecyparis thyoides—southern white cedar (S), chiefly coastal swamps.

Fig. 16 Dead black walnut (breeding American Kestrel) and white pines (nesting Mourning Doves and Common Grackles), Laurel Hollow, Nassau Co., spring of 1969. Photo by John Taylor

Juniperus virginiana—red cedar (WD), in dry soil in more open country.

J. communis—juniper (N), on dry hillsides; a prostrate or low shrub.

PART II—DECIDUOUS OR BROAD-LEAVED TYPES

Juglans nigra—black walnut (S), in rich soil.

J. cinerea—butternut (WD), in rich soil, chiefly at lower elevations.

Hicoria (Carya)—various hickories (S), chiefly in rich soil.

Populus grandidentata—large-toothed aspen (WD), in rich soil.

P. tremuloides—quaking aspen (N), up to 3000′ in Adirondacks.

P. deltoides—eastern cottonwood (W), along rivers and lakes (local).

Salix—various willows (N), along rivers and lakes and in wet soil.

Betula populifolia—gray birch (N), in poor soil and in clearings.

B. papyrifera—white or paper birch (N), chiefly in the mountains.

B. lenta—black or cherry birch (WD), in rich soil.

B. lutea—yellow birch (N), chiefly in the mountains.

Alnus—various alders (N), in wet soil, forming thickets.

Fagus americana (grandifolia)—American beech (WD), in rich soil.

Castanea dentata—American chestnut (S), in rich soil; formerly common, but nearly extirpated by disease.

Quercus—various upland oaks (S), chiefly on rich soils.

Q. ilicifolia—scrub oak (S), chiefly near the coast in sandy soil.

Q. marilandica—black-jack oak (S), chiefly near the coast in sandy soil.

Ulmus americana—American elm (WD), in moist soil along streams and in swamps, but also a shade tree along streets; many disease stricken.

U. fulva—slippery elm (WD), in and near moist soil.

Celtis—hackberries (S), local in dry soil.

Liriodendron tulipifera—tulip tree (S), in rich soil.

Platanus occidentalis—American plane-tree, sycamore, or buttonball (S), along streams and in wet woods; often planted.

Sassafras sassafras—sassafras (S), in dry soil.

Liquidambar styraciflua—sweet gum (S), local in low, damp woods.

Sorbus americana—American mountain-ash (N), chiefly in the mountains.

Malus—apples and crab-apples (WD), former introduced in orchards; latter mostly native, forming thickets.

Amelanchier canadensis—shadbush (WD), chiefly wooded hillsides.

Crataegus—hawthorns or thorn-apples (WD), forming thickets in open country, especially in pastures.

Prunus serotina—wild black cherry (WD), mostly in open country.

Robinia pseudoacacia—black locust (S), along roadsides; younger trees forming groves in light woodland.

Rhus—various upland sumacs (WD), in dry soil, often forming thickets.

Ilex opaca—American holly (S), in moist soil along the coast; now rare and local (leaves evergreen) (see Fig. 17).

Kalmia latifolia—mountain laurel (WD), in sandy or rocky soil; most numerous in hillside woods (leaves evergreen).

Nyssa sylvatica—sour gum or tupelo (S), in wet soil and in swamps.

Cornus florida—flowering dogwood (WD), on wooded hillsides; also commonly planted.

Tilia americana—American linden or basswood (WD), along river bottoms; in rich woods, especially in the mountains below 1500′.

Acer rubrum—red or swamp maple (WD), in swamps and wet soil.

A. saccharum—sugar maple (N), in rich soil and along roadsides.

A. pennsylvanicum—striped maple (N), in damp woods in the mountains.

A. spicatum—mountain maple (N), in damp woods in the mountains.

A. negundo—ash-leaved maple or box-elder (W), along streams; rare eastward but spreading; often planted.

Fraxinus—various ashes (chiefly S), *F. americana*—white ash, in rich woods; other species in swamps and river bottoms.

Other important elements are various bushes and vines forming an understory in more open woodland, in wet places, and in swamps. These include:

Fig. 17   Holly-sassafras-tupelo (sour gum), Sunken Forest, near Point O'Woods, Fire Island, Suffolk Co., summer 1950. Black-crowned Night Herons and Carolina Wrens, among other species, breed or have bred here. Photo by Robert Cushman Murphy

Fig. 18 Mixed heronry (six breeding species), Lawrence, Nassau Co., July 1969. Herons nest in pin cherry-beach plum "island" and feed in salt marshes (*Spartina patens*). Photo by Arthur Singer

Fig. 19 Interior of mixed heronry, Lawrence, Nassau Co., July 1969. Habitat chiefly of pin cherry, beach plum, bayberry, poison ivy, and Virginia creeper, with mats of *Hudsonia tomentosa* (heather) on bare sand in foreground. Photo by Arthur Singer

Viburnum—viburnums or haws; *Vaccinium*—huckleberries and blueberries; *Sambucus*—elderberries; *Benzoin aestivale*—spicebush; *Hamamelis virginiana*—witch-hazel; *Lonicera*—honeysuckles; *Rubus*—blackberries and raspberries; *Smilax*—catbriers or greenbriers; *Vitis*—wild grapes; *Cephalanthus occidentalis*—buttonbush—in swamps; *Rhus toxicodendron*—poison ivy; *Ampelopsis quinquefolia*—Virginia creeper.

Open-country Habitats: Important open-country habitats are fresh-water marshes and bogs, coastal salt marshes, and grassy fields and meadows, the last both cultivated and uncultivated.

In the marshes and bogs various grasses, sedges, and rushes are dominant and *Sphagnum* moss occurs locally in bogs, particularly northward. For the aquatic breeding birds the following are of great importance for food, shelter, and/or nest sites: *Typha*—two species of cattails, up to 1600′ in the Adirondacks; *Phragmites communis*—great reed, widespread in wet places; often a pest. Other important

aquatics are *Sparganium*—bur-reeds; *Potamogeton*—pondweeds; *Sagittaria*—arrowheads; *Peltandra*—arrow-arums; *Pontederia*—pickerel weeds; *Nymphaea*—pond- or water-lilies.

In the salt marshes, three grasses and one rush are the dominant growth: *Spartina patens* and *S. alterniflora; Distichlis spicata; Juncus gerardi;* also two exclusively coastal shrubs of the family Compositae, at the edge of the salt meadows: *Iva frutescens*—marsh-elder or hightide bush and *Baccharis halimifolia*—groundsel bush.

Forming dense, often impenetrable, thickets on the sandy coastal barrier beaches are: *Myrica carolinensis*—bayberry; *Prunus maritima*—beach plum, and wild cherries; and the aforementioned poison ivy, catbriers, and wild grapes (see Figs. 18 and 19).

Finally in the sand dunes adjacent to the ocean is beach or dune grass—*Ammophila arenaria.*

One other type of open-country environment *was* the unique and ill-fated Hempstead Plains on Long Island, perhaps the only natural prai-

Fig. 20   Open pine barrens and prairie, near Central Park, Suffolk Co. Aug. 25, 1909. Pitch pines and *Baptisia tinctoria* (wild blue lupine), breeding grounds of Pine Warblers and Grasshopper Sparrows. Photo by Roland Harper, courtesy Torrey Botanical Club, from *Torrey Botanical Club Memoirs* (1918, 17: 271)

Fig. 21 Natural prairie, Hempstead Plains area near Garden City, Nassau Co., summer of 1909. *Andropogon* (beard grass) prairie, breeding haunts of Upland Sandpiper, Bobolink, Eastern Meadowlark, and Vesper and Grasshopper sparrows. Photo by Roland Harper, courtesy American Geographical Society, from *Bull. Amer. Geogr. Soc.* (1911, 43:352)

rie in the east. Thousands of acres of beard grass (*Andropogon scoparius*) formed the prevalent climax growth of this very specialized habitat. It was officially known as "bluestem prairie" (Küchler, 1964: 74). According to Küchler, the nearest similar-type prairie is to be found west of Columbus, Ohio. Other characteristic plants of this prairie region were: *Viola pedata*—bird's-foot violet and *Baptisia*

tinctoria—wild indigo. For an excellent account of this interesting area see Harper (1911) (and see Figs. 20 and 21).

The above-mentioned vegetative types are important in the discussion of the breeding bird species accounts. Most, if not all, of the plant species are included in the habitat descriptions. Botanical names are taken from Britton and Brown (1936).

OUTSTANDING BIRDING AREAS

The following 15 New York localities are among the most productive birding areas in the state. These 15 places are indicated on Map 1. Some are of interest the year around, others primarily during the migrations, and a few in the breeding season (see Figs. 22 and 23).

The following birds are specialties of these

15 areas. In a number of instances duplication in species is involved. Therefore, it seems more expedient to list the species and then the locality(ies). Only birds of particular interest are included and the more common, widespread species are purposely omitted with the exception of localities 6 and 15.

Locality Number	Locality	County	Locality Number	Locality	County
1	Montauk	Suffolk	9	Derby Hill	Oswego
2	Moriches	Suffolk	10	Montezuma	Cayuga-Seneca
3	Jones Beach	Suffolk-Nassau	11	Manitou	Monroe
4	Jamaica Bay	Queens-Kings	12	Oak Orchard	Genesee-Orleans
5	Central Park	New York	13	Niagara Falls	Niagara-Canada
6	Slide Mtn.	Ulster	14	Buffalo	Erie-Canada
7	Chubb River Swamp	Essex	15	Allegany State Park	Cattaraugus
8	Madawaska	Franklin			

Fig. 22   Black spruce bog near Madawaska, Franklin Co., August 1969. Breeding habitat of Gray Jay, Boreal Chickadee, and Lincoln's Sparrow. Photo by Gordon Meade

Fig. 23   Madawaska Pond, Franklin Co., August 1969. Breeding habitat of Ring-necked Duck and Lincoln's Sparrow. Photo by Gordon Meade

Species	Locality No.	Season(s)	Remarks
Eared Grebe	4	Oct.–Apr.	west pond
Sooty Shearwater	1, 2, 3	May, June	offshore fishing boats
Greater Shearwater	1, 2, 3	May, June, Sept.	offshore fishing boats
Cory's Shearwater	1, 2, 3	July–Nov.	offshore fishing boats
Wilson's Storm Petrel	1, 2, 3	late May–Aug.	offshore fishing boats
Gannet	1, 2, 3	Oct.–May	ocean areas
Great Cormorant	1	Oct.–Apr.	rock jetty at fish pier
Great Egret	2, 3, 4	Apr.–Oct.	
Snowy Egret	2, 3, 4	Apr.–Oct.	
Little Blue Heron	2, 3	May–Sept.	
Louisiana Heron	3, 4	May–Sept.	
Yellow-crowned Night Heron	3	May–Sept.	
Least Bittern	10, 12	May, June	
Glossy Ibis	3, 4	May–Oct.	
Whistling Swan	13	March, Apr.	
Common Eider	1	late Nov.–March	
King Eider	1, 13, 14	Nov.–Apr.	
Harlequin Duck	1, 3	Dec.–Apr.	rocky shores, stone jetties
Goshawk	9	March, Apr.	

MAP 1 OUTSTANDING
BIRDING AREAS—See text

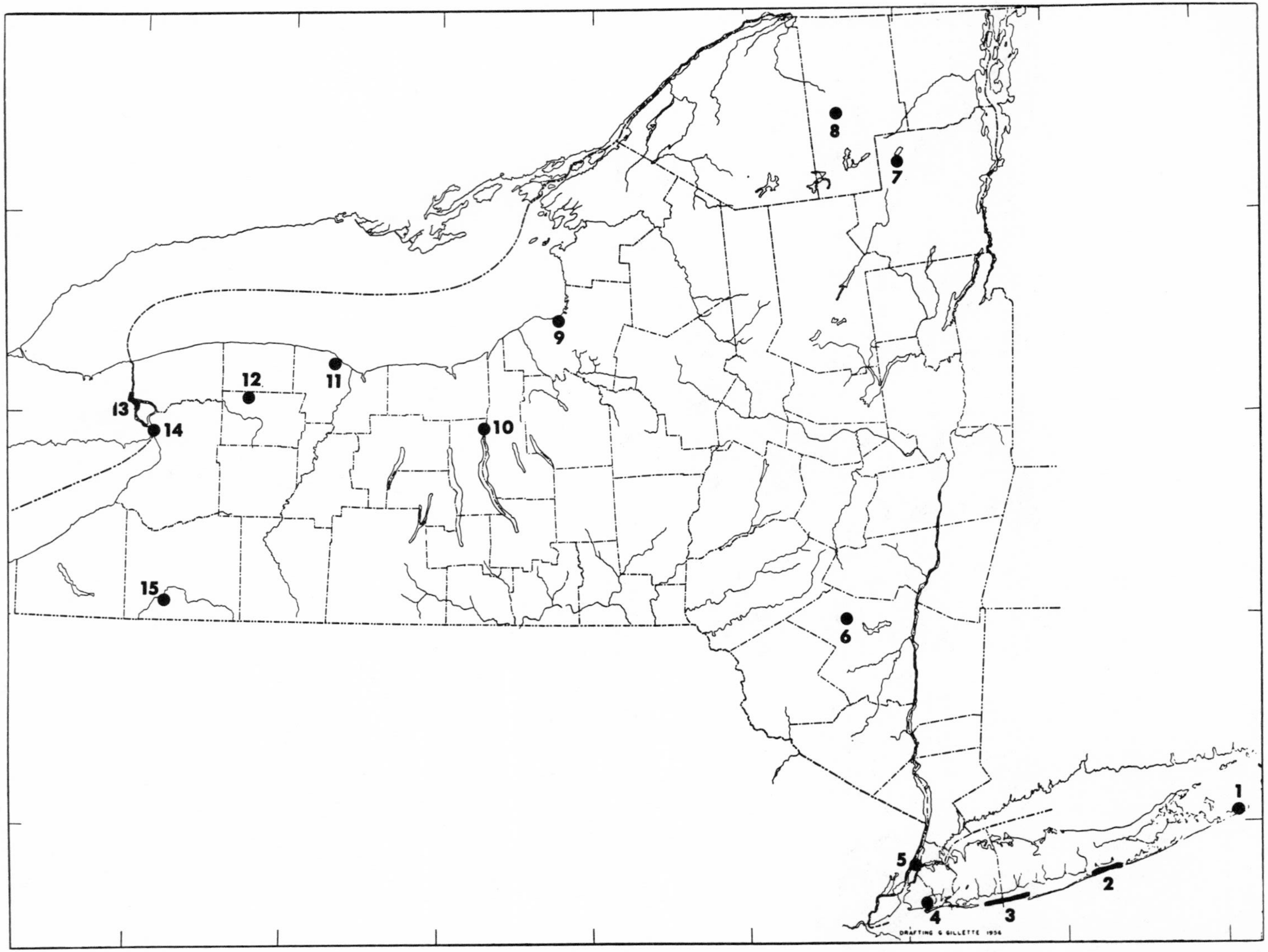

Golden Eagle	9, 11	Apr.	
Merlin	2, 3	Sept., Oct.	
Wild Turkey	15	resident	
Spruce Grouse	7, 8	resident	
Clapper Rail	2, 3, 4	Apr.–July	coastal salt marsh
Black Rail	3	May, June	Oak Beach area
Oystercatcher	2	May–Aug.	
Whimbrel	11	late May, July	
Marbled Godwit	2, 4	July–Sept.	
Hudsonian Godwit	2, 4, 10	July–Sept.	
Willet	2, 3	May–Sept.	
Curlew Sandpiper	4	May	tidal flats
Red Phalarope	1, 2, 3	chiefly May	offshore fishing boats
Pomarine Jaeger	1, 2, 3	late May–Sept.	offshore fishing boats
Parasitic Jaeger	1, 2, 3, 9, 11	late May–Sept.	offshore fishing boats
Thayer's Gull	13, 14	chiefly Dec.	
Franklin's Gull	13, 14	chiefly Sept.	
Black-headed Gull	2, 3	Nov.–March	inlets with Bonaparte's Gulls
Little Gull	13, 14	Sept.–May	with Bonaparte's Gulls
Sabine's Gull	13, 14	Sept.–Nov.	
Kittiwake	chiefly 1	Nov.–Feb.	offshore fishing boats
Roseate Tern	2, 3	May–Aug.	
Least Tern	2, 3	May–Aug.	
Royal Tern	2	Aug., Sept.	
Black Skimmer	2, 3, 4	May–Sept.	
Dovekie	1, 2, 3	Nov.–March	erratic and unpredictable
"Alcids" (sp?)	1	Dec.–Feb.	erratic and unpredictable
Black-backed 3-toed Woodpecker	7, 8	resident	
Northern 3-toed Woodpecker	7, 8	resident	very rare and local
Western Kingbird	1–4	late Aug.–Nov.	
Gray Jay	7, 8	resident	
Boreal Chickadee	7, 8	resident	
Blue Grosbeak	3, 4	Sept., Oct.	
Dickcissel	1–4	Sept., Oct.	
"Ipswich" Sparrow	2, 3, 4	Nov.–March	coastal sand dunes
Seaside Sparrow	3, 4	May–Sept.	coastal salt marsh
Sharp-tailed Sparrow	2, 3, 4	May–Sept.	coastal salt marsh
Lark Sparrow	1–4	Aug.–Oct.	
Clay-colored Sparrow	2, 3, 4	chiefly Oct.	

It will be seen from the foregoing that nothing has been mentioned about localities 5 and 6, and practically nothing pertaining to locality

15. Central Park (5) is noted for its spring warbler migration, especially, and a visit there from mid-April to early June is most reward-

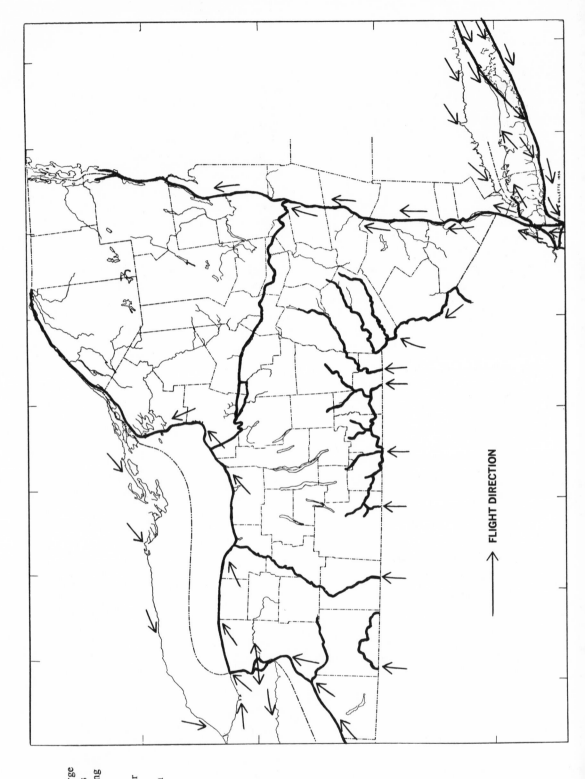

MAP 2 PRINCIPAL
MIGRATION ROUTES Large
bodies of water such as
the Atlantic Ocean, Long
Island Sound, and the
Great Lakes act as
barriers—causing major
concentrations on the
south side in spring, on
the north side in fall.

FLIGHT DIRECTION

ing, with the majority of the rarer species recorded annually.

Slide Mtn. in the Catskills (6) is at its best during the nesting season in June and July, and a climb from the base to the summit—over 4000 feet—will enable the observer to see and hear most of the Canadian zone breeding birds. Such boreal specialties as Goshawk, Sapsucker, Yellow-bellied and Olive-sided flycatchers, Red-breasted Nuthatch, Winter Wren, Swainson's and Gray-cheeked thrushes, Golden-crowned Kinglet, Myrtle, Black-poll, and Mourning warblers, and Junco and White-throated Sparrow breed there.

As for Allegany State Park (15), it is a meeting place for, in addition to Wild Turkeys, a number of southern and northern breeding species. Some examples are: Tufted Titmouse and Red-breasted Nuthatch; Carolina and Winter wrens; Wood and Swainson's thrushes; Blue-gray Gnatcatcher and Golden-crowned Kinglet; Hooded and Myrtle warblers; Louisiana and Northern waterthrushes; Cardinal and Slate-colored Junco.

Incidentally, Derby Hill, located at a strategic point on the Lake Ontario shore where the latter turns from a west-east to a south-north direction, catches or rather "traps" many northbound spring migrants, in addition to the diurnal raptors for which it has become so famous in recent years. Warm, southerly wind flows striking against the lake front, which acts as a barrier, funnel numerous individuals of migrating birds to this most productive spot and to the Manitou-Braddock's Bay area farther west on Lake Ontario, as well.

Map 2, showing the flight directions, indicates the major and minor flyways of passage migrants within the state, as well as in adjacent Canada and neighboring states.

CONSERVATION

Although we in New York may be happy with the knowledge that wildlife areas have been set aside, such as the Adirondack Forest Preserve, the Montezuma Wildlife Refuge, the Allegany State Park, and the Jamaica Bay Wildlife Sanctuary, to name but a few of the outstanding areas in the state, there is no room for complacency. Even the above-named are not inviolate. There are always threats of encroachment upon these nature reserves. Lumbering, road building, draining, filling, or airport construction are some of the evils that could mean partial or entire destruction of these areas.

Pressures on wildlife and the environment today are tremendous, only because of that most insidious of all evils, the human population explosion. For if something is not done soon about universal birth control, man himself is doomed—if not now, then in the not too distant future. He will literally starve himself into oblivion as the world's food supply becomes exhausted. As human populations grow, so do the insatiable demands for more open land for grazing, for agriculture, for road building, as well as for the destruction of forests, grasslands, wetlands, and beaches. Habitat destruction, use of pesticides in the form of lethal toxic chemicals, pollution of air, land, and water, all add up to human genocide in the final analysis.

That arch predator—man—is forever adding to the list of rare and endangered species. Indiscriminate hunting, poaching, the ever-increasing wild bird trade, the export and import of rare creatures for aviaries and of pets for private homes, the drain on the really scarce raptors for falconry, and environmental desecration are all a menace to the endangered species, not a few of which are on the road to extinction.

The continued use of toxic chemicals has doomed, at least for now, the Peregrine Falcon, Bald Eagle, and very likely the Osprey in New York State. Seriously reduced are Cooper's and Red-shouldered hawks.

Oil pollution on the high seas and in coastal waters has caused a marked diminution in loons, grebes, and especially alcids, as well as sea ducks, such as eiders and scoters.

Certain species may be saved at the eleventh hour by breeding them in captivity. This has been done for waterfowl, game birds, some passerines, and, yes, even a few hawks.

The above indictment sounds grim and ominous, but a realistic view must be taken if we are to preserve what is left today. Tomorrow will be too late.

ESCAPES

Anyone who has lived in or near a large coastal city, such as New York, Miami, or Los Angeles—all ports of entry—has from time to time observed various exotic species which occasionally escape from captivity. Whether they are imports "on the loose" (from confinement) or deliberate releases is immaterial. The fact is they are there. In the New York City region alone the number of escapes year by year is considerable. Reports of strange birds seen or captured run the gamut of a "who's who" of species from the four corners of the globe.

Importation of foreign birds into the United States today is big business. In the calendar year 1969 alone, more than a half million birds were imported (Banks, 1970) and this did not include the hordes of parrots and canaries which are specifically exempt from being declared.* The numbers of psittacine birds such as Amazon parrots (*Amazona* sp.) and Monk Parakeets (*Myiopsitta monachus*)— both from tropical America—as well as the Australian Budgerigars or Shell Parakeets (*Melopsittacus undulatus*), have been imported in large numbers and quite a few have escaped from captivity or were deliberately released. The Monk Parakeet has recently become established here and is treated separately in the species account. Nearly 12,000 individuals of this parrot were imported in 1968 alone (Banks, *op. cit.*).

The following species list, by family, includes only those not mentioned in the main list.

* As of July 1972 *all* psittacines were banned from importation into the United States without special permit, but only one year later the ban had been lifted.

Without exception all have been reported as "free flying in the wild." Many were observed on a number of occasions or caught alive; others were noted but once or twice. None of the following, insofar as the writer is concerned, deserves a rightful place in the avifauna of New York.

IBISES, SPOONBILLS—THRESKIORNITHIDAE

Scarlet Ibis (*Eudocimus ruber*), northern South America; in the same category as the Flamingo.

SWANS, GEESE, DUCKS—ANATIDAE

Members of this family are commonly kept in aviaries and are immensely popular with aviculturists. Of the non-passerines probably more species of waterfowl escape and are reported by observers than those of any other family. Jamaica Bay Refuge, in particular, is a favorite gathering place of many an exotic.

Black Swan (*Cygnus atratus*), Australia.

Black-necked Swan (*Cygnus melancoryphus*), southern South America.

Red-breasted Goose (*Branta ruficollis*), chiefly western Siberia.

Lesser White-fronted Goose (*Anser erythropus*), northern Asia, Lapland.

Bar-headed Goose (*Anser indicus*), central Asia.

Swan Goose (*Anser cygnoides*), central and eastern Asia.

Egyptian Goose (*Alopochen aegyptiaca*), Africa.

Common Shelduck (*Tadorna tadorna*), Eurasia.

Black-bellied Tree Duck (*Dendrocygna autumnalis*), tropical America.

Muscovy Duck (*Cairina moschata*), tropical America.

White-cheeked Pintail (*Anas bahamensis*), West Indies, South America.

PHEASANTS, QUAILS—PHASIANIDAE

Green Pheasant (*Phasianus versicolor*), Japan; recently introduced into Dutchess Co. (*Kingbird*, 1970, 20: 202).

CRANES—GRUIDAE

Demoiselle Crane (*Anthropoides virgo*), south-central Eurasia.

PLOVERS, LAPWINGS—CHARADRIIDAE

Spur-winged Lapwing or Plover (*Vanellus spinosus*), chiefly Africa.

GULLS, TERNS—LARIDAE

Silver or Red-billed Gull (*Larus novaehollandiae*), Australia, New Zealand, coasts of South Africa.

PIGEONS, DOVES—COLUMBIDAE

Ringed Turtle Dove (*Streptopelia risoria*), chiefly North Africa. This is considered to be the domesticated variant of the Pink-headed Turtle Dove (*S. roseogrisea*). It has bred at the Jamaica Bay Refuge.

PARROTS—PSITTACIDAE

Canary-winged Parakeet (*Brotogeris versicolurus*), South America.

Orange-chinned Parakeet (*Brotogeris jugularis*), Middle and South America.

Orange-fronted Parakeet (*Aratinga canicularis*), Mexico to Costa Rica.

Black-headed Parakeet (*Nandayus nenday*), southern South America.

Yellow-headed (Amazon) Parrot (*Amazona ochrocephala*), tropical America.

Budgerigar (*Melopsittacus undulatus*), Australia.

Cockatiel (*Nymphicus hollandicus*), Australia.

Masked Lovebird (*Agapornis personata*), tropical East Africa.

Rose-ringed Parakeet (*Psittacula krameri*), most of Africa and southern Asia.

Blossom-headed Parakeet (*Psittacula cyanocephala*), tropical southeast Asia.

All of the above psittacine species have been recorded in the New York City region, especially during the period 1969–1971.

CROWS, JAYS—CORVIDAE

Rufous Treepie (*Dendrocitta vagabunda*), southeast Asia.

American White-necked Raven (*Corvus cryptoleucus*), southwestern United States, northern Mexico. Several were brought to Long Island as captives a few years ago (Bull, 1970: 52).

BULBULS—PYCNONOTIDAE

Red-whiskered Bulbul (*Pycnonotus jocosus*), southeast Asia.

THRASHERS—MIMIDAE

Pearly-eyed Thrasher (*Margarops fuscatus*), West Indies.

THRUSHES—TURDIDAE

Black-throated Thrush (*Turdus* [*ruficollis*] *atrogularis*), chiefly Siberia.

European Robin (*Erithacus rubecula*), chiefly Europe.

Indian Robin (*Saxicoloides fulicata*), India, Ceylon.

AMERICAN ORIOLES—ICTERIDAE

Black-throated Oriole (*Icterus gularis*), Mexico to Honduras. One individual was found frozen to death at Stuyvesant Oval in lower Manhattan, Jan. 20, 1965 (Bull, 1970: 52).

Troupial (*Icterus icterus*), northern South America.

STARLINGS—STURNIDAE

Hill Myna (*Gracula religiosa*), southeast Asia.

WEAVERS—PLOCEIDAE

Masked Weaver (*Ploceus velatus*), Africa.
Red Bishop (*Euplectes orix*), Africa.

WAXBILLS—ESTRILDIDAE

Common Waxbill (*Estrilda astrild*), Africa.
Strawberry Finch (*Estrilda amandava*), southeast Asia.
Spotted Munia (*Lonchura punctulata*), southeast Asia.

Chestnut Munia (*Lonchura malacca*), southeast Asia.

Java Finch or Sparrow (*Padda oryzivora*), Java; introduced into mainland southeast Asia.

FINCHES (CARDUELINAE)—FRINGILLIDAE

Yellow-fronted Canary or Green Singing Finch (*Serinus mozambicus*), Africa.
European Greenfinch (*Carduelis chloris*), chiefly Europe.
Linnet (*Acanthis cannabina*), Europe, western Asia.
Eurasian Bullfinch (*Pyrrhula pyrrhula*), temperate Eurasia.

FINCHES (CARDINALINAE)—FRINGILLIDAE

Red-crested or "Brazilian" Cardinal (*Paroaria coronata*), southern South America.

ANALYSIS OF THE AVIFAUNA

The following lists analyze the avifauna of the state: (1) breeders, and (2) nonbreeders. Both categories are divided into the major faunal regions of the world, with the number of species found in or rather derived from each faunal region.

In addition, the breeders are further broken down into three subdivisions or points of origin (N) Northern, (S) Southern, and (W) West-

ern. In New York the majority of breeders (68) have northern or essentially boreal affinities, e.g., Common Loon and Evening Grosbeak. Forty-five breeders have southern affinities, such as Bobwhite and Cardinal, and only ten breeders, such as Ruddy Duck and Clay-colored Sparrow, have western affinities.

Widespread species have no letter after their names.

Breeders

NEARCTIC (NORTH AMERICA) ELEMENT—147 SPECIES.

1. Common Loon (N)
2. Double-crested Cormorant
3. American Bittern
4. Canada Goose (N)
5. Wood Duck

6. Black Duck
7. Baldpate (W)
8. Blue-winged Teal
9. Redhead (W)
10. Ring-necked Duck (N)

11. Lesser Scaup (W)
12. Hooded Merganser
13. Bald Eagle
14. Cooper's Hawk
15. Red-shouldered Hawk
16. Broad-winged Hawk
17. Ruffed Grouse
18. Spruce Grouse (N)
19. Heath Hen (extinct)
20. Bobwhite (S)
21. Wild Turkey (S)
22. King Rail (S)
23. Sora (N)
24. Piping Plover
25. Killdeer (also Neotropical)
26. Woodcock
27. Spotted Sandpiper
28. Willet (also Neotropical)
29. Upland Sandpiper
30. Herring Gull (also western Palearctic)
31. Ring-billed Gull (N)
32. Passenger Pigeon (N) (extinct)
33. Yellow-billed Cuckoo (also Neotropical)
34. Black-billed Cuckoo
35. Screech Owl
36. Saw-whet Owl (N)
37. Whip-poor-will
38. Chimney Swift
39. Ruby-throated Hummingbird
40. Belted Kingfisher
41. Common Flicker (also Neotropical)
42. Pileated Woodpecker
43. Red-bellied Woodpecker (S)
44. Red-headed Woodpecker (S)
45. Yellow-bellied Sapsucker (N)
46. Downy Woodpecker
47. Black-backed Three-toed
    Woodpecker (N)
48. Eastern Kingbird
49. Crested Flycatcher
50. Eastern Phoebe
51. Yellow-bellied Flycatcher (N)
52. Acadian Flycatcher (S)
53. Alder Flycatcher (N)
54. Willow Flycatcher (W)
55. Least Flycatcher (N)
56. Wood Pewee
57. Olive-sided Flycatcher (N)
58. Tree Swallow
59. Cliff Swallow (N)
60. Purple Martin
61. Blue Jay

62. Gray Jay (N)
63. American Crow
64. Fish Crow (S)
65. Black-capped Chickadee (N)
66. Boreal Chickadee (N)
67. Tufted Titmouse (S)
68. White-breasted Nuthatch
69. Red-breasted Nuthatch (N)
70. Carolina Wren (S)
71. Long-billed Marsh Wren
72. Catbird
73. Brown Thrasher
74. American Robin
75. Wood Thrush (S)
76. Hermit Thrush (N)
77. Swainson's Thrush (N)
78. Gray-cheeked Thrush (N)
79. Veery (N)
80. Blue-gray Gnatcatcher (S)
81. Golden-crowned Kinglet (N)
82. Ruby-crowned Kinglet (N)
83. Cedar Waxwing
84. Loggerhead Shrike
85. White-eyed Vireo (S)
86. Yellow-throated Vireo (S)
87. Solitary Vireo (N)
88. Philadelphia Vireo (N)
89. Black and White Warbler
90. Prothonotary Warbler (S)
91. Worm-eating Warbler (S)
92. Blue-winged Warbler (S)
93. Golden-winged Warbler (S)
94. Tennessee Warbler (N)
95. Nashville Warbler (N)
96. Magnolia Warbler (N)
97. Cape May Warbler (N)
98. Black-throated Blue Warbler (N)
99. Myrtle Warbler (N)
100. Black-throated Green Warbler
101. Cerulean Warbler (S)
102. Blackburnian Warbler (N)
103. Chestnut-sided Warbler (N)
104. Bay-breasted Warbler (N)
105. Black-poll Warbler (N)
106. Pine Warbler (S)
107. Prairie Warbler (S)
108. Ovenbird
109. Northern Waterthrush (N)
110. Louisiana Waterthrush (S)
111. Kentucky Warbler (S)
112. Mourning Warbler (N)
113. Yellow-breasted Chat (S)

114. Hooded Warbler (S)
115. Canada Warbler (N)
116. American Redstart
117. Bobolink (N)
118. Western Meadowlark (W)
119. Orchard Oriole (S)
120. Baltimore Oriole
121. Rusty Blackbird (N)
122. Common Grackle
123. Cowbird
124. Scarlet Tanager
125. Cardinal (S)
126. Rose-breasted Grosbeak (N)
127. Indigo Bunting
128. Dickcissel (formerly)
129. Evening Grosbeak (N)
130. Purple Finch (N)

131. House Finch (W)
132. Pine Siskin (N)
133. American Goldfinch
134. Towhee
135. Savannah Sparrow (N)
136. Seaside Sparrow (S)
137. Sharp-tailed Sparrow
138. Henslow's Sparrow (S)
139. Vesper Sparrow
140. Chipping Sparrow
141. Clay-colored Sparrow (W)
142. Field Sparrow
143. Slate-colored Junco (N)
144. White-throated Sparrow (N)
145. Lincoln's Sparrow (N)
146. Swamp Sparrow
147. Song Sparrow

NEARCTIC AND NEOTROPICAL (TROPICAL AMER-
ICA) ELEMENTS—39 SPECIES.

1. Pied-billed Grebe
2. Great Blue Heron
3. Snowy Egret (S)
4. Little Blue Heron (S)
5. Louisiana Heron (S)
6. Green Heron
7. Yellow-crowned Night Heron (S)
8. Least Bittern
9. Ruddy Duck (W)
10. Turkey Vulture (S)
11. Sharp-shinned Hawk
12. Red-tailed Hawk
13. American Kestrel
14. Clapper Rail (S)
15. Virginia Rail
16. Black Rail (S)
17. American Coot
18. Oystercatcher (S)
19. Laughing Gull (formerly)
20. Black Skimmer (S)

21. Mourning Dove
22. Monk Parakeet (Neotropical only)
23. Great Horned Owl
24. Barred Owl
25. Common Nighthawk
26. Hairy Woodpecker
27. Rough-winged Swallow (S)
28. House Wren
29. Short-billed Marsh Wren
30. Mockingbird (S)
31. Eastern Bluebird
32. Red-eyed Vireo
33. Warbling Vireo
34. Parula Warbler
35. Yellow Warbler
36. Yellowthroat
37. Eastern Meadowlark
38. Red-winged Blackbird
39. Grasshopper Sparrow (S)

HOLARCTIC (NORTH AMERICA AND EURASIA)
ELEMENT—24 SPECIES.

1. Mallard
2. Gadwall (W)
3. Pintail (N)
4. Green-winged Teal (N)
5. Shoveler (W)
6. Common Goldeneye (N)
7. Common Merganser (N)
8. Red-breasted Merganser (N)

9. Marsh Hawk (N)
10. Goshawk (N)
11. Golden Eagle (N)
12. Common Snipe (N)
13. Great Black-backed Gull (N)
14. Common Tern
15. Black Tern (N)
16. Long-eared Owl (N)

17. Northern Three-toed Woodpecker (N)
18. Horned Lark
19. Bank Swallow
20. Barn Swallow

21. Common Raven (N)
22. Brown Creeper (N)
23. Winter Wren (N)
24. Red Crossbill (N)

COSMOPOLITAN ELEMENT—12 SPECIES.

1. Great Egret (S)
2. Cattle Egret (S)
3. Black-crowned Night Heron
4. Glossy Ibis (S)
5. Osprey
6. Peregrine Falcon

7. Common Gallinule (S)
8. Roseate Tern
9. Least Tern (S)
10. Rock Pigeon (Old World; introduced)
11. Barn Owl (S)
12. Short-eared Owl (N)

PALEARCTIC (EURASIA) ELEMENT—7 SPECIES;
ALL INTRODUCED.

1. Mute Swan
2. Gray Partridge
3. Common Pheasant
4. Skylark (extirpated)

5. Starling
6. House Sparrow
7. Eurasian Goldfinch (extirpated)

Nonbreeders

NEARCTIC ELEMENT—72 SPECIES.

1. White Pelican
2. White-faced Ibis (also South America)
3. Whistling Swan
4. Snow Goose
5. Canvasback
6. Labrador Duck (extinct)
7. Surf Scoter
8. Bufflehead
9. Barrow's Goldeneye
10. Swainson's Hawk
11. Sandhill Crane
12. Yellow Rail
13. American Avocet
14. Semipalmated Plover
15. Long-billed Curlew
16. Eskimo Curlew (extinct?)
17. Marbled Godwit
18. Hudsonian Godwit
19. Short-billed Dowitcher
20. Long-billed Dowitcher
21. Stilt Sandpiper
22. Greater Yellowlegs
23. Lesser Yellowlegs
24. Solitary Sandpiper
25. Buff-breasted Sandpiper
26. Pectoral Sandpiper (also Siberia)
27. White-rumped Sandpiper

28. Baird's Sandpiper
29. Least Sandpiper
30. Semipalmated Sandpiper
31. Western Sandpiper
32. Wilson's Phalarope—breeds Ontario
33. Iceland Gull
34. Thayer's Gull
35. Franklin's Gull
36. Bonaparte's Gull
37. Forster's Tern—breeds New Jersey
38. Chuck-will's-widow—breeds New Jersey
39. Western Kingbird
40. Scissor-tailed Flycatcher
41. Ash-throated Flycatcher
42. Say's Phoebe
43. Brown-headed Nuthatch
44. Bewick's Wren—breeds Pennsylvania
45. Sage Thrasher
46. Varied Thrush
47. Townsend's Solitaire
48. Bell's Vireo
49. Orange-crowned Warbler
50. Black-throated Gray Warbler
51. Yellow-throated Warbler—breeds New Jersey
52. Palm Warbler—breeds Ontario
53. Connecticut Warbler

54. Wilson's Warbler
55. Yellow-headed Blackbird—breeds Ontario
56. Brewer's Blackbird—breeds Ontario
57. Boat-tailed Grackle—breeds New Jersey
58. Summer Tanager
59. Western Tanager
60. Black-headed Grosbeak
61. Painted Bunting
62. Green-tailed Towhee
63. Lark Bunting

64. LeConte's Sparrow—breeds Ontario
65. Baird's Sparrow
66. Lark Sparrow—breeds Ontario, Pennsylvania
67. Bachman's Sparrow—breeds Pennsylvania
68. Tree Sparrow
69. Harris' Sparrow
70. White-crowned Sparrow
71. Fox Sparrow
72. Chestnut-collared Longspur

HOLARCTIC ELEMENT—59 SPECIES.

1. Yellow-billed Loon
2. Arctic Loon
3. Red-throated Loon
4. Red-necked Grebe—breeds Ontario
5. Horned Grebe—breeds Ontario
6. Eared Grebe (also Africa)
7. Northern Fulmar
8. Leach's Storm Petrel—formerly bred Massachusetts
9. Brant
10. White-fronted Goose
11. Greater Scaup
12. Common Eider
13. King Eider
14. Oldsquaw
15. Harlequin Duck
16. White-winged Scoter
17. Black Scoter
18. Rough-legged Hawk
19. Gyrfalcon
20. Merlin—breeds Ontario, Quebec
21. Lesser Golden Plover
22. Black-bellied Plover
23. Whimbrel
24. Dunlin
25. Knot
26. Sanderling
27. Purple Sandpiper
28. Ruddy Turnstone
29. Red Phalarope

30. Northern Phalarope
31. Pomarine Jaeger
32. Parasitic Jaeger
33. Long-tailed Jaeger
34. Glaucous Gull
35. Sabine's Gull
36. Black-legged Kittiwake
37. Ivory Gull
38. Arctic Tern—breeds Massachusetts
39. Razorbill
40. Thick-billed Murre
41. Thin-billed Murre
42. Black Guillemot
43. Dovekie
44. Common Puffin
45. Snowy Owl
46. Hawk Owl—breeds Ontario, Quebec
47. Great Gray Owl
48. Boreal Owl
49. Black-billed Magpie
50. Northern Wheatear
51. Water Pipit
52. Bohemian Waxwing
53. Northern Shrike
54. Pine Grosbeak
55. Common Redpoll
56. Hoary Redpoll
57. White-winged Crossbill—?
58. Lapland Longspur
59. Snow Bunting

NEOTROPICAL ELEMENT—16 SPECIES.

1. Black-capped Petrel
2. Brown Pelican
3. Magnificent Frigatebird
4. Wood Stork
5. White Ibis
6. Cinnamon Teal (also western Nearctic)
7. Black Vulture (also southern Nearctic)
8. Swallow-tailed Kite
9. Purple Gallinule

10. Wilson's Plover (also eastern Nearctic)
11. Sandwich Tern (also western Palearctic)
12. Royal Tern (also West Africa)
13. White-winged Dove
14. Burrowing Owl (also western Nearctic)
15. Gray Kingbird
16. Blue Grosbeak (also southern Nearctic)—breeds New Jersey.

PALEARCTIC ELEMENT—14 SPECIES.

1. Cory's Shearwater
2. Barnacle Goose
3. Eurasian Wigeon
4. Tufted Duck
5. Smew
6. Corn Crake
7. Lapwing

8. Eurasian Curlew
9. Bar-tailed Godwit
10. Ruff
11. Curlew Sandpiper
12. Lesser Black-backed Gull
13. Black-headed Gull
14. Little Gull—breeds Ontario

PANTROPICAL ELEMENT—8 SPECIES.

1. Audubon's Shearwater
2. South Trinidad Petrel
3. Red-billed Tropicbird
4. White-tailed Tropicbird

5. Brown Booby
6. Fulvous Tree Duck
7. Sooty Tern
8. Bridled Tern

COSMOPOLITAN ELEMENT—7 SPECIES.

1. Manx Shearwater
2. Gannet
3. Great Cormorant
4. Pied or Black-necked Stilt

5. Skua
6. Gull-billed Tern
7. Caspian Tern—breeds Ontario

SOUTHERN HEMISPHERE ELEMENT—5 SPECIES.

1. Yellow-nosed Albatross
2. Sooty Shearwater
3. Greater Shearwater

4. Scaled Petrel
5. Wilson's Storm Petrel

ANALYSIS OF BREEDING LIMITS

NORTHERN ORIGIN—59 SPECIES.

A. South to the Adirondacks—22 species.
  1. Common Loon
  2. Pintail (introduced into central New York)
  3. Ring-necked Duck
  4. Common Goldeneye
  5. Golden Eagle (formerly in the Catskills?)
  6. Spruce Grouse
  7. Ring-billed Gull (Lake Ontario area)
  8. Black Tern (south to central New York)
  9. Black-backed Three-toed Woodpecker
  10. Northern Three-toed Woodpecker
  11. Gray Jay
  12. Boreal Chickadee

  13. Ruby-crowned Kinglet
  14. Philadelphia Vireo (very rare)
  15. Tennessee Warbler (very rare)
  16. Cape May Warbler (very rare)
  17. Bay-breasted Warbler
  18. Rusty Blackbird
  19. Evening Grosbeak (very rare farther south)
  20. Pine Siskin (very rare farther south)
  21. Red Crossbill (very rare farther south)
  22. Lincoln's Sparrow

B. South to the Catskills and Allegany Plateau—17 species.
  1. Green-winged Teal
  2. Common Merganser (local)

3. Goshawk
4. Yellow-bellied Sapsucker
5. Yellow-bellied Flycatcher
6. Olive-sided Flycatcher
7. Red-breasted Nuthatch (rare at lower elevations)
8. Winter Wren (rare farther south)
9. Swainson's Thrush (rare at lower elevations)
10. Gray-cheeked Thrush (absolute southern limits anywhere)
11. Golden-crowned Kinglet (rare to uncommon at lower elevations)
12. Magnolia Warbler (rare farther south)
13. Myrtle Warbler (very rare at lower elevations)
14. Black-poll Warbler
15. Mourning Warbler (also at lower elevations)
16. Slate-colored Junco (rare farther south)
17. White-throated Sparrow (rare at lower elevations)

C. South to southeastern New York mainland (chiefly higher elevations)—9 species.
1. Common Snipe
2. Passenger Pigeon (formerly)
3. Cliff Swallow
4. Solitary Vireo
5. Nashville Warbler
6. Black-throated Blue Warbler
7. Blackburnian Warbler
8. Northern Waterthrush
9. Canada Warbler (once on Long Island)

D. South to Long Island—11 species.
1. Red-breasted Merganser (rare)
2. Sora Rail (rare)
3. Great Black-backed Gull
4. Long-eared Owl
5. Saw-whet Owl (very rare)
6. Alder Flycatcher
7. Least Flycatcher
8. Brown Creeper (local)
9. Hermit Thrush
10. Rose-breasted Grosbeak
11. Purple Finch (rare)

SOUTHERN ORIGIN—49 SPECIES.

A. North to Long Island—13 species.
1. Great Egret
2. Snowy Egret
3. Little Blue Heron (rare)
4. Louisiana Heron (rare)
5. Cattle Egret (rare)
6. Yellow-crowned Night Heron
7. Glossy Ibis
8. Clapper Rail (very rare on opposite mainland)
9. Black Rail (rare)
10. Oystercatcher
11. Least Tern
12. Black Skimmer
13. Seaside Sparrow (rare on opposite mainland)

B. North to southeastern New York—3 species.
1. Fish Crow (tidewater only)
2. White-eyed Vireo
3. Kentucky Warbler (formerly)

C. North to central New York—21 species.
1. Turkey Vulture
2. Bobwhite
3. Wild Turkey
4. King Rail (rare)
5. Barn Owl
6. Red-bellied Woodpecker
7. Acadian Flycatcher (formerly)
8. Tufted Titmouse
9. Carolina Wren
10. Mockingbird
11. Blue-gray Gnatcatcher
12. Prothonotary Warbler (rare)
13. Worm-eating Warbler (eastern portion only)
14. Blue-winged Warbler
15. Cerulean Warbler
16. Prairie Warbler
17. Louisiana Waterthrush
18. Yellow-breasted Chat
19. Hooded Warbler
20. Orchard Oriole
21. Cardinal

D. North to northern New York—12 species.
1. Least Bittern
2. Common Gallinule
3. Yellow-billed Cuckoo

4. Screech Owl
5. Red-headed Woodpecker
6. Rough-winged Swallow
7. Wood Thrush
8. Yellow-throated Vireo
9. Pine Warbler
10. Towhee
11. Grasshopper Sparrow
12. Field Sparrow

WESTERN ORIGIN—7 SPECIES.

1. Gadwall
2. Baldpate
3. Shoveler
4. Lesser Scaup (very rare)
5. Willow Flycatcher
6. Western Meadowlark (very rare)
7. Clay-colored Sparrow (very rare)

SPECIES OF RESTRICTED BREEDING RANGE

Common Loon—Adirondacks
Double-crested Cormorant—eastern Lake Ontario (Gull Island)
Great Egret—Long Island
Snowy Egret—Long Island
Cattle Egret—Long Island
Little Blue Heron—Long Island
Louisiana Heron—Long Island
Yellow-crowned Night Heron—Long Island
Glossy Ibis—Long Island
Gadwall—chiefly waterfowl refuges
Pintail—chiefly waterfowl refuges
Baldpate—chiefly waterfowl refuges
Shoveler—chiefly waterfowl refuges
Green-winged Teal—chiefly waterfowl refuges
Redhead—chiefly waterfowl refuges
Lesser Scaup—Buffalo area (once)
Ring-necked Duck—Adirondacks
Common Goldeneye—Adirondacks
Common Merganser—Adirondacks, Catskills
Red-breasted Merganser—eastern Lake Ontario, Long Island
Ruddy Duck—chiefly waterfowl refuges
Golden Eagle—Adirondacks
Spruce Grouse—Adirondacks
Gray Partridge—St. Lawrence valley
Clapper Rail—Long Island
Black Rail—Long Island
Oystercatcher—Long Island
Piping Plover—Long Island, Lake Ontario
Willet—Long Island
Great Black-backed Gull—Long Island
Ring-billed Gull—Lake Ontario, Lake Champlain
Roseate Tern—Long Island

Least Tern—Long Island
Black Skimmer—Long Island
Black-backed Three-toed Woodpecker—Adirondacks
Northern Three-toed Woodpecker—Adirondacks
Yellow-bellied Flycatcher—Adirondacks, Catskills
Olive-sided Flycatcher—Adirondacks, Catskills
Gray Jay—Adirondacks
Common Raven—Adirondacks (once)
Fish Crow—Long Island, lower Hudson valley
Boreal Chickadee—Adirondacks
Gray-cheeked Thrush—Adirondacks, Catskills
Ruby-crowned Kinglet—Adirondacks
White-eyed Vireo—Long Island, lower Hudson valley
Philadelphia Vireo—Adirondacks
Prothonotary Warbler—western and central New York (very local)
Tennessee Warbler—Adirondacks
Cape May Warbler—Adirondacks
Bay-breasted Warbler—Adirondacks
Black-poll Warbler—Adirondacks, Catskills
Western Meadowlark—Monroe, Dutchess counties (once each)
Rusty Blackbird—Adirondacks
Evening Grosbeak—Adirondacks
Pine Siskin—chiefly Adirondacks
Red Crossbill—chiefly Adirondacks
Seaside Sparrow—Long Island
Sharp-tailed Sparrow—Long Island
Clay-colored Sparrow—southwestern New York (twice)
Lincoln's Sparrow—Adirondacks

TAXONOMIC TREATMENT

The recent proliferation of field guides and lavishly illustrated bird books in many parts of the world, together with the ease and speed of traveling to remote places, has aroused an exceptional interest in seeing a multitude of bird species. This has necessitated an international approach to the "Birds of New York State." Gone are the days of provincial thinking when one considered only the local list as the ultimate goal of a state bird book. Birds pay no attention to political boundaries and are free to fly from country to country. Moreover, many avian species are widespread and quite a few occur nearly throughout the world.

This brings us to the important subjects of bird names and taxonomy. In regard to taxonomy, the modern biological species concept is used throughout this book. Bird taxonomy today, like most things, is dynamic, not static. Important revisions of certain families and genera have, in the main, been followed, at times with minor modifications. All this has made it necessary to deviate somewhat from the treatment used in the American Ornithologists' Union Check-list of 1957, 5th edition (hereinafter called the A.O.U. Check-list). This is especially true at the generic and subspecific levels. Very few changes have been made at the specific level, however. Only six forms currently included in the A.O.U. Check-list as species are here merged with their presumed close relatives. Two other forms, currently included in the A.O.U. Check-list as subspecies, are here elevated to the rank of full species (see lists below). On the other hand, *52* "genera" have been merged with existing genera. Over half of these (29) consist of water birds which follow, in the main, the outdated first two volumes of Peters (1931, 1934) Check-list of the Birds of the World (hereinafter called "Peters").

For example, the A.O.U. Check-list (1957) still follows the outmoded treatment of "Peters" (1931) in using one genus apiece for each of the *11* New York heron species—or *11*

genera for *11* species! In the current state book these 11 genera are reduced to seven. A broad generic concept is, therefore, used here, following modern practice. Reasons for adopting these changes are given under the family and/or species accounts. In the family Anatidae (waterfowl) seven "A.O.U." generic names are combined with others, and in the order Charadriiformes (shorebirds, gulls, etc.) no fewer than *15* "genera" are merged. In such instances recent revisionary treatments have been followed.

To be of maximum value a genus should reflect a grouping of closely related species showing similarities in plumage pattern and coloration rather than minor external structural differences, such as presence or absence of a hind toe, or the number of rectrices, points of difference to be emphasized at the species level and not of generic significance.

The three shorebirds of the genus *Pluvialis* are similarly patterned and colored whether in breeding or nonbreeding plumage, characters that are nonadaptive and thus conservative taxonomically. The hallux or hind toe is a character that is strictly adaptive or functional and therefore of little value taxonomically. For instance, the Black-bellied Plover (*Pluvialis squatarola*) possesses the hallux, presumably as an aid in locomotion on soft, muddy terrain, whereas both the Lesser and Greater Golden plovers (*P. dominica* and *apricaria*) lack this appendage which is presumably not necessary for progressing on drier ground where these latter two species frequent.

No serious-minded taxonomist would dream of separating the Yellow-bellied Flycatcher (*Empidonax flaviventris*) into a monotypic genus merely because it nests on the ground while the three other eastern members of this genus are arboreal breeders. Nest location is, therefore, of little use at the generic level. See also reasons for placing the Wood Thrush (*Catharus mustelinus*) into the same genus with the other members, rather than treating it as monotypic (see under **Remarks** in the above species account).

Another example is that of the eleven New York species of "capped" terns. In the A.O.U. Check-list they are currently placed in four genera based mainly on differences in size and shape of bill. By reduction to a single genus (*Sterna*) similarities are stressed and minor structural differences are submerged.

Large genera, i.e., those comprising many species, are nothing new, even to the A.O.U. Check-list. The genus *Dendroica* (Wood Warblers) is a case in point. Not less than 16 species occur in New York alone and all but three of these breed in the state.

At the species level the following six New York forms are reduced to subspecies: *Branta nigricans* is merged with *B. bernicla*; *Anser hyperborea* with *A. caerulescens*; *Anas carolinensis* with *A. crecca*; *Icterus bullockii* with *I. galbula*; *Ammodramus princeps* with *A. sandwichensis*; *Junco oreganus* with *J. hyemalis*. The two New York forms elevated to species rank are: *Larus argentatus thayeri* to *L. thayeri*; *Empidonax traillii traillii* to *E. alnorum*. Reasons for the above eight changes are found in the species accounts.

As to subspecies, *57* New York races recorded in the A.O.U. Check-list are not recognized here; reasons for dropping them are found in the species accounts. Too many trivial subspecies (I call them "microsubspecies") have been named in the past and are still being described. Many are based on average differences, for instance slight color or size characters. These trivial racial names only add to an already enormously overburdened synonymy.

Amadon (1970: 10) sized up the situation correctly when he stated: ". . . only well differentiated populations [should] be admitted, that is, ones so distinct that they must be recognized in one way or another—either as races or as species."

Hale (1970: 243) speaking of clinal populations said: "There is little justification for naming any intermediate population within a cline; at most, the populations at the extremes of a cline might be named, since they have spatial [=geographical] limits." This would eliminate a large percentage of races in the A.O.U. Check-list.

A list of generic and subspecific changes from that of the A.O.U. Check-list follows:

A.O.U. genera *not* recognized

1.	*"Morus"*	= *Sula*
2.	*"Casmerodius"*	= *Egretta*
3.	*"Leucophoyx"*	= *Egretta*
4.	*"Florida"*	= *Egretta*
5.	*"Hydranassa"*	= *Egretta*
6.	*"Nyctanassa"*	= *Nycticorax*
7.	*"Olor"*	= *Cygnus*
8.	*"Chen"*	= *Anser*
9.	*"Spatula"*	= *Anas*
10.	*"Mareca"*	= *Anas*
11.	*"Oidemia"*	= *Melanitta*
12.	*"Mergellus"*	= *Mergus*
13.	*"Lophodytes"*	= *Mergus*
14.	*"Canachites"*	= *Dendragapus*
15.	*"Squatarola"*	= *Pluvialis*
16.	*"Philohela"*	= *Scolopax*
17.	*"Totanus"*	= *Tringa*
18.	*"Erolia"*	= *Calidris*
19.	*"Ereunetes"*	= *Calidris*
20.	*"Crocethia"*	= *Calidris*
21.	*"Lobipes"*	= *Phalaropus*
22.	*"Steganopus"*	= *Phalaropus*
23.	*"Catharacta"*	= *Stercorarius*
24.	*"Rissa"*	= *Larus*
25.	*"Xema"*	= *Larus*
26.	*"Gelochelidon"*	= *Sterna*
27.	*"Thalasseus"*	= *Sterna*
28.	*"Hydroprogne"*	= *Sterna*
29.	*"Pinguinus"*	= *Alca*
30.	*"Zenaidura"*	= *Zenaida*
31.	*"Columbigallina"*	= *Columbina*
32.	*"Speotyto"*	= *Athene*
33.	*"Megaceryle"*	= *Ceryle*
34.	*"Centurus"*	= *Melanerpes*
35.	*"Asyndesmus"*	= *Melanerpes*
36.	*"Dendrocopos"*	= *Picoides*
37.	*"Nuttallornis"*	= *Contopus*
38.	*"Iridoprocne"*	= *Tachycineta*
39.	*"Petrochelidon"*	= *Hirundo*
40.	*"Thryomanes"*	= *Thryothorus*
41.	*"Telmatodytes"*	= *Cistothorus*
42.	*"Ixoreus"*	= *Zoothera*
43.	*"Hylocichla"*	= *Catharus*
44.	*"Cassidix"*	= *Quiscalus*
45.	*"Richmondena"*	= *Cardinalis*
46.	*"Guiraca"*	= *Passerina*
47.	*"Hesperiphona"*	= *Coccothraustes*
48.	*"Chlorura"*	= *Pipilo*

49. *"Passerculus"*   = *Ammodramus*
50. *"Passerherbulus"* = *Ammodramus*
51. *"Ammospiza"*   = *Ammodramus*
52. *"Melospiza"*   = *Passerella*

A.O.U. subspecies *not* recognized

1. *Podiceps auritus "cornutus"*
2. *Fulmarus glacialis "minor"*
3. *Fregata magnificens "rothschildi"*
4. *Egretta tricolor "ruficollis"*
5. *Anser caerulescens "hyperboreus"*
6. *Dendrocygna bicolor "helva"*
7. *Anas discors "orphna"*
8. *Aythya affinis "nearctica"*
9. *Bucephala clangula "americana"*
10. *Oxyura jamaicensis "rubida"*
11. *Falco rusticolus "obsoletus"*
12. *Bonasa umbellus "helmei"*
13. *Dendragapus canadensis "canace"*
14. *Charadrius melodus "circumcinctus"*
15. *Capella gallinago "delicata"*
16. *Numenius americanus "parvus"*
17. *Arenaria interpres "morinella"*
18. *Larus argentatus "smithsonianus"*
19. *Sterna nilotica "aranea"*
20. *Cepphus grylle "atlantis"*
21. *Colaptes auratus "luteus"*
22. *Melanerpes carolinus "zebra"*
23. *Picoides pubescens "medianus"*
24. *Picoides pubescens "nelsoni"*
25. *Myiarchus crinitus "boreus"*
26. *Eremophila alpestris "hoyti"*
27. *Pica pica "hudsonia"*
28. *Parus hudsonicus "littoralis"*
29. *Sitta carolinensis "cookei"*
30. *Troglodytes aedon "baldwini"*
31. *Thryothorus bewickii "altus"*
32. *Cistothorus palustris "dissaeptus"*
33. *Zoothera naevia "meruloides"*
34. *Catharus guttatus "crymophilus"*
35. *Catharus ustulatus "swainsoni"*
36. *Catharus ustulatus "clarescens"*

37. *Catharus fuscescens "fuliginosus"*
38. *Catharus fuscescens "salicicola"*
39. *Lanius ludovicianus "migrans"*
40. *Dendroica petechia "amnicola"*
41. *Seiurus aurocapillus "furvior"*
42. *Seiurus noveboracensis "notabilis"*
43. *Geothlypis trichas "brachydactylus"*
44. *Setophaga ruticilla "tricolora"*
45. *Euphagus carolinus "nigrans"*
46. *Carpodacus purpureus "nesophilus"*
47. *Carpodacus mexicanus "frontalis"*
48. *Acanthis flammea "holbollii"*
49. *Acanthis flammea "islandica"*
50. *Ammodramus sandwichensis "labradorius"*
51. *Ammodramus sandwichensis "oblitus"*
*52. *Ammodramus sandwichensis "mediogriseus"*
53. *Ammodramus henslowii "susurrans"*
54. *Junco hyemalis "carolinensis"*
55. *Junco hyemalis "cismontanus"*
56. *Passerella georgiana "ericrypta"*
57. *Passerella melodia "euphonia"*

Note also that insofar as nomenclature is concerned, the following alters A.O.U. usage: Article 27 of the International Code of Zoological Nomenclature specifically prohibits the use of diaereses, umlauts, hyphens, etc.

As to vernacular name changes, only 48 species names in the present New York State list differ from existing A.O.U. names. Actually most of these are of a minor nature and involve placing modifiers before A.O.U. names. These modifiers are essential in order to distinguish different species with the same root name, such as robin. There are many kinds of robins, therefore American Robin is used here to denote the exact meaning.

Some of the above changes have already been adopted in the 32nd Supplement to the A.O.U. Check-list (*Auk*, 1973, 90: 411–419).

* Not recognized by A.O.U., but by "Peters."

TERMS AND ABBREVIATIONS

A. Biological and taxonomic

Allopatric—species ranges *separated* in breeding season.

Sympatric—species ranges *overlap* in breeding season.
Monotypic—a species *not* divided into subspecies.

Polytypic—a species divided into two or more subspecies.

Nominate—the first-named subspecies of a polytypic species.

Polymorphic—a species with two or more color or size variants (morphs).

B. Zoogeographic regions

Australasian—Australia, Tasmania, New Zealand, New Guinea, the Moluccas, and Pacific islands to the north and east.

Cosmopolitan—worldwide, or nearly so.

Ethiopian—Africa south of the Sahara; Madagascar.

Holarctic—Nearctic and Palearctic regions combined.

Nearctic—Arctic and temperate North America (including Greenland) north of tropical Mexico.

Neotropical—West Indies, and Middle and South America.

Oriental—tropical Asia and islands from India and Ceylon east to Formosa (Taiwan), the Philippines, Celebes, Lesser Sundas, etc.

Palearctic—Europe, northern Africa (including the Sahara), and arctic and temperate Asia.

C. Frequency, occurrence, and relative abundance

Very abundant—over 1000 individuals per day *per locality* (often in large flocks)

Abundant—200 to 1000 individuals per day *per locality*

Very common—50 to 200 individuals per day *per locality*

Common—20 to 50 individuals per day *per locality*

Fairly common—7 to 20 individuals per day *per locality*

Uncommon—1 to 6 individuals per day *per locality*

Rare—1 to 6 individuals per season

The above are in the regular occurrence category, i.e., reported annually.

Very rare—over 6 records, but of very infrequent occurrence

Casual—2 to 6 records

Accidental—only 1 record

The above are in the irregular occurrence category, i.e., not reported annually.

It is of paramount importance that the above be interpreted correctly. The category *"per locality"* means precisely that.

Attempts to correlate numerical abundance with such undertakings as Christmas, waterfowl, shorebird, spring, fall, and other counts are purposely omitted here, simply for the reason that the amount of area covered on these various counts is too variable and is virtually useless for *locality maxima*, although suitable enough to indicate trends.

D. Abbreviations of Museums with Important Bird Collections from New York State

AMNH—American Museum of Natural History—New York, N.Y.

BMNH—British Museum (Natural History)—formerly London (now Tring), England.

BMS—Buffalo Museum of Science—Buffalo, N.Y.

CUM—Cornell University Museum—Ithaca, N.Y.

MCZ—Museum of Comparative Zoology—Harvard University, Cambridge, Mass.

NYSM—New York State Museum—Albany, N.Y.

RMAS—Rochester Museum of Arts and Sciences—Rochester, N.Y.

USNM—United States National Museum—Washington, D.C.

E. Miscellaneous

*—Species in the following list with an asterisk after the name are based on *specimen* evidence.

B—Species in the following list with the letter B after the name are based on *breeding* evidence.

PART II

FAMILY AND SPECIES ACCOUNTS

LOONS — GAVIIDAE

Four species in New York.
One species breeds.

Appropriately called divers in the Old World, these birds are also excellent swimmers. They dive from the surface of the water for their food which is primarily fish.

The best places to see loons in numbers are the south and east shores of Long Island, especially the Montauk area, both during migration and in winter, and along Lake Ontario, particularly in the region about Rochester in spring and fall, and also on the larger inland lakes during passage.

Long Island is one of the very few places in the United States (outside of Alaska) that can boast of all four species of loons. Two of them are accidental in New York State, one is a common winter visitant, and the fourth is a local breeder.

In this exclusively Holarctic family, the two large species, Common Loon (*Gavia immer*) and Yellow-billed Loon (*G. adamsii*), are very closely related and form a superspecies. Some taxonomists even consider them to be conspecific. Their breeding ranges are essentially allopatric, the Common Loon being confined mainly to the Nearctic region, the Yellow-billed Loon breeding across northern Asia east to northwestern North America, chiefly north of the breeding range of the Common Loon.

In contrast, the two smaller species, the Arctic Loon (*G. arctica*) and the Red-throated Loon (*G. stellata*), are very distinct from each other and occur sympatrically over much of the Holarctic region. The Red-throated Loon is the most widespread of the four species, breeding nearly throughout the circumpolar regions.

Common Loon (*Gavia immer*) * B

Range: Nearctic region; Iceland. Breeds from Alaska and Canada to northern United States; in the east to the northern portions of Michigan, New York, and New England, very rarely farther south. Winters from southern Canada southward, mainly along the coast.

Status: Common to abundant migrant on larger bodies of water, both on the coast and inland, especially numerous in the Lake Ontario area; also numerous in winter at the east end of Long Island (ocean off Montauk). Common breeder in the Adirondacks and nearby region, but very rare elsewhere.

Nonbreeding: The Common Loon is, at times, a frequent sight during spring and fall passage on the Great Lakes and on the many smaller bodies of water both inland and coastwise. It is most numerous in April and November, and is regularly observed flying overhead in May. In winter, especially after severe freezes on interior waters, great numbers may be seen on the salt-water bays and inlets of Long Island and in the ocean offshore. Numbers, however, fluctuate greatly and some years very few Common Loons are reported. Summering nonbreeders are not infrequent in Long Island waters and on upstate lakes.

MAXIMA: *Inland*—275, Cayuga Lake, Nov. 9, 1969; 700, off Rochester, Nov. 18, 1967; 600, same area, Nov. 27, 1953; 550, Oneida Lake, Apr. 12, 1960; 350, Lake Ontario shore off Pultneyville, Wayne Co., Apr. 26, 1962.

MAXIMA: *Coastal*—200, off Montauk Point, Jan. 1, 1921; 300, Long Beach, Nassau Co., Apr. 11, 1933; 50, over Prospect Park, Brooklyn, May 7, 1950; 250, Jones Beach, May 20, 1950 (late for so many).

Breeding (see Map 3): Common Loons, with their wailing call, are (or were) among the most characteristic breeding birds of the Adirondack lake country. Many of the smaller lakes and ponds each had a pair of these fine birds, and only the larger lakes like George, Cranberry, and Tupper had more than a single pair, as loons are highly territorial. In more recent times, however, with the encroachment of motor boats on many of these lakes and an

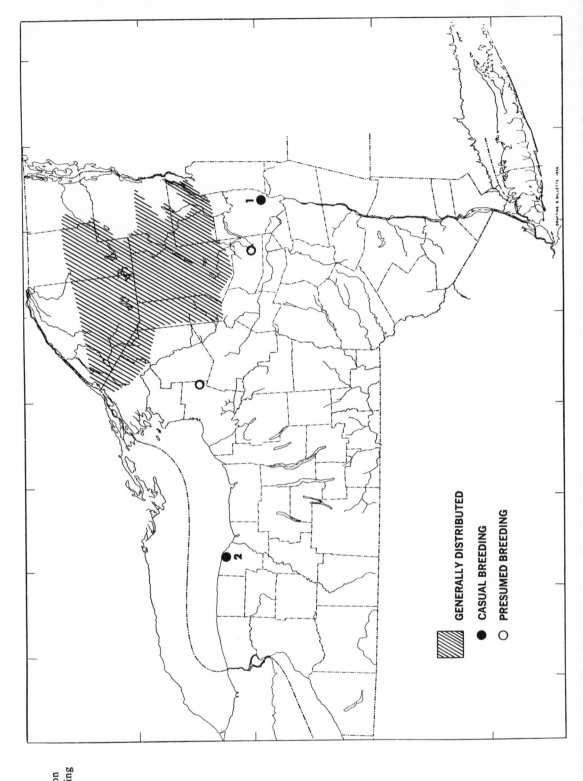

MAP 3 Common Loon
(*Gavia immer*) Breeding
distribution

GENERALLY DISTRIBUTED

● CASUAL BREEDING

○ PRESUMED BREEDING

increase of summer cottages along the shores, loons and other waterfowl have deserted for more quiet waters in wilder areas where they may nest and rear their young in relative solitude.

I have seen descriptions of only *five* New York nest sites, all in the Adirondacks: (1) on large roots of the pond lily in a lake, 100 feet from shore; (2) on sloping rocky ground partially concealed under brush three feet from the water; (3) on a boggy island; (4) on a floating nest of dead cattails; (5) on "floating" cranberry bog.

Egg clutches in 29 New York nests were invariably two. Four others contained only a single egg, but in each instance the collector or observer believed that it represented an incomplete set.

EGG DATES: May 15 to July 17 (latter may represent re-nesting because of disturbance by humans or predators, for June is more "typical").

Unfledged juveniles: June 5 to Aug. 22; fledglings: July 20 to Sept. 15.

Breeding distribution in the state is based on the various egg collections, the literature, nest record cards, and the detailed account by Arbib (1963). More than 100 breeding localities have been amassed, and there may be two or three times that number unreported, especially in little-worked areas in the Adirondack wilderness.

The center of breeding distribution is in the lake-studded counties of Franklin, Hamilton, Herkimer, and the southern half of St. Lawrence. By comparison, the largely forested mountainous counties of Essex (except the southwest portion) and Warren, with their correspondingly fewer lakes, have relatively few nesting loons. As may be seen on the map, only four localities are situated outside the Adirondack-St. Lawrence valley region, and in at least two of these breeding was suspected but not proved (Fulton and Oswego counties). Only two "extralimital" localities have details published: (1) Manning's Cove, Saratoga Lake, Saratoga Co., June 1953 (H. John), pair with one unfledged young; (2) near Shore Acres, Monroe Co., June 11, 1938 (A. Secker), pair with one young bird, "barely out of the down state." This locality is most unusual—a small pond, lying back of Lake Ontario, which was still wild and unspoiled in 1938. As for the remaining localities shown on the map in Arbib (*op. cit.*), the one on Cayuga Lake is of ancient vintage, dating back to Audubon, but whether he personally observed this supposed nesting or reported it on hearsay is not certain. The alleged breeding occurrence on Canandaigua Lake in Orleans Co. was based merely on a sighting of summering adults (Stephen Eaton, pers. comm.). Finally, the so-called nesting on Highland Lake, Orange Co., is erroneous since there were also one or two *nonbreeding*, summering individuals present, without any breeding evidence. Still another "breeding record" from Cattaraugus Co., mentioned by Beardslee and Mitchell (1965: 79), is without details. Nearly every summer Common Loons spend all or part of the season somewhere in the state, but that in itself is not proof of breeding.

Yellow-billed Loon
(*Gavia adamsii*)   *

Range: Northern Eurasia and northwestern North America, in the New World breeding east nearly to the northwest shore of Hudson Bay. The American breeding population apparently migrates west along the Arctic coast to its chief wintering grounds off the Pacific coast of Alaska.

Status: *Accidental*—the only known record in eastern North America south of Greenland (where accidental) is the remains of a specimen picked up on the beach, but only the mandible preserved; eastern Long Island, "early" 1930 (G. H. Thayer), AMNH skeletal coll. 4005. Specimen identified by Zimmer (*Auk*, 1947, 64: 145–146) and corroborated by Wetmore.

This species is so little prone to wander great distances that it is a moot question whether the above individual arrived at these shores unaided. An alternative possibility is that its carcass was carried here by strong currents.

Remarks: The Yellow-billed Loon is closely related to the Common Loon (*G. immer*).

Arctic Loon (*Gavia arctica*)   *

Range: Northern Holarctic region, but local in eastern North America, breeding south and east to Hudson Bay and southern Baffin Island. Winters commonly along the Pacific coast, the eastern American breeding population presumably migrating west to the Pacific coast. Vagrant on the Atlantic coast of Quebec, New Hampshire, and New York (Long Island).

Status: *Casual*—There is one verified record for New York, a Long Island specimen of an adult male of the race *pacifica* (smaller; in breeding plumage, throat with purplish gloss) taken at Sand's Point, Nassau Co., Apr. 29, 1893 (Merritt), AMNH 10980.

Observations of the following three individuals in breeding plumage are believed correct: (1) Montauk Point, Long Island, Mar. 30, 1941 (Helmuth); (2) Lake Ontario shore at Point Breeze, Orleans Co., Apr. 26, 1959 (Axtell); (3) Lake Ontario shore at Pultneyville, Wayne Co., May 5, 1963 (Kemnitzer).

Reports of birds in nonbreeding plumage are rejected because of difficulties in separating this species from the Red-throated Loon and small individuals of the Common Loon. Overall size and bill shape are quite variable. Even specimens have been misidentified on occasion (Bull, 1964: 72).

Remarks: Vaurie (1965: 5), and Mayr and Short (1970: 28–29) consider *arctica* and *pacifica* distinct species. Further field work in the areas where these forms meet (eastern Siberia and western Alaska) is necessary to determine their systematic relationship.

Red-throated Loon (*Gavia stellata*)   *

Range: Holarctic region, in eastern North America breeding south to James Bay, southeastern Quebec including Anticosti Island, and sporadically on the north shore of Lake Superior in south-central Ontario (Godfrey, 1966: 14). In the east winters south to the Gulf of Mexico.

Status: Common to locally abundant migrant on Lake Ontario and on the ocean; also common in winter on the ocean. Highly variable in numbers, though scarce at times. Usually rare on the smaller lakes. Very rare in summer.

Occurrence: This species sometimes outnumbers the Common Loon, and is especially numerous along the shores of Lake Ontario and off Montauk Point, Long Island. Unlike the Common Loon, however, the Red-throated Loon is seldom observed in these latitudes in breeding plumage (chestnut throat).

MAXIMA: *Coastal*—78, Montauk, Nov. 6, 1949; 100, Rockaway Point, Queens Co., Nov. 24, 1948; 480, Easthampton to Montauk, Dec. 28, 1941 (Helmuth); 75, Jones Beach, Apr. 23, 1950; *nine* in breeding plumage, Eaton's Neck, Suffolk Co. (north shore), May 15, 1936 (Cruickshank), are unusual.

MAXIMA: *Inland*—200, Hamlin, Monroe Co., Nov. 11, 1960; 500, Webster Park, Monroe Co., Apr. 14, 1952 (Kemnitzer). Unprecedented away from the Great Lakes are 150, Saratoga Lake, Nov. 18, 1962 (Schenectady Bird Club).

Eaton (1910: 104) listed specimens taken on Lake Ontario, north of Brockport, Monroe Co., June 13 and 22, 1899, and July 17, 1896. Sundell observed four on Chautauqua Lake at Dewittville, June 25–30, 1947. One in breeding plumage was seen at Southampton, Suffolk Co., June 12, 1969.

Remarks: An immature with a "very straight" bill found dead on the beach at Shinnecock Bay, Suffolk Co., Aug. 4, 1957, and now a specimen, NYSM 19012, was considered an Arctic Loon, but turned out to be a Red-throated Loon in worn plumage—a good object lesson for all as to the difficulty in identifying every individual bird seen, dead or alive.

GREBES — PODICIPEDIDAE

Four species in New York.
One species breeds.

Compared to only four species of northern hemisphere loons, the grebes are represented by 19 species found nearly throughout the world. As with the loons, the grebes are excellent divers and swimmers. Their food is more varied, the larger species being primarily fish eaters, the smaller ones more vegetarian in their diet. A curious and unique feature of this family is that its members swallow their own feathers, possibly as an aid in digestion or as a buffer against sharp fish bones.

Of the four species occurring within New York, three are Holarctic in distribution. Two of them, the Red-necked Grebe (*Podiceps grisegena*) and the Horned Grebe (*P. auritus*), winter in New York, and the latter is the most numerous grebe in the state from October through April. Horned Grebes may be seen in large numbers along the south and east shores of Long Island and upstate on Lake Ontario and on the larger inland lakes. The Eared or Black-necked Grebe (*P. nigricollis*) is more local in distribution. In North America it is confined as a breeder to the western portions. It also breeds locally in Africa, as well as in portions of Eurasia. In New York it occurs only as a rare migrant and winter visitant.

The fourth species, the Pied-billed Grebe (*Podilymbus podiceps*), breeds in New York. It is restricted to the western hemisphere, but has a broad distribution there.

Red-necked Grebe
(*Podiceps grisegena*)   *

Range: Holarctic region. The larger American race *holbollii* breeds southeast to Ontario (locally east to Burlington, near Hamilton—only 40 miles from New York). In the east winters to southern United States.

Status: Rare or uncommon to fairly common migrant and winter visitant along the coast and upstate on larger bodies of water; occasionally more numerous after severe weather. Erratic and variable in numbers.

Occurrence: The Red-necked Grebe occurs principally in March and April, and again in November and in winter depending on the amount of open water. Curiously enough, in recent years this species has been present in larger numbers upstate than on Long Island, for which I can offer no explanation. In fact during only one decade (1930–1940) has it been recorded in large numbers along the coast (see maxima below). The great irruption of February 1934 is treated separately.

MAXIMA: *Coastal*—25, Montauk Point, Dec. 31, 1936; 35, Bayville, Nassau Co. (north shore), Mar. 5, 1933; 115, Easthampton to Montauk, Apr. 7, 1940; 64, Point Lookout, Nassau Co., Apr. 11, 1939. Note lack of *fall* coastal maxima.

MAXIMA: *Inland*—30, Sandy Pond, Oswego Co., Nov. 6, 1955; during March 1959 there was a widespread flight—25, Hudson River, off New Hamburg, Dutchess Co., Mar. 6; 45, Niagara River, Mar. 22; 38, Lake Ontario, off Webster, Monroe Co., Mar. 31; also 46, off Rochester, Apr. 14, 1963.

Two late winter irruptions of this species are especially noteworthy.

(1) During the period Feb. 12 to Mar. 3, 1912, Cayuga Lake was frozen solid from end to end. At this time at the south end of the lake (Ithaca area) 28 specimens were taken, of which 11 were found alive—all stranded on the ice, unable to take off—and 17 more were found dead. All these birds were in an emaciated condition (Cahn, *Auk*, 1912, 29: 437–444).

(2) In late February 1934 with practically all fresh water ice-locked many dead and live birds were found upstate as follows: six, Seneca Lake at Geneva, Ontario Co.; ten (with ten Horned Grebes), Cayuga Lake at Ithaca; eight on the Mohawk River at Fort Plain, Montgomery Co.

(3) But the most dramatic event occurred at that time on Long Island. The following account is taken from Bull (1964: 73): "During the great winter irruption of late February 1934, when a severe freeze closed the Great Lakes, large numbers of Red-necked Grebes were reported both dead and alive along the coast of Long Island. On Feb. 22, while visiting the Montauk area, Breslau counted *225* dead —frozen carcasses—chiefly on the ocean beaches. He estimated at least another *150* alive, but in very weakened condition, including 14 waddling about on the main street of Montauk village. On the same day at Long Beach [Nassau Co.], Sedwitz saw 50 alive; also eight dead there on March 18."

The Red-necked Grebe has been recorded in the state in every month except August. Usually rare before October and after April.

Horned Grebe (*Podiceps auritus*)   *

Range: Holarctic region, in North America breeding southeast to Ontario (in 1967 sporadically southeast to Lake Simcoe—about 40 miles north of Toronto). In the east winters south to Florida.

Status: Common to abundant migrant and winter visitant along the coast and in the interior. Rare in summer.

Occurrence: The Horned Grebe is often seen in considerable numbers on the larger inland lakes, on the bays and inlets along the coast, and even on the ocean itself. It is numerous in the warmer sections of the state in the winter months and throughout the state in October, November, and April. This species is frequently observed in breeding plumage in spring.

MAXIMA: *Coastal*—250, Shinnecock and Mecox bays, Suffolk Co., Oct. 21, 1924; 1200, Montauk area, Dec. 28, 1957; 1000, Atlantic Beach to Point Lookout, Nassau Co., Mar. 8, 1959; 48, Fort Salonga, Suffolk Co. (north shore), Apr. 28, 1934; four, Jamaica Bay Refuge, summer of 1954.

MAXIMA: *Inland*—150, Rochester, Oct. 5, 1957; 350, Hamlin Beach, Monroe Co., Oct. 29, 1967; 350, Lake Ontario at mouth of Ni-

agara River, Nov. 18, 1956; 300, Saratoga Lake, Nov. 23, 1957; 350, Oneida Lake, Nov. 24, 1955; 180, Cayuga Lake, Feb. 15, 1953; 600 (about 300 each) on two lakes, about three miles apart—Bear and Cassadaga—Chautauqua Co., Apr. 19, 1962; 380, Findley Lake, also Chautauqua Co., Apr. 26, 1963.

Horned Grebes, like other water birds, are sometimes trapped at Niagara Falls and are carried to their deaths when they are swept over the cataract. Two large concentrations of these birds occurred there, the first on Apr. 21, 1949, when at least 375 were observed—300 above the falls, 75 in the gorge—of which 36 dead ones were retrieved. The second concentration was much larger; on Apr. 8, 1954, Muma estimated 700 alive in the vicinity and at least 75 dead at the foot of the cataract.

Remarks: There is no proof that the Horned Grebe has ever bred or breeds now within the state, although it has nested as near as eastern Ontario and is therefore a possibility. I found no eggs or young preserved in the many collections examined. The statements in (1) Eaton (1910: 95), (2) Beardslee and Mitchell (1965: 83–84), and (3) the *Kingbird* (1966, 16: 234) concerning alleged breeding are not substantiated by either specimen or photographic evidence. (1) The statement ". . . old birds with their young" seen on the shore of Lake Ontario is too vague to be given credence. (2) A *lone* bird seen on a pond near Westfield (Chautauqua Co.) on June 30, 1928, ". . . which behaved as though it had a nest or young nearby," is hardly proof of breeding. (3) ". . . adult with young, Lake Alice [near Chazy, Clinton Co.], late June . . . ," without details by an unknown observer is of little value. In none of these instances was there any corroboration. (4) A report of breeding in southern Saratoga Co. in 1970 and published in the *Kingbird* (1970, 20: 147) and in *Feathers* (1970, 32: 33, 48) was subsequently withdrawn and corrected in *Feathers* (1970, 32: 75). In this instance an error in identification was involved.

Subspecies: No subspecies are recognized here; the color differences in New World and Old World populations (lighter vs. darker) are of average quality only; the form "*cornutus*" is considered to be a synonym.

Eared or Black-necked Grebe
(*Podiceps nigricollis*)   *

Range: Southern Ethiopian, Palearctic, and western Nearctic regions—local throughout. In North America breeds east to southern Manitoba and central Minnesota. Winters from southern Canada to Guatemala; rarely along the Atlantic coast from Massachusetts to Florida.

Status: Rare but regular migrant and winter visitant along the coast and on the Great Lakes. This species was undoubtedly overlooked in the east until recently because of its similarity to the Horned Grebe in nonbreeding plumage.

Occurrence: In New York State the Eared Grebe was first reported from the south shore of Long Island in 1938 and again in 1941 —both observations—and a decade later, in 1948—photographs—(Bull, 1964: 74). In this last year it was seen for the first time on the Great Lakes (Beardslee and Mitchell, 1965: 85).

From 1956 on, this species has been of regular occurrence in very small numbers along the coast of Long Island, on Staten Island, and along the shores of lakes Erie and Ontario as well as in the gorge of the Niagara River. The Eared Grebe is very rare elsewhere in the state but has been reported several times from the Finger Lakes region and once from the southwestern portion (see below).

Along the coast it is most often observed at the Jamaica Bay Refuge from September to April where it has been observed each year since 1962 and where two individuals were seen on Nov. 20, 1965.

Upstate it is most frequently recorded at Niagara Falls (including two specimens—see below), on Lake Ontario in the vicinity of Rochester, and on Lake Erie between Buffalo and Dunkirk.

All of these aforementioned localities, including Long Island, are where the largest numbers of birdwatchers concentrate and undoubtedly the records reflect this. From the entire state there have been at least 70 reports through the years. During the winter of 1957–

1958 at least six were reported from various localities in the state.

EXTREME DATES: Sept. 6 (coastal) to Apr. 30 (inland specimen) and May 18 (inland).

Specimen data: Two from Niagara Falls (actually on the Ontario side)—Feb. 6, 1950 (Muma), Royal Ontario Museum 77014; Jan. 1, 1958 (Andrle), BMS 4090; one on the Allegheny River at Olean, Cattaraugus Co., Apr. 30, 1967 (Eaton), St. Bonaventure University Museum 1080. All three specimens are of the New World race *californicus* (inner primaries dusky, without white). The two from Niagara Falls were found dead at the bottom of the gorge, having come to grief (as so many water birds do) by being carried over the falls and swept to their deaths. The Olean individual, in partial breeding plumage, was collected; it was associated with seven Horned Grebes.

Still another bird was shot by a hunter on Lake Ontario at Braddock's Bay, Monroe Co., Nov. 7, 1964 (*fide* Listman), but the hunter would not relinquish the specimen.

For a photograph of a Long Island individual, see *Kingbird* (1969, 19: 2). Buckley (*Audubon Field Notes,* 1968, 22: 536–542) lists many New York occurrences.

Remarks: For use of the specific name *nigricollis* rather than *caspicus,* see Opinion 406, Intern. Comm. Zool. Nomencl. (1956, 13: 121).

[Western Grebe
(*Aechmophorus occidentalis*)

Hypothetical: Western North America, breeding east to southern Manitoba and southwestern Minnesota. Winters mainly on the Pacific coast. Accidental in eastern North America, specimens taken in eastern Ohio, western Pennsylvania, and coastal South Carolina.

No verified record of the Western Grebe exists for New York. Attempts should be made to collect or at least photograph the species.

There are at least a dozen sight reports, most of them from upstate; some with details published are probably correct.

Long Island: Suffolk Co., Acabonack and Greenport; Nassau Co., Zach's Bay and Long Beach.

Upstate New York: Lake Ontario region—Monroe Co., Rochester, Braddock's Bay, and Irondequoit Bay (2); Wayne Co., Pultneyville; other areas—Erie Co., Squaw Island (Niagara River); Yates Co., Branchport (Keuka Lake); Cayuga Co., Montezuma Marshes; Broome Co., Whitney Point Reservoir.

Dates of "occurrence" range from Oct. 25 to May 21.]

Pied-billed Grebe
(*Podilymbus podiceps*)   *   B

Range: Nearctic and Neotropical regions, ranging from Canada to Argentina, wintering nearly throughout. Sedentary and migratory.

Status: Fairly common to common fall migrant, occasionally more numerous, especially inland. Regular in winter in small numbers. Widespread breeder, locally common.

Nonbreeding: The Pied-billed Grebe is most numerous in fall. It winters in small numbers on ice-free waters and is even found on saltwater bays and inlets at that time.

MAXIMA: *Fall*—65, Shinnecock Bay, Suffolk Co., Sept. 24, 1952; 150, Montezuma Marshes, Oct. 12, 1961; 200, Oneida Lake, Nov. 13, 1955.

MAXIMA, INLAND: *Winter*—four, Niagara Falls, Jan. 2, 1950; eight, Conesus Lake, Livingston Co., Jan. 9, 1950.

Breeding: This grebe prefers quiet ponds and marshes where there is emergent shoreline vegetation, together with considerable amounts of open water. The nest is built of cattail stems or other aquatic vegetation on the water, where it is either anchored in place or free-floating.

Although somewhat secretive at this season, the species is very loquacious, its cuckoo-like notes often betraying its presence.

Egg clutches in 20 New York nests ranged from five to eight, with seven eggs found in 50% of the nests examined: five eggs (three nests); six eggs (four nests); seven eggs (ten nests); eight eggs (three nests).

EGG DATES: Apr. 21 to July 2.

Unfledged young: May 14 to Aug. 20; fledged juveniles: June 30 to Sept. 23.

Apparently double-brooded judging by the extent of dates; see also Palmer (1962: 112).

Pied-billed Grebes are fairly well distributed statewide, in suitable ponds and marshes. They are least plentiful in the higher mountains, but that may be due to lack of proper habitat, for they have been found nesting on several shallow marshy lakes in the Adirondacks. Their apparent absence in the Catskills is probably because of the prevalence of unsuitable deep-water lakes there.

Although usually from one to several pairs per locality are the norm, as many as *40* pairs were estimated at the Jamaica Bay Refuge in 1961 (Johnson), and during 1970 Clayton Hardy, refuge manager at Montezuma, estimated at least *75* pairs which produced more than *250* young.

ALBATROSSES — DIOMEDEIDAE

One species in New York.
None breed.

The inclusion of this essentially southern hemisphere family (13 species) in New York rests on the occurrence of a single individual of the Yellow-nosed Albatross (*Diomedea chlororhynchos*).

Yellow-nosed Albatross
(*Diomedea chlororhynchos*)

Range: Breeds in the Tristan da Cunha group and on Gough Island, South Atlantic Ocean; and on St. Paul Island, Indian Ocean. Vagrant in the North Atlantic Ocean; it has occurred in Quebec, New Brunswick, Maine, and off Long Island.

Status: *Accidental*—An adult, about two miles off Jones Beach, May 29, 1960, was photographed and observed by many people during a Linnaean Society pelagic trip (see Fig. 24, from AMNH collection). On this memorable date a great variety of oceanic birds was recorded, including three species each of jaegers and shearwaters, two species of petrels, and both ocean-going phalaropes (Bull, *Linnaean News-Letter,* 1960, 14: June; and Bull, *Auk,* 1961, 78: 425–426).

Fig. 24 Yellow-nosed Albatross (*Diomedea chlororhynchos*) off Jones Beach, Long Island, May 29, 1960. Photo by Joseph R. Jehl

SHEARWATERS, PETRELS — PROCELLARIIDAE

Nine species in New York.
None breed.

Members of this worldwide family (50± species) and the following subfamily (Hydrobatinae, 20± species) are sometimes the victims of hurricanes and are carried far inland by such storms, as well as to the ocean beaches or in the vicinity of marine estuaries, salt bays, coastal ponds, and tidal lagoons. Occasionally they have been caught alive exhausted and/or emaciated after having been buffeted about by powerful winds and unable to obtain food. At other times they have succumbed to the elements and been found dead.

The various species can and do originate

from the far corners of the globe and several species recorded in New York State as accidentals do not appear in the North American field guides. In addition, some of the species resemble one another and are among the most difficult of birds to identify in the *hand* and quite impossible to differentiate in the field. It is therefore of paramount importance that individuals of these families be saved for proper identification and forwarded to a *large* museum with adequate comparative material for determination. The American Museum of Natural History in New York City is the only museum in the state which has large series of these pelagic birds.

The great tropical storm of Aug. 22, 1933, resulted in a number of great rarities being found far inland. Most notable were specimens of the Black-capped Petrel (*Pterodroma hasitata*) and the only known North American record of the South Trinidad or Herald Petrel (*P. arminjoniana*). In addition, more than twenty Leach's Storm Petrels (*Oceanodroma leucorhoa*) were found upstate. Also reported after this storm, but not in New York, was a specimen of the Band-rumped or Harcourt's Storm Petrel (*O. castro*) picked up to the north of us in Ontario. This species and Leach's Storm Petrel are siblings; they are virtually impossible to distinguish from each other except in the hand. One should therefore not assume every petrel of this genus found after a storm to be Leach's Storm Petrel.

The following three members of the order Procellariiformes have *not* been recorded in New York on the basis of specimen evidence but are distinct possibilities in the future: (1) The aforementioned Harcourt's Storm Petrel, to the north and south in Ontario and Pennsylvania; (2) the Little Shearwater (*Puffinus assimilis*), recorded from Nova Scotia and South Carolina; this form has been treated as conspecific with Audubon's Shearwater (*P. lherminieri*) which has occurred in New York; (3) the White-faced Storm Petrel (*Pelagodroma marina*), recorded at sea 100 miles southeast of Montauk Point.

On the other hand, the three large and numerous shearwaters of the genus *Puffinus*, as well as the at-times-abundant little Wilson's Storm Petrel (*Oceanites oceanicus*), may be observed during the warmer months from fishing boats operating in offshore waters, south

and east of Long Island. Frequent pelagic trips are really the only way for one to become better acquainted with these interesting birds.

For a recent paper on the distribution and taxonomy of these birds, see Bourne (1971).

Northern Fulmar
(*Fulmarus glacialis*)   *

Range: Northern Holarctic region, in North America breeding south to northern Baffin Island; winters south to the Grand Banks off Newfoundland, very rarely to the fishing banks off Massachusetts. Vagrant to Ontario, New York, Connecticut, and New Jersey (specimens). Godfrey (1966: 21) lists four inland occurrences for southeastern Canada.

Status: *Casual*—There is one substantiated record for New York State: the remains of a specimen of the light morph, found on the Lake Ontario shore, near the mouth of Catfish Creek, New Haven Township, Oswego Co., Oct. 3, 1971 (P. Merritt), identified by Chris Spies; specimen preserved as a skeleton, AMNH 7838, identification confirmed by the writer.

In addition there are three observations believed correct, all from Long Island: (1) off Mecox Bay, Suffolk Co., Oct. 3, 1930 (Helmuth); (2) Rockaway Point, Queens Co., Oct. 13, 1937 (Mayer); (3) off Riis Park, Queens Co., Nov. 4, 1961 (Mayer and Rose).

Remarks: Closely related to the Southern Fulmar (*F. glacialoides*) of the subantarctic region. No North Atlantic subspecies other than nominate *glacialis* is recognized here (Bull, 1964: 77); the poorly differentiated form, "*minor,*" is considered to be a synonym.

Sooty Shearwater (*Puffinus griseus*)   *

Range: Pelagic in the nonbreeding season, breeding on islands in the southern hemisphere, chiefly in two main areas—Australia-New Zealand and southern South America. The latter populations are presumably those birds from the Falklands and the Cape Horn region that range north after the breeding season through the western Atlantic to the northeastern coast of North America, and then in late summer or early fall move out to sea toward the eastern Atlantic.

Status: Regular late spring and early summer visitant off Long Island, occasionally very common-to-abundant at the east end. Unknown elsewhere.

Occurrence: The Sooty Shearwater, unlike the other two common large species, is most numerous in our waters soon after its arrival in May. Of the three, it is certainly the most prevalent close inshore. It is apparently relatively scarce after June, as numbers decrease markedly.

MAXIMA: 50, Easthampton, May 23, 1937; 250, same locality, June 2, 1928 (Helmuth). Other maxima, also first week of June, various years: 350, Easthampton to Montauk, 1939; 280, Moriches to Shinnecock, 1955; 300, including one flock of 160, between Moriches and Mecox bays, 1957; also 25, off Easthampton, Aug. 20, 1913. All localities are in eastern Suffolk Co.

EXTREME DATES: May 11 to Oct. 24. Rare before late May and after mid-September.

Greater Shearwater (*Puffinus gravis*) *

Range: Pelagic in the nonbreeding season, breeding only in the South Atlantic Ocean on the Tristan da Cunha Islands and on Gough Island; also in 1961 in the Falkland Islands (*Ibis,* 1970, 112: 259–260). Ranges north and west after the breeding season through the western Atlantic to the northeastern coast of North America, then migrating eastward in fall toward the eastern Atlantic.

Status: Regular summer visitant off Long Island, occasionally common at the east end. Unknown elsewhere.

Occurrence: This species, like the other two common large shearwaters, is seen to best advantage from the deck of a boat. These shearwaters, and petrels as well, may be attracted alongside the boat by throwing out fish oil and fish scraps which the birds devour ravenously. At such close quarters the differing field marks and habits of the various species may be observed readily. Less satisfactory are observations from the beaches where these birds are

sometimes driven after storms. The Greater Shearwater is the least common of the three large shearwaters inshore, at least in our waters.

MAXIMA: All Suffolk Co., except Jones Beach—14, Jones Beach, May 1, 1965 (also the earliest arrival date); 20, Easthampton, May 23, 1937; 50, Jones Beach, June 8, 1957; 150, Moriches-Shinnecock area, June 9, 1957; 150, off Montauk, Sept. 1, 1968 (Kleinbaum); 100, off Mecox Bay, Sept. 23, 1918 (Helmuth).

EXTREME DATES: May 1 and May 4 to Nov. 6. Usually rare before late May and after early October.

A dead specimen (in fresh condition) was found on the beach at Point O'Woods, Fire Island, Suffolk Co., Dec. 1, 1969 (Hopkins), AMNH collection. It is the latest record by more than three weeks.

Cory's Shearwater (*Puffinus diomedea*) *

Range: Southwestern Palearctic region (for details see **Subspecies**). Whereas the Sooty and Greater shearwaters breed in the southern hemisphere, Cory's Shearwater is a species of warm-temperate waters in the eastern Atlantic and Mediterranean.

Status: Common to abundant late summer and fall visitant off eastern Long Island; usually much less numerous off the western end. Unknown elsewhere.

Occurrence: This species disperses westward into the Atlantic Ocean in late summer after the breeding season and occurs in large numbers in our waters. It may be seen from the beaches, especially after storms but, like other shearwaters and petrels, is best observed to advantage from a boat offshore. At certain times very large flocks are encountered.

MAXIMA: Unless otherwise stated, all figures are taken from Helmuth (diary) at Montauk Point—120, July 6, 1939; 300, Aug. 27, 1936; 500, Sept. 8, 1936; 750, Oct. 11, 1936; 300, Nov. 6, 1949; 200, Nov. 13, 1949; 30, Nov. 20, 1949. Note that 1936 was a big year for this species and that in 1949 there was a large, *late* flight. Most exceptional were 435 within one hour seen off Jones Beach, Oct. 16,

1966 (Davis and Houston). Ordinarily only small numbers are recorded so far west. Still farther west, 20 were observed south of Ambrose lightship (outside of New York harbor), Aug. 27, 1962, and five specimens were collected there on Sept. 9, 1918 (Murphy). Also unusual were 150, Orient Point, Suffolk Co., Oct. 17, 1969 (Raynor).

EXTREME DATES: Exceptionally early— May 29 and June 5; June 26 to Nov. 29 (specimen) and Dec. 1. Rare before July and after mid-November.

Subspecies: The larger race *borealis*, discussed above, breeds on islands in the eastern Atlantic (Azores, Madeira, Canaries, etc.). Nominate *diomedea* is smaller and breeds to the east in the Mediterranean region. This latter subspecies is accidental in North American waters where it is known only from Long Island, specimens having been taken as follows: two, Jones Beach, Oct. 4, 1902 (Chichester), AMNH; two, Montauk Point, Aug. 15, 1907 (Braislin collection), AMNH; one found dead at Montauk Point, Sept. 22, 1938, after the great hurricane (Helmuth), specimen formerly in his collection. All five specimens were identified by Murphy.

Remarks: Palmer (1962) and Vaurie (1965) use *Calonectris* and *Procellaria* respectively as the generic names for this species. The A.O.U. Check-list (1957) is followed here.

Manx Shearwater
(*Puffinus puffinus*)   *

Range: Western Palearctic region; also islands off the Pacific coast of Mexico; and in the Hawaiian Archipelago, and off New Zealand. Banded birds from Wales have been recovered at various points in the South Atlantic along the coasts of Brazil and Argentina. At least three specimens have been taken in Massachusetts, but only one in New York.

Status: *Accidental*—One specimen record from Long Island—found dead after a storm, Ocean Beach, Fire Island, Suffolk Co., Aug. 30, 1917 (Thurston), AMNH 349273.

A bird observed and color-photographed off Jones Beach, May 27, 1962 (N. Levine and P. Post), was probably but not positively this species according to Murphy (Bull, 1964: 80). More frequent observations from boats off-

Fig. 25 Bird identified as a Manx Shearwater (*Puffinus puffinus*) Cox's Ledge, east of Montauk Point, Long Island, Sept. 23, 1972. Photo by Peter Alden

shore might indicate that this species is not so rare as was formerly believed (see discussion under Audubon's Shearwater).

I have examined a black-and-white print (see Fig. 25) of a bird identified as a Manx Shearwater taken from a boat off Cox's Ledge, east of Montauk Point, Sept. 23, 1972 (Alden). Although one of the field marks, indeed a character that can be seen in the hand, is of white undertail coverts, the picture here seems to show that of a *dark* area under the tail. This is a feature of Audubon's Shearwater. I am still convinced that the two forms are difficult to identify in the field, except under the most favorable circumstances.

Audubon's Shearwater
(*Puffinus lherminieri*) *

Range: Pantropical, breeding chiefly on oceanic islands nearly throughout the world. In the western North Atlantic breeds north to the Bahamas and Bermuda. Wanders north to Long Island; once to Martha's Vineyard, Massachusetts.

Status: *Casual*—There are five specimen records in New York, all from Long Island: (1) Great South Bay, off Bellport, Suffolk Co., Aug. 1, 1887 (Dutcher collection), AMNH 64714; (2) one found dead, Point Lookout, Nassau Co., July 24, 1938 (Lind and Rorden), AMNH 4110, preserved as a skeleton; (3 and 4) two found dead in 1951 in Suffolk Co. (Costich), one at Dix Hills, July 31, AMNH 6590, preserved as a skeleton, the other at Cedar Beach, Sept. 4, specimen in the Nassau County Museum; (5) one found alive, but in weakened condition, died same day, Fire Island, opposite Blue Point, Suffolk Co., July 28, 1967 (Kessler), AMNH 788362.

An individual observed and photographed just off Oakwood Beach, Staten Island, Aug. 14, 1955 (Redjives)—two days after hurricane "Connie"—was probably but not positively this species according to Murphy (Bull, 1964: 80).

Remarks: The field identification of small black-and-white shearwaters is difficult as to species. Relative size and critical color charac-

ters of the two species (*puffinus* and *lherminieri*) are often virtually impossible to observe satisfactorily at even fairly close range (Gordon, 1955: 140, 147; Griscom and Snyder, 1955: 23). Even a third form (species?), *P. assimilis,* the Little Shearwater, is a possibility. Considerable doubt remains as to the correctness of the observations listed in Post (1964, 1967). Even the photographs published by him are probable, not positive, identifications (Bull, *op. cit.*).

Vaurie (1965: 28–29) considers *P. lherminieri* and *P. assimilis* to be conspecific.

Black-capped Petrel
(*Pterodroma hasitata*) *

Range: West Indies, breeding or formerly breeding on certain islands of the Greater Antilles; has been very rare for many years. In 1961 rediscovered breeding in the mountains of Hispaniola. Recorded principally after hurricanes north to Ontario, New Hampshire, Connecticut, and New York (all specimens).

Status: *Casual*—There are five specimen records for New York: (1) Quogue, Suffolk Co., Long Island, July 1850 (Lawrence collection), AMNH 46145; (2) Verona Beach, Oneida Lake, Aug. 28, 1893 (Biederman), AMNH 458986; (3) Cayuga Co., September 1893 (Foster), AMNH 98754 (Murphy, 1936: 693)—I have not been able to locate this specimen; (4) New Paltz, Ulster Co., Jan. 26, 1895 (Vradenburgh), mounted specimen examined by Foster and formerly in a private collection (*Auk,* 1895, 12: 179), but present whereabouts not known. The date is remarkable. This individual was found *alive* in the snow in an exhausted condition; (5) Adult male, near Owego, Tioga Co. [not near Endicott, Broome Co., as stated in the *Auk* (1940, 57: 244)], Aug. 26, 1933 (Loomis), CUM 5838. This specimen was found exhausted after the storm of Aug. 22, the same storm that "brought" *P. arminjoniana* (see account under that species).

Remarks: Murphy (verbal comm.) considers *hasitata* to be in the same superspecies with *externa,* the White-necked Petrel, and *phaeo-*

pygia, the Dark-rumped Petrel, but *not* with *cahow,* the Bermuda Petrel (*contra* his opinion in 1936: 697). However, Palmer (1962: 203–209) treats all four forms as conspecific.

Scaled or Mottled Petrel
(*Pterodroma inexpectata*)   *

Range: Breeds in New Zealand and on nearby islands, in recent years in considerably reduced numbers; in the nonbreeding season ranges eastward and northward through the Pacific Ocean to at least the Aleutian Islands (rarely).

Status: *Accidental*—One specimen record: Mt. Morris, Livingston Co., early April 1880 (Smith), MCZ collection 205224 (*fide* Paynter). "One of the laborers while ploughing an old cornfield, noticed it [the petrel] running in a freshly turned furrow and despatched it with a stick. It was apparently exhausted, for it made no attempt to escape." (Brewster, *Bull. Nuttall Ornith. Club,* 1881, 6: 91–97). An illustration of the mounted specimen of this most unexpected occurrence is found in Eaton (1910: 161).

South Trinidad or Herald Petrel
(*Pterodroma arminjoniana*)   *

Range: Pantropical, breeding on oceanic islands south of the Equator in the Atlantic, Indian, and Pacific oceans; in the South Atlantic off the Brazilian coast on South Trinidad Island.

Status: *Accidental*—The only known occurrence in North America is that of an individual of the light morph, found alive, but exhausted, near Caroline Center, Tompkins Co., after the hurricane of Aug. 22, 1933 (Westfall). The specimen, a male, died a few days later and is now in the USNM collection, 348070. This tropical storm also "transported" *P. hasitata* (see that species). This hurricane struck the North Carolina coast at Cape Hatteras, then continued north through Maryland and Pennsylvania to the Finger Lakes region and along the St. Lawrence valley (Allen, 1934: 134–135).

Remarks: This species and the closely related *P. neglecta,* the Variable or Kermadec Petrel, are highly polymorphic, ranging from all dark to very light populations throughout their wide ranges. The two forms must be examined in the hand to be certain of proper identification (Murphy and Pennoyer, 1952).

STORM PETRELS — HYDROBATINAE

Two species in New York.
None breed.

For discussion, see family Procellariidae. The storm petrels, containing 20± species with a nearly worldwide distribution, differ from the shearwaters and "typical" petrels by having a *single* tube atop the bill, instead of double tubes. This difference is here considered to be only of subfamilial distinction, following several recent authorities.

Leach's Storm Petrel
(*Oceanodroma leucorhoa*)   *

Range: North Atlantic and Pacific regions, breeding on offshore islands; in the western Atlantic locally south to Maine (no longer breeding on Penikese Island, Mass.—*fide* Greenway). Winters from tropical seas southward.

Status: Very rare visitant inshore, perhaps regular offshore, but status not well known. Vagrant inland.

Occurrence: There are over 70 reports of Leach's Storm Petrel within the state, many of the individuals found dead or seen alive after storms. For instance, after the hurricane of Aug. 22, 1933, numerous individuals were reported but, interestingly enough, all upstate. No fewer than 20 were picked up dead along the shore of Oneida Lake at Sylvan Beach, Oneida Co., from Sept. 7 to Sept. 30, 1933 (Sadler), all of these specimens identified as this species by Murphy (*Bird-Lore,* 1933, 35: 320). Also shortly after this storm, three individuals were observed: (1) Catlin Lake, near Newcomb, Hamilton Co.; (2) Poland, Herkimer Co.; (3) Niskayuna, Schenectady Co. Another inland occurrence, also the result of a storm, was that of an individual seen flying over Otsego Lake, near Cooperstown, Otsego Co., Nov. 26, 1950 (Hill), the day after the severe tempest of Nov. 25. This is also the latest fall occurrence (see below).

As mentioned elsewhere (Bull, 1964: 81–82), this species is active at night, several specimens having hit lighthouses. Further proof of nocturnal activity is provided by two individuals caught in mist nets at night and banded on Great Gull Island, Suffolk Co. (eastern Long Island), Aug. 4 and 6, 1967 (Cooper).

Another very recent record from Long Island is that of a freshly dead individual picked up at Westhampton Beach, Suffolk Co., July 3, 1965 (Davis), specimen in AMNH collection.

For additional records from the New York City region, see Bull (*op. cit.*). Six old occurrences from the upper Hudson valley were summarized by Eaton (1910: 164).

MAXIMA, OFFSHORE: 12, off Montauk, Oct. 1, 1932 (Helmuth); four, off Jones Beach, May 29, 1960 (Linnaean Society pelagic trip).

EXTREME DATES: May 4 (coastal specimen) to Nov. 13 (inland specimen) and Nov. 26 (inland observation—see above).

Remarks: This species can be confused easily with Wilson's Storm Petrel in the field and extreme caution is urged in identification.

Even more critical and of great importance is the finding of a dead specimen. It should not be assumed that every petrel found will turn out to be Leach's or Wilson's. All individuals should be sent to a large museum like the American Museum of Natural History for identification. For example, the Band-rumped or Harcourt's Storm Petrel (*Oceanodroma castro*), a pantropical species not as yet recorded from New York, although taken in Ontario and Pennsylvania, is virtually identical in appearance to Leach's Storm Petrel and must be compared directly with a large series of museum skins for correct determination.

Wilson's Storm Petrel
(*Oceanites oceanicus*) *

Range: Antarctic and sub-Antarctic zones, breeding north to islands off southern South America. After the breeding season ranges north in the Atlantic Ocean to Labrador.

Status: Variously uncommon to very abundant summer visitant off Long Island; in recent years rarely reported in the bays and harbors, or from the beaches, except after storms. Vagrant inland.

Occurrence: The best way to see Wilson's Storm Petrels is to board a fishing boat and spend time "chumming" well offshore. With luck, numbers ranging from a few individuals to hundreds may be enticed close to the boat by the odoriferous lure. Here these birds, as well as other pelagic species, may be studied to advantage (see Fig. 26). However, sometimes none may be seen, no matter how much "chumming" is done. This species is equally unpredictable as to time of arrival and numbers recorded. At times hundreds may be observed soon after arrival in late May or early June. At other times Wilson's Storm Petrels may not be reported until July or even August and then estimated in the "many thousands."

EXTREME DATES: May 18 to Oct. 22 (specimen). Rare after mid-September.

This species is apparently much rarer inland, at least upstate, than Leach's Storm Petrel, judging from the few records, and these all after storms. In fact, I am aware of only three reliable records from the interior of the state: (1) a specimen found dead at Lockport, Niagara Co., October 1875 (Davison collection), BMS 6386, was probably carried there by the tropical storm of Oct. 10–13, 1875, "originating" in Puerto Rico; (2) another specimen was captured alive at Lake Titus, Franklin Co.,

Fig. 26 Wilson's Storm Petrels, Lower New York Bay, Aug. 9, 1914. Photo by Howard H. Cleaves

Aug. 26, 1933 (Hale), NYSM 5261, undoubtedly the result of the Aug. 22 hurricane; (3) one well observed in Lake Ontario, off Charlotte, Monroe Co., Sept. 25, 1938 (Meade), after the great hurricane of Sept. 21.

The specimen mentioned by Eaton (1910: 165) from Monroe Co. in November 1882 is apparently not extant nor did Eaton presumably examine it; November is very late for this species. Leach's Storm Petrel is more likely.

TROPICBIRDS — PHAETHONTIDAE

Two species in New York.
None breed.

Two of the three world species have occurred on Long Island. Collectively they are pantropical in distribution and, like other warm water species in the Order Pelecaniformes, have for the most part occurred on our shores only after hurricanes. The two species, White-tailed Tropicbird (*Phaethon lepturus*) and Red-tailed Tropicbird (*P. aethereus*), are merely vagrants in our area.

Red-billed Tropicbird
(*Phaethon aethereus*)   *

Range: Pantropical, the race *mesonauta* (primary coverts blackish; grayish in nominate race) breeding locally in the Lesser Antilles north to the Virgin Islands. In the nonbreeding season ranges widely in the Caribbean Sea and tropical Atlantic, occasionally north as far as the Bahamas. The report off the Newfoundland Grand Banks (A.O.U. Check-list, 1957: 27) is considered unsatisfactory (Bull, 1964: 83).

Status: *Accidental*—The only known occurrence for continental eastern North America is a Long Island specimen record: Immature female found dead along the shore of Bergen Beach, Jamaica Bay, Kings Co., June 10, 1963 (Lynch), AMNH 776556. This vagrant was very likely carried to Long Island by the tropical storm of June 4 that had originated south of the Bahamas two days previously (Bull, *Auk,* 1964, 81: 433–434).

White-tailed Tropicbird
(*Phaethon lepturus*)   *

Range: Pantropical, the race *catesbyi* (primaries with black more extensive than in other races) breeding north to the Bahamas and Bermuda. Recorded as a vagrant north to New York, Massachusetts, and Nova Scotia.

Status: *Casual*—In New York State there have been six occurrences after hurricanes, five of them specimen records: (1) Immature, Knowlesville, Orleans Co., Sept. 19, 1876 (Langille), mounted specimen in exhibition collection, NYSM. This specimen was found alive, but exhausted, in a field after the hurricane of Sept. 18. The great hurricane of Sept. 21, 1938, produced all of the Long Island occurrences: (2) One observed flying over Jones Beach, Sept. 25 (Brennan, Tengwall, and Russell); (3, 4, and 5) Specimens found dead (all by Helmuth, formerly in his collection)— two, Easthampton, Sept. 22 and Oct. 3, and the remains of another at Montauk, Jan. 1, 1939. (6) An immature was found dead on the Lake Ontario shore near Ellisburg, Jefferson Co., Oct. 26, 1954 (Belknap), NYSM 17046, following the hurricane of Oct. 15.

PELICANS — PELECANIDAE

Two species in New York.
None breed.

Of the seven pelican species found in the world, all of the "white" ones feed chiefly from the surface of the water. Only the Brown Pelican (*Pelecanus occidentalis*) regularly obtains its food by diving from the air into the water. The former birds are restricted mainly to inland fresh-water areas, at least during the breeding season, whereas the latter is exclusively a salt-water species found only along the American coasts. The Brown Pelican and the American White Pelican (*P. erythrorhynchos*) are vagrants to the state.

American White Pelican
(*Pelecanus erythrorhynchos*)   *

Range: Western North America, breeding east to southwestern Ontario; winters east to the Gulf states, commonly in southwestern

Florida. Wanders rarely in migration to the Atlantic states.

Status: *Very rare*—In New York State the White Pelican has been recorded at least 25 times, mostly from Long Island, seven from upstate. Eaton (1910: 174) listed eleven occurrences, all specimen records, but only one appears to be extant: Roslyn, Nassau Co., May 11, 1885 (West), AMNH 11579. In recent years two more have been taken, one of which is extant: one was illegally shot and found dead on the shore of Lake Ontario at Shore Acres, Monroe Co., Apr. 22, 1945, NYSM 6468; the other was found dead near the shore of Pine Lake, Fulton Co., Sept. 23, 1955 (Richelieu), and photographed (*Conservationist,* 1956, 10: 45).

Usually only one individual is recorded, but on occasion more are observed. The following occurrences are noteworthy: flock of six, Shelter Island, Suffolk Co., Oct. 12, 1926 (Worthington); three, Stafford's Pond, Oak Orchard

Swamp, Genesee Co., Apr. 27–30, 1950 (Pixley and many others), and probably the same three were observed later on Lake Ontario near Rochester, May 1 (*fide* Taylor); six, on Lake Ontario, off Shore Acres, Monroe Co., Mar. 28, 1954 (Taylor and Conway, *Goshawk*, 1954, 7: 40–41).

EXTREME DATES: Mar. 28 (exceptionally early) and Apr. 22 to May 20; Sept. 2 to Nov. 13. The different summering individuals are believed to have been escapes.

Brown Pelican
(*Pelecanus occidentalis*)   *

Range: Nearctic and Neotropical regions, locally distributed—on the Pacific coast from California to Chile, on the Gulf and Atlantic coasts from South Carolina to Venezuela and the Guianas.

Status: *Very rare*—In New York this species has been recorded on Long Island at least nine times (Bull, 1964: 8, and 1970: 3), including a flock of four, Jones Inlet, Nassau Co., Sept. 7, 1954 (Bull), after hurricane "Carol" of Aug. 31, and a flock of five off the beach at Fire Island, opposite Bellport, Suffolk Co., July 6, 1962 (Alperin).

Dates range from May 10 to Sept. 12, exceptionally to Nov. 3. Most interesting is a nestling banded at Mosquito Lagoon, near Titusville, Florida, Sept. 7, 1941, and found dead at Fort Terry (=Plum Island), Suffolk Co., May 4, 1943 (*Florida Nat.*, 1944, 18: 33). The disposition of this specimen was not stated.

Brown Pelicans have occurred inland on at least two occasions: one was found alive, but exhausted, emaciated, and with one leg injured, Richland, Oswego Co., Dec. 21, 1920 (Pirnie, *Auk*, 1921, 38: 597). The present whereabouts of this specimen, formerly in the NYSM collection, is unknown. Another individual was observed on the Niagara River from June 20 to June 26, 1950 (Lyon, Seeber, Wright, *et al.*); presumably the same bird was seen at Hanford Bay, Lake Erie, July 2, 1950 (several observers).

This species is undergoing intensive study for pesticide residues found in eggs. Contamination in California is especially high resulting in few young hatching. Breeding colonies in Florida are also being investigated.

Subspecies: The race *carolinensis* of the Atlantic and Gulf coasts of the United States is larger than nominate *occidentalis* of the West Indies.

BOOBIES — SULIDAE

Two species in New York.
None breed.

All members of this family (seven species) are fish eaters and secure their food by diving, sometimes from spectacular heights. Those species called boobies—only one, the Brown Booby (*Sula leucogaster*), occurring in our area as an accidental visitant—are characteristic of tropical regions. The one species of Gannet (*S. bassana*) is, on the other hand, a representative of temperate areas. Impressive numbers of Gannets may be seen from time to time in the ocean waters off Long Island.

Although the Gannet is often placed in a separate genus (*Morus*), as by Palmer (1962), the morphological differences from *Sula* are those of degree and are relatively slight. The treatment of combining them into *Sula* is adopted by Vaurie (1965) and by Mayr and Short (1970). At the species level, all three authorities (*op. cit.*) combine the North Atlantic population of the Gannet with the two southern hemisphere representatives (South Africa, Australia) into a single species, the only marked differences in the three forms being varying amounts of black and white in the tail and wings. See especially Broekhuysen, *et al.* (*Ostrich*, 1954, 25: 19–22, and 1961, 31: 14–15).

Brown Booby (*Sula leucogaster*)   *

Range: Pantropical, breeding north to the Bahamas. Vagrant after hurricanes north to Massachusetts (specimen).

Status: *Casual*—There is one confirmed record for New York, an immature taken on Moriches Bay, Long Island, "many years ago." This specimen, examined by Dutcher, was formerly in the collection of the Long Island Historical Society. Its present whereabouts is unknown.

Two sight reports on Long Island by experienced observers are believed correct: (1) two seen off the beach at Mecox Bay, Sept. 2, 1936 (Helmuth), following a Florida hurricane; (2) one off Moriches Inlet, Sept. 3, 1949 (Mayer and Rose), after the hurricane of Aug. 29.

Gannet (*Sula bassana*)   *

Range: Three widely separated populations, one northern and two southern hemisphere (see **Remarks**). North Atlantic Ocean—in the Palearctic region (Iceland, British Isles, etc.) and in the Nearctic region with an extremely limited breeding distribution (Newfoundland and islands in the Gulf of St. Lawrence). American birds winter south to Florida, very rarely in the Gulf of Mexico.

Status: Common to abundant migrant off the south shore of Long Island, less numerous in winter, and rare but perhaps regular in summer. Extremely rare anywhere else in the state.

Occurrence: Gannets are most numerous off Montauk Point. Elsewhere they are seen to best advantage on the ocean from fishing boats and from the beaches during onshore winds. Often they may be observed diving from considerable heights into the sea for fish. Peak numbers occur from late October to early December and from late March to mid-May.

MAXIMA: *Fall*—150 in one hour, Jones Beach, Oct. 16, 1966; 500, Montauk Point, Oct. 28, 1924; 800, Montauk Point, Nov. 3, 1963; 300, Montauk region, Dec. 8, 1944.

MAXIMA: *Winter*—220, Easthampton to Montauk, Dec. 31, 1949; 125, Montauk, Feb. 7, 1937.

MAXIMA: *Spring*—300 in one half-hour, off Mecox Bay, Apr. 16, 1953; 200 (only four adults), Jones Beach, May 15, 1949; 150 (mostly immatures), Jones Beach, May 20, 1950; 30, Moriches, May 30, 1956.

Summering individuals (usually immatures) make it difficult to give "extreme" dates but the species is generally rare before September and after May. Pelagic trips in the summer months usually turn up one or more each season. Two adults were found dead on eastern Suffolk Co. beaches: one at Easthampton, July 4, 1936 (Helmuth); the other at Westhampton, July 13, 1949 (Staniford), specimen in AMNH collection.

The Gannet is extremely rare inland. As far as known all inland records are of immature birds. A few have been driven by strong gales to inshore waters, such as Long Island Sound and the lower Hudson River, but occasionally immatures are reported from upstate, particularly in the vicinity of the Great Lakes. Beardslee and Mitchell (1965: 92–93) list a dozen or more observations, especially on Lake Ontario, west of Rochester, with a maximum of six off Charlotte pier, Monroe Co., Oct. 19, 1947, and three or four more the same day, west to the mouth of the Niagara River, but these numbers are most exceptional.

There are three specimens from upstate, but only one is apparently extant: (1) one caught alive in an exhausted condition from the Grasse River near Canton, St. Lawrence Co., Dec. 10, 1879 (Lee); (2) one collected on Saratoga Lake, Nov. 11, 1880 (Rich); (3) one taken alive at Le Roy, Genesee Co., Dec. 15, 1962 (Sporer), BMS 5086.

Banding: Four nestlings banded on Bonaventure Island, Quebec, were found dead at the following Long Island localities:

Date banded	Date recovered	Locality recovered
Sept. 2, 1924	Dec. 16, 1933	Rockaway Beach
Sept. 11, 1950	Oct. 15, 1951	near Amagansett
Sept. 16, 1961	Nov. 1, 1963	Westhampton Beach
Sept. 21, 1962	May 14, 1963	Jones Beach

Note that the Gannet is a late nester with young still unfledged well into September. Note also that No. 1 above was more than nine years old when recovered.

Remarks: Both Vaurie (1965: 44) and Mayr and Short (1970: 27) merge the genus *Morus* (gannets) with *Sula* (boobies) and treat all three gannets as one species: *capensis,* ocean off South Africa, and *serrator,* ocean off Aus-

tralia and New Zealand, as well as the present northern hemisphere form, *bassana.*

This treatment is followed here. Minor points of head feathering and tarsal reticulation separate the two "genera." The slight differences in the three isolated populations involve varying amounts of black and white in the tail and are considered to be of subspecific degree only.

CORMORANTS — PHALACROCORACIDAE

Two species in New York.
One breeds.

Of this cosmopolitan family (30± species) only two occur in New York State. The Great Cormorant (*Phalacrocorax carbo*) is the most widely distributed of the group, being found on every continent except South America. It occurs locally in Long Island waters during the colder months. The second species, the Double-crested Cormorant (*P. auritus*), is restricted to North America. It is a familiar sight in coastal waters during spring and fall passage, sometimes occurring in impressive numbers. Cormorants dive from the surface of the water in the manner of loons and, like them, feed on fish.

Great Cormorant
(*Phalacrocorax carbo*)   *

Range: Widespread in the Old World, but of very limited distribution in the New World; restricted in the breeding season to the Gulf of St. Lawrence area, south to northern Nova Scotia and Prince Edward Island; in 1971 to *southern* Nova Scotia. Winters south to central New Jersey, rarely farther.

Status: Uncommon to locally very common winter visitant along the coast, but rare in many areas. The species has increased greatly in recent years.

Change in status: The Great Cormorant has become more numerous in the northeast within the past 30 years, a change noted both on the breeding and the wintering grounds.

Occurrence: This species is partial to a rocky coast and is rarely recorded along sandy shores. It is seen in numbers at such favorable localities as the bluffs of the Montauk area and the rocky islets and stone jetties in Long Island Sound. Along the flat sandy shore of southern Long Island west of Montauk Point it is relatively rare. The greatest numbers are observed from December through March, although it is regular from October to April.

MAXIMA: 17, Pelham Bay, Bronx Co., Jan. 22, 1964; 40, Larchmont, Westchester Co., Jan. 23, 1953; 30, Sands Point, Nassau Co., Feb. 13, 1954; 52, Montauk, Suffolk Co., Feb. 23, 1948.

As this cormorant winters in large numbers along the nearby coast of Rhode Island, it is not surprising to find a sizable wintering population in New York waters. On two late December trips in 1967 and 1968, approximately 350 individuals in each of those years were discovered on a rocky islet north of Gardiner's Island, called Gardiner's Point. These birds were seen by dozens of observers on the annual Christmas count. At least 114 were observed on nearby Great Gull Island, late December 1970 (Duffy, Hays, Lapham, and LeCroy).

EXTREME DATES: Sept. 6 and 14 (specimen) to May 3. No earlier fall or later spring dates have been confirmed, although in view of the recent great increase, it would not be surprising if occasional summering individuals turned up.

Remarks: No specimen or other satisfactory evidence existed for this species from inland New York, including unverified sight reports from the lower Hudson River. The Great Cormorant is often confused with its smaller, more numerous relative, the Double-crested Cormorant. For a discussion of the difficulties involved, see Bull (1964: 88).

On Nov. 2, 1969, however, an adult was shot illegally on the Hudson River at Cornwall, Orange Co., and was seized by the State Conservation Department. The specimen was preserved and is now in the State Museum collection at Albany—NYSM 24848. This individual was first observed on Oct. 19 and seen by numerous people. It represents the first confirmed inland record for the state. Cornwall is at least 40 miles from the coast (Long Island Sound).

Double-crested Cormorant
(*Phalacrocorax auritus*)   *   B

Range: Chiefly Nearctic region, in the east a very local breeder: (1) along the Atlantic coast from Newfoundland and Quebec south to Maine; locally to Massachusetts, south of which it is very local in North Carolina; not known to breed between these two states; (2) inland from southern Canada and Michigan east to islands in lakes Erie and Ontario; in the latter known only from the Canadian side except for one small island in New York waters, as noted below (see **Breeding**). In the east winters chiefly from Maryland southward.

Status: Common to very abundant coastal migrant. Regular summering nonbreeder, especially on eastern Long Island, sometimes in numbers. Rare but probably regular on the coast in winter. Inland rare to uncommon at any time. One breeding colony in eastern Lake Ontario.

Nonbreeding: Great flocks, flying overhead in long single lines, may be observed both spring and fall along the south shore of Long Island, particularly at the east end.

MAXIMA: *Fall*—all from eastern Long Island—450, Moriches Inlet, Aug. 17, 1946; 900, same locality, Sept. 2, 1951; 5500, Ram Island Shoals, Sept. 13, 1935; 15,000, Easthampton to Montauk, Oct. 18, 1930 (Helmuth); 1000, Gardiner's Bay, Nov. 8, 1949.

MAXIMA: *Spring*—5000, Jones Beach, Apr. 22, 1934; 20)0, Mecox Bay, May 7, 1932; 400, Jones Bei ch, May 23, 1948.

MAXIMA: *Summer*—nonbreeders regular on eastern Long Island, as follows—220, Montauk to Acabonack, June 20, 1936; 100, Gardiner's Bay, July 13, 1939; 300, Moriches Bay, July 23, 1949; 30, same locality, all summer of 1955.

Inland it is usually observed in very small numbers, from one to four seen perched on pilings or rocks in the Hudson River, but occasionally flocks are observed flying overhead.

MAXIMA, INLAND: *Spring*—160, Tuckahoe, Westchester Co., May 15, 1935. *Fall*—95, Bear Mountain, Rockland Co., Sept. 22, 1949.

Upstate the Double-crested Cormorant is uncommon and irregular in occurrence, usually only one or two, rarely more seen at one time.

In *winter* this species is rare even on Long Island, where a few are reported each year. I know of no extant winter specimen of *P. auritus* from the state.

Beardslee and Mitchell (1965: 93–94) list three winter observations in the Niagara Frontier region.

Breeding: Double-crested Cormorants were found breeding for the first time in New York in 1945 on tiny one-acre Gull Island in extreme eastern Lake Ontario in Henderson Bay, Jefferson Co. (Kutz and Allen, *Auk*, 1947, 64: 137). For exact location of this islet, see banding recovery map. These men found fourteen nests in elms and willows; all nests were at least 15 feet up. On June 20 some of the nests were under construction, others contained from one to four eggs.

Belknap (1950) visited Gull Island on June 11, 1950, and found 34 nests, some with eggs. Four years later, from June 24 to July 2, 1954, 11 nestlings were counted by Belknap, one of which he banded on June 24 and was found dead at Lake Apopka, Florida, about ten months later in April 1955 (see Map 4).

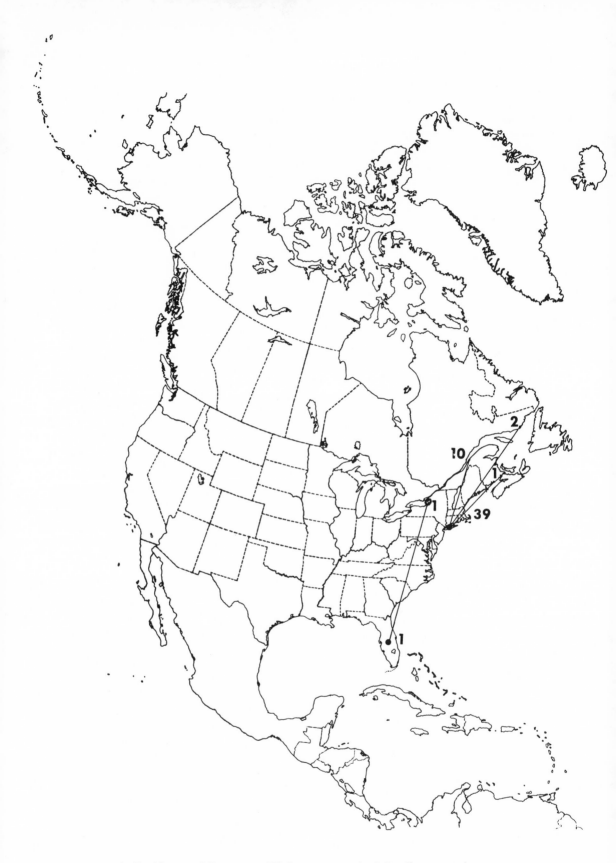

MAP 4 Double-crested Cormorant (*Phalacrocorax auritus*) Banding recoveries
0=Breeding locality

During the early and middle 1960s about 20 occupied nests were observed by Belknap.

Also breeding on this one-acre islet are Black-crowned Night Herons, and both Herring Gulls and Ring-billed Gulls.

Banding (see Map 4): Of more than fifty individuals banded as nestlings in various years and recovered the following autumn on Long Island, 39 were banded by J. Cadbury on islands off the Maine coast. Others banded were: ten on the St. Lawrence River in Quebec; one in eastern New Brunswick; two on the north shore of the Gulf of St. Lawrence in extreme eastern Quebec, opposite Newfoundland. See also juvenile recovered in central Florida (discussed under **Breeding).**

FRIGATEBIRDS — FREGATIDAE

One species in New York.
None breed.

In this exclusively tropical family (five species), the Magnificent Frigatebird (*Fregata magnificens*) is, except for a population in the Cape Verde Islands, the only species restricted to the western hemisphere. It is recorded from New York only as a vagrant.

Magnificent Frigatebird
(*Fregata magnificens*) *

Range: Chiefly tropical American coasts, on the Atlantic side breeding north to the Bahamas. As of 1969 found breeding in southern Florida on the Marquesas Keys between Key West and the Dry Tortugas (*Audubon Field Notes*, 1969, 23: 652–654). Vagrant north to Newfoundland.

Status: *Very rare*—There have been seven occurrences in New York, all but one from Suffolk Co., Long Island, only two confirmed: (1) Adult female collected on Gardiner's Island, Aug. 4, 1886 (J. P. Miller), AMNH 11705; (2) female color-photographed in flight over Great South Bay near Brookhaven, Sept. 18, 1965 (Puleston), photo on file in AMNH collection.

Five sight reports, made by observers previously familiar with the species in the field, are believed correct: (1) Easthampton, Sept. 5, 1934 (Helmuth); (2) Jones Inlet, Nassau Co., May 19, 1959 (G. and R. Rogin); (3) over West Islip, Sept. 15, 1960 (Alperin), three days after hurricane "Donna"; (4) Fisher's Island, Aug. 20, 1963 (Simmons, *fide* Ferguson); (5) Montauk, July 3, 1965 (Davis and Epstein).

Faulkner's Island, the locality of a much published specimen, is in Connecticut waters.

Remarks: No subspecies (*"rothschildi"*) recognized here. Many individuals from different parts of the range are virtually indistinguishable.

HERONS — ARDEIDAE

Eleven species in New York.
Eleven species breed.

All 11 New York members of this widespread family (over 60 species) have bred within the state at one time or another and today all but the Great Blue Heron (*Ardea herodias*) breed on Long Island.

On a trip in early summer to the coastal heronries from Jamaica Bay to Jones Beach breeding egrets of two species may be seen, as well as two night herons, the Green Heron (*Butorides virescens*), the uncommon Little Blue Heron (*Egretta caerulea*), nonbreeding Great Blue Herons, and, if the observer is lucky, the rare Tricolored or Louisiana Heron (*E. tricolor*). Of the above, only the Green Heron, Great Blue Heron, and Black-crowned Night Heron (*Nycticorax nycticorax*) bred in the state 30 or so years ago, emphasizing the phenomenal recovery made by the "southern white" herons in recent decades. The two secretive, marsh-inhabiting bitterns are also members of this family.

At the time of the 1957 A.O.U. Check-list, *all* 11 species of New York herons were included in as many genera, or one genus for each of the 11 species. Today's trend of enlarging genera to accommodate morphologically similar species into one genus is adopted here. As a result both night herons are placed in *Nycticorax* and the expanded genus *Egretta* now includes the related Little Blue and Louisiana herons, as well as the two common breeding species of egrets. Eleven genera are thus reduced to seven. With minor modifications, the treatments of Bock (1956), Dickerman and Parkes (1968), and Curry-Lindahl (1971) are followed here.

Great Blue Heron
(*Ardea herodias*)   *   B

Range: Nearctic and Neotropical regions, breeding from the southern portions of Alaska and Canada to southern Mexico and the West Indies; Galápagos Islands. Winters from southern Canada to northern South America.

Status: Sedentary and migratory. Locally common to very common migrant; less numerous in winter, chiefly near the coast. Widespread breeder but absent from many areas and rare in the southeastern section; only nonbreeders are presently known on Long Island.

Nonbreeding: Our largest heron is a familiar sight on both fresh and salt water and may be seen any day of the year, but is scarcest over most of the inland areas during the winter months. It frequents lake and river shores, ponds, marshes, swamps, and coastal estuaries.

MAXIMA: *Fall*—75, Eden, Erie Co., Aug. 23, 1965; 75, Lawrence, Nassau Co., Aug. 28, 1949.

MAXIMA: *Winter*—38, Jones Beach, Jan. 1, 1958; seven, Grand Island, Niagara River, Jan. 22, 1956.

Breeding: The Great Blue Heron is the best documented of the family in the state insofar as its breeding status and distribution are concerned. Yearly statewide surveys are undertaken by the Federation of New York State Bird Clubs and a detailed report was published by Benning (1969).

More than 100 breeding localities have been censused, many of them in recent years, others in the past, for a number had become extirpated years ago. Shooting and habitat destruction were principal causes. On Long Island there was only one known small colony, on Gardiner's Island, last reported in 1900. In 11 southeastern mainland counties only seven localities have had breeding Great Blue Herons and only two or three small colonies exist there today.

Over 60% of the nesting localities are found in central and western New York, chiefly in the Finger Lakes region, the southern tier section (near Pennsylvania), around Oneida Lake, and a number in the Adirondacks. As to the last-named, Benning (1969: 90) stated, "This area contains a vast amount of remote sections . . . Lack of coverage by observers . . . may account for at least a part of the seeming scarcity of Great Blue Herons in this part of the state."

This species nests most frequently in large, inaccessible wooded swamps, especially those of mixed hardwoods—ash, elm, and maple— with the trees tall and dense. However, not a few are to be found in upland forests of good-sized beech and oak, some of them a fair distance from water, even high on hillsides. As many as 11 nests have been found in a single large elm.

Nest heights may be as low as 25 feet above ground but most are from 40 to as high as 100 feet.

Egg clutches in 75 New York nests ranged

from three to six with five eggs each in 40 nests (53%)—the balance as follows: three eggs (eight nests); four eggs (ten nests); six eggs (17 nests).

EGG DATES: Apr. 15 to June 9.

Nestlings: May 24 to July 17; fledglings: from July 17.

Eight of the largest New York heronries, 100 nests or more, are (or were) as follows:

(1) Former years: 1896, Tonawanda Swamp (=Oak Orchard) near Alabama, Genesee Co., "several hundred"; 1906, part of the same swamp near West Barre, Orleans Co., 150; 1909, north shore of Oneida Lake near Constantia, Oswego Co., 300; 1915, north end of Honeoye Lake, Ontario Co., 100.

(2) Recent years: 1961, Grand Island, Niagara River, Erie Co., 150; 1963, near Savannah, Wayne Co., 150; subsequently abandoned, and what may well have been part of the same colony at nearby Marengo Swamp, near Clyde, 100 nests in 1966, 175 (produced 440 young) in 1967, and at least 200 in 1970. Parker and Maxwell (1969: 192) estimated 240 nests, not all active, on 18-acre Ironsides Island, St. Lawrence River, Jefferson Co., 1968. They found that alewives formed 82% of the food analyzed. In 1969 these same observers found 255 nests there, of which 130 were occupied.

Banding: A recently fledged juvenile banded June 20, 1948, on the Bruce Peninsula, Ontario, was trapped and released only ten days later, 450 miles to the southeast, on the Hudson River between Nyack and Tarrytown. This shows a tendency for young birds to wander soon after the nesting season.

Remarks: The "Great White" Heron (*Ardea "occidentalis"*) is probably a color morph as many authorities suggest; intermediates, called "Würdemann's" Herons, are found in the same areas with both blue and white individuals. This morph occurs in the Caribbean region, breeding north to the Florida Keys. Vagrants occur north to North Carolina and Pennsylvania (specimens).

An individual, believed to be this form, was observed on Long Island after the Florida hurricane of Aug. 29, 1949. It was first seen at Tobay Pond, Nassau Co., on Sept. 3 (Bull); very likely the same individual was reported later at Mecox Bay, Suffolk Co., from Sept. 17 to Oct. 15 (Helmuth and McKeever).

The Great Blue Heron is considered by some to be conspecific with the Gray Heron (*A. cinerea*) of the Old World.

Three very similar allopatric populations replace each other on the large continental land masses of the world and are best treated as superspecies: (1) the very wide-ranging *A. cinerea*, the Gray Heron, found nearly throughout Eurasia and Africa, including Madagascar; (2) *A. herodias*, the Great Blue Heron (including the white morph, *A. "occidentalis,"* the so-called "Great White Heron" of the Florida Keys, Cuba, etc.), occurring throughout North America, including the West Indies, and on the mainland south to Panama, also the Galápagos Archipelago; (3) *A. cocoi*, the White-necked Heron, ranging nearly throughout South America.

Great Egret (*Egretta alba*) * B

Range: Nearly cosmopolitan, in eastern North America breeding along the Atlantic coast north to Long Island (since 1953), rarely to Massachusetts and Maine; in the interior rarely north to Ohio and extreme southeastern Ontario (islands in western Lake Erie). Winters north to Long Island.

Status: Common to locally abundant summer visitant along the coast, much less common inland but occasionally numerous. Rare but regular in winter on the coast. Local breeder on Long Island. Greatly increased in recent years.

Change in status: Years ago this fine species was known as an "occasional summer visitant" (Eaton, 1910: 256). It was at its lowest ebb during the first two decades of the twentieth century when severely persecuted for the millinery trade. Given complete protection by 1913, it slowly recovered and by the 1920s reappeared once again on the shores of Long Island. Details of its early history in the New York City region are given in Bull (1964: 95–96).

Nonbreeding: Great Egrets, like other "southern" white herons, are found most frequently and in largest numbers on the broad salt meadows, mud flats, and coastal ponds along the outer coast. But unlike the others, they have occurred within recent years in impressive numbers far inland, especially along the lakes, rivers, and larger marshes, as can be seen from the following—particularly during the period of 1947–1949:

MAXIMA: *Coastal*—evening roosts at Tobay Pond, Nassau Co.: 280, Sept. 4, 1949, and 165, Sept. 14, 1947 (both Bull); Jamaica Bay Refuge, 1959: 70, Nov. 23 (Johnson), and 20, as late as Dec. 20 (Bull)—mild, open fall.

MAXIMA: *Inland*—18, over Wanakah, Erie Co., Apr. 18, 1962 (Able); 30, Montezuma Refuge, July 18, 1949; 50, near Buffalo, Aug. 21, 1933; 50, Montezuma, Sept. 8, 1961; 240 along 50 miles of Hudson River, from Kingston to Albany, Sept. 12, 1948 (Stoner); seven, Mendon Ponds, Monroe Co., Oct. 8, 1948.

EXTREME DATES: Mar. 2 (coastal) and Mar. 30 (inland), also Apr. 1 (inland specimen) to Nov. 10 (inland specimen), Dec. 5 (inland), and "late" December (coastal). In recent years rare before April and after November.

MAXIMA, COASTAL: *Winter*—four each at Hempstead Reservoir, Nassau Co., all January 1956, and Feb. 13, 1954. Usually one or more are reported each winter on Long Island.

Breeding (see Map 5): Great Egrets have been found breeding on coastal islands or the barrier beaches at seven different localities on Long Island, with the first recorded New York nesting in 1953 on Fisher's Island. The majority of nests in this area are placed in dense scrub thickets of catbrier, bayberry, poison ivy, and wild cherry, invariably with other species of herons. Nests have also been found in tupelos or sour gums (Fisher's Island) and in black pines (Jones Beach area). A few have been placed on the ground, but most range from four to 12 feet above ground level.

Eight Long Island nests contained three eggs each.

EGG DATES: May 23 to June 4.

Nestlings: June 25 to July 25; fledglings: July 25.

The seven known breeding colonies on Long Island, with year of first recorded nesting, are: Suffolk Co.—(1) Fisher's Island, 1953; (2) Gardiner's Island, 1967; (3) East Moriches, 1964, only year; (4) Oak Beach, 1967. Nassau Co.—(5) Tobay Pond and nearby Jones Beach,

1956; (6) Lawrence, 1961. Kings Co.—(7) Canarsie Pol, Jamaica Bay area, 1960. The maximum number of pairs breeding at one time in the four largest colonies ranged from 17 to 28, and as many as *50* pairs at a single locality in the Jones Beach area in 1973.

Subspecies: The New World race *egretta* has the bill yellow *all* year.

Snowy Egret (*Egretta thula*)   *   B

Range: Neotropical and southern Nearctic regions, in eastern North America breeding on the Atlantic coast north to Long Island, rarely to Massachusetts. Winters rarely north to Long Island.

Status: Locally common to abundant summer visitant and breeder on Long Island; rare in winter on the south shore. Rare at any time inland and virtually unknown in the extreme northern portions. Greatly increased in recent years.

Change in status: The Snowy Egret, like the previous species, is most often found in or near extensive salt meadows on the coast and along the bays, tidal estuaries, and coastal ponds. It is uncommon to rare anywhere else and is the rarest of the native "white" herons inland.

This species, more than any other heron, was valued for its ornamental plumes and consequently suffered severely. It had become almost exterminated by the early 1900s and only because of the strictest protection in 1913 and thereafter escaped possible extinction. At any rate it started to make a comeback by the 1930s and greatly increased along the coast during the next two decades. As a result, it is today the most numerous breeding heron on the south shore of Long Island, even outnumbering the formerly abundant Black-crowned Night Heron. At one or two mixed heron colonies on western Long Island it is even more numerous than all the others combined! For details of its early history on Long Island, see Bull (1964: 99).

Nonbreeding: The Snowy Egret is most numerous from August to October. The following maximum numbers undoubtedly contain, in part, some breeding individuals.

MAP 5 Great Egret
(*Egretta alba*) Breeding
distribution

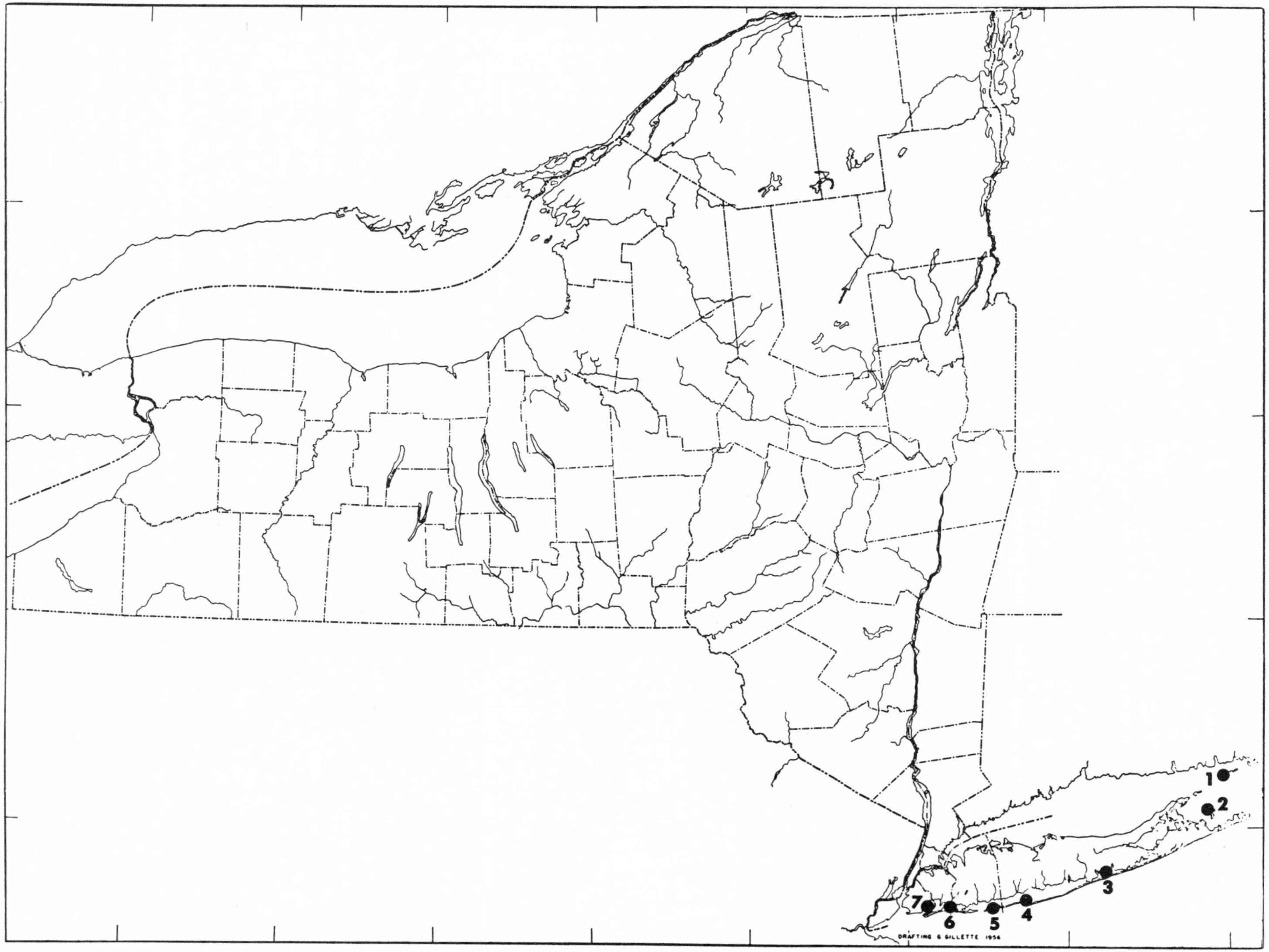

MAXIMA: Very large flight in 1964—40, Orient, Suffolk Co., Aug. 4; 175, East Moriches, Suffolk Co., Aug. 17; all the following at the Jamaica Bay Refuge—300, Sept. 1; 250, Sept. 26; 150, Oct. 28; also 40, Nov. 23, 1959; 20, Dec. 20, 1959 (fall of 1959 was mild).

The Snowy Egret in New York is essentially a coastal species and, apart from a flock of seven observed at Cornwall, Orange Co., Aug. 15, 1964 (note flight year above), usually only single individuals are reported at upstate localities.

EXTREME DATES: Mar. 14 (coastal) and Apr. 13 (inland) to Sept. 30 (inland) and "late" December (coastal). On the coast generally rare before late March and after November.

Winter: A few have been reported regularly on south shore Christmas counts since 1967; seven individuals were observed on Dec. 30, 1967, on the southern Nassau count. The latest report in midwinter appears to be that of an individual seen on Jan. 17, 1967, at Tobay Pond, Jones Beach area.

Breeding (see Map 6): Except for a breeding record in 1885 on Fire Island, opposite Sayville, Suffolk Co. (Bull, 1964: 100), the first known record of nesting in modern times on Long Island was in 1949 at Oak Beach, Suffolk Co. Since then it has multiplied prodigiously as may be seen from the following maximum densities: 1956, Tobay Pond, Nassau Co., 80 nests; 1959, Meadowbrook Causeway, Nassau Co., 100 nests; 1965, Canarsie Pol, Jamaica Bay, Kings Co., 150+ nests; 1967, Lawrence Marsh, Nassau Co., 180+ nests.

On Long Island, Snowy Egrets breed in mixed heronries, especially near Black-crowned Night Herons, and many nests have been found adjacent to those of Glossy Ibis. These colonies are often located in dense scrub thickets on coastal sand dunes close to salt marsh, mud flats, and tidal creeks, where the birds feed.

Nests are commonly placed from three to ten feet up (rarely on the ground) in wild cherry, sumac, elderberry, bayberry, catbrier (*Smilax*), and occasionally in vines of Virginia creeper, wild grape, and poison ivy. Nests at Oak Beach have been found also in pine, and others on Fisher's Island in tupelo (sour gum).

Egg clutches in 258 Long Island nests ranged from two to six, as follows: two eggs (48 nests); three eggs (106 nests); four eggs (91 nests); five eggs (12 nests); six eggs (one nest).

EGG DATES: Apr. 16 to June 25.

Nestlings: May 16 to July 14; fledglings: July 31 to Sept. 17.

The following eight breeding colonies are indicated on the accompanying map (year indicates first known nesting): Suffolk Co.— (1) Fisher's Island, 1965; (2) Gardiner's Island, 1967; (3) East Moriches, 1963; (4) Oak Beach, 1949. Nassau Co.—(5) Tobay Pond, 1951; also breeds at various spots along Jones Beach; (6) Meadowbrook Causeway, 1958 or earlier; (7) Lawrence Marsh, 1959. Queens Co. and Kings Co.—(8) Jamaica Bay area, 1953.

Banding (see Map 7): The following banding recovery information is taken from Davis (*Bird-Banding*, 1968, 39: 317). In all three instances nestlings were banded; all were recovered in the West Indies the following autumn:

Place and date of banding	Place and date of recovery
Jamaica Bay, June 22, 1963	Marie Galante Island, near Guadeloupe, Sept. 17, 1963
Jamaica Bay, July 4, 1963	Dominican Republic, Nov. 4, 1963
Lawrence Marsh, June 25, 1966	Puerto Rico, Nov. 2, 1966

Little Blue Heron
(*Egretta caerulea*)   *   B

Range: Neotropical and southeastern Nearctic regions, breeding along the Atlantic coast north to southern New Jersey and Long Island (since 1958); casually to Massachusetts; in 1971 to the Isles of Shoals, New Hampshire. Winters chiefly in the tropics north to southeastern United States, rarely farther north.

Status: Rare to uncommon summer visitant, more numerous in flight years. Local breeder on Long Island.

Change in status: The Little Blue Heron was called an "accidental summer visitant" by

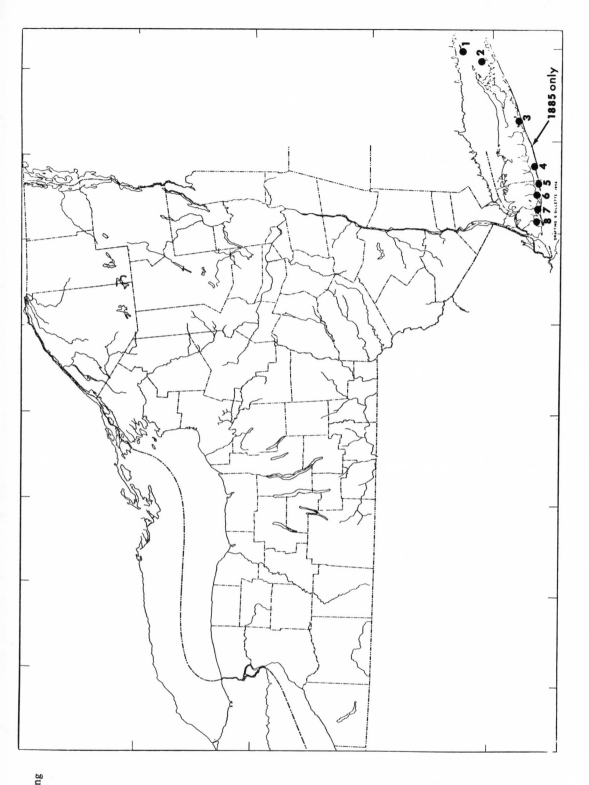

MAP 6   Snowy Egret
(*Egretta thula*) Breeding
distribution

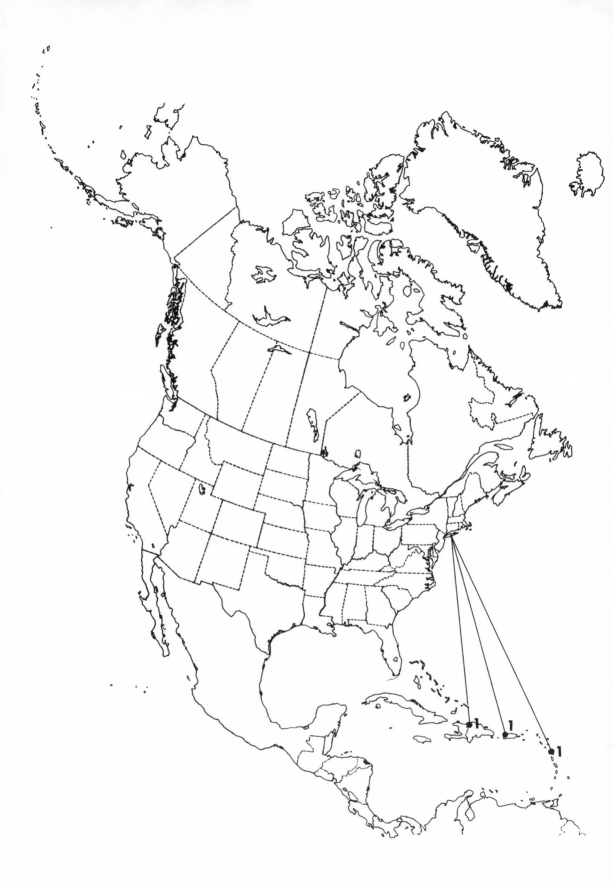

MAP 7 Snowy Egret (*Egretta thula*) Banding recoveries

Eaton (1910: 260). For many years it continued to be very rare, but by the late 1920s it had increased considerably, with marked flights in 1929–1930, 1936, and 1948. Since 1948, however, it has decreased, but not to the pre-1929 level. For details of its early history in the New York City region, see Bull (1964: 92–94).

Nonbreeding: In New York a characteristic of this polymorphic species is that the blue-plumaged adults are almost invariably seen in early spring, whereas the white immatures are greatly in the majority in fall; pied individuals, however, are rarely reported. Maximum abundance is attained in August and early September.

On the coast the Little Blue Heron inhabits salt marshes, mud flats, and ponds. Inland it is a frequenter of fresh-water marshes and wooded swamps, ponds, and streams.

MAXIMA: *Coastal*—120, between Easthampton and Shinnecock Bay, Aug. 20, 1930 (Helmuth); 50, Easthampton to Mecox Bay, Aug. 30, 1948; 54, Iona Island, Rockland Co., Sept. 6, 1936 (locality is near the coast); 19, Oak Beach, Suffolk Co., Sept. 24, 1970.

MAXIMA: *Inland*—14, Tivoli, Dutchess Co., June 21, 1930; four, Montezuma Marshes, July 18, 1948; 60, Fishkill Plains, Dutchess Co., Aug. 2, 1929 (Frost). It has been recorded as far north as Saratoga and Jefferson counties.

EXTREME DATES: Mar. 16 (coastal) and Mar. 23 (inland) to Oct. 23 (inland), and Nov. 6 (coastal), exceptionally to Dec. 13, 1964 (coastal). Rare before late April and after September.

Winter: An immature was studied carefully at Speonk, Suffolk Co., Dec. 27, 1965 (Wilcox and Terry).

Breeding (see Map 8): The first known breeding record in New York was in 1958 at Tobay Pond, Nassau Co. It has been found breeding subsequently at four additional Long Island localities. They are (with year of first known breeding) as follows: Kings Co.—(1) Canarsie Pol, Jamaica Bay, 1960. Nassau Co.—(2) Lawrence, 1961, maximum of six pairs in 1962; (3) Tobay Pond, 1958. Suffolk Co.—(4) Oak Beach, 1967; (5) Gardiner's Island, 1967.

Little Blue Herons have nested in mixed heronries at all five localities. It is the only "southern" heron in the state not showing any appreciable increase. Very little has been studied of its nesting habits on Long Island. Even nest height is unrecorded and data on only three nests with clutch size are available: two eggs (two nests); three eggs (one nest).

EGG DATE: June 18.

Nestlings: July 7; fledglings: July 4 to 18.

Tricolored or Louisiana Heron
(*Egretta tricolor*)   *   B

Range: Chiefly Neotropical region, but breeds also along the Atlantic coast north to southern New Jersey, very rarely to Long Island; winters north to the Carolinas, rarely farther. Wanders north to New Brunswick.

Status: Rare to uncommon, but regular visitant on the south shore of western Long Island, where it is also a very rare breeder; very rare to casual anywhere else in the state.

Change in status: Prior to 1953 this species was extremely rare on Long Island, but since then it has been reported annually. It is still considered a good find, however, and is to be expected each year at only three localities: (1) Jamaica Bay area; (2) Lawrence Marsh heronry; (3) Jones Beach area, especially in the vicinity of Tobay Pond. Even at these three localities single individuals are the rule. Elsewhere on Long Island the Louisiana Heron is considered a great rarity.

Nonbreeding: There are three specimen records for Long Island, all from Suffolk Co., but apparently only one is extant: (1) near Patchogue, summer of 1836 (Giraud, 1844: 282); (2) Little Reed Pond, Montauk, June 26, 1925 (Ellis), specimen examined by Griscom; (3) Fisher's Island, Apr. 14, 1963 (Ferguson), specimen in his collection, examined by the writer.

MAXIMA: Four, Jamaica Bay Refuge, Queens Co., May 13, 1955; four, Canarsie Pol, Kings Co., Aug. 25, 1965; six, Jamaica Bay Refuge, Sept. 12, 1964; 11, Oak Beach, Suffolk Co., Sept. 24–29, 1970 (Connolly and Finch), are exceptional; four, Tobay Pond, Nassau Co., Oct. 13, 1962.

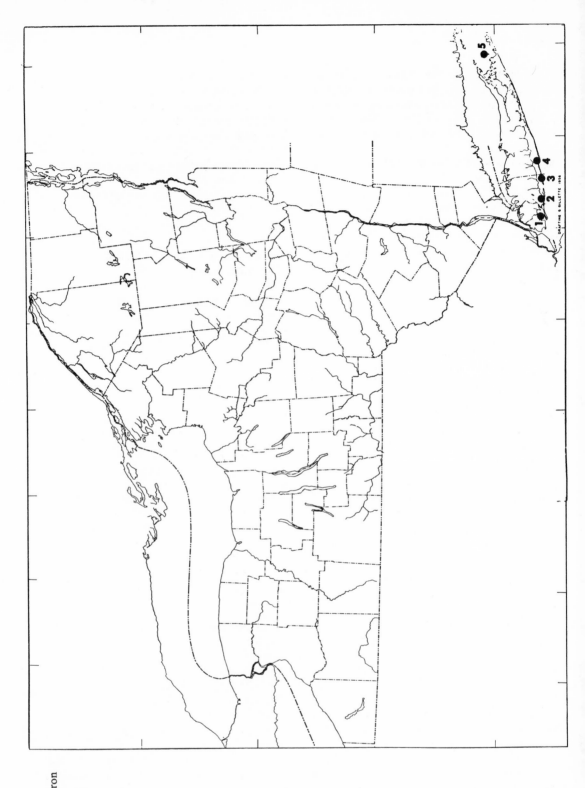

MAP 8 Little Blue Heron
(*Egretta caerulea*)
Breeding distribution

EXTREME DATES: Mar. 9 and 22 to Oct. 23, exceptionally to Dec. 1, 1940, Orient, Suffolk Co. (Latham).

As far as known, this species has been reliably recorded in upstate New York on only three occasions, one of these a specimen. (1) An adult male was collected at Allegany, Cattaraugus Co., May 21, 1959 (S. Eaton), specimen in St. Bonaventure University collection 655. Interestingly enough single individuals were reported at about the same time in Ontario and Pennsylvania. (2) A Louisiana Heron was carefully studied at Braddock's Bay, Monroe Co., May 31, 1950 (Listman, in Beardslee and Mitchell, 1965: 99). (3) Another was well seen at Montezuma Marshes, Apr. 23, 1970 (McIlroy). Other reports from inland localities by inexperienced observers are without details and considered unreliable.

Breeding: Louisiana Herons have been proved to breed only four times on Long Island: (1) A nest and three eggs were found ten feet up in a gray birch at Jamaica Bay Refuge, May 17, 1955 (Meyerriecks, *Wilson Bull.*, 1957, 67: 184–185). (2) Another nest, also in a gray birch only four feet above the ground, containing one (addled?) egg and a downy young approximately two weeks old, was located also at Jamaica Bay Refuge on nearby Canarsie Pol, Kings Co., Aug. 4, 1966 (Johnson, Hays, and Cooper). This latter nest was situated in a heronry containing breeding Snowy Egrets and Black-crowned Night Herons. Further details are given by Hays (*Kingbird*, 1969, 19: 93–94). (3) An adult with two "recently" fledged young were seen at Oak Beach, Suffolk Co., July 1970 (Buckley and B. Ward—*fide* Davis). (4) Short Beach, Nassau Co., July 19, 1971 (Gochfeld), a nest containing four nestlings was situated 3½ feet above ground in a partially dead bayberry, in *Phragmites* growth. In 1973 as many as *12* pairs were reported to have nested in the Jones Beach–Oak Beach area.

Remarks: The subspecies *"ruficollis"* is poorly differentiated from nominate *tricolor* and not recognized here. The alleged size and color differences are variable, especially the latter; there is overlap in both characters, noticeable in a large series.

Cattle Egret (*Bubulcus ibis*)　B

Range: Virtually cosmopolitan, except in the colder portions. An Old World species that crossed the Atlantic Ocean, presumably unaided, from Africa to northern South America. It has recently spread north through the West Indies into continental North America where it has been undergoing a phenomenal breeding range extension: north to southern New Jersey (1958), southeastern Ontario (1962), Rhode Island (1964), Long Island (1970), and Connecticut (1971). Withdraws in winter from northern portions.

Status: First reported in New York State in 1954. Recorded regularly since 1958, the first large invasion occurring in 1962. By 1970 a locally common visitant, chiefly in spring, with one breeding record.

Nonbreeding: The Cattle Egret first appeared in the state in 1954 when one was seen on Long Island from May 17 to 27 on the Lukert turkey farm at East Moriches, Suffolk Co. There were scattered reports, usually of single birds, mostly from Long Island, during the next seven years. The first definite record from upstate was that of an individual photographed at Niskayuna, Schenectady Co., May 25, 1957 (Tepper, *Feathers*, 1957, 19: 29).

MAXIMA: In the spring of 1962 a widespread irruption occurred, at least several hundred birds reported. The largest concentrations were as follows: 12, Claverack, Columbia Co., Apr. 26; 20, Selkirk, Albany Co., Apr. 30; 14, Scotia, Saratoga Co., May 1; 40, Remsenburg, Suffolk Co., May 2; 15, Scottsville, Monroe Co., May 17.

EXTREME DATES: Mar. 26 (coastal) to Nov. 19 (inland), exceptionally to Dec. 1, 1970, Larchmont, Westchester Co. (S. Bahrt, photographed).

Northern winter limits in the United States remain to be determined. One was recorded on Long Island at Brookhaven, Suffolk Co., Dec. 31, 1968 (Puleston).

There is no known specimen from the state. However, at least four individuals have been photographed. One of these was captured alive as it wandered around a building excavation in a "dazed" condition in downtown Manhattan, New York City, Nov. 17, 1964; it recovered and was photographed and released later that day.

Unlike other local herons, this species frequents grassy areas and cultivated fields where it feeds upon insects stirred up by livestock or plows. During the nesting season, however, Cattle Egrets associate communally with other species of herons (see **Breeding**).

In 1966 three nonbreeders spent most of the summer at the Jamaica Bay Refuge, four were observed on Gardiner's Island, Suffolk Co., July 11, 1969, and individuals were noted at Lawrence, Nassau Co., during late spring and early summer in recent years, but no evidence of nesting was found at these long-established heronries.

Breeding: Although Cattle Egrets have bred as close to New York State as Ontario (opposite Rochester), and as recently as 1968 on Pigeon Island in extreme eastern Lake Ontario (only five miles from the state line—

Jefferson Co.), this species had not been recorded as breeding in New York prior to 1970.

During the summer of 1970 Dennis Puleston (*Kingbird*, 1970, 20: 178–179) at last obtained proof of breeding in the state on extreme eastern Long Island. On June 7 on Gardiner's Island he discovered an adult at a nest containing eggs five feet up in a dense thicket of catbrier (*Smilax*). The nest was located in a mixed heronry. From July 2 to 7, 1970, Puleston, Roger Peterson, Paul Spitzer, David Duffy, and others observed two unfledged young out of the nest climbing about the bushes (see Fig. 27).

The second known breeding record for the state and for Long Island was the discovery of three nests containing five downy young, banded and color-photographed, Zach's Bay area, Jones Beach, June 9, 1973 (Davis); color photos on file, AMNH collection.

Remarks: Placed in the genus *Ardeola* by

Fig. 27 Recently fledged Cattle Egret in mixed heronry, Gardiner's Island, Suffolk Co., July 1970. First known breeding record for New York State. Photo by Dennis Puleston

some authors, but members of that genus, especially the pond herons of the Old World, behave very differently from the Cattle Egret.

Green Heron
(*Butorides virescens*)   *   B

Range: Nearctic and Neotropical regions, breeding from extreme southeastern Canada and the United States (absent from the northern Great Plains and Rocky Mountains) through the West Indies and Middle America to Panama and islands off northern South America. In the east winters north to South Carolina, casually to New York.

Status: Fairly common to common migrant; locally abundant at postbreeding roosts in late summer. Widespread breeder, but rare at higher elevations in the Adirondacks and Catskills.

Nonbreeding: This species is most numerous at summer roosts and during the fall migration.

MAXIMA: 143, Far Rockaway, Queens Co., July 31, 1949; 240, Clay Swamp, Onondaga Co., Aug. 19, 1969; *400*, Montezuma Refuge, Aug. 22, 1967 (Benning); 60, Mecox Bay, Suffolk Co., Sept. 28, 1928. These numbers are exceptional; groups of a dozen or more being usual.

EXTREME DATES: Apr. 1 (coastal) to Nov. 17 (inland) and Nov. 26 and early December (coastal); exceptionally to Dec. 21 (coastal). Rare before mid-April and after mid-October.

Winter: Green Herons are among the rarest members of the family in winter. Scarcely one-half dozen records exist for the state, mostly from coastal areas where the weather is milder. Upstate, a bird (nearly frozen) was caught alive at East Randolph, Cattaraugus Co., Dec. 15, 1921 (E. A. Wheeler, *Ool.*, 1922, 39: 4–5). The species is also recorded at Old Chatham, Columbia Co., Mar. 7, 1963 (Reilly), which is much too early for a spring arrival date. Four winter occurrences on Long Island are listed in Bull (1964: 92 and 1970: 5), including an individual that wintered near

Fig. 28   Nest and eggs of Green Heron, Little Galloo Island, Jefferson Co., June 10, 1967. Photo by Robert G. Wolk

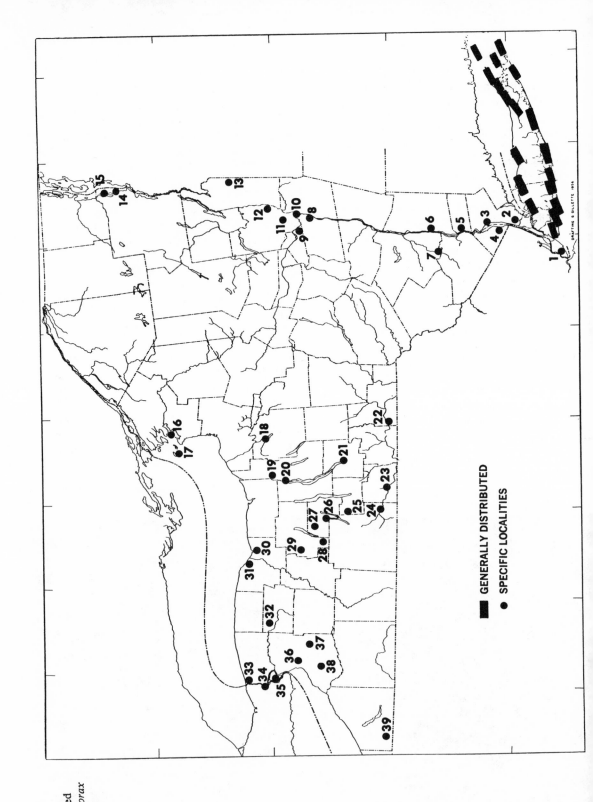

MAP 9 Black-crowned Night Heron (*Nycticorax nycticorax*) Breeding distribution

GENERALLY DISTRIBUTED

SPECIFIC LOCALITIES

Quogue, Suffolk Co., 1961–1962 (Puleston, Wilcox, *et al.*).

Breeding: The nests of this species are most often scattered in marshes, along wooded streams and ponds, and in coastal thickets. However, it sometimes nests colonially, especially in coastal areas.

Green Herons nest most often in low trees and bushes, usually from five to 20 feet up, rarely as high as 40. In 17 New York nest sites, cedar was preferred for five nests, followed by hawthorn (three nests), hemlock (two nests), and one nest in each of tupelo, tamarack, ash, maple, beech, birch, oak, and even one in a wild grape vine (see Fig. 28).

Much more rarely nests are placed on the ground, such as in reed beds (*Phragmites*).

Egg clutches in 42 New York nests ranged from three to seven, as follows: three eggs (five nests); four eggs (22 nests); five eggs (nine nests); six eggs (five nests); seven eggs (one nest).

EGG DATES: Apr. 29 to Aug. 4.

Nestlings: May 22 to Aug. 24; fledglings: July 4 to Sept. 19.

The following data are taken from Meyerriecks' detailed studies (1960) at Jamaica Bay Refuge. In 1955 he found as many as *136* breeding pairs. Most of the birds built their nests from five to ten feet up, occasionally to 15 feet, in bayberry, birch, and willow. Only six ground nests were noted. Most Green Herons used old nests of their own species, but a few also utilized those of Snowy Egrets and Black-crowned Night Herons.

In 76 nests examined, Meyerriecks found egg clutch size as follows: three eggs (25 nests); four eggs (38 nests); five eggs (11 nests); six eggs (two nests).

He determined that the incubation period in 18 out of 20 clutches was 20 days, the nestling period about 16 to 17 days and that the average number of juveniles per nest to fledge was three. Most interesting, perhaps, was his finding of actual double-broodedness in this species. By marking the nests, as well as the birds, Meyerriecks discovered that "32 pairs laid second, normal clutches." At one nest the female laid the first egg of the second clutch nine days after the first brood fledged. Interestingly enough, *all* 32 second-brood nests contained but three eggs.

Remarks: This species may prove to be conspecific with the widespread (Old World, South America), gray-necked form, the Striated Heron (*B. striatus*) which is said to hybridize with the Green Heron in Panama and on Margarita Island, off Venezuela.

Black-crowned Night Heron
(*Nycticorax nycticorax*) * B

Range: Nearly cosmopolitan, in the New World breeding from southern Canada to South America. Winters nearly throughout. Sedentary and migratory.

Status: Locally common to abundant resident near the coast, least numerous in winter; has decreased considerably as a breeder on Long Island. Rare and local inland, but common at a few breeding localities; absent in the mountains.

Nonbreeding: Black-crowned Night Herons are often heard calling as they fly over at night, especially during migration. Migrants usually arrive in mid-March. The largest concentrations are reported during the breeding season. Numerous summering nonbreeders at roosts are often mistaken for nesting birds.

Breeding (see Map 9): This species nests in colonies, often of large size, but there are fewer and smaller colonies on Long Island now than in former years due to the encroachment of New York City's rapidly expanding human population and continued growth of its suburbs. The largest colonies in the state were situated on the north shore in Nassau Co. and on Gardiner's Island in eastern Suffolk Co. (see following). Upstate these birds are, or were, very common in the Albany area and along the Niagara River. Elsewhere the colonies are relatively small, mostly under 100 pairs and many others under 50.

Black-crowned Night Herons frequently breed in wooded swamps, especially those of red maple. They nest commonly in mixed deciduous woodland near water, and on the coast in dense thickets of bayberry, cherry, poison ivy, and catbrier; also often in evergreens such as red cedar and pine. Curiously enough, although breeding inland along fresh-water streams and ponds, as well as in swamps, on

Long Island nests are almost without exception on or near tidewater.

Nest heights range from as low as two feet above ground in coastal thickets up to 60 feet in trees. One notable exception is that of a number of nests (about 25) in the Montezuma Marshes in 1970 placed on cattails over water. The refuge manager, Clayton Hardy (*in litt.*), states that these nests were built only four to ten inches above water level. The previous year's growth of cattails was bent down making a platform on which the nests were placed, supported by old upright cattail stalks (see Fig. 29).

Egg clutches in 155 New York nests range from three to six, with the great majority being three and four eggs in 66 and 67 nests respectively; also five eggs (13 nests) and six eggs (nine nests).

EGG DATES: Apr. 1 to July 12, exceptionally

to late August (renesting attempts after initial failures).

Nestlings: May 21 to July 26; fledglings: June 30 to Aug. 25.

The two largest colonies were on Long Island. One on Gardiner's Island, Suffolk Co., had as many as 1500 pairs in 1881, but only 250 pairs in 1930, and 100 pairs in 1970. The other at Great Neck, Nassau Co., had 1200 pairs in 1936, only 600 pairs in 1951.

Upstate the largest colony at Grand Island on the Niagara River had 500 pairs in 1930, 300 pairs in 1939. Another large colony due east of Saratoga Lake on the Hudson River, now presumably extinct, contained 500 pairs in 1880.

The accompanying map shows the breeding distribution of this species in the state. Nearly half of the 72 localities are on Long Island (33), the other 39 are situated in the Hudson-

Fig. 29 Nestling Black-crowned Night Herons, Montezuma Refuge, Cayuga Co., June 1968. Nest built on old cattail stems from four to ten inches above water level. Nests are made by bending down cattails into a platform and supported by old upright cattail stalks. Photo by Clayton Hardy

MAP 10   Black-crowned Night Heron (*Nycticorax nycticorax*) Banding recoveries

Champlain valley (15), and the rest in central and western New York (24). The last two areas are listed below. Some of the localities no longer have breeding birds. Note the wide gap on the map where these herons are not known to breed.

(A) Hudson-Champlain valley: Staten Island, Richmond Co.—(1) Eltingville. Westchester Co.—(2) Tuckahoe; (3) Croton Point. Rockland Co.—(4) Piermont. Putnam Co.— (5) Constitution Island. Dutchess Co.—(6) Poughkeepsie. Ulster Co.—(7) Wallkill. Albany Co.—(8) Menands. Schenectady Co.— (9) Niskayuna. Saratoga Co.—(10) Vischer's Ferry; (11) Round Lake; (12) "due east" of Saratoga Lake, Hudson River. Washington Co. —(13) Granville. Essex Co., Lake Champlain —(14) Four Brothers Islands; (15) Schuyler Island near Port Kent.

(B) Central and western New York: Jefferson Co., Lake Ontario—(16) Gull and Bass islands; (17) Little Galloo Island. Onondaga Co.—(18) Lakeside, Onondaga Lake. Cayuga Co.—(19) Howland's Island; (20) Montezuma. Tompkins Co.—(21) near Ithaca. Broome Co.—(22) Vestal. Chemung Co.— (23) near Elmira. Steuben Co.—(24) Corning. Schuyler Co.—(25) Lamoka Lake. Yates Co. —(26) Branchport, Keuka Lake; (27) Potter Swamp. Ontario Co.—(28) near Naples; (29) north end of Honeoye Lake. Monroe Co.— (30) Irondequoit Bay; (31) Buck Pond. Genesee Co.—(32) Oak Orchard Swamp near Alabama. Niagara River—(33) Youngstown; (34) Goat Island; (35) Grand Island. Erie Co.— (36) West Seneca; (37) East Aurora; (38) Boston. Chautauqua Co.—(39) Clymer.

Banding (see Map 10): Four nestlings banded in June of various years in New York were recovered the following fall or winter, as follows: Two banded on Long Island were taken in Florida; a third banded on Little Galloo Island was recovered in western Cuba; the fourth banded on Lake Champlain (Four Brothers Islands) was shot near Yablis, Nicaragua.

A juvenile banded on Long Island in 1942 was found dead 14 years later.

Subspecies: The American race *hoactli* is larger and paler than the Old World nominate form; also the superciliary is narrower, the posterior portion being dull blackish-brown.

Yellow-crowned Night Heron
(*Nycticorax violaceus*)   *   B

Range: Neotropical and southern Nearctic regions, in eastern North America breeding along the Atlantic coast north to Long Island, rarely to Connecticut and Massachusetts. Winters chiefly from Florida south, but occasionally or rarely north to Long Island.

Status: Uncommon to locally common summer visitant and breeder along the coast. Greatly increased in recent years. Rare in winter on the coast. Very rare inland.

Change in status: This species was called by Eaton (1910: 266) ". . . one of the rarest of herons in New York State." He listed five Long Island records, four of them specimens, plus a dubious inland report. It was still very rare in the 1920s. Not until the 1930s and especially the 1940s did it materially increase; the first recorded breeding was on Long Island in 1938. Further details of its history are found in Bull (1964: 104–106).

Nonbreeding: Maximum numbers for this species are found under **Breeding**. Scarcely a dozen occurrences exist upstate where never more than two individuals have been seen together. I know of no authentic inland specimen, but an adult was photographed at Five Corners, Allegany Co., by Lou Burton. This bird remained from Apr. 30 to May 15, 1967, and was seen by numerous observers. All inland records are of adults in spring, except one in fall. There are no satisfactory records from the northern part of New York.

EXTREME DATES: Mar. 19 (coastal) and Apr. 25 (inland) to Oct. 4 (inland) and Nov. 1 (coastal). On the coast it is rare before mid-April and after early October.

Winter: There are seven reliable winter occurrences to my knowledge, all on Long Island, dates ranging from Dec. 30 to Mar. 2 in various years (1942–1967). Localities, dates, and observers are found in Bull (1964: 107, and 1970: 6–7).

Breeding (see Map 11): Unlike the other "southern" herons, the Yellow-crowned Night Heron is not confined as a breeder to the south side of Long Island, but is also to be

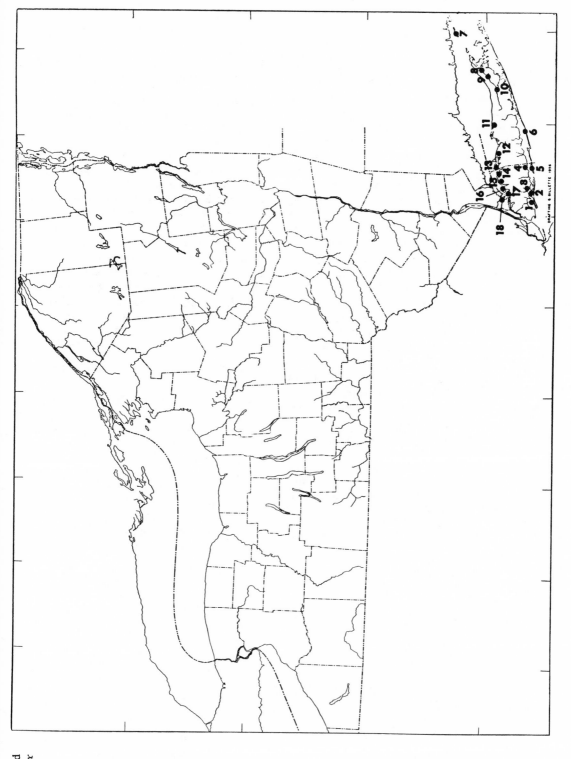

MAP 11 Yellow-crowned
Night Heron (*Nycticorax
violaceus*) Breeding
distribution

found nesting at a number of north shore localities, chiefly on or near Long Island Sound.

Nests of this species occur in two different ecological areas: (1) in mixed heronries located in coastal scrub consisting of wild cherry and dense tangles of poison ivy, catbrier, bayberry, and sumac, rarely in pine; the nests are placed low, from five to 12 feet above ground; (2) in wooded swamps or moist, or even dry, woodland consisting of such trees as maple, oak, cherry, tupelo, cedar, and other deciduous types, the nests situated from 15 to as high as 60 feet above ground. In the latter habitat this species may be found nesting alone, but more often with Black-crowned Night Herons.

Egg clutches in 15 New York nests: three eggs (four nests); four eggs (three nests); five eggs (seven nests); six eggs (one nest).

EGG DATES: Apr. 30 to June 10.

Nestlings: May 30 to June 24; fledglings: June 22 to July 4.

The three largest known colonies are: Tobay Pond, Nassau Co., 1956, 30 pairs; Lawrence Marsh, Nassau Co., 1962, ten pairs; Mt. Sinai, Suffolk Co., 1957, six nests.

The accompanying map indicates the 18 known breeding localities, 17 of which are on Long Island, number 18 on the adjacent mainland. Year following each locality denotes first known breeding at that locality: South shore, Kings and Queens counties—(1) Jamaica Bay Refuge, 1953. Nassau Co.—(2) Lawrence Marsh, 1961; (3) Woodmere Woods, 1947; (4) Massapequa, 1938—first for the state; (5) Tobay Pond and nearby Jones Beach, 1951. Suffolk Co.—(6) Sunken Forest, Point O'Woods, Fire Island, 1953 (S. Hopkins, *in litt.*), previously unpublished. North shore and eastern bays, Suffolk Co.—(7) Fisher's Island, 1958; (8) Southold, 1952; (9) Mattituck, 1952; (10) Riverhead, 1957; (11) Mt. Sinai, 1955; (12) Northport, 1960; (13) Caumsett State Park, 1965. Nassau Co.—(14) Centre Island, 1954; (15) Oyster Bay, 1954; (16) Sands Point, 1954; (17) Great Neck, 1941. Bronx Co.—(18) Pelham Bay Park, 1962.

American Bittern
(*Botaurus lentiginosus*)   *   B

Range: North America, breeding from southern Canada to central United States, rarely and locally to the Gulf states. Winters from New York southward, chiefly along the coast.

Status: Widespread breeder. Rare, but regular in winter on the coast, much rarer in the interior.

Nonbreeding: This species is encountered mostly during the fall migration, although only a few are to be seen even at that time. On a trip from Montauk to Shinnecock Bay, Suffolk Co., Oct. 9, 1932, Helmuth flushed 29 individuals in about 18 miles of suitable marsh.

On the south shore of Long Island in winter it is regularly observed on the coastal salt meadows in very small numbers. Upstate, however, it is very seldom met with at that season. A specimen in the New York State Museum collection was caught in a mink trap at Chatham, Columbia Co., Dec. 28, 1922.

Migrants usually arrive in early April.

Breeding: The American Bittern breeds in virtually every county in the state and nests in the Long Island salt marshes as well as in the inland fresh-water areas. Its booming notes in spring are among the characteristic sounds of the meadows.

Nests are placed on a platform or tussock of grass, or among cattails, rarely in a damp hayfield, from four to 18 inches above water level.

Egg clutches in 27 New York nests range from three eggs (probably incomplete sets) to six eggs, as follows: three eggs (four nests); four eggs (13 nests); five eggs (eight nests); six eggs (two nests).

EGG DATES: May 10 to June 29.

Nestlings: May 23 to July 24; fledglings: June 14 to Aug. 3.

Least Bittern
(*Ixobrychus exilis*)   *   B

Range: Nearctic and Neotropical regions, breeding from extreme southern Canada to southern South America. Winters north to Florida, in the east very rarely as far as Long Island (specimens).

Status: Rare to uncommon local breeder at lower elevations, occasionally locally common southward; absent in the mountains. Very rare in winter on the coast.

Nonbreeding: The secretive Least Bittern, the smallest member of the heron family in New York, is rarely reported in migration, or anywhere away from its breeding grounds. On rare occasions one may be found in a city park or in the heart of a large city, such as the individual found dead in lower Manhattan, New York City, May 8, 1950 (J. E. Taylor).

EXTREME DATES: Apr. 16 (coastal) and Apr. 27 (inland) to Oct. 17 (inland) and Nov. 19 (coastal); casual on Dec. 12, 1895 (coastal specimen). Rare before May and after September.

There are three midwinter specimens from the south shore of Long Island, the first two in the American Museum of Natural History collection, the last in the Nassau County Museum of Natural History: (1) Lido Beach, Nassau Co., Feb. 17, 1949 (Elliott); (2) Brookhaven, Suffolk Co., Jan. 26, 1964 (Puleston); (3) Seaford, Nassau Co., Feb. 17, 1966 (Van Sant).

Another individual was observed at Lawrence, Nassau Co., Jan. 28, 1950 (Boyajian and Ryan). Still another was present in the tidal brackish marshes of the lower Hudson River, at Iona Island, Rockland Co., from Feb. 3 to Mar. 3, 1952 (Orth).

The species is unknown in winter from upstate.

Breeding: Least Bitterns may be found in many of the marshes in the southern and western parts of the state, especially where cattails occur, and are also noted in grassy marshes inland and in the brackish meadows along the coast of Long Island. At least six breeding pairs were present at the Jamaica Bay Refuge in 1960. Least Bitterns are fairly numerous in the larger inland marshes, such as those at Montezuma and Oak Orchard.

In the more northern sections of the state this species becomes progressively less common. It is found in certain marshes along Lake Ontario, north to at least the Oswego-Jefferson Co. line, perhaps farther north. It is practically unknown in the Adirondack district. However, three birds were flushed from the marsh at the south end of Lake Champlain, near Ticonderoga, Essex Co., July 10, 1932 (Carleton), and may well have bred. It is not known as a breeder from farther north than these areas.

Least Bitterns nest from one to four feet above water level, preferably in cattails, but also on grass tussocks.

Egg clutches in 38 New York nests range from three to five eggs: three eggs (nine nests); four eggs (21 nests); five eggs (eight nests).

EGG DATES: May 15 to July 10.

Nestlings: June 10 to July 20; fledglings: July 2 to Sept. 4.

Remarks: A specimen of the rare melanistic morph, known as "Cory's" Least Bittern, was taken in the marshes near Ithaca, May 17, 1913 (Allen and Harper, *Auk,* 1913, 30: 559–561). This specimen was not in the Cornell University Museum when I examined that collection.

STORKS — CICONIIDAE

One species in New York.
None breed.

The members of this fairly widespread family (17 species) include several familiar birds. Only the Wood Stork (*Mycteria americana*) is represented in our area and it is but a vagrant here. For an excellent revision of this family, see Kahl (1971, 1972).

Wood Stork (*Mycteria americana*) *

Range: Neotropical region, breeding north to Florida, occasionally to South Carolina. Wanders widely after the breeding season, rarely north to southern Canada. Winters throughout much of the breeding range.

Status: *Very rare*—There are at least 13

known occurrences of the Wood Stork in New York, about half of these from Long Island. Eaton (1910: 245) listed three specimen records from upstate, but apparently only one of these is extant: One of two collected at Sand Lake, Rensselaer Co., June 24, 1876 (Webster), is USNM 98509; another, reported by Fisher (*Auk*, 1885, 2: 221), was taken at Glennie Falls, Ulster Co., July 8, 1884 (Tipp); the third specimen was collected at East Galway, Saratoga Co., August 1896 (Ingersoll and Brower). The species has also been observed in recent years (all single individuals) on three occasions upstate: (1) Ithaca, July 9, 1932 (Allen); (2) Waneta Lake, Schuyler Co., July 17, 1934 (Clausen and Conroe); (3) Esopus Creek, near Slide Mtn., Ulster Co., Sept. 1958 (Dunn-photographed). Other inland reports were not confirmed.

On Long Island a specimen was shot in a wooded swamp at East Marion, Suffolk Co., June 21, 1890 (Schellinger, *fide* Latham). The whereabouts of this specimen is not known. Most remarkably, 65 years later, Latham himself saw an individual in this very same swamp on June 23, 1955.

All of the above have been of single birds, but within a five-year period (1958–1962) *flocks* of Wood Storks were observed on Long Island as follows: ten, East Marion, Aug. 17, 1958 (E. Morgan) and 13 each (same flock?) at Orient (Latham), East Marion (Morgan), and Riverhead (Stoutenburgh), all on Aug. 18, 1958. All of these localities in extreme eastern Suffolk Co. are only 12 miles apart at the most and it seems quite likely that the birds seen on those two days may have been the same ones. A flock of 11 was observed flying over the Jamaica Bay Refuge, Queens Co., June 10, 1961 (Johnson); still another flock of 15 was seen alighting on the salt meadows north of Jones Beach, Nassau Co., Apr. 2, 1962 (Alperin). This last flock was associated with about 100 Snowy Egrets and 35 Great Egrets.

It seems remarkable that there was only the one record on Long Island of a single individual in over a century and that "suddenly" within five years *flocks* of Wood Storks were reported. A possible explanation of so many Wood Storks in the north during recent years may be attributed to the drying up of southern feeding grounds, forcing these birds to go elsewhere for food.

IBISES — THRESKIORNITHIDAE

Three species in New York.
One breeds.

Only the Glossy Ibis (*Plegadis falcinellus*) of this mainly tropical family (30± species) is a common bird in coastal areas and breeds on Long Island. Its phenomenal northward range extension as far as New York and its current local abundance as a breeder there occurred within the last decade (1960–1970). Its close relative the White-faced Ibis (*P. chihi*) and the White Ibis (*Eudocimus albus*) are, however, nothing more than accidental visitants to New York.

Glossy Ibis
(*Plegadis falcinellus*)   *   B

Range: Widespread, but local breeder in warm-temperate and tropical regions of the Old World; in America breeds locally in the Greater Antilles, the coast of Louisiana, and from Florida north along the Atlantic coast to Long Island, New York, and in 1971 to southwestern Connecticut. Withdraws in winter from northern portions.

Status: Formerly a very rare vagrant, but in recent years has greatly increased along the coast. Local breeder on western Long Island (since 1961). Sporadic visitant inland, but increasing.

Change in status: This primarily Old World species (if not considered conspecific with the White-faced Ibis, *Plegadis chihi*) has had a similar history, if not as spectacular as that of the Cattle Egret (*Bubulcus ibis*). Both apparently crossed the tropical Atlantic from the Old World and settled in the Caribbean area, and then spread northward along the Atlantic coast, although the Glossy Ibis became established in the New World much earlier. The Glossy Ibis has had a notable range expansion in about 20 years along the east coast of the United States—breeding for the first known time north of Florida in the early 1940s and reaching its present northernmost known breeding localities on Long Island by 1961.

In New York State it was accidental prior to 1935 and until 1939 was observed sporadically, the sighting of a single bird being considered an outstanding event. Between 1944 and 1959 Glossy Ibises were reported almost annually on the coast and on occasion even small flocks were observed. Since the early 1960s the species has been reported in considerable numbers, especially on Long Island. It is not unusual for groups to be seen flying over coastal towns to and from their breeding grounds and feeding areas which are as much as six miles apart. The birds often gather to feed on the extensive salt meadows along the south shore, particularly about the many tidal creeks and pools; also on flooded golf courses after heavy rains.

Nonbreeding: There are three old specimen records from Long Island from 1840 to 1848 (Bull, 1964: 109–110). At least seven specimens were taken in upstate New York between 1854 and 1907 (Eaton, 1910: 243) including two collected and four more observed in the Montezuma Marshes in May 1907. In recent years one was collected near Vischer's Ferry, Saratoga Co., May 8, 1958 (Burtt), NYSM 19015.

Together with the great increase and northward spread of this species along the coast of New York during the middle to late 1950s, a number of individuals and occasional small flocks also appeared inland.

MAXIMA: *Coastal*—185, marshes east of

Kennedy Airport, May 5, 1968 (Berliner and Hirschbein); 225, Jamaica Bay Refuge, Aug. 31, 1969 (Arbib); 88, Hempstead Reservoir, Nassau Co., July 26, 1970 (Dempsey).

MAXIMA: *Inland*—listed according to year —flock of 12, Oak Orchard Swamp, Apr. 29 to May 13, 1939 (Eckler and Savage), moving pictures taken, an unprecedented number both for time and place; four, Perch River Refuge, Jefferson Co., June 22, 1958; three, Lyndonville, Orleans Co., Apr. 28, 1960; seven, Derby Hill, Oswego Co., May 6, 1960; seven, Montezuma Marshes, May 15, 1960; nine, Chittenango, Madison Co., May 4, 1962; seven, Chemung River near Elmira, May 15, 1967; nine, Cedarville, Herkimer Co., May 11, 1968; seven, Hamlin, Monroe Co., May 17, 1969; 15, Braddock's Bay, Monroe Co., May 3, 1970, largest inland flock to date.

EXTREME DATES: Mar. 12 (coastal) and Mar. 26 (upstate) to Nov. 8 (upstate) and Nov. 23 (coastal), exceptionally to Dec. 12 (Long Island). Usually rare before late April and after October.

Winter: one, Jamaica Bay Refuge, Long Island, Jan. 1, 1966 (Johnson); and most exceptionally 14 there, Dec. 26, 1970 (Brooklyn Bird Club).

Breeding (see Map 12): First reported breeding in 1961 at (1) Jamaica Bay Refuge; nesting colony located on Canarsie Pol, Kings Co., an island in Jamaica Bay. The second known breeding location was at (2) Lawrence Marsh, Nassau Co., in 1964; the third at (3) Oak Beach, Suffolk Co., in 1967; the fourth and fifth at nearby (4) Jones Beach in 1968, and (5) Short Beach in 1969, both in Nassau Co.; and the sixth on (6) Gardiner's Island, Suffolk Co., in 1970.

The following table indicates growth of the two main colonies and four new ones; numbers represent occupied nests and/or pairs.

Jamaica Bay Refuge	Lawrence Marsh
1961—3 (Canarsie Pol)	
1962—6 (Canarsie Pol)	1964—3
1963—not visited	1965—13
1964—not visited	1966—24
1965—18 (Canarsie Pol)	1967—42
1966—60+ (Canarsie Pol)	1971—70+
1967—70+ (Canarsie Pol)	
1968—40 (east pond)	

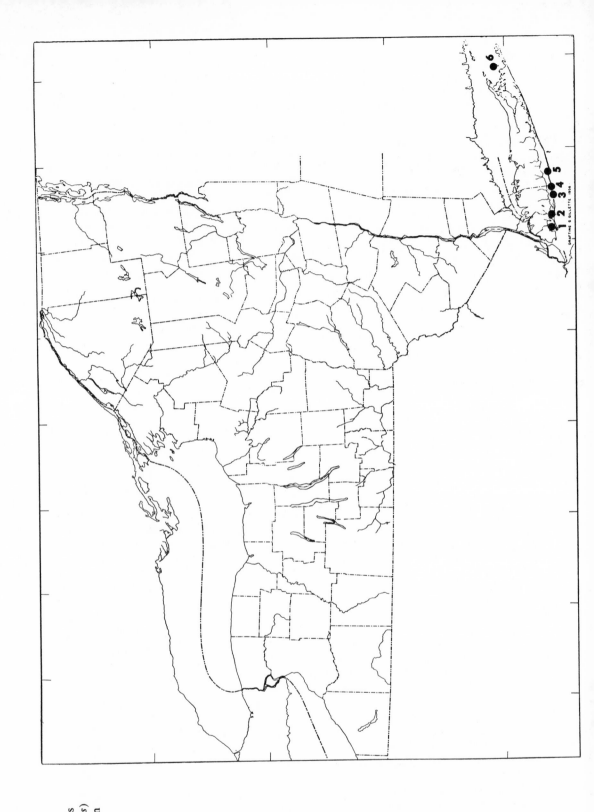

MAP 12 Glossy Ibis
(*Plegadis falcinellus*)
Breeding distribution

Oak Beach	Short Beach
1967—1	1969—11
1971—100+	1971—120+

Jones Beach	Gardiner's Island
1968—12	
1971—25	1970—1
	1971—4

The accompanying map includes the above six breeding localities: Kings and Queens counties—(1) Jamaica Bay Refuge. Nassau Co.—(2) Lawrence; (3) Short Beach; (4) Jones Beach (near Tobay Pond). Suffolk Co.—(5) Oak Beach; (6) Gardiner's Island.

Of numerous nests examined, all were situated in mixed heron colonies located chiefly on sandy islands partially covered with dense vegetation. These islands are along the inland waterway within a mile of the ocean. A few nests were found on the ground, but the majority ranged from three to nine feet up in wild cherry, poplar, willow, bayberry, alder, sumac, and beach plum often interspersed with thick tangles of catbrier, poison ivy, and Virginia creeper.

The lone Glossy Ibis nest at Oak Beach was located in a mixed heronry in a black pine grove (Enders and W. Post), as were those at Jones Beach and Short Beach (Post, et al., 1970: 7).

Egg clutches range from one to four. The 42 nests at Lawrence in 1967 contained the following clutch sizes on June 9: six nests with one egg; ten with two; 20 with three; six with four.

EGG DATES: Eggs in one or both colonies were found as early as May 3 (four nests—two with one egg, two with two) and as late as July 27.

Unfledged juveniles: June 4 to Aug. 25; fledglings: July 1 to Sept. 14. The great span of egg dates is thought to represent renesting after early unsuccessful attempts.

In 1965 at the Lawrence colony many of the ibis and heron nests were marked and the young banded. Several nests there occupied by Glossy Ibis in 1967 had been used the previous year by Snowy Egrets and Black-crowned Night Herons.

Much of the nesting information at the two large colonies was supplied by Helen Hays and Tom Davis.

In 1970 on Gardiner's Island, Dennis Puleston and others found an occupied nest in a mixed heronry on July 7, which contained four unfledged young. This Gardiner's Island locality represents a northeastward range extension of about 80 miles.

During the breeding season of 1973 it was estimated that not less than 500 pairs nested in the greater Jones Beach area and another 75+ pairs on Gardiner's Island. This reflects its tremendous increase of recent years, plus the fact that the species was recorded as breeding as far north as Maine.

White-faced Ibis (Plegadis [falcinellus?] chihi) *

Range: Western United States, breeding (mainly resident) locally east to Nebraska and coastal Louisiana (rarely in Minnesota and Florida), south to central Mexico; also southern South America. Primarily a temperate zone "species." Vagrant east to Michigan, Ohio, and western New York.

Status: Accidental—Two specimen records, curiously enough both adults from Grand Island, Niagara River: (1) August 1844 (Hurst), NYSM 205; (2) Sept. 18, 1908 (Reynolds), specimen examined by Eaton (1914: 542–543) and formerly in the BMS collection, but unfortunately discarded around 1919 (Beardslee and Mitchell, 1965: 105–106). As there have been only two records in New York in over 120 years and the latter more than 60 years ago, this bird is placed in the Accidental category.

Remarks: Palmer (1962: 515–522) treats P. falcinellus and chihi as conspecific; admittedly they are very close morphologically, at least as to plumage. However, J. Morony (MS) found a mixed breeding colony of the two forms in southern Louisiana in 1965 and 1966. He reported that breeding adults of the two forms possessed markedly different facial (soft-part) colors as well as different vocalizations and courtship displays, suggesting that the two may be distinct species. Nevertheless, he found at least three pairs that appeared to be morphologically intermediate or presumed hybrids. Clearly further field work is necessary in contact zones.

White Ibis (*Eudocimus albus*)   *

Range: Chiefly Neotropical region, breeding (resident) north to coastal South Carolina, rarely to North Carolina. Wanders north to Quebec and Vermont.

Status: *Casual*—In New York there are five occurrences, all from Long Island as follows: three old specimen records (only one extant) and two recent sight reports.

(1) Raynor South (=Freeport), Nassau Co., summer of 1836 (Giraud, 1844: 275).

(2) adult, Great South Bay, Suffolk Co., 1840 (Pike), AMNH 442374.

(3) Moriches, Suffolk Co., early March 1843 (Giraud, *op. cit.*).

(4) adult seen in flight, Jamaica Bay Refuge, Queens Co., Oct. 25, 1969 (Johnson).

(5) adult with Snowy Egrets, Cedar Beach, Suffolk Co., Mar. 29 to early April, 1970 (W. L. Graves, R. Cohen, and others).

Note that the three specimen records occurred within a span of only eight years, but that well over a century passed before the species was reported again, and that finally White Ibis were seen *twice* within six months.

In the case of (4), the observer had had previous field experience in Florida. As to (5), this bird was observed both on the ground and in flight in direct comparison with Snowy Egrets on several occasions during the period stated above.

Beardslee and Mitchell (1965: 106) discount two supposed occurrences for western New York.

FLAMINGOS — PHOENICOPTERIDAE

One species in New York (hypothetical).
None breed.

Depending on taxonomic opinion, from four to six species of these unmistakable and unique birds occur in mostly disjunct populations. Except for tropical east Africa with two species, the only other continent with more than one is South America with three or four; three forms occur in the Andean region, two of them at high altitudes (salt lakes of the puna zone).

[Greater Flamingo
(*Phoenicopterus ruber*)

Hypothetical: Caribbean area, Galápagos Archipelago, and southern Palearctic and Ethiopian regions. Nominate *ruber* (northern

Neotropical region) wanders north to southern Florida, but many individuals are believed to be escapes from the colony at the Hialeah race track near Miami.

In New York State, as in other sections of the northeast, all occurrences, including two Long Island specimen records, were most probably escapes from confinement. The species is common in captivity.

In addition to the two Long Island specimens (Bull, 1964: 471), there have been two observations of birds in 1964 and 1965, one on eastern Long Island, the other in the upper Hudson valley (Bull, 1970: 51).

Some authorities consider this form and the South American *chilensis* to be conspecific. Others would make the New World *ruber* and the Old World *roseus* two distinct species; these last two are treated here as one species, following Palmer (1962) and Vaurie (1965).]

SWANS, GEESE, DUCKS — ANATIDAE

Forty species in New York.
Eighteen breed.

This diverse, worldwide family (150± species) has been studied extensively for many years by students of waterfowl and by aviculturists. Its members are among our most familiar birds. In the swans and geese the sexes are alike, but many species of ducks have marked sexual dimorphism.

The lakes, ponds, rivers, and marshes, as well as the bays, inlets, and ocean itself are at times all frequented by both dipping and diving forms. Nearly half the species found in the state have been known to breed, fully twice as many kinds breeding today as back in Eaton's time early in this century. This is due mainly to the creation of waterfowl refuges and to the efforts of biologists and state conservation personnel in attracting these birds and encouraging them to breed. Many interesting banding recoveries have been obtained from hunters.

Waterfowl taxonomy has received much attention in recent decades, primarily due to the interest of Jean Delacour in his reassessment of relationships based on studies of morphology and behavior. The treatment followed here is, with minor modifications, that of Delacour and Mayr (1945), Delacour (1954, 1956, 1959), and Johnsgard (1965).

The following 15 genera are recognized: *Cygnus, Branta, Anser, Dendrocygna, Anas, Aix, Aythya, Histrionicus, Camptorhynchus, Somateria, Melanitta, Clangula, Bucephala, Mergus,* and *Oxyura.* One major change in generic sequence is the placing of the goldeneyes (*Bucephala*) near the mergansers (*Mergus*), because of several known hybrids between the two.

With the reduction from the 21 genera in the 1957 A.O.U. Check-list to 15, the following six are no longer recognized: *"Olor," "Chen," "Mareca," "Spatula," "Oidemia,"* and *"Lophodytes."* As a consequence they are merged as follows: (1) *"Olor"*=Cygnus; (2) *"Chen"*=Anser; (3) and (4) *"Mareca"* and *"Spatula"*=Anas; (5) *"Oidemia"*=Melanitta; (6) *"Lophodytes"*=Mergus.

Mute Swan (*Cygnus olor*)   *   B

Range: Palearctic region; introduced in 1910 into southeastern New York in the lower Hudson valley (chiefly near Rhinebeck, Dutchess Co.) and in 1912 on the south shore of Long Island (at Southampton and Oakdale, Suffolk Co.). Sedentary.

Status: *Introduced*—since about 1912 the Mute Swan has become established over much of Long Island, but is really numerous only on the bays and ponds at the east end; it is locally common inland in Dutchess and Rockland counties. Elsewhere it is rare to uncommon and of local occurrence.

This species is essentially sedentary, although wandering somewhat in winter. A juvenile **banded** Aug. 9, 1964, near Sakonnet Point, Rhode Island, was found injured nearly seven months later, Mar. 3, 1965, about 80 miles to the southwest on Great South Bay, near Bellport, Suffolk Co.

MAXIMA: All except one in eastern Suffolk Co., Long Island: 60 adults, Mill Neck, Nassau Co., July 13, 1958; 155 adults, Fort Pond, Montauk, July 15, 1958; 175, South Haven, Dec. 9, 1950; 500, Moriches Bay, Dec. 26, 1959 (many observers); 275, Mecox Bay, Dec. 31, 1949; 65, Rockland Lake, Rockland Co., Feb. 6, 1965.

Mute Swans breed along the shores of shallow ponds and in marshes. Rarely, nests have been built on muskrat houses.

Of nine New York nests examined, clutches contained from seven to ten eggs.

EGG DATES: Mar. 26 to May 26.

Unfledged young: May 16 to June 21; no New York data on fledglings.

Whistling Swan
(*Cygnus columbianus*)   *

Range: Subarctic regions of North America, breeding south to Hudson Bay (Churchill, Manitoba; Belcher Islands). On the Atlantic coast winters from Maryland to North Carolina. The eastern populations migrate via the Great Lakes; rare on the Atlantic coast north of Maryland.

Status: Common to abundant spring migrant in extreme western New York, less numerous in fall; rare to uncommon east of the Finger Lakes.

Occurrence: Among the most spectacular sights in the bird world are the large gatherings of this fine species during the spring migration on Chautauqua Lake and at Niagara Falls. Much has been written about the destruction of Whistling Swans in the past as they were forced down by severe storms in the vicinity of the falls and then swept by the strong current over the cataract to their deaths or, if they survived this ordeal, were often spun around by the violent whirlpools below the falls and dashed against the rocks. This occurred chiefly during the first quarter of the twentieth century. In more recent times fewer swans have used this precarious route. For a full account of these happenings, see Beardslee and Mitchell (1965: 107–112).

MAXIMA: *Spring*—Niagara Falls: 300+, above the falls, Mar. 14, 1908, over 100 killed the following day (42 mounted by one taxidermist alone); 200 went over the falls, Apr. 6, 1912; 200+, swept over the falls, night of Mar. 24–25, 1928; 335, Mar. 29, 1961; other spring maxima—3000, Chautauqua Lake, Mar. 20, 1955 (Beal, Parker, *et al.*), a most exceptional concentration; 1000, Conewango Valley, near Chautauqua Lake, Mar. 26, 1968; 650, Groveland, Livingston Co., Mar. 30, 1968.

MAXIMA: *Fall*—115, flying over Java, Wyoming Co., Oct. 26, 1942; 700+ near Buffalo, Nov. 6, 1966; 300, Chautauqua Lake, Nov. 9, 1956; 200 over Jamestown, Chautauqua Co., Nov. 18, 1968. "Large" coastal flight on Nov. 16, 1969—40 each at Mecox Bay and Shinnecock Inlet, Suffolk Co.

MAXIMA, INLAND: *Winter*—five, Strawberry Island, Niagara River, winter of 1952–1953; coastal—six, South Haven, Suffolk Co., winter of 1942; nine, Mecox Bay, Suffolk Co., winter of 1960.

EXTREME DATES: Sept. 15 to May 26 (specimen) and May 31. Rare before late October and after April. One summered at Oak Orchard Swamp, 1952; another summered at Montezuma Marshes, 1967. These occurrences are most unusual.

Great care must be taken by beginners not to confuse the immature Mute Swan with the present species, especially when in flight. When heard, the trumpet-like call of the Whistling Swan is diagnostic.

Specimen data: Numerous specimens, mostly from western New York, are represented in the various museums.

Remarks: Treated as conspecific with *C. bewickii* (Bewick's Swan) of the eastern Palearctic region by Delacour (1954: 71), by Mayr and Short (1970: 32), and by Palmer (in prep.), but not by Vaurie (1965: 106).

[Trumpeter Swan (*Cygnus buccinator*)

Hypothetical: Locally in western North America, formerly east to the Mississippi valley region. No definite proof exists of former occurrence on the Atlantic coast, contrary to the statement in the A.O.U. Check-list (1957: 60), ". . . on the Atlantic seaboard to North Carolina." None of the recent publications on birds from Newfoundland to North Carolina includes this species, nor does Banko (1960) mention it.

There is no specimen evidence to indicate occurrence in New York State. The few old specimens in museums, thought to have been this species and labeled as such, were re-identified as Whistling Swans (*C. columbianus*) by the writer.

Perhaps conspecific with *C. cygnus* (Whooper Swan) of the Palearctic region, and so treated by Delacour (1954: 71–82) and by Mayr and Short (1970: 32), but not by Vaurie (1965: 105), nor by Palmer (in prep.).]

Canada Goose
(*Branta canadensis*)   *   B

Range: Nearctic region, breeding from Alaska and Canada (in the east) to the central portions of Ontario and Quebec, rarely to northern United States (introduced stock). Winters from the southern portion of the breeding range to the Gulf states. See **Subspecies** for details.

Status: Very abundant migrant, especially in western New York; common to very abundant in winter on Long Island. Local breeder (semidomesticated birds).

Nonbreeding: In early spring flocks of birds flying in long V-shaped lines and honking continuously are almost certainly to be Canada Geese on their way to northern breeding grounds. Occasionally enormous numbers of these geese, often in the tens of thousands, pitch down to rest and feed in the famous Oak Orchard and Montezuma wildlife refuges. Few sights are as spectacular. Concentrations in fall are much less numerous, although no less impressive.

MAXIMA: *Spring*—12,000 Mecox Bay, Suffolk Co., Mar. 9, 1945; 60,000 Oak Orchard Swamp, Mar. 28, 1968; 85,000, same area, Apr. 7, 1963; 70,000, Montezuma Marshes, Apr. 21, 1968.

MAXIMA: *Fall*—10,000, Oak Orchard Swamp, Oct. 25, 1969; 4000, Jones Beach, Long Island, Nov. 5, 1950.

MAXIMA: *Winter*—5000, Shinnecock Bay, Suffolk Co., Jan. 1, 1922; 5000, Mecox Bay, Feb. 5, 1950.

Breeding: Frequent releases of captive birds are the only known source of breeding Canada Geese in New York. This state is considerably south of the nearest *wild* breeding populations in central Canada.

In 1961 at least 50 pairs bred in the Montezuma Refuge, the same number of pairs in 1962 at nearby Howland's Island, and in 1963 more than 20 breeding pairs were counted in the Oak Orchard Refuge. On Long Island in 1970 Dennis Puleston estimated *100* pairs on Gardiner's Island, Suffolk Co.

These birds construct their nests on mounds, such as on muskrat houses in lakes and ponds, or more rarely on dry land near water. At the Montezuma Refuge some nests were even placed on tree stumps (*Journ. Wildlife Mgmt.*, 1967, 31: 229–235).

In the few New York instances known, egg clutch size ranged from six to eight, with one of 11 reported.

EGG DATES: Mar. 28 to May 14.

Unfledged young: May 14 to June 27; fledglings: from May 18.

Banding (see Map 13): Two nestlings, banded in the wilds of northern Quebec on the coasts of Hudson and Ungava bays, were recovered the following fall near Rochester and Poughkeepsie respectively.

Seven others banded in April of various years in western New York (near Rochester and Syracuse) were recovered in the following early summer on their presumed breeding grounds along the south and east shores of Hudson Bay and on the west shore of Ungava Bay. With the exception of one taken near Cape Henrietta Maria, Ontario, and another at Cape Jones, Quebec, all others were recovered in northern Quebec on the Ungava peninsula.

An example of how even banding data are subject to error is the report of an adult female Canada Goose banded at the Oak Orchard Refuge, Apr. 13, 1955, and trapped and released in California, June 23, 1955. Canada Geese *do not* fly from coast to coast (unless deliberately transported) at any time, least of all in late spring and early summer. Clearly one of two things happened—either the bird was misidentified or, more likely, the band number was misread.

Banding data should receive the same scrutiny and skepticism as sight reports.

Subspecies: Three very distinct subspecies are known from New York. (1) Nominate *canadensis* has been discussed previously. It is the southeasternmost Canadian breeding population.

(2) The more western race *interior* (much darker below than nominate form and little or no color contrast between neck and back as in *canadensis*) is represented by seven state specimens: Three from Montauk Point—two of which were collected, Mar. 14, 1902, the third taken Dec. 3, 1909—are ali in the AMNH collection, 350133, 350134, and 350131; four

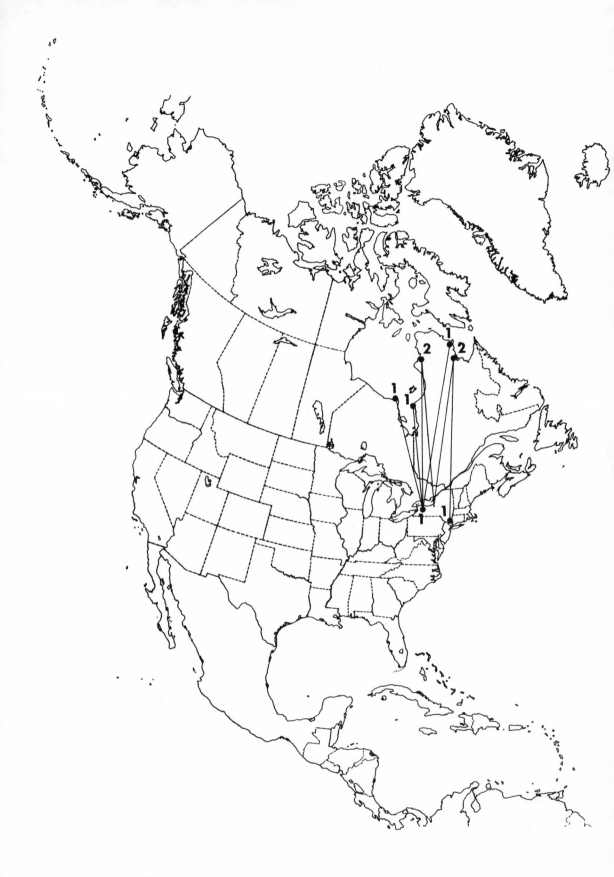

MAP 13 Canada Goose (*Branta canadensis*) Banding recoveries

other specimens, all from the east shore of Cayuga Lake near King Ferry, were taken as follows: two, Nov. 4, 1928, and two, Dec. 14,
1941, all by A. A. Allen and in the CUM collection (247 and 248, and 23244 and 23245).

(3) The subarctic race *hutchinsii* (much
smaller, only half the size of the previous races,
and with a short bill), breeding to the north of
canadensis, has been collected twice in New
York, both very recently. One from the Oak
Orchard Swamp area near Alabama, Genesee
Co., in April 1964 (Andrle and Axtell), BMS
5081. The other from Long Island was shot on
Sayre's Pond, Southampton, Suffolk Co., Nov.
20, 1968 (W. E. Logan), AMNH 789787.

There are also several excellent color photographs of an individual of this Mallard-sized
subspecies taken near Tobay Pond, Nassau
Co., Oct. 15, 1966 (Darrow), color prints on
file in the AMNH collection. The photographs
clearly show the size difference and stubby
bill of the small bird which is alongside three
individuals of the much larger common form.
These color prints have been examined by
Delacour, who concurs in the identification.

The New York specimen taken at Gaines,
Orleans Co., in 1888 and alleged to be the race
hutchinsii in much of the literature, is in the
NYSM collection, 1163. This specimen, examined by me, is too large for *hutchinsii,* as the
wing and culmen measurements greatly exceed
the maximum for this race. It appears to be an
immature of nominate *canadensis,* somewhat
smaller than adults compared with it.

Sightings as to subspecies are not accepted.

Brant (*Branta bernicla*)   *

Range: Northern Holarctic region, breeding
in high latitudes; (1) the light-bellied, eastern
North American race *hrota* (palest of the three
subspecies) south to Baffin and Southampton
islands; (2) the very dark-bellied population
nigricans (considered by some a species, called
the Black Brant) from northeastern Siberia
east to at least Melville Island in the Canadian Arctic where the two forms occasionally
interbreed. (1) Winters chiefly on the Atlantic
coast from Long Island to about Chesapeake
Bay; (2) winters on the Pacific coast from
Alaska to Baja California and is purely casual
in eastern North America.

Status: Abundant to very abundant migrant
and winter visitant on the south shore of western Long Island. Less numerous elsewhere
along the coast. Recorded every month of the
year, but summering stragglers are infrequent.
Formerly very rare inland, but has greatly increased recently and is now a locally common
to abundant n igrant.

Change in status: For details of this bird's
fluctuations in the marine region, see Bull
(1964: 114–115); it is much too long an account to include here and would be repetitious.
It may be stated briefly, though, that the main
wintering grounds in New York State are on
the south shore of Long Island from Jamaica
Bay east to the western reaches of Great South
Bay.

With a change in food from eel grass
(killed by blight) to sea lettuce and ultimately
back to eel grass and with a resultant change
in winter status and migration, the Brant's occurrence inland changed from very rare to locally common or even abundant (see maxima).
This took place around the early to mid-1950s
when the first really sizable concentrations occurred away from Long Island. Moreover, a
late spring flight by way of the Hudson valley
and the Great Lakes, thence overland through
the wilds of Quebec to the arctic breeding
grounds is now an annual phenomenon. There
is also a large inland flight in fall.

MAXIMA: *Coastal*—10,000, Jamaica Bay,
Nov. 21, 1965; 20,000, Woodmere and Hewlett bays, Nassau Co., Jan. 10, 1960; 10,000,
Jamaica Bay, Apr. 27, 1957; 4000, same locality, May 20, 1956; 500, Point Lookout,
Nassau Co., June 4, 1950; 40, Jamaica Bay,
all summer of 1961.

MAXIMA: *Inland*—4500, Cornwall, Orange
Co., May 23, 1966; 1500, Montezuma
Marshes, May 26, 1960; unprecedented inland
flight in 1965, in two days total of 12,000 at
Derby Hill, Oswego Co.—9000, Oct. 23
(Rusk) and 3000, Oct. 24; also 6000, Hamlin
Beach, Monroe Co., Oct. 29, 1966 (Listman);
finally on Nov. 3, 1962, 2600 were reported at
four different localities as follows—930, Point
Breeze, Orleans Co.; 1070, Manitou, Monroe
Co.; 100, Cayuga Lake; 500, Oneida Lake.

Specimen data: E. H. Eaton (1910: 234)
listed seven inland specimens, but apparently
none is extant. The only known existing speci-

MAP 14   Brant (*Branta bernicla*) Banding recoveries

mens from upstate are four taken in recent years: (1) Olean Creek, Cattaraugus Co., November 1950 (S. W. Eaton, 1953: 7); (2) Myer's Point, Cayuga Lake, Nov. 10, 1956 (Angel), CUM 28548; (3) Shadigee, Orleans Co., Oct. 23, 1959 (Tuttle and Reu), BMS 5082; (4) Greece, Monroe Co., Oct. 31, 1959 (Boardman), RMAS no number.

Banding (see Map 14): Of 36 Brant banded as nestlings in summer on Southampton Island in various years, 31 were recovered the following fall or winter on Long Island, and the remaining five were taken in fall upstate as follows: three from the Oneida Lake region and two from Lake Erie near Fredonia.

Subspecies: Delacour (1954: 190) is followed in treating *nigricans* as conspecific with *bernicla*. Godfrey (1966: 50) has adoped this treatment also.

In New York State three specimens of *nigricans* have been reported, all from Suffolk Co., Long Island, but none is known to be extant: (1) Islip, 1840; (2) Babylon, spring of 1889 (both examined by Dutcher); (3) Babylon, Mar. 31, 1908 (Herrick).

Another specimen, supposedly *nigricans*, but with the subspecific allocation in doubt, is also apparently not extant: Oneida Lake, at Lewis Point, Madison Co., Oct. 30, 1891 (Dexter), was not examined by an ornithologist (*Auk*, 1894, 11: 163).

Two observations of birds on Long Island believed to be this race are: Merrick Bay, Nassau Co., Mar. 30, 1946 (Bull and Komorowski), direct comparison with 2000 light-bellied birds on mud flat; Mattituck, Suffolk Co., Oct. 25, 1959 (E. Morgan), observed on open beach.

Another individual observed at Burntship Creek, near Niagara Falls, Nov. 13, 1949 (Byron, Clement, Nathan, Seeber, and Wright), was photographed by the last-named. I have examined this photo (in the BMS collection) but the picture is only fair. It *appears* to be a "Black" Brant. Other reports are much less satisfactory.

Barnacle Goose (*Branta leucopsis*) *

Range: Northwestern Palearctic region, breeding west to eastern Greenland and wintering south to the British Isles and France. Vagrant in eastern North America from Baffin Island to Long Island.

Status: *Very rare*—The Barnacle Goose is one of those species which is commonly kept in captivity and as such is virtually impossible to evaluate the dozen or so occurrences within the state. Two Long Island reports were listed (Bull, 1964: 116) as being of almost certain captive origin due either to their being wing-clipped or to their exceedingly tame behavior. The records for extreme western New York cited by Beardslee and Mitchell (1965: 118–119) were not qualified by them in this respect and the origin of some or all are highly suspect.

However, since this species has been recorded at such places as Baffin Island and Labrador, where aviaries are nonexistent, it is very likely that Canadian-based birds, at least, were genuine stragglers from the Old World.

It may be significant that all four Long Island specimen records are in fall (October to December) as are *all* coastal occurrences in eastern North America, i.e., Canada and Massachusetts; whereas the seven or more western New York occurrences—all sightings and some individuals suspiciously tame—are in early spring (late March and early April) which, to this writer, seems more than a coincidence (see discussion following).

There is apparently only one New York specimen that is extant: female collected on Jamaica Bay, Long Island, Oct. 18, 1876 (Kendall), USNM 80015.

Three other Long Island records, all specimens from Suffolk Co., are: Money Island, Great South Bay, Oct. 16, 1919 (Hollis); Orient, Dec. 11, 1926 (*fide* Latham); one with a flock of Canada Geese on Shinnecock Bay, December 1926 (*fide* Latham). These four specimens were all taken at coastal points during the hunting season and it appears likely that these birds were of wild origin but, of course, there is no absolute proof.

It is very difficult to be sure how many individuals were involved in the western New York observations, but it should be pointed out that the four counties of Monroe, Orleans, Niagara, and Genesee are involved and that the localities of Shore Acres, Shelby, Oak Orchard Swamp, Stafford's Pond, Wolcottsville, Somerset, and Yates are not much more than

30 miles from one another. In fact, Beardslee and Mitchell (*op. cit.*) stated that the first four localities mentioned above, with dates ranging from Mar. 26 to Apr. 17 in the years 1953 to 1957, represent probably not more than one individual. The species was also observed in this same general region in 1961, 1963, 1967, and 1968 with the same probability of only one or two individuals being involved.

It seems curious that all of these upstate occurrences were restricted to one general area and all within a space of 16 years and all in a short period of 23 days (Mar. 26 to Apr. 17). Axtell (*Prothonotary*, 1968, 34: April) is of the belief that all of the inland Barnacle Geese may well be escaped birds.

Finally, two different individuals seen the same day (Jan. 5, 1969) about 20 miles apart on Long Island Sound (Norwalk, Conn., and Pelham Bay, Bronx Co.), were reported on good authority to have escaped from confinement.

Greater White-fronted Goose
(*Anser albifrons*)   *

Range: Northern portions of the Holarctic region, but absent in much of the eastern Canadian arctic, Greenland (except the southwest coast), Iceland, Spitsbergen, and Scandinavia. In North America the species breeds southeast to the west shore of Hudson Bay in the District of Keewatin; migrates chiefly west of the Mississippi River; winters along the Gulf coast east to Louisiana. Vagrant on the Atlantic coast from Labrador to Georgia. See **Subspecies.**

Status: *Very rare*—This species is represented in New York by seven specimens (only one extant), six from Long Island (all from Suffolk Co.) and one from upstate. The five old Long Island specimens are listed in Bull (1964: 117).

The upstate specimen was an adult shot over duck decoys on Catfish Bay, Lake Champlain, one-quarter mile south of Rouses Point, Clinton Co., Oct. 22, 1943 (Owen). Although the specimen was not preserved, a color film of the dead bird was examined by Stoner (*Auk*, 1944, 61: 651–652). On the basis of bill color (pink) it was identified as *A. a. frontalis*, the race breeding in Canada.

Of great interest is an adult male shot among a flock of 18 Canada Geese on Long Island at Sagaponack, eastern Suffolk Co., Dec. 23, 1968 (Barbour), AMNH 789788. This specimen, examined by the writer, is also of the race *frontalis* and has the following measurements: wing (flat) 452 mm.; tail 150 mm.; culmen 52 mm. This individual had been **banded** as a juvenile at Mantario, in southwestern Saskatchewan on Sept. 28, 1962. It was therefore over six years old when recovered.

This **banding** record has an important bearing on the status of the species in New York, as it definitely establishes the White-fronted Goose as a wild bird occurring within the state. As with many other kinds of waterfowl, the White-fronted Goose is also kept in captivity. In several instances individuals of this species were known to have escaped from aviaries or game farms. In a few other cases either the date or locality confirms the likelihood of captive origin. As to yet other examples, doubt remains as to their derivation.

Upstate the White-fronted Goose has been observed at the following localities: Montezuma Refuge (at least four times); Oak Orchard Swamp (twice); near Rochester; Point Breeze, Orleans Co.; Grand Island and Newstead, Erie Co.; Beaver Lake, Onondaga Co.; Pamelia, Jefferson Co. The individual at Pamelia (*Kingbird*, 1966, 16: 112) and one of the Montezuma birds were reported as being suspiciously tame and regarded as probable escapes. Some of the others may well have been also.

EXTREME DATES: The upstate birds were from Oct. 22 (specimen) and Dec. 13 to Apr. 20. On Long Island the species has arrived as early as Oct. 18 (specimen).

However, three Long Island observations listed in Bull (1964: 117), including a flock of *11* seen at Miller's place, Suffolk Co., Apr. 5, 1883 (Helme), were almost certainly wild birds. The two individuals recorded in Bull (1970: 8–9), on the other hand, were very likely escapes as one of the localities (Mill Neck, Nassau Co.) has an aviary in the vicinity which has been the source of several exotic waterfowl. Another bird was observed in early June, a highly unlikely time of year for this species to occur in New York.

Subspecies: The southwest Greenland breeding population (*flavirostris*), with orange-yellow bill and much darker underparts than *frontalis*, winters in the British Isles. It has been collected in Quebec and several Atlantic coast states but, as yet, is unrecorded from New York.

The very large subspecies (*gambeli*), probably breeding at high latitudes in the Canadian arctic, is likewise a possibility.

Snow Goose (*Anser caerulescens*)   *

Range: Primarily the Nearctic region, breeding from northeastern Siberia east to northern Greenland; southern breeding limits as far as the coasts of southern Hudson Bay (northern Ontario) and James Bay (Akimiski Island). Eastern populations winter along the Atlantic coast from southern New Jersey to North Carolina. For further details, see **Subspecies.**

Status: Variously uncommon to very abundant migrant. Usually rare in winter on the coast.

Occurrence: The Snow Goose and "Blue Goose" are now generally considered to be color morphs of one species, with two subspecies involved. In the discussion that follows, *sight* reports are limited to either light ("Snow") or dark ("Blue") morphs. Intermediates occur also. Subspecific identification is unreliable in the field and is limited to specimen evidence (see **Specimen data**). To prevent confusion and for the sake of brevity the terms "Snows" and "Blues" are used.

These geese are a familiar sight to the active observer both along the coast and in the interior. Occasionally good-sized flocks are noted overhead in spring and fall passage to their breeding and wintering grounds respectively. Rarely these flocks—more often individuals—are seen alighting on the bays and estuaries of Long Island and on the inland lakes and rivers. On occasion they are reported grazing in fields, sometimes with Canada Geese, and are noted also on golf courses, especially after heavy rains.

From the evidence at hand it appears that "Blues" predominate in the western portion of the state (Niagara River east to Montezuma Refuge), and "Snows" are greatly in the majority in the eastern sections (Hudson-Champlain valley) and even more so near the coast and on Long Island. This is borne out by the following statistics.

MAXIMA, *eastern* New York: "Snows"— 130, Blauvelt, Rockland Co., Oct. 4, 1963; 800, Monticello, Sullivan Co., Nov. 5, 1954; 850, Tomhannock Reservoir, Rensselaer Co., Nov. 8, 1959. What was estimated to be at least *8000* "Snows" flying overhead near the north end of Lake Champlain on Nov. 26, 1950 (Anderson), was attributed to a violent easterly gale the previous day. That observer also saw a flock of 500 Canada Geese (*Feathers*, 1950, 12: 93). These Snow Geese were undoubtedly driven off course from their regular stopping-off place on the St. Lawrence River east of Quebec (city) where, according to Godfrey (1966: 53), these birds usually depart in late November and at which locality they have increased in numbers ever since 1900. 2200, Jamaica Bay, Dec. 12, 1948; 800, Mount Kisco, Westchester Co., Apr. 4, 1962; 700, Babylon, Suffolk Co., Apr. 5, 1959; seven immatures, Jamaica Bay, all summer of 1961.

MAXIMA, *eastern* New York: "Blues"—14, Tobay Pond, Nassau Co., Nov. 10, 1963; ten, Miller's Place, Suffolk Co., Apr. 28, 1883. Note how few "Blues" are present.

MAXIMA, *western* New York: "Snows"— 250, Niagara Falls, Oct. 27, 1935 (see "Blues," same date); 450, Montezuma Refuge, Apr. 30, 1969 (see "Blues," same date); four immatures, Montezuma, June 11–17, 1967.

MAXIMA, *western* New York: "Blues"— Great flight at Niagara Falls, Oct. 27, 1935 (*Auk*, 1936, 53: 204–207), when at least *5000* "Blues," but only 250 "Snows" were seen above the falls. At least 200 "Blues" were swept to their deaths over the cataract that night, of which 47 were preserved as specimens. No other concentration matches this figure. Other maxima—400, Buffalo, Oct. 29, 1934; 100, Oak Orchard Swamp, Mar. 30, 1969 (only eight "Snows").

Note the following yearly increase at the Montezuma Refuge in a single decade: 100, Apr. 15, 1961; 200, Apr. 23, 1962; 150, Mar. 26, 1964; 400, Mar. 30, 1965; 480, Apr. 15, 1966; 650, May 5, 1967 (only 250 "Snows," same date); 800, Apr. 21, 1968 (only 200 "Snows," same date); *1000*, Apr. 30, 1969 (unprecedented).

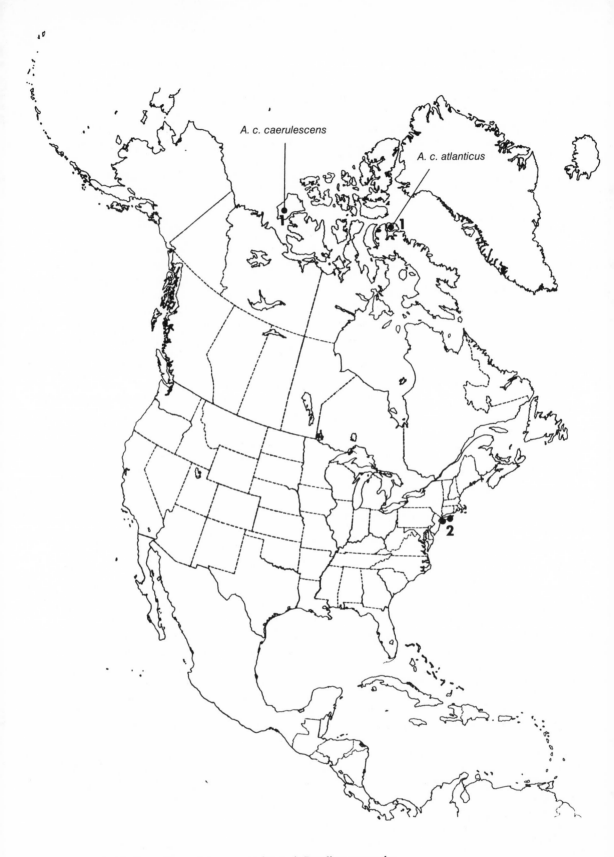

MAP 15 Snow Goose (*Anser caerulescens*) Banding recoveries

EXTREME DATES: Sept. 21 (coastal "Snow") and Oct. 3 (coastal "Blue") to May 24 (coastal "Snow") and May 30–June 10, 1954 (inland "Blue"); summer stragglers, "Snows" only.

Specimen data: Many reported taken, but relatively few extant; only 14 examined by the writer. Of these, eight (six "Snows" and two "Blues") were taken downstate—all from Long Island, details of which were published (Bull, 1964: 118–120).

The six upstate specimens are as follows: two adult "Snows" killed flying into power lines during a heavy fog, between Lake George and Glens Falls, Warren Co., Apr. 15, 1962, NYSM 20569 and 20570. Both of these are of the large eastern race *atlanticus;* juvenile "Snow" taken on the south shore of Cayuga Lake, Nov. 22, 1952 (Parkes), CUM 24066, is of the small western nominate race. The three "Blues" are: Schenevus, Otsego Co., Mar. 23, 1898 (Graham), NYSM 191; near Depew, Erie Co., Nov. 25, 1934 (Hochmuth), BMS 1834; Greene, Chenango Co., Oct. 29, 1953 (W. Bartlett), CUM 24328.

Banding (see Map 15): Nestling ("Snow," nominate *caerulescens*) banded on Banks Island, District of Franklin, July 28, 1961; found dead, Shinnecock Bay, Suffolk Co., fall of 1964. Nestling ("Snow," *atlanticus*) banded on Bylot Island, District of Franklin, Aug. 17, 1957; shot on Great South Bay, near Bay Shore, Suffolk Co., November 1958.

Subspecies: As mentioned above, two subspecies occur within the state.

(1) the larger monomorphic (blue morph unknown) high-arctic, eastern race *atlanticus* formerly called Greater Snow Goose, breeding south to northern Baffin Island and wintering on the Atlantic coast from Delaware Bay to North Carolina. Migrates in fall overland by way of Quebec and the St. Lawrence River, the Champlain-Hudson valley (probably) and south along the Atlantic coast. Spring passage is presumably in reverse over essentially the same route. Regular stopping-off places during the migrations where enormous concentrations gather are: (a) St. Lawrence River east of Quebec (city) near Cap Tourmente; (b) Delaware Bay.

(2) The smaller low-arctic dimorphic or polymorphic breeding population (nominate *caerulescens*) breeds south to Hudson and James bays; winters chiefly along the Gulf coast from Louisiana and Texas southwest to about Veracruz, Mexico, with the majority of "Blues" wintering on the Louisiana coast. The main migration route is by way of western Ontario and the Mississippi valley, but a number of "Blues" pass through western New York, especially in spring, as noted above. In recent years the blue morph has been increasing, believed due to a recent warming trend in the Arctic (Cooch, 1963), but a reversal to a cooling trend even more recently has been noted (Ryder, 1971), resulting in an increase of "Snows."

As the specific name of the "Blue Goose" (*caerulescens*) has priority over what used to be called the Lesser Snow Goose (*hyperboreus*) and, as the blue phase, or, more properly, morph, is considered to be merely a color variant of the Snow Goose and not a separate species, then *caerulescens* is the correct species name for the Snow Goose.

Remarks: Placed in the genus *Anser* by nearly all recent authorities and followed here.

Fulvous Tree Duck
(*Dendrocygna bicolor*)   *

Range: Tropical and subtropical regions in widely disjunct areas—breeding locally from California, Texas, Louisiana, and southern Florida (in 1965) to Guatemala and Honduras; northern South America from Colombia and Peru to the Guianas; from central Brazil to northern Argentina; eastern Africa from the Sudan and Ethiopia (Abyssinia) to South Africa; Madagascar; India, Burma, and Ceylon. Winters throughout.

Status: *Very rare*—In North America the Fulvous Tree Duck is subject to irruptions far north of its breeding grounds and, especially since 1960, has wandered north in *numbers* as far as New Brunswick (Baird, *Audubon Field Notes*, 1963, 17: 6–8).

All New York State records, except one, have occurred near the coast and all were from 1962 through 1966. During this five-year period this species was reported on at least eight occasions. On three of these, more than one individual were involved: Flock of six, three of which were shot on Sexton Island, Great South Bay, Suffolk Co., Dec. 22, 1962 (Kopf). One of these was preserved as a specimen, AMNH 781279. Three individuals were observed at the Jamaica Bay Refuge, Queens Co., May 29 to June 4, 1965 (Johnson, Epstein, Marshall, and Bull). Eight were seen at East Moriches, Suffolk Co., Nov. 15, 1965 (Wilcox). Another specimen, AMNH 785879, was killed near Bellport, Suffolk Co., Nov. 12, 1965 (Haas).

The only known upstate occurrence is that of an individual seen at the Montezuma Marshes on May 17 and 18, 1964 (Acland and Peakall, *Kingbird,* 1964, 14: 155).

Dates of the eight New York records range from Apr. 25 to June 4 and from Oct. 31 to Dec. 22. Details of the other downstate reports are covered in Bull (1970: 9).

Remarks: The very slightly differentiated race *"helva"* is not recognized here. Hellmayr and Conover (1948: 313) did not accept it, nor did Delacour (1954: 41–42) who stated that "plumage differences are entirely individual."

Wood Duck (*Aix sponsa*)   *   B

Range: Nearctic region, in the east breeding from southern Canada to the Gulf states, Florida, and Cuba. Winters throughout, but rare in the extreme northern portions.

Status: Locally common to abundant fall migrant inland, much less numerous in spring and elsewhere. Rare to uncommon in winter. Widespread but local breeder.

Nonbreeding: During the migrations Wood Ducks are not as particular in their feeding and resting areas as in the breeding season. They may be found in more open marshes and coastal ponds, as well as in the usual wooded portions. They are much more gregarious, too, than in summer, as may be seen by the following.

MAXIMA: *Fall*—400, Montezuma Marshes, Sept. 3, 1955; 600, same locality, Sept. 14, 1970; 900, same locality, Oct. 12, 1968; 800, Clay Swamp, Onondaga Co., Oct. 15, 1960; 450, Montezuma, Nov. 12, 1967. The largest coastal concentrations at this season are only about 100 in early October.

MAXIMA: *Spring*—150, Groveland Flats, Livingston Co., Mar. 24, 1962.

MAXIMA: *Winter*—18, Bronx Park, Bronx Co., winter of 1933–1934; eight, Baldwinsville, Onondaga Co., Jan. 4, 1968, an unusual number inland. It should be emphasized that the above numbers are exceptional, as ordinarily Wood Ducks are quite rare in winter.

Breeding: Wood Ducks may be found in secluded wooded swamps and about shaded streams and ponds. These beautiful hole-nesting ducks breed in hollow trees and stumps, also in bird boxes ranging from six to 50 feet above water or, on occasion, even above dry ground some distance from water. As many as 25 broods were counted at the Montezuma Refuge in 1971, and up to 50 nests at Howland's Island Refuge, Cayuga Co., the same year.

A departure from its usual nesting site was that of a stick nest, *not* in a tree cavity, but resting against the trunk of an oak 32 feet above water in the Montezuma Refuge (Hall, *N.Y. Fish and Game Journ.,* 1969, 6: 127).

Even more unusual is a site described by Geoffrey Carleton (*Kingbird,* 1971, 21: 212) —that of a *presumed* nest hole in a cliff. Near Climax, Greene Co., June 2, 1971, Carleton observed a female with a brood of ten downy young on the gravel shoulder of a road. He saw a hole about three-quarters of the way up the cliff and could find no suitable nest tree in the vicinity.

Egg clutches reported in 52 New York nests ranged from six eggs (five nests) to as many as 16 eggs (three nests). Eight- and 12-egg clutches were most frequent with eight nests apiece followed by 12 eggs (seven nests).

EGG DATES: Mar. 28 to July 15.

Nestlings: May 15 to Aug. 7; fledglings: May 30 to Sept. 23.

Banding (see Map 16): Two individuals banded in fall in New York were recovered the following early winter in the northern Bahamas and on the Isle of Pines, south of Cuba. Others banded during summer in New York were taken the following winter in various southeastern states (not all shown on map) west to Texas.

Two birds banded in late summer in New Brunswick were recovered during that fall on Long Island.

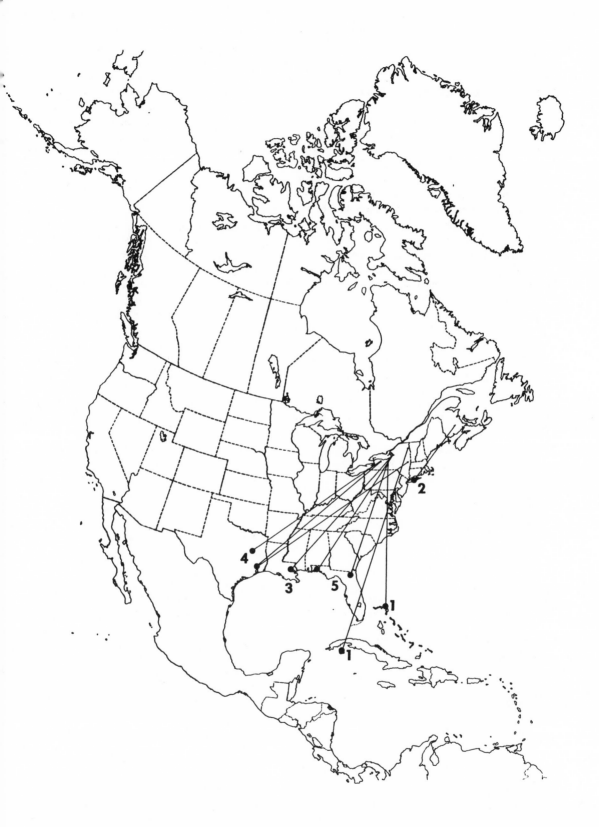

MAP 16 Wood Duck (*Aix sponsa*) Banding recoveries

Mallard (*Anas platyrhynchos*)   *   B

Range: Holarctic region, in North America widely distributed in the west—breeding from Alaska and northern Canada to Mexico, but in the east only from southern Quebec to northern Virginia. Sedentary and migratory, wintering in eastern North America south to the Gulf states and the northern West Indies.

Status: Resident throughout (chiefly semi-domesticated stock), but less numerous in winter northward. Common to locally very abundant migrant, especially in late fall.

Nonbreeding: Mallards are among our most numerous ducks, especially in the western part of the state. As can be seen from the numbers below, Montezuma Refuge has by far the largest concentration of this species in New York.

It must be emphasized that much of our Mallard population is derived from captive stock raised on game farms and released in suitable marshes; also of birds brought from elsewhere and released. However, there is no doubt that this local, chiefly sedentary, population is augmented by numerous birds from far to the north and west of us, as proved by banding recoveries (see **Banding**). The species as a whole is much more numerous in the east than formerly.

MAXIMA: *Fall*—2500, Montezuma, Sept. 13, 1957; 15,000, same locality, Nov. 12, 1967 (C. Hardy, refuge manager).

MAXIMA: *Winter*—1800, Montezuma, Jan. 1, 1958; 400, "Sapsucker Woods," Ithaca, winter of 1962–1963, consumed *five tons* of corn (*fide* Hoyt). 450, South Haven, Suffolk Co., Feb. 18, 1938.

MAXIMA: *Spring*—1000, Montezuma, Apr. 4, 1957; 1500, same place, May 1, 1967.

Breeding: Mallards commonly nest on the ground in and near marshes and along ponds and streams, but on occasion will nest some distance from water.

That they are ubiquitous nesters, however, is indicated by location of the following nest sites above ground.

Studies conducted at Montezuma (*Journ. Wildlife Mgmt.*, 1967, 31: 229–235) showed that these ducks made extensive use of stumps and dead snags for nest sites. They also utilized artificial nests made of chicken wire with hay added and placed in tree-sprout clumps. These stump nests ranged from 1½ to 15 feet above water. Tree crotches and even hollow logs were also used.

Another nest in Bronx Park, New York City, was located in a hole 20 feet up in a dead oak.

Beardslee and Mitchell (1965: 124) tell of a Mallard nest that, in addition to eleven duck eggs, contained three eggs of a Pheasant.

In 1961 at Howland's Island marsh (not far from Montezuma) 65 broods were produced. In a coastal salt marsh within the town of Hempstead, Nassau County in 1965, McNamara (*in litt.*) counted 41 broods with clutch sizes ranging from four to 13 eggs. However, the smaller ones were probably incomplete. He found nests in open salt hay (*Spartina patens*) areas, as well as in or under clumps of bayberry, groundsel bush (*Baccharis halimifolia*), high-tide bush (*Iva frutescens*), and in the giant reed association (*Phragmites communis*).

Egg clutches in 29 other New York nests ranged from seven to 14, with maxima of nine eggs (ten nests) and 11 eggs (six nests).

EGG DATES: Mar. 25 to July 1.

Juveniles: Apr. 24 to Aug. 16.

Banding (see Map 17): Fourteen individuals banded during the autumn months in New York were recovered the following winter in the southeast from the Bahamas west to Louisiana and Arkansas.

Two more banded in winter on Long Island were recovered the following summer on the breeding grounds in Manitoba; two others from western New York, banded as nestlings, were taken in Minnesota the following fall.

Still another, a juvenile banded on Aug. 3, 1962, near Watertown, flew *northeast* in fall and was shot the following December (early in the month) on the outer coast of Newfoundland.

A juvenile banded on Charlton Island, southern James Bay, was taken on Long Island the following fall.

A Mallard banded in New York was at least 12 years old when shot.

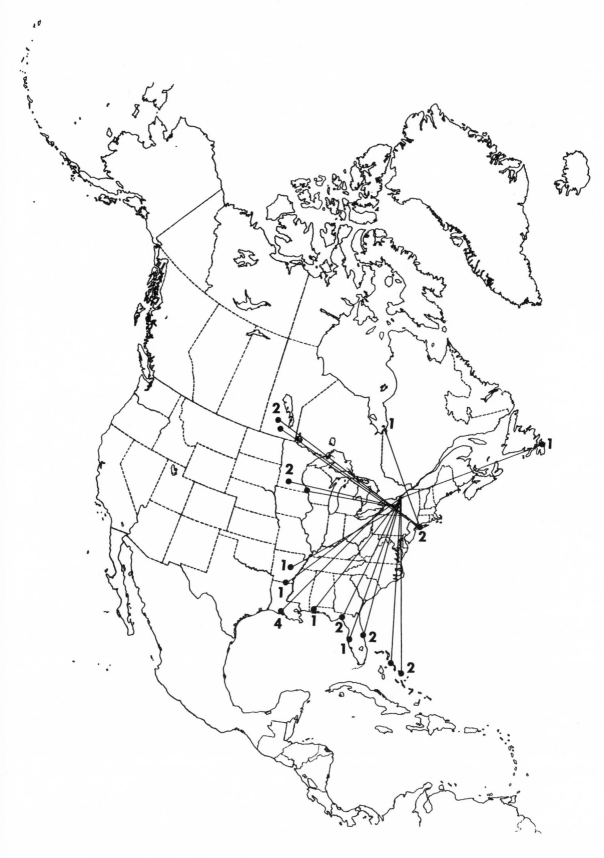

MAP 17 Mallard (*Anas platyrhynchos*) Banding recoveries

American Black Duck
(*Anas rubripes*) * B

Range: Eastern North America, breeding from northern Manitoba east to Labrador, south to the central states; in the east, south to North Carolina. Sedentary and migratory, wintering through much of the breeding range.

Status: Common to very abundant migrant and winter visitant. Widespread breeder.

Nonbreeding: The well-known Black Duck occurs from mountain lakes and wooded streams to coastal mud flats and estuaries and, when everything else freezes over, resorts to the ocean itself.

MAXIMA: *Fall*—5000, Shinnecock Bay, Suffolk Co., Oct. 16, 1924; 13,000, Montezuma Marshes, Nov. 12, 1967 (C. Hardy, refuge manager).

MAXIMA: *Winter*—6500, south end of Cayuga Lake, Feb. 15, 1953.

MAXIMA: *Spring*—2300, Montezuma, Apr. 1, 1958.

Breeding: Black Ducks are very adaptable, nesting in fresh-water marshes, coastal salt marshes, along the shores of lakes, ponds, and streams, and even in scrub fields or open woodland some distance from water.

A ground nester, the Black Duck has been known to utilize elevated sites for its nest (see stump and tree nesting account under Mallard), especially at the Montezuma Refuge.

At Orient Point, eastern Suffolk Co., Long Island, in 1968, a female Black Duck laid her eggs 20 feet above ground in an abandoned Osprey nest.

Mayer found 34 breeding pairs of Black Ducks in the Jamaica Bay area in 1949. In 1965, McNamara (*in litt.*) counted 19 broods in the town of Hempstead, Nassau Co., in salt marsh association and found clutch sizes ranging from five to 11 eggs.

In 30 other New York nests, egg clutches ranged from six eggs (three nests) to 14 eggs (one nest), with maxima of nine eggs (eight nests) and 12 eggs (five nests).

EGG DATES: Apr. 2 to June 22.

Nestlings: Apr. 28 to July 14; fledglings: in the form of nearly fully grown young, were reported as late as Sept. 22.

Banding (see Map 18): According to the *Conservationist* (1962, 16: 37) a male banded at Rochester, December 1933, was shot in Pennsylvania during the fall of 1953, 20 years later.

Another banded on Long Island, July 26, 1932, was shot in Maine 21 years later, Oct. 5, 1953.

A perusal of the map indicates *two* distinct populations. (A) A total of 32 individuals caught and banded during the fall migrations, *all* in western New York, were recovered the following winter in the southeastern states from the Atlantic coast of Florida (11) west along the Gulf coast to Louisiana (five) and north to Arkansas (seven). Even a "straggler" to central Kansas was banded in fall, Oct. 25, 1941, in western New York and shot 20 days later on Nov. 14.

(B) Eight individuals wintering on Long Island and banded there were recovered on their northernmost known breeding grounds in Labrador. Four banded in Labrador were recovered on Long Island. Four others banded in fall in Newfoundland and another on the east shore of James Bay in Quebec were likewise recovered in winter on Long Island. The circles on the Labrador coast mark the northeasternmost known limits of the Black Duck and coincide nicely with the breeding distribution map shown in Godfrey (1966: 56).

Although admittedly a relatively small sample of recoveries is indicated, it is of interest to note that two discrete populations are involved. (1) *All* of the 33 individuals banded in western New York were recovered in a southwesterly direction from place of banding. (2) *All* six individuals banded on Long Island were recovered in a northeasterly direction from place of banding, and *all* but one of 12 banded in Canada were recovered in a southwesterly direction from place of banding—and no farther than Long Island.

Reports of two Black Ducks banded in New York and shot in such unlikely places as Oregon and Axel Heiburg Island are most probably errors. The latter locality is only 600 miles south of the North Pole. These are examples of either mistaken identification or misread band numbers. Clearly great care is essential in the interpretation of these data.

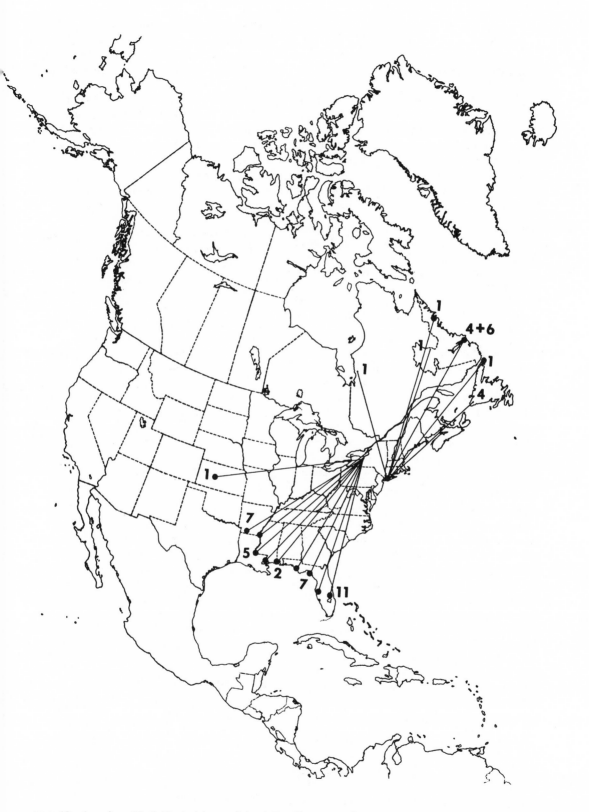

MAP 18   American Black Duck (*Anas rubripes*) Banding recoveries

Gadwall (*Anas strepera*)   *   B

Range: Holarctic region, but local in its distribution; in America chiefly in the west, breeding east to Manitoba and Wisconsin; very local in the east, from southeastern Ontario to northwestern Pennsylvania and western New York, and along the Atlantic coast from Long Island to South Carolina. Winters north to New York.

Status: Locally common to very common migrant and winter visitant on the south shore of Long Island; generally uncommon inland, but abundant to very abundant migrant at Montezuma Refuge. Recorded in winter at Niagara Falls where not rare. Locally common breeder on Long Island since 1947, and at Montezuma since 1950.

Change in status: Formerly (prior to 1940) considered very rare to rare in the east, the Gadwall has increased tremendously in New York since the early 1950s and particularly during the late 1960s. However, it is still extremely local. For instance, on Long Island, it is limited in numbers to the *south* shore ponds. Upstate it is very numerous at Montezuma, but apparently not at Oak Orchard—so attractive to other dabbling ducks.

Nonbreeding: The huge concentrations of Gadwalls at the Montezuma Refuge within the past few years, as with several other primarily western fresh-water ducks, are among the spectacular sights in the bird world.

MAXIMA: *Inland* (Montezuma, unless specified otherwise)—2000, Apr. 29, 1967; 2000, Oct. 19, 1968; *10,000, Nov. 12, 1967* (C. Hardy, refuge manager), unprecedented; 47, Niagara Falls, Dec. 31, 1966.

MAXIMA: *Coastal*—150, Babylon, Suffolk Co., Nov. 28, 1963; 130, Wantagh, Nassau Co., Jan. 11, 1964; 100, Valley Stream, Nassau Co., Mar. 5, 1959.

Nonbreeders occur infrequently in summer.

Breeding (see Map 19): Gadwalls were first found breeding in New York in 1947 at Tobay Pond, Nassau Co. Details of breeding there are given in Bull (1964: 123–124).

The second known breeding record for the state and the first for upstate was, according to Parkes (1952), in 1950 at Montezuma where a nest was discovered. Maximum density for that locality occurred in 1971 with at least 40 broods.

Maximum densities for Long Island are: 28 broods at Jamaica Bay Refuge in 1965; an estimate of *100* pairs (an astounding figure) bred on Gardiner's Island, Suffolk Co., in 1970 (Puleston).

Egg clutches in 11 New York nests ranged from six eggs (four nests) to 12 eggs (two nests). Three other nests each contained eight eggs.

EGG DATES: May 30 to July 25 (perhaps represents renesting).

Unfledged juveniles: June 16 to Aug. 25; fledged young: June 29 to Sept. 19.

On Long Island three nests were located in sand among beach grass, two others were under bayberry bushes; all five in *dry* situations, as much as 100 feet from water.

The accompanying map shows locations of the ten known breeding areas: *Upstate*—(1) Howland's Island, Cayuga Co.; (2) Montezuma; (2a) Oak Orchard complex, Genesee Co., 1971; *Western Long Island*—(3) Jamaica Bay Refuge; (4) Lawrence, and (5) Tobay Pond, Nassau Co.; *Suffolk Co., Long Island*—(6) Oak Beach and nearby Gilgo Beach and Captree Island, Great South Bay; (7) Oakdale; (8) Gardiner's Island; (9) Fisher's Island.

Banding (see Map 20): A juvenile banded in summer in North Dakota was shot the following late October on eastern Long Island. Two other juveniles banded in summer at Montezuma were recovered the following winter in Florida and Louisiana. Still another juvenile banded, Aug. 16, 1963, at the Bear River Marshes in Utah, was recovered little over a year later (fall, 1964) at the Montezuma Marshes.

Common Pintail (*Anas acuta*)   *   B

Range: Holarctic region (also islands in southern Indian Ocean), in eastern North America breeding south locally to the northern portions of Ohio, Pennsylvania, and New York, very rarely to Long Island. Withdraws from the more northern portions of the breeding range in winter.

MAP 19 Gadwall (*Anas strepera*) Breeding distribution

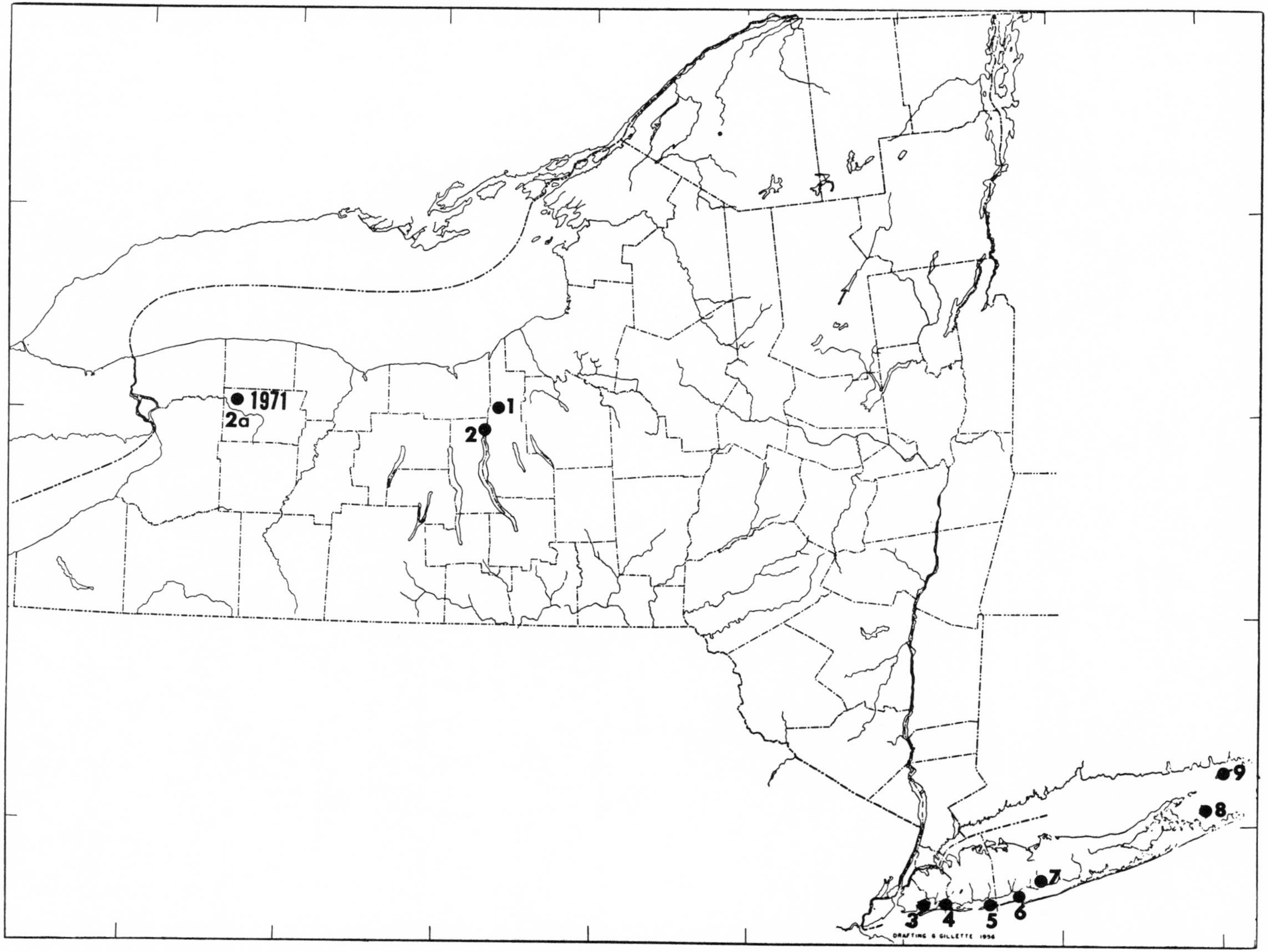

MAP 20   Gadwall (*Anas strepera*) Banding recoveries

Status: Locally common to abundant fall migrant and winter visitant on Long Island; common to very abundant migrant inland, especially numerous at the Montezuma and Oak Orchard refuges. Rare to uncommon breeder (since 1945).

Nonbreeding: Pintails are at times among our most numerous dabbling ducks and occur in very large concentrations in western New York. They were formerly rare in the northeast, but have increased markedly since the early 1920s. As with many other "fresh-water" ducks, they favor large marshy ponds and lakes, and are relatively rare on the deep-water reservoirs inland. They are also at home on coastal brackish ponds and estuaries, especially in winter.

MAXIMA: *Inland*—5000, Oak Orchard, Apr. 1, 1969; 8000 at the adjacent Wolcottsville Sinks, Niagara Co., Apr. 11, 1954; the following at Montezuma—9000, Mar. 31, 1968; 10,000, Apr. 16, 1970; 8000, Oct. 7, 1969; 6000, Nov. 12, 1967.

MAXIMA: *Coastal*—600, Jamaica Bay Refuge, Oct. 28, 1967; 600, South Haven, Suffolk Co., Dec. 26, 1934; 250, Tobay Pond, Nassau Co., Jan. 14, 1962.

Nonbreeding individuals are rarely recorded throughout summer.

Breeding (see Map 21): The first known breeding record for New York was in 1945 at (2) Perch River Refuge, Jefferson Co., where D. G. Allen and H. L. Kutz discovered a female and nine downy young on July 9 of that year, collecting one of the latter on July 11, CUM 15345.

Since 1947 Pintails have raised at least one brood each year on (3) Little Galloo Island in extreme eastern Lake Ontario, also in Jefferson Co. (J. Wilson). On June 10, 1967, the late Arthur W. Allen, John Belknap, Robert Wolk, and the writer flushed a female from a nest containing ten eggs; the nest was located under some bushes near the shore of that island.

During 1959 the State Conservation Department released Pintails at three wildlife refuges: (1) Wilson Hill Refuge, St. Lawrence Co.; (5) Montezuma; and nearby (4) Howland's Island, Cayuga Co. Broods of young were successfully raised that year at all three localities. As many as 15 and 20 broods were raised at Howland's Island in 1960 and 1961 respectively, all presumably derived from introduced stock.

The only other known inland breeding locality is (6) Oak Orchard Swamp, near Alabama, Genesee Co., where three broods of young were reported in 1967 by the refuge manager, J. Morse. Whether these birds were also artificially stocked or came in "on their own," is not certain.

The only coastal (Long Island) breeding record that I am aware of was a pair with downy young at the (7) Jamaica Bay Refuge in 1962 (Johnson).

Banding (see Map 22): Two juveniles, banded in summer on the breeding grounds in Manitoba and Prince Edward Island, were recovered in late fall on Long Island. Two others banded in late summer and early fall on the coast of Labrador, where they are not known to breed, presumably were trapped on passage there, probably originating from the northwest in the Ungava Bay region (Quebec) where they do breed; these birds were shot later in fall on Long Island. Two more banded in September on the shore of James Bay, Ontario, were recovered the following month in western New York. Another was banded in September in North Dakota and recovered the following January, also in western New York.

A Pintail banded in November on Long Island was shot two months later in Cuba.

Other individuals banded during summer or fall of various years in western New York were recaptured the following fall or winter in Missouri, Arkansas, Louisiana (two), Florida (two), and near Port au Prince, Haiti.

Finally, one banded on Sept. 16, 1953, at Montezuma was recovered more than four years later, Dec. 24, 1957, near Long Beach, Calif.

American Wigeon; Baldpate
(*Anas americana*)   *   B

Range: Chiefly western Nearctic region, rare and local breeder in the east. Breeds regularly east and south to Manitoba and Wisconsin; in recent years (since the 1950s) spreading eastward and southward, but very locally, to eastern Canada and New York (including Long Island). Winters north to Long Island.

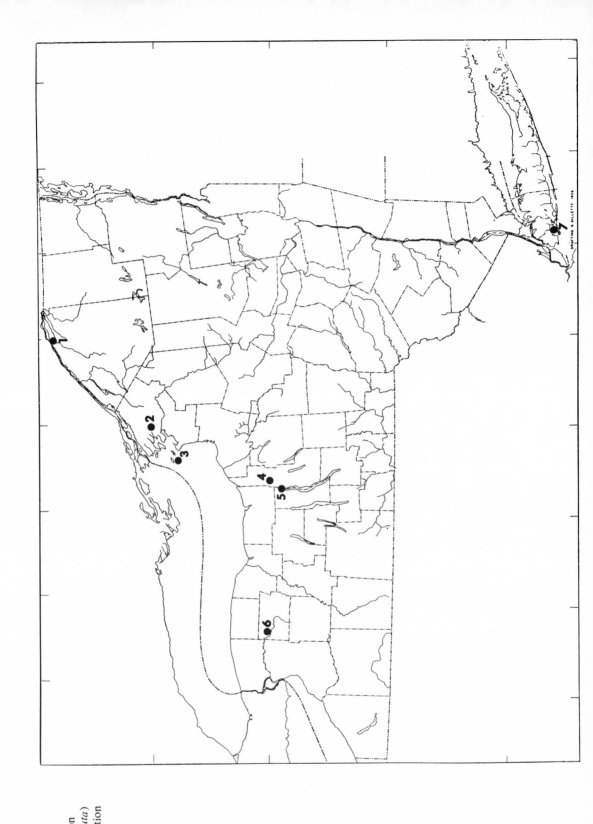

MAP 21 Common
Pintail (*Anas acuta*)
Breeding distribution

MAP 22 Common Pintail (*Anas acuta*) Banding recoveries

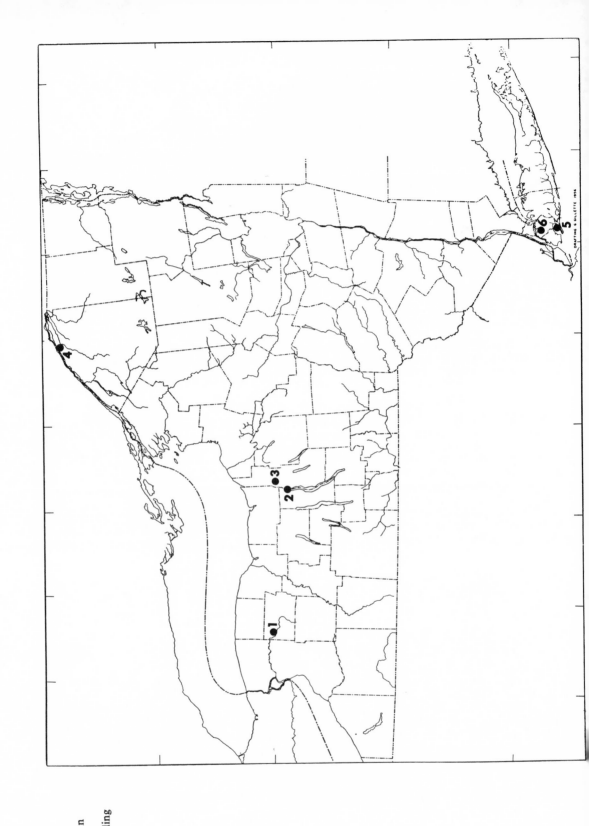

MAP 23 American
Wigeon (*Anas
americana*) Breeding
distribution

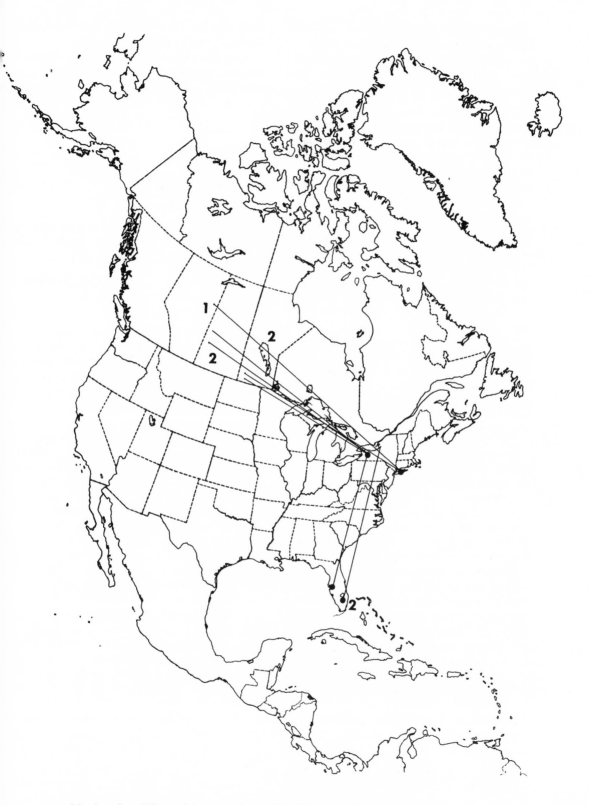

MAP 24 American Wigeon (*Anas americana*) Banding recoveries

Status: Locally common to very abundant migrant and winter visitant on Long Island; especially numerous in fall passage at Montezuma. In recent years (1959 on) a very rare and local breeder.

Change in status: This species has increased tremendously in the northeast within very recent times as may be seen from the maximum numbers listed below. Like other primarily western breeding ducks, it has been found nesting recently in a number of eastern localities, albeit widely scattered.

Nonbreeding: The American Wigeon or Baldpate is a common duck in both freshwater ponds and marshes, and in brackish estuaries and shallow bays. After the Mallard and Black Duck it is perhaps the most ubiquitous duck in winter, often resorting to coastal salt marshes, lagoons, and creeks when freshwater ponds freeze over.

MAXIMA: *Coastal,* Jamaica Bay Refuge— 5000, Sept. 28, 1960; 3000, Oct. 18, 1959; 8000, Nov. 13, 1959; Mecox Bay, Suffolk Co., 2500, Jan. 11, 1957.

MAXIMA: *Inland,* Montezuma—27,000, Sept. 28, 1965; 19,000, Oct. 30, 1959; 26,000, Nov. 23, 1966; 3300, Mar. 31, 1959.

Breeding (see Map 23): Although far more numerous than the Shoveler in migration, the American Wigeon is nevertheless the rarer (numerically) of the two during the breeding season, and was not recorded as a breeder until much later (1959). Within New York both of these species have a very similar distribution, as may be seen from the accompanying breeding map. Years following the localities indicate first known breeding dates: (1) Oak Orchard Swamp near Alabama, Genesee Co., 1961; (2) Montezuma Marshes, 1959; (3) Howland's Island Refuge, Cayuga Co., 1968; (4) Wilson Hill Refuge, St. Lawrence Co., 1960; (5) Jamaica Bay Refuge, Queens Co. portion, 1961; (6) Flushing Meadows, Queens Co., 1961. All three 1961 sites were occupied for only that year, as far as known.

Two broods at Wilson Hill consisted of six and ten young. Dates for unfledged juveniles ranged from July 7 to Aug. 6.

Banding (see Map 24): Two individuals banded in fall at Perch River Refuge, Jefferson Co., and at Montezuma Refuge were recovered later the same season in Florida at Lake Okeechobee and Tampa respectively.

Five juveniles banded on their Canadian breeding grounds in summer in Alberta (one), Saskatchewan (two), and Manitoba (two) were recovered the following autumn or early winter at Montezuma, and on Great South Bay, Long Island.

Eurasian Wigeon
(*Anas penelope*)   *

Range: Palearctic region, breeding west to Iceland. Recorded annually in eastern North America, most frequently along the coast.

Status: Rare to uncommon, but regular migrant and winter visitant on the coast; rare inland. Has decreased since 1952.

Occurrence: Prior to 1900 this species was considered to be an accidental vagrant in the state, but during the early part of this century more individuals were reported, especially from Long Island. It was most prevalent from the late 1920s to the early 1950s, but since 1952 never more than two per day at one locality have been observed. The reason for this decrease is not known. Its American counterpart and associate, the Baldpate, on the other hand, has increased enormously since the mid-1950s.

MAXIMA: 14, South Haven, Suffolk Co., Nov. 3, 1935 (Cruickshank); six, Hempstead Reservoir, Nassau Co., Nov. 6, 1938; seven, Rockville Centre, Nassau Co., Dec. 7, 1947; four, Hempstead Reservoir, Jan. 2, 1950; total of 11 from Tobay Pond to Valley Stream, Nassau Co., Dec. 20, 1952.

Upstate the Eurasian Wigeon has been recorded most frequently in the Finger Lakes region, chiefly from Cayuga Lake and the Montezuma Marshes, but never more than two per day per locality. Inland this species is recorded most often in spring, much more rarely in fall.

EXTREME DATES: Aug. 30 (inland) to June 1 (coastal). Rare before October and after early April. Casual at Montezuma Refuge, June 20 to July 5, 1970 (Benning and Doherty).

Specimen data: Eight specimens were collected on Long Island over 65 years ago, the last in 1906 (Bull, 1964: 130–131). There are three upstate specimens, two old ones from Cayuga Lake, and another taken recently at the Perch River Refuge, Jefferson Co., late November 1957 (*fide* J. Wilson).

Remarks: It is thought by some that there may be a small breeding population of this species somewhere in the Canadian Arctic. However, a few North American individuals do originate in Europe as proved by several birds banded in Iceland and taken along the Atlantic coast from Newfoundland to North Carolina (Donker, 1959).

Green-winged Teal
(*Anas crecca*)   *   B

Range: Holarctic region, in North America breeding southeast to New York and Maine; locally to Pennsylvania, New Jersey, and Massachusetts; in 1971 to Maryland. Winters north to extreme southern Canada. For discussion of races, see **Subspecies.**

Status: Variously common to locally abundant migrant, especially upstate; very abundant in the Montezuma Marshes. Fairly common in winter along the coast. Widely scattered breeder, has increased considerably in recent years.

Nonbreeding: This species frequents marshy ponds and shallow lakes; in winter it also resorts to coastal bays and estuaries. As with most dabbling ducks, Montezuma Refuge is the chief concentration area in the state.

MAXIMA: *Inland,* all from Montezuma— 5000, Oct. 25, 1962; 6500, Nov. 9, 1968 (Hardy), unprecedented numbers; 630, Apr. 16, 1970. Estimates up to 400 have been recorded at other localities in western New York.

MAXIMA: *Coastal*—450, Tobay Pond, Nassau Co., Dec. 11, 1949; 450, Hempstead Reservoir, Nassau Co., Apr. 3, 1938.

Nonbreeders infrequently occur in summer.

Breeding (see Map 25): Eaton (1910: 193) spoke of the Green-winged Teal as breeding in the Montezuma Marshes and on Strawberry Island in the Niagara River, and Parkes (1952) stated, "There is a single breeding record from Ithaca," but in no case were there any details

concerning these occurrences, not even the year.

The species has been recorded as nesting at the following 22 localities: (1) Strawberry Island, Niagara River, Erie Co.; (2) Amherst, Erie Co.; (3) Oak Orchard Swamp near Elba, Genesee Co.; (4) Batavia, Genesee Co.; (5) Riverside Marsh, Chautauqua Co.; (6) North Cuba Marsh, Allegany Co.; (7) Ithaca, Tompkins Co.; (8) Montezuma; (9) Howland's Island Refuge, Cayuga Co.; (10) Skaneateles, Onondaga Co.; (11) near Phoenix, Oswego Co.; (12) Three Rivers Refuge, Onondaga Co.; (13) Clay Swamp, Onondaga Co.; (14) near Rome, Oneida Co.; (15) Perch River Refuge, Jefferson Co.; (16) Wilson Hill Refuge, St. Lawrence Co.; (17) near Paul Smith's, Franklin Co.; (18) Oseetah Lake, Franklin Co.; (19) near Ellenburg, Clinton Co.; (20) Coxsackie, Greene Co.; (21) Jamaica Bay Refuge, Queens Co.; (22) Easthampton, Suffolk Co.

As many as five broods were counted at Oak Orchard in 1968, and five at Montezuma Refuge in 1971.

Most New York nests were placed near marshy ponds in grass or under bushes.

Six New York nests contained the following egg clutches: six eggs (one nest); seven eggs (one nest); nine eggs (two nests); ten eggs (one nest); 12 eggs (one nest).

EGG DATES: May 25 to July 15.

Unfledged young: June 16 to July 28; fledged juveniles: July 5 to Aug. 11.

Banding (see Map 26): All 24 "direct" recoveries shown are of birds banded in various years in late summer or early fall and recovered late that same fall or early winter: nine from southeastern Quebec and three from Newfoundland were taken on Long Island; another from Newfoundland and one each from James Bay and Saskatchewan were taken in Montezuma and Oak Orchard. Birds banded at either Oak Orchard or Montezuma were recovered in Minnesota (one), Kansas (one), Louisiana (one), Mississippi (two), and Florida (four).

An "indirect" recovery involved a bird banded Aug. 6, 1964, at Montezuma and shot Nov. 21, 1965, at Lake Tulare, Calif.

Subspecies: Two well-marked races occur in New York: (1) nominate *crecca* (male in

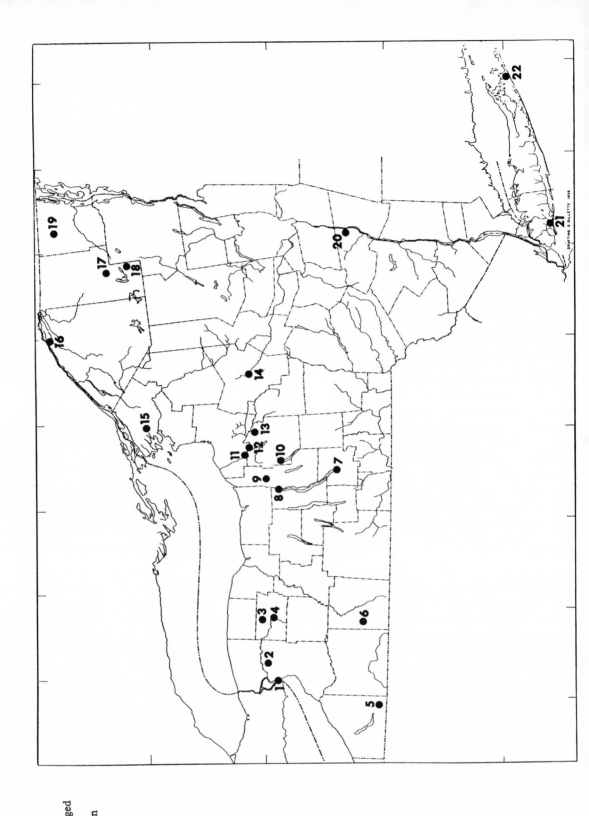

MAP 25 Green-winged
Teal (*Anas crecca*)
Breeding distribution

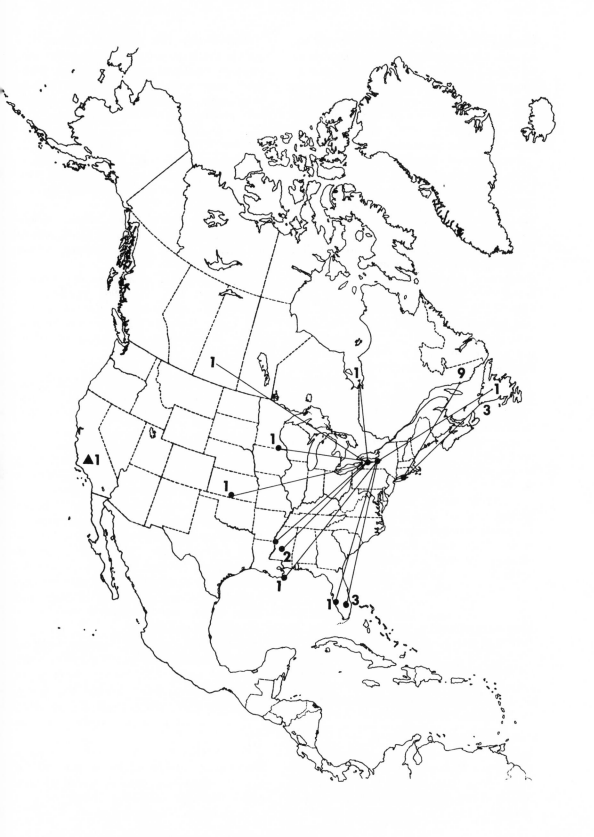

MAP 26 Green-winged Teal (*Anas crecca*) Banding recoveries

breeding plumage with a white *horizontal* bar, actually the scapulars) occurs in the Palearctic region, breeding west to Iceland, and recorded on the Atlantic coast of North America from Labrador to South Carolina and inland west to Ohio; (2) the race *carolinensis* (male in breeding plumage with a white *vertical* bar in front of wing) has been discussed.

The treatment here of making these two forms conspecific follows that of Delacour (1956: 96–100). These birds have been recorded as hybridizing in western Alaska where their ranges meet. Males of *crecca* and *carolinensis* in eclipse plumage are virtually indistinguishable, and females of the two are alike.

An old specimen of nominate *crecca* taken upstate was recorded by Eaton (1910: 192), as were two old ones from Long Island (Bull, 1964: 125). A recent specimen, a male, shot near Seaford, Nassau Co., Dec. 5, 1962 (collector?), is AMNH 787422. This subspecies is still a rarity anywhere in the state, including Long Island, and the maxima of from four to six per day per locality in the 1930s given in Bull (*op. cit.*) has never been equalled.

During April and May 1967 at least *five* different males were reported from the following localities: (1) Jamaica Bay Refuge; (2) Hempstead Lake, Nassau Co.; (3) Stockport, Columbia Co.; (4) Phoenix, Oswego Co.; (5) Rochester.

EXTREME DATES: late November to May 14 (coastal) and May 17 (inland). Note lack of records between June and November when males of the two subspecies are in eclipse plumage and thus are indistinguishable. For further details, see Bull (1964: 125–126).

Blue-winged Teal
(*Anas discors*) * B

Range: Nearctic region, in the east breeding from southern Canada to Tennessee and North Carolina. Winters north to southern Maryland, rarely to New York.

Status: Locally common to abundant *fall* migrant, occasionally very abundant in the Montezuma Marshes; much less numerous in spring. Very rare to rare in winter. Local breeder, occasionally fairly common in western and central New York, and on Long Island.

Nonbreeding: This duck occurs most frequently and in largest numbers on ponds with emergent vegetation and in the larger freshwater marshes. As with nearly all of the dabbling ducks, the Blue-winged Teal is particularly numerous in the Montezuma region.

MAXIMA: *Inland*—300, El Dorado Beach, Jefferson Co., Aug. 27, 1970; Montezuma: *8000,* Sept. 21, 1970 (C. Hardy, refuge manager), an unprecedented number; 3000, Oct. 25, 1962; 900, Nov. 12, 1967; 1100, Apr. 22, 1967.

MAXIMA: *Coastal*—150, Mastic, Suffolk Co., Aug. 20, 1952; 250, Tobay Pond, Nassau Co., Sept. 7, 1941; 115, Sagaponack, Suffolk Co., Oct. 8, 1939.

Winter: Three (including one male), Jamaica Bay Refuge, Dec. 26, 1964 (Enders and Heath). This species is ordinarily very rare at this season. There are a few upstate reports in winter. It is generally rare before April and after November.

Breeding (see Map 27): As might be expected, the Blue-winged Teal is most numerous in the vast marshes of the Montezuma Refuge, with at least *40* broods of young in 1962 (J. Morse, refuge manager). With the exception of the Oak Orchard Swamp complex, no other area in the state matches this locality in size and relative abundance of this species.

Perusal of the distribution map indicates three main areas of breeding concentration: (1) extreme western portion, the so-called Niagara Frontier region; (2) central portion, extending from Jefferson Co. south to near the Pennsylvania state line in Tioga and Chemung counties; (3) coastal portions of Long and Staten islands, with all breeding localities on the south and east shores.

Nests of this species are frequently found on dry land, some distance from a marsh or pond, and most often under bushes or in dense clumps of grass. When hatched the downy young resort to marshy ponds and to either fresh or brackish ponds and marshes along the coast.

Egg clutches in 23 New York nests range from eight to 13 with maxima of nine and ten egg sets found in six nests each, and with 11 eggs in four nests, and 13 eggs in five.

EGG DATES: May 3 to July 4.

MAP 27 Blue-winged
Teal (*Anas discors*)
Breeding distribution

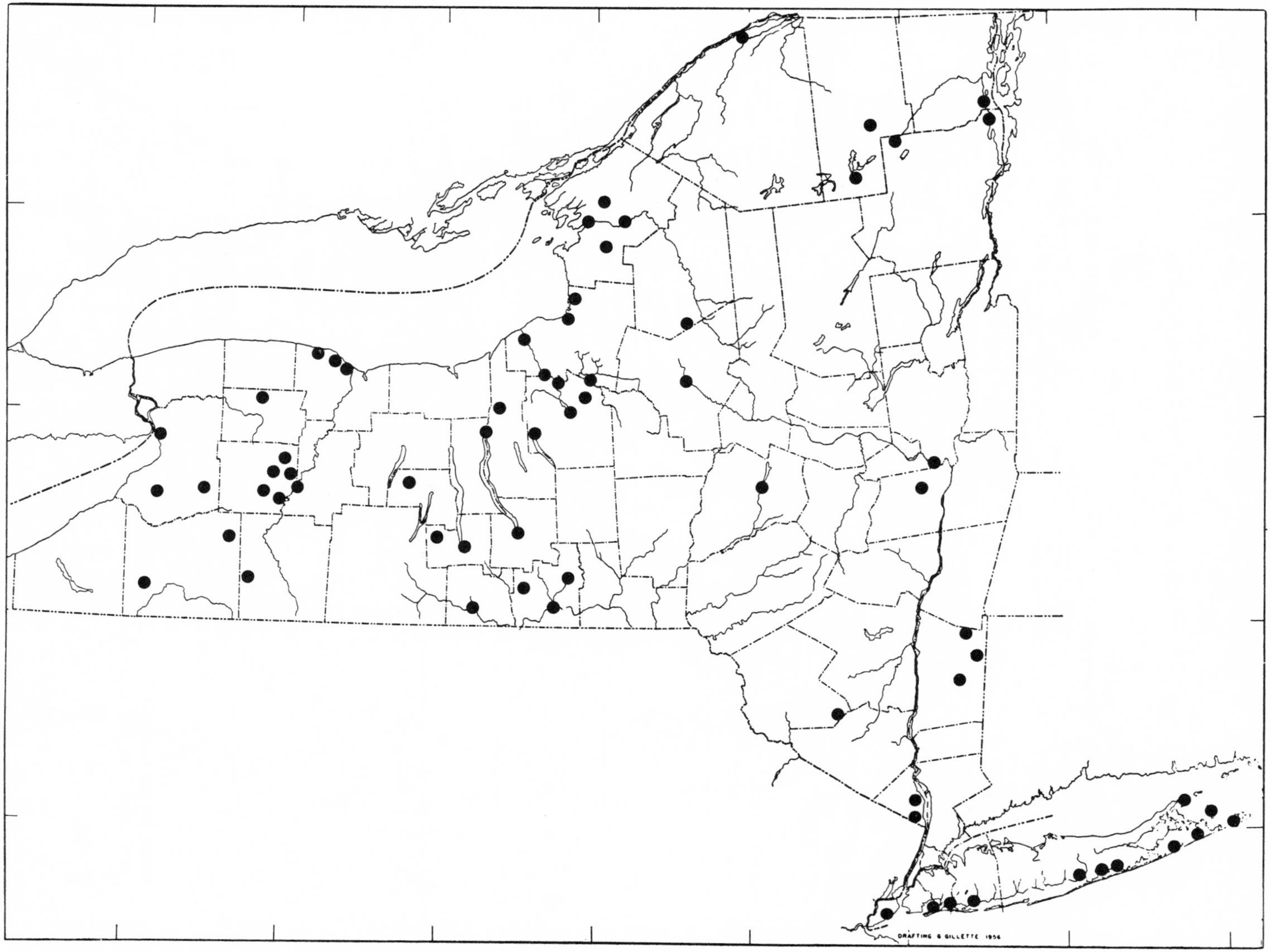

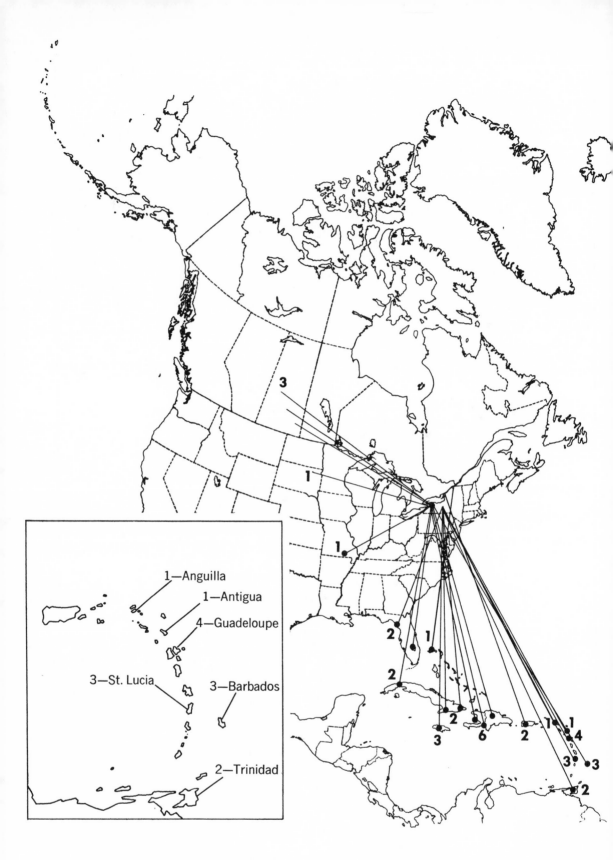

MAP 28   Blue-winged Teal (*Anas discors*) Banding recoveries

Inset legend:

1—Anguilla
1—Antigua
4—Guadeloupe
3—St. Lucia
3—Barbados
2—Trinidad

MAP 29 Blue-winged Teal (*Anas discors*) Banding recoveries

Unfledged young: May 17 to Aug. 7. No New York dates are available for fledglings.

Banding (see Maps 28 and 29): (A) North America, including the West Indies and Trinidad—Four juveniles banded on the breeding grounds, three from Saskatchewan and one from South Dakota, were all recovered the following fall in the Oak Orchard area. With the exception of three juveniles banded in western New York (chiefly Oak Orchard and Montezuma) and recovered in Missouri (one) and Florida (two), all other New York bandings (juveniles) were recovered the following fall or winter in the West Indies and Trinidad (Bahamas (one), Cuba (four), Jamaica (three), Hispaniola (six), Puerto Rico (two), and Lesser Antilles and Trinidad (14); for further details, see inset map.

(B) South America—The following 26 New York banded juveniles were taken the following fall or winter: Colombia (six), Venezuela (11), Guyana (three), Surinam (four) including an individual shot only eight days later, and Brazil, near São Luis, Maranhão (two).

Note the general recovery pattern, the great majority taken in a *southerly* or *southeasterly* direction, *none* from Middle America, and only three from the extreme eastern portion of the Gulf of Mexico.

Remarks: The weakly differentiated (only very slightly darker) Atlantic coastal population, *"orphna"* is not recognized here.

Cinnamon Teal (*Anas cyanoptera*)   *

Range: Neotropical region; western North America, the race *septentrionalium* (males distinguished from nominate race by lighter coloration of the scapulars, and almost total absence of black dots in plumage), breeding east to the western portions of Saskatchewan and Nebraska, and wintering north to southern Texas. Vagrant to eastern United States.

Status: *Casual*—One specimen record for New York State: Male taken on the shore of Seneca Lake, Yates Co., about the middle of April 1886. According to Eaton (1910: 196), this specimen was formerly in the private col-

lection of J. Flahive. Its present whereabouts is unknown.

Three occurrences of males in recent years on Long Island are as follows: (1) A tame individual on a pond in the Massapequa State Park, Nassau Co., from Jan. 12 to Feb. 10, 1957 (M. A. Nichols and many others), was probably an escape (Bull, 1964: 471). (2) Another present at Jamaica Bay Refuge, Queens Co., from May 20 to July 18, 1964 (numerous observers), was photographed in color; it too may have escaped, although there is no proof of this. (3) Still another observed at Mill Neck, Nassau Co., during the spring and summer of 1968, as well as a male Eurasian Wigeon (*Anas penelope*) during the same period, were known to have escaped from a nearby aviary (Bull, 1970: 11).

The report of a bird claimed to have been a Cinnamon Teal from the Niagara Frontier region during the fall of 1962 was published in the *Kingbird* of that period. However, neither the *Prothonotary* for that year, nor Beardslee and Mitchell (1965) mention it. Judging from the published description, it is no wonder it is omitted from the other literature.

Northern Shoveler (*Anas clypeata*)   *   B

Range: Holarctic region, in North America widespread in the west, but local in the east, breeding in southeastern Ontario, northwestern Pennsylvania, New York (including Long Island), New Jersey, and locally southward. Winters north to Long Island.

Status: Locally common to very common migrant on Long Island; abundant to very abundant in the Montezuma Marshes; generally uncommon to rare elsewhere. Rare and local breeder, occasionally numerous at Montezuma.

Nonbreeding: This fine species has increased markedly in the northeast, especially in the past 20 years or so. Very large numbers can be found in the Montezuma complex. Shovelers favor shallow ponds with muddy bottoms, marshes, coastal lagoons with aquatic vegetation, and often associate with Blue-winged Teal in these surroundings.

MAXIMA: *Coastal*—350, Jamaica Bay Ref-

MAP 30 Northern
Shoveler (*Anas clypeata*)
Breeding distribution

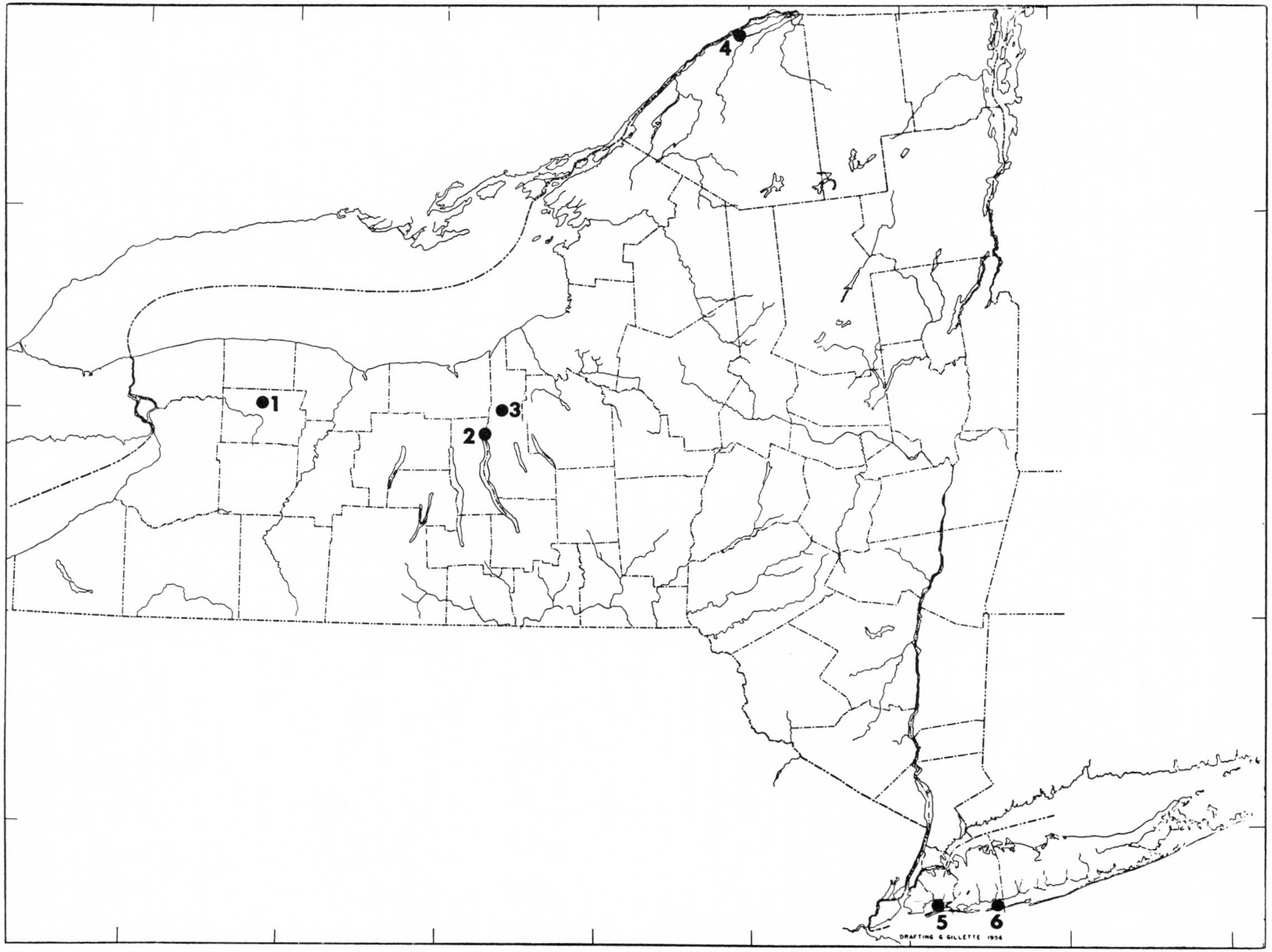

uge, Nov. 29, 1969; 20, Central Park Reservoir, New York City, all January 1963.

MAXIMA: *Inland*, all from Montezuma Marshes—500, Sept. 13, 1957; 2000, Oct. 21, 1956; *7400*, Nov. 12, 1967 (C. Hardy, refuge manager), an unprecedented number; 2000, Nov. 23, 1970; 300, Apr. 4, 1957; 900, Apr. 29, 1967.

Breeding (see Map 30): In addition to attracting the largest numbers of Shovelers in the state, Montezuma was also the first breeding location, as mentioned by Eaton (1910: 197). As many as eight broods were raised at that locality in 1962.

It has nested in six different localities, mostly widely separated from one another, as may be seen from the accompanying map. Years after the locality indicate first known breeding: (1) Oak Orchard Swamp, especially between Elba and Oakfield, Genesee Co., 1931; (2) Montezuma (see above for details); (3) Howland's Island area, Cayuga Co., 1961; (4) Wilson Hill Refuge, St. Lawrence Co., 1959; (5) Jamaica Bay Refuge, Queens Co. portion, 1956; (6) Tobay Pond, Nassau Co., 1958.

One of the Oak Orchard nests contained eggs on May 29; the young hatched on June 12. Dates for unfledged young range from June 12 to July 8, and for fledged juveniles, July 18.

Six New York brood sizes were: two of four (probably incomplete), one of nine, two of 11, and one of 13.

Banding: A juvenile banded July 16, 1964, at Montezuma was shot Nov. 27, 1964, in southern Louisiana.

Canvasback (*Aythya valisineria*) *

Range: Chiefly western North America, breeding east to southeastern Manitoba and northern Minnesota; very rarely to southeastern Ontario (Luther Marsh, 1965). In the east winters chiefly from New York to Chesapeake Bay.

Status: Common to locally very abundant winter visitant; less numerous in migration.

Occurrence: Canvasbacks, often found associating with Redheads and scaups, are most numerous in winter in upstate waters, especially in the Niagara River region and on the larger inland lakes, such as Cayuga and Oneida. On the last named, they are abundant during the migrations. These ducks are also to be found in large numbers on the bays of western Long Island. Canvasbacks have greatly increased in the state since the late 1940s.

MAXIMA: *Fall*—5000, Oneida Lake, Oct. 30, 1956. *Winter*—14,000, Niagara River, Jan. 17, 1953 (Schaffner); 30,000, Cayuga Lake, all January 1958 (Nisbet); 5300, Flushing and Little Neck bays, Queens Co., Jan. 15, 1954. *Spring*—4000, Niagara River, Mar. 12, 1967; 4000, Oneida Lake, Apr. 12, 1959.

This fine species is ordinarily rare before October and after April, but has been recorded every month of the year. At the Jamaica Bay Refuge in 1956, two individuals were observed from June 19 to July 18, and a nonbreeding pair summered there in 1964.

Banding (see Map 31): Three individuals shot at the north end of Seneca Lake in fall of various years had been banded as downy young the previous summers in southeastern Saskatchewan, south-central Manitoba, and northeastern South Dakota. Four adults, all banded on Keuka Lake near Penn Yan, Yates Co., during winter of various years, were recovered as follows: (1) north-central Iowa in mid-April; (2) near Lesser Slave Lake, Alberta, in March; (3) north end of Great Slave Lake, District of Mackenzie in late summer; (4) near Fort Yukon, Alaska, in late summer.

Of considerable interest, indicating wide dispersal and vastly different wintering areas, are three birds, all banded on Keuka Lake and recovered in Oregon, California, and Texas.

Date and Place of Banding	Date and Place of Recovery
Mar. 10, 1958, New York	Jan. 11, 1959, near Beaver, Oregon
Jan. 19, 1957, New York	Dec. 15, 1957, near Oakland, California
Feb. 18, 1957, New York	Nov. 9, 1958, north of Lubbock, Texas

Remarks: One pair and a brood of six young were reported for the Montezuma Marshes in 1962 (Morse). Breeding Canvasbacks were also reported, without details, from the same

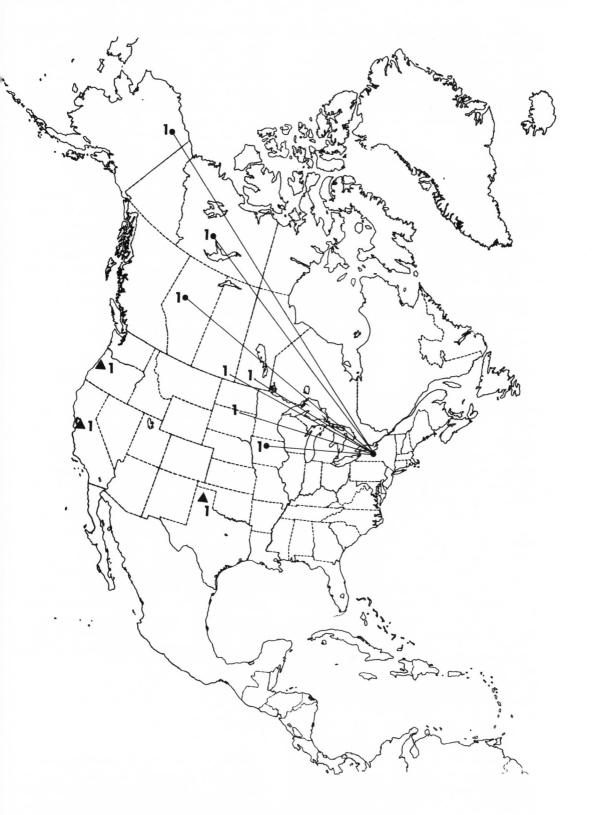

MAP 31 Canvasback (*Aythya valisineria*) Banding recoveries

locality in 1965. Despite the statement to the contrary (*Kingbird*, 1962, 12: 149), these birds undoubtedly were of introduced stock. There is no evidence to date that this species is an established breeder in New York. The Canvasback is primarily western in its breeding distribution (see **Range**).

Redhead (*Aythya americana*)   *   B

Range: Western Nearctic region, breeding east to eastern Michigan; rarely and sporadically to northwestern Pennsylvania, southeastern Ontario, southwestern Quebec, and New Brunswick. In the east winters north to Chesapeake Bay and locally to the Finger Lakes.

Status: Common to locally very abundant winter visitant and migrant in the Finger Lakes region, and formerly on eastern Long Island. Less numerous elsewhere on other inland lakes and coastal bays. Introduced locally as a breeder.

Nonbreeding: Spectacular concentrations of diving ducks, such as Redheads and Canvasbacks, are to be seen on the deep-water lakes of central New York, especially Cayuga and Seneca. Prior to the late 1920s, Redheads were present in impressive numbers on the bays and ponds of eastern Long Island, but have declined drastically there in recent decades.

MAXIMA: *Inland*—4500, Montezuma area and north end of Seneca Lake, Nov. 30, 1964; 5000, Seneca Lake, winter of 1950–1951; 5000, Cayuga Lake, Jan. 17, 1959; 3300, Cayuga Lake, Mar. 7, 1965.

MAXIMA: *Coastal*—2000, Moriches Bay, Nov. 17, 1905; 600, Great Pond, Montauk, Jan. 5, 1924. In recent years only 160, Water Mill, Suffolk Co., Dec. 2, 1950.

Breeding (see Map 32): This species has been introduced into New York in recent years by the State Conservation Department (Weller, 1964). The first known release—eggs from Delta, Manitoba—was in 1952 at the Montezuma Refuge (*Conservationist*, 1956, 11: 37). Since that time, Redheads have been stocked at nine other refuges and waterfowl preserves, chiefly during the 1950s and early 1960s. Maximum numbers of broods produced were: eight at Montezuma in 1962; nine at nearby How-

land's Island Refuge in 1961, *20* there in 1964. Also ten at Jamaica Bay Refuge in 1965, when at least 70 young hatched, of which about 50 fledged (Helen Hays, pers. comm.). According to Hays there were: one brood of 12, three broods of 11 each, the others of six and seven. In 1966 she found a brood of 14. Dates in 1965 and 1966 ranged from June 4 to July 27 for unfledged young, and various August dates for fledglings.

I have no New York data for eggs.

The accompanying map shows location of the ten breeding areas: (1) King's Bay, Lake Champlain, Clinton Co.; (2) Wilson Hill Refuge, St. Lawrence Co.; (3) Perch Lake and (4) nearby Perch River Refuge, Jefferson Co.; (5) Three Rivers Refuge, Onondaga Co.; (6) Mud or Beaver Lake, Onondaga Co.; (7) Howland's Island Refuge, Cayuga Co.; (8) Montezuma; (9) Oak Orchard Refuge portion, near Elba, Genesee Co.; (10) Jamaica Bay Refuge, Long Island.

Banding (see Map 33): All 17 bandings shown involve Montezuma during the winter months either as place of banding or point of recovery. The 14 "direct" recoveries are of birds either banded at or recovered on their presumed western breeding grounds, as follows: two in Alberta, five in Saskatchewan, four in North Dakota, and three in South Dakota. *All* of these 14 recoveries occurred within five or six months after date of banding.

Details of the three "indirect" banding recoveries, are as follows: (1) banded at Laguna Madre, Tex., Jan. 26, 1965, shot at Montezuma, early January 1966; (2) banded at Clear Lake, northern California, Aug. 27, 1951, shot at Montezuma, Nov. 8, 1952; (3) banded at Montezuma, Mar. 12, 1957, shot in the Imperial Valley, south of Salton Sea, California, early December 1957. The dates and localities indicate the great wandering tendencies of this species.

Ring-necked Duck
(*Aythya collaris*)   *   B

Range: Nearctic region, breeding south to the northern portions of New York and New England; very rarely to northwestern Pennsylvania and northeastern Massachusetts. In win-

MAP 32 Redhead
(*Aythya americana*)
Breeding distribution

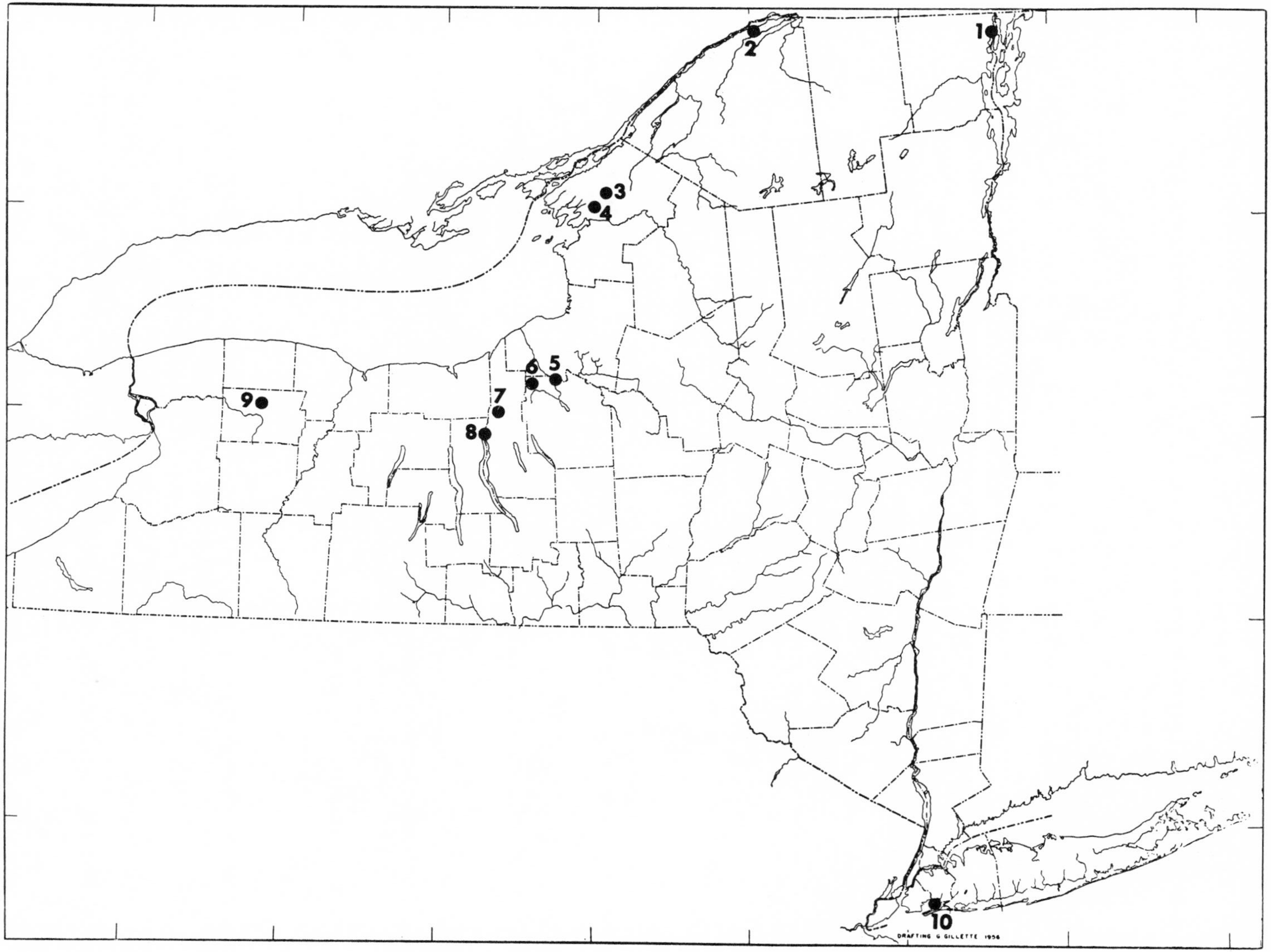

MAP 33 Redhead (*Aythya americana*) Banding recoveries

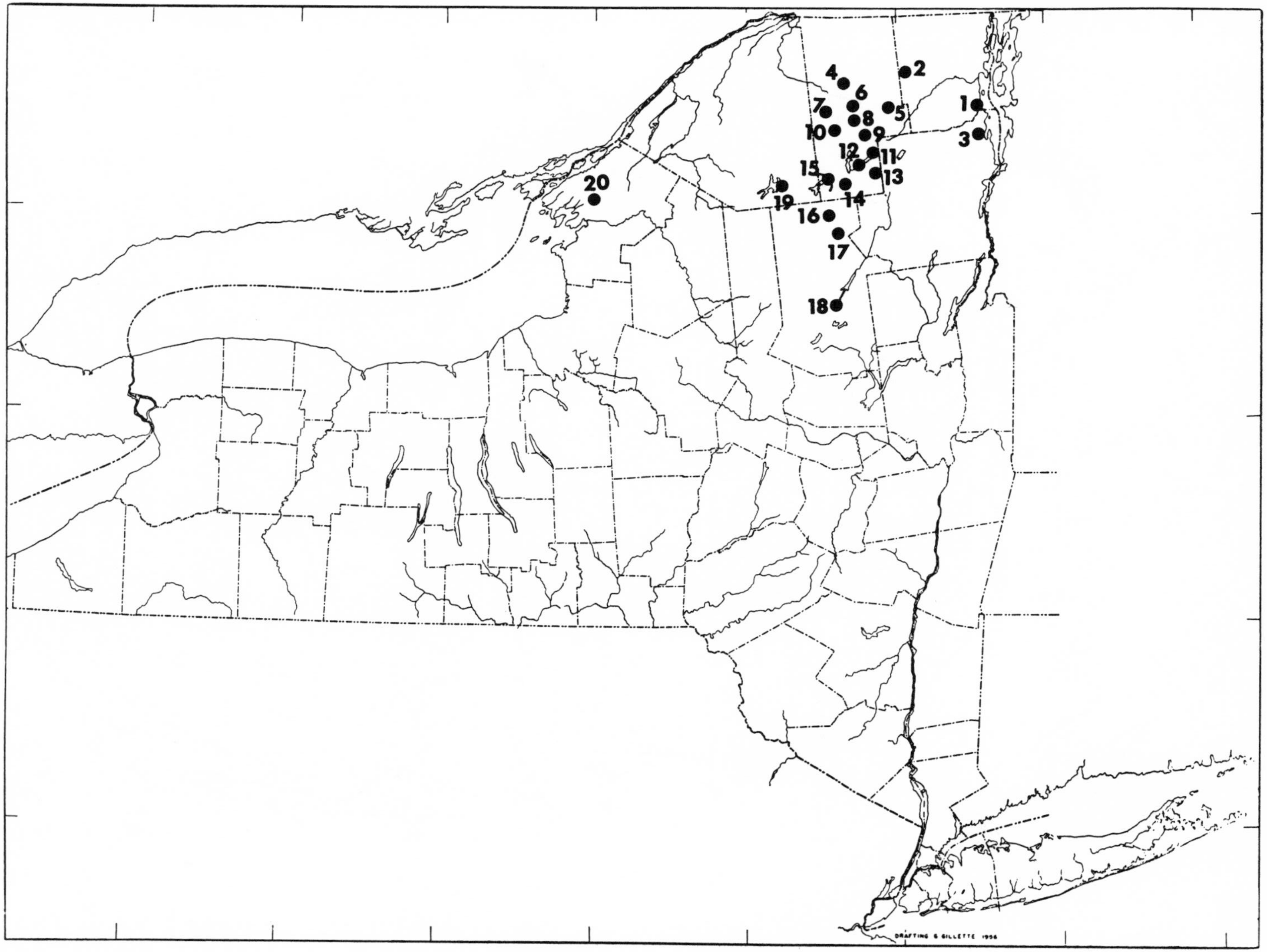

MAP 34 Ring-necked
Duck (*Aythya collaris*)
Breeding distribution

MAP 35   Ring-necked Duck (*Aythya collaris*) Banding recoveries

ter withdraws from the more northern portions of the breeding range.

Status: Locally common to abundant migrant and winter visitant, most numerous in central New York. Fairly common, but local breeder in the Adirondacks, very rarely elsewhere; most numerous in Franklin Co.

Change in status: The Ring-necked Duck was formerly an uncommon species in upstate New York and quite rare on Long Island. With the recent great increase in the northeast, it has increased correspondingly in this state and breeds in the northeastern section.

Nonbreeding: Along the coast this species frequents the deep-water lakes and reservoirs and is relatively scarce in the shallow ponds and marshes, but inland it occurs in both situations being especially numerous in and near the Syracuse region.

MAXIMA: *Inland*—1000, Montezuma Marshes, Oct. 19, 1970; 900, Mud or Beaver Lake, Onondaga Co., Nov. 1, 1962; 1200, Montezuma, Apr. 1, 1958; 200, Oneida Lake, Apr. 24, 1964.

MAXIMA: *Coastal*—340, Kensico Reservoir, Westchester Co., Feb. 5, 1950; 300, South Haven, Suffolk Co., Feb. 12, 1941.

Summering nonbreeders are infrequent, otherwise it is recorded in every month.

Breeding (see Map 34): This species was first recorded as breeding in New York in 1946 at Jones Pond, Franklin Co. (Severinghaus and Benson, *Auk,* 1947, 64: 626–627). Since that time it has been found nesting at 19 different localities, chiefly in the Adirondack district, especially in Franklin Co. Mendall (1958) summarized its status up to that time.

According to Foley (*in litt.*) this duck prefers boggy ponds "most often bordered with leatherleaf and other ericaceous plants, but often where there are also some . . . cattails or bulrush." Breeding places are sometimes found along a shoreline of dense alders with conifer forest nearby. A nest with eggs was built on flattened cattail leaves, four inches above water level (Foley and Browne, *in litt.*).

Six New York nests were found with seven to 11 eggs, with two nests holding ten eggs each.

EGG DATES: May 20 to June 30.

Unfledged young: May 29 to July 11; fledglings: July 25 to Aug. 22.

As many as six broods of young were at Upper Chateaugay Lake, Clinton Co., in 1967 (Browne).

The accompanying map shows the 20 localities, as follows: Clinton Co.—(1) Ausable River marshes, Lake Champlain; (2) Upper Chateaugay Lake. Essex Co.—(3) Butternut Pond. Franklin Co.—(4) Twin Ponds; (5) near Inman; (6) near Meacham Lake; (7) Dodge River Flow near Madawaska; (8) McColloms; (9) Jones Pond and nearby Barnum Pond; (10) Follensby Jr. Pond and nearby Slush Pond; (11) Lake Colby; (12) Middle Saranac Lake; (13) Oseetah Lake; (14) Raquette River near Axton; (15) Tupper Lake (marshes). Hamilton Co.—(16) Middle Cat Pond; (17) south end of Long Lake; (18) Lewey Lake. St. Lawrence Co.—(19) near Cranberry Lake, vicinity of Brandy Brook Flow. Jefferson Co.—(20) near Perch Lake.

A report of this duck breeding in Chenango Co. in 1958, without details, was not confirmed.

Banding (see Map 35): An individual banded in late fall near Rochester was recovered the following March in the southern Bahamas. Two juveniles banded on their Adirondack breeding grounds were shot the following winter in the northern and central portions of Florida. A fourth bird banded near Watertown, Nov. 16, 1955, was shot 18 days later in Louisiana, near the mouth of the Mississippi River.

Tufted Duck (*Aythya fuligula*)

Range: Palearctic region, breeding west to Iceland; winters in the western portion from the British Isles south to central Africa. Vagrant to Greenland and recorded in Massachusetts, New York, and New Jersey.

Status: *Very rare*—it is virtually impossible to be certain whether New York State occurrences of this species are genuine wild birds that wandered from Europe or escapes from confinement. The Tufted Duck is common in captivity and, at least in two instances (Bull, 1964: 472), a male and a female were known to have escaped. See Griscom and Snyder (1955: 253) concerning occurrences in Massachusetts. Godfrey (1966: 70) mentions no records from eastern Canada.

The following reports are all from the same general area, in or near the northern portions of Bronx Co. in the Hudson-Harlem river drainage: A female or immature male near Sputen Duyvil from Dec. 26, 1955, to Feb. 1, 1956 (numerous observers), was photographed in color by Gilliard, photos on file at AMNH; male, Jerome Reservoir, Mar. 15, 1962 (Sedwitz); a male seen by F. Lohrer and numerous other observers at various localities between the George Washington Bridge and Randall's Island, all of February 1966 and again during the winters of 1966–1967, 1967–1968, and 1968–1969 (Bull, 1970: 52). For a photograph of a male taken during the winter of 1966–1967, see *Kingbird* (1969, 19: 132).

There is also a report of a male at Oakdale, Suffolk Co., Feb. 19–21, 1970 (numerous observers).

Greater Scaup (*Aythya marila*)   *

Range: Holarctic region, in eastern America breeding south to the southern shores of Hudson Bay, and rarely to southeastern Quebec (islands in the Gulf of St. Lawrence—Anticosti and the Magdalen Islands). Winters in the eastern portions from the Great Lakes and Quebec to Florida, but chiefly in Long Island waters.

Status: Very abundant winter visitant on Long Island; much less numerous on the Great Lakes and in the Niagara River region. Recorded in largest numbers on the coast in fall and early winter, inland in winter.

Occurrence: In the coastal districts the Greater Scaup is by far the most widespread of our winter ducks and, at times, the most numerous. It is especially abundant on the saltwater bays of the south shore of Long Island and on Long Island Sound.

MAXIMA: *Coastal*—75,000, Shinnecock and Mecox bays, Suffolk Co., Oct. 24, 1929; 250,000, Great South Bay, Suffolk Co., Dec. 3, 1929 (Helmuth); 40,000, Flushing and Little Neck bays, Queens Co., Dec. 20, 1952; 60,000, Pelham Bay, Bronx Co., Dec. 31, 1953; 23,000, Jamaica Bay, Kings and Queens

counties, Jan. 15, 1956. 21 summered at the Jamaica Bay Refuge in 1965. Recorded every month of the year.

MAXIMA: *Inland*—3600, Derby Hill, Oswego Co., Oct. 26, 1968; 6000, Niagara River, Jan. 17, 1953; 7000, Oswego (harbor), winter of 1958–1959; 2500, Oneida Lake, Apr. 12, 1959 (see Lesser Scaup, this date for comparative numbers).

Banding (see Map 36): One of the breeding grounds of the Greater Scaup in America is Alaska (ten New York recoveries). That this is not strictly a one-way deal is proved by the fact that two individuals banded in the winter months in New York were recovered during summer in Alaska, as well as one each the same season from Mackenzie and Alberta.

It can thus be seen that some of these birds migrate in a northwest-southeast direction from coast to coast. Seven of ten banded Alaskan juveniles come from the Kotzebue Sound region, only 250 miles from Siberia.

An individual banded in New York was recovered in Saskatchewan 12 years later.

Remarks: No subspecies are recognized here; the darker and coarser barring of the upper parts in males, attributed to the American population (*"nearctica"*), is of average difference only.

Lesser Scaup (*Aythya affinis*)   *   B

Range: Western North America, breeding southeast to southwestern Ontario; very rarely to the Lake Erie region—southeastern Ontario (west of Toronto), northern Ohio, and extreme western New York (Buffalo). Winters commonly from Chesapeake Bay to Florida.

Status: The two scaups are so similar in appearance that they can be considered sibling species. So difficult are they to differentiate in the field, except at very close range and in extremely good light, that it is next to impossible to give the precise status of the Lesser Scaup within the state. However, it is probably more numerous inland and less so along the coast. It is also much rarer in winter than the Greater Scaup.

Nonbreeding: I am unable to vouch for the

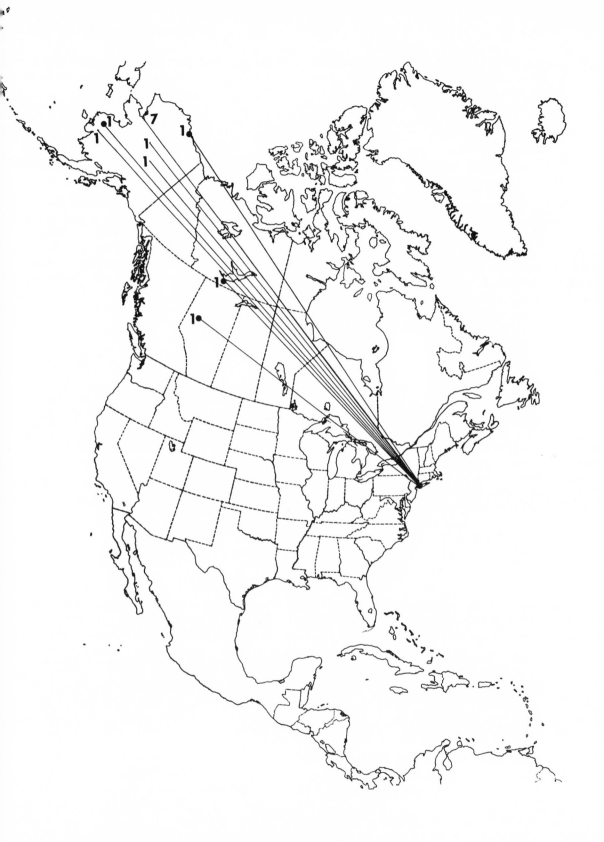

MAP 36 Greater Scaup (*Aythya marila*) Banding recoveries

MAP 37 Lesser Scaup (*Aythya affinis*) Banding recoveries

accuracy of the following three upstate maximum estimates published in the literature:

MAXIMA: 500, Lake Ontario, near Rochester, Oct. 14, 1950 (many observers); 275, Silver Lake, Wyoming Co., Nov. 8, 1959 (Rosche); 2000, Oneida Lake, Apr. 12, 1959 (Scheider)—see Greater Scaup for comparative numbers, this last date.

Three male Lesser Scaup summered at the Jamaica Bay Refuge in 1956 where they were compared directly with a small group of summering Greater Scaup.

Breeding: The only known and proved breeding record of this duck within New York was established by Harold Mitchell, who observed a female with a brood of seven downy young at the Tifft Street (Buffalo) Marsh on June 1, 1946 (Beardslee and Mitchell, 1965: 139).

Banding (see Map 37): Unlike its close relative, the Greater Scaup, the southern breeding and winter limits of the present species lie much farther south. Note the greater numbers of Lesser Scaup breeding in the Canadian prairie provinces and the lesser numbers breeding in Alaska, based on banded birds, as well as the much deeper penetration into Alaska of the Greater Scaup.

In view of the eastern breeding limits (James Bay) indicated on the distribution map in Godfrey (1966: 69), it is of interest to note the banding recoveries of presumed breeders taken during the summer months in east-central Quebec, Labrador, and New Brunswick.

The farthest south winter records of *direct* recoveries of birds banded in New York are those of one from Hispaniola and another shot on the Gulf coast of Mexico in Tamaulipas. Still another was shot near the Gulf coast of Florida only six days after date of banding.

An individual banded in New York was recovered in New Jersey 12 years later.

[Red-crested Pochard (*Netta rufina*)

Hypothetical: Palearctic region. A specimen, no longer extant, was purchased in Fulton Market, New York City, in 1872. Although it was supposed to have been collected on Long Island, no definite proof of this was ever obtained. Many birds in this market originated from places far removed from Long Island, including European localities.]

Common Eider
(*Somateria mollissima*) *

Range: Holarctic region, in eastern North America breeding south along the coast to southern Maine. Winters south to Massachusetts (in large numbers), eastern Long Island (in very much smaller numbers), and rarely to New Jersey.

Status: Uncommon to occasionally very common winter visitant at extreme eastern Long Island (Montauk area) and rare to uncommon elsewhere on Long Island; notable increase since 1942. Very rare inland.

Occurrence: On most trips to Montauk Point and vicinity Common Eiders may be seen, including one or more adult males. The following maxima undoubtedly contain some King Eiders in the flocks, especially since immatures—greatly in preponderance—are exceedingly difficult to differentiate, as are females at distant range: 1947—32, Jan. 1; and more than 140 (including 40 adult males) Feb. 23 (Helmuth); 1950—42 (nine adult males), Dec. 10; and 115 (30 adult males), Dec. 31 (Grant and Komorowski); 200, Nov. 16, 1969 (Plunkett).

Away from Long Island this species has always been extremely rare. Except for five specimen records (see **Subspecies),** only a handful of sight reports are known, three from Lake Ontario and one from Lake Erie, the latter including two individuals, one an adult male in breeding plumage, off Hamburg, Erie Co., Apr. 14, 1966 (Danner and Schafer).

Extreme dates: Sept. 2 (exceptionally early, Montauk) and Sept. 25 to Apr. 20. Usually rare before mid-November and after March.

Subspecies: (1) The race *dresseri* (lobe at base of bill broad), the southernmost breeding population in eastern North America, is presumably the dominant form in the state. Two specimens from Long Island are in the AMNH collection. A female collected at Ossining, Westchester Co., Dec. 14, 1894 (Fisher), is MCZ 300372. Another female was taken on the Niagara River, Sept. 29, 1960

(Axtell), BMS 4522. All of these were examined by the writer.

(2) The more northern coastal breeding subspecies *borealis*, breeding south to Labrador (distinguished by very narrow lobe at base of bill), has been collected at least once in the state. A female was shot at Montauk, Long Island, Dec. 15, 1945 (Lester); specimen examined by J. T. Nichols (*in litt.*), its present whereabouts unknown.

(3) The "inland" race *sedentaria*, breeding south to James Bay, differs from the other subspecies by the females and juveniles being noticeably paler and grayer. A young male was shot on the Niagara River, near Navy Island, Nov. 21, 1936 (Anderson), and is in the National Museum of Canada collection at Ottawa where it was confirmed as this race by Godfrey (Parkes, 1952).

King Eider (*Somateria spectabilis*) *

Range: Holarctic region, in eastern North America breeding "inland" along the west coast of Hudson Bay, south to islands in James Bay; but on the Atlantic coast not known to breed south of Baffin Island (Godfrey, 1966: 78). Winters south along the coast in large numbers to Newfoundland, in much smaller numbers to Massachusetts, Rhode Island, Long Island, and New Jersey; also inland on the Great Lakes.

Status: Rare to uncommon but regular winter visitant along the coast of Long Island (most numerous at Montauk) and on the Great Lakes, occasionally even fairly common.

Occurrence: Although numerically less prevalent off eastern Long Island than the Common Eider (at least in recent years) the King Eider is by far the more numerous of the two species on the Great Lakes and other inland waters. It should be emphasized, however, that adult males are definitely in the minority in these latitudes and that the identification of females and immatures as to species is problematical. This is true especially on the coast where both eiders occur. The specific determination of these birds at a distance and of immatures (except subadult males) at close range is critical and often highly dubious. As a result, flocks of eiders seen in our waters often contain individuals of both species. When perusing the maxima given below this should be kept in mind.

MAXIMA: *Coastal,* Montauk area—seven males, Dec. 18, 1945; 22 (eight males), Feb. 2 to Mar. 16, 1958; 30 (at least ten males), Apr. 8, 1887 (Dutcher, 1888). *Coastal,* elsewhere—Atlantic Beach, Nassau Co., eight, Dec. 29, 1957, to Jan. 30, 1958; eight, Mar. 23, 1952.

MAXIMA: *Inland*—20 observed, three collected, Cayuga Lake, Nov. 3, 1908 (Eaton); 18 collected, Buffalo area, Nov. 26, 1879 (*fide* J. A. Allen); 15, Niagara River, winter of 1959–1960, some of these shot, others found dead (all females and juveniles); 22, mouth of Niagara River, Jan. 14, 1967; six, Buffalo harbor, Mar. 13, 1937; eight on Lake Ontario at Sea Breeze, Monroe Co., Apr. 19, 1960.

EXTREME DATES: Sept. 5 (inland) and Sept. 30 (coastal) to May 20 (inland) and June 3, 1966 (three males off Gardiner's Island, Suffolk Co., Bull). Summer stragglers of females and/or juveniles recorded in Long Island waters on several occasions (1924, 1960, 1961, 1968) but species questionable; however, a male in breeding plumage was present on Oyster Pond, Montauk, the entire summer of 1938 (Helmuth, *et al.*). Ordinarily rare before November and after April.

Specimen data (based on extant specimens only): 32—only four adult males—in the AMNH collection from Long Island, all but nine from the Montauk area. Three inland specimens (either females or juveniles) as follows: Montezuma Marshes, Nov. 26, 1909 (Lloyd), CUM 744, a very unusual locality for a deep-water species; Charlotte (near Rochester), Dec. 15, 1921, CUM 745; Grand Island, Niagara River, Dec. 3, 1959, BMS 4504. Other inland specimens published in the literature were not available for examination.

Labrador Duck
(*Camptorhynchus labradorius*) *

Extinct: A species of very restricted range; breeding area unknown, supposedly in Labrador. Wintered on the Atlantic coast south to Long Island, possibly farther but evidence is lacking.

In New York, as far as known, this species was restricted to the south shore of Long Island. At least 15 local specimens were listed by Dutcher (*Auk,* 1891, 8: 201–216, and 1894, 11: 4–12) as being extant, including five in the AMNH collection, the remainder scattered in other collections. Most of these specimens are without detailed data. One male was shot by Colonel Nicholas Pike as it lit among decoys in Great South Bay near Quogue in 1858. The last recorded specimen was collected on Long Island in the fall of 1875 (Bell), USNM 77126.

Very little is known of this bird's habits. Greenway (1958: 173–175) stated: "The mature male was always rare, even during the first half of the nineteenth century when the birds could sometimes be found in the markets of New York. In winter the birds were found in sandy bays and estuaries. The reasons for its extinction are not known." This species was called the Sand Shoal Duck, due to its preference for sand bars where it was reputed to feed on shellfish. It was also known as the Pied Duck, and as the Skunk Duck on Long Island, both these names referring to its coloration.

A specimen, alleged to be this species, was shot near Elmira, Chemung Co., Dec. 12, 1878 (Gregg), but was ultimately lost. No experienced ornithologist ever examined the specimen and the year 1878 makes it highly unlikely, as the last known specimen was taken on Long Island in 1875 (see above). Furthermore, no authentic inland specimen is known. I agree with Eaton (1910: 218) that the evidence is too insufficient to credit this "occurrence."

Oldsquaw (*Clangula hyemalis*)   *

Range: Holarctic region, in eastern North America breeding south to James Bay and the coast of Labrador. Winters south to southern United States.

Status: Common to very abundant winter visitant along the coast and on the larger inland lakes.

Occurrence: Oldsquaws are most numerous in the Great Lakes area and at the eastern end of Long Island. They are occasionally found in large numbers on the Finger Lakes.

MAXIMA: *Coastal*—2500, Montauk, Jan. 1, 1930; 5000, Gardiner's Bay, Mar. 24, 1910 (Griscom). *Inland*—2000, Hamlin, Monroe Co., Oct. 23, 1965; 5000, Charlotte, Monroe Co., Nov. 27, 1966; 3000, Lower Niagara River, all January 1956; 1000, north end of Keuka Lake, near Penn Yan, Yates Co., Apr. 22, 1965 (Lerch); 500, Oklahoma Beach, Monroe Co., May 15, 1966, late for so many. The three Monroe Co. localities are on Lake Ontario near Rochester.

According to Bacon (*Ornith. and Ool.,* 1892, 17: 45) the Oldsquaw was formerly taken in large numbers in gill nets from great depths in Lake Erie. In November 1891 at Dunkirk between 5000 and 7000 were gathered at a single haul. Most of these ducks were caught at 15 fathoms (=90 feet).

This species has been collected inland on the Montezuma Marshes. One was taken at Oyster Bay, Nassau Co., Long Island, July 12, 1884. It has been recorded every month of the year, but is generally uncommon before October and after mid-May.

Banding: A juvenile banded at Churchill, Manitoba, on July 18, 1941, was shot from the Lake Ontario shore of Wayne Co. on Nov. 6, 1943.

Harlequin Duck
(*Histrionicus histrionicus*)   *

Range: Northeastern Asia, extreme western North America, and coasts of the North Atlantic Ocean from Baffin Island, Greenland, and Iceland, breeding south to the Gaspé Peninsula, Quebec. Winters on the Atlantic coast south to Long Island, New York; rarely farther.

Status: Rare to uncommon but regular winter visitant on the coast of Long Island, occasionally more numerous; rare and irregular on the Great Lakes and at Niagara Falls.

Occurrence: This beautiful duck frequents rocky coasts and inlets. One of the best places to see this species fairly close to New York City is off the rock jetty on the Point Lookout (west) side of Jones Inlet, Nassau Co. At that locality from late January to Mar. 8, 1968, record numbers of *16* individuals (eight of

them adult males) were seen by numerous observers. They were very tame and could be
photographed at close range. Other maxima on
Long Island are: seven, Montauk Point, Feb.
4, 1956; five, Orient, winter of 1962–1963; five,
Atlantic Beach, Jan. 28, 1961.

Inland the Harlequin Duck is ordinarily extremely rare, but is occasional in the turbulent
waters of the gorge of the Niagara River,
especially in the vicinity of the falls. Here two
males were present from Nov. 30, 1957, to
Mar. 8, 1958. More than a dozen records have
been obtained from that locality. It has been
recorded also along the Lake Ontario shore
and very rarely elsewhere. The only extant
inland specimen examined by me is that of a
female collected on the Allegheny River near
Salamanca, Cattaraugus Co., Mar. 27, 1950
(collector unknown), mounted specimen in the
Allegany State Park Museum.

EXTREME DATES: Oct. 20 and Nov. 2 to
Apr. 18, exceptionally to May 26. Rare before late November and after early April.

White-winged Scoter
(*Melanitta fusca*) *

Range: Palearctic and western Nearctic regions, in North America breeding east to
extreme western Ontario. Winters south to
southern United States. For subspecies, see **Remarks.**

Status: Very abundant migrant and winter
visitant on the coast; much less numerous
inland.

Occurrence: This species is ordinarily the
most numerous of the scoters, although occasionally outnumbered by the other two. At
times it is present in truly spectacular numbers
off Montauk Point, Long Island. Regular in
summer (nonbreeders) in Long Island waters.
Upstate it is most frequent on Lake Ontario.

MAXIMA: *Coastal*—90,000, Jones Beach,
Dec. 7, 1952; 25,000, Mount Sinai, Suffolk
Co., Dec. 25, 1910; 75,000, Montauk, Jan. 1,
1930; 180,000, Montauk, Mar. 16, 1930 (Helmuth); 150, off Mount Sinai, June 28, 1955;
100, Orient, Suffolk Co., summer of 1964.

MAXIMA: *Inland*—Unprecedented movement along Lake Ontario on Oct. 23, 1965 (see
other two scoters for comparative numbers):

2000, Hamlin Beach, Monroe Co., and 4700,
Derby Hill, Oswego Co., very large numbers
of Brant occurred on this date also; 500, Sea
Breeze, Monroe Co., Dec. 31, 1957; 500,
Manitou, Monroe Co., Feb. 2, 1966, after a
blizzard; 300, Manitou, Apr. 30, 1960; 100,
Keuka Lake, May 8, 1954, a good "inland"
number; seven, Manitou, July 4, 1964.

Remarks: The writer follows Delacour
(1959) in treating *fusca* and *deglandi* as conspecific. The frontal processes (bill knobs) appear more alike in these two forms than those
of *M. nigra* and *M. n. americana,* and yet the
latter are merged into one species in the
A.O.U. Check-list (1957), while *M. fusca* and
M. deglandi are retained as separate species.
Mayr and Short (1970) and Palmer (in prep.)
likewise consider them as a single species.

The American race *deglandi* (compared
with nominate *fusca*) has a more pronounced
knob on bill, colored portion of bill orange
rather than yellowish, feathering extends onto
bill closer to nostril, and finally the flanks are
deep brown rather than black.

Surf Scoter (*Melanitta perspicillata*) *

Range: North America, breeding southeast
occasionally to northern Ontario and islands in
James Bay, and locally in northern Quebec
and central Labrador. Winters south to southern United States.

Status: Common to very abundant migrant
and winter visitant on the coast; much less
numerous inland, but occasionally abundant
on the Great Lakes.

Occurrence: The Surf Scoter is the second
most numerous of the scoters off Montauk
Point and occasionally outnumbers the White-
winged Scoter there. It is, however, the least
numerous of the three on the Great Lakes, and
certainly the rarest on the smaller lakes and
rivers of the interior. Interestingly enough, it
is during October that the largest concentrations of all three species occur on inland waters, especially on Lake Ontario, probably indicating a regular overland migration at that
time. Along the coast all three scoters are
present in large numbers from October to
April.

MAXIMA: *Coastal*—For comparative numbers on Jan. 1 and Mar. 16, 1930, Dec. 7, 1952, and June 28, 1955—see other scoters; 5000, Jones Beach, Dec. 7, 1952; 25,000, Montauk, Jan. 1, 1930; (Helmuth) 120, Montauk, Mar. 16, 1930; 50, off Mount Sinai, June 28, 1955.

MAXIMA: *Inland*—For comparative numbers on Oct. 23, 1965, and Oct. 19, 1967—see other scoters; 1200, Derby Hill, Oswego Co., Oct. 19, 1967; 800, Hamlin, Monroe Co., Oct. 23, 1965; 150, Silver Lake, Wyoming Co., Oct. 25, 1959. One individual was observed in the Niagara Gorge on July 13, 1946.

All three scoters have been recorded every month of the year, but are much scarcer inland during summer.

Black Scoter (*Melanitta nigra*) *

Range: Palearctic region and western Alaska; the race *americana* (bill less bulbous and with much more orange) breeds from northeastern Siberia east to western Alaska, also very locally in Canada—southern Keewatin, northern Quebec, and Newfoundland (Godfrey, 1966: 80–81). Summering non-breeders occur throughout much of northern and central Canada, but without definite proof of breeding. Winters south to southern United States.

Status: Similar to the Surf Scoter, but usually less numerous than that species on the coast; however, more numerous inland, especially on the Great Lakes and in the Hudson-Mohawk valleys and on Lake Champlain.

Occurrence: This species, the smallest of the scoters, is more likely to be found on smaller bodies of water upstate, such as ponds and rivers, than are the other two, possibly because it can take off from the water with less difficulty.

MAXIMA: *Coastal*—600, Jones Beach, Sept. 25, 1955; 10,000 Montauk, Jan. 3 and Mar. 16, 1930; 18,000, Jones Beach, Apr. 5, 1936. Much rarer in summer than the other two scoters.

MAXIMA: *Inland*—On Oct. 9, 1900—156 were shot in Buffalo harbor and 175 more in Lake Erie, near Angola, Erie Co. (Eaton, 1910: 222); on Oct. 13, 1962, a total of 540

was observed at the following three "inland" localities—325, Saratoga Lake, 140, Alcove Reservoir, Albany Co., and 75, Niskayuna (near Schenectady). On Oct. 23, 1965, on Lake Ontario, a very large number was recorded at two localities—3300, Derby Hill, Oswego Co., and 1700, Hamlin Beach, Monroe Co. Also 3500 at Derby Hill, Oct. 19, 1967. An estimate of 5200 at Dunkirk, Chautauqua Co., Feb. 7, 1969 (Rew), is exceptional.

Remarks: The vernacular name Black Scoter, as translated from its scientific name *nigra*, is more appropriate than the misleading "Common" Scoter, due to the fact that the male is the only *all black* scoter. Black Scoter is used also by Delacour (1959).

All three scoters are here considered congeneric, following Vaurie (1965), Mayr and Short (1970), and Palmer (in prep.).

Bufflehead (*Bucephala albeola*) *

Range: Chiefly western North America, breeding east to the northern portions of Ontario—casually in the Sudbury district north of Georgian Bay in southeastern Ontario (Godfrey, 1966: 72). Winters south to southern United States.

Status: Locally common to abundant winter visitant and migrant.

Occurrence: The Bufflehead seems to have increased in recent years, especially within the last decade. It occurs most frequently and in the largest numbers on the coastal bays—especially those on Long Island—and on the lakes and rivers of western New York, chiefly from mid-November to mid-May—at the latter season much later than in former years. Recorded every month of the year.

MAXIMA: *Coastal*—1000, Jamaica Bay Refuge, Nov. 21, 1965 (Norse); 600, East "River" at Clason Point, Bronx Co., Dec. 22, 1963; 360, Jamaica Bay Refuge, Mar. 28, 1964; 200, same locality, May 14, 1966.

MAXIMA: *Inland*—350, Chautauqua Lake near Mayville, Nov. 14, 1962; 1100, Niagara River, Dec. 7, 1968 (Mitchell); 2200, same locality, Dec. 28, 1970 (Axtell, *et al.*); 350, same area, Jan. 21, 1962; big flight on Apr. 19, 1962—200, Cassadaga Lake and 150, Bear

MAP 38   Bufflehead (*Bucephala albeola*) Banding recoveries

Lake (both in Chautauqua Co.) and 100, near Tully, Onondaga Co.

Interestingly enough single Buffleheads were reported at opposite ends of the state on the same day in summer, Aug. 8, 1964, at Buffalo and at the Jamaica Bay Refuge.

A male was collected at the north end of Skaneateles Lake, Onondaga Co., June 23, 1882 (D. C. Smith), AMNH 461503. This species was seen in midsummer also on Long Island, July 6 and July 8, different years. It is ordinarily very rare at that season.

Banding (see Map 38): Note the four northwest-southeast flyway routes used by these ducks, three bandings involving Saskatchewan and one Alberta. The longest "direct" recovery shown is that of a juvenile Bufflehead banded Aug. 10, 1962, near Goose Lake, Alberta, and shot Dec. 1, 1962 on Great South Bay, Long Island.

Common Goldeneye
(*Bucephala clangula*)   *   B

Range: Holarctic region, in North America breeding from Alaska and Canada to extreme northern United States. Winters from southern portions of the breeding range to extreme northern Mexico and the Gulf states.

Status: Common to very abundant winter visitant on the coast and on the Great Lakes, especially numerous on eastern Long Island. Rare or perhaps uncommon breeder in the Adirondack region and the area adjacent to Lake Champlain.

Nonbreeding: This species is most numerous on the coast when the winters are at their severest, particularly during long cold spells. It is also locally common on the larger inland rivers and lakes until frozen.

MAXIMA: *Coastal*—All from eastern Suffolk Co.: 8000, Orient, Dec. 26, 1924 (Latham); 4000, Montauk, Mar. 15, 1945 (Helmuth); 10,000, Gardiner's Bay, Mar. 24, 1910 (Griscom). These numbers have not been approached in recent years, 2000 being the maximum reported.

MAXIMA: *Inland*—All from the Lake Ontario shore, except one: 1200, Derby Hill, Oswego Co., Nov. 16, 1966; 2300, Grand Island, Niagara River, Dec. 2, 1965; 2500, Manitou, Monroe Co., Jan. 26, 1961; 2500, Oswego (harbor), Oswego Co., Mar. 29, 1959.

The species is generally rare before November and after early April. Reported every month of the year, but only vagrants in summer, including a female that summered at the Jamaica Bay Refuge in 1963.

Breeding (see Map 39): Although eight New York localities have been recorded as breeding sites for the Common Goldeneye, nonetheless little is known about its nesting habits in the state. Here it is at or very near its southernmost known breeding limits. Eaton (1910: 209) was vague about its breeding in the Adirondacks, probably because his correspondents furnished him with meager information. Both Merriam and Ralph and Bagg (in Eaton, *op. cit.*) stated that this species bred in the Adirondacks, but gave few details. Bagg merely stated that it "nested" in western Hamilton Co. in June of both 1878 and 1879 at Jones Lake and nearby Deer Lake respectively. These were based on "young" birds.

The unsubstantiated breeding records that Eaton (*op. cit.*) gave for Cortland and Onondaga counties (well outside the Adirondacks and south of the known southern limits) are probably erroneous. Even today, I know of not a single egg or juvenile preserved in any collection from New York State. As far as known, an actual nest of this species has never been found in the state; but see Andrle (*Kingbird*, 1971, 21: 212–214), especially his remarks concerning the possibility of birds escaped from captivity. It is a tree nester, laying its eggs in holes or cavities, chiefly near lakes in evergreen forest.

Within the past two decades (1955–1969) biologists of the State Conservation Department have come across adults with broods of young. With the exception of a brood found by Francis Singer in 1969 at Lake Alice, Clinton Co., the northernmost known breeding record in New York (see map), and the above Hamilton Co. record, all others (1950s and 1960s) were given to me by Foley and Browne (*in litt.*) of the New York State Conservation Department. They are: Clinton Co., "inland" —(1) Lake Alice. Clinton Co. on Lake Champlain—(2) Monty Bay marshes; (3) marshes at the mouth of the Ausable River. Franklin

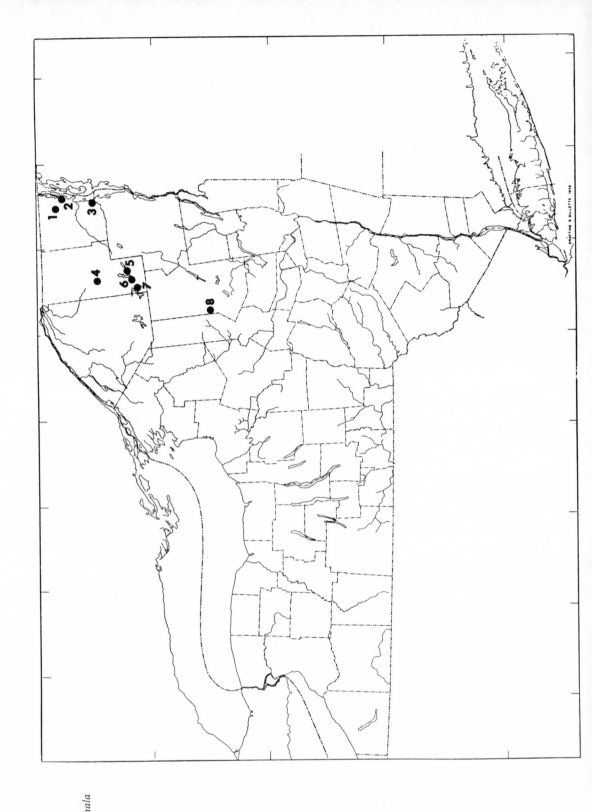

MAP 39 Common
Goldeneye (*Bucephala
clangula*) Breeding
distribution

Co.—(4) Dodge River Flow near Madawaska; (5) Middle Saranac Lake; (6) Raquette River between Axton and Simon Pond; (7) near Tupper Lake (village). Hamilton Co.—(8) Jones Lake and nearby Deer Lake.

The above information is not offered as a recent increase, but reflects incidental observations by State Conservation Department personnel, much of it done by canoe on backwaters during regular field work. Clearly more observations are needed to ascertain brood size, nest sites, and dates for eggs and young.

Banding: Two individuals banded during the winter months on Chautauqua Lake were recovered the following summer on or near their presumed breeding grounds in Saskatchewan (Quill Lakes and Frobisher Lake).

Remarks: No subspecies are recognized here; the New World population *"americana"* averages larger than birds from Eurasia but with considerable overlap in wing and bill length.

Barrow's Goldeneye
(*Bucephala islandica*) *

Range: Nearctic region, most prevalent along the Pacific slope of Alaska and Canada; rare and local in eastern North America, breeding restricted to the coast of northern Labrador; also Iceland. Winters south to New York.

Status: Very rare to rare winter visitant.

Occurrence: In the east Barrow's Goldeneye is at its southern limits in the latitude of Long Island and is seldom recorded in New York State. This species has been reported most frequently in the St. Lawrence valley and to a lesser extent in the Lake Champlain-upper Hudson valley district, along the Lake Ontario plain, and at the eastern end of Long Island.

Ordinarily only one individual at a time is reported or, more rarely, two. On occasion larger numbers have been noted: (1) on eastern Long Island at Orient, Suffolk Co., Latham observed six on Jan. 5, 1909, and three, Feb. 1, 1935; (2) in a flock of mixed goldeneyes, three Barrow's were reported of which two were shot on Lake Champlain at Ausable

Point, Clinton Co., Nov. 10, 1954 (Lesperance); (3) out of a flock of four of this species, three were shot by duck hunters on the St. Lawrence River off Stony Point, Jefferson Co., Nov. 27, 1960 (*fide* Clinch). For disposition of these birds, see **Specimen data.**

In all of the above instances one or more adult males were involved. Females and immatures are ordinarily difficult to identify in the field and some females reported as this species may have been misidentified Common Goldeneyes.

Specimen data: Eaton (1910: 211) stated that D. G. Elliot "took nearly 40 specimens" on the St. Lawrence River in 1865. I do not know the whereabouts of most of these, but five collected by Elliot in the AMNH collection, 3675–3679, of which three are males and two either females or immatures, were taken in the vicinity of Ogdensburg, St. Lawrence Co. (dates not given).

There are at least ten other specimens taken in the state including three old ones mentioned by Eaton (*op. cit.*). Of the seven remaining specimens four are extant, three adult males and one female: (1) female, Orient, Suffolk Co., Dec. 30, 1924 (Latham), NYSM 24834, previously unpublished; (2) one of the 1954 specimens (see above) is in the collection of the State University at Plattsburgh, identification confirmed by Geoffrey Carleton; (3) one of the 1960 specimens (also above) is a mount in the collection of the Case Junior High School at Watertown, identity corroborated by John Belknap; (4) one captured alive, but badly oiled, Fisher's Island, Suffolk Co., Mar. 22, 1963 (Ferguson), specimen in the Ferguson Memorial Museum, examined by the writer.

Remarks: Since about the mid-1950s Barrow's Goldeneye has been reported at least once annually and in three years it has been seen twice.

The species has been reliably observed at the following upstate localities: (1) St. Lawrence valley—Waddington, St. Lawrence Co.; (2) upper Hudson valley—Saratoga Lake and Mechanicville, Saratoga Co.; Troy, Rensselaer Co.; Albany and Green Island, Albany Co.; (3) central New York—Oneida Lake; Onondaga Lake; (4) western New York—Sodus Bay, Wayne Co.; Braddock's Bay, Brockport, and Sandy Creek, Monroe Co.; Niagara River and Buffalo.

Downstate this species has been observed at: (1) Long Island—Montauk Point and Georgica Pond, Suffolk Co.; Atlantic Beach, Nassau Co.; (2) Staten Island—off Wolfe's Pond, Richmond Co.

EXTREME DATES: Nov. 10 (specimen) to Apr. 5 and 20.

Smew (*Mergus albellus*)

Range: Northern Palearctic region, wintering in the western portion south to the British Isles and France, rarely to Spain and Portugal. Accidental in New York.

Status: *Accidental*—The only known occurrence of this species in North America is that of an individual, believed to have been an immature, observed in Buffalo harbor and at various other localities in the Niagara River region from Jan. 17 to Mar. 30, 1960 (Andrle, Coggeshall, Thill, and numerous others). Attempts to collect this bird proved unsuccessful, but good color photographs were taken by D. R. Gunn. For detailed description and illustrations, see Beardslee and Mitchell (1965: 153–154).

The species is an addition to the A.O.U. Check-list.

Hooded Merganser
(*Mergus cucullatus*)   *   B

Range: Nearctic region, in the east breeding from southern Canada locally to the Gulf states; having a much more southerly distribution than the other mergansers. Winters north to New York and New England.

Status: Locally common to very common migrant, occasionally abundant at Montezuma and on Chautauqua Lake; less numerous in winter along the coast. Uncommon and very local breeder.

Nonbreeding: This species is decidedly the least numerous of the mergansers. It is essentially a fresh-water duck and prefers more secluded waters than the other two.

MAXIMA: *Fall*—1000, Montezuma Refuge,

Nov. 23, 1970 (C. Hardy, refuge manager), an unprecedented number; 135, Rockville Centre, Nassau Co., Dec. 5, 1959.

MAXIMA: *Spring*—220, Chautauqua Lake, Apr. 5, 1964; 440, Montezuma, Apr. 30, 1969.

Breeding (see Map 40): Hooded Mergansers frequent wooded swamps, beaver ponds, and quiet stretches of water in forested regions, especially where dead trees are plentiful (see Fig. 30). They are sometimes found nesting—literally—with Wood Ducks; indeed, both species are hole nesters and on several occasions eggs of the two have been observed in the *same* nest box, ostensibly erected for Wood Ducks. It has been stated that the Hooded Merganser is "parasitic" on the Wood Duck, but the precise relationship of the two species under these conditions is not certain.

Mr. Donald Foley of the State Conservation Department states (*in litt.*), "In many areas where we have erected Wood Duck boxes, the Hooded Merganser has invaded numbers of them, sometimes alone and sometimes in company with a Wood Duck already using the box. Often we have found both species' eggs in the same box, and rarely mixed clutches have hatched, though there is some strife resulting in egg breakage and nest desertion."

According to the same authority, a nest box at Vischer's Ferry, Saratoga Co., contained a mixed clutch of 13 eggs, a female Wood Duck incubating nine of her own and four of the merganser; at still another nest box he observed a female Hooded Merganser incubating seven of her own eggs and three of the Wood Duck. In neither instance was the outcome of the mixed clutches ascertained. This would make a good research project.

In these nest boxes, height above water level ranged from two to six feet, but in tree cavities nests are usually located much higher, up to 25 feet.

In 26 New York nests, egg clutches of the Hooded Merganser ranged from seven eggs (seven nests) to 12 eggs (four nests), with a maximum of eight eggs (ten nests).

EGG DATES: Apr. 25 to July 2.

Unfledged young: May 11 to July 17; fledglings: June 21 to Aug. 18.

The breeding distribution in the state of this showy species is of considerable interest (see Map 40). Judging from the available informa-

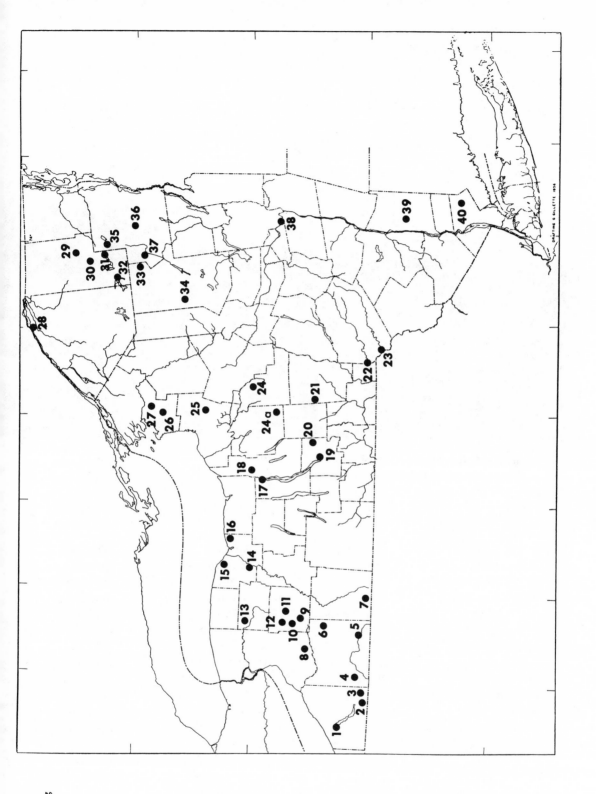

MAP 40 Hooded Merganser (*Mergus cucullatus*) Breeding distribution

Fig. 30 Beaver Meadow Refuge, Java, Wyoming Co., Sept. 29, 1954; breeding habitat of Hooded Merganser. Photo by Richard Rosche

Locality	County	Locality	County
1. Mayfield	Chautauqua	21. German	Chenango
2. Kiantone	Chautauqua	22. near Deposit	Broome
3. Riverside Marsh	Chautauqua	23. near Hancock	Delaware
4. Stillson's Pond	Cattaraugus	24. Wampsville	Madison
5. Allegany	Cattaraugus	24a. Fabius	Onondaga
6. Farmersville	Cattaraugus	25. Happy Valley Refuge	Oswego
7. Alma Pond	Allegany	26. Honeyville	Jefferson
8. East Concord	Erie	27. south of Watertown	Jefferson
9. Beaver Lake	Wyoming	28. Wilson Hill Refuge	St. Lawrence
10. Beaver Meadow Refuge	Wyoming	29. DeBar Mtn. Refuge	Franklin
11. North Java	Wyoming	30. Black Pond	Franklin
12. Wethersfield Springs	Wyoming	31. Lower Saranac Lake	Franklin
13. Oak Orchard Swamp	Genesee	32. Sunmount	Franklin
14. Scottsville	Monroe	33. Catlin Lake	Hamilton
15. Braddock's Bay	Monroe	34. Falls Pond	Hamilton
16. Nine Mile Point Creek	Monroe	35. Ray Brook	Essex
17. Montezuma	Seneca, Cayuga	36. Elk Lake	Essex
18. Howland's Island	Cayuga	37. Rich Lake	Essex
19. near Ithaca	Tompkins	38. Vischer's Ferry	Saratoga
20. Malloryville	Tompkins	39. Pleasant Valley	Dutchess
		40. near Katonah	Westchester

tion, it occurs most frequently in extreme western New York—in the Niagara Frontier region—and in the central Adirondacks. It is local elsewhere, and is very rare in the southeastern portions, although probably overlooked in the Catskill district. Eaton (1910: 181) mentioned that "It has been known to breed in the counties of . . . Ontario, Wayne . . . ," but I have seen no definite nesting records from those counties.

Both Map 40 and the foregoing table indicate the 41 known breeding localities in the state.

Common Merganser; Goosander
(*Mergus merganser*)   *   B

Range: Holarctic region, the New World race *americanus* (bill only slightly hooked; male with conspicuous black transverse bar on greater wing-coverts) in the west breeds from Alaska and Canada, south to the mountains of northern Mexico, but in the east only as far as southeastern Ontario and the northern portions of New York and New England; rarely or very rarely to the Berkshires, Catskills, and Poconos, and casually to northwestern Connecticut, southwestern New York, and northwestern Pennsylvania. Winters nearly throughout the breeding range—in the east—to the Gulf states.

Status: Common to very abundant winter visitant on the Niagara River, the Great Lakes, and the larger lakes of the interior; much less numerous on the lower Hudson River and near the coast. Common breeder in the Adirondacks, rare and local elsewhere.

Nonbreeding: Primarily a fresh-water species, the Common Merganser or Goosander is seldom numerous before cold weather sets in. It is occasional in salt-water bays and inlets during severe freezes, and is least numerous on Long Island.

MAXIMA: *Inland*—6000, Oswego harbor, Lake Ontario, Jan. 19, 1957; 8000, Niagara River between Navy Island and Erie Beach (Ontario), Jan. 21, 1962; *15,000,* Niagara River in the Grand Island area, Jan. 21, 1960 (Buffalo Ornithological Society), an unusually large number, coincident with an enormous concentration of the emerald shiner (*Notropis*

atherinoides); 5000, Dunkirk harbor, Lake Erie, Feb. 7, 1969; 3000, Cross Lake, Cayuga Co., Apr. 4, 1965.

MAXIMA: *Coastal,* lower Hudson River— 2300 between Haverstraw and Tomkins Cove, Rockland Co., Feb. 24, 1952; 1500, Croton Point, Westchester Co., Mar. 15, 1936.

Nonbreeders occasionally linger into summer.

Breeding (see Map 41): This species is one of the characteristic breeding birds of the Adirondack forest lakes and is frequently found on the same waters as the Common Loon. Like that species Common Mergansers have been adversely affected by an ever-growing number of summer vacationists and increased use of power boats, and have been disappearing from polluted areas. Very probably pesticides have contributed to their decline also. Consequently these birds, for the most part, have been forced to the more remote ponds and lakes in the wildest sections.

These fish-eating ducks nest both on the ground and in tree cavities. Foley (*in litt.*) has found nests with eggs "among tangled tree roots under overhanging stream banks," and on the ground in "thin alder cover among *Carex strictior,*" one of the sedges. Francis Harper (*Bird Lore,* 1914, 16: 338–341) located two ground nests on the Four Brothers Islands in Lake Champlain, one of the nests situated under an arbor-vitae or white cedar. Still another nest on the same islands in 1968 was three feet above ground in a six-foot stump in deciduous woodland (J. Forbes, nest record card). Several other tree nests have been located as high as 30 feet above ground, the last in an old elm.

Egg clutches in 34 New York nests ranged from seven (four nests) to 15 (two nests), with a maximum of eight eggs (seven nests) and 14 eggs (five nests).

EGG DATES: May 5 to July 10.

Unfledged young: May 15 to Aug. 18; fledged young: July 12 to Aug. 25.

The accompanying map shows two disjunct groupings within the state: (1) a widespread, long-standing Adirondack population; (2) a restricted, very recent (from 1954, but especially since 1964) peripheral aggregation, confined to the lower reaches of the western Catskills. Note also an isolated nesting in southern Allegany Co. (1968).

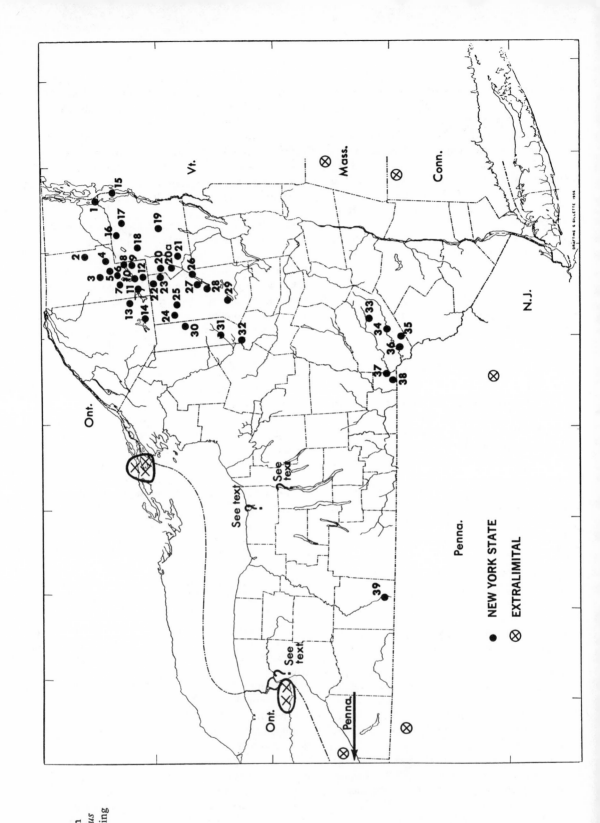

MAP 41 Common
Merganser (*Mergus
merganser*) Breeding
distribution

It should be emphasized that breeding records outside the Adirondack area were suspect (possible confusion with Hooded Mergansers) for a time by several observers including the writer, until details were submitted. However, two of the reporting parties had also recorded nesting Hooded Mergansers at or near localities where Common Mergansers were breeding. It should be pointed out also that documented breeding occurrences of *Mergus merganser* have occurred to the west, south, and east of these peripheral New York breeding localities (see map), i.e., in Ontario (Quilliam, 1965: 53, and Beardslee and Mitchell, 1965: 157), Pennsylvania (Poole, 1964: 21), Connecticut (*Audubon Field Notes,* 1962, 16: 462), and Massachusetts (Griscom and Snyder, 1955: 64).

As for alleged breeding reported by Eaton (1910: 178) for the following: (1) Buffalo area; (2) Little Sodus Bay, Wayne Co.; (3) Montezuma Marshes—no details were given.

The 40 recorded breeding localities are as follows: Clinton Co.—(1) Ausable River marshes, Lake Champlain. Franklin Co.—(2) Ragged Lake; (3) Rice Lake; (4) Rainbow Lake; (5) Lower St. Regis Lake; (6) Little Clear Pond; (7) Rat Pond; (8) Lower Saranac Lake; (9) Oseetah Lake; (10) Saranac River between Middle and Lower Saranac lakes; (11) Tupper Lake (marshes); (12) Raquette River south of Axton. St. Lawrence Co.—(13) Raquette River near Piercefield; (14) southeast side of Cranberry Lake. Essex Co.—(15) Four Brothers Islands, Lake Champlain; (16) Copperas Pond; (17) south of Jay; (18) near Mt. Jo; (19) Elk Lake; (20) Arbutus Pond and nearby Rich Lake; (20a) Goodnow Flow, 1971; (21) Boreas River near Aiden Lair. Hamilton Co.—(22) near Camp Island, Long Lake; (23) Catlin Lake; (24) Sucker Brook Bay, Raquette Lake; (25) east side of Raquette Lake; Indian Lake—(26) north end; (27) central portion; (28) south end; (29) Piseco Lake. Herkimer Co.—(30) Fourth Lake; (31) Mink

Fig. 31 Locality near site of breeding Common Mergansers, near York's Corners, about five miles south of Wellsville, Allegany Co., May 15, 1968. Photo by Lou Burton

Lake; (32) Hinckley Reservoir near Grant. Delaware Co.—(33) near Lake Delaware (34) near Pepacton Reservoir; (35) Beaverkill River between Peakville and Horton; (36) near East Branch at junction of Delaware and Beaverkill rivers. Broome Co.—(37) near Deposit; (38) Oquaga Lake. Allegany Co.—(39) Genesee River near York's Corners (see Fig. 31).

Red-breasted Merganser
(*Mergus serrator*) * B

Range: Holarctic region, in eastern North America breeding south in the interior only as far as northern New York (Jefferson Co.), but on the coast to Massachusetts and Long Island (rarely); casually farther south. Winters from the greater part of the breeding range to the Gulf of Mexico.

Status: Common to very abundant migrant on the coast and on Lake Ontario. Fairly numerous on the larger inland lakes and the lower Hudson River, but rare elsewhere. Uncommon and local breeder on islands in eastern Lake Ontario, but a rare breeder on Long Island.

Nonbreeding: This species occurs in the largest numbers in ocean waters, in the bays at the east end of Long Island, and on Lake Ontario. It occurs much less commonly on Long Island Sound, on the lower Hudson River, on the Finger Lakes, and apparently even on Lake Erie (likely due to pollution).

During the nonbreeding season this species favors salt water along the coast, whereas the Common Merganser is largely restricted to fresh water except during freezes.

MAXIMA: *Coastal*—10,000, Montauk area, Nov. 23, 1937; 25,000, Nov. 27, and 40,000, Nov. 30, 1941, from Montauk to Easthampton (all by Helmuth); 1500, Reynolds Channel, Atlantic Beach, Nassau Co., Mar. 11, 1950.

MAXIMA: *Inland*—10,000, off Sandy Pond, Oswego Co., Oct. 28, 1956; 10,000, Derby Hill, Oswego Co., Oct. 29, 1966; 10,000, Oswego, Nov. 22, 1961; 12,000, Braddock's Bay area, Monroe Co., Apr. 27, 1952; 6000, off Sandy Pond, May 8, 1957; 125, Waneta Lake, Schuyler Co., Apr. 28, 1944 (Axtell), unusually large number for a relatively small inland lake. Note that the spring flight is relatively late in the season.

Breeding (see Map 42): There seems to be a good deal of confusion and misunderstanding regarding the breeding distribution of the Red-breasted Merganser in New York.

First of all, there are two widely separated populations: (A) a local *inland* group in northern New York presumably restricted to two small islands in extreme eastern Lake Ontario; (B) a little-known *coastal* segment at the southern limits of the breeding range on islands at the east end of Long Island and beaches on its south shore.

Secondly, the earlier ornithologists confused the two mergansers (*merganser* and *serrator*) in the breeding season in the Adirondack region. Females of these two species are admittedly similar in appearance and males are in eclipse plumage (resembling females) during the breeding season.

Moreover, as explained under the Common Merganser, in northern New York the latter species is largely restricted to the taiga (coniferous forest) zone of the Adirondack-Champlain district during the breeding season. Furthermore, it nests both in trees (hole nester) and more rarely on the ground in or at the edge of the *forest*. The Red-breasted Merganser, on the other hand, nests exclusively on the ground in more *open country* and, as far as known, not in the Adirondacks or the Lake Champlain region.

Eaton (1910: 180) tersely stated: "A few are known to nest in the Adirondacks but most of the mergansers of that region belong to the preceding species [Common Merganser]." He gave no details, and apparently had no personal experience with *M. serrator* in the breeding season.

Bagg (1911: 30) completely confused the two species. Speaking of the West Canada Creek Valley (Hamilton and Herkimer counties), he called the Common Merganser, "A not common migrant," and the Red-breasted Merganser, "Common summer resident . . . Breeds." He had the status of the two species reversed.

To date, I know of not a single bona fide breeding record of the Red-breasted Merganser for "mainland" New York, i.e., the Adirondack region, based on either eggs or young birds in collections.

MAP 42 Red-breasted
Merganser (*Mergus
serrator*) Breeding
distribution

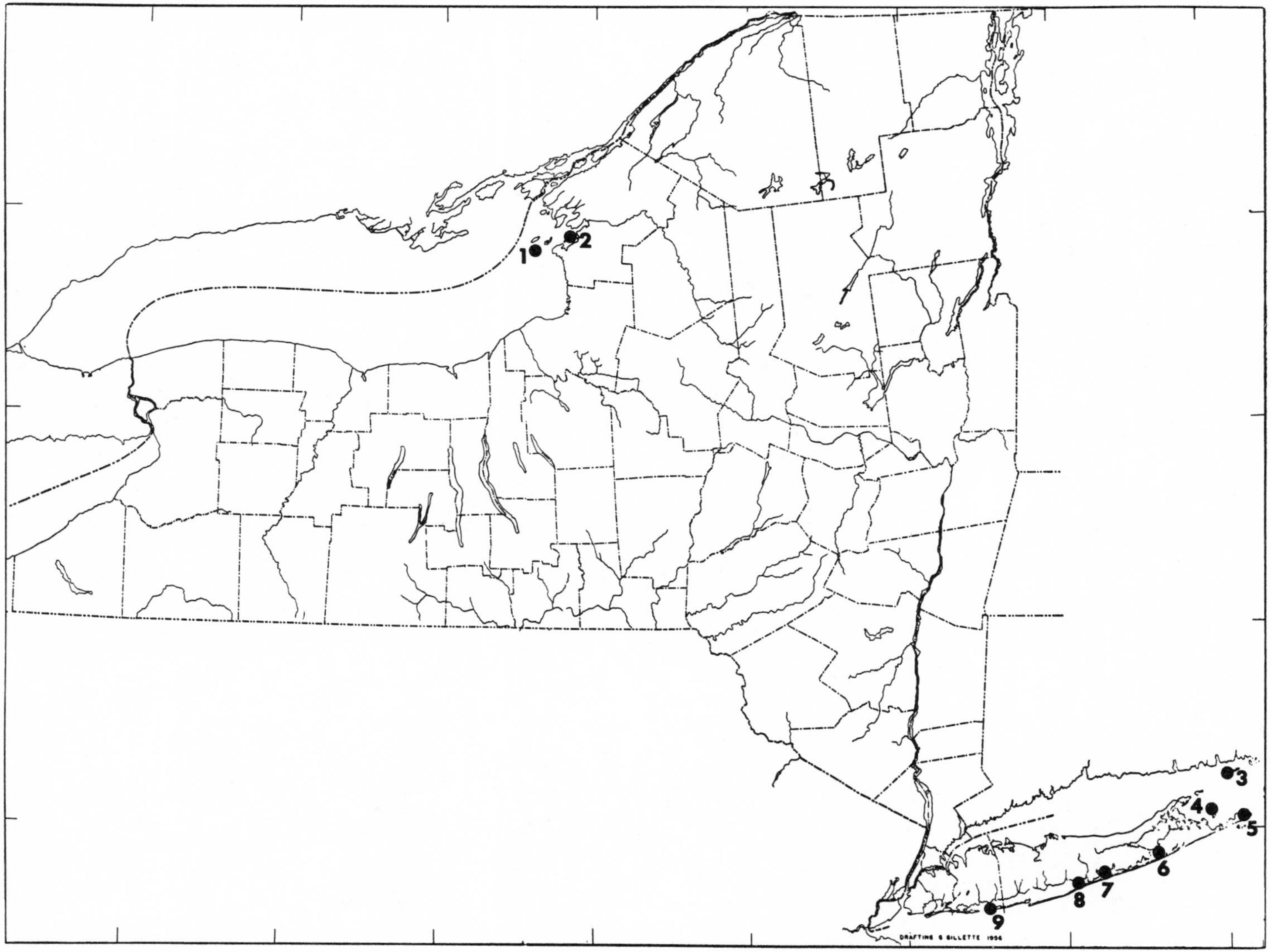

Even Parkes (1952) was misled for he stated that, "A few . . . may breed in the Adirondacks, but the metropolis of this species in New York is in the Thousand Islands region and the islands at the eastern end of Lake Ontario. Here it is a well-known and common breeding bird." It is certainly neither well known nor common there today (see below).

As to the Thousand Islands area (St. Lawrence River), I have seen no specimens or any published reference to actual breeding within that region on the New York side, although little *summer* field work has been undertaken there. However, it formerly bred on the Canadian side (Quilliam, 1965: 53–54). The three islands mentioned by her are in eastern Lake Ontario, *not* in the St. Lawrence valley.

To my knowledge, the following is "all" that is known of the breeding of this species in northern New York: Restricted to two islands in extreme eastern Lake Ontario, Jefferson Co. (see map). (1) Little Galloo Island (Hyde, 1939a; 111). That observer found a female at a nest containing 14 eggs on July 11, 1936. On June 10, 1967, the late Arthur W. Allen, John Belknap, Robert Wolk, and the writer flushed a female off a nest containing only four eggs, probably an incomplete clutch; this ground nest was under some bushes. We also saw another adult (female?) with eight downy young in the water just off the island.

(2) Gull Island, Henderson Bay (Hyde, *op. cit.*). Hyde photographed a nest with ten eggs "among nettles" (see illustration, p. 128); two of the eggs were pipped. He found two more nests with broken eggs (hatched?).

Unfortunately Cruickshank (1942: 126) gave few details (except locality) for five of the seven known breeding locations on Long Island, but merely stated: "Breeding evidence supported either by a nest or very small young has been submitted . . ."

The seven Long Island breeding localities (see map) with "details," are as follows: Suffolk Co.—(3) Fisher's Island, 1933 (Ferguson), pair with "small young"; and 1968 (Horning), adults with "young"; (4) Gardiner's Island (date and observer unknown); (5) Oyster Pond, Montauk (date?, Helmuth); (6) east end of Shinnecock Bay, 1912 (Helmuth); (7) Mastic (date?, J. T. Nichols); (8) Ridge Island, extreme east end of Great South Bay (opposite Bellport), July 20–21, 1971 (R. Rozsa

and D. Puleston)—pair of adults and six recently fledged juveniles. Nassau Co.—(9) Short Beach, Aug. 3, 1953 (Cantor and Norse), female and "four young."

The writer questioned a 1970 breeding report from Keuka Lake, alleged to be this species. However, no competent observer confirmed the identification. See retraction in the *Kingbird* (1971, 21: 223).

Another reported from Watertown during July 1971 was also without details, even the observer's name being omitted (*Kingbird,* 1971, 21: 237).

Banding: A juvenile banded along the north shore of the Gulf of St. Lawrence, at the mouth of the Natashquan River, Quebec, Sept. 10, 1949, was shot on Great South Bay, Suffolk Co., Nov. 24, 1949.

Ruddy Duck
(*Oxyura jamaicensis*)   *   B

Range: Neotropical and Nearctic regions, but local in the eastern portions of the latter area. In North America breeds east to the prairies; sporadically east to southeastern Ontario, New York, and other Atlantic coast states. In winter withdraws from the more northern sections of the breeding range.

Status: Common to locally abundant fall migrant, much less numerous in spring. In winter locally numerous on Long Island. Rare and local breeder; common at one locality. Has greatly increased in recent years.

Change in status: The Ruddy Duck frequents lakes, ponds, and marshes inland; and similar places on the coast, plus brackish estuaries and shallow bays and lagoons. Prior to the 1940s it was a decidedly uncommon bird over much of the state and still remains so in some areas, but in recent years it has become numerous in a few favorable localities, such as on Long Island, in the lower Hudson valley, and upstate at the Montezuma Refuge, and especially on Chautauqua Lake.

Nonbreeding: The recent increase is reflected in the following maximum densities:

MAXIMA: *Coastal*—1200, Mecox Bay, Suffolk Co., all October 1957; 750, Hudson River near Nyack, Rockland Co., Nov. 1, 1955; 520,

MAP 43 Ruddy Duck
(*Oxyura jamaicensis*)
Breeding distribution

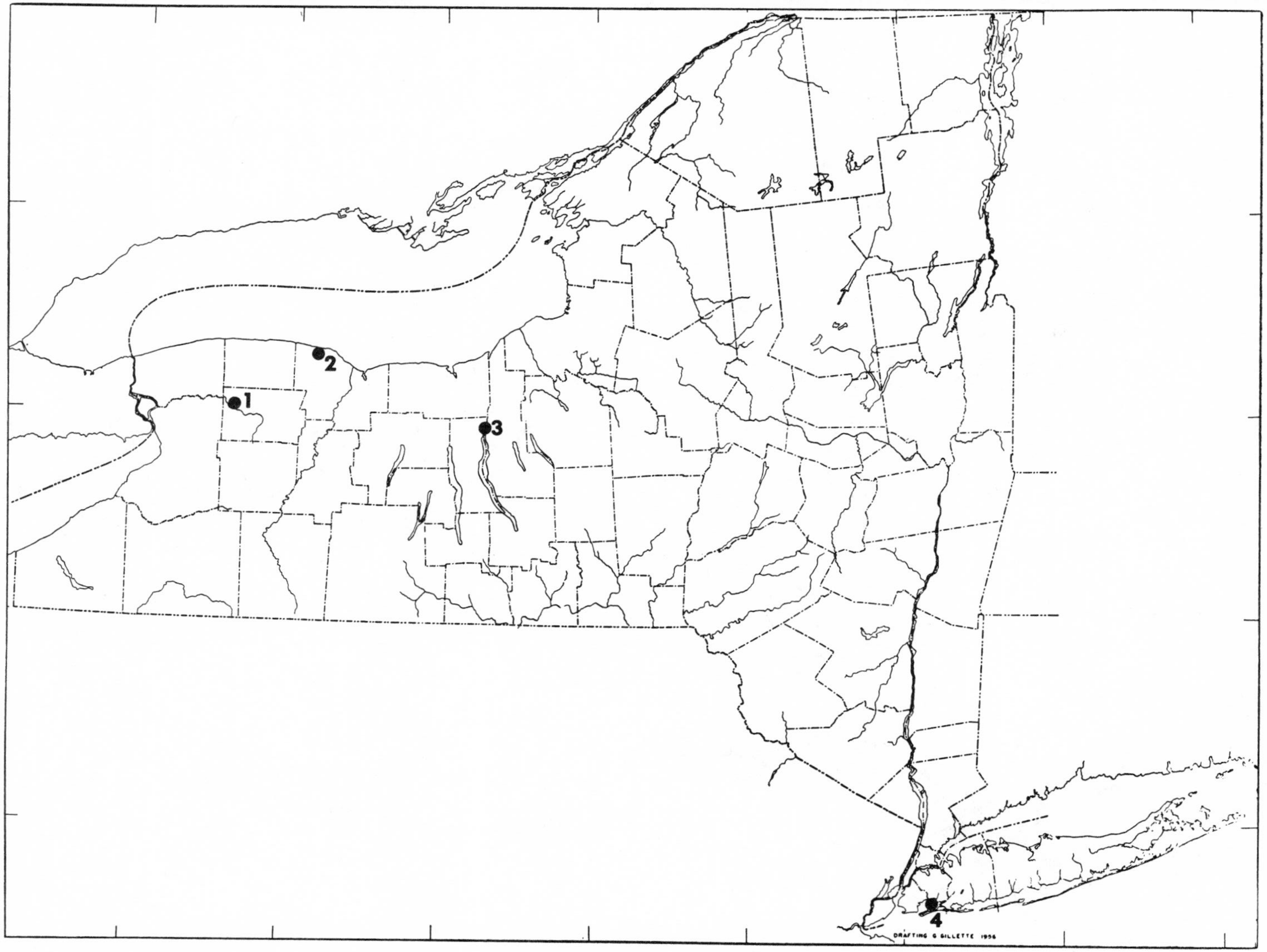

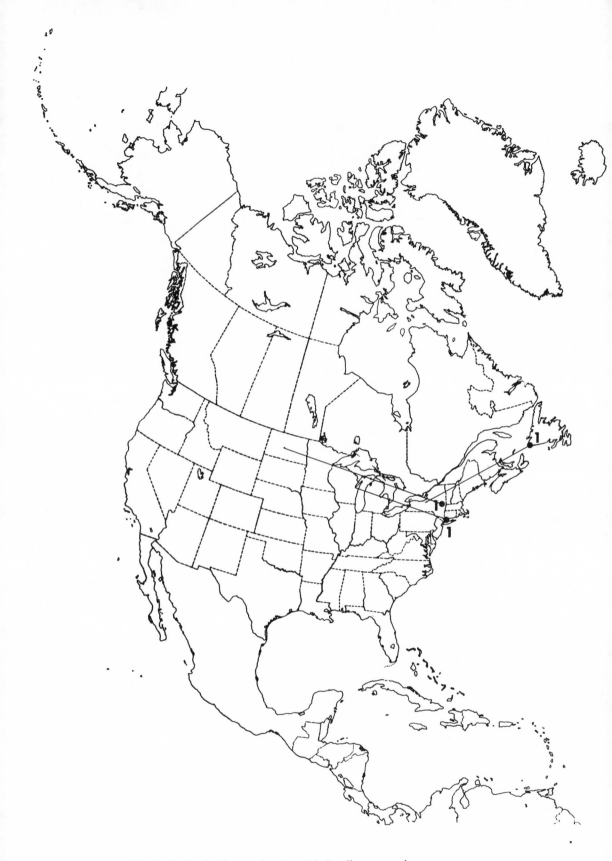

MAP 44 Ruddy Duck (*Oxyura jamaicensis*) Banding recoveries

Jerome Reservoir, Bronx Co., Nov. 15, 1963; 900, Jamaica Bay Refuge, Nov. 24, 1964; 2000, Water Mill and nearby Mecox Bay, Dec. 13, 1948; 480, Easthampton area, Suffolk Co., Dec. 31, 1949.

MAXIMA: *Inland*—1900, Chautauqua Lake, Oct. 28, 1949; 2600, same locality, Oct. 29, 1950; 500, Montezuma Marshes, Nov. 16, 1970; 200, Chautauqua Lake, Mar. 30, 1956.

Ruddy Ducks occasionally linger into late spring and early summer, especially on Long Island where nonbreeders rarely remain through summer.

Breeding (see Map 43): Known to breed regularly at only one Long Island locality and sporadically at three upstate localities, as follows:

Upstate—(1) Oak Orchard Swamp, near Alabama, Genesee Co., Aug. 14, 1961 (Meddaugh), female and brood of unfledged juveniles; (2) Lake Ontario shore, at mouth of Sandy Creek, near North Hamlin, Monroe Co., May 30, 1891 (Guelf), pair and brood of five or six unfledged young; (3) Montezuma area, Sept. 1, 1907 (Parker), adult and brood of unfledged young; in 1962 there were as many as three broods reported at Montezuma.

Long Island—(4) Jamaica Bay Refuge, first nesting in 1955 (Johnson); maxima of *25, 40,* and *26* broods in 1961, 1963, and 1965 (Helen Hays).

This species builds its nest in reeds or aquatic vegetation in or near water in marshy ponds. No completed nests of this somewhat secretive species have been observed in New York to my knowledge; therefore no data are available on eggs in this state.

As many as *40* broods of young were present at the Jamaica Bay Refuge in 1963 (Helen Hays). Both in 1965 and 1966 she observed various broods of unfledged young from June 11 to early August, and fledglings well into September. Brood sizes ranged from four and five to eight, with as many as 11 and 12 in two broods.

Banding (see Map 44): Three recoveries of juveniles, banded in late summer or early fall and shot the succeeding autumn, are as follows—(1) Banded Sept. 25, 1931, south end of Green Bay, Wisc.; recovered Nov. 18, 1931, near Port Jefferson, Suffolk Co. (2) Banded July 13, 1957 at Turtle Lake, North Dakota; recovered Oct. 23, 1957, at Green Island, Albany Co. (3) Banded Aug. 9, 1963, in the Montezuma Marshes; recovered fall of 1963, near Codroy, Newfoundland. Note that this last individual flew *northeast* in *fall*. It is rare at any time in Newfoundland.

Remarks: The North American population, called *"rubida,"* is not recognized here. It differs only slightly from nominate *jamaicensis* in being somewhat larger and averaging lighter in color. Hellmayr and Conover (1948: 400) called it a poorly marked race, and Delacour (1959: 227) did not recognize it.

NEW WORLD VULTURES — CATHARTIDAE

Two species in New York.
One breeds.

For discussion, see family Accipitridae. Best represented in tropical America, this group includes the two condors (largest members of the order Falconiformes) as well as the smaller vultures, consisting of five species; all seven are useful scavengers.

Turkey Vulture
(*Cathartes aura*) * B

Range: Neotropical and southern Nearctic regions, in eastern North America breeding north to southeastern Ontario, central New York, and southwestern Massachusetts. Sedentary and migratory, but rare in winter at the extreme north of the range.

Status: Variously uncommon to locally very common migrant or even resident, but rare in the Adirondacks. Has greatly increased in recent years. Rare breeder.

Change in status: Eaton (1914: 64) stated that the Turkey Vulture was only a summer visitor in "limited numbers" and knew of no breeding record. However, since 1925 when it was first reported breeding in the state, this species has been steadily increasing, occurring in fairly large numbers both on migration and locally at roosts.

Belknap (*in litt.*) suggests that an increase in the number of road kills of small mammals, especially woodchucks and cottontail rabbits, have been instrumental in a corresponding increase of Turkey Vultures in recent times. As stated previously (Bull, 1964: 148), it is believed that deer carcasses, as a result of starvation and disease due to overpopulation, are also a source of food; amelioration of the climate may also have been a contributing factor.

Nonbreeding: Now numerous on migration, both upstate and in the lower Hudson valley, but not on Long Island where it is rare to uncommon.

MAXIMA: *Spring*—50, Hancock, Delaware Co., Apr. 7, 1966; 66, Derby Hill, Oswego Co., Apr. 10, 1967; 64, Manitou, Monroe Co., Apr. 15, 1967.

MAXIMA: *Fall*—60, Hancock, Aug. 19, 1964; 63, Oak Orchard Swamp, Oct. 15, 1939.

MAXIMA: *Roosts*—30, near Cornwall, Orange Co., Feb. 24, 1955; 127 in hemlock grove, Fahnestock State Park, Putnam Co., Mar. 30, 1955; 75, Bear Mtn., Rockland Co., Mar. 31, 1964; 100, Oak Orchard Swamp, July 14, 1935 (Savage and Eckler), an unusually large number for the "early" years; 38, near Gouverneur, St. Lawrence Co., Sept. 28, 1962.

Breeding (see Map 45): The first known breeding record for the state occurred in 1925 when Howes (1926) discovered a "nest" in a cave at Lewisboro, Westchester Co. The second breeding occurrence, and the first reported for western New York, was in 1927 when two eggs were found in a large, hollow, decayed, moss-covered log in the Tonawanda Swamp at West Barre, Orleans Co. (W. and G. Smith).

Since then 13 additional localities have had nesting pairs.

The accompanying map shows the locations of these 15 breeding sites (see below), the first five of which lie on or near the Lake Ontario plain. These five lowland localities all have nests in densely wooded swamps and, without exception, the nests are situated in large hollow logs or hollow trees, in one case in a mixed red maple-elm-white ash swamp that was flooded to a depth of 18 inches, the actual nest log surrounded by water.

The balance of the localities are in upland situations of an entirely different character, all nests invariably among rocks in forested areas —mostly in caves—but in one instance in an abandoned granite quarry on an island in the St. Lawrence River (A. Heineman). With the exception of this last-named site, all the other upland localities are in the mountains or in hilly country, most of those in the southeastern sector—in the Catskill Mountains or the Hudson Highlands, and one in southwestern New York on the Allegany Plateau.

The 15 localities with year of first nesting are: Orleans Co.—(1) Lyndonville, 1938; (2) Tonawanda Swamp near West Barre, 1927. Genesee Co.—(3) Oak Orchard Swamp near Oakfield, 1938; (4) Bergen Swamp, 1928. Wayne Co.—(5) Marengo Swamp near Clyde, 1964. Cattaraugus Co.—(6) near Humphrey, 1962. Jefferson Co.—(7) Picton Island, St. Lawrence River, 1967. Delaware Co.—(8) Davenport, 1957. Ulster Co.—(9) northwest of Mohonk Lake, 1942; (10) Millbrook Mtn., 1939; (11) near New Paltz, 1939. Orange Co. —(12) near Blooming Grove, 1958; (13) Long Mtn., Harriman State Park, 1934. Rockland Co.—(14) West Mtn., Bear Mountain Park, 1955. Westchester Co.—(15) Lewisboro, 1925.

As with other "southern" species, the Turkey Vulture probably infiltrated the state by two routes: (1) The Lake Ontario plain population (numbers 1–5 and 7 on map) arrived from the west by way of Ontario through the Niagara Frontier corridor; (2) the lower Hudson valley population (numbers 9–15 on map) came from the south by way of New Jersey. Possibly numbers 6 and 8 followed the river valleys north from Pennsylvania.

Beardslee and Mitchell (1965: 159) list Conewango valley in Chautauqua Co. as a breeding area, but they do not give details.

MAP 45 Turkey Vulture
(*Cathartes aura*)
Breeding distribution

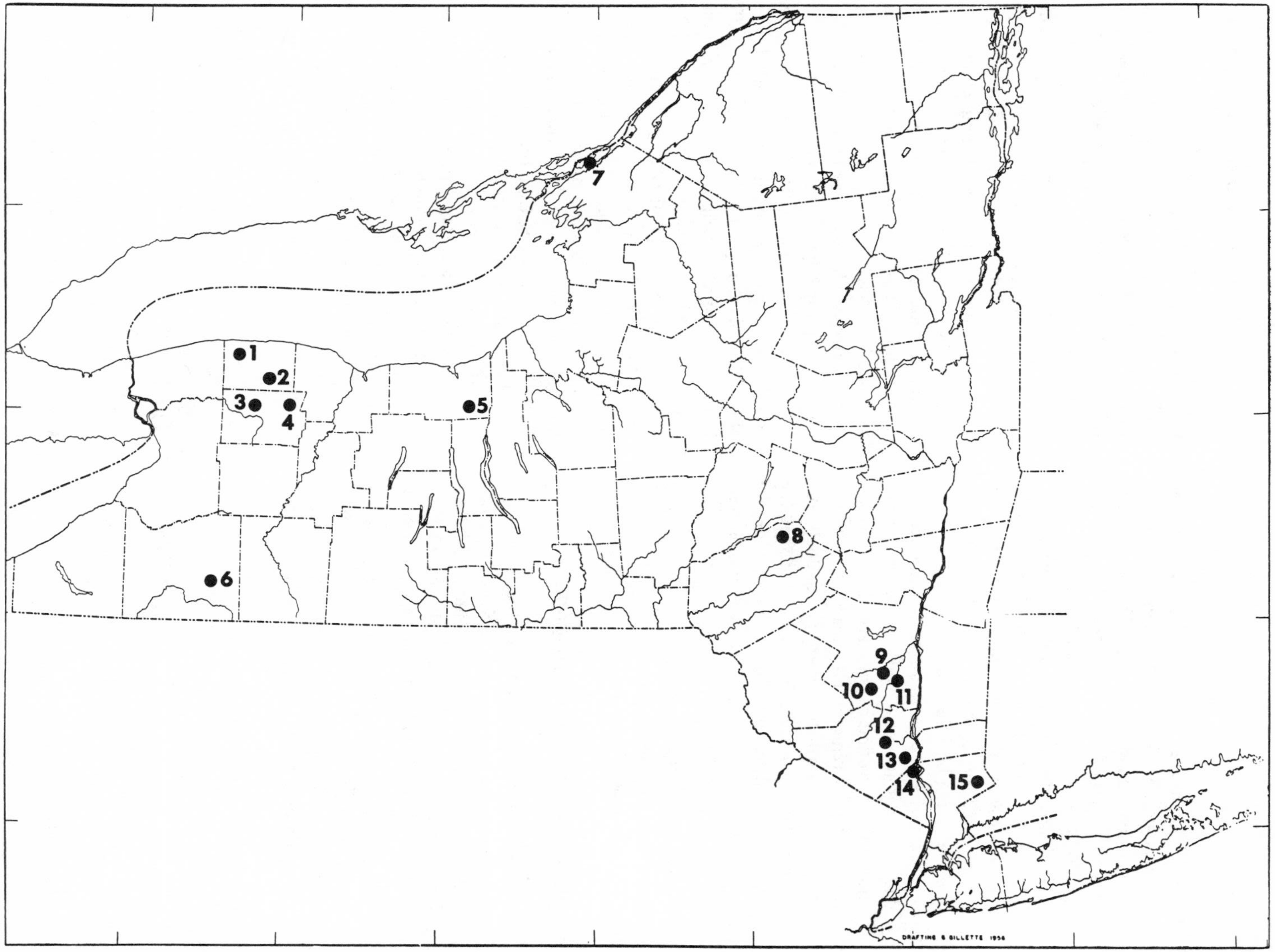

Egg clutches in 18 New York nests: one egg (six nests); two eggs (12 nests), although Brown and Amadon (1968: 177) state, "The eggs are invariably two in number."

EGG DATES: May 4 to June 20.

Nestlings: June 15 to Aug. 27; fledglings: July 14 to Sept. 24. Benning (1967b), who studied growth of a nestling at the Marengo Swamp site, found that it took 11 weeks before the young bird fledged.

Despite the recent increase in numbers of this conspicuous scavenger, nests are notoriously difficult to find as they are almost always well hidden in remote and generally inaccessible places. Nevertheless, there are undoubtedly more to be discovered. It would seem that the 15 localities listed are but a fraction of the actual number breeding, as much suitable terrain exists in the state.

Subspecies: The local race *septentrionalis* is larger than nominate *aura*.

Black Vulture (*Coragyps atratus*)   *

Range: Neotropical and southern Nearctic regions, in the eastern United States breeding (resident) north to southern Ohio and Maryland; once in southern Pennsylvania (1952). Vagrant north to southern Canada (specimens).

Status: *Very rare*—In New York State the Black Vulture has been recorded on more than three dozen occasions (at least ten specimen records), but is, nevertheless, a great rarity this far north. Nearly two-thirds of the records (all months except January) are from Long Island. All occurrences have been of single birds, except one observation of two individuals.

Following are some of the more significant records, including three extant specimens: (1) one collected while it was feeding with 11 Turkey Vultures on a dead hog, Pulteney, Steuben Co., July 11, 1909 (Burtch), specimen apparently not extant; (2) one in the NYSM collection, no number, was "found alive in a hog pen" at Victory, Cayuga Co., Apr. 11, 1911 (Parsons). It may have been the same individual reported by Eaton (1914: 66) as it was collected on the *same* day in the *same* county, although the localities reported are about 20 miles apart (Auburn) and the collectors are different (Stupp); (3) one taken on Shelter Island, Suffolk Co., Dec. 22, 1925 (Latham), NYSM 24894; (4) two seen with a small flock of Turkey Vultures at Old Chatham, Columbia Co., Aug. 24, 1964 (Reilly); (5) what may have been one and the same individual seen flying over the writer's home at Far Rockaway, Queens Co., July 6, 1966, was found shot at Central Islip, Suffolk Co., July 8 and is now a specimen, AMNH 786123; (6) one found alive, but with an injured wing, near North Burke, Franklin Co., Nov. 10, 1968 (Duheme), was photographed (Sweet, *Kingbird,* 1969, 19: 92–93).

A published report, *without details,* of 12 birds observed at an upstate locality need hardly be taken seriously.

OSPREYS — PANDIONIDAE

One species in New York.
One breeds.

For discussion, see family Accipitridae. The family Pandionidae consists of a single species, the nearly cosmopolitan fish-eating Osprey which differs from other hawks in various structural modifications including the presence of spicules on the soles of the feet for grasping fish.

Osprey (*Pandion haliaetus*)   *   B

Range: Nearly cosmopolitan, but absent as a breeder south of extreme northern Central America, the race *carolinensis* (lacks breast band) breeding from Alaska and Canada to the Gulf of Mexico. Winters in the east— north to Florida, rarely to South Carolina, and very rarely to Long Island.

Status: Fairly common to common migrant along the coast and on Lake Ontario; usually uncommon inland, but occasionally common in fall along the ridges *near* the coast. Locally common to formerly very common breeder on eastern Long Island, but has decreased considerably in recent years; local breeder in the Adirondacks and near the St. Lawrence River.

Nonbreeding: Ospreys occur chiefly near water, but may be seen flying overhead almost anywhere during migration.

MAXIMA: *Spring*—50, Orient, Suffolk Co., Apr. 1, 1944; 80, Derby Hill, Oswego Co., May 1, 1970 (several observers), an unusually large number inland; 15, Manitou, Monroe Co., May 16, 1970.

MAXIMA: *Fall*—46, Mt. Peter, Orange Co., Sept. 19, 1964; 21, Far Rockaway, Queens Co., Oct. 13, 1950.

EXTREME DATES: Mar. 10 and 16 (coastal) and Mar. 29 (inland) to Nov. 25 (inland) and Dec. 7 (coastal). Rare before late March and after early November.

Winter: Very rare at this season—no known state winter specimen—but at least *eight* coastal sightings believed correctly identified. At least two observations from upstate— (1) possibly the same individual in late winter of 1952, seen near Ithaca, Feb. 8 (Dilger), and near Elmira, Mar. 2 (Fudge); (2) Hudson River near Albany, from Dec. 31, 1967, to Jan. 21, 1968 (numerous observers).

Breeding (see Map 46): This species was formerly a numerous breeder on the islands at the east end of Long Island, but with the increased use of pesticides it has decreased alarmingly in recent years as it has over much of the northeast. In the early 1900s Gardiner's Island had the largest known colony in the world—at least *300* nests (Chapman, 1908). The low point there was in 1962 with only 21 "active" nests. However, by 1969 at least 38 "active" nests produced 25 fledged young (*Audubon Field Notes,* 1969, 23: 639), with even more hopeful signs in 1970—38 nests containing 34 young, all of which fledged (*fide* P. Spitzer), an increase of nine young over the previous year. Nevertheless, in 1971 only 25 "active" nests produced a mere 17 young (*fide* Puleston).

Another famous colony was that on nearby Plum Island, so graphically described by C. S. Allen (1892). He estimated *250* nests on that three-mile-long island, of which at least *100* ground nests were on the sandy plain. A few of these were merely "small hollows in the

Fig. 32 Osprey alighting on boulder nest, Gardiner's Island, Suffolk Co., June 9, 1911. Photo by Francis Harper

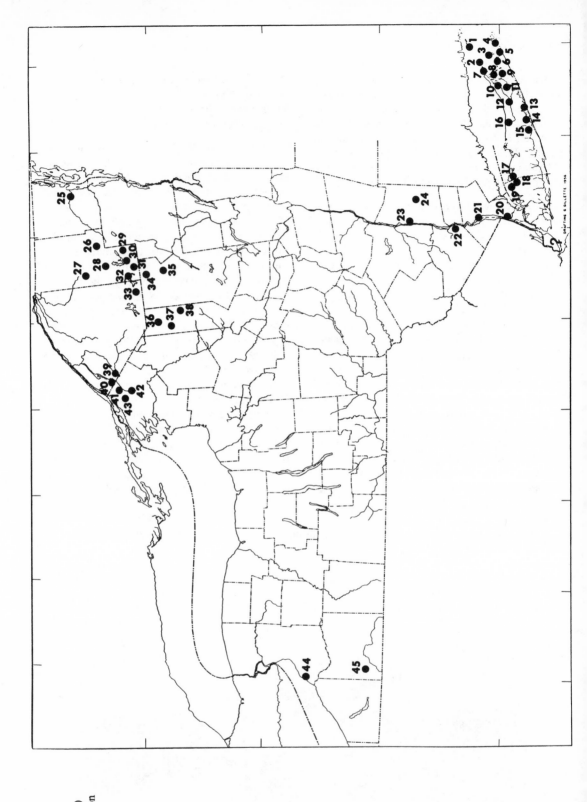

MAP 46 Osprey
(*Pandion haliaetus*)
Breeding distribution

sand." Other nests were on large boulders on the beach, and some even on rocks in the water (see Fig. 32). Still others described by Allen were placed on an old barn roof, an old pile of fence rails, on the lattice work of a buoy in the channel, and the more conventional sites atop poles and in trees. Some of the trees had as many as three nests.

An interesting aspect was the fact that a number of these Osprey nests had other species nesting within the crevices among the sticks under the edges of the nests. One Osprey nest contained as many as five Common Grackle nests (a habitat group in the Sanford Hall of the American Museum of Natural History collected by Chapman in 1901 on Gardiner's Island shows this commensalism), and one nest each of House Wren and House Sparrow. Moreover, this same Osprey nest was close to an active nest of Black-crowned Night Herons, the latter only 15 inches beneath the Osprey nest. According to Allen (*op. cit.*) nearly every Osprey *tree* nest held from two to eight grackle nests.

In recent years on the mainland of Long Island, nests have also been found on a metal radio tower, and on an abandoned, unused chimney.

Elsewhere in the state trees are used almost exclusively with nests as high as 80 feet above ground.

Egg clutches in 144 New York nests are as follows: two eggs (24 nests); three eggs (87 nests—60%); four eggs (31 nests); five eggs (two nests).

EGG DATES: Apr. 27 to June 21.

Nestlings: June 18 to July 25; fledglings: July 10 to Aug. 22.

Perusal of the map indicates that there are two main breeding areas in New York: the southeastern section; the Adirondack-St. Lawrence valley section. Two isolated and unsuccessful breeding localities are, or were, in the extreme southwest corner of the state.

Distribution of these 45 breeding localities is shown on the map; year after locality represents last known breeding at extinct sites.

Southeastern section: Suffolk Co.—(1) Fisher's Island; (2) Plum Island; (3) Gardiner's Island; (4) Goff's Point, Napeague Bay; (5) Amagansett; (6) Acabonack Harbor; (7) Orient Point; (8) Shelter Island; (9) Sag Harbor;

(10) Cutchogue; (11) Robins Island, Peconic Bay; (12) near Riverhead; (13) Quogue; (14) Mastic; (15) Brookhaven; (16) Wading River; (17) Lloyd's Harbor. Nassau Co.—(18) Oyster Bay; (19) Mill Neck. Westchester Co.—(20) near Yonkers, 1880s; (21) near Croton Point, 1890s. Orange Co.—(22) near West Point, 1870s. Dutchess Co.—(23) Hyde Park, 1896; (24) Tyrell Lake, 1923. Note that all Hudson valley locations are extinct sites. An attempt at nesting occurred near Oakwood Beach, Staten Island in the early 1900s, but the unfinished nest was abandoned (Cleaves, oral comm.).

Adirondack section: Clinton Co.—(25) Morrisonville. Franklin Co.—(26) Rainbow Lake; (27) junction of Quebec Brook and St. Regis River; (28) Ochre Pond; (29) Oseetah Lake; (30) Axton; (31) Little Clear Pond; (32) Tupper Lake (marshes). St. Lawrence Co.—(33) Horseshoe Pond. Hamilton Co.—(34) Mohegan Lake; (35) South Pond. Herkimer Co.—(36) Raven Lake; (37) southwest end of Stillwater Reservoir; (38) Big Moose Lake. St. Lawrence Co.—(39) Yellow Lake; (40) Grass Lake. Jefferson Co.—(41) Redwood; (42) Theresa; (43) Plessis. A number of other Adirondack localities was not divulged to the writer, so that this area is incomplete.

Southwestern section: Erie Co.—(44) Angola, 1880s. Cattaraugus Co.—(45) East Randolph, 1948 only (*fide* Sundell).

Banding (see Maps 47 and 48): Many years of banding nestlings on Gardiner's Island (mostly by LeRoy Wilcox) have produced some fascinating recoveries, including two birds shot from boats 60 and 73 miles off Cape Hatteras, N.C., the following fall—indicating a partial offshore migration. Another interesting recovery was of a nestling recaptured on its Gardiner's Island breeding grounds 21 years later (1914–1935). Twenty out of 22 recoveries have been during the autumn or winter immediately following date of banding (June and July of various years). The recovery pattern from place of banding is to the west (Indiana, Illinois, Kentucky—all early fall), to the southwest (Alabama—three, and Louisiana —all early fall), and to Florida (five out of six—also early fall, one in December). Seven West Indian recoveries (Cuba—three, Domini-

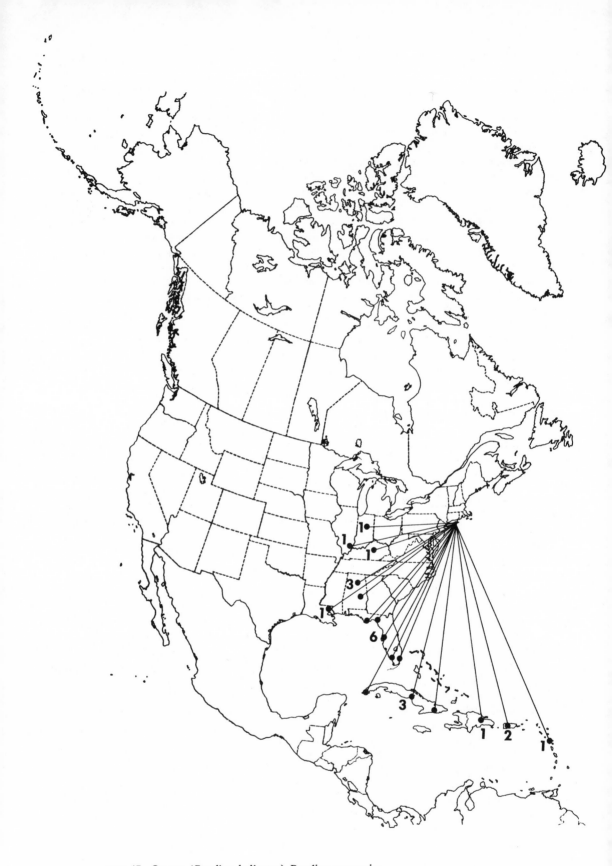

MAP 47 Osprey (*Pandion haliaetus*) Banding recoveries

MAP 48   Osprey (*Pandion haliaetus*) Banding recoveries

can Republic—one, Puerto Rico—two, and Guadeloupe—one) were in fall or early winter, except one from Puerto Rico.

Some interesting highlights of these recoveries are: Two nestlings banded the same day (June 5, 1948) were recovered the same day (Sept. 11, 1948), but far apart—one in Indiana, the other in northwestern Florida. Two others banded June 25, 1944, were recovered in November 1944—both near Tampa, Florida. Possibly the most interesting recoveries, however, were of two banded July 13, 1939,

that were recovered only a week apart (Aug. 23 and 29, 1939), one in southern Illinois, the other on the island of Guadeloupe, Lesser Antilles. Two others, banded July 3, 1941, and recovered the following December, were taken on the Gulf coast of Florida, and on the Pacific coast of Colombia, between Barbacoas and El Diviso, Department of Nariño. Finally, two nestlings were taken a year later—both summering birds—one in Puerto Rico, the .other near Bahia, Brazil. The two South American recoveries are located on Map 48.

KITES, HAWKS, EAGLES — ACCIPITRIDAE

Twelve species in New York.
Nine breed.

The order Falconiformes contains the large group of diurnal raptors or birds of prey. On a worldwide basis more than 280 species occur.

In New York 13 of 19 species breed, although the Peregrine Falcon (*Falco peregrinus*) is gone as a breeder and the Bald Eagle (*Haliaeetus leucocephalus*) now rarely nests.

With the exception of the two American vultures which feed on carrion and refuse, the others catch live prey—the Osprey (*Pandion haliaetus*) exclusively fish, the rest mammals, birds, reptiles, and amphibians, and also invertebrates (mainly insects).

Nothing in the bird world is more spectacular than the impressive numbers of these much persecuted birds in the spring and fall migrations. During periods of favorable weather in spring huge flights take place along the shore of Lake Ontario, especially at Derby Hill in Oswego Co. where numbers compare favorably with those of world-famous Hawk Mtn. in fall.

Of the breeding hawks in the state, those

species feeding largely on mammals appear to be holding their own or even increasing in numbers—Goshawk (*Accipiter gentilis*) and Red-tailed (*Buteo jamaicensis*) and Broad-winged hawks (*B. platypterus*). Many others have declined, some drastically so, in particular Bald Eagle, Osprey, and Peregrine Falcon; markedly reduced are Cooper's (*Accipiter cooperii*) and Red-shouldered hawks (*Buteo lineatus*). These population declines are believed due mainly to pesticides, resulting in egg shell thinning and unhatchability—proved in some species.

The following classification of New York species, based on Brown and Amadon (1968), is similar to that of the A.O.U. Check-list (1957), but the sequence of families and genera is somewhat different and is followed here with minor modifications. Species sequence within genera is similar.

The main reason for change in the two systems is a reassessment of relationships, based primarily on anatomical features. For instance, the Osprey is believed related to the kites on similarity in tarsal structure and the sea eagles "near to the scavenging kites, notably *Haliastur*," rather than to the unrelated buteo-like "aquiline" eagles, where they were placed formerly.

A.O.U. Check-list (1957)

Cathartidae	New World Vultures
Elanoides	Swallow-tailed Kite
Accipiter	Accipiters
Buteo	Buteos
Aquila	Aquiline Eagles
Haliaeetus	Sea Eagles
Circus	Harriers
Pandion	Osprey
Falconidae	Caracaras, Falcons

Brown and Amadon (1968)

Cathartidae	New World Vultures
Pandion	Osprey
Elanoides	Swallow-tailed Kite
Haliaeetus	Sea Eagles
Circus	Harriers
Accipiter	Accipiters
Buteo	Buteos
Aquila	Aquiline Eagles
Falconidae	Caracaras, Falcons

Swallow-tailed Kite
(*Elanoides forficatus*)   *

Range: Chiefly Neotropical region, breeding north to South Carolina, formerly to the north-central states. Vagrant north to southern Canada.

Status: *Very rare*—In New York State there are at least ten occurrences of this spectacular bird, two of which are specimen records, one of these extant: (1) Raynor South (=Freeport), Nassau Co., 1837 (Giraud, 1844: 13). (2) Male collected at West Hoosick, Rensselaer Co., July 16, 1886 (Haight), NYSM N/N; the occurrence of this latter specimen and of another seen nearby is recorded by Eaton (1914: 68–70), but alleged breeding was never proven.

The other reports are as follows:

(3) "South shore," Long Island, 1845 (Akhurst).

(4) Piermont, Rockland Co., Aug. 22, 1900 (Nicholas).

(5) Outlet of Chautauqua Lake, near Jamestown, Apr. 10, 1926 (Beal and Peterson).

(6) Orient, Suffolk Co., May 28, 1927 (Latham).

(7) Chappaqua, Westchester Co., Oct. 2, 1927 (Pangburn).

(8) University Heights, Bronx Co., Apr. 30, 1928 (Hickey and Cruickshank).

(9) Jamaica Bay Refuge, Queens Co., Sept. 2, 1956 (Mayer).

(10) West side of Cayuga Lake, near Elm Beach, Seneca Co., Aug. 20, 1967 (Baysinger, *Kingbird*, 1968, 18: 25).

Bald Eagle
(*Haliaeetus leucocephalus*)   *   B

Range: Nearctic region, breeding from Alaska and Canada to southern United States. Winters nearly throughout the range.

Status: Formerly a generally rare but locally fairly common migrant and winter visitant and a very local breeder; in recent years rare at any time and probably no longer breeding.

Change in status: The Bald Eagle was much more numerous and widespread in former years. Giraud (1844) mentioned the shooting of 60 to 70 individuals on Long Island during one winter season. Mearns (1878) stated, "In early spring when the ice breaks up, I have counted more than twenty-five that were in view at once." He was referring to the Hudson River near Cornwall, Orange Co.

The continued decrease in the east over many years has been due to (a) shooting, trapping, and egging—although protected by federal law for some time; (b) removal of nest trees; and (c) very likely an increased use of pesticides, indirectly causing sterility in adult eagles that have fed on contaminated fish.

In connection with the last, Spofford (1960: 151) reported no nesting success (eggs, but no young) after 1955 either at Montezuma, or at Selkirk Shores, Oswego Co. In 1960 the pesticide question had not been definitely linked to hatching failure, as witness the following statement by Spofford (*op. cit.*), "Why there is no nesting success is unknown."

Nonbreeding: Bald Eagles are restricted largely to lake and river shores and to coastal estuaries, although they are also found along mountain ridges during migration. Peak numbers in spring are inland along the Lake Ontario shore, in fall and winter on or near the coast. Maximum numbers are listed by *year* to show the steady decrease within ten or more years rather than by month as is usually done.

MAXIMA, INLAND: *Spring*—Manitou, Monroe Co.—18, May 18, 1949; 14, May 12, 1956; seven, Apr. 29, 1959; Derby Hill, Oswego Co.—five, Apr. 17, 1960; only 13 entire spring of 1964 from Mar. 7 to May 16.

MAXIMA, COASTAL: *Fall*—six, Van Cortlandt Park, Bronx Co., Sept. 17, 1950; five, Idlewild, Queens Co., Sept. 24, 1950.

MAXIMA, COASTAL: *Winter*—18, Croton Point, Westchester Co., Feb. 11, 1951. During the entire three-year period (1963–1965) only *one* was seen on the Christmas counts there.

Breeding (see Map 49): This magnificent species was, until recent years, a breeder chiefly in the northern and western portions of the state, nesting wherever its principal food (fish) was abundant. Almost invariably the nest was constructed in the largest trees. In many instances in open country, such as the agricultural districts of central and western New York, the most isolated trees were selected with an unobstructed view of the surrounding countryside. Very rarely a cliff site was chosen. Nest heights ranged from 30 to 65 feet or more above ground.

Egg clutches in seven New York nests: two eggs (five nests); three eggs (two nests).

EGG DATES: Mar. 16 to May 14.

Nestlings: Apr. 11 to June 30; fledglings: from May 20.

The four breeding localities shown on the accompanying map in the southeastern section are mostly of ancient occurrence, not occupied for many years: Orange Co. (39) not since the 1880s; Westchester Co. (40) not since 1890; Dutchess Co. (38) last known in 1891; eastern Long Island (41) until 1930, but not later.

The 41 former (some extinct since the 1890s) and recent breeding localities are as follows: (1) Youngstown, Niagara Co.; (2) Goat Island, Niagara Falls; (3) north end of Grand Island, Niagara River; (4) near Westfield, Chautauqua Co.; (5) Versailles, Cattar-

augus Co.; (6) near Troutburg, Monroe Co.; (7) near Scottsville, Monroe Co.; (8) near Avon, Livingston Co.; (9) south end of Hemlock Lake, Livingston Co.; (10) Sodus Bay, Wayne Co.; (11) Montezuma Refuge; (12) Union Springs, Cayuga Co. Jefferson Co.—(13) near Goose Bay; (14) Perch Lake; (15) Point Peninsula; (16) Galloo Island; (17) Stony Island; (18) near Snowshoe Bay and nearby Stony Point; (19) south of Henderson Harbor (village); (20) near Selkirk Shores and nearby Butterfly Swamp, Oswego Co.; (21) near Constantia, Oswego Co.; (22) Frenchman's Island, Oneida Lake; (23) Lakeport, Madison Co.; (24) near South Bay, Madison Co.; (25) Lebanon Reservoir, Madison Co. (26) north end of Otsego Lake, Otsego Co.; (27) County Line Island, Tupper Lake, St. Lawrence and Franklin counties; (28 Follensby Pond, Franklin Co.; (29) Taylor Pond, Clinton Co.; (30) Split Rock Mtn., Essex Co.; (31) Blue Ledge, Essex Co.—only cliff site known in the state; (32) Raquette Lake (village), Hamilton Co.; (33) Limekiln Lake, Hamilton Co.; (34) Piseco Lake, Hamilton Co.; (35) Tongue Mtn., Lake George, Warren Co.; (36) near Putnam Station, Washington Co.; (37) Niskayuna, Schenectady Co.; (38) Whaley Lake, Dutchess Co.; (39) near West Point, Orange Co.; (40) near Croton Point, Westchester Co.; (41) Gardiner's Island, Suffolk Co.

Much of the information from northern New York was provided by Greenleaf Chase and Walter Spofford (*in litt.*).

Note that *all* nest sites are, or were, either on or near water. Note also concentration of *seven* breeding sites in Jefferson Co., especially at the east end of Lake Ontario. Lack of breeding records from the southern tier section (near Pennsylvania) and from the Catskill Mountains is attributable to an absence of lakes or other suitable bodies of water. The few reservoirs in the Catskill district, as well as Chautauqua Lake, have too much human activity for nesting eagles.

Banding (see Map 50): Broley's studies (*Wilson Bull.*, 1947, 59: 4) indicated that nestlings banded on the Florida Gulf coast in winter of various years, wandered or migrated north considerable distances the *following* spring. Three of his banded birds were re-

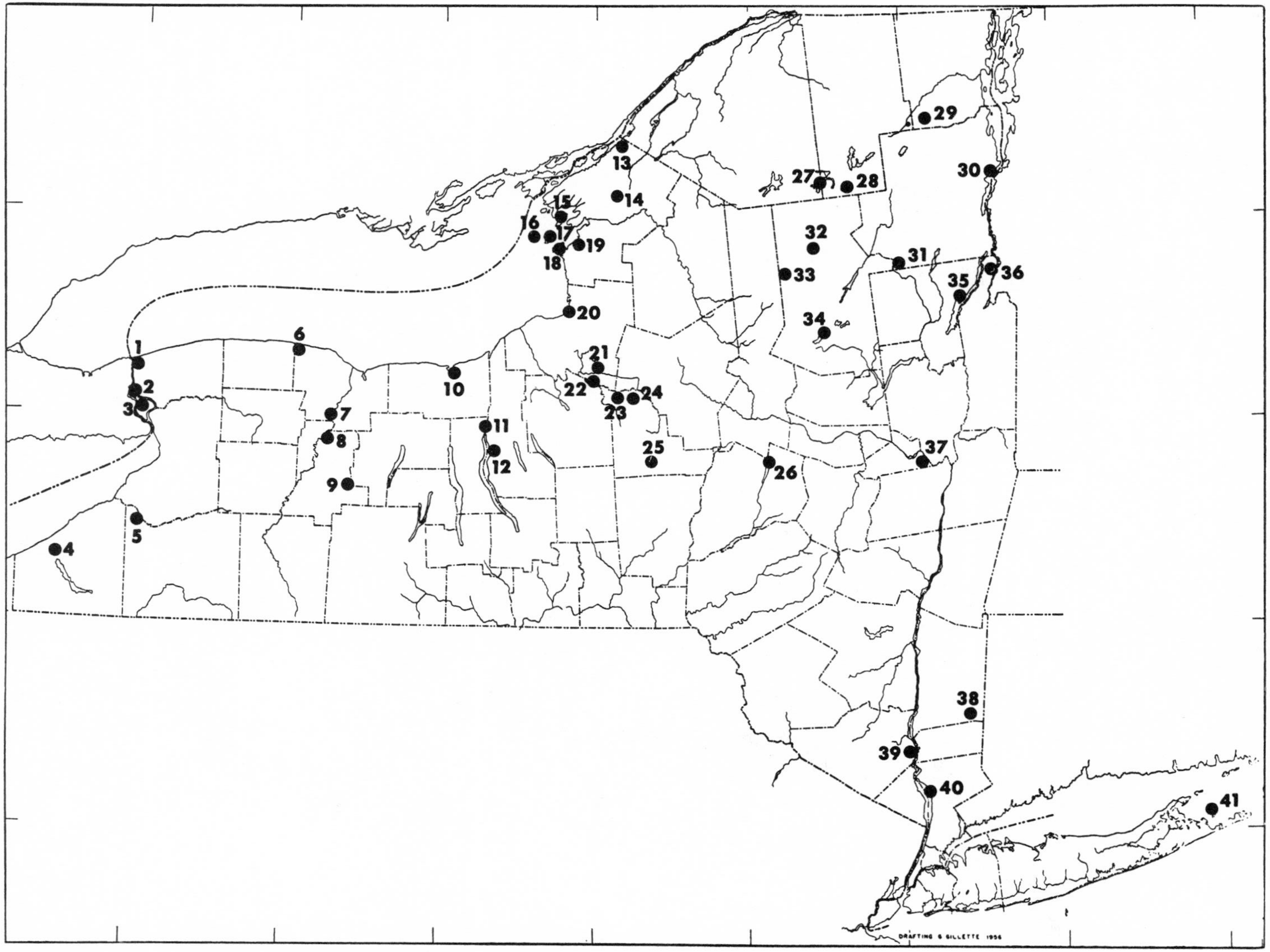

MAP 49 Bald Eagle
(*Haliaeetus leucocephalus*) Former breeding distribution

MAP 50 Bald Eagle (*Haliaeetus leucocephalus*) Banding recoveries

covered (shot or found dead) in New York: (1) Columbiaville, Columbia Co., May 8, 1939; (2) Plum Island, Suffolk Co., May 4, 1943; (3) Pine City, Chemung Co., May 21, 1945.

Another individual banded by Broley, Jan. 23, 1957, was recovered near Sayville, Suffolk Co., much later—Aug. 30, 1958.

Subspecies: Two subspecies occur in the state: the smaller southern nominate race— see **Banding**; the larger northern race *alascanus*, occurring chiefly in winter. Birds breeding within New York are probably intermediates, based on wing (chord) measurements.

The writer has examined five specimens of *alascanus*—all immatures (one male, four females)—taken in New York, as follows: (1) Highland Falls, Orange Co., Mar. 27, 1883 (male, 605 mm.), AMNH 54767; (2) Southampton, Suffolk Co., Jan. 2, 1885 (female, 637 mm.), AMNH 98726; (3) Lake View, Erie Co., Dec. 27, 1931 (female, 650 mm.), BMS 1740; (4) near Ithaca, Feb. 1, 1946 (female, 680 mm.), CUM 17844; (5) near Ilion, Herkimer Co., Dec. 1, 1951 (female, 644 mm.), CUM 23176.

Perhaps it would be better not to recognize *any* subspecies as the size difference is merely clinal. Nevertheless, extremes of wing length are very considerable. For instance, Brown and Amadon (1968: 289) give extremes of wing length of nominate *leucocephalus* as: " ♂ 515–545, ♀ 548–588; and of the northern *alascanus* as: ♂ 570–612, ♀ 605–685." Note that no overlap exists, sex for sex.

Northern Harrier; Marsh Hawk
(*Circus cyaneus*)   *   B

Range: Holarctic region, the American race *hudsonius* (adult males spotted below; immature males and females richer brown than nominate race) breeding from Alaska and Canada south to Baja California, Arizona, and Texas, but in the east only as far as Ohio and Virginia. In winter withdraws from the more northern portions.

Status: Common to occasionally very common migrant. Usually uncommon in winter, but locally numerous on the outer coastal

marshes. Widespread breeder, but has decreased considerably in recent years.

Nonbreeding: On migration these hawks are most prevalent in open country, hunting over cultivated fields in farming areas, as well as marshes and meadows. Usually seen in singles or in twos or threes, Marsh Hawks are sometimes observed in sizable flocks, such as occur in spring flights along Lake Ontario and in fall passage on the outer coast of Long Island. These birds are more often seen in flight than perched.

MAXIMA, INLAND: *Spring*—108, Derby Hill, Oswego Co., Mar. 26, 1970; on Apr. 3, 1960, 90 at Derby Hill and 50 at Manitou, Monroe Co.; in 1966 at Derby Hill, 67 on Apr. 21, and 38 on May 5.

MAXIMA, COASTAL: *Fall*—45, Fire Island Inlet, Suffolk Co., Sept. 27, 1952; 46 shot on Fisher's Island, Suffolk Co., Oct. 5, 1921.

During winter most individuals leave the inland sections of the state, although Spofford counted *ten* near the Cicero Swamp at Bridgeport, Onondaga Co., Dec. 22, 1957. In some of the larger salt marshes along the south shore of Long Island they are regular during the winter months in small scattered groups.

Breeding: Unlike other New York members of this family, Marsh Hawks are ground nesters, the nests being placed on hummocks in marshes—often in cattail marshes, in grassy meadows, and sometimes in dry upland fields (see Fig. 33). One nest was situated in an open glade in a mountain spruce bog, another in an opening among scrub oaks on the coastal plain.

Munoff (1963), in a study of six nests in Washington Co. in 1961, found all six placed in cattails with scattered growths of *Spiraea;* two nests were within 40 yards of each other. Mortality was very high due to frequent predation. Munoff found that the six nests contained a total of 28 eggs, of which only 12 hatched. Of the latter only five fledged, or less than one young per nest.

Egg clutches in 40 New York nests ranged from three to seven eggs as follows: three eggs (nine nests); four eggs (16 nests); five eggs (11 nests); six and seven eggs (two nests each).

EGG DATES: Apr. 20 to June 25, once to July 11.

Fig. 33 Marsh Hawk nest with three nestlings in *Phragmites* growth, Jones Beach area, Nassau Co., June 24, 1970. Photo by Richard Cohen

Nestlings—May 30 to July 10 and Aug. 1; fledglings—July 4 to Aug. 11.

Banding: Three "direct" recoveries of nestlings banded in June of various years in upstate New York were made the following September, as follows: near Catawba, North Carolina; Hardyville, Kentucky; and near Waco, Texas.

Sharp-shinned Hawk
(*Accipiter striatus*)   *   B

Range: Nearctic and Neotropical regions, ranging from Alaska and Canada to Argentina and Uruguay. In the northern portions, the large northern, highly migratory race *velox* chiefly withdraws southward in winter.

Status: Common to very abundant migrant, especially in spring along the Lake Ontario shoreline. Ordinarily rare to uncommon in winter. Fairly common widespread breeder, but quite secretive.

Nonbreeding: Together with the Red-tailed and Broad-winged hawks, the little "Sharpie" ranks among the most numerous of the diurnal raptors in spring, frequently observed along the lake plain country south of Lake Ontario. Like the other species, the highest counts of Sharp-shins are made at the two best hawk-watching places during migration time—the "hawk lookouts" at Manitou, Monroe Co., and at Derby Hill, Oswego Co.

MAXIMA, INLAND: *Spring*—On Apr. 20, 1957—2000 at Manitou, 1100 at Derby Hill; on two successive days at Manitou, 1200 on Apr. 20 and 1600 on Apr. 21, 1966, for a combined total of 2800 for the two days; also 2000, at Manitou, May 12, 1956 (Listman), late for so many.

MAXIMA, NEAR COAST: *Fall*—110, Van Cortlandt Park, Bronx Co., Sept. 18, 1951; 82, Mt. Peter, Orange Co., Oct. 17, 1959.

Although far more numerous than Cooper's Hawk on migration, it is scarcer than that species during winter and in the breeding season.

Breeding: Compared to Cooper's Hawk, records of New York nests of the Sharp-shinned Hawk are much fewer in number. This may be because all New York nests of *striatus* have been found in evergreen trees and are less conspicuous and more difficult to locate; also many of the nests were situated in heavy forest.

Of 25 New York nests examined, 20 (80%) were in hemlocks, only four in pines and one in a cedar. Nest heights ranged from 12 to 50 feet.

Egg clutches in 34 New York nests: two eggs (three nests); three eggs (three nests); four eggs (16 nests); five eggs (11 nests); six eggs (one nest). The two-egg clutches may represent incomplete sets.

EGG DATES: Apr. 16 to June 21.

Nestlings: June 8 to July 23; fledglings: July 3 to July 25.

Cooper's Hawk
(*Accipiter cooperii*)   *   B

Range: Nearctic region, breeding from southern Canada to northern Mexico and the Gulf states. Winters nearly throughout the breeding range southward.

Status: Fairly common to locally common migrant. Uncommon, but regular in winter; absent in the northern portions. Fairly common, widespread breeder.

Nonbreeding: Compared to the Sharp-shinned Hawk, this species is far less numerous during the migrations; one good reason is that the northern breeding limits of Cooper's Hawk lie much farther south than those of its smaller relative—therefore fewer individuals are seen on passage.

However, *cooperii* is less scarce in winter than *striatus* and much better known during the breeding season.

MAXIMA, INLAND: *Spring*—48, Derby Hill, Oswego Co., Mar. 31, 1967; 42, Manitou, Monroe Co., Apr. 17, 1960; 75, Lyndonville, Orleans Co., Apr. 21, 1966 (Smith). All of these localities lie on or near the Lake Ontario plain.

I can find no comparable *fall* data, except nine individuals observed at Mt. Peter, Orange Co., Oct. 11, 1965.

Breeding: The Cooper's Hawk is found chiefly in low, alluvial forest and wooded swamps, nesting most frequently in deciduous trees—often in old crow nests—but commonly building its own nest. It is found in country similar to that frequented by the Red-shouldered Hawk. It also occasionally breeds in wood lots adjacent to villages.

Meng (1951), in an intensive study of this species from 1948 to 1951 within a 17-mile radius in the Ithaca region, stated that it breeds most frequently in "climax beech-maple-hemlock" and "oak-chestnut-hickory" forest types, and occasionally in "pine stands." Many of the nests were situated in forest clearings or near forest edge, often near large open fields, as it hunts its prey (chiefly birds) in open areas near woodland, as well as in the depths of the forest. According to Meng, nests were spaced at least one and one-half miles apart.

In addition to 36 nests examined by Meng, I have come across 20 more from this state in museum collections and those recorded in the literature. For a total of 56 New York nests, the following tree species were used: beech (21), maple (12), oak (seven), ash (six), pine (four), birch (two), and one each for elm, cherry, hickory, and basswood. Nest heights, ranged from 30 to 70 feet.

Egg clutches in 71 New York nests are as follows: three eggs (14 nests); four eggs (37 nests); five eggs (19 nests); six eggs (one nest).

EGG DATES: Apr. 20 to June 16.

Nestlings: June 2 to July 2; fledglings: July 2 to Aug. 3.

Meng (*op. cit.*) found that incubation lasted from 34 to 36 days and that young remained in the nest from 30 to 35 days.

Food: The following prey species counted at 12 nests in the Ithaca region, were examined by Meng (*op. cit.*). Birds (mostly passerines) made up 82% of the total, mammals only 18%:

Birds

Starling	241	Pigeon	13
Flicker	134	Blue Jay	11
Meadow-		Scarlet Tanager	9
lark	118	Wood Thrush	7
Robin	79	other species (14)	32
Grackle	37		
Cowbird	17	total birds	698

Mammals

Chipmunk	109	Cottontail Rabbit	6
Red Squirrel	36	Gray Squirrel	4
		total mammals	155

Remarks: This species has decreased drastically as a breeder within the state during the past dozen years or so. Fewer and fewer nests with *young* are found and from available evidence it is believed that pesticides are the reason for the decline. The prey species (82% birds), may be affected by the various toxic chemicals used, which in turn are passed on to the predator.

Northern Goshawk
(*Accipiter gentilis*)   *   B

Range: Holarctic region, in eastern North America breeding from northern Quebec and Labrador to the mountains of Connecticut (rarely), New York, Pennsylvania, and Maryland (once). Winters nearly throughout; sedentary and migratory.

Status: Rare and irregular winter visitant; rare to uncommon but regular fall migrant along the inland ridges; fairly common but local in spring flights along the Lake Ontario shore. Formerly a very rare breeder; in recent years a greatly increased breeder in the mountains and occasionally at elevations as low as 1200 feet.

Nonbreeding: Goshawks are seldom encountered over much of the state during the migrations except at a few favorable localities. They are rarely observed in winter, but at long intervals there are southward irruptions from Canada, presumably because of food shortages in the north (scarcity of Spruce Grouse and varying hares). During these irruptions both inland and along the coast, numbers are shot or trapped at game farms and many others are killed by hunters. At that time, Ruffed Grouse, pheasants, crows, cottontail rabbits, and both red and gray squirrels are the chief prey.

MAXIMA, *"nonflight"* years: rarely more than two per *day* at a given *locality*—16 shot, Fisher's Island, Suffolk Co., late fall of 1917 (Ferguson); five adults shot at same locality, Dec. 7–10, 1926 (Ferguson), latter birds in AMNH collection. During the fall and early winter of 1944 at least eight were shot in northern Westchester Co. (*fide* Townsend) and 12 more were killed in the White Plains area alone (*fide* Grierson). A statewide irruption of this species was reported in November 1965 with a number of observations during the winter of 1965–1966, particularly upstate. Ten were seen in the Oneida Lake area; four even wintered in the Adirondack region. Six individuals were trapped at a single game farm in Dutchess Co.

MAXIMA, *"flight"* years: Fall—a few are reported each season during October and November, but in New York State no report is comparable to the numbers observed along the "hawk" ridges in Pennsylvania and New Jersey where from three to over one dozen are seen in one day.

Spring—five, Manitou, Monroe Co., Mar. 20, 1955; six each, Derby Hill, Oswego Co., Apr. 19, 1958, and Apr. 16, 1960; ten, same locality, Mar. 29, 1962 (Cade and Spofford). See Haugh (1966) for account of this latter area. The following is a summary of the flights at Derby Hill, taken chiefly from Haugh (*in litt.*), with daily maxima of five or more per day:

1963—total of 81: Mar. 16 (eight); 17 (ten); 24 (nine); 26 (eight); Apr. 6 (seven); 7 (six); 17 (five).

1964—total of 51: Mar. 3 (seven); 7 (six); Apr. 2 (five).

1965—total of 41: Mar. 28 (six); three as early as Mar. 2 and one as late as May 3.

1966—total of 93: Mar. 17 (15); 90% of the birds were seen from Mar. 10 to Apr. 18 with the first individual on Feb. 24, the last on May 5.

1967—total of 103: During the spring flight a total of 103 birds was observed from Mar. 2 to Apr. 30, 90% of these from Mar. 8 to Apr. 15, with daily maxima of 11 each on Mar. 29 and Apr. 1.

During the spring of 1969 an unprecedented total of *141* Goshawks was observed at Derby Hill, with a record tally of *23* on Apr. 4. Only 26 Cooper's Hawks were seen that day.

EXTREME DATES: Oct. 2 to May 20 (adults in both instances). Rare before late October and after April.

Beginners should use care in field identifica-

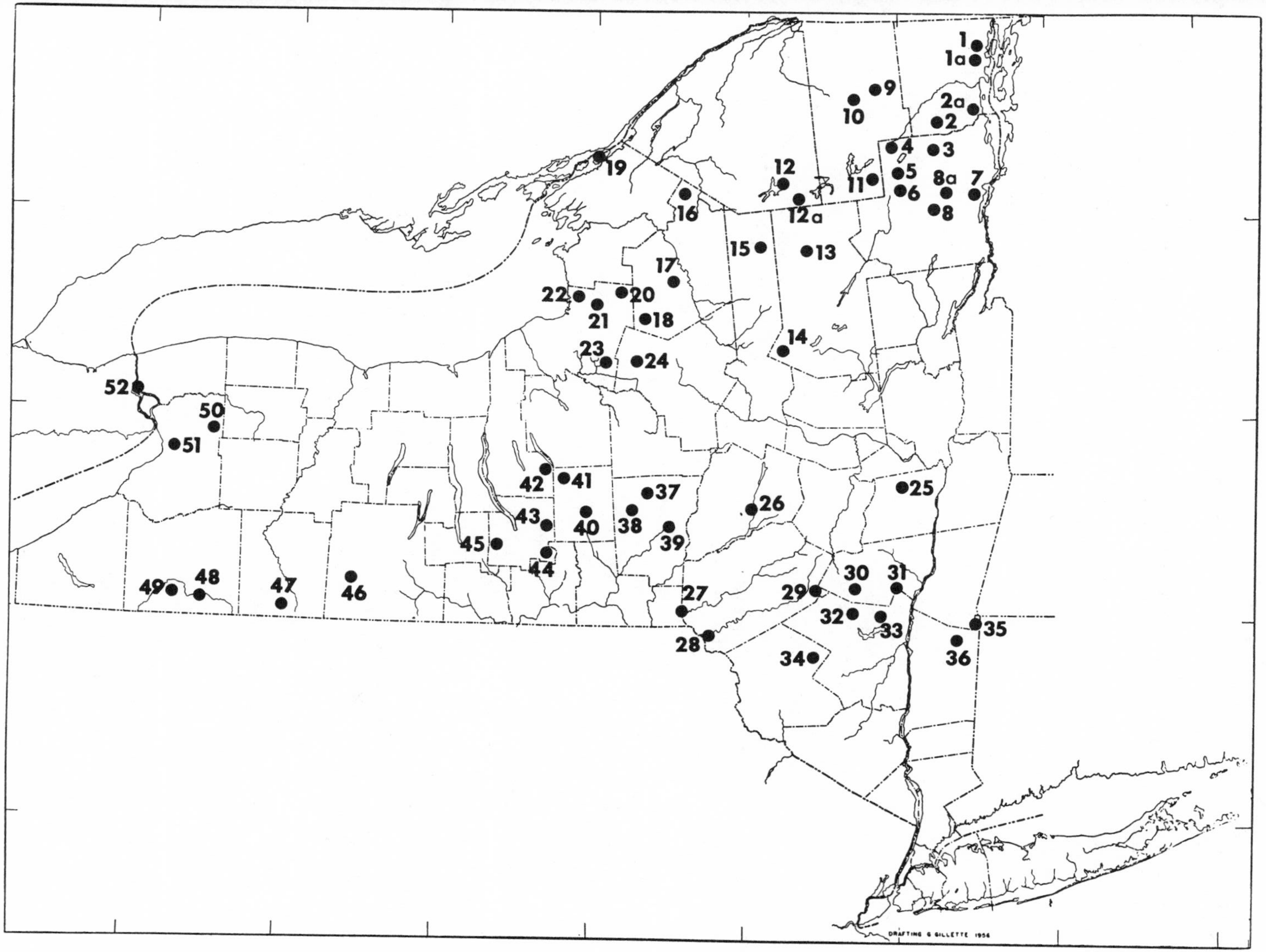

MAP 51 Northern Goshawk (*Accipiter gentilis*) Breeding distribution

tion of immatures, as confusion with the very similar immature Cooper's Hawk is likely.

Change in breeding status (see Map 51): Eaton (1914: 80) was vague about breeding Goshawks in New York. In fact, to my knowledge, only four definite breeding records were known up to that time (see following) and no additional ones until 1952. The dramatic upsurge of this fine species as a breeder in the state within the past two decades has been phenomenal, especially as regards its southward penetration into the eastern deciduous forest. It is usually a more common breeder in the boreal evergreen forest.

As may be seen on the accompanying map, this species is confined chiefly to forested areas at higher elevations in the Adirondacks, Tug Hill region, Catskills, the nearby Taconics, the uplands southeast of the Finger Lakes, and the Allegany Plateau. Elsewhere it has been reported breeding with certainty only in the St. Lawrence valley and extreme western New York in the Buffalo area. The last-named represents old records.

Of 40 New York nests examined, 34 were in deciduous trees, only six in conifers—all pines. Beech was favored with 16 nests, followed by maple (11) and birch (five). Nest heights ranged from 20 to 50 feet. One nest had been used the previous year by Red-shouldered Hawks, another by American Crows. These nest trees were variously stated to be in "heavy mixed deciduous forest," "mixed hardwoods near a large swamp," "thick second-growth maple-birch woodland," "thick maple-beech-hemlock forest," and one nest found in a white pine, in "second-growth pineland."

Egg clutches in 42 New York nests: two eggs (27 nests); three eggs (15 nests); one found by Audubon with four eggs, is dubious.

EGG DATES: Apr. 20 to May 15.

Nestlings: May 18 to July 1; fledglings: June 14 to July 27. An extremely late date for nestlings is that of one in the Adirondacks on Aug. 5, 1961—perhaps indicative of earlier nest failure.

Localities and initial years of occupancy of the 56 breeding sites are as follows: Clinton Co.—(1) four miles southwest of Chazy (village), 1966; (1a) near Lake Alice, 1971; (2) Black Brook, 1968; (2a) near Keeseville, 1971. The 1971 localities (1a), (2a), (8a), and (12a) were received too late for inclusion in

numerical order and are added here and following. Essex Co.—(3) Jay, 1960; (4) near Bloomingdale, 1969; (5) North Elba, 1968; (6) near Heart Lake, 1961; (7) near Witherbee, 1968; (8) Elk Lake, 1965; (8a) Round Mtn., 1971. Franklin Co.—(9) Debar Mtn., 1950s; (10) north of Meacham Lake, 1961; (11) near Ampersand Lake, 1963. St. Lawrence Co.—(12) near Cranberry Lake, 1970; (12a) near Bog River, 1971. Hamilton Co.— (13) near Raquette Lake, 1953; (14) near Morehouseville, 1894 and 1898. Herkimer Co. —(15) Big Moose near Twitchell Lake, 1952. Lewis Co.—(16) Lake Bonaparte, 1963; (17) Whetstone Gulf, 1964 (see Fig. 34); (18) Osceola, 1957. Jefferson Co.—(19) Wellesley Island, 1968. Oswego Co.—(20) Mad River east of Greenboro, 1962; (21) between Lacona and Orwell, 1963; (22) Sandy Creek, 1963; (23) near Panther Lake, 1964. Oneida Co.— (24) Camden, 1970. Albany Co.—(25) Thacher State Park, 1964. Otsego Co.—(26) Milford, 1970. Broome Co.—(27) Deposit, 1968. Delaware Co.—(28) Hancock, 1965; (29) Fleischmanns, 1963. Greene Co.—(30) Rusk Mtn., 1952; (31) Palenville, 1970. Ulster Co. —(32) Phoenicia, 1968; (33) Bearsville, 1969. Sullivan Co.—(34) Grahamsville, 1967. Dutchess Co.—(35) Mt. Riga, 1968; (36) Stissing Mtn., 1970. Chenango Co.—(37) Beaver Meadow, 1965; (38) Pharsalia, 1955; (39) near Norwich, 1962. Cortland Co.—(40) McGraw, 1966; (41) Scott, 1968. Cayuga Co. —(42) Bear Swamp, 1970. Tompkins Co.— (43) near Dryden, 1966; (44) near Caroline, 1967; (45) Connecticut Hill, 1967. Steuben Co.—(46) near Canisteo, 1968. Allegany Co. —(47) Alma, 1967. Cattaraugus Co.—(48) near Vandalia, 1964; (49) Allegany State Park, 1960. Erie Co.—(50) Alden, 1908; (51) Windom, 1908; (52) "near" Niagara Falls; this last record was that of a nest with (four?) eggs in a pine tree found by Audubon prior to 1835. In addition to that nest, only three other localities were reported prior to Eaton (1914): two in Erie Co. (50) and (51) above, and one in Hamilton Co. (14) as mentioned previously. Curiously enough, despite numerous egg collectors during the first quarter of the twentieth century, no additional nests were reported until 1952. During 1968 alone, *nine* new breeding sites were discovered!

Whereas only four breeding localities were

Fig. 34 Whetstone Gulf State Park, Lewis Co., showing "badlands" type erosion, May 20, 1961. A pair of Goshawks nested near here in 1964. Photo by David Gordon

known prior to 1952 (117 years), at least *52* breeding localities have been discovered since 1952 (only 19 years). In addition several more 1971 (Catskill Mtn.) nesting localities were withheld because of increased disturbance by falconers and others in that area. This strongly suggests (1) southward range extension at lower elevations in increased numbers; (2) partial niche replacement of a greatly decreased breeding population of *Accipiter cooperii*.

It is perhaps more than coincidence that within the nine-year period (1962–1970) the Cooper's Hawk was reported to have decreased considerably as a breeder (pesticides?) while the Goshawk has been found breeding in many new localities, all (except one Adirondack site) at places where the former species had nested regularly in past years and Goshawks were previously unknown as breeders. This suggests that the two species, although breeding in similar habitat on occasion, do not coexist because of a certain level of interspecific competition for somewhat similar food. However, based on stomach analyses, the Goshawk is much more of a mammal eater than the two smaller accipiters—Cooper's and Sharp-shinned hawks.

Proof of Goshawk hatching success in recent years is borne out by young birds found in 34 out of 48 nests (71%). Many of these recent nests were found by Dr. Walter Spofford who supplied much of the information concerning current breeding within the state.

Subspecies: The North American race *atricapillus* differs markedly from nominate *gentilis* of the Old World by being gray rather than brown above, by having a blackish crown, and with the barring below much finer. Some authorities believe that the two populations may have even reached the species level.

Postscript: Dr. R. J. Clark informs me (*in litt.*) that he discovered an active nest in 1972 near Charleston Four Corners, Montgomery Co. This is in the extreme southern portion of the county near the Schoharie Co. line at the northern fringe of the Catskills.

Red-tailed Hawk
(*Buteo jamaicensis*)   *   B

Range: Nearctic and northern Neotropical regions from Alaska and Canada to Panama and the West Indies. Withdraws in winter from the more northern portions.

Status: Common to abundant migrant; most numerous in spring along the Lake Ontario shore, in fall along the north-south ridges in the southeastern part of the state. Locally common in winter near the coast. Widespread breeder.

Nonbreeding: One of the features of the migrations is the spectacular flights of this species. At the hawk lookouts on Lake Ontario at Manitou, Monroe Co., and particularly at Derby Hill, Oswego Co., impressive numbers may be seen from late March to late April.

MAXIMA, INLAND: *Spring*—240, Manitou, Mar. 22, 1949; *750,* Derby Hill, Mar. 31, 1967 (Haugh)—see Red-shouldered Hawk—same place and date; 530, Derby Hill, Apr. 9, 1969; on Apr. 3, 1960, 150 at Manitou and 350 at Derby Hill; on Apr. 20, 1957, 200 at Manitou and 120 at Derby Hill.

MAXIMA, NEAR COAST: *Fall*—61, Mt. Peter, Orange Co., Oct. 20, 1968; 150 Bear Mtn., Rockland Co., Nov. 6, 1951.

The species is ordinarily scarce in winter, except in the milder coastal sections where as many as 24 were estimated on Dec. 27, 1942, in the Pelham Bay area of Bronx and Westchester counties. However, a count of *22* on Feb. 16, 1969, near the shore of Lake Ontario, at Lyndonville, Orleans Co. (Smith), would seem to be too early for spring migrants.

Breeding: Red-tailed Hawks show a preference for patches of woodland in upland, open park-like country, but are also found in such diverse terrain as the Adirondack Mountains and the pine-oak barrens of eastern Long Island, provided there are openings in the forest.

In New York the Red-tail is exclusively a tree nester, as far as known (but see following). This species was a favorite of egg collectors in the early days because of relative accessibility of the nests. As a result, perhaps more information concerning nest sites is at hand than for most other hawks. Nests are also in conspicuous places, usually before the foliage is advanced.

Of 167 New York nests, the favorite tree species was beech (70), followed by maple (45), oak (15), elm (13), basswood (nine), ash (six), birch (four), hickory (two), and one each of tupelo, tulip tree, and hemlock. Note that only one nest was in an evergreen. Height of tree nests ranged from 35 to 85 feet.

The following egg clutches reported in 119 New York nests were: two eggs (74 nests); three eggs (41 nests); and four eggs in only four nests.

EGG DATES: Mar. 8 to May 16.

Nestlings: Apr. 17 to June 20; fledglings: June 1 to July 8.

On Apr. 12, 1968, Andrle and Thill (*Canadian Field Nat.,* 1969, 83: 165) discovered a cliff nest of this species in the Niagara Gorge about five miles north of Niagara Falls on the *Canadian* side of the gorge. They reported that the nest ledge was "about 18 feet below the cliff top and approximately 280 feet above the river."

As evidence of successful breeding in this species, primarily a mammal eater, *all* seven nests at the Montezuma Refuge fledged young in 1971.

Subspecies: Two distinct races are known to occur within New York: (1) the large race *borealis* is the common subspecies over much of eastern North America and has been discussed in detail; (2) the race *calurus* (darker and more heavily marked below than *borealis,* also much more variable and highly polymorphic) ranges in the breeding season to the north and west of *borealis*).

At least 13 specimens of *calurus* have been taken within the state, chiefly in late fall of various years. Most of these, examined by the writer, are in the AMNH and CUM collections, and were listed by Parkes (1952) who,

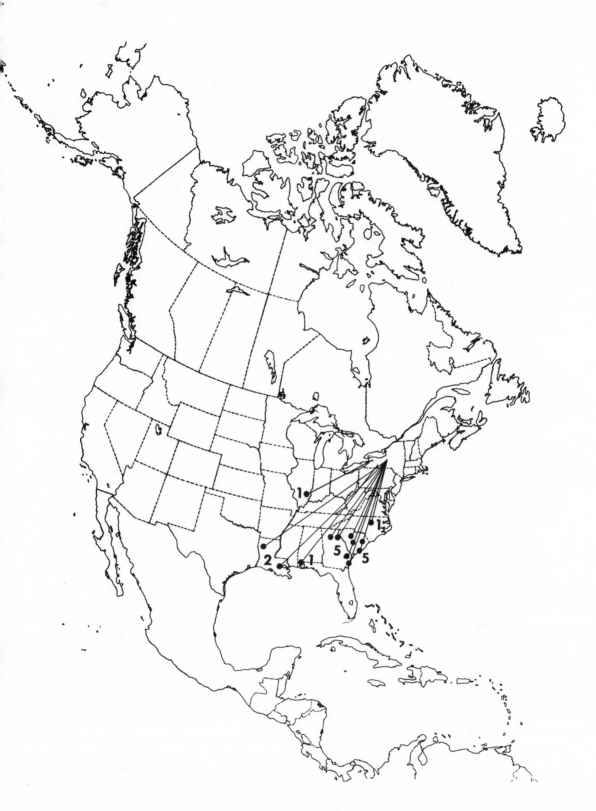

MAP 52 Red-tailed Hawk (*Buteo jamaicensis*) Banding recoveries

however, used the name *abieticola* (a synonym of *calurus*).

Banding (see Map 52): Fourteen nestlings banded in central New York in various years were recovered the following winter in five southeastern states. Another nestling banded May 26, 1934, in western New York was killed on Nov. 29, 1934, in eastern Illinois.

Red-shouldered Hawk
(*Buteo lineatus*)   *   B

Range: Chiefly eastern North America, from the extreme southern portions of Ontario and Quebec south to northern Mexico and the Gulf states, west to Nebraska and Texas; also California. Withdraws in winter from the more northern portions.

Status: Common to locally abundant migrant; most numerous in spring along the shores of the Great Lakes—especially Lake Ontario, in fall in the southeastern portions between the inner coast and the ridge slopes. Rare to uncommon in winter near the coast. Fairly common breeder in the interior lowlands, but rare to absent in the mountains, especially northward.

Nonbreeding: During the migrations great flights of "buteos" may be observed to advantage in spring along the shores of lakes Ontario and Erie, and the Red-shouldered Hawk concentrations are quite impressive, though in smaller numbers than those of its larger congener, the Red-tailed Hawk.

MAXIMA, INLAND: *Spring*—On two days in 1963 at Derby Hill, Oswego Co., 175, Mar. 17 and 200, Mar. 26 (total of 375 in two days); 420, Derby Hill, Mar. 31, 1967 (Haugh)—see Red-tailed Hawk—same place and date; 350, Derby Hill, Apr. 3, 1960; 400, Manitou, Monroe Co., Apr. 16, 1948 (Bieber and Klonick).

MAXIMA, NEAR COAST: *Fall*—46, Mt. Peter, Orange Co., Oct. 18, 1958; 120 (80 in one hour), Tuckahoe, Westchester Co., Oct. 29, 1944.

Breeding: This species prefers swampy woodlands and forested river bottoms. It also nests in patches of thickly grown woodlots adjacent to agricultural areas and villages.

There is good reason to believe that the population of Red-shouldered Hawks has greatly diminished in recent years (pesticides?—see introductory account to the hawks). Referring to "Region 5," Scheider (*Kingbird,* 1969, 19: 224) stated, "now unreported from all the wooded swamps of the Ontario lake plain."

As with some other hawks, this species was a favorite of the early-day egg collectors and we thus have an abundance of information on nest sites and clutch sizes.

Out of a total of 137 New York tree nests, beech was favored (54), followed by maple (29), chestnut (13), birch (ten), oak (nine), ash (seven), elm, basswood, cherry, and hemlock (each with three), hickory (two), and tulip tree (one). It is of interest to note that 12 of 13 chestnut tree nests were from the southeastern part of the state. In fact, Dutcher (1887–1894) stated that on Long Island, the Red-shouldered Hawk bred "almost entirely in chestnut trees." As a breeder this hawk is confined to the north shore of Long Island in low, wet woods or adjacent slopes. With the disappearance of mature chestnut trees during the present century on Long Island, hickory, oak, maple, and beech were probably used.

During his Cooper's Hawk study in the Ithaca region, Meng (1951) examined 18 nests of Red-shouldered Hawks within a 17-mile radius during the *four* year period, 1948–1951. Both of these species occur in similar habitat throughout much of the state.

In Cayuga Co., Benton (*Kingbird,* 1956, 6: 88) tells of an old Red-tailed Hawk nest utilized in succession by a Great Horned Owl (with eggs on Feb. 7) and by a Red-shouldered Hawk (with eggs on Apr. 25).

Height of 137 New York tree nests ranged from 15 to 75 feet.

The following egg clutches reported in 156 New York nests were: two eggs (only 16 nests —incomplete? clutches); three eggs (83 nests); four eggs (47 nests); five eggs (three nests).

EGG DATES: Mar. 25 to May 26.

Nestlings: May 5 to July 5; fledglings as early as June 6.

Banding (see Map 53): A total of six nestlings banded at inland New York localities in various years were recovered at inland localities in three southeastern states during the following winter or late autumn.

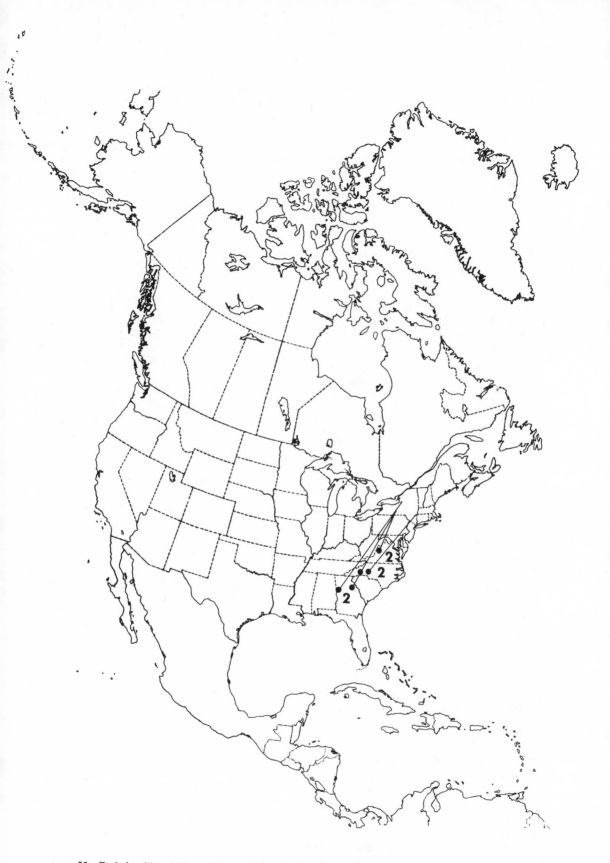

MAP 53 Red-shouldered Hawk (*Buteo lineatus*) Banding recoveries

Broad-winged Hawk
(*Buteo platypterus*) * B

Range: Chiefly eastern North America, breeding from southern Canada to the Gulf states, Florida keys, and West Indies. Continental population winters from extreme southern Florida and Mexico to Brazil and Peru.

Status: Abundant to very abundant migrant. Statewide breeder, but local in western New York.

Nonbreeding: During the migrations Broad-winged Hawks occur in spectacular numbers, both along the shore of Lake Ontario in spring and over the north-south ridges in fall. Huge flocks, sometimes numbering in the hundreds, may be seen in late April and again in late September.

MAXIMA, INLAND: *Spring*—all at Manitou, Monroe Co. and Derby Hill, Owsego Co. Note comparative numbers on two spring days.

Manitou	Derby Hill
7000, Apr. 21, 1966	10,000, Apr. 21, 1966
8000, Apr. 25, 1959	5000, Apr. 25, 1959

On Apr. 23 and 25, 1964, at Derby Hill, Haugh (1966: 15) estimated 8100 and 6700 respectively, or nearly 15,000 total for the two days. Also noteworthy were 2200 on May 12, 1956, and 200, June 4, 1949, both at Manitou.

MAXIMA: *Fall*—2300, Owego, Tioga Co., Sept. 12, 1964; 2900, Mt. Peter, Orange Co., Sept. 15, 1968; 2700, Van Cortlandt Park, Bronx Co., Sept. 22, 1945; 3000, Chestnut Ridge Park, Erie Co., Sept. 24, 1949.

Breeding: The Broad-winged Hawk is equally at home in the Adirondack wilderness or the rapidly diminishing pine barrens of eastern Long Island. It also breeds on top of the Palisades along the Hudson River. Its one important habitat requirement for breeding success is extensive woodland, either secondary or primary forest.

Perhaps because of its somewhat secretive nature or rather its adeptness at remaining still among the thick foliage, very few nests of this species have been found in New York compared with the two larger, more conspicuous buteos—the Red-tail and Red-shoulder.

Nests in New York have been found in birch, cherry, maple, and chestnut, with three in the first named. Heights of nests range from 12 to 55 feet above ground level.

Egg clutch size in 24 New York nests are as follows: two eggs (ten nests); three eggs (12 nests); four eggs (two nests).

EGG DATES: Apr. 27 to June 26.

Nestlings: May 30 to July 27; fledglings: July 4 to Aug. 16.

Remarks: As this hawk winters primarily in the tropics, there is no basis for Eaton's statement (1914: 87) "In southeastern New York the Broad-winged Hawk often remains throughout winter as it does in the Ohio and Delaware valleys . . ."

I have seen *no* winter specimen from New York in all the collections examined nor do I know of any published in the literature. The dates listed in Beardslee and Mitchell (1965: 167) of Mar. 4 and 14 are not supported by specimen evidence, nor are details given. The species is rare in the state before April and after October. There is one reliable record of a *crippled* Broad-wing that remained throughout the winter of 1933–1934 at Van Cortlandt Park, New York City. It frequented a garbage dump, probably sustaining itself on a supply of rats, and was observed by numerous birders.

The reports of Broad-wings published on many Christmas counts in recent years were in all likelihood misidentified Red-shouldered Hawks, although one or two may have been identified correctly.

Swainson's Hawk
(*Buteo swainsoni*) *

Range: Western North America, breeding east to Minnesota, rarely to Illinois. Winters mainly in Argentina, but since the early 1950s fairly common in southern Florida (chiefly immatures). Wanders in fall to eastern North America.

Status: *Casual*—there are two definite records for New York State, both specimens: (1) immature, light morph, collected in Onondaga Co., October 1877 (Rex and Lodder), mounted specimen formerly in MCZ collection, examined by Brewster (*Auk*, 1893, 10: 83), now at Phillips Academy, Andover, Mass. (*fide* Paynter); (2) immature female, dark morph, collected at Cornwall, Orange Co., Oct. 14, 1892 (Williams), examined by Howell (Dutcher, *Auk*, 1893, 10: 83–84), present whereabouts of specimen not known. Another of this species was taken on Oct. 8 of the same year in Maine.

A less satisfactory report is that of an immature caught in a trap at Brockport, Monroe Co., Oct. 1, 1889 (N. L. Davis), but this specimen was never seen by an ornithologist, nor is the specimen available for examination. Short (1896: 10), Eaton (1914: 86), and Beardslee and Mitchell (1965: 170) accepted this occurrence without reservation. As Forbush (1927: 134) pointed out, ". . . mistakes in identification [are] often made with [the] bird in hand."

I know of no basis for inclusion of Lake George, as stated in the A.O.U. Check-list (1957: 108).

A recent sighting of this species, worthy of note, is one observed at Etna, Tompkins Co., May 3, 1970 (Hance and Haugh). For details, see *Kingbird* (1970: 116).

Rough-legged Hawk
(*Buteo lagopus*) *

Range: Northern Holarctic region, the North American race *sanctijohannis* (smaller and darker than Old World races, also highly polymorphic) breeds south to southeastern Quebec (north shore Gulf of St. Lawrence) and Newfoundland.

Status: *Winter visitant*—(1) along the coast, variously rare to uncommon, occasionally fairly common; (2) inland (lake plain) more numerous, even common at times. Highly irruptive.

Occurrence: The Rough-legged Hawk inhabits chiefly open fields and marshes and is most prevalent in years of meadow mouse (*Microtus*) abundance. It is especially numerous along Lake Ontario, and in the rich agricultural country to the south of the lake.

This species is very variable in coloration;

the light morph greatly exceeds the dark morph, at least on the basis of New York specimens examined in various museums, of which there were 33 of the former and only 11 of the latter. It should be emphasized, however, that because of the great variability involved, intermediate phases (morphs) occur and, in the same collections, at least seven specimens examined were found to be in this last category.

MAXIMA: *Coastal*—seven, Fresh Kills, Richmond Co. (Staten Island), Nov. 15, 1964; nine, Gardiner's Island, Suffolk Co., Dec. 23, 1924; and on Feb. 6, 1965—ten at Jones Beach, and 15 on the Orient peninsula, Suffolk Co.

MAXIMA: *Inland*—30, Jamesville, Onondaga Co., Oct. 16, 1964; 25, Manitou, Monroe Co., Nov. 11, 1959; 20—"all in one field, feeding on mice"—Lockport, Niagara Co., Dec. 23, 1961; 39, Lockport, Jan. 24, 1962; 50, Manitou, Mar. 23, 1968; on Lake Ontario, Apr. 3, 1960—75 at Manitou (Genesee Ornith. Soc.) and 25 at Derby Hill, Oswego Co.; 58, Manitou, Apr. 21, 1962; 50, Lyndonville, Orleans Co., Apr. 22, 1965.

It can be seen from the above figures that Rough-legged Hawks are most numerous in spring along the Lake Ontario shore. The 75 birds at the Manitou hawk lookout are unprecedented.

EXTREME DATES: Sept. 25, 1966—Montezuma Refuge (Walker)—and Oct. 1 (inland) to May 21 (coastal) and to June 9, 1965— four birds at Lyndonville (Mitchell and Smith); also June 11 (inland) and one, June 26, 1965 (also at Lyndonville, Smith). Most unusual are, one near Watertown, July 9, 1966 (Meritt), and another at the Syracuse Airport, July 8, 1969 (Scheider), and possibly this latter individual at nearby Pompey, Onondaga Co., July 21 and Aug. 4 (Crumb).

Usually rare before mid-October and after April.

Golden Eagle
(*Aquila chrysaetos*) * B

Range: Holarctic region, the widespread but local race *canadensis* (darkest of all subspecies) breeds in Asia from central and eastern Siberia south to northern Mongolia; in North America from Alaska and Canada south to northern

Mexico, east to the western edge of the Great Plains; in eastern North America—rare and local—from Ontario, Quebec, and Labrador south to Maine, New Hampshire, and northeastern New York (Adirondacks); formerly south to the Great Smokies (Tennessee and North Carolina). Sedentary and migratory, with periodic movements during spring and late fall.

Status: Rare to uncommon, but perhaps regular migrant inland, much rarer in late fall and winter along the coast. Very rare breeder.

Nonbreeding: This fine species is likely to turn up almost anywhere in the state from October to April, or even May. However, years may pass at a given locality without a single record. It is singularly rare on Long Island, yet in two successive years—1967 and 1968— in late fall, single individuals were observed in the Jones Beach area, one of them photographed. Inland, the Golden Eagle is less rare.

At the two best hawk-watching spots in the state—on Lake Ontario at Manitou, Monroe Co., and at Derby Hill, Oswego Co.—it is probably regular during the spring hawk flights.

MAXIMA: three, Manitou, Apr. 17, 1949; in 1967 at Derby Hill, three each were seen on Apr. 21 and 26.

EXTREME DATES, nonbreeding: Oct. 18 and 23 (specimen) to May 3 (latest specimen) and June 1. September dates (away from the breeding grounds), although possibly correct, are not substantiated. There are at least 16 observations in May, most of them amply confirmed.

Specimen data: Of over two dozen specimens taken in the state, at least half are extant and in the larger collections. The writer has examined all of these except one. The six downstate specimens, including three from Fisher's Island on extreme eastern Long Island, have been published (Bull, 1964: 156). The six remaining extant specimens—all from upstate—

Fig. 35 Franklin Co. "burns," near Paul Smith's. Feeding area of Golden Eagle; June 16, 1968. Photo by Robert G. Wolk

Fig. 36 Golden Eagle cliff nest site with "lookout" tree on top of cliff, Adirondack Mountains, May 1961. Photo by Walter R. Spofford

are as follows: (1) Austerlitz, Columbia Co., Dec. 10, 1927 (Sweet), NYSM 4400; (2) Kingston, Ulster Co., Apr. 14, 1929 (collector?), NYSM 4845; (3) Plattsburgh, Clinton Co., Oct. 23, 1938 (Frenyea), NYSM 6060; (4) Naples, Ontario Co., May 3, 1936 (Crocker), CUM 3256; (5) Olean, Cattaraugus Co., Dec. 5, 1923 (collector?), RMAS 34; (6) near Bath, Steuben Co., Nov. 11, 1965 (Winslow), St. Bonaventure Univ. Mus. 958.

Breeding: Golden Eagles in all probability formerly bred in the mountainous portions of eastern New York—in the Adirondacks and Catskills, and possibly even in the Hudson Highlands—but in all instances without certain proof. Not until relatively recent times has this species been definitely established as breeding in New York.

The following nesting information has been obtained through the courtesy of Dr. Walter R.

Fig. 37 Golden Eagle nestling (nine weeks), Adirondacks, July 10, 1957. Remains of American Bittern and varying hare in cliff nest. Photo by Walter R. Spofford

Spofford (*in litt.*). In the interests of protecting these breeding Golden Eagles, the precise localities of the nest sites are not disclosed. Suffice it to say that four of the eight Adirondack Mtn. counties of Essex, Franklin, Hamilton, and St. Lawrence are involved (see Figs. 35 and 36).

According to Spofford (*op. cit.*) the first known New York nesting in modern times occurred in 1915 when two or more pairs occupied a site which remained active up to 1967. However, no fledglings were known since the early 1940s and no nestlings since about 1950. At another site no young were raised (fledged) after the late 1940s, and at still another site a pair had mixed success from 1950 to 1967 with one young apparently fledged in 1967. At a fourth location (1962 to 1965) a pair attempted nesting, but unfortunately laid no eggs.

At one of the above sites a nestling was actually banded on July 10, 1957, the first known banded young of this species in eastern North America (see Fig. 37).

Three of the four nest sites are on cliff ledges, two of these ranging from 50 to 85 feet above and overlooking mountain lakes. The fourth, the only known tree nest of this species in the eastern United States is, or was, situated in a tall live white pine. This tree nest was occupied from 1965 to 1967 and the "pair appeared to be incubating during April and May 1967, but there has been no nestling since 1965 and no certainty that eggs have been laid."

A cliff site that had Golden Eagle young in the late 1940s was reported to have originally belonged to a pair of Bald Eagles.

As of 1969, two pairs of Golden Eagles were reported to have fledged one young apiece; one of these was at a tree site.

It should be emphasized that more than one, sometimes three or more nests, are built by *one pair* of birds until one of these is selected as the actual nest to be used for eggs. A nest in itself, therefore, does not necessarily denote occupancy.

Spofford (*Bird-Banding*, 1964, 35: 123) stated that for eastern Golden Eagles, varying hares and grouse (sp.?) are staple food items and are available all winter, but others such as "marmot [=woodchuck] and bittern" are not.

Finally, in 1970, a fledged juvenile was photographed at a tree nest on July 24 by Spofford (1971: 4). In this very interesting account, he ends with the dismal note that "the Golden Eagle now appears well on the way to becoming a vanishing remnant."

FALCONS — FALCONIDAE

Four species in New York.
Two breed.

For discussion, see family Accipitridae. One of the structural characters supposedly separating this family (60± species) from the Accipitridae is the presence of a notched bill in many, but not all species; however, some members of the Accipitridae also possess the notch. Another difference is that the true falcons (genus *Falco*) do not build a nest, unlike most other hawks.

[Crested Caracara (*Polyborus plancus*)

Hypothetical: Neotropical region, breeding north to central Florida. Vagrant to Ontario.

An immature was observed at Alley Pond Park, Queens Co., Long Island, from Sept. 28 to Oct. 5, 1946 (Flavin, Eisenmann, Elliott, and Astle—see Eisenmann, *Auk*, 1947, 64: 470). The possibility exists that this individual was a captive, as a tame bird was reported to have escaped from its owner at Malverne, Nassau Co., in 1945 (A. Dignan, oral comm.)

For use of the genus *Polyborus* rather than *Caracara*, see Amadon (*Auk*, 1954, 71: 203).

P. cheriway is considered to be conspecific with *P. plancus*, following de Schauensee (1966: 63), and Brown and Amadon (1968: 738). The northernmost race *audubonii* differs from *cheriway* by having the cheeks, throat, and undertail coverts whitish.]

Gyrfalcon (*Falco rusticolus*) *

Range: Holarctic region at high latitudes, in eastern North America breeding south to the northern portions of Labrador and Quebec. Winters mainly in the breeding range; south to New York, casually to New Jersey. Mainly sedentary.

Status: *Very rare*—Although there have been a number of occurrences of Gyrfalcons in the state over the years, it must be emphasized that many of our very active observers have never seen this fine species in the field. Indeed, 20 or more years will pass in a given region without a single record of a Gyrfalcon. It is certainly one of the rarest of winter visitants in New York State. Nevertheless, there may be as many as *50* reliable reports, but a number of others are likely misidentified Peregrine Falcons or even dark-phased Rough-legged Hawks. In fact, one of the most recent observations upstate had the notation by the observer, ". . . resembled a dark phase Rough-leg until it flew." Harry Darrow and the writer were fortunate to witness a splendid dark-morphed Gyrfalcon feeding on a male merganser at Lawrence Marsh, Nassau Co., Feb. 7, 1948.

Of more than *20* specimens reported taken in New York, *ten* are known to be extant and all of these have been examined by the writer. Six were collected upstate, the remaining four on Fisher's Island at the east end of Long Island. Nine of ten are in the dark or intermediate "phased" plumage; one is a light-colored individual, the so-called "White" Gyrfalcon, number (6) below. Data on these ten specimens are as follows:

(1) near Lake Ontario, Monroe Co., October 1890 (Marshall), NYSM 453.

(2) Auburn, Cayuga Co., Mar. 29, 1902 (Redman), NYSM 1696.

(3) Dexter, Jefferson Co., Jan. 15, 1917 (Miller), AMNH 168803.

(4) Angola, Erie Co., Nov. 27, 1926 (Santens), BMS 1928.

(5) Sherburne, Chenango Co., Dec. 23, 1939 (Gow), CUM 6100.

(6) Found dead at Eldorado Beach, Jefferson Co., Nov. 14, 1965 (Walker), NYSM 22719.

(7), (8), (9), (10), all shot over owl decoys, Fisher's Island, Suffolk Co. (Ferguson)—Oct. 15, 1915; Oct. 28, 1925; Oct. 30, 1926; Oct. 12, 1929—all in the Ferguson Memorial Museum. Note that all four were taken in October.

During the winter of 1964–1965 three or more individuals were observed as follows: Dark morph—near Cape Vincent, Jefferson Co., Dec. 23 (Gordon), and the same or another at nearby Point Peninsula, Dec. 26 (Gordon and Clinch); two—both dark morphs— near Selkirk, Albany Co., Feb. 13, 1965 (Reilly, *Kingbird*, 1965, 15: 156); white morph—Ithaca, Feb. 24 (Pettingill, S. H. Spofford, *et al.*) and photographed by D. G. Allen (*Kingbird*, 1965, 15: 138–140) and perhaps the same individual at Clyde, Wayne Co., Mar. 7 (Benning).

EXTREME DATES: Oct. 12 (specimen) to Mar. 29 (specimen) and Apr. 7, 1963, Derby Hill, Oswego Co. (Haugh and Willoughby)—a light-morphed individual.

Remarks: No subspecies are recognized here, the form *"obsoletus"* being a synonym. Vaurie (1965: 209–210) and Brown and Amadon (1968: 843–844) are followed in treating this species as monotypic. Gyrfalcons vary greatly *individually* in various parts of their range and both light and dark birds, as well as intermediates, may be found in the same nest. Although the former tend to predominate

farther north and the latter farther south, this is by no means invariably true.

Peregrine Falcon
(Falco peregrinus) * B

Range: Virtually cosmopolitan, but absent as a breeder from tropical and subtropical America. The race *anatum* (darker than the nominate European race, especially juveniles) occurs in our area. Sedentary and migratory.

Status: Rare to occasionally fairly common fall migrant on the outer coast, rare inland migrant; formerly resident in vicinity of New York City, but rare to very rare in winter elsewhere. Former local breeder, but probably extirpated as a breeder in the state by 1961.

Nonbreeding: One of the outstanding sights of the fall migration is the occurrence of Peregrine Falcons along the beaches of Long Island, presumably birds from the arctic regions. At favorable localities one or more may be observed in flight, or perched on telephone poles, fence posts, or even driftwood among the sand dunes.

MAXIMA, LONG ISLAND: *Fall*—12, Fire Island, Suffolk Co., Sept. 28, 1963; 12 shot, Fisher's Island, Suffolk Co., Oct. 4, 1920; 23, Fire Island, Oct. 6, 1967 (C. Ward, *et al.*); 18 in six hours, Jones Beach (near Tobay), Nassau Co., Oct. 10, 1959 (Ward); ten, Far Rockaway, Queens Co., Oct. 13, 1950; 12 shot, Fisher's Island, Oct. 28, 1921, late for so many.

MAXIMA, INLAND: *Spring*—five, Manitou, Monroe Co., Apr. 22, 1954.

Winter—In former years Peregrine Falcons were not uncommon in and around New York City during the colder months. Individuals could be observed at such places as ledges of the upper stories of mid-Manhattan hotels and downtown skyscrapers, a church steeple in northern Manhattan, a gasoline storage tank in the Bronx, and a bridge tower in Brooklyn. There was probably a minimum of 20 different individuals wintering within the five boroughs of New York City, plus an unknown number of birds in the surrounding suburbs. According to Herbert and Herbert (1965), several birds banded as nestlings at eyries in the northeastern states were recovered in and near New York City in winter or late

Fig. 38 Nest site of Peregrine Falcon (eggs show slightly just to right of rock slab), Palisades on the Hudson River, about opposite Yonkers, N.Y. (Alpine, New Jersey). Date: about 1911 or 1912. Photo by Howard H. Cleaves

fall (see **Banding**). It was believed by these authors that Peregrines wintered successfully along the cliffs of the Palisades on the Hudson River, as well as in New York City, because of a "bountiful food supply" consisting primarily of "racing" pigeons and starlings.

Change in breeding status: Perhaps of all the breeding species in the state in recent times, the rapid decline and total extirpation of the Peregrine Falcon was the most dramatic event that occurred. Prior to the 1950s at least 40 Peregrine eyries were known to have been active within New York. The last known unfledged young recorded was in 1956, the last known eggs (did *not* hatch) in 1958, and the last known adult (unmated) at a nest site in 1961. The best documented and probably most thoroughly studied nesting population of this species in our area was that along the

Hudson on the cliffs of the Palisades (Herbert and Herbert, 1965, 1969). See Fig. 38.

Egging, falconry, molestation by pigeon fanciers, men and boys with firearms, picnicking above or near nesting cliff ledges, road construction, and finally pesticides—especially the last—were all contributing factors to the demise of this fine species. Pressures from these human disturbances, with the exception of egging—made illegal by 1934—militated against the chances of eggs hatching, let alone young fledging.

In New York State, the vast majority of nest sites were located on lofty cliffs overlooking rivers or lakes or, at least, not far from water. The important factor in *all* of the nest sites was that the birds have a clear, exposed view of the surroundings, unobstructed by trees in the immediate vicinity of the eyrie. Five breeding locations were man-made: three in abandoned stone quarries, one on a building, and one on a bridge. No tree or ground nests were known in this state.

Of all the cliff-nesting sites, perhaps the most remarkable was one at Lake Champlain situated on a 20-foot cliff, the nest ledge only eight feet above the water and the actual eyrie "behind" a red cedar (see Fig. 39). Another former eyrie in the Adirondacks was used by a pair of Common Ravens in 1968.

The actual nest consists of a mere "scrape" or hollow on a rocky ledge with some gravel or soil necessary to prepare the "scrape" for the eggs. On at least one occasion, however, the nest ledge contained some plant growth (Herbert and Herbert, 1965: 62–63). Even at the building (hotel) site, gravel was furnished to enable the birds to lay, after repeated unsuccessful attempts to hatch eggs on the bare stone surface. The eggs laid on the metal bridge tower were not known to hatch.

According to Herbert and Herbert (1965: 78, 81, 92), prior to the mid-1940s eight to ten pairs bred in the lower Hudson valley, plus another pair in New York City from 1943 to 1948. Clutch size "usually numbered four." There was one brood only, but if the first clutch was taken, the second and, if necessary, the third clutches "numbered two to three."

Egg clutches reported in 39 New York nests were: two eggs (ten nests); three eggs (12 nests); four eggs (15 nests); five eggs (two nests).

EGG DATES: Mar. 5 (exceptionally early) and Mar. 26 to May 31.

Nestlings: Apr. 19 to July 10; fledglings: May 21 to July 27.

Banding studies at these eyries indicated that three individuals attained the ages of at least 17, 18, and 20 years and that one pair of adults was mated for at least 14 years.

Details pertaining to many of the following breeding localities were generously contributed by Walter Spofford and Joseph Hickey.

Study of the accompanying breeding distribution map will show that all known breeding localities were in the eastern half of the state, except three nest sites in the Finger Lakes region. Other than the lower Hudson River

Fig. 39 Former Peregrine Falcon cliff nest, Valcour Island, Lake Champlain, Clinton Co., June 20, 1954. The nest cliff is only 20 feet high, the actual eyrie only eight feet above water level. Eyrie is located behind the red cedar on right side of picture. Photo by Walter R. Spofford

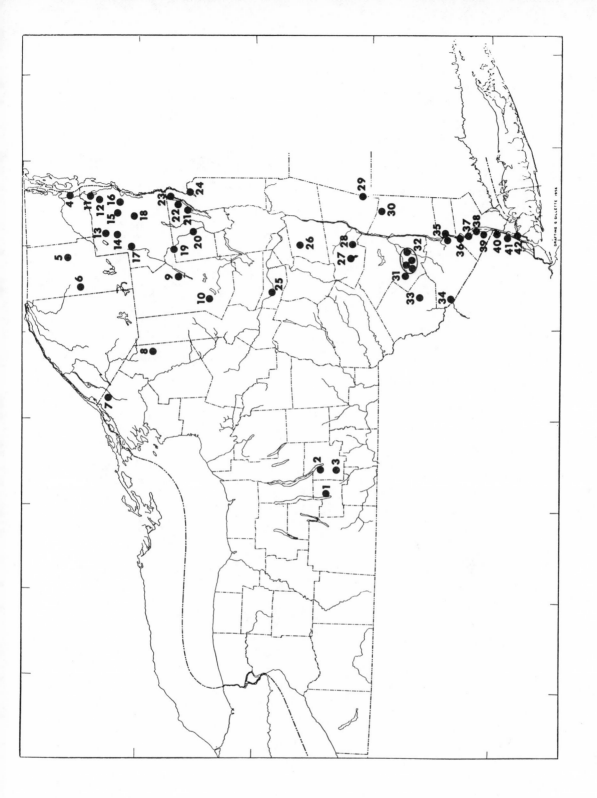

MAP 54 Peregrine
Falcon (*Falco
peregrinus*) Former
breeding distribution

MAP 55 Peregrine Falcon (*Falco peregrinus*) Banding recoveries

breeding population, most nesting locations were concentrated in the Adirondacks and to a lesser extent in and near the Catskills.

Localities of the 42 former nest sites (see Map 54) were as follows: Schuyler Co.—(1) north of Watkins Glen. Tompkins Co.—(2) Taughannock Falls; (3) Lick Brook Ravine, south of Ithaca. Clinton Co.—(4) Valcour Island, Lake Champlain. Franklin Co.—(5) Mt. Tom, Plumadore Range; (6) Azure Mtn. Jefferson Co.—(7) north end of Butterfield Lake. Lewis Co.—(8) Beaver River near Soft Maple Dam. Hamilton Co.—(9) near Griffin Brook, Indian Lake; (10) South Branch, West Canada Creek near Pine Lake. Essex Co.—(11) north end of Willsboro Bay, Lake Champlain; (12) Poke-O-Moonshine Mtn.; (13) Wilmington Notch; (14) Pitchoff Mtn.; (15) Hurricane Mtn.; (16) Cobble Hill near Elizabethtown; (17) Lake Colden; (18) Mt. Colvin, with its alternate site, Chapel Pond. Essex-Warren Co. line—(19) North River. Warren Co.—(20) The Glen; (21) Tongue Mtn., Lake George; (22) Silver Bay, Lake George. Warren-Washington Co. line—(23) Rogers Rock, with its alternate site, Anthony's Nose. Washington Co. —(24) north of Whitehall—actually on the Vermont state line, on Poulteney Creek. Montgomery Co.—(25) near Canajoharie. Albany Co.—(26) Thacher State Park, Helderberg Plateau. Greene Co.—(27) Hunter; (28) Newman's Ledge near North Lake. Columbia Co. —(29) Bash Bish Falls, Taconic State Park— actually on the Massachusetts state line. Dutchess Co.—(30) Little Stissing Mtn. Ulster Co.—(31) Napanoch; (32) New Paltz, with its alternate sites—variously known as North Trapp, Middle Trapp, South Trapp, Mill Brook, and Palmaghatt in the Mohonk Lake-Lake Minnewaska sector, Shawangunk Mountains. As many as five or more pairs nested between Napanoch and New Paltz in the 1940s. Sullivan Co.—(33) near Monticello. Orange Co.—(34) near Port Jervis. Orange and Putnam counties—(35) Storm King Mtn., with its alternate site, Breakneck Cliff, north of Cold Spring. Rockland Co.—(36) Bear Mtn. (bridge site); (37) Haverstraw; (38) Hook Mtn.; (39) Rockland Lake. Bergen Co., New Jersey—(40) Alpine; (41) Englewood. These last two are included for sake of completeness, as they are part of the Palisades complex of

eyries. New York Co. (Manhattan)—(42) St. Regis Hotel, Fifth Ave., and 55 Street.

As for Letchworth State Park in Wyoming Co., Rosche (1967) stated, "Reputed to nest . . . in the middle and late 1930s. However, definite evidence of nesting . . . records are apparently lacking." One might suppose that the species formerly nested in the Niagara gorge, but there is no definite proof of breeding there either.

Banding (see Map 55): A nestling banded at Rockland Lake, Rockland Co., June 11, 1939, was found dead at Jersey City, New Jersey in February 1943. Most extraordinary was another nestling banded at New Paltz, Ulster Co., June 18, 1929 (Smiley), and shot at Grand Island, Nebraska, Sept. 29, 1929 (only slightly over three months later). This bird flew almost due west nearly 1300 miles. A third nestling banded at its eyrie near Palenville, Greene Co., June 12, 1952, also flew west and was found injured not far west of Lansing, Michigan, Sept. 7, 1952. This last individual traveled approximately half the distance of the 1929 bird.

Merlin (*Falco columbarius*)   *

Range: Holarctic region, in eastern North America breeding south to the southern portions of Ontario and Quebec, very rarely or doubtfully in New Brunswick and Nova Scotia. No proof of breeding in northeastern United States (Bull: 1964, 163). Winters chiefly in tropical America, rarely north of the Gulf states, though a few now winter even in one part of Newfoundland (*fide* S. Temple).

Status: Common fall coastal migrant, occasionally more numerous; rare to uncommon, but regular spring inland migrant. Very rare in winter along the coast.

Occurrence: Merlins are a conspicuous part of the autumn hawk flights along the coastal sand dunes and beaches of the south shore of Long Island, where they are most numerous during the latter half of September and the first half of October. Inland in late spring small numbers may be seen along the shore of Lake Ontario.

MAXIMA: *Coastal*—66 shot on Fisher's Island, Sept. 13, 1921; 60, Easthampton, Sept. 18, 1930; 110, Jones Beach, Oct. 12, 1962 (Ward), an unusually high number; 25, Jones Beach, Oct. 17, 1935.

MAXIMA: *Inland*—four, Derby Hill, Oswego Co., Apr. 22, 1962; six, Sandy Creek, Monroe Co., May 16, 1943; five, Wilson, Niagara Co., May 19, 1945.

EXTREME DATES: *Fall*—Aug. 5 to Nov. 22 (specimen). *Winter*—see following. *Spring*—late March to May 28. *Summer*—see following. Rare any time except during the months of April, May, September, and October.

Winter: There are two specimen records for Long Island: (1) one taken at Mount Sinai, Suffolk Co., Dec. 31, 1903 (Murphy, in Griscom, 1923: 198); (2) immature female found dead on the road near Jones Beach, Apr. 12, 1969, apparently spent the entire winter in the general area (Cohen). It is now a specimen in the AMNH collection, 801459.

This species is ordinarily very rare in winter, but, within the past decade, one or more have been observed each winter along the south shore of Long Island by experienced birders. During the winter of 1964–1965 several were studied carefully at coastal localities and one was seen pursuing a small flock of Sanderlings and Dunlins at Atlantic Beach, Nassau Co., Jan. 3, 1965.

I know of no corroborated occurrence in winter away from Long Island. Beardslee and Mitchell (1965: 180–181) list five winter reports in extreme western New York, but details are lacking. Eaton (1914: 102) stated, "I saw a falcon of this species chasing the pigeons from a belfry in Canandaigua [Ontario Co.] in January 1906." However, this sounds like a Peregrine Falcon. Merlins do not ordinarily "chase" pigeons, much less hang around a "belfry" during any time of year—least of all in winter.

Summer: The status of this species in the state in summer is even less known, or rather more confused, than it is in winter. I have seen *no* specimen taken in summer in any of the museums or private collections. No authentic breeding record exists for New York despite statements to the contrary in the literature. Both Eaton, and Beardslee and Mitchell mention breeding in the state, but proof

in the form of specimens or photographs of either eggs or the birds themselves is lacking. The report by the latter authorities of alleged breeding at Batavia (Genesee Co.) in the "top of a dead stub," sounds suspiciously like an American Kestrel. Moreover, Merlins nest either on the ground or in a stick nest in a tree or bush, *not* in a tree cavity. The statement in the *Kingbird* (1959, 9: 93) that "Pigeon Hawks nest in this area [Adirondacks] but so far this year none have been observed," is completely without foundation and is definitely misleading.

In sum, *Falco columbarius* is one of the most misidentified of birds, particularly by beginners. The species most apt to be confused with Merlins are the American Kestrel and Sharp-shinned Hawk.

Remarks: The name Merlin is definitely preferred to that of Pigeon Hawk, as it neither looks like a pigeon, nor does it feed on them. Merlin is used widely in the Old World, as well as in falconry.

American Kestrel
(*Falco sparverius*)　*　B

Range: Nearctic and Neotropical regions, ranging from Alaska and Canada to southern South America. Winters nearly throughout, but rare northward.

Status: Common to abundant fall coastal migrant, common to very common spring inland migrant. Local and uncommon in winter. Widespread breeder.

Nonbreeding: This species is sometimes seen in very large numbers in fall passage along the outer beaches of Long Island. It is much less numerous in spring along the shore of Lake Ontario.

MAXIMA, COASTAL: *Fall*—notably large flight on Sept. 25, 1965—500 in *three hours,* Westhampton Beach, Suffolk Co. (Yeaton); 1000, Fire Island State Park, Suffolk Co. (Davis); 500, Riis Park, Queens Co., Oct. 1, 1956; 550, Fire Island Inlet, Oct. 1, 1960; 300, Jones Beach, Nassau Co., Oct. 12, 1962. Unusual are two days at a "hawk ridge" about 50 miles from the coast, namely at Mt. Peter, Orange Co., on Sept. 11, 1965, when over 200 were

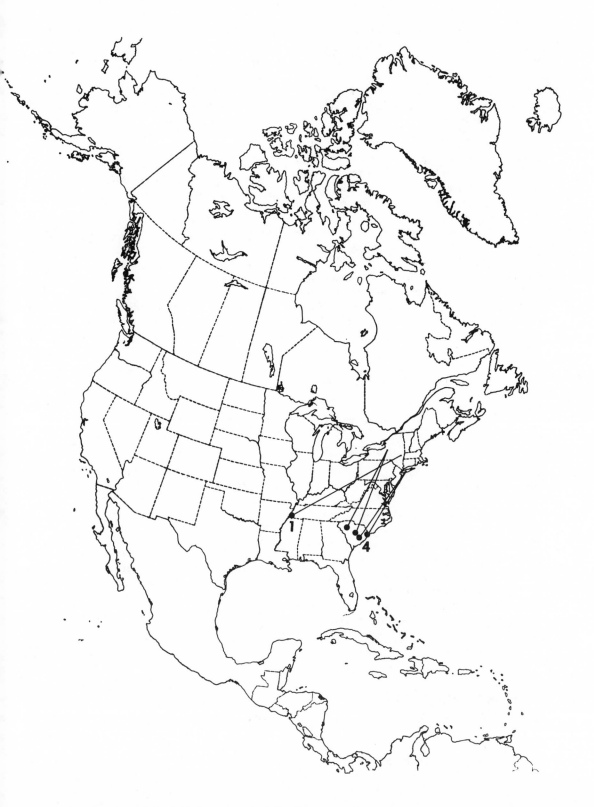

MAP 56 American Kestrel (*Falco sparverius*) Banding recoveries

estimated and again on Oct. 2, 1966, when more than 100 were observed (Bailey, *Kingbird,* 1967, 17: 129–142).

MAXIMA, INLAND: *Spring*—166, Derby Hill, Oswego Co., Mar. 31, 1967; 200, Manitou Monroe Co., Apr. 3, 1960; 113, Derby Hill, Apr. 20, 1966.

Breeding: This species is prevalent in open country, especially in agricultural districts, along roadsides, and wherever there are fields, meadows, and even swampy areas with standing dead trees. It is equally at home in such places as airports, golf courses, and city parks.

Being a hole nester, it selects such diverse sites as tree cavities, old woodpecker holes in telephone poles or fence posts, bird boxes, and building crevices. In the Rochester area one year, two pairs successfully ousted Starlings from nest boxes. In another locality a pair of these falcons bred in an abandoned Wood Duck nest box. For an unusual nesting in a Purple Martin house, see Strauss (*Kingbird,* 1968, 18: 23–24).

Heights of nest sites ranged from ten to 45 feet above ground.

Egg clutches examined in 24 New York nests were as follows: two eggs (four nests—incomplete? clutches); three eggs (two nests incomplete?); four eggs (six nests); five eggs (11 nests); seven eggs (one nest).

EGG DATES: Apr. 5 to June 29.

Nestlings: May 19 to Aug. 2; fledglings: June 13 to Aug. 10.

Banding (see Map 56): Four banded New York nestlings were recovered in South Carolina, and another near Memphis, Tennessee—all in fall or winter, following banding the preceding summer.

Remarks: Formerly called Sparrow Hawk—a group of unrelated Old World Accipiters are known as Sparrowhawks.

PHEASANTS, QUAILS — PHASIANIDAE

Seven species in New York.
Seven breed.

This family, containing more than 175 species, is of nearly worldwide distribution.

Unlike the one native turkey and three native grouse (one of them extinct) that occur in New York, two of the three members of the Phasianidae are introduced species. All seven New York species of gallinaceous birds (order Galliformes) are sedentary and breed here.

Common Bobwhite
(*Colinus virginianus*)   *   B

Range: Southern Nearctic and northern Neotropical regions east of the Rocky Mountains, ranging from Wyoming to Guatemala and from extreme southern Ontario to Cuba. Sedentary.

Status: Uncommon to rare resident at lower elevations; has greatly decreased in recent years.

Occurrence: Whereas the Ruffed Grouse has managed to hold on quite well in its woodland haunts, the Bobwhite or "Quail" has been much less fortunate. It has suffered greatly from a combination of five unfavorable factors: (1) decline of agriculture; (2) rapid destruction and subsequent development of open country; (3) excessive hunting; (4) severe winter killing (5) introduction of southern and western stock, thereby reducing the vitality of the original native population.

This species was formerly common and widely distributed, particularly at lower elevations—especially numerous on the coastal plain. It was always relatively uncommon in the interior highlands.

Eaton (1910: 361–362) stated, ". . . formerly well distributed . . . as far north as the counties of Jefferson, Oneida, Saratoga, and Washington, to an altitude of about 1000 feet, and in the southeastern portion, to an altitude of 2000 feet. At the present day [1910] it is a rare bird in all portions of the State, excepting Long Island, the lower Hudson valley, and the Delaware valley."

From the above it can be seen that it was absent from the Adirondacks and the higher Catskills.

Beardslee and Mitchell (1965: 185–186) give a good account of its former abundance, present scarcity, and numerous (mostly unsuccessful) reintroductions in extreme western New York.

Bobwhites favor farmland, brushy fields, hedgerows, and thickets, and, in winter, edges of swamps in open country.

The arched-over nest is placed on the ground, chiefly in grass or hayfields and almost always where suitable cover is available, as under bushes, among briers, and near fences or hedgerows.

Egg clutches in this species are both variable and large. In 26 New York nests, eggs range from seven to 22, with three nests each containing 11, 15, and 21 eggs.

EGG DATES: May 25 to Sept. 14.

Nestlings: June 11 to Sept. 27; fledglings: July 5 to Oct. 11. On Long Island, where there is a viable population, the species is double-brooded.

Gray Partridge
(*Perdix perdix*) * B

Range: Western Palearctic region; introduced into North America, chiefly in southern Canada and northern United States.

Status: *Introduced*—this sedentary species, often called Hungarian Partridge, has been introduced into various portions of New York State with success only in the northern parts of the St. Lawrence valley counties of Jefferson, St. Lawrence, Franklin, and a small portion of Clinton (see Map 57). This area has elevations less than 600 feet (Belknap, 1952: 80). Nearly 28,000 birds were introduced between 1927 and 1932, chiefly from Czechoslovakia (Wilson, 1959: 54). No supplemental restocking has been made since. Some of the following information has been obtained from Brown (1954), and especially from Doig (1966).

Surveys made by the New York State Conservation Department estimated 14,500 birds in 1942, and over 8000 in 1952. The most important factors in seriously reducing this population within that decade were two severe ice storms in December 1942 and again during the winter of 1946–1947.

Heavy snows, on the other hand, do not cause serious mortality, as roads are plowed after each snowfall and birds are able to obtain weed seeds and gravel on highway edges. Moreover, the area being chiefly flat, strong winds blow the snow off the ground leaving considerable portions bare, thus exposing feeding areas. However, automobiles account for some of the roadside kills.

The Gray Partridge in the St. Lawrence valley is largely restricted to lands devoted primarily to dairy farming with large acreage in grain crops, pasture, and hay. This species finds ample food in this type of agriculture and sufficient cover in the numerous hedgerows. Most favorable agricultural practices for survival of these birds is the provision of grain stubble and permanent grassland.

If summers are dry, as they most often are in the St. Lawrence River lowlands, a good breeding season is insured; but if a prolonged wet season persists, it is disastrous to breeding production.

The relatively low hunting pressure and a minimum competition from Common Pheasants in this region are conducive to Gray Partridge success.

During the ten-year period 1950–1959 a change in land use saw a general decline in harvested cropland acreage such as reduction in amount of hay, wheat, oats, and grass pasture resulting in a considerable diminution of birds. If further decline or change in agricultural methods should occur, then a corresponding decrease in the partridge population can be expected (see Belknap, *Kingbird,* 1969, 19: 96).

Midwinter roadside counts were made in a small section of Jefferson Co. where the partridge population was known to have been high (approximately two miles west to east—Depauville to Pamelia, and a similar distance north to south—Orleans Corners to Perch River). These counts were made in the eight winters of 1955–1956 to 1962–1963.

The following table (Doig, 1966) indicates

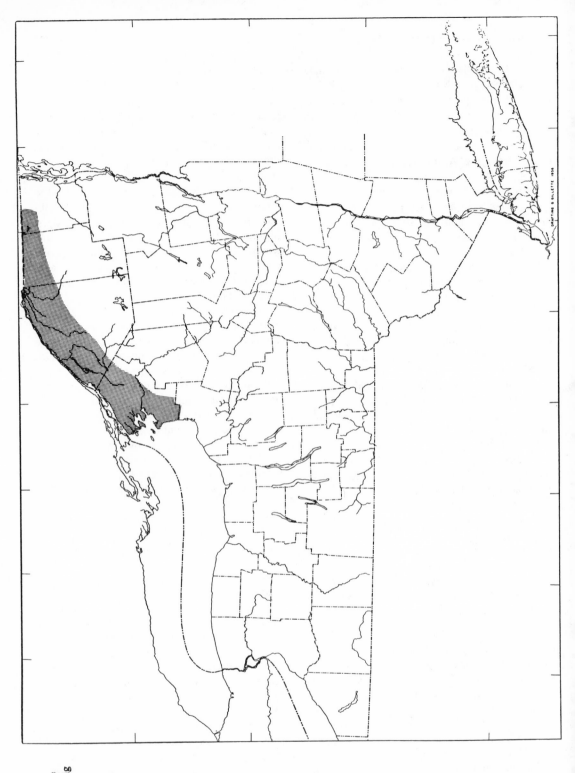

MAP 57 Gray Partridge
(*Perdix perdix*) Breeding
distribution as of 1966

considerable fluctuation from year to year, but it is important to remember that the biggest variable is the amount of snow cover.

Winter	Birds per day
1955–1956	88
1956–1957	65
1957–1958	281—peak year
1958–1959	147
1959–1960	192
1960–1961	163
1961–1962	58—low year
1962–1963	128

Farther south in the same county on the Point Peninsula, Gordon made two roadside counts: Dec. 23, 1968—188; Jan. 11, 1969—139.

Despite information on distribution and habitat within the state, I cannot find New York data on either egg dates, or those for young. However, two broods of eight and 13 juveniles have been reported.

[Chukar Partridge (*Alectoris chukar*)

Hypothetical: Southern Palearctic region from southeastern Europe east to Mongolia, China, and the western Himalayas. Introduced and established in the western United States.

Chukars were introduced in 1958 into extreme western New York in Niagara Co. and seemed to be doing fairly well up until 1962 at least (Beardslee and Mitchell, 1965: 189). However, recent releases in that area appear to be temporary and unsuccessful (Axtell, *in litt.*, 1969), contrary to the statement of Rosche (*Audubon Field Notes*, 1969, 23: 47).

The present species is considered distinct from the Rock Partridge (*Alectoris graeca*), following Watson (1962a and b) and Vaurie (1965: 47).]

Common Pheasant
(*Phasianus colchicus*)   *   B

Range: Central and eastern Palearctic region, widely introduced into various parts of the world.

Status: *Introduced*—this species was apparently first introduced into the state during the early 1890s. It has become established throughout, but is absent in the mountains, and is most numerous at lower elevations in open country, avoiding forested areas.

Pheasants frequent agricultural country, where fields with hedgerows abound, and areas bordered by swamps interspersed with numerous thickets. They breed in the former type of country but retreat into the latter during the winter months. These birds come readily to feed—especially whole and cracked corn—and are frequent visitors to well-stocked feeding stations. In many places these birds have survived heavy snows and hunting pressure.

This species is most prevalent on Long Island, in the Hudson-Mohawk valley, in the agricultural districts south of Lake Ontario, along the shore of Lake Erie, and in the Finger Lakes region.

Beardslee and Mitchell (1965: 187–188) state that the first successful introduction in western New York was in 1903 in the Genesee valley. These authors also mention that the birds are much more common in the northern lake plain counties than in the hilly regions to the south (Allegany Plateau).

In 15 New York nests examined, most of which were found in hayfields or under bushes in the vicinity of fields, egg clutch size ranged from seven to 24, with the smallest number of eggs possibly representing an incomplete clutch.

EGG DATES: Apr. 14 to July 28.

Unfledged young: June 22 to Aug. 16; fledglings: Aug. 14.

Remarks: As imported stock from several parts of Asia—involving more than one subspecies of *Phasianus colchicus*—have been liberated in New York, only the binomial is used. Much of this mixed stock represents various strains, the males of which vary from those having complete white collars to those with none. Thus the vernacular name Common Pheasant is more meaningful than Ring-necked Pheasant. Vaurie (1965: 313–314) has also used the vernacular "Common" for the same reasons.

GROUSE — TETRAONINAE

Three species in New York.
Three breed.

For discussion, see family Phasianidae. One of the above three species was the extinct Heath Hen (*Tympanuchus cupido cupido*), the eastern subspecies of the Greater Prairie Chicken (*T. c. pinnatus*).

Vaurie (1965) and Short (1967) are followed in treating the grouse as a subfamily of the Phasianidae. The 16 known species of grouse are confined to the Holarctic region.

Ruffed Grouse
(*Bonasa umbellus*)   *   B

Range: Alaska and Canada south to the United States; in the east along the coast to Virginia and in the mountains to northern Georgia. Sedentary. For distributional details in New York, see **Subspecies.**

Status: Resident throughout the wilder portions. Has become increasingly scarce in many areas.

Occurrence: The Ruffed Grouse is an inhabitant of forest clearings and edge; also cutover tracts of extensive second-growth woodland. It is equally at home in the higher Adirondack and Catskill mountains, and also at sea level in the pine-oak barrens on Long Island.

This species nests on the ground, laying its eggs usually among dead leaves at the base of a tree, near fallen timber among rock crevices, or under a brush pile.

Beardslee and Mitchell (1965: 183) tell about a nest found at East Aurora, Erie Co., May 13, 1913, that contained ten grouse eggs and eight pheasant eggs. When first discovered, a female grouse flushed off the nest. It was believed that both grouse and pheasant eggs hatched.

Egg clutches recorded in 30 New York nests ranged from seven eggs (two nests) to 15 eggs (one nest). Two nests reported to have 20 eggs apiece are most exceptional and may represent either re-nesting by the same female after initial failure, or possibly two females using the same nest.

EGG DATES: Apr. 1 to June 22.
Nestlings: May 27 to July 5; fledglings: June 15 to Sept. 4.

Subspecies: From two to four races—none of them really well differentiated—have been reported within New York. Mayr and Short (1970: 41) stressed that this species is "clinally variable and polymorphic." In these respects, the situation of the Ruffed Grouse is similar to that of the Screech Owl: (1) Both have north-south and east-west clines with the races intergrading into one another; (2) both have rufous and gray morphs with intermediates present, largely irrespective of geographical range and of sex or age.

For those interested in the subspecific variation, the revision by Aldrich and Friedmann (1943) is recommended. See also Parkes (1952) for further details.

I am not overly impressed with the differences described for the several eastern populations. Individual variation is widespread in this species. Intensity and width of ventral barring, supposedly a good character, can be matched in several "races" from different parts of the range. Other characters such as color—paler or darker—are equally variable.

I have seen "good" *togata* material, a northern subspecies, only from the Adirondack area, but no "typical" New York specimens of *monticola,* a not-very-well-marked form from the Appalachian Mountains to the south, although Parkes (*op. cit.*) examined a specimen that he assigned to *monticola* from Cattaraugus Co. As for the Long Island population called *"helmei,"* I agree with Aldrich and Friedmann (*op. cit.*) and with the A.O.U. Check-list Committee (1957) in *not* recognizing that form. In a recent paper, Hubbard and Banks (1970: 323–324) revive *"helmei,"* stating that it differs from nominate *umbellus* by having "blacker ventral barring" and by being "darker and more reddish on the breast." The barring has already been discussed; as for the darker and redder breast, a number of specimens from the adjacent mainland of Pennsylvania, New Jersey, New York, and Connecticut match or approach *"helmei"* from Long Island. The AMNH collection has eight females (males of *"helmei"* are considered inseparable from *umbellus*) of topotypical *"helmei"* from Miller's Place, Suffolk Co., taken in the 1880s and 1890s. These eight females were compared with eight females of *umbellus* from the mainland. *All* 16 specimens of the two populations are of comparable dates (both as to year and month). No marked differences could be noted, only tendencies suggesting slight variation. My colleague, Eugene Eisenmann, also examined this material and concurred.

Another factor to be considered is dilution of present-day New York stock with birds imported from other sections of the country. This admixture of several populations further complicates matters at the subspecies level.

American Spruce Grouse
(*Dendragapus canadensis*)   *   B

Range: Northern Nearctic region, breeding from Alaska and Canada to extreme northern United States. Sedentary.

Status: Local resident of the Adirondack district where rare to uncommon.

Occurrence (see Map 58): The Spruce Grouse is one of the specialties of the "north woods," and fortunate is the observer who gets more than a glimpse of it, as the bird—cryptically colored—blends into its surroundings in spruce forest. Its more numerous relative, the Ruffed Grouse, depends for survival on the element of surprise—literally flying up from under one's feet, hurtling off into the woods. However, the exceedingly tame Spruce Grouse

Fig. 40 Near Madawaska, Franklin Co., June 16, 1968. Dusting area of Spruce Grouse. Photo by Robert G. Wolk

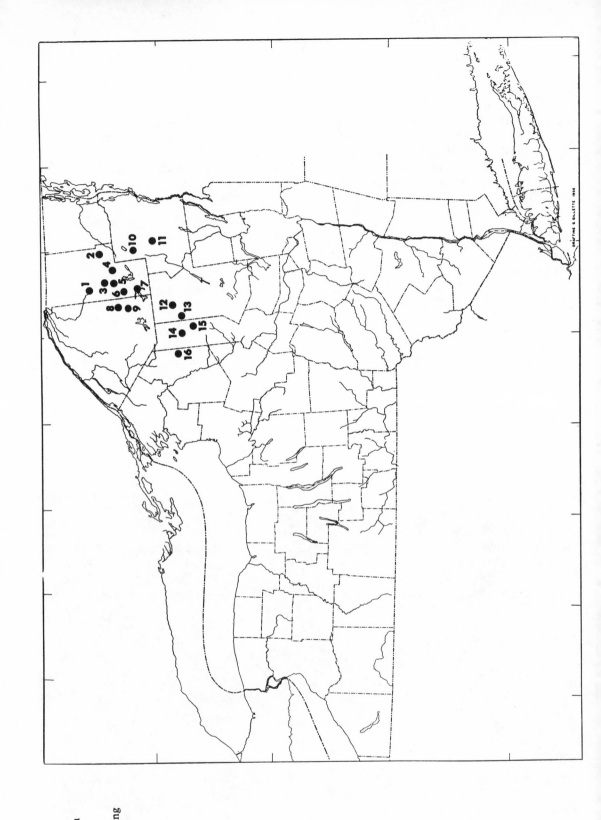

MAP 58 American
Spruce Grouse
(*Dendragapus
canadensis*) Breeding
distribution

merely walks or runs from the observer, sometimes "freezing" a short distance away, indiscernible except to the sharpest eyes. In fact, if seen at all, it is more often on the ground or low on a branch and rarely observed in flight.

In New York it is virtually confined to the wilder sections of the Adirondacks. Eaton (1910: 365) stated that ". . . it occurs only in the spruce, fir, and tamarack [larch] forests of the Adirondacks." It is not especially a bird of the high mountains, but rather of fairly level tracts at lower elevations (see Fig. 40).

A report in the *Kingbird* (1951: 35) of a "flock near Massena" is unquestionably erroneous. Spruce Grouse do not occur, let alone flock, in the mainly cultivated St. Lawrence valley lowland, at least 20 miles from the edge of the Adirondack State Park boundary. I am unaware of this species occurring even in the wild and relatively remote Tug Hill area to the west. However, there is a specimen examined by the writer in the collection of the British Museum (Natural History), 88. 10. 10. 2731, of a male taken at Watson, Lewis Co., Dec. 22, 1877, by A. J. Dayan, one of Merriam's collectors. Watson is in the Black River valley not far from Lowville. This valley separates the west slope of the Adirondacks from the eastern portion of the Tug Hill district.

Despite the *16* known New York breeding localities, I am unaware of any nest of Spruce Grouse recorded in the state. No eggs of this species from New York have been reported in the literature available, nor have I seen any eggs in numerous collections examined. Nests, if and when found in New York, are on the ground, usually at the base of a conifer—ordinarily in a dry site, but often not far from a bog or swamp. Breeding is based on both unfledged and fledged young, and of "family groups" seen by qualified observers who can tell a Spruce Grouse from a Ruffed Grouse.

Known brood size of three New York clutches are: two broods each of four young; one brood of eight young.

Dates of unfledged juveniles—June 19 to July 16; fledged young—Aug. 17 and 22.

The following *16* breeding localities are: Franklin Co.—(1) Santa Clara; (2) near Loon Lake; (3) Madawaska; (4) near Paul Smith's; (5) between Brandon and Waverly; (6) Kil-

dare; (7) near Tupper Lake (village). St. Lawrence Co.—(8) Jordan Lake; (9) near Childwold. Essex Co.—(10) Chubb River Swamp area; (11) Upper Ausable Lake. Hamilton Co.—(12) near Brandreth Lake; (13) Lake Terror. Herkimer Co.—(14) Stillwater Mtn.; (15) near Big Moose. Lewis Co.—(16) near Beaver Lake.

Remarks: The genus *Dendragapus*, rather than *Canachites*, is used here, following Short (1967). No eastern subspecies are recognized here, the poorly differentiated population called *"canace"* is based upon slight and variable characters.

[Willow Ptarmigan (*Lagopus lagopus*)

Hypothetical: Northern Holarctic region, in eastern North America breeding south to the central portions of Ontario and Quebec. Wanders casually in winter south to southern Ontario and Quebec. One record for central Maine.

In New York State what was purported to be a male in "changing plumage," was collected at Watson, Lewis Co., May 22, 1876 (R. Hough). The present whereabouts of this specimen is unknown. Coues (*Bull. Nuttall Ornith. Club,* 1878, 3: 41), who first published this report, did not examine the specimen, nor did any other ornithologist ever see it. As the specimen is unavailable, the possibility of it being an albinistic Spruce Grouse or Ruffed Grouse cannot be ruled out. Moreover, the May date is suspiciously late for a bird that is casual in *winter* in southern Canada.]

Greater Prairie Chicken; Heath Hen (*Tympanuchus cupido*) B

Extinct (eastern subspecies only): Central and eastern United States, the nominate race —known as the Heath Hen—now extinct, was resident along the coastal plain from Massachusetts to Virginia and locally inland to eastern Pennsylvania (Pocono plateau). Occurred on Martha's Vineyard until 1932.

In New York this bird was formerly common in the more open scrub oak and pine barrens of eastern and central Long Island locally west to the Hempstead Plains. It possibly occurred in similar habitat on the scrub sand plains west of Albany, but definite evidence is lacking. The Heath Hen apparently was last reported on Long Island during the late 1830s or early 1840s, but no known New York specimen exists with data.

Very little is known of this bird's disappearance within our area. Its ultimate extinction was supposedly due to excessive shooting and uncontrolled fires.

TURKEYS — MELEAGRIDINAE

One species in New York.
One breeds.

For discussion, see family Phasianidae. Only two living species of turkeys are known, the familiar one found in New York, and the very striking Ocellated Turkey (*Agriocharis ocellata*) of Yucatán and adjacent portions of Guatemala and British Honduras.

Common or Wild Turkey
(*Meleagris gallopavo*)   *   B

Range: Southern Nearctic and northern Neotropical regions, the race *silvestris* (tips of rectrices rich chestnut, primaries broadly barred with white) ranges northeast to northern Pennsylvania and southern New York (local). Formerly north to extreme southern Ontario and the central portions of New York and New England. Sedentary.

Status: Locally numerous resident in the "southern tier" counties and in the southern and western approaches to the Catskills. Very local elsewhere.

Occurrence (see Map 59): Turkeys were formerly numerous throughout much of forested New York south of a line approximating the Mohawk River valley. With the destruction of nearly all the original "southern" hardwood forest (chiefly oak-hickory-chestnut) early in the nineteenth century, this splendid species disappeared. A few individuals managed to hold on until the 1840s in the foothills of the Catskill Mountains, but these, too, vanished under heavy hunting pressure.

No "wild" turkeys were reported for the next century. Then according to Hewitt (1967: 265), "Invasion of New York State by turkeys from Pennsylvania in the late 1940s stimulated interest in management possibilities. During the 1950s, 3176 game-farm birds were released . . . The first open season was held in 1959. Releases of game-farm stock terminated in 1959, and the 1960s ushered in a period of transplanting from established wild populations. The results were gratifying. Turkeys have survived at least two winters in all areas thus far stocked . . ."

Stephen W. Eaton (1964) stated that during the spring of 1963 the four contiguous southwestern counties of Chautauqua, Cattaraugus, Allegany, and Steuben had a total of over *3300* turkeys, of which Cattaraugus alone had more than *1200*.

Eaton listed the principal autumn foods of this species as beech nuts (mast) and wild black cherries obtained from the ground; but in winter when the birds had to browse because of heavy snow cover, they fed mostly on the buds of beech and hemlock.

Turkey habitat is shown in the accompanying photograph (Fig. 40a).

Eaton was able to amass an excellent series of specimens, both adults and juveniles, but chiefly the latter for the St. Bonaventure University Museum collection—a total of 27 specimens, 21 of these from Cattaraugus Co. localities. Some of the immatures were winter-killed, probably the result of starvation, others were killed by foxes and dogs. The adults were retrieved from hunters.

That turkeys are prospering in southwestern New York is indicated by an estimate of 350

MAP 59 Wild Turkey (*Meleagris gallopavo*) Breeding distribution; hatched areas after Hewitt (1967)

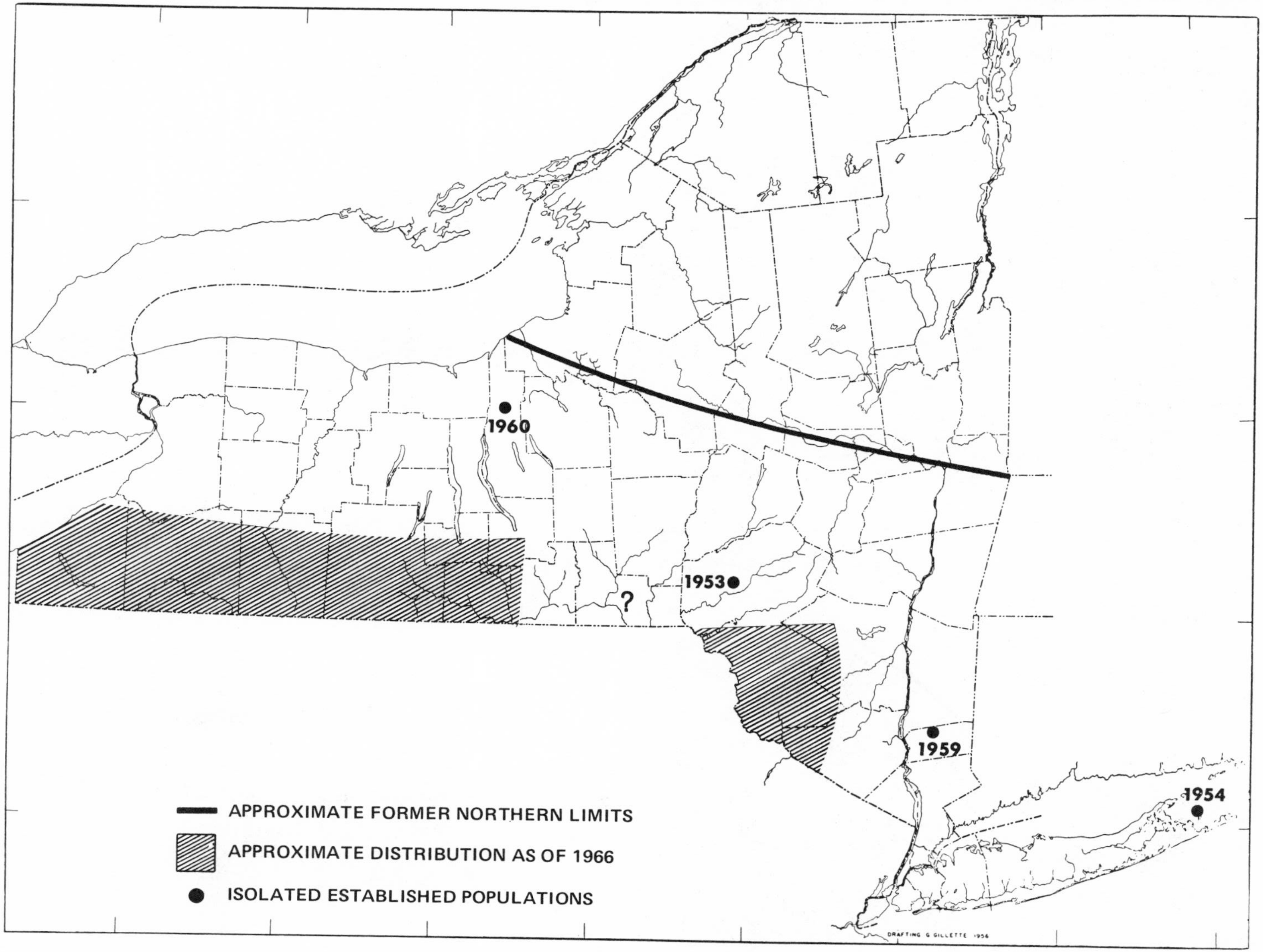
1960
1953
?
1959
1954
APPROXIMATE FORMER NORTHERN LIMITS
APPROXIMATE DISTRIBUTION AS OF 1966
ISOLATED ESTABLISHED POPULATIONS
DRAFTING G GILLETTE 1956

Fig. 40a   Bluebird nest box near Olean, Cattaraugus Co., Apr. 29, 1970. Forest edge, open slope, and fields where Wild Turkeys feed. **Photo by Ralph S. Palmer**

in the western Allegany Co. region of Cuba Lake on Nov. 11, 1966. Another 50 were observed in the Connecticut Hill area of Tompkins Co. on Mar. 15 of the same year.

In addition to the general distribution as of 1966, the accompanying map shows four peripheral localities where this species occurs today and is presumably established, with dates of reintroduction: (1) 1953, near Walton, Delaware Co.; (2) 1954, Gardiner's Island, Suffolk Co. (see Bull, 1970: 16, for details); (3) 1959, Fahnestock State Park,

Putnam Co.; (4) 1960, Howland's Island area, Cayuga Co. The question mark on the map indicates lack of detailed information on occurrence in Broome Co. and most of Tioga Co.

Turkey nests are placed on the ground in wooded regions. Fifteen New York nests contained egg clutches ranging from 10 to 20, with 12 eggs each in five nests and ten apiece in four others.

EGG DATES: Apr. 26 to July 9.

Unfledged juveniles—May 13 to Aug. 13; fledglings—June 1 to Sept. 7.

CRANES — GRUIDAE

One species in New York.
None breed.

Although this family (15 species) is widespread and is absent only from tropical America (except Cuba) and the Malayan-Indonesian subregion, nevertheless some of the species

have a relict distribution and not a few are extremely rare and on the endangered species list. The cranes are an ancient group, with over 30 fossil forms known. Today the family is best represented in Asia with no fewer than nine kinds there.

The only species occurring in New York is

the Sandhill Crane (*Grus canadensis*), merely a vagrant here.

[Whooping Crane (*Grus americana*)

Hypothetical: In recent years of local and very rare occurrence in western North America, formerly east to the Mississippi valley region.

As far as our area is concerned, there is no proof that it ever occurred. No specimen or other evidence exists. The often-quoted remarks of De Vries mentioning "White Cranes" occurring on the coast of New York Bay in the 1600s could have been white herons (egrets) which many people called, and still call, "cranes." Moreover, De Vries was an explorer and historian, not an ornithologist.]

Sandhill Crane
(*Grus canadensis*) *

Range: Breeds from northeastern Siberia east to Baffin Island; south locally, in the west to southern Colorado, and in the east to southeastern Michigan; also resident in extreme southeastern United States and Cuba. Winters north to the southern portions of California and Texas, occasionally farther. Wanders east to the Atlantic coast from Prince Edward Island to South Carolina.

Status: *Very rare*—in New York there are no less than 11 occurrences, all single individuals, ten from upstate areas, one from downstate. Of these, four are based on specimens—one of

which is extant—another was photographed: (1) collected, Utica, 1873 (Bagg); (2) collected, Albion, Orleans Co., about 1880 (Posson); (3) collected, town of Clarendon, Orleans Co., May 20, 1885 (Posson); (4) one with Great Blue Herons, Montezuma Refuge, July 30, 1948 (Fischer, Chalif, *et al.*); (5) adult near Pleasant Lake, town of Schroeppel, Oswego Co., May 16, 1965 (Scheider); (6) one near Delhi, Delaware Co., Nov. 11, 1966 (L. Clark); (7) one observed and photographed feeding chiefly in a cornfield on a dairy farm near Whitehall, Washington Co., from mid-February to Apr. 26, 1967 (Bullock, Bartlett, Sabin, *et al.*), the only winter occurrence; (8) one on a farm five miles north of Kinderhook, Columbia Co., Nov. 12–19, 1967 (Reilly, *et al.*); (9) male illegally shot at Montezuma Refuge, Nov. 13, 1968, specimen in CUM collection, 33179, prepared by A. Weisbrod and identified as the race *tabida* (larger than the northernmost nominate race and paler than the southeastern population) by G. Archibald. This bird was first seen feeding with Canada Geese in plowed fields on Oct. 20, 1968 (Sweet and Jacobs); (10) an individual at Hook Mtn., Rockland Co., Apr. 30, 1970 (E. and L. Mills); (11) one seen and heard, Virgil, Cortland Co., May 31, 1970 (K. Wood).

For photographs of the Whitehall bird and the second occurrence at Montezuma, see Scheider (*Kingbird*, 1969, 19: 74–76).

Note that *seven* of the occurrences were within only *six* years (1965–1970).

Remarks: The A.O.U. Check-list (1957: 151) mentions an occurrence "near Cohoes," Albany Co., but no details are given.

RAILS — RALLIDAE

Ten species in New York.
Seven breed.

This widespread cosmopolitan family (over 130 species) includes coots and gallinules, as well as rails. The last-named have radiated all

over the world, including many of the remotest islands in mid-ocean. However, many of these insular forms, through isolation and loss of flight, had become so specialized that when white man and other predators introduced by him arrived on these islands, many of the flightless rails succumbed to their ravages and were either exterminated or dangerously reduced in numbers. As a result more species of rails have suffered than those of any other family.

Unlike rails and gallinules, many of which are nocturnal or crepuscular, and are secretive and hide in marshes or skulk in the undergrowth of dense thickets (land rails), coots are mainly diurnal and live in open water like ducks, retiring to the reeds only to lay their eggs.

Clapper Rail
(*Rallus longirostris*)   *   B

Range: Nearctic and Neotropical regions, breeding on the Pacific coast from California to Peru and on the Atlantic and Gulf coasts from Connecticut (rarely Massachusetts) and Long Island to Brazil. Sedentary and migratory.

Status: Common to locally abundant breeder on the coast, but rare and local on eastern Long Island and in recent years rare on Staten Island, and in Bronx and Westchester counties. Regular, but uncommon in winter on Long Island. Confined to salt marsh.

Nonbreeding: A few Clapper Rails are reported each winter on the south-shore marshes of Long Island.

This species is very rarely recorded away from salt water. A specimen taken in Central Park, New York City, Oct. 17, 1888 (Richardson), CUM 1622, was apparently never previously published. Another collected many years ago on the Hudson River at Ossining, Westchester Co. (Fisher), is no longer extant. In addition there is a sight report from Central Park and three observations in Prospect Park, Brooklyn.

Breeding (see Map 60): The Clapper Rail is confined to the salt marsh environment and is particularly numerous on the south side of Long

Fig. 41 Clapper Rail nest and nine eggs, near Sayville, Suffolk Co., summer of 1954. Salt marsh growth of *Spartina alterniflora*. Actual nest about 20 inches above mud. Note runway and ramp to nest constructed by birds. Photo by William Post

MAP 60 Clapper Rail
(*Rallus longirostris*)
Breeding distribution

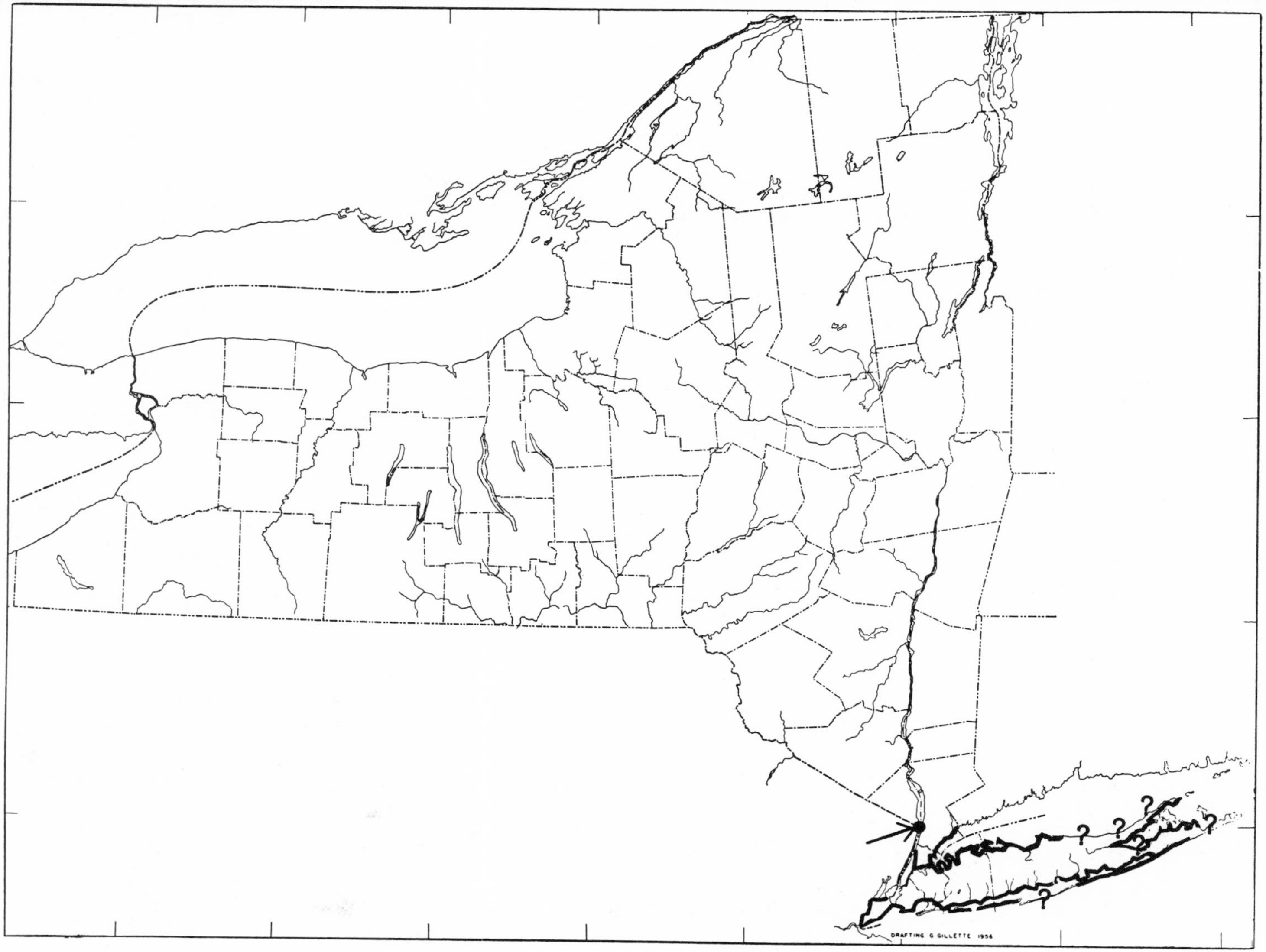

Island west of Great South Bay. The broad salt meadows stretching from the Jamaica Bay area east to Oak Beach, Suffolk Co., are the chief breeding grounds in the state, where several hundred pairs nest. The abundant fiddler crabs (*Uca*) comprise one of their chief food items. On the north shore this species is much less numerous and more local. For further details as to breeding distribution around New York City, see Bull (1964: 172–173). A pair of these birds bred on the west bank of the Hudson River at Piermont, Rockland Co., in 1959 (Gamble), its farthest known penetration inland.

In the town of Hempstead wetlands in southern Nassau Co., MacNamara and Udell (1970) found nearly *200* nests in 1965, *58* of which were discovered within a one-week period from May 9 to May 15. Of *115* nests examined by them, 39 were located in *Spartina patens,* 29 in mixed *Spartina alterniflora* and *Phragmites communis,* 21 under the shrubs *Iva, Baccharis,* and *Myrica* (bayberry), 11 in *Phragmites* in relatively "dry" situations, eight in medium or tall growths of *S. alterniflora,* and two on miscellaneous objects in the salt marsh, such as on top of a piling and on an abandoned cane chair.

MacNamara and Udell (*op. cit.*) stated that, "The nest consists of matted grass sedge and is built up to a height of from 6 to 15 inches above the floor of the meadow, and it is sometimes arched over above by the growing grass amongst which it is built."

These birds frequently construct an elevated platform for the nest up to 20 inches above water level and a runway from the ground to the nest platform (see Fig. 41).

MacNamara and Udell found *80* nests with eggs of which clutch sizes ranged from three (incomplete sets) to 13 eggs. The great majority of these 80 nests (68) contained the following clutches: seven and nine eggs (19 nests each); ten and 11 eggs (15 nests each).

Egg clutches in 23 other New York nests ranged from eight eggs (three nests) to 14 eggs (two nests), with ten eggs found in seven nests.

EGG DATES: Apr. 11 to Aug. 4 and 20 (renesting).

Nestlings: June 6 to Aug. 20; fledglings: no New York data.

Subspecies: The most northern race *crepitans,* discussed above, is like other populations from the United States in being considerably larger than nominate *longirostris* from northern South America. However, the color differences between *crepitans* and the form immediately to the south—"*waynei*" from North Carolina to Florida—are very slight and in the writer's opinion not worthy of recognition. In addition there is a great amount of individual variation.

King Rail (*Rallus [longirostris?] elegans*) * B

Range: Nearctic and northern Neotropical regions—chiefly eastern North America, breeding from the Great Lakes, New York, and Massachusetts to the Gulf coast of Mexico and Cuba. Winters nearly throughout, but rare in the northern portions. Sedentary and migratory.

Status: Rare to uncommon in late fall and winter, chiefly along the coast, but a little-known migrant. Rare and local breeder, chiefly in fresh-water marshes; perhaps overlooked.

Nonbreeding: This "species" is probably seen, caught alive, or found dead more often during the winter months than at any other time of the year. I know of at least *18* winter specimens taken in New York—15 of these from coastal areas, 11 of which were collected on the salt marshes (seven caught in muskrat traps). The writer was fortunate on one occasion (Jan. 2, 1960) to observe two King Rails and one Clapper Rail feeding together on a mud flat adjacent to salt marsh at Lawrence, Nassau Co.

Three winter specimens, two of them preserved, from the interior of the state were taken very recently: (1) one freshly killed, New York Thruway at the Montezuma Marshes, Jan. 6, 1960 (Genesee Ornith. Soc. field trip); (2) male present at Belmont, Allegany Co., from early December 1962 to Feb. 19, 1963, on which date it was found dead under the ice and snow (Burton, *Kingbird,* 1963, 13: 97–98), specimen in the St. Bonaventure University Museum collection; (3) one caught alive in a corn field at Elma, Erie Co., Dec. 31, 1967 (Schafer), specimen in BMS collection.

Presumed migrants are present in April, October, and November.

Breeding (see Map 61): The King Rail is to

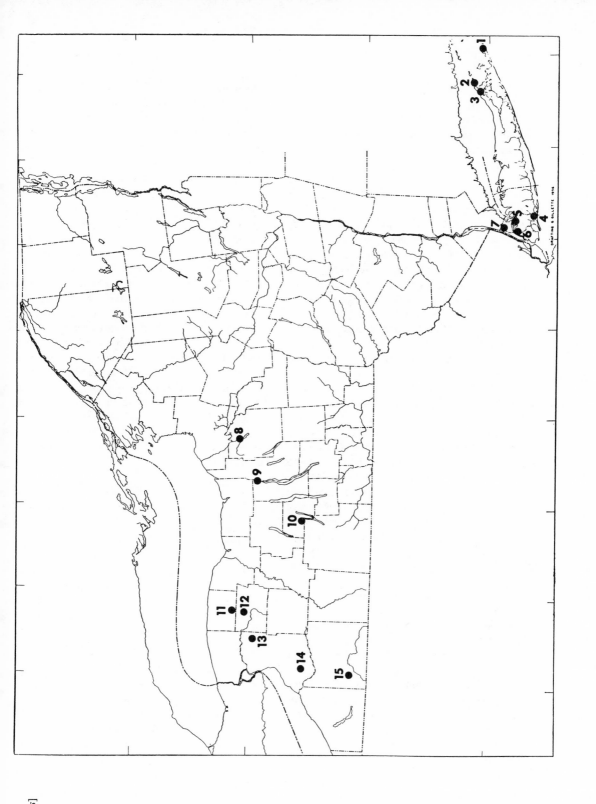

MAP 61 King Rail
(*Rallus* [*longirostris*]
elegans) Breeding
distribution

the interior fresh-water marshes what the Clapper Rail is to the coastal salt meadows; however, the former also breeds on the coast. The two forms are unquestionably closely related (see **Remarks).**

As may be seen on the accompanying map, there are two breeding populations: (A) coastal, with seven known localities; (B) inland, with eight known localities:

(A) *Coastal:* Suffolk Co.—(1) Reed Pond, Montauk, 1949 (Helmuth); (2) Orient, 1952 and 1954 (Latham); (3) Greenport, 1925 (Latham). Nassau Co.—(4) Lawrence, 1954 (Bull). Queens Co.—(5) Bayside, 1924 (Hamilton and Wright); (6) Astoria, 1922 (Schott). Bronx Co.—(7) Van Cortlandt Park, 1927 (Cruickshank). For further details, see Bull (1964: 169–171).

(B) *Inland:* Onondaga Co.—(8) North Syracuse, 1960 (Rusk). Cayuga Co.—(9) Montezuma Marshes, 1949 (Chapin). Yates Co.— (10) Keuka Lake, near Branchport, 1941 (Burtch). Orleans Co.—(11) Tonawanda Swamp, near West Barre, 1902 and 1909 (Reinecke and Frankenstein). Genesee Co.—(12) Oak Orchard Swamp, near Oakfield, 1930 (Savage, *et al.*). Erie Co.—(13) near Akron, 1953 (Beardslee, *et al.*); (14) near Langford, 1959 (numerous observers). Cattaraugus Co. —(15) East Randolph, 1918 (Wheeler), set of eggs, AMNH collection, apparently not published previously. For further details on some of these inland records, see Beardslee and Mitchell (1965: 194–195).

Of nine New York nests examined, five were situated in cattails, one in *Phragmites,* and one in a potato field near salt marsh. The habitat of the other two nests was not stated. The nests in marshes are placed a few inches above water level.

These nine nests contained clutches varying from nine eggs (two nests) to 14 eggs (one nest), with three nests containing 12 eggs apiece.

EGG DATES: May 24 to July 3.

Nestlings: June 16 to Aug. 6; fledglings: Aug. 2 to Aug. 31.

Remarks: The taxonomy and relationships of the King-Clapper Rail complex are very confused and badly in need of revision. Whether one or two species are involved is a moot question. Even those who recognize two are in disagreement as to which subspecies apply to which species. It seems to this writer that both Peters (1934) and Hellmayr and Conover (1942) were correct in placing the rufous, inland, fresh-water marsh populations of the western and southwestern United States and Mexico, with the morphologically similar King Rail, rather than with the grayish, coastal, salt-marsh populations of the Clapper Rail as was done by Ridgway and Friedmann (1941), and by the A.O.U. Check-list Committee (1957).

For those who consider the two forms conspecific on the basis of existing hybrids, see Dickerman (*Wilson Bull.*, 1971, 83: 49–50), and Ripley (in prep.). It must be admitted that these two birds are quite similar as to size, pattern, and even to color with a certain amount of overlap. The slight differences are of degree. Moreover, their vocalizations are virtually identical. The otherwise very similar eggs (size and pattern) are buffy in the Clapper Rail, whitish in the King Rail. The downy young are likewise exceedingly similar. For further discussion, see Bull (1964: 171, 173) and Meanley (1969).

More field study of these birds in contact zones is necessary to ascertain extent of hybridization.

Virginia Rail
(*Rallus limicola*)   *   B

Range: Local in the Nearctic and Neotropical regions; breeding from (1) southern Canada to California, Arizona, and New Mexico in the west, and to northern Alabama and North Carolina in the east; (2) central Mexico; (3) northwestern South America. Winters—in the eastern portions—north to Massachusetts and New York (rarely).

Status: Fairly common migrant. Rare but regular in winter on the coast, much rarer inland. Widespread breeder at lower elevations, absent in the higher mountains.

Nonbreeding: The Virginia Rail is regular in spring and fall, but as it occurs both summer and winter, it is difficult to give arrival and departure dates, though it is generally scarce before mid-April.

MAXIMA: *Spring*—eight, Round Pond, Monroe Co., May 17, 1959; *Fall*—seven, Mecox and Shinnecock bays, Suffolk Co., Sept. 7,

Fig. 42 Salt marsh (*Spartina*) breeding habitat of Virginia Rails, Oak Beach, Suffolk Co., June 17, 1969. Photo by William Post

1929; nine, Skaneateles, Onondaga Co., Sept. 8, 1957.

In *winter* this species is reported regularly in small numbers near the coast. Latham found a total of *six* dead or dying Virginia Rails in the Orient region, Suffolk Co., from Dec. 21, 1919, to Feb. 1, 1920. In the lower Hudson valley, Nolan observed *four* feeding together in a marsh on Constitution Island, Putnam Co., Jan. 2, 1956. These numbers are, however, most unusual, as ordinarily only one individual is noted at a given locality. Upstate this species is much rarer and is not recorded each winter. Nevertheless, on three occasions two individuals per locality were reported.

Breeding: Nests in both inland fresh-water marshes and coastal salt meadows (see Fig. 42). Virginia Rails are especially plentiful upstate in the extensive Montezuma Marshes and in the Oak Orchard Swamp area. Inland nests are situated in cattails or on grass tussocks from ground level to six inches above the water line.

In their study on Long Island of a 25-acre *unditched* salt marsh (chiefly *Spartina alterniflora*) at Oak Beach, Suffolk Co., Post and Enders (1970) estimated 11 breeding pairs in 1968 and discovered eight nests, six of which were domed. The nests were placed a few inches above water level on a "platform" of grass stems.

Egg clutches in 41 New York nests varied from six to 11: six eggs (five nests); seven eggs (four nests); eight eggs (nine nests); nine eggs (ten nests); ten eggs (12 nests); 11 eggs (one nest).

EGG DATES: May 5 to July 15.

Unfledged young: May 22 to Aug. 14; fledglings: July 23 to Sept. 8.

Sora Rail
(*Porzana carolina*) * B

Range: Nearctic region, breeding from central Canada to southwestern United States, but in the east only as far south as Pennsylvania, New Jersey, and Long Island (formerly); rarely farther south. Winters north to New York and New England.

Status: Fairly common fall migrant, formerly more numerous. Rare in winter on the coast, very rare inland. Local breeder, greatly decreased in recent years (since 1900) and not definitely breeding on Long Island since 1935.

Nonbreeding: In former times Sora Rails were hunted in huge numbers during fall passage, when "hundreds" were shot in a day. However, a bag of half-a-dozen would be considered good today.

MAXIMA: Seven shot, 20 more flushed by a hunter in *Spartina* salt marsh near Lattingtown, Nassau Co. (north shore), Sept. 14, 1953 (*fide* W. Post); six struck the Westhampton Air Force Base tower, Suffolk Co., Oct. 5, 1954; 18, Mecox Bay, Suffolk Co., Oct. 11, 1930; 12, Buck Pond, Monroe Co., Oct. 24, 1953.

Spring: The peak is in May but not in any numbers away from the breeding grounds. Arrival at this season is rarely before mid-April.

Winter: There are three old Long Island specimen records, two in late December, one in early January. Upstate there are two specimen records: (1) picked up in the snow at Buffalo, Mar. 6, 1900; (2) caught in a muskrat trap at Montezuma, Jan. 9, 1960.

Breeding: Soras are restricted to fresh-water marshes where they nest in cattails or sedges, the partially domed nests placed from six inches to more than one foot above water level.

Egg clutches in 34 New York nests ranged from six (incomplete set?) to 17 (two nests). Seven nests held 13 eggs each, followed by four nests containing eight eggs apiece, and four more with 14 eggs each.

EGG DATES: Apr. 30 to July 17.

Unfledged young: May 19 to Aug. 8; fledglings: June 9 to Sept. 15.

This species has decreased considerably in the northeast since the turn of the century. This is especially the case on and near the coast of Long Island, which incidentally lies near its known southern breeding limits. Only six Long Island breeding localities have been reported, four on the north shore, two on the south shore at the extreme west end: Suffolk Co.—(1) Gardiner's Island; (2) Fort Salonga. Nassau Co.—(3) Mill Neck. Queens Co.—(4) Long Island City; (5) Idlewild. Kings Co.—(6) Dyker Beach, Brooklyn. It has been unrecorded as a breeder on Long Island for over 35 years.

In Massachusetts, too, it has been steadily decreasing. Griscom and Snyder (1955: 83) stated, "Formerly nested on Martha's Vineyard and Cape Cod; no recent breeding evidence from these localities."

Although fairly widely distributed upstate in suitable marshes, it is nowhere really common, unless it be in the vast Montezuma and Oak Orchard areas. I know of no recent breeding

estimates from these two regions, however. A statewide breeding survey of this species would seem to be in order.

An idea of its former abundance in the Tonawanda Swamp (=Oak Orchard) may be seen from the account by the veteran egg collector D. C. Gillett (*Ool.,* 1897, 14: 21–23), who found *35* nests. He stated that these birds nested in habitat similar to that of the Virginia Rail, but unlike that species, the Sora was much shyer and incubating birds were very rarely seen.

Yellow Rail
(*Coturnicops noveboracensis*)   *

Range: Nearctic region, breeding chiefly in southern Canada (eastern Alberta east to New Brunswick, but *not* Nova Scotia), rarely and very locally to northeastern Ohio, but *not* New England states (Bull, 1964: 175). In the east winters mainly in the Gulf states, exceptionally north along the coast to Long Island and Rhode Island (specimens).

Status: Rare but probably regular fall migrant, undoubtedly overlooked; very rare in spring. Four winter specimens on the coast.

Occurrence: The Yellow Rail is a very elusive and secretive creature skulking in *grassy* meadows and marshes, occasionally in upland fields. Many observers have never seen one alive and the vast majority of state records are based on specimens taken primarily during the fall hunting season—usually with the aid of trained "rail" dogs. For details of sightings in coastal marshes, see Bull (1964: 175–176).

More than half of the 50 or so specimens taken in New York are extant. The majority of these are in the American Museum collection and are from Long Island. At least half of these 50 specimens were taken in the months of September and October, the period of principal occurrence. In contrast there are but eight spring specimens—only a few preserved.

During their nocturnal migrations rails sometimes get stranded in large cities and the Yellow Rail is no exception. Two instances of this in recent years are: (1) Adult caught alive in a small grassy plot at the foot of Manhattan Bridge, New York City, Oct. 18, 1962 (Cohen), banded and released at Jamaica Bay

Refuge later that day (Mrs. J. Bull), see *King-bird* (1967, 17: 2–3). (2) Immature captured alive in downtown Jamestown, Nov. 30, 1967 (Sundell and Kibler), died later—specimen in BMS collection; see *Kingbird* (1968, 18: 30). This latter record is the latest fall occurrence in the interior of the state and the second latest in fall for the entire state (see Extreme dates).

EXTREME DATES, all based on coastal specimens: *Fall*—Aug. 27 to Dec. 4. *Spring*—Mar. 30 to Apr. 29. In addition a specimen taken at Braddock's Bay, Monroe Co., "June" 1880 (collector not stated), is NYSM 283. An exceptionally early individual—with the white wing-patches observed—flushed from the marshes at the mouth of Crooked Creek, St. Lawrence Co., Aug. 11, 1936 (Hyde).

Winter—four Long Island specimens, as follows: Sayville, Suffolk Co., Jan. 17, 1894 (Dutcher); Seaford, Nassau Co., Jan. 10, 1909 (Peavey); Islip, Suffolk Co., Feb. 22, 1929 (Ritchie), all in AMNH collection; Orient, Suffolk Co., Jan. 1, 1956 (Latham), NYSM collection.

Remarks: No proof of breeding exists in New York. The following appears in the *Auk* (1962, 79: 698–701): "Several years earlier [late 1950s] Dr. Allen had found a nest in the marsh at the head of Cayuga Lake [near Ithaca] that *almost certainly* was that of a Yellow Rail" (italics mine). There is no evidence in the form of a nest, eggs, or nestlings in any collection to substantiate the above nor, as far as I am aware, were photographs taken or even birds seen, only of birds *heard*.

Finally, the famous "mystery kicker" call, for many years attributed to both the Yellow and Black rails with varying degrees of confidence—but without either species actually seen while giving this call—was proved to belong to the Virginia Rail (Callin, 1968; also Reynard and Harty, 1968).

Black Rail
(*Laterallus jamaicensis*)   *   B

Range: Locally distributed as a breeder in the Nearctic and Neotropical regions—(1) Pacific coast of Peru and Chile; also western Argentina (de Schauensee, 1966: 79); (2) Pacific

coast of southern California and Baja California; (3) Atlantic coast from Connecticut to Florida; (4) inland from Kansas east to Ohio, also in Florida.

The supposed breeding records given in the A.O.U. Check-list (1957: 158) for Hazardville, Conn., and Chatham, Mass., are erroneous (Bull, 1964: 177).

Status: Restricted to the south shore of Long Island where rare to uncommon and decidedly local. Not certainly known from elsewhere in the state.

Nonbreeding: The elusive and secretive Black Rail has been seen by relatively few observers. Only by numerous visits to the salt meadows along the south shore of Long Island—in the *Spartina* community—does the student catch a glimpse of this much-sought-after species. This bird has been reliably reported by experienced observers from Dyker Beach (Brooklyn), Kings Co., east to Napeague, Suffolk Co.

EXTREME DATES: Apr. 19 to Oct. 29.

Specimen data: Of four specimens taken on Long Island from 1879 to 1910 (Bull, 1964: 177), the only specimen apparently extant and examined by me is an adult collected at South Oyster Bay, near Gilgo Island, Suffolk Co., Aug. 1, 1884 (Foster), AMNH 64596.

Breeding: The following breeding information is taken from my book (Bull, *op. cit.*): "The only definite breeding evidence for our area is the same as that reported in Cruickshank (1942). A nest was located in 'thick sedges and narrow-leaved cattail' at Oak Beach, June 20, 1937 (Carleton). The nest contained eight eggs, of which five hatched. The young were observed on June 27. On July 5 the deserted nest and three remaining eggs were collected, and are AMNH 454. At Long Beach during the same year four young were banded on June 30 (Mrs. Beals). Mayer found a nest with nine eggs at nearby Lido Beach, July 12, 1940. These last two nests were situated in short-grass salt marsh (*Spartina patens*) resembling the habitat in southern New Jersey where numerous nests of Black Rails have been found. It seems remarkable that three nests were found in two years, and none before or since. The species has undoubtedly been overlooked."

I strongly suspect that the observations of Black Rails in the salt marshes in the Moriches

Bay area, Suffolk Co., Sept. 9, 1939 (Cadbury and Cruickshank), and Sept. 12, 1953 (Grant), were of birds reared locally, that is, family groups, because of the numbers involved—*ten* on the former date, *six* on the latter. For a species at its northernmost limits (except for two old Connecticut nesting records—both at Saybrook—1876 and 1884, Sage, *et al.*, 1913: 51), these numbers would hardly represent migrants or wanderers.

More than thirty years have elapsed since Carleton found a nest with eggs at Oak Beach (see above). Post and Enders (1969) spent much time in these marshes during the spring and summer of 1968, where they succeeded in capturing and banding *five* Black Rails. One was caught at night in a mist net on May 4; the others were trapped as follows: two on May 23 (color photographs) and one on June 17 and June 20. They saw and heard birds repeatedly through the summer. Although no nests were located, Post and Enders estimated that three pairs bred in 1968 and possibly up to five pairs in 1971. Their study area consisted of 25 acres of unditched salt marsh, 90% containing *Spartina alterniflora*, bordered by *Phragmites communis*. Virginia Rails also bred in this marsh, but in the wetter portions.

EGG DATES: June 20 to July 12.

Remarks: No satisfactory record, dead or alive, exists for the Black Rail in New York, other than on Long Island. Specimens, purportedly this species, mentioned by Eaton (1910: 282), and by Beardslee and Mitchell (1965: 199), are not known to be extant and apparently were never examined critically by a competent ornithologist.

Sight reports listed by the same authorities were not confirmed, nor were those mentioned in the *Kingbird* (1957, 7: 64; and 1960, 10: 196), the latter without details and not even the name of the observer. Still another report from the same journal (1966, 16: 34), a specimen alleged to be this species was most unfortunately accidentally destroyed and not even a photograph to substantiate the occurrence. Finally, and I am forced to repeat once again (*Kingbird*, 1962, 12: 151), an alleged breeding record for Chenango Co. made from a car by a single observer without any corroborative evidence is considered unsatisfactory also.

Needless to state, the downy black young of both the Virginia Rail and Sora Rail are frequently misidentified as Black Rails by inexperienced observers, just as downy black chicks of the Clapper Rail are often misidentified as Black Rails on Long Island by inexperienced observers.

Suffice it to say that a *preserved* specimen or a *sharp* color photograph of a Black Rail from inland New York is essential before accepting a *bona fide* record of this little-known species and admitting it to the mainland portion of the state.

Corn Crake (*Crex crex*)   *

Range: Northern and central Eurasia. Winters south to central and southern Africa. Vagrant in Greenland. Has wandered to Bermuda and along the east coast of North America south to Maryland.

Status: *Casual*—there are six specimen records from New York, five of these from Long Island: (1) Long Island (no locality or date, collected by G. Smith), AMNH 12537; (2) Oakdale, Suffolk Co., Nov. 2, 1880 (Fraser), AMNH 64959, "Shot at the foot of the uplands where they join the meadows in heavy cover"; (3) Near Cohoes, Albany Co., Nov. 5, 1883 (Drommer), NYSM 463, "Collected in a cabbage field along the Mohawk River"; (4) Amagansett, Suffolk Co., Aug. 18, 1885 (Dutcher collection), AMNH 64858, "Shot on dry upland with meadowlarks"; (5) Montauk, Suffolk Co., Nov. 1, 1888 (Dutcher collection, AMNH 64860, "Secured about three miles west of the Point in a meadow while shooting quail"; (6) Orient, Suffolk Co., Nov. 2, 1963 (Latham), NYSM 24890, "Shot by a pheasant hunter in a field of young rye 200 yards from salt marsh."

Note that four of the above specimens were taken during the first week of November and that four were taken within a nine-year period (1880–1888). The 1963 record is the first in 75 years.

No sight report has been adequately confirmed.

The Corn Crake is primarily a bird of grasslands. It has decreased markedly in the past 70 years, particularly in the British Isles and to a lesser extent on the continent (Europe).

According to Witherby, *et al.* (1941), Norris (1947), and Haartman (1958), it has become scarce chiefly because of present-day methods of mowing by machine and mowing earlier in the season when the birds are nesting. In the few areas where mowing is still done by hand, the species is reported as flourishing.

Purple Gallinule
(*Porphyrula martinica*)   *

Range: Chiefly Neotropical region, breeding north along the coast to South Carolina; locally inland to Tennessee and very rarely in central Ohio. Winters from the Gulf states southward.

Status: *Very rare*—in New York State there are over two dozen occurrences, of which only four were verified from upstate. These latter are: (1) Immature taken on the Montezuma Marshes, Oct. 1, 1931 (Parker), mounted specimen was in his collection (*Kingbird,* 1952, 2: 57); (2) adult observed at Beaver Meadow Refuge, Wyoming Co., Apr. 27 to June 9, 1963 (Busselle and numerous observers), color photographed by Mitchell; (3) adult captured alive, but exhausted, was banded near Binghamton, May 16, 1970, and subsequently released there on June 6, 1970 (Marsi, *Kingbird,* 1970, 20: 179); (4) immature caught alive near Scottsville, Monroe Co., Oct. 4, 1970 (Brown), specimen sent to the Seneca Park zoo, Rochester (*Goshawk,* 1970, 26: 65).

Most of the records from downstate are on Long Island. Details of most of these, including six specimen records, are found in Bull (1964: 179).

Since 1964 there have been four more downstate occurrences, two of them specimens within two years—details as follows: (1) Immature found alive, but injured, on the Westhampton golf course, Suffolk Co., Sept. 23, 1965 (Maxwell), taken to the Quoque Wildlife Sanctuary where it died on Sept. 27 and is now a specimen, AMNH 785878; (2) adult found dead on road—apparently freshly killed—Montauk, Suffolk Co., Nov. 18, 1967 (Hemmerich), AMNH 792679.

EXTREME DATES: Apr. 9 to Nov. 18.

Common Gallinule
(*Gallinula chloropus*)   *   B

Range: Nearly cosmopolitan, but somewhat local; in eastern North America breeding north to extreme southern Canada and northern New England. Sedentary and migratory, wintering north to New York and southern New England (rarely).

Status: Fairly common, but local migrant; rare but regular in winter on the coast. Local breeder at lower elevations, but occasionally numerous.

Nonbreeding: As gallinules frequent thick marsh growth more than coots do, they are seen in much smaller numbers. The 100 and 200 reported from the Montezuma Marshes in September of different years undoubtedly represent some breeding birds, as they are numerous there during the summer.

Ordinarily rare in winter, these birds are reported annually on the south shore of Long Island, usually only one or two being seen at one time. Even rarer upstate, nevertheless a few are reported from the Great Lakes. For instance, two were reported at the Tifft Street Marsh at Buffalo from Jan. 5 to 21, 1947; even more unusual were *five* individuals seen along the Genesee River near Rochester, Dec. 31, 1967 (Tetlow). The species usually arrives in mid-April and departs by mid-November.

Breeding: The distribution of this species in the state is similar to that of the Pied-billed Grebe, but unlike the latter it is absent as a breeder in the mountains. Although near the northern limits of the range, Common Gallinules breed commonly, but locally, in the Hudson-Mohawk valleys, and in the Lake Champlain and St. Lawrence River lowlands virtually north to the Canadian border. In the last two mentioned areas these birds breed in the marshes at King's Bay, Clinton Co., and at Wilson Hill Refuge, St. Lawrence Co. In the marshes near Ticonderoga, Essex Co., in 1932, Geoffrey Carleton found six breeding pairs, and in the Vischer's Ferry area, Saratoga Co., Guy Bartlett counted *11* nests in 1938. Naturally the larger the marsh, the greater the number of breeding pairs.

In the vast Montezuma complex in 1970, Clayton Hardy, refuge manager, estimated that *100* pairs brought off a minimum of *400* young.

Common Gallinules breed chiefly in marshes with an abundance of cattail, pickerel weed, bur-reed, arum, and buttonbush, but require a certain amount of open water in which to swim. They readily come out on land and also climb bushes as well, but less so than Purple Gallinules.

Nests are often placed in the aforementioned aquatic growths from three inches to a foot or more above water level. One New York nest was free-floating on dead cattail stalks and other debris.

Egg clutches in 43 New York nests contained from five eggs (incomplete sets) to as many as 13 eggs (one nest). The maximum clutch sizes were eight eggs (12 nests), followed by nine eggs (seven nests).

EGG DATES: May 14 to July 25.

Unfledged juveniles: June 3 to Aug. 27; fledglings: July 9 to Sept. 17.

Banding: Two juveniles banded in late summer of different years at Montezuma were recovered the following fall on the Gulf coast of Florida at Tampa and Punta Rassa.

Subspecies: In the North American race *cachinnans,* the upperparts are rich brown rather than olivaceous, as in the nominate subspecies from the western Palearctic.

American Coot
(Fulica americana)   *   B

Range: Nearctic and Neotropical regions, breeding locally from southern Canada to Ecuador and the West Indies; also the Hawaiian Archipelago. Winters north to northern United States.

Status: Common to locally abundant fall migrant, occasionally very abundant; less numerous in winter along the coast, rarer inland. Rare and local breeder in the central and western portions of the state and on Long Island, but locally common at Montezuma and Jamaica Bay.

Nonbreeding: Coots are most numerous during the fall migration, both inland and along the coast. They prefer more open water than their more secretive relatives, the gallinules and rails, and are often observed with various species of ducks.

MAXIMA: *Fall*—6500, Montezuma Marshes, Oct. 15, 1967; 4500, Chautauqua Lake, Oct. 28, 1949; 2300, Water Mill, Suffolk Co., Nov. 8, 1948.

MAXIMA: *Winter*—750, Mecox Bay, Suffolk Co., Jan. 12, 1957; 80, Cayuga Lake, Feb. 15, 1953; 20, Keuka Lake, winter of 1950–1951.

Breeding (see Map 62): Although Coots are much more conspicuous and far more numerous than Common Gallinules during migration, nevertheless, they are much scarcer as breeders over most of the state and nest at far fewer localities.

At only two localities are Coots really common breeders. At Montezuma in 1968 at least *200* broods were produced (C. Hardy), and at the Jamaica Bay Refuge in 1961 approximately 50 pairs bred. At all other places, only a single pair or, at the most, a few pairs have nested.

This species nests in more open places than gallinules. Three New York nests were found in the following situations: (1) on the open sandy shore of a pond near cattails and other vegetation; (2) on a slightly elevated mound on a grassy flat near a pond; (3) on a mass of dead vegetation, six inches above water level.

Egg clutches in 16 New York nests ranged from five (incomplete sets) to ten eggs. The maximum clutch sizes were five eggs (five nests), followed by six eggs (four nests), and nine eggs (three nests).

EGG DATES: Apr. 25 to July 14, exceptionally to late August (probably renesting).

Unfledged young: May 17 to Aug. 12; fledglings: June 29 to Aug. 21.

Perusal of the accompanying map shows that two widely separated breeding areas exist in New York: (A) Southeast—Suffolk Co.—(1) Mecox Bay. Nassau Co.—(2) Mill Neck; (3) Hewlett. Queens Co.—(4) Alley Pond; (5) Jamaica Bay Refuge. Kings Co.—(6) Dyker Beach. Mainland—Rockland Co.—(7) Congers Lake.

(B) Central and west—Jefferson Co.—(8) Perch River Refuge. Oswego Co.—(9) Sandy Pond; (10) near Oswego. Onondaga Co.—(11) Onondaga Lake near Syracuse. Cayuga Co.—

MAP 62 American Coot
(*Fulica americana*)
Breeding distribution

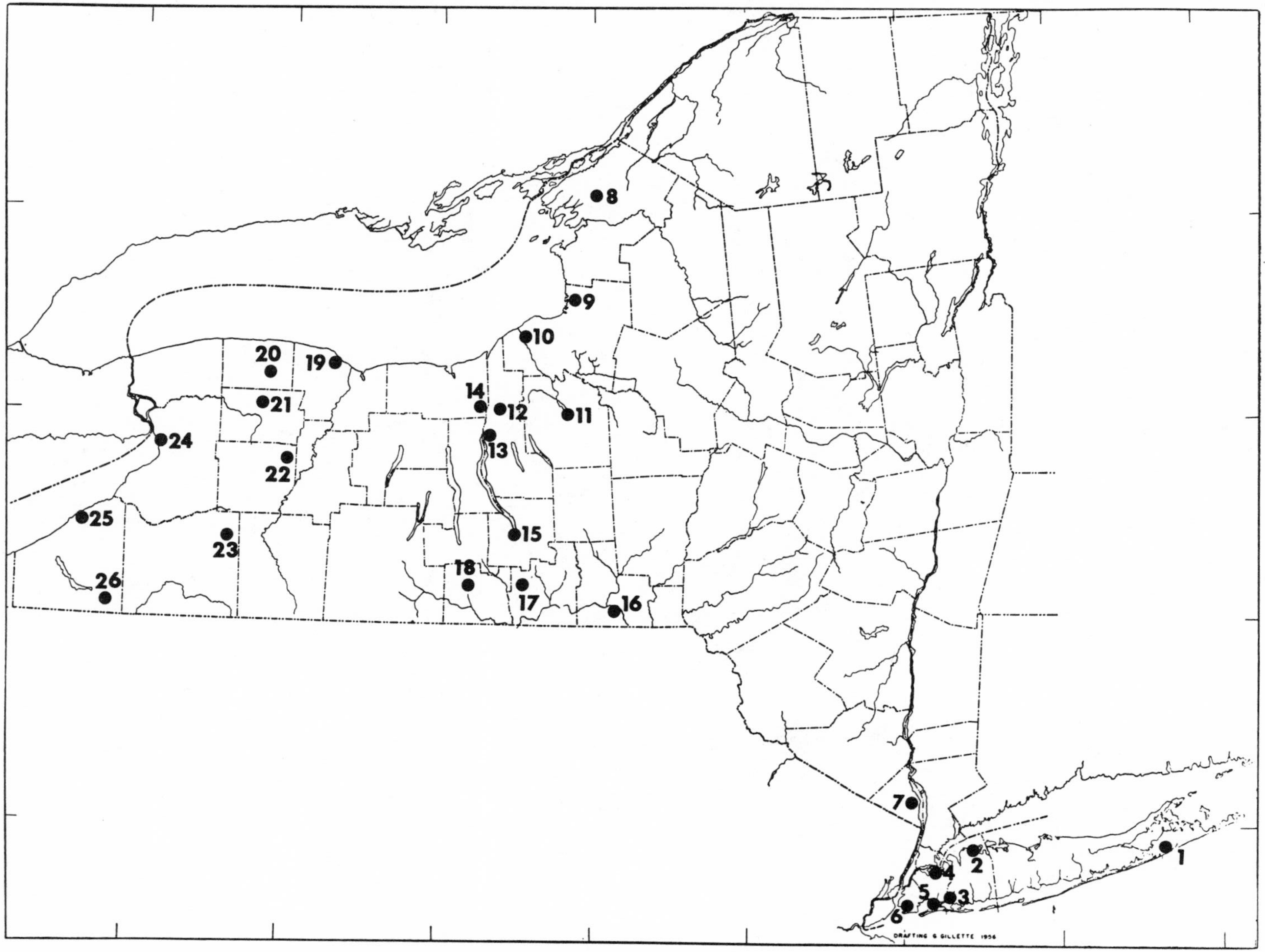

MAP 63 American Coot (*Fulica americana*) Banding recoveries

(12) Howland's Island; (13) Montezuma Refuge. Wayne Co.—(14) Seneca River marshes near Savannah. Tompkins Co.—(15) Renwick Marsh, Ithaca. Broome Co.—(16) east of Binghamton. Tioga Co.—(17) Spencer Marsh. Chemung Co.—(18) Horseheads. Monroe Co. —(19) Braddock's Bay. Orleans Co.—(20) near Albion. Genesee Co.—(21) Oak Orchard Swamp near Oakfield. Wyoming Co.—(22) Lake Le Roy. Cattaraugus Co.—(23) Elton Creek Pond. Erie Co.—(24) Buffalo, Tifft Street Marsh. Chautauqua Co.—(25) near Dunkirk; (26) Riverside Marsh south of Frewsburg.

Banding (see Map 63): Two July juveniles banded in different years at Montezuma were recovered the following autumn in Albermarle Sound, North Carolina; an individual banded in late September in extreme northern New York at the Wilson Hill Refuge, St. Lawrence Co., was shot two months later on the Gulf coast of Louisiana; another, banded Oct. 20, 1929, in southeastern Wisconsin, flew due east and was captured eleven days later in central New York near Marathon, Cortland Co.; two juveniles, banded in late summer of different years in Saskatchewan, were shot the following late fall and winter on Keuka Lake.

"SHOREBIRDS" — CHARADRII

Forty-five species in New York.
Eight breed.

Of the 45 species of this suborder occurring in New York, no fewer than 26 breed mostly in the tundra, as well as the taiga (boreal conifer forest) zones far to the north of the United States. Nearly all of these migrate tremendous distances twice yearly and spend the winter either in the tropics or in south temperate latitudes, although several even winter in the states.

One of the outstanding features of this group of birds is the variety to be found at several notable concentration spots in New York where certain species often occur in impressive numbers. Such localities as Jamaica and Moriches bays on Long Island, and Montezuma Marshes and El Dorado Beach upstate are well worth visiting both spring and fall.

The classification here adopted and sequence of both genera and species are considerably different from those of the A.O.U. Checklist (1957), although the number of species is exactly the same. The treatments of Bock (1958), Palmer (in Stout, 1967), and Jehl (1968) are followed here with minor modifications.

At the family level, the phalaropes are made a subfamily of the sandpipers. At the generic level the following eight genera are dropped or merged with existing genera: (1) *"Squatarola"=Pluvialis;* (2) *"Philohela"=Scolopax;* (3) *"Totanus"=Tringa;* (4), (5), and (6) *"Erolia," "Ereunetes,"* and *"Crocethia"=Calidris;* (7) and (8) *"Lobipes"* and *"Steganopus"* *=Phalaropus.*

Finally the turnstones (*Arenaria*) are placed with the sandpipers just prior to the phalaropes, rather than with the plovers as was formerly done.

The present sequence is as follows: oystercatchers (*Haematopus*); avocets (*Recurvirostra*); stilts (*Himantopus*); plovers (*Vanellus, Pluvialis, Charadrius*); sandpipers (*Scolopax, Capella, Numenius, Limosa, Limnodromus, Micropalama, Tringa, Actitis, Catoptrophorus, Bartramia, Tryngites, Philomachus, Calidris, Arenaria, Phalaropus*).

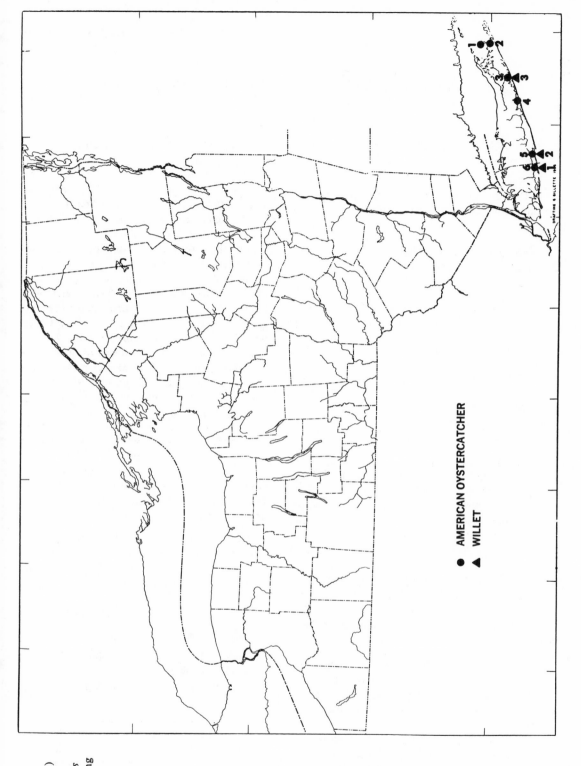

MAP 64 American
Oystercatcher
(*Haematopus palliatus*)
Breeding distribution
Willet (*Catoptrophorus
semipalmatus*) Breeding
distribution

● AMERICAN OYSTERCATCHER
▲ WILLET

OYSTERCATCHERS — HAEMATOPODIDAE

One species in New York.
One breeds.

For discussion (six to eight species), see Suborder Charadrii—"Shorebirds."

American Oystercatcher
(*Haematopus palliatus*)   *   B

Range: Southern Nearctic and Neotropical regions, but local throughout. In eastern North America breeds along the Atlantic coast north to Long Island; Massachusetts (1969). Winters north to North Carolina.

Status: Rare coastal visitant after hurricanes. Regular, but rare and local breeder on Long Island since 1957; no evidence of former breeding.

Nonbreeding: The early history of this species is found in Bull (1964: 182). Today this spectacular bird is seldom seen away from its six known breeding localities on Long Island. As a nonbreeding visitant it has been recorded most often after hurricanes, but these tropical storms have been few and far between during the last decade (since 1960). There is no known record in New York away from Long Island. Data on 11 Long Island specimens are covered in Bull (*op. cit.*).
EXTREME DATES: Mar. 9 and 26 to Nov. 15.

Breeding (see Map 64): Oystercatchers are confined largely to sandy islands with shells, pebbles, and sparse vegetation, but they frequent nearby mud banks to feed on clams, mussels, and oysters.
Egg clutches in 15 Long Island nests: two eggs (four nests); three eggs (seven nests); four and five eggs (two nests apiece).

EGG DATES: May 25 to July 22.
Unfledged young: May 30 to July 28; fledged juveniles: June 7 to Aug. 19.
A nestling banded at Moriches Inlet in 1962

was trapped on its nest at Shinnecock Inlet *seven* years later.
Maximum densities at breeding localities are: 1966—14 pairs, Gardiner's and Cartwright islands; 1970—15 pairs, Gardiner's Island (R. T. Peterson), *not* 30 pairs as reported in the *Kingbird* (1970, 20: 206).
For other breeding data on Long Island, see Post and Raynor (1964).
The accompanying map shows location of the six known breeding areas. The year following the locality represents first known breeding record for that site: Suffolk Co.—(1) Gardiner's Island, 1957—first for the state; (2) Cartwright Island, 1962; (3) *islands* in Shinnecock Bay, 1963; (4) *islands* in Moriches Bay, 1960; (5) *islands* north of Oak Beach, 1968. Nassau Co.—(6) *islands* north of Tobay Sanctuary, Jones Beach, 1966.
Note that *all* Long Island nests of these wary birds are placed in relative isolation—on *islands* in bays back of the barrier beach, rather than on the sandy beaches themselves where there is much disturbance. The birds on Gardiner's Island, which is privately owned, are protected.

Remarks: As there are a number of morphological differences between the present form and *H. ostralegus* of Eurasia, the two are here treated as separate species.

H. palliatus	*H. ostralegus*
Iris —yellow	Iris —red
Legs —pale flesh	Legs —reddish
Back —brown	Back —black
Rump—dark	Rump—white

In *palliatus,* the brown back contrasts with the black head, and only the uppertail coverts are white. In *ostralegus,* the back and head are concolorous, and both uppertail coverts and rump are white. In addition, certain vocalizations are different. Moreover, whereas *palliatus* is almost wholly coastal, *ostralegus* is not only coastal, but is also found commonly far inland in certain areas of its range.

AVOCETS, STILTS — RECURVIROSTRIDAE

Two species in New York.
None breed.

For discussion (seven species), see Suborder Charadrii—"Shorebirds."

American Avocet
(*Recurvirostra americana*)   *

Range: Western North America, breeding east to southern Manitoba and western Minnesota; formerly (prior to 1830) an isolated eastern breeding population in southern New Jersey. Winters from southwestern United States to Guatemala. Straggler on Atlantic coast except in southern New Jersey where it is a summering nonbreeder and fall visitant in relatively small numbers (ten to 40 per locality) since about 1954.

Status: *Very rare*—this showy species has apparently always been a very rare bird on Long Island and an even rarer visitant upstate (see below). On Long Island years may go by without it being reported. For instance, between 1908 and 1935—a span of 27 years—none was recorded—few observers? Even within very recent times, despite an enormous increase in the number of observers, no Avocets were seen between 1962 and 1965. With the exception of two individuals each observed at Jamaica Bay in 1959 and 1960 never more than one bird at a time has been reported. The species has been recorded most often along the south shore of Long Island in September and October.

EXTREME DATES: Aug. 2 to Nov. 15.

Specimen data: Two very old specimens in the AMNH collection were taken on Long Island in 1831 and prior to 1847 (Bull, 1964: 218).

The species has been collected twice along Cayuga Lake near Ithaca by A. A. Allen: Sept. 16, 1909, and Oct. 21, 1913, CUM 2413 and 2414.

Other records: Upstate, in addition to the two specimens listed above, Avocets have been

recorded on only six occasions, all in fall: three times on the Montezuma Marshes in 1953, 1955, and 1966; Verona Beach, Oneida Lake, Aug. 29, 1959; Lake Ontario at Shore Acres, Monroe Co., Sept. 25 to Oct. 3, 1965 (photographed); south end of Seneca Lake, Sept. 25, 1968 (photographed).

There are only two known spring occurrences, both on Long Island at Tobay Pond, Nassau Co., by numerous observers: June 9–16, 1962; May 3, 1969.

Postscript: Maximum numbers for the entire state were obtained from two localities along the shores of Lakes Ontario and Erie: (1) four, El Dorado Beach, Jefferson Co., Aug. 20, 1971 (Perrigo, Belknap, *et al.*); (2) five, Buffalo Harbor, Aug. 22, 1972 (Benham, photo, *Kingbird*, 1973, 23: 138).

Pied or Black-necked Stilt
(*Himantopus himantopus*)   *

Range: Nearly cosmopolitan, but local; absent from the colder portions of the Holarctic region. The North American race *mexicanus* (top of neck black) breeds in the west—north to the southern portions of Oregon and Idaho, but in the east—only along the Atlantic coast north to North Carolina, rarely to Delaware (1970); formerly to southern New Jersey. Winters from southern United States southward. Vagrant north to Newfoundland.

Status: *Very rare*—in New York State this striking species has been recorded only from Long Island. Seven specimens, six of them extant, were collected presumably on the south shore many years ago. Five of these in the AMNH collection are virtually without data, excepting one taken on Great South Bay in 1843 (Pike), AMNH 436941. The only known specimen taken in the present century is one from Georgica, Suffolk Co., June 4, 1924 (Latham), NYSM 24963.

Two individuals were observed at Mecox Bay, Suffolk Co., May 23–31, 1953 (McKeever, *et al.*). These birds may have come from eggs brought from Florida and hatched in southern New Jersey the previous year (Bull, 1964: 219).

In Giraud's day (1840s) the Stilt was considered much less rare than the Avocet. Today the latter is much more likely to occur.

Remarks: Following many authorities, all stilts of this genus are here considered to belong to one species (*himantopus*). Populations range from those having partially black necks

(*mexicanus*) to those with completely white heads and necks.

Postcript: An individual seen at Fairport, Monroe Co., June 3, 1973 (Tetlow), was photographed in color by Joe Taylor. This represents the first proved occurrence for inland New York. Another was observed at the Jamaica Bay Refuge, Long Island, for several days during late April of the same year by many people.

PLOVERS — CHARADRIIDAE

Seven species in New York.
Two breed.

For discussion (60+ species), see suborder Charadrii—"Shorebirds." Only the Piping Plover (*Charadrius melodus*) and Killdeer (*C. vociferus*) breed in the state.

Eurasian Lapwing
(*Vanellus vanellus*)   *

Range: Eurasia, wintering in the western portion of its range from the British Isles to northern Africa. Wanders to Greenland and Baffin Island, south to the Bahamas and Barbados.

Status: *Casual*—in New York there are three known occurrences, all from Long Island: (1) a specimen taken at Merrick, Nassau Co., Dec. 27, 1883 (Lott), is apparently not extant; (2) another specimen collected on Mecox Bay, Suffolk Co., late fall of 1905 (Beebe, *Auk*, 1906, 23: 221), is a mount in a private collection; (3) one seen near Montauk, Suffolk Co., from Dec. 3 to 18, 1966 (many observers), was photographed by Joanne Trimble—photo on file, AMNH collection (see also *Kingbird*, 1967, 17: 126–127).

A third supposed specimen is believed to be the same as the 1905 occurrence listed above (Bull, in Bagg, 1967: 87–89).

Lesser Golden Plover
(*Pluvialis dominica*)   *

Range: Holarctic region, breeding throughout the length of northern Siberia and in North America east to Baffin Island and south to extreme northeastern Manitoba. The eastern American breeding population migrates in spring chiefly through the midcontinent; in fall primarily over the Atlantic Ocean (but see Maxima below). The "Atlantic" population winters in southern South America.

Status: Variously rare to very common fall migrant statewide, more numerous inland; fairly common to very common spring migrant inland, but rare to uncommon along the coast.

Occurrence: This species frequents short-grass fields—especially those of airports—plowed and burned fields, golf courses and, along the coast, sandfill and the drier portions of salt meadows. On the coast it is most numerous after sustained easterly and southerly gales.

Formerly abundant, the Golden Plover was considered a great delicacy, and shot in large numbers for the market. It had become very scarce by the early 1890s and remained so until the 1920s when, afforded protection, it reappeared again in small numbers.

However, as may be seen from the following

figures, in more recent years the species—having been given complete protection in North America—has become numerous once more.

MAXIMA, INLAND: *Fall*—28, Fredonia, Chautauqua Co., Aug. 13, 1928; 183, Manitou, Monroe Co., Sept. 4, 1959; 200, Lima, Livingston Co., Sept. 15, 1970; 360, Grand Island, Erie Co., Sept. 26, 1954; 500, Batavia, Genesee Co., Oct. 11, 1970 (Pixley, *et al.*); 360, Syracuse Airport, Oct. 15, 1964; 87, same locality, Oct. 22, 1964; 500, Hamptonburgh, Orange Co., Oct. 17, 1970 (Getgood); 18, Rochester Airport, Nov. 1, 1952. The large numbers at the Syracuse Airport in 1964—a drought year—were attributed by Scheider (1965: 16) to a "tremendous crop of crickets." Note the widespread flight and very large numbers in 1970.

MAXIMA, COASTAL: *Fall*—all in eastern Suffolk Co., Long Island—100, Sagaponack, Aug. 22, 1921; 200, Easthampton, Sept. 16, 1944 (after hurricane); 60, same locality, Oct. 30, 1949; 15, Mecox Bay, Nov. 9, 1929.

MAXIMA, INLAND: *Spring*—12, near Hamburg, Erie Co., Apr. 3, 1963; big flight in 1954—100, Braddock's Bay, Monroe Co., Apr. 21; 100, Shore Acres, Monroe Co., May 1; 72, Grand Island, May 6.

MAXIMA, COASTAL: *Spring*—nine, Jamaica Bay, Apr. 23, 1957; six, Sagaponack, May 17, 1948. Note the much larger numbers inland in spring. These coastal maxima are exceptional, usually only one or two birds are reported each spring on Long Island.

EXTREME DATES: *Fall*—July 9 (coastal) to Dec. 4. *Spring*—Mar. 21 (observed) and Mar. 22 (specimen) to June 9 (coastal).

Rare in fall before August and after mid-November; in spring before April and after May.

The second early spring date is that of a specimen taken at King Ferry, Cayuga Co., Mar. 22, 1942 (Mengel), CUM 12626. This bird was with three Killdeers. A crippled Golden Plover was observed at Jamaica Bay, near Broad Channel, through the fall of 1956 until Dec. 30 (Mayer, *et al.*).

Remarks: The A.O.U. vernacular name "American" Golden Plover is very misleading in view of its widespread breeding distribution in northern Asia and the fact that it winters also in southeast Asia, Australia, etc. The name

Lesser Golden Plover is appropriate and has been used by Palmer (in Stout, 1967).

Black-bellied Plover
(*Pluvialis squatarola*)   *

Range: Nearctic and eastern Palearctic regions at high latitudes, in America breeding south to Southampton and Coats islands (northern Hudson Bay). Winters along the Atlantic coast north to Long Island, more rarely to Massachusetts.

Status: Very common to abundant coastal migrant, occasionally more numerous; much less numerous inland in fall, even rarer in spring. In recent years regular and locally common in winter on the outer coast where it is also a regular summering nonbreeder.

Occurrence: The Black-bellied Plover occurs in large numbers on the extensive mud flats along the south shore of Long Island, especially at the west end. It is most numerous in spring when the flight is concentrated (May) and occurs in smaller-sized flocks during the fall when the migration is protracted (August to November).

Inland this species is reported most frequently on the beaches and flats of Lake Ontario, especially in fall (principally October). It is apparently much less common in spring in the interior.

MAXIMA, COASTAL: *Fall*—67, Moriches Inlet, Suffolk Co., Aug. 13, 1967; 600, Jamaica Bay, Sept. 2, 1946; 450, Mecox Bay, Suffolk Co., Oct. 17, 1936; 200, Jamaica Bay, Nov. 4, 1944; 50, same locality, Dec. 2, 1950. *Winter* —150, Nassau, Queens, Brooklyn (Christmas counts, 1953–1954); 15, Fire Island Inlet, Suffolk Co., Jan. 23, 1949. *Spring*—1200, Jamaica Bay, May 17, 1939; 6000, Hewlett—Oceanside marshes, Nassau Co. (by boat), May 30, 1954 (Bull). *Summer*—25, Jones Beach, June 29, 1939.

MAXIMA, INLAND: *Fall*—100, Summerville, Monroe Co., Aug. 27, 1955 (O'Hara); on Oct. 2, 1966—75, Shore Acres, Monroe Co.; 34, Montezuma Marshes (good count away from Lake Ontario); 50, Salmon Creek, Monroe Co., Oct. 10, 1959; 42, Onondaga Lake, Oct. 29, 1970; 25, Hamlin, Monroe Co., Nov. 1, 1970;

four, Oneida Lake, Nov. 30, 1957. *Spring*—22, Sandy Pond, June 4, 1961—the only inland spring concentration I am aware of.

Inland it is recorded from May to November, but most often in May and especially October.

Remarks: The Black-bellied Plover and both golden plovers (*apricaria* and *dominica*) are considered congeneric and so treated here, following many recent authorities.

Piping Plover
(*Charadrius melodus*)   *   B

Range: Central and eastern Nearctic region, breeding in two separate areas—(1) coastal beaches from southeastern Quebec and southwestern Newfoundland south to Virginia; (2) inland beaches from eastern Alberta and Nebraska east to the shores of Lake Ontario (southeastern Ontario and northwestern New York). Winters chiefly on the South Atlantic and Gulf coasts, sparingly north to Massachusetts (three specimens.)

Status: Locally common migrant and breeder on the outer coast of Long Island, much less numerous on the north shore and on Staten Island. Very rare inland, and extirpated as a breeder on the east shore of Lake Ontario. Very rare in winter on the south shore of Long Island.

Nonbreeding: The Piping Plover is one of the first shorebirds to arrive in spring. In fall it departs very early, usually by early September, after which only stragglers remain.

MAXIMA: *Spring*—90, Moriches Inlet, Suffolk Co., Mar. 26, 1948. *Fall*—150, Idlewild, Jamaica Bay area, Queens Co., Aug. 10, 1944; 100, Moriches Inlet, Aug. 22, 1970.

EXTREME DATES: Mar. 3 to Dec. 10. Rare before mid-March and after September.

This species was unknown in winter on Long Island prior to 1953. Since then it has been reliably reported at least *eight* times (Bull, 1964: 186), with as many as three individuals at Montauk from Dec. 30, 1953, to Jan. 10, 1954; also one at Point Lookout, Nassau Co., as late as Jan. 27, 1957.

Fig. 43 Piping Plover settling on eggs, Oakwood Beach, Staten Island, June 2, 1941. Photo by C. Pearson

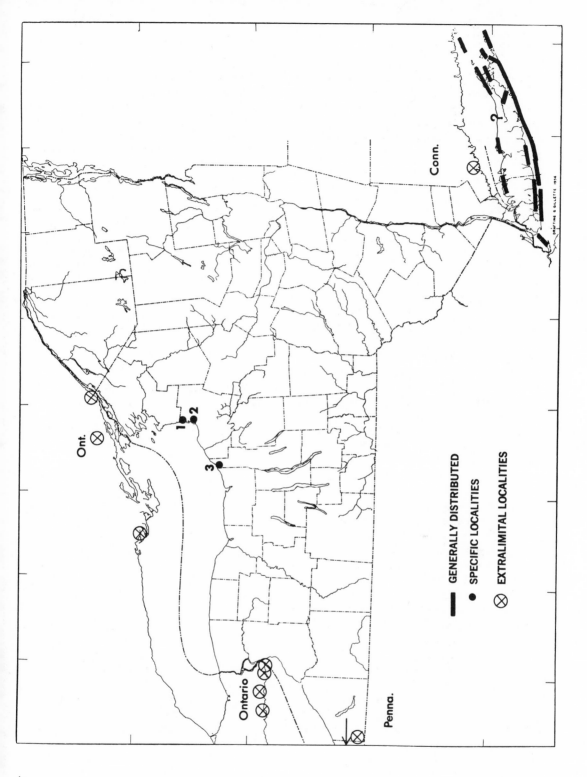

MAP 65 Piping Plover
(*Charadrius melodus*)
Breeding distribution

GENERALLY DISTRIBUTED

● SPECIFIC LOCALITIES

⊗ EXTRALIMITAL LOCALITIES

Inland it is extremely rare away from the few known breeding localities on Lake Ontario. I know of two specimen records: (1) near Ossining, Westchester Co., 1898 (Fisher), MCZ collection; (2) Hamlin Beach, Monroe Co., May 10, 1900 (Guelf), NYSM collection. As many as *four* were seen at Hamburg, Erie Co., June 30, 1966 (Bourne), and two at Montezuma Marshes, Apr. 22, 1970 (Smith, *Kingbird*, 1971, 21: 10).

Breeding (see Map 65): This attractive little plover is characteristic of ocean beaches and sandy shores of bays and inlets on Long Island. Formerly common (prior to the 1890s), its numbers were severely depleted by large-scale hunting but, with full protection by 1913, it had recovered strongly by the 1920s. In recent years it has disappeared from the more disturbed areas where an ever-increasing human population has driven it to remoter localities, such as Fire Island and Gardiner's Island.

MAXIMA: Suffolk Co.—64 nests, Moriches Bay, 1941; 55 nests, Shinnecock Bay, 1950; 50 nests, Mecox Bay, 1958 (all by Wilcox). Nassau Co.—about 75 pairs, Short Beach-Jones Inlet area, 1951 (Bull).

Piping Plovers lay their eggs on the open sand—often near Least Terns—the nests merely shallow depressions lined with bits of shell and sometimes pebbles (see Fig. 43).

Egg clutches in over 500 Long Island nests were invariably four (but see below).

EGG DATES: Apr. 18 to June 25, exceptionally to July 23. Wilcox (1959) found that July clutches contained three eggs in 70 nests and two eggs in eight nests, the result of renesting attempts after earlier failures.

Unfledged juveniles: May 21 to July 24; fledglings: June 2 to Aug. 18.

Wilcox (*op. cit.*) determined that incubation took from 26 to 30 days.

As may be seen on the accompanying map, the Piping Plover is a rare and local breeder on the north shore of Long Island, west of the Orient peninsula (Suffolk Co.—Port Jefferson and Caumsett State Park; Nassau Co.—near Oyster Bay and Bayville, the last on newly dredged sandfill).

The history of the bird as a breeder on Lake Ontario is restricted to three localities: (1) North Pond, Oswego Co.—in 1935, Hyde (1939a) found 14 nests, each with four eggs,

on bare sand in the hollows among the dunes. It last bred at that locality in 1948 according to Goodwin (*Kingbird*, 1957, 7: 81). (2) Sandy Pond, also Oswego Co. in 1935—Hyde (*op. cit.*) found 12 breeding pairs. The last known nesting at that locality was in 1955 (*fide* Scheider). (3) Little Sodus Bay, Cayuga Co.—the only known breeding evidence was procured by the indefatigable Sydney Hyde who discovered a single nest containing four eggs on a "shingle" (pebble) beach, June 18, 1936.

Banding: A nestling banded by Wilcox at Moriches, July 7, 1947, was trapped by him near its birthplace, 14 years later—June 6, 1961.

Remarks: No subspecies (*"circumcinctus"*) are recognized here (Bull, 1964: 186).

Semipalmated Plover
(*Charadrius semipalmatus*)   *

Range: Nearctic region, in the east breeding south to Nova Scotia; winters north to South Carolina, rarely to Long Island.

Status: Abundant to very abundant coastal migrant, common to very common inland migrant. Rare in winter on the coast.

Occurrence: The Semipalmated Plover is among our most numerous shorebirds on the extensive tidal mud flats along the south side of Long Island. Inland it occurs in some numbers, especially on the shore of Lake Ontario.

MAXIMA, COASTAL: *Spring*—6000, Jamaica Bay, May 17, 1939; 700, same locality, June 1, 1948. *Fall*—1000, Jamaica Bay, Aug. 6, 1936; 4000, same locality, Aug. 24, 1951; 600, Moriches Inlet, Suffolk Co., Sept. 28, 1936; 50, Easthampton, Suffolk Co., Oct. 15, 1933.

MAXIMA, INLAND: *Spring*—120, Groveland, Livingston Co., May 23, 1948; 100, Sandy Pond, Oswego Co., May 30, 1961. *Fall*—50, Sandy Pond, July 31, 1965; 100, El Dorado Beach, Jefferson Co., Sept. 2, 1961; 65, Montezuma Marshes, Sept. 14, 1965; 60, Delta Lake, Oneida Co., Sept. 28, 1969.

EXTREME DATES: *Coastal*—Mar. 23 and "early" April to Nov. 20 (specimen), Dec. 7 and 10. *Inland*—Apr. 24 to Nov. 10. Rare before late April and after October. On the coast regular in small numbers throughout the summer; inland spring and fall dates nearly overlap.

Winter: formerly very rare in winter on the coast, but since the early 1950s one or more have been recorded at that season, with maxima of three each in 1953–1954, 1957–1958, and 1965–1966, at Jones Inlet, Nassau Co. (twice), and Jamaica Bay. Although no local winter specimen has been taken, one was color-photographed on the north shore of Long Island Sound at Larchmont, Westchester Co., Feb. 7, 1969 (Bahrt); identification confirmed by the writer.

Remarks: Regarding this species and its close ally, the Ringed Plover (*C. hiaticula*) of the Palearctic region, Smith (1969) treats these forms as polymorphic populations of *one* species based on their sympatry in Baffin Island without hybridizing (no intermediates), but at the same time the progeny of mixed pairs indicates characters of either one parent or the other (never both), viz., extent of toe webbing, width of collar, and plumage pattern in downy young. He states unequivocally that eastern Baffin Island is the only area of overlap throughout the range. Clearly more field work remains to be done in eastern Baffin Island and in Siberia where both *hiaticula* and *semipalmatus* also meet.

The two forms are here treated as *separate* species in the present work.

Wilson's Plover
(*Charadrius wilsonia*) *

Range: Chiefly Neotropical region, although breeding along the Atlantic coast north to Virginia; rarely to southern New Jersey.

Status: *Very rare*—in New York State this species is confined to the south shore of Long Island. There is no confirmed inland record. A specimen from upstate New York, supposedly this species, is not extant and no details were published as to its identity. Wilson's Plover is frequently confused by beginners with the abundant and similar Semipalmated Plover.

Nine specimens have been taken on Long Island, of which the six following are extant:

(1) Flatlands, Kings Co., no date or collector, AMNH 436592; (2) Raynor South (= Freeport), Nassau Co., Apr. 24, 1833 (Lawrence collection), AMNH 45432; (3) Shinnecock Bay, Suffolk Co., May 16, 1884 (Dutcher collection), AMNH 65099; (4) Napeague, Suffolk Co., July 11, 1931 (Latham), NYSM 24905; (5) Mecox Bay, Suffolk Co., Sept. 17, 1932 (Helmuth), in his collection; (6) Moriches Inlet, Suffolk Co., Sept. 19, 1954 (Bock), CUM 443—preserved as a skeleton.

Of more than 25 reports, including specimen records, eight have occurred in May and at least nine in September, the latter mostly after hurricanes. The species has been reliably reported only once since 1954: Mecox Bay, July 1, 1968 (McKeever).

EXTREME DATES: Apr. 24 (specimen) to Oct. 2.

Killdeer
(*Charadrius vociferus*) * B

Range: Temperate North America, breeding from southern Canada to northern Mexico; local in the Neotropical region—Greater Antilles, coast of Peru. In winter withdraws from the northern portions, but regular north to Long Island.

Status: Common to very common migrant, occasionally abundant in fall inland. In winter locally numerous along the coast, but rare to uncommon inland. Widespread breeder, but rare in the Adirondack region.

Nonbreeding: Killdeers frequent open areas along lake and river shores, but are often found far from water in agricultural regions and on airports, golf courses, pastures, and gravel beds.

MAXIMA: *Spring*—100, Evans Center, Erie Co., Mar. 16, 1963; 150, Derby Hill, Oswego Co., Mar. 26, 1967.

MAXIMA: *Fall*—300, Montezuma Refuge, July 4, 1967; 125, El Dorado Beach, Jefferson Co., Aug. 26, 1965; 300, Lima, Livingston Co., Sept. 15, 1970; 260, Syracuse Airport, Sept. 16, 1965; 300, Delta Lake, Oneida Co., Sept. 28, 1969; 150, Lawrence, Nassau Co., Oct. 5, 1948; 100, Parma, Monroe Co., Nov. 12, 1967.

Fig. 44   Killdeer roof nest site,
Mann Hall, Cornell University, Ithaca,
June 10, 1970. Photo by Richard B.
Fischer

Fig. 45   Killdeer nest and eggs, roof
site, Mann Hall, Cornell University,
Ithaca, June 10, 1970. Photo by
Richard B. Fischer

MAXIMA: *Winter*—200, south shore of Long Island, from Brooklyn to Jones Beach, late December 1952.

Migrants arrive in numbers in March and depart by late November.

Breeding: This species nests on the ground either where it is bare or pebbly, with or without short clumps of grass. On two occasions nests were found on gravel rooftops. On June 22, 1953, Harold Mitchell photographed three downy young on a Buffalo roof. Both in 1958 and 1959 at Ithaca a pair bred on the roof of one of the college buildings at Cornell (Hoyt); Figs. 44 and 45 show a nest with eggs at the latter site on June 10, 1970 (Fischer).

Some idea of breeding density for this species is that of eight nests, "within a one-mile length of dirt dike at the Montezuma Refuge," all eight successfully fledged young (Mullen, *American Birds,* 1971, 25: 855).

Of 44 New York nests examined, *all* contained four-egg clutches. In one nest, Burger (1963: 14) determined an incubation period of 24 days.

EGG DATES: Apr. 3 to July 4.

Nestlings: May 3 to July 30; fledglings: May 21 to Aug. 12.

Banding: Two nestlings banded in upstate New York were recovered the following winter in North Carolina and Georgia.

SANDPIPERS — SCOLOPACIDAE

Thirty-five species in New York.
Five breed.

For discussion (90± species), see suborder Charadrii—"Shorebirds." Only the five following species of Scolopacidae are known to breed in the state: American Woodcock (*Scolopax minor*); Common Snipe (*Capella gallinago*); Upland Sandpiper (*Bartramia longicauda*); Spotted Sandpiper (*Actitis macularia*); Willet (*Catoptrophorus semipalmatus*). The last is a rare, recent breeder confined to a few localities on the south shore of Long Island.

Following Palmer (in Stout, 1967) and Jehl (1968) the three phalaropes (*Phalaropus*) and the two turnstones (*Arenaria*) are included here within the Scolopacidae. The first are considered modified sandpipers; the second, formerly placed with the plovers, are believed to be structurally nearer to the sandpipers (see also Bock, 1958).

American Woodcock
(*Scolopax minor*)   *   B

Range: Eastern North America, breeding from southern Canada to Florida and the Gulf

states. In winter throughout the range, except the extreme north.

Status: Locally common spring migrant inland; fairly common fall migrant on the coast. Rare to uncommon in winter along the coast. Widespread breeder. Formerly (prior to 1890) much more numerous in summer and on migration.

Nonbreeding: The present-day observer can scarcely credit the former abundance of this species when hundreds were shot by hunters in a single day during the height of the fall flight in late October and November. Today, if the observer sees a half-dozen Woodcock in a day, he calls it a flight. Of course, hunters with well-trained dogs will flush considerably more, but nothing like the numbers in past years.

In the 1870s, the open season started early in summer and continued until late winter. According to Mackay (1929), he shot 77 at Bridgehampton, Suffolk Co., in less than a week in early June 1870. These were presumably local breeding birds—both adults and young. Because of such hunting practices decade after decade, it is no wonder that a great decrease had occurred by the early 1900s.

Eventually with a much shorter open season and reduced bag limits, Woodcock increased, but have not regained anything like their former numbers.

This species usually arrives in late February in mild seasons, more often in early March. It ordinarily departs by late November or early December. A specimen in the AMNH collection was taken at Islip, Suffolk Co., Feb. 12, 1930.

MAXIMA, INLAND: *Spring*—1963, Monroe Co.—30, Hamlin, Mar. 26; 20, Braddock's Bay, Mar. 30; 25, near Rochester, Apr. 7, 1954.

MAXIMA, COASTAL: *Fall*—18, Easthampton, Suffolk Co., Oct. 31, 1941.

MAXIMA, COASTAL: *Winter*—nine, East Moriches, Suffolk Co., Dec. 26, 1963 (Raynor), is most exceptional.

Breeding: Woodcock nest on the ground in thickets or among thick clumps of bushes not far from moist feeding areas. They are especially fond of alder and willow thickets. The species is decidedly nocturnal, or at least crepuscular. One of the features of early spring is the spectacular aerial courtship display performed by these birds soon after their arrival from the south.

In the Ithaca area, Pettingill (1936) estimated 50 breeding pairs in 1932. During that year he actually found ten nests and in 1933 six more. One nest with eggs was placed on a "large moss-covered log partially submerged in marshy ground."

Egg clutches in 38 New York nests range from three to five, as follows: three eggs (16 nests); four eggs (20 nests); five eggs (two nests).

EGG DATES: Mar. 24 to June 17.

Unfledged young: Apr. 17 to June 29; fledglings: May 15 to Aug. 2.

Banding: One banded near Moncton, New Brunswick, Sept. 10, 1946, was recovered near Sayville, Long Island, Nov. 15 following; another banded in winter at Baton Rouge, Louisiana, was recovered the following summer near Syracuse.

Remarks: The generic name *Scolopax* is used for all species of woodcocks by many modern taxonomists, including Jehl (1968), and Mayr and Short (1970).

Common Snipe
(Capella gallinago)   *   B

Range: Holarctic region, in North America breeding from Alaska and Canada to southwestern United States; in the east locally to northern New Jersey, southeastern New York, and central Connecticut. Winters north to New York and southern New England, chiefly along the coast.

Status: Common, occasionally very common migrant inland; much less numerous on the coast. Uncommon to locally fairly common in winter on the coast; rare inland. Fairly common breeder in central and western portions, rare and local elsewhere.

Nonbreeding: This species frequents wet meadows and pastures, shallow marshes, and cultivated fields after rainstorms. Snipe fluctuate in numbers from time to time. They are rare in dry years and occasionally numerous after suitable areas become flooded.

MAXIMA: *Spring*—27, Riverside Marsh, Chautauqua Co., Mar. 30, 1959; 40, Carmel, Putnam Co., Apr. 3, 1959; 100, Watkins-Montour airport marsh, Schuyler Co., Apr. 8, 1962; 40, near Phoenix, Oswego Co., Apr. 27, 1969.

MAXIMA: *Fall*—43, Montezuma Marshes, Aug. 2, 1967; 57, Howland's Island, Cayuga Co., Sept. 10, 1966; 50, Catskill, Greene Co., Oct. 13, 1962; 150, Oak Orchard Swamp, Nov. 3, 1968 (many observers); 30, Salmon Creek marshes, Monroe Co., Nov. 23, 1956.

The species is a regular fall migrant in early July in places where it does not breed. In spring it is usually rare before mid-March.

MAXIMA: *Winter*—seven, near Poughkeepsie, Dutchess Co., winter of 1920–1921; 30 (including flock of 19 feeding on open mud flat), Mecox Bay, Suffolk Co., Jan. 12, 1964 (Raynor).

Breeding (see Map 66): The Common Snipe is an inhabitant of wet meadows, marshes, and bogs, where it often places its nest in grass or sedge tussocks (see Fig. 46). In such locations it is fairly numerous in the largest marshes, as in the Montezuma and Oak Orchard areas. In the Perch River Refuge, Jefferson Co., Belknap estimated at least eight breeding pairs in 1966.

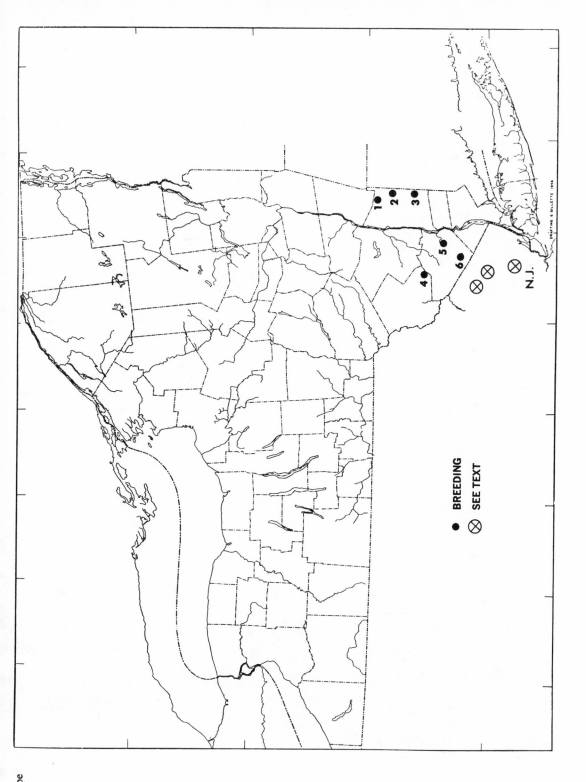

MAP 66 Common Snipe
(*Capella gallinago*)
Known southern
breeding limits

BREEDING

SEE TEXT

It is found also in suitable habitat throughout much of central and western New York, is somewhat more local in the Adirondack district, but is apparently quite rare in the Mohawk and Hudson valley regions. In fact it is virtually unknown as a breeder in the entire Catskill area. Except for the small breeding population in southeastern New York, I am aware of only *one* definite breeding record in eastern New York south of the Adirondacks—a nest and eggs found in 1939 near Galway, Saratoga Co. Clearly more field work is needed in this section, especially in and around the Catskills.

Fifteen New York nests contained four eggs apiece.

EGG DATES: Apr. 20 to June 16.

Unfledged juveniles: May 19 to June 20; fledged young: July 5.

The known southeastern breeding limits in New York are indicated on the accompanying map: Dutchess Co.—(1) Pine Plains; (2) near Wassaic; (3) near Wingdale. Sullivan Co.—(4) Basher Kill. Orange Co.—(5) Blooming Grove; (6) near Warwick.

Note also three New Jersey breeding localities even farther south (Bull, 1964: 192).

Banding: Two fall banding recoveries are noteworthy—one banded in early September on extreme southern James Bay near Moosonee, Ontario, was shot in late October following, near Jamestown, Chautauqua Co. Another banded in mid-August at Montezuma was recovered in mid-November on Merritt Island, Fla.

Remarks: For use of the generic name *Capella*, see Tuck (The Snipes, Canadian Wildlife Service, Monograph Series, No. 5, 1972: 101–102) for a detailed summation of nomenclatural treatment. *Gallinago* (as used by Brisson in his *Ornithologie*, 1760, 5: 298–310) is *not* a valid genus. The earliest available name is *Capella* Frenzel, 1801. According to Wetmore (oral comm.), who examined the original citation, Frenzel did *not* use "Kitchen Latin"

Fig. 46 Near North Java, Wyoming Co., Sept. 29, 1954. Breeding meadow site of Common Snipe. Photo by Richard Rosche

in his diagnosis of this genus, *contra* Mayr (*Ibis*, 1963, 105: 402–403); *Capella* is, therefore, a perfectly valid genus. Application is on file before the International Zoological Commission to validate the name *Capella*.

The morphological characters supposedly differentiating the New World population *"delicata"* from nominate Palearctic *gallinago*, are here considered too variable for recognition (see Witherby, *et al.*, 1940: 205).

Some authors, notably Voous (1960: 94, 120), treat the northern hemisphere *gallinago* as conspecific with the South American *paraguaiae* and the African *nigripennis*. Morphologically they appear to be very similar.

Long-billed Curlew
(*Numenius americanus*) *

Range: West-central North America, breeding east to southern Manitoba, formerly to southern Wisconsin; winters chiefly from Louisiana west to California and south to Guatemala, but locally in small numbers on the coasts of South Carolina and Florida. In recent years accidental in the east, north of South Carolina.

Status: No reliable record in New York State for more than 30 years (since 1938). This applies also to the entire northeast. Destruction of most of its former breeding grounds in the midwest and a resulting "shift" in migratory pattern further to the west are believed responsible for its disappearance.

Former occurrence: The following is taken from my account (Bull, 1964: 192–193): "The 'Sicklebill,' as it was formerly called by the gunners, was a regular fall migrant on the coast of Long Island. Giraud (1844) stated that it was also regular in spring and that it occurred in autumn as late as mid-November. According to Pike (in Dutcher, 1887–1894), he had shot 'hundreds' in the 1840s when they were very plentiful, but by 1865 they seemed to have disappeared and he had not come across a single one since. However, N. T. Lawrence (in Dutcher, *op. cit.*) stated that in 1885 in the vicinity of Far Rockaway, it was

more uncommon than the Eskimo Curlew, with only two records in 12 years, compared to four records in ten years for the latter species. According to Dutcher (*op. cit.*) a few were collected each year from the late 1870s until 1889 when the last known local specimen was taken at Montauk on Sept. 9. Griscom (1923) placed it on the extirpated list and called it a bird of the past, despite the fact that it was reported five times between 1889 and 1923. Cruickshank (1942) listed six sight reports between 1923 and 1938. The last known report for our area was of one seen at Georgica Pond, Aug. 11, 1938 (Helmuth). He saw the species on no fewer than five occasions between 1910 and 1938.

"EXTREME DATES: *Spring*—Apr. 28 and May 5 (specimen) to June 15, 1922, Amagansett (*fide* Latham). *Fall*—July 10 and 21 to Sept. 12; Oct. 15, 1924, Sagaponack (Helmuth); to 'mid-November' (*fide* Giraud)."

Specimen data: Of more than a dozen specimens reportedly taken on Long Island, only four are known to be extant—all in the American Museum of Natural History collection, as follows—three without date: one labeled "Long Island" (Arnold), 12567; two, Rockaway "Meadows" (Pike), 436677 and 436678; and the only known spring specimen, from Montauk Point, Suffolk Co., May 5, 1877 (Dwight collection), 355723.

The only confirmed inland New York record that I am aware of is that of a specimen collected at Lyons Falls, Lewis Co., Oct. 1, 1876 (A. J. Dayan), which is in the collection of the British Museum (Natural History), 88. 10. 10. 2644. I examined this specimen during a visit there in 1966. This specimen, listed in the Catalogue of Birds in the British Museum (1896, 24: 354), as being in the Salvin-Godman collection, has the erroneous date of "Jan. 10." The existence of this specimen was unknown to Eaton (1910).

Other upstate reports, supposedly of this species, are either without details (Eaton, 1910: 338) or the specimens are not extant and thus not available for examination (Beardslee and Mitchell, 1965: 211).

Remarks: No subspecies are recognized here; the poorly differentiated race *"parvus"* is based on average size differences and overlap in bill length.

Eurasian Curlew
(*Numenius arquata*)   *

Range: Northern Eurasia, in the western portion of its breeding range south to France. Winters from Iceland and the British Isles to South Africa. Accidental in Greenland and on Long Island.

Status: *Accidental*—the only known occurrence for continental North America is a Long Island specimen record of the nominate race, collected in 1853 (exact locality and collector unknown), NYSM 324.

Whimbrel
(*Numenius phaeopus*)   *

Range: Northern Eurasia and locally in northern North America, the New World race *hudsonicus* (rump barred—see also **Subspecies)** breeding south to the southern shore of Hudson Bay (extreme northern Ontario). For winter range, see **Remarks.**

Status: Variously rare to uncommon coastal migrant in spring, occasionally more numerous; usually common to very common in fall, but most flocks fly by without stopping. Inland the reverse is true, locally fairly common to common in spring, much less numerous in fall.

Occurrence: Whimbrels (formerly called Hudsonian Curlew) frequent coastal salt marshes and to a lesser extent mud flats, but most flocks of any size are observed in continuous flight overhead, the flight notes not too unlike those of the Greater Yellowlegs. Upstate these birds are occasionally to be found on the shores of the Great Lakes. However, it is along the Canadian shore of Lake Erie west of Buffalo, where large spring flights occur according to Beardslee and Mitchell (1965: 214), and in late May flocks up to several hundred may be seen there. Most of these apparently skip New York State and presumably turn north and migrate overland toward Hudson Bay.

In fall the flight is primarily coastal or rather offshore and, on occasion after easterly gales, large numbers are sometimes reported on the east end of Long Island.

MAXIMA, COASTAL: *Fall*—150, near Freeport, Nassau Co., July 27, 1911; 200, Easthampton, Suffolk Co., July 30, 1922; flocks to 30, late August and September, various southshore Long Island localities. *Spring*—250, Easthampton, May 5, 1947 (Helmuth).

MAXIMA, INLAND: *Fall*—nine, Braddock's Bay, July 25, 1954; five, Gainesville, Wyoming Co., Aug. 15, 1957. *Spring*—16, Chili, Monroe Co., May 16, 1922; 15, Montezuma Marshes, May 26, 1961—both high numbers away from the lake shore; 120, off Webster, Monroe Co., May 27, 1962 (Kemnitzer), unprecedented number inland; 47, Braddock's Bay, Monroe Co., May 28, 1963—both these last localities on Lake Ontario.

EXTREME DATES: Apr. 7 (coastal); June–July dates, but no proof of summering; to Nov. 15 (coastal).

Remarks: Winters chiefly in Middle and South America; rarely on Atlantic coast north to South Carolina.

Two Long Island occurrences in late December are believed correct: one found exhausted —died later, but not preserved—Rockaway Beach, Queens Co., Dec. 24, 1912 (Bogardus); Stony Brook (harbor), Suffolk Co., Dec. 27, 1959 (Sabin).

Subspecies: A specimen of the western Palearctic nominate race (rump white, unbarred) was collected at Jones Beach, Long Island, Sept. 4, 1912 (Van Allen), AMNH 11883 (Miller, *Auk*, 1915, 32: 226). This represents the first known record for North America. Another specimen was taken in Labrador in 1948.

Eskimo Curlew
(*Numenius borealis*)   *

Range: *Extinct?*—breeds or formerly bred on the tundra of northern Mackenzie; migrated in fall to the Atlantic coast south to Long Island (chiefly offshore) and over the ocean to eastern South America; wintered from southern Brazil to Patagonia; in spring migrated through the interior of North America. In very recent years (1960s) a few individuals have been reported in spring on the Texas coast and one was shot in fall in the Barbados (specimen preserved).

Former occurrence: Long Island—the following is taken from my account (Bull, 1964: 195–196): "The Eskimo Curlew was reported to be partial to dry upland fields adjacent to the seacoast, associating with Golden and Upland Plovers, generally avoiding the wet salt meadows and mud flats favored by Long-billed and Hudsonian Curlews. In clear weather eskimo Curlews were rarely seen. After severe easterly storms, especially during early September, occasionally 'hundreds' would be found on the fields.

"Being esteemed as a delicacy for the table, great numbers of Eskimo Curlews were shot in the past for the market, both in the west on the northbound flight and in the east on the return southward migration. This, together with constant hunting pressure on its wintering grounds in southern South America, caused this species to become virtually, if not entirely, extinct. Known by the hunters as Dough-bird (New England) and Fute (Long Island).

"Giraud (1844) reported that on Long Island it arrived in the latter part of August and remained until the first of November. He shot stragglers as late as Nov. 20. In later years (1875–91), however, the species was reported to occur from Sept. 7 to 30 (specimens in both cases) and this agrees with dates from the Massachusetts coast (Aug. 27 to Oct. 1).

"The species was definitely recorded (specimens) only from Montauk, Good Ground (= Hampton Bays), south of Amityville and Freeport, and in the vicinity of Far Rockaway. Of many local specimens reported taken, very few are in existence, and I have been able to find only three in the American Museum, all without dates: two mounts in the Lawrence collection, merely labeled Long Island, AMNH 3171 and 3348, and a skin in the Dwight collection, from Montauk Point, AMNH 355779. Two specimens in the Princeton University Museum were collected at Good Ground in 1880, and another in the University of Michigan, 121812, was shot near Amityville the same year on Sept. 11. The last known specimen from Long Island was taken at Montauk Point, Sept. 16, 1891 (Scott). The often published 'record' of Aug. 3, 1893, was an unverified sight report (see Dutcher, 1887–94). The Aug. 3 date would appear to be about a month earlier than the earliest specimen."

Upstate—There are only three reliable records from the interior of New York, all of them specimens of which two are extant, as follows: (1) Onondaga Lake, Onondaga Co. (date and collector unknown), NYSM 19177; (2) Lockport, Niagara Co., Oct. 2, 1879 (Hill) BMS 5040; (3) Manitou, Monroe Co., Sept. 23, 1890 (Hall), BMS 785 as reported by Beardslee and Mitchell (1965: 216), but the specimen cannot now be found. Eaton (1910: 342) listed several other inland occurrences, but details are lacking.

There are no authenticated spring records in New York based on specimens.

Remarks: This species is closely related to the eastern Palearctic *N. minutus* (Little Curlew), breeding in central and eastern Siberia, and wintering south to Australia.

Marbled Godwit (*Limosa fedoa*) *

Range: Central North America, breeding east to southern Manitoba and western Minnesota. Winters north to southern United States, regularly as far north as South Carolina.

Status: Rare to uncommon, but regular fall migrant on the outer coast, occasionally more numerous; very rare in spring. Very rare inland.

Occurrence: The Marbled Godwit is confined almost exclusively to the broad expanse of mud flats on the south shore of Long Island. There it may associate with Willets, both yellowlegs, and other species of shorebirds. On occasion the observer may be fortunate to find both godwits feeding together and thus obtain a direct comparison between the two species. In very recent years the Marbled Godwit has proved to be rarer in our area than the Hudsonian Godwit.

Prior to 1890, a regular migrant in small numbers in May, August, and September; then very rare until the early 1930s, when it became regular in fall, and by the late 1930s and early 1940s reported occasionally in flocks up to ten.

MAXIMA: five, Moriches Inlet, Suffolk Co., July 16, 1963; eight, Idlewild, Queens Co., Aug. 14, 1951; ten, Moriches Inlet, Sept. 14, 1944; four, Jamaica Bay Refuge, Queens Co.,

Dec. 9, 1962 (Backstrom), very late for so many.

EXTREME DATES: July 6 to Nov. 19 and Dec. 9 (see above). Usually rare after September.

Coastal, Spring: Very rare at this season— only six reliable occurrences, all in recent years, dates ranging from Mar. 27 to May 11 (Bull, 1964: 215) and exceptionally June 12, 1969, Southampton, Suffolk Co. (Queens County Bird Club).

Coastal, Winter: Only two known occurrences—one collected at Shinnecock Inlet, Suffolk Co., Dec. 22, 1952 (Wilcox), specimen in AMNH collection; another carefully observed by numerous people at the Jamaica Bay Refuge, Dec. 30, 1961.

Inland: This species is exceptionally rare upstate. There are only ten reliable reports— all singles—none of them specimens to my knowledge. Eaton (1910: 321) listed three fall occurrences. He also mentioned a spring "record" without details. The seven recent reports range from July 25 to Oct. 11 in various years. Four of the occurrences come from the Lake Ontario shore of Monroe Co., including a bird of this species and one Hudsonian Godwit, photographed at Shore Acres, Aug. 19, 1950 (Mitchell). Another photographed at Sandy Pond, Oswego Co., was present from Aug. 30 to Sept. 6, 1958.

Away from Lake Ontario the species has been recorded at Albany and on the Niagara River (Eaton, *op. cit.*) and twice at the Montezuma Refuge, Sept. 7–16, 1966, and Aug. 27 to Sept. 11, 1970.

The only reliable spring occurrence inland is one carefully observed in a pasture at Parma, Monroe Co., June 3, 1967 (Listman and O'Hara).

Bar-tailed Godwit
(*Limosa lapponica*)   *

Range: Northern Eurasia and northwestern Alaska. Winters in the Old World, in the western portion from the British Isles to central Africa. Accidental in eastern North America in Massachusetts, New York (Long Island), and New Jersey.

Status: *Accidental*—an adult of the nominate

race was collected on Moriches Bay, opposite Mastic, Suffolk Co., Nov. 15, 1946 (J. Rose), AMNH 308880 (Muller, *Auk,* 1947, 64: 326).

Hudsonian Godwit
(*Limosa haemastica*)   *

Range: Northern Nearctic region, breeding range very restricted, locally south to the shore of Hudson Bay in northeastern Manitoba; also extreme northern Ontario (Godfrey, 1966: 163–164). Spring migration chiefly through the Great Plains; in fall mainly over the Atlantic Ocean (but see below). Winters in southern South America.

Status: Rare to uncommon but regular fall migrant both coastwise and inland; occasionally more numerous. Very rare in spring.

Occurrence: The Hudsonian Godwit frequents mud flats. Formerly it was considered rare, but regular on Long Island. There were two large flights prior to 1925, both on Shinnecock Bay, the first in 1903, the second in 1922. In 1903 the flight occurred on Aug. 31, when gunners were reported to have killed a dozen or more apiece. In 1922 on Aug. 28 —after a two-day northeaster—at least 26 birds were reported, including a flock of 16, two of which were collected.

Between 1922 and 1951 no large numbers were reported on Long Island and groups up to three were the maxima recorded.

Upstate this species was formerly very rare in fall, but since the mid-1950s has become regular and appears in some numbers. It occurs most often along the shore of Lake Ontario, to a lesser extent on other inland lakes, and in the vicinity of pools and flats on the Montezuma Marshes.

RECENT MAXIMA: *Coastal* (all at Moriches Inlet, Suffolk Co.)—11, July 24, 1965; 17, Aug. 18, 1962; nine, Sept. 9, 1961.

RECENT MAXIMA: *Inland*—four, Montezuma Marshes, July 13, 1968; six, Sandy Pond, Oswego Co., Sept. 14, 1963; six, Delta Lake, Oneida Co., Sept. 15, 1963 (same? birds); ten, Sylvan Beach, Oneida Lake, Oct. 3, 1964; 12, same locality, Oct. 20, 1964 (big inland flight in 1964—see Scheider, 1965).

During the autumn of 1967 there was an unprecedented flight of Hudsonian Godwits at the Montezuma Refuge. On Sept. 28, *25* were seen and on Sept. 30 an almost unbelievable flock of *40* was recorded by many observers (*Kingbird,* 1968, 18: 28, 33, 35). These concentrations would appear to support those who believe that there is a marked overland flight of these birds in fall, which would be on an essentially direct flyway from the Hudson Bay breeding grounds to the coast of Long Island.

EXTREME DATES: July 4 (coastal) to Nov. 26 (coastal). The dates of Dec. 1–4, 1957, given by Beardslee and Mitchell (1965: 233), are erroneous. They should be *Nov.* 1–4, 1957 (see *Goshawk,* 1958, 11: 9).

Spring: Very rare at this season. A specimen was examined in the British Museum (Natural History) during the writer's visit there the summer of 1966: female in nonbreeding plumage, Long Island, May 1871 (Maynard), ex-coll. Seebohm, BMNH 92. 8. 3. 322 (Cat. Birds British Mus., 1896, 24: 390). In addition there are six recent reliable spring sight reports on Long Island with dates ranging from May 3 to 25.

Inland this species has been observed carefully in spring on three occasions: (1) Oak Orchard Swamp area in the vicinity of the Wolcottsville sinks, Niagara Co., Apr. 14–19, 1962 (Byron and numerous observers); (2) Lake Ontario shore at Hamlin Beach, Monroe Co., May 18, 1969 (Lloyd, McKinney, and Sunderlin); (3) Sandy Pond Inlet, Oswego Co., June 13, 1969 (Rusk), in breeding plumage.

Specimen data: Of at least six *inland* specimens reported, two appear to be extant: (1) Crusoe Lake, near Savannah, Wayne Co., Oct. 26, 1941 (Drummond), CUM 10873; (2) Lake Ontario at Braddock's Bay, Monroe Co., Oct. 27, 1946 (Meade), RMAS 622.

Short-billed Dowitcher
(*Limnodromus griseus*)   *

Range: Northern North America, breeding in three widely separated areas—(1) southern Alaska; (2) west-central Canada east to the west shore of Hudson Bay; (3) interior northern Quebec (Ungava district) west possibly to the east shore of James Bay. The eastern breeding population (nominate *griseus*) mi-grates mainly along the Atlantic coast and winters north to South Carolina, rarely farther.

Status: Common to very abundant coastal migrant; summering stragglers; very rare in winter (species?). Inland—much less numerous —variously uncommon to occasionally very common migrant.

Occurrence: Dowitchers are among the most numerous and conspicuous shorebirds on the outer coast of Long Island. May and July are the principal months of passage and thousands may be observed at times, especially during the spring flight. The extensive mud flats along the south shore, especially in the Jamaica Bay region, are very attractive to them.

MAXIMA, COASTAL: *Spring*—4000, Far Rockaway, Queens Co., May 7, 1950; 8000, Jamaica Bay, May 12, 1939. *Fall*—400, Jamaica Bay, July 4, 1961; 3000, Moriches Bay, Suffolk Co., July 13, 1963; 1200, Jamaica Bay, July 30, 1950.

MAXIMA, INLAND: *Spring*—May 22, 1966, 100, Medusa, Albany Co.; 75, Vischer's Ferry, Saratoga Co. *Fall*—50, Montezuma Refuge, July 24, 1964; 175, Manitou, Monroe Co., Aug. 20, 1960; 30 (species?), Montezuma, Oct. 5, 1960.

EXTREME DATES: Mar. 20 (coastal) and Mar. 30 (inland); summer coastal stragglers; to Nov. 18 (inland) and Nov. 30 (coastal).

Winter—coast only: four, Jamaica Bay, Dec. 12, 1953, to Jan. 2, 1954; two, Hempstead Reservoir, Nassau Co., Jan. 2, 1954; singles at Tobay Pond, Nassau Co., Jan. 10, 1954, also late December and early January 1956–1957, and 1962–1963.

The extreme dates and winter reports are all based on observations. It should be emphasized that in no case was the species positively determined.

Subspecies: Pitelka's treatment (1950) is followed here. The vast majority of specimens taken in New York belongs to the eastern breeding population—nominate *griseus,* number 3 above (see **Range).** Several specimens of the central Canadian breeding population (number 2 above)—the race *hendersoni* (in breeding plumage below, darker cinnamon and spotting sparser than in nominate *griseus,* but somewhat variable individually) were taken on Long Island (Bull, 1964: 210). At least **two**

inland specimens of *hendersoni* were determined by Pitelka: Cayuga Lake, Sept. 9, 1910, CUM 2091; Tonawanda, Erie Co., Aug. 5, 1949, BMS 3423.

Remarks: See discussion under next species.

Long-billed Dowitcher
(*Limnodromus scolopaceus*)   *

Range: Breeds in northeastern Siberia, western and northern Alaska, and east to extreme northwestern Canada (District of Mackenzie). Migrates and winters chiefly in western North America; in migration locally in eastern United States, in winter locally east to Florida.

Status: Regular fall migrant on the coast and probably inland.

Occurrence: The Long-billed Dowitcher frequents both inland and coastal fresh-water ponds and marshes interspersed with flats, but it is by no means confined to these, occurring also on the shores and flats of the coastal bays along with the other species. In fall it arrives and departs much later than the Short-billed Dowitcher.

Remarks: The two dowitchers are among the most difficult shorebirds to identify and this holds for identification in museum collections as well as in the field. To confirm this, one has only to read the account by Wallace (1968) regarding the difficulty of distinguishing the two forms in life.

Nonetheless, experienced observers, after long years of study, and under favorable circumstances, can identify these birds in the field. Occasionally extremely large, long-billed individuals may be recognized and the very different call attributed to *scolopaceus* is also very likely a diagnostic field "mark" in differentiating it from *griseus*. Coloration and pattern differences too may be noted sometimes when the two forms are together. Perhaps study of captive birds from known breeding grounds will settle the conflicting opinions.

Pitelka (1950) listed a number of specimens of *scolopaceus* collected on Long Island. These specimens are in several museums, chiefly the AMNH collection. He also determined as this species one taken in the Montezuma Marshes, Sept. 22, 1928, CUM 4043.

Reports of flocks up to 25 and 70 at inland fresh-water and coastal salt-water localities in October are *probably* but not definitely *scolopaceus*. Maximum numbers and dates of occurrence are given under the previous species and are intended to represent the two dowitchers collectively.

For further discussion, see *Remarks* in Bull (1964: 209–211).

Stilt Sandpiper
(*Micropalama himantopus*)   *

Range: North America, breeding locally in western and central portions southeast to the west shore of Hudson Bay; rarely to the south shore (extreme northern Ontario). Migrates in spring through the center of the continent, in fall over the spring route, also overland to the Atlantic coast from Massachusetts southward. Winters in southern South America.

Status: Variously uncommon to locally common fall migrant on the coast, occasionally even very common; very rare in spring. Inland usually rare to uncommon in fall, but on occasion even common.

Occurrence: The Stilt Sandpiper is a frequent associate of Lesser Yellowlegs and Dowitchers and, like them, wades and feeds in shallow pools and marshes interspersed with mud flats. It is, however, more particular in its choice of habitat and is rarely found on the more exposed flats. In New York although more numerous on the coast than on inland waters, this species is subject to marked fluctuations and is actually scarce some years.

MAXIMA: *Coastal*—45, Tobay Pond, Nassau Co., July 23, 1949; 80, Oak Beach, Suffolk Co., Aug. 6, 1938; 13 collected out of *200* seen, Mastic, Suffolk Co., Aug. 12, 1912 (Floyd and J. T. Nichols), specimens in AMNH collection; *150*, Jamaica Bay, Aug. 14, 1948 (Mayer and Rose); *300*, Mecox Bay to Napeague, Suffolk Co., Aug. 27, 1911 (Helmuth); 75, Easthampton, Suffolk Co., Sept. 16, 1944; 15, Jones Beach, Sept. 27, 1946.

MAXIMA: *Inland*—nine, Onondaga Lake, July 18, 1960; 12, El Dorado Beach, Jefferson Co., Aug. 1, 1964; 60, Montezuma Marshes, Sept. 6, 1965 (Benning); 40 and 30, same locality, Oct. 6 and 20, 1966, respectively—big late flight.

EXTREME DATES: July 1 (coastal) and July 7 (inland) to Nov. 8 (inland) and Nov. 17 (coastal). Rare after mid-October.

In *spring,* there are only 15 known occurrences on the coast, dates ranging from Apr. 13 to June 10 (specimen). The only spring specimens from the state that I am aware of are three taken by Roy Latham—all in NYSM collection—from extreme eastern Long Island, in Suffolk Co., as follows: (1) and (2) both at Orient, May 25, 1925, and June 9, 1940; (3) Shelter Island, June 10, 1942.

Inland this species has been reported on only three occasions in spring by experienced observers: (1) Perch River Refuge, Jefferson Co., May 6, 1968 (A. W. Allen); (2) and (3) both at Hamlin Beach, Monroe Co., May 11, 1952 (Hall), and May 18, 1969 (Foster).

Greater Yellowlegs
(*Tringa melanoleuca*) *

Range: North America, in the east breeding south to the central portions of Ontario and Quebec; and to Cape Breton Island, northern Nova Scotia (Godfrey, 1966: 149). Winters regularly north to Long Island and Massachusetts.

Status: Very common to abundant coastal migrant, common to very common inland. Uncommon, but regular in winter on the coast in recent years, formerly very rare. Probably a few summering nonbreeders occur on the coast each year.

Occurrence: The Greater Yellowlegs is very ubiquitous, inhabiting coastal flats, tidal pools, marshes, inland lake and river shores, ponds, flooded fields, and golf courses. This species is much more numerous than the Lesser Yellowlegs in spring, but is often outnumbered by the latter during the much more protracted fall migration. Quite often the two species are found together, offering the observer an opportunity for comparison.

MAXIMA, COASTAL: *Fall*—300, Jones Beach, Aug. 12, 1931; 350, Jamaica Bay, Aug. 27, 1950; 1000, same area, Sept. 27, 1965 (Norse); 150, same area, Oct. 23, 1955. *Winter*—ten, Pelham Bay, Bronx Co., Dec. 23, 1961; ten,

Jamaica Bay, Dec. 27, 1953. *Spring*—90, Easthampton, Suffolk Co., Apr. 29, 1932; 400, same locality, May 23, 1927.

MAXIMA, INLAND: *Fall*—100, El Dorado Beach, Jefferson Co., July 30, 1964; 120, Montezuma Marshes, Oct. 14, 1964; 75, Buck Pond, Monroe Co., Oct. 24, 1953. *Spring*—15, Oak Orchard Swamp, Mar. 31, 1968; 150, Hanover Center, Chautauqua Co., Apr. 25, 1965.

Inland the species has been recorded as early as Feb. 25, 1951—Tifft Street Marsh, Buffalo (Brockner)—a wintering? bird; and as late as Dec. 2. It has been recorded also along the Lake Ontario shore as late as June 9 and as early? as June 26, and arriving on July 2.

Greater Yellowlegs are usually rare before late March and after mid-November.

Remarks: The genus *Tringa* is used for both yellowlegs, in conformity with modern treatment, and is virtually universally accepted.

Lesser Yellowlegs
(*Tringa flavipes*) *

Range: Chiefly western North America, breeding south and east to extreme west-central Quebec, near James Bay. Winters north to Maryland and southern New Jersey, more rarely to Long Island. Migrates in spring chiefly through the Mississippi valley.

Status: Common to abundant fall migrant; in spring fairly common inland, but rare to uncommon, although regular on the coast. Rare and irregular in winter on the coast; rarer than the preceding species on the coast in summer, in fact no proof of actual summering.

Occurrence: The Lesser Yellowlegs is more particular in its choice of habitat than its larger relative, being less likely to occur on the open beaches and flats. It prefers grassy pools and ponds and—along the coast—salt meadows where short-grass pools have been exposed by the receding tide.

MAXIMA, COASTAL: *Fall*—40, Mastic, Suffolk Co., July 10, 1921; 500, Napeague, Suffolk Co., Aug. 24, 1924 (Helmuth); 250, Sagaponack, Suffolk Co., Sept. 17, 1932. *Winter*—four, Mecox Bay, Suffolk Co., Dec. 26, 1938, to Feb. 13, 1939. Virtually no concentrations of over a half-dozen in spring. Ten at Lawrence, Nassau Co., June 26, 1965, may represent exceptionally early southbound migrants.

MAXIMA, INLAND: *Fall*—19, Montezuma Marshes, July 1, 1964; 280, Onondaga Lake, July 18, 1969; 150, Tifft Street marsh, Buffalo, July 24, 1962; 260, Montezuma, July 30, 1967; 265, Onondaga Lake, Aug. 11, 1968; 250, Shore Acres, Monroe Co., Aug. 29, 1963; 85, Montezuma, Nov. 13, 1964. *Spring*—four, Wolcottsville, Niagara Co., Mar. 28, 1954; 18, same locality, Apr. 19, 1962; 80, same locality, May 4, 1962 (Rosche), unusual number for spring.

Inland dates range from Mar. 20 to Nov. 30; also various dates through June, but no proof of summering.

Remarks: The account in the *Auk* (1891, 8: 394) of birds believed to be this species breeding at Phelps, Ontario Co., during the summer of 1891 is unconfirmed. Neither adults, eggs, nor young were taken to substantiate the claim. Moreover, the A.O.U. Check-list (1957: 191, footnote) does not credit it. The locality is far south of the known southern limits of the breeding range (see **Range**).

[Greenshanks (*Tringa nebularia*)

Hypothetical: Breeds in northern Eurasia; winters nearly throughout the warmer regions of the Old World. No specimen record for North America.

One was observed with Lesser Yellowlegs on the shore of Onondaga Lake, near Syracuse, Aug. 30, 1962 (Peakall and Propst, *Kingbird,* 1962, 12: 141). The former observer has had previous field experience with this species in Europe.]

Solitary Sandpiper
(*Tringa solitaria*)   *

Range: North America; in the east breeds south to the central portions of Ontario and Quebec. No proof of breeding in the United States (see **Remarks**). Winters from southern United States southward.

Status: Fairly common migrant.

Occurrence: The Solitary Sandpiper fre-
quents fresh-water pools, woodland ponds and streams and, to a lesser extent, creeks and marshes—both inland and along the coast. Far from solitary at times, it is found in small aggregations as may be seen following.

MAXIMA: *Spring*—20, Jackson's Pond (near Poughkeepsie), Dutchess Co., May 14, 1922 (Crosby and Murphy); 12, Pocantico River (near Tarrytown), Westchester Co., May 20, 1949.

MAXIMA: *Fall*—nine, Prendergast Point, Chautauqua Co., July 28, 1968; 20, near Texas, Oswego Co., Aug. 9, 1956 (Scheider); 17, Otisco Lake, Onondaga Co., Sept. 8, 1963 (several observers); nine, Easthampton, Suffolk Co., Sept. 23, 1933.

EXTREME DATES: *Fall*—June 29 and July 1 (both inland) to Nov. 18 (coastal). *Spring* —Apr. 4 (coastal and inland) to June 6 (coastal) and June 11 (inland). Beardslee and Mitchell (1965: 217) give spring dates as late as June 13, 19, and 24, but these are most exceptional.

Rare before late April and after mid-October.

Remarks: Old reports of the Solitary Sandpiper supposedly breeding in the northern United States, including the Adirondack region, are entirely without foundation. These reports were based, in part, on the fact that since the bird was seen in the summer months it "must be breeding." Even Eaton (1910: 327) was misled by these erroneous reports. He stated, ". . . I have no doubt its nest will be found eventually in the Adirondack country." His further remarks attest to ignorance of the nesting habits of this species, as was prevalent in those days: "No member of this order is more mysterious in its breeding habits." The reason for the "mystery" was simply that collectors and observers had been looking for the bird's nest on the ground when, in fact, it was discovered as early as 1903 that the Solitary Sandpiper breeds arboreally in abandoned *tree* nests of passerines, such as thrushes, jays, and blackbirds, in the Canadian "wilds."

Spotted Sandpiper
(*Actitis macularia*)   *   B

Range: North America, breeding from Alaska and Canada to southwestern United

States, and on the east coast south to Virginia, and in the mountains to northern Alabama. Winters in the east—north to South Carolina, but chiefly from the Gulf of Mexico southward.

Status: Common to occasionally very common migrant inland, less numerous along the coast. Widespread breeder.

Nonbreeding: This species ranges widely from coastal beaches and marshes to mountain streams and lakes. Although numerically less prevalent than the Killdeer, the Spotted Sandpiper is better known over most of the state as it is more generally distributed.

MAXIMA: *Fall*—80, Montezuma Marshes, July 4, 1965; 70, Onondaga Lake, near Syracuse, Aug. 14, 1960. *Spring*—60, El Dorado Beach, Jefferson Co., May 22, 1965. All these numbers are exceptional, however, as groups up to a half-dozen are the norm. An estimate of 300 at a locality along the Lake Ontario shore in May, if correct, is unprecedented.

EXTREME DATES: Apr. 3 (coastal) and Apr. 6 (inland) to Nov. 14 (coastal) and Nov. 20 (inland). Usually rare before mid-April and after mid-October. An observation on the date of Mar. 22, 1969 (*Kingbird,* 1969, 19: 107), is without details.

Winter—An individual, believed correctly identified, was observed on the shore of Kensico Reservoir, Westchester Co., Dec. 21, 1947 (Oboiko and P. C. Spofford).

Breeding: Nests on the ground in open grassy fields or occasionally in cultivation where planted to grain and vegetable crops; also along ponds and streams, and in coastal sand dunes among beach grass.

Some Long Island breeding maxima are: 20 plus pairs at Short Beach in 1951, 20 pairs on Fisher's Island in 1965, and 15 nests on Great Gull Island, both in 1968 and 1969. The last-named is 17 acres in extent (=almost one nest per acre).

Of 42 New York nests examined, *all* contained four-egg clutches. In one nest, Burger (1963: 18) determined an incubation period of 18 days.

EGG DATES: May 6 to July 26.

Unfledged juveniles: June 2 to Aug. 19; fledglings: no New York data.

Banding: An individual banded Aug. 19,

1933, on Long Island, was shot the following Sept. 13 on the West Indian island of Martinique.

Remarks: Placed in the genus *Tringa* by some ornithologists, but the downy young color pattern of this species is very different from that of other tringine sandpipers (Jehl, 1968: 18–19). Although closely related to the Old World *A. hypoleucos,* the Common Sandpiper, and considered conspecific by a few taxonomists, the two forms are considered separate species by many authorities and are so treated here. Presence or absence of ventral spotting differentiates the two forms which, it is believed, have attained species level.

Willet
(*Catoptrophorus semipalmatus*) * B

Range: Nearctic and northern Neotropical regions, breeding very locally from southern Canada and northern United States to Mexico and the West Indies. In the east winters along the Atlantic coast north to Virginia, casually to Long Island. For further details, see **Subspecies.**

Status: Collectively, the Willet (both subspecies) is predominantly a *coastal* migrant, variously rare to common in spring, and fairly common to occasionally very common in fall. It is subject to marked fluctuations, but has increased in recent years. *Inland* it is a rare to uncommon migrant at any time, but is occasionally more numerous in fall. Rare and local breeder on Long Island, first recorded nesting there in 1966.

Nonbreeding: On Long Island this species delights in broad expanses of sand and mud flats. It frequently associates with Greater Yellowlegs and is often seen with godwits.

MAXIMA, COASTAL: *Spring*—all on eastern Long Island, Suffolk Co.—19, Westhampton Beach, Apr. 28, 1937; 34, Shinnecock Bay, May 16, 1958; 50, Mecox Bay area, May 18, 1947; seven, same locality, May 29, 1945.

MAXIMA, COASTAL: *Fall*—14, Moriches Inlet, Suffolk Co., July 14, 1957; 14, Easthampton, Suffolk Co., July 29, 1949; big flight, autumn of 1944 at Idlewild, Queens Co.—50,

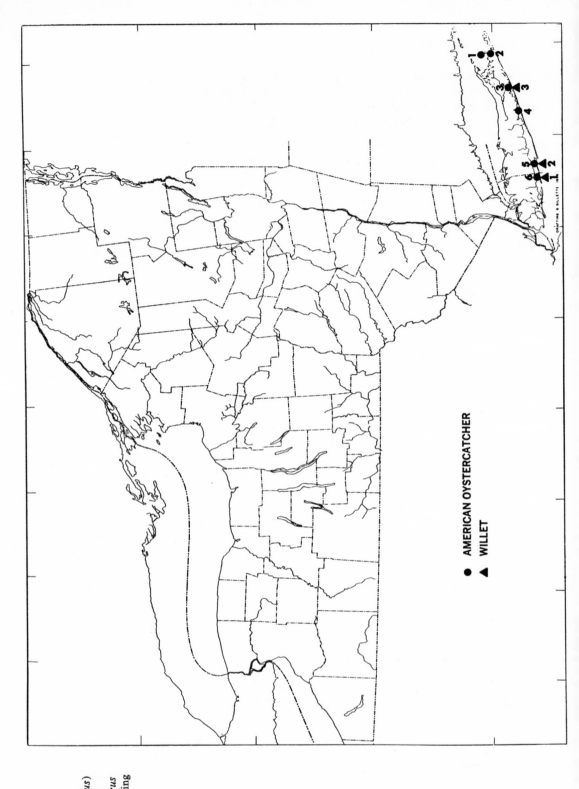

MAP 67 American Oystercatcher (*Haematopus palliatus*) Breeding distribution Willet (*Catoptrophorus semipalmatus*) Breeding distribution

● AMERICAN OYSTERCATCHER

▲ WILLET

Sept. 8; 80, Sept. 18; 45, Sept. 23; 34, Oct. 7; five, Jamaica Bay, Oct. 18, 1958.

MAXIMA, INLAND: *Spring*—four, Niskayuna, Schenectady Co., May 17, 1966.

MAXIMA, INLAND: *Fall*—four, Tonawanda, Erie Co., Aug. 16, 1946; five, Morgan Lake, Poughkeepsie, Dutchess Co., Sept. 1, 1922. Most unusual is a flock of *22* flying over Fish Gulf, near Otisco Lake, Onondaga Co., Aug. 26, 1968 (Jean Propst); unprecedented for an inland locality.

EXTREME DATES: Apr. 16 (coastal) and May 2 (inland) to Oct. 28 (inland) and Dec. 5 (coastal). On the coast rare after October.

Winter—Two eastern Long Island dates: Dec. 21, 1968; Dec. 27, 1962.

At least a dozen individuals summered in 1965 on the bay islands in the Jones Beach area, but breeding was not proved.

Breeding (see Map 67): Willets were first found nesting in the state in 1966 when at least three nests were discovered in the (1) Jones Beach area (Bull, 1970: 19). In 1967 they had spread east to (2) Oak Beach, Suffolk Co., and in 1968 were reported at (3) Tiana Beach in the eastern part of the same county.

Most of the nests were found in beach-grass clumps in sand on salt-marsh islands just back of the barrier beaches. Another nest was in a similar location in a patch of seaside goldenrod. One of these islands had a breeding colony of about 250 pairs of Common Terns. The Willet nests were at the edge of the tern colony. For further details, see Davis (*Wilson Bull.*, 1968, 80: 330). Two 1971 nests were located on the barrier beach itself.

Egg clutches in eight Long Island nests: three eggs (one nest); four eggs (seven nests).

EGG DATES: May 19 to June 30.

Nestling date: June 15; fledglings: no New York data.

Subspecies: There are two very distinct subspecies of Willet occurring in New York: (1) Nominate *semipalmatus* is *coastal* and primarily eastern in distribution. It breeds on the Atlantic coast in Nova Scotia, on Long Island (since 1966), and from southern New Jersey to Florida; on the Gulf coast from Florida to Texas and Mexico (Tamaulipas), and locally in the northern West Indies. It formerly bred

also in Massachusetts and very rarely in southern Connecticut; in 1971 in southern Maine.

(2) The race *inornatus* (much larger and paler) is an *inland* and western breeder. It nests primarily in the Great Plains area and in the prairie regions east to Manitoba, South Dakota, and Nebraska; formerly to Minnesota and Iowa.

I have examined 30 New York specimens, 29 from Long Island, only one from upstate. Of the former—all in the AMNH collection—two are of the coastal, nominate race taken in spring at Montauk Point (Bull, 1964: 200). The other 27 are *all* of the western race *inornatus* taken in fall, dates ranging from Aug. 10 to Aug. 27 in various years, all from various south-shore localities.

The one extant inland specimen is *inornatus*, and was taken near Ithaca, Aug. 8, 1921, by Arthur A. Allen, and is CUM 2040.

Another inland specimen from the Buffalo area, without date, was reported to be in the collection of the Buffalo Museum of Science (Beardslee and Mitchell, 1965: 219), but I have not seen it.

Upland Sandpiper
(*Bartramia longicauda*) * B

Range: Nearctic region, but very local and with a disruptive distribution pattern; breeds from Alaska and the Yukon south to Oklahoma and northern Texas in the west, but with a greatly compressed north-south range in the east—from extreme southern Ontario and Quebec south only as far as Virginia. Winters in southern South America.

Status: Variously rare to locally common migrant, occasionally more numerous in fall, especially inland. Fairly widespread but generally uncommon breeder in open country; locally common, but has decreased considerably in recent years.

Nonbreeding: Usually only small numbers—from one to four—are observed in most places today, but on rare occasions considerable numbers are reported.

MAXIMA: *Fall*—25, Idlewild, Queens Co., July 14, 1935; Syracuse Airport, large flight in 1964 (Scheider, 1965: 16)—*63*, Aug. 3; *87,*

Aug. 30; also *94,* Aug. 25, 1965; 17, Amherst, Erie Co., Sept. 11, 1930.

MAXIMA: *Spring*—20, Manitou, Monroe Co., Apr. 28, 1956.

EXTREME DATES: Mar. 18 (coastal specimen), Mar. 25 (coastal), and Apr. 2 (inland) to Oct. 13 (inland) and Oct. 28 (coastal).

Rare before mid-April and after mid-September.

Breeding: Upland Sandpipers (they are *not* plovers) frequent plains, prairies, short-grass fields, old pastures, golf courses, and airports. On Long Island these fine birds formerly nested in numbers on the famous Hempstead Plains (Bull, 1964: 187). As many as 25 pairs bred there in the early 1920s, just in the Garden City-Mineola-Westbury area (J. T. Nichols, pers. comm.). With the near total destruction of this unique prairie, the former numbers dwindled to a pitiful remnant and yet, as recently as 1967 on the abandoned Mitchel Field airport, at least seven pairs remained to breed. For further details regarding breeding distribution in the New York City region, see Bull (*op. cit.*).

Upstate this species is, or was, a locally common breeder, especially in the mid-Hudson-Mohawk valley region, and in the agricultural districts of central and western New York. In the former area as many as 20 pairs were seen within five miles in the Coxsackie, Greene Co., region in 1919 (Bogardus), and in the latter portion a "colony" of at least 15 pairs was present near Franklinville, Cattaraugus Co., in 1934 (Amadon).

Search of museum collections and the literature has resulted in amassing a total of more than *120* breeding localities in the state, representing nearly all sections.

Hayfields and old pastures are the favored nesting sites for the species in the agricultural areas of upstate New York as they were on most of Long Island, excepting for the natural short-grass prairie mentioned previously. At least two pairs bred in grassland habitat at Kennedy International Airport in 1969 (Cohen).

According to Yunick (*Kingbird,* 1965, 15: 221–222), a pair attempted to nest on a tarred and pebbled rooftop near Vischer's Ferry, Saratoga Co., in 1964. Although these birds often perch on fence posts, telephone poles, and rarely even on rooftops, the last-named is an unusual location for a nest.

Egg clutches are invariably four—all 14 New York nests examined containing this number.

EGG DATES: Apr. 23 to June 15.

Unfledged juveniles: May 28 to July 18; fledglings: June 15 to Aug. 11.

Buff-breasted Sandpiper
(*Tryngites subruficollis*)   *

Range: Northwestern Nearctic region, breeding in the high arctic east to King William Island (northern Keewatin). Migrates chiefly through the plains in the center of the continent (entirely so in spring) but also regularly in small numbers in fall to the Atlantic coast at least as far south as New Jersey, then presumably over the ocean to its winter quarters in southern South America.

Status: Rare but regular fall migrant, both coastal and inland; occasionally more numerous.

Occurrence: The Buff-breasted Sandpiper, one of the most sought-after shorebirds, frequents dry grassy fields, airports, moist meadows, and sandy areas, but nearly always where the grass is short and the vegetation sparse. Usually only one or two individuals are recorded each fall.

MAXIMA: *Coastal*—Flock of five collected on the shore of Gowanus Bay, Brooklyn, August 1841 (Giraud, 1844: 231); eight, Hook Pond, Suffolk Co., Sept. 8, 1944 (Helmuth).

MAXIMA: *Inland*—four, Kendall, Orleans Co., Sept. 13, 1970 (Listman).

EXTREME DATES: Aug. 3, 1963—bird hit by an airplane at Kennedy International Airport, Queens Co., specimen in USNM collection (R. H. Laybourne, *in litt.*); to Oct. 15.

Specimen data: At least 20 specimens taken on Long Island have been examined, but the only inland specimen seen by me is one collected on the shore of Owasco Lake, Cayuga Co., Sept. 12, 1909 (Wright), CUM 3988.

Remarks: No spring specimen or *verified* sight report at that season exists for the state. A good color photograph is necessary, at least, to authenticate a spring occurrence.

Postcript: Two flocks of more than *40* individuals on a plowed field near Mecox Bay, Suffolk Co., during late August 1973 (many observers), are unheard-of numbers for the northeast; and a group of 13 the following month in Bermuda (*fide* D. Wingate) is unprecedented there.

Ruff (*Philomachus pugnax*) *

Range: Palearctic region, in the western portions breeding south to France. Winters from the British Isles to South Africa. Wanders to eastern North America, perhaps regularly; also Barbados.

Status: Formerly very rare; in recent years rare but regular visitant, occasionally more numerous. Occurs both along the coast and inland.

Occurrence: One of the "prizes" of the shorebird migration is the occasional appearance of the Ruff, especially if the bird in question is a brightly colored male in breeding plumage.

Prior to 1949 this species was known only from Long Island but, since 1960, it has appeared upstate each year both spring and fall, especially during the latter season. Ruffs are most frequently observed on Long Island at the Jamaica Bay Refuge, Tobay Pond in the Jones Beach area, and at Moriches Inlet. They prefer dry fields and grassy pools to bare mud flats.

Upstate the Ruff has been reported most often at Onondaga Lake (near Syracuse), but has been observed also at the Montezuma Marshes, at nearby Howland's Island, Oak Orchard Swamp, on the Lake Ontario shore at Irondequoit Bay (near Rochester) and north of Hilton, and in the Black River valley of Lewis Co. at Castorland.

MAXIMA: *Coastal*—three, Jamaica Bay Refuge, from Apr. 21 to May 27, 1956 (numerous observers)—two differently colored males in breeding plumage, plus one female (Reeve).

MAXIMA: *Inland*—six, Onondaga Lake, from July 1 to Sept. 12, 1964 (Peakall and Propst, *Kingbird*, 1965, 15: 22); during that period what were believed to be *five* different adult males (two in breeding plumage) and one immature or female were observed also by Rusk, Scheider, Spofford, and many others.

Again at the same locality the following year, five (including three different appearing adult males) were observed from July 1 to Aug. 20, 1965 (many observers).

The frequency and numbers with which the Ruff has been recorded in fall within recent years in the vicinity of Syracuse lends credence to a Siberian origin and thence an overland passage by way of Canada. An Atlantic crossing from Europe or Africa might argue for a coastwise concentration, but certainly not for its regular appearance at a given locality 200 or more miles inland.

EXTREME DATES: *Spring*—Mar. 31 (coastal) to June 12 and 23 (both coastal). *Fall*—July 1 (inland) to Nov. 6 (inland).

Specimen data: There are five old extant New York specimens all from Long Island. Three are in the AMNH collection (Bull, 1964: 218) and two, merely labeled Long Island without date or name of collector, are in the CUM collection, 667 (male) and 706 (female). There are no known specimens from upstate.

Curlew Sandpiper
(*Calidris ferruginea*) *

Range: Eastern Palearctic region, breeding in northern Siberia; in extreme northern Alaska in 1962. Winters over a wide range from the Mediterranean region to South Africa and Madagascar, and from tropical Asia to Australia and New Zealand. Wanders occasionally or regularly to eastern North America (New Brunswick to New Jersey, but chiefly Long Island) and the Lesser Antilles.

Status: Rare but regular coastal visitant, occasionally more numerous.

Occurrence: One of the most sought-after shorebirds is the very local and usually rare Curlew Sandpiper. The only reasonably certain locality where it may be seen is on the south-shore mud flats of Long Island, especially in the Jamaica Bay area. It is most often reported during the latter half of May when it is likely to be in the rich chestnut breeding plumage. At that season it frequently associates with Dunlins from which it is easily distinguished and with Knots which it superficially resembles in color. In autumn when it is in dull plumage it is more likely to be overlooked and then does resemble the Dunlin. For this reason it may not be as rare as generally believed.

MAXIMA, all in the Jamaica Bay region: four, May 14, 1949; three, May 21, 1951; two, Sept. 13, 1966.

EXTREME DATES: May 2 to June 9 (specimen); various "summer" dates; July 8 to Nov. 25, exceptionally to Dec. 19 (specimen).

Specimen data: Of a dozen or more specimens taken on Long Island, only six are extant, of which five are in the AMNH collection and one in a private collection (Bull, 1964: 207). Exceptionally late is one collected on Fisher's Island, Suffolk Co., Dec. 19, 1923 (Fuertes), AMNH 752387.

Remarks: There are at least three theories as to why the Curlew Sandpiper, an Old World shorebird (the Ruff is probably in the same category), occurs regularly on the Atlantic coast of the northeastern United States (Massachusetts, Long Island, New Jersey).

(1) Nisbet (1959) is of the opinion that this species makes a direct east-west crossing from Europe to North America during migration.

(2) Eisenmann (1960) suggests that this species (as well as the Ruff) may be carried across the tropical Atlantic by cyclonic storms while en route to Africa during the fall migration. He further suggests that their greater frequency in spring along our coast (not proved) is the result of birds being carried by hurricanes to tropical America in preceding years, and then accompanying other shorebirds on the northward flight.

(3) Bull (1964) believes that a few individuals may migrate in fall from their Siberian nesting grounds, then east by way of Alaska and Canada to the Atlantic seaboard—a route used by certain shorebirds breeding in tundra country of northern Alaska, Yukon, and Mackenzie—i.e., Eskimo Curlew (formerly), Long-billed Dowitcher, Western Sandpiper, Buff-breasted Sandpiper. The Long-billed Dowitcher and other primarily American shorebirds also breed in northeastern Siberia.

Unlike the Ruff, however, the Curlew Sandpiper is unrecorded from upstate New York, in fact anywhere off Long Island. And yet it has been reported as occurring three times in fall in southeastern Ontario on or near the Lake Ontario shore in the Toronto and Hamilton regions (Godfrey, 1966: 155).

Dunlin (*Calidris alpina*)   *

Range: Holarctic region, in America the race *pacifica* (larger, and brighter in breeding plumage than nominate race) breeds south to extreme northern Ontario (Hudson Bay). Winters along Atlantic coast north to Massachusetts.

Status: Common to locally abundant migrant and winter visitant on the coast where it is also a regular nonbreeding summer straggler. Inland it is only slightly less numerous in migration, but is very rare in winter and virtually nonexistent in summer.

Occurrence: The Dunlin, or Red-backed Sandpiper, is the last of the migrant shorebirds to arrive in numbers during fall passage and does not become numerous until September along the coast and October inland. The Dunlin, together with the Sanderling and Purple Sandpiper, are the only really common shorebirds in winter along the south shore of Long Island, although more locally distributed. Indeed, these three species are "sorted out" very nicely on an ecological basis—the Purple Sandpiper restricted almost exclusively to rocky areas, the Sanderling to sand beaches, and the Dunlin to mud flats—especially in and near the vicinity of tidal inlets. Upstate this species favors the shores of Lake Ontario and, judging from the largest concentrations reported, the flats of the Montezuma area.

MAXIMA, COASTAL: *Fall*—225, Jamaica Bay, Sept. 9, 1944; 1800, Jones Inlet, Nassau Co., Oct. 12, 1950; 800, Jamaica Bay, Oct. 26, 1952; 475, Oak Beach, Suffolk Co., Dec. 3, 1939. *Winter*—900, Jamaica Bay, Dec. 22, 1950; 600, Jones Inlet, Jan. 16, 1960; 55, Fire Island Inlet, Suffolk Co., Feb. 19, 1939. *Spring* —900, Far Rockaway, Queens Co., May 7, 1950.

MAXIMA, INLAND: *Fall*—700, Derby Hill, Oswego Co., Oct. 16, 1970; on Oct. 17, 1964 —400, Montezuma; and 330, Sylvan Beach, Oneida Lake; 600, Montezuma, Oct. 27, 1962; 500, Shore Acres, Monroe Co., Nov. 5, 1957; 110, El Dorado Beach, Jefferson Co., Nov. 11, 1966. *Spring*—eight, Batavia, Genesee Co., Apr. 16, 1961; 1000, Montezuma, May 21, 1957; seven, Braddock's Bay, Monroe Co., June 11, 1950.

There are at least four winter occurrences for the interior: (1) near Rochester, Dec. 23, 1954, and (2) Dec. 27, 1959; (3) two birds, Lake Erie shore, near Dunkirk, Chautauqua Co., Feb. 6, 1965; (4) one shot illegally by a hunter at Prendergast Point, Chautauqua Co., Jan. 2, 1966—specimen examined by Andrle and Axtell, but not preserved.

Remarks: I know of no New York specimen of any Old World subspecies that is available for examination; the 1892 individual taken on Long Island is not extant.

Red Knot (*Calidris canutus*)   *

Range: Holarctic region at high latitudes, the race *rufa* (paler than nominate race) breeding south to Southampton Island. Winters along the coast north to South Carolina; rarely to Massachusetts (specimens).

Status: Very common to abundant coastal migrant, occasionally very abundant; generally uncommon inland migrant, occasionally more numerous. Rare and irregular on the coast in winter, but on occasion locally common.

Occurrence: Knots are among the last shorebirds to appear in the spring, not arriving in numbers until the middle or end of May. They frequent the broad coastal salt meadows and mud flats of the south shore of Long Island.

Formerly (prior to 1890) occurring by the thousands, this species decreased greatly, due to overshooting. Protected by 1913, it recovered markedly and since the 1930s is once more abundant, although not yet attaining its former numbers.

MAXIMA, COASTAL: *Spring*—2500, Jamaica Bay, May 30, 1945 (Bull and Eisenmann). *Summer*—stragglers infrequent. *Fall*—1500, Meadow Island, near Jones Inlet, Nassau Co., July 22, 1962 (Levine); 450, Jamaica Bay, Aug. 10, 1944; 450, Moriches Inlet, Suffolk Co., Sept. 21, 1936; 400, Jamaica Bay, Oct. 23, 1944. *Winter*—specimen taken, Rockaway Beach, Queens Co., Jan. 20, 1875 (Eagle), AMNH collection; 26, Jones Beach, Dec. 24, 1939 (Elliott); 18, Shinnecock Inlet, Suffolk Co., Dec. 26, 1956 (Wilcox); six, Jamaica Bay, Jan. 27 to Feb. 22, 1955; eight, Jones Inlet, winter 1968–1969.

MAXIMA, INLAND: *Spring*—36, Sandy Pond,

Oswego Co., May 25, 1969 (Sutliff); 29, Montezuma Refuge, May 28, 1967 (Benning); 39, Manitou, Monroe Co., June 1, 1964 (Listman). *Fall*—six, south end of Cayuga Lake, Tompkins Co., Aug. 4, 1912; six, Sylvan Beach, Oneida Lake, Sept. 17, 1960.

EXTREME DATES, INLAND: *Spring*—May 17 to June 16. *Fall*—July 17 to Oct. 23. Recorded on the coast every month of the year.

Sanderling (*Calidris alba*)   *

Range: High latitudes of the Holarctic region, in North America breeding south to Southampton Island. Winters on the Atlantic coast north to Massachusetts.

Status: Common to abundant migrant on the outer coast; considerably less numerous in winter and as a summering nonbreeder. Fairly common to common migrant along the Great Lakes, but relatively rare elsewhere.

Occurrence: Sanderlings are characteristic of the ocean beaches and coastal sand bars, where they occur practically the year round. Inland they are frequent in migration on the shores of the Great Lakes, especially Lake Ontario.

MAXIMA, COASTAL: *Fall*—1000, Jamaica Bay, July 28, 1945; 1300, same locality, Aug. 9, 1947; 2000, Mecox Bay, Suffolk Co., Sept. 18, 1924. *Winter*—200, Plum Beach, Kings Co., Dec. 20, 1958; 300, Atlantic Beach to Point Lookout, Nassau Co., all January 1952. *Spring*—1500, Easthampton, Suffolk Co., May 20, 1927; 800, Jamaica Bay, June 6, 1946.

MAXIMA, INLAND: *Fall*—100, Sandy Pond, Oswego Co., July 24, 1962; 100, same locality, Aug. 7, 1965; 170, El Dorado Beach, Jefferson Co., Sept. 8, 1962; 90, Hamburg, Erie Co., Oct. 8, 1959; 40, Stony Point, Jefferson Co., Nov. 11, 1966 (Gordon), late for so many. *Spring*—15, Batavia, Genesee Co., May 17, 1959; 26, Irondequoit Bay, Monroe Co., May 30, 1958.

Most exceptional are the following: One each at Manitou Beach, Monroe Co., Dec. 18, 1954 (Listman), and Lake Erie shore, near Buffalo, Jan. 6, 1944 (Nathan).

Purple Sandpiper
(*Calidris maritima*)   *

Range: Holarctic region (but not Pacific quadrant), in North America breeding south to Baffin and Southampton islands; also on the Belcher Islands in southeastern Hudson Bay.

Status: Locally a very common winter visitant on both the outer (ocean) and inner (Long Island Sound) coasts; much less numerous on the Great Lakes. Very rare inland elsewhere.

Occurrence: The Purple Sandpiper is mostly confined to rocky shores and it is unusual to find it elsewhere. It is present in largest numbers on the wave-washed rock jetties along the south shore of Long Island, the rocky promontories at Montauk Point, and on rocky islands and breakwaters in Long Island Sound. The species has been lingering later in spring in large numbers during recent years and is occasional in summer.

MAXIMA: *Coastal*—85, Rockaway Point, Queens Co., Nov. 15, 1961; 100, Rye, Westchester Co., Dec. 1, 1940; 117, Short Beach, Nassau Co., Jan. 13, 1962; 125, Point Lookout, Nassau Co., Apr. 15, 1950; 200, Jones Inlet, Nassau Co., May 17, 1966 (Trimble), an unusually large number at such a late date; 48, Long Beach, Nassau Co., May 26, 1950.

MAXIMA: *Inland*—three, Dunkirk, Chautauqua Co., Feb. 10, 1967; four, Manitou, Monroe Co., Nov. 16, 1962; five, Niagara Falls, Dec. 8, 1968; big flight along eastern Lake Ontario shore in Jefferson Co., fall of 1966 (Gordon, *Kingbird*, 1967, 17: 22)—27, Stony Point, Nov. 11; 40, El Dorado Beach, Dec. 11; 23, Stony Point, Dec. 17. The species was formerly very rare on the Great Lakes. Unprecedented away from the Great Lakes are 24, Oneida Lake, Nov. 14, 1970 (Rusk).

EXTREME DATES: *Coastal*—Sept. 7, 1936, Orient, Suffolk Co., and Sept. 29 to June 6. Summer—Gardiner's Point, Suffolk Co., July 28, 1925 (specimen examined by Griscom, but apparently not extant); Great Gull Island, Suffolk Co., July 31, 1961; Short Beach, Nassau Co., July 2 to Aug. 13, 1961.

EXTREME DATES: *Inland*—Oct. 19 to Apr. 23; one collected, Grand Island, Niagara River, June 7, 1954 (Axtell), BMS 3655 (*not* June 8 as reported by Beardslee and Mitchell, 1965: 235).

Eaton (1910: 309) gave September dates for the Keuka Lake area, but these dates are not supported by specimens. In addition to a specimen in the Cornell University Museum collection from the Lake Ontario shore at Fair

Haven, Cayuga Co., Nov. 30, 1920 (Wright), CUM 4006, there are also two others in the same collection taken inland along the shore of Cayuga Lake in Tompkins Co.—one near Ithaca, Nov. 5, 1921 (McNeil), CUM 2344 and one at Myer's Point, Nov. 27, 1949 (Allen), CUM 23702. This last bird was with a Killdeer when collected. There is also a report of a bird seen by numerous observers on the shore of Seneca Lake at Dresden, Yates Co., from Feb. 4 to Mar. 19, 1951.

Pectoral Sandpiper
(*Calidris melanotos*)   *

Range: Northern portions of the eastern Palearctic (Siberia) and Nearctic regions; in America breeding south locally to the southern shores of Hudson Bay (extreme northern Ontario). Winters chiefly in southern South America.

Status: On the coast—common to abundant fall migrant; uncommon to fairly common spring migrant. Inland—just the reverse—common to abundant in spring; much less common in fall. Most numerous upstate in western New York, much less so in the eastern portions.

Occurrence: The Pectoral Sandpiper favors grassy pools and ponds, and short-grass meadows and—especially after heavy rains—fields, golf courses, and airports.

Unlike many of the common migrant shorebirds, this species is not known to summer in our area. No winter report is acceptable in absence of a specimen; two observations were not confirmed.

MAXIMA, COASTAL: *Fall*—1200 from Montauk to Easthampton, Aug. 25, 1924 (Helmuth); 350, Mecox Bay, Suffolk Co., Sept. 15, 1935; 80, same locality, Oct. 19, 1956. *Spring* —72, Jamaica Bay Refuge, May 12, 1970 (Stout and Johnson); 40, Sagaponack, Suffolk Co., May 31, 1929 (Helmuth).

MAXIMA, INLAND: *Fall*—34, Montezuma Marshes, July 30, 1967; 100, same locality, Sept. 6, 1965; 100, Shore Acres, Monroe Co., Oct. 2, 1959; 64, Waterloo, Seneca Co., Oct. 13, 1968; seven, Montezuma, Nov. 14, 1965. *Spring*—30, Hamlin, Monroe Co., Mar. 30, 1968; 325, Wolcottsville, Niagara Co., Apr.

18, 1964; 330, Oak Orchard Swamp, Apr. 23, 1967; 40, Baldwinsville, Onondaga Co., May 19, 1963.

EXTREME DATES: *Fall*—July 1 (inland) to Nov. 24 (inland) and Dec. 11 (coastal). *Spring* —Mar. 18 (coastal) to June 5 (inland) and June 18 (coastal).

Usually rare before April and after October.

White-rumped Sandpiper
(*Calidris fuscicollis*) *

Range: High latitudes in the central Nearctic region, breeding south to Southampton Island. Winters in southern South America.

Status: Variously uncommon to locally very common fall coastal migrant, much less numerous in spring; numbers fluctuate greatly. Inland rarer in proportion to the coast at both seasons, but more frequent in fall when occasionally even common.

Occurrence: The White-rumped Sandpiper is one of the many species of shorebirds whose spring passage is chiefly by way of the center of the continent and in fall mainly along the Atlantic coast. As a consequence it is relatively rare in spring in New York and numerous in fall. This species, like some of its congeners— Pectoral, Baird's, and Least sandpipers—prefer grassy meadows, pools, and pond edges to the more exposed flats which are frequented by many other waders. However, it is also found on lake and river shores upstate and sometimes on coastal estuaries and mud flats. This species is a notably late spring migrant, flocks occurring well into June.

MAXIMA, COASTAL: *Fall*—1000, Easthampton to Shinnecock Bay, Suffolk Co., Aug. 23, 1930 (Helmuth), a very unusual number representing half a dozen localities; 75, Oak Beach, Sept. 9, 1934. *Spring*—60, Easthampton, May 29, 1927; 75, Jamaica Bay, June 5, 1949; 50, Mastic, Suffolk Co., June 10, 1934; 20, Jamaica Bay, June 19, 1959. *Summer* stragglers are not infrequent.

For remarks on apparent local decrease in the New York City region, see Bull (1964: 204).

MAXIMA, INLAND: *Fall*—20, Braddock's Bay, Monroe Co., Aug. 30, 1958; 30, Sandy Pond, Oswego Co., Sept. 8, 1957; 35, Tona-wanda, Erie Co., Oct. 8, 1945. *Spring*—12, Montezuma Marshes, May 26, 1968; seven, Manitou, Monroe Co., June 12, 1964.

EXTREME DATES: Apr. 28 (coastal) and May 8 (inland) to Dec. 4 (coastal and inland). Rare before mid-May and after early November. Inland the species has been recorded in fall as early as July 24 and in spring as late as June 18.

An upstate report of a flock of 17 in mid-December was not substantiated.

Baird's Sandpiper
(*Calidris bairdii*) *

Range: High latitudes north of the Arctic Circle in extreme northeastern Siberia east to northwestern Greenland; breeds south in Canada only to the extreme northern mainland of the District of Keewatin. Spring migrant through the Great Plains; rare east of them. Winters chiefly in South America.

Status: Rare to uncommon, but regular fall migrant.

Occurrence: Baird's Sandpiper prefers grassy areas either dry or moist and is found in fields and on golf courses, especially after rain. It also frequents shores of grassy pools and coastal lagoons.

This species is seen to best advantage when associated with the other "peep" and can then be compared directly with them. Immatures are especially difficult to identify and it should be emphasized that no other shorebird is more often misidentified. Reports of upstate flocks of 13 in September and six in late November —if correctly identified—are remarkable but, being without any details whatsoever, are omitted here.

MAXIMA: *Coastal*—five, Sagaponack, Suffolk Co., Aug. 9, 1938; five, Baxter Creek, Bronx Co., Aug. 14, 1955; six, Mecox Bay, Suffolk Co., Aug. 22, 1923; 18, Easthampton, Suffolk Co., Sept. 16, 1933 (Helmuth)—14 together and four others nearby—an exceptional concentration.

MAXIMA: *Inland*—nine, Sandy Pond, Oswego Co., Sept. 5, 1957; eight, Kendall, Orleans Co., Sept. 6, 1970; six, Shore Acres,

Monroe Co., Sept. 16, 1962; four, Onondaga Lake, Oct. 4, 1969.

EXTREME DATES: July 16 (coastal) and July 28 (inland) to Nov. 15 (coastal) and Nov. 20 (inland specimen). December dates lack confirmation. Rare before August and after mid-October.

Remarks: No spring specimens from New York are known to the writer. Numerous specimens examined in collections have all been taken in fall. Nor does Eaton (1910: 312–313) mention any collected in spring. Beardslee and Mitchell (1965: 225–226) list spring dates from May 20 to June 13 in various years, but in no case was a specimen taken. In absence of specimen evidence, spring reports are omitted. For further discussion, see Bull (1964: 205).

Least Sandpiper
(*Calidris minutilla*) *

Range: Nearctic region, in the east breeds south to islands in the Gulf of St. Lawrence, more rarely to islands off Nova Scotia (Godfrey, 1966: 155). Winters along the coast north to North Carolina, rarely to Maryland and southern New Jersey.

Status: Common to abundant coastal migrant, occasionally very abundant; very rare in winter on the coast. Fairly common to very common inland migrant, occasionally even abundant.

Occurrence: This species, the smallest of our shorebirds, is a common inhabitant of grassy shores, flats, and pools—both coastal and inland—and after rains may be seen on flooded golf courses, airports, and fields.

MAXIMA, COASTAL: *Spring*—5000, Jamaica Bay, May 19, 1939 (Mayer). *Fall*—1200, Oak Beach, Suffolk Co., July 18, 1948; 800, Sagaponack, Suffolk Co., Aug. 29, 1933; 1600, Moriches Inlet, Suffolk Co., Sept. 28, 1936; 50, Mecox Bay, Suffolk Co., Oct. 25, 1936—a notably late flight in 1936.

MAXIMA, INLAND: *Spring*—400, Montezuma Marshes, May 21, 1957; 1000, Hamlin, Monroe Co., May 21, 1967 (Foster, Listman, and Tetlow), in flooded fields—an unprecedented number for an inland locality. *Fall*—

80, Onondaga Lake, July 13, 1964; 175, same locality, July 21, 1969; 90, Shore Acres, Monroe Co., Aug. 22, 1959; 200, Oneida Lake, Sept. 3, 1961.

EXTREME DATES: Apr. 3 (coastal) and May 1 (inland) to Nov. 18 (coastal). Usually rare before May and after mid-October. Stragglers occur regularly on the coast in summer. Inland it has been reported in spring as late as June 1 and in fall as early as June 27.

The Least Sandpiper has been recorded in winter on Long Island's south shore on five occasions; single birds were seen at Sagaponack, Suffolk Co., Mar. 10, 1946; Gravesend Bay, Brooklyn, Dec. 28, 1952; Hewlett Bay, Nassau Co., Dec. 30, 1961; Shinnecock Bay, Suffolk Co., Dec. 26, 1967. Most unusual were five observed at Jamaica Bay, Jan. 2, 1955 (Mayer).

A winter specimen from New York is highly desirable to substantiate occurrence at that season.

Semipalmated Sandpiper
(*Calidris pusilla*) *

Range: Nearctic region, breeding south to the shores of Hudson and James bays. Winters along the Atlantic coast north to Maryland and southern New Jersey (rare); more rarely to Long Island and Massachusetts (specimen).

Status: Very abundant migrant on the coast where it is also a regular summering nonbreeder in small numbers, but rare and irregular in winter. Inland a common to abundant migrant.

Occurrence: The Semipalmated Sandpiper is our most numerous shorebird and, at times, thousands may be seen on the broad mud flats of the south shore of Long Island. It occurs by the hundreds on the beaches and flats of Lake Ontario and is especially numerous in the Montezuma region.

MAXIMA, COASTAL: *Spring*—25,000, Easthampton to Mecox Bay, Suffolk Co., May 19, 1924 (Helmuth). *Fall*—6000, Jamaica Bay, Aug. 24, 1951; 3000, Mecox Bay, Sept. 21, 1937.

MAXIMA, INLAND: *Spring*—500, Montezuma, May 25, 1966; 1000, Braddock's Bay, June 1, 1961; 200, Salmon Creek, Monroe Co., June 5, 1958. *Fall*—540, Montezuma, July 31, 1965; 1100, El Dorado Beach, Jefferson Co., Aug. 4, 1966; 1000, Montezuma, Aug. 9, 1967; 600, El Dorado Beach, Aug. 17, 1970; 400, Sandy Pond, Oswego Co., Aug. 31, 1958; 300, Montezuma, Sept. 7, 1963.

EXTREME DATES: Apr. 3 (coastal) and Apr. 23 (inland) to Nov. 13 (inland) and Dec. 7 (coastal). Usually rare before late April and after October. Inland it has departed in spring as late as June 16 and arrived in fall as early as June 28.

On the outer coast of Long Island this species has been recorded in winter on at least *11* occasions. Usually singles have been seen, but from two to four individuals spent most of the winter of 1953–1954 at Jamaica Bay. Most exceptional were *17* observed at Hewlett Bay, Nassau Co., Dec. 30, 1961 (Berliner).

The report of a Long Island winter specimen in Bull (1964: 213) is erroneous. The specimen, in partial breeding plumage, should be *June,* not Jan. as appears on the label. I am indebted to Dr. Allan R. Phillips for calling this to my attention.

An authentic winter specimen from New York is highly desirable to substantiate occurrence at that season.

Western Sandpiper
(*Calidris mauri*)   *

Range: Of limited breeding distribution—from extreme northeastern Siberia east only to the north and west coasts of Alaska. Winters chiefly in western North America, but in the east along the Atlantic coast north to South Carolina; rarely to New Jersey and Long Island.

Status: On the coast—fairly common to locally abundant fall migrant; rare to uncommon in spring; very rare in winter. Inland—uncommon fall migrant and usually rare in spring.

Occurrence: This species is often found associating with its very close relative, the

Semipalmated Sandpiper. They may then be compared directly. The writer knows of no state specimen taken in winter or spring. It would be highly desirable to collect one at each season to prove definitely its occurrence at those times.

MAXIMA, COASTAL: *Fall*—100, Oak Beach, Suffolk Co., Aug. 6, 1938; 200, Easthampton, Suffolk Co., Aug. 29, 1933; 250, Mecox Bay, Suffolk Co., Sept. 18, 1944. *Spring*—eight, Jones Beach, June 1, 1947 (Alperin and Sedwitz).

MAXIMA, INLAND: *Fall*—seven, Onondaga Lake, Oct. 9, 1960; five, Sylvan Beach, Oneida Lake, Nov. 13, 1960. *Spring*—five, Hamlin, Monroe Co., May 30, 1966 (Doherty, Listman, and Miller).

EXTREME DATES: *Fall*—July 2 (coastal) and July 9 (inland) to Nov. 13 (inland—see Maxima, above) and Nov. 25 (coastal, exceptionally to Dec. 5, 1968, Sandy Pond, Oswego Co. (Scheider). *Spring*—Apr. 25 (coastal) and May 16 (inland) to June 13 (inland) and June 18 (coastal).

Rare before late July, after mid-November, before May, and after early June. No proof of summering.

Known in winter only from the south shore of Long Island on but four occasions: singles in late December of 1956, 1959, and 1962; also three with Semipalmated Sandpipers at Jamaica Bay, from about Dec. 1, 1953, to Jan. 4, 1954 (many observers). As mentioned above, a winter specimen from the state is highly desirable.

Ruddy Turnstone
(*Arenaria interpres*)   *

Range: Northern Holarctic region, in America breeding south to Southampton Island. Winters along the Atlantic coast north to Long Island, more rarely to Massachusetts.

Status: Common to abundant coastal migrant; local inland, uncommon to occasionally very common in spring, much less numerous in fall. In recent years regular and locally fairly common in winter on the outer coast where it is also a regular summering nonbreeder.

Occurrence: The Ruddy Turnstone frequents sandy and pebbly beaches (shingle), rocky islands, and jetties, and is also found on mud and sand flats, and on salt meadows. In winter a few are sometimes found associating with Purple Sandpipers on the rock breakwaters along the outer coast.

MAXIMA, COASTAL: *Fall*—400, Jamaica Bay Refuge, Aug. 4, 1964; 100, same locality, Sept. 17, 1944. *Winter*—12, Montauk, Dec. 29, 1962; 12, Great Kills, Staten Island, Feb. 27, 1965; 25, same locality, winter of 1967–1968; 16, Montauk, Dec. 28, 1968. *Spring*—500, Jamaica Bay, May 24, 1946; 200, Long Beach, Nassau Co., June 3, 1949. A few are regular each summer.

MAXIMA, INLAND: *Spring*—135, Sandy Pond, Oswego Co. (Lake Ontario shore), May 29, 1961; 100, Oneida Lake, May 31, 1956; two shot out of "hundreds" seen at the north end of Canandaigua Lake, Ontario Co., June 1, 1895 (E. H. Eaton). *Fall*—55, El Dorado Beach, Jefferson Co. (Lake Ontario shore), Aug. 19, 1965; 25, same locality, Sept. 8, 1962; 11, Bird Island, Niagara River, Oct. 22, 1959.

Inland it has been recorded as early as Apr. 15 and as late as Nov. 12. Generally rare before May.

Remarks: I quite agree with Peters (1934: 271) in considering the American *"morinella"* a "very unsatisfactory" subspecies. Even in breeding plumage there is much overlap in both size and coloration. The supposedly richer chestnut upperparts attributed to *"morinella"* can be matched with specimens from Europe and Asia taken at comparable dates.

PHALAROPES — PHALAROPODINAE

Three species in New York.
None breed.

This exclusively Holarctic subfamily of three species has two members breeding throughout the circumpolar regions. The Red Phalarope (*Phalaropus fulicarius*) has the more northerly breeding distribution and is, on the whole, more pelagic on migration than the Northern Phalarope (*P. lobatus*), which is more numerous on inland waters. They both winter at sea, chiefly in the southern hemisphere.

Very different in several respects is Wilson's Phalarope (*P. tricolor*), confined to the western hemisphere, breeding inland and much farther south than the two ocean-going phalaropes, and much more of a wader and less of a swimmer than the others. It winters mainly in South America.

The suggested sequence of the three species is Red, Northern, and Wilson's, in that order, based mainly on structural differences (Bull, 1964: 222) rather than inserting Wilson's in the middle as was done in the A.O.U. Checklist (1957). The arrangement followed here is that of Hellmayr and Conover (1948) and has been used also by Vaurie (1965), Palmer (in Stout, 1967), Jehl (1968), and Mayr and Short (1970).

Many modern authorities combine all three species into the genus *Phalaropus;* this treatment is followed here.

The phalaropes are here considered to be modified sandpipers, specialized for a partial marine life. See also main discussion under suborder Charadrii—"Shorebirds."

Red Phalarope
(*Phalaropus fulicarius*)   *

Range: Holarctic region at high latitudes, in eastern North America breeding south to the northern portions of Hudson Bay. Winters chiefly at sea off South America, but occasionally north to the Gulf of Mexico; much rarer in winter farther north but status little known, recorded at this season north to New York.

Status: Regular pelagic and offshore migrant, on rare occasions even very abundant in spring; much less numerous and irregular inshore. Very rare to rare and irregular inland.

Occurrence: The Red Phalarope occurs most numerously in spring at the *east end* of Long Island and, at times, may be seen in spectacular numbers well offshore or when forced inshore after severe storms or prolonged periods of fog. On these occasions it greatly outnumbers the Northern Phalarope which is ordinarily more numerous. At other times much smaller concentrations of Red Phalaropes may be observed in May during sea trips from fishing boats off *western* Long Island.

Red Phalaropes have struck lighthouses on a number of occasions, either during periods of foggy weather, or at night. In the American Museum collection there are 19 specimens that hit the Montauk Point lighthouse on the night of Apr. 30, 1898. These range from birds in nonbreeding plumage to full breeding plumage.

MAXIMA: *Spring*—3700, Westhampton Beach to Shinnecock Bay, Apr. 29, 1958; tremendous movement in 1969—12,000, Montauk area, May 9 (Ryan), and "thousands," Westhampton to Easthampton, May 11 (Frech); 3000, Easthampton region, May 16, 1939.

The numbers in fall are much smaller, the species apparently migrating much farther offshore.

EXTREME DATES, coastal unless otherwise noted: *Spring*—Mar. 25 (specimen) to June 12 (specimen). *Summer* stragglers, but no specimens. *Fall*—Sept. 8 (specimen) to Dec. 12; Dec. 20, 1964 (Rochester).

As mentioned previously the Red Phalarope is usually very rare inland and, with one exception (see below), has been recorded only in *fall*. Most occurrences are from the shores of the Great Lakes, much more rarely on other inland lakes. Practically all upstate observations have been of single birds, but four were seen on the Lake Erie shore at Athol Springs, Nov. 6–11, 1966 (Andrle, Bourne, *et al.*), and an unprecedented *13* at Derby Hill, Lake Ontario, Oct. 22, 1969 (Crumb). The only known *spring* occurrence inland is of two individuals in breeding plumage in Buffalo harbor, June 6–9, 1941 (Byron).

There are five extant inland specimens, three from the Buffalo area in the BMS collection and two taken on the shore of Cayuga Lake in the CUM collection.

Winter—Curiously enough this species has been recorded on *five* different occasions on the Lake Ontario shore in winter by competent observers: (1) Oklahoma Beach, Monroe Co., Jan. 16, 1955 (Listman); (2) near Oswego, Dec. 29, 1957 (Rusk and Scheider); (3) near Rochester, Dec. 22, 1963 (Listman); (4) Stony Point, Jefferson Co., Dec. 28, 1966 (Gordon); (5) Irondequoit Bay, Monroe Co., Jan. 1 to Feb. 5, 1967 (Genesee Ornith. Soc.).

The only documented winter record for the state is the occurrence of one on Long Island that was color-photographed at Montauk Point, Jan. 28, 1967 (Erasmus), and observed by Astle, Yeaton, Schore, and other members of the Queens Co. Bird Club. Color photographs are on file in the AMNH collection.

A flock of *six* was observed from two to three miles off Fire Island Inlet, Dec. 21, 1968 (Ryan).

Northern Phalarope
(*Phalaropus lobatus*)   *

Range: Holarctic region, of more southerly distribution than the preceding species, in eastern North America breeding south to islands in James Bay and along the coast of west-central Quebec south to Rupert House (Godfrey, 1966: 169–170). Winters at sea, chiefly in warm waters.

Status: Variously uncommon to abundant migrant offshore, especially in spring; more frequent inshore than the preceding species but in smaller-sized flocks (see Maxima below).

Rare to fairly common fall migrant inland, but very infrequent in spring.

Occurrence: On the coast of Long Island and on upstate waters the Northern Phalarope is much more prevalent than the Red Phalarope. It is more often seen on mud flats than the Red Phalarope. Both species not infrequently occur together and offer the observer direct comparison for study.

Of interest are eight specimens in the AMNH collection that struck the Montauk Point Lighthouse the night of Aug. 26, 1892.

On one of the regularly scheduled fishing trips offshore in late spring the observer may be lucky to see both ocean-going phalaropes in breeding plumage at a close distance from the boat.

MAXIMA, COASTAL: *Spring*—500, Shinnecock Bay, Apr. 29, 1937; 900, Westhampton Beach to Shinnecock Inlet, May 2, 1958; 500, Easthampton, May 16, 1939. Note the much smaller-sized concentrations than those listed for Red Phalarope. *Fall*—165, off Montauk Point, Sept. 13, 1916.

MAXIMA, INLAND: *Spring*—three collected on a small lake near Albany, May 19, 1882; six, Parma, Monroe Co., May 30, 1964. *Fall*—ten, Montezuma Marshes, Aug. 20, 1964; 15, El Dorado Beach, Jefferson Co., Aug. 27, 1966; 12, Niagara Gorge, Sept. 4, 1949; 39, Derby Hill, Oswego Co., Oct. 19, 1967. Much more unusual in spring.

EXTREME DATES, coastal unless otherwise noted: *Spring*—Mar. 29 (specimen) to June 3 (specimen). *Summer* stragglers offshore; female in breeding plumage seen on the St. Lawrence River, off Grenadier Island, Jefferson Co., June 23, 1955 (Mason). *Fall*—July 4, 1949 (specimen), collected at sea, about seven miles off Easthampton (Murphy), AMNH collection to Nov. 19 (inland) and Nov. 23.

Wilson's Phalarope
(*Phalaropus tricolor*) *

Range: Chiefly central North America, breeding south to northern Indiana and east to southeastern Ontario—Lake Erie shore, within 25 miles west of Buffalo—at Long Beach, Ontario, summer of 1959 (Beardslee and Mitchell, 1965: 238–239). Winters in South America.

Status: Rare to uncommon, but regular fall migrant both coastal and inland, at least in recent years. Usually rarer in spring, but probably of regular occurrence.

Occurrence: Wilson's Phalarope, the most southerly of the three phalaropes, is the rarest numerically. And yet, in suitable locations, it is more frequently observed. It may be found along the shores of small ponds not inhabited by the other two species which prefer to swim in deeper water. Wilson's Phalarope is more of a wader and often comes out to feed on dry land. On the coast in fall it often associates with Lesser Yellowlegs.

MAXIMA: *Fall*—four, Jones Beach, July 29, 1934; four, Lake Ontario shore, north of Brockport, Monroe Co., Aug. 20, 1911; four, Montezuma Marshes, Sept. 15, 1962. *Spring*—three, Montezuma Marshes, May 8, 1955; three females, Jamaica Bay Refuge, most of May 1958; three also *summered* there in 1964.

EXTREME DATES: *Fall*—July 1 (inland) to Nov. 9 (coastal), exceptionally to Nov. 20, 1960—collected on Fisher's Island, Suffolk Co. (Ferguson), specimen in the Ferguson Memorial Museum examined by the writer. *Spring*—Apr. 24 (coastal) to June 12 (coastal). *Summer* stragglers, chiefly on the coast.

SKUAS, JAEGERS — STERCORARIIDAE

Four species in New York.
None breed.

This is another family in which all species are represented within the limits of New York State. The three species that breed exclusively in the northern hemisphere and winter mainly in the southern hemisphere are called jaegers by American ornithologists, but by Europeans all members of this family are known as skuas. These three species are all monotypic and present no taxonomic problem.

The "Great" Skua (*Stercorarius skua*), as the British call this largest species, is one of the few bipolar birds treated by most, but not all, taxonomists as a single species. Both the northern hemisphere form and the three or more southern hemisphere populations resemble one another quite closely. The Skua has also been variously treated at the generic level: by many modern taxonomists in the one genus *Stercorarius*, by the more conservative as a separate genus, *Catharacta*. The merger of the Skua with the three jaegers at the generic level seems justified by the great similarity of all four species in the juvenal plumages.

Some taxonomists consider this group as specialized gulls which pirate other gulls and terns for food; these ornithologists would treat them merely as a subfamily of the Family Laridae.

All the jaegers or skuas live partially by plundering other seabirds, notably terns and the smaller gulls.

Skua (*Stercorarius skua*)   *

Range: A wide-ranging species, occurring in the oceans of both the northern and southern hemispheres, but exceedingly limited in the former area. The northern nominate race breeds only on islands in the eastern Atlantic (Orkneys, Shetlands, Faeroes), west to Iceland. In American waters it winters chiefly well offshore south to the Newfoundland Grand Banks and more rarely to the shoals off the Massachusetts coast. Wanders south occasionally to at least the waters off eastern Long Island. The occurrence of this species during the summer months in these waters may be summering individuals of the northern population and/or individuals of southern populations, sometimes considered separate species.

Status: *Casual*—in New York State there are two Long Island specimen records: One found dead on the beach at Amagansett, Suffolk Co., Mar. 17, 1886 (Dutcher collection), AMNH 64633; the other struck the Montauk Point Lighthouse, Aug. 10, 1896, but only a wing of this individual is preserved, AMNH 67894. The subspecies of this latter specimen cannot, therefore, be identified with certainty. The A.O.U. Check-list (1957: 215) omitted these two specimen records, despite their inclusion in previous editions.

Less satisfactory are two specimens taken on the Niagara River, neither known to be in existence: One was collected by Linden during the spring of 1886 (note the Long Island specimen above taken the same year and season). According to Beardslee and Mitchell (1965: 242), James Savage examined this specimen. The other was picked up in the gorge below the falls on Dec. 3, 1915, and shown to O. Reinecke who published a description (*Oologist*, 1916, 33:13–14).

There are two or three observations in the Montauk area believed to be correct: off the Point—possibly the same individual—in 1937, Nov. 11 (Arbib), and Dec. 14 (Helmuth); one well observed from a boat west of Cox's Ledge on June 11, 1967 (B. and J. Trimble, *Kingbird*, 1967, 17: 245).

Finally, a bird observed harassing Herring Gulls, off Point O'Woods, Fire Island, Suffolk Co., Nov. 27, 1970 (S. V. Hopkins, *in litt.*). The observer is very familiar with Skuas, both in European waters and also off the Newfoundland Grand Banks.

Remarks: The Skua is here merged in the genus *Stercorarius*, following many authorities. Resemblance to the jaegers, especially juveniles, is very marked.

Pomarine Jaeger
(*Stercorarius pomarinus*)   *

Range: Northern Holarctic region, in eastern North America breeding south to extreme northwestern Quebec (northeast shore of Hudson Bay). Winters at sea, rarely north to North Carolina.

Status: Uncommon to fairly common, but regular pelagic migrant, occasionally more numerous. Usually rare inshore. Possibly of rare occurrence on the Great Lakes.

Occurrence: The best way to observe jaegers is to go out on a fishing boat, but sometimes one may travel offshore without seeing any.

Their numbers are largely determined by the presence or absence of fish—being most numerous when fish are plentiful.

On Long Island the Pomarine Jaeger, the largest of the three jaegers, is apparently less common than *S. parasiticus* in fall, but occurs in larger numbers in spring. Both of these species have been recorded as summering infrequently off the coast.

MAXIMA: *Long Island*—40 jaegers, "mostly" this species, Easthampton, June 3, 1928 (Helmuth); 30, off Jones Beach, June 13, 1955 (Alperin); five, off Easthampton, July 14, 1940; eight, off Mecox Bay, Aug. 29, 1936; 15, Montauk, Sept. 28, 1920.

MAXIMA: *Upstate*—two immatures, Sandy Pond, Oswego Co., Oct. 15, 1964 (Scheider, *Kingbird,* 1965, 15: 40). Scheider states that, "One was seen to cross Sandy Pond, loft higher and higher in wide circles, then head southeast inland, a lake-escaping tactic suspected for a number of years, but never demonstrated heretofore." Big flight of immatures on Lake Ontario during the fall of 1965, as follows: three, Manitou, Monroe Co., Sept. 8 (Listman); three, Derby Hill, Oswego Co., Oct. 3 (Scheider), see Parasitic Jaeger for comparison; one, Hamlin, Monroe Co., Oct. 23; one, Sodus Bay, Wayne Co., Oct. 24. It should be pointed out that jaegers, most of which are in immature plumages, possibly occur regularly on the Great Lakes, especially during October. *Parasiticus* is more common than *pomarinus*.

EXTREME DATES: Apr. 13–20, 1958, Atlantic Beach, Nassau Co. (Levine, Penberthy, and Bull); May 6 (coastal) to Nov. 12 (coastal), Nov. 24 (inland), and Dec. 1, 1937, Easthampton, Suffolk Co. (Helmuth).

Winter: The statement in the A.O.U. Check-list (1957: 213), "Winters . . . casually north to Massachusetts, New York, New Jersey," is not substantiated by specimen records. There are two upstate reports of immatures alleged to be this species seen by experienced observers: (1) off Buffalo, Jan. 16, 1960 (Mitchell, Axtell, and many others), this bird was observed both at rest and in flight; (2) near Rochester, Dec. 24, 1964 (Foster, Maley, and McNett).

Specimen data: From Long Island there are at least eight fall specimens in the AMNH collection, all of the light morph and only one

an adult. Upstate there are three immatures—all light morphs—all collected in October, in various museums. In addition, an adult—also a light morph—was taken on Red House Lake, Cattaraugus Co., June 29, 1968 (Eaton and Clark), BMS 6370.

Parasitic Jaeger
(*Stercorarius parasiticus*)   *

Range: Holarctic region, in eastern North America breeding south to extreme northern Ontario (south shore of Hudson Bay). Winters north to the Carolinas.

Status: Similar to that of the preceding species, but apparently more regular inshore and certainly more numerous on inland waters.

Occurrence: The Parasitic Jaeger is ordinarily the most numerous jaeger off the coast of Long Island and is more frequently observed both inshore and on the Great Lakes. It has been reported regularly on Lake Ontario since 1960. This may reflect, in part at least, an increase in the number of keen observers on the watch for this species.

MAXIMA: *Long Island*—12, off Jones Beach, June 13, 1955; six, Gardiner's Bay, Suffolk Co., July 8, 1911; 20, Oak Beach, Suffolk Co., Aug. 31, 1936; 30, off Moriches Inlet, Sept. 3, 1949; five, Easthampton, Oct. 25, 1936.

MAXIMA: *Upstate*—Unprecedented is the observation of *21* at the north end of Keuka Lake, Yates Co., May 13, 1945 (Burtch, *Auk,* 1946, 63: 253). This veteran field observer and collector saw three separate flocks of nine, seven, and five all flying in a northwesterly direction. This occurrence is most unusual for two reasons: (1) It is the only large number ever reported inland in spring; (2) the only large number reported at an inland locality away from Lake Ontario. Other inland maxima —all Lake Ontario in fall: four, Manitou, Monroe Co., Sept. 13, 1963 (Listman); six, including three adults and three immatures, Sandy Pond, Oswego Co., Oct. 4, 1964 (Rusk and Scheider); 19, Derby Hill, Oswego Co., Oct. 3, 1965 (Scheider). The last were observed during a gale wind of 45 miles per hour from the northwest (see Pomarine Jaeger—same day for comparison). Also 22, Derby

Hill, Oct. 19, 1967, after a strong northwest wind. It has become a regular fall migrant on Lake Ontario.

EXTREME DATES: Apr. 28 (coastal) to Dec. 5 (coastal). Later dates are unconfirmed.

Specimen data: From Long Island there are at least 14 fall specimens in the AMNH collection, all but one are of the light morph. Eight are immatures, six are adults. Also extant is an adult taken off Montauk, July 28, 1930 (Latham), specimen in NYSM collection.

Upstate there are at least five extant specimens, all immatures of the light morph in various museums. Two of these are of interest, one because it was taken "inland," away from the Great Lakes—west shore of Cayuga Lake, Oct. 15, 1937 (Brown), CUM 3248; the other because of the very late date—Niagara River off Fort Erie, Ontario, Nov. 26, 1960 (Axtell), BMS 4601.

Remarks: The statement in the A.O.U. Check-list (1957: 214), "Winters . . . from Maine . . . south . . ." is not confirmed by specimen evidence.

Banding: A nestling banded on Fair Isle, off the north coast of Scotland, July 7, 1969, was shot on Fire Island, Suffolk Co., Sept. 24, 1970 (L. Rems). The specimen is NYSM 26543.

Long-tailed Jaeger
(*Stercorarius longicaudus*) *

Range: Northern Holarctic region, in eastern North America breeding south to northern Quebec. Winters at sea, chiefly in the southern hemisphere. Pelagic in migration, seldom seen near land; very rare and little known inland migrant, probably chiefly immatures.

Status: *Very rare*—this species, by far the rarest of the three jaegers in New York State,

has been recorded at least 16 times, all but four occurrences have been on Long Island (Bull, 1964: 224–225). Three immature specimens from there are: (1) Long Island (no date), Lawrence collection, AMNH 46094; (2) Fire Island, Suffolk Co., Aug. 26, 1913 (Thurston), AMNH 358008; (3) one found dead in woodland near Mount Sinai, Suffolk Co., Sept. 26, 1963 (Walker), specimen in poor condition, preserved as a skeleton, AMNH 7319. Another immature killed by an automobile at Millbrook, Dutchess Co., Sept. 7, 1929 (*fide* Frost), was apparently not preserved as its whereabouts is not known.

All nine fall coastal records have occurred from Aug. 25 to Oct. 6, in various years. The three spring observations occurred on May 29, 1960, June 8, 1934, and June 16, 1939, all from boats off the south shore of Long Island; the 1960 individual was an adult well seen and studied by a boat load of more than thirty observers of the Linnaean Society.

There are three confirmed records from upstate New York, two of them immature specimens in the Cornell University collection: (1) one, originally identified as a Parasitic Jaeger, from Owasco Lake (west shore), Cayuga Co., Sept. 14, 1908 (Wright), CUM 3934; (2) one found dead in a mummified condition on the Ithaca lighthouse breakwater on Cayuga Lake, Tompkins Co., Mar. 8, 1942 (Mattli), CUM 12731—specimen "obviously had been dead some weeks" (*fide* Sutton), and may have been present from the previous fall; (3) remains of an immature found on the Lake Ontario shore near Sandy Pond, Oswego Co., Oct. 31, 1971 (Chris Spies), was preserved as a skeleton, and is AMNH 7837—identification confirmed by the writer.

Remarks: The bluish or blue-gray tarsi, often said to be restricted to the juvenile Long-tailed Jaeger, are found in *all* immature jaegers. The extreme difficulty involved in separating juveniles of the Long-tailed Jaeger from the Parasitic Jaeger is discussed in Bull (1963, and 1964: 225).

GULLS, TERNS — LARIDAE

Twenty-seven species in New York.
Eight breed.

Of the 27 species in this worldwide family (over 80) occurring in New York, 15 are gulls, 12 are terns. Four of each breed within the state.

For the birder, the place *par excellence* to see the greatest variety and numbers of rare gulls is the Niagara River area from Buffalo to Lewiston, especially in the vicinity of Niagara Falls. Among the better spots there to view gulls are the falls proper—best observed from the Canadian side—and across from the spillway and hydroelectric plant with its generators and turbines; also the Austin Street pier in Buffalo. In addition to the regular Glaucous, Iceland, Little, and Franklin's gulls (*Larus hyperboreus, glaucoides, minutus,* and *pipixcan*) —always in small numbers—an occasional individual of the following may be found: Thayer's (*L. thayeri*), Black-headed (*ridibundus*)—very rare upstate—Sabine's (*sabini*), and even the normally pelagic Black-legged Kittiwake (*tridactylus*)—immatures.

As for tern specialties, the Moriches Bay area on the south shore of Long Island offers the greatest variety in the state. In addition to such regular breeders as Common, Roseate (*Sterna hirundo, dougallii*)—the latter very local, and Least terns (*S. albifrons*), and such regular nonbreeders as Forster's and Black terns (*S. forsteri* and *Chlidonias niger*), occasional Caspian and Royal terns may be seen (*Sterna caspia* and *maxima*). After hurricanes the very rare Gull-billed, Sandwich, and Sooty terns (*S. nilotica, sandvicensis,* and *fuscata*) have been reported from this area.

The classification of Moynihan (1959), with minor modifications, is followed here: (1) All of the gulls with the exception of the Ivory Gull (*Pagophila eburnea*) are included within the expanded genus *Larus*. This means that the genera *"Rissa"* and *"Xema"* are not recognized. The former is merely a specialized cliff-nesting *Larus*, the latter a fork-tailed, hooded gull. (2) All of the terns with the exception of the Black Tern are included within the expanded genus *Sterna*. This means that the genera *"Gelochelidon," "Thalasseus,"* and *"Hydroprogne"* are also not recognized. They are merely capped terns with heavier bills and/or crests, characters not considered to be of generic importance.

The juvenal plumage of the Ivory Gull is so different (spotted) from that of other juvenile gulls, that a monotypic genus seems justified. As for the Black Tern, the distinctive adult breeding plumage, together with its quite different feeding and nesting behavior would appear to warrant a separate genus, although one of the other two Old World species, *Chlidonias hybrida*—the Whiskered Tern—with its white cheeks and black cap would seem to bridge the gap with *Sterna*.

Glaucous Gull
(*Larus hyperboreus*)   *

Range: Northern Holarctic region, in America breeding south to the east coast of Hudson Bay (northwestern Quebec). Winters south to the Great Lakes and the coast of Long Island; more rarely farther south.

Status: Rare to uncommon, but regular winter visitant; occasionally fairly common in the vicinity of the Great Lakes.

Occurrence: The Glaucous Gull is found chiefly in the vicinity of garbage dumps and consequently the greatest numbers are concentrated around the larger cities. At times these birds also frequent the fish-cleaning pier at Montauk (village) on eastern Long Island. Ordinarily they are much less numerous along beaches and shores. This and the Iceland Gull, with which it may be confused, are primarily winter gulls.

MAXIMA: *Coastal*—six, Montauk, Dec. 26, 1937 (see Iceland Gull for comparative numbers); five, Pelham Bay, Bronx Co., Feb. 17, 1935.

MAXIMA: *Inland*—ten, Squaw Island, Niagara River (near Buffalo), Jan. 16, 1969; 14 on the Oswego River, from Lake Ontario to about 24 miles upstream, Jan. 14, 1968, and Jan. 17, 1960—most exceptionally—20, Feb. 22, 1969 (see Iceland Gull, same dates and locality).

"EXTREME" DATES, *coastal:* Usually present from November to April. Collected at Rockaway Beach, Queens Co., May 1, 1904 (Peavey), AMNH collection. Reported every month of the year, but very rare in summer. An immature summered at Oakwood Beach, Staten Island, in 1932 (Wiegmann).

EXTREME DATES, *inland:* Immature found dead on Lake Ontario shore at Sodus Bay, Wayne Co., May 12, 1950 (Dewey), CUM collection. Beardslee and Mitchell (1965: 242) give extreme dates from Sept. 18 to May 23 for the Niagara Frontier region.

Remarks: Barth (1968: 30) reports extensive hybridization with the Herring Gull in Iceland. Elsewhere these two gulls behave as "good" species.

Iceland Gull
(*Larus glaucoides*)   *

Range: Northeastern Nearctic region—with a limited breeding distribution—coasts of Greenland (except in the north), eastern and southern Baffin Island; also the extreme northwest tip of Quebec (Godfrey, 1966: 175–176). Winters south to the Great Lakes and the coast of Long Island; more rarely farther south.

Status: Rare to uncommon, but regular winter visitant; occasionally fairly common, especially near the Great Lakes.

Occurrence: This species is most often found in association with the ever-present Herring Gulls. The best places to see Iceland Gulls are at city dumps, sewer outlets, and fish-process-

ing plants and piers. They are relatively scarce along beaches and shores.

MAXIMA: *Coastal*—ten, Montauk, Dec. 26, 1937 (see Glaucous Gull for comparison); eight, Clason Point, Bronx Co., Jan. 11, 1934; six, Croton Point, Westchester Co., Jan. 26, 1963; seven, Central Park (reservoir), New York City, Feb. 7, 1957.

MAXIMA: *Inland*—12, Niagara Falls to Lewiston (about six miles on the Niagara River), Jan. 9, 1965; 11, Oswego River (24-mile stretch); Jan. 17, 1960, and 15, Jan. 14, 1968 (see Glaucous Gull, same dates and locality); 12, Oswego (harbor), Feb. 23, 1964.

"EXTREME" DATES, *coastal:* Usually present from November to March, but reported every month of the year. Very rare in summer.

EXTREME DATES, *inland:* Eaton (1910: 124) gives dates from Sept. 10 to Apr. 14 for specimens taken in western New York, and Beardslee and Mitchell (1965: 243–244) give extreme dates (observations) from Aug. 16 to May 22 for the Niagara Frontier region.

Subspecies: Two subspecies are found in New York State: (1) nominate *glaucoides* (adults completely white-winged) of Greenland; and (2) the race *kumlieni* (adults having the wingtips with gray markings) of Baffin Island and northern Quebec.

Juveniles of the two races are quite impossible to distinguish from each other even in the skin. Two specimens originally identified as *kumlieni* taken in the Buffalo area and now in the BMS collection were submitted to Godfrey who determined both as *Larus thayeri* (see Thayer's Gull for details). Adults and subadults, however, may be readily differentiated. On the basis of specimens collected in the state, *kumlieni* appears to be the prevailing form.

The following five specimens—three adults and two subadults—examined by me, all pertain to *kumlieni:* (1) subadult, captured alive, Jones Beach, Aug. 2, 1936 (Hickey, *et al.*), AMNH 448094—this specimen lived in the Bronx Zoo for nearly two years; (2) subadult, Mohawk River at Green Island, Albany Co., Jan. 27, 1884 (Root), NYSM 42; (3), (4), (5) adults—all taken on the Niagara River, near Buffalo, and in the BMS collection—1817, Mar. 25, 1934 (Mitchell); 1840, Mar. 24, 1935 (W. A. Davis); 5001, Jan. 30, 1963 (Andrle).

Great Black-backed Gull
(*Larus marinus*)   *   B

Range: Northwestern Palearctic and north-eastern Nearctic regions, restricted chiefly to the North Atlantic area in the breeding season; in North America breeds south to Long Island, very rarely to southern New Jersey (1966) and Virginia (1970); also inland to the Great Lakes (1954, Lake Huron; 1962, Lake Ontario at Presqu'ile Park, Ontario—opposite Rochester—see breeding map—x; 1963, St. Lawrence River near Montreal—see breeding map—⊗. In America winters from Newfoundland to southern United States. Sedentary and migratory.

Status: Common to abundant, occasionally even very abundant, winter visitant on the coast; much less numerous inland, but has increased greatly in recent years. Local breeder on Long Island.

Change in status: This species was formerly common only in *winter* along the outer coast but, with its steady southward advance as a breeder, first to New England, then Long Island (1942 on) it became more numerous on the coast at all times of year and increased steadily on the Great Lakes and the smaller interior lakes. By 1970 it had been recorded in *summer* at many inland localities, albeit rare to uncommon (including one that summered on Cayuga Lake in 1964) and a breeder on Long Island in as many as *nine* different areas.

Nonbreeding: Peakall (1967) summarized the steady increase in the state.
MAXIMA: *Coastal*—400, Jones Inlet, Nassau Co., Sept. 7, 1947; 900, Owl's Head Park, Brooklyn, Sept. 20, 1961; 3000, Spring Creek garbage dump, Dec. 26, 1964 (Heath), and 2000, Edgemere garbage dump, Feb. 7, 1965 (Bull)—both in the Jamaica Bay area of Queens Co., during the same winter.
MAXIMA: *Inland*—(1) Great Lakes region —550, Oswego, Lake Ontario, Feb. 18, 1962; 215, Dunkirk, Lake Erie, Mar. 3, 1968; (2) elsewhere—450, Ogdensburg, St. Lawrence River, Jan. 19, 1969; 100, Hudson, Hudson River, Mar. 5, 1961; 42, south end of Cayuga Lake (vicinity of Ithaca), Jan. 1, 1962.

Breeding (see Map 68): Great Black-backed Gulls breed on Long Island in sandy areas with scattered vegetation, often in beach grass. Nests are placed invariably in or near Herring Gull colonies.

Egg clutches in 26 New York nests: one egg (four nests—probably incomplete sets); two eggs (three nests); three eggs (19 nests).
EGG DATES: Apr. 25 to June 19.
Unfledged young: May 30 to June 27; fledged juveniles: July 10 to July 26.
MAXIMA: Suffolk Co.—ten pairs, Cartwright Island, 1955; 35 pairs, Gardiner's Island, 1957; perhaps 100 pairs there in 1966; ten pairs, Plum Island, 1965; 25 pairs, Captree State Park, 1971; 36 pairs there in 1972 and 70 pairs in 1973.
The accompanying map indicates the ten known breeding localities on Long Island, with year of first recorded breeding: Suffolk Co.—(1) Cartwright Island, 1942—first for the state; (2) Gardiner's Island, 1948; (3) Plum Island, 1963; (4) Orient Point, 1958; (5) Shinnecock Bay, 1954; (5a) Moriches Bay, 1971; (6) Fire Island State Park, 1960; (7) Captree State Park, 1958. Nassau Co.—(8) Meadow Island north of Jones Beach, 1970, and nearby Short Beach, 1971. Kings Co.—(9) Canarsie Pol, Jamaica Bay, 1960.

Banding: A nestling banded in 1950 in Massachusetts was recovered 15 years later (1965) in New York.

Lesser Black-backed Gull
(*Larus fuscus*)   *

Range: Western Palearctic region, the race *graellsii* (back and wings much paler than nominate race) breeding in Iceland, British Isles, and northern France. Winters south to central Africa. Vagrant in eastern North America (New York, New Jersey, Maryland—all specimens are *L. f. graellsii*).

Status: Very rare to rare winter visitant, but from 1954 on has been regular along the coast in very small numbers; more local upstate.

Occurrence: The only known New York State specimen is that of an adult collected at the Tifft Street dump, Buffalo, Mar. 14, 1949 (Andrle), BMS 4084.

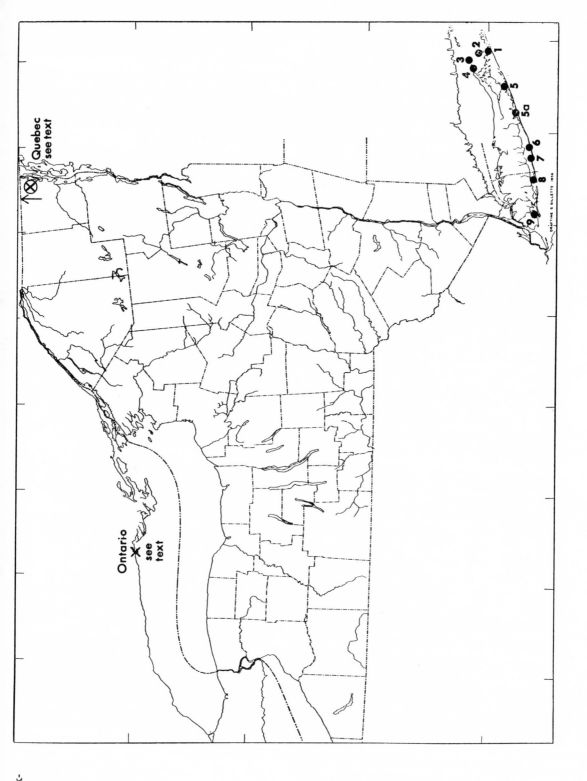

MAP 68 Great Black-
backed Gull (*Larus
marinus*) Breeding
distribution

Lesser Black-backed Gulls frequent garbage dumps (e.g., the above specimen) and sewer outlets in the harbors of the larger cities, and also the coastal beaches of Long Island. One of the better localities to observe this species is at the huge municipal dump at Fresh Kills, Staten Island. Another place is at or near Ithaca (see below). For details of occurrence in the New York City region, see Bull (1964: 232, and 1970: 22).

In upstate New York, in addition to the aforementioned Buffalo specimen, this species has occurred at two other localities. For seven consecutive years, an adult appeared at the Ithaca dump, first on Mar. 2, 1964 (McIlroy). What is presumed to be the same individual, was recorded each succeeding winter (from 1964 to 1970) on Cayuga Lake in the same vicinity and was studied by hundreds of observers. The extreme dates of occurrence there were from Nov. 11 to Mar. 25. Another adult was seen at Oswego harbor on Jan. 2, 1967 (Rusk and Peakall, *Kingbird*, 1967, 17: 85–86). Opportunities were available to compare this species directly with Great Black-backed Gulls and Herring Gulls at both these localities. A few other inland reports are without details.

EXTREME DATES: Aug. 30 to Apr. 14.

Herring Gull
(*Larus argentatus*)   *   B

Range: Nearctic and northwest Palearctic regions, in eastern North America breeding from northern Canada locally south to the coast of Virginia. Winters throughout much of the breeding range and southward.

Status: Very abundant resident, especially near the coast; most numerous in winter. Locally common breeder on Long Island and in northern New York, especially the Adirondack region.

Nonbreeding: The ubiquitous and extremely successful Herring Gull is one of our most numerous birds. Enormous numbers may be seen during the colder months when the local population is vastly augmented by arrivals from more northern areas. The largest concentrations are found about New York harbor, especially in the vicinity of sewer outlets and garbage dumps, as well as in harbors along the

Great Lakes; also in the vicinity of Niagara Falls. Great throngs are to be seen also along the ocean, bays, and the numerous tidal estuaries and inlets. Lesser numbers frequent the larger inland lakes and reservoirs until the freeze-up. After heavy rains considerable numbers visit flooded fields, golf courses, and even empty parking lots.

MAXIMA: Estimates as high as 30,000 to 40,000 around New York harbor during some winters; also 12,000, Oswego harbor, Jan. 19, 1957; 20,000, Rochester area, Dec. 11, 1965; 30,000, Niagara Falls, Dec. 17, 1968; 10,000, Buffalo harbor, Dec. 26, 1954.

Breeding (see Map 69): In New York this species breeds in two widely separated areas:

(A) Inland—on *islands* in mountain lakes in the Adirondack district, ever since ornithological records were first kept over a century ago; also on *islands* in extreme eastern Lake Ontario and in the St. Lawrence River, and on *islands* in Lake Champlain and in Oneida Lake.

(B) Coastal—much more recently, first reported on eastern Long Island in 1931; chiefly on *islands* along the south and east shores of Long Island.

Islands are emphasized—both inland and coastal—as these birds usually require relative solitude and little disturbance (but see Figs. 47 and 48); on the mainland they apparently cannot adapt to humans and other predators.

Herring Gulls place their nests on the ground, either in sand (with scattered vegetation) or grassy areas (in the open or under bushes). See Figs. 49 and 50. In the Adirondacks nests are frequently located on rocks in lakes, and under trees; or next to stumps and bushes. No tree nests are recorded in this state.

Egg clutches in approximately 900 New York nests invariably held either two or three eggs: two eggs (200 nests); three eggs (700 nests, about 78%).

EGG DATES: Apr. 27 to June 22.

Unfledged: May 17 to July 24; fledged: July 5 to Aug. 31.

As with many Larids, this species is highly colonial and nests in sizable colonies, especially on the coast. Because islands in the interior of the state are considerably smaller, the colonies are proportionally smaller.

Surveys made in recent years indicate the

MAP 69 Herring Gull
(*Larus argentatus*)
Breeding distribution

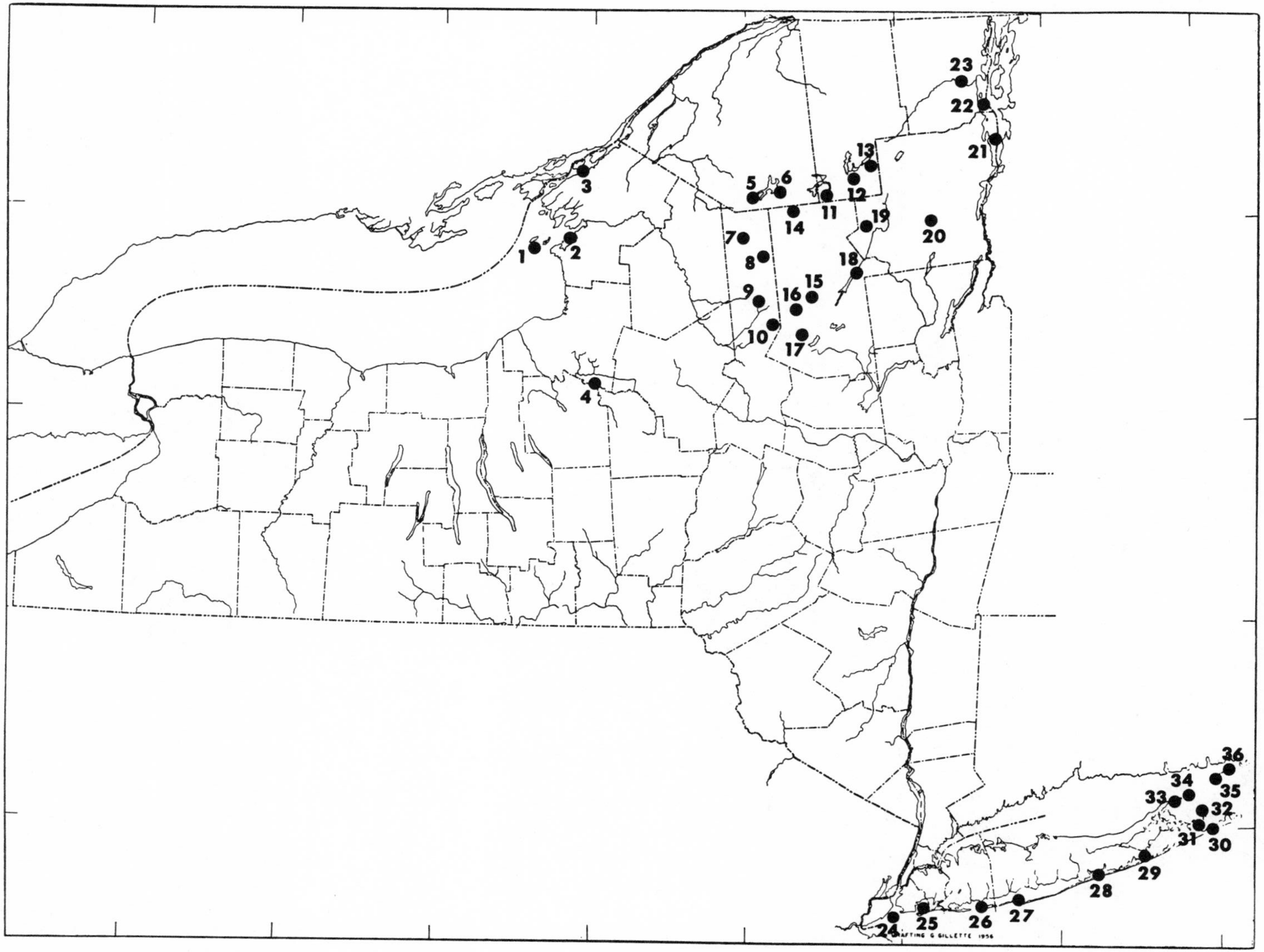

Fig. 47   Herring Gull's nest, Crooke's Point, Great Kills, Staten Island, June 4, 1948. Photo by Howard H. Cleaves

Fig. 48   Nest and eggs of Herring Gull, Little Galloo Island, Jefferson Co., June 10, 1967. Compare this nest with that of Ring-billed Gull (Fig. 52). Photo by Robert G. Wolk

two largest colonies are on Long Island in Suffolk Co.: 2000 nests, Gardiner's Island—1967; 1000 pairs, Captree Island and nearby Captree State Park—1969; 2000+ pairs in the Captree locations in 1972.

Upstate: 100 nests, Little Galloo Island in Lake Ontario—1965; 60 nests, Four Brothers Islands in Lake Champlain—1967; there were 300 pairs at the last-named in 1922. On little Galloo Island the breeding Herring Gulls are in the midst of an enormous Ring-billed Gull colony.

The accompanying map shows distribution of the 36 known breeding localities in the state: (A) northern New York—Jefferson Co. —(1) Little Galloo Island; (2) Gull and Bass islands, Henderson Bay; (3) Eaglewing Rocks, off Grindstone Island, St. Lawrence River. Oswego Co.—(4) Long and Wantry Islands, Oneida Lake. St. Lawrence Co.—(5) Cranberry Lake-Wanakena; (6) Cranberry Lake-Barber Point. Herkimer Co.—(7) Raven Lake; (8) Big Moose Lake; (9) Canachagala Lake; (10) Honnedaga Lake. Franklin Co.—(11) Jenkins Pond; (12) near Axton; (13) Lower Saranac Lake. Hamilton Co.—(14) near Sabattis; (15) Cedar Lake; (16) West Canada Lakes; (17) Metcalf Lake; (18) north end of Indian Lake. Essex Co.—(19) Wolf Pond; (20) Elk Lake; (21) Four Brothers Islands, Lake Champlain. Clinton Co.—(22) islet (Garden Island) south of Valcour Island, Lake Champlain; (23) near Morrisonville.

(B) coastal New York—Lower New York Bay—(24) adjacent Swinburne and Hoffman islands. Long Island—Kings Co.—(25) Canarsie Pol, Jamaica Bay. Nassau Co.—(26) Meadow Island, north of Short Beach. Suffolk Co.—(27) Captree Island and nearby Captree State Park; (28) islet in Moriches Bay; (29) islet in Shinnecock Bay; (30) Goff's Point, Napeague Bay; (31) Cartwright Island; (32) Gardiner's Island; (33) Orient Point; (34) Plum Island; (35) Fisher's Island; (36) Wicopesset Island, northeast of Fisher's Island.

Eaton (1910: 128) listed "North Pond" in the Adirondacks as a breeding locality in 1907, but he did not specify which North Pond. There are six with this name, three of them in Essex Co. alone, listed by Douglas (1931).

Fig. 49 Herring Gull nest and eggs in washtub. Captree State Park, Suffolk Co., June 1968. Photo by Tom Davis

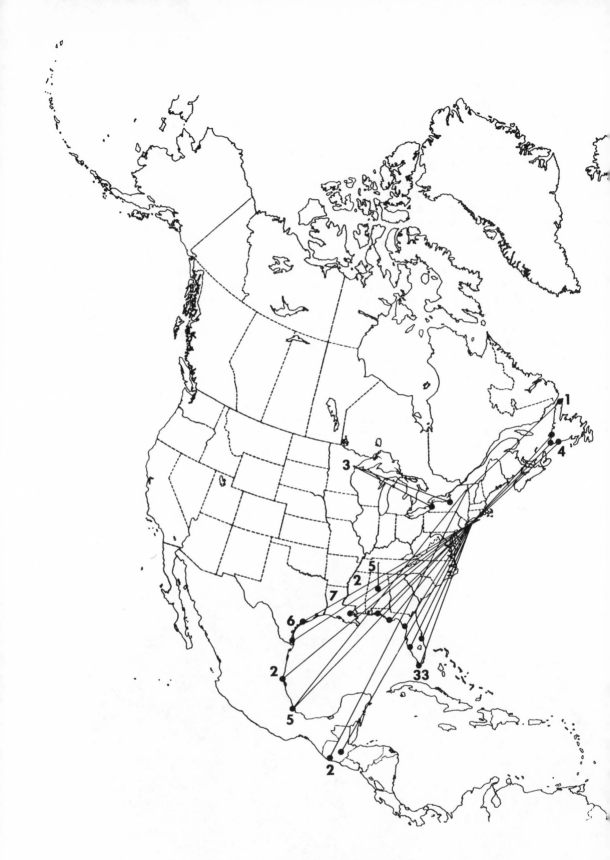

MAP 70 Herring Gull (*Larus argentatus*) Banding recoveries

Fig. 50 Herring Gull incubating at base of picnic table, Captree State Park, Suffolk Co., May 31, 1969. Photo by Tom Davis

Banding (see Map 70): Three nestlings banded in summer of various years near Duluth, Minn., were recovered the following winter in western New York. Four Long Island nestlings and another from Lake Champlain were recovered in southwestern and extreme northern Newfoundland respectively—all five in early fall following, after hurricanes.

A total of 53 nestlings banded in various years on Long Island were recovered the following late fall or winter, as follows: Florida—33, chiefly Gulf coast areas, but also the upper keys; Alabama—five; Mississippi—two; Louisiana—seven; Texas—six.

Five Long Island nestlings were recovered the following winter along the Mexican Gulf coast in Tamaulipas—two, and Veracruz—three, as were two more from Lake Champlain—both recovered in Veracruz.

Another Long Island juvenile was taken the following winter near the capital city of Guatemala; still another from Lake Champlain was shot the following April on the Pacific coast of Guatemala.

The published report (*Ebba News,* 1971, 34: 148) of a nestling banded on Long Island and recovered more than five years later in California—proved to be a "duck," according to the same publication (*Ebba News,* 1971, 34: 298–299). This shows that all very unusual recoveries should be verified. One wonders how many other faulty banding data appear in the literature without being corrected.

A banded nestling from New York was recovered in Massachusetts 22 years later.

Remarks: The American form, called "*smithsonianus*," is here considered to be a synonym of nominate *argentatus* of western Europe. It is barely separable from the latter, with overlap in both color and wing length.

Thayer's Gull
(*Larus thayeri*)   *

Range: Arctic North America, breeding south to Southampton and Coats islands, northern Hudson Bay. Winters mainly on the Pacific coast south to California. Vagrant in eastern North America south to Ohio, Kentucky, Massachusetts, New York, and New Jersey (all specimens).

Status: *Casual*—in New York there are six specimen records, all from the extreme western part of the state in the BMS collection as follows: (1) 2857—immature, Buffalo (Fuhrmann Blvd. dump), Feb. 4, 1945 (Filor); (2) 4107—immature, Buffalo (Squaw Island dump), Dec. 24, 1957 (Andrle); (3, 4, and 5) 5107, 5108, and 5109—all collected on the Niagara River at Lewiston, Niagara Co., in 1967 by Andrle and Clark, the first on Dec. 11, the others on Dec. 17. 5107 and 5108 are adult females and 5109 is a subadult, and were verified as *thayeri* by the writer and Eisenmann with direct comparison of breeding material from Baffin Island in the AMNH collection.

2857 and 4107 were both originally identified and published as *kumlieni* (Beardslee and Mitchell, 1965: 244), but subsequently reidentified as *thayeri* by Godfrey (*in litt.*), who compared them with the large series of immatures in the collection of the National Museum of Canada. Finally, (6) another adult female (6371) was also taken at Lewiston, Dec. 21, 1968, by Andrle and Clark. For further details of these occurrences in the Niagara Frontier region, see Andrle (*Auk,* 1969, 86: 106–109).

These six specimens, three of them taken within *one* week at the same locality, and a fourth at the same locality within two years, would indicate that this form is not as rare as believed, that it undoubtedly has been overlooked until recent years and that the juvenile stages, at least, are easily confused with *kumlieni*. Even the adults of these two forms would be difficult to differentiate in life, except under extremely favorable conditions at close range, and then only with familiarity of the existing variation within *thayeri* and *kumlieni*.

I provisionally follow Smith (1966) in treating *thayeri* as a species separate from *argentatus* and *glaucoides*. The three are sympatric in southern Baffin Island, where they apparently do not interbreed. However, further field work in other contact zones is needed before the status of the three forms is settled. Vaurie (1965: 474) tentatively includes *thayeri* with *glaucoides,* but questions this treatment. On the other hand, Barth (1968: 42) would be "inclined" to lump *thayeri, kumlieni, glaucoides,* and even the Pacific coast Glaucous-winged Gull—*glaucescens,* as races of *argentatus*.

Ring-billed Gull
(*Larus delawarensis*)   * B

Range: Chiefly central North America, local in the east; breeds from southern Canada—in the east, very locally south to the Great Lakes and central New York (Oneida Lake). Winters north to open water in southern Canada.

Status: Great increase in recent years; common to very abundant migrant and winter visitant on the Great Lakes and the Niagara River, much less numerous on the coast and on the larger lakes and rivers of the interior. Local,

MAP 71 Ring-billed Gull
(*Larus delawarensis*)
Breeding distribution

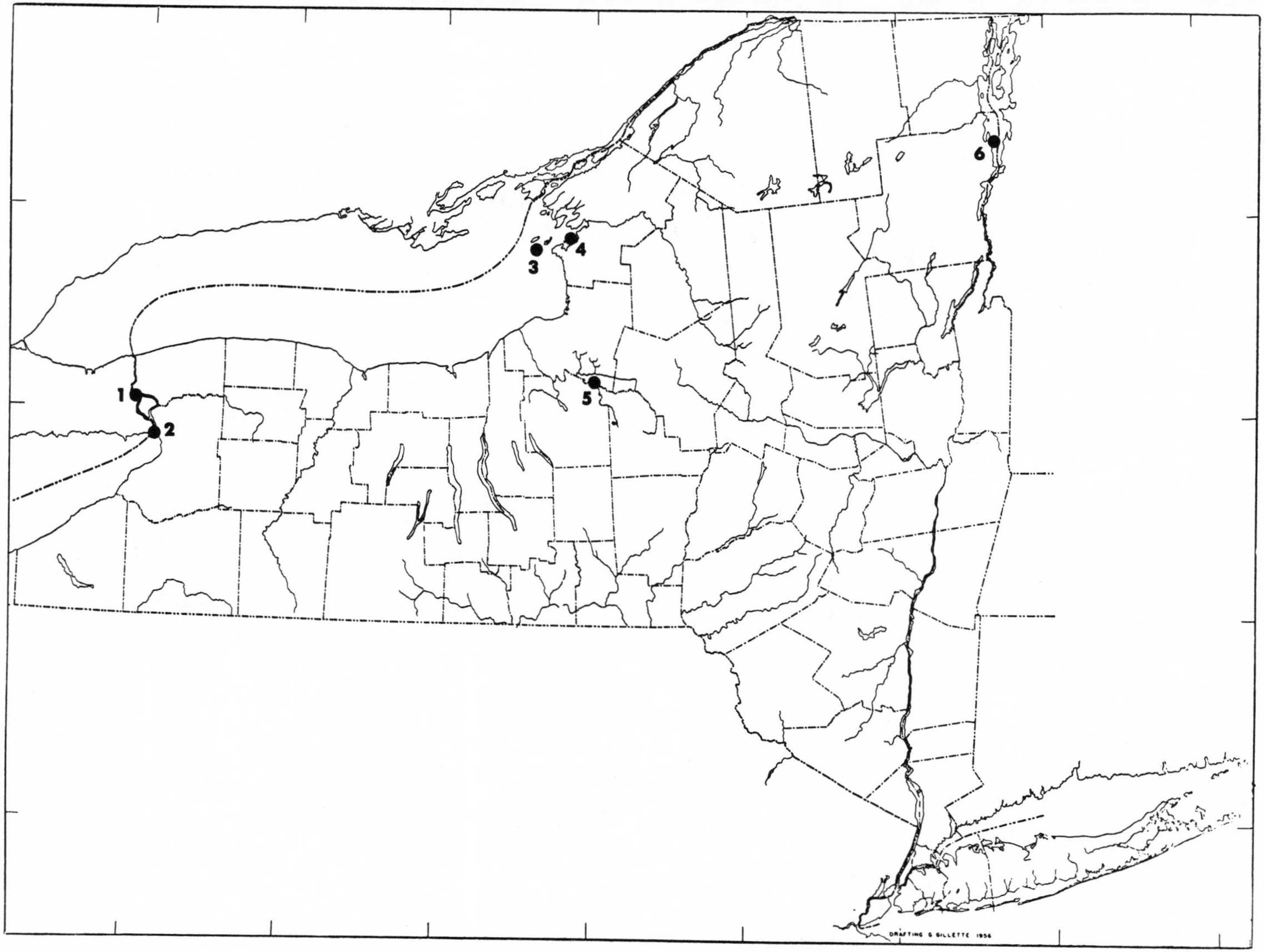

but common to very abundant breeder (since 1936, see **Breeding**).

Change in status: Few species in the state have increased in numbers as has the Ring-billed Gull. This is attributable mainly to an eastward extension of the breeding range, both in Canada and in New York within the past 40 years or so. Eaton (1910: 131) spoke of it mostly as a rare to uncommon visitant in upstate New York, chiefly during the migrations. The recent tremendous concentrations reported, in eastern Lake Ontario especially, has resulted in a gradual increase of this species during the summer months and actual breeding in this area by 1936. On one small island alone in the 1960s, estimates ranged from *75,000* to *100,000* pairs.

Nonbreeding: This species is found both on inland lakes and rivers, and on coastal bays, inlets, and estuaries. Like the Herring Gull, it frequents flooded fields, golf courses, and airports after rains; it also follows the plow for grubs which are avidly consumed.

MAXIMA: *Inland*—14,000, Derby Hill, Oswego Co., Oct. 19, 1967; 15,000, Oswego harbor, Dec. 1, 1957; 9000, Niagara River, Dec. 23, 1962; 8000, Dunkirk harbor, Chautauqua Co., Jan. 28, 1967; 10,000, Sandy Pond, Oswego Co., May 20, 1956. A count of 270 on Attica Reservoir, Wyoming Co., Sept. 7, 1960, is a good-sized number for an "inland" locality away from the Great Lakes.

MAXIMA: *Coastal*—1500, Dyker Beach, Kings Co., Sept. 10, 1950; 1500, Jamaica Bay, the same day; 2300, Jamaica Bay, Dec. 27, 1952.

Breeding (see Map 71): Ring-billed Gulls were first found nesting in the state in extreme eastern Lake Ontario on Gull Island (number 4 on map), Jefferson Co., in 1936 (Hyde, 1939a), although they had been breeding on islands not far away in Canadian territory in 1927 (Quilliam, 1965: 91). In 1938 these birds were observed nesting on nearby Little Galloo Island (number 3 on map). This 43-acre island has received considerable attention from John Belknap (1955, 1968), who made periodic visits there and witnessed the phenomenal population increase over the years. He estimated the build-up in the number of nests or pairs to be from about 1000 in 1945 to 19,000 in 1950,

45,000 in 1955, 63,000 in 1961, and between 75,000 and 85,000 in the period 1965–1967. This mainly grassy island, with few trees, is reputed to be the site of the largest nesting colony in existence. The writer had the opportunity of visiting this island during June 1967 with Belknap, Arthur W. Allen, and Robert Wolk. Wolk's photographs (Figs. 51 and 52) are here reproduced giving the "feel" of the place far better than words can express.

The five other localities contain insignificant numbers of these birds compared to Little Galloo Island. These localities with the year of first recorded arrival and maximum numbers of pairs with year are: (1) small island near Goat Island, Niagara Falls (1956)—400 pairs, 1959; (2) Donnelly's pier, Buffalo harbor (1964), "many" pairs breeding in Common Tern colony (Andrle, *in litt.*); (3) Little Galloo Island, described above; (4) Gull Island, also described previously—1400 pairs, 1950; (5) Long and Wantry islands, Oneida Lake (1952)—700 pairs, 1957; (6) Four Brothers Islands, Lake Champlain, Essex Co. (1949)—2500 pairs, 1967.

The reports of single pairs of breeding Ring-billed Gulls at Hermon, St. Lawrence Co., in 1886, and near Axton, Franklin Co., in 1902, were very likely misidentified Herring Gulls. A report of a nest of Ring-billed Gulls at Sabattis, Hamilton Co., in 1965 is erroneous; it was a Herring Gull nest (*fide* Rusk). Only Herring Gulls have been proved to breed in the Adirondack region.

Note that all six breeding localities of *Larus delawarensis* are located on *islands*.

Egg clutches in 234 New York nests: two eggs (20 nests); three eggs (200 nests—85%); four eggs (nine nests); five eggs (five nests).

EGG DATES: May 16 to July 10.

Unfledged young: May 16 to July 10; fledglings: June 25 to July 24. It is obvious that the date of May 16 for eggs could not be the earliest, as unfledged birds were reported on the *same* date. This also applies to the latest date of July 10 for unfledged juveniles as eggs were still reported on that date.

Banding (see Map 72): Nestlings banded in various years on Little Galloo Island by Belknap and Allen were recovered the following winter in Louisiana (one), Florida (27), Bahamas (one), and western Cuba (two).

Fig. 51 Ring-billed Gull colony with downy chicks in the foreground, Little Galloo Island, eastern Lake Ontario, Jefferson Co., June 10, 1967. Photo by Robert G. Wolk

Fig. 52 Nest and eggs of Ring-billed Gull, Little Galloo Island, Jefferson Co., June 10, 1967. Compare this nest with that of Herring Gull (Fig. 48). Photo by Robert G. Wolk

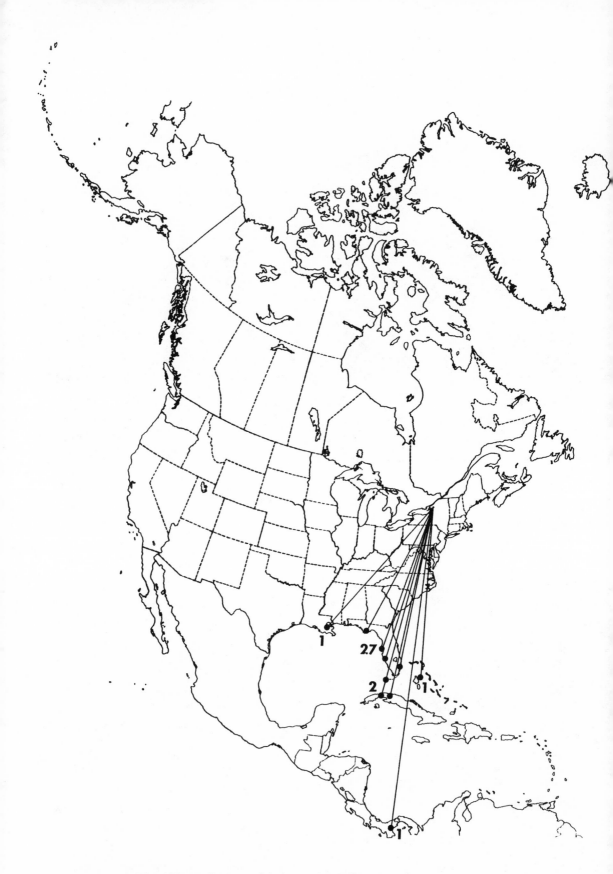

MAP 72 Ring-billed Gull (*Larus delawarensis*) Banding recoveries

Another banded nestling (June 14, 1953) was recovered the following summer (July 11, 1954) on the *Pacific* coast of Panama near Agua Dulce, province of Coclé. This is further proof of juvenile birds of the order Charadriiformes, in particular, summering in the tropics.

Laughing Gull
(*Larus atricilla*) * B

Range: Local breeder—Caribbean region, both coasts of Mexico, Gulf and Atlantic coasts of United States, north to southern New Jersey; also Massachusetts and Nova Scotia; formerly on Long Island. Winters north to North Carolina, uncommonly but regularly to New York.

Status: Common to locally abundant coastal migrant and summer visitant. Rare to uncommon in winter, but occasionally more numerous in and near New York harbor. Very rare upstate except after tropical storms.

Occurrence: Although the Laughing Gull has not been recorded as breeding on Long Island since 1890, it is locally numerous on passage and as a summering nonbreeder. By early April numbers have arrived in the harbor and bays of the New York City region and the birds attract attention by their vociferousness and their conspicuous black hoods. Where most of the local population of adult Laughing Gulls goes during the breeding season is a mystery, in view of their apparent rarity north of Long Island (see **Remarks**). Nevertheless, great numbers are observed each year in the area of Long Island Sound and the lower reaches of the Hudson River.

MAXIMA: *Spring*—800, Narrows (Brooklyn) Apr. 28, 1949; 200, Centre Island, Nassau Co., May 15, 1960.

MAXIMA: *Summer*—100, Piermont (Hudson River), Rockland Co., June 25, 1933; 1000 (mostly immatures), Setauket, Suffolk Co., June 27, 1934.

MAXIMA: *Fall*—300, Idlewild, Queens Co., Aug. 24, 1951; 1000, Little Neck Bay, Queens Co., Aug. 27, 1946; 400, after hurricane, Easthampton region, Suffolk Co., Sept. 16, 1944; 2000, Lower Bay, New York City, Oct. 28, 1951; 2000, Pelham Bay, Bronx Co., Oct.

30, 1938; 250, Narrows, Nov. 16, 1945; 75, same locality, Dec. 14, 1947.

MAXIMA: *Winter*—14, New York harbor, Jan. 26, 1948; 39, same area, late December 1952.

This species was formerly very rare in winter, in fact was unknown prior to 1925. Only since the early 1930s has more than a single individual been reported at this season.

Upstate the Laughing Gull has always been very rare at any time of year. The only known inland specimen extant is an adult collected at Buffalo, Sept. 15, 1888 (Bergtold), and examined by Mitchell in the collection of the University of Colorado Museum, 2391 (Beardslee and Mitchell, 1965: 250).

The species was not reported again from upstate until the 1930s. Usually only one or two at a time have been observed on the Great Lakes. However, after severe storms numbers have been seen. After the great cyclonic storm of Nov. 25, 1950, no fewer than *50* were observed on Otsego Lake, Otsego Co., Nov. 26 (Hill), who had been familiar with the species in Massachusetts. This number is unprecedented away from the coast. After hurricane "Hazel" of Oct. 15, 1954, Laughing Gulls were reported in numbers (possibly as many as 24) along the shore of Lake Ontario, as follows: eight each—between Hamlin and Charlotte, Monroe Co., Oct. 16; from Oswego to Selkirk Shores, Oswego Co., Oct. 17; and at Sandy Pond, same county and date.

EXTREME INLAND DATES: *Spring*—Apr. 15 to June 17. *Fall*—Aug. 9 to Dec. 1.

Remarks: Nisbet (*in litt.*) stated that, as of 1970, the Laughing Gull as a breeder has decreased "alarmingly" on the New England coast since 1966 chiefly due to depredations by Herring Gulls. In 1970 there were only 50 pairs of Laughing Gulls reported breeding on Muskeget Island, Mass.

Very little is known of the Laughing Gull's former breeding status on Long Island, other than it had nested on certain islands in Great South Bay and, according to Griscom (1923: 74), "formerly bred" in the Orient region in extreme eastern Suffolk Co. As to this latter locality, Latham (*Univ. State New York Bull. Schools*, 1936, 22: 135–136), stated that prior to 1880 there was a ". . . restricted nesting

colony on a gravel flat between salt marshes."
The last known set of eggs from Long Island
was taken on Cedar Island (north of Cedar
Beach), Great South Bay, June 14, 1890
(Marshall), AMNH 1091.

Egg dates and clutch size on Long Island
are known from only two sets of three eggs
each, dates of June 14 and 28.

Despite the great decrease in size of known
breeding colonies in the northeast in recent
years, paradoxically great numbers of this species are seen yearly on passage both spring and
fall. More intensive search is needed during
the breeding season of the numerous islands
and marshland along both coasts of Long Island.

Franklin's Gull (*Larus pipixcan*)   *

Range: Central North America, breeding
east to the western portions of Manitoba and
Minnesota. Winters north to Texas and Lou-
isiana. Migrates chiefly through the Great
Plains; regularly in small numbers east to the
Great Lakes, but casually to the Atlantic coast
—Massachusetts (two specimens), New York
(one specimen).

Status: Unrecorded in the state before 1939.
Since the 1940s a rare to uncommon but regular fall migrant in western New York in the
vicinity of the Great Lakes; occasionally more
numerous. Very rare in spring.

Change in status: Franklin's Gull was not
recorded by Eaton (1910, 1914). It was first
reported in the state in 1939 (see **Specimen
data**). From the early 1940s this species was
reported at least once each fall in the Buffalo
area. Since 1964 small flocks have been seen
from time to time on the Niagara River during
October and November. Most of the several-
dozen occurrences have been from the Lake
Erie portion of Buffalo, along the Niagara River
to its mouth on Lake Ontario, and east along
Lake Ontario to the vicinity of Rochester. Elsewhere upstate it has been recorded only along
the Lake Erie shore southwest of Buffalo—as
at Hamburg and Dunkirk—and east of Rochester on Lake Ontario—at Oswego. Inland
(away from the lake shore) it has been reported but twice—once at Ithaca (specimen)
and a flock of *six* at Montezuma.

It is unknown elsewhere in the state except
for one Long Island specimen record and two
Long Island observations in 1948 and 1954
(Bull, 1964: 239–240).

MAXIMA: *Fall*—four, Niagara River near
Buffalo, Sept. 30, 1966; seven, same locality,
Oct. 2, 1968; six, Niagara Falls to Lewiston,
Niagara Co. (six miles), Oct. 22–29, 1967; and
as many as *11* there on Nov. 1 (Hess). *Spring*
—six in breeding plumage, Montezuma
Marshes, Apr. 11, 1964 (Ives and Farnham,
Kingbird, 1964, 14: 153), are most excep-
tional.

EXTREME DATES: *Fall*—July 19 to Dec.
8. *Winter*—Buffalo, Dec. 23, 1967 (several observers); Niagara River at Tonawanda, Dec.
26, 1955 (Mitchell); Oswego (harbor) on Lake
Ontario, Jan. 3, 1960 (Scheider). *Spring*—
Mar. 15 to June 10. The early spring occurrence was that of an adult in breeding plumage
with a nearly complete hood at Oswego (harbor) on Mar. 15, 1959 (Seaman and Spofford,
Kingbird, 1959, 9: 23).

Specimen data: There are *five* specimen records for the state—four from western New
York, one from Long Island—(1) immature
found dead on the shore of Lake Ontario
near the mouth of the Genesee River, Oct.
15, 1939 (Meade), CUM 13758; (2) adult collected on the Niagara River off Bird Island,
Buffalo, Nov. 10, 1941 (Mitchell), BMS 2031;
(3) and (4) two immatures taken at the latter
locality, Oct. 6 and 13, 1966 (Andrle), BMS
5074 and 5075; (5) adult with black hood
collected at Shelter Island, Suffolk Co., June
2, 1940 (Latham), NYSM 24988; this record
not previously published.

Bonaparte's Gull
(*Larus philadelphia*)   *

Range: Alaska and western and central Canada, breeding east to extreme eastern Ontario
(southern James Bay and south to about Lake
Abitibi). Winters from southern portions of
the breeding range southward.

Status: Common to very abundant migrant
and winter visitant; regular summering nonbreeder in small numbers.

Occurrence: The attractive Bonaparte's Gull frequents Long Island waters, the lower Hudson River, and the Great Lakes region, but is especially numerous in the Buffalo-Niagara Falls area and to a lesser extent, New York harbor. It is relatively uncommon on small inland lakes and ponds.

MAXIMA: *Coastal*—2500, Lower Bay (New York harbor), Nov. 2, 1941; 4500, Montauk Point, Long Island, Jan. 5, 1936; 10,000, Gravesend Bay, Brooklyn, early January 1962 (many observers); 2500, Narrows (New York harbor), Apr. 12, 1947; 1000, Upper Bay (New York harbor), Apr. 26, 1931; 100, Jamaica Bay, May 25, 1957; five, Long Beach, Nassau Co., June–July 1937.

MAXIMA: *Inland*—3000, Buffalo, Aug. 28, 1965; 15,000, lower Niagara River, Oct. 22, 1967 (Klabunde); 30,000, Niagara Falls, Nov. 26, 1959 (numerous observers); 12,000, same locality, Dec. 23, 1967; 5000, Dunkirk, Chautauqua Co., Apr. 23, 1967; 10,000, Niagara Falls, May 3, 1930; 200, Cayuga Lake, May 14, 1965; 30, Montezuma Refuge, summer of 1967 (Benning); 200, Ontario Beach, Monroe Co., July 27, 1969 (O'Hara).

For a more detailed regional status within the state, see Burger and Brownstein (1968a).

Specimen data: Five summer specimens have been collected in the state—Great Gull Island, Suffolk Co., July 8, 1889 (Chapman and Dutcher), AMNH collection; four in the Rochester area by Dilger (two at Manitou Beach, July 24, 1946, CUM collection; two at nearby Braddock's Bay, July 27, 1948, RMAS collection).

Black-headed Gull
(*Larus ridibundus*)   *

Range: Palearctic region, breeding west to Iceland, recently in southwestern Greenland (*fide* Salomonsen); in the western portion of its range winters south to Africa. Regular visitant to the Atlantic coast of North America (Labrador to New Jersey) since the 1930s; much rarer inland to the eastern Great Lakes.

Status: Unrecorded in the state before 1937. Since the 1940s a rare to uncommon, but regular winter visitant along the coast; casual or very rare in western New York.

Change in status: This species was first reported in the state in 1937 when Helmuth saw two adults at Montauk, Long Island, from Dec. 27, 1937, to Jan. 4, 1938. It was next observed in New York harbor during the winter of 1943–1944. Since that time these birds have been reported regularly in the vicinity of sewer outlets and where refuse has accumulated in the bays and estuaries. These gulls are almost invariably seen associating with Bonaparte's Gulls which they closely resemble. The Black-headed Gull is most numerous during the colder months, especially from late November to March.

MAXIMA: *Coastal*—four, Narrows (New York harbor), winter of 1949–1950; six (possibly as many as nine), Upper Bay (New York harbor), Dec. 23, 1961 (Ryan, *et al.*); six, Moriches Inlet, Suffolk Co., Nov. 22, 1964 (Raynor and Puleston); three still present there Jan. 4, 1965.

Black-headed Gulls (they actually have *brown* hoods), first reliably reported near Niagara Falls in late fall of 1953, have been noted irregularly in the Niagara River region since at least 1959, but never more than one at a time. In fact they have been recorded only seven times between Buffalo and the mouth of the Niagara River at Lake Ontario. Elsewhere they have been reported upstate only twice in the vicinity of Rochester, once in May, once in January, and at Sandy Pond, Oswego Co., July 22, 1967 (Rusk).

A specimen—the only one known for the state, an adult female—was taken on the Niagara River between Buffalo and Fort Erie, Ontario, on Oct. 13, 1966 (Andrle), BMS 5073.

"EXTREME" DATES: July 22 (inland), Aug. 18 (coastal), and Sept. 11 (inland) to May 19 (inland) and May 30 (coastal). One bird was reported most of the summer of 1963 at Jamaica Bay, Long Island.

Little Gull (*Larus minutus*)   *

Range: Palearctic region, breeding west to Sweden, Denmark, and Germany; recently to Holland. Winters from the British Isles to the Mediterranean Sea. Regular visitant to the Atlantic coast of North America (Maine to New Jersey) and to the interior (eastern Great

Lakes). In 1962 bred in southeastern Ontario (three pairs at Oshawa, north shore of Lake Ontario); and again in 1971, two nests near there—also three nests at Rondeau Park, north shore of Lake Erie.

Status: Rare to uncommon but regular visitant, both along the coast and in western New York.

Occurrence: The Little Gull, like the Black-headed Gull, is most often found with Bonaparte's Gulls. On the coast all three species frequent the bays and inlets, especially in the vicinity of sewer outlets. As a result the waters of New York harbor are among the best places to look for rare Old World gulls. Inland, Little Gulls are most frequently reported in the Buffalo-Niagara Falls area, very likely derived from the above-mentioned Canadian breeding localities, relatively nearby.

Interestingly enough this species is rarer than the Black-headed Gull in the New York City region, but is much the commoner of the two in the Great Lakes area. For instance, never more than two Little Gulls at one time have been reported in the coastal waters of New York. Unlike *L. ridibundus,* which is chiefly a cold-weather gull, the Little Gull has been recorded every month of the year.

MAXIMA: *Inland*—five, Buffalo, Sept. 11, 1965; six, Niagara Falls, Nov. 11, 1958; five, same locality, Dec. 23, 1967; three, Lewiston, Niagara Co., Apr. 25, 1968; four, Braddock's Bay, Monroe Co., all summer, 1965.

Specimen data: At least *eight* specimens of *L. minutus* have been collected in the state, of which *six* are from upstate. The two old Long Island specimens—often published—are found also in Bull (1964: 240). The six from upstate New York are: (1) immature, Cayuga Lake, May 20, 1916 (Griscom), CUM 2524; (2) immature, Buffalo, Nov. 10, 1941 (Mitchell), BMS 2030; (3) adult, Braddock's Bay, Monroe Co., July 27, 1948 (Boardman and Klonick), RMAS, no catalog no.; (4) immature, Oneida Lake, July 7, 1951 (Loomis), specimen in his collection—confirmed by A. A. Allen; (5) adult, Buffalo, Nov. 25, 1959 (Andrle), BMS 5085; (6) adult, Buffalo, Oct. 6, 1966 (Andrle), BMS 5078. For further details of these western New York occurrences, see Burger and Brownstein (1968b).

Remarks: It is possible that some or all of the Little Gulls recently reported from the interior of the state are from additional New World breeding colonies, as yet undiscovered.

Postscript: According to Andrle (*in litt.*), an unprecedented number of these birds was present on the Niagara River between Niagara Falls and Queenston, Ontario (about five miles of river), on Nov. 4, 1973. On that day *28,* including *21* in a single flock, were observed by P. Benham and D. Salisbury; at least five were in immature plumage. As usual they were associating with Bonaparte's Gulls.

Sabine's Gull (*Larus sabini*) *

Range: Holarctic region, locally distributed at high latitudes; in America breeding south to Southampton Island. Winter range poorly known, but in the Pacific Ocean ranges south to Peru; in the Atlantic off the southwest coast of Africa. Some adults may winter in the breeding range. Migrations not well known, but probably pelagic, coastal, and overland.

Status: *Very rare*—Sabine's Gull is a great rarity in this state and yet there may be as many as 30 recorded occurrences here. Nevertheless, relatively few of these have been adequately confirmed (i.e., by specimen evidence). Confusion of this species with the immature Black-legged Kittiwake is possible.

Sabine's Gull is a very rare fall migrant on Long Island, but is apparently less rare in western New York.

Seven specimens have been taken in the state, three on Long Island, two of which are extant; and four from upstate, also two extant: (1) Raynor South (=Freeport), Nassau Co., July 1837 (Giraud, 1844: 363); (2) immature, Gardiner's Bay, Suffolk Co., Oct. 6, 1899 (Worthington), and (3) adult in nearly full breeding plumage, Oyster Pond, Montauk, Sept. 15, 1931 (Latham)—both of these latter specimens are NYSM 24984 and 24987; (4) adult in breeding plumage, Montezuma Marshes, about 1887 (Parker, in Eaton, 1910: 137); (5) immature, Keuka Lake, near Branchport, Yates Co., Oct. 29, 1921 (Burtch, *Auk*, 1922, 39: 277); (6) immature, Niagara River, above the Peace Bridge at Buffalo, Sept. 27, 1966 (Andrle), BMS 5079; (7) immature, Niagara River, between Buffalo and Fort Erie, Ontario, Nov. 29, 1967 (Andrle), BMS 6321.

On at least three occasions, *two* individuals at one time have been observed in western New York: two, Manitou, Monroe Co., Oct. 1, 1962 (Listman), and two, Niagara Falls, Oct. 21, 1962 (Able and Rosche), may represent the same two individuals rather than four; two, Niagara Falls, Oct. 17, 1964 (Andrle).

EXTREME DATES: Other than the July specimen record reported above, the dates range from Aug. 25 (coastal) to Dec. 3 (inland). A winter report at sea and another in early spring on Long Island—both by single observers—may be correct, but lack corroboration.

Black-legged Kittiwake
(Larus tridactylus)   *

Range: Holarctic region, in eastern North America breeding south to islands in the Gulf of St. Lawrence; in 1971 on an island off northern Nova Scotia. Winters south to New Jersey (mainly offshore).

Status: Variously uncommon to very common late fall and winter pelagic visitant. Occasional along the outer coast after storms. Rare visitant to the Great Lakes.

Occurrence: Kittiwakes are seldom seen at coastal areas, except after severe easterly gales, or off Montauk Point. But even then these pelagic gulls rarely come close to land and the observer may consider himself fortunate if he sees one. Offshore trips during the colder months will increase the observer's chances for studying this species.

MAXIMA: *Coastal*—usually up to a dozen individuals; 40, ten miles off Long Beach (= Cholera Banks), Dec. 19, 1913; big flight in 1956–1957—110, Montauk Point, Nov. 10, and 65, Jones Beach, Nov. 12 (after strong gale); 200+, Montauk Point, Jan. 26, 1957 (several observers). The species is most often recorded from November to February.

MAXIMA: *Inland*—of more than two dozen occurrences from western New York (chiefly Lake Ontario-Niagara River area), at least 11 are specimen records. Eaton (1910: 121) listed three specimens, none of which is extant. The other eight—*all* immatures except one

—taken within nine years (1959–1967) are extant: (1) Bird Island, Niagara River (near Buffalo), Nov. 25, 1959 (Andrle), BMS 4923; (2 and 3) two found dead along the shore of Lake Ontario, near Oswego, Jan. 10, 1965 (Spies, *Kingbird,* 1965, 15: 116); (4) adult, same locality, Dec. 22, 1966 (Spies, *Kingbird,* 1967, 17: 104)—these last three specimens examined by the writer; (5) Buffalo harbor, Jan. 11, 1967 (Andrle), BMS 5076. The following three were found dead during the fall of 1967—(6) Ramona Beach (near Derby Hill), Oswego Co., Sept. 3, (Rusk), exceptionally early (*Kingbird,* 1968, 18: 42); (7) shore of Lake Erie at Athol Springs, Erie Co., Nov. 30 (Bourne), BMS 6147; (8) Buffalo harbor, Dec. 5 (Clark), BMS 6146.

The only proved record "inland" (i.e., away from the Great Lakes area) is that of an immature photographed by P. Trail on Seneca Lake at Geneva, Ontario Co., Dec. 31, 1968 (photos in *Kingbird,* 1969, 19: 95–96, and *Audubon Field Notes,* 1969, 23: 279).

Despite its rarity upstate, at least five different Kittiwakes were observed on Nov. 14, 1965, at the following Lake Ontario localities: one at Sandy Pond, Oswego Co., and two each at Derby Hill, and Sodus Bay, Wayne Co. Five days earlier on Nov. 9, also on Lake Ontario, three were seen at Manitou, Monroe Co. The upstate maxima—also on Lake Ontario—are *five* each observed at Hamlin Beach, Monroe Co., Oct. 29, 1966, and Sodus Bluff, Wayne Co., Nov. 24, 1970 (both by Listman).

EXTREME DATES: Sept. 1, 1963, immature off Montauk Point (Kleinbaum) and Sept. 3 (inland specimen—see above)—both very early —Sept. 20 (coastal) to May 14 (coastal specimen) and May 23 (coastal).

The species is rare before late October and after March. No summer reports have been confirmed.

Ivory Gull *(Pagophila eburnea)*   *

Range: Northern Holarctic region, in eastern North America breeding at high latitudes, questionably south to northern Baffin Island; winters south only to the edge of the pack ice, rarely to Newfoundland and the Gulf of St. Lawrence. Vagrant south to New Jersey.

Status: *Casual*—in New York there are only two confirmed records, both specimens from Long Island, and only one of these is extant: (1) adult collected on Great South Bay near Sayville, Suffolk Co., Jan. 5, 1893 (Goldsworth); (2) immature found dead on the beach at Orient, Suffolk Co., Feb. 17, 1945 (Latham), NYSM 24989.

There are four sight reports by single observers, believed to be correct: Mount Sinai, Suffolk Co., "years ago" (Helme); two in February 1934—immature, Niagara Falls, Feb. 10 (Vaughan)—adult, Orient Point, Feb. 21 (Latham); immature, Coney Island, Kings Co., Feb. 13, 1964 (Ryan).

Gull-billed Tern (*Sterna nilotica*)   *

Range: Nearly cosmopolitan, but very local in distribution, as is true of many species of terns. In eastern North America breeds north to southern Maryland, and sporadically to Delaware and southern New Jersey; winters from Gulf of Mexico southward. Vagrant north to Maine and New Brunswick.

Status: *Very rare*—the Gull-billed Tern is a very rare, irregular summer and fall visitant to the outer coast of Long Island, chiefly after hurricanes, when occasionally more numerous. It is virtually unknown elsewhere (one Staten Island record) and is unrecorded inland.

The first definite record for our region is that of two specimens taken on South Oyster Bay (opposite Jones Beach), Nassau Co., July 4, 1882 (Dutcher collection), AMNH 64666 and 64667. They appear to be the only local extant specimens. For the next half-century hardly any were reported.

In recent years the species has been observed chiefly after hurricanes as follows: Sept. 1, 1934—individuals seen at Jones Beach, Mecox Bay, and Sagaponack; after hurricane "Donna," of Sept. 12, 1960, at least *28* along the south shore of Long Island from Jones Inlet to Sagaponack, with at least *16* in the Short Beach, Nassau Co. area alone (numerous observers). For additional occurrences, see Bull (1964: 243–244, and 1970: 23).

EXTREME DATES: May 14 to Sept. 17. Casual at Mecox Bay, Nov. 29, 1954 (Boyajian, Penberthy, and Wilcox). Note that 1954 was a

hurricane year, when vagrants of several species were reported as remaining long after the actual storm (see especially Black Skimmer).

Remarks: The New World population, called "*aranea,*" supposedly differs from nominate *nilotica* by its smaller size (shorter wing and thinner bill), but at best these differences are of average quality only.

[Trudeau's Tern (*Sterna trudeauii*)

Hypothetical: Southern South America, breeding near the Pacific coast of northern Chile and near the Atlantic coast of central Argentina. Winters and migrates to southern Chile and from southern Argentina to southeastern Brazil (Rio de Janeiro). No proved records from farther north are known.

The supposed occurrence of this species on the coast of southern New Jersey (including Audubon's alleged type locality of Great Egg Harbor) is here considered erroneous, although his type specimen is preserved (Bull, 1964: 479). Peters (1934: 334) did not specifically question the type locality, but the exclamation mark after it indicates his surprise. Stone (1937: 588) stated, "The original specimen . . . which was supposed to have come from Great Egg Harbor seems to have been obtained in Chile."

Nor is its "occurrence" on Long Island, based on old sight reports, satisfactory. Trudeau's Tern and the nonbreeding plumage of Forster's Tern are virtually indistinguishable, especially in the field.

The species should be deleted from the North American list.]

Forster's Tern
(*Sterna forsteri*)   *

Range: North America—of local breeding distribution in three widely disjunct areas, one inland and two coastal—(1) chiefly fresh-water lakes of western and central United States and south-central Canada east to southeastern Wisconsin and northwestern Indiana; (2) western Gulf coast from northeastern Mexico east to

Louisiana; (3) Middle Atlantic coast of Virginia and southern Maryland, rarely north to southern New Jersey (1956 on). For winter range, see **Remarks.**

Status: Variously uncommon to common fall coastal migrant, occasionally more numerous after hurricanes; fairly common fall migrant along the Great Lakes. Very rare in spring.

Occurrence: The numbers of this tern fluctuate widely, especially on the coast. It was reported to be very scarce prior to 1924, but that was before the days of modern field guides and the species was possibly overlooked. However, in 1925 there was a large irruption throughout the northeast and since then it has appeared regularly on the coast. Whether this represented an actual increase is not known.

Forster's Terns frequent a wide variety of terrain from coastal bays and estuaries to inland lakes and marshes.

MAXIMA: *Coastal*—700, Easthampton to Montauk, Sept. 15, 1944 (Helmuth), day after hurricane; 200, Mecox Bay, Suffolk Co., Sept. 23, 1928 (Helmuth), following a hurricane; 50, Rockaway Point, Queens Co., Nov. 6, 1936— late for so many.

MAXIMA: *Inland*—five, Hudson River, near Peekskill, Westchester Co., Aug. 28, 1960; 16, Niagara River, Sept. 13, 1953; 14, Lake Ontario at Sandy Pond, Oswego Co., Sept. 27, 1958; 12, Buffalo harbor, Oct. 1, 1949; five, Hudson River at Croton Point, Westchester Co., Oct. 7, 1928.

EXTREME DATES: *Fall*—July 10 (coastal) to Nov. 30 (coastal).

The Forster's Tern is very rare in spring, barely a dozen reports at that season. There is one spring specimen: adult, Cayuga Lake, May 15, 1914 (F. S. Wright), CUM 3954. Most exceptional are four seen on Lake Erie at Dunkirk, Chautauqua Co., May 19, 1967 (Benham and Brownstein).

EXTREME DATES: *Spring*—Apr. 23 (inland) to May 26 (inland) and June 9 (coastal).

Remarks: This species winters along the coast rarely north to southern New Jersey, casually to Rhode Island. During the great flight in the autumn of 1925, an individual remained at Manhattan Beach, Kings Co., until Dec. 26 (Hix and Nathan).

Common Tern (*Sterna hirundo*)   *   B

Range: Holarctic region, but absent as a breeder on the Pacific coast of North America. Breeds from Canada south, locally inland to northern United States and on the Atlantic coast to North Carolina. Winters north to South Carolina, casually to New York and Massachusetts.

Status: Locally abundant breeder and migrant on Long Island; less numerous in the interior, breeding locally in the northwestern, central, and western portions of the state.

Nonbreeding: The Common Tern is most numerous and widespread in fall, but occurs in large numbers also in spring, especially on the coast.

MAXIMA, COASTAL: *Spring*—1500, Oak Beach, Suffolk Co., May 10, 1936. *Fall*—5000, after a hurricane, Moriches Inlet, Suffolk Co., Sept. 3, 1949.

MAXIMA, INLAND: *Spring*—450, Buffalo, Apr. 18, 1958 (Mitchell), early for so many. *Fall*—750, Sodus Bay, Wayne Co., Sept. 3, 1966; 600, east end of Oneida Lake, Oct. 4, 1964; 200, Niagara Falls, Oct. 31, 1965.

EXTREME DATES: Apr. 2 (inland) and Apr. 15 (coastal) to Dec. 5 (coastal) and Dec. 7 (inland); exceptionally on the coast as early as Mar. 20 (two different years). On the coast it is rare before May and after mid-October, but inland it is rare before mid-April and after mid-November, arriving much earlier and departing later than on the coast. Usually the reverse is true. The inland population may migrate mainly by way of the Mississippi valley and the Great Lakes.

Winter—Extremely rare at this season, but there are at least three occurrences: Montauk Point, Long Island, Dec. 27, 1957 (Ryan); twice in the Buffalo area—Dec. 27, 1964, to Jan. 2, 1965 (Mitchell and Rew), and Dec. 16, 1965, to Jan. 5, 1966 (Axtell and Freitag); single birds in all instances.

Breeding (see Map 73): Variously rare to abundant. Nearly completely extirpated in the early 1900s during the height of the plume trade, until given full protection in 1913; recovered again by the 1920s. In more recent

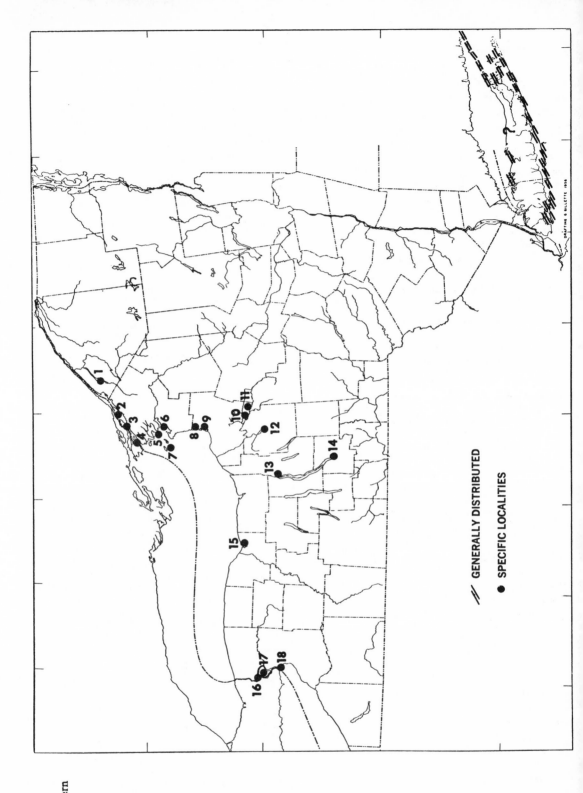

MAP 73 Common Tern
(*Sterna hirundo*)
Breeding distribution

GENERALLY DISTRIBUTED

SPECIFIC LOCALITIES

times these terns have been partially displaced at nest sites, by the ever-increasing and aggressive Herring Gulls, especially on Gardiner's Island and in the Moriches Bay area.

The Common Tern breeds on ocean beaches, on various islands in the bays along the south shore, on islands at the east end of Long Island, and since 1917 in various upstate localities (see below).

On Long Island nests are commonly placed on the sand among scattered clumps of grass and are often lined with shell fragments and pebbles. On the north shore where sand beaches are rare, eggs are laid on gravel bars. In 1967 at Lawrence, Nassau Co., McCauley, Hays, and LeCroy found nests constructed of *Phragmites* stems on salt marsh hay (*Spartina patens*) (see Fig. 53).

On islands in Oneida Lake a number of pairs nested in grassy areas, others among pebbles or gravel, still others in thick growths of sedge and other vegetation. A few nests on islets in the St. Lawrence River were found on bare rock; others were situated on the stone jetties near Niagara Falls, at Buffalo harbor, and at the south end of Cayuga Lake near Ithaca. At Montezuma Marshes, Common Tern nests have frequently been built on the tops of muskrat houses and a few even on duck blinds.

By all odds the most unusual nest site was of one discovered at Huntington harbor, Suffolk Co., June 4, 1951, by Geoffrey Gill (*Auk*, 1953, 70: 89). A nest and eggs were found inside a coil of rope on the roof of a small cabin cruiser anchored in the harbor.

Egg clutches in 1770 New York nests—all from Great Gull Island, Suffolk Co., in 1969 (Helen Hays and Mary LeCroy)—are as follows: one egg (353 nests); two eggs (900 nests —51%); three eggs (513 nests); four eggs (four nests).

EGG DATES, from all parts of the state:

Fig. 53 Common Tern nest with two downy young and one pipped egg; nest built of *Phragmites* stalks on *Spartina patens* growth in salt marsh, Lawrence, Nassau Co., Aug. 1, 1967. Photo by Mary LeCroy

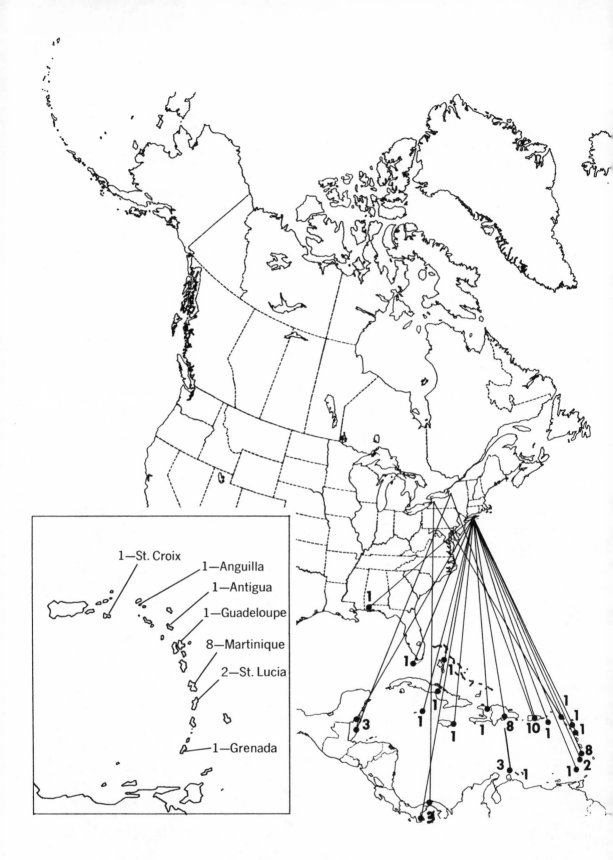

MAP 74 Common Tern (*Sterna hirundo*) Banding recoveries

WEST AFRICAN COAST (GULF OF GUINEA)

40 – Trinidad

7

5

5

6

27

3

1

2

1

1

1

MAP 75   Common Tern (*Sterna hirundo*) Banding recoveries

May 12 to Aug. 15 (latter represents renesting after initial failure).

Unfledged young: June 11 to Sept. 3; fledged juveniles: July 10 to Sept. 9.

The largest colonies (estimated number of pairs or nests) on Long Island are all in eastern Suffolk Co.—years representing the period of known maximum abundance: 4000, Great Gull Island, 1886 (much fewer in recent years—not more than 2500 in 1971, *fide* Helen Hays); 6000, Orient Point, 1930; 6000, islands in Moriches Bay, 1963.

Upstate the colonies are much smaller: 1000, Little Galloo Island, Jefferson Co., 1952; four different colonies of 800 pairs each—Buffalo and Niagara River, both in 1948, nearby Grand Island in 1962, and Sandy Pond, Oswego Co., 1967; and the same year at an "inland" locality, i.e., away from the Great Lakes, 300 nests on two small islands in western Oneida Lake.

Compared to Long Island, the upstate history of this species is much more recent (since 1917). For instance, Eaton (1910: 145) stated, ". . . is not known to breed within our limits, except on the seacoast . . ."; and again he says, ". . . formerly bred on the Canadian shore of Lake Erie, not far from Buffalo . . ."

As a matter of fact, although it was first known definitely as a breeder as early as 1917 on one of the islands in the St. Lawrence River, next in 1929 on Oneida Lake, and in 1936 on Gull Island in eastern Lake Ontario, nevertheless it was not until 1944 that breeding was reported in the Buffalo area (Beardslee and Mitchell, 1965: 260).

As may be seen on the accompanying map, two widely separated breeding populations are evident: (A) Coastal, restricted to Long Island, on which at least two dozen localities have, or had, breeding *Sterna hirundo*.

(B) Inland, with a total of 18 known breeding localities. These latter are: St. Lawrence Co.—(1) small island in Lonesome Bay, Black Lake. Jefferson Co.—St. Lawrence River—(2) island in Eel Bay; (3) Eaglewing Rocks, off Grindstone Island; (4) Featherbed Shoals, near Cape Vincent. Jefferson Co.—eastern Lake Ontario—(5) Point Peninsula; (6) Gull Island; (7) Little Galloo Island. Oswego Co.—(8) North Pond; (9) Sandy Pond. Oneida Lake—(10) Wantry and Long islands; (11) Leete Island. Onondaga Co.—(12) Onondaga Lake near Syracuse. Cayuga Lake—north end—(13)

Montezuma Marshes; south end—(14) near Ithaca. Monroe Co.—(15) Irondequoit Bay, Rochester. Niagara River—(16) small island near Goat Island, Niagara Falls; (17) Grand Island. Erie Co.—(18) Buffalo harbor.

Banding (see Maps 74 and 75): Relative to long-distance recoveries, out of a total of 160 juveniles banded on the breeding grounds in New York, all but ten were from Long Island (most of these banded by LeRoy Wilcox), the balance from breeding grounds in Buffalo, Montezuma, Oneida Lake, and Sandy Pond. With few exceptions these juveniles were taken the following fall or winter, the exceptions being birds that remained the following summer in the tropics, a common phenomenon in the Charadriiformes. All but two of the 160 banded birds were recovered at or near coastal points, the two exceptions are noted in detail below.

With the exception of seven islands in the Lesser Antilles (see inset map), the following localities of recovery are listed by name from north to south and from west to east. Numbers in parentheses indicate recoveries.

(A) North America, including the West Indies and Central America: Alabama, near Mobile (one); Florida, Boca Chica Key, near Key West (one); Bahamas, near Nassau (one); Cuba, near Camaguey (one); Little Cayman Island, south of Cuba (one); Jamaica (one); Hispaniola—Haiti, near Cap Haïtien (one)—Dominican Republic, near Ciudad Trujillo (eight); Puerto Rico (ten); Lesser Antilles (15)—see breakdown of seven islands on inset map; British Honduras (three); Panama (three, including two in the Canal Zone, Atlantic coast, the third on the Pacific coast near Chitré).

(B) South America, including islands off the north coast: Curaçao (three); Aruba (one); Trinidad (*40*, including *13* that summered); Colombia (six, including four on the Atlantic coast, two on the Pacific coast); Venezuela (seven, including one that summered); Guyana —formerly British Guiana (*27*); Surinam or Dutch Guiana (five, including one that summered); Cayenne or French Guiana (five); Ecuador (three); Brazil (15, including three that summered—eight of the 15 were recovered in the vicinity of the Amazon delta, six more near the east hump, and one far *inland* near Pirapora on the Rio Velhas, state of Minas

Gerais); Bolivia (one—even farther *inland* near Tarija on the river of the same name—bird banded on Oneida Lake); Chile (one, banded on Long Island, July 21, 1962, taken near Valdivia, Aug. 30, 1963—it presumably summered somewhere along the Pacific coast —a distance of more than *6500* miles from place of banding to place of recovery).

It will thus be seen that Trinidad with 40 recoveries and nearby Guyana with 27, for a total of 67 out of 160 (nearly 42%), are probably two of the chief wintering grounds for New York juveniles of this species. Most of the Long Island birds were banded by LeRoy Wilcox.

The most remarkable recovery of this species concerns a nestling banded on an island in Moriches Bay, Suffolk Co., June 28, 1969, by Gilbert Raynor (*Bird-Banding,* 1970, 41: 310–311). It was caught alive aboard a fishing boat on Dec. 12, 1969, off the West African coast in the Gulf of Guinea, at approximately 4°30′ north latitude, 6°20′ west longitude! According to Raynor (*op. cit.*), "This is apparently the first transatlantic recovery of a North American banded Common Tern . . ." He postulated that, "The most likely supposition is that the bird joined a flock of Arctic Terns and accompanied them to the Gulf of Guinea . . ."

A 14-year-old bird, banded as a nestling, July 8, 1939, at Moriches Bay, was trapped and released, June 29, 1953, at Plymouth, Mass.

Arctic Tern (*Sterna paradisaea*)   *

Range: Northern Holarctic region, in eastern North America breeding south along the Atlantic coast to Martha's Vineyard, Massachusetts. Pelagic in migration, the western Atlantic population migrates east in fall to the coasts of western Europe and Africa, then south to the southern oceans in winter. This species is virtually unrecorded in North America south of Long Island. After the breeding season the birds presumably migrate well offshore and do not visit coastal areas.

Status: *Casual*—there are three proved occurrences for New York State, all collected specimens: (1) adult male taken on Ram Island Shoals (=Cartwright Island), eastern

Long Island, July 18, 1884 (Worthington), AMNH 64696; (2) immature male taken on Long Island (locality and collector unknown), Oct. 7, 1897, NYSM 1707; (3) adult female shot at the north end of Cayuga Lake, May 20, 1916 (Griscom), CUM 2574.

This last specimen was with a mixed flock of Common Terns, Black Terns, Bonaparte's Gulls, and a single Little Gull—the last also collected. Not a bad haul for one day!

A specimen alleged to be this species from the Buffalo area, reported by Beardslee and Mitchell (1965: 261), is not extant. It was not critically examined by an ornithologist.

No sight reports of Arctic Terns in New York are accepted. This species is easily confused with the Common Tern, even in breeding plumage, as was amply demonstrated by a specimen collected several miles off Jones Beach, Long Island, May 29, 1960. This individual, "identified" as an Arctic Tern—even when in the hand—proved to be a Common Tern, after an examination of a large series of study skins of both species. The specimen is in the AMNH collection. For further discussion, see Bull (1964: 247–248).

Despite the article in *British Birds* (1969, 62: 297–299 and Plate 53), the field identification of Common Terns versus Arctic Terns remains extremely difficult, as already mentioned.

Roseate Tern
(*Sterna dougallii*)   *   B

Range: Of local distribution chiefly in warmer regions of the Old World and even more limited in America; in the latter restricted to the North Atlantic coast and the Caribbean Sea, breeding on coastal islands and ocean beaches from Nova Scotia to Virginia, Dry Tortugas (Florida), and the West Indies. Winters chiefly in the West Indies and Caribbean region.

Status: Variously uncommon to locally abundant breeder and fall migrant on Long Island, chiefly at the east end. Rare and local elsewhere on the coast. No satisfactory record for the interior of the state.

Nonbreeding: Away from the breeding grounds the Roseate Tern is ordinarily a decidedly uncommon migrant. Numbers fluctuate from year to year even in the Montauk and Orient regions. Flocks of over a dozen are the exception rather than the rule.

MAXIMA: 20, Rockaway Beach, Queens Co., May 19, 1956; 500, Montauk Point, Aug. 21, 1950 (Darrow and Helmuth); 25, Mecox Bay, Suffolk Co., Sept. 22, 1937.

EXTREME DATES: Apr. 29 to Oct. 9. Rare before mid-May and after September.

Reports of Roseate Terns upstate have not been corroborated. Eaton (1910: 147) listed three occurrences from the interior of the state, but did not mention whether they were specimens, nor did he give details. Beardslee and Mitchell (1965: 261) mentioned three observations from the Niagara River area within a four-year period (1935–1938), all by single observers only. In absence of specimen evidence, there is no satisfactory inland record for New York of this coastal species.

Breeding (see Map 76): The Roseate Tern breeds in situations similar to those of the Common Tern, but the nests are generally placed in thicker vegetation. Locations in dense grass are preferred to open sandy areas with scattered grass. On Great Gull Island, in extreme eastern Suffolk Co., it nests also under boulders and in rock crevices (see Figs. 54 and 55). Thus interspecific competition is avoided, or at least reduced, by nest site selection, as well as by possible food preference and by a slight difference in breeding schedule. Great Gull Island, incidentally, has the largest numbers of breeding Roseate Terns in New York, more than all other Long Island colonies combined—all *large* colonies being restricted to Suffolk Co.

MAXIMA: 1500 pairs, Great Gull Island, 1971; 400 pairs, Orient Point, 1934; 100 pairs, Cartwright Island, 1938; 100 pairs, Moriches Bay, 1963; 200 pairs, Fire Island State Park, 1960; 150 pairs, Cedar Beach, 1960.

The accompanying map indicates locations

Fig. 54 Great Gull Island, Suffolk Co., July 1968. Nesting sites of Common Terns, mainly in open areas and on concrete strips; and of Roseate Terns, among and under rocks along the shore and also in the grass. Photo by Mary LeCroy

MAP 76 **Roseate Tern**
(Sterna dougallii)
Breeding distribution

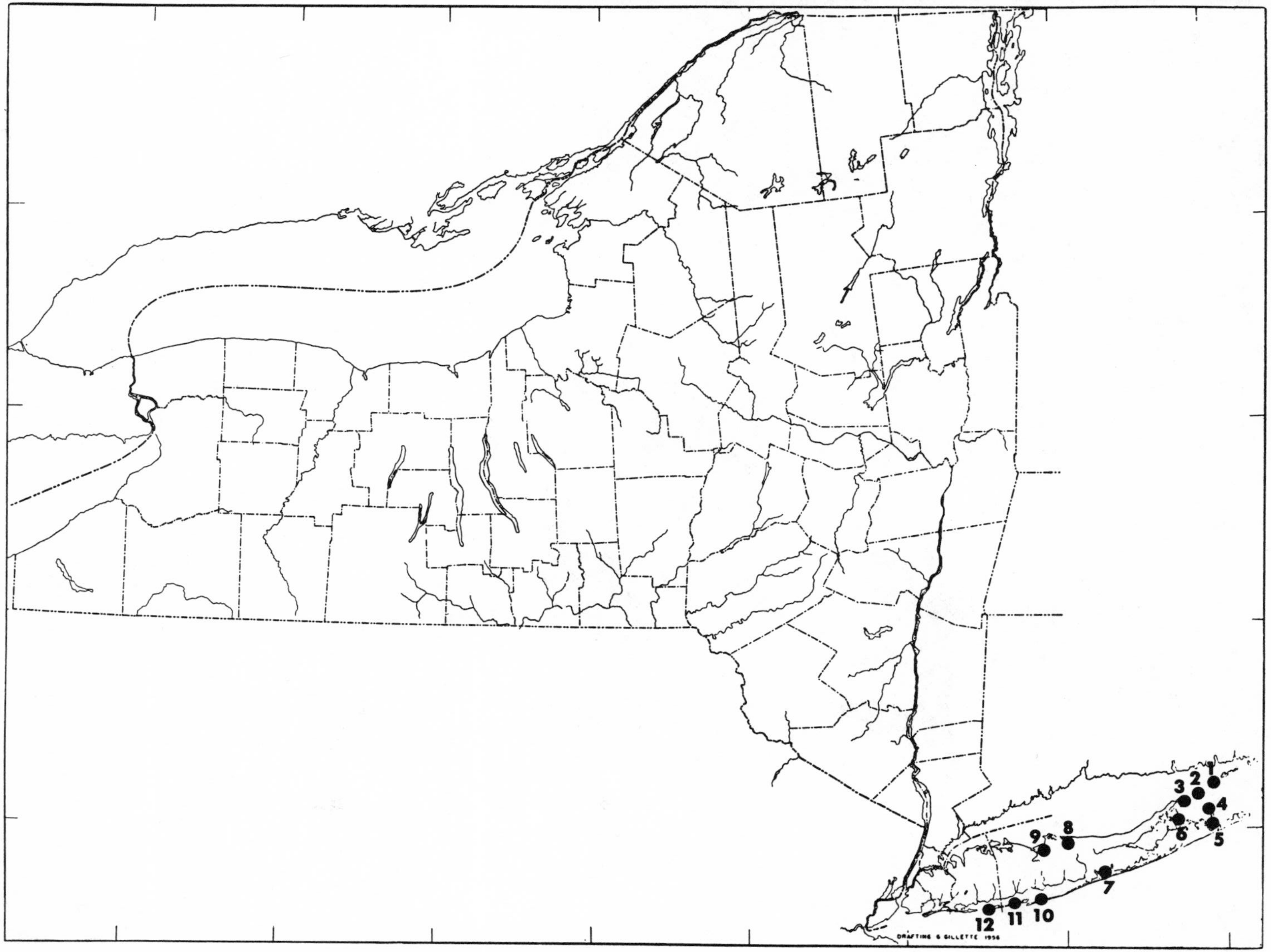

Fig. 55 Roseate Terns, Great Gull Island, Suffolk Co., Long Island, June 1967. On this small island at the east end of Long Island exists a thriving breeding colony of these attractive birds. Photo by Frederick R. Schaeffer

of the 12 known breeding areas on Long Island with year of known initial occupancy recorded for each. Localities are all in Suffolk Co. with the exception of one. I am not aware of a definite breeding record for Fisher's Island, despite Eaton's reference to one (1910: 147).

(1) Great Gull Island, 1889; (2) Plum Island, 1878; (3) Orient Point, 1924; (4) Gardiner's Island, 1912; (5) Cartwright Island, 1930; (6) Shelter Island, 1952; (7) Moriches Bay, 1947; (8) Mount Sinai—north shore, 1934; (9) Stony Brook—north shore, 1968; (10) Fire Island State Park, 1958; (11) Cedar Beach, 1958; (12) Short Beach, Nassau Co., 1951.

Egg clutches in 1240 New York nests: one egg (616 nests); two eggs (574 nests); three eggs (44 nests); four eggs (six nests)—all in 1969. During 1970, however, one-egg and two-egg clutches were 870 and 310 nests respectively, illustrating the great variation present in clutch size.

EGG DATES: May 20 to July 27.

Unfledged juveniles: June 13 to Aug. 31; fledged young: July 11 to Sept. 9.

All egg and juvenile data are from Great Gull Island, courtesy of Helen Hays and Mary LeCroy. According to Donaldson (*Bird-Banding,* 1971, 42: 300), a banded individual bred when only *two* years old.

Banding (see Map 77): Details of three long-distance recoveries of nestlings banded on Long Island are as follows:

(1) Cedar Beach, June 22, 1957 (Wilcox); recovered near Bayamon, Puerto Rico, Aug. 27, 1957.

(2) Great Gull Island, July 9, 1966 (*fide* Helen Hays); recovered near Barahona, Dominican Republic, Sept. 21, 1966.

(3) Great Gull Island, Aug. 8, 1969 (Hays); recovered on Gorgona Island, off the *Pacific* coast of Colombia, Oct. 27, 1969. This appears to be the first record for the Pacific

MAP 77 Roseate Tern (*Sterna dougallii*) Banding recoveries

coast of South America and possibly one of the very few occurrences of the Roseate Tern in the eastern Pacific; see Hays (*Bird-Banding*, 1971, 42: 295).

An unfledged juvenile banded on Great Gull Island, Aug. 19, 1967, was trapped on a nest on Ram Island, Plymouth Co., Massachusetts, three years later, June 16, 1970 (Harlow, *Bird-Banding*, 1971, 42: 50).

Postscript: During the summer of 1972 at least two mixed pairs of Common and Roseate terns successfully hybridized on Great Gull Island (Hays, *et al.*, verbal comm.). This is apparently the first known instance of interbreeding between these species.

Sooty Tern (*Sterna fuscata*)   *

Range: Pantropical, breeding north to the Bahamas and the Dry Tortugas (west of the Florida keys). Ranges widely in the nonbreeding season over tropical and subtropical seas. Vagrant north to Nova Scotia.

Status: *Very rare*—a visitant along the outer coast of Long Island, chiefly after tropical storms; casual elsewhere.

Occurrence: Most of the Sooty Tern records in New York have been the result of hurricanes. This is not surprising in view of the fact that these birds range far and wide in the track of these tropical disturbances. Many of the occurrences in the state are specimen records, a number of which are extant in the larger museums and others in private collections.

MAXIMA—all in hurricane years, as follows:

1878—hurricane on Sept. 12: A number of individuals found dead and alive, including a specimen taken at Highland Falls, Orange Co., Sept. 13 (Mearns), USNM collection, and two at Lake Ronkonkoma, Suffolk Co., the same day (Dutcher), AMNH collection.

1928—hurricane on Sept. 19, biggest invasion in our area (all on Long Island): *16* records, including *ten* specimens, mostly from eastern Suffolk Co.

1955—hurricane "Connie," Aug. 12: Ten occurrences, only one specimen, mostly from western Long Island, including three seen flying through the Narrows (Brooklyn side) on Aug. 13.

1960—hurricane "Donna," Sept. 12: 12 Long Island occurrences, seven of these specimens, five on Sept. 13 alone, plus two banded birds found (see below).

Eaton (1910: 149) listed two upstate specimen records, both in 1876, one from Lake Champlain, Sept. 6, the other from Owasco Lake, Cayuga Co., Sept. 20. In addition, one reported as found dead on the road near Lake Ontario at Irondequoit Bay, Monroe Co., June 5, 1963, is supposedly in the Rochester Museum of Arts and Sciences, but I did not locate it when examining that collection in 1968.

Banding (see Map 78): Two individuals banded on the Dry Tortugas, Florida: one, a juvenile, banded on July 14, 1960, was found dead—suspended from a telephone wire—near Shinnecock Bay, Suffolk Co., Sept. 14, 1960, two days after hurricane "Donna"; the other, an adult banded on May 11, 1964, was caught alive on a hook from a fishing boat off Great Kills, Staten Island (Richmond Co.), Aug. 13, 1964.

An immature found alive and banded in 1960 during a lull in hurricane "Donna" of Sept. 12 at Quogue, Suffolk Co., was caught alive on Block Island, Rhode Island, three days later.

Robertson (1969: 633) has shown that many juveniles banded on the Dry Tortugas have been recovered in West African waters.

Note that the circles on the banding recovery map are not intended as the "lines" of flight (actually unknown), but merely to point out localities of banding and recovery. It is even quite possible that one or both birds were at sea immediately prior to recovery.

Bridled Tern (*Sterna anaethetus*)   *

Range: Pantropical, the race *recognita* (has considerably more white—less gray on outermost [longest] rectrices than the nominate race). Breeds north to the Bahamas. Ranges widely in the nonbreeding season over tropical and subtropical seas, rarely to Florida and South Carolina. Reported after tropical storms north to Massachusetts.

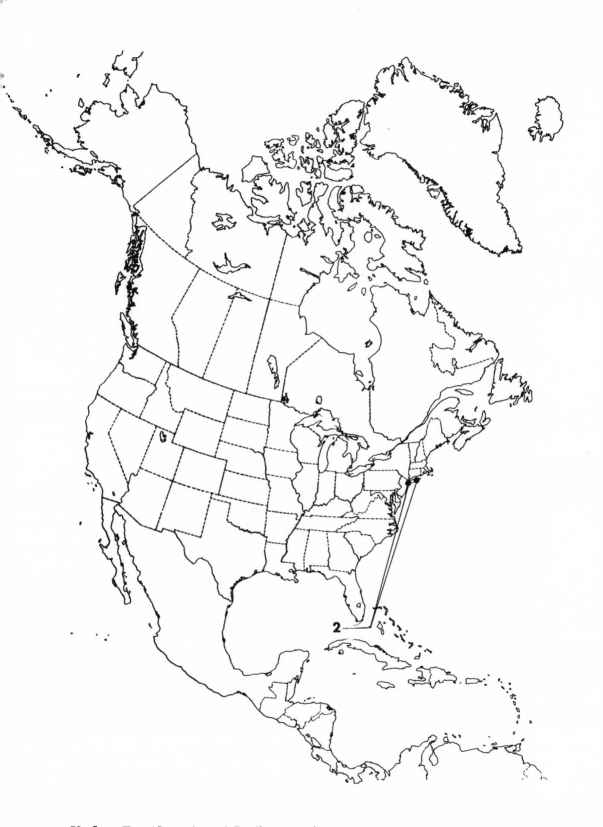

MAP 78 Sooty Tern (*Sterna fuscata*) Banding recoveries

Status: *Casual*—there are two specimen records for New York, both from Long Island: (1) immature found alive on the beach at Quogue, Suffolk Co., Dec. 11, 1950 (Wilcox), is in his collection. The specimen was examined by Amadon who confirmed the identification. The severe tropical storm of Nov. 25 may have caused the presence of this individual. (2) A tern wing found along the stone jetty at Short Beach, Nassau Co., Jan. 22, 1967 (Ward), was identified as this species by the writer and also by Parkes. The specimen is AMNH 786360. By what means and how long the bird was in the area is purely conjectural.

Least Tern (*Sterna albifrons*) * B

Range: Nearly cosmopolitan, widespread but local; in eastern North America the race *antillarum* (rump and tail *gray;* nominate race rump and tail *white*) breeds along the Atlantic coast north to Massachusetts. Winters along the north and east coasts of South America from Venezuela to Brazil.

Status: Common to abundant migrant on the outer coast, much less numerous elsewhere on Long Island, and very rare in the lower Hudson valley. Local breeder on Long Island.

Nonbreeding: As the Least Tern breeds to the north of us only as far as Massachusetts, the following maxima may represent birds chiefly from nearby nesting grounds in our area, and postbreeding wanderers from more southern regions.

MAXIMA: 300, Atlantic Beach, Nassau Co., May 6, 1945; 175, Moriches Inlet, Suffolk Co., Aug. 20, 1946; 500 after a tropical storm, same locality, Sept. 3, 1949 (Mayer and Rose).

EXTREME DATES: Apr. 20 to Oct. 10. Rare before May and after early September.

Least Terns were recorded at two localities on the lower Hudson River after hurricane "Connie" of Aug. 14, 1955: 13, West Point, Orange Co., and six, Piermont, Rockland Co. (numerous observers).

Upstate this species is exceedingly rare. Eaton (1910: 148) questioned all records from the interior of the state; specimens that he examined proved to be juvenile Black Terns.

However, two recent records from the Finger Lakes region are believed correct: (1) An individual color-photographed on Keuka Lake, near Branchport, Yates Co., Aug. 14, 1955 (Fudge, *Kingbird*, 1957, 7: 13–14). Note that this is the same date and tropical storm that produced the inland Least Terns mentioned above. (2) One studied carefully at the Montezuma Marshes, July 3, 1965 (Benning, Scheider, and Williams, *Kingbird*, 1965, 15: 220).

Breeding (see Map 79): The following is taken from Bull (1964: 253)—"The Least Tern, like the Piping Plover, nests on the open sand. It is found on the ocean beaches, and especially the sand flats where new fill has been dredged and pumped in the vicinity of bays and inlets.

"Formerly common (prior to 1880), its numbers were severely depleted by the millinery hunters. With full protection in 1913, the species recovered strongly by the 1920s and is now once more numerous. Its future depends upon the preservation of beaches from being developed into bathing resorts."

It is also found in suitable habitat along the north shore (Long Island Sound) and in the vicinity of the bays at the east end of Long Island.

Nests are most often placed on the sand where there are patches of grass, some pebbles, and shell fragments.

Egg clutches in 58 New York nests: one egg (four nests—incomplete?); two eggs (37 nests); three eggs (11 nests); four eggs (six nests).

EGG DATES: May 9 to July 27.

Unfledged young: June 4 to Aug. 11; fledglings: July 15 to Aug. 29.

Maximum breeding densities including years are: 200 pairs, Short Beach, Nassau Co., 1951; 200 pairs, Gilgo Island, Suffolk Co., 1936; 200 pairs, Westhampton Beach, Suffolk Co., 1966—all on the south shore; 120 pairs, Stony Brook, Suffolk Co., 1968 (Cioffi and Davis)—very unusual number for the north shore.

The accompanying map shows the 26 known breeding localities: Staten Island, Richmond Co.—(1) Great Kills. Balance on Long Island—Kings Co.—(2) Canarsie Pol, Jamaica Bay. Queens Co.—(3) Rockaway Point; (4) Idlewild. Nassau Co.—(5) Baldwin; (6) Long Beach; (7) Short Beach; (8) Seaford. Suffolk Co.—(9) Gilgo Island; (10) Oak Beach; (11) Heckscher State Park; (12) near Point O'Woods, Fire Island; (13) Moriches Inlet;

MAP 79 Least Tern
(*Sterna albifrons*)
Breeding distribution

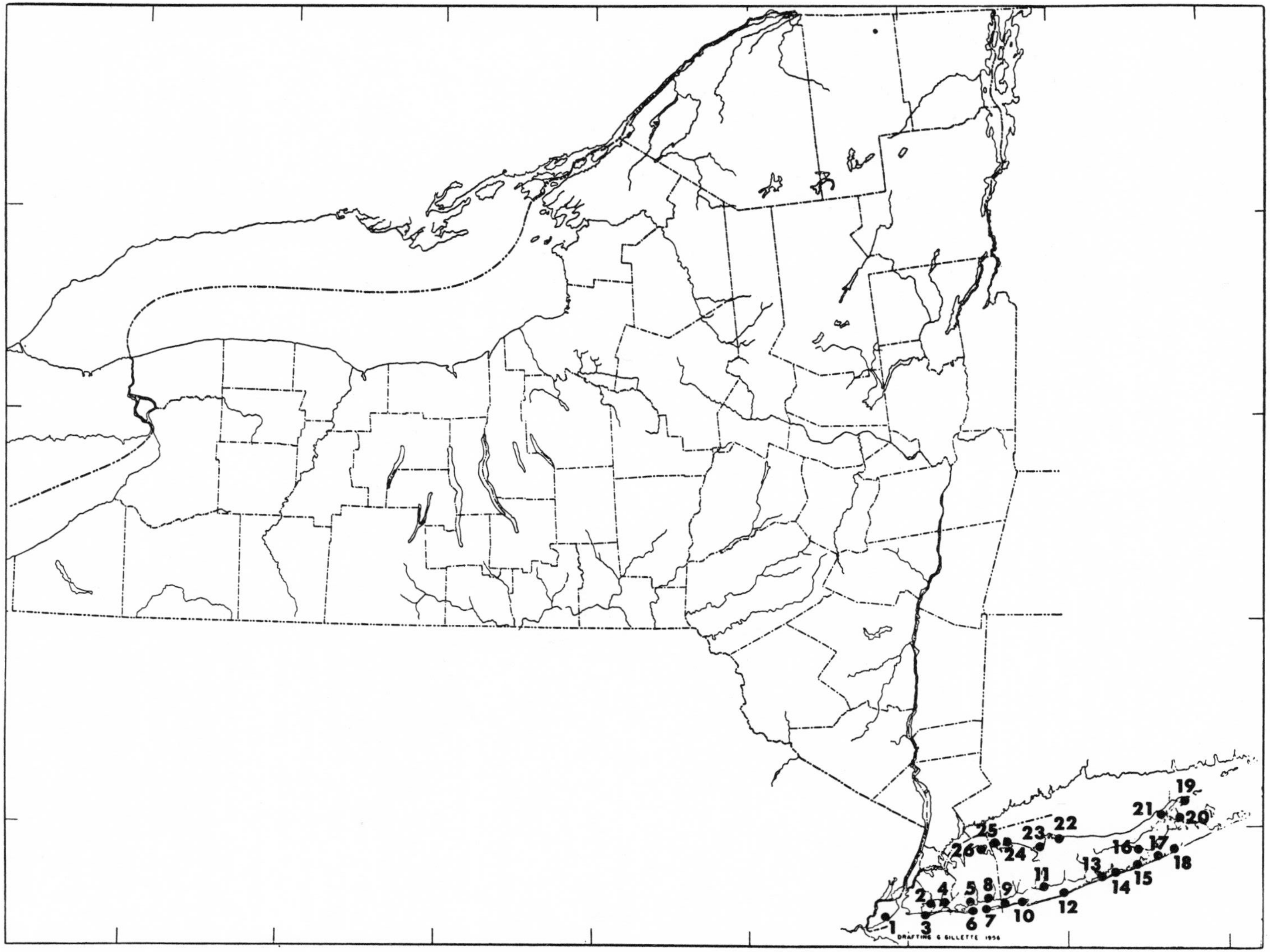

(14) Westhampton Beach; (15) Tiana Beach; (16) Red Cedar Point, Flanders Bay; (17) Shinnecock Inlet; (18) Mecox Bay; (19) Orient Point; (20) Shelter Island; (21) Southold; (22) Port Jefferson; (23) Stony Brook; (24) Eaton's Neck; (25) Caumsett State Park. Nassau Co. —(26) Bayville.

Banding: A juvenile banded at Fire Island, June 22, 1940 (Herrick), was recovered there *17* years later on July 4, 1957.

Sandwich Tern
(*Sterna sandvicensis*) *

Range: Chiefly western Palearctic region and warm-temperate portions of the Nearctic region, in the latter area the race *acuflavidus* (undersurface of primaries with noticeably more gray [less white] than nominate race). Breeds locally and sporadically in the Caribbean, Gulf of Mexico, and on the Atlantic coast of North and South Carolina, rarely to southern Virginia (1967). Winters from the Gulf of Mexico southward. Vagrant north to southern Ontario.

Status: *Very rare*—in New York State recorded only from Long Island, after tropical storms. The first definite record is that of a female in nonbreeding plumage taken at Mecox Bay, Suffolk Co., June 30, 1957 (Buckley), AMNH 707775. This occurrence was very likely the result of hurricane "Audrey" of June 27.

In 1960, after the passage of hurricane "Donna" on Sept. 12, at least *nine* individuals were observed by many people from Sept. 13 to 16 at six different south-shore localities from Jones Beach east to Sagaponack.

An adult was observed at Gilgo Beach, Suffolk Co., Oct. 22, 1968 (Buckley), after hurricane "Gladys" of Oct. 20 had passed well offshore.

Royal Tern
(*Sterna maxima*) *

Range: Very local, with a discontinuous breeding distribution—Pacific coast of Mexico; Gulf coast of Texas and Louisiana; Atlantic coast from Georgia to Maryland; West Indies and southern Caribbean region; West African

coast. Winters from southern United States southward. Vagrant north to Nova Scotia.

Status: Variously rare to uncommon summer and fall visitant to the outer coast, but sometimes numerous, especially after hurricanes. Great increase in recent years with northward breeding range extension.

Change in status: The Royal Tern, formerly considered accidental, for many years was known only from an old specimen taken at Raynor South (=Freeport), Nassau Co., Aug. 27, 1831 (Ward), AMNH 46008—the oldest known specimen of any species collected in the state with full data. Except for another specimen collected at Gardiner's Bay, Suffolk Co., July 6, 1896 (Worthington), NYSM 24990, the species was not recorded again until 1936 when one was seen at Mecox Bay, Suffolk Co., on Sept. 19 (Helmuth) after a tropical storm. These three records represent the only known occurrences in more than a century. Another specimen was found dead at Moriches Bay, Suffolk Co., Sept. 4, 1954, after hurricane "Carol" of Aug. 31 (Carleton and Grant), AMNH 648729.

The species has been of regular occurrence on the south shore of Long Island, especially since 1950, coinciding with the great increase in the south.

MAXIMA: nine, Shinnecock Inlet, Suffolk Co., Aug. 22, 1953; 32, Moriches Inlet, Suffolk Co., Sept. 4, 1954 (after hurricane "Carol" of Aug. 31); 60, Jones Inlet to Shinnecock Inlet, Sept. 12, 1954 (after hurricane "Edna" of Sept. 11); 300, Jones Inlet to Sagaponack, Sept. 14, 1960 (after hurricane "Donna" of Sept. 12); 28, off Great Kills, Staten Island, Oct. 24, 1965 (Barber), late for so many.

EXTREME DATES: June 7, 13, and 18 (see below), to Oct. 27.

Remarks: The only substantiated inland report is that of an individual found dead near Lake De Forest, Rockland Co., June 18, 1960 (Irving), specimen identified by Orth—in the collection of the Trailside Museum at Bear Mountain.

Spring dates earlier than those listed above and other inland reports have not been confirmed by experienced observers. More than likely this species was confused with the Caspian Tern.

Caspian Tern
(*Sterna caspia*)   *

Range: Nearly cosmopolitan, but virtually absent from Central and South America. Breeds at widely scattered localities, being extremely local in northeastern North America: (a) on *inland* lakes east to southeastern Ontario (approximately 150 nests in 1968 on Pigeon Island in extreme eastern Lake Ontario, Canada, five miles from the international boundary—about ten miles west of Grenadier Island, Jefferson Co.); (b) on the *coasts* of southeastern Quebec and Virginia (Cobb's Island). Winters north to South Carolina, casually to Long Island, New York.

Status: Variously uncommon to common migrant on the outer coast of Long Island and on the shore of Lake Ontario, occasionally more numerous, especially in fall; relatively rare to uncommon elsewhere. Subject to marked fluctuations.

Occurrence: The Caspian Tern is found in the largest numbers on the coast in fall after hurricanes. Inland it is also more numerous in fall, but it is more regular there than on the coast and is not affected by tropical storms. The greatest concentrations upstate at either season are to be found at two localities along Lake Ontario: (1) Braddock's Bay, Monroe Co.; (2) Sandy Pond, Oswego Co. It is, however, of statewide occurrence, but local and unpredictable in appearance.

MAXIMA, INLAND: *Spring*—30, Braddock's Bay, Apr. 18, 1964; 26, Sandy Pond, May 5, 1956; 12, Sandy Pond, May 30, 1954. *Fall* —15, El Dorado Beach (also on Lake Ontario), Jefferson Co., July 30, 1964; 55, Braddock's Bay, Aug. 12, 1966; 100, Sandy Pond, Aug. 31, 1967; 45, Sandy Pond, Sept. 18, 1965.

MAXIMA, COASTAL: *Spring*—nine, Easthampton, Suffolk Co., May 6, 1932; 19, Idlewild, Queens Co., May 16, 1953; five, Mecox Bay, Suffolk Co., June 4, 1962. *Fall*—hurricane of Sept. 14, 1944—20, Jones Inlet, Nassau Co., to Oak Beach, Suffolk Co., Sept. 16; 32, Easthampton to Mecox Bay, the same day. Hurricane "Donna" of Sept. 12, 1960—"huge invasion" on Sept. 13—100, Jones Inlet to Tobay Pond, Nassau Co., (about seven miles);

400 estimated between Jones Inlet and Sagaponack, Suffolk Co. (distance of approximately 70 miles).

EXTREME DATES: Apr. 3 and 10 (inland); summer stragglers; to Nov. 4 (inland) and, exceptionally, Nov. 23, 1952, Atlantic Beach, Nassau Co. (Bull).

Winter: One observed on Prospect Park Lake, Brooklyn, Mar. 3, 1940 (Fleisher, Brennan, and Tengwall); another seen from a fishing boat off Jones Beach, Dec. 28, 1958 (Ryan).

Banding: A nestling banded on Beaver Island, Michigan, July 2, 1935, was recovered more than nine years later at Montauk Point, Long Island, where it was found—the day of the great hurricane on Sept. 14, 1944. Another nestling banded July 15, 1961, on the Bruce Peninsula, Ontario (Lake Huron), was recovered only a month later, Aug. 16, 1961, near Rochester.

Black Tern
(*Chlidonias niger*)   *   B

Range: Holarctic region, the New World race *surinamensis* (underparts distinctly darker than nominate race) breeds exclusively inland from southern Canada—locally in the east— to northwestern Pennsylvania, western and northern New York, and northern New England. Winters chiefly in northern South America.

Status: Common to locally abundant fall migrant in the interior of the state and on Long Island; occasionally very abundant on the Niagara River. Locally numerous breeder on and near the Lake Ontario plain, rare elsewhere.

Nonbreeding: The fall migration of Black Terns along the upper Niagara River, especially in the vicinity of the Peace Bridge, is truly spectacular. These birds are also to be found at that season in large numbers along the south shore of Long Island and even on the ocean itself.

MAXIMA: *Inland*—all Niagara River—5000 each on July 26, 1958, Aug. 23, 1961, Sept. 9, 1953.

MAXIMA: *Coastal*—1000, Easthampton,

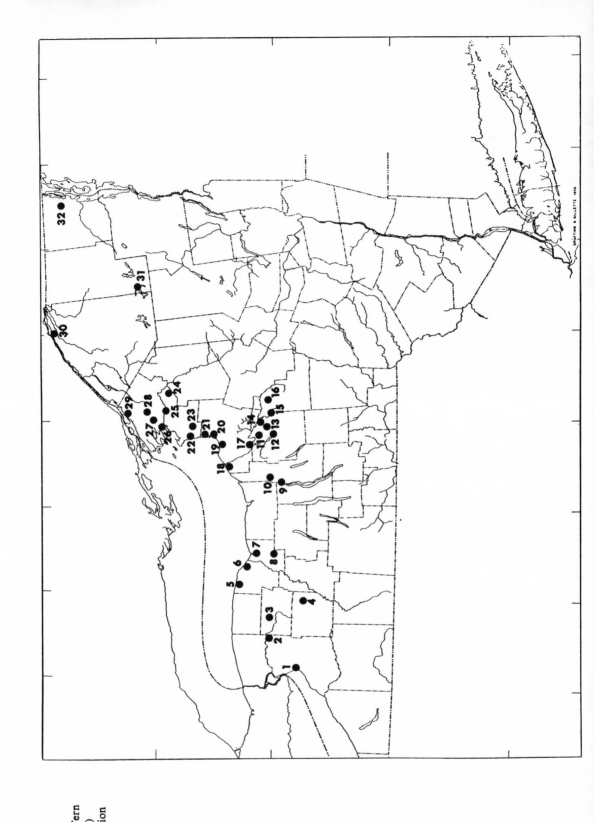

MAP 80 Black Tern
(*Chlidonias niger*)
Breeding distribution

Suffolk Co., Aug. 25, 1933; 1500, Jamaica Bay, Sept. 6, 1955; 450 in one hour, ocean off Jones Beach, Sept. 16, 1951.

EXTREME DATES: Apr. 23 (inland) and May 3 (coastal) to Oct. 27 (coastal) and Nov. 13 (inland), exceptionally to Nov. 20 (coastal —hurricane year). Rare before mid-May and after early October, but inland it usually arrives earlier in spring and departs later in fall, than along the coast where it is decidedly uncommon in spring passage.

Breeding (see Map 80): The Black Tern is most plentiful as a breeder in the fresh-water marshes of Jefferson Co., along the Lake Ontario shore in Oswego and Monroe counties, the region south and west of Oneida Lake, and in the Montezuma Refuge and Oak Orchard Swamp. Elsewhere it is very local and sporadic. It is a rare breeder in the Adirondacks (two localities).

At most sites only a few to a dozen pairs nest. Only three localities have colonies of 100 pairs or more: 200 pairs, Montezuma, 1960; 150 pairs, near the mouth of Big Sandy Creek, Jefferson Co., 1903 (this colony gone); 100 pairs, Perch River Refuge, Jefferson Co., 1957.

Nests are often placed in cattails or among other aquatic vegetation, especially where matted down. Hyde 1939a: 137–138) described a small colony of 14 birds in North Pond, Oswego Co., where some of these birds nested in rushes (*Juncus*) in stagnant water, some built on small mounds of wet, decaying vegetation, others on higher heaps of dead, broken cattail stalks, a few had floating nests directly on the shallow water, others on the mud bottom, and still other nests were resting on partially submerged logs. At another locality one or two nests were placed on floating boards and other debris.

The tops of muskrat houses were used in at least *ten* of the 32 known New York localities.

Egg clutches in 114 New York nests were either two (29 nests) or three (85 nests— 75%).

EGG DATES: May 27 to July 23.

Unfledged young: June 13 to Aug. 5; fledglings: July 3 to Aug. 25.

The accompanying map shows location of the 32 known New York breeding stations: Erie Co.—(1) Buffalo, Tifft Street marsh; (2) near Tonawanda Creek, about five miles north of Akron. Genesee Co.—(3) Oak Orchard Swamp near Oakfield. Wyoming Co.—(4) Prairie Slough. Monroe Co.—(5) near mouth of Sandy Creek; (6) adjacent Round and Buck ponds; (7) Tryon Park; (8) Mendon Ponds. Seneca-Cayuga counties—(9) Montezuma. Cayuga Co. —(10) Howland's Island Refuge. Onondaga Co.—(11) Clay Swamp; (12) near Syracuse; (13) North Syracuse; (14) Cicero Swamp. Madison Co.—(15) Boliver Swamp; (16) near Canastota. Oswego Co.—(17) Scott's Swamp near Phoenix; (18) near Southwest Oswego; (19) Sage Creek Marshes; (20) Sandy Pond; (21) North Pond. Jefferson Co.—(22) near mouth of Big Sandy Creek; (23) Ellisburg; (24) Pleasant Lake; (25) Beaver Meadows, south of Watertown; (26) mouth of Perch River; (27) Perch River Refuge; (28) Perch Lake; (29) near Alexandria Bay. St. Lawrence Co.—(30) Wilson Hill Refuge. Franklin Co. —(31) Tupper Lake (marshes). Clinton Co. —(32) Lake Alice.

SKIMMERS — RYNCHOPIDAE

One species in New York.
One breeds.

This small family (three species) has an interesting distribution. One species in tropical Asia—the Indian Skimmer (*Rynchops albi-collis*)—is presumably restricted to inland rivers. A second in tropical Africa—the African Skimmer (*R. flavirostris*)—is supposedly found both on rivers and along the coasts, as is the third species—the American Black Skimmer (*R. niger*)—in South America. In North

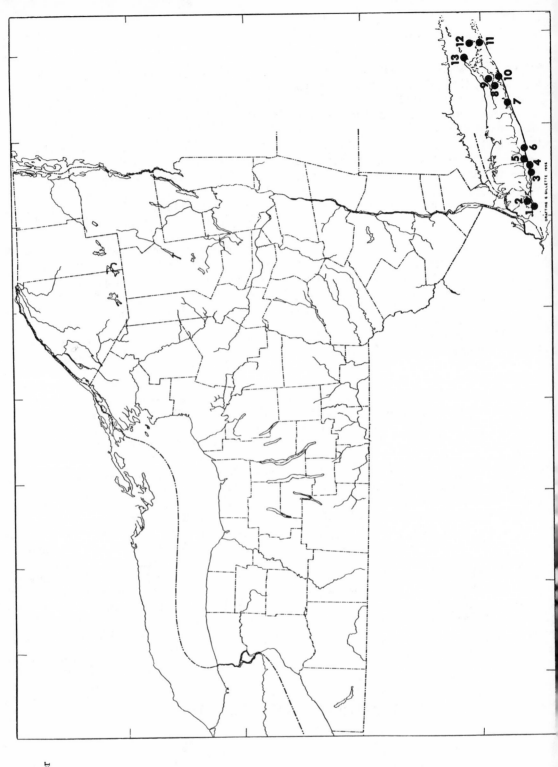

MAP 81 Black Skimmer
(*Rynchops niger*)
Breeding distribution

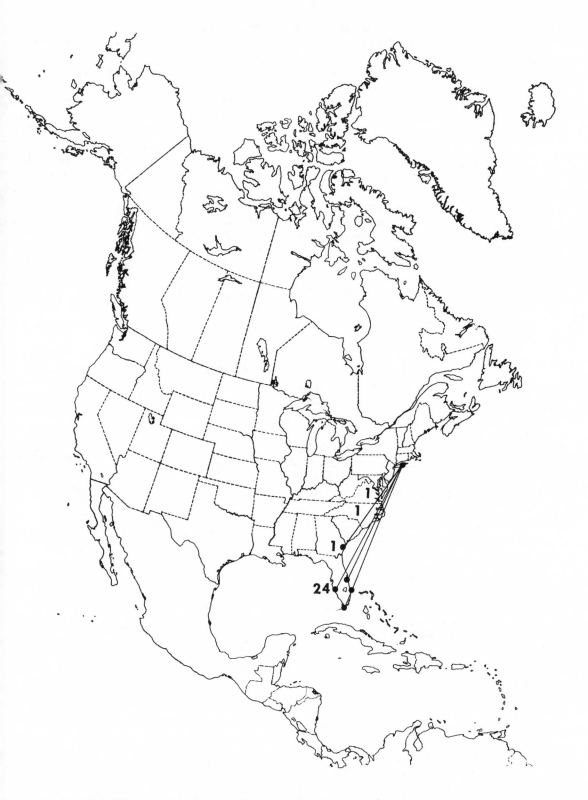

MAP 82 Black Skimmer (*Rynchops niger*) Banding recoveries

America, however, *niger* is known as a *breeder* from only along the coasts, and is unreported on rivers.

The skimmers are treated by some taxonomists as highly specialized terns or gulls and as such would be entitled to no more than subfamily rank of the Laridae.

Black Skimmer
(*Rynchops niger*)   *   B

Range: Neotropical and southern Nearctic regions, on the Atlantic coast breeding north to Long Island; very rarely to Massachusetts. Winters north to South Carolina, rarely to Long Island.

Status: Locally common to abundant breeder on the south side of Long Island; rare to very rare elsewhere. Has greatly increased in recent years.

Change in status: The Black Skimmer was called by Eaton (1910: 153) ". . . an occasional summer visitant off the shores of Long Island . . ." but he gave less than a half-dozen records. Even as late as Griscom's book (1923) it was very rare.

It started to increase by the late 1920s and early 1930s with the first breeding record obtained in 1934. Today it is a conspicuous sight on the beaches of the south shore, most numerous in hurricane years, at which times it even appears or rather lingers into early winter—on occasion in considerable numbers.

Nonbreeding: This striking bird with its curious bill and interesting method of fishing cannot fail to attract the attention of even the most blasé observer and is one of the most sought-after species by the inland birder.

MAXIMA: After 1944 *hurricane*—850, Easthampton to Mecox Bay, Suffolk Co., Sept. 16; 450, Plum Beach, Kings Co., Sept. 23; 300, Moriches Inlet, Suffolk Co., Oct. 15. After 1954 *hurricane*—800, Mecox Bay to Shinnecock Bay, Sept. 9; *2000,* east pond, Jamaica Bay Refuge, Queens Co., Sept. 29, 1965 (Bull), *no* hurricane; 100, same locality, Nov. 15, 1964; 350, Flushing Bay, Queens Co. (north shore), Nov. 3, 1968 (Sedwitz), very unusual number—both for place and date.

Winter: After 1944 *hurricane*—unprecedented numbers—*200,* Narrows, Brooklyn, Dec. 22 to Jan. 4, 1945 (Elliott, Soll, *et al.*); 40, Plum Beach, Jan. 7, 1945 (Grant); for other winter occurrences, including specimens, see Bull (1964: 260).

EXTREME DATES: Apr. 14 to early December; later in hurricane years. Ordinarily rare before May and after October.

Black Skimmers are exceedingly rare upstate, apparently recorded only after hurricanes. I know of but four occurrences: (1) one collected near Whitesboro (Utica area), Oneida Co., fall of 1893, specimen examined by Egbert Bagg; (2) one collected on Braddock's Bay, Monroe Co., Sept. 15, 1924 (Bauer), specimen in RMAS collection (no catalog no.), without further data, is believed to be this record; (3) one seen on the Mohawk River at Niskayuna, Schenectady Co., Aug. 27, 1933 (Bartlett); (4) one observed near Norwich, Chenango Co., Oct. 17, 1954 (several observers).

Breeding (see Map 81): This species prefers to breed in broad open sandy areas, such as occur along the south shore of Long Island. Nests are located near beaches, and on newly dredged fill. It also nests in tern colonies in open places, but if the grass or other vegetation becomes too dense, Black Skimmers eventually move to other areas. They nest along the causeways at Jones Beach, undisturbed by passing cars.

Egg clutches in 57 New York nests: two eggs (nine nests); three eggs (33 nests); four eggs (15 nests).

EGG DATES: May 31 to Sept. 3.

Unfledged juveniles: June 20 to Sept. 24; fledglings: July 17 to Oct. 11.

Most of the above data on egg clutches and dates were received through the courtesy of Michael Gochfeld and Robert Wolk.

The following represent the largest known colonies (pairs) on Long Island, with year of maximum abundance: 120 pairs, Jamaica Bay Refuge, 1962; 120 pairs, Short Beach and nearby Meadow Island, Nassau Co., 1963; 100 pairs, Cedar Beach, Suffolk Co., 1972; 200 pairs, Moriches Bay, Suffolk Co., 1963; 150 pairs, Robins Island, Peconic Bay, Suffolk Co., 1965.

The accompanying map shows location of all known breeding colonies (13) on Long Is-

land, with year of first nesting if known:
Queens Co.—(1) Rockaway Point; (2) Jamaica Bay Refuge, 1953. Nassau Co.—(3)
Short Beach, 1951; (4) Tobay Beach, 1946;
also a small colony halfway between these
last two, 1971. Suffolk Co.—(5) Gilgo Island,
1934—first for the state; (6) Oak Beach,
1935; (7) Moriches Bay, 1936; (8) Red Cedar
Point, Flanders Bay; (9) Robins Island, Peconic Bay; (10) Shinnecock Bay; (11) Cartwright Island, 1964; (12) Gardiner's Island;
(13) Orient Point, 1944—the only year.

As this goes to press, reports were received
of breeding in 1972 on the north shore at two
additional localities in Suffolk Co.: (1) Southold (Dove); (2) Eaton's Neck (Ruppert).
Both were reported to me by David Duffy (verbal comm.), but too late for inclusion on the
breeding distribution map. Other than the single nesting record in 1944, at Orient (see

above), these represent the only known breeding reports on the north shore of Long Island.

Banding (see Map 82): 24 nestlings banded
on Long Island in various years were recovered
in Florida the following winter; 16 from lower
east coast localities and four each from the
keys and the Gulf coast. Two more were taken
in Georgia and Virginia, as indicated. Another
nestling banded near Oregon Inlet, North Carolina, June 29, 1960, was found dead in the
Moriches Bay area, Sept. 14, 1960—two days
after hurricane "Donna."

Still another juvenile banded in the Jones
Beach area in 1948 was recaptured 12 years
later (1960) near locality of banding.

Remarks: The current species name, *nigra*,
is changed to the masculine *niger*, by reason of
Article 30 (a) (i) (2), amend. *Bull. Zool. Nomencl.*, 1972, 29(4): 182.

AUKS, MURRES, PUFFINS — ALCIDAE

Six species in New York.
None breed.

The six members of this exclusively northern
hemisphere family (22 species) occurring
within the state are thick-set, black-and-white
birds of deep, cold seas and rocky coasts. Generally avoiding warmer shallow waters along
sandy shores, nevertheless, occasionally they
are forced into such places—a matter of necessity, not of choice. Violent gales often drive
them onto the beaches or they become stranded
—victims of waste oil discharged by tankers
offshore—their feathers matted with the vis-
cous fluid, thus rendering them virtually helpless.

Preferring rocky areas, they are rare and
local anywhere in our area except at Montauk

Point. During mild winters few are seen even
at Montauk. The colder, more severe, and
stormier the weather, the better the chances of
finding alcids. The next best place to seek
them out is at the entrances to inlets along the
south shore of Long Island, adjacent to the pro-
tective stone jetties jutting into the ocean.

It is of interest to note that the most northerly
breeding alcid—the little Dovekie (*Alle alle*)—
is the most frequent and numerous visitant to
our shores or, to state it more correctly, the
least rare; the most southerly breeding species
—the Common Puffin (*Fratercula arctica*) and
Black Guillemot (*Cepphus grylle*)—are the
rarest, especially the Puffin which is extremely
rare in our region. The explanation for this
seemingly anomalous situation is that the Dovekie, a far northern species breeding south only

to central Greenland, is highly migratory, literally forced out of its inhospitable and bleak surroundings by ice-bound waters to find food in more southern ice-free areas, whereas the Puffin and Black Guillemot breeding south to the coast of Maine are essentially sedentary species—able to feed the year around.

Interestingly the "intermediate" breeding alcids—the Razorbill (*Alca torda*) and Thick-billed Murre (*Uria lomvia*)—nesting chiefly between Greenland and Maine, are also "intermediate" in occurrence along our coast, that is in numbers and frequency of visitations. They are generally rarer than the Dovekie, and certainly much less rare than the Black Guillemot and particularly the Puffin.

[Great Auk (*Alca impennis*)

Hypothetical: Extinct—formerly bred on islands in the North Atlantic Ocean, south to Funk Island off Newfoundland and, to Bird Rocks, Gulf of St. Lawrence; wintered primarily at sea south to the Massachusetts coast as far as Martha's Vineyard. Accidental in Florida (Brodkorb, *Auk*, 1960, 77: 342).

There is no basis for including this species on the New York list. No specimen or other firm evidence exists (Bull: 1964, 479–480), though it wandered south to Florida during the Ice Age.

Greenway (1958: 271) believes that, "This species is closely related to the razor-billed auk, the differences being due to loss of the power of flight, degeneration of the wing and keel. Its retention in the genus *Alca* expresses its relationship." Witherby, *et al.* (1941:142) also use the generic name *Alca* on similar grounds. The writer concurs.]

Razorbill (*Alca torda*)   *

Range: Northeastern Nearctic and northwestern Palearctic regions, in the former area breeding south to islands in the Gulf of St. Lawrence and to northern Nova Scotia; very exceptionally to southern New Brunswick. Winters south to Long Island, rarely to New Jersey; casual farther south.

Status: Rare and irregular winter visitant on the outer coast, occasionally in numbers at Montauk Point. Perhaps more regular offshore.

Occurrence: Razorbills, like most alcids, prefer rocky coasts. During most winters few individuals are recorded and occasionally none are seen. As is true with other members of this family, individuals are often found in an oiled condition and washed up on the beach—either alive or dead.

MAXIMA: In January 1932 at Montauk Point, there was an unprecedented flight of Razorbills. After a severe easterly gale that lasted for three days numerous individuals were found driven ashore in the Montauk area —80, Jan. 1 (Walsh); 100, Jan. 3 (Helmuth); 50, Jan. 10 (Helmuth, Walsh, *et al.*).

EXTREME DATES: Nov. 2 to May 11 (specimen) and May 18. Rare before late December and after early March. The species has also been reported on Long Island on three exceptional summer dates: one found dead on the beach at Moriches Inlet, Suffolk Co., June 3, 1950 (Eisenmann and Grant); one seen from a boat at Cox's Ledge—about 30 miles southeast of Montauk Point—July 2, 1966 (B. & J. Trimble); and another dead individual found in fresh condition, but badly oiled, at Moriches Inlet, Aug. 25, 1939 (Helmuth).

Remarks: Dubiously reported from the interior of the state, but see following. Eaton (1910: 111) listed two individuals, purported to be this species, collected from Saratoga Lake, Saratoga Co., Nov. 26, 1893 (Ingersoll and Brower), but Eaton did not state whether he himself examined these two specimens, neither did he mention the disposition of them, nor give any details of their capture. I have no reports of Razorbills from inland waters in this state in nearly 80 years subsequent to the above date; there is always the possibility that they were, in fact, misidentified Thick-billed Murres of which there are numerous records for inland New York.

As this goes to press, the following information has been received from Dr. Noel Cutright of Cornell University: An immature Razorbill was found by Mr. C. Gallo near the Montezuma Marshes in Seneca Co., Nov. 5, 1972. It was seen swimming in a small drainage ditch and later caught alive by hand and placed in a small pond, where it finally died on Nov. 10 following. It was found to be emaciated and was prepared as a mounted specimen for display at the Montezuma Refuge. Photographs were taken of the Razorbill when alive and were examined by the writer. This is the first known confirmed occurrence for inland New York. See also photo in the *Kingbird* (1973, 23: 139).

Thick-billed Murre
(*Uria lomvia*)   *

Range: Holarctic region, in eastern North America breeding south to northern Newfoundland; also Magdalen Islands in the Gulf of St. Lawrence. Winters south to Long Island; more rarely to Maryland. Occasional inland— usually storm-driven.

Status: Rare and irregular winter visitant on the outer coast. Perhaps more regular offshore. Usually very rare inland, but on occasion large numbers are blown inland by storms.

Occurrence: This species occurs inland more than any other alcid, especially on the Great Lakes. During and after the great northeast storm of Nov. 25, 1950, a great many Thick-billed Murres were reported both dead and alive from numerous upstate localities. A severe wind storm from the northeast reached velocities up to 75 miles per hour. According to Belknap (1951: 13–14): "The birds are presumed to have come from the Gulf of St. Lawrence, their path being up the St. Lawrence River valley." As many specimens (50+) were found dead from this 1950 storm alone, as Eaton (1910: 108–109) recorded for the half-century—1854 to 1907. Apparently the great 1950 storm did not blow any of these birds along the coast. At any rate none was reported during that time on Long Island.

MAXIMA: On the coast rarely more than three or four of these murres are to be found together. During some winters very few or none are reported.

EXTREME DATES: Nov. 13 to Apr. 15.

During the late *summer* of 1966 at least seven Thick-billed Murres were found alive, but oiled, sick, and/or exhausted along the south shore of Long Island. Five of these birds eventually died and are now specimens in the AMNH collection. These individuals were found from July 25 to Aug. 30—an unprecedented occurrence. Three of them were in breeding plumage.

Remarks: Great care must be taken in separating immature Razorbills from this species, as the former have relatively thin bills and are often mistaken for murres by inexperienced observers.

Thin-billed Murre
(*Uria aalge*)   *

Range: North Atlantic and North Pacific oceans of both the Nearctic and Palearctic regions. In eastern North America breeds south to islands in the Gulf of St. Lawrence. Winters mainly offshore in the breeding range, south to Maine, more rarely to Massachusetts, and exceptionally to Long Island and New Jersey.

Status: *Very rare*—in New York State the Thin-billed Murre has been reliably reported only from the south and east shores of Long Island. There are at least 13 occurrences, of which two are preserved specimens (see below).

This species was first recorded in 1936. Most individuals were found in an oiled condition, either caught alive or picked up dead. Localities from east to west are: Fisher's Island, Montauk area, Moriches Inlet, Fire Island, Oak Beach, Jones Beach, Short Beach, and Long Beach. Dates range from Dec. 23 to Apr. 4. Further details are found in Bull (1964: 261).

The two extant specimens are: (1) found dead on Fisher's Island, Suffolk Co., Feb. 12, 1951 (Ferguson), mounted specimen in his collection—examined by the writer; (2) oiled bird found dead on the beach at Hither Hills State Park near Montauk, Jan. 3, 1970 (Wellander), AMNH 708671.

There are three photographs, two published and one on file: (1) caught alive at Oak Beach, Suffolk Co., Jan. 16, 1938 (Kimball, *Bird-Lore*, 1938, 40: 300); (2) oiled individual at Short Beach, Nassau Co., Jan. 26, 1965 (Friton and Rafferty, *Kingbird*, 1966, 16: 190–191); (3) one captured alive at Montauk Point, Feb. 9, 1970 (Buckley and Davis), photo on file, AMNH collection.

Remarks: Although breeding somewhat farther south than the Thick-billed Murre, it wanders much less in winter, is much the rarer of the two species in our region and in many other sections of its range, and has never been reported inland in New York. The A.O.U. usage of the name "Common" Murre is, therefore, very misleading.

Black Guillemot (*Cepphus grylle*) *

Range: Holarctic region, in eastern North America breeding south to eastern Maine. Winters chiefly in the breeding range, in lesser numbers to Massachusetts and Rhode Island; very rarely south to Long Island and New Jersey.

Status: *Very rare*—like the Great Cormorant and Harlequin Duck this species is virtually restricted to rocky coasts. It is casual along sandy beaches except in the vicinity of the numerous stone jetties which dot the south shore of Long Island.

Of more than two dozen occurrences in New York, three are specimen records—two of which are extant, the third an old record without details: (1) Orient, Suffolk Co., Jan. 3, 1918 (Latham), NYSM 25005; (2) Quogue, Suffolk Co., Nov. 27, 1949 (Federico), AMNH 348699.

Other than a sight report from Rye, Westchester Co., Jan. 30, 1932 (Kuerzi), there are no reliable reports in New York away from Long Island. Eaton (1910: 106) mentioned the supposed occurrences of this species along the shore of Lake Ontario, but the information is too vague in the absence of confirmatory evidence, nor are any inland specimens known.

EXTREME DATES: Oct. 26 to Apr. 2.

Remarks: The poorly differentiated race *"atlantis"* is not recognized here (Bull, 1964: 264–265).

Dovekie (*Alle alle*) *

Range: Northern Holarctic region at high latitudes, breeding from extreme northeastern Canada (Ellsmere Island) east to islands off north-central Siberia, and south to Iceland and

southern Greenland. Winters chiefly at sea—in the western Atlantic south to Long Island—less commonly to New Jersey, and sporadically farther south, as far as Cuba.

Status: Rare to uncommon but regular winter visitant on the outer coast, occasionally numerous after strong easterly gales when large numbers are sometimes driven ashore.

Occurrence: The Dovekie is the most pelagic of the alcids occurring in our waters. On very rare occasions violent storms transport great numbers to coastal beaches, bays and inlets, or even far inland. It is at these times that the little birds are picked up in an exhausted condition, often starved or emaciated, or even found dead; others, badly oil-soaked and in a helpless state, eventually succumb.

This species is most frequently reported from mid-November to early March, but on Long Island it has been reported every month of the year. In 1929, from late June to mid-July, Latham saw as many as a dozen individuals in the Montauk region on one day and collected two in breeding plumage. Wilcox found a dead one in breeding plumage at Speonk, Suffolk Co., June 15, 1957.

MAXIMA: Ordinarily only a few Dovekies are observed along the coast of Long Island in winter, but in late December 1928, over 50 oiled birds—all dead—were found between Montauk and Westhampton. Again during late December 1940, between Montauk and Easthampton, Helmuth found over 150 alive and dead, many badly oil-soaked.

During the raging northeast gale of Nov. 19, 1932, a tremendous flight of Dovekies occurred along the Atlantic coast. This great storm brought "thousands" of these birds to our shores. On the afternoon of the aforementioned date Wilcox estimated 3000 just between Moriches and Shinnecock inlets and at about the same time Drescher reported more than 1000 in the Jones Beach region. For a detailed account of this great irruption, see Murphy and Vogt (1933) and Nichols (1935).

Inland: The two dozen or so Dovekies found at various upstate localities through the years all came to grief soon after they were discovered and most ended up as museum specimens. Those found alive were in a greatly weakened state and exceedingly emaciated as a result of battling the elements. A few individuals were found in the most unexpected locations completely helpless and unable to leave their strange surroundings. For instance, one in a garden was easily caught by a cat, another was taken alive in the *cellar* of a house, while a third stopped traffic completely as it waddled clumsily along the main street of a village.

The species has been recorded as far inland as Cayuga Lake; Saratoga Lake; Sodus Bay, Wayne Co.; and Sweden, Monroe Co.

Remarks: The genus *Alle* is used here, following *Bull. Zool. Nomencl.* (1970, 27: 110–112). Adoption of this name by the International Commission on Zoological Nomenclature was recently passed by the commission and by suppression of the name *Plautus,* used by the A.O.U. (1957) —*fide* E. Eisenmann.

Common Puffin
(*Fratercula arctica*)   *

Range: Breeds from Greenland east to Novaya Zemlya (northwestern USSR) south to the coasts of Maine and France; chiefly sedentary, but on the American side of the Atlantic winters to New Jersey (casually).

Status: *Very rare*—this species, an inhabitant of rocky coasts, is a great rarity south of Maine (where very local), even in winter.

There are eight known occurrences in New York State. With one notable exception, all records—including four specimens—are from Suffolk Co., eastern Long Island. The four specimen records and three sight reports from Long Island are: (1) adult, ocean beach opposite Center Moriches, Dec. 15, 1882 (Foster), AMNH 64613; (2) adult male found dead on beach at Hither Hills, Montauk, Mar. 30, 1902 (A. Miller), AMNH 359599; (3) another badly decomposed, Montauk, Apr. 30, 1915 (Weber); (4) adult male, Shelter Island, Apr. 15, 1941 (Latham), NYSM 25013; (5) Orient, Apr. 7, 1931 (Latham); (6) two, Montauk Point, Mar. 19, 1940 (Helmuth); (7) one, same locality, Feb. 7, 1953 (Mayer and Rose).

The eighth record is from Dutchess Co. An immature was caught alive near Rhinebeck, Sept. 27, 1963. This bird was reported (*Kingbird*, 1964, 14: 28) to be in a weakened and emaciated condition and died the following day. It was mounted and is in the collection of the State University at New Paltz, Ulster Co. For a photograph of this individual, see *Conservationist* (1964, 18: 35). The inland locality and the remarkably early date raises the question of a possible captive bird.

PIGEONS — COLUMBIDAE

Four species in New York.
Three breed.

In this widespread, cosmopolitan family (about 290 species), only four species are known from the state; one is extinct, another introduced, the third a vagrant (one record), and the last is the common Mourning Dove (*Zenaida macroura*).

Members of this family, together with the Sandgrouse (Pteroclidae), are among the very few birds known to drink by sucking up water, rather than by tilting the head back. Many pigeons lay two white eggs, others only one.

The terms pigeon and dove are interchangeable. Pigeons usually refer to the larger species, doves to the smaller ones.

Rock or Domestic Pigeon
(*Columba livia*)   *   B

Range: Palearctic, Oriental, and Ethiopian regions, widely introduced into various parts of the world.

Status: *Introduced*—abundant resident, except forested portions.

Nonbreeding: Unlike other foreign species, date of introduction into our area appears to be unknown. For many years this pest has been well established and is all too familiar. Beardslee and Mitchell (1965: 269) mentioned that the Buffalo Department of Public Works destroyed over 94,000 individuals during the six-year period 1946–1951, "with little apparent effect on their overall abundance." Abundant in all of the large cities, it is almost as numerous in the smaller suburban towns and villages, and also in the agricultural districts of rural New York.

It avoids forest, but perches freely in trees in city parks and in suburban yards. At the other extreme it frequents ocean beaches, provided there are buildings nearby on which to nest.

Breeding: Nests are commonly placed on window sills and building cornices and in many other man-made sites. Smiley (1964: 207) reports these pigeons breeding on *rocky* cliffs in the Mohonk Lake area of Ulster Co. Beardslee and Mitchell (*op. cit.*) likewise report nesting on *rock* ledges of the steep cliff sides in the Niagara gorge, thereby living up to their name. Pigeons are resident wherever found and eggs have been reported both in New York City and in Buffalo every month of the year. The species is triple-brooded in the state and a clutch of two eggs is the norm.

Remarks: The treatment here in using a binomial follows that of the A.O.U. Check-list (1957: 260) which states in part: "The mongrel wild stock found in our New World cities includes so many of the characters of . . .

races and variants that it is listed only under the specific name *livia*."

Passenger Pigeon
(*Ectopistes migratorius*)   *   B

Extinct: Chiefly eastern North America, formerly breeding from southern Canada south to the mountains of northern Georgia and at lower elevations in the east to southeastern New York. Wintered north to North Carolina, occasionally farther. Highly migratory.

Migration: Formerly an abundant migrant, except in the southeastern portions of the state where it was common only in fall. Migration was mainly along the Appalachian Mountains and to the west of them; relatively uncommon to rare along the coast. The Passenger Pigeon was most numerous in the great upland oak-beech forests where, in fall, an abundant crop of acorns and beech-mast was available as the principal source of food.

MAXIMA: *Early years*—"thousands," near Albany, Mar. 25, 1830 (Munsell); "millions" reported arriving to feed at the "salt springs," near Montezuma between Apr. 1 and June 15, 1854 (*fide* Mershon). *Later years*—200, Lowville, Lewis Co., Apr. 12, 1884 (J. H. Miller); 300, Constableville, Lewis Co., May 22, 1896 (Felshaw).

EXTREME DATES: Mar. 3 (earliest specimen, Mar. 23) to Nov. 6 (specimen).

The last known extant specimen from the state was a male taken at Canandaigua, Ontario Co., Sept. 14, 1898 (Wilbur), a mount in the CUM collection; the last known New York specimen was collected at Bolivar, Allegany Co., Aug. 10, 1899 (Mealy). Later reports proved to be Mourning Doves, but see under **Breeding.**

Winter: No confirmed record from the state. No specimen taken at this season has been reliably reported.

Breeding: The following accounts taken from (A) Schorger (1955: 90) and (B) Eaton (1910: 382–383) indicate the former extraordinary abundance of this species during the breeding season in New York: (A) In 1823 an enormous nesting ". . . began near the Allegheny River, Cattaraugus County, and extended north to the town of Collins, Erie County. It covered part or all of the townships of South Valley, Cold Spring, Napoli, New Albion, Dayton, and Tonawanda. The length was thirty miles and the average width was said to be six miles."

"About the year 1847 there was a nesting that extended from the vicinity of Annsville, Oneida County, nearly to Watertown, Jefferson County. It [too] was thirty miles in length and averaged three in width."

(B) "The last great pigeon nesting on New York soil evidently occurred in 1868, when millions of birds occupied the timber along Bell's Run, near Ceres, Allegany County, on the Pennsylvania line. This nesting tract was about 14 miles in length. The birds began laying in April and the height of the nesting season was reached about the tenth of May, when hundreds of thousands occupied the hemlock, pine, and hardwood trees extending several miles into Pennsylvania. A large hemlock would frequently contain 30 or 40 nests with eggs or young. Both male and female birds took part in incubation and in feeding the squabs [young]."

"Pigeons continued to nest in the general locality until 1872, but no nesting of any considerable size occurred subsequent to 1875 . . ."

"In 1875 there was an immense roost at Cooper's [=Cooper's Plains, near Painted Post], Steuben County, and on May 5 the birds seemed about to nest, but I have been unable to find evidence that a nesting actually occurred there at that time; although the time of year would indicate its probability."

The writer has seen *no* eggs with data from New York State in any of the large or small collections examined, and very few specimens of juveniles. In fact, in only *seven* instances, have I come across information with precise details as to clutch size, and of these, *five* were obtained from the literature. In only a single instance was the tree name and nest height given. From the meager evidence at hand it will be seen that in New York State this species was limited to one egg as the invariable clutch size.

The following is all that is known about exact breeding data in New York insofar as details are concerned. Note that three of these records occurred in 1878.

(1) Three specimens in the British Museum (Natural History), all taken at Locust Grove, Lewis Co., in 1878 by Merriam, as follows: nestling, June 4, and two fledglings, June 11— all BM (NH) 88. 10. 10. 2885–2887.

(2) Nest and one egg collected, near McKeever, Herkimer Co., May 18, 1878 (Pennock); nest was 30 feet up in a spruce; three other nests, also in spruce, each contained a single egg. The breeding area was located in mixed evergreen-deciduous forest.

(3) Several nests, one with one juvenile nearly fledged, the others with one egg apiece, near Fourth Lake, Herkimer Co., early June 1878 (Ralph).

(4) One fledgling collected, Springville, Erie Co., July 21, 1882 (E. H. Eaton).

(5) One fledgling taken at Alder Creek, Oneida Co., July 15, 1886 (Green), AMNH 69796.

(6) Nestling collected, Mayville, Chautauqua Co., May 30, 1889 (Kibbe).

(7) Adults observed feeding one fledgling at Scottsville, Monroe Co., May 30, 1904 (E. H. Short). This, the last known New York breeding record, occurred in an "open glade in the great Cedar Swamp" (*Oologist*, 1904, 21: 92).

The southernmost known breeding occurrences within the state were in the Hudson Highlands of Orange and Putnam counties.

Destruction of the forests plus wholesale slaughter of adults and young for the market and taking the eggs as well were too much for what must have been one of the most numerous birds of all time. The species was highly gregarious during the breeding season. When the large colonial nestings were broken up the Passenger Pigeon was apparently unsuccessful in small aggregations. This, together with the fact that it was not only single-brooded, but also laid only one egg (many pigeons lay two eggs), helped speed its downfall and ultimate extinction.

Mourning Dove
(*Zenaida macroura*)   *   B

Range: Nearctic and northern Neotropical regions, the eastern race *carolinensis* occurring in our area (larger than nominate *macroura* of the West Indies). Winters nearly throughout.

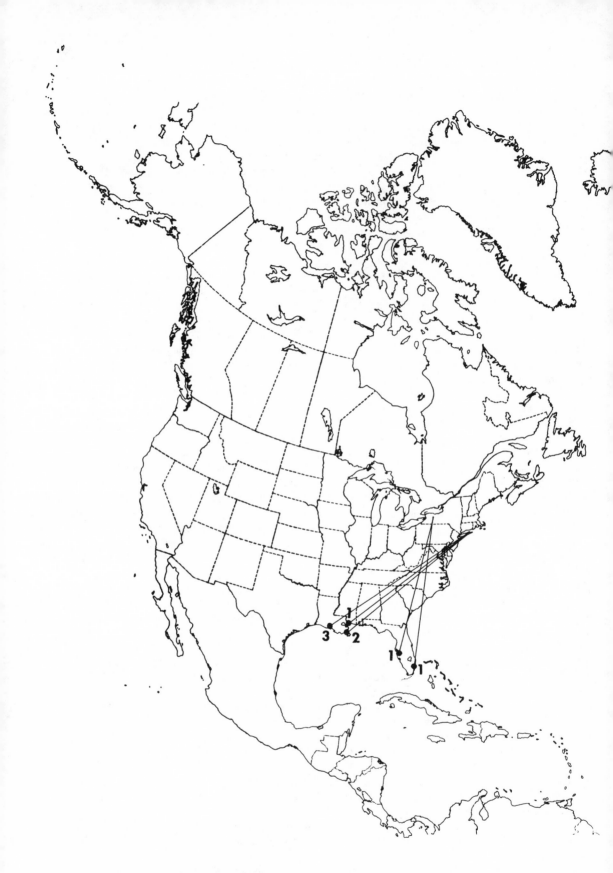

MAP 83   Mourning Dove (*Zenaida macroura*) Banding recoveries

Fig. 56 Unfledged juvenile Mourning Doves in nest among cattails, Renwick Marsh, Ithaca, Tompkins Co., June 11, 1909. Photo by Francis Harper

Status: Common to locally abundant migrant at lower elevations, especially numerous on the coastal plain of Long Island; common to very common in winter, particularly at feeding stations. Rare to absent in the mountains. Sedentary and migratory.

Nonbreeding: Mourning Doves inhabit open country and are especially numerous in agricultural areas, fields interspersed with thickets, and less commonly in open woodland. In recent winters these birds have greatly increased at an ever-growing number of feeding stations. Years of banding have proved that certain individuals are highly migratory and others have remained the year around at or near their breeding places.

MAXIMA: *Spring*—100 passing over Lake View, Erie Co., Mar. 25, 1967. *Fall*—600, Kennedy Airport, Aug. 8, 1965 (Bull); 300, Idlewild, Queens Co., Aug. 24, 1946; 500, Bridgehampton, Suffolk Co., Sept. 2, 1924; 140, Grand Island, Erie Co., Oct. 1, 1960. *Winter*—150, Oneida, Madison Co., Dec. 26, 1960; 400, Orient, Suffolk Co., Dec. 30, 1968; 150, Fayetteville, Onondaga Co., winter of 1957–1958; 200, Rush, Monroe Co., Jan. 11, 1963.

Note how much more numerous this species is on Long Island than upstate. Migrants are generally rare before mid-March and after mid-November, but this varies with the season.

Breeding: Nests most frequently in open country around agricultural areas, in fields with second-growth thickets, and suburban districts and estates having both deciduous and evergreen trees.

Some unusual breeding sites of this species were reported by Reed and Wright (1909: 425). "In the Renwick [Ithaca] marshes they nest in colonies varying from three or four to a dozen pairs. The nests are only a few feet apart, built upon stumps, brush piles, logs and heaps of debris." One nest was even "among" cattails (see Fig. 56).

Lesperance (*Kingbird*, 1960, 10: 166–167) mentions that he found a nest in Clinton Co. placed on a "hummock of saw grass" in a small swamp, the hummock surrounded by water and that the nest itself was under some black alder bushes.

Maxon (*Auk*, 1903, 20: 264) mentioned that in Madison Co. "Out of more than 25 nests found the majority were in apple trees, but occasionally in a pine, a white cedar, or upon a fallen log."

Stoner (1932: 497) said that "all" nests in

the Oneida Lake area were situated in willows near water. Latham (*in litt.*) stated that of 11 nests he found on May 10, 1938, at Greenport, Suffolk Co., *all* were in hawthorns, with one tree containing *three* nests. Referring to Chemung and Schuyler counties, Axtell (1947) listed evergreens and hawthorns as the preferred nesting sites.

During the 1969 breeding season at Delmar, Albany Co., State Conservation Department personnel found that out of 19 nest trees selected, spruce was first with 12, followed by pine with five.

In four instances, Mourning Doves have been found using old nests of Robins and one nest previously used by a Cedar Waxwing. Perhaps the oddest nesting place recorded was that of one found at Ovid, Seneca Co. in 1935 (Spiker)—incubating in an old Robin nest on a beam in a shed.

In this state, ground nests are uncommon but not unusual, at least a dozen having been reported—principally in open fields, far from bushes or trees. Benton (*Kingbird*, 1961, 11: 201) mentions one in a wheat field at Ira, Cayuga Co.

Height of nests above ground most often ranges from four to 12 feet, with extremes from one to 20 feet.

Egg clutches in more than 50 New York nests examined were invariably two. In New York this species is double-brooded and on occasion may even be triple-brooded, judging from the great span of dates, but this has not been proved to my knowledge.

EGG DATES: Mar. 9 to Sept. 28.

Nestlings: Apr. 6 to Oct. 5; fledglings: Apr. 24 to Oct. 26.

Banding (see Map 83): Over 50 Mourning Doves banded in New York during the breeding season of various years have been recovered in the southeastern states the following winter, chiefly in southern Georgia (20) and northern Florida (11).

Two individuals from western New York flew as far south as Miami and Tampa, Florida, while six others from Long Island were taken on or near the Gulf coasts of Alabama (two), Mississippi (one), and Louisiana (three).

The most remarkable state recovery was recorded in the *Auk* (1971, 88: 924): a juvenile

banded on Aug. 25, 1969, near Palmyra, Wayne Co., was shot a year later (Sept. 1970) in the Shasta valley, Siskiyou Co., extreme northern California! This most unusual report was authenticated upon receipt of the band by the U. S. Fish & Wildlife Service.

Remarks: The generic name *Zenaida* is used here, following de Schauensee (1966) and Goodwin (1967).

White-winged Dove
(*Zenaida asiatica*)   *

Range: Chiefly Neotropical region, in the eastern portion of its range breeding north to the Bahamas. Wanders occasionally to southern Florida. Accidental north to Ontario, Maine, Massachusetts (Nantucket), and New York (Long Island).

Status: *Accidental*—a specimen was collected at Water Mill, Suffolk Co., Nov. 14, 1929 (Wilcox), and is in his collection. It was verified as this species by Chapin. Although the record was included in the fourth edition of the A.O.U. Check-list (1931: 155), it was unaccountably omitted from the fifth edition (1957).

[Common Ground Dove
(*Columbina passerina*)

Hypothetical: Neotropical region and southern United States, breeding north to South Carolina. Wanders north to southern New Jersey (specimen).

In New York State the only report is that of a bird shot in New York City "many years ago." The specimen was not preserved and no competent ornithologist ever examined it (Griscom, 1923: 387).

The above generic name, adopted by de Schauensee (1966), Goodwin (1967), and Wetmore (1968), is used here.]

PARROTS — PSITTACIDAE

One species in New York.
One breeds.

This very large family (nearly 320 species) is best developed in the tropics, especially in the Australasian region, followed by the Neotropical region, but is poorly represented in Africa.

It is included here because of the introduced Monk Parakeet (*Myiopsitta monachus*) from South America.

The extinct Carolina Parakeet (*Conuropsis carolinensis*) may possibly have strayed to New York in the early days, but positive proof is lacking.

[Carolina Parakeet
(*Conuropsis carolinensis*)

Hypothetical: *Extinct*—formerly central and southeastern United States, in the eastern portion ranging north to Maryland; wandered casually to southern Pennsylvania. No definite proof of occurrence for New York.

The only reports of this species for New York State are those of DeKay (1844: 183) and Bergtold on hearsay (*Auk*, 1927, 44: 252). In neither instance were specimens taken nor did an ornithologist observe the species. Nor is there any basis for the statement in Beardslee and Mitchell (1965: 273–274) that this species ". . . was once well established here." No known specimen exists for New York.]

Monk Parakeet
(*Myiopsitta monachus*) * B

Range: Southern Neotropical region, breeding (resident) from Bolivia and southern Brazil to central Argentina.

Status: *Introduced*—escaped from captivity in the New York City region; present since at least 1968 and apparently becoming established. Sedentary.

A preliminary account of this parrot in our area is found in Bull (1971). Suffice it to say that the birds and their *stick* nests have been photographed by many people and seen by numerous observers. Photos of both birds and nests are on file in the AMNH collection. A recently fledged juvenile that had fallen from its nest and died of injuries is now a specimen, AMNH 802522. It is from Valley Stream, Nassau Co., June 21, 1971 (Mrs. A. Derkasch). Another from the same brood was raised in captivity.

The Monk Parakeet is about the size and shape of a Mourning Dove, with a long pointed tail, but a large head, is bright green, and has blue wings, and a gray head and breast; the sexes are alike.

This South American species is becoming increasingly popular as a pet and cage bird. Since the summer of 1968 reports have come from as far as Northport and Babylon, Suffolk Co., Long Island, and once as far east as Quogue.

More important, they have survived two consecutive cold winters and have nested. Unlike many parrots they are able to withstand relatively low temperatures, as happens in their native Argentine pampas—south to the Río Negro district—a distance south of the equator [40°S.], as New York is north of the equator [40°N.].

The bulky stick nests (the only parrot in the world known to build a stick nest) have been found in New York from seven to nearly 100 feet above ground, not only in trees and in a rosebush only seven feet up, but also on buildings, on telephone poles, in broken street lamps and lampposts, on the steel structures of an abandoned crane, and even on a U. S. Coast Guard microwave tower, nearly 100 feet up (see Figs. 57 and 58). Roger Peterson (pers. comm.) says that he has seen these birds building nests on telephone poles, as well as in trees, in the Argentine.

Fig. 57 Nest of Monk Parakeet (*Myiopsitta monachus*) atop a partly dislodged screen on the third floor of the residence of Mr. and Mrs. William Crane, Richmond Valley, Staten Island, mid-May 1971. Photo by Philip Benjaminson

These stick nests are domed with entrances at the bottom and on the sides. One or two pairs have been variously reported at each of these nests. Actual breeding dates, clutch size, and other detailed nesting activity in the New York region remain to be determined, although the aforementioned date of June 21 for fledglings would suggest that egg laying occurs in May and hatching perhaps by early June. However, a set of six eggs was taken from the chamber of a house nest that was blown down by a wind storm at Richmond Valley, Staten Island, July 4, 1971, and at the same locality two young from a tree nest fledged as late as Sept. 1, 1971 (*fide* Cleaves). Examination of the nest chamber of one of the Valley Stream tree nests that had contained two young, revealed a lining of grasses, paper, and goose and duck feathers from a nearby ornamental waterfowl pond.

Location of all known New York nests as of 1971 was as follows: Long Island, Suffolk Co.—Babylon; Nassau Co.—Valley Stream and Glen Cove; Queens Co.—Fort Totten, Middle Village, near Ozone Park, Fort Tilden, Rock-

away Point, Rockaway Beach, and nearby Riis Park; also Riker's Island in the East River. Kings Co.—Brooklyn (Bay Ridge and Flatbush). New York (other than Long Island), Bronx Co.—City Island, Pelham Bay area; New York Co.—Central Park, Manhattan; Richmond Co.—Great Kills and Richmond Valley, Staten Island. Recently fledged young have been observed as of 1971 only on Long Island at Valley Stream and on Staten Island at Richmond Valley.

Howard Cleaves (*in litt.*), referring to Staten Island, said of these interesting birds: "Only two parakeets built and occupied the roosting nest reported to you. They retire before dusk, visit feeders together eating sunflower seed, peanut butter, suet, and they worked on remains of a leg of lamb put out for them by one party. They are sensitive to human approach, uttering a chattering sound when flying away. They used mulberry twigs exclusively in nest building, biting them off at the base, twigs about ten to fifteen inches in length, the nest equal to a bushel basket in size, entrance hole on the *side* about five inches

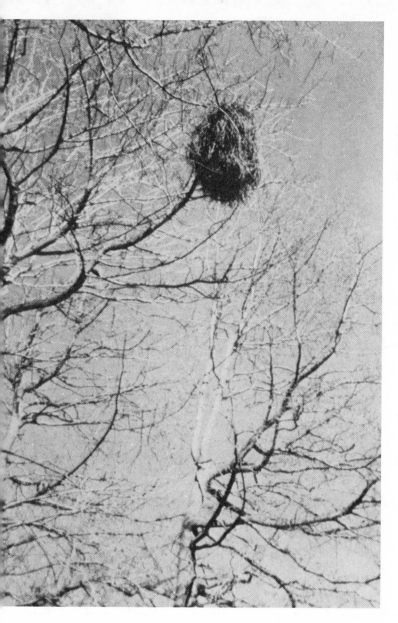

Fig. 58 Monk Parakeet tree nest, Valley Stream, Nassau Co., November 1970. Photo by Arthur Singer

in diameter. They seemed unperturbed by the big snow, perching on snow-covered twigs of Norway spruce in which the nest is located about 30 feet up."

At another nest at Rockaway Point, only eight feet from the ground under the eaves of a bungalow, the thorny twigs from a rosebush were used.

According to Mrs. Eleanor Nagel (*in litt.*) of City Island, Bronx Co.: "They [the parakeets] live in a large cavity in a broken-off limb of a *Paulownia* tree! The opening . . . is stuffed with small branches and twigs. They break twigs off my apple and mulberry trees . . . I have also seen them rob . . . nesting material out of the starling nests. Good work!"

In addition to the foods listed in Bull (*op.*

cit.) these omnivorous birds have been seen feeding on barberries and the seed pods of an ornamental mimosa (*Acacia*-sp.). As many as eight have been present at a single feeder at Fort Tilden at one time. Mixed wild bird seed, suet, bread, various fruits, and other staples are favored.

Remarks: Banks (1970: 26) stated that nearly *12,000* of these birds were imported into the United States during 1968 alone, the year this species was first reported in the "wild" in New York.

As of 1973, Monk Parakeets have been reported as far distant as the Buffalo region. Both federal and state officials are concerned about their increase and spread, and are trying to eliminate these birds.

CUCKOOS — CUCULIDAE

Two species in New York.
Two breed.

Although there are about 125 species found nearly throughout the world, most are tropical in distribution. Our two look-alike cuckoos are nonparasitic, building nests of their own, though very loosely constructed. Although not shy birds by any means—they are quite sluggish—they are secretive and hard to observe, and are more often heard than seen.

Yellow-billed Cuckoo
(*Coccyzus americanus*)   *   B

Range: Nearctic and Neotropical regions, breeding from extreme southern Canada to Mexico and the West Indies. Winters in South America.

Status: Uncommon migrant, occasionally numerous. Local breeder at low elevations. Rare northward and absent in the mountains. Subject to marked fluctuations.

Nonbreeding: Both cuckoos are unobtrusive in habits and rarely seen in any numbers at one time, especially this species (but see below). They are more numerous in years of tent caterpillar infestations.

MAXIMA: six, Rockaway Beach, Queens Co., Oct. 5, 1956.

In late September and October 1954, there was a veritable flood of both cuckoos on eastern Long Island. Many were picked up dead or alive on Fisher's Island (Ferguson) and at Orient (Latham). It was estimated that altogether over *1000* of both species were passing through and that approximately two-thirds were Black-billed Cuckoos. A number were killed by cars, others hit obstructions, while many of those seen alive were in such a weakened (emaciated?) condition that they were approached within a few feet. Not only were they observed in woodland, but also in open fields, salt marshes, and along the beaches.

Many individuals were seen feeding on the ground. This remarkable flight was probably the result of hurricane "Edna" of Sept. 11. They were recorded in numbers north to Newfoundland.

EXTREME DATES: Apr. 19, 1952, Manhasset, Nassau Co., (Ricks)—after southerly storm—Apr. 29 (coastal) and May 2 (inland) to Nov. 13 (coastal) and Nov. 16 (inland).

Unusual was an injured *albino* caught alive at Arverne, Queens Co., Nov. 29, 1965 (T. Eicher). This bird died and was preserved as a specimen, AMNH 785880.

Usually rare before mid-May and after mid-October.

A dead Yellow-billed Cuckoo that had struck a window at Lake Placid, Essex Co., July 1, 1942 (Benton), was also preserved. This record is notable because the species is extremely rare in the Adirondack region.

Breeding: Nests in light, open, second-growth woodland, fields with scattered bushes and small trees, thickets, and overgrown or abandoned orchards and farmland. Saunders (1938:45) stated that it occupied the cherry-aspen zone in Allegany State Park, Cattaraugus Co.

The nest is placed from about two to ten feet, rarely up to 20, in bushes and saplings, sometimes in fruit trees.

Egg clutches in 15 New York nests number from two to four: two eggs (five nests); three eggs (six nests); four eggs (four nests).

EGG DATES: May 26 to Aug. 19 (second? brood).

Nestlings: June 21 to Sept. 17; fledglings: June 23 to Sept. 23.

Black-billed Cuckoo
(*Coccyzus erythropthalmus*)   *   B

Range: Chiefly eastern North America, breeding from southern Canada to South Carolina. Winters in northwestern South America.

Status: Similar to preceding species, but more widely distributed as a breeder; absent in the higher mountains.

Nonbreeding: This species is slightly more numerous in migration than the Yellow-billed Cuckoo as it breeds farther north.

MAXIMA: eight, near Rochester, May 22, 1959; nine, struck the Fire Island lighthouse, Suffolk Co., Sept. 30, 1883.

EXTREME DATES: Apr. 15, 1961, Bronx Park, New York City (Maguire and Hackett), Apr. 25 (inland), and Apr. 28 (coastal) to Oct. 28 (inland) and Nov. 4 and 13 (coastal). Rare before mid-May and after mid-October.

Breeding: Throughout much of the southern half of the state both cuckoos are about equal in numbers, but the Black-billed Cuckoo is more numerous in the highlands and is the only one known to breed in and around the valleys of the Catskill and Adirondack districts. Curiously it is the "only" species of cuckoo found breeding on the barrier beaches of the south side of Long Island, whereas over most of the island and the adjacent mainland both occur in about equal numbers.

Habitat similar to the previous species, but also breeds in evergreens, as well as in low trees, bushes, and vines. Referring to Allegany State Park in southwestern New York, Saunders (1938: 44) stated that this species prefers the cherry-aspen zone, but is also found in clearings of the maple-beech association.

The nest is placed from about one to 11 feet up. However, a nest at Nyack, Rockland Co., June 4, 1893 (Brownell), was only two inches above the ground in a weed clump.

Another nest with two eggs (BMS collection) at Glenwood, Erie Co., June 6, 1915 (Frankenstein), was located *"on the ground in grass twelve inches high, in a willow patch"* [Italics mine].

Egg clutches in 32 New York nests are as follows: two eggs (nine nests); three eggs (14 nests); four eggs (seven nests); five and six eggs (one nest each).

EGG DATES: May 20 to Aug. 28 (second? brood).

Nestlings: June 1 to Sept. 10; fledglings: June 20 to Sept. 27.

Both cuckoos, although they are not known to be parasitic, do lay eggs in other birds' nests, including each other's, on rare occasions.

OWLS — STRIGIDAE

Twelve species in New York.
Seven breed.

Members of this nearly cosmopolitan family (130± species), including the Barn Owls (Tytoninae), are popularly known as the nocturnal raptors or birds of prey. However, two species—the Snowy Owl (*Nyctea scandiaca*) and Short-eared Owl (*Asio flammeus*)—birds of open country, are mainly diurnal, active at dusk and on overcast days.

Conversely, most of the nocturnal species are forest-inhabiting owls and spend the daylight hours in winter roosting in groves of evergreens. In such places pellets cast up by the owls after digestion—bones and fur, or feathers—are found at the base of the trees.

Nest sites vary from hollow trees and old bird nests to buildings (Barn Owl—*Tyto alba*) and even the ground (Short-eared Owl).

Of the 12 species known to occur in New York, seven are Holarctic in distribution, four of which are circumpolar and boreal nonbreeders in the state—Snowy, Hawk, Great Gray and Boreal owls (*Nyctea scandiaca, Surnia ulula, Strix nebulosa,* and *Aegolius funereus*)—whereas the other three that breed in the state are more southern in distribution—Barn, Long-eared (*Asio otus*), and Short-eared owls—indeed the Barn Owl is widespread in the tropics as well. The remaining five species are restricted to the New World, but with the possible exception of the Burrowing Owl (*Athene* [*Speotyto*] *cunicularia*), the other four have closely related congeneric counterparts in Eurasia—Screech, Great Horned, Barred, and Saw-whet owls (*Otus asio, Bubo virginianus, Strix varia,* and *Aegolius acadicus*).

Common Barn Owl
(Tyto alba)   *   B

Range: Nearly cosmopolitan in temperate and tropical regions, but presumably absent over much of temperate Asia. Mainly sedentary, but juveniles sometimes wander considerable distances (see **Banding**). The mainland North American race *pratincola* (larger than nominate race of western Europe; ventral spotting conspicuous) occurs from northern United States (casually extreme southern Canada) to Guatemala and southern Florida.

Status: Uncommon, local resident at low elevations, rare to absent in the mountains and generally northward.

Nonbreeding: The Barn Owl is one of a number of "southern" species that have spread northward during the past half century or more. It is local in our area and subject to mortality in severe winters. It is virtually nonmigratory and has been reported as breeding every month of the year.

Unless one visits a breeding site or a winter roost, Barn Owls are rarely observed. They are prevalent in the vicinity of garbage dumps where they are attracted by numerous rodents. Small concentrations are sometimes located in conifer groves during the winter months, especially along the coast.

MAXIMA: four, Pelham Bay Park, Bronx Co., winters of 1953 and 1960; four, Montauk, Suffolk Co., late December 1957.

Breeding (see Map 84): This species nests in the vicinity of man—in large cities, in small villages, and frequently in farming country. Nesting places are situated most often in old and abandoned buildings, as follows: eight

Fig. 59 Barn Owl flying from pigeon cote, Vanderbilt Farm, New Dorp, Staten Island, June 1912. The owls nested regularly in the cote, causing no conflict with the pigeons. Photo by Howard H. Cleaves

MAP 84 Common Barn
Owl (*Tyto alba*)
Breeding distribution

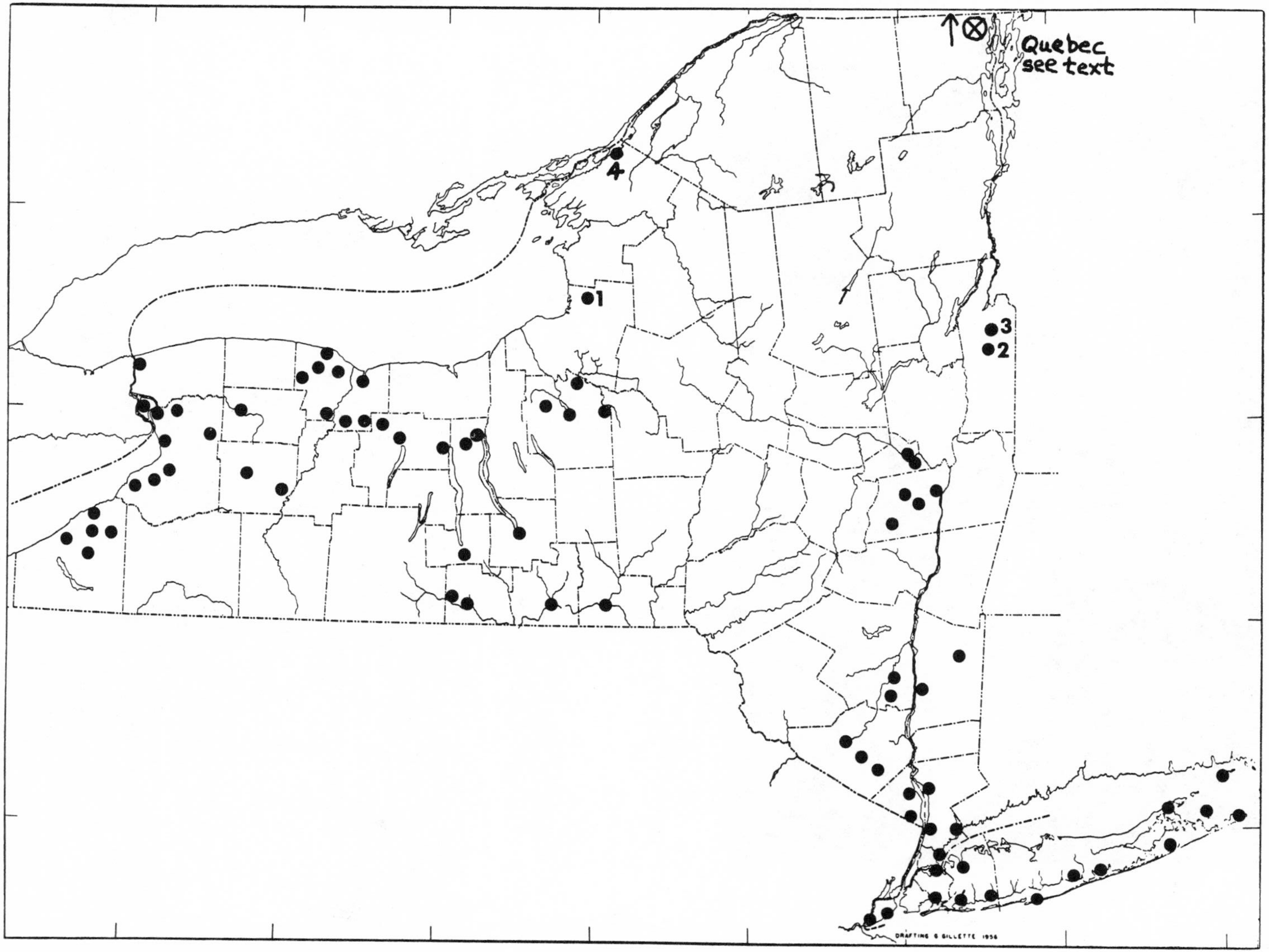

Fig. 60 Nestling Barn Owls, removed from nest inside dovecote, New Dorp, Staten Island, 1908. Photo by Howard H. Cleaves

were in barns and five in water storage towers; also 14 were located in abandoned or unused silos, six were in church steeples, two in bridge abutments, one in a lighthouse (on an exterior window ledge) and one in cable housing on a canal lock (see Figs. 59 and 60). Only three New York sites were in tree cavities.

Egg clutches in 51 New York nests ranged from three eggs—incomplete? (eight nests) to ten eggs (one nest). Most common clutch sizes were: four eggs (14 nests), five eggs (13 nests), and six eggs (nine nests).

EGG DATES: Eggs have been recorded in all months except January—from early February to early December—most frequently from April to early June (17 out of 31 nests).

Unfledged and fledged young have been found in *all* months.

The species is double-brooded, at least in southern New York, as proved by banding. In a nest site at Hunt's Point, Bronx Co., in 1938, Irving Kassoy banded a female which laid six eggs in March and another five in November. In 1939 the same female had five nestlings on July 27 and three more on Dec. 5—all eight young were banded.

The two largest broods were found in silos: (1) Nine nestlings were banded at Kirkville, Onondaga Co., May 21, 1961 (Burtt). (2) A brood of ten was reported as completely suc-

cessful—*all* fledged—near Manitou, Monroe Co., in 1967. The two observers, Doherty and O'Hara, made repeated visits to watch the progress of this brood. The following table graphically illustrates this event.

Date	Status
Aug. 6	6 eggs, 4 nestlings
Aug. 30	6 remaining eggs hatched
Sept. 10	10 nestlings
Oct. 8	4 of 10 fledged
Oct. 15	7 of 10 fledged
Nov. 5	all 10 "gone"

The above clearly indicates that eggs are laid at intervals and that young of different ages occupy a given nest. It is also obvious that considerably more than three months elapse between the time of the first eggs and that of the last fledgling.

The accompanying map shows distribution of the 77 known nesting localities in the state. The species is most prevalent on Long Island and Staten Island, in the Hudson valley, in and near the Finger Lakes, in the Genesee valley (especially near Lake Ontario), and in or near the Lake Erie lowlands. Note the absence of breeding records from the mountainous areas of the Catskills, Adirondacks, and the Allegany plateau, as well as in the northern low-lying areas of the St. Lawrence (with one exception below) and Lake Champlain valleys. The four northernmost-known nesting localities are: Oswego Co.—(1) Sandy Creek. Washington Co.—(2) near Adamsville; (3) near Comstock. Jefferson Co.—(4) near Alexandria Bay, 1972 (*Kingbird*, 1972, 22: 184). This last breeding record is not extraordinary in view of the fact that Godfrey (1966: 211–212) reported it as a casual breeder in Quebec in the St. Lawrence valley northeast of Montreal.

Banding: Two banded nestlings from the Rochester area were recovered the following winter in West Virginia and Tennessee. A third from Rye, Westchester Co., was recovered in North Carolina.

Common Screech Owl
(*Otus asio*)   *   B

Range: Locally resident from southeastern Alaska and southern Canada to central Mexico and southern Florida. The northeastern race *naevius* (larger than nominate *asio*) occurs in our area.

Status: Fairly common resident, but rare to absent at higher elevations and decreasing northward.

Nonbreeding: The Screech Owl, although essentially nonmigratory, is found in largest numbers during the winter months, indicating considerable dispersal at that season.

MAXIMA: *Coastal*—18, Queens and southern Nassau counties, Dec. 30, 1950. *Inland*—nine, Syracuse area, Dec. 26, 1960; seven, Rochester area, Feb. 25, 1954.

Breeding: This species breeds in orchards, farmland, open woodland groves, and shade trees in village streets and city parks. There is some evidence to indicate that Screech Owls are much less numerous than 20 years ago (1950s). In addition to increased road kills at night, and spraying of fruit trees with pesticides, there are fewer nest sites available. Orchard and shade trees are systematically pruned, holes and cavities are filled with cement, and dead trees are removed. Erecting bird boxes will help, however. Screech Owls nest in tree holes and bird houses from about seven to 25 feet up.

Examination of 27 New York egg sets revealed clutches ranging from three to eight eggs as follows: three eggs (nine nests); four eggs (ten nests); five eggs (six nests); six eggs (one nest); eight eggs (one nest).

EGG DATES: Mar. 23 to May 11.

Nestlings: Apr. 24 to June 25; fledglings: May 6 to Aug. 17.

Banding: An individual banded at Hamburg, Erie Co., May 29, 1959, was found dead near place of banding, Aug. 26, 1970—at least 11 years later (Avery).

Remarks: As is well known, this species is dimorphic, having both rufous and gray phases (more correctly morphs); these color morphs are neither age nor sex-linked, but are often found in the same nest. There are also, on occasion, individuals in intermediate plumage.

Localities	Rufous	Gray	Mixed	Totals
Long Island	28	9	2	39
Southeastern New York (Staten Island; Westchester, Putnam, Rockland, Orange counties)	12	7	1	20
Balance of eastern New York (*south* of Adirondacks)	8	17	0	25
Western New York (west of Syracuse and Cortland)	8	51	1	60
State totals	56	84	4	144

What is not so well known is that these color morphs are geographically distributed in the state. As indicated by the table (p. 329), the rufous morph is predominant in or near the coastal districts, especially on Long Island; the gray morph increases in the interior areas, particularly in western New York. Western New York is that portion of the state west of an arbitrary north-south line through Syracuse and Cortland.

Note that all 25 specimens from the balance of eastern New York, occur *south* of the Adirondacks. The Screech Owl is quite rare in northern New York.

The writer has examined 144 New York specimens in eight museum collections. Of these, 84 are gray-morphed, 56 rufous-morphed, and only four are considered to be intermediate.

Great Horned Owl
(*Bubo virginianus*)   *   B

Range: Alaska and Canada to southern South America.

Status: Local and uncommon to fairly common resident, occasionally more numerous in winter concentrations.

Nonbreeding: This species is fairly evenly distributed throughout the state, occurring chiefly in the wilder sections, but occasionally may be found in winter in the larger city parks, such as those in New York and Buffalo. Usually found singly; roosts may contain several individuals, especially in extensive groves of evergreens. On rare occasions flights occur during the cold months and these owls are quite numerous locally. For instance, 26 individuals were trapped at a single Cortland Co. game farm during the winter of 1951–1952 (*fide* Gustafson).

Breeding: The Great Horned Owl is one of our earliest, if not *the* earliest, species to breed in the state. Nesting activity may start as early as the latter part of January with snow on the ground. The species nests from the Adirondack Mountains to the pine barrens of eastern Long Island. Nests have been found in the densest and remotest wooded swamps

and, at the other extreme, in relatively small wooded tracts on the outskirts of large cities or even in such terrain within the cities themselves.

In 1920 Goelitz found five occupied nests in the vicinity of Rochester. In 1968 on Long Island Heck found the same number within six or seven miles in northern Nassau Co. Grand Island in the Niagara River with its formerly extensive woodland had eight nests in 1948 (Nathan). On this same island and nearby on much smaller Navy Island, at least 12 nesting pairs were present in 1952 (Gamble).

Nest sites are most often located in tall trees, usually in deserted stick nests of crows, hawks, and herons; more rarely in tree hollows or cavities. Of 39 stick nests examined by W. A. Smith in the general area of Lyndonville, Orleans Co., 65% were in old nests of Red-tailed Hawks, 25% in old Crow nests, and 10% in old nests of Red-shouldered Hawks (Beardslee and Mitchell, 1965: 279). A pair of these owls bred in an abandoned Osprey nest on Shelter Island, Suffolk Co., and another used an old Great Blue Heron nest near Candor, Tioga Co. Nest sites are occasionally found on cliff ledges and at least three of this type occur on the basalt cliffs of the Palisades, one of which is at or near a former Peregrine Falcon eyrie. In fact, at the long-deserted Peregrine cliff nest at Taughannock Falls, near Ithaca, two unfledged Great Horned Owl young were present on April 8, 1953. For many years a pair of these birds bred on a narrow slate ledge overlooking Keuka Lake near Branchport, Yates Co. A photograph of this cliff nest may be found in Bent (1938: Plate 71). Still another similarly situated nest site was discovered by Helme at Allaben, Ulster Co. The actual nest was on the ledge of an abandoned quarry. Finally, one was located on a cliff overlooking a gorge at Clarksville, Albany Co., from 1966 to 1971 (R. S. Palmer, see Fig. 61).

Of 67 tree nests examined, 56 were in deciduous trees, only 11 in evergreens (four each in pine and hemlock and one each in spruce, cedar, and larch). Of the 56 deciduous or so-called hardwood species, no less than 34 nests were situated in beech, eight in maple, four in oak, three in elm, two in hickory, and one each in cherry, chestnut, linden, ash, and birch.

Fig. 61 Great Horned Owl at cliff nest, Onesquethaw Creek Gorge, Clarksville, Albany Co., Mar. 14, 1966. Site last occupied in 1971, but bird deserted because of cliff erosion. Photo by Ralph S. Palmer

Height of tree nests ranged from 20 to 70 feet.

Egg clutches examined in 78 New York nests were: two eggs (51 nests); three eggs (19 nests); and only one egg (eight nests). The last category may represent incomplete clutches.

EGG DATES: Jan. 28 to Apr. 18, exceptionally to May 8 (incubation "far advanced").

Nestlings from Mar. 8 to June 12; fledglings from Apr. 9 to July 9. Unusually late were two fledged juveniles "nearly fully grown" on Aug. 1, 1914, Allaben, Ulster Co. (Helme).

Banding: An individual, at least ten years old, was banded as an adult on Aug. 1, 1947, near Chatham, Columbia Co., and found dead in October 1956 near Springfield, Mass. (about 50 miles to the southeast).

Subspecies: Three subspecies have occurred in the state: (1) Nominate *virginianus,* is the breeding form. (2) A pale, whitish race (*wapacuthu*) breeding southeast to northern Ontario, has been taken three times: Bronx Park, Bronx Co., Feb. 15, 1919 (*fide* Crandall), AMNH 144845; Orient, Suffolk Co., Feb. 20, 1929 (Latham), NYSM 25034; Forest Lawn Cemetery, Buffalo, Jan. 1, 1947 (Thorpe), collected Jan. 8 by Mitchell, BMS 2157. (3) A very dark, large race (*heterocnemis*) breeding along the humid east coast of Quebec, Labrador, and Newfoundland, has been collected three times also: Fisher's Island, Suffolk Co., Dec. 15, 1918 (Ferguson), specimen in his collection, recently examined by the writer—previously unpublished; Connecticut Hill, Tompkins Co., Dec. 5, 1933 (Cameron), CUM 3562; Ithaca, Tompkins Co., captured alive—

date not known but died in captivity, April 1941 (Allen), CUM 10072. Both of these last two specimens were examined also by Parkes (1952).

Snowy Owl (*Nyctea scandiaca*)   *

Range: Holarctic region, in eastern North America breeding on the arctic tundra south to the northern portions of Manitoba, Quebec, and Labrador. Winters irregularly south to southern United States.

Status: Rare and irregular winter visitant; occasionally there are great irruptions, both coastal and inland.

Occurrence: Snowy Owls are found in open country where they may be seen on the ground on a hillock or on some other low perch, such as a tree stump, fence post, or rock. These fine birds have also been observed in and around cities where they inhabit rat-infested garbage dumps. At other times, they may even perch on buildings attracted by the resident pigeons. Large winter irruptions have been reported following periods of decrease in the arctic lemming population. Great numbers of Snowy Owls were formerly shot, as they are inviting targets. The following maxima are noteworthy:

1876–1877—40+ specimens received by one Rochester taxidermist; many of these birds had been feeding primarily on stranded fish along the Lake Ontario shore.

1890–1891—20 shot at Montauk, Long Island, in a two-week period prior to Dec. 6; over 70 shot on eastern Long Island between Nov. 24 and Dec. 12 (mounted by one taxidermist).

1901–1902 (inland)—Boonville, Oneida Co., 15 shot of which ten were mounted by a single taxidermist; the stomachs of five of these contained meadow mice (*Microtus*).

1901–1902 (coastal)—Fisher's Island, Suffolk Co., 15 (12 shot), feeding on Belgian hares, the latter introduced on the island.

1905–1906—Boonville, 15 shot, mounted by one taxidermist; "many" others killed, but not preserved.

1926–1927 (inland)—three Rochester taxidermists received *235* specimens and another in Gloversville, Fulton Co., 35.

1926–1927 (coastal)—the greatest Long Island flight on record—40 killed on Fisher's Island during November and December, and a single taxidermist received 36 additional birds from eastern Long Island. At Long Beach, Nassau Co., eight were shot the morning of Dec. 5 and at least 75 more were shot elsewhere in the New York City region. Many others were seen through January 1927.

1945–1946—61 specimens sent to one Buffalo taxidermist.

1960–1961—Snowy Owl protected by state law. All the following are observations: nine, Buffalo area, Mar. 11; 16, Point Peninsula, Jefferson Co., Mar. 17; seven, same locality, Mar. 25.

1964–1965—seven trapped and banded, Jones Beach, Dec. 5 and 6; five, Kennedy Airport, January and February, one of these killed by a plane.

EXTREME DATES: Oct. 12 (coastal) and Oct. 20 (inland) to May 4 (coastal) and May 7, 12, 18, and 31 (all inland); exceptionally to June 6, 1968, Evans Mills, Jefferson Co. (*fide* Gordon). Rare before November and after early April.

A crippled bird with a broken wing was found at Wales, Erie Co., July 29, 1938 (Creighton).

Northern Hawk Owl
(*Surnia ulula*)   *

Range: Holarctic region, the American race *caparoch* (considerably darker than nominate race, ventral barring wider) breeds south to the southern portions of Ontario and Quebec. Chiefly sedentary, but at rare intervals southward irruptions occur. Winters irregularly south to northern New York, much rarer farther south.

Status: *Very rare*—the long-tailed, diurnal Hawk Owl avoids the densely forested areas, and prefers instead the more open semiwooded spaces. It is a great rarity with us and scarcely three dozen reliable reports exist for the state. However, at least one dozen of these are specimen records and another four have been photographed. Except for two old Long Island specimens (Bull, 1964: 272), no other occurrences are known in New York south of Ulster Co.

Of the specimen records, only two are known to be extant: (1) Bay Ridge, Brooklyn, about 1863 (collector?), AMNH 437332; (2) Conquest, Cayuga Co., Nov. 14, 1903 (Ashbury), NYSM 1744.

An excellent photograph of a bird at Millersport, Niagara Co., present from Dec. 28, 1962, to Feb. 10, 1963, and seen by numerous observers, is depicted in Beardslee and Mitchell (1965: 281), and also in the *Kingbird* (1969, 19: 187).

EXTREME DATES: Oct. 24 to Mar. 16.

Burrowing Owl
(*Athene cunicularia*) *

Range: (1) Neotropical region, north to central Florida—sedentary; (2) western North America, the migratory race *hypugaea* (axillars and base of underwing coverts rich buff and unbarred) breeds east to Minnesota. Vagrant east to Ontario, New Hampshire, Massachusetts, New York, and Virginia (all specimens).

Status: *Casual*—there are two records for New York, 75 years apart: (1) one caught alive in New York City, Aug. 8, 1875, was suspected of having been an escaped cage bird (Griscom, 1923: 387); (2) one collected on Long Island at Westhampton, Suffolk Co., Oct. 27, 1950 (Cooley), identity verified by Zimmer. The specimen is in the private collection of LeRoy Wilcox. This individual may well have wandered from the west, but definite proof is lacking.

Parkes (1952) mentioned that Arthur Allen had kept one of these birds as a pet at Ithaca for one year, but that it ultimately escaped.

Remarks: Following Voous (1960: 159–160), and Mayr and Short (1970: 51–52), the genus "*Speotyto*" is here merged with the partially terrestrial, Old World *Athene*, the two being closely related. The widespread Little Owl (*A. noctua*) of Eurasia is, in the eastern portions of its range, ground-inhabiting and nests in burrows, as does the Spotted Owlet (*A. brama*) of tropical southeast Asia. The latter species especially bears a striking resemblance to the Burrowing Owl, even to the long tarsi, but particularly as to color and pattern. Meinertzhagen (*Bull. Brit. Orn. Club*, 1950, 70: 8–9) presented an especially compelling case for making them congeneric, although he consistently referred to the specific name *cunicularia*, when he actually meant *Speotyto*.

Barred Owl (*Strix varia*) * B

Range: Chiefly central and eastern Nearctic and northern Neotropical regions, from southern Canada to Honduras, the Gulf states, and southern Florida. Sedentary.

Status: Locally uncommon to fairly common resident throughout, but very rare on Long Island.

Nonbreeding: The Barred Owl is essentially a sedentary species, but wanders about during late fall and winter. As with all our local owls, the largest concentrations are to be found at those seasons. Barred Owls often roost in dense stands of evergreens, preferably in hemlocks and pines.

MAXIMA: five, Bronx Park, New York City, late December 1943.

Breeding: This species is partial to low, wet woods, forested stream bottoms, and heavily wooded swamps or at least woodland adjacent to swamps. Its breeding habitat is thus similar to that of Cooper's and Red-shouldered hawks. Nests are placed either in tree cavities or in the deserted stick nests of hawks or crows.

The statement in Bull (1964: 273), as to 11 nests found on Staten Island in 1908, should be amended to read 11 nests in four years from 1905 to 1908.

In contrast to its former local abundance on Staten Island and its locally numerous status today on the adjacent mainland, it is curious that the Barred Owl is extremely rare on Long Island (Bull, *op. cit.*). I know of only *five* breeding records—one from Nassau Co. near Jericho and four from Suffolk Co.—(west to east) Heckscher State Park, East Patchogue, Sag Harbor, and Shelter Island.

While conducting studies on Cooper's Hawks, Meng (1951) found six occupied Barred Owl nests in the four-year period 1948 to 1951 within a 17-mile radius in the Ithaca area.

Ten New York nests were placed in deciduous trees: five in hollows or cavities of dead trees, the other five in live trees of chestnut (two), oak, birch, and linden or basswood. Nest heights ranged from 20 to 40 feet.

Of 22 New York nests examined, the following egg clutches were noted: two eggs (14 nests); three eggs (seven nests); four eggs (one nest).

EGG DATES: Mar. 23 to May 3.

Nestlings: Apr. 14 to June 11; fledglings: May 13 to July 1.

Great Gray Owl (*Strix nebulosa*) *

Range: Holarctic region, but absent as a breeder in North America east of Hudson Bay and Ontario; breeds southeast to southeastern Ontario (north of Georgian Bay). Sedentary, but wanders southward in winter at rare intervals to northern New York, more rarely farther south.

Status: *Very rare*—this species, the largest of American owls, lives in the taiga zone (conifer forest) of the north. It is even rarer with us than the Hawk Owl and very few ornithologists have ever seen a live *wild* one in New York. As a result, most, or nearly all, of the records are of birds that have been collected. Indeed, of nearly two dozen occurrences in the state, no fewer than *18* are specimen records. Except for two old Long Island specimens (Bull, 1964: 274), and one old specimen from Steuben Co. (Eaton, 1914: 117), this species is virtually unrecorded in the state south of the Adirondack and Lake Ontario regions.

Of these 18 specimens, however, only *two* are known to be extant: (1) Locust Grove, Lewis Co., Apr. 11, 1873 (Merriam), BM (NH) 88. 10. 10. 543; this specimen was not included in the Catalogue of Birds in the British Museum, 1875, 2; it was unknown to Eaton (*op. cit.*). (2) Gull Pond, near Tupper Lake, Franklin Co., autumn of 1919 (Crowninshield), NYSM 5967. A third specimen taken near Niagara Falls, date and collector unknown, was reported by Beardslee and Mitchell (1965: 283) to be 4925 in the Buffalo Museum of Science collection, but I did not see

the specimen when visiting that museum in 1967.

I cannot vouch for the authenticity of two or three sight reports as they were not confirmed by experienced observers, nor were details published. The Great Gray Owl is *not* unmistakable and both Barred Owls and juvenile Great Horned Owls have been misidentified as the rare bird. However, one was trapped, banded, photographed, and released in extreme southeastern Saratoga Co. in late winter of 1970–1971 (R. Yunick, *in litt.*). For photo, see *Kingbird* (1972, 22: 5).

EXTREME DATES: Nov. 15 to Apr. 11 (both specimens).

Long-eared Owl
(*Asio otus*) * B

Range: Holarctic region, in eastern North America the race *wilsonianus* (generally darker above than nominate *otus* of Eurasia; belly with transverse barring) breeds from southern Canada to Arkansas and Virginia. Winters north through most of the breeding range. Sedentary and migratory.

Status: Uncommon to locally fairly common winter visitant, more numerous in the southeastern portions. Rare to uncommon and local breeder, perhaps overlooked. Breeding status in the mountainous sections is little known and needs investigation.

Nonbreeding: The Long-eared Owl is our most gregarious woodland owl, roosting in conifer plantings in late fall and winter. Usually only one to four, but on occasion much higher numbers are found.

MAXIMA: *36*, Pelham Bay Park, Bronx Co., Jan. 18, 1968; 18, near Poughkeepsie, Dutchess Co., Feb. 10, 1968; 20, Blooming Grove, Orange Co., winter 1968–1969.

Breeding (see Map 85): Although the Long-eared Owl is fairly widely distributed as a breeder in central and western New York, and is found locally in the southeastern section of the state (including Long Island), it is nevertheless little known at this season in other areas, especially the mountains and northern New York in general. However, this may be due, in part, to lack of observers in those

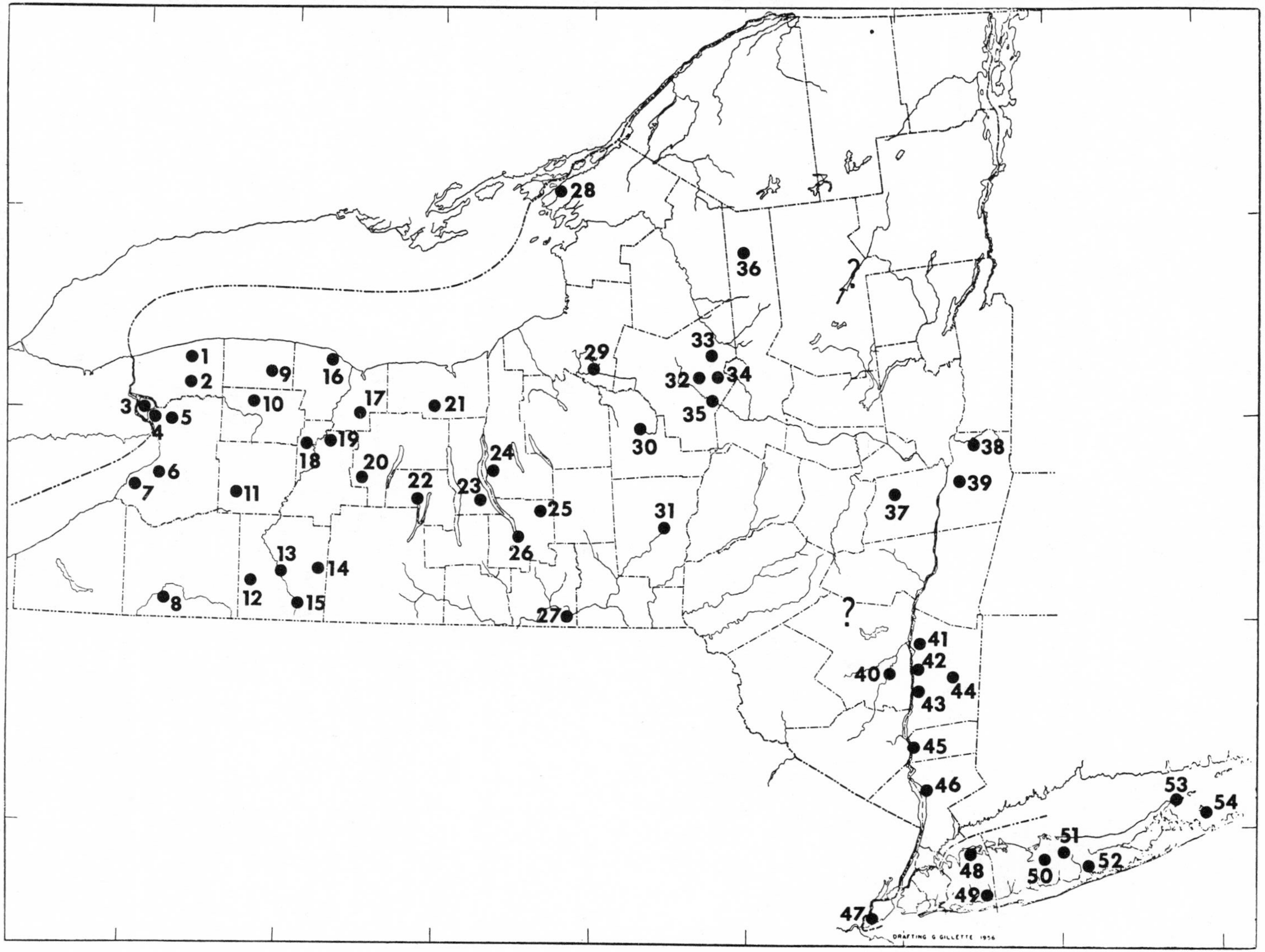

MAP 85 Long-eared Owl
(*Asio otus*) Breeding
distribution

areas. The species is secretive and is probably overlooked. Even Eaton (1914: 112) was vague as to its breeding status, for he says, ". . . not very uncommon in most parts of the state, but is apparently uncommon in the Adirondack forests."

That it is not exclusively a forest species is evidenced by the fact that nests have been found in New York City (on Staten Island) and in an apple tree in an abandoned orchard in Niagara Co.

New York nests range from 12 to 45 feet above ground. They are situated chiefly in evergreen trees—six in pine, three in hemlock, and two in cedar. Only four were in deciduous trees, two in maple, and one each in apple and sassafras. Old, deserted crow and hawk nests are frequently utilized, and one nest of the Long-eared Owl was in a "natural hollow" in a maple. The breeding habitat is largely in wooded swamps, evergreen plantings, and in open woodland.

Egg clutches in 32 New York nests ranged from three to five, as follows: three eggs (seven nests); four eggs (12 nests); five eggs (13 nests).

EGG DATES: Mar. 21 to May 23.

Nestlings: May 5 to June 24; fledglings: June 1 to Aug. 8.

The accompanying map indicates distribution of the 54 known New York localities: Niagara Co.—(1) Newfane; (2) near Lockport. Erie Co.—(3) Grand Island; (4) Tonawanda; (5) Amherst; (6) Hamburg; (7) Evans. Cattaraugus Co.—(8) near Red House, Allegany State Park. Orleans Co.—(9) Albion. Genesee Co.—(10) near Oakfield. Wyoming Co.—(11) Java Center. Allegany Co.—(12) Cuba; (13) Belvidere; (14) Alfred; (15) Wellsville. Monroe Co.—(16) Salmon Creek near Braddock's Bay; (17) Mendon Ponds. Livingston Co.—(18) York; (19) Avon. Ontario Co.—(20) Canadice Lake. Wayne Co.—(21) Newark. Yates Co.—(22) near Branchport. Seneca Co.—(23) Interlaken. Cayuga Co.—(24) near Aurora. Tompkins Co.—(25) McLean Bog; (26) near Ithaca and nearby Varna. Tioga Co.—(27) Apalachin. Jefferson Co.—(28) near Riverview. Oswego Co.—(29) Constantia. Madison Co.—(30) Peterboro. Chenango Co.—(31) Norwich. Oneida Co.—(32) Steuben; (33) Floyd; (34) Holland Patent; (35) near Utica. Herkimer Co.—(36) Stillwater Mtn.

Albany Co.—(37) Altamont. Rensselaer Co.—(38) Schagticoke; (39) east of Rensselaer. Ulster Co.—(40) New Paltz. Dutchess Co.—(41) Rhinebeck; (42) Hyde Park; (43) near Poughkeepsie; (44) Millbrook. Putnam Co.—(45) Constitution Island, Hudson River. Westchester Co.—(46) near Ossining. Richmond Co.—(47) south of Fresh Kills, Staten Island (for details, see Bull, 1970: 26). Nassau Co.—(48) Lattingtown; (49) Massapequa. Suffolk Co.—(50) Lake Grove; (51) Selden; (52) near Mastic; (53) Orient; (54) Gardiner's Island.

Banding: A banded adult from eastern New York was taken in nearby Connecticut *15* years later.

Short-eared Owl
(*Asio flammeus*) * B

Range: Holarctic and Neotropical regions, also certain Pacific islands; in North America breeding from Alaska and Canada, in the east only to central New Jersey, rare farther south. In winter withdraws from the northern portions of the breeding range.

Status: Generally uncommon migrant and winter visitant along the coast and upstate, but very irregular in occurrence, occasionally locally common. Local breeder, greatly decreased in recent years.

Nonbreeding: Although this species is the most gregarious of our owls, at times appearing in large concentrations, it is nevertheless quite erratic in its visitations. If rodents (especially *Microtus*) appear in large numbers these owls are often in evidence and remain as long as this food supply is plentiful. Marshes, meadows, old fields, refuse dumps, airports, and similar terrain are favored habitats of the largely diurnal Short-eared Owl.

MAXIMA: *Coastal*—40, Canarsie Pol, Jamaica Bay, late December 1959, appears to be the only large aggregation on the coast.

MAXIMA: *Inland*—three big years, as follows: 1962—50, near Waterloo, Seneca Co., Feb. 12; 40, Lockport, Niagara Co., Feb. 24. 1965—40, Lyndonville, Orleans Co., Mar. 31. 1969—75, Alden, Erie Co., Dec. 30 (Wolfling), many birds seen perched on trees and

MAP 86 Short-eared Owl
(*Asio flammeus*)
Breeding distribution

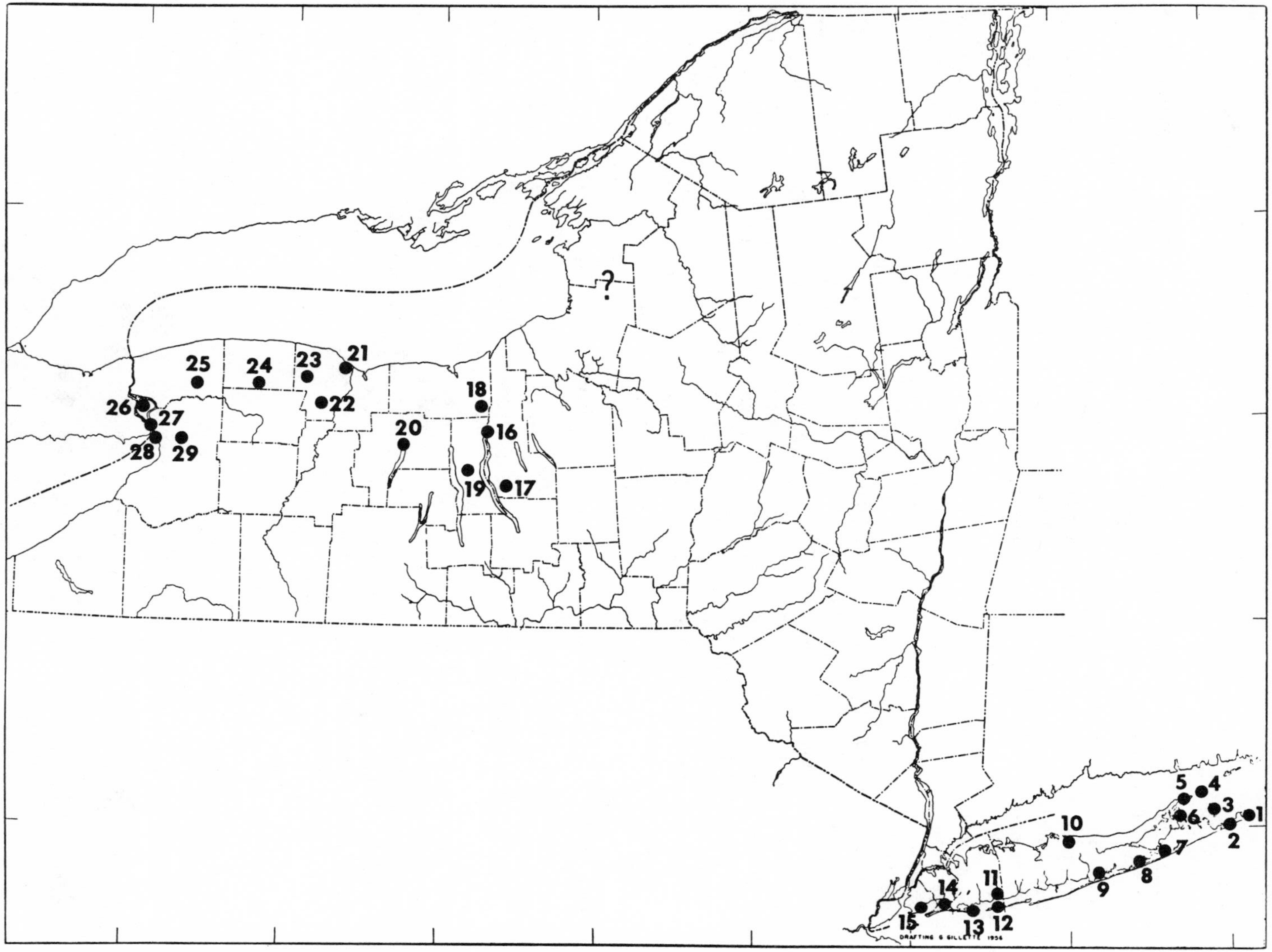

fence posts; 55, near Niagara Falls, Jan. 28; 40, Galeville, Ulster Co., most of February.

Breeding (see Map 86): Despite being numerous at times during the colder months, the Short-eared Owl is apparently scarce in the nesting season, at least in recent years. Judging from the relatively few nests (exclusively on the ground) found in the state, and even fewer eggs (see below), it is not surprising how little is known or published about its precise breeding habitat requirements in New York. Descriptions of only four nest sites from the state are before me: (1) a nest found many years ago on eastern Long Island was described as a slight hollow in the bare sand with a scattered growth of beach grass; (2) a nest in extreme western New York was placed on a clump of dried, flattened cattails in a low swampy tract; (3) another nest from the central portion of the state was located in an uncultivated field among "alfalfa stubble"; (4) also in central New York was one described as being in a "fallow field of wheat stubble." These last two nests were reported by R. J. Clark (*in litt.*)—see Fig. 62.

Egg clutches in only *six* New York nests ranged from six to nine, with six and seven eggs in two nests each and eight and nine eggs in one nest apiece.

EGG DATES: Apr. 2 to May 19.

Nestlings: May 7 to June 19; fledglings: June 11 to July 15.

Perusal of the accompanying map shows 29 breeding localities in two main areas: (A) Long Island with 15 and (B) western New York with 14.

(A) Suffolk Co.—(1) Montauk Point; (2) Napeague; (3) Gardiner's Island (see Fig. 63); (4) Plum Island; (5) Orient; (6) Shelter Island; (7) Shinnecock Hills; (8) Westhampton Beach; (9) Mastic; (10) Miller's Place. Nassau Co.—(11) Massapequa; (12) Jones Beach; (13) Long Beach. Queens Co.—(14) Idlewild. Kings Co.—(15) Bergen Beach.

(B) Cayuga Co.—(16) Montezuma Marshes (17) near King Ferry. Wayne Co.—(18) near Savannah. Seneca Co.—(19) near Romulus. Ontario Co.—(20) north end of Canandaigua Lake. Monroe Co.—(21) Rigney's Bluff; (22) near Chili; (23) near Brockport. Orleans Co. —(24) Tonawanda Swamp near West Barre. Niagara Co.—(25) Lockport. Erie Co.—(26) Grand Island; (27) Strawberry Island; (28) near Buffalo; (29) Cheektowaga.

Eaton (1914: 114) stated, ". . . its commonest breeding grounds are . . . on the wet lands near the eastern end of Lake Ontario." However, I have been unable to find a single instance of its nesting in that area. Moreover, Belknap (*in litt.*) knows of no definite breeding record for Jefferson Co., nor does Rusk (*in litt.*) for Oswego Co.

Cruickshank (1942: 270) stated, "It breeds . . . casually on Staten Island and along the

Fig. 62 Short-eared Owl nesting area in old field of goldenrod, *Spiraea,* and grass, near Lockport, Niagara Co., summer of 1969. Photo by Richard Clark

Fig. 63 Downy young Short-eared Owls, Gardiner's Island, Suffolk Co., 1912. Photo by Howard H. Cleaves

[Long Island] Sound in Bronx [and] Westchester . . . counties." However, no details are given, nor is there any published information regarding definite breeding in those areas. Furthermore, Cleaves (*in litt.*) knows of none for Staten Island.

Boreal Owl (*Aegolius funereus*)   *

Range: Holarctic region, the New World race *richardsoni* (darker below than nominate race, especially the lower belly) breeds south to the central portions of Ontario and Quebec; casually on Grand Manan Island, southern New Brunswick. Sedentary, but wandering in winter south to northern New York, very rarely to the central part of the state; once in northern New Jersey (specimen).

Status: *Very rare*—the little Boreal Owl is virtually unknown in the state outside the Adirondack region, except for two Monroe Co. occurrences (see below). It is the rarest of the three northern nonbreeding species of forest-inhabiting owls within New York. Never-

theless, this species is much better documented than are either the Hawk Owl or the Great Gray Owl. The records bear this out. There are about one dozen occurrences, of which *nine* are specimen records and three more of birds photographed. Of the *nine* specimen records, *six* are extant.

These six specimens are: (1) near Hecla (=Lowell), Oneida Co., February 1893 (Allwood), NYSM 1144; (2) and (3) Fort Covington, Franklin Co., Nov. 16, 1914, and Jan. 19, 1916 (both by Macartney), AMNH 126935 and 129290; (4) Plattsburgh, Clinton Co., Dec. 16, 1922 (Wolfe), NYSM 9467; (5) Saranac Lake, Franklin Co., December 1922 (Dickert), CUM 3505; (6) Ogdensburg, St. Lawrence Co., Mar. 13, 1958 (Mayhood), NYSM 19022.

The three recent instances of birds photographed are: (1) east of Pulaski, Oswego Co., Mar. 17–18, 1962 (Rusk, Allen, *et al.*); (2) Hamlin, Monroe Co., Feb. 22–29, 1964 (Foster and many others); (3) near Webster, Monroe Co., Feb. 24–26, 1965 (Kemnitzer and many others). Photographs of the 1962 and 1965 birds were published in the *Kingbird* (1965, 15: 74–76).

EXTREME DATES: Nov. 16 to Mar. 18.

Saw-whet Owl
(*Aegolius acadicus*)   *   B

Range: Nearctic region, breeding from the southern portions of Alaska and Canada to the mountains of southern Mexico in the west, but in the east only as far as the coastal plain of Cape Cod and Long Island (once in southern New Jersey), and in the mountains to Virginia; North Carolina (1965). Sedentary and migratory, wintering nearly throughout the breeding range south to the Gulf coast.

Status: Variously rare to fairly common migrant and winter visitant, occasionally more numerous in "flight" years, such as the great coastal irruptions in fall of 1965 and 1967. Generally a rare and local breeder, but unquestionably overlooked (see **Breeding**).

Nonbreeding: The little Saw-whet Owl occurs most frequently in conifers or evergreen groves along the south shore of Long Island and in city parks where these trees are concentrated and where observers are numerous. It occurs in small numbers in other areas of the state where one or two may be seen by chance.

With the increased use of mist nets in recent years these very tame birds have been caught frequently. The following numbers are all of mist-netted individuals, unless stated otherwise.

MAXIMA, COASTAL: *Fall*—1965—six each at Atlantic Beach and Tobay Beach, Nassau Co., Oct. 17; five, Huntington, Suffolk Co., Oct. 31; total of 55 netted and banded at these three stations from Sept. 30 to Nov. 10. In several pine groves from Cedar Beach to Oak Beach, Suffolk Co., Oct. 29, 1967, Ward and other observers estimated 26 individuals. Seven were netted and banded at Fire Island State Park, Suffolk Co., Nov. 27, 1969.

MAXIMA, INLAND: *Spring*—ten observed, Lake Ontario shore from Island Cottage to Salmon Creek, Monroe Co., Apr. 3, 1952 (Barry and Listman).

EXTREME DATES, coastal: Sept. 22 to May 13; summer vagrants. Rare before October and after April.

Breeding (see Map 87): That this species was not as rare a breeder in the state as gen-erally believed was borne out by the fact that during the spring of 1886 those two indefatigable collectors William Ralph and Egbert Bagg discovered *four* nests within little more than three weeks and two of these in one day within approximately five miles of wooded swamp between Holland Patent and Trenton Falls, Oneida Co. According to Bagg's account·(*Ornith. and Ool.*, 1887, 12: 56–57), the finding of these nests was the "result of a good deal of hard work in exceedingly unpleasant weather . . ." All four nests were located in deserted woodpecker holes in dead stubs from 20 to 50 feet above ground. Three of the nests each contained seven eggs, the other, one egg and five downy young, dates ranging from Apr. 7 to Apr. 30.

Five breeding localities in Monroe Co. (see map) does not mean that Saw-whet Owls are more common there than elsewhere, as these five localities represent a period of over 60 years (1901–1964).

The Saw-whet Owl is a cavity or hole nester, judging from 13 nest sites described—11 of these in dead trees, two others in birdhouses—one in a Wood Duck box, the other in a box ostensibly erected for Screech Owls. Most of the nest sites were in wooded swamps or at the edge of forest, but one was in a spruce-sphagnum bog, one in an old apple orchard, and another (the "owl" box) in the open, adjacent to salt marsh.

Nest heights ranged from 18 to 65 feet above ground, but the "owl" box was only five and one-half feet up.

Egg clutches in ten New York nests: four eggs (one nest) and five, six, and seven eggs (three nests each).

EGG DATES: Mar. 31 to June 11.

Nestlings: Apr. 21 to July 16; fledglings: May 28 to Aug. 22.

Location of the 29 known breeding stations are as follows: Niagara Co.—(1) Middleport. Erie Co.—(2) Como Lake Park. Cattaraugus Co.—(3) near Salamanca. Wyoming Co.—(4) Beaver Meadow Refuge. Allegany Co.—(5) Short Tract. Monroe Co.—(6) near Brockport; (7) Ling Road Swamp; (8) south of Coldwater; (9) near Rochester; (10) Scottsville. Cayuga Co.—(11) Howland's Island Refuge. Tompkins Co.—(12) near Ithaca. Oswego Co.—(13) near Oswego. Onondaga Co.

MAP 87 Saw-whet Owl
(*Aegolius acadicus*)
Breeding distribution

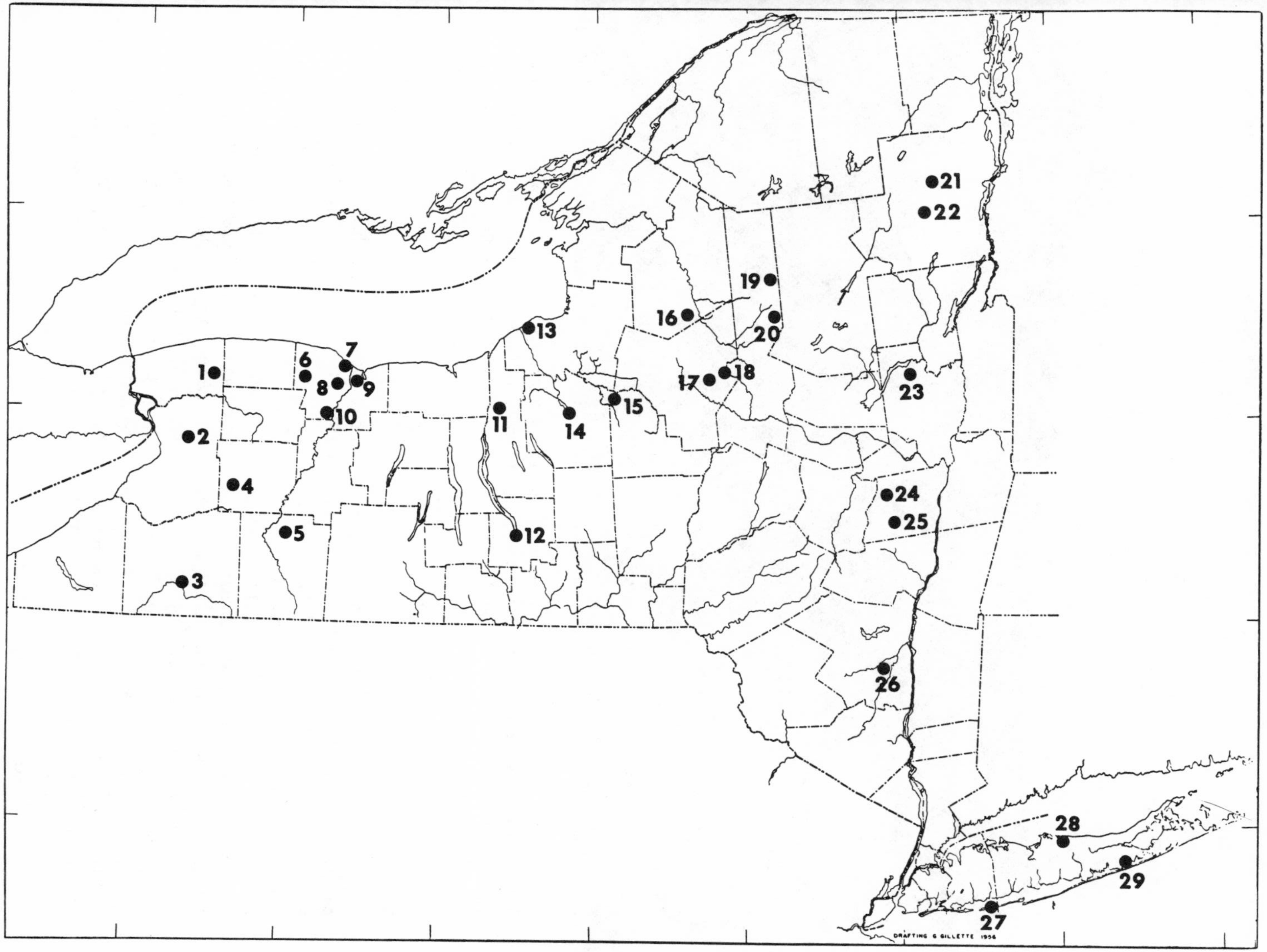

Fig. 64 Nest box used by Saw-whet Owls, Tobay Sanctuary, Nassau Co., May 1968. Six young fledged from this site. Habitat is open sand dune with bayberry, wild cherry, and poison ivy thickets. In vicinity are patches of beach grass and salt marsh. Photo by Frederick R. Schaeffer

—(14) near Syracuse. Madison Co.—(15) southwest of Lakeport. Lewis Co.—(16) Locust Grove. Oneida Co.—(17) Holland Patent; (18) Trenton Falls. Herkimer Co.—(19) Fourth Lake; (20) Honnedaga Lake. Essex Co.—(21) Keene; (22) the divide between Elk Lake and Upper Ausable Lake. Saratoga Co.—(23) Jenny Lake. Albany Co.—(24) Berne Swamp; (25) Rensselaerville. Ulster Co. —(26) Mohonk Lake. Nassau Co.—(27) near Tobay Pond, Jones Beach (see below for details). Suffolk Co.—(28) Miller's Place; (29) Westhampton Beach.

The last-mentioned locality relates to an injured juvenile, with traces of natal down, which was found perched on a fence, July 21, 1966 (Puleston); the bird died the same day and is now a specimen, AMNH 786124.

Banding: Full details of the Jones Beach breeding record have been published by Schaeffer (*Ebba News,* 1968, 31: 174–177, and *Kingbird,* 1968, 18: 143–144). Schaeffer and Barth banded both the female and young in the nest box located in coastal scrub (Fig. 64). All five young were fledged by June 16. The female, which was last seen alive on June 15, was found shot nearly seven months later, Jan. 12, 1969, almost 300 miles to the *northeast* at South Portland, Maine.

NIGHTJARS — CAPRIMULGIDAE

Three species in New York.
Two breed.

In this family of 70± species most are nocturnal or at least crepuscular, although the Common Nighthawk (*Chordeiles minor*) is active in daylight, especially on overcast days. The Whip-poor-will (*Caprimulgus vociferus*), on the other hand, is seldom seen, but often heard during spring and summer.

Chuck-will's-widow
(*Caprimulgus carolinensis*) *

Range: Chiefly southeastern United States, breeding north to southern New Jersey (Cape May Co.). Winters from the Gulf states to northern South America. Has occurred as a straggler north to southern Canada.

Status: *Very rare*—the only certain records within New York State are two from Long Island and two from Monroe Co.

(1) A specimen was taken at Riverhead, Suffolk Co., May 2, 1933 (Latham), NYSM 25049.

(2) One heard calling near the home of Joe Taylor, near Rochester, May 19, 1959, responded to his recording of its call (Taylor, *in litt.*).

(3) Another netted, banded, measured, color-photographed, and released near Braddock's Bay, June 1, 1961 (Leubner and Listman), remained until July 2 (Foster, Lloyd, Miller, Tetlow, *et al.*). This bird was observed frequently in flight and on the ground, and was often seen perched on a branch of a pear tree. For further details of these two Monroe Co. occurrences, see *Kingbird* (1959, 9: 78, and 1961, 11: 149).

(4) An individual was heard at Islip, Suffolk Co., from May 27 to 30, 1969 (Mona Boch). This bird called frequently during its stay and remained in a patch of oak woods with an understory of greenbrier (*Smilax*). Mrs. Boch

was able to record the bird's voice on tape and submitted the tape recording to W. E. Lanyon for confirmation. A copy of the tape and sonagram are on file in the AMNH collection. See *Kingbird* (1969, 19: 148).

Postscript: This species, formerly casual, is now *very rare,* in view of its being recorded nearly every year within the past five years. The following are the more outstanding records since those listed above: 1972—Central Park, New York City, May 13 (many observers), photographed in color by Bahrt and Swoger, Whip-poor-will present nearby, also photographed. 1973—(1) Fire Island State Park, Suffolk Co., May 11 (Ford), female—also female Whip-poor-will netted, banded, color-photographed, and released, both carefully measured. (2) Kennedy Airport, May 21 (A. S. Moorhouse and R. W. Dickerman), female hit obstruction, specimen in AMNH collection, 810371. (3) Near Cedar Beach, Suffolk Co., Nov. 18 (Gochfeld), road kill—remains only, wing and skull preserved, AMNH 819462, "probably dead for at least two weeks."

Whip-poor-will
(*Caprimulgus vociferus*) * B

Range: Chiefly eastern North America, breeding from southern Canada to the mountains of northern Georgia and on the coast to Virginia; also in the mountains from southwestern United States to Honduras. In the east winters north to the Carolinas.

Status: Widespread and locally common breeder, most numerous on the coastal plain of Long Island; local over much of upstate New York. Rare to absent at higher elevations in the Adirondacks, especially where heavily forested.

Nonbreeding: This species is recorded annually by the active birdwatcher in such localities as the city parks, where individual Whip-poor-wills may be observed perched lengthwise on some tree limb, or flushed from the ground. It is a rare occasion, however, when more than one individual is *seen* in any one locality, as they are nocturnal. Nevertheless, most people who have never seen one are familiar with the distinctive song—chiefly at dusk or just before dawn—which gives the bird its name. Whip-poor-wills feed on moths to a large extent.

EXTREME DATES: Apr. 2 and 8 (both coastal) to Oct. 16 (inland) and Oct. 20 (coastal); Nov. 6, 1945, Northport, Suffolk Co. (Elliott). Rare before late April and after early October.

Breeding: This species prefers dry woodland where it nests on the ground. It is locally numerous in the pine barrens of eastern Long Island and in deciduous woodland near the coast, but is decidedly local in western and central New York.

As to eastern Long Island—in Suffolk Co.—Howell recorded 15 birds calling in two miles of pine barrens at Lake Grove on May 30, 1890; Helmuth estimated *50* calling birds between Mecox Bay and Montauk on May 9, 1942. On western Long Island in Nassau Co., Elliott heard at least 30 in the Seaford-Massapequa area in mid-May, 1945.

The Whip-poor-will still manages to hold on as a breeding bird within New York City limits. On Staten Island in the summer of 1969, Cleaves (*in litt.*) stated that at least three pairs nested in the section from Woodrow to Richmond Valley.

The nest is placed on the ground, usually in open or light woodland. Raynor (1941) studying three nests at Manorville, Suffolk Co., found the nests in extensive second-growth oak woodland, with some pitch pine present. The rather dense undergrowth consisted primarily of laurel and huckleberry. On the basis of marked birds, Raynor discovered that one pair raised *two* broods, the second nest being placed about 100 feet from the first. He also determined that the female incubated by day, both sexes by night. Incubation lasted from 18 to 20 days.

Of 15 New York nests examined, two eggs constituted the invariable clutch.

EGG DATES: May 3 (early) and May 16 to June 30.

Nestlings or, more properly, unfledged young: June 2 to July 14; fledglings: June 16 to Aug. 8.

Common Nighthawk
(*Chordeiles minor*) * B

Range: Nearctic and Neotropical regions, breeding from Alaska and Canada to the West Indies and Central America. Winters in South America.

Status: Common to abundant fall migrant, especially near Long Island Sound; less numerous in spring. Statewide breeder, but much less common on and near the coast than formerly.

Nonbreeding: Among the highlights of the fall migration in late August and early September are the spectacular flocks of these conspicuous birds, particularly near Long Island Sound. They are mostly crepuscular in habits, but are sometimes diurnal, especially on cloudy days.

MAXIMA: *Fall*—1000 in two hours (6 to 8 P.M.) Bayside, Queens Co., Aug. 20, 1969; 670, Buffalo, Sept. 3, 1965; 1500, Port Chester, Westchester Co., Sept. 7, 1968.

MAXIMA: *Spring*—200, Forest Lawn Park, Buffalo, May 20, 1959.

EXTREME DATES: Apr. 6 (inland tornado and high winds prior to occurrence) and Apr. 12 (coastal) to Nov. 1 (inland) and Nov. 11 (coastal—possibly a crippled bird). Rare before mid-May and after September. March dates are not substantiated.

Breeding: This species breeds in two distinct habitats: (1) on the ground in open country; (2) on flat gravel rooftops in cities and towns.

(1) Formerly common and widespread as a ground nester, the Nighthawk has decreased in recent times. For instance, on eastern Long Island it was found breeding in such diversified ecotypes as sandy openings in mixed pine–scrub-oak barrens, on bare ground in pastures and fields, on sand dunes, on gravel beaches,

and on flat rocks and logs in the open. Up-state it formerly nested most often on bare flat rocks in fields and pastures, or on the ground itself devoid of vegetation. It has decreased greatly in these habitats. It breeds in mountainous country as well, provided the forest has openings or clearings.

(2) But it is in the heart of large or small cities and some villages that Nighthawks are most familiar, and on almost any summer evening and into the night, these birds may be heard calling their characteristic notes as they hunt flying insects attracted to the bright lights. Nighthawks have learned to adapt to the flat, gravel-surfaced roofs of buildings and, in years gone by, even nested in uptown Manhattan and in Brooklyn. Today, such large cities as Buffalo, Rochester, Syracuse, and Albany have their nesting Nighthawks. In 1957 at least *33* pairs were estimated as breeding in Syracuse, with 23 pairs there in 1971.

Egg clutches in New York are invariably two (27 nests examined).

EGG DATES: May 25 to July 25.

Nestlings: June 14 to Aug. 14; fledglings: July 7 to Aug. 30.

SWIFTS — APODIDAE

One species in New York.
One breeds.

This wide-ranging family of nearly 70 species has only one representative in New York. It was only relatively recently that the winter home of the Chimney Swift (*Chaetura pelagica*) was located—chiefly in the upper Amazon basin of Peru and Brazil.

Chimney Swift
(*Chaetura pelagica*)   *   B

Range: Eastern North America, breeding from southern Canada to Texas and Florida. Known to winter in Amazonian Peru and western Brazil; locally on the Pacific coast of Peru.

Status: Common to abundant migrant, especially inland, occasionally very abundant. Widespread breeder.

Nonbreeding: On occasion in spring, Chimney Swifts may be seen in impressive numbers during the evening hours, entering chimneys for nocturnal roosting. The following maxima listed include these evening roosts.

MAXIMA: *Spring*—50, Binghamton, Apr. 25, 1961; 1000, Derby Hill, Oswego Co., May 6, 1961; 1000, Rochester, May 12, 1956.

MAXIMA: *Spring roosts*—1000, near Buffalo, May 20, 1937; Ithaca, 1948—1000, May 4; 3000, May 10; 2500+ banded at chimney, May 19; total of 4000+ banded the entire spring.

MAXIMA: *Fall*—1000, Peekskill, Westchester Co., Aug. 15, 1962; 1500, Fort Tryon Park, New York Co., Aug. 30, 1947; 1000, Poughkeepsie, Dutchess Co., Sept. 15, 1968; 520, Buffalo, Sept. 28, 1970, and 450, same locality, Oct. 4, 1966 (late dates for so many).

EXTREME DATES: Apr. 3 (coastal) to Oct. 23 (inland) and Oct. 28 and Nov. 4 (both coastal). Rare before late April and after early October.

Breeding: Before the advent of white man, this species very likely nested inside hollow trees, and perhaps cave walls. Today it rarely does so, although there are a few authenticated records in the state. Bagg (1911) took a nest from a hollow tree at New Hartford, Oneida Co., about 1870. Along the trail to Slide Mountain, Ulster Co., July 10, 1960, Walton Sabin found an unfledged juvenile inside a large hollow tree in which several pairs were nesting. Near Sargent Pond, Hamilton Co., Kelsey

Fig. 65 Chimney Swift on its nest in hollow pine tree, Sargent Pond, Hamilton Co., July 1, 1964. Nest located about 30 feet above ground. Photo by Paul M. Kelsey

Fig. 66 Chimney Swift nest with adult and nestlings, Livingston Manor, Sullivan Co., July 8, 1951. Nest placed on couch cover tacked onto barn rafters. Photo by Richard B. Fischer

(*Kingbird*, 1964, 14: 90, with Fig. 65) relates that these birds bred for three years in a very large, dead white pine, the nests 25 to 30 feet above ground. At Elk Lake, Essex Co., Schetty found them breeding in hollow trees in 1969.

Even today in some localities, chimneys are by no means exclusively utilized. In fact, Fischer (1958), referring to the area about Beaver Kill, Sullivan Co., stated that Chimney Swifts occupied interior building walls more often than chimneys.

Elsewhere in New York, walls and rafters of barns (see Fig. 66), silos, deserted farmhouses, and campsites, as well as the side walls of an old lime kiln and an old flour mill —even the side of a stone well—were used as nest sites.

In his study of this species, Fischer (*op. cit.*) found a number of nests attached to barn walls ranging from seven to 28 feet above floor level. Incubation averaged 19 days in 27 nests. He noted that hatching success was as high as 90.7% and fledging success 86%.

Out of a total of 45 New York nests, the following represent clutch size: three eggs (eight nests); four eggs (22 nests); five eggs (15 nests).

EGG DATES: May 30 to July 27.

Nestlings: June 25 to Aug. 12; fledglings: July 18 to Sept. 1.

Banding: An individual of this species banded in Georgia was recovered in New York *ten* years later.

HUMMINGBIRDS — TROCHILIDAE

One species in New York.
One breeds.

In this exclusively American family (320± species) are some of the most brilliant birds known. The family is best represented in South America with many species in the Andean region. In contrast only 16 species are known north of Mexico and the West Indies, with only one species in the northeast, the Ruby-throated Hummingbird (*Archilochus colubris*).

Ruby-throated Hummingbird
(*Archilochus colubris*) * B

Range: Central and eastern North America, breeding from southern Canada to the Gulf of Mexico. Winters north to the Gulf states.

Status: Fairly common to occasionally common migrant, especially inland. Widespread breeder.

Nonbreeding: The Ruby-throated Hummingbird is greatly attracted to flowers, especially *red* ones like trumpet creeper, jewel weed, beebalm, salvia, and others, and during late fall to petunias. Ordinarily only one or two are observed around a flowerbed, but on occasion many more.

MAXIMA: *Spring*—25, Delaware Park, Buffalo, May 12, 1956; *43*, Derby Hill, Oswego Co., May 16, 1970 (G. Smith); 15 at a flowering cherry tree, Green Haven, Dutchess Co., May 21, 1967; 20, Camillus Valley, Onondaga Co., May 23, 1969.

MAXIMA: *Fall*—15, Fire Island, Suffolk Co., Aug. 31, 1963; 30, Jamestown, Chautauqua Co., Sept. 2, 1947; 24, mist-netted and released at Vischer's Ferry, Saratoga Co., Sept. 5, 1970, and 23 more there on Sept. 19 (both by Yunick); 18, Bayside, Queens Co., Sept. 8, 1941; 14, Sandy Pond, Oswego Co., Sept. 13, 1958.

EXTREME DATES: Apr. 14 and 19 (coastal) to Nov. 11 (coastal), Nov. 21 (inland), and Nov. 23 (coastal); also one at Riis Park, Queens Co., from Nov. 26 to Dec. 13, 1961

(Enders, Carleton, and Steck); see Bull (1964: 281) for details.

Rare before May and after mid-October.

Breeding: This species prefers rural areas, nesting in a variety of situations, such as gardens, orchards, roadside thickets and trees, and forest clearings—often near streams.

Eaton (1914: 175) stated that it was a common breeding species in the Adirondacks, nesting on Mt. Marcy up to at least 3500 feet.

Saunders (1936: 136) referring to Allegany State Park in southwestern New York, stated that this species nested chiefly in beech-maple forest near streams and especially where the flowering plant, bee-balm (*Monarda*), was prevalent.

Of 31 New York tree nests examined, heights ranged from five to 30 feet above ground. Tree preference was as follows: beech and hornbeam (six each); maple (five); apple, birch, and oak (three each); and one each in elm, horse-chestnut, pine, larch, and hemlock.

These 31 nests invariably contained two eggs.

EGG DATES: May 21 to Aug. 16.

Nestlings: June 24 to Sept. 4; fledglings: July 12 to Sept. 30.

KINGFISHERS — ALCEDINIDAE

One species in New York.
One breeds.

This well-defined family (90± species) is best developed in the Australasian region where many diverse types occur, including a number of forest-inhabiting forms living on lizards and insects. One aberrant New Guinea species even digs for earthworms with its shovel-shaped bill. Many species are brilliantly colored, among them the striking racket-tailed, paradise king-fishers.

Only six species occur in the New World, the most familiar being our Belted Kingfisher (*Ceryle alcyon*).

Belted Kingfisher
(*Ceryle alcyon*) * B

Range: Nearctic region, breeding from Alaska and Canada to the southern limits of the United States. In the east, winters north to the Great Lakes and New England.

Status: Fairly common migrant. Rare to uncommon in winter. Widespread breeder in suitable habitat.

Nonbreeding: Usually from two to six individuals a day are found during the spring and fall migration, and perhaps from one to three in winter, chiefly along the coast.

MAXIMA: *Spring*—nine, Derby Hill, Oswego Co., Apr. 25, 1962. *Fall*—ten, Jones Beach, Long Island, Oct. 1, 1963.

Breeding: Kingfishers are dependent upon suitable cutbanks for nesting along streams, lakes, and coastal estuaries, but occasionally removed some distance from water. The actual nest is a chamber at the end of a burrow dug into a vertical cutbank, the nest sites located at times in sand or gravel pits.

This species is considered to be a solitary breeder, that is, somewhat territorial, although Rawson Wood (*in litt.*) stated that he observed "*three* [italics mine] active nest holes in a gravel pit spaced about 40 yards apart" in the Hempstead Harbor, Nassau Co., area in 1943.

S. W. Eaton (1953: 13) found "six fresh holes along an eight-mile stretch of River [Allegheny] from Vandalia to South Carrollton [Cattaraugus County] on June 22, 1951."

Clutch size in 31 New York nests varied from four (perhaps incomplete clutches) to seven eggs, as follows: four eggs (five nests), five eggs (four nests); six eggs (five nests); seven eggs (17 nests).

EGG DATES: May 1 to June 10.

Nestlings: June 8 to July 14; fledglings: July 29 to Aug. 9.

Banding: An individual banded on Sept. 13, 1966, at Patchogue, Long Island, was caught alive on Mar. 31, 1967, near the north coast of Hispaniola, on the Río Yuna, Dominican Republic.

Remarks: The genus *Ceryle* is used here, following Peters (1945: 165).

WOODPECKERS — PICIDAE

Nine species in New York.
Nine breed.

This distinctive family (about 210 species) is absent from Madagascar, the Australasian region, and *oceanic* islands.

In New York all nine species breed within the state, but two of them (both three-toed woodpeckers) are restricted to the Adirondacks. All are strictly arboreal or, more properly, trunk climbing, except the Common Flicker (*Colaptes auratus*) which is also terrestrial, foraging on the ground for ants.

The classification adopted here at the generic level is somewhat different from that of the A.O.U. Check-list (1957). Three fewer genera are recognized. With minor modifications, the treatments of Peters (1948), Delacour (1951), de Schauensee (1966), Goodwin (1968), Mayr and Short (1970), Short (1971), and Bock and Short (MS) are followed.

The following genera are merged: (1) *"Centurus"* and *"Asyndesmus"* (latter on hypothetical list) with *Melanerpes*; (2) *"Dendrocopos"* with *Picoides*.

"Centurus" is connected or bridged with *Melanerpes* through the Neotropical, morphologically intermediate grouping formerly called *"Tripsurus."* As for Lewis' Woodpecker (*"Asyndesmus" lewis*), it is no more different in appearance, say from the Red-headed Woodpecker (*Melanerpes erythrocephalus*), than are two West Indian species (*herminieri*) of Guadeloupe, and (*portoricensis*) of Puerto Rico, currently placed in *Melanerpes* by Bond (1961).

In respect to merging *"Dendrocopos"* with *Picoides*, presence of three versus four toes is an adaptive character, not considered to be of generic significance. The Oriental woodpecker genus, *Dinopium,* moreover contains species with three and four toes. Insofar as yellow versus red crown patches are concerned, both *auriceps* and *mahrattensis* of the Himalayan subregion possess yellow, yellowish, or orange patches and thus bridge the gap from red to yellow, *contra* Parkes (1952). Furthermore, a number of other "dendrocopine" species from southeast Asia, Africa, and South America have neither red nor yellow in the crown— but rather patches of gray or brown. Finally, our own White-headed Woodpecker (*"Dendrocopos" albolarvatus*) of the western mountains, for many years placed in this genus, is far more different-looking from any of the 33 species of *"Dendrocopos,"* than are the two species of three-toed woodpeckers (*Picoides*).

Common Flicker
(*Colaptes auratus*) * B

Range: Nearctic and northern Neotropical regions, breeding from Alaska and Canada to Cuba and in the mountains to northern Nicaragua. Withdraws in winter from the northern portions.

Status: Common to abundant migrant. Regular, but uncommon in winter, more numerous along the coast. Widespread breeder.

Nonbreeding: Flickers are our most numerous woodpeckers, inhabiting chiefly open and semiopen country. They are quite terrestrial in habits, often feeding on ants. Migrants usually arrive in early March and depart in late No-

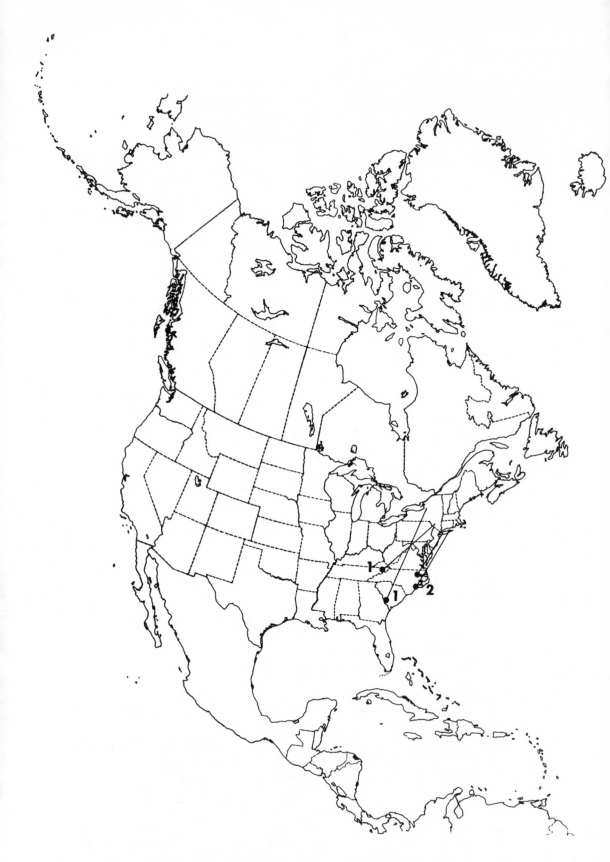

MAP 88 Common Flicker (*Colaptes auratus*) Banding recoveries

vember. Most numerous inland in spring, on the coast in fall. Great flights occur both seasons.

MAXIMA: *Spring*—150, Atlantic Beach, Nassau Co., Apr. 6, 1947; 1200, Derby Hill, Oswego Co., Apr. 23, 1959; 1000, Manitou, Monroe Co., Apr. 25, 1965; 450, Dunkirk, Chautauqua Co., May 2, 1965. Note that the largest inland flights occur along the shores of the Great Lakes, as is the case with hawks and many other species.

MAXIMA: *Fall*—800 in two hours, Far Rockaway, Queens Co., Sept. 24, 1949; 2000, Saltaire, Fire Island, Suffolk Co., Sept. 29, 1953; 1000 within one hour, Short Beach, Nassau Co., Sept. 30, 1951.

MAXIMA: *Winter*—40, Easthampton area, Suffolk Co., Dec. 31, 1949; eight, Syracuse area, Dec. 31, 1956; 15, Howland's Island, Cayuga Co., Jan. 1, 1968.

Breeding: This widespread species nests in trees, sometimes in poles, generally in open country, also in woodland clearings, and regularly in city parks and suburban yards. Many nest sites in these last two locations are taken over by Starlings, however.

In nine out of 18 New York tree nests reported, maple was the favorite site. These tree heights ranged from four to 40 feet. The lowest at four feet was in a dead stub, and only ten inches below an active nest of a pair of Downy Woodpeckers. Another nest in a telephone pole was only two feet above the ground. By all odds, the strangest location was that of a *ground* nest on Fisher's Island, Suffolk Co., June 9, 1916. H. L. Ferguson found this nest a slightly scooped-out hollow in the sand; it contained seven eggs. An illustrated account of this remarkable nest is found in *Bird-Lore* (1916, 18: 399–400).

Egg clutches in 23 New York nests ranged from three to nine eggs, although the three- and four-egg clutches may represent incomplete sets. The breakdown: three eggs (four nests); four eggs (six nests); five eggs (two nests); six eggs (one nest); seven eggs (three nests); eight eggs (three nests); nine eggs (four nests).

EGG DATES: Apr. 20 to June 19.

Nestlings: May 18 to July 26; fledglings: June 19 to Aug. 15.

Banding (see Map 88): Four New York ju-

veniles banded during the nesting season were recovered the following winter in the Carolinas and Tennessee.

Remarks: The writer follows Short (1965) in treating the Yellow-shafted (*Colaptes auratus*) and Red-shafted (*C. cafer*) flickers as a single species. The two forms hybridize extensively in a wide zone of sympatry along the western border of the Great Plains; intermediates are numerous.

So-called hybrid flicker occurrences in New York, including published reports, are not true hybrids according to Short and are better called "introgressants." Of numerous eastern flicker specimens examined by Short with various combinations of characters present, *none* would be treated by him as a "hybrid." Banders handling live birds and persons finding dead ones should consult a recent paper by Short (*Ebba News,* 1971, 34: 4–8).

No eastern mainland races (*"luteus"*) are recognized here other than nominate *auratus.* There is a north-south cline of decrease in size, with some overlap present.

Pileated Woodpecker
(*Dryocopus pileatus*)   *   B

Range: North America, breeding (resident) in southern Canada and nearly all the United States. The larger northern race *abieticola* occurs in our area.

Status: Resident in nearly all of the more heavily forested sections of the state, but absent from Long Island.

Nonbreeding: An account of the occurrence of this fine woodpecker in the early part of this century was ably stated by Eaton (1914: 152): "In New York it was formerly rather generally distributed throughout the State, but at the present time it is almost entirely confined to the evergreen forests of the Adirondacks and Catskills. A few are still found in the highlands along the Pennsylvania border and in various localities throughout central and western New York where there are mixed forests of unusual extent . . . More than any of our native species, with the possible exception of the Spruce Grouse and some of the larger hawks, this bird disappears with the destruction of the forests, and it probably will never be reestablished in the State except in the larger evergreen forests of the Canadian zone . . ."

Its "recovery" since Eaton's time has been phenomenal and its present status is in startling contrast—for the better.

Far from being confined to primary forest of the Adirondacks and Catskills, the Pileated Woodpecker is now found adjacent to or even on the outer edges of large cities. For instance, there were four occurrences within recent years in four different parks in the northern limits of New York City (Bull, 1964: 282).

Within the past two decades (1950–1970) these splendid birds have appeared at feeding stations. Here and in city parks, the one essential element is the presence of large trees. The following upstate occurrences are especially noteworthy:

(1) Nestling **banded** at Ithaca, June 4, 1942, was found dead *nine* years later about 20 miles to the north at Sherwood, Cayuga Co., June 20, 1951.

(2) Two pairs each at two different Ithaca feeders, winter of 1954–1955.

(3) Three individuals at Watkins Glen, Schuyler Co., January 1962, foraging on diseased elms in the main streets.

(4) Four presumably different individuals present in the Schenectady city parks, winter of 1962–1963.

There have been only two reliable records on Long Island—one a specimen—within the past 90 years (Bull, 1964: 283).

Breeding: There have even been *breeding* records of this woodpecker within city parks. In southern Westchester Co., two suburbs of New York City boast nesting records—one near Tarrytown in 1958, the other in Silver Lake Park, north of White Plains in 1963.

For three years in a row (1963–1965) a pair bred in Stewart Park, Ithaca.

Pileated Woodpeckers usually nest in old and very large trees, both coniferous and deciduous, from as low as eight feet and as high as 70. Incubation takes 18 days (Hoyt).

Egg clutches recorded in nine New York nests: three eggs (four nests); four eggs (five nests).

EGG DATES: Apr. 22 to May 19.

Nestlings: May 10 to June 21: fledglings: June 9 to July 15.

Red-bellied Woodpecker
(*Melanerpes carolinus*)   *   B

Range: Chiefly southeastern United States, resident north to southern Michigan, southeastern Ontario, and western and southeastern New York.

Status: Formerly uncommon and local in western New York, very rare elsewhere; since the early 1960s greatly increased and locally common in the Genesee valley and Finger Lakes regions, but rare and local in the southeastern portion of the state. Sedentary, but wanders in winter and irrupts in spring flights.

Change in status: Eaton (1914: 157) knew of "numerous" records of this species for the western part of the state chiefly in fall and winter, although he listed only three or four breeding occurrences in Erie and Yates counties. However, his statement that "it evidently was common on Long Island and in the lower Hudson valley fifty years ago" is contrary to the known facts and is presumably unsubstantiated in view of its casual occurrence in adjacent areas (see Bull, 1964: 283–285 for history in southeastern New York).

By the late 1950s and early 1960s the Red-bellied Woodpecker had become a locally, fairly common species, as may be seen below.

Nonbreeding: With the great increase in observers and feeding stations in recent years, more and more of these birds have been recorded, especially on Christmas counts. Upstate the many diseased and dying elms, particularly in the river swamps, attract wood borers and other insects, creating an abundant food supply.

MAXIMA: 18, Avon, Livingston Co., Jan. 4, 1958; 22, Montezuma Marshes, Dec. 26, 1966; 17, Port Byron, Howland's Island area, Cayuga Co., late December 1966.

There was a spring irruption of this species in 1969 on Long Island with at least 16 individuals reported in as many localities, dates ranging from Apr. 12 to June 1.

The species has been collected as far north as Locust Grove, Lewis Co., winter of 1871–

MAP 89 Red-bellied
Woodpecker (*Melanerpes
carolinus*) Breeding
distribution

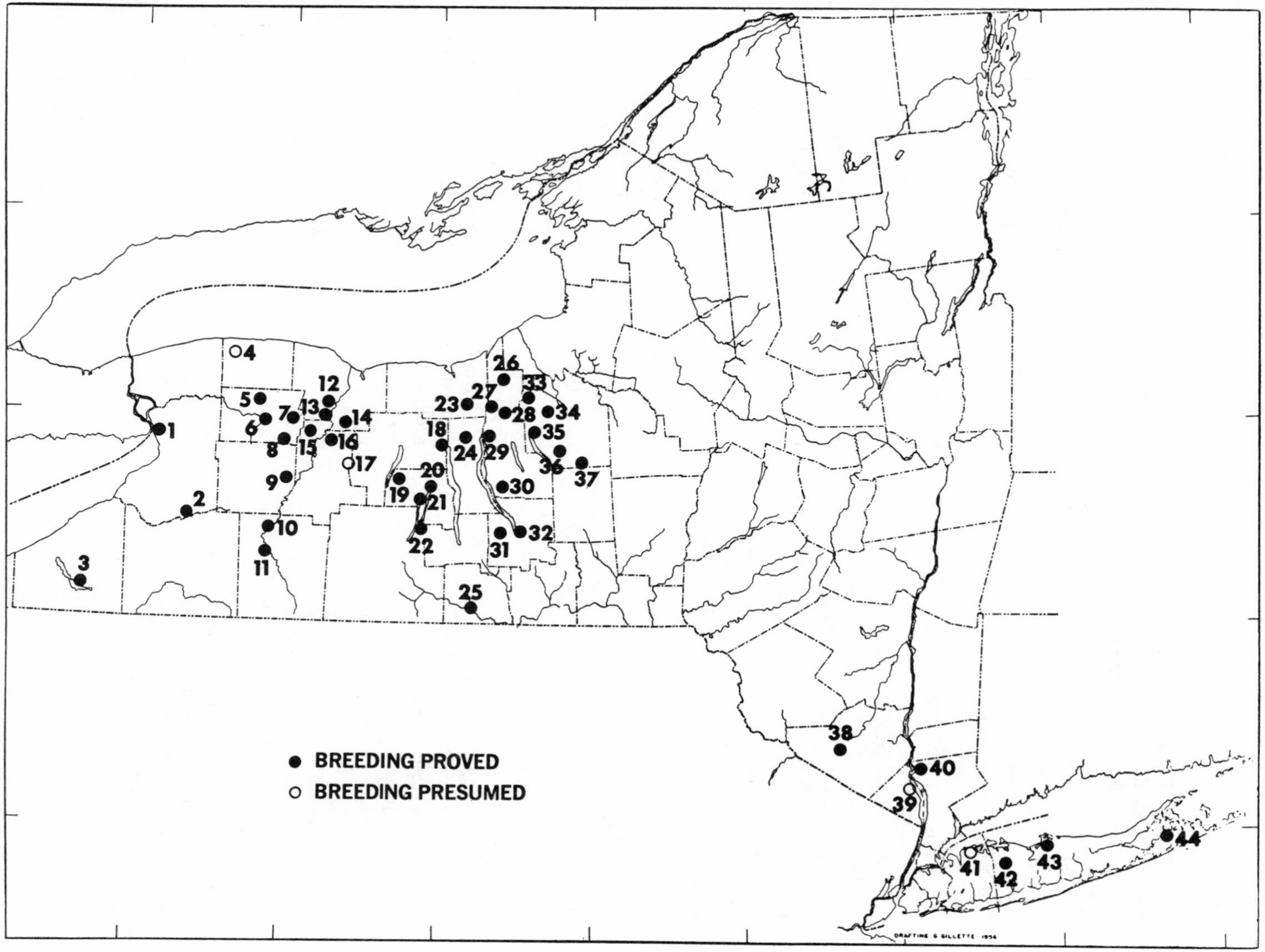

● BREEDING PROVED
○ BREEDING PRESUMED

1872 (C. L. Bagg), BM(NH) collection. It has been reliably observed as far north as Watertown, Jefferson Co., May 12, 1968 (Gordon).

Breeding (see Map 89): From a glance at the breeding distribution map, it is evident that the Red-bellied Woodpecker (1) occurs in two widely disjunct areas, and (2) is concentrated in the Finger Lakes region and to the west in the Genesee valley section. In between these two latter areas there is a narrow gap. West of the Genesee valley exists a much wider gap where the species is unaccountably very rare as a breeder. The two nesting records for Erie Co. date back to the 1890s. In contrast, the single known breeding occurrence for Chautauqua Co. is as recent as 1968. There are no known, or at least no published, breeding records for either Niagara or Cattaraugus counties.

I am at a loss to explain this erratic distribution, but it should be borne in mind that, of 37 breeding localities for western New York, no fewer than *27* were reported within the decade 1961–1971. In other words eastward dispersal into New York is mostly very recent. As the species is a rare breeder immediately to the south in *northern* Pennsylvania and, as it is equally rare or absent from the Lake Erie plain south of Buffalo, it follows that the origin of this species was from the *west*—through the Niagara Frontier corridor between lakes Erie and Ontario, originating from the southwest up the Mississippi-Ohio rivers by way of Illinois, Indiana, Ohio, and southern Michigan—thence into extreme southeastern Ontario, and finally into New York State—where, incidentally, the species is at its northeasternmost known breeding limits.

Note also that, as a breeder in upstate New York, the species has not reached the area *east* of a line stretching from Syracuse, Ithaca, and Elmira, except for the 1971 station (37) at Labrador Pond, Onondaga Co.

In western New York, as Seeber (1963) has suggested, the Red-bellied Woodpecker follows the watercourses—lakes, streams, creeks, and swamps.

Breeding habitat in western New York has been variously described as: (1) flooded, wooded swamps; (2) openings in mature oak forest; (3) roadside sugar maples and shagbark

hickories in open pastureland; (4) forested stream bottoms, and (5) dry upland maple-beech woodland. Nest heights ranged from 20 to 30 feet above ground.

The seven breeding and/or presumed breeding localities in southeastern New York (1964–1971) undoubtedly owe their origin to the South Atlantic coastal states by way of New Jersey, as the species has been spreading northward in recent years.

Only two New York egg-clutch records are before me: one of three, the other of four eggs.

EGG DATES: Apr. 26 to June 28.

Nestlings: May 18 to July 14; fledglings: June 23 to Aug. 13.

The 44 New York breeding localities, with recent years included, are: Erie Co.—(1) near Buffalo; (2) Springville. Chautauqua Co.—(3) Bemus Point, 1968. Orleans Co.—(4) Yates, 1963. Genesee Co.—(5) Oak Orchard Swamp near Oakfield, 1965; (6) Batavia, 1963; (7) Le Roy, 1965; (8) Pavilion, 1963. Wyoming Co.—(9) west side of Silver Lake, 1961. Allegany Co.—(10) Fillmore, 1969; (11) Caneadea, 1966. Monroe Co.—(12) Reed Road Swamp, 1969; (13) near Scottsville, 1948; (14) West Rush, 1954. Livingston Co.—(15) Caledonia, 1963; (16) Avon, 1963; (17) Hemlock, 1968. Ontario Co.—(18) Geneva, 1968. Yates Co.—(19) Potter Swamp; (20) Benton Center; (21) Keuka Park, 1965. Steuben Co.—(22) Keuka, 1965. Wayne Co.—(23) Clyde, 1969. Seneca Co.—(24) Waterloo, 1967. Chemung Co.—(25) Elmira, 1969. Cayuga Co.—(26) near Victory, 1969; (27) Howland's Island, 1947; (28) Port Byron; (29) Montezuma, 1954; (30) King Ferry, 1962. Tompkins Co.—(31) Enfield, 1970; (32) near Ithaca, 1970. Onondaga Co.—(33) Plainville, 1961; (34) Camillus, 1965; (35) Skaneateles, 1968; (36) near Amber, 1970; (37) Labrador Pond, 1971. Orange Co.—(38) Ridgebury, 1971. Rockland Co.—(39) Garnerville, 1964. Westchester Co.—(40) Peekskill, 1971. Nassau Co.—(41) Mill Neck, 1971. Suffolk Co.—(42) near Huntington, 1971; (43) Setauket, 1969; (44) Noyack, 1971.

Remarks: The form *"zebra"* is here considered a synonym of nominate *carolinus* (Bull, 1964: 285).

Red-headed Woodpecker
(*Melanerpes erythrocephalus*)   *   B

Range: Chiefly eastern North America, breeding from extreme southern Canada to the Gulf states. Sedentary and migratory.

Status: Formerly common to abundant fall migrant on and near the coast; now rare to uncommon, but regular there. Fairly common but local migrant in central and western New York. Local breeder in lowland areas north to the St. Lawrence valley, but now rare in the southeastern portions. Most plentiful in the Oneida Lake region.

Nonbreeding: For an account of its past history and abundance in the New York City region, see Bull (1964: 285–286). Suffice it to say that nothing in the state today remotely resembles the magnitude of the fall flights formerly occurring along the coast—viz., ". . . several hundred," principally immatures, at Miller's Place, Suffolk Co., Sept. 24, 1881 (Helme), all *prior* to 10 A.M.

Today if the observer should see from one to four at a given locality on the coast in September, he may consider himself fortunate.

MAXIMA, INLAND: *Spring*—eight, Derby Hill, Oswego Co., May 12, 1964. *Fall*—15, Grand Island, Niagara River, Sept. 1, 1944; 14, Point Gratiot (Dunkirk), Chautauqua Co., Sept. 8, 1955.

Winter: The following inland concentrations emphasize the fact that this species is also sedentary in nature and that food, not climate, is the controlling factor: (A) nine (eight adults, one immature) collected at Leyden, Lewis Co., Dec. 23–31, 1875 (Merriam), "beech mast and chestnuts abundant"—these specimens in the BM(NH) collection; (B) eight in an oak grove, Rhinebeck, Dutchess Co., winter of 1914–1915 (Crosby), "good acorn crop"; (C) six, near Canton, St. Lawrence Co., winter of 1922–1923 (Ayers), "beech nuts plentiful": (D) six at feeding station, Avon, Livingston Co., winter of 1962–1963 (Genesee Ornith. Soc.) —"sunflower seeds and peanuts eaten."

Breeding: Red-headed Woodpeckers were formerly more numerous and widespread in suitable areas in New York, especially in farm-

ing country. The decrease in recent years is believed due to two main reasons: (1) roadside mortality as a result of the bird's flycatching habits, i.e., darting down to the roadside to pick up insects; (2) increase of the Starling and the latter's ability to usurp nest holes.

This handsome woodpecker breeds in two distinct habitats: (a) in river bottoms, beaver ponds, and open wooded swamps where dead trees and stumps are plentiful; (b) in open savanna-like country with extensive grassland and scattered trees; also in cleared upland areas, such as on golf courses, around farms, open groves in pastures, and along roadsides. It frequently nests in hickory, oak, and elm; also in telephone poles and fence posts. Nest holes are placed from 12 to 50 feet above ground.

The greatest density of nesting Red-headed Woodpeckers in New York that I am aware of is that reported by Dorothy Ackley (*Kingbird*, 1966, 16: 214). She made an actual count of 27 occupied nest holes during the summer of 1966 within a ten-mile radius of Oneida, Madison Co., and adjacent Oneida Co. plus an additional five nesting pairs in the Canastota, Madison Co. area. Miss Ackley stated that all 32 breeding sites "are within ten miles of Oneida, with the heaviest concentration being south and southwest of that city."

Egg clutches in 21 New York nests: three eggs (four nests); four eggs (four nests); five eggs (11 nests); six and seven eggs (one nest apiece).

EGG DATES: May 16 to June 19.

Nestlings: May 31 to Aug. 26; fledglings: July 5 to Sept. 15.

[Lewis' Woodpecker (*Melanerpes lewis*)

Hypothetical: Western North America, breeding east to the western portions of South Dakota and Nebraska. Casual east to Manitoba and Illinois. Accidental in Rhode Island in November 1928 (specimen).

Two sight reports from New York (both interestingly enough during the fall of 1954) are: (1) an individual carefully studied at the Swope feeding station, Ossining, Westchester Co., Oct. 27 to Nov. 6 (Grierson, Kieran, Nolan, and Walsh)—unfortunately no photographic evidence was obtained of this well-marked species; (2) another reported, without details, Cohocton, Steuben Co., Nov. 6 (Mrs. I. Sick, *Audubon Field Notes*, 1955, 9: 23).]

Yellow-bellied Sapsucker
(*Sphyrapicus varius*)   *   B

Range: Nearctic region, breeding from Canada to southwestern United States and in the east to the Berkshires, Catskills, and Poconos; in the higher mountains to northern Georgia. Winters north to southern New Jersey, rarely to New York and Massachusetts.

Status: Common to very common spring migrant inland and fairly common to occasionally common fall migrant coastwise. Rare in winter. Common breeder in the Adirondacks, Tug Hill area, and the higher Catskills; uncommon but fairly widespread at higher elevations in the central and western portions, but very rare to absent southeastward; no known breeding records south of the Catskills (see Map 90).

Nonbreeding: This species fluctuates greatly in numbers, particularly in spring. At this season it is numerous upstate, but usually uncommon or even rare along the coast. In fall, however, the migration is mainly coastal. It is almost entirely silent on migration.

Sapsuckers drill numerous holes in both evergreen and broad-leaved trees to feed on the soft cambium layer, the sap, and insect borers. By doing this they often girdle the trees, however, rarely killing them.

MAXIMA, INLAND: *Spring*—75, near Binghamton, Broome Co., Apr. 11, 1959; *150,* Dunkirk, Chautauqua Co., May 2, 1965 (Grzybowski)—an unusually large number.

MAXIMA, COASTAL: *Fall*—Fire Island State Park, Suffolk Co.—25 netted and banded, Sept. 29, 1969; 28, Sept. 30, 1956; 24, Bronx Park, New York City, Oct. 4, 1925.

Various *summer* (June–August) dates of nonbreeders along the coast, but usually rare before mid-September and after mid-May.

Winter: Usually rare at this season. One was collected at Lowville, Lewis Co., Mar. 3, 1885 (J. H. Miller), specimen in NYSM collection. Beardslee and Mitchell (1965: 296)

list 13 winter occurrences between 1938 and 1962 for the Niagara Frontier region.

Breeding (see Map 90): Perusal of the breeding distribution map indicates not only the generally wide nesting range in the montane areas of the Adirondack and Catskill districts, as well as the less numerous nestings in the highlands of the central and western portions of the state, but more important the apparent gaps in distribution designated by question marks (?). Especially mystifying is the presumed lack of breeding records (except one) in the north-south corridor stretching from south of the Lake Ontario plain to the Pennsylvania state line and encompassing the counties of Wayne, Seneca, Ontario, Livingston, Schuyler, Steuben, and Tioga. This is particularly noticeable in view of seemingly suitable habitat directly to the east and to the west of this corridor. I suspect the answer is a lack of observers, not a lack of sapsuckers. That the species is not entirely absent in this section is evident from its breeding at (5) Potter Swamp, Yates Co.

Another anomalous situation is the lowland breeding population south of Lake Ontario on the Niagara escarpment in the counties of Monroe, Orleans, and Niagara (see encircled area on map)—the last named having breeding birds near (6) Lockport, only 600 feet above sea level, and 350 feet above lake level. At this spot the "northern" sapsucker and the "southern" Cerulean Warbler practically breed side by side, and at Chili, Monroe Co., Carolina Wrens breed "with" sapsuckers.

Still another low-lying breeding locality is in Oswego Co. on the north side of Oneida Lake at (4) Constantia at only 500 feet elevation.

Near or at the edge of the montane forest areas are: (3) Cherry Valley, Otsego Co., just outside the Catskills; (1) Berlin Mtn. and (2) near Grafton, both in Rensselaer Co.; (7) Austerlitz, Columbia Co., 1971—all these localities at the edges of the Berkshires and Taconics.

This species should be looked for in the breeding season at higher elevations in the southern portions of Ulster and Sullivan counties.

The supposed breeding occurrence published in Bull (1964: 288) on the Connecticut state

MAP 90 Yellow-bellied Sapsucker (*Sphyrapicus varius*) Breeding distribution

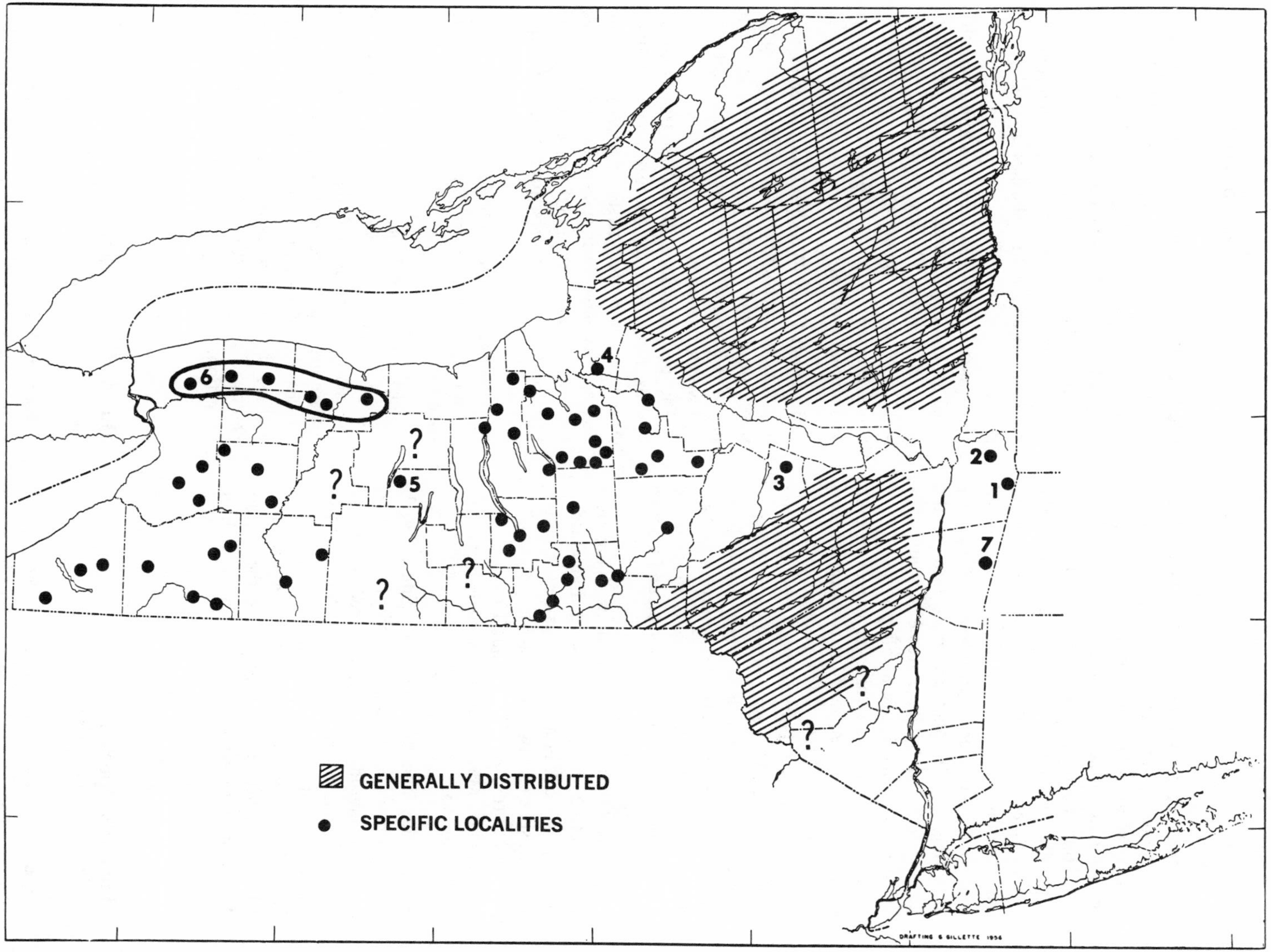

GENERALLY DISTRIBUTED
SPECIFIC LOCALITIES
1
2
3
4
5
6
7
?
DRAFTING G. GILLETTE 1956

line, adjacent to Westchester Co., should be deleted due to the lack of firm evidence. No eggs or young were ever seen. Moreover, the species is a casual breeder even in the Litchfield Hills of northwestern Connecticut.

Finally, it should be emphasized that the species is common in spring passage *west* of the Hudson valley where these birds breed commonly and that a corresponding scarcity in spring in the southeastern section of the state is reflected by its extreme scarcity as a breeder *east* of the Hudson valley.

The Yellow-bellied Sapsucker breeds in both deciduous and mixed deciduous-evergreen forest. As Eaton (1914: 151) pointed out, nests are almost always built in the forest and not in the clearings. However, one nest at Oneonta, Otsego Co., was in a dead sugar maple in an old orchard. Rosche (1967), referring to Wyoming Co., stated that it breeds in hemlock woods, "mature" conifer plantings, and wooded beaver ponds.

Nesting cavities are in dead or living trees from ten to 45 feet above ground. Egg clutches in 12 New York nests: four eggs (eight nests); five and six eggs (two nests each).

EGG DATES: Apr. 29 to June 19.

Nestlings: May 29 to July 8; fledglings: June 12 to Aug. 15.

Remarks: This and the quite different-looking Red-breasted Sapsucker complex (*ruber*) are here considered separate species, following Mayr and Short (1970: 57), but not from the very similar-appearing *nuchalis,* here considered conspecific with *varius.* More field work is needed in the west where the various forms meet to establish frequency of hybridization.

is essentially a resident species of deep woods, it does appear in more open country during winter, also coming into city parks and visiting feeding stations. On rare occasions it occurs in flights during fall, when it may be seen even on the outer coast with often nothing more to perch on than bushes and telephone poles.

MAXIMA: *Fall*—35 moving south along the ridge at Anthony's Nose, Westchester Co., Oct. 23, 1954 (Queens County Bird Club). *Winter* —35 feeding in dying elm swamps, Montezuma Marshes, Jan. 1, 1967. These are both exceptional numbers.

Breeding: Hairy Woodpeckers prefer to nest in extensive tracts of forest with plenty of large trees, dead stubs, and fallen logs. In such places it is found in mountains, river bottoms, and wooded swamps.

The nest is placed in a dead tree from as low as three feet to 40 feet above ground. Apparently very few nests or sets of eggs of this species have been taken in the state, as I know of only seven. Of these seven nests, two contained three eggs, four held four eggs, and one had five.

EGG DATES: Apr. 23 to May 19.

Nestlings: May 5 to June 14; fledglings: June 13 to Aug. 1.

Subspecies: The larger and whiter northern subspecies, *septentrionalis,* breeding south to the central portions of Ontario and Quebec, is apparently quite rare in New York in winter. At least one specimen from this state, examined by me, is assignable to this race: Danby, Tompkins Co., Jan. 8, 1949, CUM collection.

Hairy Woodpecker
(Picoides villosus) * B

Range: Nearctic and northern Neotropical regions, breeding from Alaska and Canada to Florida, the Bahamas, and in the mountains to Panama. Both sedentary and migratory.

Status: Fairly common resident in the wilder portions, occasionally more numerous in fall irruptions.

Nonbreeding: While the Hairy Woodpecker

Downy Woodpecker
(Picoides pubescens) * B

Range: Alaska and central Canada to extreme southern United States. Both sedentary and migratory.

Status: Common migrant along the coast. Locally common in winter throughout. Widespread breeder.

Nonbreeding: At such places as the outer beaches, where the Downy Woodpecker is rare both summer and winter, it is easy to discern marked migratory movements. Banding has proved that considerable numbers pass through in some years (see below).

MAXIMA: *Fall*—At Tobay Beach, Nassau Co., in 1966, Davis and Schaeffer netted and banded a total of *36* individuals from Sept. 1 to Oct. 29, with as many as eight each on Sept. 28 and Oct. 29; also, six banded, same locality, Nov. 8, 1958. 25, Far Rockaway, Queens Co., Oct. 9, 1970.

MAXIMA: *Winter*—26, Avon, Livingston Co., Jan. 4, 1958; 60, "mostly in dying elm swamps," Howland's Island area, Cayuga Co., Jan. 1, 1967 (Scheider, *et al.*), an unusual concentration. This species has become fairly common at an ever-increasing number of feeding stations.

MAXIMA: *Spring*—28, Prospect Park, Brooklyn, Mar. 25, 1945.

Breeding: The ubiquitous Downy Woodpecker nests in city parks, suburban yards, orchards, and other cultivated areas, and also in open woodland, forest edge and clearings, but not in the depth of the forest. The nest site—usually in dead trees, more rarely in living ones—ranges from as low as three feet to 30 feet above ground.

Egg clutches range from four to seven in 13 New York nests examined: four eggs (three nests); five eggs (seven nests); six eggs (one nest); seven eggs (two nests).

EGG DATES: May 6 to June 31.

Nestlings: May 31 to July 3; fledglings: June 9 to July 16.

Banding: A Downy Woodpecker banded at Ocean City, Maryland, Oct. 9, 1967, was trapped 450 miles away at Clayton, Jefferson Co., June 1, 1968. Two others banded during the fall of 1959 on the island of Martha's Vineyard, Mass., were recaptured the following autumn near Port Chester, Westchester Co., about 170 miles away. Another two, banded in the fall of 1956 at Ithaca, were recovered three and five years later, both near Birmingham, Ala., at least *800* miles distant. Two individuals banded in New York State each lived for eight years.

Remarks: No eastern races are recognized here. A north-south decrease in size from *"nelsoni"* in southern Canada, through *"medi-*

anus" in northeastern United States, to nominate *pubescens* of southeastern United States, is only of clinal significance. Nor are color differences of value. Godfrey (1966: 245) considers *"nelsoni"* as poorly characterized also, being only slightly larger.

Black-backed Three-toed Woodpecker (*Picoides arcticus*)   *   B

Range: Nearctic region, breeding (resident) from Alaska and Canada south—in the west to the mountains of California and Nevada, but in the east only as far as extreme northern United States. In the northeast wanders in winter to Long Island and northern New Jersey. Sedentary and irregularly migratory.

Status: Rare and irregular winter visitant, occasionally uncommon upstate. Uncommon breeder (resident) in the Adirondacks.

Nonbreeding: Both boreal species of *Picoides* are fond of feeding on wood-boring beetles in dead and dying trees. The larvae of these insects infest both evergreen and deciduous trees, often killing them. Among the evergreens, spruce, pine, larch, hemlock, and balsam fir are especially prone to attack. Of the deciduous trees, elm in particular, but also birch, are subject to infestation. Strips or flakes of bark beneath the diseased and dying or dead trees are usually indications of the birds' presence.

Within recent years the winters of 1960–1961 and 1965–1966 have produced southward irruptions of these woodpeckers from their boreal breeding grounds.

MAXIMA, 1960–1961: four, Buffalo area; five, Syracuse area. 1965–1966: four, Syracuse area.

EXTREME DATES: Sept. 28 (coastal) and Sept. 30 (inland), earliest specimen—Oct. 4 (coastal) to Apr. 21 (coastal) and May 13 (inland); exceptionally to May 31, 1961, Ithaca (many observers).

Usually rare before late October and after early April.

Breeding (see Map 91): According to Eaton (1914: 145), "This species is confined to the

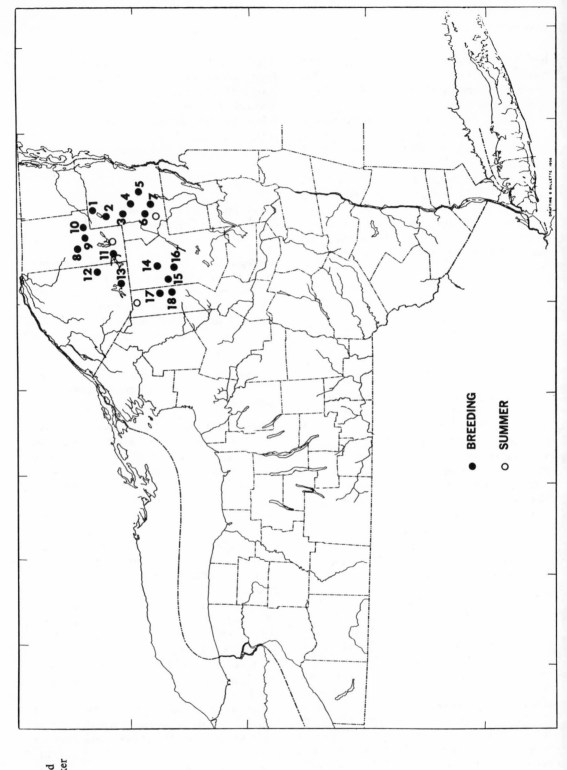

MAP 91 Black-backed
Three-toed Woodpecker
(*Picoides arcticus*)
Breeding distribution

● BREEDING

○ SUMMER

spruce and balsam belt [of the Adirondacks] . . . during the breeding season." The same author stated that it also was "reported as breeding" in the higher Catskills and in Tioga Co., which, however, has never been proved.

Black-backed Three-toed Woodpeckers have fairly wide altitudinal distribution, as low as 1700 feet, breeding in spruce and tamarack swamps, up to over 4000 feet on forested slopes of spruce and fir. They also frequent clearings, stands of freshly burned timber, and lake and river shores in evergreen forest. Ferdinand La France (*in litt.*) found these birds "attracted to dead spruce and hemlock [=balsam] trees in spongy sphagnum bogs, especially where there are active beaver colonies."

In addition to spruce, larch, and fir, nests have been found in white birch on two occasions. Almost invariably dead trees are chosen for nest sites. Height of nest holes above ground ranges from four to 40 feet.

In the three known New York nests with eggs, one contained three eggs, two others held four each.

EGG DATES: May 18 to June 12.

Nestlings: May 30 to June 20; fledglings: June 20 to July 23.

The accompanying map shows the breeding and summer distribution. The breeding localities of the present species, *P. arcticus,* outnumbers those of the other species, *P. tridactylus,* by two to one (18 to 9).

The 18 breeding localities are: Essex Co.— (1) Whiteface Mtn.; (2) Chubb River Swamp; (3) Arnold Lake; (4) Bartlett Ridge near Mt. Marcy; (5) Elk Lake; (6) Wolf Pond (7) Sand Pond. Franklin Co.—(8) Madawaska; (9) near Jones Pond; (10) near Paul Smith's; (11) near Tupper Lake (village). St. Lawrence Co. —(12) Jordan Lake and nearby Mt. Matumbla; (13) Barber Point, Cranberry Lake. Hamilton Co.—(14) Eldon Pond, Raquette Lake; (15) Seventh Lake and about three miles north on Eagle Creek; (16) near Lost Ponds. Herkimer Co.—(17) Big Moose Lake and nearby Woods Lake; (18) Third Lake Creek.

Summer occurrences, but breeding not proved: Axton, Franklin Co.; near Aiden Lair, Essex Co.; Five Ponds, Herkimer Co.

It is certain that with more field work, this species, as well as others, will be found to have a wider breeding distribution within the Adirondacks than is presently known.

Northern Three-toed Woodpecker
(*Picoides tridactylus*)   *   B

Range: Holarctic region, in America generally ranging farther north than the preceding species; resident from Alaska and Canada, south—in the west to the mountains of Arizona and New Mexico, but in the east only as far as extreme northern United States. Sedentary and virtually nonmigratory.

Status: Very rare winter visitant upstate, unknown downstate. Rare, possibly very rare resident in the Adirondacks, formerly less rare.

Nonbreeding: Other than a specimen taken at Waterville in extreme southern Oneida Co. (Eaton, 1914: 147), I know of only three reliable occurrences outside the Adirondack region, all from western New York. These were of birds feeding on dead and dying elms: (1) near Rochester, from Dec. 27, 1956, to Mar. 1, 1957, and possibly the same individual on May 11; (2) one seen and photographed on Grand Island, Niagara River, from Dec. 16, 1962, to Mar. 3, 1963; (3) near Rochester, from Nov. 28, 1965, to Mar. 13, 1966. All three individuals were seen by numerous observers. The Rochester birds of 1956–1957 and 1965–1966 occurred simultaneously with the irruptions of *P. arcticus.*

The inclusion of Long Island in the range of this species (A.O.U. Check-list, 1957: 331) is erroneous.

Breeding (see Map 92): Field work in recent years has shown this species to be much scarcer than formerly. Only three nesting pairs have been reported within the past 30 years. Compared with the previous species, the Northern Three-toed Woodpecker has been found breeding in only half as many localities. Altitudinal distribution and habitat preference appear to be similar, and even nesting habits are apparently alike, as the range of nest hole heights are virtually the same, as are also clutch size and egg dates (but see **Remarks).** In addition to the same evergreen trees used for nest sites by *P. arcticus,* the present species has utilized one each of red pine and white cedar.

Two New York nests contained four eggs apiece.

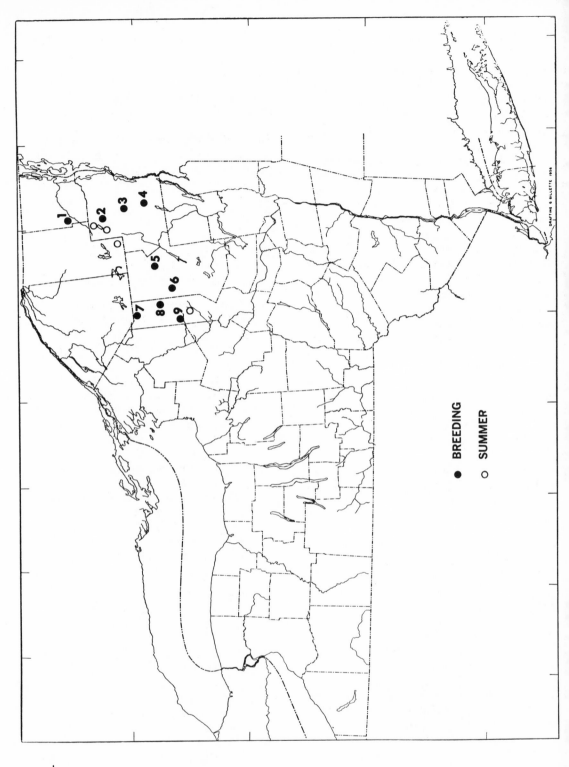

MAP 92 Northern Three-
toed Woodpecker
(*Picoides tridactylus*)
Breeding distribution

BREEDING

SUMMER

EGG DATES: May 14 to June 14.

Nestlings: July 2; fledglings: July 9 to July 24.

The nine known breeding localities of *P. tridactylus* are: Clinton Co.—(1) Upper Chateaugay Lake. Essex Co.—(2) Copperas Pond; (3) Mt. Marcy; (4) Upper Ausable Lake. Hamilton Co.—(5) Marion River at Raquette Lake; (6) Sixth Lake and nearby Seventh Lake. Herkimer Co.—(7) Big Shallow Pond; (8) Big Moose Lake; (9) Moose River near McKeever; also see below.

There are four localities where this species has occurred during late spring and summer, but definite evidence of nesting is lacking: Essex Co.—Whiteface Mtn. and Chubb River Swamp (a pair in 1961 quite possibly nested at the latter locality). Franklin Co.—Ampersand Mtn. Herkimer Co.—Sand Lake.

Remarks: It is surprising to note that the two morphologically similar three-toed woodpeckers (*P. arcticus* and *P. tridactylus*) are not only sympatric, but occur together ecologically. As stated above, even nesting times are roughly the same. The all-important question is: What, if anything, reduces interspecific competition between these two bog-loving and evergreen forest-inhabiting woodpeckers, as well as with the similar-sized Hairy Woodpecker (*P. villosus*)?

Perhaps the somewhat longer and heavier bill of the more numerous and larger Black-backed Three-Toed Woodpecker may be an adaptation for larger-sized insect prey, as well as for digging into harder wood, whereas the somewhat shorter and lighter bill of the rarer and smaller Northern Three-toed Woodpecker may be for probing less deeply for its food and for digging into softer or rotten wood. Analyses of stomach contents may give us the answer. These differences in bill size might also apply for excavating nest sites, or perhaps even for scaling bark. Foraging heights may differ between these species, also. As a result, interspecific competition would be, at least, reduced, if not eliminated.

Todd (1963: 473), in speaking of habitat differences of the two species in Labrador, stated that *tridactylus* was ". . . much less common than" *arcticus,* and was ". . . rather quiet by comparison and seems to prefer low growth in muskeg country [=spruce-sphagnum bogs] instead of dead high timber, thus it more readily eludes observation."

Subspecies: The northeastern race *bacatus* tends to have narrower white dorsal barring than the two western subspecies. It is also smaller than nominate *tridactylus* of Europe which has the back nearly solid white rather than barred as in *bacatus*. In addition, the Asiatic races vary greatly, from almost melanic, "black-backed" to barred, to essentially "white-backed" subspecies. This suggests that the Holarctic species *tridactylus* evolved in Eurasia, subsequently reinvaded North America, only to find the New World species *arcticus* already established. In other words a double invasion occurred in North America with *arcticus* the earlier arrival and having differentiated to the species level.

Postscript: On July 2, 1972, Ferdinand La France and I were so fortunate to discover a pair of this species feeding a nearly full-grown young about ready to leave the nest hole approximately 20 feet up in a dead spruce at Ferd's Bog (near Eagle Bay) on the Hamilton-Herkimer Co. line. Mr. La France had previously found *P. arcticus* breeding here also. This is one of the very few localities in New York where both three-toed woodpeckers are known to breed "side by side" (see Fig. 15).

TYRANT FLYCATCHERS — TYRANNIDAE

Fifteen species in New York.
Ten breed.

In this exclusively American family (over 300 species), the vast majority of species occurs in South America, but a good many (85+) inhabit Middle America and the West Indies.

Of the five New York nonbreeders, four are accidental or casual vagrants, the fifth (*Tyrannus verticalis*), the Western Kingbird, is a regular fall migrant in small numbers on the outer coast.

Although five of the ten breeders are easy enough to identify at any time of year, the other five species—all in the genus *Empidonax* —are notoriously difficult to separate on migration. However, during the summer months while on the breeding grounds, they can be told by the habitat they frequent, plus their vocalizations (primary songs, not call notes). Each of five species may be sorted out on an ecological basis: (1) Yellow-bellied Flycatcher (*E. flaviventris*) in boreal spruce forest; (2) and (3) Traill's Flycatcher (*E. traillii* and *E. alnorum*)—both song types—nearly throughout the state in bogs, swamps, or wet pastures, occasionally in dry, overgrown fields; (4) Least Flycatcher (*E. minimus*) generally north of Long Island—in shade trees in rural and agricultural country, and in open woodland; (5) the now very rare Acadian Flycatcher (*E. virescens*) in beech forest or sometimes in oak-hickory areas, usually near water, and with undergrowth present.

Eastern Kingbird
(*Tyrannus tyrannus*)   *   B

Range: North America, breeding from southern Canada to southern United States. Winters in South America.

Status: Common to very common migrant, occasionally abundant in fall on the outer coast. Widespread breeder.

Nonbreeding: This species sometimes occurs in spectacular numbers in fall along the south shore of Long Island. In spring the flight is chiefly inland.

MAXIMA: *Spring*—60, Lake View, Erie Co., May 12, 1962; 40, Derby Hill, Oswego Co., May 24, 1966.

MAXIMA: *Fall*—110, Easthampton, Suffolk Co., Aug. 16, 1923; 300, Mastic, Suffolk Co., Aug. 24, 1912; *900,* Riis Park, Queens Co., Aug. 29, 1965 (Davis)—an unusually high number—"observed between sunrise and late morning, mostly loose flocks of five to 20 birds"; 250, Far Rockaway, Queens Co., Sept. 10, 1969; 100, near Baldwinsville, Onondaga Co., Sept. 18, 1959.

EXTREME DATES: Apr. 10 and 14 (both inland) to Oct. 24 (coastal). Casual, Apr. 4, 1931, Eastport, Suffolk Co. (Wilcox), after a strong southerly storm; also very unusual, Nov. 7–11, 1954, Riis Park, Queens Co. (many observers), one with four Western Kingbirds.

Ordinarily rare before May and after September.

Breeding: The Eastern Kingbird breeds in generally open country, especially in cultivated areas—farms, orchards, along rural roadsides—and also along lake and river shores, and in open woodlands, swamp edges, and clearings.

The nest is often placed in fruit trees, occasionally on telephone poles, at heights from eight to 30 feet above ground.

An unusual site (see Fig. 67) is that of a nest with young on the winch of a moored houseboat on the shore of Oneida Lake near Bridgeport, Madison Co., July 10, 1962 (Fischer).

Egg clutches in 22 New York nests: three eggs (eight nests); four eggs (12 nests); five eggs (two nests).

EGG DATES: May 22 to July 16.

Nestlings: June 3 to Aug. 5; fledglings: June 21 to Aug. 21.

Fig. 67 Eastern Kingbird nest with young, on winch of moored houseboat, Oneida Lake, near Bridgeport, Madison Co., July 10, 1962. Photo by Richard B. Fischer

Gray Kingbird
(*Tyrannus dominicensis*) *

Range: Neotropical region, breeding north to southern Florida; very rarely to South Carolina. Winters from the West Indies to northern South America. Vagrant north to Massachusetts, often after tropical storms.

Status: *Casual*—in New York State recorded only from Long Island. There are two specimen records, one of them extant: According to Griscom (1923: 228), one was taken at Setauket, Suffolk Co., about 1874, but is without further details; another was collected at Orient, Suffolk Co., Apr. 29, 1921 (Latham), NYSM 25091.

Three sight reports by experienced observers are believed correct: Jones Beach, June 7, 1930 (Hix); Dyker Beach, Kings Co., Aug. 22, 1930 (Johnston); Westhampton Beach, Suffolk Co., Sept. 18 and 19, 1960 (Dunning, Yeaton, and Wilcox), after hurricane "Donna" of Sept. 12.

Western Kingbird
(*Tyrannus verticalis*) *

Range: Western North America, breeding east to western Minnesota; very rarely to southern Ontario (western Lake Erie), southern Michigan, and northwestern Ohio. Winters chiefly from Mexico to Nicaragua, but regularly in small numbers in southern Florida, and occasionally north to coastal South Carolina; casually as far as Nova Scotia.

Status: Rare to uncommon, but regular fall migrant on the outer coast; very rare in winter. Very rare inland.

Occurrence: On the south shore of Long Island the active observer may see one or more Western Kingbirds each fall from the end of August to early December or even later. The species is very rare anywhere else. This bird may be seen along the coast perched on telephone wires, fence posts, bushes, or even in isolated trees, as it is a species of open

country. It is conspicuous and not easily overlooked.

MAXIMA: three, Fire Island, opposite Mastic, Suffolk Co., Sept. 10, 1955; four, Riis
Park, Queens Co., Nov. 13, 1954; four, Montauk, Dec. 8, 1956. As many as *23* were reported in the autumn of 1954.

EXTREME DATES: Aug. 14 to Jan. 14. The
species is very rare in winter, the above January date (1957) representing an individual
that remained at Riis Park. In late December
1956, three Western Kingbirds were reported
at Riis Park, Jones Beach, and Montauk. Winter individuals have been observed feeding on
Eleagnus berries.

There are only two spring occurrences con-
sidered reliable: (1) Easthampton, Suffolk Co.,
June 3, 1950 (Helmuth); (2) Pleasant Plains,
Richmond Co., Staten Island, June 16, 1958
(Cleaves).

Change in inland status: Eaton (1914: 184)
knew of no inland occurrence. In 1927 two
apparently different individuals were observed
in Dutchess Co.—one on Oct. 8 at Pine Plains
in the eastern sector and the other on Oct. 14
at Barrytown close to the Hudson River in the
western portion.

Including the two aforementioned reports
there are scarcely a dozen observations for the
interior of the state. Not until Sept. 3, 1951,
was another seen—near Sherrill, Oneida Co.
(*Kingbird,* 1951, 1: 110). The other upstate
sightings are scattered.

EXTREME DATES, inland: Aug. 25 to Oct.
15; Nov. 21, 1965, Poughkeepsie, Dutchess
Co. (Waterman Bird Club). Casual at Bear
Mountain, Rockland-Orange Co. line, Dec. 6–
26, 1953 (Orth and Kenney).

Specimen data: I know of only two specimens
taken in the state, one of which I have seen:
(1) Riverdale, Bronx Co., Oct. 19, 1875 (Bicknell); (2) Miller's Place, Suffolk Co., Sept. 6,
1912 (Helme), AMNH 802433.

Scissor-tailed Flycatcher
(*Muscivora forficata*)   *

Range: Chiefly south-central United States,
breeding northeast to western Missouri. Winters chiefly in Middle America, but small num-

bers regular in southern Florida. Recorded during migration in the east, north to southern
Canada, especially in recent years.

Status: *Very rare*—there appear to be thir-
teen reliable occurrences of this striking species
in New York, of which only two are reported
from upstate. Nine of the 11 downstate records are from Long Island, including one specimen: Sag Harbor, Suffolk Co., June 11, 1939
(Latham), NYSM 25087. This is also the first
known record for the state.

The other ten downstate occurrences are
found in Bull (1964: 292 and 1970: 28), plus
one observed as recently as Oct. 16, 1969.
One of these, a beautiful adult, present at Atlantic Beach, Nassau Co., from Oct. 30 to
Nov. 7, 1960 (Buckley, Cashman, Isleib, and
numerous others), was studied at leisure and
many color photographs were taken (see also
Kingbird, 1966, 16: 130). This bird was observed feeding not only on grasshoppers and
dragonflies, but also on the fruit of *Eleagnus*
and bayberry.

The two upstate observations are: One seen
flying along the Lake Ontario shore at Rigney's
Bluff near Rochester, May 18, 1952 (Kemnitzer and McKinney); another at Tomhannock Reservoir, Rensselaer Co., Nov. 11, 1956
(Merritt and 14 other observers of the Schenectady Bird Club).

Seasonal distribution is as follows: May (six
records—earliest, May 7); June (two records—
June 11 and 12); Sept. (one record—Sept. 11–
16); Oct.–Nov. (four records—Oct. 16–Nov.
23).

[Fork-tailed Flycatcher
(*Muscivora tyrannus*)

Hypothetical: Neotropical region, breeding
north to southern Mexico; the races from
southern South America are highly migratory
and winter north to the southern Lesser Antilles. Vagrant north to Pennsylvania, New
Jersey, and Maine (all specimens).

Two Long Island observations and one from
upstate New York are believed correct: (1)
East Quogue, Suffolk Co., Sept. 14, 1944 (Mrs.
H. Walter and Mrs. H. Ward), seen the day of
the great hurricane; (2) Heckscher State Park,
Suffolk Co., Sept. 23, 1947 (Eckelberry); (3)

Clermont, Columbia Co., Oct. 7, 1954 (Ingersoll, *Audubon Field Notes*, 1955, 9: 13).

Remarks: The two species of the genus *Muscivora* are merged with *Tyrannus* by Smith (1966), who considers them to be merely long-tailed members of the kingbird group, with similar vocalizations.]

Great Crested Flycatcher
(*Myiarchus crinitus*)   *   B

Range: Eastern North America, breeding from southern Canada to the Gulf states. Winters chiefly from southern Texas and Mexico to northern South America, occasionally or uncommonly in southern Florida.

Status: Fairly common migrant in the southern portions, but uncommon northward and rare to absent in the higher mountains; numbers subject to marked fluctuations. Widespread breeder in the lowlands, more numerous southward, but local on the south shore of Long Island.

Nonbreeding: A few Great Crested Flycatchers may be seen during the spring and fall migrations on the *south* shore of Long Island where this species is uncommon or local as a breeder.

MAXIMA: *Spring*—18, Easthampton, Suffolk Co., May 18, 1929. *Fall*—9, Far Rockaway, Queens Co., Sept. 8, 1956.

EXTREME DATES: Apr. 24 (inland) to Oct. 27 (inland) and Nov. 3 and 8 (both coastal). Casual, Apr. 17, 1919, Orient, Suffolk Co. (Latham), after a southerly storm.

Rare before May and after September.

Late fall and early winter individuals of this genus should be collected to determine the species (Bull, 1964: 293, and 1970: 29). See next species.

Breeding: Great Crested Flycatchers are primarily birds of woodland and keep pretty much to the foliage, but their characteristic

Fig. 68   Cowbird egg and Great Crested Flycatcher nestling in bird box, Ithaca, Tompkins Co., July 5, 1969. Photo by Richard B. Fischer

call reveals their presence. They breed also in orchards and in large deciduous trees in cultivated districts. Our only local hole-nesting flycatcher, it occupies birdhouses (see Fig. 68), rarely fence posts and telephone poles, as well as tree cavities and dead stubs. Apple trees are much preferred in some areas, but are used less extensively nowadays as orchards have been abandoned or cut down, and Starlings preempt available holes early in the spring. Nest heights range as low as four feet above ground (fence posts), more often from ten to 30 feet up.

Nests of this species are often lined with shed snakeskin and, in recent years, cellophane wrappers have been found.

Egg clutches in 23 New York nests ranged from four to seven: four eggs (eight nests); five eggs (11 nests); six eggs (three nests); seven eggs (one nest).

EGG DATES: May 22 to July 11.

Nestlings: June 10 to July 26; fledglings: June 27 to Sept. 14.

Remarks: No subspecies are recognized here. The differences in wing length and bill size are quite variable and considerable overlap exists in northern and southern specimens. The form *"boreus"* is thus considered to be a synonym.

Ash-throated Flycatcher
(*Myiarchus cinerascens*)

Range: Western United States, breeding from Washington and Idaho to northern Mexico, east to the Rocky Mountains of Colorado. Winters from Arizona and California to El Salvador. Vagrant east to Rhode Island (specimen), New York (color photographs), and Maryland (two specimens).

Status: *Casual*—On Nov. 21, 1970 at Larchmont, Westchester Co., Sid Bahrt color-photographed a smallish, very pale *Myiarchus* flycatcher which he realized was different from the familiar Great Crested Flycatcher. It was seen subsequently and tentatively identified as an Ash-throated Flycatcher by Robert Arbib. This individual was present until Nov. 23.

The color photographs were seen by the writer and Wesley Lanyon who concurred in

the identification. Color photos are on file in AMNH collection.

It is noteworthy that both Maryland specimens were secured also in late November. The mid-September Rhode Island specimen was taken just east of New York on Block Island.

Postscript: An adult female, discovered at Ridge, Suffolk Co., Dec. 1, 1973 (J. Ruscia and G. Raynor), was mist-netted on Dec. 5 (W. E. Lanyon). The bird was placed in an aviary, but it died 12 hours after capture. Upon dissection, Lanyon found the stomach and intestine empty, its muscle masses much reduced, and its plumage heavily infested with *Mallophaga*. The specimen was preserved and is AMNH 819464. This represents the first state specimen and the second state record.

Eastern Phoebe
(*Sayornis phoebe*)   *   B

Range: Chiefly eastern North America, breeding from southern Canada south—in the east to the mountains of northern Georgia. In the east winters north to Maryland; rarely to Long Island and southern coastal New England.

Status: Common to very common coastal migrant, especially in fall; less numerous inland. Rare in winter on the coast. Widespread breeder inland, but local on the coastal plain.

Nonbreeding: This species is sometimes present in large numbers on the coast during the southward migration.

MAXIMA: *Spring*—35, Atlantic Beach, Nassau Co., Mar. 27, 1949; 30 each, Derby Hill, Oswego Co., Apr. 4, 1969, and Apr. 22, 1962.

MAXIMA: *Fall*—65, Idlewild, Queens Co., Sept. 25, 1949; 85, Jones Beach, Nassau Co., Oct. 5, 1963; 40, same locality, Oct. 13, 1962.

"EXTREME" DATES: Mar 10 (coastal and inland) to late November or early December. Usually arrives in mid-March and departs after October.

Winter: Although still a rare bird at this season, Phoebes have been regular in recent years on the coast. Usually one or two are reported on the Long Island Christmas counts, but in 1952 at least *five* different individuals were observed along the south shore. They probably do not survive the entire winter, unless the bayberry crop or other fruiting shrubs persist. The species is much rarer in winter upstate. A report of 11 listed in *Audubon Field Notes* on one Long Island Christmas count in 1968 is certainly a typographical error as undoubtedly the number "one" was intended.

Breeding: This species is exceedingly adaptable in its nesting habits and breeds in a great variety of situations. Nests have been found in such diverse locations as under bridges, eaves of barns, overhanging edges of road banks, upturned tree roots, on wooden ledges of country houses, and on rock ledges and cliffs. Mearns (1878), speaking of the Hudson Highlands, stated that "a pair for several years built their nest in a shaft of an iron mine, in a dark and extremely humid situation."

On at least two occasions this species has utilized other bird nests. One pair used an old Robin nest at Mohonk Lake, Ulster Co., in 1936 (Smiley) and another pair laid eggs in an abandoned nest of a Barn Swallow at Voorheesville, Albany Co., during the summer of 1935 (Stoner).

Egg clutches in 21 New York nests ranged from four to six: four eggs (seven nests); five eggs (11 nests); six eggs (three nests).

EGG DATES: Apr. 20 to Aug. 4.

Nestlings: May 13 to Aug. 10; fledglings: June 9 to Aug. 24.

The species is double-brooded in New York. Mrs. Irving (*Kingbird*, 1953, 3: 35), in her banding studies of two nests at West Nyack, Rockland Co., found that in both 1951 and 1952 the incubation period was 17 days, but in the latter year the second clutch of eggs laid by the same female was incubated for only 14 days. The first clutch contained five eggs, that of the second only four; both clutches hatched.

Say's Phoebe (*Sayornis saya*) *

Range: Western North America, breeding east to Manitoba and Nebraska. Vagrant east to Massachusetts, Connecticut, and New York (specimens).

Status: *Casual*—there is one confirmed record for New York: male collected at Montauk, Long Island, Oct. 9, 1933 (Latham),

NYSM 25522. This record was not previously published.

Four observations, including three from Long Island, are believed correct: (1) Dyker Beach, Kings Co., Sept. 25–28, 1926 (W. Eaton and Nathan); (2) Gilgo Beach, Suffolk Co., Sept. 16, 1958 (Buckley and Restivo); (3) Greece, Monroe Co., Dec. 13–19, 1959 (Listman and Lloyd); (4) Point O'Woods, Fire Island, Suffolk Co., Oct. 12, 1969 (S. Hopkins).

Yellow-bellied Flycatcher
(*Empidonax flaviventris*) * B

Range: Chiefly central and eastern North America, breeding from central Canada south to the northern portions of New York and New England; rarely to the Catskills and Poconos. Winters from Mexico to Panama.

Status: Regular but uncommon, occasionally fairly common migrant. Local breeder in the mountains; common in the Adirondacks, but rare to uncommon in the Catskills.

Nonbreeding: This species is a late spring and early fall migrant, most numerous in late May and early June, and again in late August and the first half of September. Although generally unobtrusive, it is not rare at these times. It may be found in thickets and light woodland, in either moist or dry areas.

MAXIMA: *Spring*—nine netted and banded, Fire Island State Park, Suffolk Co., May 20, 1970; 12 netted and banded, Manitou, Monroe Co., June 6, 1965 (Leubner).

MAXIMA: *Fall*—two big years, 1966 and 1968.

1966—netted and banded, Tobay Sanctuary, Nassau Co.—seven, Aug. 20, and five, Sept. 11; also four hit the Elmira TV tower, Sept. 20, specimens, CUM collection.

1968—netted and banded, Huntington, Suffolk Co.—six each on Aug. 20 and Aug. 23; also 11 netted and banded, Vischer's Ferry, Saratoga Co., Aug. 24 (Yunick). Also eight netted and banded, Fire Island State Park, Suffolk Co., Sept. 1, 1970.

EXTREME DATES: *Spring*—May 8 (coastal) to June 19 (coastal specimen).

EXTREME DATES: *Fall*—July 29 (coastal)

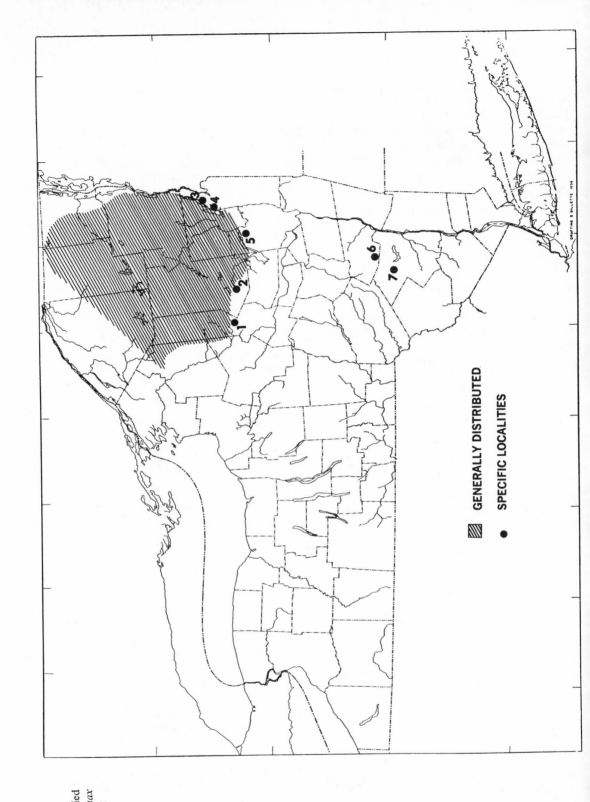

MAP 93 Yellow-bellied Flycatcher (*Empidonax flaviventris*) Breeding distribution

GENERALLY DISTRIBUTED

SPECIFIC LOCALITIES

and Aug. 4 (coastal specimen) to Oct. 11 (inland specimen).

Usually rare before late May and after mid-September. Spring dates earlier than those given above are rejected in absence of specimen evidence. The species is not always easy to identify, either in the field or in the hand. More than one museum specimen has been misidentified.

Breeding (see Map 93): Eaton (1914: 193–194) described the breeding habitat and nest site of the Yellow-bellied Flycatcher in its Adirondack home: ". . . inhabiting mostly the damp shady slopes and mountains where the rocks and soil are covered with a dense mat of green mosses and the atmosphere is continually laden with moisture . . . here it constructs its nest hidden among the moss on some fallen log or thickly covered rock or steeply sloping bank. It is almost impossible to discover the nest except when the bird is driven from it."

This species differs from all other members of the genus in New York in that it is a ground nester, the nest being on or near the ground. In parts of Essex Co. it is locally common in spruce forest.

In the higher Catskills (above 2800 feet) Hough (*in litt.*) says that it "prefers steep inclines that are boulder strewn and with rocky outcroppings, all covered with various kinds of moss, Canadian flora, and a moderate tree growth of stunted birch, balsam, and spruce."

Two Adirondack nests and one from the Catskills are as follows: (1) on ground in swampy woodland of spruce and larch—the nest in the side of a small mound covered with sphagnum moss; (2) the nest 14 inches above ground in a small hollow in some moss growing on the roots of an overturned spruce tree; (3) the nest nine inches up in a cavity (partially hidden in overhanging roots) scooped in moss facing the side of a low rock in mixed balsam-spruce bog forest.

Egg clutches in five New York nests were four apiece.

EGG DATES: June 10 to June 27.

Nestlings: no New York data; fledglings: July 25.

Known limits of breeding distribution in New York are indicated on the map. Only two definite breeding localities are reported for the Catskills. The species is generally distributed

throughout the higher Adirondacks and at lower elevations in suitable terrain in the northern and western portions of the Adirondack State Park. Although reported in summer in the Tug Hill area, no proved breeding is known from there; nor is the report of two singing individuals in Thacher Park (Helderbergs), Albany Co., July 14, 1971 (D. Allen, *Kingbird,* 1971, 21: 241) proof of breeding, although at both these locations breeding is within the realm of possibility, especially in the Tug Hill district.

The five southernmost Adirondack and two Catskill localities shown are: Herkimer Co.—(1) Wilmurt. Hamilton Co.—(2) south of Piseco Lake. Washington Co.—both on Lake George—(3) Black Mtn.; (4) Pilot Knob. Saratoga Co.—(5) Jenny Lake. Greene Co.—(6) Hunter Mtn. Ulster Co.—(7) Slide Mtn. and nearby Cornell and Wittenberg mountains.

The alleged breeding occurrences at low elevations in the bogs of western and central New York, listed by Eaton (1914: 193) and by Beardslee and Mitchell (1965: 303–304), were not confirmed. Even the eggs reported as collected near Chili, Monroe Co., are not in the BMS collection or available for examination. To my knowledge, no proved breeding exists in New York outside the Adirondack and Catskill districts.

Acadian Flycatcher
(*Empidonax virescens*)   *   B

Range: Eastern North America, breeding from the Gulf states north to the southern Great Lakes, including extreme southern Ontario, and to central New Jersey; formerly north to western and southeastern New York, and southwestern Connecticut, casually farther (also recently in southern Connecticut; see *Audubon Field Notes,* 1968, 22: 588–589). Winters from Panama to Ecuador.

Status: Formerly a local breeder; since 1900 has greatly decreased; now a rare migrant only; no definite breeding for over 45 years.

Nonbreeding: Because of extreme difficulty

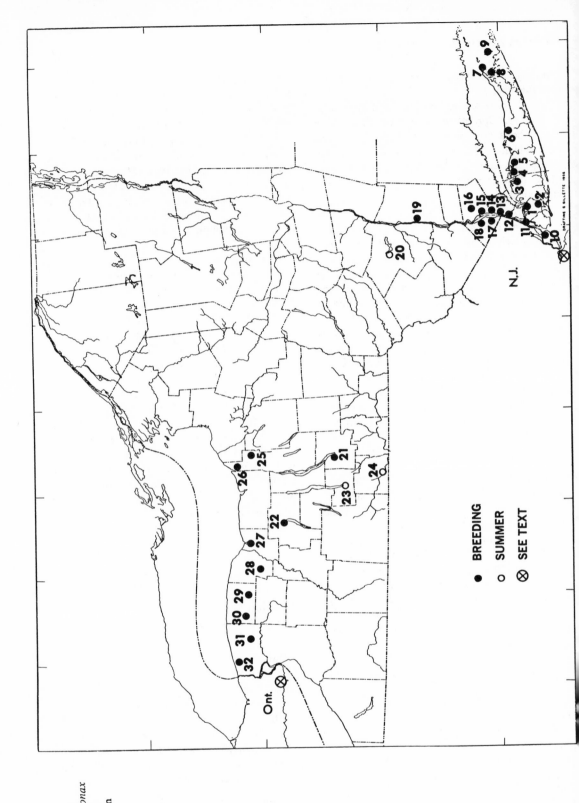

MAP 94 Acadian
Flycatcher (*Empidonax
virescens*) Former
breeding distribution

in identification of members of the genus *Empidonax,* the following dates of occurrence are based entirely on (1) specimens; (2) banded birds carefully examined and measured; (3) singing individuals reported by observers familiar with vocalizations of the various species. All dates are from coastal localities unless specified otherwise.

EXTREME DATES: May 8 (singing bird), May 10 (specimen), and May 18 (inland specimen) to Sept. 19 and 30 (specimens). Rare before late May.

Either a very late spring migrant or a vagrant was netted and banded by Fred Schaeffer and Kenneth Parkes, June 20, 1968, on Great Gull Island, Suffolk Co. (Bull, 1970: 29). Near Huntington, Suffolk Co., June 8–9, 1969, a female was netted, in response to a playback of a tape recording, and was preserved as a specimen (*fide* Lanyon). The following are especially noteworthy: Spring of 1970—"11 were netted at Fire Island [Suffolk Co.] 20 May–7 June. Two were caught at Atlantic Beach [Nassau Co.] on 24 May and 6 June . . . This total of 13 individuals of an inconspicuous, hard-to-identify species might represent a northerly incursion or could be a regular, but overlooked occurrence during late May–early June on the outer coast. Continued mist-netting, especially the large-scale Fire Island operation, should provide an answer within a few years. It should also be noted that all these Acadians were identified by a combination of wing-formula and measurements, easily applied to this species in the hand" (Davis and Morgan, *Kingbird,* 1970, 20: 157).

Breeding (see Map 94): Eaton (1914: 195) described the Acadian Flycatcher as a common inhabitant of the lower Hudson valley, and fairly common on western Long Island, but rare to uncommon elsewhere. However, Griscom (1933: 122) stated that "Since 1900 . . . is definitely known to have abandoned the greater part of its northeastern breeding range." Reasons for its disappearance are apparently not known.

As may be seen from the accompanying map, there are, or were, two widely separated populations, in turn subdivided into two geographical units, as follows: (1) southeastern—(a) Long Island; (b) lower Hudson valley. (2) western—(c) Finger Lakes region; (d) Lake

Ontario plain. These units will be discussed presently.

It is obvious that this lowland species is divided by the Appalachian Mountains and that population (1) is derived from the coastal plain region to the south of New York, and that population (2) originated from the Mississippi River and its tributaries by way of the southern portions of Michigan and Ontario. It should be noted that the species is unknown as a breeder in extreme western New York *south* of the Lake Ontario plain, and that the ever-increasing elevations just to the south of the Niagara escarpment act as a barrier to its southward penetration. This is further borne out by the fact that even today this species is found breeding in the corridor in Canadian territory (⊗ on map) to the west of New York between lakes Ontario and Erie—the Niagara "Frontier." Furthermore, the absence of breeding Acadian Flycatchers in New York south of Buffalo along the Lake Erie shore would suggest that these birds invaded western New York by way of the corridor *north* of Buffalo and Lake Erie rather than along the narrow Lake Erie plain to the south of Buffalo.

(a) It is of interest to note that this population was confined to the north shore of Long Island or, at least, north of the terminal moraine. It was known to have bred at the following localities: Queens Co.—(1) Flushing; (2) Jamaica. Nassau Co.—(3) Oyster Bay. Suffolk Co.—(4) Cold Spring Harbor; (5) Northport; (6) Miller's Place; (7) Orient; (8) Shelter Island; (9) Gardiner's Island. It was last known to breed on Long Island in 1926 at (7) Orient (Latham) in "oak woodland."

(b) Formerly common in the Hudson River lowlands of Westchester and Rockland counties, especially the former (Bull, 1964: 296–297). Note that all known breeding sites were within a few miles of the Hudson. Breeding (●) or summer (○) localities were: Staten Island (Richmond Co.)—(10) West New Brighton (1887)—today breeds south of the Raritan River in New Jersey (see map—⊗). New York Co.—(11) Central Park (at least until 1892). Westchester Co.—(12) near Riverdale; (13) Grassy Sprain (until 1925); (14) Dobbs Ferry; (15) Ossining; (16) Croton Lake. Rockland Co.—(17) Nyack; (18) Lake DeForest (1957) —for details of unsuccessful nesting, see Bull (*op. cit.,* 297). Dutchess Co.—(19) Poughkeepsie (1913). Ulster Co.—(20) Rondout Creek near West Shokan (1957)—Hough and Smiley reported two singing birds on June 15 in mature beech-maple forest at about 1200 feet, but no proof of breeding was obtained. Note that 1957 was the year of the abortive breeding in Rockland Co., as well as the only recent New York summer occurrences since 1926.

(c) Only two certain breeding records from this area: Tompkins Co.—(21) near Ithaca (1913)—later reports of breeding there not substantiated. Ontario Co.—(22) Canandaigua. Also summer occurrences for Schuyler Co.—(23) Watkins Glen, two singing birds, June 24, 1954 (Carleton). Chemung Co.—(24) Lowman, a singing bird in June of 1945 and 1946 (Axtell). With the exception of the breeding pair at (22) Canandaigua, which probably arrived by way of the Lake Ontario plain, the three others may have come from Pennsylvania from the south by way of the river valleys.

(d): Cayuga Co.—(25) Meridian; (26) Fair Haven. Monroe Co.—(27) near Rochester (1909); (28) Chili (1900). Orleans Co.—(29) Barre Center; (30) Medina. Niagara Co.—(31) Lockport; (32) Wilson.

Note that no known breeding occurrence in the state has taken place since 1957 and that was an abortive attempt. No proved breeding has occurred in extreme western New York in more than 60 years, and yet the species breeds regularly in extreme southern Ontario along the *north* shore of Lake Erie from Point Pelee and Rondeau Park east to Abino Bay, the last-named locality only ten miles west of Buffalo (see map—⊗).

Acadian Flycatchers nest from about three to ten feet above ground in deep, shady, moist or dry, deciduous forest, in wooded ravines, and along stream bottoms. Beech and formerly chestnut forest with extensive undergrowth were frequented.

In eight New York nests examined, seven contained three eggs and one held four.

EGG DATES: May 28 to July 4.

No New York information is available on nestling or fledgling dates.

Postscript: An abortive nesting occurred on eastern Long Island in 1972 near Noyack, Suffolk Co. (Puleston and Raynor). The unfinished nest was deserted.

Traill's Flycatcher
(*Empidonax traillii*)   *   B

Willow Flycatcher
(*E. traillii*)   *   B

Alder Flycatcher
(*E. alnorum*)   *   B

Range: Nearctic region, breeding from Alaska and Canada to southwestern United States; in the east, in the mountains to northern Georgia and along the coast to New Jersey. Winters from Mexico to Argentina.

Status: Fairly common fall coastal migrant, as proved by banding. Fairly common to locally common breeder statewide, least numerous on Long Island.

Nonbreeding: This complex, considered as one species in the last A.O.U. Check-list (1957), but probably consisting of two extremely similar (sibling) species, may be identified positively in the field only when singing, which happens on rare occasions in spring. The following data are based on singing birds, banding records, and collected specimens. Traill's Flycatchers are among the latest of spring migrants (see maxima, below).

Thanks to modern methods of capturing *Empidonax* flycatchers with mist nets, and by checking wing formulae in the hand, we have more detailed information on relative abundance and peak dates than was formerly possible.

MAXIMA, COASTAL: *Fall*—nine netted and banded, Tobay Sanctuary, Jones Beach area, Aug. 28, 1966 (Davis and Schaeffer); 11 netted and banded, Fire Island State Park, Suffolk Co., Sept. 1, 1970 (Buckley and Davis). *Spring*—ten netted and banded, Great Gull Island, Suffolk Co., June 6, 1970 (Parkes and Duffy). Note especially the lateness of the spring migration.

EXTREME DATES: May 11 (coastal—singing bird) to Sept. 23 (inland specimen) and Sept. 26 (coastal specimen). Rare before late May and after early September.

The early dates of May 4, 5, 6, as given in Beardslee and Mitchell (1965: 306), are not

Fig. 69 St. Regis River, between Madawaska and Santa Clara, Franklin Co., August 1969. Stream bordered by alders; breeding habitat of Traill's Flycatcher ("fee-be-o" song type). Photo by Gordon Meade

supported by either specimens or singing birds, for these authorities state that, "We cannot determine whether they were based on vocal records or not."

Breeding: Traill's Flycatcher (in the broad sense) breeds from the cold, boreal, tree-lined bogs and swamps of the high altitude Adirondack Mountains ("fee-bee-o" song type) (see Fig. 69) to the hot, coastal thickets among sand dunes adjacent to salt marsh at sea level on Long Island ("fitz-bew" song type). Thus, it is today far and away the most widespread breeder in the state among the members of the singularly difficult genus *Empidonax*. This latter area is, however, represented by a recent eastward penetration of range from the midwestern prairie "fitz-bew" breeding population.

Perhaps the first field ornithologists in New York to distinguish two song types in the state were: (1) C. J. Spiker (1931: 57), who was familiar with the "fee-bee-o" song type in the mountains, recognized the other song type

nesting at Peterboro, Madison Co., in 1927 in "brush-grown areas of the open marshes, showing a preference for the alder, willow, aspen, and dogwood growths." He said that they called " 'Fitzhugh' or 'vitzyeou' the first syllable strongly accented." This is quite clearly the equivalent of the more usual current verbalization, "fitz-bew." (2) Roger Peterson (1934) who stated that, "The regular song in New York . . . is a three-syllabled *wee-be-o* with a hoarse burry quality, the accent on the middle syllable. The Ohio bird contracts this into a sneezy *fitz-bew* . . . as distinctly different as that of any other two species of the genus." Peterson (oral comm.) learned these two song types near his boyhood home of Jamestown, in the southwestern portion of the state—nearest to the Ohio population mentioned above.

Peterson further stated (*in litt.*), "I collected three 'fitz-bew' birds in the extreme southwestern tip of New York on the shore of

Lake Erie at Ripley, Chautauqua Co., and three hill-country birds of the other song type near Jamestown, and submitted them to John Aldrich [then at the Cleveland Museum] for examination. He [Aldrich] at a much later date identified them as being of two different forms." Aldrich (1951) used these specimens in his discussion of the various races. "It was this distinction of two song types that later stimulated Stein [1958, 1963] to engage in field and laboratory studies of these birds" (Peterson, oral comm.).

Collectively—both song types—nest from one to eight feet above ground in various shrubs; in New York most often in hawthorn (11), viburnum (nine), spiraea (six), and buttonbush (six). Alder, dogwood, willow and numerous other types are used as well.

Ecologically they are very tolerant, breeding in bogs, swamps, brushy meadows, moist open pastures, thickets, dry fields and hillsides, and even open young pine plantings.

Egg clutches in 52 New York nests were equally divided: three and four eggs in 26 nests apiece.

EGG DATES: June 11 to July 29.

Nestlings: June 21 to Aug. 14; fledglings: July 11 to Aug. 24.

According to Stein (1958) the incubation period in five nests was from 12 to 14 days. He found that, on the whole, "fitz-bews" nested earlier than "fee-bee-o's." In the Ithaca area he was told by Arthur A. Allen that only "fee-bee-o's" were present prior to 1940, but that shortly thereafter the area was infiltrated by "fitz-bews," and that, especially since 1950, the former was being displaced by the latter.

According to collectors and observers familiar with both song types, "fee-bee-o's" in New York are largely restricted as breeders to montane or hill country ("Canadian zone") areas, especially the Adirondacks, Tug Hill Plateau, Catskills, and generally northward, where there are streams and lakes in wooded areas. "Fitz-bews," on the other hand, breed mostly at lower elevations, particularly the Hudson valley, the lake plains, and the valleys of the southern tier and southwestern portions, in the more open brushy areas with grassland type habitat; on Long Island only the "fitz-bew" has been recorded breeding.

"Fitz-bews" have nested at least as far north as southern Saratoga Co.—not far from Albany; "fee-bee-o's" as far south as the Hudson Highlands of Rockland and Orange counties—in the Bear Mountain-Harriman Park section. At both of these localities, the opposite song types predominate. Both song types are sympatric also at and near such places as Ithaca, and certain portions of the following counties—Erie, Cattaraugus, Onondaga, and Delaware—to name a few—all areas which have varied habitats suitable for both song types.

For further details of breeding status in the New York City region, see Bull (1964: 298, and 1970: 29).

Remarks: It should be stressed that the two song types discussed above very likely represent *two* sympatric sibling species, following Stein's investigations (1958, 1963), a summary of which is found in Bull (1964: 299–300).

Suffice it to say here that for those who recognize *two* species of Traill's Flycatcher, appropriate vernacular names suggested by Stein (*op. cit.*) for the two song types are: Willow Flycatcher (=fitz-bew); Alder Flycatcher (=fee-bee-o). As to scientific species names, Eugene Eisenmann (unpublished paper delivered at the 1969 A.O.U. meeting) has investigated this matter, and states that *E. traillii* and *E. alnorum* are the correct specific names for "fitz-bew" and "fee-bee-o" respectively.

Needless to state, the field observer is cautioned about differentiating as to song type those individuals singing on the breeding grounds, unless thoroughly familiar with *both* song types.

For banders, the only safe procedure is to identify birds in the hand as merely Traill's Flycatchers—*Empidonax traillii* (*sensu lato*). As to the difficulties involved, see Phillips, Howe, and Lanyon (1966, 1970).

The A.O.U. Check-list Committee has voted to recognize two species (*Auk*, 1973, 90: 411–419). The "fitz-bew" or prairie breeding populations will bear the species name *E. traillii* (Audubon), and the English name Willow Flycatcher. The "fee-bee-o" or northern, Canadian zone breeding populations will bear the species name *E. alnorum* Brewster, and the English name Alder Flycatcher. When circumstances do not permit identification of the two species or, if an author does not consider the two of species rank, the name Traill's Flycatcher can continue to be used in the broad sense to embrace both.

Least Flycatcher
(Empidonax minimus) * B

Range: North America, breeding from central Canada south and east to the edge of the coastal plain in southeastern New York (Long and Staten islands) and central New Jersey (Princeton); in the mountains to northern Georgia. Winters in Middle America from Mexico to Panama.

Status: Fairly common migrant. Widespread breeder, but on Long Island restricted to the north shore where it is local.

Nonbreeding: This is the earliest species of the genus to arrive in spring. Because of the difficulty in field identification of the species of *Empidonax,* except when in song or as otherwise noted, dates of occurrence and maximum numbers are listed only when birds are either collected, or banded and carefully measured with wing formulae noted.

MAXIMA: *Fall*—four each netted and banded on Aug. 19, 1964, and Aug. 25, 1963, at Huntington, Suffolk Co. (Lanyon); 13 netted and banded, Fire Island State Park, Suffolk Co., Sept. 1, 1970 (Buckley and Davis).

EXTREME DATES: Apr. 20 (coastal) and Apr. 24 (inland) to Oct. 4 (coastal specimen) and Oct. 9 (coastal banding); exceptionally to Nov. 8, 1970, Fire Island (specimen—verified by Lanyon), AMNH collection. Sight reports through October but the species is in doubt. Usually rare before May.

Breeding: The Least Flycatcher nests in shade trees along roadsides and about farms, in orchards, and woodland borders. In the mountains it is more an inhabitant of open woodland, and in old "burns" and clearings in the forest. Peakall and Rusk (*Kingbird,* 1963, 13: 218) called it the "commonest flycatcher of the taller deciduous woods of the Tug Hill —a count of 35 per seven miles there June 28." In 1970 Scheider found it more than twice as numerous there, estimating *80* within the same distance.

It is a local breeder on the north shore of Long Island, from west to east as follows:

Queens Co.—Flushing (Kissena Park); Nassau Co.—Manhasset, Oyster Bay, Syosset, Woodbury; Suffolk Co.—Cold Spring Harbor, Lloyd's Neck, Northport, Miller's Place, Greenport, Gardiner's Island, Fisher's Island, and at Manorville—halfway between the north and south shores.

Although it has been stated (Bull, 1964: 301) that this species is not known to nest on Staten Island, there is, in fact, a nest and three eggs in the AMNH collection, 14617, taken at Egbertville, Staten Island, June 17, 1905 (Chapin), apparently not published previously.

All of the above records are at or near the known southern breeding limits on the Atlantic coastal plain.

Least Flycatchers nest in trees, mostly deciduous, from 12 to 35 feet up. Egg clutches in ten New York nests: three eggs (three nests); four eggs (six nests); five eggs (one nest).

EGG DATES: May 16 to June 28.

Nestlings: June 22 to Aug. 6; fledglings: July 8 to Aug. 16.

Eastern Wood Pewee
(Contopus virens) * B

Range: Eastern North America, breeding from southern Canada to the Gulf states. Winters from Costa Rica to Peru.

Status: Fairly common migrant, occasionally more numerous. Widespread breeder.

Nonbreeding: During the migrations this species is found throughout, even along the outer coast, wherever there are trees or even clumps of scrub vegetation.

MAXIMA: *Spring*—20, Sandy Pond, Oswego Co., May 20, 1969; 12, Prospect Park, Brooklyn, June 3, 1945.

MAXIMA: *Fall*—27, Fish Gulf, near Otisco Lake, Onondaga Co., Sept. 18, 1968; 15, Far Rockaway, Queens Co., Sept. 21, 1952.

EXTREME DATES: May 2 (coastal) to Oct. 30 and Nov. 15 (coastal specimens). Rare before mid-May and after early October.

April sight reports are highly suspect and are very likely misidentified Least Flycatchers.

A specimen mist-netted and collected at Fire Island, Suffolk Co., Nov. 15, 1969 (Davis),

AMNH 793548, is definitely the eastern form (*virens*) and was determined as such by the writer; identification confirmed by W. E. Lanyon and L. L. Short.

Breeding: The adaptable Eastern Wood Pewee breeds in mature forest and open woodland, both deciduous and coniferous, and is found nesting also in orchards, and in large shade trees in city parks and along village streets.

The nest is placed at heights varying from seven to 40 feet. Eleven New York nests contained clutches of three eggs (eight nests) and four eggs (three nests).

EGG DATES: May 30 to July 20 and Aug. 6. The date of Sept. 8 for eggs given in Beardslee and Mitchell (1965: 308) is almost certainly an error.

Nestlings: June 22 to Aug. 13; fledglings: Aug. 31.

Remarks: Some authorities consider this form and the Western Wood Pewee (*C. sordidulus*) conspecific, but extensive field studies in the contact zone are necessary before a sound decision can be made.

Olive-sided Flycatcher
(*Contopus borealis*)   *   B

Range: Nearctic region, breeding from Alaska and Canada to southwestern United States; in the east, to the higher mountains south to Massachusetts, southeastern New York, and Pennsylvania; locally to the Great Smokies in Tennessee and North Carolina. Winters in the mountains of northwestern South America.

Status: Regular but uncommon migrant, more numerous in fall, especially on the coast. Fairly common breeder in the higher mountains, but local and uncommon to rare in the Catskills.

Nonbreeding: Olive-sided Flycatchers prefer the uppermost dead branches of tall trees, darting out for insect prey. They are, therefore, more conspicuous than Wood Pewees which usually stay below the canopy and within the foliage.

MAXIMA: *Fall*—all coastal—five, Prospect Park, Brooklyn, Aug. 19, 1944; six, Far Rockaway, Queens Co., Sept. 10, 1969; three collected, Ossining, Westchester Co., Sept. 15, 1879, specimens, MCZ collection.

EXTREME DATES: *Spring*—May 4 (inland specimen) and May 8 (coastal) to June 12 (coastal).

EXTREME DATES: *Fall*—July 27 and Aug. 3 (both coastal) to Sept. 26 (coastal specimen) and several early October dates (coastal and inland).

Usually rare before late May and after mid-September. Birds seen in April and after early October are probably misidentified Phoebes, and/or Wood Pewees in the latter month.

Breeding (see Map 95): This species is a fairly common breeder over much of the Adirondacks and is not rare in the Tug Hill district to the west. It is much less numerous and more local in the higher Catskills. Of the last-named area, Hough (*in litt.*) states that it is "not common" and "occurs in montane environment of cool, deep ravines at the edge of and within the coniferous zone. It favors tall, partially dead balsam and spruce trees at the edge of the forest."

Six Adirondack nests were equally divided between spruce and balsam; four bog nests contained *Usnea* lichen in their construction, the other two in forest openings near bogs or swamps lacked the "beard moss." The nests were from 25 to 45 feet above ground.

All six nests contained three eggs apiece.

EGG DATES: June 9 to June 27.

Nestlings: June 22; fledglings: July 10 to July 24.

The accompanying map shows general distribution within the Adirondack State Park, several localities at its southern limits, and all known breeding localities in the Tug Hill and Catskill districts. Two other localities on the map outside the above areas, indicated by open circles, are presumed breeding sites only.

Eaton (1914: 190) mentioned the east end of Oneida Lake and the vicinity of Albany as nesting localities of this species, but no details were given.

An even more unlikely breeding locality at a low elevation in the Hudson valley (Newburgh, Orange Co. area), with unsuitable habitat, was included by Bull (1964: 302). More than likely Wood Pewees were involved.

MAP 95 Olive-sided
Flycatcher (*Contopus
borealis*) Breeding
distribution

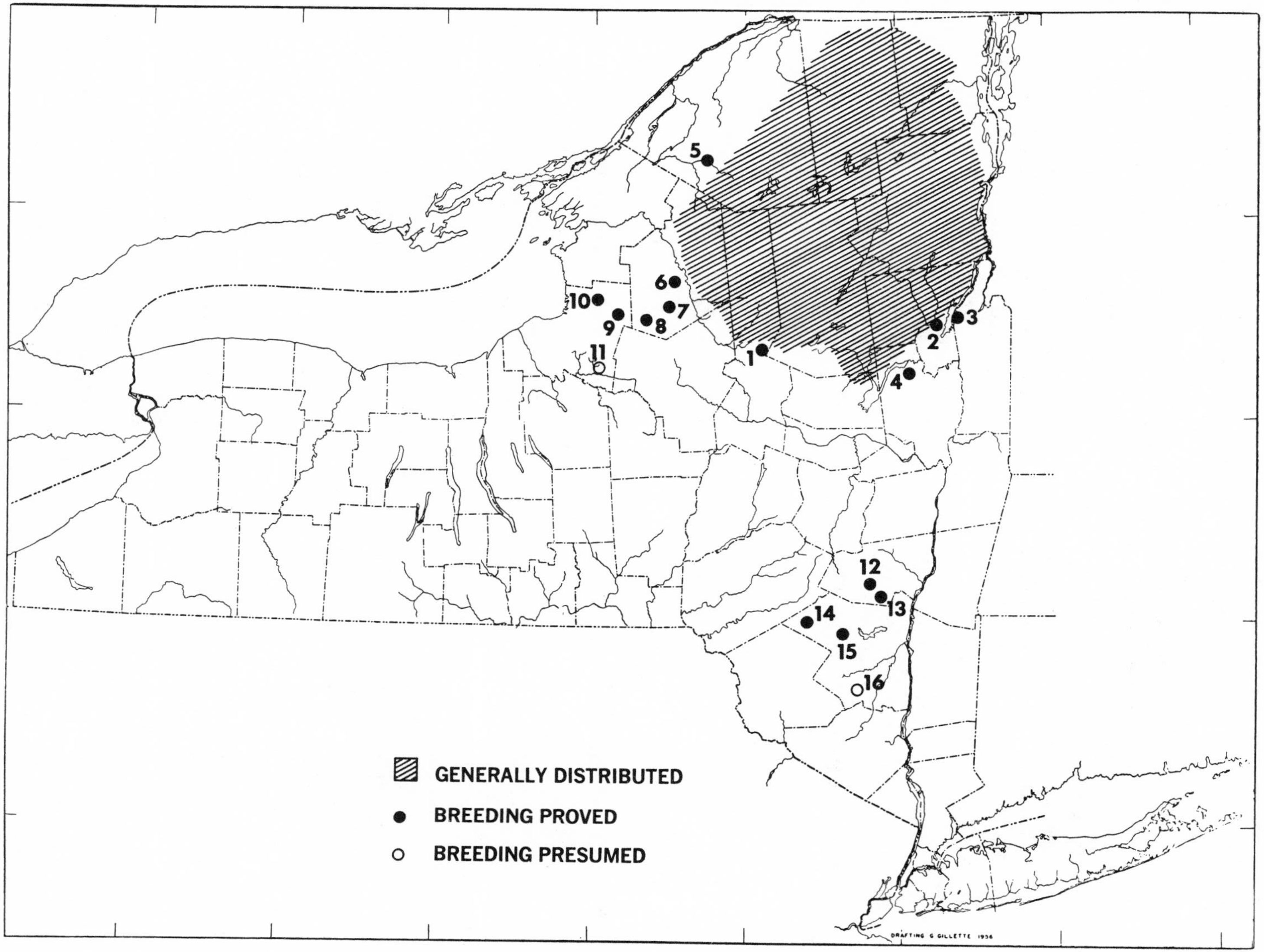

GENERALLY DISTRIBUTED

● BREEDING PROVED

○ BREEDING PRESUMED

The 16 specific localities on the accompanying map are: (A) Adirondack district—Herkimer Co.—(1) Wilmurt. Warren Co.—(2) Warrensburg. Washington Co.—(3) Pilot Knob, Lake George. Saratoga Co.—(4) Jenny Lake. St. Lawrence Co.—(5) Edwards.

(B) Tug Hill district—Lewis Co.—(6) Whetstone Gulf; (7) near Highmarket and nearby Michigan Mills; (8) near Osceola. Oswego Co. (9) near Redfield; (10) Boylston; (11) near Constantia, Oneida Lake—breeding *not* proved.

(C) Catskill district—Greene Co.—(12) Hunter Mtn.; (13) Plateau Mtn. Ulster Co.—

(14) Balsam Round Top Mtn.; (15) Slide Mtn. and nearby Cornell Mtn.; (16) near Lake Awosting—breeding *not* proved.

Remarks: Mayr and Short (1970: 60) are followed here in merging the monotypic genus "*Nuttallornis*" with *Contopus* (the pewees). The Olive-sided Flycatcher (*C. borealis*) especially resembles *C. pertinax*—ranging from southwestern United States to Nicaragua, the latter considered by several authorities to be conspecific with the wide-ranging *C. fumigatus* (Greater Pewee), extending south to northern Argentina.

LARKS — ALAUDIDAE

One species in New York.
One breeds.

This almost exclusively Old World family (75± species) is represented in America by the Horned Lark (*Eremophila alpestris*). This species occurs south to Mexico, with an isolated population in the mountains of Colombia. It is widespread also in the northern portions of the Old World. Another species, the introduced Skylark (*Alauda arvensis*), is no longer found in New York.

Horned Larks are familiar birds in the state, one race breeding in suitable habitat over much of the state, another subspecies from the north wintering with us, occasionally in very large flocks. They are birds of open country, nesting on the ground.

Horned Lark
(*Eremophila alpestris*) * B

Range: Holarctic region; isolated population near Bogotá, Colombia. For details, see **Subspecies.** Sedentary and migratory.

Status: Very common to abundant migrant and winter visitant. Locally common breeder statewide.

Nonbreeding: Large roving flocks of Horned Larks may be seen from November to March both along the outer coast and at many inland points, especially near the Great Lakes. They favor open agricultural country where both plowed and uncultivated fields are found; also beaches, golf courses, airports, bare ground with scattered vegetation, and short grass fields.

MAXIMA: 1000, Montauk, Suffolk Co., Nov. 7, 1924; 900, Sandy Pond, Oswego Co., Nov. 16, 1957; 1500, Orient, Suffolk Co., Dec. 27, 1934; 700, Syracuse, Feb. 12, 1956; 800, Jones Beach, Mar. 11, 1956.

Breeding: Horned Larks nest on the ground where suitable open terrain exists, such as airports, golf courses, fields, pastures, sandy areas, and barren wastes. When much of the forest was cleared by the middle of the nineteenth century, these birds took advantage of the newly created openings, and moved from the prairie regions of Ohio and Ontario eastward into New York.

The first definite breeding record for New York was in 1875 when a nest with eggs was found near Buffalo. The following year the Horned Lark nested near Rochester and even as far east as the Black River region near

Lowville, Lewis Co. By 1879 it had reached western Long Island where young birds were collected at Long Island City, Queens Co. It was recorded in the Albany area in 1881 and had penetrated the eastern Adirondacks by 1900, where it was reported at Jay, Essex Co. By 1905 it was breeding in extreme northeastern New York at Rouses Point, Clinton Co., near the Canadian border. Today it breeds in virtually every county of the state.

Eggs have been found in stubble fields of wheat and rye, in newly planted corn, among young tomato, potato, and strawberry plants, on overturned sod clumps, bare ground, gravel road shoulders, sand dunes with beach grass, and on the short-grass strips of airports and golf links.

Egg clutches in 67 New York nests: three eggs (28 nests); four eggs (31 nests); five eggs (eight nests).

EGG DATES: Feb. 28 to July 31.

Nestlings: Mar. 11 to Aug. 4; fledglings: Mar. 31 to Sept. 13. The species is believed to be triple-brooded. It certainly is the earliest passerine to nest and has a long breeding season. According to Pickwell (1931), incubation takes 11 days.

Subspecies: The geographical and individual variation in this species is very great and like other widespread continental forms there is a blending of races (clines) from region to region with the result that a number of populations with intermediate characters would be better off unnamed. Such a population is *"hoyti,"* not recognized here.

Two races occur in New York: (1) nominate *alpestris* which breeds southeast to east-central Ontario, southeastern Quebec, and islands in the Gulf of St. Lawrence. This is the race which is highly migratory and winters in large numbers, especially in the coastal districts.

(2) The well-marked race *praticola* (much paler than the preceding, the superciliary whitish instead of yellow) is the local breeding population which has spread eastward and southward, ranging in the east from Nova Scotia to North Carolina and inland from southeastern Ontario to northern Alabama. This subspecies is at least partially sedentary as proved by banding. As discussed above, *praticola* has greatly spread over the state within a century.

Skylark (*Alauda arvensis*) * B

Range: Palearctic region, introduced into Long Island, Vancouver Island, Hawaii, and New Zealand.

Status: *Introduced*—the Skylark, a bird of open grassland, was introduced in 1887 into Brooklyn, especially the sections of Flatbush and Flatlands. It was well established by 1898 and was still present in numbers in 1907. However, destruction of open land throughout this area caused it to disappear by 1913.

Three specimens, all extant, were taken in Flatbush: two fledglings in 1887, one on June 13, the other on July 1; and an adult on Feb. 22, 1888 (all by Marshall), are AMNH 68248, 68249, and 65319. In addition, a nest and eggs were collected on July 28, 1895 (Proctor), AMNH collection. On July 14, 1887, Marshall found a nest in Flatbush that contained five half-grown young being fed by an adult. The nest was situated in a tuft of grass in a "long-grass field."

Birds liberated in the Hudson valley failed.

SWALLOWS — HIRUNDINIDAE

Six species in New York.
Six breed.

This compact cosmopolitan family (80± species) occurs nearly everywhere except in the polar regions and on some Pacific islands.

Like the swifts, these birds obtain their food —flying insects—entirely on the wing. More than any other family in New York, all six species wholly or partially depend on man for nest sites. Buildings are used by Barn and Cliff swallows (*Hirundo rustica* and *H. pyr-*

rhonota). Birdhouses are utilized by Tree Swallows and Purple Martins (*Tachycineta bicolor* and *Progne subis*), although the former species also nests in holes in dead trees. Bank Swallows (*Riparia riparia*) nest in cutbanks, and Rough-winged Swallows (*Stelgidopteryx ruficollis*) breed there also and, in addition, lay their eggs in pipes, culverts, and crevices in stone walls.

Tree Swallow
(*Tachycineta bicolor*)   *   B

Range: North America, breeding from Alaska and Canada—in the west, south to southern California—in the east only to Virginia. In the east winters along the coast north to Long Island occasionally and to Massachusetts rarely.

Status: Common to very abundant migrant, especially in fall along the outer coast. Usually rare in winter on the coast, but occasional flocks are reported; much rarer inland. Widespread breeder, especially northward.

Nonbreeding: The following is taken from Bull (1964: 304–305)—"The first swallow to arrive in spring—regularly by late March, sometimes earlier. The first and last to depart in fall, one of the first birds to move south, regularly by the first week in July; the fall migration is of long duration—into early November, or even later. On the coast, it is regular into December.

"Occurs in truly extraordinary numbers in fall on the outer coast; perhaps one of the most abundant birds in our area. At times it literally swarms by the thousands, certainly one of the most spectacular events of the fall migration. The height of this movement is from late August to the middle of September. On the south shore of Long Island, estimates of 50,000 to 100,000 or more are frequently noted."

MAXIMA, INLAND: *Fall*—11,000, Sandy Pond, Oswego Co., Aug. 11, 1957; 15,000, Waterloo, Seneca Co., Oct. 10, 1968.

MAXIMA, INLAND: *Spring*—1000, Castile, Wyoming Co., Apr. 9, 1951; 12,000, Montezuma Marshes, Apr. 26, 1961.

The earliest known spring arrival date inland is Mar. 12.

Winter: Along the coast Tree Swallows are reported every month of the year. In winter these birds feed extensively on bayberries and are rare to absent when the crop is poor.

MAXIMA: *Coastal*—73, Montauk, Suffolk Co., Dec. 30, 1966; 100+, Oak Beach, Suffolk Co., winter of 1950–1951.

MAXIMA: *Inland*—12, Montezuma Marshes, Jan. 20, 1967 (most exceptional).

Breeding: Tree Swallows breed in a variety of situations—most often in holes in dead trees and stubs near lakes and in wooded swamps; in nest boxes erected specifically for Tree Swallows, but also in Purple Martin and Bluebird houses; occasionally in dock pilings, in metal pipes (including those on a "moving ferryboat," *Auk*, 1942, 59: 437), in a mailbox, once in an opening in an unused fire hydrant only a few feet from the ground; and according to Colonel L. R. Wolfe (*Auk*, 1923, 40: 623)—on the Four Brothers Islands in Lake Champlain—several nests in "cavities behind roots in upturned trees," and "behind loose pieces of shale along the banks and just over the water."

Egg clutches in 55 New York nests varied from three eggs (perhaps incomplete sets) to eight eggs: three eggs (five nests); four eggs (nine nests); five eggs (21 nests); six eggs (15 nests); seven eggs (four nests); eight eggs (one nest).

EGG DATES: May 5 to June 29.

Nestlings: May 22 to July 14; fledglings: June 14 to July 27.

Banding: A juvenile banded in Massachusetts was trapped in New York 11 years later. Another juvenile banded during the summer of 1956 at Oneida Lake was recovered the following winter near Boca Raton, Florida.

Remarks: Here placed in the genus *Tachycineta* following Peters (1960: 81), as it is considered closely related to the western Violetgreen Swallow (*T. thalassina*), as well as to several other members of the genus in tropical America. *"Iridoprocne"* is thus considered to be a synonym.

Bank Swallow
(*Riparia riparia*) * B

Range: Holarctic region, in eastern North America breeding in the mountains south to the Carolinas, on the coast to Virginia. Winters in South America.

Status: Very abundant migrant inland, much less numerous along the coast. Widespread, but local breeder.

Nonbreeding: This species is especially numerous in fall on the Lake Ontario plain, as may be seen from the following concentrations:

MAXIMA: *Spring*—9000, Derby Hill, Oswego Co., Apr. 26, 1960; 8000, Montezuma Marshes, May 6, 1961; 5000, Derby Hill, May 19, 1959.

MAXIMA: *Fall*—10,000, Montezuma, July 10, 1964 (Benning); 27,000, Manitou, Monroe Co., July 26, 1969 (Listman); 15,000, Sandy Pond, Oswego Co., Aug. 11, 1957 (Scheider); 1350, same locality, Sept. 5, 1965.

An estimate of 400, Jones Beach, Long Island, Aug. 28, 1953, is the highest known coastal figure.

EXTREME DATES: Apr. 2 (coastal and inland) to Oct. 11 (coastal) and Oct. 24 (inland).

Rare before late April and after mid-September.

Breeding: The Bank Swallow or, as it is called in the Old World, Sand Martin, is a colonial breeder, nesting in sand or clay banks and gravel pits, usually but not always near water, often in road cuts or, on rare occasions, even in piles of hardened sawdust or coal dust.

Several colonies in the interior of the state contained from as many as 500 to 800 nest holes apiece, with one colony near Falconer, Chautauqua Co., reported to have as many as 1000 nesting pairs in 1956 (Beal). Another near Sandy Pond, Oswego Co., was estimated to contain at least 2000 pairs in 1966 (Barker).

On eastern Long Island, Latham estimated 350 nest holes in a bluff on the seaward side of Gardiner's Island in 1936.

In his extensive studies of the Oneida Lake colonies, Stoner (1936) found the largest numbers concentrated along steep, sandy banks of creeks and streams.

On the basis of his banded birds, relatively few pairs were double-brooded. He also determined that the incubation period was from 14 to 16 days.

Egg clutches in 22 New York nests ranged from three to six eggs: three eggs (one nest); four eggs (four nests); five eggs (15 nests); six eggs (two nests).

EGG DATES: May 15 to July 13 (second brood).

Nestlings: May 31 to Aug. 12 (second brood); fledglings: June 28 to Sept. 1.

Rough-winged Swallow
(*Stelgidopteryx ruficollis*) * B

Range: Nearctic and Neotropical regions, from Argentina north to southern Canada in the west—in the east locally to the St. Lawrence valley; west-central New Brunswick (1969). Rare, but has increased recently northeastward. Winters north to southern United States as far as coastal South Carolina. The local breeding race is *serripennis* (considerably darker than *psammochrous* of southwestern United States and northern Mexico).

Status: Rare to uncommon migrant along the coast, but variously fairly common inland to even locally abundant in western New York. Local breeder at lower elevations, but uncommon northward and on the coastal plain.

Nonbreeding: This species is surprisingly scarce where it does not nest, as along the south shore of Long Island. Inland numbers range from 20 to 40 or so, chiefly in late April or May.

MAXIMA, INLAND: *Spring*—25, Lake View, Erie Co., Apr. 15, 1961; the following numbers, all at Derby Hill, Oswego Co.—500, Apr. 26, 1960; 1000, May 1, 1967 (Scheider); 500, May 16, 1966.

MAXIMA, INLAND: *Fall*—the following numbers on the Niagara River, near Buffalo—500, Oct. 10, 1948; 150, Oct. 17, 1948.

EXTREME DATES: Mar. 24 (coastal) and Mar. 31 (inland) to Sept. 10 (coastal) and Oct. 30 (inland). Rare before mid-April; in fall it is rare on the coast after mid-August, but inland it remains well into October (see above numbers). Mitchell took a specimen near Buffalo on Oct. 11, 1931, BMS 1737.

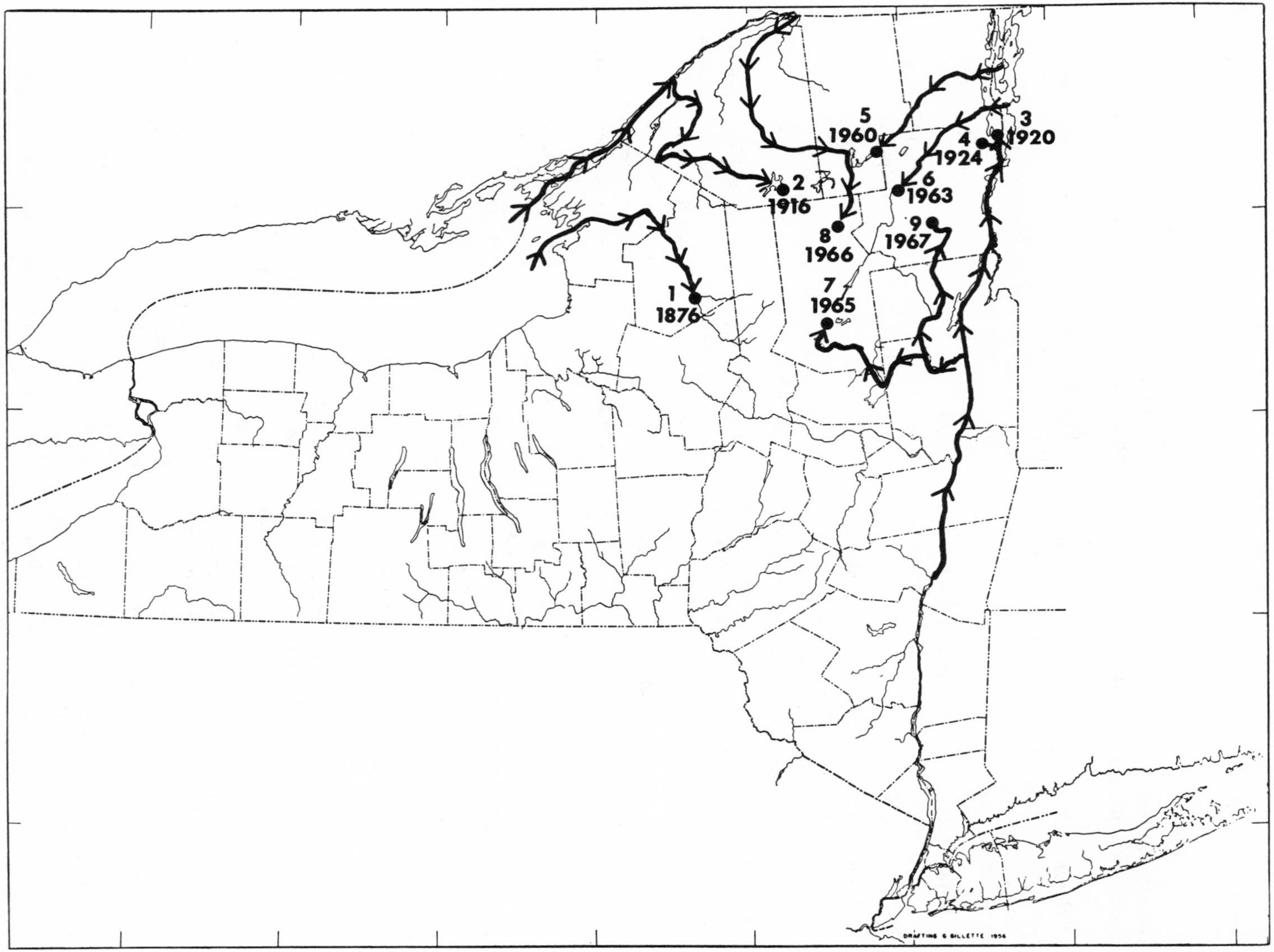

MAP 96 Rough-winged Swallow (*Stelgidopteryx ruficollis*)—Postulated arrival routes by rivers to known northern breeding limits. Years indicate first known breeding occurrences at specified localities.

It is surprising to note the great difference in time of fall departure of this species in the southeastern portion of the state, where it is one of the earliest birds to depart, as compared with western New York, although this may be partly related to its much greater abundance in the latter area.

Breeding (see Map 96): The Rough-winged Swallow was unknown to both DeKay (1844) and Giraud (1844). In fact it was unrecorded from the state prior to 1870. The first known breeding records came from the lower Hudson valley and Long Island in 1872. Just four years later the first definite report of breeding in northern New York was that of a recently fledged juvenile collected along the Black River at (1) Lyon's Falls, Lewis Co., July 26, 1876 (A. J. Dayan), USNM collection (see map).

By the 1880s this species had penetrated the Hudson-Mohawk valley as far north as the south end of Lake George, Warren Co., and to Trenton Falls, Oneida Co. It had also come into the state from the west via the Great Lakes, nesting in Buffalo by 1889 and extending northeastward to the St. Lawrence River by the early 1890s or before (but see 1876 Black River locality on accompanying map).

At the turn of the century Rough-winged Swallows were found nearly statewide, even to the edge of the mountains. Silloway (1923: 454) found a nest as early as 1916 at (2) Barber Point, Cranberry Lake, St. Lawrence Co. (probably by way of the Oswegatchie River). Nests were discovered in the Lake Champlain region on (3) the Four Brothers Islands in 1920 and at (4) Long Pond in 1924, both these localities in eastern Essex Co. (see map).

Eaton's breeding map (1910: 24) shows western Essex and Hamilton counties included in the range, but he gives no particulars as to years or localities.

Today the Rough-winged Swallow breeds in practically all of the river valleys and lake shores of the state, except those in the heart of the Catskill and Adirondack mountains. However, it breeds right up to their edges. For example, in 1960 a pair bred at the village of (5) Saranac Lake, Franklin Co. (via the Saranac River from Lake Champlain), and in 1963 another pair was present at (6) Heart Lake, Essex Co. (probably up the Ausable River from the same direction—see map).

Further recent breeding records from the Adirondacks show a still deeper penetration: 1965—(7) Piseco (via the Sacandaga River), and 1966—(8) Long Lake (by way of the Raquette River from the north), both in Hamilton Co.; 1967—(9) Elk Lake (up the Hudson and Schroon rivers) in Essex Co. (see map). In the last-named county the species had reached Lake Placid by 1968.

This species prefers the vicinity of water but is by no means restricted to it. Unlike the Bank Swallow, it is not a colonial breeder but rather nests singly or in small aggregations. It is, however, much more of a diversified breeder than that species, not only nesting in sand banks—often in Bank Swallow colonies and sometimes in abandoned Belted Kingfisher holes—but also in gravel pits, shale cliffs, hardened sawdust piles, rock crevices, tile culverts, stone bridges, and metal drainpipes.

Beardslee and Mitchell (1965: 313) state that along the shore of Lake Erie, "where there are many shale cliffs, the Rough-winged Swallow is much more common [as a breeder] than the Bank Swallow."

Egg clutches in 20 New York nests ranged from three eggs (three nests) to eight eggs (one nest). The majority held five eggs (nine nests) and six eggs (seven nests).

EGG DATES: May 19 to July 5.

Nestlings: June 14 to July 11; fledglings: July 6 to July 28.

Barn Swallow
(*Hirundo rustica*) * B

Range: Holarctic region, the New World race *erythrogaster* (a well-marked race; compared to nominate *rustica* usually much darker below, chest band broken and narrow, and outermost rectrices much shorter) breeding from Alaska and Canada south to Mexico and the Gulf states. Winters chiefly in South America.

Status: Common to very abundant migrant. Widespread breeder.

Nonbreeding: The species is most numerous in late April, May, and August.

MAXIMA: *Spring*—12,000, Derby Hill, Oswego Co., Apr. 26, 1960; 4000, same locality, May 19, 1959.

MAXIMA: *Fall*—800, Orient, Suffolk Co., Aug. 1, 1965; 9000, Sandy Pond, Oswego Co., Aug. 17, 1957; 25,000, Jones Beach, Suffolk Co., Aug. 23, 1958 (Nisbet, *Kingbird,* 1959, 8: 111); 20,000 at roost, Clay Swamp, Onondaga Co., Aug. 24, 1965 (Propst).

EXTREME DATES: Mar. 15 (coastal) and Mar. 19 (inland) to Nov. 17 (inland) and Dec. 1 (coastal specimen); exceptionally to Dec. 19, 1937, Jones Beach (Cruickshank). Usually rare before mid-April and after October.

Breeding: Barn Swallows breed in open country, nesting on beams, rafters, and ledges of old buildings, barns, sheds—usually on the *insides* of these structures. The most unusual nest site reported in this state is located on a cliff ledge of shale outcrop, the actual nests about fifteen feet above the water. This site overlooks Lake Ontario about two miles west of Nine Mile Point, Oswego Co. (Rusk, *in litt.*)—see Fig. 70.

Egg clutches in 56 New York nests: three eggs (four nests—incomplete?); four eggs (17 nests); five eggs (31 nests); six eggs (four nests).

EGG DATES: May 11 to Aug. 3.

Nestlings: May 24 to Aug. 28; fledglings: June 25 to Sept. 22.

According to Saunders (1929: 408) the species is double-brooded at North Elba, Essex Co., and in the Elmira region may even be triple-brooded according to observers there, but this needs confirmation.

Banding (see Map 97): Two nestlings banded in New York in late July were recovered in Louisiana in early September following. Another nestling was shot in Mexico the following March (on return migration?). A most interesting recovery is that of an immature mist-netted and banded by Yunick in the Sche-

Fig. 70 Shale cliff ledges on Lake Ontario near Nine Mile Point, Oswego Co., late summer of 1967. Breeding site of Barn Swallows; actual nests were 15 feet above the water. Photo by Margaret Rusk

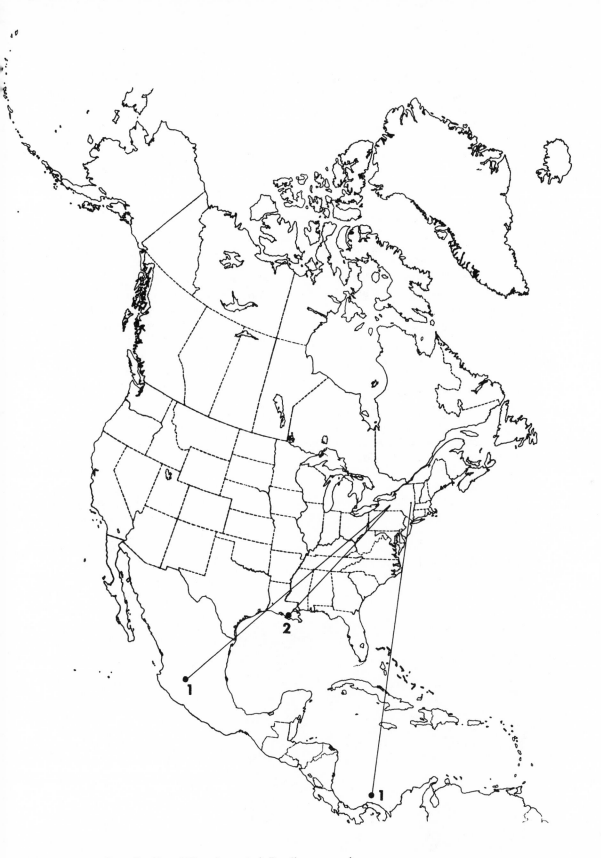

MAP 97 Barn Swallow (*Hirundo rustica*) Banding recoveries

nectady area on Aug. 29, 1964, and picked up aboard a ship off the Atlantic or Caribbean coast of Panama (at about 10° north latitude, 80° west longitude) on Oct. 12 following.

Cliff Swallow
(*Hirundo pyrrhonota*)   *   B

Range: Nearctic region, widely distributed in the west, breeding from Alaska to central Mexico; very local in the east, breeding from southern Canada to the mountains of North Carolina and near the coast to New Jersey, but absent from the coastal plain. Winters in southern South America.

Status: Rare to fairly common coastal migrant, infrequently occurring in large numbers; much more numerous in the interior but erratic. Locally common breeder upstate, especially in the mountains and at higher elevations, but rare southeastward; formerly more numerous and widespread.

Nonbreeding: This species is scarce where it does not breed, particularly along the coast. Large concentrations are recorded only from inland localities.

MAXIMA: *Spring*—125, Manitou, Monroe Co., May 2, 1964; 500, near Peekskill, Westchester Co., May 22, 1948 (Walsh), an unusual number *near* the coast.

MAXIMA: *Fall*—800, Cranberry Lake (village), St. Lawrence Co., Aug. 17, 1957; 1000, near Lake Placid, Essex Co., Aug. 19, 1940; 100, Manitou, Sept. 19, 1959. Note the large postbreeding concentrations at or near montane breeding localities.

EXTREME DATES: Mar. 27 and Apr. 4 (both inland) and Apr. 7 (coastal) to Oct. 11 (coastal) and Oct. 16 (inland); casual Nov. 5, 1963, Manitou (Listman). Generally rare before late April and after mid-September.

Breeding: Cliff swallows were formerly much more numerous throughout the state, at least in certain portions, although they seem to be common enough today in various upstate sections. Southeast of the Catskills, however, they have largely disappeared from many a former breeding locality and from Long Island where they have always been rare—last known breeding there 1924 at Cutchogue, Suffolk Co. (Bull, 1964: 308).

As is true over much of the breeding range the species was most numerous in mountainous sections. For instance, Trippe (*Amer. Nat.*, 1872, 6: 48) wrote that it was ". . . the commonest swallow in the Catskills, far outnumbering all the other species combined. It breeds in great numbers under the eaves of every barn and deserted house. In no other eastern locality have I noticed it in such great abundance as in these mountains."

However, in southwestern New York even within *recent* years, Saunders (1942: 194) called it our most common swallow, and S. W. Eaton (1953: 15), the most generally distributed swallow.

In addition to nesting under the eaves of wooden buildings, colonies have been found

Fig. 71 Cliff Swallow nest in active Bank Swallow colony, Powder Mill Park, Monroe Co., June 30, 1970. Photo by Reginald W. Hartwell

with their gourd-shaped nests on the stone-work of buildings, bridges, and dams. In New York the last report of nesting on cliffs that I am aware of was in 1932 near Cornwall, Orange Co. (Bull, 1964: 307).

Upward of 100 nests have been found on a single barn. Axtell (1945, 1947) has seen Cliff Swallows add material to, and nest successfully on, old nests of Robins and Phoebes. He stated that there were five factors responsible for re-ducing or limiting Cliff Swallow populations in western New York: (1) poor adhesion of nests on new or freshly painted barns; (2) destruc-tion of nests by misinformed farmers—fortu-nately in the great minority; (3) destruction of nests by Starlings; (4) eviction of rightful owners from their nests or the breaking of their eggs by House Sparrows; (5) prolonged cold or rainy spells during the nesting period.

On one barn in the Albany district, these swallows deserted when the barn was painted, but returned when wood strips were nailed several inches below the eaves.

At Prattsburg, Steuben Co., 36 artificial plas-ter nests placed under house eaves were used by these birds (*Kingbird*, 1964, 14: 141–143).

An unusual site was that of a single Cliff Swallow nest in the middle of an active Bank Swallow colony in a sandpit—see Fig. 71 (Davis, *Kingbird*, 1971, 21: 67). This was lo-cated at Powder Mill Park, Monroe Co., June 30, 1970.

Egg clutches examined in only nine New York nests were: four eggs (eight nests); five eggs (one nest).

EGG DATES: May 9 to July 14.

Nestlings: May 29 to Aug. 15; fledglings: June 23 to Aug. 23.

Banding: A nestling banded June 22, 1950, near Plattsburgh, Clinton Co., was recovered seven months later, Jan. 20, 1951, not far from the coastal city of Florianopolis, in the state of Santa Catarina, near extreme south-eastern Brazil.

Remarks: Here placed in the genus *Hirundo* following Mayr and Bond (*Ibis*, 1943: 334–341), and Vaurie (1959). The morphological differences separating *"Petrochelidon"* from *Hirundo* are here considered too slight to war-rant generic recognition of the former name. There is overlap in several characters, such as color, pattern, and tail shape. All members (23

species on a worldwide basis) are known to construct mud nests attached to rock surfaces or buildings.

Purple Martin (*Progne subis*)   *   B

Range: Nearctic region, breeding from southern Canada to northern Mexico and the Gulf states. Winters in South America.

Status: Variously rare to common migrant; locally very abundant in late summer roosts. Local but widespread breeder at lower eleva-tions. Absent in the higher mountains.

Nonbreeding: In many areas where this spe-cies does not breed it is usually a rare migrant. While numerous enough at times during the migrations, it is far and away most abundant at tree roosts in late August and early Septem-ber when really spectacular numbers may be observed flying in and settling down for the night.

MAXIMA: *Spring*—1000, Derby Hill, Os-wego Co., Apr. 26, 1960. *Fall*—2000, Lake Ronkonkoma, Suffolk Co., Aug. 30, 1952.

MAXIMA: *Roosts*—100,000, Strawberry Is-land, Niagara River, Aug. 30, 1970 (Axtell). These birds were seen flying west across the river into Canada. The following table vividly shows the enormous numbers present at the long-established roost at Jamestown, Chautau-qua Co., during 1960 when periodic estimates were made by Clarence Beal. Note especially the steady decrease every few days.

Date	Number	Date	Number
Aug. 29	100,000	Sept. 14	15,000
Sept. 2	75,000	Sept. 18	5,000
Sept. 9	30,000	Sept. 23	200

On the evening of Oct. 1, only a single bird was observed.

EXTREME DATES: *Casual*—Mar. 9, 1963, Montauk, Long Island (Puleston and Raynor), and Mar. 12 (coastal specimen); Mar. 21 (in-land) and Mar. 27 (coastal) to Oct. 9 (coastal) and Oct. 21 (inland). Rare before mid-April and after September.

Breeding: Although in prehistoric times the Purple Martin undoubtedly bred in hollow trees, and in suspended gourds before the advent of white men, I am not aware of their doing so today in New York. Prior to the introduction of the Starling, Purple Martins nested in wall crevices and building cornices in such cities as Buffalo, Rochester, Syracuse, and Utica, and occasionally still do so in Buffalo. But the multichambered birdhouses are most frequented by Purple Martins today and many a farmer and bird lover have erected martin houses on their grounds hoping to attract these useful and delightful birds (see Fig. 72). These birds are even nesting within the limits of New York City—on Staten Island at Princess Bay, near Lemon Creek, where Howard Cleaves has been watching their progress for many years (Bull, 1964: 310). According to Cleaves (*in litt.*) as many as 75 pairs nested in 1963; in 1970 there were 56 pairs.

One of the largest colonies in the state was that of more than 100 pairs nesting in a *230-room* house at Branchport, Yates Co., in 1960 (G. Sutherland).

These adaptable birds also nested 25 feet up on a crosspiece inside the shade of a street lamp at Oneida, Madison Co., in 1895 (Maxon, *Auk*, 1903, 20: 265), and 30 feet up in holes in grain elevators near Auburn, Cayuga Co., (Benton, 1949). In 1965 Carleton (*in litt.*) found 25 pairs nesting in holes under the eaves of an abandoned hotel at Speculator, Hamilton Co. Finally at Round Lake, Saratoga Co., one pair built a nest on the cylinder head at the entrance to the cowling of an airplane! A photograph of this unusual site is in *New York State Conservationist* (1956, 11: 34).

Egg clutches examined in only 13 New York nests were: three and four eggs (six nests each); five eggs (one nest).

EGG DATES: May 21 to July 13.

Fig. 72   Rome Sand Plains, Oneida Co., June 1969. Farm scene with Purple Martin nest box. Savannah and Vesper sparrows breed here also. Photo by Ken Hanson

Nestlings: June 22 to Aug. 15; fledglings: July 30 to Aug. 22.

Martins, being exclusively aerial insect feeders, are subject to severe mortality during extended periods of cold, wet weather, especially in April and May. The disastrous spring season of 1966 reduced populations in western New York by as much as 75% to 80% (Benton and Tucker, 1968: 751); see also Rusk (1964, 1967). Control of Starlings and House Sparrows in the vicinity of Purple Martin houses will insure success of occupancy by the desired swallows.

This species, although a statewide breeder, is virtually lacking from the higher Adirondacks and Catskills, and is absent from extensive areas elsewhere. In the Adirondacks, although it has nested at such montane localities as Ray Brook and Newcomb in Essex Co. and Speculator in Hamilton Co., nevertheless these localities are all at relatively low elevations.

JAYS, CROWS — CORVIDAE

Six species in New York.
Five breed.

This very adaptable and successful family (over 100 species) has succeeded in colonizing almost every major land mass outside Antarctica, with the notable exception of New Zealand. In fact, the crows and ravens (*Corvus*) have penetrated such distant places as Tasmania, Hawaii, Guam, and the Solomon Islands, each of these four islands or island groups having an endemic species.

The jays and magpies, on the other hand, aside from occupying some of the continental land masses, are found only on *continental* islands; none is known from an oceanic island. Moreover, there are no jays in the West Indies, despite the fact that North, Middle, and South America are rich in jays; there are none in Africa south of the Sahara, nor are there jays in Australia or in the New Guinea subregion.

Interestingly, there are four species of crows in the West Indies (all in the Greater Antilles), but curiously enough none in South America; in fact there are none south of Nicaragua—the southern limits of the Common Raven (*Corvus corax*) in the higher mountains. This last species, incidentally, is the largest passerine in the world, or at least the largest oscine ("song bird").

Of the five New York breeding species, the Blue Jay (*Cyanocitta cristata*) and American Crow (*Corvus brachyrhynchos*) are widespread, the Gray Jay (*Perisoreus canadensis*) and Common Raven are restricted to the Adirondacks, and the Fish Crow (*Corvus ossifragus*) is confined to the southeastern sections near tidewater.

Blue Jay (*Cyanocitta cristata*)   *   B

Range: Chiefly eastern Nearctic region from southern Canada to Texas and Florida. The northern race *bromia* (larger than nominate race) occurs in New York.

Status: Sedentary and migratory. Common to very abundant migrant; locally common in winter and as a breeder.

Nonbreeding: As proved by banding, Blue Jays are both resident and migratory, certain individuals remaining the year around or moving but short distances, while others banded in summer in New York have been recovered in late fall or winter in the southern states (see **Banding**). Years of observation have proved that large flocks to occasional tremendous concentrations pass overhead in the spring migration, especially along the shores of lakes Ontario and Erie, and also on Long Island. This spring migration is sometimes concentrated *late* in May. The fall passage is particularly noteworthy along the coast, but much less so inland.

MAXIMA: *Spring*—3300, Lake View, Erie Co., May 6, 1966; 5000, Derby Hill, Oswego Co., May 10, 1970; 1000, Orient, Suffolk Co.,

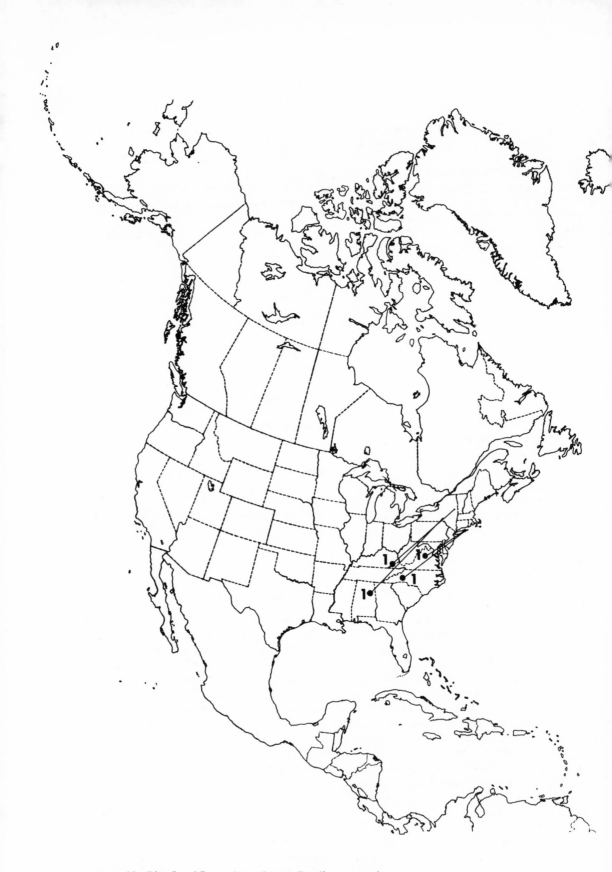

MAP 98   Blue Jay (*Cyanocitta cristata*) Banding recoveries

May 12, 1947; 2000, Braddock's Bay, Monroe Co., May 16, 1958; 2000, Derby Hill, May 16, 1964, and 3000, same locality, May 26, 1970. In 1969 there was a very late flight along Lake Ontario. At Braddock's Bay on May 29, Listman observed at least *6000,* and on June 6 at the same place, McKinney saw about 200. Over 2000 were estimated at Derby Hill on May 30 (several observers). During a Linnaean Society pelagic trip on June 7, 1964, members saw three Blue Jays migrating in a northeasterly direction eight miles off Jones Beach.

MAXIMA: *Fall*—3500, Port Chester, Westchester Co., Sept. 18, 1969; 3000, Riis Park, Queens Co., Sept. 27, 1957; 500, Montauk Point, Oct. 14, 1950. Aaron Bagg (*in litt.*) describes an interesting flight, or rather an exodus of these birds, at the south end of Central Park, New York City, on Oct. 1, 1967. From his hotel window during an hour's observation between 9 A.M. and 10 A.M. he saw over 350 Blue Jays, including two flocks of about 100, flying out of the park and up and over the tall buildings in a southwesterly direction.

The writer has noted on a number of occasions during fall passage that Blue Jays, perhaps more than any other species, become temporarily "confused" at coastal points, hesitating to make a water crossing when they reach the last bit of land. The flocks circle around, mount higher and higher in the air and fly in the *opposite* direction from whence they were headed, only to reapproach the water barrier and finally, after one or more attempts, "reluctantly" make the crossing.

That Blue Jays are locally numerous in early winter is indicated by the following maxima on four Christmas counts taken in 1968, the species being more numerous along the coast: 140 each on the Albany and Buffalo counts, and 500, Bronx-Westchester count, and 400 on the Captree count in southern Suffolk Co. The widespread use of feeding stations undoubtedly helps in swelling the totals.

Breeding: This species is most prevalent where oaks are numerous, the acorns providing one of the staple food items throughout the year, supplemented by seeds. Blue Jays are widely distributed throughout the state, although relatively scarce in the more heavily forested portions at higher elevations. They

breed in such widely diverse surroundings as city parks and suburban yards to woodland swamps.

Nests are found both in hardwood trees and in coniferous growth, the nests themselves ranging in height from about six feet to over 20 feet. For notes on an unusual location of a Blue Jay nest, see Rosche (*Kingbird,* 1966, 16: 212). Not only did this pair use an old Robin nest as a base for its own nest, but the nest site was "located inside a small shed on a rafter under the roof about ten feet above the ground."

Egg clutches in 21 New York nests ranged from four eggs (ten nests) and five eggs (nine nests) to six eggs (two nests).

EGG DATES: Apr. 28 to June 17.

Nestlings: May 18 to July 5; fledglings: June 1 to July 31.

Banding (see Map 98): Two individuals banded in upstate New York during late summer were recovered in eastern Kentucky and northeastern Alabama the following winter. Two others banded on Long Island in July and early September were taken in northern Virginia and western North Carolina the following October and November, respectively.

An adult Blue Jay banded in 1939 in New York was recovered *14* years later in Maryland.

Gray Jay
(*Perisoreus canadensis*) * B

Range: North America, resident from Alaska and Canada—in the west—to the mountains of California, Arizona, and New Mexico; but in the east only to extreme northern portions of United States.

Status: Sedentary, but very rarely wanders southward (Quebec, see below) in flight years. In New York virtually confined to the Adirondack region where strictly resident.

Nonbreeding: Eaton (1914: 211) stated that the Gray Jay ". . . is confined to the Adirondack district and is scarcely if ever, seen outside the spruce and balsam belt." He gave no records from outside this area. Parkes (1952a) listed two "records" from the Mo-

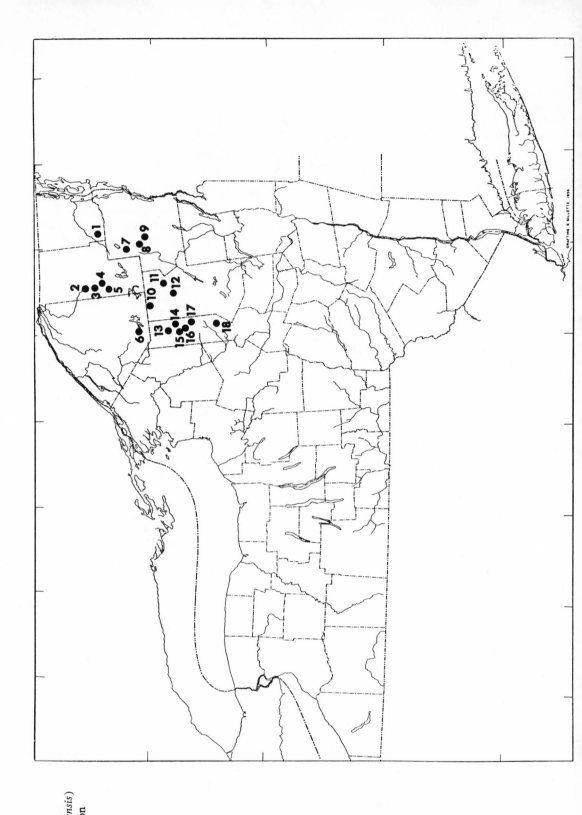

MAP 99 Gray Jay
(*Perisoreus canadensis*)
Breeding distribution

hawk valley at Utica and Little Falls, but gave no details.

I am not aware of any records for the Tug Hill region, although it is possible that it has occurred there. That indefatigable collector, A. J. Dayan, however, took a specimen in the Black River valley—between the Adirondacks and the Tug Hill plateau—at Lyon's Falls, Lewis Co., Nov. 11, 1878, BM(NH) 88.10.-10.579.

Various sight reports of birds reputed to be this species from elsewhere in the state were not documented, with two exceptions; (1) an individual filmed in color at the Jones feeder, Rhinebeck, Dutchess Co., from Oct. 15 to Nov. 1, 1963 (*fide* O. Waterman); (2) an immature photographed in color at the Craighead feeder, Cross River, Westchester Co., from Nov. 27 to Dec. 6, 1968 (P. Wolf), photo on file, AMNH collection.

It is noteworthy that during the late summer of 1968 Gray Jays irrupted in southern Quebec. In the vicinity of Quebec (city) *46* Gray Jays were counted on Aug. 31 and *54* more on Sept. 2 (*Audubon Field Notes,* 1968, 22: 592).

Breeding (see Map 99): This species together with the Spruce Grouse, Boreal Chickadee, and both three-toed woodpeckers are specialties of the Adirondack region, the desiderata of the visiting birder.

Eaton (1914: 211) said of it, "In the denser portion of this Adirondack forest it is a fairly common resident, both in the spruce and tamarack [larch] swamps and on the wooded mountain slopes." Again, he stated, ". . . breeds very early in the season, . . . evidently making its nest late in February or early in March. The young are out of the nest and flying about foraging for themselves by the middle of June."

And yet despite all this, I know of not a single nest, with either eggs or young, having been found in New York or, at least, it has not been published to my knowledge. All of the following 18 breeding records are based on parents with *fledged* juveniles observed chiefly in *late* summer—even well into August. Perhaps these represent second broods.

Dates of fledglings range from June 6 to Aug. 17. The former date is of an adult and two young taken at Limekiln Creek, Herkimer Co., in 1878 (Merriam), specimens in the

BM(NH) collection. The latter date represents an adult and an immature collected at Eldon Pond, Raquette Lake, Hamilton Co., in 1955 (Dilger), specimens in the NYSM collection.

Brood size in five New York "family parties" of adults and known fledged juveniles, ranged from two to four: two young (one brood); three young (two broods): four young (two broods).

Breeding has been recorded in six New York counties, with *18* localities, as follows (see map): Clinton Co.—(1) Silver Lake. Franklin Co.—(2) Santa Clara; (3) Jenning's Swamp; (4) Madawaska; (5) south of Long Pond. St. Lawrence Co.—(6) Wanakena. Essex Co.— (7) Chubb River Swamp; (8) Mt. Marcy (9) Ausable Lakes. Hamilton Co.—(10) Sabattis; (11) near Long Lake (village); (12) Eldon Pond, Raquette Lake. Herkimer Co.— (13) Beaver River (village); (14) Big Moose Lake; (15) Big Moose (village); (16) Fourth Lake (village); (17) Limekiln Creek; (18) near Black Creek Lake.

Postscript: A Gray Jay remained at the Garvin feeder in the Ithaca area during the second half of January 1973 and was seen and photographed by several observers (Kibbe, *Kingbird,* 1973, 23: 83).

Black-billed Magpie (*Pica pica*) *

Range: Eurasia and western North America, in the latter region breeds east to central Manitoba; mainly sedentary, but some migrational movement, especially in fall and early winter. Wanders east to southeastern Ontario and to the Atlantic seaboard from Massachusetts to Virginia.

Status: *Very rare*—this species, perhaps more than any other, is most difficult to evaluate because of its frequency in confinement. As a result, an attempt to enumerate occurrences within the state as wild or captive birds is futile. In a number of instances, however, presumed origin is inferred, but in only very few cases is it proved.

(1) The following three examples of more than 40 records in New York may be con-

veniently categorized as suspected escapes: (a)
An individual present in the Greenwood Cemetery in Brooklyn for at least *nine* consecutive
years (1960–1968) was reported almost annually on the Christmas counts. (b) One
found dead in Delaware Park, Buffalo, May
17, 1964—specimen supposedly in the collection of the Buffalo Museum of Science (not
seen by me)—was subsequently "found" to be
an escape. (c) An individual seen near Albany,
Apr. 22, 1955, may have been one of several
Magpies released in Vermont during the summer of 1954.

Others "known" to have escaped in northern
New Jersey during the fall seasons of 1952 and
1957 were reported from adjacent New York
shortly thereafter.

(2) The following three specimens examined
by me are in *fresh, unworn* plumage suggesting wild, uncaged birds: (a) male caught in a
mink trap, Island Pond, Orange Co. (not Iona
Island, Rockland Co., as stated in Bull, 1964:
311), Nov. 14, 1935 (Carr), AMNH 300598;
(b) female, Orient, Suffolk Co., Dec. 20, 1927
(Latham), NYSM 25159; (c) female, Islip,
Suffolk Co., Mar. 28, 1951 (Latham), NYSM
25160.

(3) A number of Magpies have been observed in sustained flight during the migrations
in the New York City region (Bull, 1964:
312). More recently *two* birds were seen flying
westward along the outer beach on Fire Island,
Suffolk Co., Oct. 2, 1964 (Pembleton and
Ward). Upstate, one was observed off Braddock's Bay, Monroe Co., Mar. 20, 1949 (Listman), ". . . following a flock of Crows which
were migrating in an easterly direction over
Lake Ontario . . ." (Beardslee and Mitchell,
1965: 319).

For additional occurrences, see Bull (*op.
cit.* and 1970: 30), also Beardslee and Mitchell (*op. cit.*), as well as recent issues of *Audubon Field Notes* and the *Kingbird*.

Remarks: The alleged difference, supposedly
distinguishing the American population known
as *"hudsonia"* (throat feathers spotted white,
or with white bases) from that of nominate
pica of western Europe (throat feathers black,
without white) does not hold in large series. A
number of specimens of the latter, examined
by the writer, also had white spotting in the
throat region.

Common Raven
(*Corvus corax*)   *   B

Range: Holarctic region, the race *principalis*
(compared to nominate *corax* of the western
Palearctic—larger, with longer wing and heavier bill) breeds in North America—in the east
from Greenland and arctic Canada south to
Maine and northern New England, northern
New York (rarely), and in the mountains to
northern Georgia. Formerly also along the
coast from southern New Jersey to Virginia.
Sedentary and migratory.

Status: Very rare to rare vagrant over much
of the state, but local and uncommon in the
Adirondacks.

Nonbreeding: There are at least a dozen Raven specimens from New York preserved in
various museums, of which three were taken
in recent years, two in 1962 and one in 1969,
from Orleans, Madison, and Jefferson counties.

Recent maxima, Adirondack area: ten, High
Falls, St. Lawrence Co., Feb. 23, 1954 (Wilson); eight, Wright Peak, Essex Co., Oct. 26,
1968 (Carleton).

One was seen migrating with American
Crows at Derby Hill, Oswego Co., Apr. 17,
1964 (many observers). Two more were observed flying over Bear Mtn. on the Rockland-
Orange county line, Nov. 10, 1946 (Komorowski). There have been a number of other
recent sightings outside the Adirondacks during the migrations and winter season.

Breeding: Formerly distributed widely over
the state before the virgin forest was lum-
bered, this species had become very scarce
many years ago, although Merriam (1881:
231) still called it a "Common resident,
throughout the Adirondacks."

Eaton (1914: 212–213), referring to that
area, stated, "At the present time a few may
be seen in the western Adirondack region, especially in the northern portions of Hamilton
and Herkimer counties, the southern portion
of St. Lawrence County, and the eastern portion of Lewis County. In this part of the North
Woods the Raven still breeds, but in constantly
diminishing numbers."

No further reports of its breeding were obtained until 1968 when adults were seen and

heard on May 27 in the vicinity of Chapel Pond, Essex Co., by Geoffrey Carleton and Greenleaf Chase. On June 1 they found a huge stick nest on a cliff opposite Chapel Pond. This nest contained three nestlings fairly well grown. By June 14 the young had fledged and were seen in the vicinity of the cliff. This cliff site, interestingly, was the location of a former Peregrine Falcon eyrie.

No other nesting record in New York within recent times has come to my attention, although a nest was discovered in 1970 in Vermont just east of the New York line—east of Granville, Washington Co. (W. R. Spofford, *in litt.*). A report, entirely without details, in the *Kingbird* (1971, 21: 239) from Region 7, merely states:—"1 nesting—", is about as vague as one could wish for; needless to state an unsatisfactory occurrence as published.

Remarks: This species is often confused with the much smaller American Crow and many misidentifications are made by inexperienced observers. The vocalizations of the two are quite distinctive, but size is very deceptive unless both species are together—an altogether seldom event in our area.

American Crow
(*Corvus brachyrhynchos*) * B

Range: Nearctic region—Canada and nearly the entire United States. Migratory and sedentary, partially migratory in the northern portions.

Status: Common to very abundant migrant and locally in winter roosts. Widespread breeder.

Nonbreeding: Crows in New York are most numerous during spring passage along Lake Ontario at the two best-watched localities in the interior—Manitou, Monroe Co., and Derby Hill, Oswego Co.—and locally at winter roosts, both upstate and along the coast. Numbers in fall, although impressive, are much smaller, as may be seen below.

MAXIMA: *Spring*—20,000, Manitou, Mar. 11, 1956 (Dobson). During a total of six days

in March 1964 (Mar. 5–28), Haugh estimated more than 37,000 passing Derby Hill. The two largest days (Mar. 7 and 24) produced 11,000 and 15,000 birds respectively.

MAXIMA: *Fall*—3600, Sandy Pond, Oswego Co., Oct. 22, 1964; 2500, Orchard Park, Erie Co., Nov. 20, 1966.

MAXIMA: *Winter roosts*—without going into exact details, it may be said that inland winter roosts during the early 1960s numbered in the tens of thousands (up to at least 30,000), the largest being found in the Lake Ontario lowlands—near the cities of Rochester and Syracuse, the famed Montezuma Marshes, and near the communities of Canandaigua, and Phelps, both in Ontario Co.

In former years (*circa* 1930s) as large or even larger numbers (up to 50,000 at one Long Island roost) were to be found on or near the coast. With the human population explosion after World War II, these roosts were destroyed or rather the localities were (Bull, 1964: 313–314). See also Emlen (1938).

Breeding: Crows are most numerous in agricultural districts with a great variety and plentiful supply of food, and adjacent woodland with the necessary cover for suitable nesting sites. Because of these two favorable factors, the species has thrived and undoubtedly will continue to prosper.

In this state 61 tree nests examined ranged in height from six to 60 feet, chiefly in hardwoods, with 18 in beech, 17 in oak, 12 in apple, five in maple, six in four other hardwood types; and only three in evergreens—two in hemlock, one in pine.

Egg clutches based on 103 New York nests ranged from three to eight eggs, as follows: three eggs (20 nests); four eggs (25 nests); five eggs (44 nests); six eggs (ten nests) and seven and eight eggs (two nests each).

EGG DATES: Mar. 30 to June 14.

Nestlings: May 1 to July 28. No New York information available for fledgling dates.

Banding (see Map 100): Three individuals banded at Quebec (city), Nova Scotia, and Cape Cod, were all recovered at relatively short distances in New York, but a fourth (nestling) banded in late May near Poughkeepsie was shot the following fall as far away as the coast of Georgia.

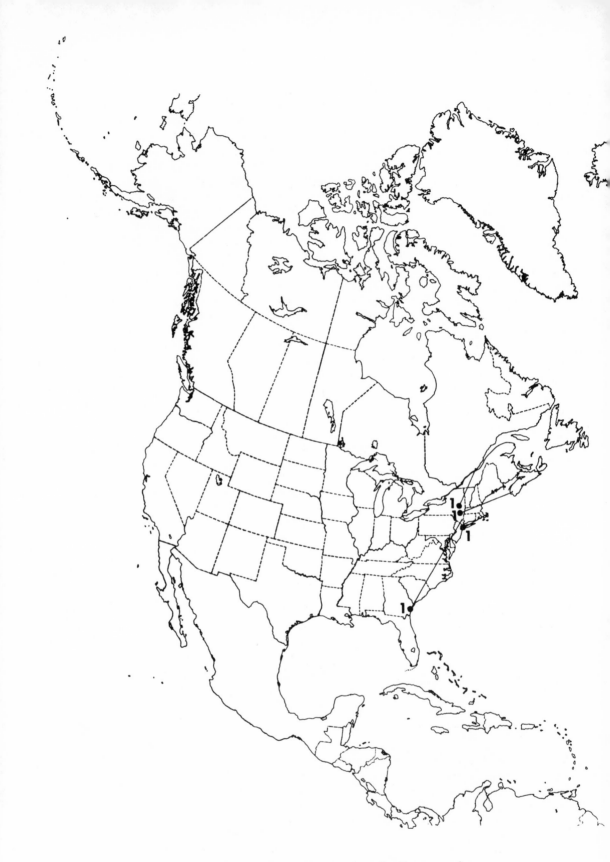

MAP 100 American Crow (*Corvus brachyrhynchos*) Banding recoveries

Fish Crow
(*Corvus ossifragus*)   *   B

Range: Chiefly Gulf and Atlantic coasts of the United States, ranging north to Rhode Island. Sedentary and migratory.

Status: Uncommon to locally very common resident or migrant in tidewater areas in the southeastern portion of the state. Unknown elsewhere.

Nonbreeding: This species arrives regularly in mid-March and departs early, usually by late August, except for a relatively small winter population.

MAXIMA: *Spring*—175, Easthampton, Suffolk Co., Mar. 31, 1914; *Fall*—200, same locality, Aug. 30, 1922; *Winter*—60, Staten Island, Dec. 26, 1959; 75 at roost, Pelham Bay Park, Bronx Co., Dec. 27, 1964.

Breeding (see Map 101): The Fish Crow is restricted to the New York City area, Long Island, and the lower Hudson valley. It is virtually unknown elsewhere.

Although common enough on the south shore of Long Island during the migrations, it is very local and decidedly uncommon there in the breeding season. It is frequent as a breeder on Staten Island, on the north shore of Long Island, and on the mainland opposite in Westchester Co.

It ascends the Hudson River on the east bank as far as Poughkeepsie, Dutchess Co. (1), and along the west bank to Esopus, Ulster Co. (2). It has not been recorded as *breeding* farther north than these localities.

Eaton (1914: 218–219) mentioned occurrences as far north as Troy, Rensselaer Co., but no specimens were taken. Crows that look small and sound like Fish Crows at many inland points are most likely young American Crows with very similar calls. Few species are more misidentified by the beginner.

Fish Crows nest in evergreen trees much more than do their larger relatives. Pine, cedar, and spruce are favored in drier localities, although oak, ash, maple, and tupelo (sour gum) are utilized in low, wet woodland. Nests range from 15 to 40 feet above ground.

Of eight New York nests examined, four each contained four and five eggs.

EGG DATES: Mar. 20 to June 5.

No New York dates are available for either unfledged or fledged juveniles.

TITMICE — PARIDAE

Three species in New York.
Three breed.

This large family (65± species) has its stronghold in the Palearctic region, but is fairly well represented in North America and Africa. It is absent everywhere in tropical America and also in the Australian region.

All three members of this family in New York are in the genus *Parus* and all breed in different zones: (1) *P. hudsonicus*, the Boreal or Brown-capped Chickadee, in the boreal spruce-fir zone in the Adirondacks; (2) *P. atricapillus*, the Black-capped Chickadee, is widespread throughout the state; (3) *P. bicolor*, the Tufted Titmouse, in the southern and central deciduous woodland zone. The last named is one of a number of southern species that has been extending its range northward in recent years.

The tits are hole nesters; of the three, *atricapillus* is the tamest, not only utilizing bird boxes and coming readily to feeding stations, but on occasion taking food from the hand and even perching on humans.

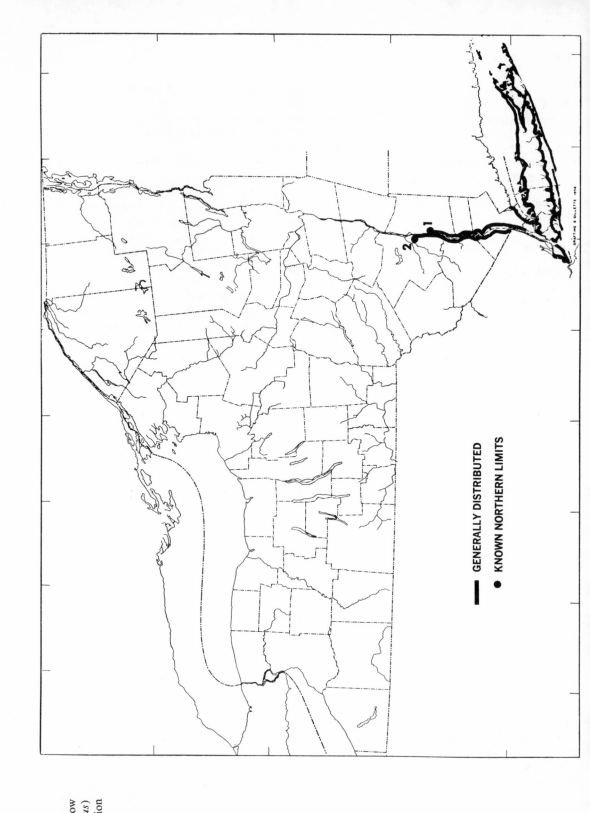

MAP 101 Fish Crow
(*Corvus ossifragus*)
Breeding distribution

GENERALLY DISTRIBUTED

● KNOWN NORTHERN LIMITS

Black-capped Chickadee
(*Parus atricapillus*) * B

Range: North America—in the east breeding south to the central portions of Pennsylvania and New Jersey, in the mountains to Tennessee and North Carolina.

Status: Sedentary and migratory. Occasionally very abundant in fall irruptions, especially inland. Widespread breeder.

Nonbreeding: During the winter months especially, the Black-capped Chickadee is one of the tamest and most confiding of birds, a frequent visitor at the feeding station, sometimes taking food from the hand.

At irregular intervals, this species irrupts southward in great numbers in fall and at such times is abundant. During these irruptions individuals have been found in small patches of shrubbery in the midst of large cities and have even flown in through open windows of Manhattan skyscrapers!

In recent years two enormous flights occurred along the Lake Ontario shore in the vicinity of Rochester. During three days in October 1954, near Manitou Beach, Monroe Co., Listman and Van Beurden estimated nearly *27,000* birds flying from *west* to *east*. The breakdown follows: 10,000, Oct. 9; 12,-000, Oct. 12; 4500, Oct. 17. An even larger invasion took place during October 6–12, 1961, at nearby Oklahoma Beach, when more than *42,000* flew by from *east* to *west* and were seen by numerous members of the Genesee Ornithological Society. More than *17,000* were observed in ten hours on Oct. 8 and another *8500* the following day in just over four hours.

Breeding: The Black-capped Chickadee breeds in open woodland, near habitations, and sometimes in city parks. Regarding the Adirondacks, Saunders (1929: 374) said that it occurs chiefly below 4000 feet.

The nest is generally located in tree holes and cavities in dead stubs, and fairly often in bird boxes, from four to seven feet above ground.

A most unusual nest site at Fayetteville, Onondaga Co., was described by Spofford (*Kingbird,* 1958, 8: 87). The nest, an open affair, was "cupped in a knot-hole on an upper rail of a split-rail fence, roofed over only by thick *multiflora* rose."

Egg clutches in 23 New York nests range from five to ten: five eggs (four nests); six eggs (four nests); seven eggs (eight nests); eight eggs (five nests); nine and ten eggs (one nest apiece).

EGG DATES: Apr. 29 to July 15.

Nestlings: May 21 to July 20, and Aug. 15 (second brood); fledglings: June 4 to Aug. 3.

According to Eaton (1914: 505), both sexes construct the nest, incubate, and feed the young.

Banding: An individual banded at Mohonk Lake, Ulster Co., in 1955, was retaken there *nine* years later (Smiley).

Remarks: The relationships of this form with the very similar Carolina Chickadee (*P. carolinensis*) of more southern distribution, as well as with the Willow Tit (*P. montanus*) of the Palearctic region (extending from western Europe to eastern Siberia), remain to be worked out. Recent field investigations suggest that vocalizations of Alaskan and Siberian birds may not be so different from one another.

[Carolina Chickadee
(*Parus carolinensis*)

Hypothetical: Southeastern United States, breeding north to southern Pennsylvania and central New Jersey. Sedentary.

There is no substantiated record for New York State. No known specimen has ever been taken. From time to time individuals reported to be this form have been seen and/or heard, as for instance (*Kingbird,* 1963, 13: 23–24), but good evidence is lacking.

There is even doubt as to whether the Carolina Chickadee is specifically distinct from its very close relative, the Black-capped Chickadee (*P. atricapillus*). The two forms have been found hybridizing in Virginia where they meet altitudinally (Johnston, 1971). One of the most pressing needs is for a sound, modern biological study of these forms where their ranges meet.]

Boreal or Brown-capped Chickadee
(*Parus hudsonicus*) * B

Range: Nearctic region, breeding (resident) from Alaska and Canada to extreme northern United States. In the northeast wanders in winter to southeastern New York and northern New Jersey, casually farther south. Sedentary and irregularly migratory.

Status: Rare to uncommon winter visitant in upstate New York, much rarer downstate. Uncommon breeder (resident) in the Adirondacks.

Nonbreeding: Unrecorded during most winters, the Boreal or Brown-capped Chickadee occasionally irrupts southward from its northern breeding grounds. Within recent years, large irruptions occurred during the winters of 1951–1952, 1954–1955, 1961–1962, and 1965–1966. Small flocks have been observed in upstate New York. Rarely more than one or two at once have been reported along the coast where the species is at, or very near, its southern limits. In nearly all of these flights, heavy irruptions of Black-capped Chickadees occurred, sometimes preceding the arrival of *P. hudsonicus*.

MAXIMA: five, Braddock's Bay, Monroe Co., Nov. 11, 1951; 15, Westmoreland, Oneida Co., Nov. 11, 1965 (Paquette), and at least 12 wintered there through 1966 in a spruce plantation (many observers)—a most unusual concentration; six, Norwich, Chenango Co., Nov. 28, 1954; four, Savin feeder, Rensselaerville, Albany Co., Mar. 27, 1962.

EXTREME DATES: Casually, Sept. 14–17, 1965 (note flight year), at a feeder, Scotia, Saratoga Co. (many observers); and from Oct. 9 (inland) and Oct. 29 (coastal) to Apr. 18 (coastal) and May 10 (inland), exceptionally to May 31, 1952 (flight year), Rochester.

A report in Beardslee and Mitchell (1965: 324) of an individual observed Aug. 25 was not confirmed.

Breeding (see Map 102:) Boreal Chickadees are confined to the Adirondacks during the nesting season. They are often found in spruce-larch (tamarack) swamps, or at their edges. According to Saunders (1929: 373), the spe-

cies occurs chiefly above 4000 feet nearly to tree line, mostly in balsam (fir) forest. Nest holes in New York have been located from six to 15 feet above ground in dead or rotten yellow birch, sugar maple, and in spruce saplings.

Two New York nests contained four eggs each, another held five.

EGG DATES: June 11 to July 17 (late).

Nestlings: June 27 to July 26; fledglings: July 2 to Aug. 27.

Judging from the available evidence, the Boreal Chickadee is more prevalent in the eastern Adirondacks than elsewhere. Half of the 20 known breeding localities are in Essex Co. (see accompanying map). They are: Franklin Co.—(1) Madawaska; (2) Bay Pond; (3) Paul Smith's; (4) near Saranac Lake (village). Essex Co.—(5) Whiteface Mtn.; (6) near Jay; (7) Ray Brook; (8) Chubb River Swamp; (9) near Keene; (10) Mt. McIntyre at 3900 feet; (11) Mt. Marcy; (12) inlet above head of Upper Ausable Lake; (13) Elk Lake and nearby Boreas Mtn.; (14) Schroon Lake (village). Hamilton Co.—(15) Lake Terror; (16) Snowy Mtn. at 3900 feet. Herkimer Co.—(17) Nick's Lake; (18) Woods Lake; (19) Big Moose Lake; (20) near Honnedaga Lake. St. Lawrence Co.—(21) near Mt. Matumbla.

Remarks: No eastern subspecies are recognized here; the poorly marked form *"littoralis"* is of average color and size differences only —part of a cline (Bull, 1964: 318).

Tufted Titmouse
(*Parus bicolor*) * B

Range: Chiefly southeastern United States and eastern Mexico, ranging northeast to extreme southeastern Ontario (rare), central New York and Connecticut, rarely Massachusetts. Sedentary.

Status: Common to locally very common resident in the lower Hudson valley; less numerous east to western Long Island, but rare eastward; in recent years extending north to western and central New York. Absent in the mountains.

Change in status: Eaton (1914: 502–503) knew of only one breeding record for the state

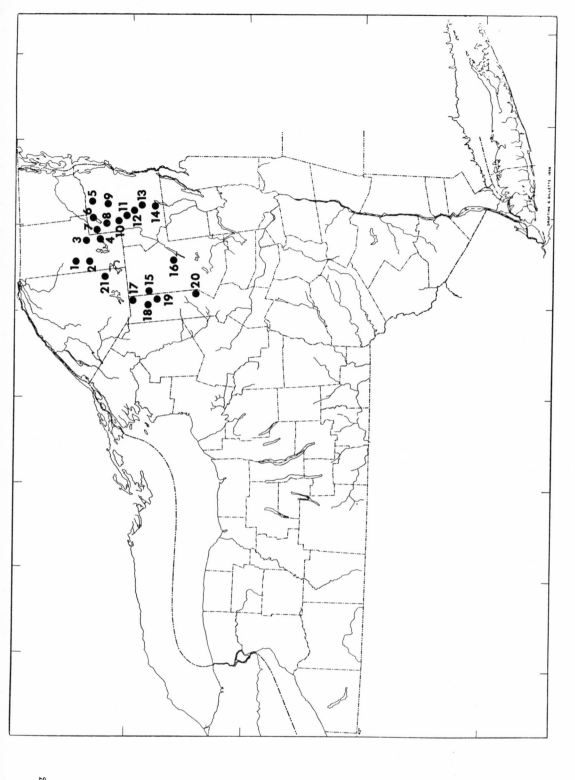

MAP 102 Boreal
Chickadee (*Parus
hudsonicus*) Breeding
distribution

(Staten Island) and considered it rare in upstate New York. Bull (1964: 318–320, and 1970: 31) gave its history in the New York City region where, prior to the 1950s, it was rare and local north and east of New Jersey, especially east of the Hudson River, and extremely rare on Long Island.

As of 1971 it had greatly increased and spread east to western Suffolk Co. and locally in the Hudson valley north to the Schenectady area.

In western and central New York it has invaded the state from the south by way of Pennsylvania; to quote Poole (1964: 48), "now nests or occurs in summer in practically every county," in that state. A southern, rather than western, origin is proved by its presence along the *south* shore of Lake Erie, south of Buffalo, but only very rarely north of that city, with only one known breeding record for Niagara Co. at Lewiston in 1966 (see map). Moreover it is an extremely rare breeder in southeastern Ontario; not known in the corridor west of the Niagara River, except at Hamilton—more than 40 miles to the west (Godfrey, 1966: 281).

According to Axtell (1947) it was unknown as a breeder in Chemung and Schuyler counties at that time. S. W. Eaton (1959: 59–62) gave a detailed account of its recent range expansion in the western portions of the state.

Nonbreeding: Tufted Titmice, like several other resident species, visit feeding stations during the fall and winter months, sometimes in numbers as seen by the following concentrations at two feeders along the Lake Erie shore: (1) six at the Stanley feeder, Dunkirk, Chautauqua Co., February 1954; (2) seven banded at the Czont feeder, Athol Springs, Erie Co., Oct. 16–31, 1965. Incidentally, both of these localities are also breeding stations. As many as *16* were observed along the Lake Ontario shore near Rochester during the second week of October 1961 (Genesee Ornith. Soc.).

The species has been reported in the state as far north as Theresa, Jefferson Co., Nov. 1, 1961 (Gordon)—remarkably on the *same* day that an individual appeared at a feeder across the St. Lawrence River at Kingston, Ontario (Quilliam, 1965: 131). It has been observed also along the shore of Lake Cham-

plain, about five miles south of Westport, Essex Co., Oct. 28, 1968 (Carleton).

Although by no means rare on the south side of Long Island—at the west end—it is virtually unknown on the barrier beach. However, one was banded at Atlantic Beach, Nassau Co., Apr. 13, 1970 (Cohen).

That this species wanders considerable distances on occasion is illustrated by an individual banded at Springfield, Mass. (where very rare), July 23, 1963, and recovered more than 130 miles to the southwest at Port Jervis, Orange Co., Feb. 1, 1964.

Breeding (see Map 103): Tufted Titmice occur most frequently in low rich woodland, wooded swamps, and more rarely in suburban areas with plenty of large trees. They are ordinarily less tame and confiding than Blackcapped Chickadees and keep more to the forest than the latter, at least during the breeding season, although in recent years they have tended to become somewhat "suburbanized." Nest holes in trees are located as high as 60 feet in wooded swamps. However, bird boxes are occasionally utilized and then nest heights may be as low as four or five feet above ground.

This species has even bred in Central Park, New York City, first in 1968 (Carleton). On May 5, 1970, Helen Lapham (verbal comm.) found a most unusual nest site—only two feet above the ground in a metal lamppost. The actual nest entrance was inside a small "door" left ajar, with a one-inch opening. On the above date the pair was observed constructing a nest but, as the breeding site was situated along a busy footpath and subject to disturbance, the birds deserted.

Egg clutches in ten New York nests: four eggs (six nests); five and six eggs (two nests each).

EGG DATES: Apr. 29 to May 27.

Nestlings: May 13 to June 30; fledglings: May 30 to Aug. 4.

The species is more or less generally distributed in the counties of Westchester, Putnam, and Rockland, and in the southern portions of Orange and Dutchess.

As may be seen on the accompanying map there are some anomalies in the breeding distribution. Why are there apparent gaps in the

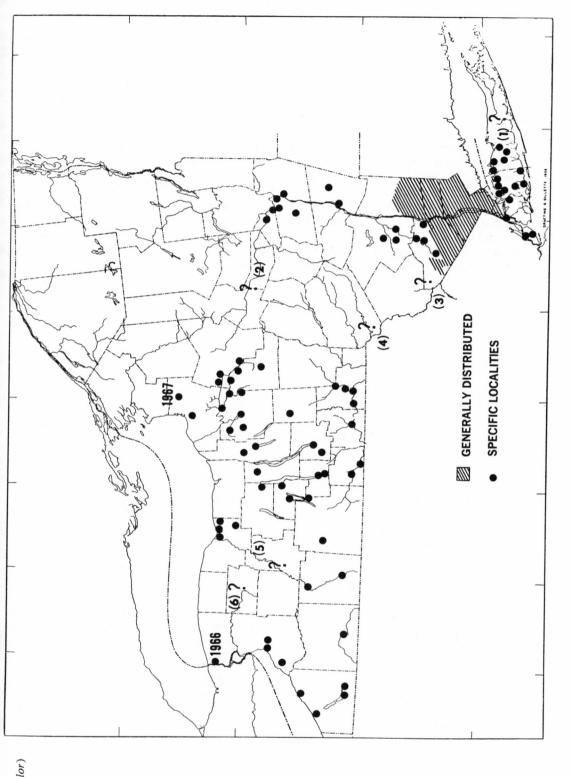

MAP 103 Tufted
Titmouse (*Parus bicolor*)
Breeding distribution

GENERALLY DISTRIBUTED

SPECIFIC LOCALITIES

six areas indicated with question marks (see map)?

I suspect that breeding sites are overlooked. On Long Island the species had bred as early as 1964 at Smithtown (1), but not east of there; in the central Hudson valley—in the Albany-Schenectady region (2)—as early as the late 1950s, but not in the Mohawk valley farther west; in 1969 at least *30* individuals were reported on the Christmas count at Monticello, Sullivan Co. (3). They should be found breeding at the latter locality, as well as in the river valleys in adjacent Delaware Co. (4); also at (5) in the Genesee valley between Rochester and Fillmore, Allegany Co., and at (6) in the Oak Orchard Swamp-Tonawanda Creek area where there is plenty of suitable habitat.

The most northerly known penetration (1967) is at Orwell, Oswego Co.—at the very edge of the Tug Hill Plateau.

Banding: See **Nonbreeding.**

Remarks: Here considered conspecific with the southwestern *atricristatus*, the Black-crested Titmouse, following several recent authorities. The two forms interbreed freely where their ranges meet.

NUTHATCHES — SITTIDAE

Three species in New York.
Two breed.

Omitting the aberrant members from the Old World tropics—which may not even be related—there are 17 species, all in the genus *Sitta*. They occur mostly in the mountains of central Asia, but are found in the temperate zone throughout the Holarctic region, in America ranging only as far south as the mountains of southern Mexico.

Most nuthatches are sedentary, but the Red-breasted Nuthatch (*Sitta canadensis*) is highly migratory, though irregular in its movements. In the breeding season and during winter it is practically confined to pines, where it feeds mainly among the smaller branches and twigs, whereas the larger White-breasted Nuthatch (*S. carolinensis*) inhabits broad-leaved trees and does most of its foraging on the trunks and larger branches. Nuthatches are hole or cavity nesters. The third species (*S. pusilla*), the Brown-headed Nuthatch, is accidental in New York.

White-breasted Nuthatch
(*Sitta carolinensis*)   *   B

Range: North America, resident from southern Canada to the mountains of Mexico and the Gulf states.

Status: Sedentary and migratory. Fairly common coastal migrant, more numerous upstate. Local but widespread breeder, rare on the coastal plain and in the higher mountains.

Nonbreeding: Although considered a resident species, being commonplace at winter feeding stations, the White-breasted Nuthatch is nevertheless quite migratory at times, as the following data indicate. For instance, one banded Nov. 13, 1959, on Long Island at Huntington, Suffolk Co., was found dead May 2, 1960, near Portland, Maine—some 400 miles distant.

MAXIMA, COASTAL: *Fall*—14, Jones Beach, Oct. 5, 1963; 12, Central Park, New York City, Oct. 9, 1943. *Spring*—ten, Central Park, Apr. 23, 1962.

MAXIMA, INLAND: *Fall*—28, Oklahoma Beach, Monroe Co., Oct. 8, 1961, coinciding with a big movement of Black-capped Chickadees. *Spring*—30, Point Gratiot (near Dunkirk), Chautauqua Co., Apr. 26, 1962; *65,* Derby Hill, Oswego Co., Apr. 26, 1964 (many observers). Note that the upstate flights occurred on the shores of lakes Ontario and Erie.

Breeding: The White-breasted Nuthatch breeds in deciduous woodland and near habitations with a quantity of large trees. It nests in tree holes and bird boxes from as low as five feet up to about 50 feet.

Clutch size in 14 New York nests ranges from four to nine: four eggs (three nests); five eggs (one nest); six eggs (three nests); seven eggs (one nest); eight eggs (two nests); nine eggs (four nests).

EGG DATES: Apr. 13 to June 6.

Nestlings: May 8 to June 11; fledglings: June 3 to June 22.

Remarks: No eastern subspecies are recognized here. Females of the northeastern population, *"cookei,"* are supposedly distinguished from males, as well as from females, of the southern nominate population on the basis of their grayish instead of blackish crowns; but in large series examined of both northern and southern individuals, the crown color of females ranged from gray to black in both populations.

Red-breasted Nuthatch
(*Sitta canadensis*)   *   B

Range: Nearctic region, breeding from Alaska and Canada to southwestern United States; in the east to the Berkshires, Catskills, and Poconos, and the higher mountains to Tennessee and North Carolina. Winters north to southern Canada. Sedentary and irregularly migratory.

Status: Variously rare to very common migrant, most numerous in fall along the coast; much less common in winter. Common breeder in the mountains, less numerous and local at lower elevations, but absent from the southeastern sections.

Nonbreeding: The Red-breasted Nuthatch is found chiefly in pines, particularly during winter. It is very erratic and unpredictable, sometimes rare or almost absent in fall, in other years very numerous. Usually rare (sometimes unreported) in spring, except after a flight the preceding fall. Its time of arrival and length of stay are equally unpredictable, in most years not common until late September or October, at long intervals arriving as early as mid-August or even July. Numerous in winter on the outer coast, if there has been a flight the preceding fall, otherwise uncommon or rare.

MAXIMA, COASTAL: *Fall*—45 in one half hour, Montauk, Suffolk Co., Sept. 18, 1948 (Fischer); *120,* Far Rockaway, Queens Co., Sept. 19, 1969 (Bull); "hundreds," Point O'Woods, Fire Island, Suffolk Co., Sept. 22, 1906 (Dutcher); over 100 netted and banded at Fire Island State Park in two successive days in 1969—53 on Oct. 19, and 49 on Oct. 20 (Davis, *et al.*)— note flight at Far Rockaway above on Sept. 19 of same year.

MAXIMA: *Winter*—36, Easthampton, Suffolk Co., Jan. 1, 1917; 16 in a spruce plantation, Westmoreland, Oneida Co., Jan. 9, 1966.

MAXIMA: *Spring*—28 netted and banded, Fire Island State Park, May 9, 1970 (note return spring movement after big fall irruption of previous year—see above); good inland flight in central New York on May 16, 1966—25, Syracuse, and 25, Phoenix, Oswego Co.

Migrants are recorded every month of the year, but the species is scarce in summer (late June–August).

Change in breeding status (see Map 104): This species has always been known as a common breeding bird of the Adirondacks and higher Catskills (mostly above 3000 feet in the latter), chiefly in the balsam-spruce zone. Outside of the mountains, Eaton (1914: 500) knew of definite breeding records only at (x on map) Holland Patent, Oneida Co.; Peterboro, Madison Co.; near Branchport, Yates Co.; West Falls, Erie Co. That there has been considerable range extension to lower elevations since Eaton's time is obvious from the following.

All localities shown on the map outside the mountains (=diagonal lines) are indicated by solid circles. In addition, the seven numbered circles (from one to seven) signify breed-

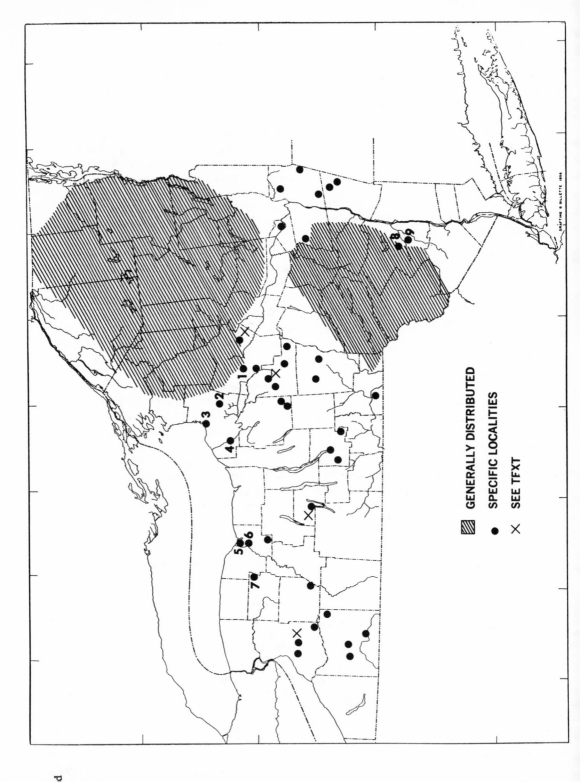

MAP 104 Red-breasted
Nuthatch (*Sitta
canadensis*) Breeding
distribution

GENERALLY DISTRIBUTED

● SPECIFIC LOCALITIES

✕ SEE TEXT

ing localities in the low-lying Lake Ontario-Oneida Lake plain, as follows: Oneida Co.—(1) Rome Sand Plains. Oswego Co.—(2) Happy Valley Refuge; (3) Selkirk Shores State Park; (4) Fulton. Monroe Co.—(5) Rochester—Durand Eastman Park; (6) Rochester—Highland Park. Genesee Co.—(7) Bergen Swamp.

Although not, by any means, restricted to evergreen forest in the breeding season, the Red-breasted Nuthatch is to the boreal spruce-fir belt what the White-breasted Nuthatch is to the deciduous forest biotope. The former also forages mainly among the twigs and smaller branches, whereas the latter feeds chiefly on the trunks and larger tree branches.

Outside montane areas, *Sitta canadensis* has been recorded as nesting in a mixed pine-hemlock bog; in pine and spruce reforestation plantings; at the above-mentioned Rome Sand Plains in "open pitch pine-aspen-white oak woods" (Rusk, 1968), as well as in "hemlock"; and at another nest site at Nassau, Rensselaer Co. (elev. 450 feet), in mixed coniferous-deciduous woodland. More unusual was a nest in an ornamental spruce in a village cemetery, at Hamburg, Erie Co., and another in one of the Rochester city parks in a birdhouse on a light pole situated in a stand of thick hemlocks.

With the exception of the bird-box location, all known New York nest sites have been in dead trees, or living ones with dead tops, from 15 to 50 feet above ground.

Egg clutches examined in only six New York nests were five and six in three nests each.

EGG DATES: Apr. 30 to June 17.

Nestlings: May 15 to July 11; fledglings: June 6 to Aug. 18.

The known southeastern breeding limits in New York are in Ulster Co.—(8) near Liebhardt (650 feet elev.); and (9) near Mohonk Lake—(1250 feet elev.). Both these localities are southeast of the Catskills and are situated at the northern extremity of the Shawangunk Mountains.

No proof of breeding exists at Poundridge Reservation, Westchester Co., *contra* Arbib, *et al.* (1966: 108); nor for Long Island, as claimed in the A.O.U. Check-list (1957: 399), for which see Bull (1964: 323).

Brown-headed Nuthatch
(*Sitta pusilla*) *

Range: Southeastern United States, breeding north to southern Delaware. Resident throughout. Accidental in New York.

Status: *Accidental*—the only known record in New York is that of an adult male collected near Elmira, Chemung Co., May 24, 1888 (Swift), CUM 13512. This is a most surprising record of a sedentary species of southern pine forests.

Remarks: Probably conspecific with the Pygmy Nuthatch (*S. pygmaea*) of western North America and so considered by many authorities. The only sharply defined difference between the two forms is color of the crown; gray in *pygmaea*, brownish in *pusilla*. Their vocalizations, behavior, and ecology are very similar.

CREEPERS — CERTHIIDAE

One species in New York.
One breeds.

Of the five "typical" creepers or tree-creepers of the genus *Certhia* only one species is known from North America—the Brown Creeper (*C. familiaris*)—also occurring in temperate Eurasia; the other four are strictly Palearctic, three of them mostly confined to the mountains of central Asia.

Brown Creepers are one of the familiar members of mixed flocks that forage on tree trunks, associating with woodpeckers and nuthatches during the migrations. The Brown Creeper is certainly the most inconspicuous species of these assemblages. Being cryptically colored, it is difficult to detect as it crawls up the matching bark. In recent years it has extended its breeding range south to Long Island where a number of nests have been found.

Brown Creeper
(*Certhia familiaris*)   *   B

Range: Chiefly Holarctic region, in North America breeds from southeastern Alaska and Canada to the high mountains of Nicaragua in the west; in the east to the mountains of North Carolina and to the coastal plain of Long Island. Sedentary and migratory, withdrawing in winter from the northernmost portions of the breeding range. The local breeding race *americana* is darker and grayer above than western Palearctic races, but not markedly different from adjacent American subspecies.

Status: Common to very common migrant; usually rare to uncommon in winter, but locally numerous. Common breeder in the mountains, but decidedly local at lower elevations, such as the lake plains of central and western New York, and rare and local southward, especially on Long Island.

Nonbreeding: Although ordinarily inconspicuous and with relatively small numbers occurring at one time, Brown Creepers are seen in good numbers on occasion. During flights these birds may be seen climbing up fence posts, telephone poles, and even rock walls—in the absence of trees—as on the outer beaches of Long Island. However, they are most often associated with good-sized trees—spiraling up the trunks in their never-ending search for insects in bark crevices and then flying to the base of another tree where the process is repeated.

MAXIMA: *Spring*—75, Manitou, Monroe Co., Apr. 14, 1960; 60, Selkirk Shores, Oswego Co., Apr. 22, 1961; 50, Syracuse, Apr. 28,

1956; 35, Far Rockaway, Queens Co., May 6, 1950.

MAXIMA: *Fall*—60, Manitou, Sept. 28, 1963; 75, Easthampton, Suffolk Co., Oct. 5, 1946; 33 netted on *each* of two days in 1969 at Fire Island, Suffolk Co., Oct. 10 and 26.

MAXIMA: *Winter*—from 20 to 50 individuals were present in the Montezuma region during January of three successive years, 1966–1968. These birds were feeding in swampy areas on diseased and dying elms.

Migrants usually arrive in early April, depart by mid-May, then arrive in mid-September and depart by mid-November.

Breeding (see Map 105): This species is fairly common and widespread in suitable habitat at higher elevations and throughout much of upstate, but is decidedly local on the Lake Ontario plain and in the southeastern sections of the state. Here it reaches its southernmost known breeding limits along the Atlantic coast and, as may be seen on the accompanying map, is decidedly rare on the coastal plain of Long Island—a recent range extension from the north. The following Long Island localities, all situated in Suffolk Co., are:

(A) north shore—Orient (1947); Smithtown (1947); south of Huntington (1963).

(B) south shore—East Quogue (1950); Yaphank (1963); Sayville (1963); nearby Oakdale (1970 and 1971)—two different nests in the latter year at the last locality, and at least *five* there in 1972 (R. Giffen and C. Kessler).

Details for the above, except those at Huntington and Oakdale, are found in Bull (1964: 324–326).

The 1963 Huntington record involved an adult and two recently fledged juveniles netted and banded on July 10 (Lanyon, *et al.*, 1970: 38). The 1970 Oakdale occurrence was that of a nest behind loose bark in a dead oak, only four feet above ground in dry pitch pine-scrub oak forest adjacent to swampy woodland, containing three unfledged young on June 16 (Giffen and Kessler); nest in AMNH collection.

The Brown Creeper usually places its nest behind slabs or strips of loose bark in dead or dying trees. Although many nests are found in wet areas, such as in boreal bogs in the higher mountains and in wooded swamps at low eleva-

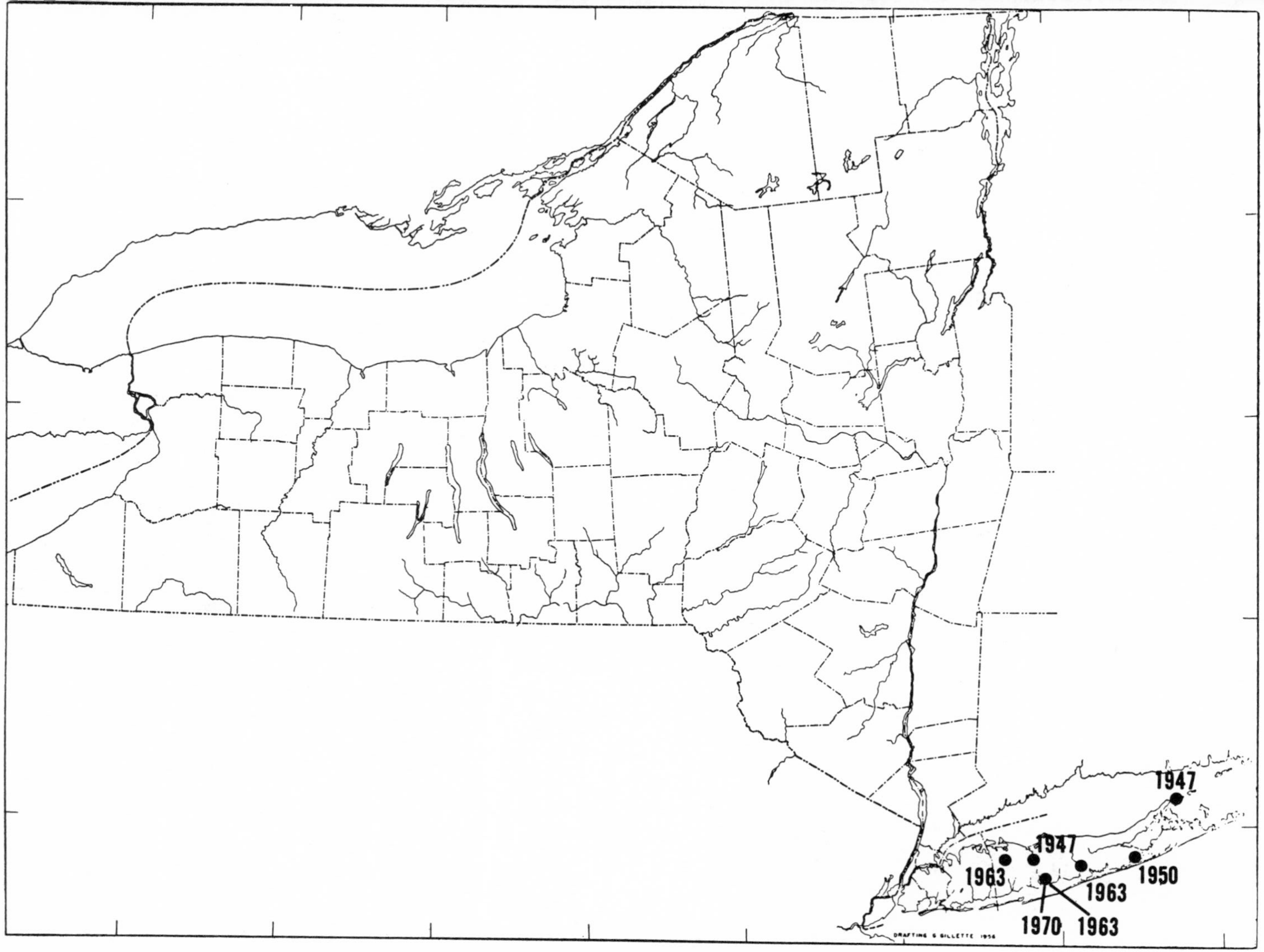

MAP 105 Brown Creeper
(*Certhia familiaris*)
Recent southward
breeding range extension
to Long Island

tions, others have been located in both deciduous and evergreen forest or at their edges
in dry uplands, as long as suitable trees are
available. Scheider, *et al.* (*Kingbird,* 1966,
16: 228), suggest that, in central New York,
breeding sites for these birds "probably will
increase as more and more elm swamps succumb to Dutch elm disease, since these dying
woods provide ideal nesting sites and super-
abundant food."

Of 28 New York nest sites examined, 26
were located in the conventional loose-bark
situation. The remaining two, however, were
in decidedly unorthodox locations—behind
wooden house shutters. One of these was in
northeastern Westchester Co. in 1965 (Bull,
1970: 32). The other was in the Adirondack
foothill village of Elizabethtown, Essex Co.,

in 1969 (Carleton). Nest heights have ranged
from four to over 16 feet.

Egg clutches in 24 New York nests ranged
from four to seven: four eggs (six nests);
five eggs (ten nests); six eggs (seven nests);
seven eggs (one nest).

EGG DATES: Apr. 24 to June 30.

Nestlings: May 27 to July 28; fledglings:
June 24 to Aug. 20.

Postscript: On June 6, 1972, Messrs. Bergen,
Giffen, and Kessler showed the writer *four*
active nests—all within one-half mile—all nests
were situated on dead or dying pitch pines, in
swampy woods at the Oakdale, Long Island,
location—along the *south* shore at the southern periphery of the species' range along the
coast. The species was unknown as a breeder
anywhere on Long Island prior to 1947.

WRENS — TROGLODYTIDAE

Six species in New York.
Five breed.

This almost exclusively New World family
(about 60 species) reaches its highest development in the Neotropics—nearly half that number being found only in Middle America.

The Winter Wren (*Troglodytes troglodytes*)
alone has crossed into the Old World from
Alaska to Siberia by way of Bering Strait, and
has colonized virtually all of temperate Eurasia. It has penetrated as far as Formosa
(Taiwan), the Himalayas, and various Mediterranean islands; one population has even
reached the north African coast, and another
to the island of St. Kilda, off the Scottish
coast. No fewer than 27 Old World subspecies
have been described.

Both marsh wrens (*palustris* and *platensis*)
have been merged into the genus *Cistothorus,*
following Hellmayr (1934), Paynter (in
"Peters," 1960), and Mayr and Short (1970).
For reasons why Bewick's and Carolina wrens
(*bewickii* and *ludovicianus*) have been combined in the genus *Thryothorus,* see species
account.

House Wren
(*Troglodytes aedon*)   *   B

Range: Nearctic and Neotropical regions,
breeding from southern Canada to southern
South America. In the east winters north to
North Carolina, rarely to Maryland, and once
in northern New Jersey (specimen).

Status: Fairly common fall migrant. Widespread breeder, but rare in the higher mountains.

Nonbreeding: Though found nearly throughout the state during migration, the House Wren
is not reported in large numbers, even in fall
—ordinarily only a few individuals at any one
locality.

MAXIMA: 12, near Rochester, Sept. 19,
1959; 12, Easthampton, Suffolk Co., Sept. 26,
1927; eight netted and banded, near Huntington, Suffolk Co., Oct. 1, 1967.

EXTREME DATES: Apr. 9 (inland) and
Apr. 12 (coastal) to Oct. 29 (inland) and
Nov. 3 (coastal specimen); exceptionally to
late November and early December along the

coast. Rare before late April and after mid-October.

Winter: No state specimen or other adequate confirmation exists. However, in recent years a few have been observed lingering into late December or early January on Long Island, but have never survived the winter, as far as known. Some of these sight reports were made by experienced observers, while others were probably misidentified Winter Wrens, mostly on Christmas counts.

Breeding: The House Wren breeds in rural and suburban areas in gardens, orchards, and estates, also in dense thickets, forest clearings, and swampy woodland. It is a very adaptable species in nesting habits. The nest is placed in a variety of situations such as tree cavities, upturned tree roots, stone walls, birdhouses, tin cans, coat pockets, iron pipes, mailboxes, old shoes, nail kegs, fence posts, and once in a human skull. Old paper-wasp nests have been utilized at least five times. Even old avian nests may be used—two each of Barn Swallow and Baltimore Oriole—and once a pair of House Wrens nested in one compartment of a Purple Martin house. Even more unusual is a record (Allen, 1892: 319) of several pairs of House Wrens on Plum Island, Suffolk Co., nesting in *occupied* Osprey nests. More than once Allen "found nests of the House Wren in the deeper interstices" (of Osprey nests).

In 31 New York nests, egg clutches ranged from four to eight: four eggs (four nests); five eggs (seven nests); six eggs (11 nests); seven eggs (six nests); eight eggs (three nests).

EGG DATES: May 15 to July 31 (second brood).

Nestlings: May 22 to Aug. 25 (second brood); fledglings: June 26 to Sept. 11 (second brood).

Banding: Two individuals banded in late summer and early fall in New York were recovered the following winter in Florida.

Remarks: No eastern subspecies (*"baldwini"*) are recognized here: much individual variation occurs within this species and alleged differences between eastern and midwestern birds are too slight to warrant recognition.

The House Wren and the wide-ranging Neotropical form, *T. musculus,* are here consid-

ered to be conspecific, following Bond (1961) and de Schauensee (1966).

Winter Wren
(*Troglodytes troglodytes*) * B

Range: Holarctic region, in North America breeding from Alaska and Canada, in the east rarely to the highlands of southeastern New York; also in higher mountains to northern Georgia. Winters throughout except the more northern portions of the breeding range.

Status: Uncommon to fairly common migrant, especially inland; less numerous in winter. Common breeder in the mountains, local elsewhere at higher elevations, and rare southeastward.

Nonbreeding: During migrations and in winter this secretive species frequents brush piles and dense thickets, but may be "squeaked" out of hiding and thus more easily observed. Ordinarily only one to three Winter Wrens are observed, but sometimes more are seen.

MAXIMA: *Spring*—seven, Hamburg, Erie Co., Apr. 9, 1962; 13, Manitou, Monroe Co., Apr. 20, 1954; 14, Sandy Pond, Oswego Co., Apr. 25, 1954.

MAXIMA: *Fall*—18, Island Cottage, Monroe Co., Sept. 28, 1958; 18, Sandy Pond, Oct. 8, 1961; 15, Inwood Hill Park, New York City, Oct. 11, 1965; 15, Sandy Pond, Oct. 18, 1958.

MAXIMA: *Winter*—six, Ellison Park, Rochester, Feb. 25, 1951.

EXTREME DATES: Sept. 5 (inland) and Sept. 11 (coastal) to May 21 (coastal) and May 25 (inland). Rare before late September and after early May.

Breeding (see Map 106): This species, considered by some to be the finest singer in the state, occupies two distinct nesting habitats: (1) It is a well-known inhabitant of montane evergreen forest consisting primarily of spruce and balsam fir. (2) It is also less well known as a dweller in the more lowland areas in "cold" bogs and swamps, especially hemlock-white cedar bogs upstate and even more rarely in hemlock-rhododendron swamps in the lower

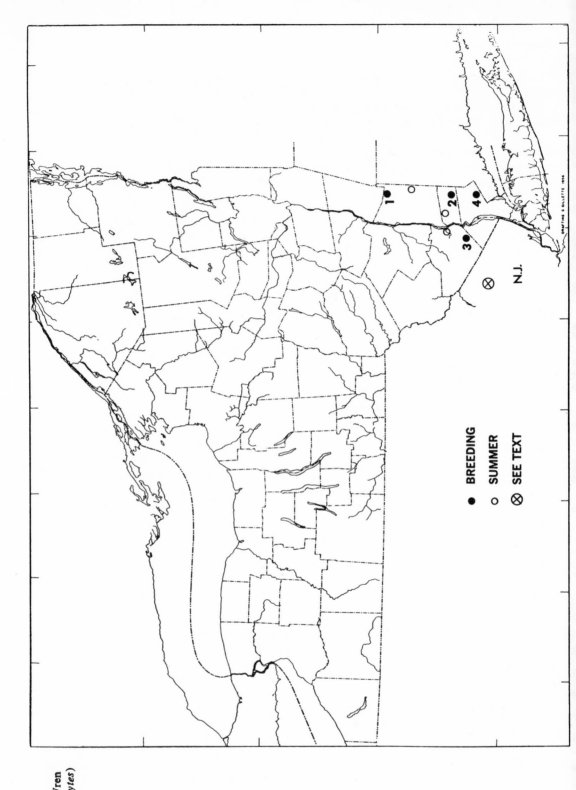

MAP 106 Winter Wren
(*Troglodytes troglodytes*)
Known southern
breeding limits

BREEDING
SUMMER
SEE TEXT

N.J.

Catskills and to the southeast of them (see below).

Winter Wrens are quite numerous in both the Adirondacks and in the Tug Hill region to the west. In the former area at Elk Lake, Essex Co., Frank Schetty counted 22 singing males in 1965 along the trails, and in 1967 he found *17* nest sites. In the Tug Hill area 18 individuals were counted on July 3, 1960 (Scheider).

Whether occurring in the higher mountains or at lower altitudes, this species' favorite nest site is among the roots of overturned trees. It occasionally places its nest in a stump cavity or in an earthen bank. In such places height above ground level ranges from nine inches to about two and one-half feet.

Egg clutches in 14 New York nests ranged from four to six: four eggs (eight nests); five and six eggs (three nests each).

EGG DATES: May 22 to July 7 and July 29 (second brood).

Nestlings: June 3 to Aug. 4; fledglings: June 15 to Aug. 16.

The accompanying map shows the four known southeasternmost breeding localities in New York, as well as three summer occurrences—breeding not proved: (1) near Pine Plains, Dutchess Co.; (2) Peach Lake, Putnam Co. portion; (3) Surebridge Swamp, Harriman State Park, Orange Co.; (4) Westmoreland Sanctuary (only 700 feet elevation) between Bedford and Mount Kisco, Westchester Co. (see Bull, 1964: 327). The three summer occurrences were at Turkey Hollow near Wassaic, Dutchess Co., near Cornwall, Orange Co., and Fahnestock State Park, Putnam Co. See also breeding locality to the south in New Jersey.

Remarks: The eastern race *hiemalis* is considerably paler than the western race *pacificus*. However, *"pullus"* from the southern Appalachians hardly differs from *hiemalis* and is not considered separable.

Carolina Wren
(*Thryothorus ludovicianus*)   *   B

Range: Chiefly eastern United States and northeastern Mexico, ranging north to extreme southeastern Ontario and the central portions of New York and New England. Sedentary.

Status: Locally fairly common resident on Long Island and in the lower Hudson valley; uncommon resident at lower elevations elsewhere, but has increased in recent years. Virtually absent in northern New York and in the mountains.

Change in status: Eaton (1914: 479) called the Carolina Wren a rare visitant over most of western and central New York, and knew of only seven localities where it occurred, and but two breeding records—one each for Genesee and Tompkins counties. In 1925 Roger Peterson discovered a nesting pair in Chautauqua Co. near Jamestown. It was unknown as a breeder in Chemung and Schuyler counties prior to 1947 (Axtell, 1947).

However, it was not until the 1950s that this species increased greatly upstate, especially in the mid-Hudson and eastern Mohawk valleys, the Syracuse region, the western Finger Lakes, the river valleys in the "southern tier" counties (adjacent to Pennsylvania), and near Rochester and the lower Genesee valley.

Nonbreeding: This species is very sensitive to severe winters, being decimated by ice storms, heavy snows, and long periods of sub-zero weather. With a succession of mild winters, it gradually recovers and re-establishes itself. Numbers of these birds have survived even the rugged upstate weather by remaining at feeding stations for part of the winter, at least. One banded at an Essex Co. feeder at Essex on Lake Champlain, Nov. 9, 1952, remained until Dec. 28 (Mason). Another visited a feeder at Saranac Lake, Franklin Co., from Nov. 28 to Dec. 13, 1954 (Meade).

A large population has been present on Gardiner's Island, Suffolk Co., for many years —no doubt due to the milder climate of an insular locality, plus a good amount of forest and thick undergrowth. On Dec. 25, 1908, and again on Dec. 30, 1967, observers recorded the maximum known numbers—15 individuals—*60* years apart.

Breeding (see Map 107): Carolina Wrens are very adaptable, occurring in such diverse terrain as thickets in sand dunes in the Sunken Forest on Fire Island, on cliff ledges of the

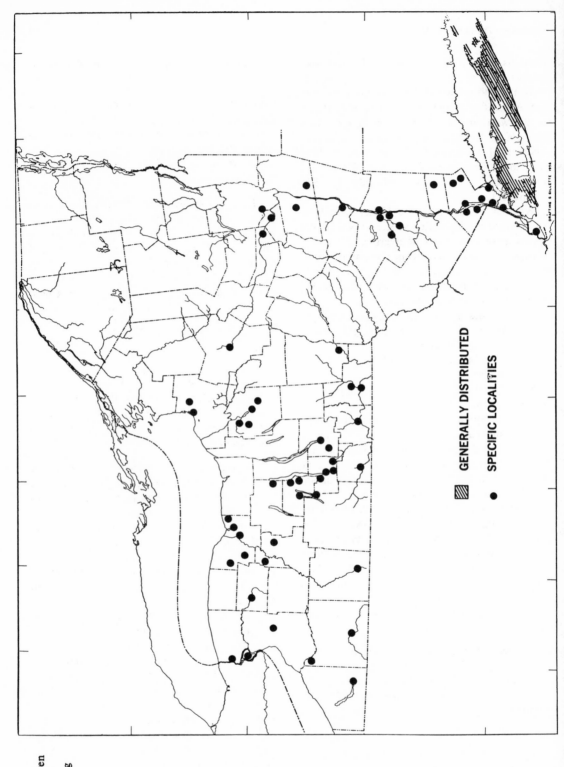

GENERALLY DISTRIBUTED

SPECIFIC LOCALITIES

MAP 107 Carolina Wren (*Thryothorus ludovicianus*) Breeding distribution

Palisades, and in wooded ravines and in dense tangles near streams and swamps in upstate New York. One partially domed nest was even on the ground in a tiny hummock at the base of a cinnamon fern.

The nest is placed in a vast assortment of situations, such as in bird boxes, stone walls, hollow tree stumps, tin cans, old hats or coat pockets, privies, shelves of houses and garages, crevices of a log house, crate in tool house, mailboxes, metal pipes, ivy on wall, on the side of an abandoned well, and even in an enclosed bird feeder.

Egg clutches in 18 New York nests contained the following: four eggs (six nests); five eggs (11 nests); six eggs (one nest).

EGG DATES: Apr. 1 to Aug. 5 (at least double-brooded in southern New York).

Nestlings: Apr. 21 to Aug. 18; fledglings: May 8 to Aug. 29. As many as *three* broods were reported near Watkins Glen, Schuyler Co., in 1971 (J. Brubaker, *Kingbird*, 1971, 21: 225).

In this state the highest breeding densities are on eastern Long Island: 12 pairs, Easthampton to Montauk, summer of 1932 (Helmuth); *26* singing birds, Gardiner's Island, June 1939 (Helmuth); six pairs, Orient to Southold, summer of 1956 (Latham).

More than 90 localities in the state have had breeding birds. Almost without exception, upstate sites are located at, or near, lake and river shores. The northernmost known nesting record for New York is at Pulaski, Oswego Co. (see map).

Banding: See **Nonbreeding.**

Bewick's Wren
(*Thryothorus bewickii*)   *

Range: Chiefly western, central, and southeastern United States, south to central Mexico; absent from the Atlantic coastal plain; breeds northeast to central Pennsylvania; also extreme southern Ontario (Point Pelee). Sedentary. Apparently scarce where the House Wren is common, at least at the periphery of its range. Vagrant to New York, Rhode Island (Block Island), and New Hampshire (specimens).

Status: *Very rare*—there are two confirmed records for New York. (1) A male was collected on eastern Long Island at Riverhead, Suffolk Co., Sept. 21, 1930 (Latham), NYSM 25297; this record previously unpublished. (2) An individual was present at the Coalson and Daboll feeders, Auburn, Seneca Co., from November 1953 to late February 1954 and a color movie was taken by H. Daboll. The film is on file at the Cornell University Laboratory of Ornithology, *fide* S. H. Spofford (see also *Kingbird*, 1954, 4: 3–4).

The following six reports of birds observed are believed to be correct: (1) Central Park, New York City, Apr. 10–May 8, 1928 (Capen, Griscom, *et al.*); (2) north of Brockport, Monroe Co., June 16, 1940 (Guelf and G. Morgan); (3) Prospect Park, Brooklyn, May 13, 1946 (Soll and Whelen); (4) same locality, Apr. 15–23, 1952 (Carleton, Grant, *et al.*); (5) Croton Point, Westchester Co., May 8, 1952 (Walsh); (6) near Braddock's Bay, Monroe Co., Apr. 21–23, 1954 (Van Beurden, Corcoran, and McKinney).

An individual netted and collected on Block Island, Rhode Island, Oct. 4, 1969 (E. Lapham), was confirmed as this species by the writer; the specimen is AMNH 793543 (*Auk*, 1971, 88: 168). This specimen record was published *prior* to the discovery of the above 1930 Long Island specimen.

Remarks: The genus *"Thryomanes"* is here merged with *Thryothorus*. Ridgway (1904: 478) gave relative length of hallux (hind toe) and bill width as generic distinctions. Hellmayr (1934: 210) said of *Thryomanes*, "doubtfully separable from *Thryothorus*."

A cursory examination of members of the largely Neotropical genus *Thryothorus* indicates that some of the many species currently placed in that genus are far more different in appearance from one another than the Bewick's and Carolina wrens are to each other.

No eastern races are recognized here; the birds of the southern Appalachians, called *"altus,"* are too slightly differentiated to warrant recognition.   •

Long-billed Marsh Wren
(*Cistothorus palustris*)   *   B

Range: North America, breeding from southern Canada to southern United States and northern Mexico. Withdraws from northern portions in winter.

Status: Locally common to abundant breeder, much less numerous northward and rare at higher elevations. Rare to uncommon in winter, but very rarely reported as a migrant.

Nonbreeding: As it occurs both summer and winter, migration dates are difficult to determine; but this species usually arrives on the breeding grounds by early May and departs in October. Being a night migrant and very secretive during the day, it is rarely reported away from the breeding grounds.

MAXIMA: *Winter*—seven, Buck Pond, Monroe Co., Dec. 30, 1951 (Barry), squeaked up from cattail marsh; six, Oak Beach, Suffolk Co., winter of 1967–1968 (Enders and W. Post), coastal salt marsh. These numbers, especially the upstate ones, are exceptional. Usually only one or two individuals are reported in winter.

Breeding: The Long-billed Marsh Wren breeds colonially in cattails inland and along the larger tidal rivers—for example, approximately 100 pairs bred in the Hudson River marshes at Croton Point, Westchester Co., in 1942 (Bull, 1964: 329)—and to a lesser extent in *Phragmites* and other grasses in both brackish and salt marshes on the coast. Naturally the number of pairs depends upon the size of the marsh.

According to Welter (1935) in the Ithaca area this species prefers to nest in narrow-leaved cattail (*Typha angustifolia*) rather than broad-leaved cattail (*T. latifolia*). Saunders (1938) also found this to be the case for the Syracuse region and in Allegany State Park.

These birds also breed in coastal salt and brackish marshes, nesting in cattails, *Phragmites,* occasionally in *Spartina alterniflora,* and at least twice in the salt meadow shrub (*Iva frutescens*) at Tobay Beach, Nassau Co., in 1967 and 1971 (see Fig. 73).

Fig. 73   Long-billed Marsh Wren nest, four feet up in *Iva frutescens* bush, Tobay Pond, Nassau Co., June 1971. Photo by Adrian Dignan

The nest is ordinarily attached to stems of one of the above-mentioned plants from three to five feet above water level. The nest is domed with the entrance on the side. Many dummy nests are also constructed, which may be used for sleeping.

Egg clutches in 30 New York nests: three eggs (seven nests); four eggs (ten nests); five eggs (seven nests); six eggs (six nests).

EGG DATES: May 22 to Aug. 7 (second brood).

Nestlings: June 21 to Aug. 12; fledglings: July 2 to Aug. 31.

Remarks: No northeastern subspecies are recognized here. This species is another good example of a continental east-west cline, the inland fresh-water population *"dissaeptus"* not being markedly different from nominate *palustris* of the coast, and intermediate in appearance between the latter and more western birds. The color differences are of average quality only as individual variation exists within the same population.

Short-billed Marsh Wren
(*Cistothorus platensis*)   *   B

Range: Nearctic and Neotropical regions, but very local throughout, breeding from southeastern Canada to Arkansas and Virginia; also from southern Mexico to extreme southern South America. The northern population winters north to Maryland, very rarely to Long Island. The species is absent from western North America and the West Indies.

Status: Rare and little-known migrant; very rare in winter. Rare to uncommon and local breeder, absent in the higher mountains.

Nonbreeding: The Short-billed Marsh Wren is exceptionally secretive and about as easy to study as a mouse. Rare and little known as a migrant, it is very difficult to state accurately its arrival and departure dates. This species is extremely rare away from breeding localities.

It may be that it is chiefly nocturnal during passage. A specimen taken at Batavia, Genesee Co., Oct. 9, 1941 (M. I. Kinley), NYSM 6267, was labeled by the collector as "found dead under a street light."

EXTREME DATES: Apr. 18 (coastal) and May 4 (inland) to Oct. 27 (inland specimen) and Nov. 22 (coastal). However, these dates may not be at all representative. The October date referred to above is a specimen taken on the breeding grounds—New Bremen, Lewis Co., Oct. 27, 1887 (R. B. Hough), RMAS 4723.

The only positive winter record for the state that I am aware of is a specimen collected at Jones Beach, Long Island, Dec. 28, 1913 (Griscom), AMNH 142895. Otherwise reported very rarely and irregularly at this season in coastal salt marshes. A number of unconfirmed sight reports by inexperienced observers are probably misidentified Long-billed Marsh Wrens. I know of no winter occurrence inland.

Breeding: This species is extremely particular in its choice of nest sites. It avoids the cattail marsh which is frequented by its congener, the Long-billed Marsh Wren. Instead it is restricted to *moist* meadows with scattered low bushes, or grass and sedge bogs, also coastal brackish marshes consisting of *Spartina patens* (salt hay), interspersed with herbs and low shrubs. But even in these places it is found only if it is not too wet or not too dry, disappearing and reappearing from a known breeding locality when the water table fluctuates. In such localities this hard-to-see bird may be found. However, its characteristic song, once known, will reveal its presence.

The few domed nests found in New York were situated in coarse grass clumps or grass hummocks from a few inches to a foot above ground or water level.

Egg clutches examined in only six New York nests ranged from three (incomplete set?) to seven: three, five, and seven eggs (one nest each); four eggs (three nests).

EGG DATES: May 28 to July 30.

Nestlings: June 30 to Aug. 22; fledglings: Aug. 4 to Sept. 15.

The distribution of this little-studied species is as local today as it was in Eaton's time. It is least rare in the southeastern portions and in parts of central and western New York. It bred on Long Island prior to 1962, but only along the south shore where it was known from six stations—three from central Suffolk Co., two in Nassau Co., and one in Queens

Co. It is, or was, locally fairly common on the east side of the Hudson River from West-chester Co. north to Dutchess Co., but like Long Island, a number of former breeding localities were destroyed. Small "colonies" of up to six pairs were reported from these areas, as well as in Orange Co., west of the Hudson.

Short-billed Marsh Wrens today are present in small numbers in the following upstate areas: lower St. Lawrence River, shore of Lake On-tario, Oneida Lake region, the Finger Lakes and to the south of them, the lower Genesee valley, the Oak Orchard Swamp region, and from Niagara Falls locally south to Chautauqua Lake.

These wrens are generally scarce in the mountains—including much of the Allegany Plateau—and are virtually absent from the entire Catskill district.

Although very rare in the Adirondacks, there are at least two localities where breeding has been proved: (1) western Adirondacks at Heath Point (elevation 1500 feet) north of Wanakena near Cranberry Lake, St. Lawrence Co., in 1940 (Terres); (2) "high peak" coun-try at Heart Lake (elevation 2000 feet), Essex Co., in 1950 (Elliott).

The Short-billed Marsh Wren has been found breeding in at least 90 New York localities.

Subspecies: The local breeding population, belonging to the isolated North American race *stellaris,* differs from the nearest Mexican races (*elegans* and *tinnulus*) by possessing a buff breast band.

THRASHERS, MOCKERS — MIMIDAE

Four species in New York.
Three breed.

This exclusively American family (30± species) is well represented in the West Indies, Mexico (including southwestern United States), Central America, and chiefly tem-perate South America. There is also a distinct mockingbird genus (*Nesomimus*) confined to the Galápagos Islands.

In New York two of the species—Gray Cat-bird (*Dumetella carolinensis*) and Brown Thrasher (*Toxostoma rufum*) are well-known breeders in most of the state, one—Common Mockingbird (*Mimus polyglottos*)—is a recent arrival and is spreading northward, and the fourth—Sage Thrasher (*Oreoscoptes mon-tanus*)—is merely a vagrant from the west.

Gray Catbird
(*Dumetella carolinensis*)   *   B

Range: Breeds in southern Canada and through much of the United States (except the southwest). Winters chiefly in southern United States south to Panama and the Greater Antilles; a few regularly north to Long Island.

Status: Common to very common migrant. Uncommon but regular in winter along the coast; much rarer inland. Widespread breeder, but rare to absent in the mountains at high elevations.

Nonbreeding: Catbirds usually arrive the first few days in May and depart in late October.

MAXIMA: *Spring*—58 netted and banded, Fire Island, Suffolk Co., May 9, 1970; 35, Syracuse, May 10, 1956; 100, Bronx Park, Bronx Co., May 14, 1953 (Komorowski); 50, Sandy Pond, Oswego Co., May 15, 1965; 100, same locality, May 27, 1961 (Scheider), a very late spring.

MAXIMA: *Fall*—150, Far Rockaway, Queens Co., Sept. 23, 1953 (Bull); 35, Syra-cuse, Sept. 29, 1964.

During the winter months this species has increased correspondingly in recent years with the great increase in the number of feeding stations. As with many other species that over-winter, Catbirds are much less rare near the

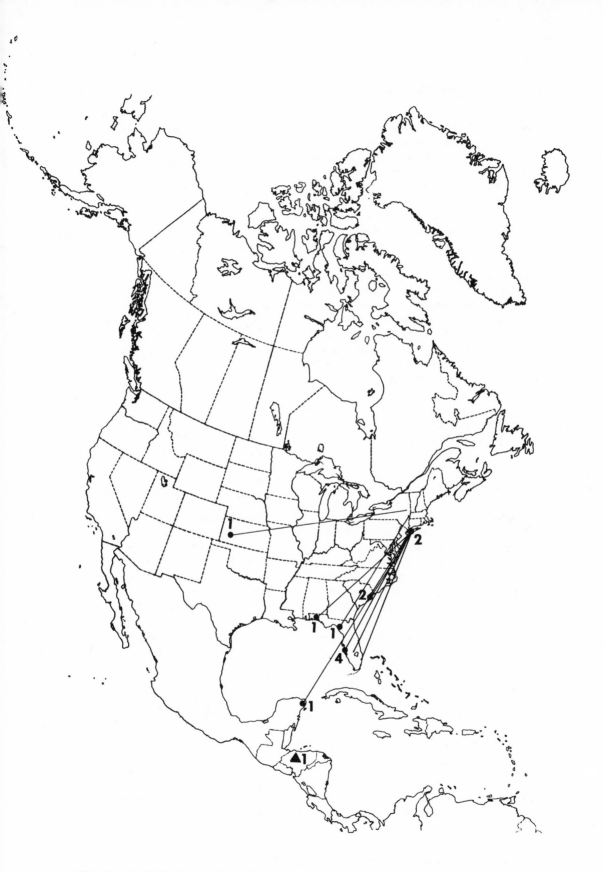

MAP 108 Gray Catbird (*Dumetella carolinensis*) Banding recoveries

milder coastal areas than upstate. See Brown Thrasher.

Breeding: A common species nesting wherever thickets or shrubbery occur, from suburban yards and city parks to farmland, along swamp borders, at the edge of, but not in, forest (except clearings), and frequently in coastal sand dunes. During a breeding survey in 1965 at Van Cortlandt Park, Bronx Co., Heath and Zupan found 30 pairs nesting in a 19-acre tract. Most nests were located in viburnum bushes.

The nest is placed low, from three to ten feet up. Of 22 additional New York nests examined, hawthorn was a favorite site with *ten* nests, three in swamp rose, followed by one each in choke cherry, lilac, forsythia, honeysuckle, Virginia creeper, hydrangea, and saplings of willow, elm, maple, and hackberry, as well as such evergreens as hemlock, spruce, pine, and arbor-vitae.

Egg clutches in 41 New York nests numbered as follows: three eggs (six nests); four eggs (26 nests); five eggs (eight nests); six eggs (one nest).

EGG DATES: May 5 to June 13, exceptionally to Aug. 12 (second brood).

Nestlings: May 29 to Aug. 20; fledglings: June 6 to Sept. 21.

Benton (*Kingbird,* 1961, 11: 81–82 and 137) gives an interesting account of nest sharing by a pair of Robins and a pair of Catbirds near Albany. Apparently both species participated in nest construction (started by the Catbirds), and shared in incubation and feeding of the young. Seven eggs were laid, three—Catbird, four—Robin. Only three hatched, however, two —Robin, one—Catbird. All three fledged successfully. In another instance, McIlroy, *et. al.* (*Kingbird,* 1965, 15: 234), tell about another nest near Ithaca, built by a Catbird, "in which the first of four eggs was laid on June 1, was taken over by a Robin which incubated the four Catbird eggs and raised two young to successful fledging, continuing to feed the young out of the nest."

Banding (see Map 108): An individual banded in early September 1964 on Long Island was recovered the following winter in the state of Quintana Roo, Mexico. Another banded in 1927 upstate was recovered more than two years later at the end of October in Honduras.

Unusual was a Catbird banded on Sept. 21, 1956, at Amsterdam, Montgomery Co., and recovered only a month later—Oct. 24—in a *southwesterly* direction at Ensign, Kansas.

Too late for inclusion on the banding map is that of another individual banded and recaptured on Sept. 11 and 26, 1970, respectively in the Schenectady area (R. P. Yunick), and reported shot Nov. 4, 1970, on the coast of British Honduras.

Brown Thrasher
(*Toxostoma rufum*)   *   B

Range: Chiefly central and eastern North America, breeding from southern Canada to the Gulf states. Winters chiefly in southern United States, a few regularly north to Long Island.

Status: Common migrant near the coast and rare to uncommon there in winter. Much less numerous upstate at all seasons. Widespread breeder, but rare to absent in the mountains and in the northeastern sections.

Nonbreeding: Brown Thrashers usually arrive in late April and remain until early November, but the season is shorter upstate by as much as one week, both spring and fall.

MAXIMA, COASTAL: *Spring*—23, Prospect Park, Brooklyn, May 12, 1945. *Fall*—50, Far Rockaway, Queens Co., Sept. 17, 1949.

No comparable figures are at hand for *inland* maxima *per day, per locality.* However, Beardslee and Mitchell (1965: 336–337) give comparisons for several localities—all-day spring and fall "counts" for both Catbird and Brown Thrasher. It is obvious from a perusal of these "counts" that in fall, Catbirds outnumber Thrashers by nearly five to one, and in spring even more so—from six to one, up to eight to one.

In *winter,* this species has increased in recent years with a proportionate increase in feeding stations. Formerly much less numerous at this season than the Catbird, since about 1962 the Brown Thrasher has outnumbered the Catbird, at least according to Long Island Christmas counts.

Breeding: This species breeds in dry open country, especially in thickets and scrubby fields. It is particularly numerous on the coastal plain of Long Island and least common in the mountains; in the Adirondacks it is much less numerous than the Catbird.

In western New York, where it is much less common than along the coast, Benton (1949) stated that in Cayuga Co., the Brown Thrasher prefers "brushy hillsides covered with *Crataegus*" (hawthorn). According to Parkes (1952a) in southeastern New York it is generally tamer than upstate and nests closer to habitations, as in suburban yards. In the Ithaca region, however, it prefers "scrubby hillsides, old pastures, and abandoned orchards." S. W. Eaton (1953: 17) says that in Cattaraugus Co. it nests mainly in thorn apples (hawthorns) in deserted pastures.

At least three ground nests have been reported in New York. However, this species usually builds low, from seven inches to rarely eight feet up. Thorn growth is definitely preferred. Of 12 nests with details as to location, five were in viburnum, four in hawthorn, two in *Smilax* (catbrier), and another in scrub cedar.

Of 38 New York nests, all had from three to five eggs, with the following breakdown: three eggs (18 nests); four eggs (13 nests); five eggs (seven nests).

EGG DATES: May 6 to June 26.

Nestlings: May 19 to July 14; fledglings: June 19 to July 26.

Banding: Three individuals banded in summer in New York were recovered the following fall or winter in southern Georgia, northern Florida, and near New Orleans, Louisiana.

Sage Thrasher
(*Oreoscoptes montanus*)　*

Range: Western North America, breeding east to southeastern Wyoming. Casual east to the Great Plains. Vagrant to Ontario and New York (specimens).

Status: *Very rare*—the only known substantiated records in New York are: (1) a female collected at Braddock's Bay, near Rochester, Apr. 12, 1942 (Meade), CUM 12789; (2)

an individual caught in a mist net was banded, color-photographed, and released at Shinnecock Inlet (near the Tiana Coast Guard station), Suffolk Co., Oct. 18, 1958 (Wilcox and W. Terry). Confirmation was made by Eisenmann and the writer by comparison of the color slide with museum skins; photo on file, AMNH collection.

Remarks: This species perhaps would be best merged with the genus *Toxostoma* (thrashers). Ridgway (1907: 183–184, key) gave two characters supposedly separating these genera: (1) a difference in wing formula—relative lengths of fifth, ninth, and tenth primaries, a character sometimes used in separating species (within *Empidonax* [flycatchers], for instance); (2) presence or absence of "subterminal notch to maxillary tomium," barely discernible in some specimens.

On the other hand, the tail pattern—white patches—suggests a possible relationship with *Mimus* (mockingbirds).

Postscript: A bird originally identified by many people as a Bendire's Thrasher (*Toxostoma bendirei*) at Massena, St. Lawrence Co., Dec. 27, 1971, was subsequently photographed by Douglas Allen and reidentified as a Sage Thrasher (third state occurrence) by comparing the photographs with skins at the American Museum of Natural History; photos on file, AMNH collection. Prior to this photographic evidence, it had been published in one of the regional journals as a "sure" sight identification of an improbable Bendire's Thrasher (a sedentary species of the arid southwest), an especially dangerous procedure, as published errors tend to become perpetuated.

Another was observed and photographed at the Jamaica Bay Refuge, Long Island, Jan. 13–17, 1973 (numerous people); see photo, *Kingbird* (1973, 23: 72).

Common Mockingbird
(*Mimus polyglottos*)　*　B

Range: Southern Nearctic and Neotropical regions, in the east breeding north to the northern portions of New York and New England, very rarely to extreme southern Canada, and casually north along the St. Lawrence River in

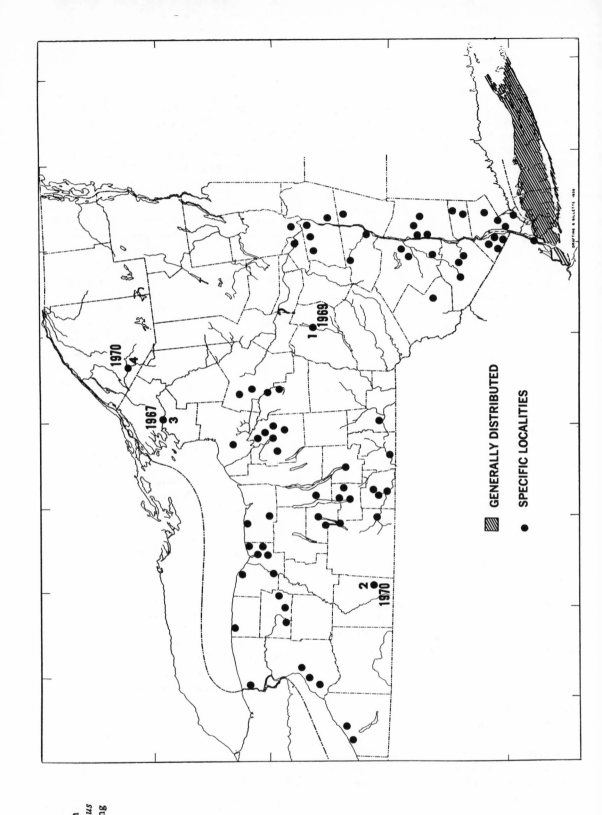

MAP 109 Common
Mockingbird (*Mimus
polyglottos*) Breeding
distribution

GENERALLY DISTRIBUTED

SPECIFIC LOCALITIES

Quebec, and even to Newfoundland (Godfrey, 1966: 292); spreading north in recent years. Mostly sedentary.

Status: Locally common resident in southeastern New York, especially on Long Island. Much less numerous elsewhere, but steadily increasing. Very rare in northern New York, local in the St. Lawrence valley. Unrecorded in the mountains prior to 1966, and still very rare even at the edges and in the foothills.

Change in status: Few species have increased in the state as has the Mockingbird. Eaton (1914: 471–472) did not know of a single authentic breeding record for New York, and considered it merely a rare visitant. The first definite breeding record was obtained in 1925 at Orchard Park, Erie Co., where a nest and eggs were collected (C. G. Smith, *Ool.,* 1927, 44: 44). No further nesting evidence was obtained for many years.

Not until the early 1950s did any appreciable increase take place. In the two decades (1951–1970) Mockingbirds increased prodigiously and spread far and wide—more than *100* breeding localities recorded within only *20* years.

Nonbreeding: Prior to the mid-1950s when the Mockingbird first bred along the outer coast, it was a regular fall migrant from mid-August (chiefly September) to late November, but as it now breeds commonly there and as individuals are recorded every month of the year, it would be virtually impossible to distinguish migrants from residents (see Bull, 1964: 331).

In the late 1960s vagrants were recorded for the first time in and near the Adirondack district, as follows: Essex Co.—Lake Champlain at Willsboro; Herkimer Co.—Old Forge; Hamilton Co.—Sabael, and Little Tupper Lake; Franklin Co.—Saranac Lake.

Breeding (see Map 109): This species frequents open country in both agricultural and residential districts. It nests commonly in thickets and hedgerows, and is particularly fond of rosebushes and vines—especially *Rosa multiflora* and *R. rugosa.* Pine trees are often utilized as nest sites, particularly *Pinus mugo*—the introduced Japanese black pine—on Long Island. Holly, bayberry, lilac, and privet are also used.

Nest heights range from two to ten feet above ground. Egg clutches in 34 New York nests: three eggs (14 nests); four eggs (18 nests); five eggs (two nests).

The species is occasionally triple-brooded in New York, as proved by banding.

EGG DATES: Apr. 27 to July 21.

Nestlings: May 5 to Aug. 11; fledglings: May 25 to Aug. 29. Both incubation and nestling periods were determined to be 12 days.

Details of breeding distribution in the New York City region are given in Bull (1964: 331–333 and 1970: 32–33). It is now a common breeder on Long and Staten islands, especially along the outer beaches, nesting all the way to Montauk and Orient points. In 1969 at least *three dozen* pairs were estimated on the Rockaway peninsula from Far Rockaway to Rockaway Point, a distance of 12 miles, or about three pairs per mile (Bull). In this area singing Mockingbirds are familiar sights on rooftops and on television antennae. Only 14 years before (1956) the first known nests were discovered on Long Island.

In the lower and mid-Hudson valley Mockingbirds are more local, but fairly common and increasing, nesting as far north as southern Saratoga Co. Their "absence" in much of the Mohawk valley is probably more apparent than real (lack of observers?).

Elsewhere in the state these birds are local but spreading, as follows: (A) Oneida Lake—Syracuse region; (B) southern Finger Lakes to the Pennsylvania state line; (C) Rochester—lower Genesee valley, southwest to Lake Erie.

Four recent isolated and peripheral breeding localities are: (1) Cooperstown, Otsego Co., 1969, at the headwaters of the Susquehanna River; (2) Alfred, Allegany Co., 1970, "penetration" into the Allegany Plateau via the Genesee River; (3) near Watertown, Jefferson Co., 1967, Black River via Lake Ontario; (4) near Gouverneur, St. Lawrence Co., 1970, Oswegatchie River, by way of the St. Lawrence River. The last is the northernmost known breeding record in the state, based on three nestlings found there on July 3 by John Belknap.

Remarks: This and the tropical American *gilvus,* the Tropical Mockingbird, are here considered conspecific following several recent authorities. The two interbreed in Mexico where their ranges meet.

THRUSHES — TURDIDAE

Ten species in New York.
Seven breed.

This complex is sometimes considered to be a subfamily of the Muscicapidae, (Old World Flycatchers, etc.) but for convenience is here treated as a family. The nearly worldwide and successful thrush group (300± species), though absent from New Zealand, has reached some of the remotest oceanic islands, such as the mid-Pacific Hawaiian Archipelago and the Tristan da Cunha group in the mid-south Atlantic, each with an endemic genus and species.

Some of the world's finest singers are thrushes. In New York the brown-backed members of the genus *Catharus* (Veery, Hermit Thrush, etc.) are in this category. The beautiful Eastern Bluebird (*Sialia sialis*) is our only hole-nesting thrush, all the others building open cup-shaped nests.

American Robin
(*Turdus migratorius*)   *   B

Range: North America south to Mexico and the Gulf states. Winters from New York south. The nominate subspecies breeds in our area.

Status: Very abundant migrant and abundant breeder. Rare to uncommon in winter, but occasionally numerous.

Nonbreeding: The Robin is one of our most numerous species and certainly the most widespread and familiar bird in the state. Great flocks pass through the state both spring and fall, and in late summer they congregate in large roosts. Even in winter Robins may be found in sheltered thickets near swampy places where there is an abundance of berries.

MAXIMA: *Spring*—4500 (3500 in two hours, 7–9 A.M.) migrating along the shore of Lake Erie at Wanakah, Erie Co., Mar. 27,

1961 (Clark); 5000, Manitou, Monroe Co., Apr. 10, 1970; 3800, Derby Hill, Oswego Co., Apr. 15, 1965; 2400, Lake View, Erie Co., Apr. 20, 1966.

MAXIMA: *Summer* roost—5000, Jamestown, Chautauqua Co., Aug. 26, 1959 (Beal).

MAXIMA: *Fall*—1000, Far Rockaway, Queens Co., Sept. 10, 1969; 1500, Sandy Pond, Oswego Co., Sept. 17, 1964; 1500, Fire Island State Park, Suffolk Co., Oct. 25, 1969.

MAXIMA: *Winter*—100, Ithaca, 1950–1951; 300, Rural Grove, Montgomery Co., Jan. 29, 1951; 500, northern Nassau Co. Christmas count, Dec. 29, 1968.

Migrant Robins usually arrive in New York in late February or early March and depart by late November.

Breeding: This is easily the most adaptable of our native breeding species, being found almost everywhere. It nests from city parks and suburban yards to forest clearings in the Adirondack wilderness. In the forest, its ancestral home—for the Robin was originally a forest thrush—it is inordinately wary, in startling contrast to its tameness around man's dwellings.

Just as variable is its choice of nest sites. Robins often build their nests on ledges under the eaves of houses and on window sills, in a honeysuckle vine on the side of a porch, in various types of trees—especially deciduous, on top of a decayed wood stump, in a balsam sapling on the summit of Slide Mtn. in the Catskills, on the crossbar of a movable railroad signal gate (see photograph, *Bird Lore*, 1920, 22: 287–288), and even on the ground. I know of at least *three* published records of New York ground nests: (1) at the base of an alder bush in a thicket; (2) on a rock at ground level; (3) along a road bank among ferns.

Nest heights above ground usually range from four to 25 feet, although Eaton (1914:

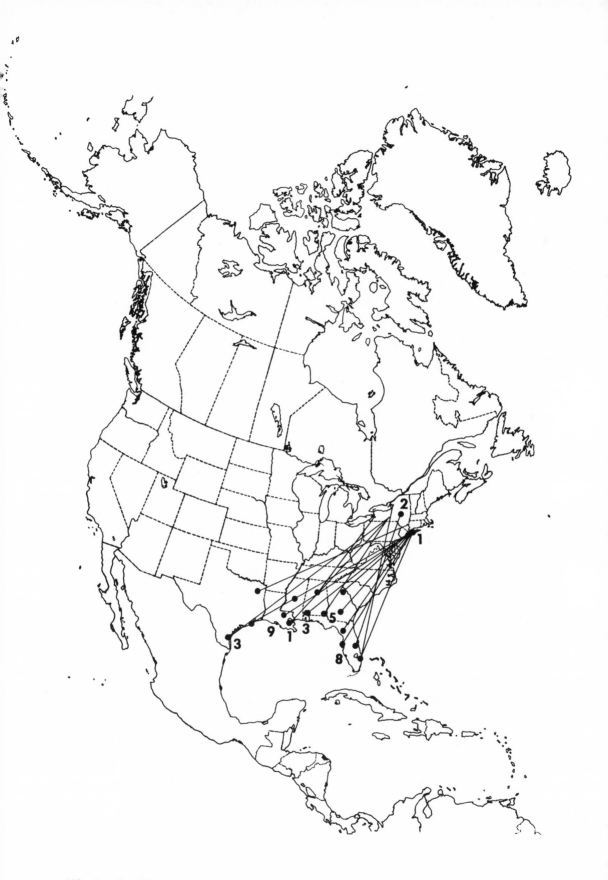

MAP 110   American Robin (*Turdus migratorius*) Banding recoveries

530) saw two nests—one in an elm about 60 feet above ground and another *80* feet up on the beams of a water tank.

The species is usually double-brooded and occasionally raises three broods. Egg clutches examined in 37 New York nests were: three eggs (12 nests); four eggs (24 nests); six eggs (one nest).

EGG DATES: Mar. 23 to July 19, exceptionally to Aug. 8.

Unfledged juveniles: Apr. 21 to Aug. 30; fledged young: May 25 to Sept. 10.

In some suburban communities excessive spraying with pesticides has resulted in a greatly decreased population of Robins in recent years.

Subspecies: The well-marked race *nigrideus* (darker and more richly colored than the nominate race—especially noticeable in males) breeds in humid coastal areas of Quebec, Labrador, and Newfoundland. It has been taken on migration and in winter in New York on a number of occasions. I have examined at least a dozen specimens of *nigrideus* in the larger museum collections from various portions of the state. Dates based on these specimens range from Nov. 1 to Apr. 23; exceptionally to May 13, 1941, CUM collection.

Banding (see Map 110): A total of 29 winter recoveries (from Georgia and Florida west to Texas) of birds banded in New York during the preceding summer is shown. Also indicated are three summer recoveries in New York of Robins banded on their winter grounds in Florida. The longest distance recorded for a Robin banded in New York is of one recovered near Rockport, Texas.

A banded New York Robin was retrapped *11* years later not far from place of banding.

Varied Thrush
(*Zoothera naevia*)   *

Range: Western North America, breeding from Alaska southeast to northwestern Montana. Winters chiefly south of the breeding range. Wanders east to the Atlantic coast from Quebec to New Jersey.

Keith (1968: 275) has suggested "—that the extralimital wandering documented may be a trait originally responsible, in part, for the species' colonization of the western hemisphere from Asia."

Status: *Very rare*—in New York there are at least 29 reports of this far western species, of which 18 are from Long Island. Its occurrence here is well substantiated. Four are specimen records, three from Long Island of which only one is extant: adult male caught in a rabbit trap, Port Jefferson, Suffolk Co., Dec. 20, 1889 (Helme), AMNH 802432; two others were taken in 1874 and 1905 (Bull, 1964: 336). The fourth specimen was collected upstate at Watertown, Jefferson Co., Dec. 9, 1958 (Belknap), NYSM 18665.

Of 25 sight reports in the state (nearly all at feeding stations), *nine* are of birds that were photographed; three of these photos are either published or available for examination: (1) Candor, Tioga Co., Jan. 8 to Mar. 6, 1968 (Weber and Pantle, *Kingbird*, 1968, 18: 85); (2) Bedford Hills, Westchester Co., Jan. 30 to Mar. 13, 1966 (Pierson); (3) South Haven, Suffolk Co., Jan. 5 to Mar. 2, 1969 (Wilcox). Photographs of these last two individuals are on file in the AMNH collection.

In addition to those named above, the distribution is as follows: (1) downstate—Staten Island; (2) upstate—Sullivan, Schenectady, Rensselaer, Washington, Livingston, Erie, and Cattaraugus counties; these last seven upstate occurrences took place during a six-year period (1965–1970).

EXTREME DATES: Nov. 10 to Apr. 17. Most of the records are in December and January.

Remarks: No subspecies are recognized here. Males of the two supposed races are virtually indistinguishable. Females of *"meruloides"* have the back only slightly paler and grayer than the nominate form.

The genus *Zoothera* is used here, following Ripley (in "Peters," 1964), and Mayr and Short (1970).

[Redwing (*Turdus iliacus*)

Hypothetical: Palearctic region, breeding west to Iceland. Vagrant in Greenland.

.The only known occurrence for continental North America is that of an individual present on Long Island at the Jamaica Bay Refuge (adjacent to Kennedy Airport), Feb. 20–24, 1959. It was first noted by H. Johnson, refuge manager, identified by C. Young (*Wilson Bull.,* 1959, 71: 382–383), and seen subsequently by hundreds of observers; several color photographs were taken.

Although there is no proof that this bird escaped from confinement, suspicion is unavoidable that it did so. Its congener, the Black-throated Thrush (*Turdus ruficollis atrogularis*) —chiefly from eastern Russia and Siberia— and seen at Kennedy Airport on Mar. 6, 1968, was "known to have escaped from an air shipment" (*fide* Ryan). The Brambling (*Fringilla montifringilla*), also seen at Kennedy Airport on Feb. 11, 1965 (Ryan), is in the same category. These three species, therefore, are almost certainly not genuine wanderers from the Palearctic region.]

Wood Thrush
(*Catharus mustelinus*) * B

Range: Eastern North America, breeding from extreme southern Canada and Maine to the Gulf states. Winters from southern Texas to Panama; very rare at this season in Florida and collected once in North Carolina.

Status: Fairly common to occasionally common spring migrant along the coast; fairly common fall migrant inland. Widespread breeder at lower elevations, but rare to uncommon northward and absent in the higher mountains.

Nonbreeding: The Wood Thrush is present in smaller numbers on migration than the other species which breed much farther north.

MAXIMA, COASTAL: *Spring*—a flight occurred on May 5–6, 1950, in the New York City parks, as follows—40, Central Park; 35 each in Bronx and Prospect parks; 40, Far Rockaway, Queens Co., May 8, 1961.

MAXIMA, INLAND: *Fall*—13 struck the Elmira television tower, Sept. 20, 1966; 15, Ithaca, Sept. 24, 1964; 12, Sandy Pond, Oswego Co., Oct. 3, 1961.

EXTREME DATES: Apr. 14 (inland) and Apr. 17 (coastal) to Nov. 25 (coastal and inland). Rare before May and after mid-October.

Winter: Although the writer (Bull, 1964:

338) listed six winter observations of Wood Thrush from the southeastern portion of the state, all between the years 1944 and 1961, no corroboration (specimen or photograph) was submitted by the various observers. The species has not been reported in winter since 1961. Any future report should be supported by solid evidence to remove any doubt as to its occurrence at this season in the northeast.

Breeding: This species nests in moist open woodland with plenty of undergrowth; also in towns and villages where numerous shade trees and shrubbery occur, especially in the southeastern portions of the state.

Wood Thrushes breed on the lower slopes of both the Catskills and Adirondacks, and in recent years have been extending their range northward in the latter area, penetrating deeper into the wilder deciduous forests. They generally avoid mixed evergreen areas.

Nests are usually placed in saplings or trees from four to 23 feet above ground.

An examination of 25 New York nests revealed the following egg clutches: three eggs (14 nests); four eggs (11 nests).

EGG DATES: May 17 to July 7.

Nestlings: May 22 to Aug. 1; fledglings: June 9 to Aug. 31. The species is double-brooded, at least in the warmer portions of the state.

Remarks: Dilger (1956 a, b, c) separated *Hylocichla* from *Catharus* on behavioral grounds, retaining only the Wood Thrush in the genus *Hylocichla*. To the writer this appears to be a tenuous procedure at the generic level based on a single character. However, color and pattern suggest close relationship of the Wood Thrush with the more northern North American members of *Catharus;* moreover the primary songs of Wood and Hermit thrushes are quite similar. Finally, comparison in the field should be made with the Neotropical members of *Catharus.* Otherwise, *all* boreal North American members should either be retained in the genus *Hylocichla,* or *all* merged into *Catharus.* Dr. S. Dillon Ripley (oral comm.) would revert to his earlier treatment (1952) of merging *all* into one genus (*Catharus*) rather than his later treatment (in "Peters," 1964) of following Dilger (*op. cit.*). A few taxonomists would even go so far as placing the Wood Thrush in the genus *Turdus;* indeed, Dorst (*L'Oiseau,* 1950: 212–248) did just that, combining all of the North American members of *Hylocichla* into *Turdus.* It must be admitted that the Wood Thrush bears a resemblance, although smaller, to the Song Thrush (*Turdus philomelos*) of Eurasia. Dorst (*op. cit.,* 222–223) placed them "near" each other.

Very recently, Hendrickson and Yow (*Condor,* 1973, 75: 301–305), on the basis of blood protein analysis, concluded that the Wood Thrush "cannot be included in the genus *Turdus,* but is a member of the genus *Catharus.* The genus *Hylocichla* should be eliminated and considered a synonym of *Catharus.*"

Hermit Thrush
(*Catharus guttatus*)   *   B

Range: Nearctic region, breeding from Alaska and Canada to southwestern United States; in the east to the mountains of West Virginia and Maryland, and to the coastal plain of Long Island. Winters north to southern Canada (rarely).

Status: Common to abundant coastal migrant, less numerous inland; rare to uncommon but regular in winter on the coast, rarer inland. Locally common breeder at higher elevations, especially numerous in the mountains; local breeder in the lowlands, but common in the Long Island "barrens."

Nonbreeding: The Hermit Thrush is most numerous during October and April. In fall it is actually numerous only on the coast.

MAXIMA, COASTAL: *Fall*—300, Orient, Suffolk Co., Oct. 12, 1952; 350, Prospect Park, Brooklyn, Oct. 15, 1950; 170, same locality, Oct. 28, 1944.

MAXIMA: *Spring*—75, Braddock's Bay, Monroe Co., Apr. 20, 1954; 250, Far Rockaway, Queens Co., to nearby Woodmere Woods, Nassau Co., May 6, 1950—a notably late spring.

Winter: Hermit Thrushes overwinter either where fruiting shrubs and vines persist or at well-stocked feeding stations. As many as *five* wintered near New Rochelle, Westchester Co., 1939–1940.

Nonbreeders are rare during the summer months.

Breeding: The Hermit Thrush, one of the state's finest singers, is fairly widely distributed from the cool, moist, wooded slopes of the Adirondack and Catskill mountains to the hot, dry, sandy pine-oak barrens of Long Island, the latter area at its southern breeding limits on the coast.

For the Catskills, Hough (1964: 141) gave an excellent description of its nesting haunts: Hermit Thrushes nest "on the lower boulder-strewn slopes . . . , in the deep wooded areas of cool ravines or depressions." He stated that on Slide and other mountains it occurs from as low as 600 feet up to 3200 feet, "seeming to draw its upward line at the beginning of the balsam zone. Here it shares the woods with Swainson's Thrush."

Saunders (1938: 85) stated that it is the most common and widely distributed thrush in Allegany State Park (Cattaraugus Co.) and occurs there in maple-beech forest on the cooler northward-facing slopes, but not in oak-chestnut forest on the warmer southward-facing slopes where it is replaced by the Wood Thrush.

In Wyoming Co., Rosche (1967) found Hermit Thrushes most frequently on "hemlock knolls" and in "black spruce and tamarack bogs."

In the Oneida Lake region it is found in mixed evergreen-deciduous forest types.

All this should not be construed as meaning that the species is found statewide in suitable woodland; far from it. The distribution is sporadic and many areas are without breeding Hermit Thrushes. For example, in western New York the species is virtually lacking along the entire south shore of Lake Ontario, in fact on the whole low-lying lake plain it is known as a breeder at only three localities: (1) near Albion, Orleans Co.; (2) Bergen Swamp, Genesee Co.; (3) Chili, Monroe Co.

Nor is it known to breed on the mainland south and east of the Island Pond-Pine Swamp area in the Orange Co. section of Harriman State Park.

On Long Island it is known only from Suffolk Co., where it is absent from the entire north shore, but is found on the south shore from Hither Hills on the Montauk peninsula west to at least Patchogue, and in the center of the island from near Riverhead west to Commack, Pinelawn, Wyandanch, and formerly Dix Hills (south of Huntington).

Nests are placed mostly on the ground, occasionally up to three feet (in a spruce sapling). In New York there are at least two broods.

EGG DATES: May 12 to Aug. 24.

Nestlings: May 30 to Aug. 31; fledglings: June 9 to Sept. 23. On a carefully watched nest at·Long Lake, Hamilton Co., Schetty determined that the nestling period was 11 days.

It appears that Eaton (1914: 528) erred, or had some other species in mind, when he stated that, "The eggs are four to six in number, usually four . . ." This is considerably at variance with the following: Saunders (*op. cit.*) found 20 nests with three eggs and only five with four. The latter is in line with the writer's findings—namely, egg collections, the pertinent literature, and nest-record cards thusly—55 New York egg clutches ranged from three to five: three eggs (*40* nests—73%); four eggs (13 nests); five eggs (two nests).

Banding: An individual, banded Oct. 25, 1969, on Long Island, was recovered Nov. 10 following near Winston-Salem, North Carolina.

Subspecies: The local breeding race *faxoni* differs from nominate *guttatus* in having brownish, rather than grayish flanks. This is obvious in skins comparable as to age and season. As for the population from Labrador and Newfoundland called "*crymophilus*," the differences are too slight to warrant recognition.

Swainson's or Olive-backed Thrush
(*Catharus ustulatus*)   *   B

Range: Nearctic region, breeding from Alaska and Canada to southwestern United States; in the east to the Berkshires, Catskills, and Poconos, and rarely in the higher mountains to West Virginia and Maryland. Winters from southern Mexico to Argentina.

Status: Common to very common migrant, occasionally abundant nocturnal migrant, especially in fall. Common breeder in the mountains; uncommon and local at lower elevations.

Nonbreeding: This species is the most numerous member of the genus on migration and greatly outnumbers the Gray-cheeked Thrush both spring and fall (see MAXIMA under Gray-cheeked Thrush). These comparisons (in bold face) are made at the *identical* localities on the *same* days and are based on tower kills, banded birds, and observations.

MAXIMA: *Spring*—200, Central Park, New York City, May 11, 1914 (Helmuth), early for so many; 175, Buffalo, May 20, 1957; 80, Syracuse, May 26, 1960.

MAXIMA: *Fall*—2000, Far Rockaway, Queens Co., Sept. 7, 1953 (Bull), nocturnal migration; "thousands," **Syracuse, Sept. 16, 1965** (Scheider), nocturnal migration; 1000, **Far Rockaway, Sept. 20, 1952** (Bull), nocturnal migration; 44 netted and banded, **Huntington,** Suffolk Co., **Sept. 26, 1965;** 173, **Colden** TV tower, Erie Co., **Sept. 29, 1962;** 458 banded at **Huntington** in a **ten-year period, spring and fall** (Lanyon, *et al.*, 1970: 41).

EXTREME DATES: *Spring*—Apr. 24 (coastal) and Apr. 26 (inland) to June 11 (coastal).

EXTREME DATES: *Fall*—July 25 (inland specimen, Buffalo), various August dates to Oct. 29 (inland) and Nov. 6 (coastal specimen) and Nov. 10 (coastal).

Rare before mid-May and after early June, and before September and after mid-October.

Winter observations, including those on Christmas counts, published in *Audubon Field Notes* (various years), are considered to be unsatisfactory. No winter specimen is known from anywhere in the northeast.

Breeding (see Map 111): In the Adirondacks and Catskills, Swainson's Thrush nests mainly below the zone where the Gray-checked Thrush breeds and usually higher than that of the Hermit Thrush, but some overlap occurs in both areas.

Both Dilger (1956b: 177) and Hough (1964: 16) state that red spruce-balsam fir forests are preferred at higher altitudes in the Adirondacks and Catskills, and that mixed beech-maple-birch-hemlock woodland is utilized on the lower slopes, as well as at lower elevations elsewhere.

The actual nest site, however, is almost invariably in evergreens from two to 15 feet up. In 17 New York nests, ten were in hemlock, four in balsam, and three in spruce.

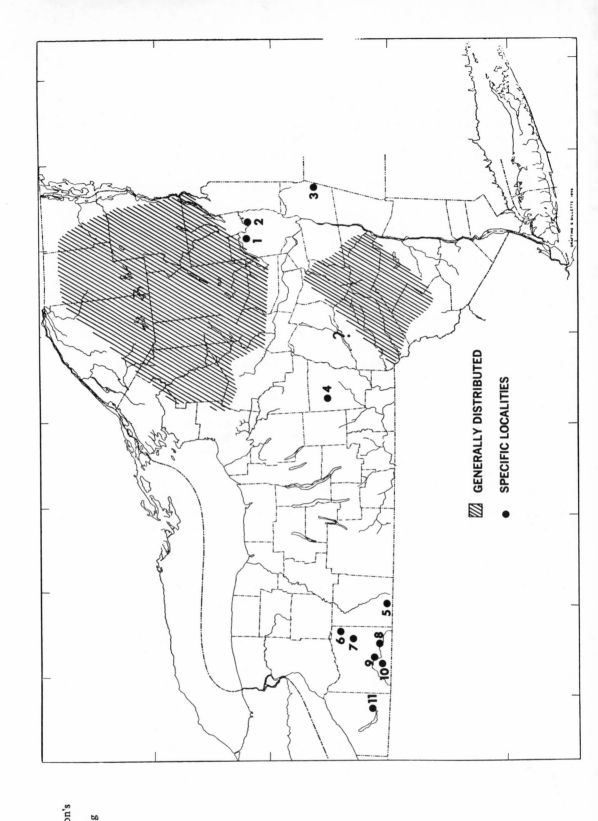

MAP 111 Swainson's
Thrush (*Catharus
ustulatus*) Breeding
distribution

GENERALLY DISTRIBUTED

SPECIFIC LOCALITIES

Egg clutches in 13 New York nests: three eggs (five nests); four eggs (eight nests).

EGG DATES: June 10 to July 11.

Nestlings: June 30 to July 22; fledglings: July 10 to Aug. 10.

Reference to the distribution map indicates how sparse breeding records are outside the Catskill and Adirondack-Tug Hill districts. With the exception of southwestern New York, only four other localities report breeding Olivebacks. In all probability this species will be found breeding west of the Catskills and along the "southern tier" section now "vacant" on the map.

The 11 extra-montane breeding localities are: Saratoga Co.—(1) Jenny Lake; (2) Mt. McGregor. Rensselaer Co.—(3) Berlin Mtn. Chenango Co.—(4) Pharsalia. Allegany Co.—(5) Alma. Cattaraugus Co.—(6) Freedom Bog; (7) near Franklinville; (8) Allegany; (9) Carrollton; (10) Big Basin, Allegany State Park. Chautauqua Co.—(11) north of Jamestown.

Alleged breeding near the north shore of Oneida Lake at Cleveland, Oswego Co, in 1968 was not proved. The terrain is apparently unsuitable. Alleged breeding reports based on eggs (no longer available for examination) at Gaines, Orleans Co., and other low-lying areas along the Lake Ontario shore (Beardslee and Mitchell, 1965: 341) are not acceptable either. Eaton (1914: 525) himself doubted these records. More than likely the birds were Veeries.

Remarks: Morphological differences (color) in the various eastern populations are too slight to warrant subspecific recognition here. These differences are clinal in nature and considerable individual variation exists. Even Ridgway (1907: 55) considered *"swainsoni"* as doubtfully distinct from nominate *ustulatus*. As to the northeastern *"clarescens,"* see Bull (1964: 340–341).

Gray-cheeked Thrush
(*Catharus minimus*) * B

Range: Breeds in northeastern Siberia and in the Nearctic region from Alaska and northern Canada southeast to the mountains of northern New York and northern New England; locally on Mt. Greylock in the Berkshires and on the highest mountains in the Catskills (see also **Subspecies).** Winters chiefly in South America.

Status: Fairly common to common coastal spring migrant; common to very common in fall, both coastal and inland, when reported as a nocturnal migrant in larger numbers than in spring. Common breeder in the higher Adirondacks; local, but fairly common on the highest peaks of the Catskills.

Nonbreeding: There is abundant evidence to show that the Gray-cheeked Thrush is much less numerous both spring and fall than the Swainson's Thrush, as proved by a direct comparison with that species (see MAXIMA under Swainson's Thrush). These comparisons (in bold face) are made at the *identical* localities on the *same* days, and are based on tower kills, banded birds, and observations.

MAXIMA: *Spring*—50, Central Park, New York City, May 20, 1924 (Helmuth), an unusually large number for spring.

MAXIMA: *Fall*—"hundreds," **Syracuse, Sept. 16, 1965** (Scheider), nocturnal migration; 300, **Far Rockaway,** Queens Co., **Sept. 20, 1952** (Bull), nocturnal migration; 14 netted and banded, **Huntington,** Suffolk Co., **Sept. 26, 1965;** 29, **Colden** TV tower, Erie Co., **Sept. 29, 1962;** 190 banded at **Huntington** in a **ten-year period, spring and fall** (Lanyon, 1970: 41).

EXTREME DATES: *Spring*—May 1 to June 7 (inland) and June 12 (coastal).

EXTREME DATES: *Fall*—Aug. 25 (coastal) and Sept. 1 (inland) to Nov. 14 (coastal) and Nov. 21 and 28 (coastal specimens—Bull, 1964: 341). Casual at the Brooklyn Botanic Garden, Dec. 16, 1910, specimen, AMNH collection.

Rare before mid-May, and before mid-September and after October. Sight reports in April and before late August are considered unsatisfactory.

Winter observations, published in *Audubon Field Notes* (various years), are also unsatisfactory. No winter specimen is known from anywhere in the northeast.

Breeding (see Map 112): The Catskill Mountains in southeastern New York are at the southernmost known breeding range of the Gray-cheeked Thrush in North America. Here they are confined to near the summits of the

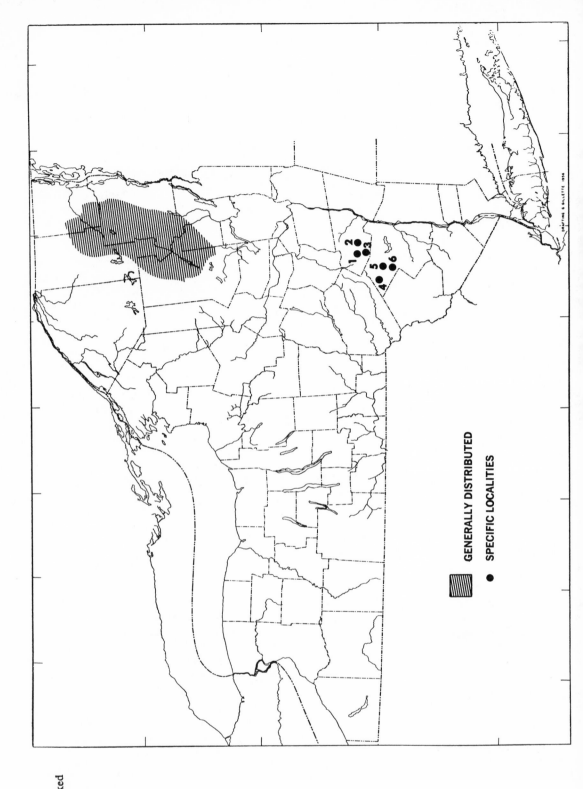

MAP 112 Gray-cheeked
Thrush (*Catharus
minimus*) Breeding
distribution

GENERALLY DISTRIBUTED

● SPECIFIC LOCALITIES

Fig. 74 Summit of Slide Mtn., Ulster Co., type locality of *Catharus minimus bicknelli,* the Gray-cheeked (Bicknell's) Thrush with stunted mixed growth of balsam and spruce at 4200 feet elevation. Summer of 1960. Photo by Richard Rosche

highest peaks (3300 to 4400 feet—see Fig. 74). In the Adirondacks they are more generally distributed, but even there are found chiefly above 3000 feet up to at least 5000 feet (tree line).

The breeding distribution closely parallels that of the Blackpoll Warbler with virtually identical habitats, that is, dense stands of stunted balsam fir and spruce. Details of this thrush's ecology and nesting habits are found in Dilger (1956b: 177–178) and Hough (1964: 18). Nest heights reported in New York range from one to seven feet above ground.

I have seen only two reports of New York nests containing eggs: one nest with three eggs, the other with four.

EGG DATES: June 12 to June 27.

Nestlings: July 1 to July 25; fledglings: July 12 to Aug. 7.

The known Catskill breeding localities are found on the accompanying map: Greene Co. —(1) Hunter Mtn.; (2) near Tannersville; (3) near Lanesville. Ulster Co.—(4) Balsam Lake Mtn.; (5) Slide Mtn., and nearby Cornell, Friday, and Wittenberg mountains; (6) Peekamoose Mtn., and nearby Balsam Cap Mtn. Peekamoose Mtn. is the southernmost known breeding locality anywhere.

Slide Mtn. is the type locality of the race *bicknelli,* the type specimen of which was collected on the summit, June 15, 1881 (Bicknell), and described by Ridgway in 1882; it is USNM 95545.

Subspecies: Two subspecies occur in New York—(1) the larger, widespread nominate race, breeding south and east to central Quebec and Newfoundland, and (2) the smaller, more southern race, *bicknelli,* breeding locally in the mountains from the Gaspé peninsula in Quebec, Nova Scotia, Maine, New Hampshire, Vermont, and northeastern New York, locally south to western Massachusetts (Mt. Greylock) and southeastern New York (Catskills).

Banding studies on Long Island of carefully measured birds indicate that nominate *minimus* is the more common of the two subspecies, which is not surprising considering the very wide breeding range of that race and the relatively restricted one of *bicknelli*.

During an eight-year period at Elmhurst, Queens Co., out of a total of 378 individuals banded, nominate *minimus* outnumbered *bicknelli* by 237 to 141 (Beals and Nichols, 1940); and in a ten-year span at Huntington, Suffolk Co., of 654 banded, 458 were nominate *minimus*, only 196 were *bicknelli* (Lanyon, *et al.*, 1970: 41).

Veery (*Catharus fuscescens*)   *   B

Range: North America, breeding from southern Canada—in the west to the mountains of northern Arizona; in the east to the mountains of northern Georgia, and on the coastal plain to Long Island and central New Jersey. Winters in northern South America.

Status: Common migrant; occasionally abundant nocturnal fall migrant. Widespread breeder, mainly at lower elevations, but local on the coastal plain and absent in the higher mountains.

Nonbreeding: Veeries are seldom seen in large numbers during the day but, especially in fall, their characteristic calls are heard as they pass over at night. They are at maximum abundance during the first half of September.

MAXIMA: *Spring*—25, Central Park, New York City, May 5, 1950; 50, Goat Island, Niagara River, May 21, 1943.

MAXIMA: *Fall*—500, Sept. 3, 1949; 700, Sept. 10, 1946—both at night, Far Rockaway, Queens Co. (Bull); 100 in one hour, Syracuse, Sept. 19, 1966 (Scheider); 29 hit the Fire Island Lighthouse, Suffolk Co., Sept. 30, 1883 (Dutcher), very late for so many.

EXTREME DATES: Apr. 20 (coastal) and Apr. 24 (inland) to Oct. 11 and 16 (both coastal). Rare before May and after September.

Earlier and later dates than those given above are not substantiated by specimens or color photographs.

Reports of Veeries in winter on Christmas counts in the northeast are unconfirmed. Specimen evidence is necessary for such an unlikely occurrence of a species that winters in South America.

Breeding: The Veery is an inhabitant of mostly moist or wet lowland .forest. Dilger (1956b: 177) said, ". . . reaches its greatest concentrations in rather damp areas, either deciduous or coniferous. Moist bottomland woods with a lush understory of ferns and other plants seem to provide optimum conditions."

Speaking of the Catskill district (Hough, 1964: 12) stated that, "The bird [Veery] as a nesting species avoids the slopes of ridges and mountains unless there is a situation in the terrain that harbors a deep wooded ravine." He further added, ". . . a sizable stand of tall trees with dense understory vegetation on moist ground." Also, "The Veery and Wood Thrush will sometimes nest in close proximity . . . and, more rarely, a Hermit Thrush may share the same general area as a Veery."

Axtell (1947) estimated 66 pairs present in one-half mile between Alpine and Odessa, Schuyler Co.

This species is also a local breeder near the south shore of Long Island in suitable terrain.

Veeries nest on or near the ground (rarely as high as six feet in a hemlock), most often in saplings, tree sprouts, or among roots and dead or fallen branches, also in low shrubs.

Egg clutches in 28 New York nests: three eggs (eight nests); four eggs (18 nests); five eggs (two nests).

EGG DATES: May 16 to June 25.

Nestlings: June 14 to July 22; fledglings: June 20 to July 31.

Banding: One banded on the north shore of Long Island, Sept. 3, 1963, was found dead near the Florida Gulf coast in the vicinity of St. Marks only two weeks later.

Remarks: No subspecies are recognized here. The population described as *"fuliginosus"* is but very slightly differentiated from nominate *fuscescens;* the alleged differences stated for the more western form *"salicicola,"* such as intensity of spotting and differences in color barely exist. Making allowance for "foxing" in old specimens, rufous or tawny, versus grayish morphs, do not hold in large series taken at comparable dates (both year and month).

Eastern Bluebird (*Sialia sialis*) * B

Range: Central and eastern North America, breeding from southern Canada to the Gulf states and in the mountains to northern Nicaragua. Withdraws from the extreme northern portions in winter.

Status: Generally an uncommon spring migrant, common to locally very common fall migrant; occasionally abundant in fall. Variously rare to locally common in winter. Widespread breeder upstate. Numbers fluctuate greatly at all seasons.

Nonbreeding: Depending on weather conditions, Bluebirds arrive from late February to mid-March; in fall they usually depart by late November excepting, of course, wintering birds.

Ordinarily this species is observed only in very small numbers during migration and the spring flight is virtually nonexistent. In fall, however, large flocks are, on all too rare occasions, seen and heard passing overhead. Only fall and winter maxima are listed below.

MAXIMA: *Inland*—200, Brocton, Chautauqua Co., Oct. 26, 1962 (Bates and Buck, *Kingbird,* 1963, 13: 25).

MAXIMA: *Coastal*—During the autumn of 1944, there was an unprecedented flight on Long Island—500, Long Beach, Nassau Co., Oct. 26 (Komorowski); 400, Orient, Suffolk Co., Nov. 5 (Latham).

MAXIMA: Winter—200, Rye, Westchester Co., Feb. 12, 1934 (Drescher). Much smaller numbers are the rule at this season.

Breeding: This attractive species, our state bird, is today largely restricted to rural areas in upstate New York and is most plentiful in agricultural districts; it is found also in forest clearings and open glades in the wilder portions of the state. Of recent years it has greatly decreased in suburban regions and near the larger cities. Even about farms and orchards it has become much scarcer. Dead trees are cut down, dead limbs are removed, and cavities and holes are cemented over, thus removing potential nesting sites for Bluebirds, our only hole-nesting thrush.

Competition from Starlings and House Sparrows are also serious factors in keeping down the Bluebird breeding population, as these introduced pests are well established in nearly all available nest sites by the time Bluebirds return from the south.

To overcome the shortage of natural nest sites, a number of "Bluebird projects," or extensive programs of erecting nest boxes in favorable country throughout various areas of the state, has resulted in attracting and increasing sizable Bluebird populations.

The writer disagrees with the premise that winter-killing in the south is the *most* severe limiting factor in reduced populations. The Bluebird is thus often referred to as a "disaster" species. This is true for only a temporary period—for a year or two after severe winters. Bluebirds have "always" recovered in the past after a series of mild winters and undoubtedly will recover in the future. Even Eaton (1914: 538) mentioned this phenomenon and was in disagreement with those who believed that winter-killing was "disastrous" to the species.

As mentioned above, this species is exclusively a cavity nester. Nests have been found from five to 17 feet up in tree holes and telephone poles (most exceptionally as high as 35 feet up in a pitch pine), somewhat lower down in fence posts and bird boxes (sometimes in Purple Martin houses) and on two occasions even in old Cliff Swallow nests under building eaves (in one instance, "but a few inches away" from active swallow nests). For details, see *Bird-Banding* (1935, 6: 137) and *Auk* (1938, 55: 539).

In a Bluebird nest-box project in the vicinity of Olean, Cattaraugus Co. (*Kingbird,* 1963, 14: 26–27), two broods were raised. In the first brood (31 boxes occupied) only 25% of the eggs laid produced fledged young, whereas in the second brood (28 boxes occupied) 68% were successful.

In another project in Dutchess Co. (*Kingbird,* 1965, 15: 96), in which 20 out of 42 boxes were occupied, five pairs successfully fledged two broods.

In his behavioral studies of this species at Olean within the four-year period, 1963–1966, Krieg (1971: 3) erected 236 nest boxes with 88 boxes occupied—about 38% occupancy.

Egg clutches reported in 45 New York nests ranged from three to eight, with the following breakdown: three eggs (three nests, probably incomplete sets); four eggs (18 nests); five eggs (16 nests); six eggs (three nests); seven eggs (three nests); eight eggs (two nests).

EGG DATES: Apr. 1 to Aug. 18 (as many as three broods have been raised).

Nestlings: Apr. 30 to Sept. 6; fledglings: May 10 to Sept. 17.

Banding: Three juveniles banded during the breeding season in New York were recovered the following fall or early winter in Virginia (one) and North Carolina (two).

Northern Wheatear
(*Oenanthe oenanthe*)   *

Range: Holarctic region, the race *leucorhoa* (larger than nominate race; males in nonbreeding plumage are deeper buff [tawny] below) breeds south to extreme northern Quebec and along the coast of Labrador. The North American populations winter mainly in the Old World. Those individuals breeding in the eastern Canadian arctic migrate across the Atlantic Ocean to Europe and then south through western Europe to winter quarters in tropical west Africa, except for occasional stragglers to New York, rarely farther south.

Status: *Very rare*—in New York there are at least *16* occurrences, of which four are old specimen records. These latter are: (1) adult female taken on Long Island, fall of 1863 (Elliot collection, AMNH 1236; (2 and 3) two females collected at Jamaica, Queens Co., in

1885 (Akhurst), AMNH 439561 and 439562; (4) one obtained at Junius, Seneca Co., Sept. 9, 1872 (Hampton), is in the Hobart College collection (Eaton, 1914: 536).

Of 12 state observations, eight are from downstate—all in the New York City region (Bull, 1964: 345, and 1970: 33), including one at Upton, Suffolk Co., Sept. 28, 1970 (several observers). The four upstate sightings are: (1) near Rochester, Sept. 30–Oct. 1, 1934 (Miller, *et al.*); (2) Piseco Lake, Hamilton Co., Sept. 25, 1963 (McIlroy); (3) Grand Island, Niagara River, Sept. 25, 1965 (Benham, Brownstein, Mitchell, and Ulrich); (4) two, Hamburg, Erie Co., Sept. 27, 1967 (Bourne).

Seven of the dozen observations occurred in September, two in fall and early winter (Nov. 15, Dec. 27), and three in spring (May 13 to June 8).

Townsend's Solitaire
(*Myadestes townsendi*)   *

Range: Western North America, breeding east to the western portions of South Dakota and Nebraska; winters east to western Kansas. Vagrant east to Ontario, Michigan, Ohio, New York, and New Brunswick.

Status: *Casual*—there are two positive records in New York State, both specimens taken in the southeastern section, as follows: (1) male, Kings Park, Suffolk Co., Nov. 25, 1905 (Weber), AMNH 377452; (2) female, Amenia, Dutchess Co., Mar. 16, 1953 (J. L. George), AMNH 707718. This latter individual had also been observed on Mar. 14.

OLD WORLD WARBLERS — SYLVIIDAE

Three species in New York.
Three breed.

Like the previous grouping, this assemblage (nearly 290 species) is often treated as a subfamily of the Muscicapidae (Old World Fly-

catchers, etc.), but is here retained as a family for convenience. As the name implies, most members are found in the eastern hemisphere. Only the kinglets (*Regulus*) are found throughout the Holarctic region (two species each in the new and old worlds), while the gnatcatchers are restricted to America, chiefly in the tropical portions.

Although in New York the Ruby-crowned Kinglet (*Regulus calendula*) is confined as a breeder to the Adirondacks, the Golden-crowned Kinglet (*R. satrapa*) within recent years has spread from the mountainous areas, to conifer plantings in much of the cooler portions upstate. The Blue-gray Gnatcatcher (*Polioptila caerulea*) is a southern species that has been extending its breeding range northward in recent times.

Blue-gray Gnatcatcher
(*Polioptila caerulea*)   *   B

Range: Southern Nearctic and northern Neotropical regions, breeding northeast to extreme southeastern Ontario, central New York, and Massachusetts; central New Hampshire (1965). Winters north to southern United States.

Status: Uncommon to fairly common spring migrant; rare to uncommon in fall on the coast. Local, but greatly increased breeder at lower elevations; absent in northern New York.

Change in status: Prior to the 1940s this species was a rare visitant to the state. There was one old breeding record—a nest and eggs at Coldwater, Monroe Co., June 1890 (E. H. Short in Beardslee and Mitchell, 1965: 347–348).

The first known modern breeding occurrence was in 1943 along Lake Erie in Chautauqua Co. Three big flight years produced a multitude of records, both migration and breeding— 1947, 1954, and 1963. The state was probably invaded from the south by way of New Jersey and from the west via Ohio and southern Ontario along the shores of Lake Erie.

Nonbreeding: Gnatcatchers are relatively early migrants in spring, arriving in numbers during the latter half of April. They are much less often recorded in fall.

Fig. 75 Pair of Blue-gray Gnatcatchers at nest in walnut tree, about 12 miles southeast of Rochester, Monroe Co., July 1966. Three nestlings were present. Photo by Franklin Enos

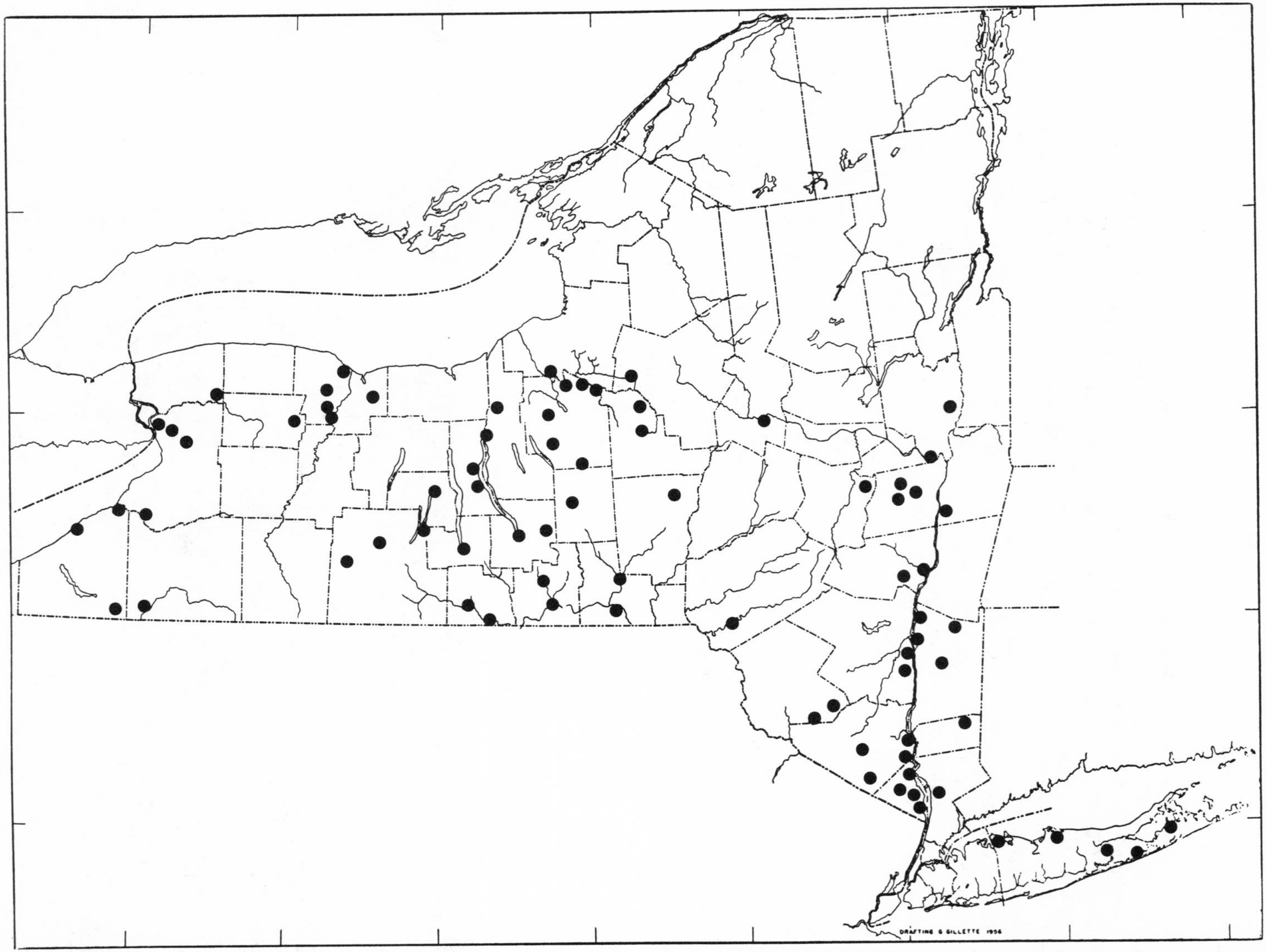

MAP 113 Blue-gray
Gnatcatcher (*Polioptila
caerulea*) Breeding
distribution

MAXIMA: *Spring*—nine, Bronx Park, New York City, Apr. 18, 1947; 12, Portland, Chautauqua Co., Apr. 29, 1962; 20, Ithaca, May 12, 1958 (Nisbet); 16, near Syracuse, May 18, 1968.

MAXIMA: *Fall*—five, Central Park, New York City, Aug. 24, 1953; six, Montauk Point, Suffolk Co., Sept. 18, 1948.

EXTREME DATES: Apr. 3 (coastal) and Apr. 7 (inland) to Nov. 27 (coastal). Rare before mid-April and after mid-October.

Breeding (see Map 113): The Blue-gray Gnatcatcher nests in both secondary and primary forest, often where it is wet, as in elm-maple swamps, in willows and sycamores along streams, but occasionally in upland areas with a mixed oak-hickory association (see Fig. 75 of nest in black walnut). Tall trees are preferred, nest heights in New York ranging from 15 to 50 feet above ground. The vast majority of the 77 recorded breeding localities in the state are along or near lakes and rivers.

Only five New York nests with *eggs* have been examined to my knowledge. Three nests contained three eggs each, two others held four and five apiece.

EGG DATES: May 14 to June 17.

Nestlings: June 1 to July 11; fledglings: June 28 to July 25.

As may be seen on the map, the species is most prevalent in the Hudson valley, having penetrated as far north as the outlet of Lake Lonely, Saratoga Co., just north of Saratoga Lake. It is fairly widely distributed from Oneida Lake south through the Finger Lakes to the Pennsylvania state line. It is also locally distributed in the lower Genesee valley south of Lake Ontario, and from the area near Buffalo southwest along Lake Erie.

It is noteworthy that, although the six breeding localities in the "southern tier" counties of Broome, Tioga, and Chemung are situated in the Appalachian highlands, nevertheless all six are in river bottoms, as are also the other localities near the Pennsylvania border.

There seems to be a lack of breeding records for the Mohawk valley (except two stations— Vischer's Ferry, Saratoga Co., and Jacksonburg, Herkimer Co.) where relatively little observation is done, as well as for most of Long Island and much of the immediate New York City region where, however, there is an abundance of observers. For the last-named areas, since my publications (Bull, 1964: 346–348, and 1970: 34), three additional localities are indicated on the accompanying map—Briarcliff Manor, Westchester Co.; Quogue and Mount Sinai, Suffolk Co.

Golden-crowned Kinglet
(*Regulus satrapa*)   *   B

Range: Nearctic region, breeding from Alaska and Canada to the mountains of Guatemala in the west; in the east to the mountains of Tennessee and North Carolina; also since 1950 at lower elevations in New York. Winters nearly throughout the breeding range and southward. Sedentary and migratory.

Status: Variously uncommon to very common migrant and winter visitant. Common breeder at higher elevations in the Adirondacks and Catskills; in recent years greatly increased at lower elevations outside the mountains (see **Breeding**).

Nonbreeding: The Golden-crowned Kinglet is subject to marked fluctuations, appearing in great numbers in certain years and in very small numbers in others. In winter it frequents conifers, and is usually more prevalent at that season inland than along the coast.

MAXIMA: *Fall*—big movement in 1967 at Selkirk Shores State Park, Oswego Co., east shore of Lake Ontario—200, Sept. 25, and an unprecedented estimate of *450,* Oct. 20 (many observers); 200, of which 125 were netted and banded, Fire Island State Park, Suffolk Co., Oct. 13, 1969 (Davis, *et al.*); 100, Prospect Park, Brooklyn, Nov. 10, 1946; 100, Oneonta, Otsego Co., Nov. 20, 1960.

MAXIMA: *Winter*—85, Bear Mtn., Rockland Co., Dec. 27, 1952; 30, Phoenix, Oswego Co., Feb. 11, 1962.

MAXIMA: *Spring*—100, Bronx Park, New York City, Apr. 3, 1946; 60 in one hour, Syracuse, Apr. 18, 1959; 40, Selkirk Shores, Apr. 28, 1962.

EXTREME DATES: Casual, Aug. 15 (coastal) and Aug. 25 (inland); Sept. 8 (coastal) to May 19 (coastal) and May 22 (inland). Rare before mid-September and after April.

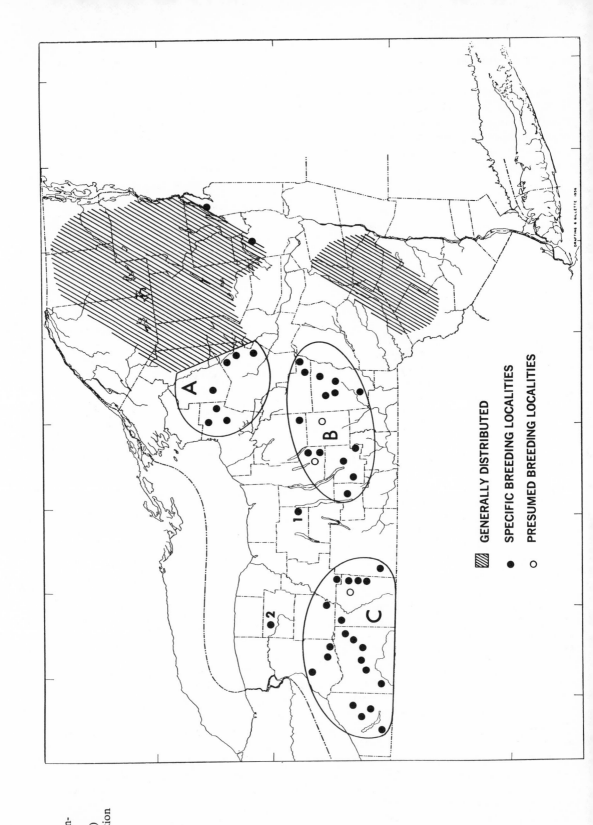

MAP 114 Golden-
crowned Kinglet
(*Regulus satrapa*)
Breeding distribution

GENERALLY DISTRIBUTED

● SPECIFIC BREEDING LOCALITIES

○ PRESUMED BREEDING LOCALITIES

Change in breeding status (see Map 114):
Prior to 1950 this species was considered as
limited in the breeding season to the spruce
forests of the higher Adirondacks and Catskills, with a scattering of records at the southern perimeter of the Adirondacks in Washington, Saratoga, and Oneida counties.

Within the last two decades, however, artificial planting of Norway and white spruce in
central and western New York by the State
Forestry Department has created new habitat.
As a result, at least *40* additional breeding localities as well as considerable range extension
(see below and accompanying map) are now
known.

Andrle (1971b) stated that this "new" breeding habitat consists almost entirely of tall,
dense Norway and white spruce, mostly in
state reforestation areas (see Fig. 75a). Elevations of most plantations are over 1000 feet
above sea level, and many lie above 2000 feet.
Altitude apparently is not a critical factor affecting breeding occurrence of kinglets in these
areas. He found that their presence is related
to the existence of suitable habitat with certain
microclimatic conditions differing from surrounding habitats, such as those with cool,
moist, and densely shaded stands of spruce.
Tracts vary from about two to over 60 acres,
and contain from one to three pairs of kinglets
each, a density less than in some natural evergreen and mixed forests in the species' normal
range. Andrle (*op. cit.*) further stated that
these disjunct New York populations appear to
be persisting, and many will probably continue
to do so indefinitely unless habitat is removed
or significantly altered by forest practices. The
new breeding areas represent a rather extensive range expansion of the species, and
younger plantations in some counties are potential future expansion areas. However, his map
(p. 314) should show more extensive shading
than it does for the Catskill district.

As to natural breeding sites, in addition to
spruce forest, balsam and white cedar bogs
are utilized. Speaking of the Adirondacks, Sil-

Fig. 75a Breeding habitat of Golden-crowned Kinglet, elevation about 2100 feet near Farmersville, Cattaraugus Co., July 1969; 38 acres of pure dense stand of Norway spruce and some
white spruce; trees 40–50 feet high, planted in 1932; Photo by Robert F. Andrle

loway (1923: 443) stated that these kinglets breed chiefly in "spruce, balsam, tamarack, and hemlock; . . . prefer well established second growth to undisturbed primeval forest." However, according to Saunders (1929: 372), they nested chiefly in *mature* spruce, hemlock, balsam, and tamarack, as well as in second-growth spruce only 10–15 feet high.

Heights of other recorded nests range from 18 to 35 feet. Egg clutches in only six known New York nests: six eggs (one nest); seven and eight eggs (two nests apiece); ten eggs (one nest).

EGG DATES: May 28 to June 26.

Nestlings: June 11 to July 25; fledglings: June 17 to Aug. 30.

The breeding distribution map indicates the two long-established montane populations, plus the three recent disjunct breeding areas. The latter with *44* localities are: (A) Tug Hill region; (B) Finger Lakes region and the area immediately to the east; (C) southwestern section.

Most of these localities are found in Andrle (*op. cit.*). All but two are at elevations over 1000–1500 feet. The two exceptions are just under 1000 feet: (1) near Geneva, Ontario Co., May 28, 1929 (F. A. Young and E. H. Eaton) —active nest in large spruce in cemetery; (2) near Alabama, Genesee Co., June 3, 1967, and July 26, 1969 (Andrle and McKale)—a pair present both years.

Remarks: By some authorities variously considered conspecific with the Palearctic *R. regulus,* the Goldcrest, and *R. ignicapillus,* the Firecrest. However, to this writer it most nearly resembles the latter.

Ruby-crowned Kinglet
(*Regulus calendula*) * B

Range: Nearctic region, breeding from Alaska and Canada to the southern portions (mountains) of California, Arizona, and New Mexico in the west; but in the east only to the extreme northern portions of the United States. Winters north to northern United States (rarely).

Status: Fairly common to very common migrant. Rare but regular in winter near the coast, much rarer upstate. Very rare breeder in the Adirondacks.

Nonbreeding: The Ruby-crowned Kinglet arrives earlier in fall and departs later in spring than the Golden-crowned Kinglet. Its numbers are more stable than the latter and less subject to wide fluctuations.

MAXIMA: *Spring*—100, Bronx Park, New York City, Apr. 17, 1944; 200, Syracuse, Apr. 27, 1957; 60, Prospect Park, Brooklyn, May 5, 1950; 100, Syracuse, May 11, 1962; 30, Selkirk Shores, Oswego Co., May 18, 1960, a late spring.

MAXIMA: *Fall*—150, Selkirk Shores, Sept. 25, 1967; 140, Jones Beach, Nassau Co., Oct. 5, 1963; 100, Syracuse, Oct. 9, 1955; 75 netted and banded near Huntington, Suffolk Co., Oct. 12, 1964; 60, Grand Island, Niagara River, Oct. 17, 1961; 70 netted and banded, Fire Island State Park, Suffolk Co., Oct. 26, 1969.

EXTREME DATES: Aug. 22 (coastal) and Sept. 1 (inland) to May 31 (coastal) and June 8 (inland). Rare before mid-September and after early May. Migrants arrive in early April and depart by late November.

Winter: Rare, but regular, usually frequenting conifer groves or dense thickets near the coast. Ordinarily only one to three individuals are reported in winter, but with more feeding stations in recent years, this species has become less rare. Upstate the species is more unusual at this time of year. However, an individual appeared at a feeder on Feb. 13, 1962, at Watertown.

Breeding (see Map 115): The first published account of this species in summer in the Adirondacks was that of Eaton (1914: 511) who observed an individual on July 19, 1905, on Mt. Marcy. It was next reported in 1922 by J. Kittredge who saw a singing male on June 16 on Whiteface Mtn. at 3900 feet in a dense growth of balsam fir. Breeding evidence, however, was not obtained at the latter locality until 30 years later.

The first definite record of breeding in New York was that of a nest (the only known nest from the state) containing young at Bay Pond, Franklin Co., June 1942, and photographed by A. A. and D. G. Allen (Parkes, 1952a). The nest is in the Cornell University collection.

Of the following 16 known localities re-

MAP 115 Ruby-crowned
Kinglet (*Regulus
calendula*) Breeding
distribution

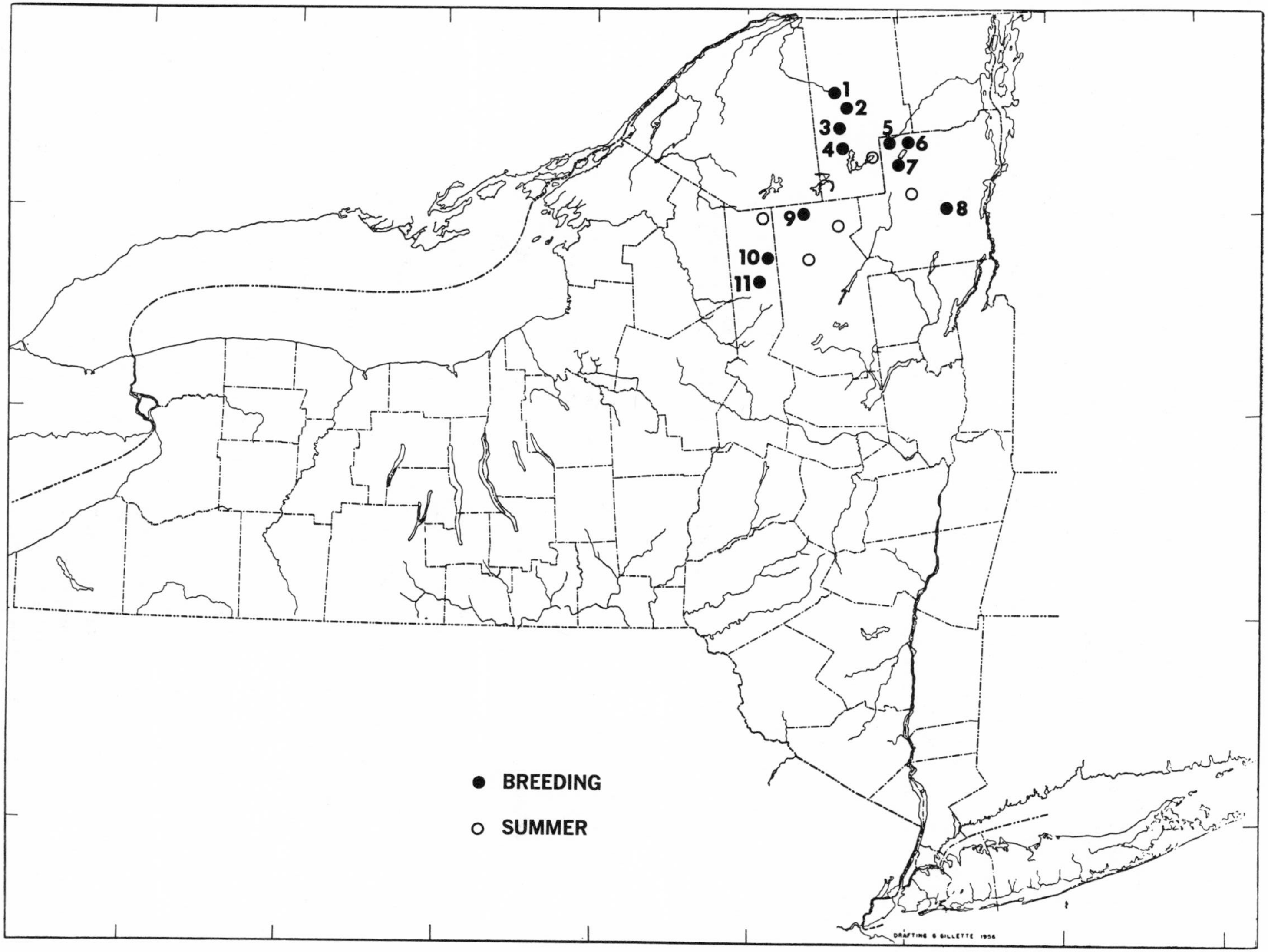

● BREEDING

○ SUMMER

corded in the Adirondacks during the summer, breeding has been proved at 11 by observations of fledged juveniles or of suspected, or probable, nesting by repeated sightings of adults. The other five are merely summer occurrences. Breeding habitat is evergreen forest where nests are very likely difficult to find.

Franklin Co.—(1) near Santa Clara; (2) near Madawaska; (3) Bay Pond; (4) Floodwood. Essex Co.—(5) Bloomingdale; (6) Whiteface Mtn.; (7) Chubb River Swamp; (8) Elk Lake.

Hamilton Co.—(9) Sabattis. Herkimer Co.—(10) Big Moose Lake; (11) Little Moose Lake.

The five summer localities are: Franklin Co.—Saranac Lake (village). Essex Co.—Mt. Marcy. Hamilton Co.—Lake Eaton; Raquette Lake (village). Herkimer Co.—Dart Lake.

Further field work should produce more breeding records—especially in St. Lawrence and Hamilton counties; there has not even been a summer report in the former county to my knowledge.

WAGTAILS, PIPITS — MOTACILLIDAE

One species in New York.
None breed.

This primarily Old World family (over 50 species) is represented in New York only by the widespread, Holarctic species, *Anthus spinoletta,* the Water Pipit. This bird inhabits open country in habitat similar to that occupied by the Horned Lark (*Eremophila alpestris*)—namely fields, pastures, and shores. It occurs with us chiefly during the migrations, much more rarely in winter.

Water Pipit (*Anthus spinoletta*)   *

Range: Holarctic region; in North America east of the Rocky Mountains the wide-ranging subspecies *rubescens* (buffy underparts compared to white in nominate race of southern Europe—see also **Additional subspecies**) breeds south to the eastern shores of James Bay (western Quebec) and to Newfoundland; rarely to southeastern Quebec—Mt. Albert, Gaspé peninsula (Godfrey, 1966: 308), and possibly on the summit of Mt. Katahdin, Maine. Winters chiefly along the coast north to Maryland; rarely and irregularly to New Jersey and Long Island.

Status: Variously uncommon to abundant migrant; usually rare and irregular in winter on Long Island and in the lower Hudson valley. Erratic and unpredictable in its occurrence, numbers fluctuating widely.

Occurrence: Water Pipits inhabit open treeless country, frequenting recently plowed and freshly burned fields, lake and river shores, inland and coastal mud flats and beaches, and short-grass areas such as airports.

MAXIMA: *Fall*—100, Rochester, Aug. 31, 1952; 150, Grand Island, Niagara River, Sept. 21, 1955; 500, Hicksville, Nassau Co., Oct. 16, 1935; 800, near Tully, Onondaga Co., Oct. 28, 1965; 500, Idlewild, Queens Co., Nov. 2, 1946; 200, Jones Beach, Nov. 14, 1964.

MAXIMA: *Spring*—35, Syracuse, Mar. 19, 1954; 125, Warsaw, Wyoming Co., Apr. 1, 1963; 500, Braddock's Bay, Monroe Co., May 1, 1954; 1000, same locality, May 12, 1959 (Listman).

MAXIMA: *Winter*—125, Jamaica Bay, Dec. 25, 1934 (Sedwitz); 50, Croton Point, Westchester Co., Jan. 22, 1949 (Darrow)—both unusual numbers.

EXTREME DATES: Aug. 2 (inland) and Aug. 13 (coastal) to June 7 (inland). Rare before late August and after mid-May. Very rare inland in winter. A specimen was collected at the

Ithaca city dump, Jan. 1, 1948 (Dickerman and Kessel), CUM 21437. Migrants occasionally arrive in early March and depart by late November.

Additional subspecies: A specimen of the Rocky Mountain race *alticola* (distinguished from *rubescens* by greatly reduced ventral streaking) was found by Parkes (*in litt.*) in the American Museum collection. It was taken at Miller's Place, Suffolk Co., May 10, 1882 (Helme), AMNH 25964. I have examined this specimen and concur in the identification. According to the range given in the A.O.U. Check-list (1957: 458), this race has not been recorded east of western Texas.

WAXWINGS — BOMBYCILLIDAE

Two species in New York.
One breeds.

If this family is restricted to the three members of the genus *Bombycilla,** it is confined to the Holarctic region. All three are quite similar in pattern and coloration: *cedrorum*, the Cedar Waxwing, is strictly North American; *garrulus*, the Bohemian Waxwing, is found nearly throughout northern Eurasia, as well as in Alaska and western Canada; and *japonica*, the Japanese Waxwing, is confined to extreme eastern Asia.

Only the Cedar Waxwing is common in New York, the Bohemian Waxwing being one of the rarest of winter visitants. These are among the tamest birds, often allowing a close approach. They are chiefly fruit eaters, but also take insects during the warmer months, at that time indulge in flycatching.

Bohemian Waxwing
(*Bombycilla garrulus*) *

Range: Northern Eurasia and northwestern North America, the New World race *pallidiceps* (much paler and grayer than nominate race) breeds southeast to northern Manitoba. Winters south irregularly to the southern portions of Ontario and Quebec, more rarely to Pennsylvania, New York, and New England.

* Not including the subtropical American silky-flycatchers ("Family" Ptilogonatidae) or the somewhat aberrant *Hypocolius* of the Old World.

Status: Highly erratic winter visitant and subject to irruptive flights on rare occasions. Usually very rare to uncommon northward, occasionally more numerous; very rare southward.

Occurrence: The Bohemian Waxwing is one of the very rarest of winter visitors to New York State and the observer may consider himself extremely fortunate to see even one in these parts. In some years the species is unrecorded. On rare occasions when small numbers are reported, they are more often than not accompanied by the far more numerous Cedar Waxwings and thus provide the observer with ready comparison.

MAXIMA: At least four flights of considerable proportions have occurred within New York, the first three spaced about 40 years apart—(1) 1879–1880; (2) 1919–1920; (3) 1961–1962; (4) February 1969.

(1) 23 shot from a flock of about *200* with "numerous" Cedar Waxwings, as they were feeding on mountain-ash berries at Mexico, Oswego Co., Feb. 2, 1880 (Davis); some of these specimens examined by Ruthven Deane and at least one preserved (see following); two collected out of 16 near Sterling, Cayuga Co., late December 1879 (*Ornith. and Ool.*, 1882, 7: 132–133).

(2) 24 observed at Branchport, Yates Co., Jan. 20, 1920 (Stone); up to 65 seen near Rochester, from Feb. 28 to Mar. 26, 1920 (Edson and Horsey), frequently seen with Cedar Waxwings feeding on crab apples.

(3) 18 near Buffalo, Feb. 18, 1962 (Able); *300* near Watertown, Jefferson Co., Mar. 17–18, 1962 (Allen, Clinch, Dake, and Ross), with Cedar Waxwings—color photographs taken (*Kingbird,* 1962, 12: 24).

(4) A great irruption on Feb. 12, 1969, occurred near Watertown, when *500* were estimated by Walker (*Kingbird,* 1969, 19: 117); 250 were still present on Apr. 5 (Walker).

EXTREME DATES: Nov. 7 and 15 (earliest specimen) to Apr. 18 (latest specimen) and Apr. 26.

Specimen data: Of a number of specimens taken in the state, eight with data are extant, six from upstate, two from Long Island, as follows—(1) Niagara Falls, Nov. 15, 1851 (J. Gould), BM (NH) 81. 51. 5285; (2) Utica, 1869 (Davis), BM (NH) 88. 10. 10. 4502; (3) Mexico, Oswego Co., Feb. 2, 1880 (Davis), RMAS 4786; (4) North Haven, Suffolk Co., Apr. 18, 1889 (Lucas), AMNH 66001; (5) Waterford, Saratoga Co., Feb. 24, 1904 (Richard), NYSM 1200; (6) Ithaca, Nov. 28, 1914 (Allen), CUM 14441; (7) Fisher's Island, Suffolk Co., Feb. 17, 1918 (Latham), NYSM 25250; (8) Lyndonville, Orleans Co., Dec. 2, 1961 (Mitchell), BMS 4926.

Remarks: The report of one, supposedly this species, seen at Tupper Lake (village), Franklin Co., July 22, 1962 (*Audubon Field Notes,* 1962, 16: 462), "should be disregarded" (J. Carleton, *in litt.*).

Cedar Waxwing
(*Bombycilla cedrorum*)   *   B

Range: Breeds from central Canada to central United States. Winters in the breeding range south to Panama and the Gulf coast.

Status: Sedentary and migratory. Common to abundant early fall coastal migrant; very common in late fall inland; very common throughout the state in spring; local and irregular in winter, although occasionally numerous. Numbers fluctuate from season to season, however, and the species is unpredictable and erratic, except in late spring and early fall. Statewide breeder.

Nonbreeding: Although feeding chiefly on fruit through much of the year, the Cedar Waxwing supplements this diet with insects during the warmer months, especially in late summer, often flycatching along the edges of lakes and streams.

MAXIMA: *Fall*—1000 each at Far Rockaway, Queens Co., Sept. 8, 1953, and Sept. 10, 1969; 700, Riis Park, Oct. 1, 1967; 500, Ilion, Herkimer Co., Oct. 28, 1964.

MAXIMA: *Winter*—300, Easthampton, Suffolk Co., Dec. 28, 1946; 600, near Rochester, Feb. 26, 1955; 600, near Syracuse, Feb. 28, 1964.

MAXIMA: *Spring*—1000, Camillus, Onondaga Co., Mar. 14, 1965 (perhaps overwintering concentration rather than genuine spring migrants); 350, Pleasantville, Westchester Co., Apr. 18, 1947; 250 in one hour, Derby Hill, Oswego Co., May 28, 1969; in 1970, at same locality—560, May 29, and 380, May 31; 300, Boonville, Oneida Co., June 9, 1969.

Breeding: This species and the American Goldfinch are our two latest nesting passerines, breeding as late as October. Cedar Waxwings nest in a variety of trees, both deciduous and evergreen in semiopen country, often near water and not uncommonly in cultivated districts.

Saunders (1929: 405), speaking of the Adirondacks, stated that this species was a "semicolonial" nester near North Elba, Essex Co. He found six nests within a radius of 100 yards. On Long Island, Puleston (*in litt.*) at Noyack, Suffolk Co., in 1964 found seven pairs nesting "in a small grove of locusts and honeysuckle."

Occasionally these birds breed very close to other species. One nest in an apple tree was within five feet of a Chipping Sparrow nest. Another in a maple was only 15 feet from the nest of a Baltimore Oriole.

Nests range in height from four to 25 feet up, rarely as high as 50 feet. Of 29 New York nest sites reported, apple trees were favored by nine, followed by maple (eight) and spruce (five). The balance selected were one each in willow, locust, beech, sumac, bayberry, and wild grape; also pine, larch, hemlock, cedar, yew, and balsam.

Egg clutches examined in 50 New York

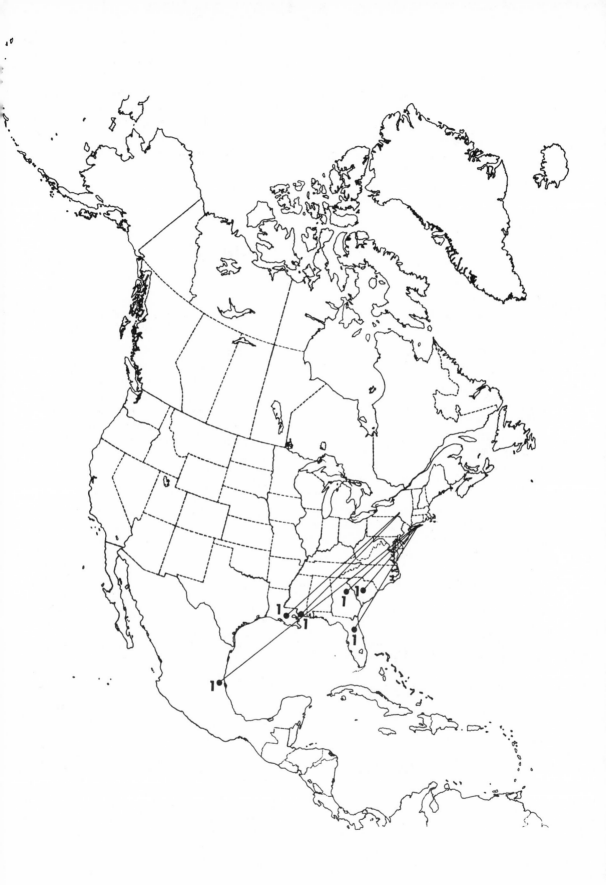

MAP 116   Cedar Waxwing (*Bombycilla cedrorum*) Banding recoveries

nests were: three eggs (eight nests); four and five eggs (20 nests each); six eggs (two nests).

EGG DATES: June 5 to Sept. 25.

Nestlings: June 12 to Oct. 1; fledglings: June 16 to Oct. 8. The species is double-brooded.

Banding (see Map 116): Nestlings and fledglings banded in summer or early fall in New York were found the following winter in five southeastern states, while a sixth was recovered in Mexico—near Panuco, Veracruz.

SHRIKES — LANIIDAE

Two species in New York.
One breeds.

This family (over 70 species), so rich in variety in the Old World, especially Africa, is poorly represented in the New World and is absent from South America. In North America only two species occur, both in the genus *Lanius*. The Holarctic species, *L. excubitor*, the Northern or Great Gray Shrike, is larger and paler than the more southern, allopatric, and strictly Nearctic *L. ludovicianus*, the Loggerhead Shrike. The latter is the breeding form in New York. It probably represents an earlier invasion from the Old World, and has achieved specific distinctness in isolation from the similar *excubitor* which is a more recent arrival.

Neither of the two can be called anything but rare or uncommon in New York and during migration or winter it is unusual to see more than one or two individuals at a time. They are not easily overlooked as they are conspicuous whether perched or in flight, being birds of open country and usually quite tame, often allowing a fairly close approach.

Northern or Great Gray Shrike
(*Lanius excubitor*)   *

Range: Holarctic region, in eastern North America breeding south to northern Quebec and central Labrador. Winters south to central United States.

Status: Rare to uncommon, irregular winter visitant; occasionally more numerous.

Occurrence: This species may be seen in semiopen country wherever there are scattered trees and bushes. It perches also on telephone wires, fence posts, and other exposed vantage points. On occasion Northern Shrikes visit feeding stations where they prey on small birds.

The Northern Shrike irrupts southward at irregular intervals after a diminution in the food supply (small mammals and birds) on its northern breeding grounds. At rare intervals these southward irruptions comprise up to six individuals. The brownish juveniles outnumber the adults in our area.

MAXIMA: Five, Ellery Center, Chautauqua Co., Nov. 11, 1958; eight banded at the Fitzgerald feeder, Amsterdam, Montgomery Co., all December 1956; eight, Montauk, Long Island, Dec. 11, 1949; 12 between Montauk and Easthampton, Jan. 1, 1950; eight, Rochester area, Jan. 29, 1956.

EXTREME DATES: Oct. 6 (inland specimen) to Apr. 28 (coastal specimen), and May 2 (inland specimen). Ordinarily rare before November and after March.

Reports of Northern Shrikes observed and or banded in September are rejected as none has been verified. The closely related Loggerhead Shrike occurs regularly in September and is sometimes misidentified. The two closely resemble each other.

Subspecies: The American race *borealis*, as well as the north Asiatic form *sibiricus*, have the adults barred or vermiculated below, whereas adults of nominate *excubitor* of Europe are virtually immaculate beneath.

Loggerhead Shrike
(*Lanius ludovicianus*)   *   B

Range: Chiefly southern Nearctic region, breeding from southern Canada to southern Mexico (chiefly highlands) and the Gulf states; local in the northeast. Winters north to Long Island (rarely).

Status: Rare to uncommon migrant, but regular in spring along the Great Lakes and in fall along the coast; occasional in winter on the coast. Local breeder at low elevations in western, central, and northwestern New York, but has decreased in recent years.

Nonbreeding: This species inhabits open country and may be observed on telephone wires, fence posts, and exposed twigs of bushes and small trees.

MAXIMA, INLAND: *Spring*—six, Sodus Bay, Wayne Co., Apr. 4, 1956; six, Derby Hill, Oswego Co., Apr. 12, 1970.

MAXIMA, COASTAL: *Fall*—four each at three different Long Island south-shore localities, late August and September, various years.

EXTREME DATES (coastal only, where unknown as a breeder): Aug. 2 to May 28. Rare before mid-August and after April.

Winter: There are three January *coastal* specimens (Bull, 1964: 353), and one known *inland* specimen at this season—female taken at Castleton, Columbia Co., February 1962, by J. Cook, NYSM 20576.

Although a number of winter sight reports are undeniably correct, others are highly questionable, especially from upstate where this species is rare in winter and the Northern Shrike is not uncommon. The two are often confused.

Change in breeding status (see Map 117): Eaton (1914: 362–364) called the Loggerhead Shrike a "fairly common breeder," stating that with the clearing of the forest prior to 1870, this species had increased and moved eastward into western and central New York, as had the Horned Lark. The high point of its abundance was apparently during the last two decades of the nineteenth century judging from the activities of the oölogists of that day. For example, N. F. Posson collected 19 sets of

eggs within the six-year period 1887–1892 in the vicinity of Medina, Orleans Co. In the two-year period 1897–1898, C. H. Johnston took eight sets near Rome, Oneida Co., and in the same two-year period at Phelps, Ontario Co., Beecher Bowdish did even better, collecting ten sets—six in 1897, four more in 1898. The writer examined these ten sets in the collection of the New York State Museum at Albany.

The species continued to be fairly common during the first quarter of the twentieth century. Agriculture was at its zenith and pastureland with an abundance of hawthorn or thornapple (*Crataegus*) was plentiful, as were apple orchards, the two preferred breeding habitats of shrikes. The hawthorn, liberally supplied with thorns, the apple with sharp-pointed terminal twigs, as well as the many roadside barbed-wire fences, were greatly desired by these predatory passerines for impaling their prey.

Be that as it may, for reasons not obvious, Loggerhead Shrikes progressively decreased during the 1930s and 1940s and have, as yet, not recovered their former numbers. Possibly abandonment of many farms and orchards, overgrown from neglect, created unfavorable nesting habitat. However, the late E. H. Eaton (*Kingbird,* 1953, 3: 55) suggested that the automobile was a likely factor (road kills) in the decrease of this species, because of the shrike's predilection for diving down to road surfaces for insects. Wetmore (pers. comm.) was of the same opinion, noting that these birds had become scarce in Maryland and Virginia. To the north of New York, a similar story, but reason(s) not stated: "Have become rare birds in the Toronto area, with none reported in a 100-mile survey" (*Audubon Field Notes,* 1966, 20: 566).

Nevertheless, Belknap (*in litt.*) mentions that ". . . this section of New York State [Jefferson and St. Lawrence counties] probably has the largest current breeding population, due partly to extensive hawthorn growth in the numerous old pastures bordered by fences." He considers this shrike to be a "regular but not common breeder, holding its own" and that it is "rather secretive during the nesting season, with nests not easy to find."

On the opposite side of the St. Lawrence River, in the Kingston, Ontario region, Quil-

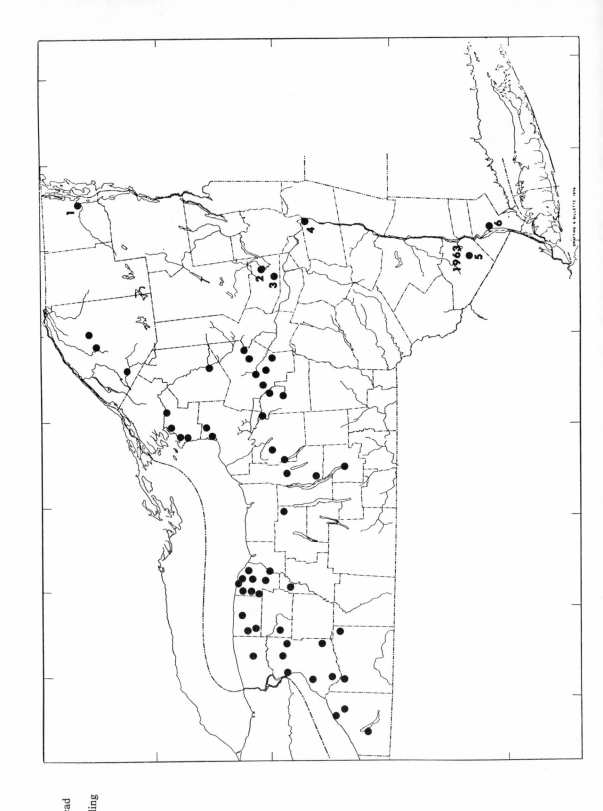

MAP 117 Loggerhead
Shrike (*Lanius
ludovicianus*) Breeding
distribution

liam (1965: 146) called it a "fairly common summer resident."

From a perusal of the breeding distribution map it is evident that this species is, or was, most prevalent in the region east of Lake Ontario, the area south and east of Oneida Lake, the eastern Finger Lakes, the Lake Ontario shore region west of the Genesee River, and the lands east of Lake Erie. Monroe Co. leads with *nine* breeding localities, followed by Erie and Oneida counties each with six.

There are two peculiar apparent gaps in western New York: (1) the Lake Ontario shore between the Genesee River and Sandy Pond, Oswego Co.—a distance of more than *100* miles of "shrikeless" breeding range; (2) around the western portion of the Finger Lakes where there is a virtual absence of breeding shrikes.

The species is notably absent from the southern tier area (adjacent to Pennsylvania) and on Long Island. It is also a very rare breeder throughout the Hudson valley. It is entirely absent from the mountains which might explain its scarcity as a breeder in the highlands between the Pennsylvania state line and the Finger Lakes—Cattaraugus Creek district— the last forming a county boundary (Erie-Cattaraugus).

The two peripheral and four isolated breeding localities in eastern New York are indicated by number. Five of these six are old records (prior to 1930): (1) Plattsburgh, Clinton Co.; (2) and (3) Mayfield and Gloversville, Fulton Co.; (4) Cohoes, Albany Co.; (5) Blooming Grove, Orange Co.—1963 (see Bull, 1964: 354); (6) Sing Sing (=Ossining), Westchester Co.

Nest heights ranged from four to 20 feet; 32 New York nests were situated in hawthorns and 20 in apples, with one each in elm, pine, and spruce.

Egg clutches in 58 New York nests ranged from four to seven: four eggs (eight nests); five eggs (13 nests); six eggs (36 nests— 62%); seven eggs (one nest).

EGG DATES: Apr. 18 to June 28 (known to be partially double-brooded in western New York—based on color-marked birds).

Nestlings: May 18 to June 25; fledglings: May 25 to July 26. The dates for nestlings and fledglings are obviously not representative.

Remarks: The weakly differentiated northern population *"migrans"* is not recognized here. Supposed difference in bill size from that of the nominate race varies considerably.

VIREOS — VIREONIDAE

Seven species in New York.
Six breed.

This strictly American family (37± species) ranges from southern Canada to the subtropical portions of South America.

All seven New York species are members of the genus *Vireo*. Six of these breed in the state, the seventh, Bell's Vireo (*V. bellii*), is a vagrant from the west. Four of the six breeders, Yellow-throated, Solitary, Red-eyed, and Warbling vireos (*V. flavifrons, solitarius, olivaceus, and gilvus*), are fairly widespread; one is a rare breeding bird of the Adirondacks, Phila-

delphia Vireo (*V. philadelphicus*), and the other is confined as a breeder to the southeastern section, White-eyed Vireo (*V. griseus*).

White-eyed Vireo
(*Vireo griseus*)   *   B

Range: Chiefly southeastern United States and northeastern Mexico, the race *noveboracensis* (not well differentiated, but tends to be more extensively yellow below than nominate *griseus*) breeding north to southeastern New York, Connecticut, and Rhode Island; casual breeder in extreme southeastern Ontario in 1971 (*American Birds,* 1971, 25: 853). Winters from the Gulf states to Central America.

Status: Ordinarily rare to uncommon spring migrant in the extreme southeastern section, but apparently more numerous in fall there (see following). Locally common breeder on Long Island and in the lower Hudson valley (Westchester and Rockland counties), but has decreased considerably in recent years in the latter area and on western Long Island. Very rare visitant elsewhere and absent in northern New York.

Nonbreeding: This species is rare to uncommon on migration. Usually only one or two a season are seen by an active observer away from breeding areas. This is not surprising as the White-eyed Vireo is at its northern limits in our area. It has also decreased considerably since about 1900 over much of the northeast, and has shown little signs of increasing.

MAXIMA: *Fall*—"flight" in 1964—seven, Northport, Suffolk Co., Sept. 7 (Mudge); four netted and banded, Brookhaven, Suffolk Co., Sept. 13 (Puleston and Terry); on Sept. 30, 1883—a very late fall—*20* struck the Fire Island Lighthouse, Suffolk Co. (Dutcher, *Auk,* 1884, 1: 174). Nothing remotely resembling this number has ever been reported in the state since then.

EXTREME DATES: Apr. 15 (coastal) to Oct. 30 (coastal). Uusally rare before May and after early October.

In 1969, record arrival and departure dates were set: *Spring*—Mar. 29, Staten Island (N. Wagerik and H. Fischer); Mar. 31, Mill Neck, Nassau Co. (L. Schore, *et al.*); one netted and banded, Apr. 9, Huntington, Suffolk Co. (Lanyon).

Fall—one netted, banded, and color-photographed, Nov. 4, Fire Island State Park, Suffolk Co. (Davis); also a male collected, Nov. 6, 1955, Forest Lawn Park, Buffalo (Mitchell), BMS 4119—specimen examined by the writer.

A report of one seen Nov. 22, 1969, on Long Island was not verified.

Breeding (see Map 118): White-eyed Vireos breed in open country in lowland areas, nesting in thickets in and near swamps, more rarely in thickets in drier regions as on hillsides and along rural roads.

Nests in this state are placed near the ground from one to three feet up, rarely to ten feet—in hickory and maple saplings, and in mountain laurel, hazel, lilac, blackberry, and catbrier.

Egg clutches in 11 New York nests: three eggs (four nests); four eggs (seven nests).

EGG DATES: May 17 to July 17.

Nestlings: June 18; fledglings: June 30

This species is at its northernmost known breeding limits in the state in southeastern New York. The accompanying map shows extent of distribution northward in the lower Hudson valley, the known breeding localities situated mostly near the river.

As it has nested once as far north as Troy, Rensselaer Co., in 1900 (nest and eggs in NYSM collection), it would not be surprising to find breeding birds to the south in the counties of Columbia, Greene, and Albany—all without definite breeding records.

White-eyed Vireos were formerly locally distributed in the greater New York City region, but with wholesale habitat destruction in recent years, they have largely disappeared from a number of former localities.

Contrary to the statements of Griscom (1923: 310) and Cruickshank (1942: 363) that this species is a "rare" breeder on eastern Long Island, some of the highest breeding densities occur there. For example, in extreme eastern Suffolk Co., Helmuth found five pairs at Three Mile Harbor in 1910, and on Gardiner's Island, Lanyon and the writer estimated at least ten pairs, based on singing males, June 2, 1966, while in the summer of 1965, Ferguson located seven pairs on Fisher's Island.

In 1963 members of the Rockland County Audubon Society found five nesting pairs in the New City area.

Reports in the older literature of this species breeding in western and central New York at or near such localities as Buffalo, Auburn, Dunkirk, Brockport, Lockport, Rochester, and Herkimer, have never been proved to my knowledge. I have seen no unquestioned specimens of eggs, nests, or breeding adults in any museum collection. Critical determination of eggs in the Buffalo Museum of Science, alleged to be this species, proved to be those of the Solitary Vireo (see Beardslee and Mitchell, 1965: 357). Nor have any nests of *V. griseus* been found in western New York by present-day observers. However, two observed in the

MAP 118 White-eyed
Vireo (*Vireo griseus*)
Breeding distribution

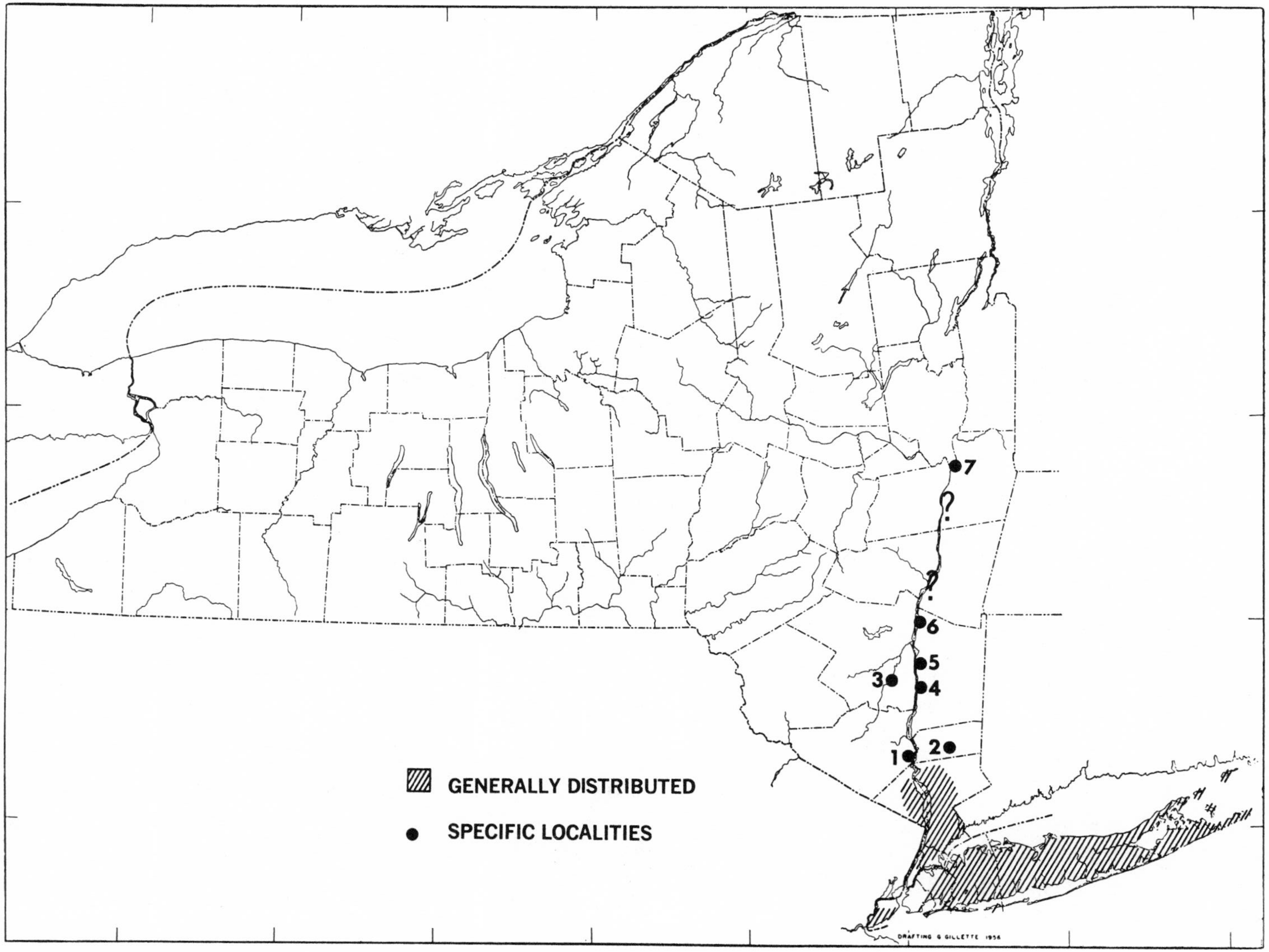

GENERALLY DISTRIBUTED

● SPECIFIC LOCALITIES

Cattaraugus Indian Reservation, in southwestern Erie Co., July 2, 1971 (Axtell), may have been breeding. Note also casual breeding in Ontario, likewise in 1971 (see **Range**).

Even immediately to the south of New York the species is unknown as a breeder—in northern Pennsylvania (Poole, 1964).

Nesting localities in the Hudson valley north of Westchester and Rockland counties are shown on the map: Orange Co.—(1) Highland Falls. Putnam Co.—(2) Lake Secor. Ulster Co.—(3) New Paltz. Dutchess Co.—(4) Poughkeepsie; (5) near Hyde Park; (6) Cruger's Island. Rensselaer Co.—(7) near Troy.

Bell's Vireo (*Vireo bellii*) *

Range: Chiefly southwestern United States and northern Mexico, breeding east to central Indiana; southwestern Ohio (1968). Winters from Mexico to Nicaragua. Vagrant in New Hampshire, New York (Long Island), and New Jersey.

Status: *Casual*—the only substantiated occurrences in New York for this dull-colored species are: (1) One caught in a mist net, banded, color-photographed, and released at Tiana Beach, near Shinnecock Inlet, Suffolk Co., Sept. 25, 1959 (Wilcox); corroboration was made by Eisenmann and the writer by comparing the color slide with museum skins; photo on file, AMNH collection. (2) One collected at Fire Island State Park, Sept. 26, 1970 (D. Ford), specimen examined by the writer; in USNM collection, 566493.

A number of observations, alleged to be this species, have been made, chiefly in the New York City parks during spring migration. Some or all of them may be correct, but because this is such a difficult species to identify in the field, and one which can be confused with the similar White-eyed and Solitary vireos, these sightings are omitted (Bull, 1964: 356). Buckley (*Kingbird*, 1970, 20: 57–60) attempted to revive these observations, but his arguments add nothing that would alter my reasons for excluding the observations; see also Carleton (*Proc. Linn. Soc. N.Y.,* 1970, 71: 141).

Yellow-throated Vireo
(*Vireo flavifrons*) * B

Range: Eastern North America, breeding from extreme southern Canada to the Gulf states. Winters chiefly from southern Mexico to Panama.

Status: Uncommon to fairly common migrant upstate, but rare and erratic on and near the coast. Locally common breeder at lower elevations, but rare to uncommon in the extreme northern portions, rare on the north shore of Long Island, and absent on the coastal plain and in the mountains.

Nonbreeding: This species has been quite rare near the coast for many years and has shown no signs of increasing. It was formerly more numerous (prior to 1900).

MAXIMA: *Spring*—six, Central Park, New York City, May 11, 1913; 22, Camillus Valley, Onondaga Co., May 14, 1970 (probably some local breeders). *Fall*—eight, Boonville, Oneida Co., Sept. 20, 1964.

EXTREME DATES: Apr. 21 (coastal) and Apr. 23 (coastal specimen) to Oct. 8 (inland), Oct. 12 (coastal), and Oct. 18 (coastal, banded). Rare before May and after September.

Unconfirmed reports of birds seen during the first half of April, as well as *"flocks"* in late April, are probably misidentified Pine Warblers. For instance, Beardslee and Mitchell (1965: 358) list maximum numbers from May 15 to May 22 in their table, and give Apr. 29 as the earliest arrival date; both of these are in harmony with migration schedules for the rest of the state, but at the same time they credit a report of "eight" on Apr. 29.

Breeding: The Yellow-throated Vireo is, today, more numerous in much of upstate New York, particularly in the Finger Lakes region, than it is in the southeastern portion where it is decidedly rare to uncommon and very local in distribution.

Downstate it is primarily a bird of rich open woods and swampy woodland, whereas in upstate New York it is also found breeding in orchards, and in shade trees along village streets.

Eaton (1914: 372) found it nesting in shade trees of Buffalo and Rochester, but Beardslee and Mitchell (*op. cit.*) state that it "is more often found in woodland areas, particularly along streams . . ."

Axtell (1947) in Chemung Co. estimated an average of four pairs per mile along the Chemung River ". . . wherever bordered with good-sized trees."

Benton (1949) found it a common breeder in Cayuga Co. around "houses and dooryards . . . for virtually every town in the county."

In Wyoming Co., Rosche (1967) said that formerly it was fairly common in tall shade trees bordering village streets and around farmhouses, but that it had decreased and its distribution was somewhat spotty.

During a survey of the southern portion of the Tug Hill area in 1968, Scheider found this species "usually confined to mature beech woodland or maple-edged riverine areas."

On Long Island it is restricted to the north shore and has been known to breed at the following localities: Queens Co.—Flushing. Nassau Co.—Manhasset; Mill Neck; Oyster Bay; Syosset. Suffolk Co.—Cold Spring Harbor; Smithtown; Peconic; Southold; Orient; Shelter Island.

This species builds its nest from 20 to 60 feet up in deciduous trees.

Egg clutches in eight New York nests: three eggs (two nests); four eggs (five nests); five eggs (one nest).

EGG DATES: May 24 to June 18.

Nestlings: June 16 to July 30; fledglings: July 1 to Aug. 14.

Solitary Vireo
(*Vireo solitarius*)   *   B

Range: Nearctic and northern Neotropical regions, breeding from central Canada, in the west through the higher mountains to El Salvador; in the east to the mountains of northern Georgia, and rarely at lower elevations to eastern Massachusetts and southern Connecticut. Winters occasionally north to central North Carolina, casually to Long Island (specimen).

Status: Uncommon to fairly common migrant. Common breeder at higher elevations (Adirondacks and Catskills), but local in the highlands of southern and southeastern New York.

Nonbreeding: With the exception of the Red-eyed Vireo, the most common member of the genus during migration is the Solitary Vireo. Its numbers fluctuate more often—in some seasons it is quite scarce. It is the earliest vireo to arrive in spring and the last to depart in fall.

MAXIMA: *Spring*—12, Prospect Park, Brooklyn, May 6, 1950; eight, Syracuse, May 6, 1959; 13 netted and banded, Fire Island State Park, Suffolk Co., May 9, 1970.

MAXIMA: *Fall*—12, Jamestown, Chautauqua Co., Sept. 14, 1957; 20, Prospect Park, Oct. 15, 1947.

EXTREME DATES: *Spring*—Apr. 8 (coastal) and Apr. 15 (inland) to June 2 (coastal).

EXTREME DATES: *Fall*—Sept. 1 (coastal) to Nov. 19 (inland) and Dec. 1 (coastal), exceptionally to Dec. 10 (coastal).

Rare before late April, after mid-May, before mid-September, and after October.

Winter: One found dead after a severe cold wave, Great Neck, Nassau Co., Dec. 27, 1958 (Heck and Yeaton), AMNH 763822.

Breeding (see Map 119): Solitary or Blue-headed Vireos are common nesting birds in mixed evergreen-deciduous forest at considerable elevations. In the Adirondacks, Eaton (1914: 374) found them breeding on Mt. Marcy up to 3000 feet. In the Tug Hill district of southern Lewis Co. on June 10, 1957, Scheider (1959a) counted approximately 28 birds in 14 miles, or an average of two per mile.

Eaton (*op. cit.*) found the species absent as a breeder from western New York, except for two Ithaca nesting records in 1893 and 1913.

However, in recent years at least, it has not been a rare breeder in the Allegany Mountains of southwestern New York, having been recorded in the counties of Cattaraugus, Allegany, Steuben, and Schuyler, as well as in Tompkins Co. Saunders (1938: 102) reported that it was fairly common in the Allegany State Park in mixed maple-beech-hemlock forest.

The nest is placed low, from one to 15 feet above ground in saplings of either conifers or hardwoods.

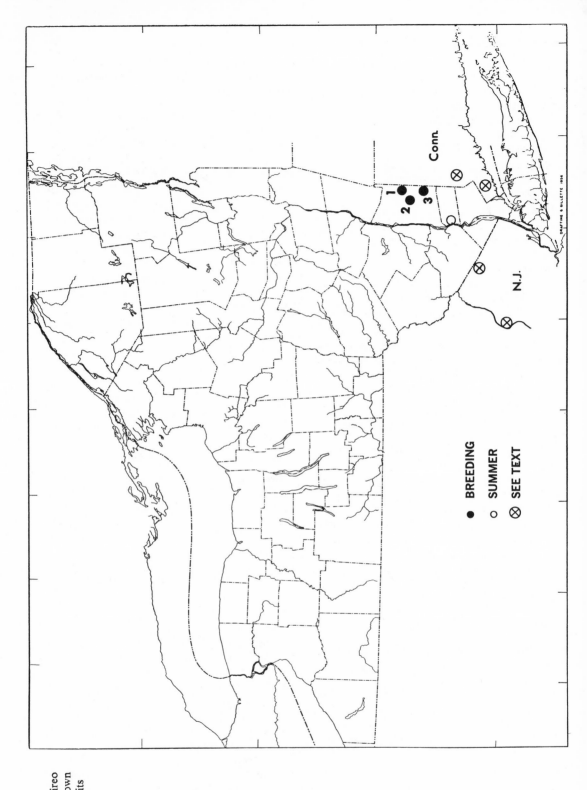

MAP 119 Solitary Vireo
(*Vireo solitarius*) Known
southern breeding limits

Egg clutches in 13 New York nests are either three or four: three eggs (four nests); four eggs (nine nests).

EGG DATES: May 14 to July 22.

Nestlings: June 7 to Aug. 13; fledglings: June 28 to Aug. 31.

The breeding limits of this species in the southeastern portion of the state are poorly understood (see map). It probably breeds at higher elevations in Orange, Rockland, and Putnam counties in New York—all in places where birds either have been heard singing or have been seen during the nesting season, but positive breeding evidence from those areas is lacking. It nevertheless has been found nesting on at least two occasions, to the *south*—in northern New Jersey—and twice to the *southeast*—in southern Connecticut (see map).

The Dutchess Co. breeding localities are located in or near the Taconic Mountains: (1) Turkey Hollow near Wassaic; (2) Washington Hollow Glen near Millbrook; (3) Bald Mtn. near Wingdale.

Although singing birds were present during the summer of 1929 near Cold Spring, Putnam Co., definite nesting evidence was lacking.

It is clear that more field work is needed during the breeding season to determine current status in the areas south and southeast of the Catskills, especially in southern Sullivan, southern Ulster, and Orange, Rockland, and Putnam counties.

Remarks: In the older literature (A.O.U. Check-list, second edition, 1895: 265, and Eaton, 1914: 375) there is a record of a New York specimen purported to be the western subspecies *plumbeus,* and so published in the *Auk* (1894, 11: 79). It was collected at Peterboro, Madison Co., Sept. 24, 1893 (G. S. Miller). This specimen, a female, is in the collection of the British Museum (Natural History), 1906. 12. 7. 1580. The writer had an opportunity to examine it there on a visit in 1966 and can state the following: Although the paler coloration agrees with that of the western race, the distinctly smaller measurements (wing, tail, culmen) are in line with those of nominate *solitarius.* In fact, the collector and the author of the note himself (Miller) made similar comments. Dr. Allan R. Phillips, who also examined this specimen, agrees with me that it is merely an aberrant *V. s. solitarius.*

Red-eyed Vireo
(*Vireo olivaceus*) * B

Range: Nearctic and Neotropical regions, breeding mainly from southern Canada to southern South America. Northern populations winter in South America.

Status: Common to very common migrant. Widespread breeder.

Nonbreeding: In New York the Red-eyed Vireo outnumbers all the other species of this genus combined.

MAXIMA: *Spring*—50, Prospect Park, Brooklyn, May 17, 1945; 57, Sandy Pond, Oswego Co., May 20, 1969; 60, Syracuse, June 6, 1956—a big, late flight.

MAXIMA: *Fall*—50, Selkirk Shores State Park, Oswego Co., Aug. 30, 1966; 59 netted and banded, Fire Island, Suffolk Co., Sept. 1, 1970 (Buckley and Davis). 91 struck the Fire Island Lighthouse, Sept. 23, 1887 (Dutcher); 39 struck the Westhampton Air Force Base tower, Suffolk Co., Oct. 5, 1954; eight struck the Colden television tower, Erie Co., Oct. 10, 1962.

EXTREME DATES: May 1 (coastal) to Nov. 5 (inland) and Nov. 10 and 14 (both coastal). Casual, Apr. 18, 19, 22, and 24 (all coastal) to Nov. 27, 1952, Durand-Eastman Park, Rochester (Listman and Van Beurden). Rare before mid-May and after mid-October.

Breeding: This species breeds in deciduous woodland and in large shade trees in city parks and suburban areas. It is the most numerous and widespread member of its family in the state. Nests are placed in shrubs and trees from two to 18 feet above ground.

The Red-eyed Vireo is the second commonest species parasitized by the Cowbird in New York. See that species for details.

In 23 New York nests, clutch size ranged from three to five eggs: three eggs (eight nests); four eggs (14 nests); five eggs (one nest).

EGG DATES: May 13 to July 7 and Aug. 1 (second brood).

Nestlings: June 8 to Aug. 17 and Sept. 4 (second brood); fledglings: Aug. 6 to Sept. 13.

Remarks: The Red-eyed Vireo together with the tropical American forms *flavoviridis* and *chivi*—Yellow-green and Chivi vireos—are here considered conspecific, following most recent authorities. The south Florida and West Indian *altiloquus*—Black-whiskered Vireo—may well belong here also.

Philadelphia Vireo
(*Vireo philadelphicus*)   *   B

Range: North America, breeding chiefly in central and southern Canada, very rarely south to extreme northern United States. Winters from Mexico to northwestern Colombia. Migrates in spring chiefly through the Mississippi valley; in fall also east of the Appalachians.

Status: Rare to uncommon migrant, more numerous in western New York; very rare in spring along the coast. Very rare breeder in the Adirondacks.

Nonbreeding: The Philadelphia Vireo is seldom seen except by the more active and experienced observers. May and September are the principal months of occurrence, but the species is quite rare in spring in southeastern New York. In fall ordinarily only one or two per day are seen, but on occasion more are reported.

MAXIMA: *Fall*—five hit television tower, South Wales, Erie Co., Sept. 11, 1968; big flight in 1970—ten netted and banded, Fire Island, Suffolk Co., Sept. 20 (Buckley and Davis); *17* hit TV tower, Colden, Erie Co., Sept. 24 (Clark), specimens in BMS collection —an unprecedented number, a "big" year in the northeast; six hit the Empire State Building, New York City, Sept. 27; also six hit TV tower, Colden, Sept. 29, 1962.

MAXIMA, INLAND: *Spring*—four, Elma, Erie Co., May 17, 1956 (Coggeshall); six, Selkirk Shores State Park, Oswego Co., May 20, 1968 (Scheider).

I have examined at least 20 *spring* specimens, all from upstate, dates ranging from May 12 to May 28, various years. Half of these are in the Cornell University collection; four others, in the collection of the British Museum (Natural History), were taken at Geneva, Ontario Co., within two days—May 17 and 19, 1888 (Miller), two on each day.

EXTREME DATES: *Fall*—Aug. 18 (inland) and Aug. 20 (coastal) to Oct. 23 (coastal).

Spring—May 6 (inland) and May 11 (coastal) to June 1 (coastal) and June 10 (inland—near Rochester). Rare before September, after early October, and before mid-May.

Breeding (see Map 120): The Philadelphia Vireo is at its southern known breeding limits in the Adirondack Mountains. Eaton (1914: 369 and 543) searched in vain for the bird's presence in that area in summer.

Finally, a singing male was found at about 2100 feet elevation near (1) Mt. Jo, Essex Co., July 12, 1926 (Saunders), for the first known summer occurrence. Saunders saw this individual in an aspen grove in second-growth maple-aspen-cherry association. During the first week in July of both 1932 and 1933, Geoffrey Carleton likewise found a singing male at about the same location. But it was not until *thirty* years later, a short distance to the south of Mt. Jo, near Marcy Dam, that evidence of breeding was obtained. On June 19 and 20, 1963, Robert and Mary Sheffield were fortunate to discover a pair of these birds constructing a nest 18 feet up in a maple in open secondary forest along a creek at about 2360 feet elevation. The fate of this nest was not reported to my knowledge. This remains the only positive evidence of nesting or, at least, attempted nesting.

As far as I am aware, only two other summer occurrences in Essex Co. (see map) are known. In one instance breeding probably occurred, in the other it might have, but in neither case was definite evidence obtained.

(2) North fork of the Bouquet River between Lewis and Elizabethtown at approximately 1500 feet; on July 3, 1927, Livingston and Weyl found *three* Philadelphia Vireos, one of which was singing. These birds were in a mixed grove of aspen and birch.

(3) At the south end of Upper Cascade Lake, altitude about 2000 feet, an adult male with enlarged testes was collected on June 19, 1954 (Dilger), specimen NYSM 16937. The collector's notation on the specimen label states that the male was with a second individual and that, "Both birds were very much agitated by my presence." Dilger found these birds in white birch woodland.

During the summer of 1960, Dorothy McIlroy found birds "present" at two localities—

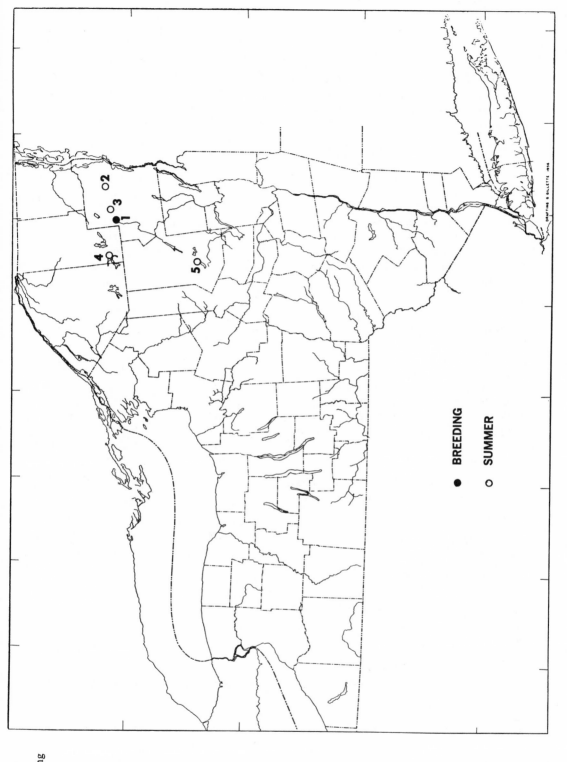

MAP 120 Philadelphia
Vireo (*Vireo
philadelphicus*) Breeding
distribution

(4) near the villages of Tupper Lake, Franklin Co., and (5) Piseco Lake, Hamilton Co. At the latter locality she also saw individuals of both Tennessee and Cape May warblers, quite a feat in itself.

Remarks: The report of a nesting pair of birds, alleged to be this species (*Kingbird,* 1970, 20: 42) at only 400 feet altitude, near Ghent, Columbia Co., during the summer of 1969, was unfortunately not substantiated by specimens or photographs, and, most surprising, not even verified by other observers. The locality, approximately 20 miles *southeast* of Albany, is an unlikely locale for breeding Philadelphia Vireos.

Warbling Vireo
(*Vireo gilvus*)   *   B

Range: Nearctic and Neotropical regions, widespread in the west—breeding from central Canada to Bolivia; but local in the east— breeding from extreme southeastern Canada and Maine only to the highlands of Tennessee and North Carolina, and to the coastal plain of Virginia (rare). Winters from Mexico south.

Status: Rare to uncommon and little-known migrant. Fairly widespread but local breeder; rare on the coastal plain; absent in the higher mountains, but sometimes present at their edges.

Nonbreeding: Were it not for its melodious song, a warble not unlike that of the Purple Finch, this vireo would go unnoticed in the thick foliage of tall shade trees, for it is dull-colored and generally unobtrusive in demeanor.

MAXIMA: *Spring*—four, Dunkirk, Chautauqua Co., Apr. 29, 1964. The figures of 20 at Ithaca, May 12, 1954, and 12 near Syracuse, May 14, 1970, undoubtedly include some or mostly local breeders, as the regions about these localities have sizable breeding populations.

MAXIMA: *Fall*—three netted and banded at Tobay Beach, Nassau Co., Sept. 23, 1967.

EXTREME DATES: Apr. 23 (inland) to Oct. 30 (coastal-netted) and Nov. 7 (inland). Rare before May and after September.

Breeding: Warbling Vireos favor tall shade trees, such as elms and maples in city parks, along rural village streets, and about farmhouses; they are found also in willows, locusts, and sycamores along streams, lakes, and swamps, and once nested in a cherry tree in an open field. Referring to Chemung and Schuyler counties, Axtell (1947) reported these birds as nesting in "open groves of large hardwood trees." Nests are placed from 20 to over 50 feet above the ground.

Only seven New York nests with eggs are known to me: three eggs (five nests); four eggs (two nests).

EGG DATES: May 16 to June 16.

Nestlings: May 31 to June 29; fledglings: June 21 to July 24.

This species has decreased considerably in many sections because of spraying diseased elms. In other areas where most of the elms have died, maples are often used for nesting.

Maximum breeding densities per acre are: six pairs in 20 acres, Van Cortlandt Park, Bronx Co., 1962; eight pairs in 30 acres, Ithaca, Tompkins Co., 1967.

Although Warbling Vireos are recorded as having bred in extreme northern Ulster Co. in the Catskill Mountain villages of Big Indian, Pine Hill, and Allaben, all are located at relatively low elevations in the Esopus Creek valley section. The species breeds also in the village of Saranac Lake, Franklin Co., virtually in the heart of the Adirondacks, but at a low altitude.

Remarks: Following most recent authorities, this form and the tropical American *leucophrys* (Brown-capped Vireo) are here considered conspecific. The two are connected by the morphologically intermediate population *amauronotus* of southern Mexico.

WOOD WARBLERS — PARULIDAE

Thirty-seven species in New York.
Thirty-one breed.

In this exclusively American family (about 120 species) nearly one-third of the total occurs within the state and of 37 species recorded from New York more than 80% breed. The genus *Dendroica* alone has 16 species in the state, 13 of them breeding.

The vernacular family name is a misnomer, as hardly any of the species can be said to warble. Most species have little more than dry, buzzy "songs," more insect-like than bird-like. What they lack in voice, however, is made up by beauty of plumage, many of them being brightly colored or attractively patterned. In spring these birds are the favorites of bird watchers, as they are then easily identified in their breeding dress. In fall when they are in dull plumage, with few exceptions, they test the most experienced observers in identification. During the height of the migrations (spring or fall) it is possible to observe more than 25 species in a day in favorable warbler localities.

Black and White Warbler
(*Mniotilta varia*)   *   B

Range: Chiefly central and eastern North America, breeding from southern Canada to southern United States. Winters in tropical America north to Florida, very rarely farther north along the Atlantic coast.

Status: Common to occasionally very common migrant. Widespread breeder.

Nonbreeding: This species is one of the more numerous warblers during the migrations, especially along the coast. It often crawls on tree trunks in search of food.

MAXIMA: *Spring*—36 netted and banded, Fire Island, Suffolk Co., Apr. 26, 1970; 30, Inwood Hill Park, New York City, Apr. 30, 1965; 100, Woodmere Woods, Nassau Co., May 6, 1950; 50, Rochester, May 24, 1917—a notably very late spring statewide.

MAXIMA: *Fall*—25, Far Rockaway, Queens Co., Aug. 14, 1954; 40, Jones Beach, Nassau Co., Sept. 10, 1969; 66 struck the Empire State Building, New York City, Sept. 27, 1970; 13, Sandy Pond, Oswego Co., Oct. 2, 1966.

EXTREME DATES: Apr. 3, 1967 (Latham), exceptionally early; Apr. 10 (coastal) and Apr. 19 (inland) to Nov. 30 (inland) and Dec. 2 (coastal specimen). Rare before late April and after October.

Winter: Most unusual are two Long Island observations by experienced observers—(1) Baldwin, Nassau Co., Jan. 2, 1950 (Pettit); (2) Cold Spring Harbor, Suffolk Co., Dec. 27, 1964 (John Taylor).

Breeding: The Black and White Warbler breeds in woodland from near sea level on Long Island to near the tops of the highest mountains in the Adirondacks. Eaton (1914: 378) found it nesting up to tree line on Mt. Marcy, Essex Co. Despite this wide range both altitudinally and latitudinally, apparently very few nests have been found in New York. Beardslee and Mitchell (1965: 362) state that, "The finding of its nest is seldom reported." Perhaps many of them are well concealed from human eyes.

Nests are placed on the ground at the base of trees, among overturned tree roots, or under the edges of logs and stones.

The contents of only nine New York nests with eggs are as follows: three eggs (two nests); four eggs (three nests); five eggs (four nests).

EGG DATES: May 10 to June 30.

Nestlings: June 5 to July 23; fledglings: June 19 to July 31.

Prothonotary Warbler
(*Protonotaria citrea*)   *   B

Range: Southeastern Nearctic region, breeding north to extreme southeastern Ontario, western and central New York, northern New Jersey, and once in southwestern Connecticut. Winters north to southern Mexico.

Status: Rare but regular migrant, scarcer in fall. Local breeder in western and central portions.

Change in status: The Prothonotary Warbler was called by Eaton (1914: 381), as "only an accidental visitant." Not until the late 1920s or early 1930s was it reported with any degree of regularity—a few observed each spring. The first state breeding record was in 1931.

Nonbreeding: This species is restricted to wet areas even during migration and may be found along wooded ponds and streams, and particularly in swamps. Most reports are during the last week in April and in May. It is most often observed in western, central, and southeastern New York, in the last-named section in the New York City region. Ordinarily only one or two individuals are seen each spring, but in recent years more have been reported. As many as *nine* were recorded in the New York City area during the spring of 1970, seven of these from Apr. 27 to May 24.

EXTREME DATES: Casually as early as Mar. 27 and Apr. 2, 1970; on the first date one was found exhausted at Manorville, Suffolk Co. (Raynor); it died later that day, specimen saved. There was a "tropical" storm the night of Mar. 24. Apr. 19 (coastal) and Apr. 23 (inland) to Sept. 30 (inland) and Oct. 4 (coastal); also a male at Babylon, Suffolk Co., Oct. 13–15, 1963 (Eckelberry).

The species has been observed as far north as Saratoga and Oswego counties.

Breeding (see Map 121): The beautiful Prothonotary Warbler is the only member of this family within our area that is a hole-nester. It is an inhabitant of swampy woods or streams,

often nesting in dead trees or stumps standing in water.

In 1931 the first New York nests were discovered in the Oak Orchard Swamp. At least *four* different nests were found there in an area of partially submerged willows and buttonbushes (*Cephalanthus*). The species has nested there annually since, with at least *ten* individuals seen on June 15, 1961 (Mitchell). It commenced breeding in the Montezuma Marshes in 1948 when the first nest was found and has been present there since then, usually every year, with two pairs in 1969. The habitat at Montezuma is a red maple-elm swamp.

Most nests found in New York were in dead stubs or live trees with cavities, usually willows, and at low heights ranging from two to eight feet above water.

Two other nests were situated near swamps, one in a birdhouse, the other in a mailbox.

Egg clutches in 11 New York nests ranged from three to seven; three eggs (four nests); four eggs (three nests); five eggs (two nests); six and seven eggs (one nest each).

EGG DATES: May 17 to June 29.

Nestlings: June 8 to July 6; fledglings: July 10 to Aug. 6.

Distribution of the six known nesting localities with initial year of arrival is shown on the accompanying map: Genesee Co.—(1) Oak Orchard Swamp near Alabama, 1931; (2) Le Roy, 1933, only year. Seneca and Cayuga counties—(3) Montezuma Marshes, 1948. Onondaga Co.—(4) Oneida Lake at Short Point, 1944, and nearby Muskrat Bay, 1957, only year. Chautauqua Co.—(5) Ashville, 1952, only year; (6) Riverside Marsh, 1963, only year.

"Permanent colonies" exist only at Oak Orchard, Montezuma, and Oneida Lake.

A pair of these birds was present at Alden, Erie Co., June 17–24, 1947, but no nest was found.

It is quite obvious from the map that this species arrived in New York from the west (by way of the Niagara Frontier corridor via Ontario—⊗), and from the southwest (by way of Ohio and Pennsylvania—⊗).

Despite the fact that Prothonotary Warblers have been breeding in adjacent northern New Jersey and once to the east in Connecticut—⊗ (Bull, 1964: 361–362), no nesting as yet has been reported from southeastern New York.

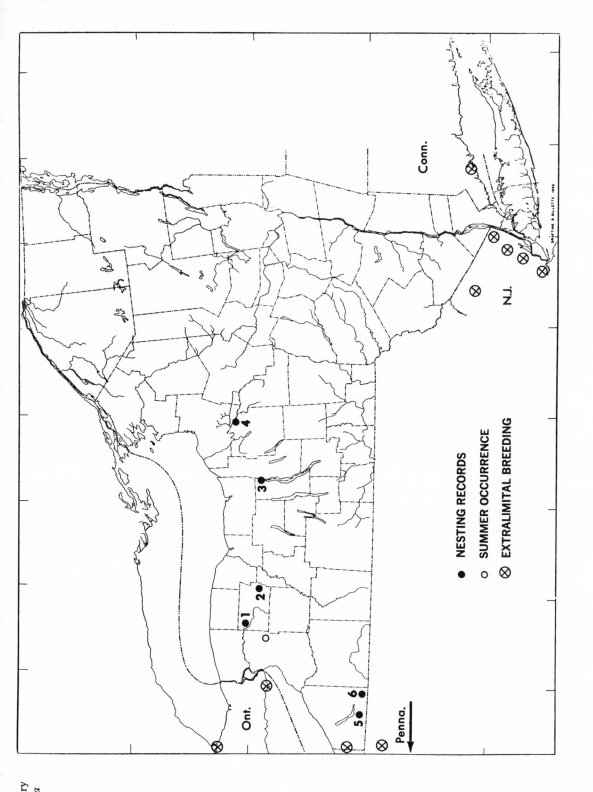

MAP 121 Prothonotary Warbler (*Protonotaria citrea*) Breeding distribution

● NESTING RECORDS

○ SUMMER OCCURRENCE

⊗ EXTRALIMITAL BREEDING

[Swainson's Warbler
(*Limnothlypis swainsonii*)

Hypothetical: Southeastern United States, breeding north to southeastern Maryland and western West Virginia.

Two reports of birds seen in New York City by experienced observers are believed correct: (1) An individual was observed at Prospect Park, Brooklyn, May 5 and 6, 1950 (Carleton, Helmuth, Alperin, and Grant, *Wilson Bull.,* 1952, 64: 109–110); (2) another was carefully studied at the Bronx Botanical Garden, May 6, 1963 (Carleton, Hackett, Horowitz, Maguire, and Post).]

Postscript: This species can now be placed on the New York State list in view of the following: an individual was netted, banded, photographed, and released at Tobay Beach, Nassau Co., May 20, 1973 (Lauro)—see photo by Buckley in *American Birds* (1973, 27: 841).

Another was observed in Central Park, Manhattan, the same year, on May 11, by many people.

Worm-eating Warbler
(*Helmitheros vermivorus*)   *   B

Range: Southeastern United States, breeding north to east-central New York, northern Connecticut, and western Massachusetts. Winters in the tropics north to Mexico and the West Indies, rarely to Florida.

Status: Variously rare to fairly common migrant on the coast. Locally common breeder in the lower Hudson valley and in the Susquehanna-Chemung river watershed from Binghamton to Elmira; rare and local breeder on the north shore of Long Island and in the upper Hudson valley north to Albany Co.

Nonbreeding: This species may be seen to best advantage in the New York City parks in late April and early May when the foliage is still sparse.

MAXIMA: *Spring*—five, Central Park, New York City, Apr. 27, 1925; 1950—12, Prospect Park, Brooklyn, May 5; ten, Van Cortlandt Park, Bronx Co., May 6.

MAXIMA: *Fall*—seven, Inwood Hill Park, Manhattan, Aug. 2, 1963; five, Central Park, Aug. 9, 1964; five struck the Fire Island Lighthouse, Suffolk Co., Aug. 28, 1898.

EXTREME DATES: Apr. 10 (coastal) to Oct. 9 (inland) and Oct. 17 (coastal). Rare before late April and after mid-September. This species departs early in fall—two individuals were banded on July 11 and 17 on Long Island at localities where they are not known to breed.

According to Parkes (1952a) it has been reported as far north as Watertown, Jefferson Co.

Breeding (see Map 122): The Worm-eating Warbler breeds among dense undergrowth in or near ravines on heavily wooded hillsides, chiefly along river valleys. The nest is placed on the ground usually at the base of a tree or bush, or next to a log or rock.

Egg clutches in five New York nests: five eggs (three nests); four and six eggs (one nest each).

EGG DATES: May 24 to June 18.

Nestlings: June 6 to July 15; fledglings: June 16 to July 29.

That these warblers are locally common may be seen from the following densities: (1) ten pairs on a 40-acre tract, Grassy Sprain, Westchester Co., summer of 1941 (Hickey); (2) 12 pairs, along the Chemung River near Elmira, 1943 (Axtell, 1947).

The accompanying map shows the 28 known breeding localities in the state: Long Island—Suffolk Co.—(1) Port Jefferson; (2) Cold Spring Harbor. Queens Co.—(3) Bayside. Hudson valley—Westchester Co.—(4) near Yonkers; (5) Grassy Sprain; (6) Hartsdale; (7) Elmsford area; (8) near Bedford; (9) Mianus Gorge. Rockland Co.—(10) Nyack; (11) Bear Mtn. area; it undoubtedly nests elsewhere in that county. Orange Co.—(12) near Lake Kanawauke, Harriman Park; (13) Highland Falls; (14) Cornwall; (15) near Newburgh. Putnam Co.—(16) Piano Mtn. Dutchess Co.—(17) Mt. Beacon; (18) Bald Mtn. near Wingdale; (19) Rhinebeck. Ulster Co.—(20) Mohonk Lake; (21) Lomontville. Greene Co.—(22) near Catskill. Albany Co.—(23) Ravena; (24) Indian Ladder, Thacher State Park; (25) near Cohoes; "southern tier" area

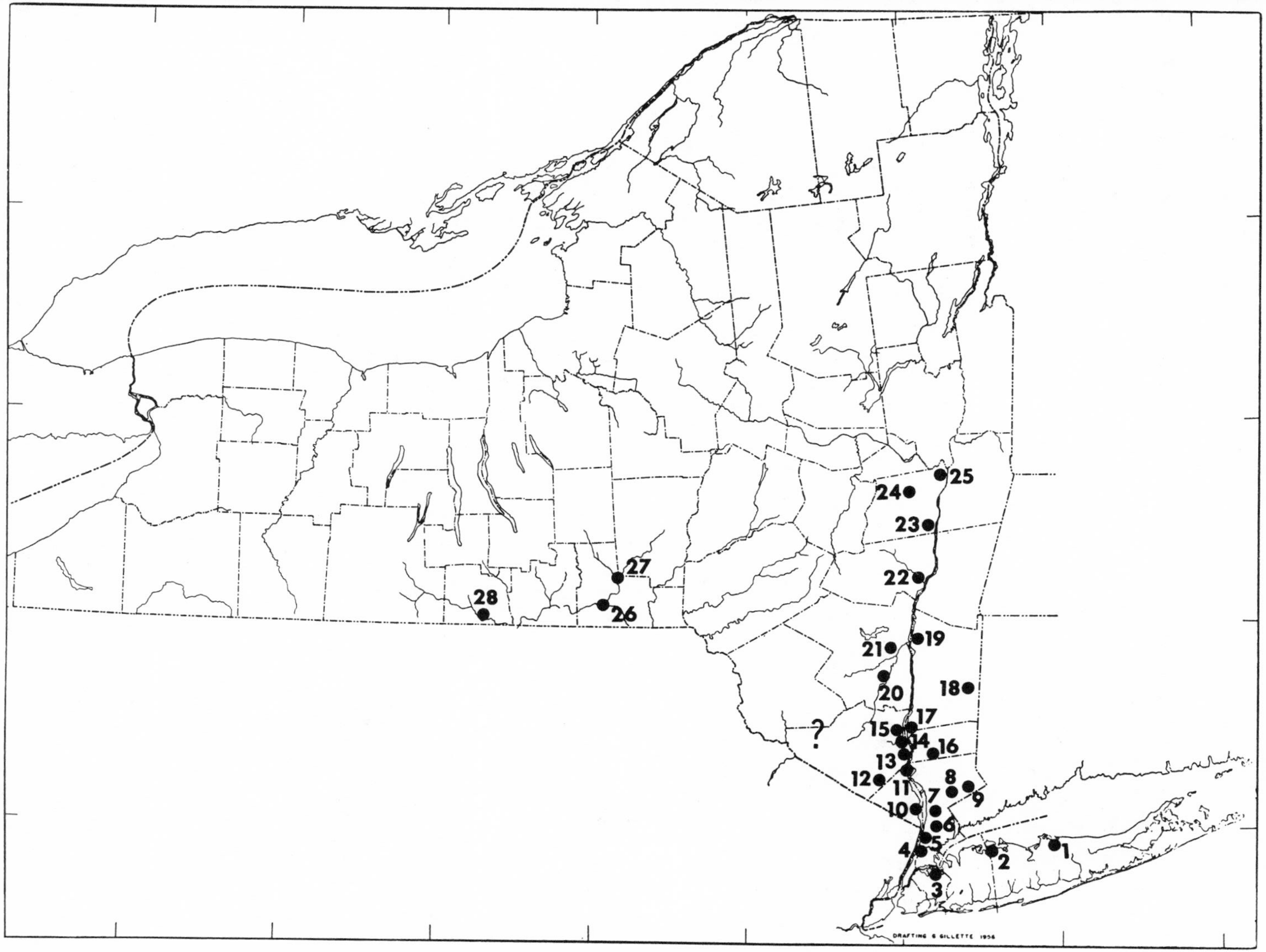

MAP 122 Worm-eating
Warbler (*Helmitheros
vermivorus*) Breeding
distribution

—Broome Co.—(26) near Binghamton; (27) Chenango Valley State Park. Chemung Co.—(28) near Elmira.

Eaton (1914: 383) included as a breeding locality, Bellport, Suffolk Co. (*south* shore of Long Island), but on what evidence I am not aware. The habitat there is utterly unsuitable.

Blue-winged Warbler
(*Vermivora pinus*)   *   B

Range: Chiefly eastern United States, breeding from Nebraska and Iowa east to extreme southeastern Ontario, central New York, and Massachusetts; south to Arkansas, the mountains of northern Georgia, and the coast of Delaware. Winters from Mexico to Panama.

Status: Uncommon to fairly common migrant on and near the coast, occasionally more numerous; rare to uncommon upstate, but increasing. Common breeder at lower elevations near the coast, but rare to absent in the mountains; increasing in the interior and spreading northward, but not certainly known as a breeder north of the central portions.

Nonbreeding: This species occurs in numbers apparently only in the New York City parks and is relatively scarce elsewhere.

MAXIMA: *Spring*—25, Prospect Park, Brooklyn, May 4, 1953.

MAXIMA: *Fall*—12, Inwood Hill Park, Manhattan, Aug. 2, 1963; 12, Bronx Park, Bronx Co., Aug. 9, 1963; ten, same locality, Aug. 18, 1946. As can be seen from the above fall dates, the peak is early in the season.

EXTREME DATES: Casual Apr. 7, 1947, West Falls, Erie Co. (Matlock), same date as a Hooded Warbler—following a heavy storm in the Oklahoma-Texas region; Apr. 15 (coastal) to Oct. 12 (coastal), exceptionally to Oct. 30 (coastal); also Nov. 29, 1958, near Cross River, Westchester Co. (Grierson)—male caught by cat, specimen preserved; still another Nov. 30, 1960, Hamburg, Erie Co. (Bacon and Lillie)—freshly dead, picked out of a snowdrift. The specimen is BMS 5042. Rare before May and after early September.

An individual was observed as far north as Watertown, Jefferson Co., May 18, 1968 (Gordon).

Winter: An individual seen alive in the Bronx Botanical Garden, Dec. 10, 1899, was found dead on Jan. 6, 1900 (Britton). The specimen—examined by Chapman, but not seen by me—is not at present in the AMNH collection.

Breeding (see Maps 123 and 124): Blue-winged Warblers nest on the ground in dry or moist areas, in thickets in clearings—especially those with *Smilax* (catbrier); also in scrubby overgrown fields and pastures, often near streams; and along woodland borders.

Eaton (1914: 385) called this bird ". . . extremely rare as a breeding species in central and western New York . . ." Beardslee and Mitchell (1965: 366) considered it very rare in former years in western New York, but that it had started to increase there by about 1938, and that recently it had become fairly common in the "southern tier" counties (bordering Pennsylvania). Rosche (1967) speaking of Wyoming Co. said that it was a presumed regular breeder since 1960 in "subclimax" habitat in aspen and pin cherry, gradually spreading into the central portions up to 1500 feet.

Egg clutches in 12 New York nests: four and five eggs (five nests each); six eggs (two nests).

EGG DATES: May 18 to June 17.

Nestlings: June 4 to July 11; fledglings: June 16 to Aug. 12.

Remarks: For relationship with Golden-winged Warbler, see that species.

Golden-winged Warbler
(*Vermivora chrysoptera*)   *   B

Range: Chiefly eastern United States, breeding from southeastern Manitoba (rarely), Minnesota, and Iowa east to extreme southeastern Ontario, southwestern Quebec, 1971 (see map), central and northwestern New York, and southern Vermont; south to Illinois, and to the mountains of northern Georgia. Ranges farther north and at higher altitudes than *V. pinus*, and not as far south in the midwestern states, nor along the Atlantic coastal plain. Winters from Guatemala to northwestern South America.

Status: Variously rare to uncommon but regular spring migrant near the coast, but rare anytime on Long Island; more numerous up-state. Fairly common, but local breeder up-state and in the highlands downstate, but absent on Long Island, in the mountains, and generally in the northern portions. Extending its breeding range northward in recent years (see map).

Nonbreeding: This attractive warbler, like the Blue-winged Warbler, is reported in numbers apparently only in the New York City Parks, although usually much scarcer than the latter species. The spring concentrations recorded at Hamburg, Erie Co., and at Camillus Valley, Onondaga Co., undoubtedly include chiefly local breeders as both of these localities are breeding stations.

MAXIMA: *Spring*—12, Bronx and Van Cortlandt parks, Bronx Co., May 8, 1943; seven, Prospect Park, Brooklyn, May 10, 1946 —both unusual numbers. The Golden-winged Warbler is ordinarily rarely observed where it does *not* breed.

EXTREME DATES: Apr. 26 (coastal) and Apr. 30 (inland) to Oct. 10 (coastal). Rare before May and after early September.

Most unusual is a singing male recorded at Jay, Essex Co., June 5, 1965 (Hagar); but see map for possible breeding record in adjacent Vermont.

Breeding (see Maps 123 and 124): Golden-winged Warblers nest in habitats similar to those of Blue-winged Warblers, but often at higher elevations and are somewhat more northerly in range. However, the two forms are widely sympatric and interbreed freely. Both are ground nesters. One nest was located in the center of a fern clump among skunk cabbage in open swampy woods in Potter Swamp, Yates Co. In contrast these birds have been found breeding in dry, open oak-pine barrens near Phoenix, Oswego Co. Like the Blue-winged Warbler, the Golden-winged Warbler tends to occur in "colonies" which may be scattered about the countryside.

Egg clutches in 14 New York nests: four and five eggs (seven nests each).

EGG DATES: May 18 to June 16.

Nestlings: June 8 to July 6; fledglings: June 27 to Aug. 6.

Braislin (1907: 90–91) specifically stated that on Long Island the Golden-winged Warbler was only a "Rare transient visitant," and the

Blue-winged Warbler was a "Common summer resident in suitable localities on the western end of Long Island; elsewhere rare." I do not know the basis of the following statements concerning the Golden-wing's alleged breeding on Long Island, which stems from (1) Eaton (1914: 386): "Rare summer resident on Long Island"; (2) K. C. Parkes (1952a), "is limited [in the breeding season] to the western end, chiefly along the north shore." (3) Short (1963; 152), ". . . occasional reports of 'Brewster's' Warblers breeding on the north shore of Long Island ([Irene] Parks, pers. comm.)." I am unaware of any definite breeding record of either the "Brewster's" Warbler or the Golden-winged Warbler on Long Island, although a male Golden-wing was observed feeding two recently fledged juvenile Blue-wings at Oyster Bay, Nassau Co., from July 2 to July 10, 1969 (Barbara Spencer, Lanyon, Bull, *et al.*). The female, however, was never observed.

As may be seen on the accompanying maps, the Golden-wing has been extending its breeding range to the north. By the late 1950s and early 1960s this bird had been found breeding as far north as southern Saratoga Co., northeastern Oneida Co., southwestern Lewis Co., and northern Oswego Co.—the last three counties at the edge of the Tug Hill plateau.

In Canada (Ontario) the Golden-wing had reached Kingston as early as 1961 and by 1967 had even penetrated northwest as far as the Muskoka district (see map). Two years later (1969) in New York it had made its farthest north advance to Gouverneur, St. Lawrence Co. (Belknap). In 1971 it was found breeding in Jefferson Co. at Watertown (Belknap), and in Quebec, southeast of Montreal (see map).

Meanwhile the Blue-winged Warbler had been extending its range northward also—well into the breeding range of the Golden-winged Warbler, as is obvious by comparing the pre-1910 and post-1970 maps. Wherever the two forms have met, interbreeding has occurred on a fairly extensive scale, and the zone of overlap is expanding.

Short (1962: 63) collected 32 individuals in 1961 in central New York, 23 of these in Tompkins Co. (Ithaca region). Of these 23, five were "pure" *pinus*, only two were "pure" *chrysoptera*, four were "Brewster's" type, and the remaining 12 were as follows: eight were

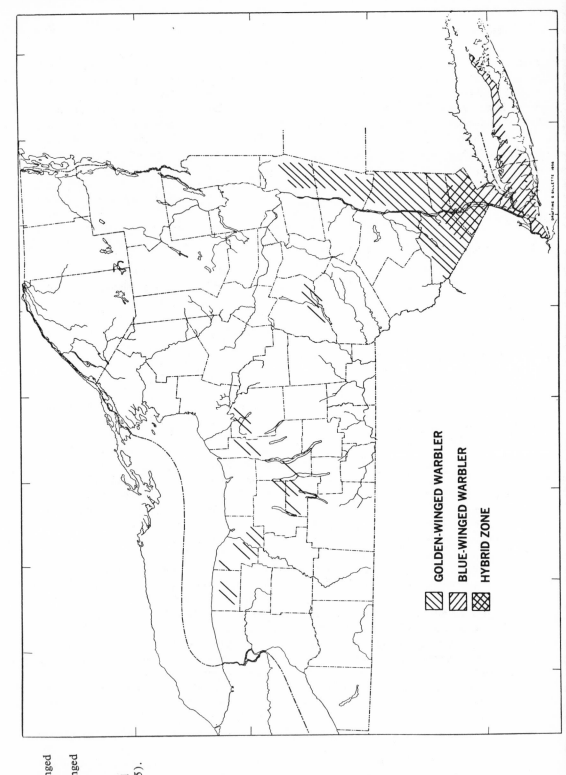

MAP 123 Golden-winged Warbler (*Vermivora chrysoptera*) Blue-winged Warbler (*Vermivora pinus*) Breeding distribution as of the early 1900s. Adapted from Eaton (1910: 25).

GOLDEN-WINGED WARBLER

BLUE-WINGED WARBLER

HYBRID ZONE

MAP 124 Golden-winged
Warbler (*Vermivora
chrysoptera*)
Blue-winged Warbler
(*Vermivora pinus*)
Breeding distribution as
of 1971; based chiefly on
specimen and
color-banding evidence.

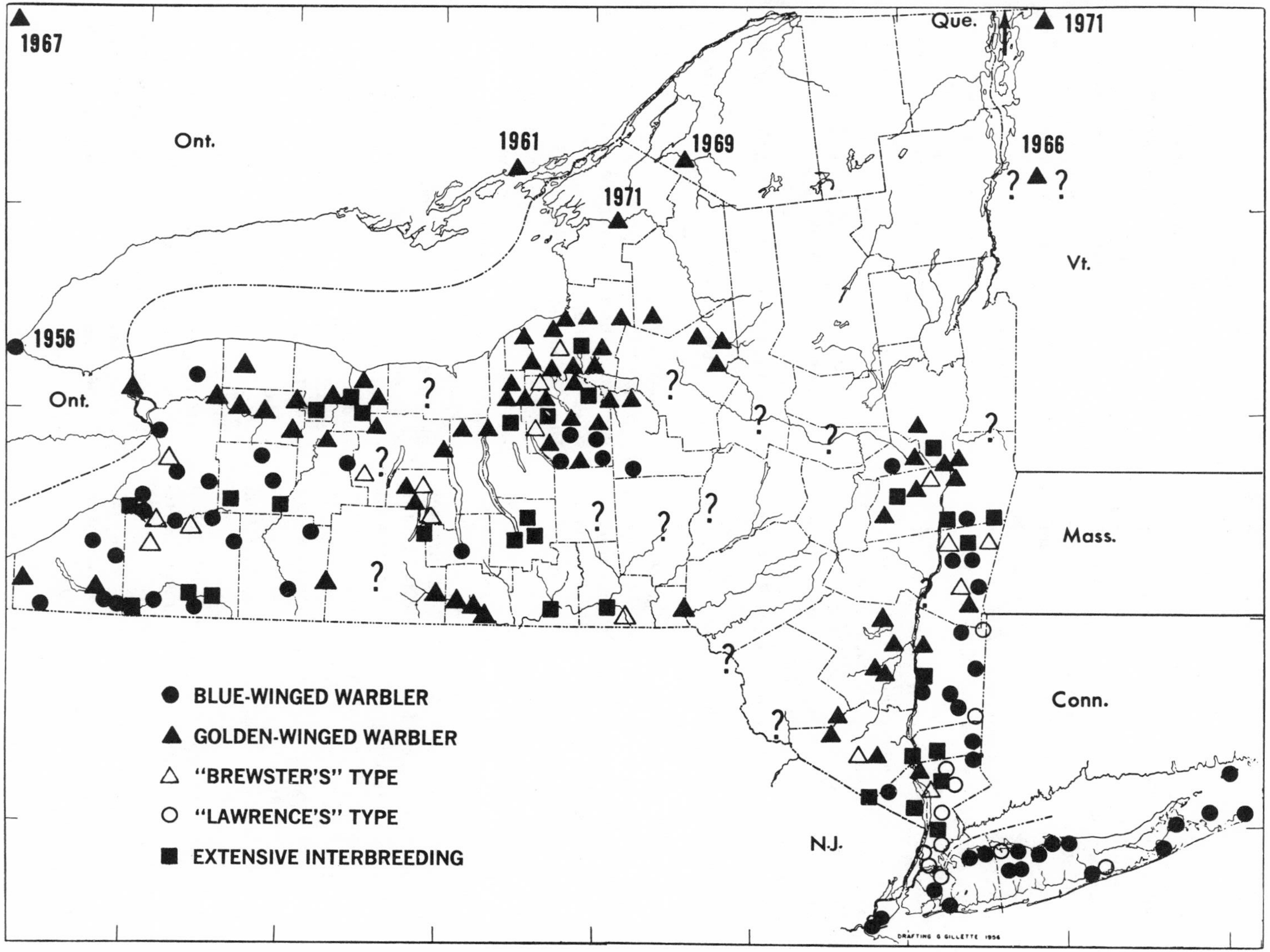

● BLUE-WINGED WARBLER

▲ GOLDEN-WINGED WARBLER

△ "BREWSTER'S" TYPE

○ "LAWRENCE'S" TYPE

■ EXTENSIVE INTERBREEDING

Que.

▲ 1971

▲ 1966

? ▲ ?

Vt.

Mass.

Conn.

N.J.

1969

1971

1961

1956

Ont.

Ont.

▲ 1967

designated as *pinus* with traces of *chrysoptera;* only four as *chrysoptera* with traces of *pinus.* In sum, 13 were of predominant *pinus* "strain," the other ten of chiefly *chrysoptera* "strain."

Of seven individuals collected by Short in Onondaga Co., all seven were from Camillus (Syracuse region), plus two more in nearby Cayuga Co. at Howland's Island. However, *none* of the nine was *pinus* or even predominantly *pinus.*

Of great significance is the fact that Short (*op. cit.:* 67) found, "Song is so variable that it cannot be used alone to identify warblers as Blue-wings or Golden-wings." He further stated (1963: 159), "and those [songs] of both forms are occasionally given by the same bird." Short (1963: 154) said of the central New York birds, "The original *chrysoptera* population is now shifting toward *pinus* as a result of hybridization." He postulated (1963: 160) that, "Continued interbreeding at the present time may lead to swamping of the differences between the two as they merge, or may result in the establishment of some form of polymorphism."

Remarks (see Color Plate 9): Based on present distribution and range expansion, it is possible that at one time these two warblers were allopatric (geographic isolates), and that with recent amelioration of the climate both forms have been extending their ranges northward. The more southerly breeder—the Blue-winged Warbler—has spread northward more rapidly than has the more northerly Golden-winged Warbler, as may be seen by a comparison of the two breeding distribution maps, more than *60* years apart.

This acceleration of northward penetration of Blue-wings into Golden-wing range has resulted in a wide zone of sympatry (overlap) which in turn has initiated extensive and widespread interbreeding between these closely related forms. This large-scale introgression or gene flow has created a situation in which these two morphologically different forms appear to behave like conspecifics rather than two separate species, as currently recognized. It is not inconceivable that we are witnessing a complex evolution of polymorphism within one species. If, on the one hand hybridization has in fact taken place, producing "Brewster's" (F_1) type and "Lawrence's" (backcross) type

warblers—as is commonly believed—these two hybrid types are themselves as morphologically different from one another as are their parental forms—the Blue-wing and the Golden-wing—which is a distinctly different situation than normally associated with two populations that hybridize; for example, a blending of characters as exist between the Yellow-shafted and Red-shafted flickers, or between the Baltimore and Bullock's orioles, where the hybrids themselves tend to appear intermediate morphologically. In the case of the mixed Blue-wing x Golden-wing matings, however, the morphological characters of the offspring are *not* intermediate or of a blending nature, but in themselves appear to be so different, that originally they ("Brewster's" and "Lawrence's" warblers) were described as new *species.*

If, on the other hand, this is a situation of secondary contact, whereby originally this complex of warblers occurred sympatrically as a *single* highly polymorphic species, and at a later stage became separated because of climatic vicissitudes (glaciation) and at a still later period came "together again" (secondary contact) due to a warming trend, then polymorphism is a likelihood in this dynamic situation.

The genetics and interactions of these warblers are, however, so complex that it is idle to do more than speculate, even though cognizant of what is happening; it is tempting to treat these forms as *one* highly variable species. Perhaps rearing birds in captivity may help solve the dilemma.

The interested reader is referred to Parkes (1951), Berger (1958), and Short (1962, 1963). For an earlier summation in the New York City area, see Bull (1964: 365–368).

Finally, the field observer is urged to identify the hybrid types with caution, especially the variable "Brewster's" type. It is not scientific to categorize every individual hybrid that one sees in the field as a "Brewster's." After all it may not be one.

Orange-crowned Warbler
(*Vermivora celata*)   *

Range: Chiefly western North America, rare and local breeder and migrant eastward; breeds southeast to the central portions of Ontario and Quebec and, according to Godfrey (1966: 324), even to southwestern Labrador. In the east winters along the south Atlantic coast north to South Carolina; very rarely to Massachusetts (specimens). Migrates in spring through the Mississippi valley; in fall mainly over the spring route, but regularly along the Atlantic coast in small numbers.

Status: Rare but regular fall migrant; very rare spring migrant, although less rare in western New York. Rare winter visitant.

Occurrence: The dull-colored and inconspicuous Orange-crowned Warbler is scarcely ever noticed except by the active, discerning observer. During autumn this species frequents overgrown weedy fields and scrub. In spring it rarely ever occurs except on days of big warbler movements. Being more arboreal at that season, it may be located in the taller trees by its somewhat junco-like song. It has been recorded to winter occasionally at feeding stations.

MAXIMA: *Fall*—three, Old Chatham, Columbia Co., Oct. 21, 1962; *Winter*—three, Nichols feeder, Babylon, Suffolk Co., all January 1955, one of these wintering; *Spring*—three, Syracuse, May 7, 1962; three, Geneva, Ontario Co., May 18, 1958.

Single individuals of this species have been recorded wintering at feeders at the following localities: New Dorp, Richmond Co., Dec. 25, 1923, to Mar. 8, 1924; Baldwin, Nassau Co., Jan. 1 to Mar. 3, 1947; Wellsburg, Chemung Co., Dec. 4, 1953, to Jan. 9, 1954; Penn Yan, Yates Co., Dec. 28, 1968, to Feb. 28, 1969. The individual at Baldwin fed chiefly on suet.

Of special interest is an individual found dead on a fishing boat, approximately 30 miles southeast of Montauk, Long Island, Oct. 6, 1967 (Jensen and Livingstone, 1969: 6).

EXTREME DATES: Sept. 7 (earliest specimen, Sept. 15) to May 29 (specimen). This latter specimen was taken in 1926 at Conquest, Cayuga Co. (Wright), CUM 16026. Rare before October.

Remarks: August reports are considered unsatisfactory and have been rejected because of confusion with dull or immature Yellow Warblers and Tennessee Warblers. A number of years ago, a warbler thought to be an Orange-crowned was picked up dead in late August and brought to a Linnaean Society meeting for identification. It was variously identified by those present as: Orange-crowned, Nashville, Tennessee, Yellow, and female Wilson's warblers. Upon examination of skins, it proved to be an immature Yellow Warbler.

Tennessee Warbler
(*Vermivora peregrina*)   *   B

Range: North America, breeding from southern Alaska and central Canada to extreme northern United States (where very rare). Winters from southern Mexico to northern South America.

Status: Variously uncommon to very common migrant. Most numerous in spring in western New York and in fall in the southeastern portion. Very rare breeder in the Adirondacks.

Nonbreeding: This species, like the Cape May Warbler, fluctuates greatly in numbers and, like it, is much more numerous today than in the last century.

MAXIMA: *Spring*—all inland—12, Syracuse, May 5, 1955; 20 in one hour, Oakwood, Cayuga Co., May 13, 1964; 100, Syracuse, May 17, 1957; 75, same locality, May 20, 1955; 20, Niskayuna, Schenectady Co., May 29, 1956. It is apparent that the species is especially numerous at Syracuse.

MAXIMA: *Fall*—all coastal—12, Prospect Park, Brooklyn, Aug. 19, 1944; 30, including 12 in one tree, Far Rockaway, Queens Co., Sept. 7, 1949; 35, Central Park, New York City, Sept. 20, 1958; 42 struck the Empire State Building, New York City, Sept. 22, 1953; 15, Idlewild, Queens Co., Oct. 8, 1949.

EXTREME DATES: *Spring*—Apr. 29 (coastal) and May 2 (inland) to June 9; singing birds at inland, non-Adirondack localities, June 15 and 29.

EXTREME DATES: *Fall*—exceptionally early, July 14, 1970, Great Gull Island, Suffolk Co. (A. Poole), adult banded and color-photographed, color slides in AMNH collection; Aug. 5 (inland) and Aug. 9 (coastal) to Oct. 29 (coastal); exceptionally to Nov. 15 (coastal) and Nov. 22–26, 1959, banded bird at Nassau, Rensselaer Co.

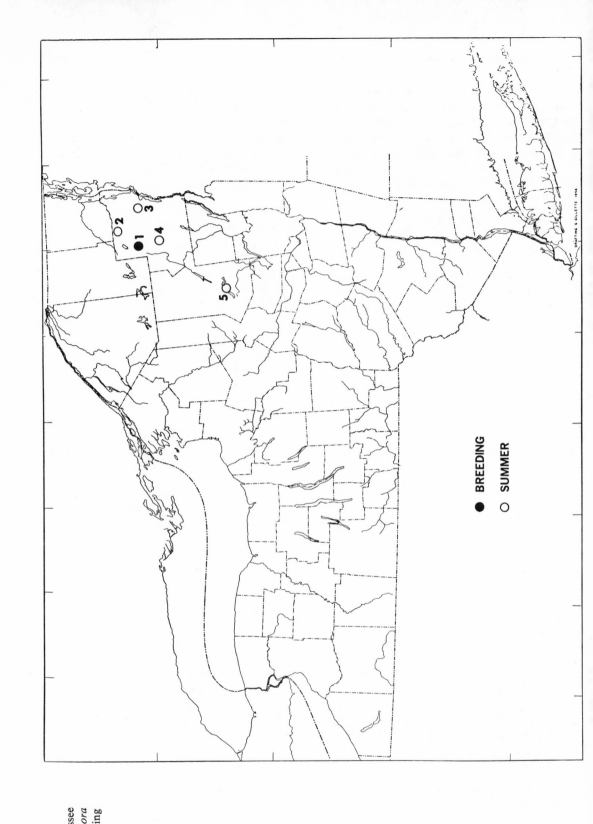

MAP 125 Tennessee
Warbler (*Vermivora
peregrina*) Breeding
distribution

● BREEDING

○ SUMMER

Usually rare before mid-May and after early October.

Winter: An adult present at the Wood feeding station, Ossining, Westchester Co., Jan. 12, 1955, was found dead there on Jan. 30 and was preserved as a specimen, AMNH 788901 (Bull, *Auk,* 1961, 78: 263–264). The only known confirmed winter records north of Mexico are the above New York occurrence and, appropriately enough, a specimen from Tennessee.

Breeding (see Map 125): The only definite instance of breeding in New York to my knowledge is that of an adult feeding two recently fledged juveniles along a stream in aspen-willow association, south of (1) North Elba, Essex Co., July 1926 (Saunders).

There are four other *summer* occurrences in the Adirondack region, of which three are from Essex Co.—(2) Wilmington Mtn. at about 3000 feet, at Cooper Kill Pond, June 4–10, 1966 (Hagar and Young), pair present—may well have bred; (3) Hurricane Mtn. at about 2000 feet, July 10, 1930 (Carleton and L. Williams), singing male in second growth woodland; (4) one mile north of Mt. Marcy, near Indian Falls, July 13–16, 1949 (R. Stone), several birds—may have nested; (5) Piseco Lake region, Hamilton Co., summer of 1960 (Dorothy McIlroy), a few individuals present, may have bred also. Most unusual, she also reported Philadelphia Vireos and Cape May Warblers in the same general area. There is also a report of a singing male at Indian Lake, Hamilton Co., July 3, 1971 (McKinney, *Kingbird,* 1971, 21: 239), but the exact locality is not stated.

Nashville Warbler
(*Vermivora ruficapilla*) * B

Range: Southern Canada and northern United States, in the east breeding south to the mountains of Maryland; rarely to the lowlands of southern Connecticut and Rhode Island. Winters north rarely to the Gulf states; casually to Long Island (photograph) and Massachusetts (specimen).

Status: Common to very common migrant inland, but only uncommon to fairly common along the coast. Locally numerous breeder in the mountains and in central New York, but uncommon in the western portions and rare southeastward.

Nonbreeding: This species is much more numerous upstate than along the coast as may be seen from the numbers listed below.

MAXIMA, INLAND: *Spring*—50, Syracuse, May 4, 1965; 60, same locality, May 14, 1962; 80, Avon, Livingston Co., May 21, 1961.

MAXIMA, INLAND: *Fall*—seven, Forest Lawn, Buffalo, Aug. 8, 1944; 110, Syracuse, Sept. 24, 1966 (Propst); 30, same locality, Oct. 4, 1967.

MAXIMA, COASTAL: *Spring*—five, Central Park, New York City, Apr. 28, 1924; nine, Far Rockaway, Queens Co., May 3, 1953; 14 netted and banded, Fire Island State Park, Suffolk Co., May 9, 1970.

MAXIMA, COASTAL: *Fall*—18 struck the Empire State Building, New York City, Sept. 27, 1970.

It is obvious from the above that Syracuse lies astride a main migration route.

EXTREME DATES: *Spring*—Apr. 20 to June 16 (coastal specimen). *Fall*—July 24 (coastal) to Nov. 10 (inland) and Dec. 4 (coastal); exceptionally to Dec. 9, 1951, Buck Pond, Monroe Co. (Barry, *et al.*).

Rare before and after May, before mid-August, and after mid-October.

Winter: An individual was well seen at Van Cortlandt Park, Bronx Co., from Dec. 16, 1917, to Jan. 9, 1918 (Chubb and W. DeW. Miller); another that remained at the Ruppert feeder, Lloyd's Neck, Suffolk Co., from Jan. 5 to Feb. 7, 1967 (many observers), was photographed. Other winter reports were without details and unconfirmed.

Breeding (see Map 126): The Nashville Warbler is common enough in the Adirondacks and Catskills. In the former region Silloway (1923: 451) reported it as an inhabitant of open bushy tracts in dry locations, and Saunders (1929: 397) stated that this bird showed a preference for alder, willow, and birch thickets in old burns and at the edges of tamarack swamps.

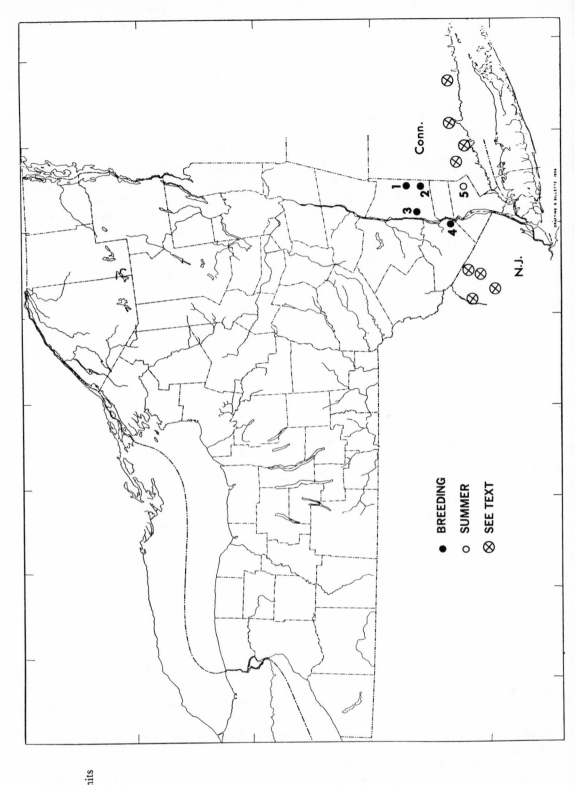

MAP 126 Nashville
Warbler (*Vermivora
ruficapilla*) Known
southern breeding limits

BREEDING
SUMMER
SEE TEXT

Conn.

N.J.

Over much of the central portions of the state, however, spruce-sphagnum bogs are its choice. In the Allegany State Park in Cattaraugus Co., mixed aspen-cherry groves seem to be favored.

Some samples of breeding densities based chiefly on singing males are: 25 in bogs of the Rome Sand Plains, Oneida Co., June 9, 1956; 15 at edge of a spruce-fir planting, Highland Forest, Onondaga Co., July 19, 1960 (both by Rusk and Scheider); 18 in 50 acres, Edwards, St. Lawrence Co., June 30, 1960 (A. W. Allen).

This species is a ground nester, eight New York nests recorded as being among low bushes—in clearings, in scrubby fields, and in bogs.

Egg clutches in 14 New York nests ranged from three to five: three eggs (two nests); four and five eggs (six nests each).

EGG DATES: May 19 to June 10.

Nestlings: May 30 to June 22; fledglings: June 15 to Aug. 17.

The Nashville Warbler is apparently absent as a breeder from the lowlands of the lake plain and some distance back from the Great Lakes as well. I have not heard of any nesting records from either Niagara or Wayne counties, and only one each from Genesee (Bergen Swamp) and Monroe (near Chili) counties.

The southeasternmost known breeding limits in the state are shown on the accompanying map: Dutchess Co.—(1) Schaghticoke Mtn. near Dover Plains; (2) Bald Mtn. near Wingdale; (3) hills near Poughkeepsie [presumably based on the fact that Mearns (1878: 50) credited C. L. Bagg with taking eggs at that locality]. The writer examined an adult female shot at the nest containing one egg from the same place, May 31, 1876, by Bagg, himself, BM(NH) 88. 10. 10. 4828, although this specimen is not listed in the Catalogue of Birds in the British Museum (1885: 10). Orange Co. (4) Bear Mtn. near Queensboro Lake. Westchester Co.—(5) Poundridge Reservation, summer of 1947; pair present, but definite breeding evidence lacking.

In view of the extralimital breeding records to the south and southeast in New Jersey and Connecticut (see map), the species should be sought during the nesting season in Putnam, Orange, Rockland, and northern Westchester counties.

Parula Warbler
(*Parula americana*) * B

Range: Nearctic and Neotropical regions, in eastern North America breeding from southern Canada to the Gulf states. Winters in Middle America and the West Indies, rarely north to southern Florida.

Status: Common to very common coastal migrant, especially in spring; uncommon inland. Fairly common but local breeder in the Adirondacks; rare to very rare elsewhere on the mainland, greatly decreased; formerly very common on eastern Long Island, but extirpated by the early 1950s.

Nonbreeding: This species is, at times, one of our most numerous spring warblers, especially on and near the coast. Its distinctive buzzy song is often heard at this season.

MAXIMA: *Spring*—Prospect Park, Brooklyn, 1950—200, May 14 (several observers); 75, May 20; 12, Far Rockaway, May 28, 1967, a very late spring.

MAXIMA: *Fall*—seven, Sandy Pond, Oswego Co., Sept. 28, 1960; 34 struck the Westhampton Air Force Base tower, Suffolk Co., Oct. 5, 1954.

EXTREME DATES: *Casual,* Apr. 1, 6, 9, and 13—all coastal localities, some storm-driven —to Nov. 26 (coastal), Dec. 3 (inland specimen), Dec. 9 (coastal), and Dec. 13 (coastal specimen); also one observed eating suet at a feeding station, Noyack, Suffolk Co., Dec. 1–23, 1965 (many observers)—first known winter occurrence in the state.

Rare before late April and after mid-October. Coastal migrants in fall usually appear by late August.

Change in breeding status (see Map 127): With the possible exception of the Adirondack region, where Parula Warblers are still fairly common—although local—breeders, the nesting population in the balance of the state has crashed badly in recent years and has even disappeared from Long Island. That this sorry state of affairs is by no means restricted to New York, but is true of much of the northeast, is evidenced by its former abundance and present scarcity in Massachusetts (Griscom and Snyder, 1955: 195). A likely explanation

Fig. 76 Long Pond, south of Sag Harbor, Suffolk Co., 1968. Sour gum, swamp maple, various oaks made up most of the tree growth. Parula Warblers formerly nested in this type of habitat prior to disappearance of *Usnea* lichen. Photo by Edgar M. Reilly.

for the warbler's decrease is the disappearance of its favored nesting material, the swamp- and bog-loving *Usnea* lichen or "beard moss," possibly due to drainage, disease, or other causes (see Fig. 76).

That it was a common breeder at one time on Long Island, especially at the east end, is borne out by the following: on Shelter Island, Suffolk Co., two egg collectors secured *40* sets of eggs just within the four-year period, 1879–1882. One collector took 24 sets—"all in beard moss [*Usnea* lichen] clumps in wet situations" (from data in USNM nest and egg collection); the other collector secured 16 sets under similar conditions (*Ornith. and Ool.*, 1881, 6: 62). For a more recent history on Long Island, see Bull (1964: 372).

As to its former abundance in western New York, as well as to its general distribution, I can do no better than quote in entirety from Eaton (1914: 396–397). "This species breeds throughout New York State, but is local in distribution during the nesting season, being confined to swamps and gullies [or glens] which produce a growth of gray moss or usnea. It is probably commoner as a breeding species in the swamps of Long Island and in the Catskill and Adirondack districts than in other portions of the state, although I have noticed a few pairs nesting in the gullies of the Finger Lakes region and in various scattered peat swamps [=glacial bogs] of western New York. In the North Woods [=Adirondacks] it is fairly common, as I noticed in the swamps [=spruce-sphagnum bogs] about the Ausable Lakes, Elk Lake, and the Boreas ponds and as my assistants found in nearly every portion of the Adirondacks, yet it is by no means generally distributed in the North Woods, but almost entirely confined to the swamps . . . It is practically confined to the localities where usnea moss is fairly abundant, although in the ravines on Canandaigua and Seneca and Cayuga lakes I have found it nesting where the atmosphere was damp on the south side of the gully and the hemlocks rather abundant, but almost no usnea was visible. In the Adirondacks we found it in the spruce swamps where this

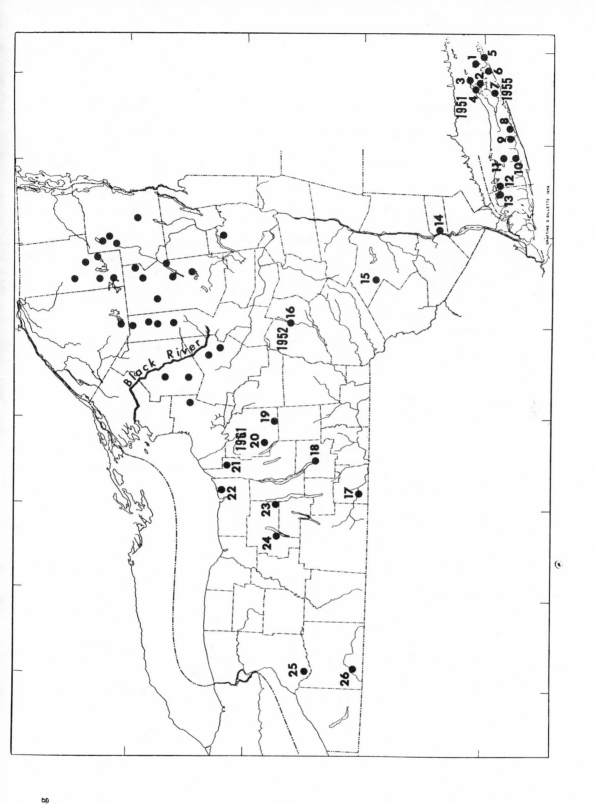

MAP 127 Parula Warbler (*Parula americana*) Breeding distribution

moss was particularly abundant. The nest is almost always concealed in a large hanging bunch of usnea . . ."

That *Usnea* is not used exclusively for nesting is evidenced by a nest found in a clump of "drift grass" on a maple branch overhanging the Chemung River west of Elmira, summer of 1942. This nest was photographed *in situ* by A. A. Allen (Axtell, 1947). Allen himself found another nest at Ithaca in 1918, located in a hemlock, the nest composed "entirely of leaf skeletons." Still another nest in a pine at Collins, Erie Co., in 1921, according to Perkins, was built of skeletonized leaves and pine needles.

Nest heights range from as low as three feet to as high as 25 feet. Egg clutches in 46 New York nests ranged from three to six, as follows: three eggs (five nests—incomplete?); four eggs (24 nests); five eggs (14 nests); six eggs (three nests).

EGG DATES: May 17 to June 27.

Nestlings: June 6 to July 4; fledglings: July 4 to Aug. 5.

Perusal of the breeding distribution map readily indicates the apparent scarcity of the species outside the Adirondack and Tug Hill districts. Its presumed, almost total, "absence" from the Catskills may be more imaginary than real, although the "necessary" spruce-balsam swamps—so plentiful in the Adirondack Mountains and in the Tug Hill plateau—may be at a premium in the Catskills.

All 26 localities outside the Adirondacks (east of the Black River) and the Tug Hill area (west of the Black River) are numbered on the map—13 former breeding localities on Long Island (A), and 13 former (mostly) localities in the rest of the state (B). Recent (since 1950) breeding records are designated by the last-known year alongside the numbers.

(A) Suffolk Co.—(1) Gardiner's Island; (2) Shelter Island; (3) Orient; (4) Greenport, 1951; (5) Hither Hills; (6) near Easthampton; (7) North Sea, 1955; (8) Mastic; (9) Brookhaven; (10) Oakdale; (11) Lake Ronkonkoma; (12) Cold Spring Harbor. Nassau Co.—(13) Oyster Bay.

(B) Putnam Co.—(14) Garrison. Ulster Co.—(15) Frost Valley, about four miles southwest of Slide Mtn. Otsego Co.—(16) Cooperstown, 1952. Chemung Co.—(17) near Elmira. Tompkins Co.—(18) near Ithaca. Onon-

daga Co.—(19) Tully; (20) near north end of Otisco Lake, 1961. (1985 correction: erroneous report.) Cayuga Co.—(21) Ira. Wayne Co.—(22) between East Bay and Port Bay. Ontario Co.—(23) Kashong Glen; (24) Seneca Glen. Erie Co.—(25) Collins. Cattaraugus Co.—(26) Holt Brook Valley, Allegany State Park.

Note that there have been no certain breeding records outside northern New York since 1961.

Remarks: This form and the morphologically similar *P. pitiayumi*, the Olive-backed Warbler or Tropical Parula, ranging from Mexico to Argentina, are here considered conspecific following Phillips, *et al.* (1964: 149). The vocalizations of the two forms are said to be very similar, also (Phillips, pers. comm.). See also comments of Mayr and Short (1970: 73).

Yellow Warbler
(*Dendroica petechia*)   *   B

Range: Nearctic and Neotropical regions, breeding from Alaska and Canada to northern South America. Winters in tropical America.

Status: Common migrant. Widespread breeder.

Nonbreeding: This is one of our more numerous warblers, although numerically less so than, for example, Ovenbird, Yellowthroat, and Redstart.

MAXIMA: *Spring*—50, Montezuma area, May 1, 1962; 25, Central Park, New York City, May 23, 1954.

MAXIMA: *Fall*—50, Syracuse, Aug. 23, 1964; 40, Sandy Pond, Oswego Co., Aug. 29, 1968.

EXTREME DATES: Apr. 19 to Oct. 2 (inland) and Oct. 11 and 24 (coastal specimens, see **Subspecies**). No later sight reports are accepted, as confusion with the Orange-crowned Warbler is likely (see discussion under that species).

Rare before late April and after mid-September.

Breeding: The Yellow Warbler is quite adaptable in its breeding locations. It nests in shrubbery in rural and suburban gardens; in bushes and trees, often in willows along streams, lakes, swamps, and marshes; also in dense thickets of poison ivy and bayberry on coastal sand dunes. Nest heights range from 18 inches to ten feet above ground.

This species is more frequently parasitized by the Cowbird than any other bird in New York. However, it often "outwits" the Cowbird by relining the nest on top of the eggs and laying a new set of eggs.

In 32 New York nests, egg clutches ranged from three to five: three eggs (nine nests); four eggs (20 nests); five eggs (three nests).

EGG DATES: May 15 to July 3.

Nestlings: June 4 to July 23; fledglings: June 12 to Aug. 1.

Subspecies: Nominate *petechia* (chestnut crown) occurs on Barbados; other West Indian races have entire head rufous (Martinique) o varying amounts of rufous in the crown; he eastern continental population, *aestiva* (without rufous in crown), but otherwise like hose populations, i.e., bright yellow, breeds in eastern North America from extreme southern Canada to southern United States and is the subspecies which has been discussed above.

The race *rubiginosa* (much darker, duller, and noticeably greener above) breeds to the north of *aestiva* from Alaska and Canada and —in the east—south to central Ontario, southeastern Quebec, and Newfoundland. This race has been collected on a number of occasions in New York and probably is of regular occurrence. It is a notably late migrant in fall, the October 11 occurrence listed above under extreme fall date, was a specimen that struck the Empire State Building in New York City, Oct. 11, 1962, and is AMNH 701818.

A specimen, also of the race *rubiginosa*, was collected near the Fire Island Lighthouse, Suffolk Co., Oct. 24, 1970 (D. B. Ford), AMNH 802429. It was suffering from such a heavy infestation of "foot pox" that it was unable to stand and was barely alive, which might account for the extremely late date.

The population known as *"amnicola"* is here considered a synonym of *rubiginosa;* it is barely distinguishable from the latter.

Magnolia Warbler
(*Dendroica magnolia*)   *   B

Range: Nearctic region, in the west breeding in central and southern Canada, but entirely north of the United States; in the east, south to the Berkshires, Catskills, and Poconos, and in the higher mountains to Virginia; rarely at high elevations in New Jersey. Winters mainly in Middle America and the West Indies, rarely north to southern Florida; casually in Virginia (specimen).

Status: Common to very common migrant. Widespread breeder in the mountains and at higher elevations in southwestern New York; uncommon to rare and local elsewhere in highland areas.

Nonbreeding: Magnolia Warblers are, at times, among the most numerous members of this family.

MAXIMA: *Spring*—51 netted and banded, Fire Island State Park, Suffolk Co., May 8, 1970; 70, Prospect Park, Brooklyn, May 10, 1948; 75, Rochester, May 24, 1917; 14 netted and banded, Huntington, Suffolk Co., May 30, 1967. A spring estimate of 250 given in Bull (1964: 373) is here considered as questionable—being much too high.

MAXIMA: *Fall*—25, Sandy Pond, Oswego Co., Aug. 27, 1960; 63 struck the Empire State Building, New York City, Sept. 14, 1964; in 1970, 60 struck the television tower at Colden, Erie Co., Sept. 24, and 64 hit the Empire State Building, Sept. 27; 30, Syracuse, Oct. 7, 1968.

EXTREME DATES: *Spring*—Apr. 26 (inland) to June 11, 18, and 23 (all coastal).

EXTREME DATES: *Fall*—July 25 (coastal) to Nov. 27 (inland) and Nov. 30 (coastal); exceptionally to Dec. 12–13, 1954, at the May feeder, Westernville, Oneida Co.

Rare before May, after early June, before late August, and after mid-October.

Winter: An individual was carefully studied at Smithtown, Suffolk Co., Dec. 28, 1940 (Fischer).

Breeding: The Magnolia Warbler is mainly an inhabitant of mixed evergreen-deciduous forest at higher elevations. It is numerous in the Adirondacks, up to 4000 feet, according to Saunders (1929: 392), and in the Catskills. It is likewise plentiful in the Tug Hill district, 75 having been estimated within 14 miles of trail in southern Lewis Co., June 10, 1957 (Scheider, 1959a). In central New York, it is also common in suitable habitats. In a young spruce plantation at Highland Forest, southern Onondaga Co., July 19, 1960, several observers estimated 25 males. At and near Branchport, Yates Co., in 1904, at least 12 pairs bred in hemlock ravines bordering Keuka Lake (C. F. Stone). In the gorges of the beech-birch-maple-hemlock forest along Owasco Lake, Cayuga Co., it is a common breeder (Benton, 1949), as it is in mature hemlock groves at higher elevations of the Letchworth State Park in Wyoming Co. (Rosche, 1967). Andrle (1971) found 11 breeding pairs in 150 acres of spruce-pine plantings at McCarty Hill near Ellicottville, Cattaraugus Co.

It is virtually absent as a breeder from the lake plain of western New York and from all low elevations in the southeastern sections. Curiously enough it is unrecorded as a nesting species in the Hudson Highlands, despite the fact that it has bred to the *south* of us in northwestern New Jersey (Bull, 1964: 373–374). The farthest southeast nesting record from New York that I am aware of is at Lomontville, Ulster Co., in 1960, virtually in the foothills of the Catskills. More field work during the breeding season in the Taconics of eastern Dutchess Co., as well as in the Shawangunks bordering Sullivan and Orange counties, might produce a few nesting pairs.

Most New York nests are placed in spruce and hemlock, rarely in deciduous shrubs, from two to 30 feet above ground.

Egg clutches in 24 New York nests: three eggs (three nests); four eggs (19 nests); five eggs (two nests).

EGG DATES: May 25 to July 11.

Nestlings: June 5 to July 24; fledglings: June 15 to Aug. 26.

Cape May Warbler
(*Dendroica tigrina*)   *   B

Range: Chiefly central and eastern North America, breeding from Canada to extreme northern United States (where very rare). Winters chiefly in the West Indies north to the Bahamas, rarely to southern Florida.

Status: Variously uncommon to common migrant, more numerous in spring upstate, and in fall along the coast. Very rare breeder in the Adirondacks.

Nonbreeding: The Cape May Warbler is noted for its fluctuating numbers. Some seasons it is fairly numerous, in others quite scarce.

MAXIMA: *Spring*—12, Highland Falls, Orange Co., May 6, 1959; 23, Syracuse, May 8, 1959; 15 (14 males), Far Rockaway, Queens Co., May 16, 1954; 20, Syracuse, *same date;* four, Buffalo, May 31, 1953.

MAXIMA: *Fall*—on Sept. 3, 1944—ten, Central Park, New York City, and 12, Seaford, Nassau Co.; 45, Easthampton, Suffolk Co., Sept. 15, 1946 (Helmuth); nine, Spring Brook, Erie Co., Oct. 4, 1967.

EXTREME DATES: *Spring*—Apr. 23 (coastal) and Apr. 26 (inland specimen) to June 6; casual, July 3, 1960, Arkwright, Chautauqua Co., singing male (Rew).

EXTREME DATES: *Fall*—Aug. 3 (inland) and Aug. 10 (coastal) to Nov. 10 (inland) and Nov. 16–22 (coastal-banded bird); exceptionally to Dec. 5 (coastal).

Rare before May, before late August, and after mid-October.

Winter: three occurrences, including a specimen, *all* males in late December, as follows: (1) one at the Henderson feeder, Geneva, Ontario Co., early Dec. to Dec. 28, 1918 (E. H. Eaton, *et al.*); (2) one collected at a feeder, Poughkeepsie, Dutchess Co., from early Dec. to Dec. 31, 1946 (Palmer), MCZ 275788 —notation on specimen label—"Bird so dirty it had to be shot for identification"; (3) one well observed at Point Lookout, Nassau Co., Dec. 30, 1956 (Bull and Eisenmann).

Breeding (see Map 128): There are three known summer occurrences for this attractive species in New York, all from the Adirondack region, but only two of them are breeding records: (1) on July 4, 1947, Carleton, Poor, and Scott (*Auk*, 1948, 65: 607) discovered a female feeding two recently fledged juveniles in black spruce forest at 1900 feet altitude, near North Elba, Essex Co.; (2) a female was observed carrying food to "begging" young, also recently fledged, in a mixed spruce-larch forest at Madawaska, Franklin Co., June 23, 1962 (Rusk and Scheider); (3) Dorothy McIlroy, a keen and veteran observer, saw birds "present" in Hamilton Co. in the Piseco Lake area during the summer of 1960, but without evidence of breeding. She was also fortunate in finding both Philadelphia

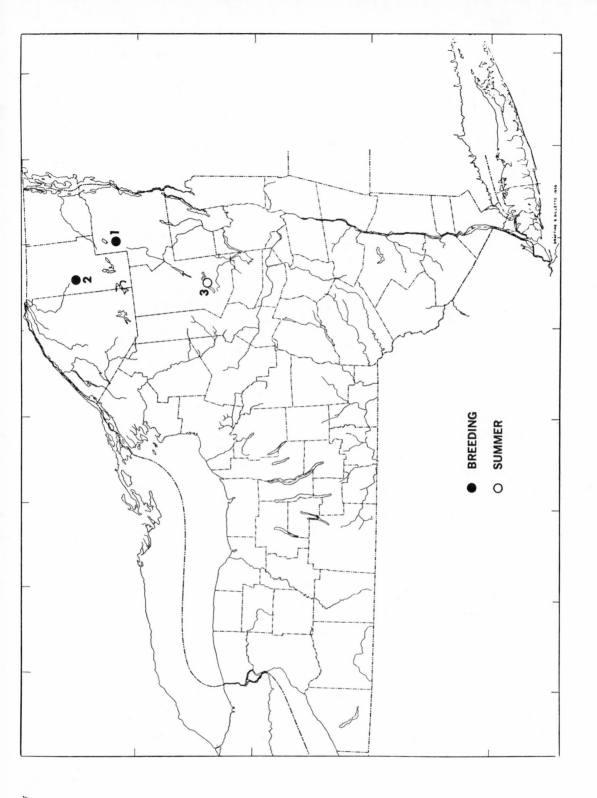

MAP 128 Cape May
Warbler (*Dendroica
tigrina*) Breeding
distribution

BREEDING

SUMMER

Vireos and Tennessee Warblers in the same region, also in 1960—but again without proof of nesting.

Banding: Three interesting recoveries of banded birds, all involving Long Island: (1) banded at Elmhurst, Queens Co., Sept. 12, 1937 (Beals), caught by a cat at Cleveland, Tennessee, Oct. 15, 1937; (2) banded at Tiana Beach, Suffolk Co., Oct. 2, 1963 (Wilcox), found dead at Raleigh, North Carolina, Mar. 12, 1964—possibly wintered in North Carolina, as the March date is much too early for a spring migrant; (3) banded at Ocean City, Maryland, Sept. 13, 1966 (Robbins), was trapped and released near Patchogue, Suffolk Co., Sept. 29, 1966 (Terry). Note that this individual flew *northeast* in fall.

Black-throated Blue Warbler
(Dendroica caerulescens) * B

Range: Eastern North America, breeding from southern Canada to northern New Jersey, southeastern New York, and Connecticut; at higher elevations to the mountains of Georgia and South Carolina. Winters mainly in the West Indies, occasionally north to southern Florida.

Status: Variously uncommon to common migrant. Widespread breeder at higher elevations, but local in the southeastern section.

Nonbreeding: This species, like many other warblers, fluctuates in numbers from time to time and is decidedly uncommon in certain years.

MAXIMA: *Spring*—50, Bronx Park, New York City, May 6, 1953; 30 (29 males), Far Rockaway, Queens Co., May 16, 1954; 100, Rochester, May 24, 1917 (Edson)—a very late spring; 45, Sandy Pond, Oswego Co., May 27, 1961—also a late spring.

MAXIMA: *Fall*—25, Sandy Pond, Sept. 17, 1960; 51 hit the Empire State Building, New York City, Sept. 27, 1970; 48 struck the Fire Island Lighthouse, Suffolk Co., Oct. 12, 1883 —an exceptionally late fall.

EXTREME DATES: *Spring*—male, Apr. 11,

1955, Tobay Pond, Nassau Co., exceptionally early; Apr. 24 (coastal) and Apr. 27 (inland) to June 14 (coastal).

EXTREME DATES: *Fall*—Aug. 7 to Nov. 21 (coastal); exceptionally to Dec. 11 (coastal).

Rare before and after May, and before late August and after mid-October.

Winter: Two Long Island occurrences, both males at feeding stations in Suffolk Co.: (1) Northport, from Nov. 13, 1954, to Jan. 13, 1955 (Mudge); (2) Brookhaven, Dec. 27, 1962 (Stoutenburgh).

Breeding (see Map 129): The Black-throated Blue Warbler is one of the more numerous breeding warblers in the mixed ever-green-deciduous forests of the Adirondacks and Catskills. It nests as well in secondary forest with clearings in those same mountains, and at lower elevations in other portions of the state. Of 42 New York nests found in this mixed growth, 19 were located in mountain laurel bushes, 13 in hemlock, and five each in spruce and maple.

Some idea of densities may be seen from the following: (1) 22 singing males in four miles of logging road near Osceola, Lewis Co., June 11, 1960; (2) 58 in the Highland Forest of southeastern Onondaga Co., July 19, 1960 (both of these by Rusk and Scheider); (3) 21 singing males along eight miles of road in the Arnot Forest of southeastern Schuyler Co., June 25, 1946 (Axtell).

Nests are placed from as low as four inches above ground to as high as 20 feet.

Egg clutches in 63 New York nests: three eggs (six nests); four eggs (55 nests); five eggs (two nests).

EGG DATES: May 29 to July 16.

Nestlings: June 14 to July 29; fledglings: June 22 to Aug. 14.

Like other warblers with northern affinities, this species is absent or quite rare in the generally low-lying agricultural region of the lake plain in western New York.

Its southeastern nesting limits in the state are shown on the accompanying map: Putnam Co.—(1) near Carmel; (2) near Cold Spring. Orange Co.—(3) Lake Kanawauke.

In view of its breeding in adjacent Connecticut and New Jersey, it should be found in Rockland and northern Westchester counties, and elsewhere in Orange Co.

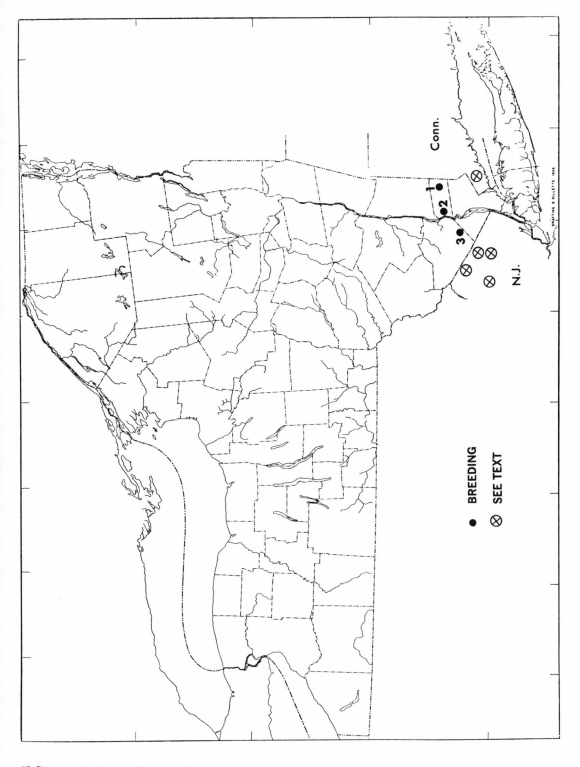

MAP 129 Black-throated
Blue Warbler (*Dendroica
caerulescens*) Known
southern breeding limits

Myrtle or Yellow-rumped Warbler
(*Dendroica coronata*)   *   B

Range: Nearctic region, breeding from Alaska and Canada to northern Mexico in the west, but in the east only to the Berkshires, Catskills, and Poconos. Winters north to near the northern limits of the breeding range.

Status: Common to abundant migrant, most numerous inland in spring, on the coast in fall. Variously rare to very common in winter along the coast, but usually very rare inland. Common breeder at higher elevations, but rare southward; most numerous in the Adirondacks.

Nonbreeding: This species is our most numerous migrant warbler, often outnumbering all other warblers combined. In winter, if the bayberry crop is plentiful, these warblers may be present in considerable numbers on the outer coast.

MAXIMA: *Spring*—300, Manitou, Monroe Co., Apr. 30, 1960; 1000, Rochester, May 7, 1964; 200, near Syracuse, May 20, 1967.

MAXIMA: *Fall*—500, Syracuse, Sept. 18, 1955; 1000, Prospect Park, Brooklyn, Oct. 15, 1950; 550 netted and banded, Tobay Beach, Nassau Co., Oct. 16, 1965; 700, also netted and banded, same locality, Oct. 22, 1967, with an estimate of at least another 1800 observed.

MAXIMA: *Winter*—800, Montauk to Easthampton, Long Island, January and February 1924; 10, Alden, Erie Co., Feb. 14, 1959— a good number for an inland locality.

EXTREME DATES: Aug. 2 (coastal) and Aug. 6 (inland) to June 9, 12, 17, and 23 (all coastal). Rare before September and after mid-May.

Change in breeding status (see Map 130): Regarding the Myrtle Warbler as a breeder in New York, Eaton (1914: 406) stated that it was confined to the Adirondacks and Catskills, although it is much more local and scarcer in the latter area. In the Adirondacks it is found mostly in spruce and balsam forest up to tree line where it is an associate of the Blackpoll Warbler.

It was first discovered outside the mountains in 1922 when Colonel L. R. Wolfe found a nest with eggs near Plattsburgh, Clinton Co. However, it was not until 30 years later (early 1950s) that this warbler was found at lower elevations—see following for list of localities. This species, like the Golden-crowned Kinglet, was discovered nesting in spruce and red pine plantings, although not as widespread as that bird. Nests were found to a lesser extent in white pine and hemlock.

Height of ten New York nests ranged from four to ten feet—all in evergreens.

Egg clutches in eight New York nests were invariably four.

EGG DATES: May 19 to July 10.

Nestlings: June 2 to July 22; fledglings: June 9 to Aug. 17.

The 25 known localities outside the Adirondack-Catskill area, with year of "arrival," are: Clinton Co.—(1) Plattsburgh, 1922. Rensselaer Co.—(2) Berlin Mtn., 1967. Ulster Co.—(3) Mohonk Lake, 1952; (4) Lake Awosting, 1952—both of these in the Shawangunk Mountains, the most southern known records in the state. Oswego Co.—(5) Sandy Creek, 1963; (6) Sandy Pond, 1957; (7) Smartville, 1969; (8) near Redfield, 1954; (9) Selkirk Shores, 1954; (10) near Pulaski, 1954; (11) Happy Valley Refuge, 1968; (12) Cleveland, 1966. Oneida Co.—(13) Rome Sand Plains, 1958. Madison Co.—(14) Brookfield, 1961. Onondaga Co.—(15) Fabius, 1968; (16) Highland Forest, 1958. Cayuga Co.—(17) Summer Hill, 1970. Cortland Co.—(18) near Preble, 1970. Chenango Co.—(19) Pharsalia, 1960. Tompkins Co.—(20) near Varna, 1961; (21) Connecticut Hill, 1960. Broome Co.—(22) Chenango Forks, 1966. Allegany Co.—(23) Foster Lake near Alfred, 1967. Cattaraugus Co.—(24) McCarty Hill near Ellicottville, 1967; (25) Allegany State Park, 1962.

Banding: Five individuals banded in October of various years on Long Island were all recovered the following winter at coastal points in North Carolina (2) and South Carolina (3). Still another individual banded on Oct. 17, 1959, at Tiana Beach, Suffolk Co. (Wilcox), was recovered in November 1959, near St. John's, Newfoundland. This bird flew *northeast* in fall. Was this an instance of reverse

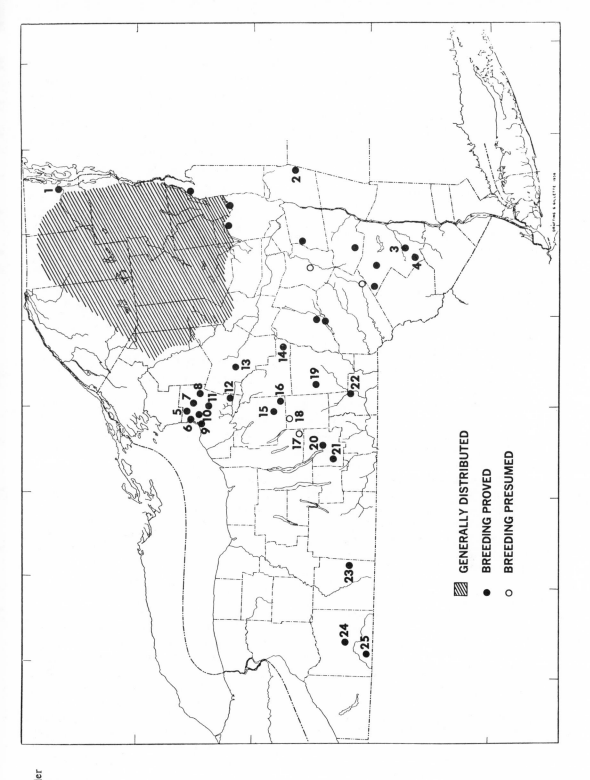

MAP 130 Myrtle or
Yellow-rumped Warbler
(*Dendroica coronata*)
Breeding distribution

GENERALLY DISTRIBUTED

● BREEDING PROVED

○ BREEDING PRESUMED

migration or was it carried or blown off course by a storm?

Remarks: This and the western *D. auduboni* (Audubon's Warbler) are treated here as conspecific, following Hubbard (1970).

A report of an immature male *auduboni* netted, banded, color-photographed, and released on Long Island during the fall of 1970, was *not* critically examined or checked with museum specimens to my knowledge. A specimen is desirable before placing it on the state list.

Black-throated Gray Warbler
(*Dendroica nigrescens*)   *

Range: Western United States, breeding east to central Colorado. Vagrant east to New York and Massachusetts (specimens).

Status: *Casual*—there is one confirmed record for New York: A male was collected at Ithaca, Nov. 15, 1932 (A. A. Allen), CUM 16326.

At least six observations of this species have been reported by competent people, four of these within three years (1961–1963): (1) male, Oak Orchard Creek, Genesee Co., May 11, 1930 (Beardslee, Mitchell, and Verrill); (2) female or immature male, Jones Beach, Nassau Co., Sept. 22, 1961 (Kleinbaum and Tudor); (3) male, Portland, Chautauqua Co., Apr. 28–29, 1962 (Mitchell, Rew, *et al.*); (4) male, Katonah, Westchester Co., Aug. 9, 1962 (Russell); (5) male, Central Park, New York City, Sept. 21, 1963 (Huber); (6) singing male, Central Park, May 24, 1970 (Pasquier, Goelet, Baumann, *et al.*).

[Townsend's Warbler
(*Dendroica townsendi*)

Hypothetical: Western Canada and northwestern United States, breeding southeast to Montana and Wyoming. Vagrant east to Pennsylvania (specimen).

This species has been reported in New York on six occasions, all in the southeastern portion of the state and, curiously enough, five times in spring, four of these during the first half of May. Most vagrants from the west occur in the east during fall. It is highly desirable to

secure specimen or photographic evidence, as confusion of this species in nonbreeding plumage with Blackburnian and Black-throated Green warblers in similar plumage is possible.

The occurrences, all males believed correctly identified, are as follows: (1) Prospect Park, Brooklyn, May 8, 1947 (Alperin, Carleton, Jacobson, and Sedwitz); (2) Central Park, New York City, May 4, 1963 (Cantor, Gilbert, *et al.*); (3) Bronx Park, New York City, May 9, 1964 (six observers); (4) near Pine Plains, Dutchess Co., Apr. 24–25, 1965 (Pink, Van Wagner, *et al.*); (5) Jamaica Bay Refuge, May 9, 1970 (P. Post, Holloway, and Longyear); (6) the single fall occurrence—Hewlett Harbor, Nassau Co., Nov. 10, 1963 (Berliner, Sloss, *et al.*).]

Black-throated Green Warbler
(*Dendroica virens*)   *   B

Range: Chiefly central and eastern North America, breeding from central Canada to northern United States; in the east to the mountains of northern Georgia, along the coast to central New Jersey (rare), and an isolated population along the coast from Virginia to South Carolina. Winters north to southern Florida, rarely farther north.

Status: Fairly common to very common migrant. Widespread breeder, especially in evergreen forest.

Nonbreeding: This species is one of the more numerous warblers on migration.

MAXIMA: *Spring*—15, Clymer, Chautauqua Co., Apr. 28, 1957; 50, Bronx Park, New York City, May 6, 1953; 75, Prospect Park, Brooklyn, May 10, 1946; 100, Rochester, May 24, 1917; 100, Sandy Pond, Oswego Co., May 25, 1960. In both of these last two years spring was very late.

MAXIMA: *Fall*—60, Sandy Pond, Sept. 15, 1960; 135, Pompey, Onondaga Co., Sept. 19, 1969 (Crumb), an unusually large number for fall; 45, Ithaca, Sept. 28, 1960; 22, Easthampton, Suffolk Co., Oct. 6, 1946; 17, Pelham Bay Park, Bronx Co., Oct. 20, 1927, a very late fall.

EXTREME DATES: Mar. 30, Apr. 4 and 9 (all coastal) to Dec. 9 (coastal). Inland it arrives much later (Apr. 19) and departs much earlier (Nov. 4). Rare before late April and after October.

There is one local winter occurrence: An individual remained in a pine grove at Van Cortlandt Park, Bronx Co., from Nov. 8, 1943, to Jan. 1, 1944 (Komorowski, *et al.*).

Breeding: This species is common and widely distributed throughout the state in suitable habitat, breeding from the coniferous forests of the Adirondack Mountains to the pitch pine barrens of Long Island. It is known to breed in all counties except those five comprising New York City.

On Long Island it is, or was, commonly distributed on the north shore from Manhasset, Nassau Co., east to Miller's Place, Suffolk Co., and in extreme eastern Suffolk Co. at Peconic, Southold, and Orient. In 1939 Latham recorded eight pairs breeding within three miles on the Orient peninsula. In the center of Long Island it is locally common in Suffolk Co. from Melville east to Coram and Riverhead, but on the south shore of the coastal plain, where nominate *virens* is near its southern limits, it is known from only three localities —all in Suffolk Co.—Sayville, Mastic, and Georgica.

In New York State most nests by far (30, or nearly 80%) have been found in hemlocks. But the species breeds also in pitch pine (chiefly Long Island), in red, white, and Scotch pines, spruce, fir, and red and white cedars. During a 1970 breeding survey in Allegany Co. near Alfred, members of the Allegany Bird Club estimated 21 breeding pairs in 38 acres of "maturing upland red pine-white pine plantation" (Klingensmith, *Audubon Field Notes*, 1970, 24: 754–755).

In certain upstate localities this species is found breeding also in mixed hemlock-maple forest, and on Long Island in western Suffolk Co. it is a local breeder in oak-hickory woodland. Two inland nests were found in birch and elm. In these instances, where deciduous trees were predominant, hemlock or pine occurred in the vicinity.

Nests in New York are placed from ten to 40 feet up, but in one instance as low as three feet from the ground.

Egg clutches in 24 New York nests: four eggs (21 nests); five eggs (three nests).

EGG DATES: May 24 to July 2.

Nestlings: June 11 to July 29; fledglings: June 23 to Aug. 15.

Cerulean Warbler
(*Dendroica cerulea*)   *   B

Range: Chiefly southeastern United States, breeding north to extreme southeastern Ontario, and west-central and southeastern New York. Generally absent from the Atlantic coastal plain, including migration. Winters in South America.

Status: Rare to uncommon migrant in western and central New York; usually very rare along the coast. Locally common breeder at lower elevations in central and western portions and in the lower Hudson valley; rare and sporadic elsewhere (see map).

Nonbreeding: As the Cerulean Warbler in New York is at the northeastern limits of its breeding range, it follows that it is rare to uncommon on migration. The numbers reported near Syracuse in mid-May (up to 30–40 per day) undoubtedly represent chiefly local breeders.

EXTREME DATES: Apr. 27 (coastal) to Oct. 5 (coastal). Rare before mid-May and rarely reported in fall.

Change in breeding status (see Map 131): The history, distribution, and recent range expansion of the Cerulean Warbler in New York is exceedingly interesting and quite complex.

Eaton (1914: 412) knew this species as a locally common breeder "in various localities of central and western New York . . ." (A and B on map). He knew of only one "summer date" from the isolated population in the lower Hudson valley—"Hyde Park [Dutchess Co.], July 4, 1895" (C on map). This last area as well as other peripheral localities are discussed below. Eaton postulated that, "Evidently it has invaded this State from the Mississippi valley and its migrations each year follow this route."

The species, at least populations A and B, quite obviously arrived from the west, as did a number of others (Red-bellied Woodpecker, for example), by way of the Niagara Frontier region—the corridor in Ontario west of the Niagara River separating Lake Ontario to the

north from Lake Erie to the south. That A
and B did not originate from the south is
evident by the lack of breeding records in
the river valleys in the southern tier counties
adjacent to Pennsylvania and in northern Pennsylvania itself (Poole, 1965: 56, 79).

The two principal breeding grounds of the
Cerulean Warbler in New York are (A) the
lowland plain to the south of Lake Ontario,
extending from the Niagara River east to the
Wayne Co. line; and (B) the Finger Lakes
region extending from Keuka Lake in the
southwest, northeastward as far as Oneida
Lake and beyond to the border separating
Madison and Oneida counties. A glance at
the distribution map shows that the center of
abundance is Onondaga Co., with at least a
dozen known breeding localities, and possibly
with the highest breeding density in the state,
at least in recent years—south and west of
Syracuse, especially the Camillus Valley area—
41 singing males, May 25, 1953 (Scheider,
1959b). In his account, Scheider warns, however, that with the continued disappearance of
the elms due to disease—the principal nest tree
in that section—the Cerulean Warbler may decrease rapidly as a breeder unless other tree
species are utilized.

In most of New York the Cerulean Warbler
breeds in wooded swamps, in deciduous forest
in stream bottoms, and along lake and river
shores with an abundance of tall trees. Of
trees selected for nests in this state, elm leads
(22), followed by maple (ten), oak (nine), and
sycamore (six). Nest heights range from 20 to
over 60 feet above ground.

Egg clutches in 35 New York nests: three
eggs (nine nests); four eggs (18 nests); five
eggs (eight nests).

EGG DATES: May 19 to June 23.

Nestlings: June 12 to July 6; fledglings:
June 22 to July 22.

The isolated population in southeastern New
York (C) is located on the east bank of the
Hudson River in western Dutchess Co. It is
of long-standing establishment, dating back at
least to 1922. The early history of this population is given in detail by Griscom (1933:
146–149), and more recently by Pink and
Waterman (1967: 83). The latter authors
state that the species no longer breeds (since
1940) at the two southern stations at Wap-
pinger's Creek (near Poughkeepsie) and at

Hyde Park because of continued housing developments. It is still present, however, at the
three northern localities of Rhinebeck, Barrytown, and Tivoli—the last named near the
Columbia Co. line. Actually the Rhinebeck
and Barrytown breeding sites are adjacent to
the extensive marshes of Cruger's Island.

That this Hudson valley population very
probably originated also from the *west*, quite
possibly by way of the Mohawk valley—
although curiously there are no known breeding records from the latter area (lack of observers and/or suitable habitat?)—is suggested
by two plausible hypotheses: (1) no known
breeding records immediately to the *south*, in
northern New Jersey prior to the early 1950s;
(2) no known breeding records at all to the
southwest, in northern Pennsylvania (Poole,
op. cit.).

Additional recent New York breeding localities are (see map): (1) in 1964 Allen and
Belknap (*Kingbird*, 1964, 14: 215) discovered
an active nest near Pamelia, Jefferson Co.
Although at first glance this locality appears
to be far removed from the "main" breeding
ranges (A and B), it should be noted that the
species was found breeding in Canada to the
northwest at Canoe Lake, Ontario (⊗), as
early as 1961 (Quilliam, 1965: 157). (2) near
Lawtons, Erie Co., 1951; (3) Zoar valley, Cattaraugus Co., 1959. Note lack of breeding
along the narrow Lake Erie plain southwest of
Buffalo, which suggests that the breeding birds
of these last two localities may have derived
from population (A). (4) Onoville, Cattaraugus Co., 1968, three or four birds present in
June, but no evidence of breeding. (5) Fox
Creek near Gallupville, Schoharie Co., 1958, a
"colony" of four or five birds, but breeding not
proved. (6) Castleton, Rensselaer Co., 1966,
pair bred and again at nearby Schodack Land-
ing, 1968. (7) Sterling Forest, and (8) Wey-
ant's Pond, both in Orange Co. (9) Clear Lake,
Putnam Co., all late 1960s, as well as (10)
Pawling, Dutchess Co., three singing males
only. It is anyone's guess as to whether these
birds originated from the long-established population (C) to the north, or from the more
recent population to the south in New Jersey.
Perhaps they came from both directions. (11)
Cheningo, Cortland Co., 1970, an adult on
June 23, may presage a future range extension
from population (B).

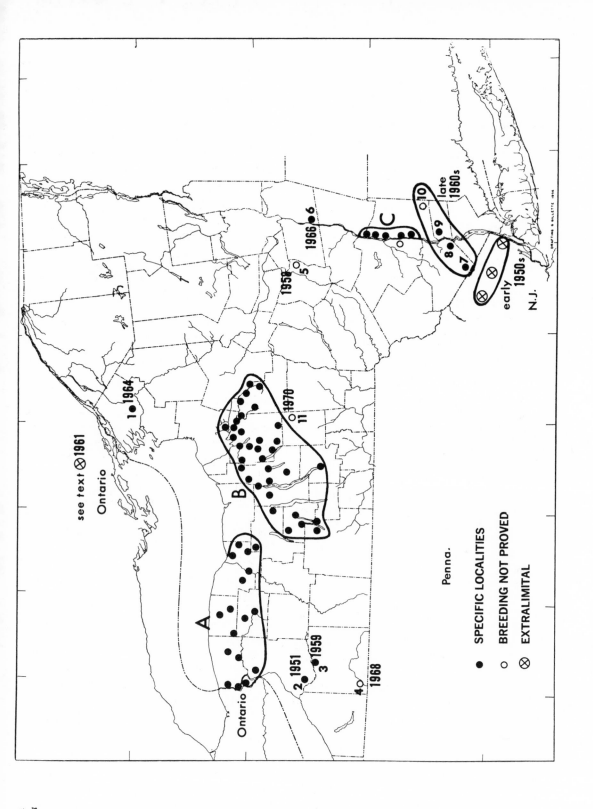

MAP 131 Cerulean Warbler (*Dendroica cerulea*) Breeding distribution

It is curious that there has been no overflow of population (C) to the *west* bank of the Hudson, except for a short-lived occurrence in Ulster Co. on Black Creek near West Park, 1939, two singing males only (see open circle on map for location).

Blackburnian Warbler
(*Dendroica fusca*)   *   B

Range: Chiefly central and eastern North America, breeding from southern Canada to northern New Jersey and southeastern New York; in the mountains to northern Georgia and South Carolina. Winters from Guatemala to Peru, but chiefly in northern South America.

Status: Common migrant inland, occasionally more numerous; uncommon to fairly common along the coast. Widespread breeder at higher elevations, especially numerous in the mountains.

Nonbreeding: This fine species is much more numerous in central and western New York than it is downstate as may be seen from the relative numbers below:

MAXIMA, INLAND: *Spring*—35, Syracuse, May 12, 1954; 55, Camillus Valley, Onondaga Co., May 19, 1966; an almost unbelievable *200* at Rochester, May 24, 1917 (Edson, *Auk,* 1920, 37: 142), feeding on flies at sewage beds; 1917 was a notably late spring.

MAXIMA, INLAND: *Fall*—20, Hamburg, Erie Co., Aug. 24, 1961; 35, Pompey, Onondaga Co., Sept. 11, 1969; 21 found dead at the Albany Airport ceilometer, Sept. 15, 1956; 12 struck the Elmira television tower, Sept. 26, 1968.

MAXIMA, COASTAL: *Spring*—15, Bronx Park, New York City, May 6, 1953 (Komorowski), unusually early for so many; 15, Woodmere Woods, Nassau Co., May 23, 1954.

MAXIMA, COASTAL: *Fall*—six, Far Rockaway, Queens Co., Aug. 14, 1954; 17 hit the Empire State Building, New York City, Sept. 14, 1964.

EXTREME DATES: *Spring*—Apr. 16 (inland) and Apr. 19 (coastal) to June 9 (in-land), June 13 (coastal), and June 18 (coastal, banded).

EXTREME DATES: *Fall*—Aug. 3 (coastal) and Aug. 6 (inland) to Oct. 20 (coastal) and Nov. 17, 1967, Jamestown (Sundell), one found dead.

Rare before mid-May and after September.

Breeding (see Map 132): In New York the Blackburnian Warbler is one of the most common of its family in mixed evergreen-deciduous forest at higher elevations, although all 37 nests were situated in evergreens, of which 30 were in hemlock, five in spruce, and three in pine. Nests are placed from 15 to over 80 feet above ground.

Egg clutches in 19 New York nests: three eggs (three nests); four eggs (15 nests); five eggs (one nest).

EGG DATES: June 1 to June 24.

Nestlings: June 17 to July 1; fledglings: July 13 to Aug. 4.

Although most numerous in the Adirondacks and Catskills, this species is plentiful enough at much lower elevations in central and western New York as may be seen from the following: (1) Scheider (1959a) estimated 65 within 14 miles of trail in the southern Lewis Co. section of the Tug Hill region on June 10, 1957. (2) Benton (1949) called it a fairly common breeder in hemlocks in the Howland's Island area of Cayuga Co.; (3) Axtell (1947) estimated 35 scattered pairs breeding in Chemung and Schuyler counties; (4) Rosche (1967) said that it was perhaps the most abundant breeding warbler in hemlocks and other conifers in Letchworth State Park in Wyoming Co.; (5) Klingensmith (*Audubon Field Notes,* 1970, 24: 754–755) counted 13 breeding pairs in 38 acres of "maturing upland red pine-white pine plantation" near Alfred, Allegany Co.

This is still another warbler with "northern" affinities that is rare to absent over much of the lake plain in western New York.

Its southeastern limits in New York are shown on the accompanying map: Putnam Co.—(1) Fahnestock State Park; (2) near Cold Spring. Westchester Co.—(3) Peach Lake. Orange Co.—(4) Lake Tiorati and nearby Island Pond. It probably breeds in northern Rockland Co. and elsewhere in Orange Co.

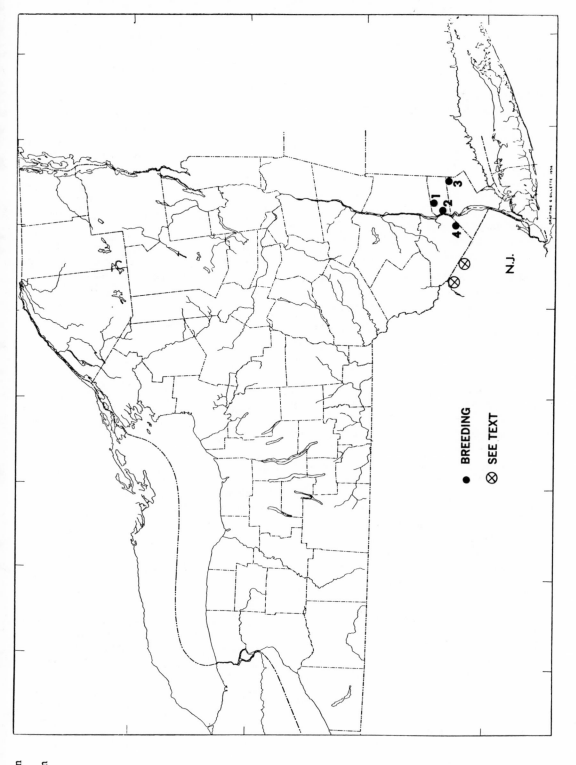

MAP 132 Blackburnian
Warbler (*Dendroica
fusca*) Known southern
breeding limits

● BREEDING

⊗ SEE TEXT

N.J.

Yellow-throated Warbler
(*Dendroica dominica*)   *

Range: Chiefly southeastern United States, nominate *dominica* (lores yellow) breeding mainly on the coastal plain north to central Delaware; the inland race *albilora* (lores white) breeding northeast to southern Ohio, more rarely to western New Jersey (Delaware River valley). In migration north to New York and southern New England. Winters north to southern United States.

Status: Rare, but regular spring migrant along the coast, much rarer in fall; very rare inland, but has increased in recent years.

Occurrence: The Yellow-throated Warbler is one of the rarest warblers to visit New York with any degree of regularity, but it has increased somewhat since the early 1950s, although this may be reflected, in part, by an enormous increase in observers. Most of the occurrences are in late April and May. Except for specimen records (see below) all other reports are based at the species level. Observations of birds, alleged to be subspecifically identified, are here discounted owing to the difficulty or impossibility of correct determination in the field. Even some specimen identifications are questionable and a few are nothing more than intermediates.

Along the coast and in the larger New York City parks one or two are seen annually, but on occasion more are reported. In 1956 at least 12 were observed, eight in the New York City region, and four at upstate localities.

EXTREME DATES: Apr. 15 to June 6 and 15; twice in July (see **Specimen data);** Sept. 2 to Sept. 26 (specimen) and Oct. 6. All the above dates, except June 15, are from the coast.

Casual at Sandy Pond, Oswego Co., Nov. 23–30, 1962 (Wyman and Reed), with a color photograph of the bird at a suet feeder taken by Dake and examined by the writer—print on file at AMNH. Two other November reports from western New York were not confirmed.

Specimen data: Of eight extant state specimens identified as to subspecies, six are from Long Island. Five specimens [A] are of the

nominate race, the other three [B] are *albilora.* I have examined all these.

[A] (1) Brooklyn, "mid 1800s" (Akhurst), AMNH 440264; (2) Fire Island, Suffolk Co., May 9, 1883 (Akhurst), in collection of F. T. Pember Museum, Granville, Washington Co., N.Y.—previously unpublished; (3) Oyster Bay, Nassau Co., July 8, 1907 (T. Roosevelt), AMNH 99697; (4) Orient, Suffolk Co., May 11, 1927 (Latham), NYSM 25375; (5) Sag Harbor, Suffolk Co., July 15, 1933 (Wilcox), in his collection.

[B] (1) Albany, "prior to 1888" (Hurst), BM(NH 88.7.12.821—the only known upstate specimen; (2) Central Park, New York City, Apr. 18, 1919 (Valentine), AMNH 240958; (3) Garden City, Nassau Co., Sept. 26, 1953 (McAllister), AMNH 787433.

Chestnut-sided Warbler
(*Dendroica pensylvanica*)   *   B

Range: Chiefly eastern North America, breeding from southern Canada, south in the mountains to northern Georgia, but along the coast only to central New Jersey and Long Island. Winters in southern Central America.

Status: Fairly common to common migrant. Widespread breeder, but rare and local on the coastal plain.

Nonbreeding: This species is usually more numerous in spring than in fall, although in very recent years the reverse has been the case.

MAXIMA: *Spring*—30, Prospect Park, Brooklyn, May 10, 1946; 25, Syracuse, May 14, 1962; 45, Central Park, New York City, May 23, 1954, a notably late spring.

MAXIMA: *Fall*—16, Redfield, Oswego Co., Aug. 19, 1968; 20, Selkirk Shores, Oswego Co., Sept. 2, 1966; 50, Pompey, Onondaga Co., Sept. 11, 1969; 47 struck the Colden television tower, Erie Co., Sept. 24, 1970, late for so many; five hit the Montauk Point Lighthouse, Suffolk Co., Oct. 7, 1950, also late for so many.

EXTREME DATES: Apr. 25 (coastal) and Apr. 29 (inland) to Oct. 20 (inland). Rare before May and after early October.

Casual in Central Park, Apr. 16, 1967 (H. and B. Dresher), and Nov. 13, 1958 (Messing).

Breeding: The Chestnut-sided Warbler favors overgrown scrubby fields, bushy hillsides and pastures, roadside thickets, and open second-growth deciduous woodland; also clearings at higher elevations wherever cutting and burning of the forest has taken place.

The nest is placed in vines, bracken ferns, low bushes, and saplings from one to six feet above the ground.

Egg clutches in 28 New York nests range from three to five: three eggs (five nests); four eggs (21 nests); five eggs (two nests).

EGG DATES: May 20 to July 25.

Nestlings: June 15 to Aug. 6; fledglings: June 22 to Aug. 20.

A high density upstate was obtained when approximately *60* singing males were found along one and one-half miles of roadside in the Rome Sand Plains of Oneida Co. on June 10, 1956 (Scheider).

At the other extreme, on the south shore of Long Island where this species is very local during the nesting season, only two breeding pairs could be found in the entire Seaford-Massapequa area in Nassau Co. in 1940 (Elliott). As mentioned above under **Range,** this bird in New York is at its southern breeding limits on the coastal plain of Long Island.

Bay-breasted Warbler
(*Dendroica castanea*) * B

Range: Chiefly central and eastern North America, breeding from central Canada to extreme northern United States. Winters from Panama to northwestern South America.

Status: Variously uncommon to very common migrant in western New York, less numerous elsewhere but has increased. In recent years a rare breeder in the Adirondacks, especially in Essex Co., but probably less rare and more widely distributed than supposed.

Nonbreeding: The Bay-breasted Warbler is another species that fluctuates in numbers, in some years quite numerous, in others even scarce, especially southeastward. It is much commoner in western New York.

MAXIMA: *Spring*—45, Camillus, Onondaga Co., May 14, 1970; 85, same locality, May 18, 1960; 42, Grassy Sprain, Westchester Co.,

May 19, 1948; 75, Sandy Pond, Oswego Co., May 27, 1961.

MAXIMA: *Fall*—100, Durand Eastman Park, Rochester, Sept. 2, 1962; Hamburg, Erie Co., 1961—110, Sept. 12, and *175,* Sept. 15 (Able); 63 struck the Empire State Building, New York City, Sept. 22, 1953; 43 hit the Elmira television tower, Sept. 26, 1968; 25, Oakdale, Suffolk Co., Sept. 28, 1964.

EXTREME DATES: *Spring*—Apr. 30 (inland) to June 11 (coastal); June 23, 1870 (coastal specimen—Bull, 1964: 384).

EXTREME DATES: *Fall*—July 23 (inland) and July 26 (coastal) to Nov. 2 (coastal). Casual, Riis Park, Queens Co., Nov. 25 to Dec. 1, 1956 (many observers)—male with rufous sides.

Rare before mid-May, after early June, before late August, and after early October.

Change in breeding status (see Map 133): Eaton (1914: 416 and 543) and his associates, as well as the earlier ornithologists, were unsuccessful in locating even a summering Bay-breasted Warbler, let alone a breeding pair, in the Adirondack region.

It was not until 1924 that the species was recorded in summer when, on July 14, C. E. Johnson collected a male at Pillsbury Lake, Hamilton Co. The following year in July he observed a singing male in the same county at Grampus Lake.

Finally in 1926 breeding was established when a female was found feeding fledged young—one of the latter collected by J. A. Weber—specimen in USNM collection. This was on July 23, 1926, near North Hudson, Essex Co.

No New York nests with eggs are known, and only four with nestlings, dates ranging from June 25 to July 6, various years. No New York data on heights above ground, tree species (except one nest in a hemlock), or even the habitats were given with these nests, but the species prefers mixed evergreen-deciduous forest ranging from about 1200 feet to over 3000 feet altitude. It seems to be replaced at higher elevations by the Blackpoll Warbler, but more field work remains to be done to determine this.

Of the following 15 known localities in the Adirondacks recorded during the summer, 11 of these are where breeding has been proved.

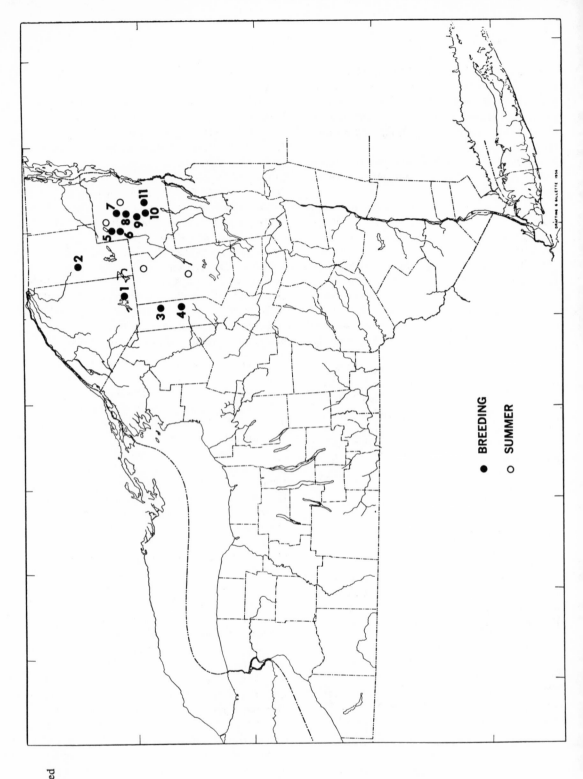

MAP 133 Bay-breasted
Warbler (*Dendroica
castanea*) Breeding
distribution

● BREEDING

○ SUMMER

The remaining four are merely summer occurrences.

St. Lawrence Co.—(1) east of, but "near," Cranberry Lake. Franklin Co.—(2) near Madawaska. Herkimer Co.—(3) north of Big Moose Lake; (4) Little Moose Lake. Essex Co.—(5) Chubb River Swamp; (6) Indian Pass; (7) Keene Valley; (8) near St. Hubert's at 1200 feet; (9) near Upper Ausable Lake at 2000 feet; (10) Elk Lake at about 2000 feet; (11) near North Hudson.

The four summer localities from north to south are: Essex Co.—Wilmington Notch at 1700 feet; near Giant Mtn. at 2400 feet. Hamilton Co.—Grampus Lake; Pillsbury Lake.

It is certain that with more intensive field work, definite breeding records will be obtained for Hamilton Co. and that more breeding localities will be found in Franklin, St. Lawrence, and Herkimer counties—all with an abundance of suitable habitat, but with a dearth of observers.

Blackpoll Warbler
(*Dendroica striata*)   *   B

Range: Northern Nearctic region, breeding from Alaska and Canada southeast to the higher mountains of northern New York and northern New England; locally south on Mt. Greylock in the Berkshires and on the highest mountains in the Catskills. Migrates through the West Indies. Winters chiefly in South America.

Status: Most numerous in migration in southeastern New York, especially on Long Island where common to very common in spring, often abundant in fall; much less numerous in the interior of the state. Common breeder in the higher Adirondacks and local but fairly common on the highest peaks of the Catskills.

Nonbreeding: The Blackpoll Warbler is one of the most numerous members of the family, especially in the southeastern section, and on certain days on autumn passage outnumbers all other warblers excepting only the Myrtle Warbler.

MAXIMA: *Spring*—100, Woodmere Woods, Nassau Co., May 16, 1953; 130, Prospect Park, Brooklyn, May 17, 1945; 55, Sandy Pond, Oswego Co., May 27, 1961; 30, Manitou, Monroe Co., June 1, 1968.

MAXIMA: *Fall*—(all Suffolk Co.) Fire Island Lighthouse kill—*356*, Sept. 23, 1887; 230, Sept. 30, 1883; Westhampton Air Force Base tower kill—114, Oct. 5, 1954.

EXTREME DATES, *all coastal: Spring*—Apr. 28 to June 26; several early July dates. *Fall* —Aug. 23 to Dec. 2 (specimen) and Dec. 3.

Rare before mid-May and after mid-October. Early and mid-August dates are rejected because of confusion with the very similar Bay-breasted Warbler which arrives much earlier.

The Mar. 30 report in Bull (1964: 384) is dubious. The specimen, which the writer never saw, apparently is not extant and cannot now be examined; the report should be nullified. The possibility that the bird in question may have been a Black-throated Gray Warbler (*D. nigrescens*) cannot be ruled out.

Breeding (see Map 134): This species and the Gray-cheeked Thrush are unique in that both are found breeding in North America at their southernmost-known limits in southeastern New York on the tops of the highest mountains in the Catskills. Elsewhere in the state they are confined as breeders to the higher Adirondacks. Unlike many other breeding warblers of boreal or northern affinities, the Blackpoll Warbler is restricted to the *upper* slopes of the mountains, mostly above 3500 feet in the Adirondacks and usually above 3700 feet in the Catskills.

Speaking of the Adirondacks, Eaton (1914: 418) said that this species was "found on all the higher peaks . . . where there are stunted spruces and balsam firs." Silloway (1923: 448) stated ". . . seems to prefer the open bog forest where there is an association of young and medium-sized conifers in sphagnum ground and of low bog shrubs in cleared spots . . . This preference for small growth leads the Blackpoll higher on the mountainsides than other warblers associated with coniferous forest." Saunders (1929: 389) stated that in the Adirondacks it was to be found above 3500 feet in balsam forest and in balsam swamps.

As to the Catskills it is also found in low, stunted spruce and fir forest where it is the most common warbler on the summits of the

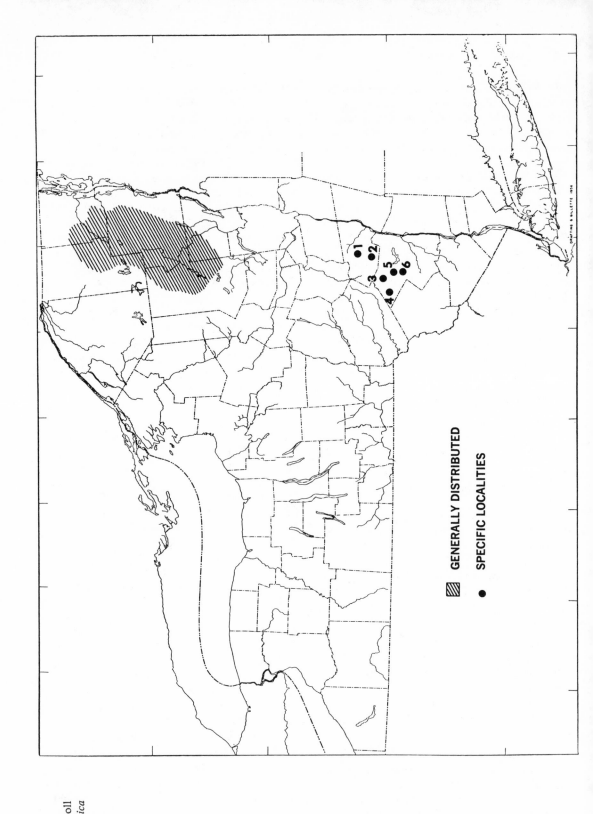

MAP 134 Blackpoll
Warbler (*Dendroica*
striata) Breeding
distribution

GENERALLY DISTRIBUTED

SPECIFIC LOCALITIES

highest peaks—as many as ten singing males recorded at two localities (several observers).

Fifteen New York nests ranged from three to eight feet above ground, rarely up to 15 feet.

Egg clutches in ten New York nests were four and five, each in five nests.

EGG DATES: June 5 to July 10.

Nestlings: no New York data; fledglings: June 30.

The six known Catskill breeding localities are found on the accompanying map: Greene Co. —(1) High Peak; (2) Hunter Mtn. Ulster Co.—(3) Balsam Mtn.; (4) Balsam Round Top Mtn.; (5) Slide Mtn.; (6) Peekamoose Mtn. The last-named is the southernmost-known breeding locality anywhere.

This species may prove to breed on other high peaks in the Catskill district.

Pine Warbler (*Dendroica pinus*) * B

Range: Eastern North America, breeding from extreme southern Canada to the Gulf states; also the Bahamas and Hispaniola. Winters throughout but rare northward. Rare and local inland.

Status: Variously rare to fairly common migrant on the coast, but rare inland. Very rare in winter. Locally common breeder in the pine barrens of eastern Long Island, but has decreased in recent years; rare to uncommon and local breeder inland in pine forest. Absent in the mountains and at higher elevations generally.

Nonbreeding: In recent years, at least, this species has become quite scarce. Its numbers fluctuate markedly and on migration it is very erratic, some years fairly common in spring, but for some reason almost always rare in fall. It is our earliest spring warbler, arriving regularly the first week in April.

The Pine Warbler in the Syracuse-Oswego-Oneida area (Region 5), according to Rusk and Scheider (*Kingbird,* 1970, 20: 32), ". . . is rarely seen, spring or fall, away from its few local breeding stations." This is applicable anywhere in the state except during spring passage in the New York City parks, as seen below.

MAXIMA, COASTAL: *Spring*—eight, Van

Cortlandt Park, Apr. 8, 1950; 15, Bronx Park, Apr. 23, 1955.

An estimate of *20* from Easthampton to Montauk (=approx. 30 miles), Oct. 8, 1932 (Helmuth), is unusual. Today it is extremely rare in fall—even along the coast. During an 11-year period of banding in the late 1930s and early 1940s at Elmhurst, Queens Co., Mrs. Beals recorded only four individuals in fall (Oct. 1–14) and *none* in spring. During a similar period—1960s—near Huntington, Suffolk Co., Lanyon banded but one bird—Oct. 7, 1967. Nevertheless, during a one-month period —Sept. 26 to Oct. 25, 1970—at the Fire Island State Park, Suffolk Co. banding station, as many as *six* individuals were reported by Davis and others.

Winter: Ordinarily very rare at this season when it has been recorded visiting feeding stations. On the south shore of Long Island at least a dozen wintering individuals have been reported.

The following five upstate winter occurrences are noteworthy: (1) one collected in pine woods near Schenectady, February 1881 (Eaton, 1914: 428); (2) two at Branchport, Yates Co., Jan. 9 to Feb. 8, 1932 (Stone), from time to time at a feeder, otherwise in red pine-hemlock forest; (3) two at the Taylor feeder, Penn Yan, Yates Co., winter of 1950–1951; (4) one banded at the Wolfling feeder, Alden, Erie Co., Dec. 20, 1952, to Jan. 3, 1953; (5) one at a Dunkirk, Chautauqua Co. feeder, winter of 1966–1967 (many observers); this individual was photographed, and during its stay, fed on suet, seeds, and doughnuts.

Breeding (see Map 135): Well named, the Pine Warbler breeds exclusively in pines (see Figs. 77 and 78). In the ever-shrinking pine barrens of Suffolk Co. (central and eastern Long Island) it was formerly much more numerous. Today it still is a characteristic bird of the taller, denser stands of pitch pine, but is becoming progressively scarcer in the remaining pinelands. Elsewhere the species is very local and quite rare. Nevertheless, in the Karner barrens of Albany Co. in 1954, at least a dozen pairs were found within four miles (Benton). Upstate the Pine Warbler is not restricted to pitch pine but nests as frequently in stands of both red and white pine.

Nest heights range from 20 to 60 feet above

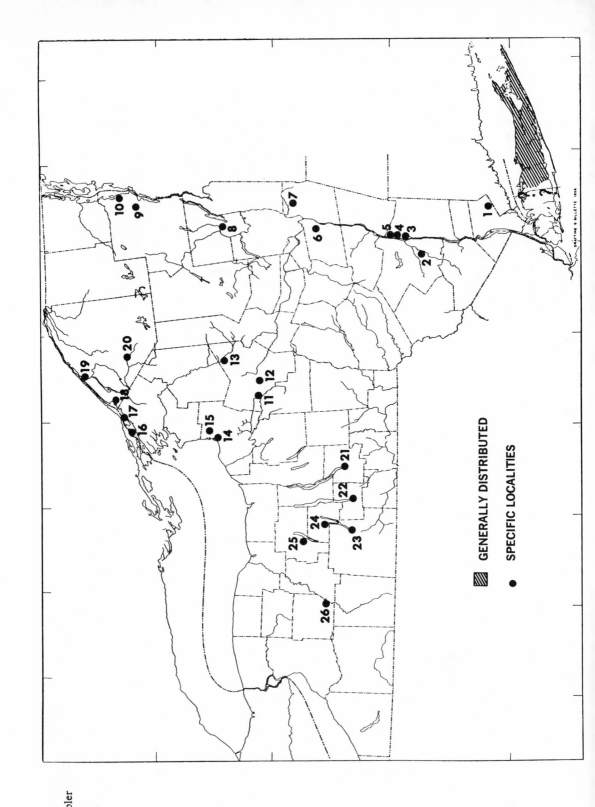

MAP 135 Pine Warbler
(*Dendroica pinus*)
Breeding distribution

GENERALLY DISTRIBUTED

SPECIFIC LOCALITIES

Fig. 77 Rome Sand Plains, Oneida Co., June 1969; mixed pitch-red pine woods, breeding habitat of Pine Warbler. Photo by Ken Hanson

Fig. 78 Pitch pine-scrub oak, Baiting Hollow, Suffolk Co., 1968. Breeding habitat of Pine Warbler. Photo by Edgar M. Reilly

ground. Egg clutches in eight New York nests were three eggs each in three nests and four eggs apiece in five nests.

EGG DATES: May 4 to June 6.

Nestlings: May 19 to June 17; fledglings: May 30 to Aug. 8.

Four disjunct populations occur in New York (see map):

(A) Long Island—generally distributed in the eastern third, but fast dwindling in western Suffolk Co.; vaguely reported as having formerly bred at Oyster Bay, and at Valley Stream (in extreme western Nassau Co.) but details are lacking.

(B) Hudson-Champlain valley: Westchester Co.—(1) Bedford. Ulster Co.—(2) Mohonk Lake. Dutchess Co.—(3) Rhinebeck; (4) Cruger's Island; (5) Tivoli. Albany Co.—(6) Karner. Rensselaer Co.—(7) Tomhannock. Warren Co.—(8) Warrensburg. Essex Co.—(9) Elizabethtown; (10) Willsboro.

(C) Lake Ontario-St. Lawrence lowlands: Oneida Co.—(11) Sylvan Beach, Oneida Lake;

(12) Rome Sand Plains; (13) Boonville, Black River valley. Oswego Co.—(14) Selkirk Shores State Park; (15) Centerville. Jefferson Co.—(16) Grindstone Island; (17) Lake of the Isles, Wellesley Island. St. Lawrence Co.—(18) mouth of Crooked Creek; (19) Ogdensburg; (20) Edwards.

(D) Finger Lakes region: Tompkins Co.—(21) Ithaca. Schuyler Co.—(22) Watkins Glen. Steuben Co.—(23) near Hammondsport. Yates Co.—(24) near Branchport. Ontario Co.—(25) Seneca Glen. Wyoming Co.—(26) Letchworth State Park near Portageville.

Prairie Warbler
(Dendroica discolor) * B

Range: Eastern North America, breeding north to *northern Michigan* and *southern Ontario,* but only to the central portions of New York and New England. Winters north

Fig. 79 Pitch pine-scrub oak woodland; habitat of Pine and Prairie warblers. Riverhead, Suffolk Co., 1968. Photo by Edgar M. Reilly

to central Florida; casual in Massachusetts (specimen).

Status: Fairly common to common migrant and breeder on Long Island; less numerous on the adjacent mainland, but decidedly uncommon north of the lower Hudson valley (Albany area) and rare and local elsewhere at lower elevations. Absent in the mountains.

Nonbreeding: The Praire Warbler is one of the very few members of this family that is more numerous on Long Island than on the mainland.

MAXIMA: *Spring*—30, Prospect Park, Brooklyn, May 5, 1946; 30, Woodmere Woods, Nassau Co., May 6, 1950.

MAXIMA: *Fall*—five netted and banded, Tobay Beach, Nassau Co., Sept. 25, 1965.

EXTREME DATES: Apr. 16 to Nov. 29 (specimen) and Dec. 2 (all coastal); casual Dec. 26, 1967, East Moriches, Suffolk Co. (Stoutenburgh, who knows this species very well); this is the only known winter occurrence

in the state. Rare before late April and after October.

Breeding (see Map 136). This species is particularly numerous in the scrub oak and pine barrens of Long Island where Elliott (1951) stated, "Scrub fires appear to be beneficial in making up the habitat. When scrub oaks and pines become high and dense, this species usually vacates" (see Figs. 79 and 80). Inland it nests in open scrubby fields and on hillsides with a scattering of red cedars and brier tangles. It has greatly increased in the past 40 or 50 years in these latter environments.

On Long Island it is widely distributed over the central and eastern portions. The Prairie Warbler formerly bred as far west as the Nassau-Queens county line.

The only breeding "density" that I have heard about is that of approximately 20 pairs within four miles of sand plain in the famous Karner barrens between Albany and Schenec-

Fig. 80 Pine barrens between Pinelawn and Wyandanch, Suffolk Co., 1908. Trees consist chiefly of pitch pine and two species of scrub oaks. Breeding habitat of Pine and Prairie warblers. Photo by Francis Harper

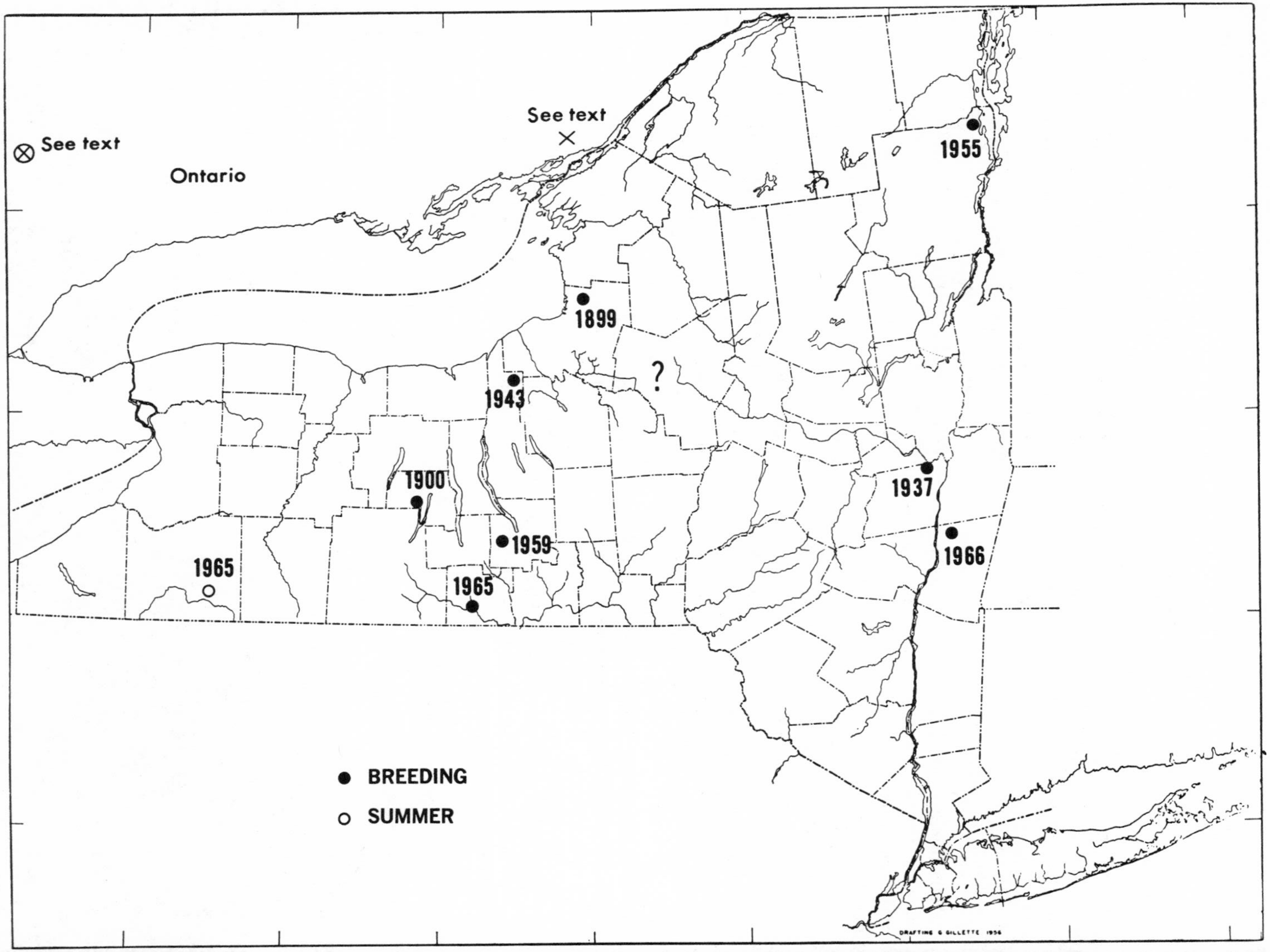

MAP 136 Prairie
Warbler (*Dendroica
discolor*) Known
northern and western
breeding limits

⊗ See text

Ontario

See text
×

?

● 1955

● 1937 1966 ●

● 1899

● 1943

● 1959

● 1965

1900 ●

1965
○

● BREEDING
○ SUMMER

tady, 1939 (Bedell). This flat sandy area is not unlike the Long Island barrens and has a mixture of pitch pine, various scrub oaks, and an understory of blueberry bushes.

The habitat in most inland areas is overgrown pastures and fields with scattered red cedars. A breeding locality near Binghamton was described as an "abandoned meadow with thorn apples and young white pines." Another site was located in a young spruce plantation, and yet another had an admixture of juniper (red cedar) and staghorn sumac.

Despite its predilection for stunted evergreen cover in various sections of the state, whether in the sandy areas of Long Island or the Karner barrens with their pitch pine, or on overgrown upland hillsides with red cedars, nevertheless nine New York nests of this warbler were found in non-evergreen vegetation. The nine nests ranged in height from only one inch above ground in a clump of wild lupine to nine feet up in a birch sapling. The other seven nests were located in two each of oak and maple, and one each of hazel, elderberry, and huckleberry.

Egg clutches in 12 New York nests: three eggs (three nests); four eggs (five nests); five eggs (four nests).

EGG DATES: May 25 to June 29.

Nestlings: June 19 to July 4; fledglings: June 30 to July 14.

The breeding distribution of the Prairie Warbler is erratic and irregular except on Long Island and in the Hudson valley as far north as Albany. Despite a specimen cited by Eaton (1914: 433) as taken at Paul Smith's, Franklin Co., May 17, 1908 (E. B. Woodruff), AMNH 22990, no other record exists for the Adirondack region to my knowledge.

The accompanying map indicates how erratic in distribution this species is in New York and, like the Orchard Oriole but unlike most other species with southern affinities, it has *not* penetrated northward except for one locality on Lake Champlain. Note that the Prairie Warbler is absent as a *breeder* from extreme western New York, is virtually absent from the Great Lakes area, but at the same time is present as a breeder to the *north* and *northwest* in Ontario in the region lying between Kingston and Westport (x) and at Wasaga Beach (⊗) respectively (see map). This northward penetration into Canada but, at the

same time, absence far to the *south* in New York confirms the belief that this species has come not from the south, but from the *west* by way of Michigan (see **Range**), probably via the Mississippi valley.

The New York breeding localities, with years of "arrival" shown on the map, are: (1) east of the Catskills and Adirondacks—Kinderhook Lake, Columbia Co., 1966; Karner, Albany Co., 1937; near Port Douglas, Essex Co., 1955. (2) west of the Catskills and Adirondacks—Elmira, Chemung Co., 1965; Connecticut Hill, Tompkins Co., 1959; Branchport, Yates Co., 1900; Ira, Cayuga Co., 1943; Sandy Creek, Oswego Co., 1899. Also a summer occurrence about five miles north of Allegany, Cattaraugus Co., 1965. In 1970 an estimated *nine* pairs bred in the Elmira region.

Certain comments are in order concerning some of the above. It should be emphasized that the older stations (1899, 1900, and 1943) are *not* regular localities for breeding, the 1899 one in Oswego Co. being based on a nest and eggs collected that year (Eaton, 1914: 433). It is of considerable interest that, although the species is common enough in the sandy Karner pine-oak barrens (1937), it is unknown in similar habitat in Oneida Co. in the Rome Sand Plains. The late Arthur A. Allen discovered *four* nests in a young spruce plantation on 2100-foot Connecticut Hill in 1959—"breeding with Magnolia Warblers."

Beardslee and Mitchell (1965: 385) expressed grave doubt about the identity of two eggs in the BMS collection taken at Glenwood, Erie Co., in 1907, and the writer, having examined these eggs, concurs. Similar skepticism may be felt for a nest taken in Orleans Co. in 1904; neither nest nor eggs are available for examination.

Palm Warbler
(*Dendroica palmarum*)   *

Range: Chiefly central and southern Canada, the nominate western race breeds southeast to southeastern Ontario and central Michigan; the eastern race *hypochrysea* (brighter than nominate race; yellow below more extensive, including belly; ventral streaking chestnut) breeds south to central Maine and east-central New Hampshire. Nominate *palmarum* migrates *southeastward* in fall toward the Atlantic coast and winters chiefly in Florida and the West Indies, rarely north along the coast to Massachusetts; in spring migrates chiefly *west* of the Appalachians, rare in the east. The race *hypochrysea* migrates *southwestward* in fall toward the Gulf coast, its chief wintering grounds; rarely north to the middle Atlantic states; in spring migrates *northeastward* along the Atlantic coast, rare farther west. In other words the two subspecies essentially "cross" each other's migration routes both spring and fall.

Status: Variously uncommon to abundant migrant; especially numerous along the coast, in much smaller numbers inland. Rare to locally uncommon in winter on the outer coast.

Occurrence: The Palm Warbler (collectively) arrives regularly in April and, with the exception of the Pine Warbler, is our earliest spring warbler. It prefers open country and is usually found on or near the ground. Although the two subspecies can often be identified in the field, the observer should realize that a number of individuals are intermediate in appearance and are not separable even in the hand.

The following maxima and extreme dates are based on the species as a whole; no attempt is made to differentiate the races. Notice how relatively scarce the species is inland.

MAXIMA, COASTAL: *Fall*—80, Easthampton, Suffolk Co., Sept. 15, 1946; 30, Montauk Point, Oct. 14, 1950.

MAXIMA, COASTAL: *Winter*—five, Oak Beach, Suffolk Co., Jan. 2, 1965; ten, Captree, Suffolk Co. Christmas count, Dec. 31, 1966.

MAXIMA, COASTAL: *Spring*—200, Central Park, New York City, Apr. 21, 1929; 300, Van Cortlandt Park, Bronx Co., May 1, 1950; 80, Woodmere Woods, Nassau Co., May 6, 1950.

MAXIMA, INLAND: *Spring*—15, Derby Hill, Oswego Co., Apr. 29, 1969; 36 in one hour, same locality, May 4, 1963; 12, Syracuse, May 19, 1957, late for so many.

It should be pointed out that most of the birds listed in the fall coastal maxima above were of the nominate, western race, whereas the vast majority, if not all, of the spring coastal birds were of the eastern "Yellow Palm" type.

EXTREME DATES: Aug. 26 (earliest specimen, Sept. 8—nominate *palmarum*) to May 27. Rare in fall before mid-September and after November; in spring, before April and after mid-May. Reports as early as mid-August have not been corroborated.

Specimen data: I know of only one corroborated winter occurrence of this species from the interior: one hit a window near Schenectady, Jan. 25, 1967, but the specimen spoiled before it could be preserved. Fortunately it was examined and identified as the race *hypochrysea* (Reilly, *in litt.*). Another winter specimen (race *palmarum*) was collected at Orient, Suffolk Co., Jan. 14, 1932 (Latham), NYSM 25391.

Occasional specimens of *hypochrysea,* much the rarer of the two races in western New York, have been collected there—including three from the Finger Lakes region in the Cornell University collection—one in spring and two in fall; and even as far west as Buffalo where one was taken on Apr. 22, 1948 (Mitchell), BMS 3588. I have examined all of the above.

Banding: An individual banded as a "Yellow Palm" Warbler, Oct. 13, 1932, at Elmhurst, Queens Co. (Beals), was recovered Jan. 15, 1933, at Dunn, North Carolina.

Ovenbird
(*Seiurus aurocapillus*)   *   B

Range: North America, chiefly the eastern portions, breeding from central Canada south in the mountains to northern Georgia. Winters in the east, north to Florida, rarely to coastal South Carolina; vagrant north to Massachusetts (specimen).

Status: Common to very common spring migrant; less numerous in fall. Widespread breeder.

Nonbreeding: The Ovenbird is one of our best known and most numerous warblers.

MAXIMA: *Spring*—big coastal early May flight in 1950—160, Prospect Park, Brooklyn, May 5; 100, Woodmere Woods, Nassau Co., May 6; 200, Central Park, New York City, May 11, 1914; 200, Madison Square Park, New York City, May 15, 1921, after a heavy fog and rain the previous night; 200, Goat Island, Niagara River, May 21, 1943.

MAXIMA: *Fall*—79 struck the Empire State Building, New York City, Sept. 11, 1948; 63 hit the Elmira television tower, Sept. 20, 1966; 175 struck the Colden TV tower, Erie Co., Sept. 24, 1970 (Clark), a record number for fall; 85 hit the Empire State Building, Sept. 27, 1970; 22 hit the Westhampton Air Force Base tower, Suffolk Co., Oct. 5, 1954—late for so many.

EXTREME DATES: Apr. 10 (specimen), 15, and 19 (all coastal) to Nov. 24 (coastal). The upstate arrival date is considerably later, about Apr. 26; the fall departure date much earlier, about Oct. 28, excepting one very late date— Nov. 29, 1964, Rochester (Weld).

Rare before May and after early October.

Winter: Exceedingly rare, no state specimen, but *eight* well-corroborated sightings (all but one coastal) as follows: (1) Inwood Hill Park, New York City, Dec. 21, 1935 (Karsch and Norse); (2) one caught alive on a porch, Ithaca, Dec. 19, 1951 (Kellogg); (3) one at a feeding station, Baldwin, Nassau Co., up to Dec. 31, 1955 (Teale, *et al.*); (4) Poundridge (village), Westchester Co., Dec. 21–30, 1961 (Grierson, *et al.*); (5) one at a feeder, Lloyd's Harbor, Suffolk Co., Jan. 26 to Feb. 19, 1968 (Cooke and many others); (6), (7), and (8) all on Long Island, late December 1969, Christmas counts at Brooklyn, Captree (Suffolk Co.), and Montauk.

Breeding: The Ovenbird builds a domed nest on the ground in both deciduous and evergreen forest and is statewide in distribution, being one of the most common members of the family. Eaton (1914: 435–436) states that it breeds in spruce and pine forest as high as 3500 feet in the Adirondacks. In June 1955, Scheider estimated *80* Ovenbirds within two miles of dry, open pine-oak woodland in the Rome Sand Plains area of Oneida Co.

Clutches in 26 New York nests ranged from three to six eggs: three eggs (five nests); four eggs (12 nests); five eggs (seven nests); six eggs (two nests).

EGG DATES: May 17 to July 22.

Nestlings: June 8 to Aug. 8; fledglings: June 18 to Aug. 22.

Banding: One banded Sept. 2, 1962, at Huntington, Suffolk Co., was taken late that *same* month near St. Augustine, Florida.

Remarks: No eastern subspecies are recognized here, the differences between the Newfoundland population *"furvior"* and nominate *aurocapillus* are too insignificant to warrant recognition.

Northern Waterthrush
(*Seiurus noveboracensis*) * B

Range: Nearctic region, breeding from Alaska and Canada to northern United States —in the east as far as Pennsylvania, northern New Jersey, southeastern New York, and southern New England; in the mountains to West Virginia and Maryland. Winters chiefly in the tropics, rarely north to Bermuda and southern Florida.

Status: Fairly common to common migrant, more numerous on the coast than inland, especially in fall. Widespread breeder at higher elevations; local on the lake plain and in the southeastern portions.

Nonbreeding: The Northern Waterthrush is widespread during migration, occurring from inland bogs, swamps, lake and river shores, as well as in woodland, to coastal ponds, salt creeks, and even thickets along the outer beaches.

MAXIMA: *Spring*—15, Syracuse, Apr. 27, 1957, early for so many; 25, Manitou, Monroe Co., Apr. 30, 1960 (Listman), early for so many—not Apr. *20* as stated by Beardslee and Mitchell (1964: 388); 12, Central Park, New York City, May 6, 1950; 12, Eaton, Madison Co., May 13, 1967; 21 netted and banded, Huntington, Suffolk Co., May 28, 1967.

MAXIMA: *Fall*—six netted and banded, Brookhaven, Suffolk Co., Aug. 6, 1965; 12 more there, Aug. 12; 23, Prospect Park, Brooklyn, Aug. 29, 1944; 55, same locality, Sept. 13, 1964 (Yrizarry); 28 struck the Shinnecock Lighthouse, Suffolk Co., Sept. 17, 1890; 38 hit the Westhampton Air Force Base tower, Suffolk Co., Oct. 5, 1954.

EXTREME DATES: *Spring*—Apr. 14 (coastal) and Apr. 19 (inland specimen) to June 7 (coastal).

EXTREME DATES: *Fall*—one of the first warblers to depart—July 12 (coastal) to Oct.

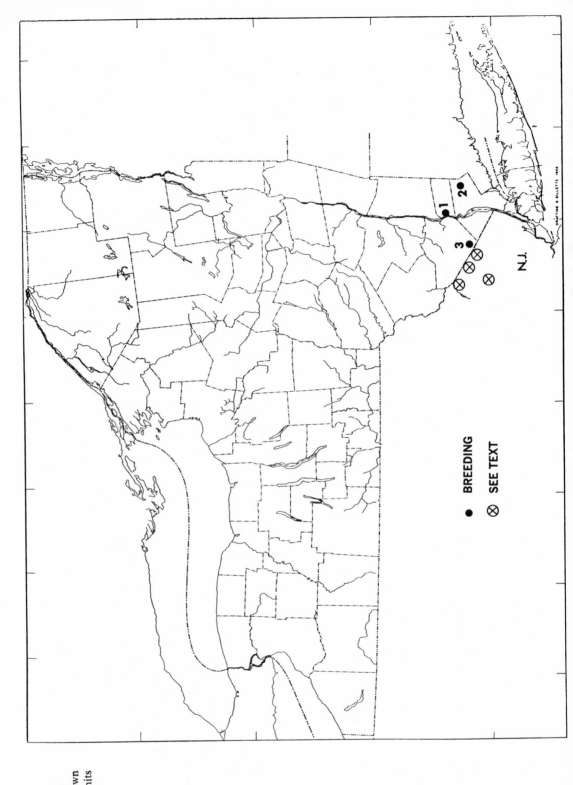

MAP 137 Northern
Waterthrush (*Seiurus*
noveboracensis) Known
southern breeding limits

BREEDING

SEE TEXT

N.J.

20 (inland) to Nov. 2 (coastal); exceptionally to Nov. 15 and 30 (both coastal).

Rare before late April and after mid-October.

Winter: There are *three* occurrences at this season, all reported by experienced observers competent to identify the species: (1) Tifft Street marsh, Buffalo, Jan. 4–24, 1947 (Mitchell, Wright, Andrle, Seeber, *et al.*); (2) Mill Neck feeder, Dec. 26–27, 1965 (Dunning, Astle, *et al.*); (3) one along the edge of a spring-fed pond, Mastic, Suffolk Co., Dec. 26, 1968 (W. F. Nichols, Weld, *et al.*). It would be most desirable to collect a specimen to authenticate occurrence here in winter.

Breeding (see Map 137): The Northern Waterthrush is to the wooded *swamp,* what the sibling Louisiana Waterthrush is to the wooded *stream.* For these two very similar species—in morphology, vocalizations, and general habits—avoid competition for nest sites and food by breeding in two *different* aquatic habitats, *noveboracensis* favoring generally stagnant water of wooded swamps, bogs, and beaver ponds, while *motacilla* frequents fast-flowing streams and mountain brooks (see, however, habitat on Long Island under *motacilla*). Whereas the two species are mainly allopatric over much of their respective ranges —one essentially northern in distribution as witness its name, the other principally southern —nevertheless in certain localities in New York they are truly sympatric, but in effect sort out their separate ways ecologically.

I know of at least seven localities in New York State (there are probably others) where the two may be found "together"—in Albany, Oneida, Onondaga, Cortland, Tompkins, Yates, and Cattaraugus counties—and in one of these localities, at least, near Cincinnatus in Cortland Co., they may be heard within earshot of each other, but the Northern Waterthrush is in a red maple swamp, the Louisiana Waterthrush within 100 yards in a hemlock-clad ravine with a running stream.

The present species occurs chiefly in the aforementioned habitats through much of the mountains and highlands, but can be found also frequenting such low-lying localities on the Lake Ontario plain as: Oak Orchard and Bergen swamps in Orleans and Genesee counties; Reed Road and 1000 Acre swamps, Monroe Co.; Montezuma Marshes in Seneca and Cayuga counties; Snake Creek, Oswego Co.; Stony Point and Henderson Pond, Jefferson Co.

Some density figures are: (1) Tug Hill district of southern Lewis Co.—52 in 14 miles of trail, June 10, 1957 (Scheider, 1959a); (2) Sapsucker Woods, Ithaca area—four pairs in 45 acres of elm-maple-ash swamp (Owen, 1950).

S. W. Eaton (1957) made an intensive study of this species in the Ithaca area. He found a total of nine nests, most of which were among fallen tree rootlets above the water and three others in clumps of cinnamon ferns.

Nearly all Northern Waterthrush nests were found on the ground, rarely up to two feet above water level. Some were placed among bushes, in overturned tree stumps, and at the bases of rotten, moss-covered logs.

Egg clutches in 18 New York nests: three eggs (two nests); four eggs (13 nests); five eggs (three nests).

EGG DATES: May 10 to June 28.

Nestlings: May 24 to July 5; fledglings: June 4 to July 20.

Southeastern limits in the state are shown on the accompanying map: Putnam Co.—(1) near Cold Spring. Westchester Co.—(2) Lake Waccabuc. Orange Co.—(3) Sterling Forest. Future field work should find this species breeding in highland swamps of Rockland Co., and certainly elsewhere in Orange Co. in view of its nesting immediately to the south in New Jersey (see map).

Banding: In 1966 a bird banded on Aug. 18 near Tawas City, Michigan, was found dead on Aug. 28 at Buffalo. This individual flew *east* in *fall* for nearly 300 miles in ten nights, or an average of 30 miles per night.

One of the most exciting long-distance recoveries involving a passerine bird—especially a warbler—was that of a Northern Waterthrush banded on Long Island. This individual was netted and banded by LeRoy Wilcox on Sept. 27, 1958, at Tiana Beach, Suffolk Co., and was netted by Paul Schwartz on Nov. 29 following, near Caracas, Venezuela.

Remarks: No northern subspecies (including *"notabilis"*) are recognized here, following Eaton (1957); see also Bull (1964: 389).

Louisiana Waterthrush
(*Seiurus motacilla*)   *   B

Range: Southeastern United States, breeding north to the central portions of New York and New England. Winters in tropical America.

Status: Rare to uncommon migrant, more numerous inland. Widespread but somewhat local breeder, mainly at lower elevations; absent in the higher mountains and on the coastal plain.

Nonbreeding: Being at the northern limits of its range in New York, the Louisiana Waterthrush is by necessity uncommon in migration. Even in such excellent warbler localities as Central and Prospect parks, the Louisiana Waterthrush, though regular in spring, is an uncommon species. The maxima appear to be three to four per day in late April.

It has always been a very rare bird on the outer coast of Long Island (Bull, 1964: 390). Even near the north shore it is rare. In ten years of banding (1960–1969) near Huntington, Suffolk Co., of more than *400* waterthrushes processed by Lanyon and his assistants, only *13* were Louisianas.

EXTREME DATES: Mar. 25 (coastal) and Apr. 12 (inland) to Oct. 1 (inland) and Oct. 12 (coastal).

Rare before mid-April and after mid-September.

Breeding (see Map 138): This species prefers wooded streams and brooks in shaded ravines with swift-flowing water, but see below (Long Island). Many of these streams in the eastern mountains have large boulders while some of those in the central and western part of the state flow through glens and gorges with shale banks.

Most nests are well concealed under the roots of bushes, behind boulders, or in banks, and range from 20 inches to four feet above water level.

Despite being so well hidden, many more nests of this species have been found (*109*) than of the Northern Waterthrush (only 18) for reasons that escape me. In their many years of collecting in the Keuka Lake region of Yates

and northern Steuben counties, during the last 20 years of the nineteenth century and nearly as many years in the early twentieth, Burtch and Stone accounted for *61* of the *109* nests.

Egg clutches in these *109* New York nests ranged from three to six, as follows: three eggs (six nests—perhaps incomplete clutches); four eggs (17 nests); five eggs (56 nests); six eggs (30 nests).

EGG DATES: Apr. 25 to June 20.

Nestlings: May 20 to July 6; fledglings: June 9 to July 25.

The species is well represented along the streams of central and western New York, but lacking from the Lake Ontario plain where fast-flowing streams are generally wanting and where the swamp-loving Northern Waterthrush replaces it. Reports of breeding Louisiana Waterthrushes along the Lake Ontario shore of Oswego and Jefferson counties have proved to be misidentified Northerns.

Although absent from most of the Catskill Mountains, the Louisiana Waterthrush ranges up to 1900 feet in the vicinity of Big Indian in northern Ulster Co.

Very different conditions prevail in the extreme southeastern part of the state where only Louisianas breed—south of the known breeding range of Northerns. I am referring to the north shore of Long Island where rapid streams are lacking and the habitat is that of wooded swamps or sluggish or slow-moving streams; here Louisianas are known to nest, or have had nests, at seven localities: Nassau Co.—Mill Neck (wooded swamp). Suffolk Co.—Cold Spring Harbor and nearby Huntington (slow-moving stream); Nissequogue River near Smithtown (sluggish stream); Mt. Sinai (swamp); Miller's Place (swamp); Manorville (bog); Greenport (swamp). All seven localities, except Manorville, are situated on the north shore. Manorville, halfway between the north and south shores, is north of the coastal plain and the terminal moraine.

The accompanying map shows the known northern breeding limits of this species in New York: south end of Lake George near Lake George (village), Warren Co., 1914; east side of Lake George near Brayton, Washington Co., 1918; Port Henry, near Lake Champlain, Essex Co., both in 1941 and 1947 (Carleton); near Boonville on the Black River, Oneida Co., 1964; western slope of Tug Hill plateau near

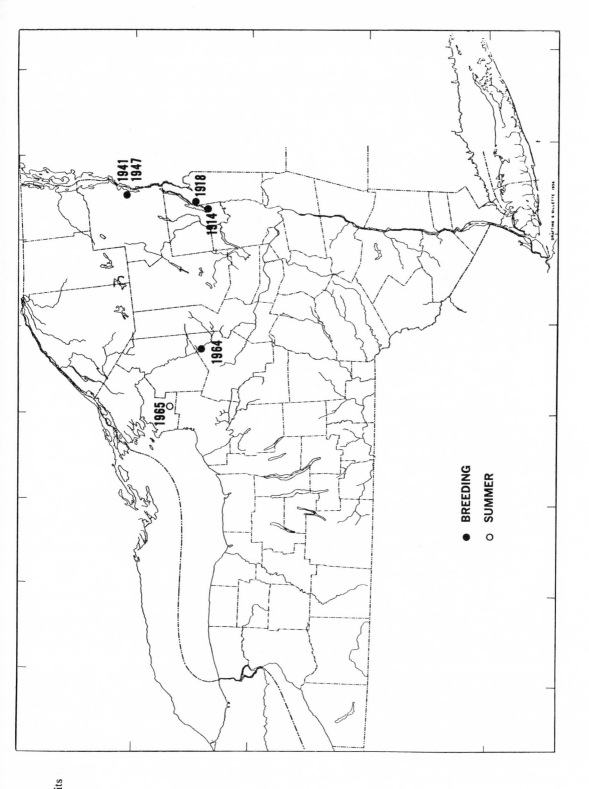

MAP 138 Louisiana
Waterthrush (*Seiurus
motacilla*) Known
northern breeding limits

1941
1947

1918

1914

1964

1965

● BREEDING
○ SUMMER

Lorraine, Jefferson Co:—pair present in late July 1965, but breeding not proved (D. Gordon).

Kentucky Warbler
(*Oporornis formosus*)   *   B

Range: Southeastern United States, breeding northeast to southern Pennsylvania and central New Jersey; formerly to northern New Jersey, southeastern and south-central New York, and extreme southwestern Connecticut. Winters from southern Mexico to extreme northwestern South America.

Status: Very rare to rare migrant. Formerly a local and not uncommon breeder in the southeastern section.

Nonbreeding: The Kentucky Warbler is now one of our rarest warblers. Away from the coast it is virtually unrecorded except during spring and early summer. A singing male at Elizabethtown, Essex Co., May 17–18, 1969 (Carleton), is unprecedented. Also very unusual were *three* banded individuals (two males, one female) at Frewsburg, Chautauqua Co., May 4, 11, and 13, 1970 (Elderkin).

Even on the coast it is extremely rare in fall and rare but regular (a few) in spring: three, Freeport, Nassau Co., May 22, 1960 (Dignan and Ward), appear to be the maxima.

EXTREME DATES: Apr. 26, 1970, Central Park, New York City (many observers), and May 1 (coastal) to Oct. 2 (coastal). Rare before mid-May and after mid-September. November and December dates lack confirmation.

Breeding: This species is at its northern limits here, has greatly decreased since about 1900, and has withdrawn over much of its former northeastern nesting range, for reasons apparently unknown. The likelihood of its being overlooked as a breeder is slight, as it is a loud and persistent singer, the song similar to that of the Carolina Wren.

Its favored haunts are rich, moist, usually hilly woodlands, especially those having ravines with stream bottoms and an understory of dense, luxuriant vegetation. There are still areas of such habitat.

For details of its former breeding in the New York City region, see Bull (1964: 392).

I know of no definite breeding record for the entire state in over *30* years (since 1942). In New York it was confined to the east side of the Hudson River in Westchester Co., formerly breeding near Riverdale, Grassy Sprain (Yonkers), in the Woodlands-Worthington-Irvington-Elmsford sector, and near Ossining. Much of this area has been destroyed.

The only other proved breeding localities in the state were in southeastern Cortland Co. in the nearly adjacent communities of Taylor and Cincinnatus, where two nests with eggs were found in 1903 and 1906 by H. C. Higgins (Eaton, 1914: 445). In recent years nests of two other "southern" warblers (Worm-eating and Hooded) have been found in similar habitat at or near those two localities, but none of Kentucky Warbler.

Nests of this species are usually situated on or near the ground in thick undergrowth. Three New York nests contained four eggs each in two nests and five eggs in the other.

EGG DATES: June 1 to June 27.

Dates June 20 and June 29 represent nestlings and fledglings respectively.

Postscript: Pair of adults, nest, and three fledged young, Kalbfleisch Research Station, near Huntington, Suffolk Co., July 1, 1973 (D. Ewert, W. E. Lanyon, and C. Wunderle). The nest was on the ground in a dense honeysuckle thicket, in moist, second-growth woodland. The female was mist-netted, banded, color-photographed, and released; she was observed feeding the young, as was the male. This constitutes the *first* proved breeding record for Long Island, and it is the first known nesting occurrence in New York State in more than 30 years.

Mourning Warbler
(*Oporornis philadelphia*)   *   B

Range: Nearctic region, breeding from Alaska and Canada to southwestern United States; in the east to the Berkshires, Catskills, and Poconos—but not *southeast* of the mountains—and at higher altitudes to Virginia and West Virginia. Winters from Mexico to northern South America.

Status: Rare to uncommon but regular migrant, occasionally more numerous inland. Fairly common to locally common breeder in the mountains and higher regions generally, but rare and local in many places in the southern tier section except the southwest, and absent south and east of the Catskills.

Nonbreeding: The following is taken from Bull (1964: 394): "The best times and places to look for this species are during the last ten days of May and the first week in June, in city parks wherever plantings of thick shrubbery occur, usually near ponds and swampy situations. Elsewhere inland the Mourning Warbler may be found in low, wet woods where extensive growths of skunk cabbage, nettle, and jewel-weed abound. While it is particularly retiring and secretive in such places, individuals may be heard singing, sometimes for long periods. Its song, similar to that of the Kentucky Warbler, or Carolina Wren, has certain notes and phrases not unlike those of the Yellowthroat, and on several occasions I have traced an off-Yellowthroat song to discover that it was actually a Mourning Warbler."

This species is exceedingly difficult to observe in autumn because of the dense vegetation at that season and because the bird does not sing then. It is rare at all times on the coastal plain.

MAXIMA: *Spring*—four, Central Park, New York City, June 2, 1930. Concentrations of seven on May 21, 1967, and 16 on May 27, 1956, in the Syracuse-Camillus region undoubtedly represent local breeders, as well as migrants.

MAXIMA: *Fall*—12 netted and banded near Huntington, Suffolk Co., Aug. 20 to Sept. 10, 1964 (Lanyon, *et al.*)—proof that this secretive species is not as rare on Long Island as was generally supposed.

EXTREME DATES: May 7 (inland specimen) and May 8 (coastal) to Oct. 8 (inland) and Oct. 12 and 19 (coastal). On the coast, where it does not breed, it has arrived in fall as early as Aug. 5 and has departed in spring as late as June 14.

Rare before late May and after mid-September. Reports the first few days in May are unconfirmed. Even more remarkable is a winter "occurrence" at Keuka Park, Yates Co., published in the *Auk* (1948, 65: 127–128), of a bird banded, but most unfortunately not collected; positive identity as to species, therefore, must remain forever in doubt.

The writer has examined four females in the CUM collection from Tompkins Co., two of which were taken in late May, the other two in September, various years; in addition, two Adirondack females in the BM(NH) collection were shot at their nests. All have *conspicuous* or *virtually complete* eye rings. In the field they would have been identified almost certainly as Connecticut Warblers. For the difficulties involved, see Lanyon and Bull (1967), field guides to the contrary, notwithstanding.

Breeding: This species, like the Chestnut-sided Warbler, undoubtedly benefited from the cutting of the forest in the early nineteenth century, for both of these birds breed in second-growth areas and in clearings. In the Adirondacks, Merriam (1881: 228) called the Mourning Warbler common, breeding chiefly in dense growths of blackberry and raspberry bushes in nearly all the burned districts. For the Catskills, Bicknell (1882: 152) said that it was locally distributed from the valleys to near the summits, inhabiting chiefly old cleared or burned-over land grown up to weeds, briers, shrubbery, and saplings.

In more recent times Saunders (1923: 280–281 and 1938: 120), referring to Allegany State Park, called this species an inhabitant of aspen-birch-cherry thickets, and in brier patches in open groves of maple-beech and oak-chestnut (later hickory) forest types. Roger Peterson (*in litt.*) referring to adjacent Chautauqua Co., remarked that Mourning Warblers breed in two distinct habitats: (1) brushy hillsides with dense tangles of blackberries; (2) wet bottomland woods among skunk cabbage.

The species is evidently a common breeder in portions of the Tug Hill sector. For instance, Rusk and Scheider (*Kingbird*, 1963, 13: 220) called it the second commonest warbler after the Redstart and about as numerous as the Canada Warbler. Near Redfield, Oswego Co., they estimated *40* singing males within ten miles, or about four per mile.

Nests of the Mourning Warbler are placed on or near the ground—rarely up to two and one-half feet in saplings. Most ground nests are located in clumps of flowers or ferns in dense thickets.

Egg clutches in 34 New York nests: three

eggs (seven nests); four eggs (18 nests); five eggs (nine nests).

EGG DATES: May 28 to July 7.

Nestlings: June 22 to July 28; fledglings: June 27 to Aug. 16.

Although generally distributed in suitable habitat throughout nearly all of the mountains and highlands, the Mourning Warbler has not been recorded as a breeder, to my knowledge, in the three southern tier counties of Chemung, Tioga, and Broome. This is not especially surprising, as the species is also unrecorded as a breeder in the Pennsylvania counties adjacent to them to the south (Poole, 1964: 82). There are apparently no breeding Mourning Warblers recorded for either of the two Mohawk valley counties of Montgomery or Schenectady, and the same is true of *all* the counties east of the Hudson River with their high elevations —Washington, Rensselaer, Columbia, and Dutchess, despite the fact that the species nests directly to the east, in northwestern Massachusetts in the higher Berkshires and Taconics (Griscom and Snyder, 1955: 208)—in fact it has bred at Hancock, Mass., within only one mile of the New York border adjoining Rensselaer Co. Very likely better coverage in the future will produce breeding birds, as Washington Co., in particular, has very few observers.

The species is entirely lacking—as a breeder —from all the southeastern mainland counties of Orange, Rockland, Putnam, and Westchester. In fact, the Mourning Warbler is absent "everywhere" as a breeding species near the coast south of Maine.

Remarks: Probably conspecific with the western *O. tolmiei* (MacGillivray's Warbler). The two forms are very similar in appearance.

Connecticut Warbler
(*Oporornis agilis*)   *

Range: Chiefly central North America; breeds east to extreme western Quebec and south to northern Michigan. Migrates in spring through the Mississippi valley, in fall mainly along the Atlantic coast. Winters in northern South America.

Status: Rare to uncommon, but regular fall migrant, chiefly on or near the coast; occasionally more numerous. Formerly much more numerous on the coast—fairly common to occasionally common. Very rare in spring.

Occurrence: The Connecticut Warbler occurs most often during the latter half of September and the first two weeks of October. At this time, the active observer, if alert and cautious, will see this species regularly in the proper places.

Relatively uncommon inland, it frequents moist, young woodland thickets where swamp maple, shadbush, and *Clethra* (white alder) tower above a rank growth of jewel-weed and other herbs; in drier localities where wooded edges adjoin overgrown weedy fields and pastures; and occasionally in groves of gray birch.

Along the coast it is partial to dense tangles of ragweed, sunflowers, and asters, especially in waste areas; and on the outer coast it is found among impenetrable thickets of *Smilax* (catbrier), poison ivy, and bayberry, as confirmed recently by mist-net operations.

There is abundant evidence that the Connecticut Warbler was much more numerous formerly (prior to 1910) and that it has not as yet regained this former abundance. It was eagerly sought by collectors who took many specimens in the late nineteenth century, as well as high mortality at lighthouses during that time that may have caused a decline.

Of more than *180* specimens taken in the New York City area, at least *44* are in the American Museum collection, and *many* others have been recorded in the literature. About *130* were collected between 1880 and 1910, only 30 since then, as there has been much less collecting in recent years.

MAXIMA, early period (prior to 1910): Reported by Dutcher in his field notes as having struck the Fire Island Lighthouse—1877—*57*, Sept. 23; 1883—16, Sept. 30, and 18, Oct. 12 (a notably late migration that fall). During the last few days of September 1900, Cherrie collected ten just south of Jamaica and reported that he had seen "many" others. The number reported above on Sept. 23, 1877, is unique. Most present-day observers would not see that many in ten years.

MAXIMA, recent period (since 1910): *Coastal*—ten hit the Empire State Building, Sept. 11, 1948; 13 struck the Westhampton

Air Force Base tower, Suffolk Co., Oct. 5, 1954. *Inland*—eight, Woodlawn, Erie Co., Sept. 7, 1946 (Nathan and Wright), early for so many; seven, Selkirk Shores, Oswego Co., Oct. 10, 1955.

EXTREME DATES: Aug. 15 (coastal) to Nov. 26 (coastal). Rare before September and after mid-October.

As mentioned above, the Connecticut Warbler is very rare in spring in this state, perhaps less rare in the western portions. There are four undoubted spring specimen records, all from the interior of New York: (1) male, Buffalo, May 30, 1889 (Bergtold), Univ. Colorado Mus. 2784; (2) male, Fleming, Cayuga Co., June 1, 1900 (Wright), CUM 16709; (3) female, McLean bog, near Ithaca, June 4, 1924 (Leffingwell), CUM 1895; (4) female, Springville, Erie Co., May 25, 1929 (Aldrich), BMS 1124. All the above specimens were examined by Lanyon and/or the writer. Determination of females was by wing-tail ratio (Lanyon and Bull, 1967).

EXTREME DATES based on specimens, or singing males identified by experienced observers: May 11 (singing male) to June 4 (specimen).

Remarks: A report in *Audubon Field Notes* (1968, 22: 593) of this species breeding in adjacent Vermont was not corroborated. More than likely it was the Mourning Warbler. The Connecticut Warbler is not known to breed east of western Quebec and Michigan (see **Range).**

Common Yellowthroat
(*Geothlypis trichas*) * B

Range: Nearctic and northern Neotropical regions, breeding from Alaska and Canada to southern Mexico. Winters—in the east—north to South Carolina; rarely to New York and Massachusetts (two specimens in latter state).

Status: Common to abundant coastal migrant, especially in spring; much less numerous inland, but usually common. Rare but regular in winter on the coast, very rare inland. Widespread breeder.

Nonbreeding: Yellowthroats are among our best known, most numerous, and widely distributed warblers.

MAXIMA: *Spring*—250, Central Park, New York City, May 11, 1914 (Helmuth); 150, Prospect Park, Brooklyn, May 14, 1950; 200, Kennedy Airport, Queens Co., May 17, 1964 (Carleton); 133 hit the Fire Island Lighthouse, Suffolk Co., May 19, 1891; 25, Central Park, May 30, 1950 (very late for so many). From 35 to 60 per day (mid-May) per locality represent the inland *spring* maxima.

MAXIMA: *Fall*—71 struck the Empire State Building, New York City, Sept. 14, 1964; 63 hit the tower at Westhampton Air Force Base, Suffolk Co., Oct. 5, 1954.

"EXTREME" DATES: Apr. 7 (coastal specimen) to late October, rarely to November and early December (both coastal and inland). Generally rare before May and after October.

Winter: No state specimen known, but reported annually along the coast in recent years with the great increase in feeding stations. At least *11* were reported on the south shore of Long Island from Brooklyn to Montauk during late December and early January (Christmas count period) 1969–1970. Inland, *two* spent the winter at feeders in Watkins Glen, Schuyler Co., 1967–1968.

Breeding: This species breeds throughout in wet, moist, and occasionally dry areas in thickets, dense shrubbery, and undergrowth in open woodland. The nest is placed on the ground or, at the most, but a few inches above it, exceptionally to 18 inches.

Egg clutches in 24 New York nests range from three to five: three eggs (three nests); four eggs (17 nests); five eggs (four nests).

EGG DATES: May 15 to July 12.

Nestlings: June 2 to Aug. 22; fledglings: June 15 to Sept. 11.

Banding: One banded in early September 1964, on the south shore of Long Island, was caught by a cat the following month on the east coast of Florida.

Remarks: No northeastern subspecies ("*brachydactylus*") is recognized here—there is much overlap in color and mensural characters between northern and southern individuals, making the two populations inseparable.

Yellow-breasted Chat
(*Icteria virens*)   *   B

Range: Southern Nearctic region, breeding from extreme southern Canada (very local) to central Mexico in the west and to the Gulf states in the east. Winters chiefly in Middle America, but in recent years rarely though regularly north to the coasts of New York and Massachusetts.

Status: Uncommon coastal migrant and rare in winter there. Local breeder on Long Island and elsewhere near the coast, but rare northward and westward. Absent at higher elevations.

Nonbreeding: Chats are adept at skulking and keeping out of sight and, during the migrations, are difficult to observe. Usually not more than one or two are seen in a day, but mist-netting operations and casualties at building obstructions give us a true picture of density figures.

MAXIMA: All in *fall*—five, Empire State Building, New York City, Sept. 11, 1948; six, Mitchel Air Force Base tower, Nassau Co., Sept. 19, 1950; four netted and banded, Tiana Beach, Suffolk Co., Sept. 25, 1964; four, Montauk Point Lighthouse, Oct. 7, 1950.

EXTREME DATES: Apr. 26 (coastal) and Apr. 30 (inland) to Nov. 19 (coastal) and Nov. 29 (inland feeder). Rare before mid-May and after mid-October.

Winter: Formerly (prior to 1950) very rare along the coast, but since then regular in small numbers, chiefly at feeding stations. It is still extremely rare at this season, however, away from coastal areas. There is at least one winter specimen—Orient, Suffolk Co., Feb. 7, 1950 (Latham), NYSM 25438.

Breeding: The Yellow-breasted Chat, an aberrant warbler—if it is actually a parulid—has about the same distribution today as in Eaton's time (1914), namely its northernmost known breeding limits are at or near Holland Patent, Oneida Co., and Granville, Washington Co.

Belknap (*in litt.*) states that for Jefferson Co. there is no proof of breeding, merely three records of single birds only, two in June, one in July, in various years.

Breeding densities: *Upstate*—eight pairs in the Ithaca region, 1909 (Allen). *Downstate*—12 pairs within four miles, between Chappaqua and Mount Kisco, Westchester Co., 1937 (Pangburn); 12 pairs, Fisher's Island, Suffolk Co., 1958 (Ferguson); "colony" of between five and eight pairs on a 125-acre abandoned, overgrown golf course, near Northport, Suffolk Co., 1961 (Mudge).

On Long Island, at least, this species is often found associating with White-eyed Vireos.

Chats nest in almost impenetrable thorn scrub and dense thickets of catbrier, wild rose, blackberry, hawthorn, as well as in other plant types without thorns such as hazel, dogwood, bayberry, viburnum, etc., and also in saplings of maple, oak, cherry, and locust. Its unwarbler-like song often betrays its nesting place, however.

The nest is placed near the ground (once on the ground) from three inches up to five feet.

Although among the more difficult nests to locate, they were favorites of the early-day egg collectors and, as a result, considerable data exist for Chat nests in the state, as may be seen from the following.

Egg clutches in 37 New York nests range from three to five, as follows: three eggs (nine nests); four eggs (26 nests); five eggs (two nests).

EGG DATES: May 25 to July 13.

Nestlings: June 8 to July 17; fledglings: June 22.

Hooded Warbler
(*Wilsonia citrina*)   *   B

Range: Chiefly southeastern United States, breeding north to central and southeastern New York, Connecticut, and Rhode Island; rarely to extreme southeastern Ontario. Winters in Middle America.

Status: Rare to uncommon migrant. Locally common breeder at low elevations in the lower Hudson valley; the lowland plain of Lake Ontario, as well as to the south and southeast; extreme western New York south and southeast of Buffalo; apparently rare in much of the Finger Lakes area, especially to the west; rare and local in the southwestern portions, but ap-

MAP 139 Hooded
Warbler (*Wilsonia
citrina*) Breeding
distribution

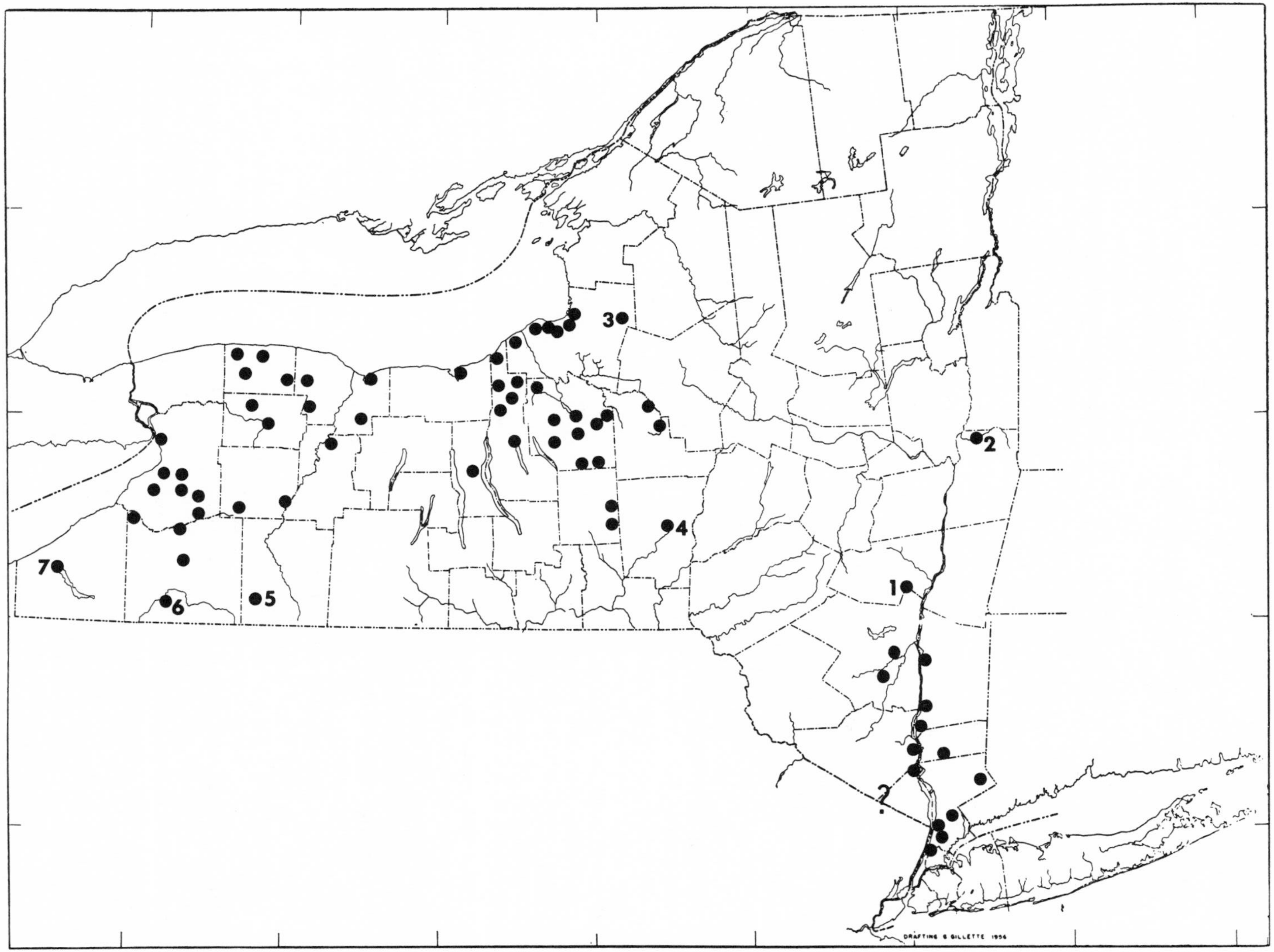

parently absent over much of the southern tier counties; entirely absent from Long Island.

Nonbreeding: This species is rare on migration, except on western Long Island where somewhat less rare. Reports of up to five and six individuals per day in spring and fall from two localities in Erie and Oswego counties are very likely based on local breeders rather than true migrants, as the two localities involved are situated at, or near, the breeding grounds, and are also at, or near, the known northern breeding limits of the species.

MAXIMA, COASTAL: *Spring*—four, Woodmere Woods, Nassau Co., May 6, 1950; five, Prospect Park, Brooklyn, May 12, 1945. Rare in fall.

EXTREME DATES: Apr. 6 (inland) and Apr. 12 (coastal—both after severe southerly storms —to Oct. 18 (coastal) and Nov. 7 (inland); exceptionally to Dec. 3–7, 1954, Northport, Suffolk Co. (Mudge), male photographed in color. Rare before May and after September.

Breeding (see Map 139). The beautiful Hooded Warbler is of peculiarly local and interrupted distribution in the state, and yet in some localities it is not at all rare.

For instance, as many as six breeding pairs each have been found in single localities in northeastern Westchester and southwestern Dutchess counties (Poundridge Reservation and Mt. Beacon respectively); seven pairs at Mayville, Chautauqua Co.; and, according to Benton (1949), "Rathbun took 66 specimens in the summer of 1878 in northern Cayuga and Wayne counties,"—an unusual number!

The habitat varies somewhat in different parts of the state, although generally the species prefers to nest in the undergrowth of moist, rich woodland, chiefly on hillsides. In the lower Hudson valley, mountain laurel thickets are often chosen, whereas in central and western New York, open maple forest with an understory of maple saplings and shrubs is preferred. In the Big Basin area of Allegany State Park, Saunders (1942: 264) stated that Hooded Warblers bred in the undergrowth of both mature oak-hickory and maple-beech forest.

Nests are placed near the ground up to a height of four feet. Egg clutches in 30 New York nests: three eggs (nine nests); four eggs (21 nests).

EGG DATES: May 26 to July 10.

Nestlings: June 14 to Aug. 12; fledglings: July 3 to Sept. 10.

The accompanying map best illustrates the discontinuous breeding distribution of this species in New York. It breeds as far north in the Hudson valley as northern Rensselaer Co. and in central New York to northern Oswego Co. Peripheral localities are indicated by number.

1—Palenville, Greene Co.; 2—Schaghticoke, Rensselaer Co., nest and eggs collected June 16, 1901 (J. P. Ward), NYSM collection; 3—near Fox Brook, south side of Salmon River Reservoir, Oswego Co.; 4—Norwich, Chenango Co.; 5—West Clarksville, Allegany Co., 6—Big Basin, Cattaraugus Co.; 7—Mayville, Chautauqua Co.

Numbers 4 through 7 represent relatively high-altitude localities for this "southern" breeding warbler.

Wilson's Warbler (*Wilsonia pusilla*)   *

Range: Nearctic region; in the east breeding south to central Maine and the northern portions of New Hampshire and Vermont, but *not* New York.

Status: Uncommon to fairly common migrant, occasionally more numerous. Numbers fluctuate markedly. Apparently more numerous inland than on the coast.

Occurrence: Despite the fact that the bog-inhabiting Wilson's Warbler breeds south to central Maine and the northern sections of New Hampshire and adjacent Vermont, no summering—let alone breeding—has been substantiated in New York to date. Reports in mid-summer from the Adirondacks are unconfirmed.

In spring this species is usually one of the later warblers to migrate.

MAXIMA: *Spring*—eight, Prospect Park, Brooklyn, May 14, 1950; 35, Sandy Pond, Oswego Co., May 20, 1969; 20, Manitou, Monroe Co., May 28, 1952; 18, same locality, June 1, 1968.

MAXIMA: *Fall*—20, Sandy Pond, Sept. 3, 1960; ten, Prospect Park, Sept. 16, 1964; ten, Sandy Pond, Sept. 20, 1963.

EXTREME DATES: *Spring*—Apr. 29 (coastal) to June 10 (inland). *Fall*—July 26 (coastal) to *seven* November dates (all coastal) to Nov. 30. Casual on Dec. 19, 1961, Stony Point, Rockland Co. (Kennedy). Rare before mid-May, before mid-August, and after mid-October.

Remarks: Winters chiefly from Mexico to Panama. Accidental at this season in Maryland (specimen). A male was present at a feeding station, Katonah, Westchester Co., from Nov. 30 to Dec. 25, 1936 (Wheeler).

A report of a female found dead at Endwell, Broome Co., Mar. 15, 1957 (Bemont), and supposedly in the CUM collection (*Kingbird,* 1957, 7: 25), is *not* there now (S. A. Temple, *in litt.*).

Canada Warbler
(*Wilsonia canadensis*)   *   B

Range: Chiefly central and eastern North America, breeding from southern Canada to northern New Jersey and southeastern New York, and in the higher mountains to northern Georgia; rarely to the coast of southern New England, and once on Long Island (1971). Winters from Honduras to southern Peru.

Status: Common to very common migrant, especially along the coast. Widespread breeder at higher elevations.

Nonbreeding: The Canada Warbler is one of the commoner members of this family, appearing in largest numbers during late May and again in August. It is usually much more numerous on the coast than inland.

MAXIMA, COASTAL: *Spring*—25, Central Park, New York City, May 7, 1964, unusually early for so many; 55, Van Cortlandt Park, Bronx Co., May 13, 1964 (a notably early spring); 50, Mill Neck, Nassau Co., May 20, 1956; 75, Central Park, May 23, 1954; 49 netted and banded, Huntington, Suffolk Co., May 28, 1967.

MAXIMA, COASTAL: *Fall*—25, Prospect Park, Brooklyn, Aug. 12, 1953; 74 netted and banded, Huntington, Aug. 20, 1964; 35, Far Rockaway, Queens Co., Aug. 23, 1958.

MAXIMA, INLAND: *Spring*—24, Camillus Valley, Onondaga Co., May 19, 1966; 75, Selkirk Shores, Oswego Co., May 25, 1960.

MAXIMA, INLAND: *Fall*—six dead at Albany Airport ceilometer, Sept. 15, 1960.

EXTREME DATES: *Spring*—Apr. 23 (coastal) and Apr. 29 (inland) to June 12 (coastal).

EXTREME DATES: *Fall*—casual July 1 and July 6 (both coastal); July 26 to Oct. 31 (both coastal), exceptionally to Nov. 13 (coastal).

Rare before mid-May; and before August and after mid-September.

Breeding (see Map 140): Of the northern warblers, this species is the most widely distributed in the state, being found from the higher elevations in the mountains to the bogs and swamps of western New York, and south to the low wooded hills not far north of the upper reaches of New York City. Its habitat too is far more diversified than the other northern breeding warblers.

In the Adirondacks it is found, according to Saunders (1929: 382), along streams in thickets of willow, alder, and elderberry; also in old "burns" of aspen and cherry.

Stoner (1932: 670–672) says that in the Oneida Lake region, in addition to alder and blueberry thickets, it favors mixed hemlock-white cedar bogs.

Scheider (*Kingbird,* 1958, 8: 88) speaking of "region five" (Syracuse, Rome, etc.) states that the Canada Warbler breeds in spruce bogs, alder swamps, hemlock glens, and weedy ravines.

In Allegany State Park, Saunders (1942: 266) found it nesting variously in mixed bogs of tamarack-balsam-black spruce, and in drier locations, such as at the edge of maple-beech-hemlock forest, in young oak-hickory clearings, and also in cherry-aspen thickets.

In the Ithaca region, in the famous, well-worked Sapsucker Woods, Owen (1950) found three pairs nesting in elm-maple-ash swamp with shaded pools of sphagnum moss and a luxuriant growth of ferns and dense low shrubs. In 1960 seven pairs bred in this wooded swamp.

Rosche (1967) in Wyoming Co. met with this species in the undergrowth of mixed wood-

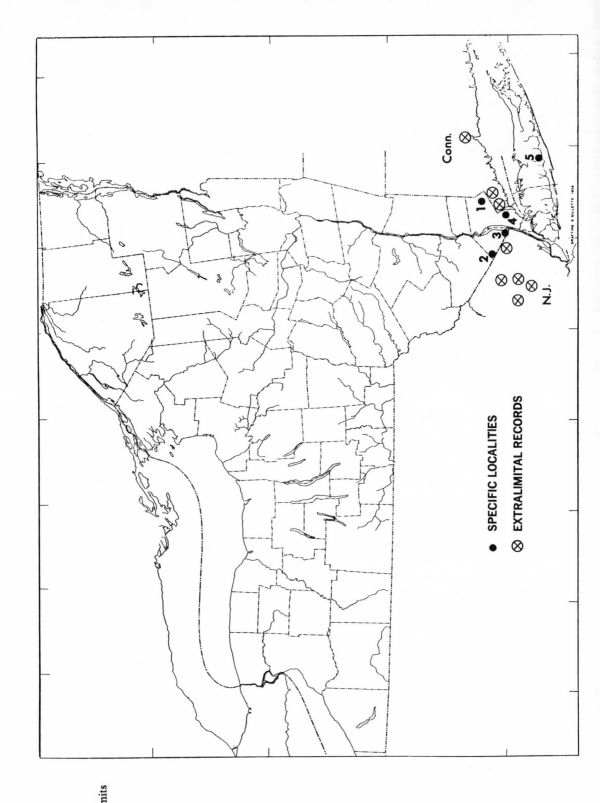

MAP 140 Canada
Warbler (*Wilsonia
canadensis*) Known
southern breeding limits

● SPECIFIC LOCALITIES

⊗ EXTRALIMITAL RECORDS

land especially where hemlock was prevalent; it was common also in bogs and shaded ravines.

In the Catskill region and to the south in portions of Orange and Rockland counties, Canada Warblers occur in hemlock-rhododendron swamps; and finally to the east of the Hudson River, from Dutchess Co. south to Westchester Co., these birds favor rich, moist woodland on hilly slopes covered with mountain laurel.

In this last-named habitat during June 1947, Harry Darrow and the writer found at least five breeding pairs of this northern warbler in the Poundridge Reservation in northeastern Westchester Co., along with six pairs of the southern Hooded Warbler.

This association was observed also in the well-known Bergen Swamp in the Monroe Co. portion during the same year (1947) by members of the Genesee Ornithological Society.

Some other breeding densities are: (1) Tug Hill district of southern Lewis Co.—64 in 14 miles of trail, June 10, 1957 (Scheider, 1959a); (2) Cicero Swamp, Onondaga Co.—26 per mile in 1968 (Rusk and Scheider); (3) Arnot Forest, southeastern Schuyler Co.—33 singing males (Axtell, 1947); (4) East Branch, Delaware Co.—11 breeding pairs in 30 acres in 1970 (Margaret Bowman).

The southernmost known breeding localities in the state are: Rockland Co.—(2) Suffern; (3) Tallman Mtn. Westchester Co.—(1) Poundridge Reservation; (4) Silver Lake Park near White Plains.

A most unusual and completely unexpected find was the discovery of a nest with five young in a wooded swamp on June 21, 1971, by Robert Giffen (in litt.)—of all places—on Long Island at (5) Oakdale, Suffolk Co. (south shore). Mr. Giffen sent me the empty nest and it is now in the AMNH collection. This breeding record is not only the first for Long Island, but also the first for the coastal plain.

Nests of this species are placed on the ground, rarely as high as two feet among bushes, at the base of logs or rocks especially where moss-covered, in earthen banks, or in cavities of stumps.

Egg clutches examined in 17 New York nests were: four eggs (nine nests); five eggs (eight nests).

EGG DATES: May 31 to June 30.

Nestlings: June 14 to July 29; fledglings: June 20 to Aug. 15.

American Redstart
(*Setophaga ruticilla*)   *   B

Range: Nearctic region, in the east breeding south to Georgia and coastal Virginia. Winters in tropical America, rarely north to southern Florida.

Status: Very common *spring* inland migrant; very common to abundant *fall* coastal migrant. Widespread breeder, but rare and local on the coastal plain.

Nonbreeding: This is one of our most numerous warblers, at times outnumbering all others, especially on the coast during late August and early September.

MAXIMA: *Spring*—50, Camillus, Onondaga Co., May 12, 1962; 60, Central Park, New York City, May 23, 1954; 125, Rochester, May 24, 1917; 100, Sandy Pond, Oswego Co., May 27, 1961.

MAXIMA: *Fall*—30, Far Rockaway, Queens Co., Aug. 14, 1954; 150, same locality, Sept. 4, 1952; 300, Jones Beach, Nassau Co., and 200, Mamaroneck, Westchester Co., Sept. 10, 1969; 111 struck the Empire State Building, New York City, Sept. 14, 1964; 50, same locality, Sept. 27, 1970; 25 hit the Westhampton Air Force Base tower, Suffolk Co., Oct. 5, 1954.

EXTREME DATES: Apr. 22 (coastal) and Apr. 28 (inland) to Nov. 4 and 21 (both inland) and Nov. 23 and 30 (both coastal); rarely to Dec. 14, 1967, Keuka, Steuben Co. (several observers). Rare before May and after mid-October.

Winter: Casual, adult male well seen at Inwood Hill Park, New York City, Dec. 10–27, 1931 (Meyers and Cruickshank).

Breeding: The American Redstart breeds commonly in deciduous second-growth woodland, occasionally in evergreen and mixed forest in the mountains, especially where burned over. At the edge of the Tug Hill region, near Osceola, Lewis Co., June 11, 1960, along four miles of an old logging road, 60 singing males were estimated (Scheider).

On Long Island, the following breeding densities were obtained—eastern Suffolk Co.: 25 pairs on Gardiner's Island in 1938; 12 pairs on Fisher's Island in 1965; western Suffolk Co.—

three pairs on Fire Island in the Sunken Forest in 1950, where this species is rare and local during the nesting season.

Nests are placed in vines and saplings from five to 18 feet above ground.

Clutches in 16 New York nests ranged from three to five eggs: three eggs (six nests); four eggs (seven nests); five eggs (three nests).

EGG DATES: May 22 to July 16.

Nestlings: June 4 to Aug. 4; fledglings: June 26 to Aug. 19.

Remarks: No subspecies are recognized here, the alleged color differences in females and juveniles of the northern *"tricolora"* are of average quality only, with considerable individual variation present; males are indistinguishable.

BLACKBIRDS — ICTERIDAE

Twelve species in New York.
Nine breed.

This exclusively American family (about 90 species) contains such diverse types as the Bobolink (*Dolichonyx oryzivorus*), meadowlarks, orioles, caciques, oropendolas, blackbirds, grackles, and cowbirds. As for the American orioles, they are in no way related to their Old World namesakes—the orioles—which belong to the Oriolidae.

Icterids are found from Alaska and Canada to southern South America but are most numerous in the tropics.

Members of this family in New York are diverse in their nest sites and breeding habitats: the Bobolink and meadowlarks (*Sturnella*) are ground nesters in open-country grassland; the Red-winged Blackbird (*Agelaius phoeniceus*) often in cattail marshes; Rusty Blackbird (*Euphagus carolinus*) in Adirondack spruce-sphagnum bogs; orioles (*Icterus*) and grackles (*Quiscalus*) in trees; and finally the Cowbird (*Molothrus ater*) in any habitat as long as there are nests of various host species to parasitize.

Bobolink
(*Dolichonyx oryzivorus*)   *   B

Range: North America, breeding from southern Canada to central United States, in the east to the mountains of North Carolina and along the coast to southern New Jersey. Winters chiefly in southern South America.

Status: Common to very abundant fall migrant, especially plentiful on the outer coast; much less numerous in spring, although locally even abundant inland. Widespread breeder, locally common upstate, but has greatly decreased and become rare and local over much of downstate, especially on Long Island.

Nonbreeding: Bobolinks are both diurnal and nocturnal migrants, the diagnostic call note being heard in flight at all times during fall passage. Spectacular numbers may be observed on the southbound flight—particularly on the south side of Long Island—many hundreds seen and heard flying overhead, but comparatively few alighting. They are on their way to the fields and wild rice marshes of the southern states, prior to resuming the long trip to the pampas of southern South America for their winter sojourn.

The return passage in spring is much less impressive, relatively small numbers observed at any one time and rarely in flocks. However, the handsome males in breeding plumage and in song are conspicuous at this season.

MAXIMA, COASTAL: *Spring*—60, Brookhaven, Suffolk Co., May 16, 1960; 100, Lattingtown, Nassau Co., May 16, 1967.

MAXIMA, INLAND: *Spring*—400, Derby Hill, Oswego Co., May 6, 1966; 250, Syracuse, May 12, 1957; 150, Selkirk Shores, Oswego Co., May 25, 1960—a notably late spring.

MAXIMA, INLAND: *Fall*—150, Vischer's Ferry, Saratoga Co., July 27, 1957; *5000,* Montezuma Marshes, Aug. 20 to Sept. 18, 1955 (many observers), feeding on planted millet—an unusual concentration inland; 93, South Dayton, Cattaraugus Co., Sept. 26, 1948, late for so many.

MAXIMA, COASTAL: *Fall—8000,* Mastic, Suffolk Co., Aug. 24, 1912 (J. T. Nichols), within four hours (4 A.M. to 8 A.M.); *5000,* Far Rockaway, Queens Co., Sept. 8, 1953 (Bull), within three hours (7 A.M. to 10 A.M.); 3000, same locality and observer, Sept. 16, 1947, within three hours (9 P.M. to midnight).

EXTREME DATES: Apr. 19 (coastal) and Apr. 23 (inland) to Oct. 25 (inland) and Nov. 2 (coastal). Upstate, at Cortland, one was picked up alive in the snow with an injured wing on Nov. 10, 1961. Another very late individual downstate was collected at Fresh Kills, Staten Island, Nov. 26, 1960 (Jehl), specimen in AMNH collection.

Usually rare before May and after early October.

Breeding: With the destruction of much open habitat—namely grassland—the Bobolink has become a much scarcer breeder than in former times. This is especially true on Long Island where it formerly nested commonly on the vast Hempstead Plains (a natural prairie), as well as on the north shore from Great Neck, Nassau Co., to Orient, Suffolk Co.; and on the south shore (both in fallow fields and on the upper brackish marshes—where dry—adjacent to the salt meadows) from Idlewild, Queens Co. to Amagansett, Suffolk Co.

It is best known as an inhabitant of lush grassy fields and meadows on the uplands, planted to alfalfa, clover, and various grains. It is perhaps most numerous in the agricultural districts of the Finger Lakes region and south of the Lake Ontario plain.

Elon H. Eaton found 25 pairs breeding in 300 acres of grassland, near Geneva, Ontario Co., in 1932.

The oologist, E. G. Tabor, collected 31 sets of Bobolink eggs within a three-year period (1888–1890) in the vicinity of Meridian, Cayuga Co., a noteworthy feat, as the nest of this species is usually difficult to locate—on the ground hidden in tall grass.

Clutch size in 44 New York nests (including the 31 nests collected by Tabor) ranged from four to seven eggs: four eggs (11 nests); five eggs (25 nests); six eggs (seven nests); seven eggs (one nest).

EGG DATES: May 18 to June 20.

Nestlings: May 30 to July 20; fledglings: no New York data available.

Eastern Meadowlark
(*Sturnella magna*)   *   B

Range: Nearctic and Neotropical regions, breeding chiefly in eastern North America from extreme southern Canada to the Gulf states and Cuba; and from Mexico to northern South America. Winters nearly throughout the breeding range.

Status: Sedentary and migratory. Common to locally abundant migrant. Fairly common inland in winter in the milder districts, more numerous on the coast. Widespread breeder.

Nonbreeding: This species is sometimes seen in impressive numbers on spring passage along the Lake Ontario shore. It was formerly more numerous on the coastal salt meadows in winter, but in recent years the concentrations have been much smaller.

MAXIMA: *Spring*—300, Manitou, Monroe Co., Mar. 15, 1964; 465, Derby Hill, Oswego Co., Mar. 27, 1968; 550, same locality, Apr. 4, 1969; 350, same locality, Apr. 16, 1960.

MAXIMA: *Fall*—200, Jones Beach, Nassau Co., Oct. 20, 1964; 200, Holland Patent, Oneida Co., Oct. 24, 1967.

MAXIMA: *Winter*—375, Orient region, Suffolk Co., Dec. 25, 1911 (Latham); 50, Wellsville, Allegany Co., Dec. 20, 1963; 20, Lancaster, Erie Co., Jan. 29, 1966.

Migrants usually arrive in early March and depart in late October.

Breeding: Meadowlarks nest on the ground in grassy fields and meadows, building a domed or arched-over nest. Many former breeding haunts, especially on Long Island, have disappeared because of housing developments.

Clutches in 26 New York nests range from four to six eggs, as follows: four eggs (12 nests); five eggs (11 nests); six eggs (three nests).

EGG DATES: May 9 to Aug. 1 (two broods). Nestlings: May 24 to Aug. 12; fledglings: June 5 to Aug. 24.

Western Meadowlark
(*Sturnella neglecta*) * B

Range: Chiefly western North America, breeding from southern Canada to northern Mexico, locally east to Ontario and Ohio, and very rarely to New York, but extending its range eastward. Mostly sedentary.

Status: Rare spring and summer visitant to western New York, very rare in the southeastern portion, and unreported on Long Island. Has bred twice.

Nonbreeding: The first definite record of the Western Meadowlark in New York was that of a specimen collected near North Hamlin, Monroe Co., Apr. 18, 1948 (A. S. Klonick), RMAS 4; specimen examined by W. E. Lanyon and the writer.

Starting with the early 1950s singing individuals, believed to be this species, were recorded from various areas in western New York almost on an annual basis. In fact, from 1953 on, these birds were not only reported yearly, but in some years—notably 1963— Western Meadowlarks, including some whose songs were tape-recorded, appeared in seven different localities. Practically all individuals of this species have been recorded during the four months of April, May, June, and July— when the birds are likely to be in song or uttering the characteristic call note, both very different from those of the Eastern Meadowlark. Nevertheless, on appearance, the two look very much alike—sibling species.

Breeding (see Map 141): Western Meadowlarks apparently have bred in New York on two occasions—(1) between Manitou and Braddock's Bay, Monroe Co., 1957 (Miller, *Kingbird*, 1958, 7: 115). A male was heard singing first on Apr. 19, and was seen subsequently in the company of a presumed female giving the "western" call note. This pair was continually present throughout the spring and summer, but the nest was not searched for, so as "not to disturb the birds." However, on Aug.

25, an adult heard giving the "typical" call was observed "feeding young out of the nest."

(2) near Bangall, Dutchess Co., 1962 (Jones, *Kingbird*, 1963, 13: 152–153); see also Lanyon (1966). On June 18 a singing male of this species and a presumed female Eastern Meadowlark were observed "together" in an open hayfield. The pair was watched closely and on June 23 an arched-over ground nest of dry grass contained five young. On June 26 the young were about "ready to fledge" and, together with both adults, were captured for study and placed in an aviary (Lanyon, *op. cit.*). The hybridization proved successful.

The accompanying map shows these two breeding localities (1957, 1962), plus four extralimital Canadian breeding sites, plus 22 additional localities in New York where singing birds were reported, but breeding not proved. In all instances birds were present from one week to as much as several months.

Of the following 22 localities, all but five were recorded since 1961: Chautauqua Co. —(1) near Dunkirk. Erie Co.—(2) Marilla. Genesee Co.—(3) Batavia. Monroe Co.— (4) Hamlin; (5) Parma Center and nearby Hilton and Spencerport; (6) near Rochester and nearby Greece; (7) Webster. Livingston Co.—(8) Retsof; (9) Lima. Yates Co.—(10) Guyanoga—song and call notes tape-recorded; (11) Penn Yan. Steuben Co.—(12) Keuka. Oswego Co.—(13) Lacona; (14) near Selkirk Shores; (15) Phoenix. Onondaga Co. —(16) Brewerton; (17) west shore Otisco Lake; (18) near Tully. Madison Co.—(19) Canastota. Tioga Co.—(20) near Newark Valley. Columbia Co.—(21) near Kinderhook Lake. Orange Co.—(22) Hamptonburgh.

The area in and near Rochester has had the most reports of this species. Western Meadowlarks have penetrated New York from the west, most likely by way of the Niagara Frontier corridor from Ontario.

Yellow-headed Blackbird
(*Xanthocephalus xanthocephalus*) *

Range: Western and central North America, breeding east to northwestern Indiana; rarely and locally in northwestern Ohio and southeastern Ontario. Winters north to southern

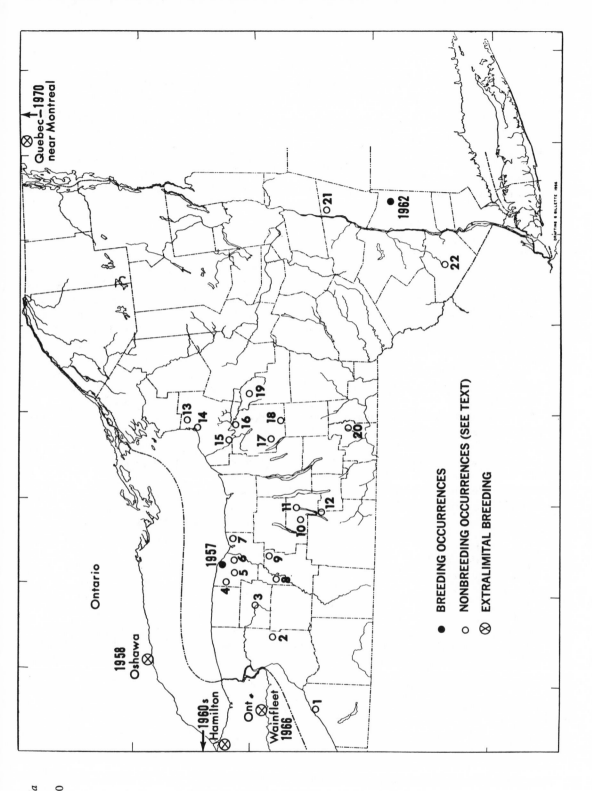

MAP 141 Western
Meadowlark (*Sturnella
neglecta*) Breeding
distribution as of 1970

● BREEDING OCCURRENCES

○ NONBREEDING OCCURRENCES (SEE TEXT)

⊗ EXTRALIMITAL BREEDING

Louisiana. Wanders east to the Atlantic coast from Quebec to Florida.

Status: *Very rare*—there are at least two dozen occurrences of this very striking and conspicuous species in New York. About half of these are from upstate, the remainder from the coastal districts—chiefly Long Island.

Of three known specimens taken in the state, two are extant: (1) Westbury, Nassau Co., date unknown (Hicks), cannot be found; (2) male, Irondequoit Bay, Monroe Co., Sept. 15, 1898 (Werden), NYSM 1142—not the year 1899 as reported by Eaton (1914: 229); (3) female, Orient, Suffolk Co., Sept. 9, 1943 (Latham), NYSM 25463.

A female at the Dewey feeder, Tonawanda, Erie Co., May 8–17, 1967 (many observers), was photographed in color by Mitchell.

EXTREME DATES: *Fall*—Aug. 5 to Oct. 30 (both coastal). *Spring*—Mar. 24 to June 23 (both inland).

A midsummer occurrence is that of a male seen at a feeder at Lacona, Oswego Co., July 6–13, 1969 (Clinch, Rusk, and Scheider).

The only known winter report for the state is a female well observed with other "blackbirds" at a feeder in Hewlett, Nassau Co., Jan. 13–16, 1962 (Sloss and Berliner).

Red-winged Blackbird
(*Agelaius phoeniceus*) * B

Range: Nearctic and Neotropical regions, breeding from southern Canada to the Bahamas, Cuba, and Costa Rica. Winters nearly throughout, but highly migratory in the north; rare in Canada in winter.

Status: Common to very abundant migrant. Locally numerous in winter, especially in the milder southeastern portion. Widespread breeder.

Nonbreeding: The Red-winged Blackbird is surely one of our most abundant birds, perhaps the most numerous native species. It swarms by the tens of thousands during the migrations and in immense concentrations at roosts, especially upstate. In winter it is often common at feeding stations.

MAXIMA: *Fall*—25,000, Jamestown roost,

Aug. 26, 1959; 300,000, Clay Swamp roost, Onondaga Co., Oct. 12, 1960 (many observers); 100,000, Montezuma Marshes, Nov. 9, 1955.

MAXIMA: *Winter*—50,000, near Tivoli (Cruger's Island marshes), Dutchess Co., Dec. 28, 1963 (*fide* Meanley).

MAXIMA: *Spring*—100,000, Montezuma, Mar. 22, 1958; 100,000, Manitou, Monroe Co., Apr. 4, 1956; 80,000, Derby Hill, Oswego Co., Apr. 9, 1961; 45,000, same locality, Apr. 21, 1970.

Breeding: This ubiquitous species breeds in marshes, open swamps, and at their edges, and in upland grassy fields, often some distance from water. The nests in the last situation are placed on the ground, those in marshes from a few inches to several feet above water in cattails, *Phragmites,* grass tussocks, buttonbush (*Cephalanthus*), willows, alders, and even in *Spartina* growth in coastal salt marshes. Nests in bushes and trees range as high as 12 feet above ground and have been found in such diverse types as spruce, pine, elderberry, hawthorn, witch hazel, lilac, cherry, viburnum, blackberry, swamp rose, and salt marsh bushes (*Baccharis* and *Iva*). For a note and photograph of a pensile nest, see *Wilson Bull.* (1942, 54: 255–256).

Some breeding densities in New York are: 11 nests in 17 acres on Great Gull Island, Suffolk Co., 1967—all in bayberry (Hays); 14 pairs in 25 acres of coastal scrub, at Tobay Sanctuary, Nassau Co., 1967 (Enders); 70 pairs in 19 acres of cattail marsh at Van Cortlandt Park, Bronx Co., 1965 (Heath and Zupan).

Allen (1914) found 51 nests in 450 acres in the Renwick (Ithaca) cattail marsh in 1910. Nests ranged from eight to ten inches above water. Most nests contained from three to four eggs, some had five and rarely as many as six.

In 45 other New York nests there is the following breakdown: three eggs (14 nests); four eggs (26 nests); five eggs (five nests).

EGG DATES: Apr. 26 to July 9.

Nestlings: May 21 to July 19; fledglings: June 20 to July 30.

Banding (see Map 142): Of numerous nestlings banded at Branchport, Yates Co., through the years by C. F. Stone and V. Burch, 28 were recovered the following win-

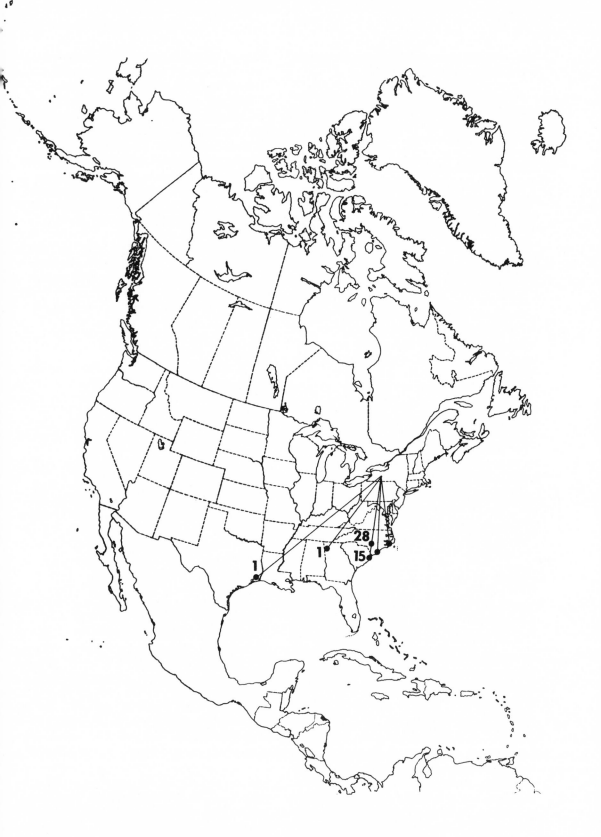

MAP 142   Red-winged Blackbird (*Agelaius phoeniceus*) Banding recoveries

ters in North Carolina, 15 in South Carolina, and one each in Georgia and Texas.

Subspecies: The race *arctolegus* (larger than nominate race) breeds to the north and west of nominate *phoeniceus,* and has occurred in central New York. Parkes (1952a) listed seven specimens of *arctolegus* from Cayuga and Tompkins counties in the collections at Cornell University and the University of Michigan. Six of the seven were collected in spring of various years, dates ranging from Mar. 17 to May 8; the seventh was taken in fall on Oct. 23, 1924.

Orchard Oriole
(*Icterus spurius*)   *   B

Range: Eastern and central North America, breeding from extreme southern Canada and northern United States to northern Mexico and the Gulf states. Winters from southern Mexico to northwestern South America.

Status: Rare to uncommon coastal spring migrant. Uncommon and local breeder, but very rare in the extreme north and absent in the mountains.

Nonbreeding: The Orchard Oriole is reported regularly in spring in the warmer portions of the state by the active observer, but even then only one or two individuals are usually recorded on any one day. Occasionally more are seen on the south shore of Long Island.

MAXIMA: five in one tree, Point Lookout, Nassau Co., May 4, 1958; six, Easthampton, Suffolk Co., May 14, 1950.

EXTREME DATES: Apr. 18 (inland) and Apr. 20 (coastal) to Sept. 22 and 27 (both coastal). Rare before May and after August.

Exceptionally late was an immature male present at Riis Park, Queens Co., from Nov. 20 to Dec. 11, 1966 (numerous observers). On the last date the bird was netted, banded, measured, and released (Davis, *Kingbird,* 1967, 17: 84). Winter reports are unsubstantiated.

Breeding (see Map 143): There is evidence that the Orchard Oriole has decreased in the state since about 1920. It was formerly more numerous and widespread in the southeastern sections, especially on Long Island (Bull, 1964: 405), in and around New York City,

and in the lower Hudson and Delaware valleys. Elsewhere it has always been uncommon and local to rare, depending on location.

Although this species has been recorded as breeding in virtually every county in central and western New York, nevertheless in the lowland agricultural counties along the lake plains and Mohawk valley it is a sparse breeder. In the southern tier counties (along the Pennsylvania state line) it is restricted to the river valleys, and is likewise rare and local in the Catskill region—at low elevations only.

The Orchard Oriole is entirely lacking as a breeder at higher altitudes and barely reaches the foothills of the Adirondacks even as a summer visitor. The alleged breeding record at Wilmington, Essex Co., in 1927 (*Auk,* 1931, 48: 606) in the Canadian zone near the "high peak" country is, according to Carleton (*in litt.*), highly unlikely and very probably based on a misidentification.

The accompanying map shows its northernmost known penetration to date, that is, by way of the Hudson-Champlain and St. Lawrence lowlands.

The situation in the extreme eastern portion remains unchanged since Eaton (1914: 237). The map localities (south to north) with dates are: Saratoga Springs, Saratoga Co., 1910—pair bred; Granville, Washington Co., 1890—nest, this locality on the Mettawee River—a tributary of the Hudson—is near the Vermont state line. The following two localities represent specimens taken in summer of the same year (1905) but without evidence of breeding: North Creek, Warren Co., on the upper Hudson River within sight of 3600-foot Gore Mountain; Port Henry, Essex Co., on Lake Champlain.

According to Godfrey (1966: 356) the Orchard Oriole breeds in southeastern Ontario along the St. Lawrence River northeast to at least Gananoque (see map). Directly across the river in Clayton, Jefferson Co., a pair of these birds was present in June 1958. Definite breeding evidence was, however, lacking.

It will thus be seen that this species, quite unlike several other "southern" birds, such as the Rough-winged Swallow and Cardinal, has *not* penetrated the Adirondack foothills. This situation is nicely correlated with prior mention of the Orchard Oriole's decrease not long after the period when it was at its northernmost

MAP 143 Orchard Oriole
(*Icterus spurius*) Known
northern breeding limits

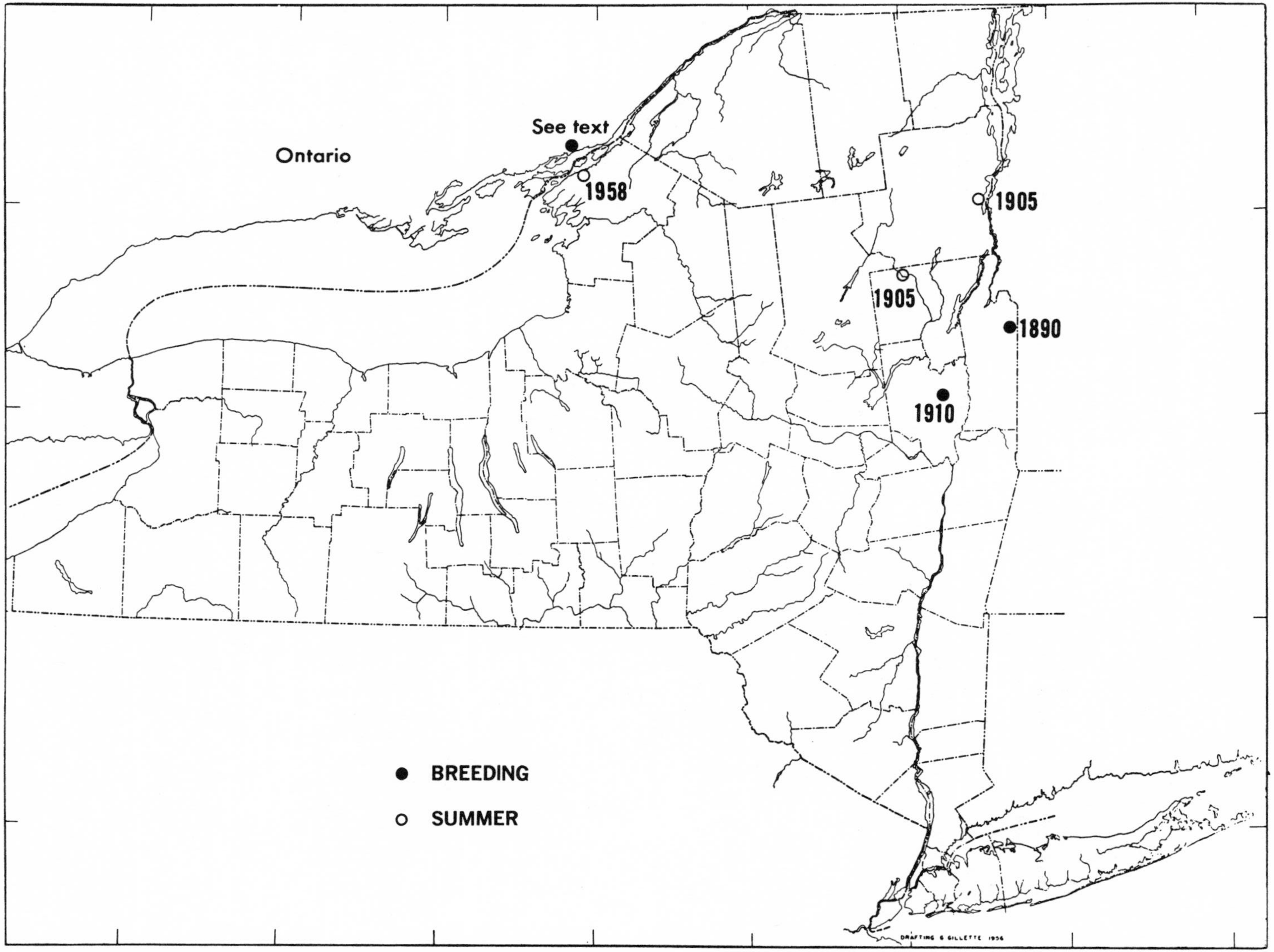

1890

1905

1910

1905

1958

See text

Ontario

● BREEDING

○ SUMMER

known advance in New York (see map). In sum, no evidence of breeding is known within the past *60* years anywhere near the Adirondack district.

This species nests in gardens and orchards, in shade trees in farming country, in suburban estates and nurseries, and in scattered trees near ponds and streams.

The pendant, purse-shaped nest is frequently placed in fruit trees and other deciduous trees, but occasionally in ornamental spruces. Heights of nests range from nine feet above ground to 35 feet, rarely up to 60 feet.

Hough (*in litt.*) described a nest at Stone Ridge, Ulster Co., in 1954, which was 50 feet up in the very top of a medium-sized elm. In the same tree at the same time was a nest of Baltimore Orioles and another of Common Grackles.

Palmer (pers. comm.) speaks of a pair of Orchard Orioles using an old Baltimore Oriole nest, also in an elm, at Delmar, Albany Co., in 1959.

An unusual nest site was that of a pair found by John Taylor (*in litt.*) in 1962 and 1963 at Cold Spring Harbor, Suffolk Co., that nested 15 feet above ground in a privet hedge.

Egg clutches in 16 New York nests: four eggs (12 nests); five eggs (three nests); six eggs (one nest).

EGG DATES: May 18 to June 22.

Nestlings: May 28 to July 26; fledglings: June 19 to Aug. 21.

Baltimore or Northern Oriole
(*Icterus galbula*)   *   B

Range: North America, breeding from southern Canada to southern United States. Winters chiefly from Mexico to northern South America, more rarely in the southern states and, in recent years, very rarely but regularly north to Massachusetts.

Status: Common to occasionally abundant migrant. Very rare to rare, but regular in winter in recent years—especially near the coast. Widespread breeder, but absent in the higher mountains.

Nonbreeding: This beautiful species arrives in spring regularly during the first week in May, usually the first few days of that month, at least in the southern portions. As may be seen from the following figures, the spring flight is mainly inland, the fall passage is coastal.

MAXIMA, INLAND: *Spring*—165, Lake View, Erie Co., May 7, 1961; *550,* Derby Hill, Oswego Co., May 16, 1966 (Haugh), a tremendous flight; 93 netted and banded at Fire Island State Park, Suffolk Co., May 8, 1970 (Davis, Buckley, *et al.*), is a very high number for the *coast* in *spring.*

MAXIMA, COASTAL: *Fall*—200, Tobay Sanctuary, Nassau Co., Aug. 22, 1965; *300* in *two* hours (7 to 9 A.M.), Far Rockaway, Queens Co., Sept. 10, 1969 (Bull and Hirschbein), a spectacular movement.

Winter: With the advent and increase of feeding stations, particularly since the early 1950s, the Baltimore Oriole has become regular and, on Long Island especially, it may be observed merely by visiting the various feeders. In fact, as many as three *different* individuals were present at one feeder at Easthampton, Suffolk Co., all January 1959 (Latham).

Four out of five winter specimens were taken at feeding stations. Two from Long Island are in the AMNH collection. Two others in the BMS collection are from the Buffalo area: Bourne feeder, Hamburg, Erie Co., Dec. 19, 1963; Rose feeder, Lake View, Erie Co., Feb. 12, 1968. A fifth specimen, found dead at the Vosburg feeder at Ithaca, Jan. 19, 1941, is in the CUM collection.

Even in the northern part of the state, in Jefferson Co., an individual was present at the Allen feeder at Watertown from Nov. 22 to Dec. 30, 1966.

Breeding: Although best known as a breeder in roadside elms, the Baltimore Oriole places its hanging, bag-shaped nest in numerous other trees, preferably deciduous, but occasionally in evergreens. However, it nests not uncommonly in fruit trees in orchards and also along streams, lakes, and at the edge of woodland.

Its nest is found from 11 to 35 feet up although Eaton (1914: 242) saw nests as low as seven feet and as high as 60.

Clutches in 11 New York nests: four eggs (three nests); five eggs (five nests); six eggs (three nests).

EGG DATES: May 15 to June 13.

Nestlings: June 6 to July 9; fledglings: June 15 to July 14.

Banding: An individual banded at Poughkeepsie, Dutchess Co., Aug. 30, 1964, was recovered the following December near Houston, Mississippi.

Subspecies: Nominate *galbula* of eastern North America has been discussed above. The western form *bullockii*—"Bullock's" Oriole (male with extensive white wing patch, black of head restricted mainy to crown and throat; female duller than female *galbula,* underparts much whiter) is treated here as conspecific, following Mayr and Short (1970: 78). Hybridization is frequent over a broad zone of sympatry in the Great Plains region.

In New York there are only three records, all from Long Island, either *bullockii* or hybrids.

(1) Immature male at the Robinson feeder, Eastport, Suffolk Co., from Dec. 12, 1963, to Mar. 4, 1964, banded and color-photographed by Wilcox; color photos examined and compared with skins at the American Museum (see also *Ebba News,* 1964, 27: 58).

(2) Adult male at the Sternberg feeder, Woodmere, Nassau Co., from early January to Apr. 2, 1966, color-photographed by Dignan; photos on file, AMNH collection (see also *Kingbird,* 1968, 18: 122).

(3) Female netted and collected at Fire Island State Park, Suffolk Co., Nov. 30, 1969 (Davis), AMNH 793547. This specimen was determined by Short (*in litt.*) as nearest to *bullockii,* but "possibly *bullockii* x *galbula*"; memorandum on file with specimen.

The record of a specimen, alleged to be *bullockii* and mentioned by Eaton (1914: 242), is not satisfactory. The individual was taken somewhere in Onondaga Co., May 17, 1875 (Dakin), but the specimen is lost. Neither Eaton himself nor any other competent ornithologist examined it.

Rusty Blackbird
(*Euphagus carolinus*)   *   B

Range: Northern portions of the Nearctic region, breeding in Alaska and Canada, reaching the United States only in the extreme northern parts of New York and New England (chiefly in the mountains). Winters mainly in the southern states, but sparingly north to extreme southern Canada.

Status: Very common to locally abundant migrant in western New York; much less numerous eastward and relatively uncommon in southeastern portions. Rare and local but regular in winter, chiefly near the coast. Uncommon breeder in the Adirondacks.

Nonbreeding: Rusty Blackbirds generally are found in wooded swamps and other wet habitats on migration. They occasionally visit feeding stations in winter, but even at that season prefer aquatic surroundings.

MAXIMA: *Spring*—1000, Waterloo, Seneca Co., Mar. 10, 1955; 1000, Clay Swamp, Onondaga Co., Apr. 23, 1959; 500, Manitou, Monroe Co., Apr. 30, 1960.

MAXIMA: *Fall*—1000, Jamestown roost, Chautauqua Co., Sept. 27, 1957; 2000, Riverside, Chautauqua Co., Nov. 12, 1967 (Sundell). A report of 6000 in the Oak Orchard Swamp area, Oct. 20, 1935 (Verrill), represents an aggregation of several estimates at various places.

MAXIMA: *Winter*—up to 25–30 at several coastal localities; eight, Ling Road Swamp, Monroe Co., winter of 1955–1956, appears to be the high count upstate.

EXTREME DATES: Sept. 6 (inland) and Sept. 9 (coastal) to May 26 (coastal) and May 29 (inland). Rare before mid-September and after mid-May. Migrants usually arrive during late February and depart by early December.

Breeding (see Map 144): The Rusty Blackbird is one of a number of species whose southernmost known breeding limits are in the Adirondack district. In that region these birds are to be found nesting in or near spruce-sphagnum swamps, bogs with alder and willow thickets, in the vicinity of beaver ponds with dead standing timber, and on wooded islands in lakes.

The nest is placed at low heights above the ground or water level, in the few New York nests discovered, from one to five feet up in spruce saplings and once in a winterberry bush (*Ilex verticillata*).

In seven New York nests, four eggs apiece were found in six nests and five eggs in one nest.

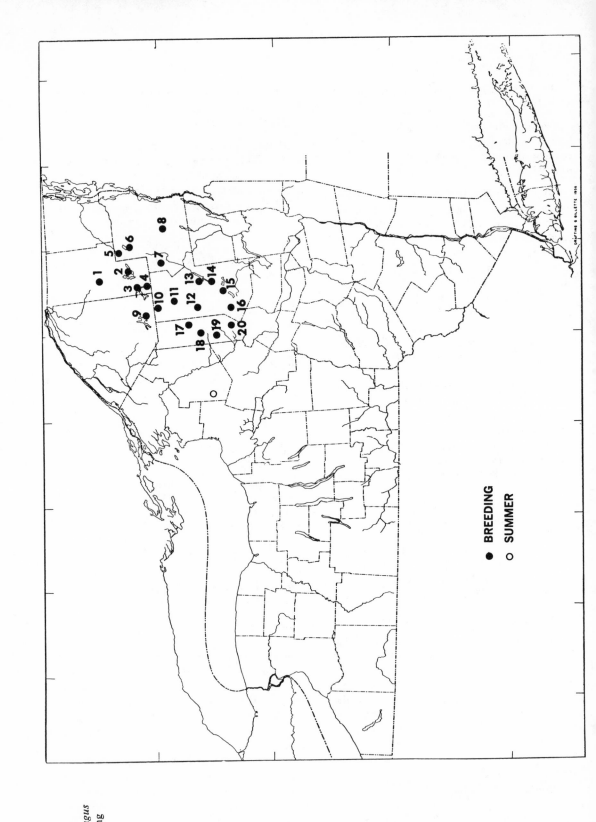

MAP 144 Rusty
Blackbird (*Euphagus
carolinus*) Breeding
distribution

● BREEDING

○ SUMMER

EGG DATES: May 7 to June 15.

Nestlings: May 30 to July 8; fledglings: July 7 to July 24.

The following 20 New York breeding localities are: Franklin Co.—(1) Madawaska; (2) Little Weller Pond near Middle Saranac Lake; (3) near Tupper Lake (village); (4) Little Simon Pond. Essex Co.—(5) Bloomingdale; (6) Chubb River Swamp; (7) Wolf Pond; (8) Elk Lake. St. Lawrence Co.—(9) Barber Point, Cranberry Lake. Hamilton Co.—(10) Sabattis; (11) Eldon Pond, Raquette Lake; (12) Falls Pond; (13) Indian Lake (west side at center); (14) Indian Lake (south end); (15) Fawn Lake; (16) Pine Lake. Herkimer Co.—(17) North Branch of Moose River near Big Moose Lake; (18) Second Lake near Old Forge; (19) near Chub Pond; (20) near Wilmurt and nearby Black Creek Lake.

Several birds were present in the Tug Hill district at Monteola Bog (see map), in southwestern Lewis Co., June 12, 1966 (Rusk), but no breeding evidence was obtained.

Banding: Six individuals banded by Burtch and Stone in fall (all during October) of various years at Branchport, Yates Co., were recovered during late fall or early the following winter at inland localities in Tennessee, South Carolina (three), Georgia, and Mississippi.

Remarks: The very slightly differentiated form "*nigrans*" from the Canadian maritime provinces is not recognized here.

Brewer's Blackbird
(*Euphagus cyanocephalus*) *

Range: Chiefly western North America, in recent years extending its breeding range eastward to southeastern Ontario (near Oshawa, 1968); in migration and winter east to North Carolina. Vagrant in New York.

Status: *Very rare*—one proved record—a male collected at the Andrle feeding station, Hamburg, Erie Co., Dec. 14, 1966, BMS 5077.

During 1953 birds reported to be this species were observed at two localities: (1) two at a feeder, Monticello, Sullivan Co., from Sept. 26 to Oct. 10 (Niven); (2) a male with

livestock in a barnyard, one mile east of Kiantone, Chautauqua Co., Dec. 26 (Beal and Sundell).

Another male was studied carefully at Somerset, Niagara Co., Apr. 23, 1967 (Curry), as was a female at a feeder at Hamburg, May 16, 1970 (Bourne).

Still another observation—on Long Island—a male and, either a female or immature male, with both Rusty and Red-winged blackbirds for comparison, carefully studied at Point O'Woods, Fire Island, Suffolk Co., Oct. 17, 1970 (S. V. Hopkins). Finally, a male was well seen at a feeder, Pelham, Westchester Co., Dec. 30–31, 1970 (A. B. Klots). Both observers were previously familiar with Brewer's Blackbird in the west.

Other reports are considered unsatisfactory, either because details were lacking or the observers were unfamiliar with the differences between this species and the Rusty Blackbird. In fall, iridescent male Rusty Blackbirds are frequently misidentified as Brewer's Blackbirds. Immatures of both forms have dark eyes and thus would be indistinguishable from female Brewer's Blackbirds.

Boat-tailed Grackle
(*Quiscalus major*)

Range: Gulf and Atlantic coasts from Louisiana east to Florida and north to southern New Jersey, the race *torreyi* (iris pale yellow rather than brownish) breeding along the Atlantic coast in salt marshes from Georgia north to southern New Jersey, where first reported breeding in 1952.

Status: *Casual*—the only confirmed record north of southern New Jersey is that of a male that appeared repeatedly at the Berman and Sorman feeding stations, Far Rockaway, Queens Co., Long Island, during *five* successive years, 1967–1971, and once at the writer's feeder during a sleet storm. This male arrived as early as Feb. 24 (with Common Grackles) and departed as late as Nov. 20. It associated with Common Grackles much of the time and fed on lawns and in trees, also perched on rooftops and television antennae where it called frequently during the daylight hours. Its nightly roosting place was believed to be in nearby salt marshes where it was observed at dusk on at least two occasions. This individual was studied by hundreds of observers and a number of photographs were taken, including one by Mrs. Sorman—photo on file, AMNH collection. Another photo by Joanne Trimble was published in the *Kingbird* (1968, 18: 182), showing direct comparison with a male Common Grackle. For further details, see Bull (1970: 43–44).

A female observed at Brookhaven, Suffolk Co., Sept. 1, 1954 (Puleston), the day after hurricane "Carol," is believed correct.

Remarks: Following Selander and Giller (1961) *C. major* is treated as a separate species from the southwestern United States and Neotropical *C. mexicanus,* the Great-tailed Grackle. Blake (in "Peters," 1968: 189) also recognized these two species; he is also followed here in the use of the genus *Quiscalus* rather than *"Cassidix."* Selander *et al.* (*Condor,* 1969, 71: 435–436) mentioned a further eastward breeding extension of *mexicanus* along the Gulf coast of Louisiana into that of *major,* thus widening the zone of sympatry.

Common Grackle
(*Quiscalus quiscula*)   *   B

Range: Central and eastern North America, breeding from southern Canada south to Texas and Florida (for details, see **Subspecies**). Winters rarely north to extreme southern Canada.

Status: Common to very abundant migrant, especially inland. Locally common in winter along the coast, much less numerous inland. Common breeder statewide, but rare at higher elevations.

Nonbreeding: This species is very numerous upstate both spring and fall, whereas near the coast very large flights are confined to the autumn season. In winter, however, it is regular in small numbers on the coast and is relatively scarce inland. Of the three widespread black icterids, it is the least numerous in winter, considerably outnumbered by Cowbirds, and greatly exceeded by Red-winged Blackbirds.

MAXIMA: *Spring*—25,000, Manitou, Monroe Co., Mar. 29, 1960; 100,000, Derby Hill,

Oswego Co., Apr. 9, 1961 (Scheider, *et al.*); 60,000, same locality, Apr. 22, 1967.

MAXIMA: *Fall*—10,000, Jamestown, Chautauqua Co. (roost), Sept. 23, 1968 (Beal); 10,000, Orient, Suffolk Co., Sept. 29, 1951; 100,000, Clay Swamp, Onondaga Co. (roost), Oct. 12, 1960 (many observers); 75,000, Catskill, Greene Co., Oct. 13, 1965 (Sabin, *et al.*); 50,000, Derby Hill, Oct. 28, 1967; 10,000, Waterloo, Seneca Co., Nov. 28, 1963.

In winter more than 200 were estimated on the Northern Nassau Christmas count, Dec. 29, 1968. Upstate the maxima were only nine each at Buffalo and Watkins Glen, also in late December 1968.

Breeding: Common Grackles nest singly or in small colonies, preferably wherever tall ornamental conifers occur, especially spruce and pine. Thus they are most numerous in the suburbs, parks, golf courses, estates, nurseries, and around farms. This decided preference for evergreens in which to nest applies throughout the state and is also true for the wilder areas.

Speaking of the Adirondack region, Saunders (1929: 429) mentioned that this species bred chiefly in black spruce and occasionally in holes in dead tree stumps.

Rosche (1967) referring to Wyoming Co., and Axtell (1947) for Chemung and Schuyler counties, both stated a partiality for ornamental and "plantation" conifers, the latter observer also finding them occasionally in deciduous growth in river bottoms.

Hamilton (*Auk,* 1951, 68: 214), relative to the Ithaca area, stated that on high ground Norway spruce and red pine were favored. He found ten nests in a thick stand of the latter in one-half acre. In another stand of 20 Norway spruce were seven grackle nests and nests of Green Herons and Mourning Doves, often within a few feet of the grackle nests. In low, wet places, Hamilton stated that grackles ". . . occasionally build . . . in dead cattail stalks in the same habitat chosen by Red-winged Blackbirds." And further, ". . . also build thirty or more feet high in [wild] grape tangles or willows."

An unusual location was described by Benton (*Kingbird,* 1961, 11: 201) of a grackle nest at Tomhannock Reservoir, Rensselaer Co. This nest, "in the metalwork of a steel bridge,

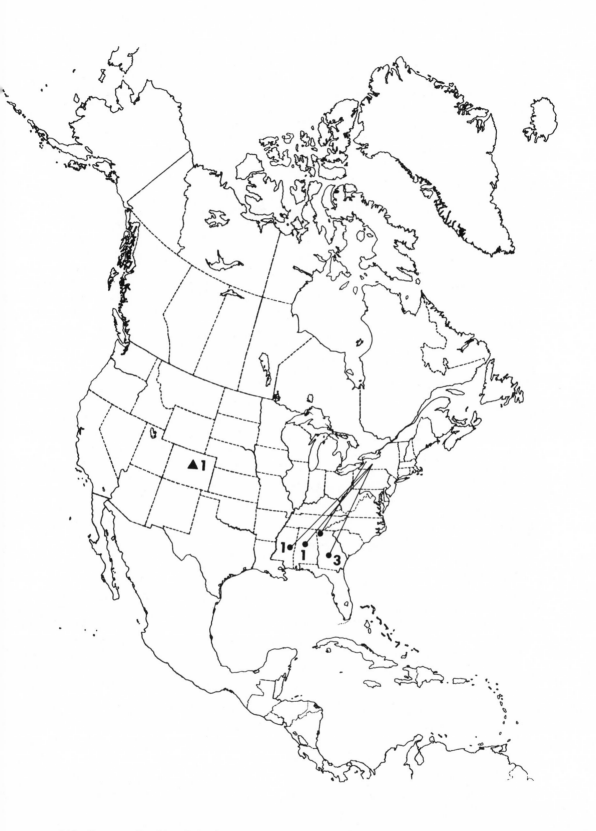

MAP 145   Common Grackle (*Quiscalus quiscula*) Banding recoveries

. . . was hidden in a recess at the side of the bridge and was surrounded by girders." Amadon (oral comm.) has seen these birds nesting on the "ledges of a brick house" near Franklinville, Cattaraugus Co.

Clark (*Prothonotary,* 1971, 37: 158) reported a nest and eggs in a Wood Duck box at Farmersville Station, Cattaraugus Co.

Probably the most unique site was that of three grackle nests found by Frank M. Chapman in the side of an *active* Osprey nest on Gardiner's Island on eastern Long Island on June 3, 1901. Chapman collected the entire structure for a habitat group which is on exhibit in the American Museum of Natural History.

Heights of nests ranged from only four feet in a willow over water, up to fifty feet in a pine.

Egg clutches in 35 New York nests: three eggs (five nests); four eggs (14 nests); five eggs (12 nests); six eggs (four nests).

EGG DATES: Apr. 12 to June 4.

Nestlings: May 3 to June 28; fledglings: May 18 to July 29.

Subspecies: Two occur in the state—(1) the race *stonei* (considerably larger than nominate *quiscula* of the south) is at its northern limits in our region, breeding only on western Long Island, in New York City proper, and in the extreme lower Hudson valley. Intermediates of this and the next race occur on eastern Long Island, in the Hudson valley north to about Troy, and in the Delaware and Susquehanna valleys northwest to about Binghamton.

(2) The grackles breeding in the balance of New York and in central and northern New England belong to the race *versicolor* (males with the back uniformly bronze-colored rather than the purple and blue iridescence of *stonei*).

Based on a number of state specimens taken in winter, the race *versicolor* prevails, as would be expected.

Banding (see Map 145): Of five individuals banded during the summer months in western New York, *all* presumably migrated along the mountain ridges in a southwesterly direction and were recovered the following fall or winter as shown on the map (three in Georgia and one each in Alabama and Mississippi).

Still another grackle (fledged juvenile) banded on July 5, 1964, at Wilton, Saratoga

Co., by P. J. Garland, was found dead on May 6, 1969, in Denver, Colorado. This information was kindly forwarded to me by Mr. Garland in a letter dated Aug. 23, 1970. See also *Ebba News* (1970, 33: 190) which, however, does not mention either date of recovery or age of bird when banded.

Two banded grackles each lived for 11 years.

Brown-headed Cowbird
(*Molothrus ater*) * B

Range: North America, breeding from southern Canada to northern Mexico and the Gulf states. Winters throughout, but scarce in the extreme north and at higher elevations generally.

Status: Common to very abundant inland migrant; locally abundant in winter at coastal roosts. Widespread breeder.

Nonbreeding: Cowbirds are among our most familiar and, at times, numerous species in open country, often following cattle and other livestock for insect food in pastures and fields. They may also be seen along roadsides feeding in short grass fields, and on lawns, golf courses, and airports. In winter this species is often a visitor at feeding stations, occasionally becoming very tame. In recent years it has even wintered in small numbers at feeders in the heart of the Adirondacks.

MAXIMA: *Spring*—15,000, Manitou, Monroe Co., Apr. 3, 1960; 30,000, Derby Hill, Oswego Co., Apr. 9, 1961.

MAXIMA: *Fall*—3500, Jamestown (roost), Chautauqua Co., Aug. 29, 1961; 70,000, Clay Swamp (roost), Onondaga Co., Oct. 12, 1960.

MAXIMA: *Winter*—1400, Syracuse (roost), winter of 1964–1965; 1000, Albany (roost), Feb. 5, 1966. Up to 5000 have been reported at several Long Island roosts.

Breeding: This parasitic species has the well-known habit of laying its eggs in other birds' nests, chiefly passerines, as it builds none of its own. Arboreal, terrestrial, and even hole-nesting species are not immune. Birds of city parks and suburban yards, farmland, open country, swamp, and forest are all parasitized by the Brown-headed Cowbird.

I have recorded a total of 75 New York species of more than 1100 individuals that have been parasitized. These have been taken from the literature (especially Friedmann, 1929 and 1963), museum collections, and nest-record cards. These 75 species encompass 14 families, chiefly flycatchers, thrushes, vireos, warblers, icterids (a few individuals of each species), and finches; all but nine species belong to these six families. The three species most commonly parasitized are: Yellow Warbler, Red-eyed Vireo, and Song Sparrow, in that order. The following 14 families are involved, with the number of species in parentheses: Cuculidae (one); Tryannidae (seven); Alaudidae (one); Sittidae (one); Troglodytidae (one); Mimidae (two); Turdidae (six); Bombycillidae (one); Vireonidae (five); Parulidae (26); Icteridae (six); Thraupidae (one); Ploceidae (one); Fringillidae (16).

The following table lists all 75 species in order of decreasing frequency—numbers represent nests parasitized, either with Cowbird eggs or young and/or fledgling Cowbirds actually being fed by the host species. Species preceded by asterisks are hole nesters.

Species	No. of nests
Yellow Warbler	148
Red-eyed Vireo	116
Song Sparrow	97
American Redstart	70
Chipping Sparrow	65
Common Yellowthroat	46
Chestnut-sided Warbler	44
Rufous-sided Towhee	41
Eastern Phoebe	37
Ovenbird	34
Veery	31
Louisiana Waterthrush	30
Indigo Bunting	28
Hooded Warbler	27
Field Sparrow	25
Wood Thrush	22
Northern Waterthrush	21
Warbling Vireo	20
Hermit Thrush	16
Blue-winged Warbler	16
Purple Finch	15
Eastern Wood Pewee	14
Yellow-throated Vireo	14
Black-throated Green Warbler	14
Scarlet Tanager	12
Golden-winged Warbler	11
Yellow-breasted Chat	11
Canada Warbler	11
American Goldfinch	11
Prairie Warbler	10
Rose-breasted Grosbeak	10
American Robin	9
Traill's Flycatcher	8
Solitary Vireo	8
Black and White Warbler	8
Cardinal	8
Slate-colored Junco	8
Least Flycatcher	7
Catbird	7
Cedar Waxwing	7
Black-throated Blue Warbler	7
Vesper Sparrow	7
Eastern Kingbird	6
*Eastern Bluebird	6
Magnolia Warbler	6
Baltimore Oriole	6
Nashville Warbler	5
Myrtle Warbler	5
Cerulean Warbler	5
Eastern Meadowlark	5
Red-winged Blackbird	5
*Great Crested Flycatcher	3
*White-breasted Nuthatch	3
White-eyed Vireo	3
Blackburnian Warbler	3
Bobolink	3
House Sparrow	3
House Finch	3
Savannah Sparrow	3
Swamp Sparrow	3
White-throated Sparrow	3
Horned Lark	2
Brown Thrasher	2
Swainson's Thrush	2
Worm-eating Warbler	2
Parula Warbler	2
Pine Warbler	2
Mourning Warbler	2
Common Grackle	2
Black-billed Cuckoo	1
Acadian Flycatcher	1
*House Wren	1
Blackpoll Warbler	1
Orchard Oriole	1
Evening Grosbeak	1

Unlike other species which form pair bonds, construct their own nests, and in which *one* fe-

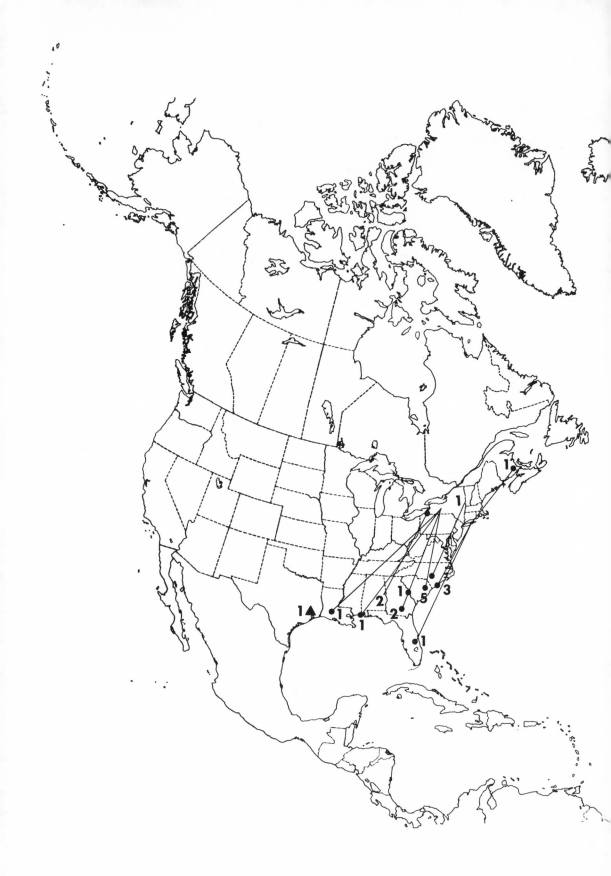

MAP 146 Brown-headed Cowbird (*Molothrus ater*) Banding recoveries

male lays her own eggs, cowbirds are poly-androus. Females sometimes lay eggs in more than one host's nest; moreover one host nest may contain more than one female Cowbird's eggs. Therefore clutch size in this species is very difficult to determine. The only alternative is to state the number of host nests containing one or more Cowbird eggs: one egg (825 nests —74%); two eggs (246 nests); three eggs (40 nests); four eggs (three nests). The last cate-gory may represent *two* female Cowbirds per nest.

EGG DATES: Apr. 23 to July 31.

Nestlings: May 19 to Aug. 2; fledglings: May 30 to Aug. 19.

Banding (see Map 146): Fourteen individu-als banded in summer or fall in New York were recovered the following winter in six southeastern states. Two others, banded in winter in Alabama, were taken the following spring at Jamestown, New York.

A bird banded in late March at Montauk, Long Island, was taken three weeks later near Moncton, New Brunswick. Still another banded at Rochester, New York, was shot more than a year later near Dayton, Texas.

STARLINGS — STURNIDAE

One species in New York.
One breeds.

This entirely Old World family (100± spe-cies) is represented in New York by the intro-duced Common Starling (*Sturnus vulgaris*). Such diverse types as mynas and oxpeckers be-long to this family, rich in species in the Ethi-opian and Oriental regions.

Common Starling
(*Sturnus vulgaris*)   *   B

Range: Palearctic region, widely introduced into various parts of the world.

Status: *Introduced*—very abundant through-out the state, except the forested portions. Sedentary and migratory.

Nonbreeding: First introduced into Central Park, New York City, in 1890, the Starling spread rapidly and multiplied throughout the state within the following 30 years. By 1922 it was firmly established except in the mountains.

Following are some of its "arrival" dates: 1905—Newburgh, lower Hudson valley; 1908 —Gardiner's Island, off extreme eastern Long

Island; 1911—Albany; 1912—Utica; 1914— Buffalo and Niagara Falls; 1916—Ithaca; 1917 —Plattsburgh, Lake Champlain.

An idea of the enormous abundance of this species in the state may be obtained from estimates of roosts in some of the large cities in 1960: Manhattan, New York City —200,000; Syracuse—300,000; Rochester— 250,000; Jamestown, Chautauqua Lake—150,-000. During the same year on Apr. 16, at least 20,000 Starlings were estimated passing the hawk lookout on Lake Ontario at Derby Hill, Oswego Co.

Breeding: Unfortunately, even more than that other introduced pest—the House Spar-row—this species, being almost exclusively a hole or cavity nester, usurps breeding sites of the far more desirable native species, all hole nesters themselves. Crested Flycatcher, vari-ous woodpeckers—such as the Downy, Red-headed, and Flicker—and other birds like Tree Swallow, Purple Martin, and Bluebird, all fall victim to the hordes of Starlings which are al-ready established on territory before most of the native species have returned from their winter quarters.

Equally obnoxious is their habit (along with

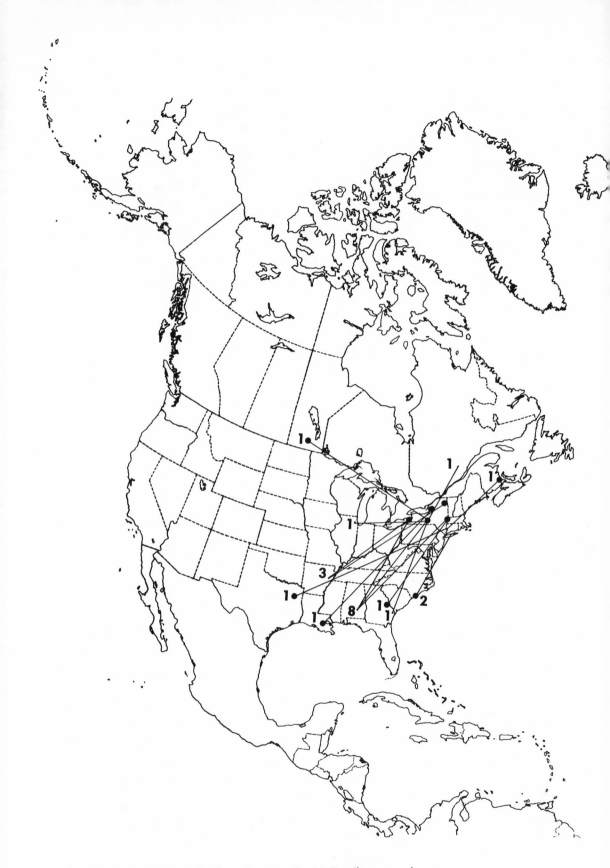

MAP 147   Common Starling (*Sturnus vulgaris*) Banding recoveries

pigeons) of fouling public buildings and side-walks with their excrement, to say nothing of their noise.

Starlings nest in a variety of places. In addition to utilizing bird boxes and natural tree cavities, they have been recorded as breeding in such diverse sites as under house eaves, among loose bricks in an old chimney, in an air-conditioning unit, in deserted holes of a former Bank Swallow colony in a gravel pit, and three pairs even nested in the base of an *occupied* Osprey nest on eastern Long Island—unusual for a hole nester.

Egg clutches in 16 New York nests: three eggs (five nests); four eggs (six nests); five eggs (one nest); six and seven eggs (two nests each).

EGG DATES: Apr. 10 to June 15.

Nestlings: May 11 to July 30; fledglings: May 19 to Aug. 30.

Although Stoner (1932) stated that this species was triple-brooded in the Oneida Lake region, Kessel (1957) reported only two broods in New York. As to the birds she studied, Kessel (*op. cit.*) remarked that better than 86% of the eggs hatched and 85% of the young fledged.

Banding (see Map 147): Years of banding have proved that some Starlings are highly migratory. Some individuals have flown hundreds of miles, a few as far as Manitoba and Texas. Eight individuals that had wintered in various years in or near Montgomery, Alabama, where they were banded, were recovered the following spring at various upstate New York localities. One of three banded Mar. 4, 1963, near Chatfield, Arkansas, was taken two weeks later, Mar. 18, 1963, near Plattsburgh, Clinton Co. A bird banded in Ohio in 1927 was trapped in New York in 1937, ten years later.

WEAVERS — PLOCEIDAE

One species in New York.
One breeds.

This family of over 150 species (not including the waxbills, Estrildidae) is most abundantly represented in Africa but occurs also in the Palearctic and Oriental regions. The introduced House Sparrow (*Passer domesticus*) is a member of this family.

House Sparrow
(*Passer domesticus*) * B

Range: Palearctic, Oriental, and northern Ethiopian regions, widely introduced into various parts of the world. Sedentary.

Status: *Introduced*—abundant resident, except the forested portions.

Nonbreeding: In this state the House Sparrow was first introduced into Brooklyn in the early 1850s. Within the next twenty years the species had spread to the western portions of New York, and Eaton (1914: 258) stated that by 1888 it "had occupied practically every hamlet in the state."

By the 1890s it was probably at its peak of abundance. During the summer of 1892 Chapman estimated *4000* bathing in one little pool in Central Park, New York City.

Supposedly because of the passing of the horse, arrival of the automobile, and competition with the Starling, the House Sparrow rapidly declined after 1913, especially in the larger cities. It is still widespread and all too numerous in city parks, suburbs, and agricultural areas, in fact wherever man dwells. It is often a pest at feeding stations, sheer numbers keeping desirable species away, and a particular scourge during the breeding season, like the Starling utilizing the vast majority of nest sites, particularly in suburban and farming areas.

The House Sparrow is a sedentary species.

Fig. 81 House Sparrows at nest between building walls, about seven feet above ground, Central Park South, New York City, June 1972. Photo by Sid Bahrt

Out of 32 banded at Ithaca in December 1936, all except one were recovered within one mile or so from place of banding. The one exception, an adult, was banded on Dec. 18, 1936, and recovered in April 1937 near Jamestown, about 140 miles to the west. This record is so remarkable that one suspects it was transported by rail on a grain shipment.

Breeding: This species breeds in a variety of situations, such as in dense vines growing on building walls (see Fig. 81). It sometimes builds globular or domed nests in trees. House Sparrows often utilize bird boxes, especially those of the Purple Martin, Tree Swallow, and Bluebird, as well as vacated nests of Barn and Cliff swallows, not infrequently usurping occupied nests of the last-named species. On at least two occasions on extreme eastern Long Island, House Sparrows raised young in nests situated at the bases of *occupied* Osprey nests, and others built nests in the huge stick nests of the introduced Monk Parakeet at Valley Stream, Nassau Co., in 1971. Other unusual breeding locations were in a haystack and in a willow stump in a cattail marsh.

The House Sparrow is double- or triple-brooded; on Long Island a color-banded female at Garden City, Nassau Co., raised three broods (J. T. Nichols).

Egg clutches in 21 New York nests: three eggs (three nests); four eggs (eight nests); five eggs (six nests); six eggs (four nests). It is possible that the nests with three eggs were incomplete clutches.

EGG DATES: Mar. 23 to July 16.

Nestlings: Apr. 15 to Aug. 4; fledglings: June 24 to Sept. 6.

TANAGERS — THRAUPIDAE

Three species in New York.
One breeds.

This is yet another strictly American family* (200± species), with the greatest variety of species by far in tropical and subtropical South America. Members of this family are among the most brilliant and gaudy of birds. The tanagers are considered by some taxonomists to be merely a subfamily of the Emberizidae; here they are given familial status.

All three species of New York tanagers belong to the genus *Piranga*. The Scarlet Tanager (*olivacea*) is a fairly widespread breeder; the other two—Summer Tanager (*rubra*) and Western Tanager (*ludoviciana*)—are rare visitants from the south and west, respectively.

Western Tanager
(*Piranga ludoviciana*) *

Range: Western North America, breeding east to central Saskatchewan and western Nebraska. Winters chiefly from southern Mexico to Costa Rica. Vagrant east to the Atlantic coast from Nova Scotia to New Jersey, though occurring more frequently in recent years.

Status: *Very rare*—in downstate New York there are at least 20 reports of this species —four of them specimens and one a color

* Does not include the honeycreepers (Coerebidae).

photograph—all from the southeastern portion of the state.

The four specimen records are: (1) immature male, Highland Falls, Orange Co., Dec. 21, 1881 (Mearns), USNM 235651; (2) female, near Accord, Ulster Co., mid-March 1960 (Hough), in collection of the State University at New Paltz (*fide* Heinz Meng)—I have not seen this specimen; (3) female, Riis Park, Queens Co., Dec. 26, 1966 (Schaeffer), AMNH 786269, first observed Nov. 20 (many observers), netted and banded, Dec. 11 (Davis), and found dead, Dec. 26 (Schaeffer), apparently a victim of the Dec. 24 snowstorm; (4) male collected near Fire Island Lighthouse, Suffolk Co., Nov. 21, 1970 (D. B. Ford), AMNH 802430.

An adult male with the red head was photographed in color at Central Park, New York City, May 9, 1970 (S. Bahrt), color photo examined by the writer.

Details of other occurrences in the New York City region are covered in Bull (1964: 410, and 1970: 44).

The following four upstate sightings of males are believed to be correct: (1) at feeder, Watkins Glen, Schuyler Co., Jan. 12, 1958 (Champion and Hope); (2) Black Lake, St. Lawrence Co., June 1, 1963 (Ives); (3) Wolf Hollow, near Hoffmans, Schenectady Co., May 16, 1965 (Angst); (4) Silver Bay, Warren Co., Oct. 23, 1965 (Yrizarry).

Other reports are without details and are omitted. August and early September dates require confirmation.

EXTREME DATES: Sept. 17 to June 1.

Scarlet Tanager
(*Piranga olivacea*)   *   B

Range: Eastern North America, breeding from extreme southern Canada to the northern portions of the Gulf states and on the east coast to Virginia. Winters in northwestern South America.

Status: Fairly common to common migrant, apparently more numerous in the southern portions. Widespread breeder, but rare on the coastal plain.

Nonbreeding: The strikingly colored males are especially conspicuous in backward seasons before the trees are in full leaf, or when occasionally seen on or near the ground during cold and rainy springs.

MAXIMA: *Spring*—16 males in two oak trees, Far Rockaway, Queens Co., May 9, 1951; 25, same locality, May 13, 1956.

MAXIMA: *Fall*—25, Inwood Hill Park, New York City, Sept. 13, 1964; 17 struck the television tower at Colden, Erie Co., Sept. 29, 1962; 24 hit the Westhampton Air Force Base tower, Suffolk Co., Oct. 5, 1954; 50, South Nyack, Rockland Co., Oct. 6, 1959 (Deed, *Audubon Field Notes,* 1960, 14: 19), an exceptional number; 7 hit the Fire Island Lighthouse, Oct. 12, 1883.

EXTREME DATES: Apr. 8 (coastal specimen), Apr. 12, 17, and 19 (all coastal), and Apr. 22 (inland) to Nov. 7, 11, 15, 17, and 21 (all coastal); some or all of the April birds may have been driven north by early spring storms. Rare before May and after mid-October.

Breeding: In the southern portion of the state the Scarlet Tanager prefers oak forest, but it is rare and local over much of the sandy coastal plain, even where oaks predominate. Upstate, however, this species nests in mixed deciduous growth, occasionally in hemlock or pine.

The nest is placed from six to 50 feet above ground, sometimes even higher.

Clutches in 15 New York nests were either three or four eggs: three eggs (four nests); four eggs (11 nests).

EGG DATES: May 20 to July 23.

Nestlings: June 9 to Aug. 14; fledglings: July 4 to Sept. 19.

Remarks: No winter reports are accepted in absence of specimen evidence. Cardinals are not infrequently misidentified as Scarlet Tanagers by beginners, but even experienced observers have difficulty in identifying obscurely colored tanagers in winter at the species level (Bull, 1964: 411).

Postscript: An adult male was found dead near Van Cortlandt Park, Bronx Co., Dec. 3, 1973 (Mrs. Cass Gallagher); specimen is AMNH 819465. This is the first New York December record for the species that has been substantiated.

Summer Tanager (*Piranga rubra*)   *

Range: Central and southern United States to northern Mexico; in the east breeding north to the central portions of Ohio, Maryland, and Delaware; casually to southern New Jersey. Winters from Mexico to South America. Vagrant north to southern Canada.

Status: Rare but regular spring migrant along the coast; very rare in fall. Casual inland.

Occurrence: The Summer Tanager is reported at least once or twice each spring along the south shore of Long Island and in the larger New York City parks. Elsewhere it may go unrecorded for years at a time. It arrives early in spring, rarely as early as the first week in April, but most frequently during the month of May.

It is a red-letter day when the observer spots one of these birds in the foliage. Perhaps because of a great increase in the number of observers the species has been reported each spring since 1947. The greatest number of individuals observed in one year has been five each in 1955, 1959, and 1965. The combined extreme dates for those three years ranged from Apr. 23 to May 29. However, there was a notable irruption of Summer Tanagers during the spring of 1969. At least a dozen individuals were reported in the New York City parks and on Long Island, with dates ranging from Apr. 27 to May 18.

EXTREME DATES: *Spring*—Apr. 6 to June 12; reported July 6, 1940, Central Park, New

York City (Wiegmann). *Fall*—Sept. 3 (specimen) to Oct. 6 and 19.

Where the fall birds come from is a mystery as none breed north of us. Possibly some individuals are storm-driven as in spring. There are at least a dozen records in September and five in October.

Upstate, or even 100 miles north of New York City, this species is extremely rare, all reports occurring in the month of May. There are only two confirmed records—both specimens: (1) one collected at Cincinnatus, Cortland Co., May 11, 1900 (*fide* Tanner, in

Parkes, 1952a); (2) immature male caught by a cat at Irondequoit Bay, Monroe Co., May 7, 1960 (Leubner), specimen supposedly in RMAS collection, but neither this nor the Cortland Co. specimen was seen by the writer.

Two inland sight reports with details given are believed correct: (1) a "changing male," Forest Lawn, Buffalo, May 14–16, 1958 (Webster and many others); (2) female, Braddock's Bay, Monroe Co., May 19, 1969 (Listman).

Other upstate observations reported were either without details or made by inexperienced observers.

FINCHES — FRINGILLIDAE

Forty-six species in New York.
Twenty-five breed.

This heterogeneous grouping (450± species), as here understood, consists of an array of forms that may possibly be unrelated. But since there is little agreement as to which group of species belongs where, the Wetmore sequence (i.e., A.O.U. Check-list, 1957) is adhered to—in other words, the "grosbeak-bunting-finch-sparrow" assemblage so familiar to the amateur. Moreover, this is not the place to discuss in detail extremely intricate and complex interrelationships of the various taxa involved. The interested reader is referred to Mayr, Paynter, and Storer (in "Peters," 1968, 1970) who also list additional references. Therefore three main stems or subfamilies are recognized here for convenience: (1) cardinalines, of America; (2) carduelines, absent from Australasia and the Pacific islands; (3) emberizines, nearly cosmopolitan, but not found in Indonesia or Australasia.

The sequence of genera and species followed here is in accordance with the A.O.U. Check-list (1957) for the most part, except for the sparrows of the genus *Ammodramus* in the emberizines (see following).

The following genera of the A.O.U. Check-list (1957) are herewith changed or merged:

"*Richmondena*" is a synonym of *Cardinalis* to conform with the subfamily name Cardinalinae; "*Guiraca*" is merged with *Passerina*; "*Hesperiphona*" with *Coccothraustes*; "*Chlorura*" with *Pipilo*; "*Passerculus*," "*Passerherbulus*," and "*Ammospiza*" with *Ammodramus*; "*Melospiza*" with *Passerella*—a reduction of seven genera.

Two species are merged: (1) Ipswich Sparrow with Savannah Sparrow; (2) Oregon Junco with Slate-colored or Dark-eyed Junco.

Although on anatomical evidence Robins and Schnell (1971) advocated two genera for the short-tailed grassland sparrows—using *Ammodramus* for the "grassland" species and *Ammospiza* for the "marshland" species, it is believed that they did not go far enough. Dickerman (*Auk*, 1968, 85: 312–313) suggested that only one genus be recognized—*Ammodramus* for *all* of the short-tailed, grassland species. Paynter (in "Peters," 1970: 70–78) adopted this view also. His sequence of species is followed here: *sandwichensis* (Savannah); *maritimus* (Seaside); *caudacutus* (Sharp-tailed); *leconteii* (Le Conte's); *bairdii* (Baird's); *henslowii* (Henslow's); *savannarum* (Grasshopper). The result is that four genera have been reduced to one to accomodate seven presumably related species.

However, as there is much disagreement

about generic limits in the cardueline finches, a conservative treatment is used here, following the A.O.U. Check-list (1957): *Carpodacus* (rosefinches); *Pinicola* (Pine Grosbeak); *Acanthis* (redpolls); *Spinus* (siskins, goldfinches); *Loxia* (crossbills).

At the other extreme one could merge all or most of the above into *Carduelis*. Even the crossed bills of *Loxia* are only special adaptations for extracting seeds from cones and may not be of generic importance. The genera *Chloris* (greenfinches) and *Serinus* (canaries, serins) could also be lumped into an enlarged genus *Carduelis* without too much imagination.

This writer cannot understand the rationale of those taxonomists who merge *Spinus* with *Carduelis*, but at the same time retain the related *Acanthis* as a "good" genus. One should either lump all of these genera or recognize each one.

As to the merger of *"Melospiza"* with *Junco* or even with *Zonotrichia*, it seems a bit premature on the basis of a few reported intergeneric hybrids. It is in the right direction, however, to lump *"Melospiza"* with *Passerella*, as the two appear to be morphologically similar, at least. The genera *Junco*, *Zonotrichia*, and *Passerella* (including *"Melospiza"*) appear to be morphologically distinct groups and, as such, warrant recognition, at least for the present.

Common Cardinal
(*Cardinalis cardinalis*)   *   B

Range: Southern Nearctic and northern Neotropical regions, in the east from extreme southern Canada to the Gulf of Mexico, in the west from southwestern United States to Guatemala. Sedentary.

Status: Common to locally resident in the southeastern lowlands; much less numerous northward and westward at low elevations, but steadily increasing and extending its range. Rare to absent at higher elevations.

Change in status: More than any other species in New York, the Cardinal has increased and spread markedly, especially within the past twenty years or so. Its loud whistled song and sharp penetrating call-note are now characteristic sounds of many a suburban yard.

Eaton (1914: 325–326) listed the two southernmost counties *west* of the Hudson River—Richmond (Staten Island) and Rockland—as the only areas in the state where this species was "well established"; and "common" only in the latter county. He considered it rare elsewhere. For its history in the New York City region, see Bull (1964: 412–416, and 1970: 44–45).

Its phenomenal increase and range extension throughout the rest of the state is given following.

Nonbreeding: I cannot help but feel that the tremendous increase in the number of feeding stations in recent years has been of the utmost importance in sustaining a very large number of Cardinals during the winter months, when they are more concentrated than at any other season. This is abundantly proved by banding —particularly color-banding—many individuals wintering over.

MAXIMA: All banded birds at feeders—20, Burtt feeder, Syracuse, winter of 1957–1958; six, Allen feeder, Watertown, January 1958— a good number so far north; *27*, Hoyt feeder, Etna, Tompkins Co., from mid-November 1961 to Mar. 30, 1962; *30*, Burgess feeder, Ithaca, winter of 1962–1963.

Another example of increase is taken from the Schenectady area Christmas counts. In 1942 and 1952 none was recorded, but in 1957 four Cardinals were counted, in 1962 there were *22*, and in 1967 at least *36*.

Although Cardinals are sedentary and there is no migration as such, they do have a tendency to wander at times. On tiny Great Gull Island (off eastern Long Island), on June 16, 23, and 27, 1969, three Cardinals were netted and banded—very likely vagrants from the adjacent "mainland" portion of Long Island, or from nearby Connecticut, places where the species breeds commonly. As this goes to press, I have learned that the June 27 individual was caught by a cat at Old Lyme, Conn., Sept. 19, 1972 (Duffy, Hays, and Janvrin), 13 miles from Great Gull Island in a northwesterly direction, although a good ten miles over the open water of Long Island Sound.

Breeding (see Map 148): It is a far cry from 1914, when this attractive species was known to breed in only *two* counties (see preceding)

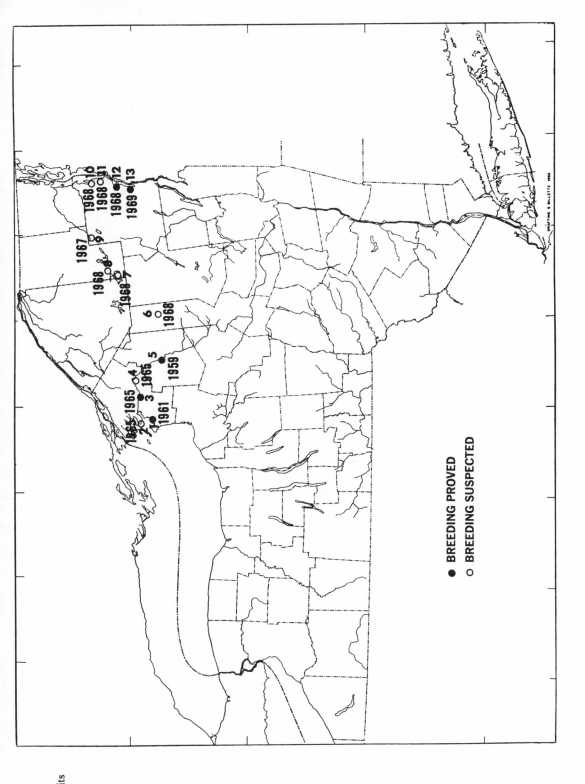

MAP 148 Common
Cardinal (*Cardinalis
cardinalis*) Known
northern breeding limits

● BREEDING PROVED
○ BREEDING SUSPECTED

1968 ○ 10
1968 ○ 11
1968 ● 12
1969 ● 13

1967 ○
1968 ○ 8
1968 ○ 7
6 ○ 1968
5 ● 1959
○ 4
1965 1965 ● 3
1965 2 ●
1 ● 1961

DRAFTING & GILLETTE 1966

and today when it has been recorded nesting in 59 of the 62 counties, excepting only St. Lawrence, Hamilton, and Clinton.

The accompanying map indicates the northernmost known penetration to date, with the following 13 localities, including year of first reported breeding or suspected breeding: Jefferson Co.—(1) Henderson Harbor; (2) Pillar Point; (3) Watertown; (4) Great Bend. Lewis Co.—(5) Lowville. Herkimer Co.—(6) Big Moose. Franklin Co.—(7) Moody; (8) Tupper Lake (village). Essex Co.—(9) Bloomingdale; (10) Willsboro; (11) Essex; (12) Westport; (13) Port Henry. Note that the last four localities are situated on Lake Champlain, the first two on Lake Ontario, three on the Black River, and the remaining four on or near relatively low-altitude lakes, although situated in the "heart" of the Adirondacks.

Cardinals presumably became locally numerous in parts of western New York rather early. According to Beardslee and Mitchell (1965: 413), Dr. Perkins estimated 20 pairs within four miles of the Gowanda State Hospital, Cattaraugus Co., as early as 1930, a decided increase over the 1920s.

Axtell (1947) believed that the species "arrived" in Chemung and Schuyler counties during the mid-1930s, with three nesting pairs in the Elmira region in 1939. As of 1947 he estimated a minimum of 45 pairs in both counties, half of which were within four miles of Elmira.

The Cardinal is quite adaptable, frequenting low, rich, but open woodland, brushy swamps, woodland borders, thickets and—in recent years—has become common in suburban yards and even city parks, provided dense shrubbery is available. The nest is often placed in bushes, hedges, and vines, more rarely in saplings, from three to 12 feet above ground.

Nests of this species are not difficult to locate. In 118 New York nests examined, egg clutches ranged from three to five, as follows: three eggs (85 nests—71%); four eggs (32 nests); five eggs (only one nest).

Based on color-banded females, the Cardinal is triple-brooded in New York.

EGG DATES: Apr. 10 to Sept. 9.

Nestlings: Apr. 23 to Sept. 23; fledglings: Apr. 30 to Oct. 20. This three-broodedness is very likely a contributing factor toward the continued success of this species.

Rose-breasted Grosbeak
(*Pheucticus ludovicianus*)   *   B

Range: Chiefly eastern North America, breeding from southern Canada to the mountains of northern Georgia and to the edge of the coastal plain on Long Island and in central New Jersey. Winters from Mexico to northern South America; rarely north to the Gulf states and in recent years casually to New York (at feeding stations).

Status: Fairly common to common migrant, but uncommon and local on the coastal plain, except at the west end of Long Island. Widespread breeder north of the coastal plain, but rare on Long Island. Very rare in winter.

Nonbreeding: This species, like the Baltimore Oriole and Scarlet Tanager, is very conspicuous with its bright colors and is eagerly awaited each spring.

MAXIMA: *Spring*—18 males, Atlantic Beach, Nassau Co., May 1, 1966 (Cohen), a very high number for such an early date; 111, netted and banded, Fire Island State Park, Suffolk Co., May 9, 1970 (Buckley, Davis, *et al.*), is an unprecedented number at any season anywhere in the state. 35, Bronx Park, Bronx Co., May 12, 1950; 38, Camillus, Onondaga Co., May 14, 1970; 22, Sandy Pond, Oswego Co., May 21, 1961.

MAXIMA: *Fall*—25, Tully, Onondaga Co., Sept. 10, 1961; 60, Owego, Tioga Co., Sept. 23, 1966 (Ruth Williams); 19 hit the television tower at Colden, Erie Co., Sept. 29, 1962.

EXTREME DATES: Casual—one found dead at Falconer, Chautauqua Co., Apr. 1, 1948 (Crosby); Apr. 16 (coastal) and Apr. 23 (inland), after southerly storms, to Nov. 2 (inland) and Nov. 5 (coastal); also a male at a Long Island feeder, Nov. 18 to Dec. 5, 1967. Usually rare before May and after early October.

Winter: With the tremendous increase in feeding stations in recent years this species, like many others unreported in former times, has been recorded during the winter months. However, very few reports have been corroborated and no winter specimen has ever been collected in the state to my knowledge. Actually some reports may have been the western Black-headed Grosbeak (see that species) which closely resembles the eastern Rose-breasted Grosbeak, especially females and young males.

Nevertheless, at least two reports appear to be the present species: (1) male with "partial rose breast" at the Stanley feeder, Dunkirk, Chautauqua Co., from December 1965 to late January 1966 and seen by numerous observers; (2) male filmed in color at the Key feeder, Poughkeepsie, Dutchess Co., from Dec. 25, 1966, to Jan. 12, 1967. There may be others also.

Three winter reports in New York City parks (Bull, 1964: 417) appear to have been escaped zoo birds.

Breeding: Rose-breasted Grosbeaks nest in rich, moist secondary forest with much undergrowth, and in swampy woodland; occasionally in shade trees along rural roads with extensive thickets and shrubbery.

This species has always been rare and local as a breeder on Long Island and practically confined to the north shore. It has not been proved to breed on the south shore or on Staten Island as far as I know. Definite Long Island breeding localities are: Queens Co.—Astoria. Nassau Co.—Great Neck; Manhasset; Port Washington; Sea Cliff. Suffolk Co.—Huntington; Smithtown; East Marion; Noyack (west of Sag Harbor).

These birds place their nests in bushes and trees from four to about 30 feet up.

Egg clutches in 29 New York nests: three eggs (11 nests); four eggs (18 nests).

EGG DATES: May 6 and 15 to June 24 and July 19.

Nestlings: May 30 to June 29 and July 26; fledglings: June 11 to Aug. 15. The July dates for eggs and nestlings are exceptionally late and may represent renesting, rather than second clutches.

Black-headed Grosbeak
(*Pheucticus melanocephalus*)

Range: Western North America, breeding east to central Nebraska. Winters chiefly in Mexico, occasionally north and east to Louisiana (since about 1950). Vagrant east to the Atlantic coast from Massachusetts (color photograph) to South Carolina (specimen).

Status: *Very rare*—although never collected within New York, the occurrence of the Black-headed Grosbeak is well substantiated by color photographs of three different individuals—all at feeding stations: (1) male, Watertown, Jefferson Co., Apr. 30, 1959 (A. W. Allen), color photo examined by the writer; (2) female, Holland, Erie Co., from Jan. 1 to Apr. 20, 1962 (Duttweiler), trapped and banded by Boynton and color-photographed by Coggeshall, Hall, and Mitchell (Beardslee and Mitchell, 1965: 415); (3) male, Pleasant Valley, Dutchess Co., from Jan. 23 to Apr. 15, 1965 (Pink), color photos on file, AMNH collection.

In addition, there are four sight reports of birds believed to be this form from the New York City region, in Nassau, Queens, Westchester, and Rockland counties (Bull, 1964: 417).

Remarks: Hybridizes *infrequently* with the Rose-breasted Grosbeak (*P. ludovicianus*) in the Great Plains region from Saskatchewan to Kansas, and considered to be conspecific by West (1962). Here the two forms are treated as separate species.

Blue Grosbeak (*Passerina caerulea*) *

Range: Chiefly southern United States and Middle America, breeding north to Maryland and Delaware, rarely to the southern portions of Pennsylvania and New Jersey; in recent years twice in central New Jersey. Winters from Mexico to Panama. Wanders north to southern Canada.

Status: Rare but regular coastal migrant.

Occurrence: The Blue Grosbeak was considered an extremely rare bird in New York prior to the late 1940s. It is still a good find, however, and only the active observer records the species each year. The best place to observe this bird is the outer coast along

the south shore of Long Island where it inhabits thickets and hedgerows. There it is reported most often in September and October,
and again in late April and May. With luck,
during a flight of birds, the much-sought-for
Blue Grosbeak may be seen. Ordinarily only
one or two are observed each season, but as
many as seven were reported during the spring
of 1961 and at least six in the fall of 1957.

EXTREME DATES: *Fall*—July 27 to Nov. 25,
exceptionally to Dec. 15, 1963, Jones Beach
(Garland). *Spring*—Mar. 25 to May 21. Rare
before September, after mid-October, and before late April.

Specimen data: Five specimens are known,
of which two old ones—neither extant—were
taken in the mid-nineteenth century.

The three recent occurrences, all males from
eastern Long Island in Suffolk Co., are: (1)
Moriches Inlet, Sept. 20, 1934 (Wilcox), in
his collection; (2) Orient, Apr. 26, 1929
(Latham), NYSM 25539; (3) Montauk,
Apr. 28, 1944 (Latham), NYSM 25540.

In addition, the late Walter Terry banded
three males at Patchogue, Suffolk Co., during
the spring of 1961—Apr. 27, May 1, and May
13—the last of which he photographed in
color; photo on file, AMNH collection.

Remarks: Indigo Buntings are frequently
misidentified as Blue Grosbeaks. The report of
a "flock of 12" seen near Oneonta, Otsego Co.,
in July 1899 (Eaton, 1914: 330), should not
be taken seriously, as even Indigo Buntings do
not flock in such numbers in July.

Beardslee and Mitchell (1965: 415–416)
wisely placed the Blue Grosbeak on their hypothetical list in absence of confirmatory evidence.

As far as I am aware, the only upstate report of a Blue Grosbeak with details is that of
a male observed near Lake Champlain at Port
Kent, Essex Co., June 17, 1964 (Delafield,
Kingbird, 1964, 14: 215–216).

Taxonomy: The Blue Grosbeak is merely an
overgrown, large-billed Indigo Bunting with
similar vocalizations and tail-flicking habits. It
is for these reasons, also following several recent authorities (Phillips, *et al.,* 1964: 179;
Blake, 1969: 138–139; and Paynter, in "Peters," 1970: 237), that the generic name *"Guiraca"* is merged with *Passerina.*

Indigo Bunting
(Passerina cyanea)   *   B

Range: Eastern North America, breeding
from extreme southern Canada to Texas and
Florida. Winters in tropical America south to
Panama and north to Florida; casually along
the Atlantic coast to Long Island and Massachusetts.

Status: Fairly common migrant, numbers
fluctuating somewhat from year to year. Fairly
widely distributed breeder, but local on Long
Island and rare in the higher mountains.

Nonbreeding: This species, though usually
seen singly or in groups of two or three, sometimes occurs in larger numbers. In May and
October it may be seen also on lawns with
scattered shrubs, particularly in city parks, and
in the same environment on the coast just back
of the beaches.

MAXIMA: *Spring*—16, Derby Hill, Oswego
Co., May 12, 1964; 18, Van Cortlandt Park,
Bronx Co., May 19, 1946.

MAXIMA: *Fall*—six struck the Fire Island
Lighthouse, Suffolk Co., Sept. 23, 1887; 15,
Jones Beach, Long Island, Sept. 30, 1951;
eight, Prospect Park, Brooklyn, Oct. 10, 1947.

EXTREME DATES: Apr. 10 and 15 (coastal)
and Apr. 18 (inland)—some of these storm-
driven—to Nov. 14 (coastal), casually to Dec.
7 (inland and coastal). Usually rare before
mid-May and after mid-October.

Breeding: The Indigo Bunting nests in bushy
fields, abandoned overgrown farmland, second-
growth   clearings   and   woodland   edge,
and thickets along country roads. The species is local on Long Island and on the coastal plain generally.

Near Elmira, Axtell (1947) counted 21 singing
males in two miles of steep hillside.

Eaton (1914: 331) stated that the Indigo
Bunting was to be "found about the edges of
the Catskill and Adirondack districts, but does
not enter the Canadian zone."

Parkes (1952a), however, said that, "Its
penetration into the Adirondack area has been
quite recent." He called it "completely unknown prior to 1947" in the vicinity of Newcomb, Essex Co., but it had become common

there by 1950, and was also common at that time at Bay Pond, Franklin Co.

The nest is placed in saplings and bushes near the ground, from about 20 inches to four feet up.

Egg clutches in 17 New York nests ranged from three eggs (eight nests) to four eggs (nine nests).

EGG DATES: May 26 to July 12 and Aug. 3. Nestlings: June 18 to Aug. 14; fledglings: June 21 to Sept. 20. The species is double-brooded in New York.

Remarks: I am aware of only a single winter occurrence in New York—on Long Island—one remained at a feeding station at Riverhead, Suffolk Co., all through December 1957 (Latham).

Painted Bunting (*Passerina ciris*) *

Range: Southeastern United States, breeding north to coastal North Carolina. Winters from the Gulf states to Panama. Vagrant north to Massachusetts.

Status: *Very rare*—as in the case of the Black-billed Magpie (*Pica pica*), it is quite impossible to evaluate the status of the Painted Bunting here. In New York all old records were assumed to be escaped cage birds. Two specimens, both extant, are in this category: (1) male, Riverdale, Bronx Co., July 13, 1875 (Bicknell), NYSM 23672; (2) male, Long Island, June 10, 1899 (Leutloff), AMNH 72045.

Even in recent years, although protected by federal law, this brilliantly colored species has been illegally imported from Mexico and Central America and confined to cages from time to time, with a number of releases made in New York City and Brooklyn. The birds seen in the New York City parks are also likely in this category: two in Central Park—male, Sept. 9–23, 1927 (Samek, *et al.*), and female, Oct. 19, 1949 (Helmuth)—and one in Van Cortlandt Park—female, Sept. 29, 1937 (Peterson). However, two birds recorded on Long Island may have been "wild"; female observed at Easthampton, Suffolk Co., May 13, 1947 (Helmuth); male found dead on road, East

Hempstead, Nassau Co., May 28, 1952 (Holmes), AMNH 748473.

Beardslee and Mitchell (1965: 417) mention, but question, the validity of three observations in western New York of birds reported to be this species. The most recent reports are: a "resplendent" male at several feeders in Hudson, Columbia Co., from late December 1966 through mid-March 1967, seen by numerous observers. It very likely escaped from confinement, as did a pair observed at Sidney, Delaware Co., May 26–28, 1967, reported feeding on dandelion seeds. Still another male was present at the Stone feeder, Williamsville, Erie Co., May 18–21, 1970, and was photographed in color by Mitchell.

Dickcissel (*Spiza americana*) * B

Range: Chiefly central North America, breeding from extreme southern Canada to the Gulf states; sporadically northeast to southern Ontario, west-central New York, Ohio, Pennsylvania, southern New Jersey, and Maryland. Formerly (prior to 1880) bred on the Atlantic coastal plain from Massachusetts to South Carolina. Two recent breeding records ascribed to Massachusetts (A.O.U. Check-list, 1957: 555) are erroneous. Winters from southern Mexico to northern South America, rarely north to the Gulf states; in recent years (1952 on) regular in small numbers at *feeding stations* north to New York and New England.

Status: Rare to uncommon, but regular fall coastal migrant, occasionally more numerous. Much less frequent in spring and at any time inland, but recorded regularly in winter at feeders, both on the coast and inland. Has bred twice in the present century.

Nonbreeding: Along the coast Dickcissels frequent dry grassy fields and lawns with hedgerows and thickets. Occasionally in fall, flights occur on the outer coast of Long Island.

MAXIMA: 1963—all in Suffolk Co.—*14*, Montauk Point, Sept. 28 (Yeaton, *et al.*); six, Smith's Point, Fire Island, Sept. 29; three at one feeder, Fisher's Island, Nov. 5. Usually one or two per locality are the rule.

There are two winter specimens for the state, both taken at feeders: (1) female, Fisher's

Island, Suffolk Co., Jan. 22, 1961 (Ferguson), specimen in his collection; (2) female, Chatham, Columbia Co., Jan. 14, 1964 (Thurston), AMNH 781845. In recent years winter Dickcissels have become regular, if scarce, inhabitants at feeders, upstate as well as along the coast.

The species has been recorded every month of the year but is rare in spring and very rare in summer. A supposed flock of 25 reported on July 19, 1922, at Garland, Monroe Co. (Beardslee and Mitchell, 1965: 417–418), was not verified. Dickcissels do *not* flock in mid-July, at least not in New York.

Breeding: This species formerly ranged widely in the breeding season over the Atlantic states from Massachusetts to South Carolina, being found in open country. It was restricted mainly to lowland areas where it nested on or near the ground in lush grassy fields and meadows grown up to alfalfa, clover, daisies, timothy, etc., avoiding the drier sections. There is no exact information as to how numerous it was in the early and middle nineteenth century, except that the early writers stated that it was "common" or "abundant." Nor do we know why or exactly when it disappeared from much of this region. It had apparently become very rare by the 1870s in the northeast.

Eaton (1914: 335) gave the last of the old breeding records for the state—Junius, Seneca Co., summer of 1875. More than 60 years were to elapse before the first modern breeding record was established. Benton (1949) stated that an adult was seen at a nest in a hayfield at Meridian, Cayuga Co., in May 1937 by Tabor, who collected two eggs. According to the collector (Tabor), the pair renested later that season and raised four young.

The only recent New York nesting record known to the writer was that of a nest containing four eggs, near Victor, Ontario Co., June 29, 1955 (Genesee Ornith. Soc.). The nest was later destroyed when the field was mowed.

Note that the above three nestings occurred in the contiguous counties of Cayuga, Seneca, and Ontario—located in the agricultural lowlands north of the Finger Lakes and south of Lake Ontario.

The Dickcissel has thus shown little sign of becoming re-established as a breeder in New York, although it is a regular visitant during certain other times of the year.

[Brambling (*Fringilla montifringilla*)

Hypothetical: Northern Eurasia, in the western portion wintering from Scotland to Portugal.

A male seen at Kennedy Airport, Long Island, Feb. 11, 1965 (Ryan), was believed to have been an escape from an air shipment.

A male collected in New Jersey in 1958 and two more captured alive in Massachusetts in 1962 were considered escapes also, as was one seen at the Delehanty feeder at Tupper Lake (village), Franklin Co., N.Y., Apr. 6, 1962.

All occurrences in the northeast are suspect, the article by Banks (*Auk*, 1970, 87: 165–167) notwithstanding. Ryan (*in litt.*) states that, "Bramblings are not infrequently imported into the United States by dealers."—*contra* Banks (*op. cit.*), who feels that these birds were "wild." Arrival in this country by assisted passage (ship) is a distinct possibility, also.]

Evening Grosbeak
(Coccothraustes vespertinus) * B

Range: Nearctic region, breeding from southern Canada to the mountains of southern Mexico in the west, but in the east (in recent years) only as far as northern and east-central New York, rarely to Massachusetts, and casually to southeastern New York, southern Connecticut, and northern New Jersey. Winters north to the edge of the breeding range. Formerly much rarer. Sedentary and irregularly migratory.

Status: Somewhat irregular, but locally common to abundant migrant and winter visitant; most numerous inland. Generally uncommon but fairly widespread breeder in and near the Adirondacks, very rare elsewhere.

Change in status: More than any other species in the history of New York ornithology, the Evening Grosbeak has changed from "an occasional winter visitant—usually in very small numbers" (Eaton, 1914: 252) to an occasionally numerous visitant, as stated above. In other words, within the past half century or more, this species has increased tremendously. Prior to the 1890s it was considered a vagrant from the west, with the first flight of any consequence during the winter of 1889–1890. In the latter year a number of specimens were taken at various points in the state. When in the early 1950s the species gradually spread eastward as a breeder, from western Ontario and Michigan to Nova Scotia and Maine, it became more numerous throughout the northeast during fall, winter, and spring. When, however, during the 1950s and especially the 1960s, it also moved *south* as a breeder into New York and central New England, it became an abundant statewide visitor at feeding stations and a breeder south almost to the Mohawk valley. As of 1971 it was recorded as breeding or probably breeding at *50* New York stations.

Nonbreeding: Evening Grosbeaks are best known as prodigious consumers of sunflower seeds at an ever-growing number of winter feeding stations. They are less well known as avid eaters of the fruit of *Acer negundo,* the ash-leaved maple or box-elder, and also the fruit of several species of *Eleagnus,* the "Russian olives," so-called.

Great irruptions of these colorful finches take place at irregular intervals, especially at inland points. Oddly enough they occur chiefly during October and especially in early *May;* with large numbers occurring, of course, also in winter.

MAXIMA: *Fall*—500 in *one flock* flying along the Lake Ontario shoreline at Webster Park, Monroe Co., Oct. 7, 1961 (Lloyd); a big migration of chickadees at the same time.

MAXIMA: *Winter*—1200 banded at the Fitzgerald feeder, Amsterdam, Montgomery Co., winter of 1955–1956; 1300 banded at the Wilson feeder, Deposit, Broome Co., winter of 1959–1960.

MAXIMA: *Spring*—2500, flying by the Lake Ontario shore at Derby Hill, Oswego Co., in *two* days in 1969 (Propst)—1300 on May 7 in only two hours, and 1200 on May 8 in four hours.

EXTREME DATES: Sept. 6 (coastal) and Sept. 9 (inland) to May 26 (inland) and

June 7 (coastal); also casual July 3, Orient, Long Island. The above dates are from Buffalo and the immediate New York City region—at which places the species is not known to breed.

Breeding (see Map 149): The first summer occurrences for the state were reported in 1942 and again in 1945, but it was not until 1947 that the first breeding evidence was obtained. During that year fledged young were fed by adults at feeding stations in the Saranac Lake area, Franklin Co. As a matter of fact the vast majority of the *50* breeding localities have been near feeders. In reality very few nests of this species have been found in New York (see following).

From 1947 on, during each year one or more additional breeding localities have been reported. The biggest single year was 1953 when *11* "new" localities were tallied, followed by 1967 with seven more.

But it was during the year 1962, following the largest autumnal (1961) flight on record, that the Evening Grosbeak really "went places." It was the first and *only* time that the species bred far outside the usual boreal evergreen forest zone, or at least the "greater" Adirondack region.

Study of the breeding distribution map conveys far more than words. The 1962 irruption is illustrated as follows: (1) Schenectady feeder, at that time the southernmost known breeding record in the state. Then in rapid succession—and in all instances young at feeders—breeding was reported at (2) Pittsford, Monroe Co.; (3) Ithaca; and (4) Stissing, Dutchess Co.; as well as at Wallingford, Conn., and at two localities in northern New Jersey (Bull, 1964: 423).

As mentioned previously, very few nests of this species have been discovered in New York (difficult to find?). In fact only four, two in spruce and one each in pine and maple, ranging from 40 to 50 feet above ground, were located at the edge of primary forest. Two of the four nests held three eggs apiece, the other two had four each.

EGG DATES: May 19 to June 4.

Nestlings: May 31 to June 17; fledglings: June 15 to Sept. 5. The great spread of fledgling dates probably represents two broods. In one instance color-banded adults brought three

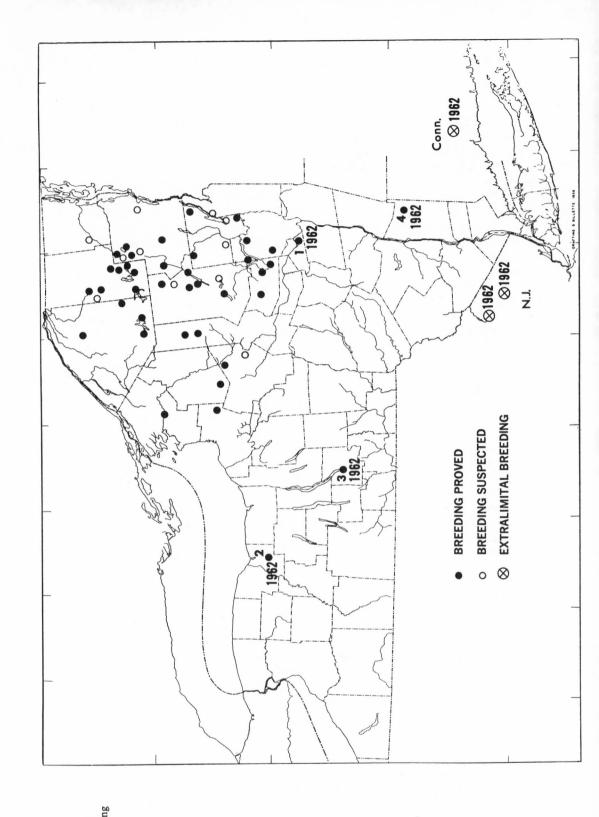

MAP 149 Evening
Grosbeak
(*Coccothraustes
vespertinus*) Breeding
distribution

BREEDING PROVED

BREEDING SUSPECTED

EXTRALIMITAL BREEDING

1 1962

2 1962

3 1962

4 1962

Conn. 1962

N.J. 1962

1962

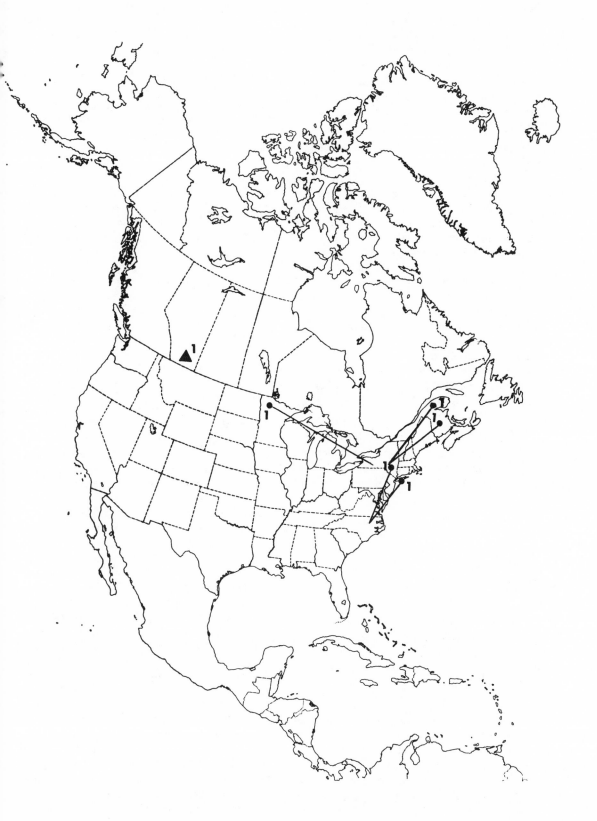

MAP 150 Evening Grosbeak (*Coccothraustes vespertinus*) Banding recoveries

fledged juveniles to a feeder in *early* July and two more in *late* August.

At Saranac Lake, July 2, 1949, a male Evening Grosbeak was seen feeding a fledgling Brown-headed Cowbird (Schaub). This is the only known case of parasitism in this species (Friedmann, 1963: 143–144).

Banding (see Map 150): Two individuals banded in late winter and spring in eastern New York were recovered the following June on their presumed breeding grounds near the Matapedia River, Rimouski Co., Quebec, and near Salmon Creek, New Brunswick. Two others were banded in winter and spring at Ithaca. One was recovered the following spring at Red Lake, Minnesota, while the other was found nine months later in *January* east of Lethbridge, Alberta. This last recovery is proof that the species may remain in winter in the north or far northwest. Two more banded in late winter and early spring at Rocky Mount, North Carolina, were recovered the following May at Deposit, Delaware Co., and at Westhampton, Long Island. Still another, an adult, banded in New York, was at least 11 years old when found.

Remarks: The genus *"Hesperiphona"* is here merged with *Coccothraustes* (the Palearctic group of Hawfinches), following Paynter (in "Peters," 1968: 299), and Mayr and Short (1970: 80).

Purple Finch
(*Carpodacus purpureus*)   *   B

Range: Nearctic region, breeding from Canada to southwestern United States, but in the east only as far as the mountains of West Virginia and Maryland (rare), near the coast in northern New Jersey and southeastern New York, and on the coast to Long Island (rare). Winters north to southern Canada.

Status: Erratic and unpredictable migrant and winter visitant, common to abundant in fall on the coast, sometimes numerous in spring both coastwise and in the interior, and usually rare in winter except on the coast where occasionally numerous. Widespread and common breeder, especially at higher eleva-

tions, but uncommon and local southeastward, and rare on Long Island.

Nonbreeding: Purple Finches are irregular in their movements and length of stay, and are exceedingly variable in numbers. During some seasons they are common to abundant, in others rare or locally absent for long periods.

MAXIMA, COASTAL: *Fall*—200, Bronx Park, New York City, Oct. 5, 1943; 400, New Rochelle, Westchester Co., Oct. 24, 1943; 400, Far Rockaway, Queens Co., Oct. 25, 1952.

MAXIMA, COASTAL: *Winter*—100, Van Cortlandt Park, Bronx Co., Jan. 19, 1928.

MAXIMA, COASTAL AND INLAND: *Spring*—330, Easthampton, Suffolk Co., Mar. 22, 1939; 300, Manitou, Monroe Co., Apr. 30, 1960; 30, Prospect Park, Brooklyn, May 10, 1946.

Breeding: Purple Finches are largely restricted to evergreen growth in the breeding season both at the edge of, but not in, spruce forest in the Adirondack and Catskill mountains, and also at lower elevations in ornamental conifers in suburban yards, parks, and nurseries, and in recent years in conifer plantings of reforestation projects. In all these habitats spruce is far and away most often chosen for nest sites. More than 60 spruce trees in the state held nests, followed by pine (22) and cedar (11). Fruit trees are rarely used, only two each of apple and pear. Nest heights ranged from five to 60 feet above ground.

Egg clutches in 28 New York nests ranged from three to five: three eggs (nine nests); four eggs (18 nests); five eggs (one nest).

EGG DATES: May 13 to July 16.

Nestlings: June 2 to July 24; fledglings: June 10 to Aug. 1.

The species is partially double-brooded in New York based on color-banded adults at Amsterdam, Montgomery Co., in 1953 (Mrs. Fitzgerald). She observed a pair of adults feeding fledged young of the first brood on June 28 and fledglings of the second brood on Aug. 1.

The Purple Finch is one of a number of species with northern affinities whose breeding range in New York has as its southern limits the coastal plain of Long Island. It should be emphasized, however, that only three known nesting localities are recorded on the *south* shore, all in eastern Suffolk Co., none west of

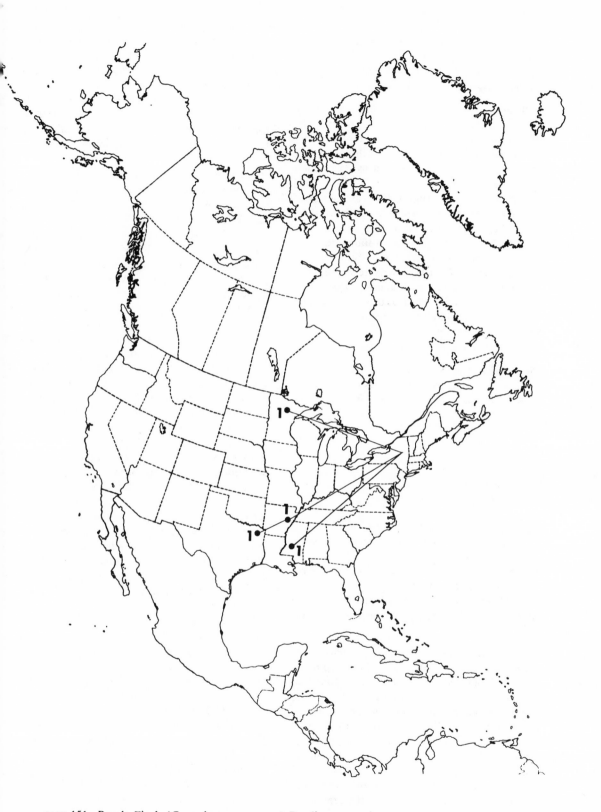

MAP 151 Purple Finch (*Carpodacus purpureus*) Banding recoveries

Mastic. The species is unknown as a breeder on Staten Island. For details of its breeding status in the New York City region, see Bull (1964: 424–427, and 1970: 46).

Banding (see Map 151): Thanks to an intensive trapping and banding program by Mrs. Margaret Fitzgerald at Amsterdam (Mohawk valley), we know something of the longevity of this species as well as its wanderings. An adult banded by her in April 1954 was found dead in August 1967 at an age of at least 14 years. Another that she banded on Mar. 11, 1954, was recovered exactly two months later in northeastern Minnesota. This bird flew northwest in *spring*. Still another banded Sept. 30, 1952, was recovered the following February in Arkansas. Two more banded in 1954 in April and July were also recovered the following February, one near Jackson, Mississippi, the other near the Red River section in northeastern Texas.

Remarks: The Newfoundland breeding population, known as *"nesophilus,"* is not separable from nominate *purpureus,* and is not recognized here.

House Finch
(*Carpodacus mexicanus*)   *   B

Range: Western Nearctic region, breeding (mainly resident) from southern British Columbia to the highlands of southern Mexico, east to western Nebraska. Introduced into the eastern United States (Long Island) in 1942. As of 1971—northeast to Massachusetts and south to the Carolinas. Both sedentary and migratory.

Status: *Introduced*—the present population descended from illegally caged birds from the west and released on western Long Island in the early 1940s. The history of the House Finch on Long Island and nearby areas is given in detail in Elliott and Arbib (1953), and in Bull (1964: 427–432, and 1970: 46–47). Only a summary is presented here (see following). It is a tame and familiar species around man's dwellings and a frequent visitor to feeding stations throughout much of the area it inhabits.

At the present time it is a common to very common resident on Long Island and on the adjacent mainland of Westchester and Rockland counties. It is more local and slightly less numerous elsewhere in the New York City region, and decreases progressively northward in the Hudson valley. These birds are still very rare elsewhere in the state but are increasing.

Nonbreeding: Although essentially sedentary, the House Finch is reported to be partially migratory in the east, as proved by banding recoveries (see **Banding).**

With the steady population increase radiating out from Long Island, this species has greatly expanded its range in the southeastern portion of New York. By 1965 it had become established throughout most of Long Island, extending even to Montauk and Orient points, although as of 1971 it was still unreported on the islands to the east—Gardiner's and Fisher's islands.

By the late 1960s House Finches were firmly established to the north in Westchester and Rockland counties, at least in the low-lying sections adjacent to Long Island Sound and near the Hudson River, as well as in all five boroughs of New York City.

As early as 1952 vagrants began to appear at feeding stations in outlying sections, for example at Monticello, Sullivan Co., and in 1956 as far west as Rochester. Other "first" arrivals upstate were: 1963—Binghamton; 1964—Schenectady; 1965—Buffalo; 1968—Syracuse; 1969—Elmira; 1970—Ithaca. A number of these birds were with Purple Finches for direct comparison and several were banded and color-photographed.

Breeding (see Map 152): The range extension of the House Finch in New York to the east, north, and west is graphically illustrated on the accompanying map. Years indicate first *proved* breeding: extreme eastern Long Island —1965—(1) Montauk and (2) Orient points, Suffolk Co. Hudson-Mohawk valleys—1965—(3) Poughkeepsie, Dutchess Co.; 1966—(4) Kingston; 1967—(5) New Paltz, both in Ulster Co.; 1968—(6) Catskill, Greene Co.; (7) Niskayuna, Schenectady Co.; 1970—(8) Schenectady; also near Herkimer, but breeding not proved. Elsewhere—1970—(9) Monticello, Sullivan Co.; (10) near Binghamton;

MAP 152 House Finch
(*Carpodacus mexicanus*)
Breeding distribution

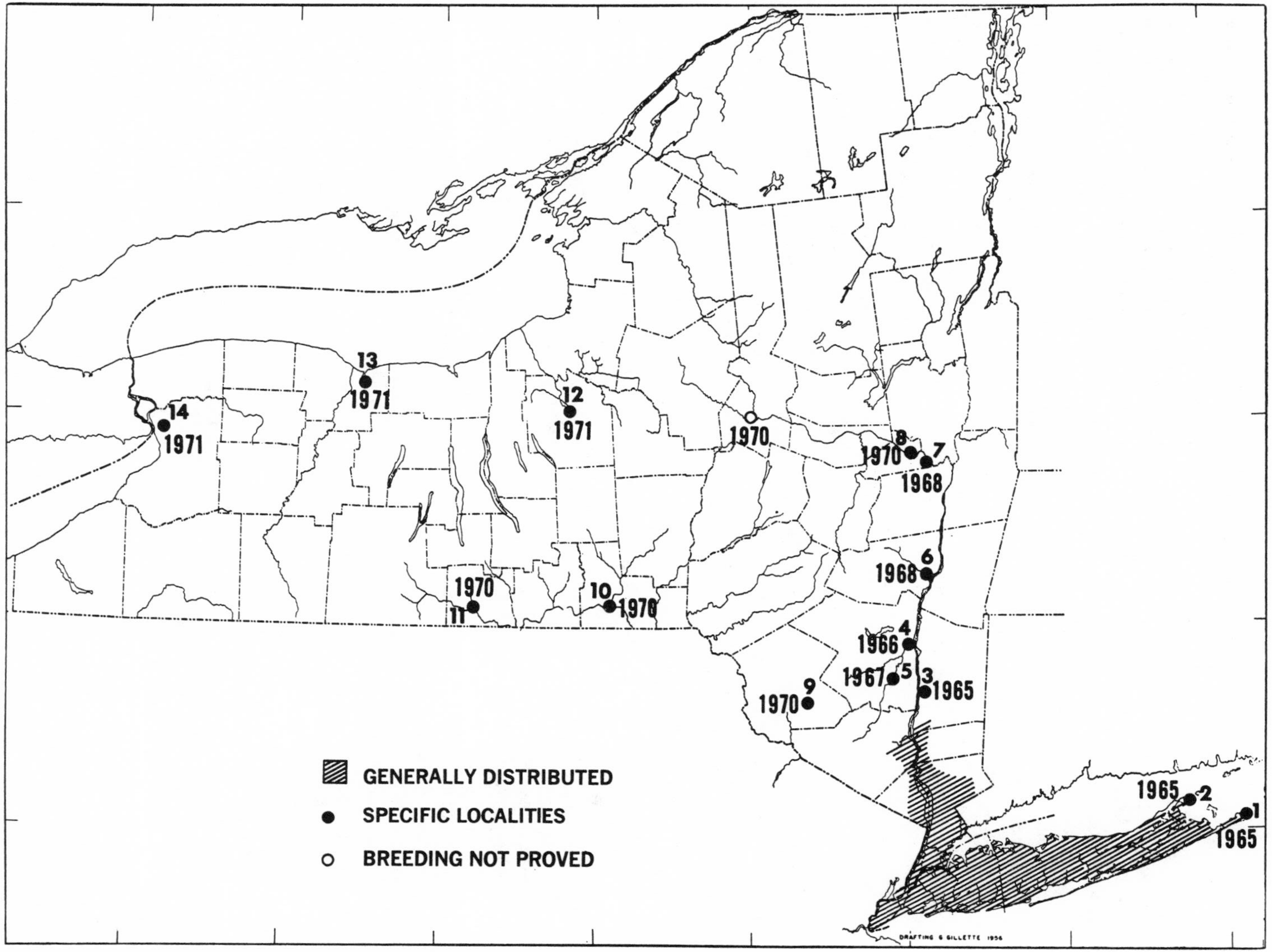

GENERALLY DISTRIBUTED

● SPECIFIC LOCALITIES

○ BREEDING NOT PROVED

(11) Elmira; 1971—(12) Syracuse; (13) Rochester; (14) near Buffalo.

House Finches are very adaptable, breeding around cultivated and residential areas, in city parks, and in landscaped districts along the ocean front, such as the vicinity of buildings at Jones Beach, Long Island.

Nest sites are varied, often in evergreen trees such as spruce, cedar, pine, and .yew; many others in ivy growing on building walls, also in rose trellises, privet hedges, hanging flower baskets, broken lampposts, mailboxes, on building ledges and under eaves, behind house shutters and screens, and other unusual places.

As House Sparrows nest in similar locations, it would be of great interest to determine if competition exists for nest sites, especially in localities where House Finches have recently become established.

Nest heights are from three to 20 feet above ground. Egg clutches in 22 New York nests range from four to six, as follows: four eggs (eight nests); five eggs (12 nests); six eggs (two nests).

EGG DATES: Apr. 11 to July 20.

Nestlings: Apr. 24 to July 27; fledglings: May 18 to Aug. 11.

Gill and Lanyon (1965) found these birds to be double-brooded on Long Island and, in one instance in 1963, the same pair (color-banded) raised two broods and laid a third clutch of eggs which were, however, unsuccessful. They stated that the same nest was *never* reused by one pair, but a new nest was always built. They found that incubation lasted from 13 to 14 days and the nestling period from 14 to 16 days. They further stated, "Nesting pairs exhibited remarkable tolerance of other House Finches. In June 1963 there were three active nests on one ivy-covered wall; one nest was only eight feet from another."

Banding: Although a great amount of color-banding by Gill and Lanyon (*op. cit.*) indicated that many individuals were essentially resident, numerous others have been recovered at considerable distances (see especially Cant and Geis, 1961; also Cohen, *Bird-Banding*, 1971, 42: 50). Several birds banded by Cohen at Atlantic Beach, Nassau Co., were recovered in Virginia; one, banded by him in the summer of 1969, was recovered approximately 550

miles to the south at Gastonia, North Carolina (near the South Carolina border), the following winter, remaining from Nov. 17, 1969, to Mar. 26, 1970. This individual was also color-banded.

Remarks: The form known as *"frontalis"* is not well differentiated from adjacent populations to the south in Mexico. Size and color characters are chiefly clinal in nature and, in addition, considerable individual variation exists, discernible in large museum series.

Postscript: The writer was informed late in 1971 that "several pairs" of House Finches were making daily visits to a feeder on a 17th-floor penthouse at West 96 Street, overlooking Central Park. The species had begun nesting in that park in 1968.

By 1973 these birds were found breeding in the vicinity of the American Museum wherever there was sufficient vegetation such as ivy, vines, or evergreen shrubs to hold the nests. It is now commonplace to hear singing House Finches in many side streets of midtown and upper Manhattan!

Pine Grosbeak (*Pinicola enucleator*)   *

Range: Holarctic region (for details, see **Subspecies**).

Status: Rare, irregular winter visitant, especially southward—more numerous inland than near the coast. At long intervals during flight years even very common.

Occurrence: The Pine Grosbeak is the rarest of the "winter" finches in the state, excepting only the Hoary Redpoll. It appears much less frequently and is more erratic in occurrence than either of the crossbills or the Common Redpoll, and irrupts in much smaller numbers than does the Evening Grosbeak.

Unlike the last named, the Pine Grosbeak does not visit feeding stations but is attracted to the fruits and seeds of various trees and shrubs. It is especially fond of apple seeds and feeds to a large extent on the fruits of sumac, mountain ash, viburnum, and many others, and the buds and seeds of spruce, larch, and other conifers as well.

MAXIMA: Usually in small groups, occasionally in flocks to 40 or more—100, Durand, Eastman Park, Rochester, Nov. 11, 1957; 100+, Katonah, Westchester Co., Nov. 23, 1961; 90, Watertown, Jefferson Co., Jan. 16, 1966; 100, Oak Orchard Swamp area, Feb. 18, 1934. These numbers are exceptional, however.

EXTREME DATES: Female collected, Albany, Sept. 29, 1869 (Rothschild collection), AMNH 516809, is extremely early; Oct. 8 (coastal) to Apr. 20 (coastal) and May 9 (inland specimen—Niagara Falls, 1876, W. C. Osborn, AMNH 234182, is very late) and exceptionally to May 18 (inland—see Beardslee and Mitchell, 1965: 421).

Usually rare before November and after March.

Remarks: No *summer* occurrence in the Adirondack region, or elsewhere in the state, has been substantiated, despite the fact that Pine Grosbeaks have bred in Maine and northern New Hampshire. The report of this species allegedly breeding in southern Connecticut is erroneous (for details, see Bull, 1964: 433).

Subspecies: Two subspecies are known to occur within New York—both differing from nominate *enucleator* of the western Palearctic by being shorter billed (13–14.5 mm. as against 15–16 mm. for nominate *enucleator*):

(1) The race *leucura* (with longer wing, 115–128 mm.) breeds in Canada south to the central portions of Ontario, Quebec, and Labrador.

(2) The race *eschatosus* (with shorter wing, 105–117 mm.) breeds south of *leucura* to central Maine and northern New Hampshire.

The writer has measured numerous specimens of both races in the extensive series of the larger museum collections and has found that the great majority of the specimens taken in New York belongs to the more southern population, *eschatosus*.

Eurasian Goldfinch
(Carduelis carduelis) * B

Range: Palearctic region, east to central Siberia and northern Mongolia. Introduced into various parts of the United States.

Status: *Introduced*—temporarily established

on western Long Island where it was sedentary, but extirpated since the late 1950s.

History: This species was first found in Central Park, Manhattan, in 1879, where it increased for some time, but had disappeared there by 1907.

In 1910 these birds were discovered in Nassau Co. in the vicinity of Massapequa where they had soon increased and spread to surrounding areas—Seaford, Merrick, Freeport, Baldwin, Garden City, and Westbury—and east into Suffolk Co. to Amityville and Babylon. But it was principally in the Massapequa-Seaford sector that this species prospered; as many as a dozen pairs were found there during the mid-1940s. With the boom in real estate after World War II, however, and resultant destruction of its haunts, the birds finally disappeared by the late 1950s.

These birds, presumably sedentary on Long Island, were found in cultivated country, inhabiting gardens, orchards, nurseries, and shade trees and hedgerows along village streets. In winter they resorted to weed fields, but were not known to visit feeding stations.

John Elliott (in Bent, 1968: 387–390), who was more familiar with the bird on Long Island than anyone else, found a total of 15 nests. Twelve of these were situated in Norway maples, and one each in red maple, pitch pine, and arbor-vitae. Height of nests above ground ranged from six to 27 feet. Clutches ranged from four eggs (two nests) to five eggs (six nests).

EGG DATES: Apr. 20 to July 5,

Nestlings: May 25 to July 12; fledglings: June 14 to July 24.

According to Elliott (*op. cit.*) incubation lasted from 12 to 13 days, with young in the nest up to 18 days. He also stated that the species was apparently double-brooded, as an individual was observed building a nest as late as July 16, 1944, while the same or another pair had hatched a clutch of five eggs on the previous May 26. Elliott also mentioned considerable nest predation by Common Grackles.

The Eurasian Goldfinch is common in captivity and is frequently imported and caged. Numerous recent sightings of this bird from the New York City region and at any time period from elsewhere in the state are suspected to be nothing more than escapes.

Remarks: No attempt is made here to go into the subspecies problem. Various "imported" specimens examined by the writer belong to one or more races—either from the continent (Europe) or from the British Isles (see Bull, 1964: 434 for details).

Common Redpoll
(*Acanthis flammea*)   *

Range: Holarctic region (for details, see **Subspecies**).

Status: Irregular winter visitant, absent or very rare some years, common to occasionally very abundant in others.

Occurrence: This species often associates with Pine Siskins and Goldfinches during large irruptive flights in winter. January, February, and March are the principal months of occurrence. Redpolls frequent stands of alder and birch where they feed on the fruiting catkins, and in open fields where the seeds of various grasses and herbs abound. During flight years especially, they may be found at feeding stations. In the late winter of *1960* a large statewide irruption occurred.

MAXIMA: 200, Hamlin Beach, Monroe Co., Nov. 6, 1965; 550, Pompey, Onondaga Co., Nov. 12, 1969; 750, near Buffalo, Dec. 28, 1952; 1000, Elmira, Jan. 29, *1960;* 2000, west end of Jones Beach, Nassau Co., Jan. 30, *1960;* 2500, Pomona, Rockland Co., Feb. 7, *1960;* 1400, *on passage* at Derby Hill, Oswego Co., Apr. 20, 1966 (many observers), late for so many.

EXTREME DATES: Oct. 18 (coastal) to May 4 (coastal specimen) and May 16 (inland). Usually rare before mid-November and after early April.

Banding: One banded at Hastings, Westchester Co., Mar. 27, 1960, was recovered near Montreal, Quebec, Mar. 31, 1960—four days later, approximately 340 miles to the north.

Subspecies: Two races of this species occur in our state. (A) Nominate *flammea* breeds south to the central portions of Ontario and Quebec and to Newfoundland; also rarely on the Magdalen Islands in the Gulf of St. Lawrence (Godfrey, 1966: 375). This is the common subspecies discussed previously.

(B) The more northern race *rostrata* (larger, darker, more heavily streaked, and with a thicker bill) breeds south to Baffin Island. It is extremely rare in New York and I know of only four definite records, all specimens examined by the writer, as follows: (1) female, Shelter Island, Suffolk Co., Feb. 11, 1879 (Worthington), AMNH 65579; (2) and (3) two specimens from Sing Sing (=Ossining), Westchester Co., Feb. 12 and 13, 1883 (Fisher), MCZ 305783 and 305784; (4) male, seven miles east of Ithaca, Jan. 22, 1947 (Warner), CUM 21120.

It is possible that *A. f. rostrata* occurs in our area less rarely than supposed, particularly during flight years. Only careful collecting will determine this point. No sight reports of this subspecies are accepted. The remarks pertaining to the Hoary Redpoll concerning field identification apply even more to *A. f. rostrata* (see Hoary Redpoll for discussion).

The poorly differentiated subspecies "*holbollii*" and "*islandica*" are not recognized here. The differences are of average degree only and much individual variation is present.

Remarks: According to Williamson (1961) the Common Redpoll and Hoary Redpoll occur sympatrically in parts of Iceland and Norway where interbreeding takes place and hybrids or intermediates are "frequent." They also occur together in parts of Greenland where hybridization is reported (Salomonsen, 1950). The two forms are thus considered as conspecific by those authors.

However, in North America the high-arctic *hornemanni* and the low-arctic *flammea* meet on Baffin Island and in the northern portions of Manitoba (Churchill region) and Quebec (Ungava); in these areas they are reported *not* to interbreed and thus "behave" as "good" species. For this reason these two forms or populations are here treated as separate species. More field work is needed in other areas of sympatry on the Canadian mainland to ascertain interaction of the two forms.

Hoary Redpoll
(*Acanthis hornemanni*) *

Range: Northern Holarctic region, in America breeding south to the extreme northern portions of Manitoba and Quebec. Winters south rarely to the southern parts of Connecticut, New York, northern New Jersey, and once in Maryland (all specimens).

Status: *Casual*—there are three proved occurrences for the Hoary Redpoll in New York, two of them specimen records, the third a photograph: (1) immature male collected at Tuckahoe, Westchester Co., Mar. 24, 1888 (Dwight), AMNH 366587, was apparently unknown to Eaton (1914: 270); (2) female taken at Ithaca, Feb. 28, 1960 (N. G. Smith), CUM 30182, the same year a specimen was taken in northern New Jersey (Bull, 1964: 435)—an irruption year for Common Redpolls; (3) immature at a feeder—color-photographed, banded, and released, Schenectady, Mar. 20, 1966 (Yunick, *Kingbird*, 1966, 16: 204–205, and 1967, 17: 66–68), photos on file, AMNH collection.

The above two specimens belong to the more southerly breeding population *exilipes* (smaller and somewhat darker than the nominate race). The photographed individual appears to be this species.

For discussion of relationship with the Common Redpoll, see that species.

I am unable to vouch for the correctness of *any* observations of Hoary Redpolls within the state. Nearly every winter, reports are made of individuals alleged to be this species. Needless to state, the *ten* observed on the 1946 Rochester Christmas count, plus *50* "Greater" Redpolls (*Acanthis flammea rostrata*) out of a total estimate of 500 redpolls (10%) for the day, should not be taken seriously.

The difficulties involved in separating the Common Redpoll from the very similar Hoary Redpoll in the field have been stressed many times (see especially Bull, *op. cit.*). The writer urges all banders, as well as observers, to read the relevant articles by Houston (*Bird-Banding*, 1963, 34: 94–95) and Havens (*Feathers*, 1966, 28: 27–29).

Selective collecting is needed to determine frequency of the Hoary Redpoll within the state.

American Goldfinch
(*Spinus tristis*) * B

Range: North America, breeding from southern Canada to southern United States. Winters nearly throughout the breeding range.

Status: Sedentary and migratory, variously common to very abundant during migration and winter; subject to marked fluctuations. Widespread breeder.

Nonbreeding: The American Goldfinch, although regular in spring in small numbers, is notably erratic in fall and winter, common to occasionally very abundant some years, rare in others. Its presence in winter is largely dependent upon the available food supply, chiefly weed seeds, and the fruit of birch, alder, pine, and others.

MAXIMA: *Fall*—1200, Manitou, Monroe Co., Oct. 24, 1954; 2000, Atlantic Beach, Nassau Co., Nov. 10, 1946.

MAXIMA: *Winter*—4000, Retsof, Livingston Co., Feb. 9, 1964 (Listman), a very high number; usually not more than several hundred in winter.

MAXIMA: *Spring*—1000, Derby Hill, Oswego Co., May 9, 1968; 2500, same locality, May 16, 1970; 2000, Manitou, May 18, 1963.

Migrants usually arrive in late March and depart by November.

Breeding: This species and the Cedar Waxwing are our two latest breeders—often nesting as late as September and October. Goldfinches nest in open country—in agricultural districts, overgrown fields, hedgerows, orchards, and woodland borders. They are inordinately fond of thistles, using the seeds for food and the silky down to line their nests. Nests are placed from four to 20 feet above ground in bushes and trees. During a breeding survey on Grand Island in the Niagara River in 1966, ten nests of this species were found, *all* in hawthorns.

Clutches in 28 New York nests ranged from four to seven eggs, as follows: four eggs (nine nests); five eggs (11 nests); six eggs (six nests); seven eggs (two nests).

EGG DATES: July 3 to Sept. 16.

Nestlings: Aug. 3 to Sept. 24; fledglings: Aug. 17 to Oct. 10.

Pine Siskin (*Spinus pinus*)   *   B

Range: Nearctic region—widespread in the west—breeding from Alaska and northern Canada to the mountains of Guatemala but—in the east—only from southern Canada to northern United States, rarely and erratically as far as northern Pennsylvania, southern New York, and southern New England. Winters throughout the breeding range, except the extreme northern portions.

Status: Regular fall migrant and irregular winter visitant, numbers varying greatly, rare some years, common to occasionally very abundant in others. Present in numbers in spring provided a flight occurred the preceding fall, otherwise rare to absent. Rare and very erratic breeder in various sections of the state, but lacking on Long Island; most numerous in the mountains, but even in the Adirondacks it is local and highly unpredictable, sometimes abundant (following flights), at other times absent for years in succession.

Nonbreeding: This species feeds extensively on the seeds of conifers, birches, alders, various weeds, and, in the southern portions, fruit of the sweet gum (*Liquidambar*).

MAXIMA: *Fall*—huge coastal flight, Oct. 19, 1969—5000, Fire Island State Park, Suffolk Co. (Buckley and Davis); 4000, Riis Park, Queens Co. (Kemp). 1500 in two hours, Jones Beach, Nov. 9, 1946. *Winter*—1000, Watkins Glen, Schuyler Co., Jan. 11, 1961; 1500, near Rockland Lake, Rockland Co., Jan. 24, 1958. *Spring*—680, Derby Hill, Oswego Co., May 16, 1966.

EXTREME DATES: Sept. 5 (coastal) and Sept. 9 (inland) to June 10 (coastal) and June 18 (inland); summer vagrants.

Rare before October and after mid-May.

Breeding (see Map 153): Like the Red Crossbill, the Pine Siskin is little known as a breeder in the state and, if possible, even more erratic and unpredictable in its time of nesting than that species. First of all, only *two* nests (with eggs) have been found in the state—both over 80 years ago (Bull, 1964: 436–437). Breeding is most likely to occur following southward irruptions the preceding fall.

Secondly, siskins and crossbills are notorious wanderers and are present only during certain years when and where their food supply is plentiful, such as the cone crop on evergreens in which these birds nest exclusively. During other years, when these trees do not produce seeds, the birds are absent.

Even in the vast evergreen forests of the Adirondacks they are abundant some years, completely absent in others (Eaton, 1914: 279). Although undoubtedly they are occasionally locally common breeders in the Catskills, I know of not one published nesting record *with details*. The only two firm breeding records for western New York, to my knowledge, occurred after the large irruption of 1960–1961.

Three New York nests were in pine, cedar, and hemlock, from 25 to 35 feet above ground, two of which contained four eggs each, the other's contents were not noted.

EGG DATES: April 25 to May 25, and one nest near Elmira had a single egg on *July* 20, 1893, CUM collection.

Nestlings: Apr. 13 to June 10; fledglings: June 11 to July 16. Obviously these dates are not representative.

In addition to the higher Adirondack breeding areas where, through the years, nesting is presumed to have occurred, the accompanying map shows all of the known extramontane localities in the state. Without exception, *all* 13 breeding localities had a one-year-only nesting occurrence: (1) Sing Sing (=Ossining), Westchester Co., 1883; (2) Cornwall, Orange Co., 1887; (3) Jenny Lake, Saratoga Co., 1968; Lewis Co., 1878—(4) Lyons Falls and (5) Locust Grove; (6) Gilbertsville, Otsego Co., 1910; (7) Deposit, Broome Co., 1959; (8) Chenango Forks, Broome Co., 1966; (9) Ithaca, Tompkins Co., 1925; (10) near Elmira, Chemung Co., 1893; (11) Penn Yan, Yates Co., 1941; (12) near Rochester, Monroe Co., 1961; (13) Jamestown, Chautauqua Co., 1961.

Eaton (1914: 279) lists Remsen, Oneida Co., 1889, as a breeding locality and cites Ralph and Bagg as authorities, but they give no evidence of breeding in their county lists.

Banding: A juvenile, banded June 2, 1963, at Winnipeg, Manitoba, was recovered the following Apr. 22, 1964, at South Salem, Westchester Co.; an individual, banded Apr. 11,

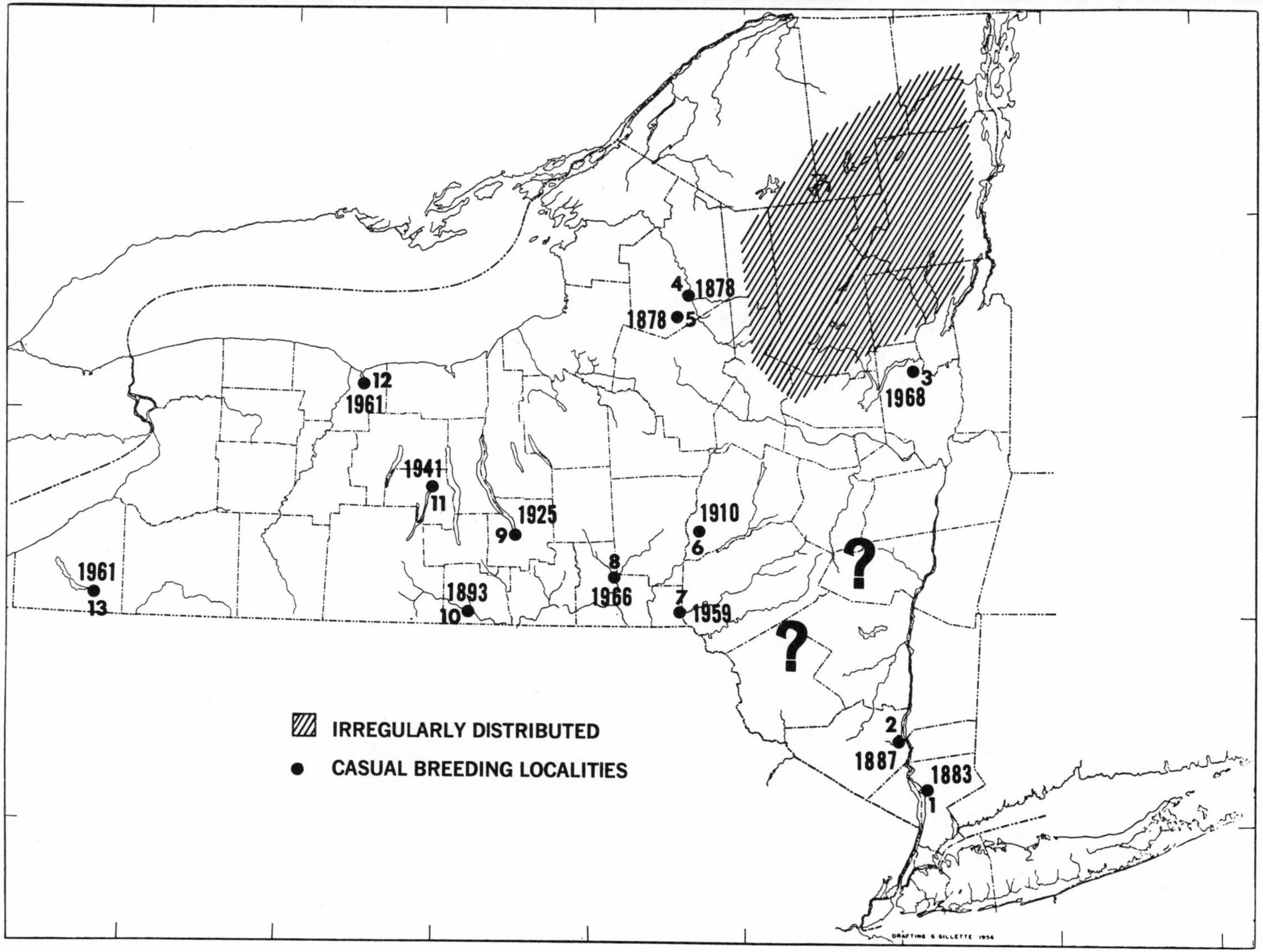

MAP 153 Pine Siskin
(*Spinus pinus*) Breeding
distribution

IRREGULARLY DISTRIBUTED

● CASUAL BREEDING LOCALITIES

● 3
1968

? ●

?

● 2
1887

1883 ●
1

● 4 1878
● 5
1878

● 1910
6

● 1959
7

● 8
1966

● 1925
9

1883
10

● 11
1941

● 12
1961

1961
13

1963, near Binghamton, Broome Co., was found dead in July of that year north of Kamsack, Saskatchewan.

Red Crossbill
(*Loxia curvirostra*) * B

Range: Chiefly Holarctic region, in the New World breeding from Alaska and Canada to the mountains of Nicaragua in the west, to the mountains of Tennessee and North Carolina in the east, and along the Atlantic coast to Long Island. Sedentary and erratically irruptive. For further details, see **Subspecies.**

Status: The most erratic and irregular of New York birds. Chiefly a migrant and winter visitant, but recorded every month of the year; variously rare to locally very common. Rare breeder.

Nonbreeding: Red Crossbills occur most often from November to March; they are sometimes present in flocks during late spring. This species occasionally associates with White-winged Crossbills in big flight years but ordinarily will be found in pure flocks, feeding on seeds extracted from the cones of spruce, hemlock, and various pines. These flights are believed to be due to failure of the cone crop in the north, especially that of spruce.

MAXIMA: In recent years, large irruptions occurred during 1960–1961 and 1969–1970. During the former flight this species was numerous in the interior but virtually absent in southeastern New York. In the latter flight, the largest numbers were reported on the coast of Long Island.

1960–1961—125, Allegany State Park, Cattaraugus Co., Nov. 6; 220, Cooperstown, Otsego Co., Apr. 1; 125, Allegany State Park, June 4; 25, Ithaca, July 10.

1969–1970—1200, Nov. 15, and 1000, Nov. 16, Fire Island State Park, Suffolk Co. (Buckley, Davis, and Ford); 500, Montauk, Suffolk Co., Nov. 22; 150, south end of Saratoga Lake, May 18; 25, Huntington, Suffolk Co., June 11; 13, Short Beach, Nassau Co., July 26.

Breeding (see Map 154): The Red Crossbill is as erratic and unpredictable in the breeding season as it is on passage and during winter. Generally speaking it breeds in the state chiefly

in years following large irruptions the preceding fall. For instance, nearly half of the two dozen breeding occurrences recorded in New York took place in the spring of 1970. Moreover, *all* of the 1970 breeding records occurred in localities outside the "normal" Adirondack spruce forest area.

Eight New York nests were found in evergreens: five in spruce, two in pine, one in cedar. Nest heights ranged from five to 65 feet above ground.

Egg clutches in ten New York nests: three eggs (seven nests); four eggs (three nests).

EGG DATES: Mar. 30 to Apr. 30.

Nestlings: Apr. 24 to May 27; fledglings: May 14 to June 19.

The accompanying map indicates location of the 23 known New York nesting records. The species has probably bred also in the four Adirondack counties of Clinton, Franklin, St. Lawrence, and Warren, as well as in the four Catskill Mtn. counties of Delaware, Greene, Ulster, and Sullivan, but actual breeding has never been proved.

Eastern New York—Essex Co.—(1) near Mt. Marcy. Hamilton Co.—(2) Forked Lake; (3) Brandreth Lake; (4) near Morehouseville. Herkimer Co.—(5) Big Moose Lake; (6) Black Creek Lake. Lewis Co.—(7) Locust Grove. Schenectady Co.—(8) Mariaville; (9) Scotia; (10) near Schenectady. Schoharie Co. —(11) near Gilboa. Orange Co.—(12) near Cornwall. Westchester Co.—(13) near Riverdale. Suffolk Co.—(14) Miller's Place; (15) Yaphank.

Western New York—Tompkins Co.—(16) Ithaca. Schuyler Co.—(17) Watkins Glen. Allegany Co.—(18) Alfred; (19) Belmont. Erie Co.—(20) Eden; (21) East Aurora; (22) Lancaster. Niagara Co.—(23) Pendleton.

Subspecies: Four subspecies occur in New York:

(1) *L. c. minor* (characterized by smaller size, relatively slender bill, and lighter, paler coloration than next race) is the breeding form over much of the northeast from Ontario east to Nova Scotia, south in the mountains to Tennessee and North Carolina, and along the coast to Long Island—has been discussed previously.

(2) *L. c. pusilla* (larger size, heavier bill, and darker coloration) breeds in Newfound-

MAP 154 Red Crossbill
(*Loxia curvirostra*)
Breeding distribution

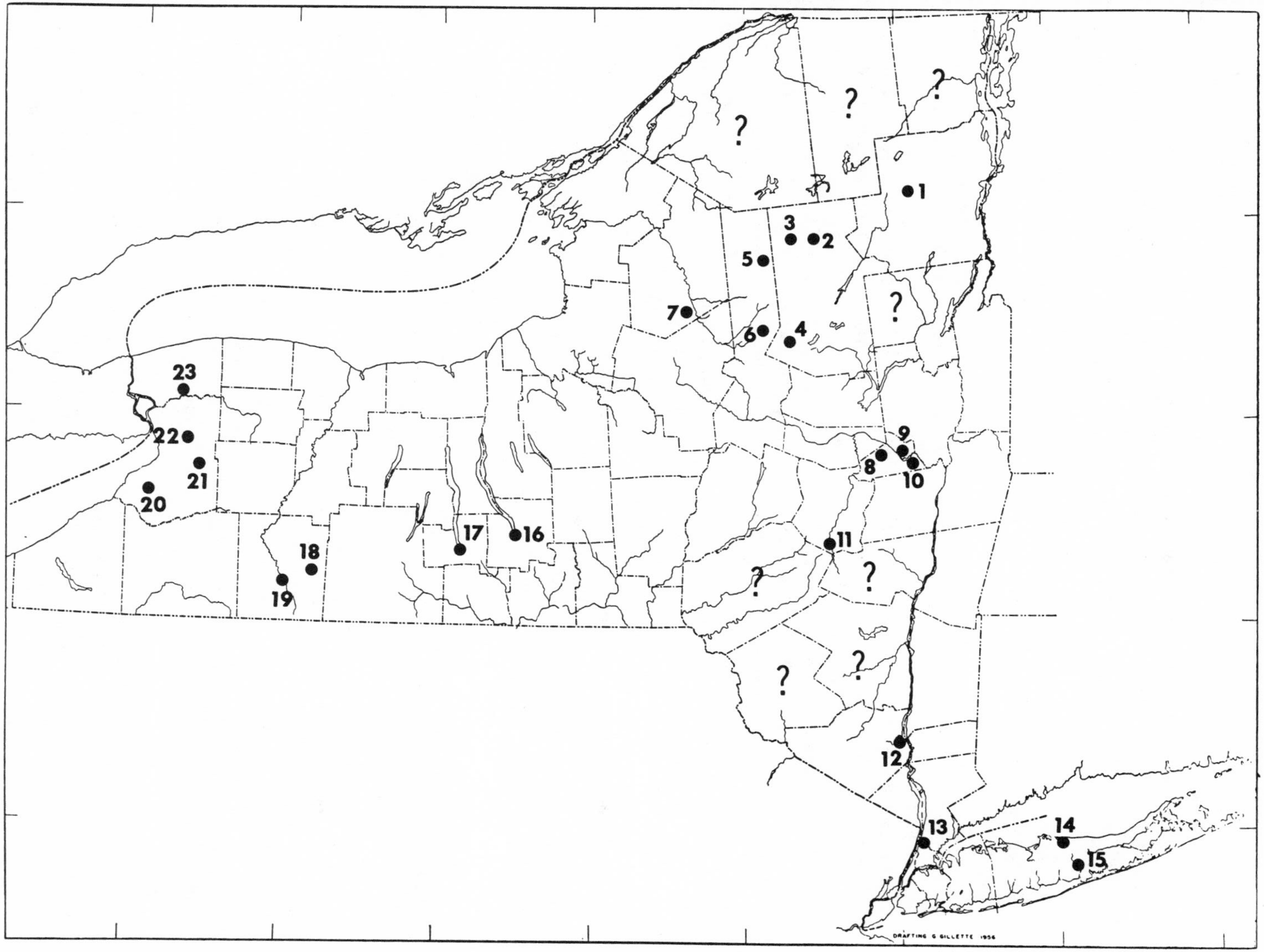

land. It is mainly sedentary, but flights have occurred in New York, chiefly late winter and
early spring—at least nine state specimens, examined by the writer, are assignable to this
race.

(3) *L. c. sitkensis* (even smaller than
minor with short, stubby bill) breeds along the
Pacific coast from southern Alaska to northern
California. This subspecies is mainly resident
but not infrequently wanders as far east as the
Atlantic seaboard. Numerous specimens were
taken in the flight of 1888 and again during
the irruption of 1961, with several collected in
other years. At least *40* specimens from New
York have been examined by the writer, taken
between November and April of various years.

(4) *L. c. benti* (characterized by very long,
slender bill basally [Griscom, 1937: 129]; also
females are lighter and brighter yellowish-green
below with a whiter throat). It breeds in the
Rocky Mountains from Montana and Wyoming
east to the Black Hills of South Dakota; wanders east to Michigan. One specimen, a female,
found dead at Jones Beach, Long Island, Dec.
29, 1963 (Leffler), specimen in Univ. Kansas
collection; see Bull (1964: 439) for details.

White-winged Crossbill
(*Loxia leucoptera*)   *   B?

Range: Holarctic region, in North America
breeding from Alaska and Canada to extreme
northern United States—where very rare; an
isolated, relict population in mountain pine
forest of Hispaniola. Chiefly sedentary, but
wanders south in winter to the Middle Atlantic
states (Ohio, North Carolina).

Status: Rare and irregular winter visitant,
occasionally common in flight years. Much less
frequent than the Red Crossbill, though sometimes outnumbering that species. Doubtful
breeder in the Adirondack region.

Nonbreeding: White-winged Crossbills feed
extensively on the seeds of hemlock and larch
cones in inland areas, and on those of pitch and
black pines along the coast. If conditions are
right (for the observer) and cones are lacking
in the north (Canada) but are in profusion in
our latitude, these birds are likely to visit us
and, on rare occasions, they irrupt in consider-

able numbers. At very long intervals these
irruptions take place both upstate and on the
coast. Within the past 20 years, three major
flights occurred.

MAXIMA (1954–1955): *Coastal*—80, Montauk area, Nov. 13; 35, Oak Beach, Suffolk
Co., March 8.

MAXIMA (1960–1961): *Inland*—120, Allegany State Park, Cattaraugus Co., Jan. 20; 100,
Saranac Lake (village), Franklin Co., Jan. 21;
75, near Java, Wyoming Co., May 21 (Rosche);
seven, Hamburg, Erie Co., June 7 (Czont).
Note the large numbers on exceptionally late
dates.

MAXIMA (1963–1964): *Chiefly inland*—
30, Durand Eastman Park, Rochester, Oct. 19;
100, Prospect Park, Kings Co. and 110, Riis
Park, Queens Co., both on Nov. 25; 150,
Fish Gulf, Oneida Lake, Nov. 27; 100, Sherburne, Chenango Co., Dec. 8; 200, Eaton,
Madison Co., Dec. 23.

EXTREME DATES: Oct. 6 (coastal) and Oct.
13 (inland) to May 29 (coastal) and June 7
(inland—see above maxima). Ordinarily rare
before late October and after April.

Breeding? (see Map 155): Although the
White-winged Crossbill very likely has bred in
the Adirondacks, I have been unable to find a
single positive breeding record for New York
State, either eggs or young in museum collections, or adequate details in the literature.

Eaton (1914: 268) stated, "It breeds in the
Adirondack forest according to Merriam . . ."
but no details as to localities or dates are
given. Taber (in Bent, 1968; 543) mentions,
"eastern Lewis County, Long Lake" (=Long
Pond) as a breeding locality, but without date
or other details.

The following seven localities are represented by summer dates ranging from June 10
to July 13 of various years. But these June and
July dates are not indicative of nesting time,
as this species is an early nester with eggs
dating from February to April, even in latitudes as far north as Labrador and Nova
Scotia. This early breeding season may account for nests being overlooked in New York
—long before most of the visiting summer
ornithologists arrive.

However, it does not explain why juvenile
White-winged Crossbills have not been discovered in the Adirondacks, even *fledged* juven-

MAP 155 White-winged
Crossbill (*Loxia
leucoptera*) Breeding (?)
distribution

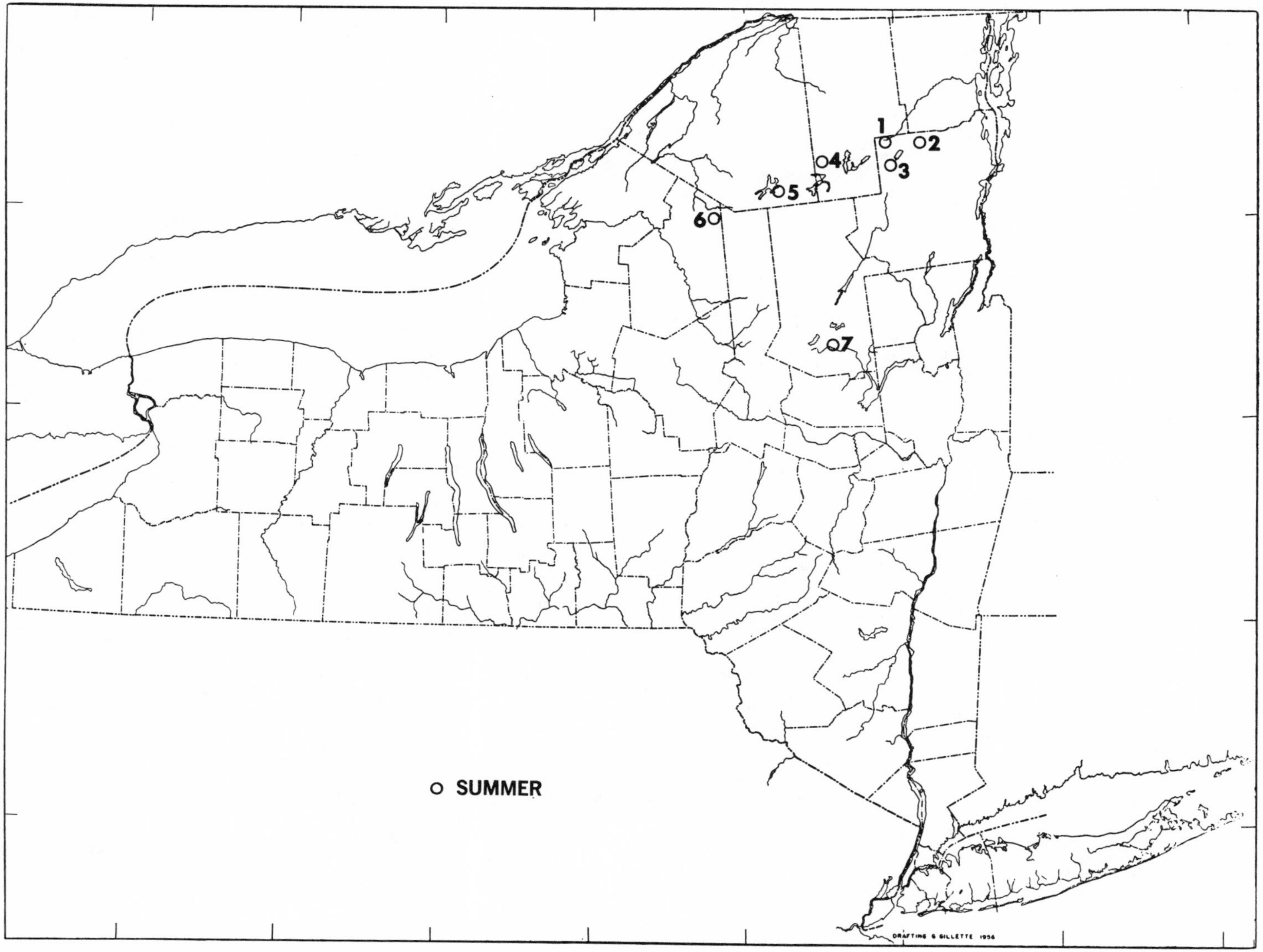

O SUMMER

iles which should be in evidence by early summer if the species breeds there.

The seven summer localities are: Essex Co.—(1) Bloomingdale (Carleton); (2) Wilmington Notch (Elliott); (3) Chubb River Swamp (Carleton), June 10, 1953—eight birds. Franklin Co.—(4) Kildare (Carleton). St. Lawrence Co.—(5) Barber Point, Cranberry Lake (Silloway). Lewis Co.—(6) Long Pond (observer unknown). Hamilton Co.—(7) Whitehouse (McIlroy).

Greenleaf Chase (*in litt.*) feels that ". . . these birds could be breeding in some of the larger white spruce stands."

Perhaps some day a sharp-eyed observer will discover a nest hidden away among the thick foliage of an evergreen, or find adults in the act of feeding young birds.

Rufous-sided Towhee
(*Pipilo erythrophthalmus*)   *   B

Range: Breeds from extreme southern Canada south to the Gulf states and in the mountains to Guatemala. In winter chiefly south of the northern breeding limits.

Status: Common to very common migrant on and near the coast, especially in spring; less numerous elsewhere. Uncommon but regular in winter, chiefly on the coast. Common breeder at lower elevations, especially on the coastal plain of Long Island. Rare to absent in the higher mountains; decidedly uncommon and local in northern New York, but has been increasing within recent years.

Nonbreeding: Migrant Towhees usually arrive in early April and depart by mid-November. Wintering individuals have been increasing in recent years, particularly at feeding stations.

MAXIMA: *Spring*—35, Manitou, Monroe Co., Apr. 28, 1956; 110, Central Park, New York City, Apr. 30, 1947; 200, Lawrence to Woodmere, Nassau Co., May 6, 1950; 50, Madison Square Park, New York City, May 15, 1921.

No fall maxima are available as the migration at this season is much more protracted (late August to November).

MAXIMA: *Winter*—six, Chatham area, Columbia Co., Jan. 27, 1959 (at *several* feeders —exceptional number for upstate); in January

1962 in eastern Suffolk Co. at two different feeders, eight at Orient and seven *males* at Brookhaven.

One individual was found dead at Victor, Ontario Co., Jan. 18, 1958, and another wintered at a feeder at Watertown, Jefferson Co., 1960–1961.

Breeding: This species nests on or near the ground in dry open woodland and in clearings, especially in brushy fields, thickets, and hedgerows. On Long Island it is most numerous in coastal scrub along the outer beaches, and in sandy areas of scrub-oak and pitch pine in the "barrens."

The nest is placed on the ground and at elevations from a few inches to as high as six feet in a clematis vine. Other elevated nests were in hemlocks (twice) and in a dogwood. Yet another was placed two feet up on top of a beech stump.

Egg clutches in 31 New York nests: three eggs (21 nests); four eggs (eight nests); five eggs (two nests).

EGG DATES: May 15 to Aug. 4 (two broods).

Nestlings: May 18 to Aug. 15; fledglings: June 2 to Aug. 31.

In recent years, Towhees have "invaded" the more northern portions of the state, especially the Adirondack region. In 1954 in the Cicero Swamp area of northern Onondaga Co., Scheider found the species "notably common in spruce-bog openings—a wet area of northern plant associations." During June 1964 Rusk found a "high concentration" at the edge of the Tug Hill district, near Redfield, Oswego Co., and during the summer of 1965 she saw the species in northern Hamilton Co. in the Sabattis area. As many as five singing males were present in late June 1963 at Wilmington, Essex Co. In 1968 a pair bred at Black Brook, Clinton Co., not far from Lake Champlain. In 1970, Carleton (*Audubon Field Notes,* 1970, 24: 668) reported these birds "nesting up to altitudes of 2700 feet on Bald and Spotted mountains in Essex County . . . [they] were in brushy fields resulting from forest fires some 65 years ago."

Subspecies: The nominate race of the northeast has been discussed above. The more western race *arcticus* (back and wings with extensive white spotting) has occurred in New

York on three occasions, all in the southeastern portion, as follows: two females collected by Buckley—(1) Zach's Bay area, Jones Beach, Nassau Co., Feb. 16, 1957, NYSM 19019; (2) Bronx Park, New York City, Dec. 23, 1958, AMNH 707778. For further details, see Buckley (1959) and Bull (1964: 442). (3) A male color-photographed by Puleston at a feeder in Bellport, Suffolk Co., during the winter of 1964–1965, was present from Dec. 3 to Feb. 1 and was seen by numerous observers; color photo on file, AMNH collection.

Banding: Six birds banded in summer or fall in New York were recovered in late fall or winter following in the southeastern states: twice each in the Carolinas and once each in Georgia and northern Florida.

Green-tailed Towhee
(*Pipilo chlorura*) *

Range: Western North America, breeding east to southeastern Wyoming, migrating east to western Kansas, and wintering northeast to southern Texas. Vagrant to eastern North America—Quebec, Nova Scotia, and New York (specimens); Massachusetts and New Jersey (photographs).

Status: *Casual*—in New York there are two confirmed records: (1) one at the Anderson feeder, Ithaca, from mid-December 1962 to Apr. 25, 1963. This bird was seen by hundreds of observers during its long stay and was photographed in color by D. G. Allen; photo examined by the writer. (2) specimen netted at Scarsdale, Westchester Co., Oct. 19, 1971, died of "unknown causes," Nov. 3, 1971 (F. R. Haeni), AMNH 808899.

One was observed south of Cazenovia, Madison Co., May 10–14, 1969 (Morrison and many other observers, *Kingbird,* 1969, 19: 166–167).

Remarks: This species is placed in the genus *Pipilo,* following Sibley (*Auk,* 1955, 72: 420–423) and Paynter (in "Peters," 1970: 168–169). It resembles especially the Mexican form, *P. ocai.* the Collared Towhee.

Lark Bunting
(*Calamospiza melanocorys*)   *

Range: West-central North America, breeding in the Great Plains region of southern Canada and northern United States east to western Minnesota. Winters in southwestern United States and northern Mexico. Vagrant to the Atlantic coast from New Brunswick to Georgia.

Status: *Very rare*—there have been at least *14* occurrences of the Lark Bunting in the state, *12* of them from Long Island. Eight reports are during the month of September, and eight are within seven years (1964–1970). Coincidentally, a huge irruption occurred in 1964 at the eastern end of the breeding range (western Minnesota). This increase in reports may also reflect an increase in the number of competent observers.

The following records include 12 from Long Island, four of them specimens:

1. Montauk Point, Suffolk Co., Sept. 4, 1888 (Evans), AMNH 65941.

2. Miller's Place, Suffolk Co., Sept. 11, 1896 (Helme), AMNH 802436.

3. Mount Sinai, Suffolk Co., Sept. 13, 1901 (Helme), AMNH 802437; not previously published.

4. Wainscott, Suffolk Co., Nov. 27, 1937 (Helmuth).

5. Easthampton, Suffolk Co., Aug. 31, 1939 (Helmuth), specimen in his collection.

6. Jamaica Bay Refuge, June 6, 1959 (Carleton, Harrison, Mayer, and Bull).

7. Riis Park, Queens Co., Sept. 6, 1964 (Robben and Hirshberg, *Kingbird,* 1965, 15: 23).

8. Westhampton Beach, Suffolk Co., Oct. 17, 1965 (Raynor).

9. Short Beach, Nassau Co., Sept. 10, 1966 (Davis, Hirschbein, Levine, and Ward); photographed in color by Daly.

10. Riis Park, Sept. 24, 1967 (Brennan, Daly, and O'Hare, *Kingbird,* 1968, 18: 61).

11. Riis Park (third report from this locality), Oct. 6–14, 1968 (Clermont and many others).

12. Belmont, Allegany Co., Nov. 30, 1966— a male appeared at the Burton feeder and was

present until May 13, 1967. During this time it was photographed; hundreds of observers saw it and the Burtons noted the plumage changes as the season progressed. By May 13 it had attained practically full breeding plumage.

What was almost certainly the same male was observed at the Wright feeder, Ithaca, Tompkins Co., May 19, 1967 (McIlroy). Belmont and Ithaca are only 75 miles apart.

13. Stissing, Dutchess Co., May 12–13, 1970 (Porter, Pink, and Waterman)—male in breeding plumage at the Haight feeder.

14. Orient, Suffolk Co., Sept. 16, 1970 (Connolly, Dove, and Melum)—immature or female feeding with House Sparrows in a potato field.

For illustrations of the Lark Buntings at Short Beach and Belmont, see *Kingbird* (1968, 18: 2–3). Other reports were not substantiated.

Savannah Sparrow
(*Ammodramus sandwichensis*)   *   B

Range: Nearctic and northern Neotropical regions, breeding from Alaska and northern Canada—in the west to the mountains of Guatemala—but in the east only south to the coastal plain of New Jersey, rarely to Maryland. Winters from Massachusetts and New York southward.

Status: Very abundant fall coastal migrant; very common spring inland migrant. Occasionally numerous in winter on the coast, rare inland. Widespread but local breeder, most prevalent on the coast.

Nonbreeding: Savannah Sparrows are occasionally found in very large concentrations along the coast, especially in fall passage.

MAXIMA: *Fall*—1200, Easthampton, Suffolk Co., Oct. 2, 1930 (Helmuth); 2000, Orient, Suffolk Co., Oct. 12, 1955 (Latham). *Winter*—210, Jamaica Bay, Long Island, Dec. 20, 1952. *Spring*—200, Derby Hill, Oswego Co., Apr. 1, 1969; 65, Syracuse, Apr. 17, 1965.

Note that the numbers in winter on the coast are greater than those in spring inland.

Migrants usually arrive in late March and depart by mid-November.

Breeding: The Savannah Sparrow is most numerous on Long Island, especially along the south shore. The once-large breeding population on the former Hempstead Plains was wiped out by destruction of that area after World War II. Although it nests locally along the coast on sand dunes, especially where beach grass (*Ammophila*) is prevalent, the Savannah Sparrow is most numerous on filled-in grassy areas adjacent to bays and inlets. In the Jamaica Bay area in 1953, Mayer estimated at least 100 breeding pairs from Idlewild to Canarsie, including the bay islands. The birds were nesting chiefly on sand fill that had grown up to grass and weeds.

Upstate this species is more local, though common in suitable fields even at higher elevations in the mountains wherever the forest has been removed and replaced by grassy swales and meadows. Nests are frequently placed in grass tufts in low moist meadows, occasionally in drier grassland, but usually *not* in short grass in which Vesper Sparrows nest, or in tall dry grassland preferred by Grasshopper Sparrows.

In the Finger Lakes region, Spiker (1935: 538) found it to be a common breeder in pastures and in alfalfa and clover fields.

Egg clutches in 20 New York nests: four eggs (15 nests); five eggs (five nests).

EGG DATES: May 11 to July 16 (second? brood).

Nestlings: May 30 to July 23; fledglings: June 12 to Aug. 30.

Banding: A fall migrant banded on the south shore of Long Island was recovered the following summer on its breeding grounds in Newfoundland. Another fall migrant banded near Ithaca was recovered the following winter in South Carolina.

Subspecies: The local breeding race *savanna* (much smaller than nominate *sandwichensis* of coastal Alaska) has been discussed above. The form known as *"labradorius,"* breeding to the north and east of *savanna,* is a weakly defined population alleged to be darker but, in fact, when examined in a large series is of average difference only. Other populations from the eastern mainland of southern Canada and northern United States, named *"mediogriseus"* and *"oblitus,"* are also poorly differentiated—part of an east-west continental cline—and are here regarded as synonyms. However, the well-marked insular race *princeps* (larger and paler than *savanna*), formerly considered to be a separate species and still thought to be such by some—the Ipswich Sparrow—is here treated as conspecific This bird, restricted in the breeding season to sandy, treeless Sable Island—nearly 100 miles off Nova Scotia—matches quite closely certain pale Pacific coast populations of the Savannah Sparrow, notably the subspecies *rostratus* of the dry sandy areas of Baja California and Sonora. Vocalizations of the Savannah and Ipswich sparrows are considered to be very similar (Elliott, 1955). The race *princeps* winters on the Atlantic coast, chiefly from Georgia to Long Island, rarely farther north.

The recognition of *princeps* as a well-marked insular race of *sandwichensis* rather than a separate species emphasizes how poorly characterized are the nearby mainland subspecies when compared with the local breeding race *savanna*.

In New York *princeps* is confined almost exclusively to coastal sand dunes and beaches of Long Island, and is most likely to be seen where beach grass (*Ammophila*) grows. In such places it is a regular, but rare to uncommon, occasionally fairly common migrant and winter visitant. It is very rare along the shores of Long Island Sound except on the Orient peninsula at the east end, where it is uncommon; there are no authentic records away from the immediate seacoast.

Recent maxima are: ten, Gilgo Beach, Suffolk Co., Nov. 11, 1950; nine, Moriches, Suffolk Co., Mar. 24, 1951.

EXTREME DATES: Sept. 20 and 28 (specimen) to Apr. 8 (specimen), and various other dates to Apr. 25. Sight reports during early September and May, although possibly correct, are rejected because of probable confusion with pale individuals of the Savannah Sparrow. Rare before late October and after March.

For a history of the Ipswich Sparrow on Long Island, see Bull (1964: 443).

Postscript: For a note and photographs of an alleged "hybridization" between *A. s. savanna* and *A. s. princeps* on the Nova Scotia mainland, see *American Birds* (1971, 25: 836).

Seaside Sparrow
(*Ammodramus maritimus*) * B

Range: Salt marshes of Atlantic and Gulf coasts from Massachusetts south to Florida, and west to Texas. Resident, except in extreme north.

Status: Locally common to very common breeder along the coast, but rare and local at the extreme eastern end of Long Island and on Long Island Sound. Regular but uncommon to fairly common in winter, occasionally more numerous. Confined to salt marsh.

Nonbreeding: The Seaside Sparrow is casual away from its saline environment. A specimen was taken at the mouth of the Croton River (where it joins the Hudson), Westchester Co., Oct. 2, 1885 (Fisher), MCZ collection. In addition there are five observations from three New York City parks: three from Central Park and one each from Prospect and Van Cortlandt parks.

It is ordinarily less numerous in winter than the Sharp-tailed Sparrow, up to a dozen being recorded per day per locality. However, in a very wet, unditched portion of the Oak Beach marshes in Suffolk Co. during the winter of 1967–1968, Enders and W. Post, by mist-netting and color-marking, recorded as many as *44* individuals, as against only eight Sharp-tails.

Breeding (see Map 156): The Seaside Sparrow occurs exclusively on the salt meadows and is casual anywhere else. It nests in the wetter portions almost invariably, according to Elliott (1953) and Woolfenden (1956), the former stating that it "occupies the wetter areas of taller, coarser grasses . . . ," such as *Spartina alterniflora*. However, it occasionally breeds in dry sandy areas among beach grass very close to the salt marsh, as at the Jamaica Bay Refuge.

Some idea of breeding density may be seen from the following: note the very much higher density in wet, *unditched* marsh—Tobay Beach, Nassau Co., 1966, only 17 pairs in 25 acres of "dry" *ditched* salt marsh (Enders and Heath); Oak Beach, Suffolk Co., 1968, *140* nests in 32 acres of "wet" *unditched* salt marsh (Post and Enders, in press). According to them 120 nests were located in, or rather attached

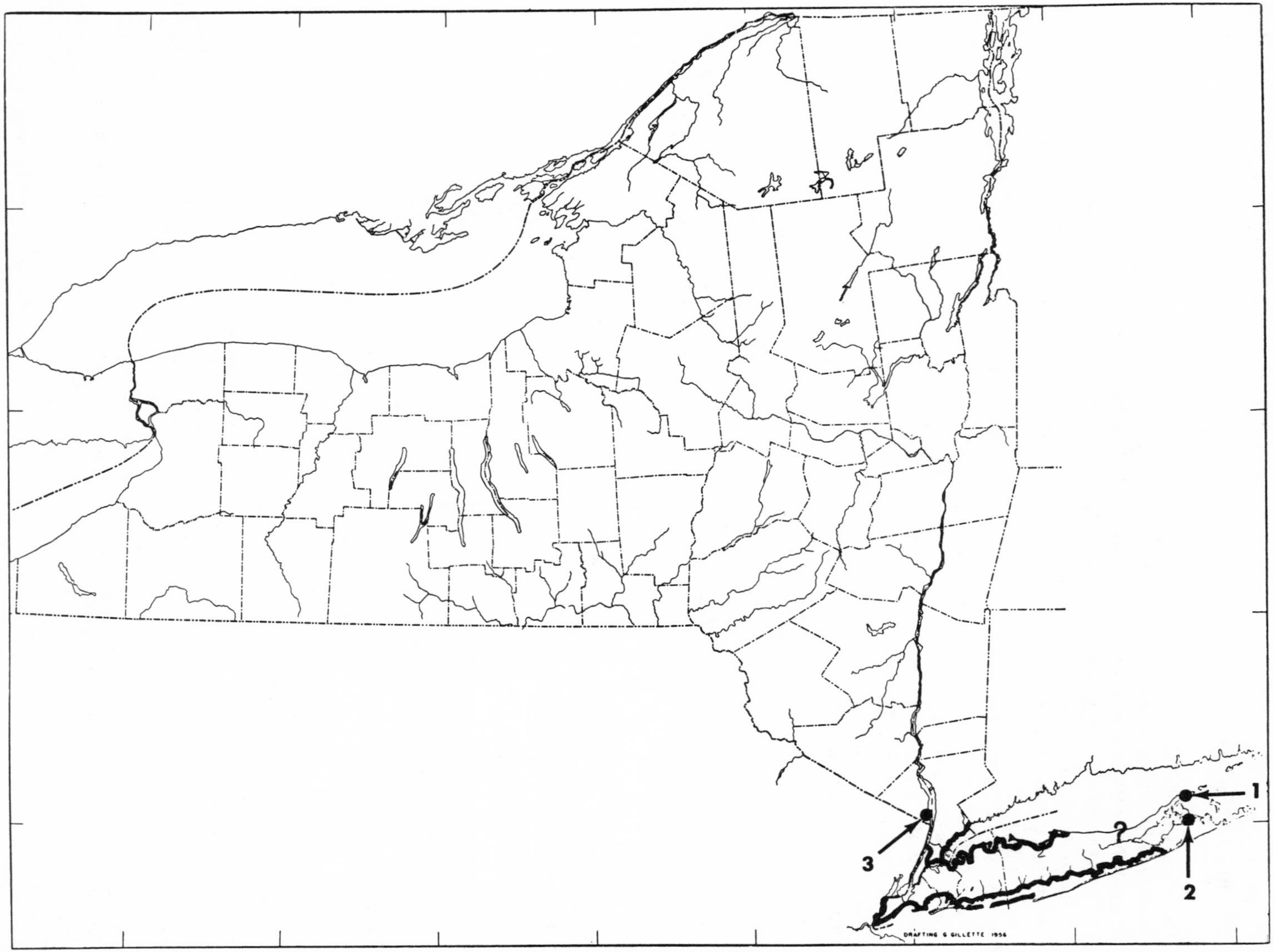

MAP 156 Seaside
Sparrow (*Ammodramus
maritimus*) Breeding
distribution

to, the stems of *Spartina alterniflora,* all nests suspended from five to ten inches above water or mud level. The heights of these dense masses of *Spartina* ranged from 18 to 45 inches, but usually averaged about 30 inches. For habitat and nests, see Fig. 82. Post and Enders (*op. cit.*) stated that these birds were ". . . not evenly dispersed over the marsh, but nested together in colonies."

Two entirely different nest sites are: (1) nest one foot above ground in tussock of beach grass (*Ammophila*) in dry sand, Jamaica Bay Refuge, June 1965 (Cooley); (2) nest one foot above ground in hightide bush (*Iva frutescens*), among relatively dry clumps of salt marsh "hay" (*Spartina patens*), in which other nests were located, Jones Beach area, June 1966 (Davis).

Egg clutches in 54 New York nests: three eggs (21 nests); four eggs (31 nests); five eggs (two nests).

EGG DATES: May 25 to July 10.

Nestlings: June 8 to July 23; fledglings: no New York data.

For further details of breeding distribution in the New York City region, see Bull (1964: 452–453) and accompanying map. Suffice it to say that the species is today very rare away from the south shore of Long Island. It was formerly reported nesting in extreme eastern Suffolk Co. at Orient (1) and until 1947 at Sag Harbor (2); also many years ago on the west bank of the Hudson River in Rockland Co. at Piermont (3). Perhaps it still nests at some or all of these localities; this needs investigation.

Fig. 82 Clapper Rail breeding habitat, Oak Beach, Suffolk Co., June 1969. Both *Spartina alterniflora* and *S. patens* are utilized for nesting. Seaside Sparrows also breed here. Photo by William Post

Sharp-tailed Sparrow
(*Ammodramus caudacutus*)   *   B

Range: Nearctic region, breeding chiefly in inland fresh-water marshes in Canada and in coastal salt marshes south to North Carolina. Winters north along the coast to Long Island, occasionally farther north. For details, see **Subspecies.**

Status: Common to locally abundant coastal migrant, especially in fall. Regular but uncommon to fairly common in winter, occasionally more numerous. Common to locally abundant breeder in coastal salt marsh. Very rare fall migrant inland, virtually unknown there at other seasons.

Nonbreeding: In New York State this species is very rarely reported away from its saline environment. For instance, there are only four observations in the New York City parks, three from Central Park and one from Prospect Park, all in May.

MAXIMA, COASTAL: *Fall*—1000, Orient region, eastern Suffolk Co., Sept. 22, 1938 (Latham), day after the great hurricane—a most exceptional number; 300, East Rockaway, Nassau Co., Oct. 10, 1962 (K. Berlin). Ordinarily only up to 50 or 60 per day per locality are observed.

MAXIMA, COASTAL: *Winter*—32, Jones Beach area, winter of 1940–1941 (Elliott), but see Seaside Sparrow for comparison.

Breeding (see Map 157): The Sharp-tailed Sparrow breeds in the drier portions of the salt meadows, preferring the higher sections where there is a growth of the shorter grasses, such as *Spartina patens* and *Distichlis spicata*.

A density of 13 breeding pairs in 15 acres of *ditched* salt marsh at Tobay Beach, Nassau Co., in 1970 (W. Post), appears to be the maximum recorded.

Egg clutches in 30 New York nests: three eggs (seven nests); four eggs (23 nests).

EGG DATES: May 30 to July 21.

Nestlings: June 11 to Aug. 5; fledglings: Aug. 1.

The Sharp-tailed Sparrow is more generally distributed than the Seaside Sparrow, breeding farther east on Long Island, as far as Gardiner's Bay and on the Montauk peninsula to Napeague Bay; also locally common on both shores of Long Island Sound.

For further details of breeding distribution in the New York City region, see Bull (1964: 449) and accompanying map. Today this species is really numerous only on the south shore of Long Island. It formerly nested, at least until 1908, on the west bank of the Hudson River in Rockland Co. at Piermont. It may still do so, but only a thorough search of these tidal marshes will determine this.

Subspecies: Four races occur in New York State:

(1) Nominate *caudacutus,* breeding exclusively in Atlantic coastal salt marshes from extreme southwestern Maine to southern New Jersey, and the only *breeding* race in New York, has been discussed above.

(2) The race *subvirgatus* (back grayer; both dorsal and ventral streaking indistinct) breeds locally in salt and brackish marshes in extreme southeastern Quebec (south shore of the lower St. Lawrence River); and from Nova Scotia, Prince Edward Island, and New Brunswick—see map in Godfrey (1966: 386) for Canadian breeding range—south to southwestern Maine, where it intergrades with nominate *caudacutus.* Common coastal migrant; winters on the south Atlantic coast.

All New York specimens of Sharp-tailed Sparrows of the subspecies *caudacutus* and *subvirgatus* examined by me are confined to the coastal region and up the Hudson valley to the Croton River marshes in Westchester Co. No *bona fide* specimen of either of these two races is known from upstate. The only known New York winter specimens of this species are of nominate *caudacutus* from Long Island. Based on specimens, the migration dates of *subvirgatus* on Long Island are: *Fall*— Sept. 29 to Oct. 19, also Nov. 24; *Spring*— May 26 to June 8.

(3) The race *alterus* (like *subvirgatus,* but more buffy below—the least well-marked race) breeds in brackish marshes of James Bay in west-central Quebec and northeastern Ontario. Fall migrant, both inland and along the coast. Winters on the coast of the south Atlantic states.

(4) The race *nelsoni* (breast rich buff, dorsal streaking conspicuous) has a wide range

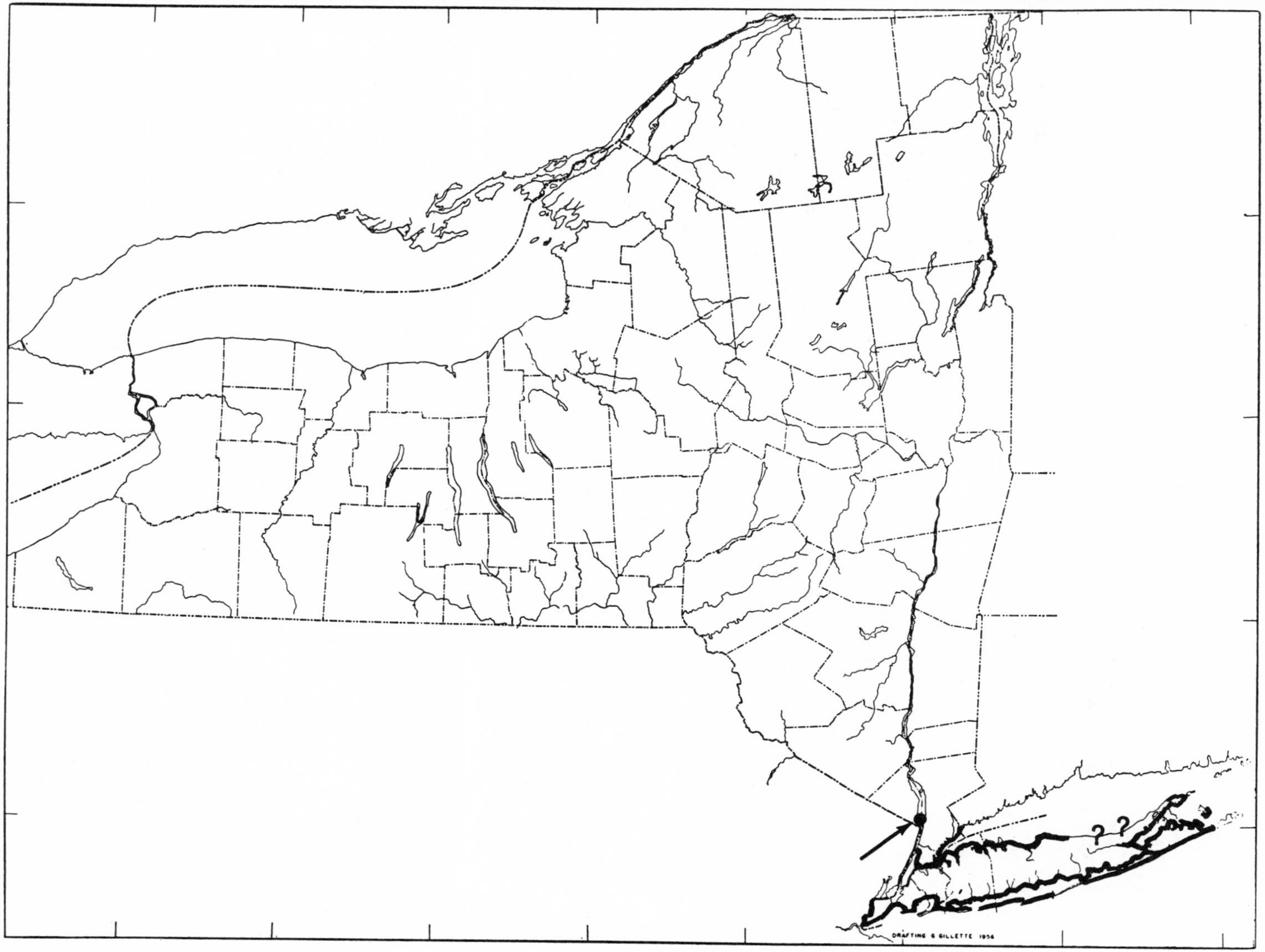

MAP 157 Sharp-tailed
Sparrow (*Ammodramus
caudacutus*) Breeding
distribution

and breeds in inland fresh-water prairie marshes from southern Mackenzie and eastern British Columbia east to southeastern Manitoba, the Dakotas, and northwestern Minnesota. Winters along the Gulf and south Atlantic coasts.

Both *alterus* and *nelsoni* have been taken quite frequently in the Ithaca area. More than 30 specimens of both races, about equally divided, were taken there in various years during the autumn migrations, with dates ranging from Sept. 23 to Oct. 24, specimens in CUM collection. The only spring specimen of either race examined by the writer is that of an individual of *nelsoni* collected at Dunkirk, Chautauqua Co., May 29, 1930 (R. T. Peterson), BMS 1622.

In sum, all previous reports in the literature of specimens from western New York identified as *subvirgatus* proved, upon re-examination, to be *alterus*.

Although there are numerous fall observations of Sharp-tailed Sparrows from upstate New York, it seems useless to give extreme dates, as this species is easily confused with its close relative, Le Conte's Sparrow (*A. leconteii*), which it resembles closely. Le Conte's Sparrow has been taken once at Ithaca and might occur again.

For the difficulties in separating the various subspecies in the museum, let alone in the field, see Bull (1964: 450–451).

Le Conte's Sparrow
(*Ammodramus leconteii*)   *

Range: Chiefly central North America, breeding east locally to southeastern Ontario —north of Toronto; rarely to south-central Quebec—Saguenay River region (Godfrey, 1966: 385). Winters mainly in southeastern United States north along the Atlantic coast to South Carolina. Vagrant in New York.

Status: *Casual*—two proved records for New York: (1) specimen collected at the head of Cayuga Lake, near Ithaca, Oct. 11, 1897 (Fuertes), CUM 19455; (2) one mist-netted, banded, color-photographed, and released at Tobay Sanctuary, Nassau Co., Oct. 18, 1970 (A. Lauro); color photo by P. Buckley—on file, AMNH collection.

In view of its breeding to the north and northeast of New York and wintering in the southeastern United States, it is surprising that this secretive species has been *reliably* recorded only twice within the state. However, it may migrate both spring and fall primarily by way of the Mississippi valley or, at any rate, west of the Appalachians. Vagrant sparrows of the genus *Ammodramus* should be collected or color-photographed to determine which species are involved. Critical identification in the hand is essential. No sight reports have been accepted as this species bears a striking resemblance to the Sharp-tailed Sparrow. They are now believed to be closely related, rather than in different genera (Murray, 1968) and Mayr and Short (1970: 83).

Remarks: The former species name *caudacutus* (Latham 1790), used for Le Conte's Sparrow, is preoccupied by *caudacutus* (Gmelin 1788), the latter name used for the Sharp-tailed Sparrow. The two species are here considered congeneric, thus necessitating the specific name change to *leconteii*.

Baird's Sparrow
(*Ammodramus bairdii*)   *

Range: Central North America, breeding east to southern Manitoba and western Minnesota; in migration through the Great Plains. Winters in southwestern United States and northern Mexico. Vagrant to New York (Long Island).

Status: *Accidental*—one proved occurrence —immature taken at Montauk, Suffolk Co., Nov. 13, 1899 (Helme), AMNH 802438.

Several recent sight reports in southeastern New York were not substantiated. However, a bird, which may well have been this species, was observed in Central Park, New York City, Oct. 24, 1949 (Helmuth), and at Short Beach, Nassau Co., Oct. 31 following (Alperin, Jacobson, and Sedwitz), and was possibly the same individual (see *Linnaean News-Letter*, 1950, 3: January).

Henslow's Sparrow
(*Ammodramus henslowii*) * B

Range: Chiefly northeastern United States, in the east breeding from southeastern Ontario, northern New York, and central New England, south to Kentucky and North Carolina. Winters from Florida north to coastal South Carolina.

Status: Rare and little-known migrant. Rare to uncommon and local breeder at lower elevations, but occasionally more numerous; absent in the higher mountains.

Nonbreeding: The Henslow's Sparrow is very seldom reported away from breeding localities, principally because of its secretive nature. Based on specimen and banding records, it is recorded most often during October.

EXTREME DATES: Apr. 2 (inland) and Apr. 4 (coastal) to Nov. 6 (inland) and Nov. 20 (coastal specimen) and Nov. 27 (coastal).

Although never collected in New York during winter, the following Long Island observation of a bird carefully studied is believed correct: one present at the Gilmore feeding station, Patchogue, Suffolk Co., from Dec. 26, 1963, to Jan. 14, 1964 (Puleston and Terry).

Breeding: Although referring specifically to the New York City region, the following (Bull, 1964: 447) is applicable to most sections of the state: "The Henslow's Sparrow breeds on the ground in grassy fields and meadows with scattered bushes and herbaceous plants, both in wet and dry situations. In such places the species' presence may be determined by its insect-like song; otherwise it is usually overlooked. However, the species is decidedly local and unpredictable; many areas which appear to be ideal for it are untenanted, and other localities are deserted after one or more years. Usually only one or two pairs are found breeding at a single locality, but in a few places small 'colonies' have been reported."

The two largest "colonies" (each with about 20 pairs) reported for the state were located at Thacher State Park, Albany Co., 1925 (Bedell), and on the St. Lawrence River at the mouth of Crooked Creek, St. Lawrence Co. (Hyde, 1939b).

Regarding its vocalizations, Rosche (1967)

had this to say: "Song period from April 26 to about August 20; commonly sings at night. This sparrow seldom appears to reach its maximum abundance [Wyoming Co.] until mid-July, probably when singing is at its peak."

Nests are usually in clumps of grass or weeds on or very close to the ground.

Egg clutches in 14 New York nests: three eggs (four nests); four eggs (nine nests); five eggs (one nest).

EGG DATES: May 17 to July 5.

Nestlings: June 1 to July 22; fledglings: June 16 to July 30. In two carefully watched New York nests, the nestling period was determined as 10–11 days. The egg date of "May 1" as stated in Eaton (1914: 294) is erroneous. The correct date is May 17 (*Ornith.* and *Ool.* 1891, 16: 27).

Despite its being recorded at 117 nesting localities in the state, the distribution of Henslow's Sparrow is spotty. On Long Island it formerly bred at ten localities—on the south shore from Idlewild, Queens Co., to Napeague (Montauk peninsula), Suffolk Co.; and in Suffolk Co. at Orient, but not elsewhere on the north shore; also on Gardiner's Island. Not since 1952 has this species been definitely recorded as a breeder on Long Island. It was locally distributed in the lower Hudson valley but there too has decreased in many former nesting areas.

Farther north in the Hudson valley, however, it is locally common. Curiously enough it appears to be absent north of Glenville, Schenectady Co., being unreported from Fulton, Saratoga, and Washington counties, and "lacking" also in the Mohawk valley to the west, between Glenville and Westmoreland, Oneida Co. A general scarcity of observers in these areas rather than a lack of *henslowii* is more than likely the answer.

The species is apparently lacking from the entire Adirondack-Champlain region and from most of the Tug Hill district. It reappears to the west in the St. Lawrence valley and is probably most generally distributed in the state along the southeast shore of Lake Ontario, especially in the counties of Oswego, Cayuga, Onondaga, Oneida, and Madison.

It is found locally in the balance of central and western New York and is not rare in suitable habitat in the southern highlands along the Pennsylvania line. According to Rosche (*op.*

cit.) it is found up to 2000 feet in Wyoming Co.

The species does not occur in the higher Catskills and is rare even in the foothills, although recorded at such localities as Oneonta, Otsego Co.; Durham and Greenville, Greene Co.; and Kripplebush, Ulster Co.

Remarks: Here regarded as monotypic. The form named *"susurrans"* does not appear to me to be well differentiated. There is overlap in both color and bill length.

Grasshopper Sparrow
(*Ammodramus savannarum*)   *   B

Range: Southern Nearctic and Neotropical regions, breeding locally from extreme southern Canada to the West Indies and Ecuador. Winters north to southern United States, very rarely to New York and Massachusetts (specimens).

Status: Rare to uncommon coastal migrant, much less numerous inland. Very rare in winter. Fairly common but local breeder on Long Island and in the lowlands of the interior, but rare northward and absent in the mountains.

Nonbreeding: The Grasshopper Sparrow is rarely reported during migration, except by those who visit the outer coast in October. Even there, however, it is unusual to find more than one or two in a day at any given locality. On rare occasions, "flights" are reported.

MAXIMA, COASTAL: *Spring*—eight, Madison Square Park, New York City, May 15, 1921, after heavy fog and rain the previous night. *Fall*—eight, Oct. 1; six, Oct. 14, 1933, Easthampton, Suffolk Co.; four netted and banded, Tiana Beach, Suffolk Co., Oct. 25, 1961.

EXTREME DATES: Mar. 20 (coastal specimen), Apr. 1 (coastal) and Apr. 12 (inland) to Nov. 19 and 23 (coastal). Rare before late April and after October.

Winter: The species has been recorded in the state in December at least five times, but rarely if ever survives the winter. One individual was reported at Nassau, Rensselaer Co., Dec. 24, 1959 (Bartlett), where it was trapped and banded.

There are two confirmed records of birds that remained into January—both at feeders: (1) Female, Livingston, Columbia Co., Jan. 16, 1958 (Munson), NYSM 18312. This specimen was found dying at a feeder after a heavy snowstorm. (2) An individual was seen and photographed at the Helms feeder, Quogue Wildlife Refuge, Suffolk Co., from Dec. 25, 1967, to Jan. 7, 1968 (Cooley, Puleston, Raynor, *et al.*).

Breeding: Grasshopper Sparrows are, or more correctly were, actually numerous only on Long Island. After World War II or about 1950, the beginnings of a human population explosion necessitated housing on an unprecedented scale, which in turn destroyed irrevocably most of the open grassland habitat of this bird.

The once extensive Hempstead Plains held over *100* pairs of Grasshopper Sparrows in the 1920s (J. T. Nichols, *in litt.*). Today only a pitiful remnant survives on the mainland portion of the island. Gardiner's and Fisher's islands off the east end of Long Island still support "colonies" of these birds. In 1967 at least 30 pairs were estimated on the former island and about a dozen pairs on the latter.

On the mainland this species is far less numerous. Only in the region bordering the lower Hudson valley are the numbers at all comparable. In 1959, 11 breeding pairs were counted in the Poundridge Reservation, Westchester Co.

The species is fairly widely but locally distributed at low elevations in upstate New York. It decreases rapidly northward and is rare and local in the St. Lawrence and Lake Champlain valleys.

Nests are placed on the ground in dry grassy fields and pastures, often well concealed in tufts or clumps of grass.

Egg clutches number from three (perhaps incomplete sets) to five, with the following in 20 New York nests: three eggs (three nests); four eggs (eight nests); five eggs (nine nests).

EGG DATES: May 27 to Aug. 6 (second brood).

Nestlings: June 29 to Aug. 19; fledglings: July 21 to Sept. 5.

Subspecies: The local breeding race is *A. s. pratensis* (decidedly larger than nominate *A. s.*

savannarum of the West Indies, and lighter in color above than *A. s. floridanus* of northern Florida).

Vesper Sparrow
(*Pooecetes gramineus*)   *   B

Range: North America, breeding from Canada to southern United States. Winters north to New York and New England.

Status: Common to very common inland migrant, much less numerous on the coast. Rare to uncommon in winter coastwise, occasionally more numerous; very rare inland. Widespread breeder, but now rare and local on Long Island; less numerous upstate than formerly.

Nonbreeding: Although less numerous inland in summer than formerly, the Vesper Sparrow occurs in large concentrations there during the migrations as may be seen below. It occurs in much smaller numbers on passage along the coast.

MAXIMA: *Spring*—25, Busti, Chautauqua Co., Mar. 30, 1963; 300, Binghamton, Broome Co., Apr. 14, 1962 (Marsi), an exceptional number; 200, Derby Hill, Oswego Co., Apr. 15, 1965.

MAXIMA: *Fall*—60, Phoenix, Oswego Co., Sept. 19, 1965; 100, Binghamton, Oct. 27, 1957; 50, Idlewild, Queens Co., Nov. 15, 1952.

Migrants usually arrive in late March and depart by late November.

MAXIMA: *Winter*—30, Bayside, Queens Co., Feb. 1, 1930; 35, near Woodmere, Nassau Co., Dec. 29, 1946. It must be emphasized that even on Long Island the Vesper Sparrow is ordinarily a rare bird in winter.

Breeding: This species favors dry, short-grass fields, pastures, and stony, cultivated ground. The nest is placed on the ground in grass tufts, under bushes, and not infrequently in agricultural country under potato and strawberry plants. Regarding the Finger Lakes region, Spiker (1935: 540) stated that he found nests in potato fields and in old fields with foxtail grass.

Egg clutches in 23 New York nests: three eggs (nine nests); four eggs (12 nests); five eggs (two nests).

EGG DATES: May 5 to Aug. 16 (second brood).

Nestlings: June 11 to July 16; fledglings: July 11 to July 31. It is obvious that data are lacking on *late* dates for nestlings and fledglings in view of the mid-August record for eggs.

Lark Sparrow
(*Chondestes grammacus*)   *

Range: Chiefly the western portions of central North America, breeding rarely east to southeastern Ontario, central Pennsylvania, western Maryland, Virginia, and North Carolina. Winters chiefly from the southern United States south to Mexico, Guatemala, and El Salvador; very rarely in the east, north to New Jersey, and southeastern New York.

Status: Rare but regular fall coastal migrant; much rarer in spring. Very rare in the interior.

Occurrence: The Lark Sparrow prefers dry, sandy fields along the outer coast during fall migration. It occurs chiefly from August to October. As many as seven individuals have been seen during one fall season; three at Jones Beach, Long Island, Sept. 13, 1958, is the maximum number for one day.

EXTREME DATES: *Fall*—July 7 and 25 to Nov. 27 (specimen), exceptionally to Dec. 5–18, 1965, at Pleasantville, Westchester Co. (Augustine and Howe). Rare before mid-August and after mid-October.

This species is extremely rare in *spring*, with only *16* known records, ten from the coast. Six from upstate are the *only* known occurrences in the interior including the only known spring specimen (see below).

EXTREME DATES: *Spring*—Apr. 11 (coastal) to June 13 (inland). Nine of the spring dates are in May.

Winter: There are two winter occurrences of the Lark Sparrow in the state, both from the southeast: (1) one photographed at a feeder, Salt Point, Dutchess Co., from Feb. 5 to Apr. 2, 1965 (Waterman and many others); (2) one also photographed at a feeder, near Mastic, Suffolk Co., from Dec. 26, 1967, to Jan. 5, 1968 (Puleston and Raynor).

Specimen data: Of six specimens taken on Long Island, only three appear to be extant and were examined by me: (1) Miller's Place, Suffolk Co., Nov. 27, 1899 (Helme), AMNH 802439; (2) Easthampton, Suffolk Co., Aug. 17, 1934 (Helmuth), in his collection; (3) Fisher's Island, Suffolk Co., Sept. 30, 1963 (Ferguson), in his collection.

The only known inland specimen and the first collected in spring is that of one taken near Allegany, Cattaraugus Co., Apr. 29, 1956 (S. W. Eaton), St. Bonaventure Univ. Mus. 451.

All extant New York specimens appear to be the somewhat darker, eastern nominate race.

Remarks: Although Eaton (1914: 300–301) credits a breeding record from Monroe Co. in 1911, no adequate confirmation exists. No specimens were taken, nor did any ornithologist corroborate the observation. The *lone* observer did not give details.

Bachman's Sparrow
(*Aimophila aestivalis*)   *

Range: Southeastern United States, the race *bachmani* (dorsal surface more rusty, less gray than nominate race) breeding north to southwestern Pennsylvania. Vagrant in New York and New Jersey (specimens).

Status: *Casual*—there is one confirmed record for New York, not previously published: male collected on extreme eastern Long Island at Greenport, Suffolk Co., June 4, 1930 (Latham), NYSM 25683; examined by the writer.

There are two sight reports of singing birds made by experienced observers with details published: (1) Mendon Ponds Park, near Rochester, May 8–12, 1940 (Meade, Hall, *et al., Auk,* 1941, 58: 103–104); (2) Prospect Park, Brooklyn, Apr. 21 and 22, 1948 (Carleton, Jacobson, Sedwitz, and Whelen, *Kingbird,* 1952, 2: 82).

Tree Sparrow (*Spizella arborea*)   *

Range: North America, in the east breeding south to the northern portions of Ontario and Quebec, and to Labrador. Winters north to southern Canada.

Status: Common to abundant winter visitant, especially numerous in the interior.

Occurrence: The Tree Sparrow is sometimes found in great numbers during severe winters and much less commonly in mild, open seasons. It occurs in open country and is particularly fond of weedy and brushy fields but is also a frequent visitor at feeding stations. Coastal maxima are much smaller than those from upstate, as may be seen from the following:

MAXIMA: 140, Fish Gulf, Oneida Lake, Nov. 9, 1966; 600, Tully, Onondaga Co., Dec. 19, 1968; 280, Orient, Suffolk Co., Dec. 25, 1909; 400, Elmira, Jan. 15, 1958; 500, Wilson, Niagara Co., Feb. 11, 1968; 500, Jamestown, Mar. 19, 1964.

EXTREME DATES: Oct. 10 (coastal specimen) to May 11 (inland—banded and photographed). Rare before late October and after early April.

September and late May dates lack confirmation and require substantiation—preferably by specimen evidence.

Banding: Two individuals banded in New York and recovered in Ontario, each lived at least *ten* years.

Chipping Sparrow
(*Spizella passerina*)   *   B

Range: North America, breeding from Alaska and Canada to the mountains of Nicaragua; in the east to northern Florida. Winters north along the coast (occasionally inland) to New York and New England (rarely).

Status: Common to very common migrant, occasionally more numerous. Rare but regular in winter on the coast, much rarer inland. Widespread breeder.

Nonbreeding: Chipping Sparrows are very fond of lawns and short-grass fields with areas of bare ground. During migration they are often found in such places, feeding with other sparrows.

MAXIMA: *Spring*—200, Prospect Park, Brooklyn, May 2, 1945; 160, Selkirk Shores, Oswego Co., May 6, 1961.

MAXIMA: *Fall*—200, Lima, Livingston Co., Sept. 15, 1970; 250, Bronx Park, Bronx Co.,

Oct. 15, 1950; 150, Allegany, Cattaraugus Co., Oct. 16, 1966.

Winter: On the coast four were banded at Freeport, Nassau Co.—one, Jan. 19, 1957, and three more, Feb. 3, 1957 (Penberthy and Arbib). Upstate the Chipping Sparrow is much rarer at this season; however, two were present at one Syracuse feeder during the winter of 1964–1965 (many observers).

Breeding: The Chipping Sparrow breeds around farms, gardens, orchards, suburban yards, city parks, estates, and in much of the settled rural country. Its nest is placed in trees, bushes, vines, and often in low ornamental conifers. In former years nests were often lined with horse hair.

A pair nested on the summit of Slide Mtn., Ulster Co., in 1965 and 1966 (Hough).

One unusual nest site was only two inches above ground in a clump of clover. Otherwise heights range from one to 13 feet, exceptionally to 30 feet.

A density of 26 pairs in a 35-acre planting of four-to-nine-foot Scotch pine near Alfred, Allegany Co., in 1969 was estimated.

Clutches in 41 New York nests held from three to five eggs, as follows: three eggs (16 nests); four eggs (23 nests); five eggs (two nests).

EGG DATES: May 2 to June 20 and July 19 (second brood).

Nestlings: May 23 to Aug. 7 and Sept. 3; fledglings: June 4 to Aug. 13 and Sept. 21.

Clay-colored Sparrow
(*Spizella pallida*)   *   B

Range: Chiefly central North America, breeding from southern Canada to central United States east of the Rockies; locally east to southeastern Ontario and casually to western New York (1960 on). Winters chiefly in Mexico. Regular fall migrant on the outer coast from Massachusetts to New Jersey.

Status: Rare but regular fall coastal migrant; much rarer in spring inland, but increasing. Casual breeder.

Nonbreeding: The first definite record for the Clay-colored Sparrow in New York was that of a specimen collected at Ithaca, Apr. 28, 1935, by Allan R. Phillips, CUM 20088. Next was a report of a singing bird at Tonawanda, Erie Co., May 20, 1943 (Beardslee and Mitchell, 1965: 441). Except for a fall sighting in 1952 in the Buffalo region, the species was rarely reported in the interior of the state for nearly a decade (see below).

Along the coast, meanwhile, this western species was nothing more than a vagrant prior to 1950, after which it was reported annually in fall on the outer coast of Long Island. For detailed status there, see Bull (1964: 458–459). A specimen was taken at Riis Park, Queens Co., Oct. 12, 1956 (Buckley), AMNH 707782. On the coast it prefers sandy fields with short grass and scattered bushes.

The increase in New York as a migrant within the two decades (1950–1971) was most likely the result of the species extending its breeding range eastward into Ontario and ultimately into this state. In spring it was recorded chiefly from the interior, in fall almost entirely on Long Island.

EXTREME DATES: Apr. 16 (inland and coastal); summering nonbreeders; to Nov. 30 (coastal). There is a report (*Kingbird*, 1971, 21: 20) of an individual that struck the Elmira television tower, Oct. 18, 1970—"specimen saved," but I have not seen it. If extant, the specimen should be examined critically for substantiation.

Breeding (see Map 158): This species rates as a New York breeder on the basis of the following two records: (1) Ithaca—an individual was seen and heard (voice tape-recorded by Kellogg) in a field in the spring of 1959. The following year a singing male of this species mated with a female Chipping Sparrow. On June 13, 1960, a nest with three eggs was discovered 12 feet up in a red cedar in an open field with scattered cedars. On June 22 the eggs hatched. The male Clay-colored Sparrow not only fed the incubating female Chipping Sparrow, but also helped feed the juveniles of the mixed mating—see photograph (*Kingbird*, 1960, 10: 105). For an account of this mixed pairing, see McIlroy (1961: 7–10). Witnesses to this attempted hybridization were Arthur Allen, Sally Hoyt, and Dorothy McIlroy among numerous other observers. Most unfortunately, only two days later—June 24—the nest was empty, the young presumably

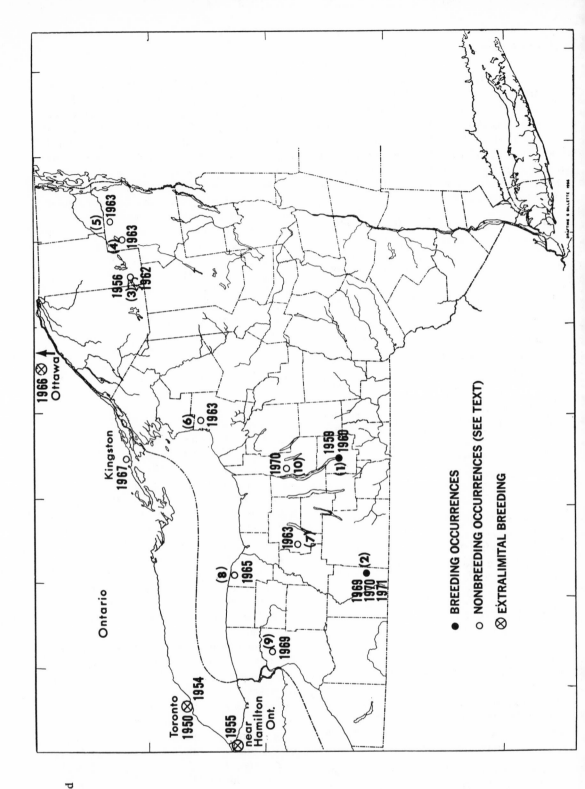

MAP 158 Clay-colored Sparrow (*Spizella pallida*) Breeding distribution

● BREEDING OCCURRENCES

○ NONBREEDING OCCURRENCES (SEE TEXT)

⊗ EXTRALIMITAL BREEDING

Ontario

Ottawa
1966 ⊗

Kingston
1967 ○

Toronto
1950 ⊗ 1954

near
Hamilton
Ont.
1955 ⊗

(5) ○1963
(4) ○1963
1956 1962
(3)

(6) ○
1963

1959 1960
1970 ○ ●(1)
(10)

1963 ○ (7)

(8) ○1965

(2)
1969 ●
1970
1971

(9) ○
1969

taken by some predator. For a successful hybridization in Michigan, see Storer (*Wilson Bull.*, 1954, 66: 143–144).

(2) Even less conclusive was the presumed nesting of a pair of these birds in a Scotch pine planting at Foster Lake near Alfred, Allegany Co., during May and June 1970 (Klingensmith and Burton, *Prothonotary*, 1971, 37: 27). The latter observer tape-recorded the song of this male. Although no nest was found, "two adult Clay-colored Sparrows were observed on June 24 and 25 in the same location carrying larvae and responding to the feeding calls of the young."

However, during 1971, the first proved successful New York breeding record occurred there (Brooks, *Prothonotary*, 1971, 37: 99). "A pair of Clay-colored Sparrows returned to the Scotch Pine . . . plantation . . . where they had been studied the year before." The nest, two feet above ground in a five-foot Scotch pine, contained three young on June 15 and presumably fledged on June 20 when the nest was found empty; the adults were observed nearby and the fledglings heard in the adjacent undergrowth. Both photographs and tape recordings substantiated this notable occurrence.

The accompanying map indicates localities of breeding and nonbreeding in the state, as well as in adjacent Ontario, with years of occurrence. In addition to the two aforementioned New York *breeding* localities (1) and (2), the following eight *nonbreeding* localities in the state, with details, are listed in chronological sequence: 1956 and 1962—(3) Tupper Lake (village), Franklin Co.—June 1 to July 4, 1956 (Amstutz and Kingsbury), and July 5–10, 1962 (Cohen and Carleton), in both instances singing birds in a grassy field with scattered, planted pines.

1963—Essex Co.—(4) Lake Placid, June 24–25, and (5) Wilmington, June 28–29 (Kemnitzer and Delafield), singing birds in both cases: (6) Sandy Creek, Oswego Co., June 29 (Scheider), singing bird; (7) Honeoye Lake, Ontario Co., June 29 to July 6 (Foster and Tetlow), singing bird.

1965—(8) Shore Acres, Monroe Co., July 4–10 (Doherty, Miller, *et al.*).

1969—(9) Amherst, Erie Co., all July (Inskip), singing bird.

1970—(10) Oakwood, Cayuga Co., May 13 to late June (many observers), singing bird.

Further evidence of breeding was made in 1972 in the Rochester area (Claffey, *Goshawk*, 1972, 28: 50–52). An adult was observed feeding two recently fledged young between July 7 and 15. The other parent was not seen.

It should be emphasized that this species and the Chipping Sparrow are difficult to distinguish, and caution should be used in accepting records.

[Brewer's Sparrow (*Spizella breweri*)

Hypothetical: Western North America, breeding east to the western portions of the Dakotas and Nebraska. In migration east to western Kansas. Accidental in Massachusetts (specimen).

In New York State this species has been reported twice on Long Island by experienced observers: (1) Gilgo Beach, Suffolk Co., Oct. 26, 1947 (Alperin, Carleton, Jacobson, and Sedwitz); (2) Montauk Point, Suffolk Co., Oct. 14, 1950 (Eisenmann, Grant, *et al.*). These observations were published in the *Linnaean News-Letter* (1947, 1: November, and 1950, 4: December).

A specimen is greatly desired. The three *Spizella* species (*passerina, pallida,* and *breweri*) are not easy to distinguish from each other, even in the hand, especially juveniles.]

Field Sparrow (*Spizella pusilla*)   *   B

Range: Chiefly eastern North America, breeding from extreme southern Canada to southern United States. Winters nearly throughout, except the extreme northern portions.

Status: Common to very common fall migrant. Rare to uncommon in winter. Widespread breeder at lower elevations, but rare northward and absent in the higher mountains.

Nonbreeding: The Field Sparrow is a common migrant, both inland and along the coast, often associating with other sparrows. On rare occasions in winter small flocks are noted in swampy thickets.

MAXIMA: *Fall*—60, Selkirk Shores, Oswego Co., Sept. 13, 1967; 50, Allegany, Cattaraugus Co., Oct. 16, 1965; 55, Easthampton, Suffolk Co., Nov. 2, 1930.

MAXIMA: *Winter*—24 at a manure pile, Clinton, Oneida Co., Dec. 30, 1967 (several observers), is an exceptional inland record; 40, Grassy Sprain, Westchester Co., Jan. 14, 1949.

No spring maxima are available.

Breeding: This species breeds in open country on or near the ground (up to one foot) in brushy fields, thickets, overgrown pastures, and thorn scrub. The nest is often placed in fairly thick tangles.

Egg clutches in 43 New York nests ranged from three to five, as follows: three eggs (12 nests); four eggs (29 nests); five eggs (two nests).

EGG DATES: May 16 to July 7 and Aug. 17 (second brood).

Nestlings: May 26 to Aug. 10; fledglings: June 17 to Aug. 20.

Banding: Three New York individuals banded in summer or fall of various years were recovered the following winter in North Carolina, South Carolina, and Georgia.

Slate-colored or Dark-eyed Junco
(*Junco hyemalis*)   *   B

Range: Nearctic region, breeding from Alaska and Canada to the mountains of southwestern United States and in the east to the mountains of northern Georgia; at lower elevations to northern and northeastern United States. Winters through much of the breeding range except in extreme north.

Status: Common to abundant migrant, less numerous in winter. Widespread breeder at higher elevations, rare and local to absent elsewhere.

Nonbreeding: This species is one of the most numerous of the sparrows on migration, occurring in large flocks at times. It is regular in much smaller numbers in winter, often at feeding stations.

MAXIMA: *Fall*—800, Webster, Monroe Co., Oct. 5, 1968; 800, Prospect Park, Brooklyn, Oct. 15, 1950; 1000, Waterloo, Seneca Co., Oct.

17, 1966; 1000, Riis Park, Queens Co., Oct. 25, 1953; 850, Easthampton, Suffolk Co., Nov. 2, 1930.

MAXIMA: *Winter*—500, Wilson, Niagara Co., Feb. 11, 1968.

MAXIMA: *Spring*—1000, Karner, Albany Co., Apr. 2, 1957; 350, Tully, Onondaga Co., Apr. 19, 1962.

Nonbreeding vagrants are reported through summer.

Breeding (see Map 159): Juncos are among the most numerous nesting birds in the Adirondacks and the higher Catskills. That they are plentiful in other areas also is proved by the following densities: (1) 35 in 14 miles of trail, Tug Hill area of southern Lewis Co., June 10, 1957 (Scheider, 1959a); (2) 12 singing males in three and one-half miles of predominantly hemlock forest between 1000 and 1350 feet, near Owego, Tioga Co., July 17, 1968 (Ruth Williams, *Kingbird,* 1968, 18: 200); (3) ten pairs in 38 acres of "maturing red pine-white pine plantation," near Alfred, Allegany Co., summer of 1970 (Klingensmith, *Audubon Field Notes,* 1970, 24: 755).

Many New York ground nests are located in cutbanks along roads, others are under bushes, or among fallen tree roots. These nests range from ground level up to two feet.

More unusual are two tree nests, one in an arbor-vitae two feet up; the other, eight feet above ground in a yellow birch *cavity* on Slide Mtn. in the Catskills (Hough, *Kingbird,* 1970, 20: 204).

S. W. Eaton (1965) described five nests in southern Allegany Co. that were all about two feet high in hemlock hedges near houses and five others ranging from six to eight feet "on ledges of the vertical faces of large conglomerate boulders."

The most extraordinary nest sites of this species, however, are those of three in manmade structures: (1) Olean, Allegany Co.— eight feet up in the triangular apex of a windvane bird feeder (*fide* Wilkinson); (2) Big Moose, Herkimer Co.—two nests in successive years, 15 and 18 feet above ground under the eaves of an old house on top of abandoned Barn Swallow nests (*fide* Fisk); (3) Mohonk Lake, Ulster Co.—on the second-floor steelwork of a building (Smiley, *Kingbird,* 1957, 7: 103).

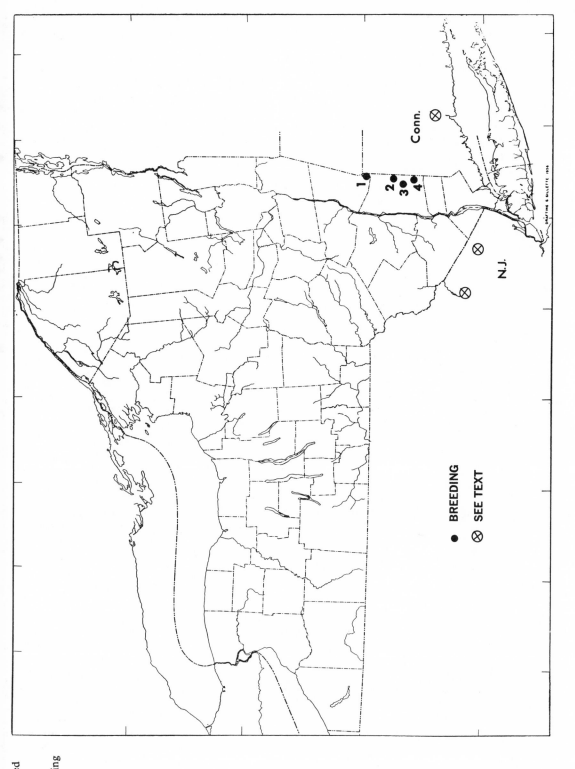

MAP 159 Slate-colored
or Dark-eyed Junco
(*Junco hyemalis*)
Known southern breeding
limits

BREEDING

SEE TEXT

Egg clutches in 70 New York nests: three eggs (five nests, incomplete); four eggs (58 nests—85%); five eggs (seven nests).

Juncos are double-brooded in New York.

EGG DATES: Apr. 28 to Aug. 15.

Nestlings: May 16 to Aug. 17; fledglings: June 7 to Aug. 27.

In a study of 21 New York nests S. W. Eaton (*op. cit.*) determined that the incubation period was from 12 to 13 days and fledging from nine to 12 days.

The breeding distribution limits of this species in western New York are most interesting. Juncos are found up to, but not beyond, the northern and western edges of the Portage escarpment (for precise location, see map in Beardslee and Mitchell, 1965: 16–17). In other words breeding juncos are virtually lacking on the Great Lakes lowland plain. There are apparently no breeding records for Niagara, Orleans, Genesee, Monroe, or Wayne counties. In fact, northern breeding limits appear to extend no further than Orchard Park and Wales Center in Erie Co., Stony Brook Glen in Wyoming Co., and Gannett Hill in Ontario Co. The western breeding limits in Erie Co. appear to be— from northeast to southwest—Orchard Park, Hamburg, and Eden.

The accompanying map indicates the southeastern known breeding limits in New York which, curiously, are restricted south and east of the Catskills to four eastern Dutchess Co. localities in the Taconic range near the Connecticut state line: (1) Mt. Riga; (2) near Wassaic; (3) Dover Plains; (4) Bald Mtn. near Wingdale. As the species has been recorded breeding twice to the south of us in northern New Jersey and once in southern Connecticut (see map), it should be found nesting in suitable habitat at higher elevations in Putnam, Orange, and Rockland counties.

Banding (see Map 160): Four birds banded in fall of various years in different New York localities were recovered the following winter in North Carolina, South Carolina, Georgia, and Alabama. A fifth individual banded in March in South Carolina was recovered nearly a month later in east-central New York.

An individual banded at Oliverea, Ulster Co., lived for at least eight years.

Remarks: As the Slate-colored Junco (*hye-*

malis) and Oregon Junco (*oreganus*), formerly considered separate species, interbreed and hybridize extensively over a broad area of the Rocky Mountains, they are treated here as conspecific.

The well-marked race, *J. h. montanus* (males with convex black hood, chestnut back, and rufous sides), has been collected in New York on four occasions:

(1) Branchport, Yates Co., Feb. 25, 1932 (C. F. Stone), USNM 331300. This individual was first seen on Feb. 7.

(2) Poundridge (village), Westchester Co., Dec. 2, 1946 (F. C. Scott), AMNH 344035.

(3) Fisher's Island, Suffolk Co., Jan. 2, 1961 (Ferguson), specimen now in Peabody Museum collection, Yale University, identified by George Watson.

(4) Williamsville, Erie Co., Jan. 22, 1965 (Andrle), BMS 5071.

Other New York specimens in various museums purported to be "Oregon" Juncos were examined independently by Lester Short and the writer, and found to belong to the intermediate hybrid population known as "*cismontanus*," a form not recognized here as a taxonomic entity.

Numerous observations of birds variously called "Oregon" Juncos, a lesser number of "Pink-sided" Juncos, and one or two "White-winged" Juncos are summarily rejected as unidentifiable, although it must be admitted that a considerable number of these sightings (including those of this writer)—principally at feeders—of "good" adult males of the plumage type described above were very likely identified correctly.

The reader should consult the important article by Andrle and Axtell (*Prothonotary*, 1965, 31: 5) for the difficulties involved.

The poorly differentiated and variable form "*carolinensis*" (somewhat larger and paler than nominate *hyemalis*) from the southern Appalachians is not recognized here. According to Parkes (1952a) intermediates between the two forms breed in the southern and western portions of the state.

Harris' Sparrow (*Zonotrichia querula*)

Range: West-central Canada, breeding southeast to northern Manitoba. Winters south and

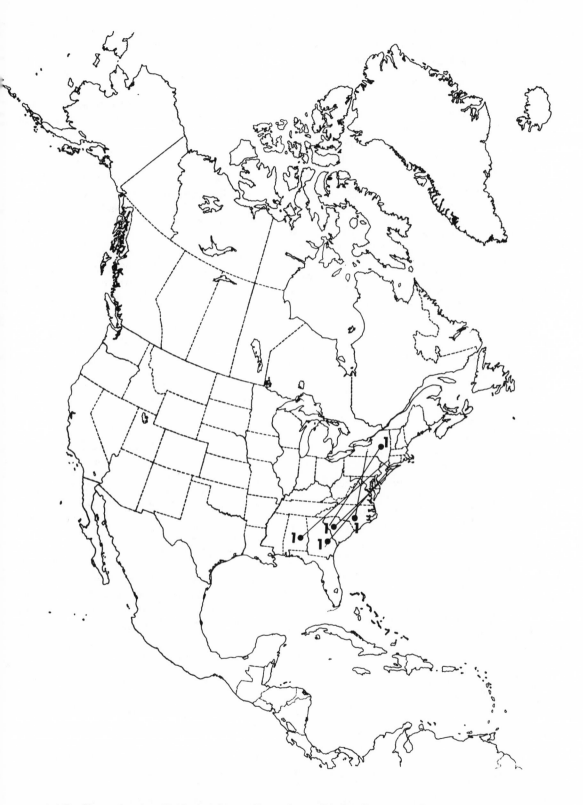

MAP 160 Slate-colored or Dark-eyed Junco (*Junco hyemalis*) Banding recoveries

east to Louisiana and Tennessee. Wanders east to the Atlantic coast of Massachusetts (specimen) and New York (photographs).

Status: *Very rare*—this species was reliably reported in New York for the first time in 1951. Since then it has been observed on at least *23* occasions by numerous competent people. An enormous increase of feeding stations in the state is directly responsible for a corresponding increase in a number of rarities, such as Harris' Sparrow—no fewer than *16* recorded at feeders.

Seasonal distribution is as follows: Eight each in fall and winter, and seven in spring. Several individuals overwintered at feeders (as many as three different individuals, winter of 1964–1965) and lingered into May when they were photographed in their breeding plumage. Most occurrences (*18*) are from upstate localities, only five from coastal areas. Several other upstate reports were not confirmed.

Although apparently never collected in the state, its occurrence is well substantiated by three photographs, including two eastern Long Island individuals photographed by Dennis Puleston: (1) adult at the Helms feeder, Quogue, Suffolk Co., Oct. 31 to Nov. 3, 1965 —photo on file, AMNH collection; (2) immature netted and banded at Brookhaven, Suffolk Co., Oct. 28, 1966—for photo, see *Kingbird* (1967, 17: 190); (3) the third photograph, also in the *Kingbird* (1967, 17: 193), was of an individual at the Czont feeder, Lake View, Erie Co., from mid-December 1964 (trapped and banded on Mar. 10) to May 6, 1965—when the bird was photographed by Mitchell.

EXTREME DATES: Sept. 28 to May 28.

White-crowned Sparrow
(*Zonotrichia leucophrys*)   *

Range: Nearctic region, in the east breeding south to northern Ontario, central and southeastern Quebec, and northern Newfoundland. Winters north sparingly to New Jersey and New York, rarely to Massachusetts (specimen).

Status: Variously uncommon to very common migrant, occasionally even abundant inland; most numerous in fall. Formerly very

rare in winter, but has greatly increased at this season in recent years.

Occurrence: The White-crowned Sparrow is especially fond of lawns with hedges and thickets in city parks and suburban areas, but is also found in great numbers in open fields in agricultural districts.

MAXIMA: *Spring*—40, Voorheesville, Albany Co., May 5, 1963; 70, Jones Beach, Long Island, May 9, 1961; 80, Central Park, New York City, May 10, 1956; 150, Syracuse, May 12, 1956 (Scheider); 110, Sandy Pond, Oswego Co., May 15, 1960; six, Jamaica Bay Refuge, May 28, 1967.

MAXIMA: *Fall*—300, Webster, Monroe Co., Oct. 5, 1968 (Lloyd); 200, Syracuse, Oct. 8, 1955 (Scheider); 150, North Boston, Erie Co., Oct. 15, 1970; 100, Jones Beach, Oct. 22, 1966, and 46 netted and banded at nearby Tobay Beach, the same day.

MAXIMA: *Winter*—20, Culver feeder, Scottsville, Monroe Co., winter of 1961–1962 (many observers); 20 in brush pile, Old Brookville, Nassau Co., Dec. 31, 1968 (Bell). These numbers are very unusual for winter.

The following is without precedent in this state. In a letter to me dated Jan. 18, 1968, Harold Mitchell of Buffalo stated that during the winter of 1965 very large numbers of this species were present on a truck farm at Newfane, Niagara Co. This truck farm planted mainly tomatoes, had an extensive growth of pigweed (*Amaranthus*) and goosefoot (*Chenopodium*), the seeds of which were eaten by numerous Slate-colored Juncos, Tree, White-throated, and White-crowned sparrows. When these seeds had been consumed, the sparrows departed. Many observers saw these birds and careful estimates were kept throughout the winter. White-crowned Sparrow totals were: 50, Jan. 10; 75, Jan. 17; *100,* Jan. 23; 75, Jan. 31 to Feb. 21.

EXTREME DATES: Sept. 14 (inland) to early December (rarely); winter; Apr. 10 (coastal specimen) and Apr. 17 (coastal) to June 14 (coastal); June 30, 1958, Irondequoit Bay, Monroe Co. (Kemnitzer and McNett). Usually rare before mid-May and after May. The spring migration is "hurried," whereas fall passage is greatly protracted.

Subspecies: The more western subspecies

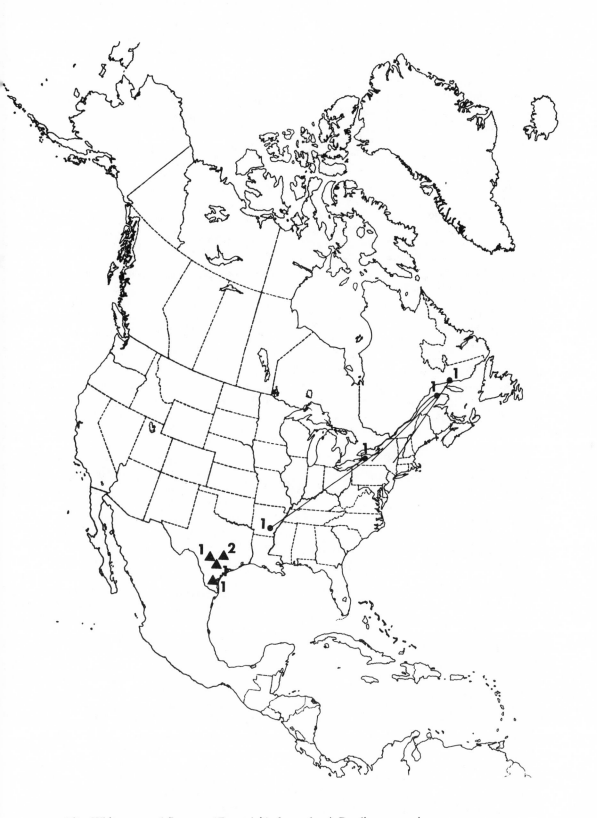

MAP 161   White-crowned Sparrow (*Zonotrichia leucophrys*) Banding recoveries

gambelii (with white lores, or, more correctly, the white superciliary extending to the base of the bill) breeds east to northern Manitoba and has been collected in Massachusetts.

The specimen from Ithaca, Apr. 30, 1898, taken by Fuertes, and reported by Eaton (1914: 303) to be "perfectly typical" of *Z. l. gambelii* was examined at Cornell by Parkes (1952a) and found by him to be intermediate in appearance between nominate *leucophrys* and *gambelii.*

The first definite state record of *gambelii* is that of an adult netted, banded, photographed, and released at Tobay Sanctuary, Nassau Co., Oct. 5, 1969 (Lauro and Schaeffer). The color slide, on file in the AMNH collection, was examined by Lanyon, Short, and the writer, and the identification confirmed.

Banding (see Map 161): Note the generally northeast-southwest direction of this species in migration. Of six birds banded in New York in various years and recovered in winter, five were from Texas—all in subsequent years (=indirect recoveries), as follows: two from near Waco, and one each—north to south— from Mason, Austin, and Alice. The sixth winter recovery (direct recovery) was a bird banded Oct. 14, 1959, at Watertown, N.Y., and recovered Jan. 1, 1960, near Varner, Ark.

Two individuals banded in upstate New York on May 15, 1947, and May 6, 1955, were recovered on or near their breeding grounds at Mingan and Mont Joli, Quebec, on June 11, 1947, and June 10, 1955, respectively.

Still another banded May 4, 1963, at Cleveland, Ohio, was captured two days later at Buffalo.

[Golden-crowned Sparrow
(*Zonotrichia atricapilla*)

Hypothetical: Alaska and western Canada, breeding southeast to western Alberta; winters east to eastern Colorado. Vagrant east to Massachusetts (specimen) and Pennsylvania (photograph).

In New York there is one report of an immature seen at Jones Beach, Long Island, from Jan. 31 to Apr. 24, 1954 (Carleton and many other observers). Permission to collect the bird

was refused and photographs taken proved unsatisfactory.]

White-throated Sparrow
(*Zonotrichia albicollis*)   *   B

Range: Nearctic region, breeding from central Canada to northern United States; in the east to the Berkshires, Catskills, and Poconos, very rarely to the mountains of West Virginia and Maryland; also at lower elevations in northwestern Connecticut (rarely) and in central and western New York. Winters north to southern Canada (rarely).

Status: Common to abundant migrant, occasionally more numerous; locally common in winter along the coast, less numerous inland. Common breeder in the mountains, but local and sporadic elsewhere at lower elevations.

Nonbreeding: This species is probably the most numerous sparrow on migration, often occurring in very large flocks both spring and fall. In winter it is a frequent visitor at feeding stations, most numerous near the coast.

MAXIMA: *Spring*—big inland flight on Apr. 30, 1960—2500, Manitou, Monroe Co. (Listman); 500, Syracuse; 700, Central Park, New York City, Apr. 30, 1947; 1000, Washington Park, Albany, May 5, 1941; 650, Greenwood Cemetery, Brooklyn, May 10, 1964.

MAXIMA: *Fall*—1200, Jones Beach, Long Island, Oct. 5, 1963; 1000, Prospect Park, Brooklyn, Oct. 15, 1950.

Unusual is an individual that spent the winter of 1952–1953 at the Meade feeder, in the Adirondack village of Saranac Lake. Also unusual is one that summered in 1964 on eastern Long Island at Orient (Latham). There are a number of other summer nonbreeders from the southern part of the state.

Change in breeding status (see Map 162): Eaton (1914: 304) said of this species, "It nests in the Canadian Zone of the Catskills and Adirondacks, and is one of the commonest birds breeding in our north woods." As to his statement, "A few also breed in the higher forests along the Pennsylvania border of southwestern New York," he gave no details, nor am I aware of any definite nesting record for that section today where one would expect to

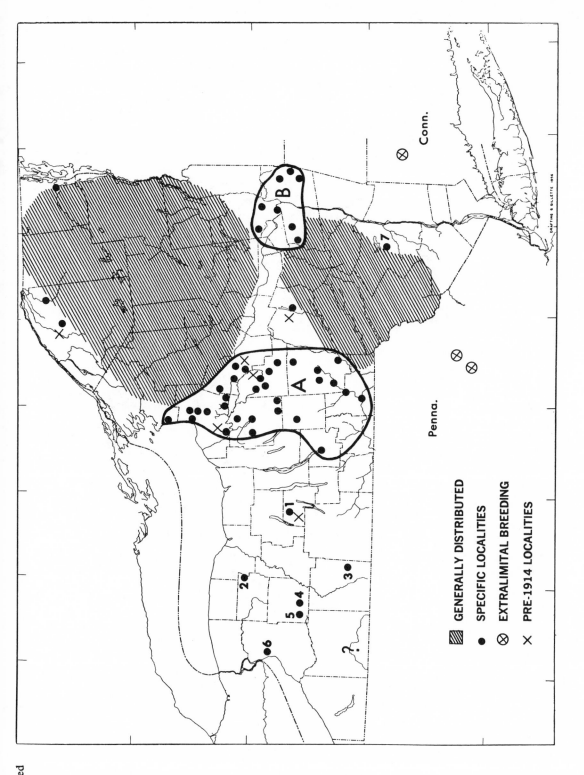

MAP 162 White-throated
Sparrow (*Zonotrichia
albicollis*) Breeding
distribution

GENERALLY DISTRIBUTED
SPECIFIC LOCALITIES
EXTRALIMITAL BREEDING
PRE-1914 LOCALITIES

Conn.

Penna.

A

B

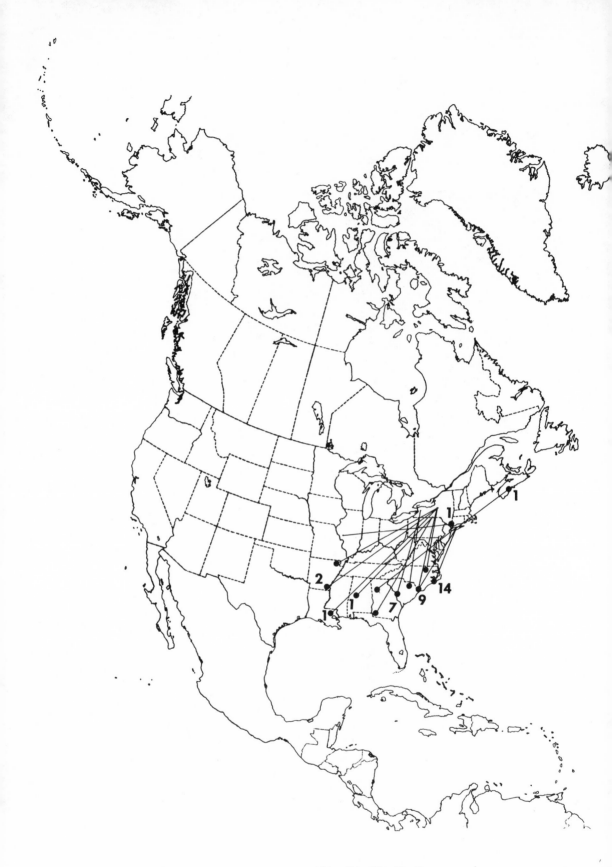

MAP 163 White-throated Sparrow (*Zonotrichia albicollis*) Banding recoveries

find it, and especially so, in view of the discussion below.

Since his time the White-throated Sparrow has expanded its range to other areas at lower elevations (see A and B on map).

A—south and west of the mountains this species now breeds in a relatively narrow east-west corridor extending all the way from El Dorado Beach, Jefferson Co., on the shore of Lake Ontario, south to near Binghamton, Broome Co., virtually on the Pennsylvania state line. The most interesting aspect of region A is the fact that a number of breeding localities lie in the low altitude belts along Lake Ontario and in the vicinity of Oneida Lake.

B—a much smaller area "squeezed in" among the Adirondacks on the northwest, the Catskills on the southwest, and the Berkshires in Massachusetts on the east. Except three localities near the state line in the Taconics of Rensselaer Co., and another in the Helderbergs of western Albany Co., the remaining four breeding localities are also in low country in the Hudson-Mohawk valleys.

The six small x's on the accompanying map represent *"pre*-Eaton" (=1914) breeding localities, as follows: Potsdam, St. Lawrence Co.; three in section A above—Phoenix, Oswego Co.; Steuben, Oneida Co.; Peterboro, Madison Co.; also Cooperstown, Otsego Co.; and Potter Swamp, Yates Co. (=no. 1 on map).

All the other solid circles (45) on the map are *"post*-Eaton" breeding localities, and of these 45, all except five are since 1950, so that areas A and B on the map essentially represent recent range expansion for the most part, as do six of the seven following isolated and peripheral breeding localities—years represent "arrival": (1) Potter Swamp, Yates Co., 1909; (2) Bergen Swamp, Genesee Co., 1967; (3) near Alfred, Allegany Co., 1969; (4) Java Lake Bog, 1960; (5) Wethersfield Springs, 1970—both in Wyoming Co.; (6) Buffalo, 1969—see below; (7) Krumville, Ulster Co., 1953. This last-named locality on the east slope of the Catskills is at the southeastern known limits of the breeding range in New York. A nesting pair was found there in 1953 in a "cold bog" at only 650 feet elevation (Hough). See Anderson and Maxfield (*Bird-Banding,* 1966, 37: 191–193) for recent low altitude breeding in Massachusetts and Rhode Island.

Breeding habitat outside montane areas includes white cedar, balsam, tamarack-alder and spruce-sphagnum bogs; swamps with white pine and yew; a small clearing in "mature" spruce planting; and a "grassy hummock" at the edge of the forest. In the Adirondacks, Catskills, and the higher portions of the Tug Hill Plateau, openings in the taiga (evergreen coniferous forest) and in mixed evergreen-deciduous woodland are preferred. In the Tug Hill area in July 1960, Scheider estimated 250 birds within eight miles.

Nests are placed on or near the ground, at the base of, among, or in thick bushes.

Egg clutches in 14 New York nests: three eggs (five nests); four eggs (seven nests); five eggs (two nests).

EGG DATES: May 30 to July 21 (second brood).

Nestlings: June 14 to Aug. 16; fledglings: June 27 to Aug. 31.

The most remarkable breeding site in the state was that described by Andrle and Rew (*Auk,* 1971, 88: 172–173, with photo) of a pair that successfully fledged two young in "border shrubbery by main library in the heart of Buffalo's business section."

Banding (see Map 163): 34 individuals banded in the autumn of various years in New York were recovered the following winter in six southern states: North Carolina (14); South Carolina (nine); Georgia (seven); one each in Alabama and Louisiana, and two in Arkansas.

Two recoveries are noteworthy: (1) an individual banded Apr. 26, 1966, at Blue Point, Long Island, was recovered 12 days later (May 8) at Chester, Nova Scotia; (2) another banded May 9, 1965, at Jacksonville, Illinois, was recovered "later" that month near Yonkers, Westchester Co.; this latter bird flew almost due *east* in spring.

Fox Sparrow (*Passerella iliaca*) *

Range: Nearctic region, in the east breeding south to northern Ontario, central and southeastern Quebec (islands in the Gulf of St. Lawrence), and Newfoundland; rarely to northwestern New Brunswick; in 1971 to central Nova Scotia. Winters north to southern Canada (rarely).

Status: A migrant in varying numbers, some years uncommon, in others common to very common. Regular, but usually uncommon in winter along the coast; much rarer inland at that season.

Occurrence: Fox Sparrows frequent thickets, hedgerows, shrubbery, and undergrowth in woodland; in winter they are not rare at feeding stations near the coast. In spring, especially, this species is noted for its rapid passage, often remaining for only a few days.

MAXIMA: *Fall*—16, near Rochester, Oct. 23, 1955; 150, Suffern, Rockland Co., Nov. 18, 1934. *Spring*—100, Central Park, New York City, Mar. 31, 1933; 35, Manitou, Monroe Co., Apr. 17, 1963; 28, Highland Park, Rochester, Apr. 20, 1966.

EXTREME DATES: Sept. 13 (coastal, see **Banding**) and Sept. 15 and 22 (inland) to May 11 (coastal) and May 15, 18, 19, 22—various years—all inland, Beardslee and Mitchell (1965: 445–446). Casual, Central Park, Aug. 9, 1913 (Griscom). The September and mid-May dates are unprecedented; the Fox Sparrow is ordinarily rare before mid-October and after April upstate and before late October and after early April downstate.

Banding (see Map 164): An individual banded at Elmhurst, Queens Co., Sept. 13, 1937 (Beals)—an extremely early arrival—was recovered at Columbus, North Carolina, Jan. 23, 1938. Another banded at Portland, Maine, Nov. 12, 1959, was recovered at Patchogue, Suffolk Co., January 1960. Still another New York individual was recovered in coastal Virginia in winter.

Two Fox Sparrows banded in New York in different years were recovered in late April on their Newfoundland breeding grounds.

Note that all five bandings and recoveries were on or near the coast.

Subspecies: An adult female was mist-netted at Fire Island State Park, Suffolk Co., May 12, 1971 (Buckley). It was collected because of its extremely dark coloration and the fact that it was very late. This writer has not seen the specimen, but it was determined as the race *altivagans* by Ned Johnson, Roxie Laybourne, and John Weske; the specimen is USNM 566277. This subspecies breeds in the southern Canadian Rockies and winters chiefly in California. It is stated in the A.O.U. Checklist (1957: 623) to be "Casual in Manitoba." This is the first known record for eastern North America.

Lincoln's Sparrow
(*Passerella lincolnii*)   *   B

Range: Nearctic region, breeding from Alaska and Canada to the mountains of California, Arizona, and New Mexico in the west, but in the east only as far as extreme northern United States. Winters north to the southern states, rarely farther north (Massachusetts specimen).

Status: Rare to uncommon but regular migrant, occasionally more numerous. Very rare in winter. Rare breeder in the Adirondacks.

Nonbreeding: Lincoln's Sparrow, a shy and usually secretive species, favors thickets, hedgerows, and brush bordering wet areas. However, it is often found on lawns adjacent to shrubbery. The species is most prevalent in spring inland and in fall on the coast.

MAXIMA: *Spring*—ten, Manitou, Monroe Co., May 19, 1967; 14, Sandy Pond, Oswego Co., May 20, 1969 (Scheider), an unusual number.

MAXIMA: *Fall*—eight netted and banded, Fire Island State Park, Suffolk Co., Sept. 20, 1970; ten, Jones Beach, Nassau Co., Oct. 1, 1963; six, Amsterdam, Montgomery Co., Oct. 20, 1957.

EXTREME DATES: *Spring*—Apr. 29 (coastal specimen) and May 1 (inland) to June 2 (inland) and June 10 (coastal banding).

EXTREME DATES: *Fall*—Sept. 2 (coastal specimen) to Dec. 4 (coastal).

Usually rare before mid-May; and before late September and after October. Most, if not all, April sight reports remain unconfirmed, as do those in August. Immatures of both Swamp and Song sparrows are undoubtedly misidentified at those times.

Winter: No positively verified winter record exists for the state, that is, specimen evidence. However, there is a photograph of an in-

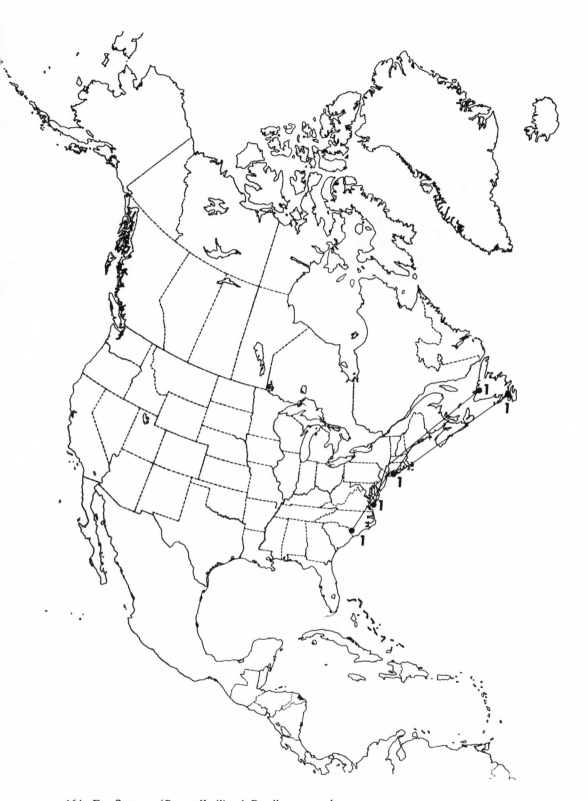

MAP 164 Fox Sparrow (*Passerella iliaca*) Banding recoveries

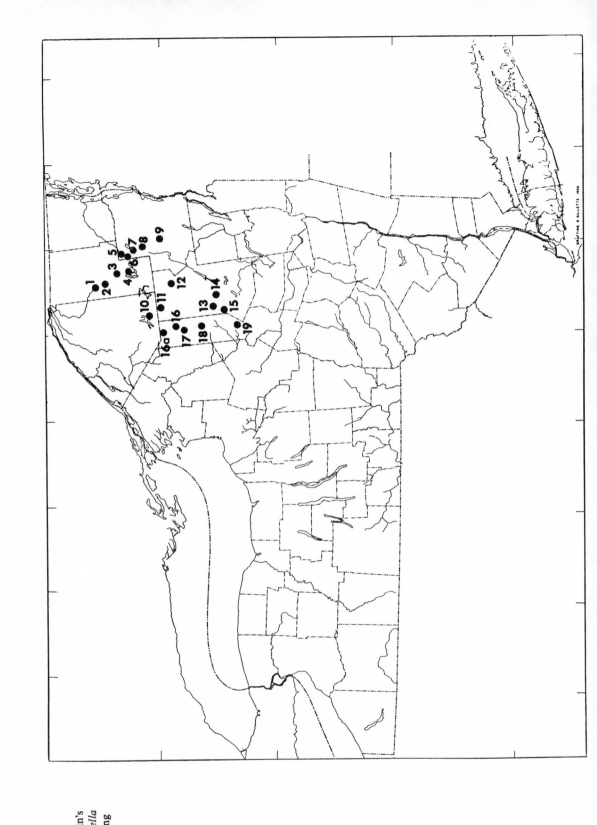

MAP 165 Lincoln's Sparrow (*Passerella lincolnii*) Breeding distribution

dividual that appeared after a heavy snowstorm at the Klein feeder, Little Neck, Queens
Co., Mar. 5–13, 1960 (Yeaton, Bull, et al.).

Three other winter observations are believed
correct: (1) one present at the Rohner feeder,
Greece, Monroe Co., from Jan. 1 to Mar. 30,
1960 (many observers from the Genesee Ornith. Soc.); (2) one well observed at Bay-
chester, Bronx Co., Dec. 22, 1963 (Tudor and
Horowitz); (3) one at a feeder, Cropseyville,
Rensselaer Co., from Jan. 27 to Feb. 10,
1966 (Sabin, Wickham, et al.).

Breeding (see Map 165): Saunders (1929:
416–417) perhaps best described the breeding
habitat of Lincoln's Sparrow in the Adirondacks, as sphagnum bogs with Labrador tea,
sheep laurel, blueberry, and with scattered
tamarack, black spruce, and alder.

Nests are placed on the ground. One New
York nest was situated at the foot of a small
huckleberry bush in a wet bog near the edge
of forest.

Of five New York nests containing eggs, one
nest held three eggs and four others had four
eggs each.

EGG DATES: June 10 to June 28.

Nestlings: June 18; fledglings: July 21.

The following 20 breeding localities in five
counties shown on the accompanying map are:
Franklin Co.—(1) Santa Clara; (2) Madawaska; (3) near Paul Smith's and nearby
Barnum Pond; (4) Lake Clear. Essex Co.—
(5) Bloomingdale; (6) Ray Brook; (7) Chubb
River Swamp; (8) North Elba; (9) Marcy
Swamp near Upper Ausable Lake. St. Lawrence Co.—(10) Barber Point, Cranberry Lake.
Hamilton Co.—(11) Sabattis; (12) Long Lake
(village); (13) Falls Pond; (14) Twin Lakes
near West Canada Lakes; (15) Moose Pond
and nearby Otter Pond. Herkimer Co.—(16)
Beaver River (village); (16a) Five Ponds,
1971; (17) Woods Lake and nearby Big Moose
(village); (18) Little Moose Lake; (19) Wilmurt.

Reports of this species breeding in Monroe
Co. in 1903 (Friedmann, 1963: 167) and in
Tioga Co. in recent years (based on 1967 nest
record cards) are erroneous. These reports are
unquestionably misidentifications. As breeders
Lincoln's Sparrows are confined to the Adirondacks.

Swamp Sparrow
(*Passerella georgiana*)   *   B

Range: Chiefly central and eastern North
America, breeding from Canada—in the west
to Missouri; in the east to Maryland. Winters
north to New York and New England.

Status: Common to very common fall migrant, less numerous in spring. Usually uncommon in winter on the coast, rare inland.
Widespread breeder.

Nonbreeding: In migration Swamp Sparrows are found in parks, on lawns, and in
fields and thickets with other sparrows, but
during the winter they retire to swampy places.

MAXIMA: *Spring*—40, Central Park, New
York City, May 14, 1933. *Fall*—200, Cuba
Marsh, Allegany Co., Oct. 1, 1966 (Burton);
219 netted and banded at Brookhaven, Suffolk
Co., Oct. 19, 1964 (Puleston and Terry).
Winter—65, Easthampton, Suffolk Co., Dec.
31, 1949 (Helmuth).

Migrants usually arrive in early April and
depart in early November.

Breeding: The Swamp Sparrow breeds in
fresh-water marshes, wooded swamps, and
along the edges of streams and ponds; more
rarely and locally in coastal brackish meadows
on the south shore of Long Island. Referring
to the Oneida Lake region, Stoner (1932)
stated that it was an abundant breeder in
cattail marshes and in alder-willow-aspen bogs.

The nest is placed on or very close to the
ground under bushes, in cattails, tussocks of
marsh grass, or the undergrowth of swampy
woods.

Egg clutches in 12 New York nests: four
eggs (four nests); five eggs (seven nests); six
eggs (one nest).

EGG DATES: May 5 to July 22 (second
brood).

Nestlings: May 21 to July 30; fledglings:
June 28 to Aug. 3.

Banding: Two Long Island individuals
banded in fall at Patchogue, Suffolk Co., were
recovered later on in fall and in late winter
following, at Charleston, South Carolina, and
near Punta Rassa, Florida.

Remarks: No subspecies are recognized here; the more northern form, *"ericrypta"* is poorly differentiated, the differences in color being only of average quality.

Song Sparrow
(*Passerella melodia*) * B

Range: North America—in the west with an extensive breeding range—from southern Alaska and central Canada to central Mexico, but in the east only from southern Canada to the coast of North Carolina and in the mountains to northern Georgia. Nominate *melodia* breeds in New York. In the east winters from extreme southern Canada to the Gulf of Mexico and southern Florida.

Status: Common to abundant migrant. Locally common in winter, especially near the coast. Widespread breeder.

Nonbreeding: Although rarely occurring in such large flocks as the Slate-colored Junco and White-throated Sparrow, nevertheless the Song Sparrow is one of our more numerous species on migration. It winters regularly in small numbers, often at feeders.

The species is most plentiful in late March and mid-October. Curiously I have seen no maxima for inland areas on a per *locality* basis.

MAXIMA: *Spring*—125, Flushing, Queens Co., Mar. 30, 1940. *Fall*—75, Central Park, New York City, Oct. 13, 1953; 400, Easthampton to Montauk, Suffolk Co., Oct. 14, 1929. *Winter*—185, Orient region, Suffolk Co., Dec. 22, 1918.

Migrants ordinarily arrive in early March and depart in late November.

Breeding: The Song Sparrow, one of our more numerous birds, is ubiquitous, breeding in a great variety of habitats from the interior mountains to the coastal beaches. It nests in woodland clearings, thickets and hedgerows in farming country, brushy fields, at the edge of marshes, swamps, streams, and lakes, in city parks and suburban yards with plenty of shrubs, and in thickets on coastal sand dunes. It is absent only in the depths of primary forest and in open fields and marshes devoid of bushes.

This species is almost entirely a ground nester, often laying the eggs in grass tussocks or at the bases of bushes. Eaton (1914: 317) stated that "99 per cent of their nests are placed upon the ground." Nevertheless, I know of at least seven New York nests above ground: (1) six inches up in catbriers; (2) two feet up in a rosebush; (3) and (4) each two and one-half feet up in Scotch pines; (5) three feet up in an apple tree cavity; (6) five feet up in a hollow apple tree; (7) eight feet up in the stub of a dead witch hazel—in a former Downy Woodpecker nest hole.

Egg clutches range from three to six in 42 New York nests as follows: three eggs (six nests); four eggs (18 nests); five eggs (16 nests); six eggs (two nests).

EGG DATES: Apr. 17 to Aug. 11.

Nestlings: May 5 to Sept. 3; fledglings: May 18 to Sept. 23. The species is sometimes three-brooded in this latitude.

Banding (see Map 166): An individual banded in New York was recovered in Ontario *11* years later. Direct recoveries of seven New York banded birds were made in late fall or winter in southeastern United States in South Carolina, Georgia, Alabama, and Mississippi. Three others banded in winter in New York were recovered the following summer (presumed breeders) in Nova Scotia, while still another banded as a fall migrant on Long Island was recovered the following spring on the Gaspé peninsula, Quebec. But the most surprising recovery was that of a bird banded on Mar. 27, 1927, in northeastern Iowa, and recovered on Apr. 26, 1927, near Branchport, Yates Co. (flew *east* in spring).

Remarks: The Song Sparrow is a highly polytypic species with much variation present in the west. In the northeast the well-marked coastal subspecies, *Passerella melodia atlantica*, extends from North Carolina to about southern New Jersey. As explained in my book (Bull, 1964: 464–465), I am unaware of any "pure" *atlantica* specimen from New York. As to the poorly differentiated inland race, *P. m. "euphonia"* (Bull, *op. cit.*), this form is merely part of an east-west cline extending from New England and New York (nominate *P. melodia*) through several slightly differentiated populations including the more western

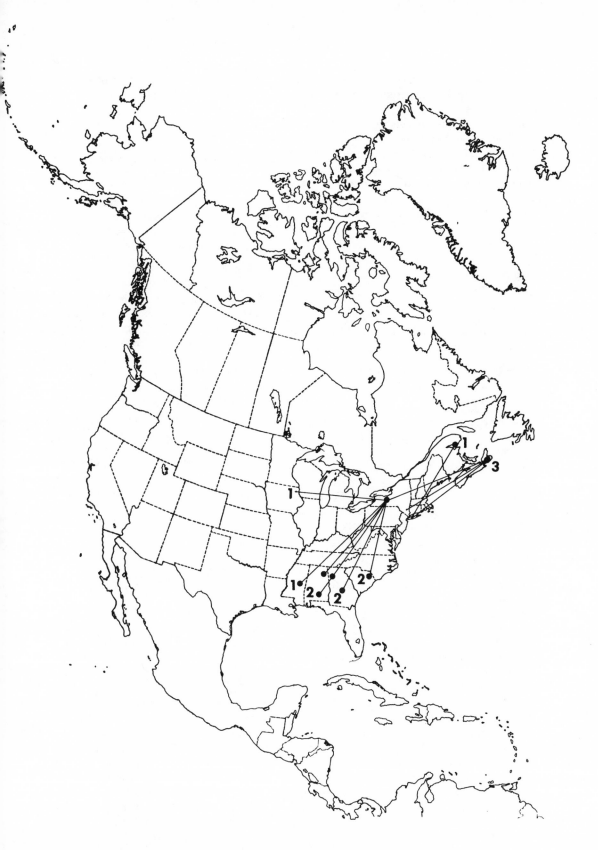

MAP 166 Song Sparrow (*Passerella melodia*) Banding recoveries

P. m. "*juddi*" (itself part of the cline) until other populations in the Rocky Mountains are reached.

In sum, the only populations examined by me from New York State are specimens of "pure" *melodia,* intermediates taken on Long Island with the more southern coastal race *atlantica,* and certain other specimens from central and western New York of or approaching what has been called "*euphonia.*"

Lapland Longspur
(*Calcarius lapponicus*)   *

Range: Holarctic region, in eastern North America breeding south to the northern parts of Ontario, Quebec, and Labrador.

Status: Winter visitant, varying from uncommon to locally abundant. Most numerous along Lake Ontario.

Occurrence: A species of open country, inhabiting short-grass fields especially in agricultural districts of the Lake Ontario plain; also airports, golf courses, and along coastal beaches and close-cut grassy strips in the vicinity of salt bays and lagoons. Frequently found in the company of Horned Larks and Snow Buntings. Lapland Longspurs on occasion may be seen quite late in spring and at this time the males are often observed in their handsome breeding plumage.

MAXIMA: *Inland*—110, Shore Acres, Monroe Co., Oct. 23, 1949; 120, Olcott, Niagara Co., Nov. 26, 1950; 220, Yates, Orleans Co., Jan. 26, 1969; 300, Elma, Erie Co., Feb. 22, 1967; 880, Braddock's Bay, Monroe Co., Mar. 28, 1954 (Bieber and Van Beurden); 500, Shore Acres, May 1, 1954 (Schaffner and Thorpe). The exceptionally high numbers during the spring of 1954 were especially noteworthy.

MAXIMA: *Coastal*—75, Idlewild, Queens Co., Nov. 11, 1951; 125, Jamaica Bay area, Dec. 20, 1952. It will be noted that the coastal concentrations are much smaller than those of western New York, particularly those along Lake Ontario.

EXTREME DATES: Sept. 16 and 23 (inland) and Oct. 3 (coastal) to May 9 (both inland and coastal); exceptionally to May 26 and

May 31 (both inland). Rare before mid-October and after early May.

Chestnut-collared Longspur
(*Calcarius ornatus*)   *

Range: Central North America, breeding east to southwestern Minnesota; winters east to Louisiana. Vagrant along the Atlantic coast from New Brunswick to Maryland.

Status: *Casual*—there are four known occurrences in New York—all from Long Island—three of which are specimen records, as follows: (1) male collected at Long Island City, Queens Co., Feb. 16, 1889 (Hendrickson), AMNH 65626; (2) female taken at Miller's Place, Suffolk Co., Sept. 14, 1891 (Helme), AMNH 802440; (3) male in nearly full breeding plumage taken at Orient, Suffolk Co., Apr. 27, 1923 (Latham), NYSM 25664—first seen on Apr. 21; (4) male in breeding plumage observed at Dyker Beach, Kings Co., Apr. 29, 1944 (Grant, *et al., Auk,* 1945, 62: 463).

Reports of individuals observed in *nonbreeding* plumage are considered unsatisfactory due to possible confusion with the very similar Lapland Longspur.

Snow Bunting
(*Plectrophenax nivalis*)   *

Range: Holarctic region, in eastern North America breeding south to northern Quebec and Labrador.

Status: Winter visitant, varying from uncommon to very abundant.

Occurrence: Snow Buntings are most numerous during the coldest months in the open farm country and grassland of western New York, and somewhat less numerous along the ocean beaches and sand dunes of the outer coast, as well as on short-grass fields around the saltwater bays and inlets. They often occur in pure flocks but frequently associate with Horned Larks and Lapland Longspurs.

MAXIMA: *Inland*—1000, Hamlin, Monroe Co., Nov. 8, 1958; 4000, Mendon Ponds, Mon-

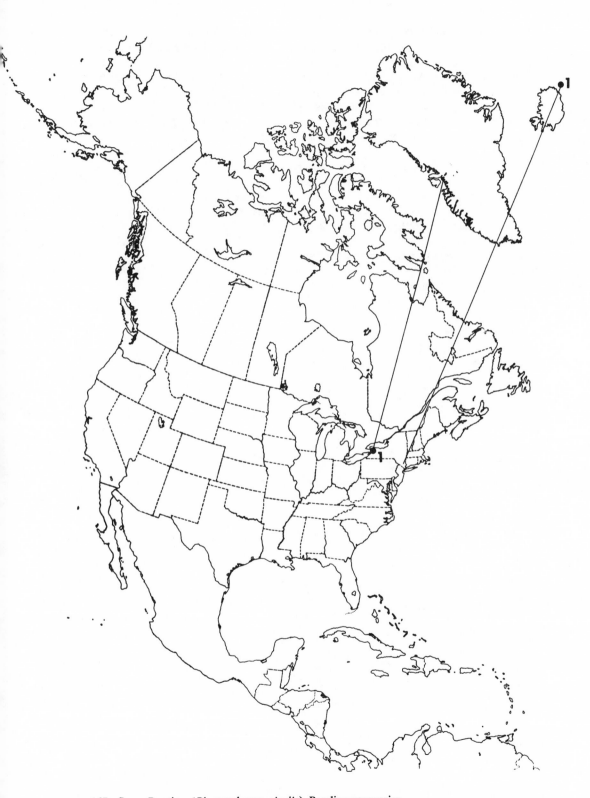

MAP 167 Snow Bunting (*Plectrophenax nivalis*) Banding recoveries

roe Co., Jan. 15, 1955; 4000, Gainesville, Wyoming Co., Mar. 16, 1961; a spectacular irruption occurred near East Aurora, Erie Co., Mar. 24, 1962, when Wright estimated *10,000* passing on migration in a nearly continuous flight within only one-half hour (Beardslee and Mitchell, 1965: 450); 1000, Arcade, Wyoming Co., Apr. 1, 1959; 1500, Pompey, Onondaga Co., Apr. 5, 1970.

MAXIMA: *Coastal*—1000, Long Beach, Nassau Co., Dec. 27, 1919; 1500, Orient, Suffolk Co., Feb. 10, 1956.

EXTREME DATES: Sept. 28 (inland) to Apr. 21 (coastal) and May 9, 1948, Oak Beach, Suffolk Co. (Elliott).

Rare before mid-October and after mid-April.

The supposed occurrence of ten of these birds reported by a single observer on Aug. 10, 1947, in western New York was not confirmed (Beardslee and Mitchell, 1965: 450–451). The date is seven weeks earlier than the earliest fall date above.

Banding (see Map 167): One banded at Millbrook, Dutchess Co., Jan. 20, 1941 (F. W. Trevor), was caught alive on a *westbound* ship, 20 miles off Iceland (63°80′N., 13°80′W.), Apr. 18, 1941 (*Bird-Banding,* 1945, 16: 129); another banded in western Greenland, Jakobshavn district, June 19, 1959, was found dead near Buffalo, Mar. 18, 1960 (Salomonsen, *Dansk Ornith. Foren. Tids.,* 1961, 55: 204). This latter individual is now a specimen in the collection of the Buffalo Museum of Science, 5126.

PART III

APPENDICES

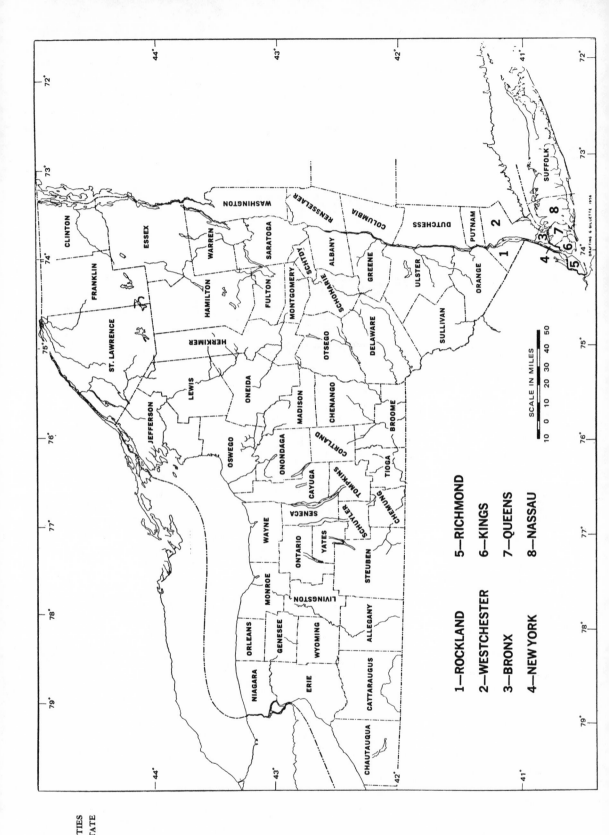

MAP 168 COUNTIES
OF NEW YORK STATE

1—ROCKLAND   5—RICHMOND

2—WESTCHESTER 6—KINGS

3—BRONX   7—QUEENS

4—NEW YORK   8—NASSAU

SCALE IN MILES

10 0 10 20 30 40 50

GAZETTEER

Localities mentioned in the text in connection with the breeding distribution maps are included here, as follows: (1) locality; (2) county; (3) coordinates to the nearest minute. Some of the place names are well known and may be found on the physiographic map inside the end covers. Many other place names, however, will have to be sought on road or county maps, and especially the topographic or quadrangle maps issued by the U. S. Geological Survey.

Many of the lakes and ponds were located only after consulting Douglas (1931). His listing was particularly helpful, in view of the fact that well over 2000 ponds and lakes exist in the state and especially as there are at least 70 bodies of water called "Mud" Pond or Lake, 60 "Little," and 43 "Long." See also Greeson and Robison (1970).

Locality names also change through the years. Few birders of today are aware that the present Oak Orchard Swamp is but a fraction of a formerly vast wetland complex known as the Tonawanda Swamp covering an enormous area encompassing parts of four counties, more than twice its current size.

Approximately 900 *breeding* localities are listed here. The list was compiled while preparing the breeding maps. All *latitudes* within New York State are *north* and all *longitudes* are *west*, so for the sake of brevity the abbreviations "N." and "W." will be omitted on all coordinates. Thus, "44°30′N., 74°55′W.," will be indicated as, "44°30′–74°55′."

COUNTIES OF NEW YORK STATE

1. Albany	22. Herkimer	43. Richmond
2. Allegany	23. Jefferson	44. Rockland
3. Bronx	24. Kings	45. St. Lawrence
4. Broome	25. Lewis	46. Saratoga
5. Cattaraugus	26. Livingston	47. Schenectady
6. Cayuga	27. Madison	48. Schoharie
7. Chautauqua	28. Monroe	49. Schuyler
8. Chemung	29. Montgomery	50. Seneca
9. Chenango	30. Nassau	51. Steuben
10. Clinton	31. New York	52. Suffolk
11. Columbia	32. Niagara	53. Sullivan
12. Cortland	33. Oneida	54. Tioga
13. Delaware	34. Onondaga	55. Tompkins
14. Dutchess	35. Ontario	56. Ulster
15. Erie	36. Orange	57. Warren
16. Essex	37. Orleans	58. Washington
17. Franklin	38. Oswego	59. Wayne
18. Fulton	39. Otsego	60. Westchester
19. Genesee	40. Putnam	61. Wyoming
20. Greene	41. Queens	62. Yates
21. Hamilton	42. Rensselaer	

Locality	County	Coordinates
Acabonack Harbor	Suffolk	41°02′–72°08′
Adamsville	Washington	43°20′–73°25′
Aiden Lair	Essex	43°85′–74°00′
Akron	Erie	43°05′–78°30′
Alabama	Genesee	43°05′–75°25′
Albany	Albany	42°10′–73°50′
Albion	Orleans	43°15′–78°15′
Alden	Erie	42°54′–78°30′
Alexandria Bay	Jefferson	44°20′–75°55′
Alfred	Allegany	42°15′–77°45′
Alice, Lake	Clinton	44°55′–73°30′
Allegany	Cattaraugus	42°06′–78°30′
Allegany State Park	Cattaraugus	42°05′–78°45′
Alley Pond	Queens	40°50′–73°45′
Alma	Allegany	42°00′–78°10′
Altamont	Albany	42°45′–74°00′
Amagansett	Suffolk	41°00′–72°15′
Amber	Onondaga	42°50′–76°15′
Amherst	Erie	43°02′–78°45′
Ampersand Lake	Franklin	44°12′–74°12′
Ampersand Mtn.	Franklin	44°14′–74°15′
Angola	Erie	42°39′–79°02′
Apalachin	Tioga	42°03′–76°08′
Arbutus Pond	Essex	44°00′–74°15′
Arnold Lake	Essex	44°07′–73°56′
Arnot Forest	Tompkins-Schuyler	42°22′–76°36′
Ashville	Chautauqua	42°05′–79°25′
Astoria	Queens	40°45′–73°45′
Aurora	Cayuga	42°45′–76°43′
Ausable Lakes	Essex	44°15′–73°50′
Ausable River (marshes)	Clinton	44°30′–73°40′
Austerlitz	Columbia	42°20′–73°25′
Avon	Livingston	42°55′–77°44′
Awosting, Lake	Ulster	41°42′–74°17′
Axton	Franklin	44°20′–74°25′
Azure Mtn.	Franklin	44°30′–74°30′
Bald Mtn.	Dutchess	41°40′–73°35′
Baldwin	Nassau	40°45′–73°35′
Balsam Lake Mtn.	Ulster	42°01′–74°36′
Balsam Mtn.	Ulster	42°05′–74°05′
Balsam Round Top Mtn.	Ulster	42°02′–74°38′
Bangall	Dutchess	41°54′–73°41′
Barber Point	St. Lawrence	44°13′–74°50′
Barnum Pond	Franklin	44°27′–74°12′
Barre Center	Orleans	43°15′–78°15′
Barrytown	Dutchess	42°00′–73°55′
Bash Bish Falls	Columbia	42°05′–73°30′
Basher Kill	Sullivan	41°35′–74°30′
Bass Island	Jefferson	43°55′–76°10′
Batavia	Genesee	43°00′–78°11′
Bay Pond	Franklin	44°25′–74°15′

Locality	County	Coordinates
Bayside	Queens	40°50′–73°45′
Bayville	Nassau	40°55′–73°34′
Beacon, Mt.	Dutchess	41°29′–73°56′
Bear Mtn.	Orange	41°18′–74°01′
Bear Mtn. State Park	Orange-Rockland	41°33′–74°30′
Bearsville	Ulster	42°03′–74°10′
Bear Swamp	Cayuga	42°15′–76°25′
Beaver Lake	Lewis	43°52′–75°10′
Beaver Lake	Onondaga	43°15′–76°22′
Beaver Lake	Wyoming	42°45′–78°36′
Beaver Meadow Refuge	Chenango	42°40′–75°45′
Beaver Meadow Refuge	Wyoming	42°40′–78°22′
Beaver River (village)	Herkimer	43°55′–74°55′
Bedford	Westchester	41°14′–73°37′
Bellport	Suffolk	40°45′–72°55′
Belvidere	Allegany	42°15′–78°10′
Bemus Point	Chautauqua	42°20′–79°25′
Benton Center	Yates	42°45′–77°05′
Bergen Beach	Kings	40°30′–73°45′
Bergen Swamp	Genesee	43°10′–77°52′
Berlin Mtn.	Rensselaer	42°42′–73°18′
Berne Swamp	Albany	42°40′–74°10′
Big Basin	Cattaraugus	42°00′–79°00′
Big Indian	Ulster	42°06′–74°27′
Big Moose	Herkimer	43°50′–74°55′
Big Moose Lake	Herkimer	43°50′–74°50′
Big Sandy Creek	Jefferson	43°45′–76°10′
Big Shallow Pond	Herkimer	44°03′–74°56′
Binghamton	Broome	42°06′–75°55′
Black Brook	Clinton	44°35′–73°45′
Black Creek Lake	Herkimer	43°26′–74°54′
Black Lake	St. Lawrence	44°40′–75°30′
Black Mtn.	Washington	43°35′–73°30′
Black Pond	Franklin	44°34′–74°20′
Bloomingdale	Essex	44°30′–74°05′
Blooming Grove	Orange	41°25′–74°12′
Blue Ledge	Essex	43°45′–74°05′
Bog River	St. Lawrence	44°10′–74°45′
Boliver Swamp	Madison	43°04′–75°56′
Bonaparte, Lake	Lewis	44°10′–75°20′
Boonville	Oneida	43°28′–75°20′
Boreas Mtn.	Essex	44°00′–73°50′
Boreas River	Essex	44°00′–73°50′
Boston	Erie	42°40′–78°45′
Bouquet River (north fork)	Essex	44°05′–73°40′
Boylston	Oswego	43°40′–76°00′
Braddock's Bay	Monroe	43°20′–77°45′
Branchport	Yates	42°36′–77°11′
Brandon	Franklin	44°45′–74°25′
Brandreth Lake	Hamilton	43°50′–74°45′
Brayton	Washington	43°25′–73°40′

Locality	County	Coordinates
Brewerton	Onondaga	43°15′–76°09′
Briarcliff Manor	Westchester	41°10′–73°50′
Brockport	Monroe	43°13′–77°56′
Bronx Park	Bronx	40°50′–73°50′
Brookfield	Madison	42°50′–75°18′
Brookhaven	Suffolk	40°46′–72°49′
Buck Pond	Monroe	43°20′–77°40′
Buffalo	Erie	42°52′–78°55′
Butterfield Lake	Jefferson	44°20′–75°45′
Butterfly Swamp	Oswego	43°35′–76°14′
Butternut Pond	Essex	44°26′–73°20′
Caledonia	Livingston	42°58′–77°49′
Camden	Oneida	43°21′–75°45′
Camillus	Onondaga	43°05′–76°18′
Canachagala Lake	Herkimer	43°36′–74°53′
Canadice Lake	Ontario	42°45′–77°35′
Canajoharie	Montgomery	42°50′–74°35′
Canandaigua	Ontario	42°53′–77°19′
Canandaigua Lake	Ontario-Yates	42°53′–77°19′
Canarsie Pol	Kings	40°40′–73°58′
Canastota	Madison	43°05′–75°45′
Caneadea	Allegany	42°24′–78°11′
Canisteo	Steuben	42°16′–77°37′
Cape Vincent	Jefferson	44°05′–76°50′
Captree Island	Suffolk	40°38′–73°15′
Captree State Park	Suffolk	40°38′–73°15′
Carmel	Putnam	41°25′–73°40′
Caroline	Tompkins	42°20′–76°20′
Carrollton	Cattaraugus	42°10′–78°45′
Cartwright Island	Suffolk	41°02′–72°07′
Castleton	Rensselaer	42°32′–73°44′
Catlin Lake	Hamilton	44°02′–74°16′
Catskill	Greene	42°14′–73°52′
Caumsett State Park	Suffolk	40°55′–73°28′
Cedar Beach	Suffolk	40°38′–73°20′
Cedar Island	Suffolk	40°38′–73°20′
Cedar Lake	Hamilton	43°37′–74°32′
Centerville	Oswego	43°35′–76°04′
Central Park	New York	40°47′–73°58′
Centre Island	Nassau	40°55′–73°30′
Chapel Pond	Essex	44°08′–73°45′
Chazy	Clinton	44°53′–73°29′
Cheektowaga	Erie	42°50′–78°45′
Chenango Forks	Broome	42°14′–75°53′
Chenango Valley State Park	Broome	42°38′–75°25′
Cheningo	Cortland	42°40′–76°00′
Cherry Valley	Otsego	42°49′–74°46′
Childwold	St. Lawrence	44°20′–74°38′
Chili	Monroe	43°06′–77°48′
Chubb River Swamp	Essex	44°15′–74°00′
Chub Pond	Herkimer	43°31′–75°03′

Locality	County	Coordinates
Cicero Swamp	Onondaga	43°12′–76°09′
Cincinnatus	Cortland	42°33′–75°55′
Clay Swamp	Onondaga	43°13′–76°11′
Clayton	Jefferson	44°15′–76°06′
Clear, Lake	Franklin	44°22′–74°16′
Clear Lake	Putnam	41°25′–73°50′
Cleveland	Oswego	43°15′–75°50′
Clyde	Wayne	43°05′–76°53′
Clymer	Chautauqua	42°05′–79°40′
Cobble Hill	Essex	44°13′–73°38′
Cohoes	Albany	42°45′–73°43′
Colby, Lake	Franklin	44°20′–74°09′
Colden, Lake	Essex	44°08′–73°59′
Cold Spring	Putnam	41°25′–73°55′
Cold Spring Harbor	Suffolk	40°53′–73°27′
Coldwater	Monroe	43°21′–77°45′
Collins Center	Erie	42°30′–78°59′
Colvin, Mt.	Essex	44°25′–73°20′
Como Lake Park	Erie	42°50′–78°45′
Comstock	Washington	43°27′–73°29′
Congers Lake	Rockland	41°08′–73°57′
Connecticut Hill	Tompkins	42°25′–76°40′
Constantia	Oswego	43°15′–76°00′
Constitution Island	Putnam	41°25′–73°55′
Cooperstown	Otsego	42°43′–74°56′
Copperas Pond	Essex	44°19′–73°53′
Cornell Mtn.	Ulster	42°00′–74°25′
Corning	Steuben	42°10′–77°04′
Cornwall	Orange	41°26′–74°02′
County Line Island	Franklin-St. Lawrence	44°15′–74°30′
Coxsackie	Greene	42°21′–73°47′
Cranberry Lake	St. Lawrence	44°14′–74°52′
Crooked Creek	St. Lawrence	44°22′–75°53′
Croton Lake	Westchester	41°15′–73°47′
Croton Point	Westchester	41°10′–73°55′
Cruger's Island	Dutchess	42°00′–73°55′
Cuba	Allegany	42°13′–78°16′
Cutchogue	Suffolk	41°02′–72°30′
Dart Lake	Herkimer	43°47′–74°52′
Davenport	Delaware	42°26′–74°55′
Debar Mtn. Refuge	Franklin	44°35′–74°11′
Deer Lake	Hamilton	43°17′–74°42′
DeForest, Lake	Rockland	41°06′–73°58′
Delaware, Lake	Delaware	41°53′–75°07′
Delmar	Albany	42°40′–73°50′
Deposit	Broome	42°04′–75°26′
Dobbs Ferry	Westchester	41°01′–73°52′
Dodge River Flow	Franklin	44°30′–74°21′
Dover Plains	Dutchess	41°44′–73°34′
Dryden	Tompkins	42°29′–76°17′
Dunkirk	Erie	42°29′–79°21′

Locality	County	Coordinates
Dyker Beach	Kings	40°35′–74°00′
Eagle Bay	Herkimer	43°45′–74°50′
East Aurora	Erie	42°45′–78°36′
East Bay	Wayne	43°15′–76°50′
East Branch	Delaware	41°59′–75°08′
East Concord	Erie	42°35′–78°40′
Easthampton	Suffolk	40°58′–72°11′
East Moriches	Suffolk	40°48′–72°46′
East Quogue	Suffolk	40°48′–72°36′
East Randolph	Cattaraugus	42°10′–78°55′
Eaton, Lake	Hamilton	43°58′–74°27′
Eaton's Neck	Suffolk	40°57′–73°24′
Eden	Erie	42°39′–78°56′
Edwards	St. Lawrence	44°19′–75°15′
Eel Bay	Jefferson	44°18′–76°03′
Elba	Genesee	43°04′–78°12′
Eldon Pond	Hamilton	43°50′–74°37′
Eldorado Beach	Jefferson	43°47′–76°12′
Elizabethtown	Essex	44°13′–73°38′
Elk Lake	Essex	44°01′–73°49′
Ellenburg	Clinton	44°59′–73°40′
Ellicottville	Cattaraugus	42°16′–78°40′
Ellisburg	Jefferson	43°45′–76°08′
Elmira	Chemung	42°06′–76°50′
Elmsford	Westchester	41°03′–73°49′
Eltingville	Richmond	40°33′–74°08′
Elton Creek Pond	Cattaraugus	46°26′–78°18′
Enfield	Tompkins	42°25′–76°40′
Esopus	Ulster	41°48′–73°58′
Evans	Erie	42°40′–79°50′
Fabius	Onondaga	42°50′–75°58′
Fahnestock State Park	Putnam	41°25′–73°47′
Fair Haven	Cayuga	43°26′–76°44′
Falls Pond	Hamilton	43°37′–74°41′
Farmersville	Cattaraugus	42°20′–78°22′
Fawn Lake	Hamilton	43°43′–74°48′
Ferd's Bog	Hamilton-Herkimer	43°45′–74°50′
Fillmore	Allegany	42°31′–78°05′
Fire Island State Park	Suffolk	40°36′–73°11′
Fisher's Island	Suffolk	41°17′–72°00′
Five Ponds	Herkimer	44°03′–74°57′
Flanders Bay	Suffolk	40°54′–72°37′
Fleischmann's	Delaware	42°10′–74°32′
Floodwood	Franklin	44°20′–74°24′
Floyd	Oneida	43°15′–75°20′
Flushing	Queens	40°46′–73°50′
Flushing Meadows	Queens	40°45′–73°50′
Follensby Jr. Pond	Franklin	44°27′–74°21′
Follensby Pond	Franklin	44°11′–74°22′
Forked Lake	Hamilton	43°50′–74°40′
Fort Salonga	Suffolk	40°55′–73°19′

Locality	County	Coordinates
Foster Lake	Allegany	42°15′–77°45′
Four Brothers Islands	Essex	44°25′–73°25′
Fourth Lake	Herkimer	43°45′–74°50′
Fourth Lake (village)	Herkimer	43°45′–74°50′
Fox Brook	Oswego	43°30′–78°50′
Franklinville	Cattaraugus	42°20′–78°28′
Freedom Bog	Cattaraugus	42°28′–78°20′
Frenchman's Island	Onondaga	43°10′–76°05′
Fresh Kills	Richmond	40°35′–74°20′
Frewsburg	Chautauqua	42°03′–79°11′
Frost Valley	Ulster	41°55′–74°30′
Fulton	Oswego	43°20′–76°26′
Galloo Island	Jefferson	43°55′–76°25′
Gallupville	Schoharie	42°35′–74°15′
Galway	Saratoga	43°02′–74°02′
Gannett Hill	Ontario	42°44′–77°25′
Garden City	Nassau	40°35′–73°40′
Gardiner's Island	Suffolk	41°05′–72°05′
Garnerville	Rockland	41°12′–73°58′
Garrison	Putnam	41°22′–73°57′
Geneva	Ontario	42°53′–76°59′
George, Lake	Warren-Washington-Essex	43°30′–72°30′
German	Chenango	42°27′–75°55′
Giant Mtn.	Essex	44°13′–73°40′
Gilbertsville	Otsego	42°27′–75°20′
Gilboa	Schoharie	42°23′–74°28′
Gilgo Beach	Suffolk	40°36′–73°22′
Gilgo Island	Suffolk	40°37′–73°22′
Glen, The	Warren	42°50′–74°20′
Gloversville	Fulton	43°03′–74°21′
Goat Island	Erie	43°06′–79°04′
Goodnow Flow	Essex	43°55′–74°13′
Goose Bay	Jefferson	44°22′–75°50′
Gouverneur	St. Lawrence	44°21′–75°29′
Grafton	Rensselaer	42°47′–73°26′
Grahamsville	Sullivan	41°52′–74°34′
Grampus Lake	Hamilton	44°01′–74°29′
Grand Island	Niagara	43°06′–79°04′
Grant	Herkimer	43°20′–75°08′
Granville	Washington	43°24′–73°16′
Grass Lake	St. Lawrence	44°20′–75°42′
Grassy Sprain	Westchester	40°56′–73°54′
Great Bend	Jefferson	44°04′–73°42′
Great Gull Island	Suffolk	41°13′–72°05′
Great Kills	Richmond	40°35′–74°15′
Great Neck	Nassau	40°49′–73°73′
Greece	Monroe	43°15′–77°43′
Greenboro	Oswego	43°40′–75°50′
Greenport	Suffolk	41°10′–72°15′
Griffin Brook	Hamilton	43°43′–74°24′
Grindstone Island	Jefferson	44°15′–76°10′

Locality	County	Coordinates
Gull Island	Jefferson	43°55′–76°10′
Guyanoga	Yates	42°40′–77°11′
Hamburg	Erie	42°44′–78°50′
Hamlin	Monroe	43°17′–77°56′
Hammondsport	Steuben	42°24′–77°15′
Hamptonburgh	Orange	41°30′–74°15′
Hancock	Delaware	41°58′–75°17′
Happy Valley Refuge	Oswego	43°27′–76°00′
Harriman State Park	Rockland-Orange	41°15′–74°10′
Hartsdale	Westchester	41°01′–73°37′
Haverstraw	Rockland	41°12′–73°58′
Heart Lake	Essex	44°10′–73°58′
Heckscher State Park	Suffolk	40°45′–73°13′
Hemlock	Livingston	42°48′–77°40′
Hemlock Lake	Livingston	42°45′–77°40′
Hempstead	Nassau	40°42′–73°37′
Henderson	Jefferson	43°48′–76°10′
Henderson Bay, Harbor, & Pond	Jefferson	43°50′–76°10′
Herkimer	Herkimer	43°02′–74°59′
Hewlett	Nassau	40°51′–73°46′
Highland Falls	Orange	41°22′–73°58′
Highland Park	Onondaga	42°48′–75°55′
Highmarket	Lewis	43°34′–75°28′
High Peak	Greene	42°23′–74°10′
Hilton	Monroe	43°16′–77°46′
Hinckley Reservoir	Herkimer	43°20′–75°08′
Hither Hills	Suffolk	41°02′–72°01′
Holland Patent	Oneida	43°15′–75°15′
Holt Brook Valley	Cattaraugus	42°05′–78°45′
Honeoye Lake	Ontario	42°45′–77°31′
Honeyville	Jefferson	41°15′–76°00′
Honnedaga Lake	Herkimer	43°32′–74°50′
Hook Mtn.	Rockland	41°10′–73°55′
Horseheads	Chemung	42°11′–76°51′
Horseshoe Pond	St. Lawrence	44°12′–74°40′
Horton	Delaware	41°58′–75°00′
Howland's Island	Cayuga	43°03′–76°38′
Humphrey	Cattaraugus	42°15′–78°32′
Hunter	Greene	42°13′–74°15′
Hunter Mtn.	Greene	42°11′–74°15′
Huntington	Suffolk	40°53′–73°25′
Hunt's Point	Bronx	40°49′–73°52′
Hurricane Mtn.	Essex	44°14′–73°40′
Hyde Park	Dutchess	41°47′–73°56′
Idlewild	Queens	40°39′–73°47′
Indian Falls	Essex	44°07′–73°56′
Indian Lake	Hamilton	43°30′–74°25′
Indian Pass	Essex	44°13′–74°00′
Inman	Franklin	44°35′–74°06′
Interlaken	Seneca	42°40′–76°45′

Locality	County	Coordinates
Ira	Cayuga	43°13′–76°35′
Irondequoit Bay	Monroe	43°15′–77°40′
Ironsides Island	Jefferson	44°25′–75°50′
Irvington	Westchester	41°03′–73°52′
Island Pond	Orange	41°11′–74°04′
Ithaca	Tompkins	42°26′–76°30′
Jacksonburg	Herkimer	43°00′–74°50′
Jamaica	Queens	40°32′–73°48′
Jamaica Bay Refuge	Queens-Kings	40°45′–73°50′
Jamestown	Chautauqua	42°05′–79°15′
Java Center	Wyoming	42°43′–78°25′
Java Lake Bog	Wyoming	42°40′–78°20′
Jay	Essex	44°28′–73°40′
Jenkins Pond	Franklin	44°07′–74°28′
Jenning's Swamp	Franklin	44°14′–74°30′
Jenny Lake	Saratoga	43°15′–73°55′
Jo, Mt.	Essex	44°13′–73°58′
Jones Beach	Nassau-Suffolk	40°35′–73°30′
Jones Lake	Hamilton	43°21′–74°38′
Jones Pond	Franklin	44°27′–74°12′
Jordan Lake	St. Lawrence	44°23′–74°35′
Junius	Seneca	43°00′–76°50′
Kanawauke, Lake	Orange	41°15′–74°10′
Karner	Albany	42°43′–73°55′
Kashong Glen	Ontario	42°45′–76°59′
Katonah	Westchester	41°17′–73°40′
Keene	Essex	44°15′–73°49′
Keene Valley	Essex	44°13′–73°49′
Keeseville	Clinton	44°31′–73°30′
Kennedy International Airport	Queens	40°39′–73°47′
Keuka	Steuben	42°30′–77°15′
Keuka Lake	Steuben-Yates	42°30′–77°15′
Keuka Park	Yates	42°30′–77°15′
Kiantone	Chautauqua	42°02′–79°13′
Kildare	Franklin	44°18′–74°30′
Kinderhook Lake	Columbia	42°27′–73°39′
King Ferry	Cayuga	42°40′–76°38′
King's Bay	Clinton	44°57′–73°41′
Kingston	Ulster	41°55′–74°00′
Kirkville	Onondaga	43°06′–75°59′
Krumville	Ulster	41°49′–74°16′
Labrador Pond	Onondaga	42°47′–76°03′
Lacona	Oswego	43°40′–76°05′
Lake George (village)	Warren	43°25′–73°45′
Lake Grove	Suffolk	40°49′–73°07′
Lakeport	Madison	43°10′–75°50′
Lakeside	Onondaga	43°15′–77°18′
Lamoka Lake	Schuyler	42°24′–77°05′
Lanesville	Greene	42°07′–74°18′
Langford	Erie	43°37′–78°50′

Locality	County	Coordinates
Lattingtown	Nassau	40°55′–73°40′
Lawrence	Nassau	40°36′–73°46′
Lawtons	Erie	42°32′–78°58′
Lebanon Reservoir	Madison	42°48′–75°36′
Leete Island	Oneida (Lake)	43°12′–75°55′
Le Roy	Genesee	42°59′–78°01′
Le Roy, Lake	Wyoming	42°47′–77°59′
Letchworth State Park	Wyoming-Livingston	42°33′–78°03′
Lewey Lake	Hamilton	43°39′–74°23′
Lewisboro	Westchester	41°15′–73°31′
Liebhardt	Ulster	41°50′–74°17′
Lima	Livingston	42°55′–77°37′
Limekiln Creek	Herkimer	43°42′–74°50′
Limekiln Lake	Hamilton	43°42′–74°48′
Ling Road Swamp	Monroe	43°16′–77°37′
Little Clear Pond	Franklin	44°21′–74°17′
Little Galloo Island	Jefferson	43°50′–76°22′
Little Moose Lake	Herkimer	43°40′–74°56′
Little Simon Pond	Franklin	44°13′–74°28′
Little Sodus Bay	Cayuga	43°27′–76°44′
Little Stissing Mtn.	Dutchess	42°00′–73°40′
Little Weller Pond	Franklin	44°17′–74°16′
Lloyd's Harbor	Suffolk	41°05′–73°30′
Lloyd's Neck	Suffolk	41°05′–73°30′
Lockport	Niagara	43°11′–78°39′
Locust Grove	Lewis	43°34′–75°20′
Lomontville	Ulster	41°50′–74°13′
Lonely, Lake	Saratoga	43°03′–73°45′
Lonesome Bay	St. Lawrence	44°40′–75°30′
Long Beach	Nassau	40°35′–73°40′
Long Island	Oneida (Lake)	43°13′–76°00′
Long Island City	Queens	40°46′–73°50′
Long Lake	Hamilton	43°57′–74°26′
Long Lake (village)	Hamilton	43°57′–74°26′
Long Mtn.	Orange	41°21′–74°01′
Long Pond	Essex	44°23′–73°27′
Long Pond	Franklin	44°27′–74°29′
Long Pond	Lewis	43°59′–75°11′
Loon Lake	Franklin	44°33′–74°04′
Lorraine	Jefferson	43°46′–75°55′
Lost Ponds	Hamilton	43°41′–74°39′
Lower St. Regis Lake	Franklin	44°25′–74°17′
Lower Saranac Lake	Franklin	44°17′–74°11′
Lowman	Chemung	42°02′–76°44′
Lowville	Lewis	43°47′–75°30′
Lyndonville	Orleans	43°20′–78°23′
Lyons Falls	Lewis	43°36′–75°22′
Madawaska	Franklin	44°31′–74°23′
Mad River	Oswego	43°40′–74°48′
Malloryville	Tompkins	42°34′–76°47′
Manhattan	New York	40°45′–73°58′

Locality	County	Coordinates
Manitou	Monroe	43°20′–77°45′
Manning's Cove	Saratoga	43°04′–73°47′
Manorville	Suffolk	40°53′–72°49′
Marcy, Mt.	Essex	44°07′–73°56′
Marengo Swamp	Wayne	43°05′–76°53′
Mariaville	Schenectady	42°48′–74°10′
Marilla	Erie	42°48′–78°35′
Marion River	Hamilton	43°50′–74°38′
Massapequa	Nassau	40°40′–73°29′
Mastic	Suffolk	40°45′–72°50′
Mattituck	Suffolk	40°59′–73°33′
Matumbla, Mt.	St. Lawrence	44°20′–74°33′
Mayfield	Fulton	43°10′–74°15′
Mayville	Chautauqua	42°15′–79°32′
McColloms	Franklin	44°30′–74°15′
McGraw	Cortland	42°36′–76°04′
McGregor, Mt.	Saratoga	43°16′–73°47′
McIntyre, Mt.	Essex	44°12′–73°59′
McKeever	Herkimer	43°40′–75°10′
McLean Bog	Tompkins	42°35′–76°48′
Meacham Lake	Franklin	44°33′–74°18′
Meadow Island	Nassau	40°35′–73°20′
Mecox Bay	Suffolk	40°55′–72°17′
Medina	Orleans	43°14′–78°23′
Menands	Albany	42°42′–73°45′
Mendon Ponds	Monroe	43°00′–77°30′
Meridian	Cayuga	43°10′–76°32′
Metcalf Lake	Hamilton	43°27′–74°40′
Mianus Gorge	Westchester	41°14′–73°37′
Michigan Mills	Lewis	43°34′–75°38′
Middle Cat Pond	Hamilton	44°02′–74°31′
Middleport	Niagara	43°13′–78°27′
Middle Saranac Lake	Franklin	44°15′–74°14′
Milford	Otsego	42°35′–74°57′
Millbrook	Dutchess	41°47′–73°42′
Millbrook Mtn.	Ulster	41°40′–74°15′
Miller's Place	Suffolk	40°58′–73°00′
Mill Neck	Nassau	40°58′–73°20′
Mineola	Nassau	40°45′–73°38′
Mink Lake	Herkimer	43°28′–75°01′
Mohegan Lake	Hamilton	44°03′–74°29′
Mohonk Lake	Ulster	41°45′–74°09′
Montauk	Suffolk	41°02′–71°57′
Monteola Bog	Lewis	43°36′–75°40′
Montezuma Marshes or Refuge	Cayuga-Seneca-Wayne	43°00′–76°45′
Monticello	Sullivan	41°39′–74°41′
Monty Bay	Clinton	44°44′–73°25′
Moody	Franklin	44°13′–74°22′
Moose Pond	Hamilton	43°56′–74°34′
Morehouseville	Hamilton	43°20′–74°45′

Locality	County	Coordinates
Moriches Bay	Suffolk	40°50′–72°50′
Morrisonville	Clinton	44°40′–73°35′
Mount Kisco	Westchester	41°13′–73°44′
Mount Sinai	Suffolk	40°56′–73°02′
Muskrat Bay	Onondaga	43°13′–76°06′
Napanoch	Ulster	41°44′–74°22′
Napeague	Suffolk	41°00′–72°03′
Napeague Bay	Suffolk	41°03′–72°00′
Naples	Ontario	42°36′–72°25′
Nassau	Rensselaer	42°31′–73°36′
Newark	Wayne	43°03′–77°06′
Newark Valley	Tioga	42°14′–76°12′
Newburgh	Orange	41°30′–74°00′
Newfane	Niagara	43°17′–78°42′
New London	Oneida	43°13′–75°38′
New Paltz	Ulster	41°45′–74°05′
Niagara Falls	Niagara	43°06′–79°04′
Nick's Lake	Herkimer	43°40′–74°59′
Nine Mile Point Creek	Monroe	43°16′–77°26′
Niskayuna	Albany-Schenectady	42°50′–73°45′
North Creek	Warren	43°42′–73°59′
North Cuba Marsh	Allegany	42°15′–78°16′
North Elba	Essex	44°15′–73°58′
North Hamlin	Monroe	43°20′–77°52′
North Hudson	Essex	43°59′–73°42′
North Java	Wyoming	42°41′–78°20′
North Lake	Greene	42°11′–74°02′
North Pond	Oswego	43°40′–76°10′
Northport	Suffolk	40°55′–73°21′
North River	Essex-Warren	43°45′–74°04′
North Sea	Suffolk	40°57′–72°28′
North Syracuse	Onondaga	43°10′–76°09′
Norwich	Chenango	42°33′–75°33′
Noyack	Suffolk	41°00′–72°17′
Nyack	Rockland	41°05′–73°56′
Oak Beach	Suffolk	40°37′–73°18′
Oakdale	Suffolk	40°44′–73°07′
Oakfield	Genesee	43°08′–78°17′
Oak Orchard Swamp	Erie-Niagara-Orleans-Genesee	43°05′–75°25′
Oakwood	Cayuga	42°50′–76°42′
Oakwood Beach	Richmond	40°35′–74°10′
Ochre Pond	Franklin	44°13′–74°20′
Ogdensburg	St. Lawrence	44°42′–75°31′
Old Forge	Herkimer	43°44′–74°59′
Oneida Lake	Oneida-Oswego-Onondaga-Madison	43°10′–76°00′
Onondaga Lake	Onondaga	43°06′–76°14′
Onoville	Cattaraugus	42°02′–78°58′
Oquaga Lake	Broome	42°01′–75°27′
Orchard Park	Erie	42°46′–78°45′

Locality	County	Coordinates
Orient	Suffolk	41°09′–72°18′
Orient Point	Suffolk	41°07′–72°19′
Orwell	Oswego	43°34′–76°01′
Osceola	Lewis	43°30′–75°45′
Oseetah Lake	Franklin	44°17′–74°09′
Ossining	Westchester	41°10′–73°52′
Oswego	Oswego	43°27′–76°31′
Otisco Lake	Onondaga	42°52′–76°17′
Otsego Lake	Otsego	42°45′–74°55′
Oyster Bay	Nassau	40°53′–73°31′
Oyster Pond	Suffolk	41°03′–71°53′
Palenville	Greene	42°10′–74°01′
Palmaghatt	Ulster	41°45′–74°08′
Pamelia	Jefferson	44°08′–75°50′
Panther Lake	Oswego	43°19′–75°54′
Parma Center	Monroe	43°15′–77°46′
Paul Smith's	Franklin	44°26′–74°15′
Pavilion	Genesee	42°53′–78°02′
Pawling	Dutchess	41°34′–73°37′
Peach Lake	Putnam-Westchester	41°22′–73°35′
Peakville	Delaware	41°59′–75°08′
Peekamoose Mtn.	Ulster	41°56′–74°25′
Peekskill	Westchester	41°12′–73°56′
Pelham Bay Park	Bronx	40°50′–73°50′
Penn Yan	Yates	42°41′–77°03′
Pepacton Reservoir	Delaware	42°04′–74°53′
Perch Lake	Jefferson	44°11′–75°56′
Perch River Refuge	Jefferson	44°08′–76°00′
Peterboro	Madison	42°58′–75°42′
Pharsalia	Chenango	42°38′–75°46′
Phoenicia	Ulster	42°04′–74°20′
Phoenix	Oswego	43°14′–76°19′
Piano Mtn.	Putnam	41°21′–75°47′
Picton Island	Jefferson	44°15′–76°07′
Piercefield	St. Lawrence	44°15′–74°34′
Piermont	Rockland	41°02′–73°55′
Pillar Point	Jefferson	43°56′–76°10′
Pillsbury Lake	Hamilton	43°35′–74°32′
Pilot Knob	Washington	43°31′–73°40′
Pine Lake	Hamilton	43°25′–74°40′
Pine Plains	Dutchess	41°58′–73°38′
Piseco	Hamilton	43°24′–74°33′
Piseco Lake	Hamilton	43°24′–74°31′
Pitchoff Mtn.	Essex	44°14′–73°52′
Pittsford	Monroe	43°06′–77°33′
Plainville	Onondaga	43°10′–76°28′
Plateau Mtn.	Greene	42°07′–74°13′
Plattsburgh	Clinton	44°42′–73°29′
Pleasant Lake	Jefferson	43°56′–75°40′
Pleasant Valley	Dutchess	41°45′–73°49′
Pleasantville	Westchester	41°10′–73°47′

Locality	County	Coordinates
Plessis	Jefferson	44°15′–75°50′
Plum Island	Suffolk	41°11′–72°10′
Point O'Woods	Suffolk	40°36′–73°13′
Point Peninsula	Jefferson	44°00′–76°15′
Poke-O'-Moonshine Mtn.	Essex	44°30′–73°31′
Portageville	Wyoming	42°33′–78°03′
Port Bay	Wayne	43°20′–76°50′
Port Byron	Cayuga	43°03′–76°38′
Port Douglas	Essex	44°27′–73°26′
Port Henry	Essex	44°03′–73°28′
Port Jefferson	Suffolk	40°57′–73°04′
Port Jervis	Orange	41°22′–74°40′
Port Kent	Essex	44°30′–73°25′
Potsdam	St. Lawrence	44°40′–75°01′
Potter Swamp	Yates	42°45′–77°00′
Poughkeepsie	Dutchess	41°43′–73°56′
Poundridge Reservation	Westchester	41°13′–73°34′
Prairie Slough	Wyoming	42°45′–78°03′
Preble	Cortland	42°43′–76°13′
Pulaski	Oswego	43°34′–76°06′
Putnam Station	Washington	43°45′–73°20′
Quebec Brook at St. Regis River	Franklin	44°31′–74°26′
Quogue	Suffolk	40°48′–72°37′
Ragged Lake	Franklin	44°42′–74°04′
Rainbow Lake	Franklin	44°29′–74°10′
Raquette Lake	Hamilton	43°49′–74°41′
Raquette Lake (village)	Hamilton	43°53′–74°35′
Rat Pond	Franklin	44°21′–74°18′
Ravena	Albany	42°28′–73°48′
Raven Lake	Herkimer	43°55′–75°02′
Ray Brook	Essex	44°18′–74°06′
Redfield	Oswego	43°32′–74°48′
Red House	Cattaraugus	42°10′–78°47′
Redwood	Jefferson	44°17′–75°47′
Reed Pond	Suffolk	41°04′–71°54′
Reed Road Swamp	Monroe	43°08′–77°44′
Rensselaer	Rensselaer	42°37′–73°44′
Rensselaerville	Albany	42°32′–74°09′
Retsof	Livingston	42°48′–77°55′
Rhinebeck	Dutchess	41°57′–73°54′
Rice Lake	Franklin	44°30′–74°18′
Rich Lake	Essex	43°59′–74°13′
Ridgebury	Orange	40°22′–74°28′
Riga, Mt.	Dutchess	42°00′–73°30′
Rigney's Bluff	Monroe	43°16′–77°37′
Riverdale	Bronx (formerly Westchester)	40°55′–73°55′
Riverhead	Suffolk	40°55′–72°40′
Riverside Marsh	Chautauqua	42°02′–79°11′
Riverview	Jefferson	44°10′–76°15′

Locality	County	Coordinates
Robins Island	Suffolk	41°01′–72°30′
Rochester	Monroe	43°12′–77°37′
Rockaway Point	Queens	40°35′–73°50′
Rockland Lake	Rockland	41°09′–73°55′
Rogers Rock	Warren-Washington	43°53′–73°26′
Rome	Oneida	43°13′–75°28′
Rome Sand Plains	Oneida	43°13′–75°38′
Romulus	Seneca	42°45′–76°50′
Ronkonkoma, Lake	Suffolk	40°48′–73°07′
Round Lake	Saratoga	42°55′–73°50′
Round Mtn.	Essex	44°05′–73°40′
Round Pond	Monroe	43°16′–77°38′
Rusk Mtn.	Greene	42°11′–74°20′
Sabattis	Hamilton	44°07′–74°44′
Sage Creek Marshes	Oswego	43°32′–76°15′
Sag Harbor	Suffolk	40°59′–72°18′
St. Hubert's	Essex	44°12′–73°45′
Salamanca	Cattaraugus	42°11′–73°43′
Salmon Creek	Monroe	43°20′–77°45′
Salmon River Reservoir	Oswego	43°32′–78°50′
Sand Lake	Herkimer	43°44′–75°00′
Sand Pond	Essex	43°56′–73°53′
Sands Point	Nassau	40°51′–73°44′
Sandy Creek	Monroe	43°20′–77°52′
Sandy Creek	Oswego	43°40′–76°05′
Sandy Pond	Oswego	43°36′–76°10′
Santa Clara	Franklin	44°37′–74°30′
Saranac Lake (village)	Franklin	44°19′–74°06′
Saratoga Lake	Saratoga	43°04′–73°47′
Saratoga Springs	Saratoga	43°07′–73°48′
Savannah	Wayne	43°06′–76°45′
Sayville	Suffolk	40°44′–73°05′
Schaghticoke	Rensselaer	42°51′–73°34′
Schaghticoke Mtn.	Dutchess	41°42′–73°32′
Schenectady	Schenectady	42°48′–73°57′
Schodack Landing	Rensselaer	42°28′–73°46′
Schroon Lake (village)	Essex	43°50′–73°45′
Scotia	Schenectady	42°50′–73°51′
Scott	Cortland	42°45′–76°15′
Scott's Swamp	Oswego	43°14′–76°19′
Scottsville	Monroe	43°02′–77°45′
Seaford	Nassau	40°40′–73°29′
Second Lake	Herkimer	43°45′–74°55′
Secor, Lake	Putnam	41°22′–73°47′
Selden	Suffolk	40°52′–73°03′
Selkirk Shores State Park	Oswego	43°35′–76°14′
Seneca Glen	Ontario	42°47′–77°20′
Seneca River Marshes	Seneca-Wayne	43°06′–76°45′
Setauket	Suffolk	40°57′–73°07′
Seventh Lake	Hamilton	43°44′–74°45′
Shelter Island	Suffolk	41°05′–72°17′

Locality	County	Coordinates
Shinnecock Bay, Hills, & Inlet	Suffolk	40°58′–72°32′
Shore Acres	Monroe	43°16′–77°46′
Short Beach	Nassau	40°35′–73°40′
Short Tract	Allegany	42°28′–78°01′
Silver Bay	Warren	43°42′–73°30′
Silver Lake	Clinton	44°31′–73°51′
Silver Lake	Wyoming	42°42′–78°01′
Silver Lake Park	Westchester	41°02′–73°45′
Simon Pond	Franklin	44°09′–74°26′
Sixth Lake	Hamilton	43°44′–74°46′
Skaneateles	Onondaga	42°57′–76°27′
Skaneateles Lake	Onondaga-Cayuga	42°56′–76°25′
Slide Mtn.	Ulster	42°00′–74°25′
Slush Pond	Franklin	44°28′–74°19′
Smartville	Oswego	43°40′–75°58′
Smithtown	Suffolk	40°52′–73°13′
Snowshoe Bay	Jefferson	43°49′–76°12′
Snowy Mtn.	Hamilton	43°42′–74°22′
Sodus Bay	Wayne	43°16′–76°59′
Soft Maple Dam	Lewis	43°57′–75°13′
South Bay	Madison	43°12′–75°15′
Southhold	Suffolk	41°08′–72°28′
South Pond	Hamilton	43°55′–74°28′
Southwest Oswego	Oswego	43°25′–76°35′
Spencer Lake	Tioga	42°14′–76°29′
Spencer Marsh	Tioga	42°12′–76°30′
Spencerport	Monroe	43°15′–77°47′
Split Rock Mtn.	Essex	44°07′–73°40′
Springville	Erie	42°31′–78°41′
Sterling Forest	Orange	41°10′–74°16′
Steuben	Oneida	43°18′–75°17′
Stillson's Pond	Cattaraugus	42°10′–78°56′
Stillwater Mtn.	Herkimer	43°50′–75°02′
Stillwater Reservoir	Herkimer	43°53′–75°03′
Stissing	Dutchess	41°54′–73°41′
Stissing Mtn.	Dutchess	41°54′–73°41′
Stone Ridge	Ulster	41°52′–74°09′
Stony Brook	Suffolk	40°56′–73°08′
Stony Island	Jefferson	43°55′–76°23′
Stony Point	Jefferson	43°49′–76°12′
Storm King Mtn.	Orange	41°25′–74°00′
Strawberry Island	Erie	43°06′–79°04′
Suffern	Rockland	41°07′–74°19′
Summer Hill	Cayuga	46°40′–76°19′
Sunken Forest	Suffolk	40°39′–73°08′
Sunmount	Franklin	44°13′–74°28′
Surebridge Swamp	Orange	41°17′–74°18′
Swinburne Island	Richmond	40°34′–74°03′
Sylvan Beach	Oneida	43°14′–75°45′
Syracuse	Onondaga	43°03′–76°10′

Locality	County	Coordinates
Tallman Mtn.	Rockland	41°00′–73°56′
Tannersville	Greene	42°12′–74°09′
Taughannock Falls	Tompkins	42°28′–76°31′
Taylor	Cortland	42°33′–75°54′
Taylor Pond	Clinton	44°29′–73°52′
Terror, Lake	Hamilton	43°54′–74°50′
Thacher State Park	Albany	42°10′–74°00′
Theresa	Jefferson	44°14′–75°49′
Third Lake Creek	Herkimer	43°45′–74°50′
Three Rivers Refuge	Onondaga	43°13′–76°17′
Tiana Beach	Suffolk	40°50′–72°40′
Ticonderoga	Essex	43°51′–73°26′
Tiorati, Lake	Orange	41°17′–74°18′
Tivoli	Dutchess	42°04′–73°55′
Tobay Beach & Pond	Nassau	40°37′–73°20′
Tomhannock	Rensselaer	42°50′–73°31′
Tom, Mt.	Franklin	44°20′–74°10′
Tonawanda	Erie	43°01′–78°54′
Tonawanda Swamp (=Oak Orchard Swamp)		43°05′–75°25′
Tongue Mtn.	Warren	43°40′–73°40′
Trenton Falls	Oneida	43°16′–75°10′
Troutburg	Monroe	43°18′–78°00′
Troy	Rensselaer	42°43′–73°43′
Tryon Park	Monroe	43°12′–77°37′
Tuckahoe	Westchester	40°57′–73°49′
Tully	Onondaga	42°47′–76°06′
Tupper Lake	Hamilton-Franklin	44°14′–74°29′
Tupper Lake (marshes)	Franklin	44°15′–74°28′
Tupper Lake (village)	Franklin	44°15′–74°28′
Twin Lakes	Hamilton	43°37′–74°38′
Twin Ponds	Franklin	44°42′–74°20′
Twitchell Lake	Herkimer	43°50′–74°50′
Tyrell Lake	Dutchess	41°45′–73°45′
Union Springs	Cayuga	42°51′–76°42′
Upper Ausable Lake	Essex	44°05′–73°51′
Upper Cascade Lake	Essex	44°13′–73°52′
Upper Chateaugay Lake	Clinton	44°44′–73°58′
Utica	Oneida	43°06′–75°15′
Valcour Island	Clinton	44°37′–73°25′
Valley Stream	Nassau	40°40′–73°42′
Van Cortlandt Park	Bronx	40°55′–73°54′
Vandalia	Cattaraugus	42°05′–78°32′
Varna	Tompkins	42°27′–76°27′
Versailles	Cattaraugus	42°31′–79°00′
Vestal	Broome	42°05′–76°03′
Victor	Ontario	42°59′–77°26′
Victory	Cayuga	43°13′–76°40′
Vischer's Ferry	Saratoga	42°50′–73°50′
Waccabuc, Lake	Westchester	41°17′–73°34′
Wading River	Suffolk	40°57′–72°50′

Locality	County	Coordinates
Wales Center	Erie	42°45′–78°30′
Wallkill	Ulster	41°36′–74°11′
Walton	Delaware	42°10′–75°10′
Wampsville	Madison	43°06′–75°45′
Wanakena	St. Lawrence	44°12′–74°55′
Wantry Island	Oneida (Lake)	43°13′–76°00′
Warrensburg	Warren	43°28′–73°47′
Warwick	Orange	41°15′–74°21′
Wassaic	Dutchess	41°48′–73°32′
Waterloo	Seneca	42°55′–76°53′
Watertown	Jefferson	43°57′–75°56′
Watkins Glen	Schuyler	42°23′–76°53′
Waverly	Franklin	44°44′–74°24′
Webster	Monroe	43°13′–77°27′
Wellesley Island	Jefferson	44°20′–76°00′
Wellsville	Allegany	42°07′–77°56′
West Barre	Orleans	43°10′–78°10′
Westbury	Nassau	40°46′–73°34′
West Canada Lakes	Hamilton	43°36′–74°38′
West Clarksville	Allegany	42°07′–78°16′
West Falls	Erie	42°42′–78°41′
Westfield	Chautauqua	42°20′–79°34′
Westhampton Beach	Suffolk	40°39′–72°39′
Westmoreland Sanctuary	Westchester	41°15′–73°38′
West Mtn.	Rockland	41°18′–74°00′
West New Brighton	Richmond	40°39′–74°18′
West Park	Ulster	41°48′–73°56′
West Point	Orange	41°23′–73°58′
Westport	Essex	44°13′–73°39′
West Rush	Monroe	43°00′–77°43′
West Seneca	Erie	42°52′–78°55′
West Shokan	Ulster	41°58′–74°18′
Wethersfield Springs	Wyoming	42°43′–78°11′
Weyant's Pond	Orange	41°19′–74°01′
Whaley Lake	Dutchess	41°34′–73°39′
Whetstone Gulf	Lewis	43°44′–75°30′
Whiteface Mtn.	Essex	44°23′–73°54′
Whitehall	Washington	43°32′–73°26′
Whitehouse	Hamilton	43°20′–74°24′
White Plains	Westchester	41°02′–73°46′
Wicopesset Island	Suffolk	41°07′–72°00′
Willsboro	Essex	44°23′–73°25′
Willsboro Bay	Essex	44°22′–73°26′
Wilmington	Essex	44°22′–73°50′
Wilmington Mtn.	Essex	44°25′–73°52′
Wilmington Notch	Essex	44°24′–73°51′
Wilmurt	Herkimer	43°20′–74°53′
Wilson	Niagara	43°18′–78°50′
Wilson Hill Refuge	St. Lawrence	44°54′–75°00′
Windom	Erie	42°46′–78°50′
Wingdale	Dutchess	41°39′–73°34′

Locality	County	Coordinates
Witherbee	Essex	44°05′–73°32′
Wittenberg Mtn.	Ulster	42°00′–74°25′
Wolf Pond	Essex	44°02′–74°14′
Wolf Pond	Essex	43°56′–73°58′
Woodmere	Nassau	40°38′–73°42′
Woods Lake	Herkimer	43°51′–74°57′
Yaphank	Suffolk	40°50′–72°54′
Yates	Orleans	43°16′–78°23′
Yellow Lake	St. Lawrence	44°18′–75°37′
Yonkers	Westchester	40°56′–73°54′
York	Livingston	42°52′–77°55′
York's Corners	Allegany	42°03′–77°55′
Youngstown	Niagara	43°15′–79°03′
Zoar Valley	Cattaraugus	42°29′–78°39′

BIBLIOGRAPHY

Adams, C. C.
1923. "Notes on the relation of birds to Adirondack forest vegetation." *Roosevelt Wildlife Bull.*, 22: 487–519

Aldrich, J. W.
1951. "A review of the races of the Traill's Flycatcher." *Wilson Bull.*, 63: 192–197.

Aldrich, J. W. and Friedmann, H.
1943. "A revision of the Ruffed Grouse." *Condor,* 45: 85–103.

Allen, A. A.
1914. "The Red-winged Blackbird: a study in the ecology of a cattail marsh." *Abstr. Proc. Linn. Soc. N.Y.*, 24–25: 43–128.
1934: "A new bird for North America." *Univ. State N.Y. Bull. Schools,* 20: 134–135.

Allen, C. S.
1892. "Breeding habits of the Fish Hawk on Plum Island, New York." *Auk,* 9: 313–321.

Amadon, D.
1970. Taxonomic categories below the level of genus: theoretical and practical aspects." *Journ. Bombay Nat. Hist. Soc.*, 67: 1–13.

Andrle, R. F.
1971a. "The birds of McCarty Hill, Cattaraugus County, N.Y." *Prothonotary,* 37: 90–93.
1971b. "Range extension of the Golden-crowned Kinglet in New York." *Wilson Bull.*, 83: 313–316.

Arbib, R. S.
1963. "The Common Loon in New York State." *Kingbird,* 13: 1–8.

Arbib, R. S., Pettingill, O. S., and Spofford, S. H.
1966. *Enjoying birds around New York City.* Boston: Houghton Mifflin.

Axtell, H. H.
1945. "The Cliff Swallow in Cortland County." *Univ. State N.Y. Bull. Schools,* 31: 232–236.
1947. "Distribution of the vertebrate animals of Chemung and Schuyler counties, New York." Cornell Univ. Ph.D. thesis, unpubl., 350 pp. (170–307, birds only).

Bagg, A. M.
1967. "Factors affecting the occurrence of the Eurasian Lapwing in eastern North America." *Living Bird,* 6: 87–122.

Bagg, E.
1911. "Annotated list of the birds of Oneida County, N.Y., and of the West Canada Creek Valley." *Trans. Oneida Hist. Soc.,* 12: 17–86.

Bailey, S. F.
1967. "Fall hawk watch at Mt. Peter, New York." *Kingbird,* 17: 129–142.

Banko, W. E.
1960. "The Trumpeter Swan—its history, habits, and population in the United States." *North Amer. Fauna,* U. S. Fish and Wildlife Serv., 63.

Banks, R. C.
1970. "Birds imported into the United States in 1968." *Spec. Sci. Rep., Wildlife,* U. S. Fish and Wildlife Serv., 36: 64 pp.

Barth, E. K.
1968. "The circumpolar systematics of *Larus argentatus* and *Larus fuscus* with special reference to the Norwegian populations." *Nytt. Mag. Zool.,* 15, Suppl., 1: 1–50.

Beals, M. V. and Nichols, J. T.
1940. "Data from a bird-banding station at Elmhurst, Long Island." *Birds of Long Island,* 3: 57–76.

Beardslee, C. S. and Mitchell, H. D.
1965. "Birds of the Niagara Frontier Region." *Bull. Buffalo Soc. Nat. Sci.,* 22: 478 pp.

Belknap, J. B.
1950. "Bird colonies in eastern Lake Ontario." *Kingbird,* 1: 3–6.
1951. "Incursion of Brunnich's Murres in northern New York." *Kingbird,* 1: 13–14.
1952. "The Hungarian Partridge in New York State." *Kingbird,* 2: 80–82.
1955. "The expanding range of the Ring-billed Gull." *Kingbird,* 5: 63–64.
1968. "Little Galloo Island—a twenty year summary." *Kingbird,* 18: 10–81.

Benning, W. E.
1965–1968. "Survey of heronries in upstate New York 1964–1968, plus various titles." *Kingbird,* 15–19: various pages.
1967. "Nesting of the Turkey Vulture in Wayne County, New York." *Kingbird,* 17: 20–21.

Bent, A. C.
1938. "Life histories of North American birds of prey (part 2)." *Smiths. Inst. Bull.,* 170.
1968. "Life histories of North American finches, etc. (part 1)." *Smiths. Inst. Bull.,* 237.

Benton, A. H.
1949. "The breeding birds of Cayuga County, New York." Cornell Univ. M.S. thesis, unpubl., 100 pp.
1950. "Notes on the breeding birds of Cayuga County, New York." *Kingbird,* 1: 8–10.
1951. "Bird population changes in a central New York county since 1870." *Kingbird,* 1: 2–11.
1960. "Southern warblers in central New York: historical review." *Kingbird,* 10: 137–141.

Benton, A. H. and Tucker, H.
1968. "Weather and Purple Martin mortality in western New York." *Kingbird,* 18: 71–75.

Berger, A. J.
1958. "The Golden-winged-Blue-winged Warbler complex in Michigan and the Great Lakes area." *Jack-Pine Warbler,* 36: 37–73.

Bicknell, E. P.
1882. "A review of the summer birds of a part of the Catskill Mountains, with prefatory remarks on the faunal and floral features of the region." *Trans. Linn. Soc. N.Y.,* 1: 115–168.

Blake, C. H.
1969. "Notes on the Indigo Bunting." *Bird-Banding,* 40: 133–139.

Bock, W.
1956. "A generic review of the family Ardeidae (Aves)." *Amer. Mus. Novit.,* 1779: 49 pp.
1958. "A generic review of the plovers (Charadriinae, Aves)." *Bull. Mus. Comp. Zool.,* 118: 27–97.

Bock, W. and Short, L. L.
In press. "A generic review of the woodpeckers (Aves: Picidae)." *Bull. Amer. Mus. Nat. Hist.*

Bond, J.
1961. *Birds of the West Indies.* Boston: Houghton Mifflin.

Bourne, W. R. P.
1971a. "Some recent revisions of the classification of seabirds." *Sea Swallow,* 21: 42–44.
1971b. "Threats to seabirds." *I.C.B.P. Bull.,* 11: 200–218.

Braislin, W. C.
1907. "A list of the birds of Long Island, New York." *Abstr. Proc. Linn. Soc. N.Y.,* 17–19: 31–123.

Britton, N. L. and Brown, A.
1936. *An illustrated flora of the northern United States and Canada.* New York: New York Botanical Garden, 2nd ed., 3 vols.

Brown, C. P.
1954. "Distribution of the Hungarian Partridge in New York." *New York Fish and Game Journ.,* 1: 119–129.

Brown, L. and Amadon, D.
1968. *Eagles, hawks, and falcons of the world.* London: Country Life, 2 vols.

Bull, J.
1963. "On leg color in immature jaegers." *Linnaean News-Letter,* 17: April.
1964. *Birds of the New York Area.* New York: Harper and Row.
1970. "Supplement to birds of the New York Area." *Proc. Linn. Soc. N.Y.,* 71: 1–54.

1971. "Monk Parakeets in the New York City region." *Linnaean News-Letter,* 25: 1–2.

Burger, J.
1963. "Comparative behavior of the Killdeer and the Spotted Sandpiper." *Kingbird,* 13: 14–17.

Burger, J. and Brownstein, R.
1968a. "The status of Bonaparte's Gull in New York State." *Kingbird,* 18: 9–20.
1968b. "The Little Gull in western New York." *Kingbird,* 18: 187–194.

Callin, E. M.
1968. "Vocalization of the Virginia Rail: A mystery solved." *Blue Jay,* 26: 75–77.

Cant, G. B. and Geis, H. P.
1961. "The House Finch: A new east coast migrant?" *Ebba News,* 24: 102–107.

Carleton, G.
1970. "Supplement to the birds of Central and Prospect parks." *Proc. Linn. Soc. N.Y.,* 71: 132–154.

Chapman, F. M.
1908. "The Fish Hawks of Gardiner's Island." *Bird Lore,* 10: 153–159.

Cooch, F. G.
1963. "Recent changes in distribution of color phases of *Chen c. caerulescens.*" *Proc. 13th Int. Ornith. Congr.,* 1182–1194.

Cruickshank, A. D.
1942. *Birds around New York City.* New York: Amer. Mus. Nat. Hist.

Curry-Lindahl, K.
1971. "Systematic relationships in herons (Ardeidae), based on comparative studies of behavior and ecology; a preliminary account." *Ostrich,* suppl., 9: 53–70.

DeKay, J. E.
1844. *Zoology of New York.* Part 2, Birds. New York: D. Appleton, and Wiley and Putnam.

Delacour, J.
1951. "The significance of the number of toes in some woodpeckers and kingfishers." *Auk,* 68: 49–51.
1954. *The waterfowl of the world.* Vol. 1. London: Country Life.
1956. *Ibid.* Vol. 2.
1959. *Ibid.* Vol. 3.

Delacour, J. and Mayr, E.
1945. "The family Anatidae." *Wilson Bull.,* 57: 3–55.

Dickerman, R. W. and Parkes, K. C.
1968. "Notes on the plumages and generic status of the Little Blue Heron." *Auk,* 85: 435–440.

Dilger, W. C.
1956a. "Hostile behavior and reproductive isolating mechanisms in the avian genera *Catharus* and *Hylocichla.*" *Auk,* 73: 313–353.
1956b. "Adaptive modifications and ecological isolating mechanisms in the thrush genera *Catharus* and *Hylocichla.*" *Wilson Bull.,* 68: 171–199.
1956c. "Relationships of the avian genera *Catharus* and *Hylocichla.*" *Syst. Zool.,* 5: 174–182.

Doig, H. E.
1966. "Ecological implications relating to a local population of Hungarian Partridge in northern New York." Unpubl. *Proc. Northeast Sec. Wildlife Soc.,* Boston.

Donker, J. K.
1959. "Migration and distribution of the Widgeon, *Anas penelope* L. in Europe, based on ringing results." *Ardea.* 47: 1–27.

Douglas, E. M.
1931. "Gazetteer of the lakes, ponds, and reservoirs of the State of New York." U. S. Geol. Surv., mimeogr., 57 pp.

Dutcher, W.
1887–1894. Long Island notes, vol. 1—water birds; vol. 2—land birds (handwritten account). In library of the American Museum of Natural History.

Eaton, E. H.
1910. *Birds of New York.* Part 1. New York: Univ. State of New York.
1914. *Ibid.* Part 2.

Eaton, S. W.
1953. "Birds of the Olean and Salamanca quadrangles." *Science Studies,* 15: 1–27 (St. Bonaventure Univ.).
1957. "A life history study of *Seiurus noveboracensis.*" *Science Studies,* 19: 7–36 (St. Bonaventure Univ.).
1958. "A life history study of the Louisiana Waterthrush." *Wilson Bull.,* 70: 211–236.
1959. "The Tufted Titmouse invades New York." *Kingbird,* 9: 59–62.

1964. "The Wild Turkey in New York State." *Kingbird*, 14: 4–12.

1965. "Juncos of the high plateaus." *Kingbird*, 15: 141–146.

Eisenmann, E.

1960. "Palearctic waders in eastern North America." *British Birds*, 53: 136–140.

Elliott, J. J.

1951. "The Prairie Warbler on Long Island." *Proc. Linn. Soc. N.Y.*, 58–62: 72–73.

1953. "The nesting sparrows of Long Island. 1. sparrows of the marshes." *Long Island Naturalist*, 2: 15–24.

1955. "The Ipswich Sparrow on the northeastern seaboard." Part 1. *Kingbird*, 4: 91–96.

1961. "Recent history of the Barrow's Goldeneye in New York." *Kingbird*, 11: 131–136.

Elliott, J. J. and Arbib, R. S.

1953. "Origin and status of the House Finch in the eastern United States." *Auk*, 70: 31–37.

Emlen, J. T.

1938. "Midwinter distribution of the American Crow in New York State." *Ecology*, 19: 264–275.

Fischer, R. B.

1958. "The breeding biology of the Chimney Swift." *New York State Mus. and Sci. Serv. Bull.*, 368: 141 pp.

Foley, D. D.

1960. "Recent changes in waterfowl populations in New York." *Kingbird*, 10: 82–89.

Forbush, E. H.

1925. *Birds of Massachusetts and other New England states*. Vol. 1. Mass. Dept. Agric., Boston.

1927. *Ibid.* Vol. 2.

1929. *Ibid.* Vol. 3.

Friedmann, H.

1929. *The cowbirds*. C. C. Thomas, Springfield, Ill., Baltimore.

1963. "Host relations of the parasitic cowbirds." *U. S. Natl. Mus. Bull.*, 233.

Gill, D. E. and Lanyon, W. E.

1965. "Establishment, growth, and behavior of an extralimital population of House Finches at Huntington, New York." *Bird-Banding*, 36: 1–14.

Giraud, J. P.

1844. *Birds of Long Island*. Wiley and Putnam, New York.

Godfrey, W. E.

1966. *The birds of Canada*. Nat'l. Mus. Canada Bull., 203.

Goodwin, D.

1967. *Pigeons and doves of the world*. London: British Mus. (Nat. Hist.), Publ., 663.

1968. "Notes on woodpeckers (Picidae)." *Bull. British Mus. (Nat. Hist.), Zool.*, 17: 1–44.

Gordon, M. S.

1955. "Summer ecology of oceanic birds off southern New England." *Auk*, 72: 138–147.

Greenway, J. C.

1958. *Extinct and vanishing birds of the world*. New York: Amer. Comm. Internatl. Wildlife Protection.

Greeson, P. E. and Robison, F. L.

1970. *Gazetteer of lakes, ponds, and reservoirs*. New York: U. S. Dept. Interior & N. Y. State Conserv. Dept., Bull., 68: 124 pp.

Griscom, L.

1923. *Birds of the New York City region*. New York: Amer. Mus. Nat. Hist.

1933. "The birds of Dutchess County, New York." *Trans. Linn. Soc. N.Y.*, 3: 184 pp.

1937. "A monographic study of the Red Crossbill." *Proc. Boston Soc. Nat. Hist.*, 41: 77–209.

Griscom, L. and Snyder, D.

1955. *Birds of Massachusetts*. Salem, Mass: Peabody Mus.

Haartman, L. von

1958. "The decrease of the Corncrake (*Crex crex*)." *Soc. Scient. Fennica Comment. Biol.*, 18: 1–29.

Hale, W. G.

1970. "Infraspecific categories in birds." London: *Biol. Journ. Linn. Soc.*, 2: 239–255.

Harper, R. M.

1911. "The Hempstead Plains: a natural prairie on Long Island." *Bull. Amer. Geogr. Soc.*, 43: 351–360.

Haugh, J. R.

1966. "Some observations on the hawk migration at Derby Hill (N.Y.)." *Kingbird*, 16: 5–16.

Hellmayr, C. E.

1934. *Catalogue of birds of the Americas and the adjacent Islands*. Field Mus. Nat. Hist. Zool. Series, 7.

Hellmayr, C. E. and Conover, B.
1942. *Ibid.*, No. 1.
1948. *Ibid.*, Vol. 13 (1), (2).

Herbert, R. A. and K. S.
1965. "Behavior of Peregrine Falcons in the New York City region." *Auk,* 82: 62–94.
1969. "The extirpation of the Hudson River Peregrine Falcon population." In *Peregrine Falcon populations,* ed. by J. J. Hickey, Madison: Univ. Wisconsin Press, pp. 133–154.

Hewitt, O. H. (ed. by)
1967. "The Wild Turkey and its management." *Wildlife Soc.,* Washington, D.C.

Hough, F. N.
1964. "The thrushes (Turdidae): their occurence in Ulster County, N.Y." *Burroughs Nat. Hist. Soc. Bull.,* 7: 19 pp.

Howes, P. G.
1926. "A Turkey Vulture's nest in the State of New York." *Bird Lore,* 28: 175–180.

Hubbard, J. P.
1970. "Geographic variation in the *Dendroica coronata* complex." *Wilson Bull.,* 82: 355–369.

Hubbard, J. P. and Banks, R. C.
1970. "The types and taxa of Harold Bailey." *Proc. Biol. Soc. Wash.,* 83: 321–323.

Hyde, A. S.
1939a. "The ecology and economics of the birds along the northern boundary of New York State." *Roosevelt Wildlife Bull.,* 7: 61–215.
1939b. "The life history of Henslow's Sparrow, *Passerherbulus henslowii* (Audubon)." *Misc. Publ. Mus. Zool.,* Univ. Michigan Press, 41: 72 pp.

Jehl, J. R.
1968. *Relationships in the Charadrii (shorebirds): a taxonomic study based on color patterns of the downy young.* San Diego Soc. Nat. Hist., Mem. 3: 1–54.

Jensen, A. C. and Livingstone, R.
1969. "Offshore records of land birds." *Kingbird,* 19: 5–10.

Johnsgard, P. A.
1965. *Handbook of waterfowl behavior.* Ithaca: Cornell Univ. Press.

Johnson, C. E.
1937. "Preliminary reconnaissance of the land vertebrates of the Archer and Anna Huntington wildlife forest station." *Roosevelt Wildlife Bull.,* 6: 556–609.

Johnston, D. W.
1971. "Ecological aspects of hybridizing chickadees (*Parus*) in Virginia." *Amer. Midl. Nat.,* 85: 124–134.

Kahl, M. P.
1971. "Social behavior and taxonomic relationships of the storks." *Living Bird,* 10: 151–170.
1972. "A revision of the family Ciconiidae (Aves)." *Journ. Zool. (Proc. Zool. Soc. London),* 167: 451–461.

Keith, A. R.
1968. "A summary of the extralimital records of the Varied Thrush, 1848 to 1966." *Bird-Banding,* 39: 245–276.

Kendeigh, S. C.
1945. "Community selection by birds on the Helderberg Plateau of New York." *Auk,* 62: 418–436.

Kessel, B.
1957. "A study of the breeding biology of the European Starling (*Sturnus vulgaris*) in North America." *Amer. Midl. Nat.,* 58: 257–331.

Klonick, A. S.
1951. "Acquisition of a natural habitat area (Reed Road Swamp, Monroe County)." *Kingbird,* 1: 19–22.

Krieg, D. C.
1971. "The behavioral patterns of the Eastern Bluebird (*Sialia sialis*)." *New York State Mus. Bull.,* 415: 139 pp.

Küchler, A. W.
1964. "Potential natural vegetation of the coterminous United States." *Amer. Geogr. Soc. Spec. Publ. No. 36.*

Lanyon, W. E.
1966. "Hybridization in meadowlarks." *Bull. Amer. Mus. Nat. Hist.,* 134: 3–25.

Lanyon, W. E. and Bull, J.
1967. "Identification of Connecticut, Mourning, and Macgillivray's Warblers." *Bird-Banding,* 38: 187–194.

Lanyon, W. E., Van Gelder, R. G., and Zweifel, R. G.
1970. *The vertebrate fauna of the Kalbfleisch Field Research Station.* New York: Amer. Mus. Nat. Hist.: 78 pp. ("Birds," 25–60).

Mackay, G. H.
1929. *Shooting journal (1865–1922)*. New York: Cosmos Press.

MacNamara, E. E. and Udell, H. F.
1970. "Clapper Rail investigations on the south shore of Long Island." *Proc. Linn. Soc. N.Y.*, 71: 120–131.

Mayr, E. and Short, L. L.
1970. "Species taxa of North American birds." *Publ. Nutt. Ornith. Club*, 9: 127 pp.

McAtee, W. L.
1926. "The relation of birds to woodlots in New York State." *Roosevelt Wildlife Bull.*, 25: 7–148.

McIlroy, D. W.
1961. "Possible hybridization between a Clay-colored Sparrow and a Chipping Sparrow at Ithaca." *Kingbird*, 11: 7–10.

Meanley, B.
1969. "Natural History of the King Rail." *North Amer. Fauna*, 67: 108 pp.

Mearns, E. A.
1878. "A list of the birds of the Hudson Highlands." *Bull. Essex Inst.* (issued in 7 parts up to 1881).

Mendall, H. L.
1958. *The Ring-necked Duck in the northeast*. Orono: Univ. Maine Press.

Meng, H.
1951. "The Cooper's Hawk." Ithaca: Cornell Univ., unpubl. Ph.D. thesis.

Merriam, C. H.
1878–1879. "Remarks on some of the birds of Lewis County, northern New York." *Bull. Nutt. Ornith. Club*, 3: 52–56 and 123–128, 4: 1–7.
1881. "Preliminary list of birds ascertained to occur in the Adirondack region, northeastern New York." *Bull. Nutt. Ornith. Club*, 6: 225–235.

Meyerriecks, A. J.
1960. "Comparative breeding behavior of four species of North American herons." *Publ. Nutt. Ornith. Club*, 2.

Mitchell, H. D. and Andrle, R. F.
1970. "Supplement to 'Birds of the Niagara Frontier Region.'" *Bull. Buffalo Soc. Nat. Sci.* 22, Suppl., 10 pp.

Moynihan, M.
1959. "A revision of the family Laridae (Aves)." *Amer. Mus. Novit.*, 1928: 42 pp.

Muller, E. H.
1965. "Quaternary geology of New York." In Wright, H. E. and D. G. Frey, *The quaternary of the United States*, Princeton: Princeton Univ. Press, 99–112.

Munoff, J. A.
1963. "Food habits, growth, and mortality in nesting Marsh Hawks." *Kingbird*, 13: 67–74.

Murphy, R. C.
1936. *Oceanic birds of South America* (2 vols.). New York: Macmillan for Amer. Mus. Nat. Hist.

Murphy, R. C. and Pennoyer, J. M.
1952. "Larger petrels of the genus *Pterodroma*." *Amer. Mus. Novit.*, 1580: 43 pp.

Murphy, R. C. and Vogt, W.
1933. "The Dovekie influx of 1932." *Auk*, 50: 325–349.

Murray, B. C.
1968. "The relationships of sparrows in the genera *Ammodramus*, *Passerherbulus*, and *Ammospiza* with a description of a hybrid LeConte's x Sharp-tailed Sparrow." *Auk*, 85: 586–593.

Nichols, J. T.
1935. "The Dovekie incursion of 1932." *Auk*, 52: 448–449.

Nisbet, I. C. T.
1959. "Wader migration in North America and its relation to transatlantic crossings." *British Birds*, 52: 205–215.

Norris, C. A.
1947. "Report on the distribution and status of the Corn Crake. Part 2—a consideration of the causes of the decrease." *British Birds*, 40: 226–244.

Owen, O. S.
1950. "The bird community of an elm-maple-ash swamp in central New York." Ithaca: Cornell Univ., unpubl. Ph.D. thesis.

Palmer, R. S. (ed.)
1962. *Handbook of North American birds— loons to flamingos*. Vol. 1. New Haven: Yale Univ. Press.

Parker, J. E. and Maxwell, G. R.
1969. "Selected maintenance behavior in a Great Blue Heron colony on Ironsides Island, New York." *Kingbird*, 19: 192–199.

Parkes, K. C.
1951. "The genetics of the Golden-winged x Blue-winged Warbler complex." *Wilson Bull.,* 63: 5–15.
1952a. "The birds of New York State and their taxonomy. Part 1—non-passerines: 1–302; Part 2—passerines: 303–612." Ithaca: Cornell Univ., unpubl. Ph.D. thesis.
1952b. "Notes on some birds of the Cayuga Lake Basin." *Kingbird,* 2: 56–59.
1953. "The Yellow-throated Warbler in New York." *Kingbird,* 3: 4–6.
1954a. "Traill's Flycatcher in New York." *Wilson Bull.,* 66: 89–92.
1954b. "Notes on some birds of the Adirondack and Catskill mountains, New York." *Ann., Carnegie Mus.,* 33: 149–178.
1955a. "Critically needed bird specimens from New York." *Kingbird,* 4: 96–99.
1955b. "Systematic notes on North American birds: the herons and ibises (Ciconiiformes)." *Ann., Carnegie Mus.,* 33: 287–293.

Peakall, D. B.
1967. "Recent changes in the status of the Great Black-backed Gull." *Kingbird,* 17: 69–73.

Peters, J. L.
1934. *Check-list of birds of the world.* Cambridge, Mass.: Harvard Univ. Press, 2: 401 pp.
1945. *Ibid.,* 5: 306 pp.
1948. *Ibid.,* 6: 259 pp.
1960. *Ibid.,* 9: 506 pp., Mus. Comp. Zool. (ed. by E. Mayr and J. C. Greenway).
1964. *Ibid.,* 10: 502 pp. (ed. by E. Mayr and J. C. Greenway).
1968. *Ibid.,* 14: 433 pp. (ed. by E. Mayr and R. A. Paynter).
1970. *Ibid.,* 13: 443 pp. (ed. by R. A. Paynter).

Peterson, R. T.
1934. *A Field guide to the birds.* Boston: Houghton Mifflin.

Pettingill, O. S.
1936. "The American Woodcock." *Memoirs Boston Soc. Nat. Hist.,* 9: 169–391.

Pettingill, O. S. and Hoyt, S. F.
1963. *Enjoying birds in upstate New York.* Ithaca, New York: Cornell Univ. Lab. Ornith., 89 pp.

Phillips, A. R., Lanyon, W. E., and Howe, M. A.
1966. "Identification of the flycatchers of eastern North America, with special emphasis on the genus *Empidonax.*" *Bird-Banding,* 37: 153–171.

Phillips, A. R. and Lanyon, W. E.
1970. "Additional notes on the flycatchers of eastern North America." *Bird-Banding,* 41: 190–197.

Phillips, A. R., Marshall, J., and Monson, G.
1964. *The birds of Arizona.* Tucson: Univ. Arizona Press.

Pickwell, G. B.
1931. "The Prairie Horned Lark." *Trans. Acad. Sci. St. Louis,* 27: 153 pp.

Pink, E. and Waterman, O. T.
1967. "Birds of Dutchess County: 1933–1964." unpubl. mimeogr. report, 124 pp.

Pitelka, F. A.
1950. "Geographic variation and the species problem in the shorebird genus *Limnodromus.*" *Univ. Calif. Publ. Zool.,* 50: 1–170.

Poole, E. L.
1964. *Pennsylvania birds: an annotated list.* Narberth, Penn.: Livingston.

Post, P. W.
1964. "The occurence and field identification of small black and white shearwaters in New York." *Kingbird,* 14: 133–141.
1967. "Manx, Audubon's, and Little Shearwaters in the northwestern North Atlantic." *Bird-Banding,* 38: 278–305.

Post, P. W. and Raynor, G. S.
1964. "Recent range expansion of the American Oystercatcher into New York." *Wilson Bull.,* 76: 339–346.

Post, W. and Enders, F.
1969. "Reappearance of the Black Rail on Long Island." *Kingbird,* 19: 189–191.
1970. "Notes on a salt marsh Virginia Rail population." *Kingbird,* 20: 61–67.
In press. "Breeding density and social system of a Seaside Sparrow population."

Post, W., Enders, F., and Davis, T. H.
1970. "The breeding status of the Glossy Ibis in New York." *Kingbird,* 20: 3–8.

Quilliam, H. R.
1965. *History of the birds of Kingston, Ontario.* Privately printed: 216 pp.

Raynor, G. S.
1941. "The nesting habits of the Whip-poor-will." *Bird-Banding,* 12: 98–104.

Reed, H. D. and Wright, A. H.
1909. "The vertebrates of the Cayuga Lake Basin, N.Y." *Proc. Amer. Phil. Soc.,* 48: 371–459.

Reynard, G. B. and Harty, S. T.
1968. "Ornithological 'mystery' song given by male Virginia Rail." *Cassinia,* 50: 3–8.

Ridgway, R.
1904. "The birds of North and Middle America." *Smithsonian Inst. Bull.,* 3.
1907. *Ibid.,* 4.

Ridgway, R. and Friedmann, H.
1941. *Ibid.,* 9.

Ripley, S. D.
1952. "The thrushes." *Postilla,* 13: 48 pp.

Robertson, W. B.
1969. "Transatlantic migration of juvenile Sooty Terns." *Nature,* 223: 632–634.

Robins, J. D. and Schnell, G. D.
1971. "Skeletal analysis of the *Ammodramus-Ammospiza* grassland sparrow complex: a numerical taxonomic study." *Auk,* 88: 567–590.

Rosche, R. C.
1967. "Birds of Wyoming County, New York." *Bull. Buffalo Soc. Nat. Sci.,* 23.

Rusk, M. S.
1964. "An Oneida Lake Purple Martin census." *Kingbird,* 14: 81–83.
1967. "Follow-up Oneida Lake Purple Martin census." *Kingbird,* 17: 83.
1968. "Birds of the Rome Sand Plains." *Kingbird,* 18: 124–127.

Ryder, J. P.
1971. "Distribution and breeding biology of the Lesser Snow Goose in central Arctic Canada." *Wildfowl,* 22: 18–28.

Sage, J. H., Bishop, L. B., and Bliss, W. P.
1913. "The birds of Connecticut." *State Geol. & Nat. Hist. Surv. Bull.,* 20; Hartford.

Salomonsen, F.
1950. *Birds of Greenland.* Copenhagen: Munksgaard.

Saunders, A. A.
1923. "The summer birds of the Allegany State Park." *Roosevelt Wildlife Bull.,* 22: 239–354.

1926a. "The summer birds of central New York marshes." *Roosevelt Wildlife Bull.,* 25: 335–475.
1926b. "Additional notes on the summer birds of Allegany State Park." *Roosevelt Wildlife Bull.,* 25: 477–497.
1929. "The summer birds of the· northern Adirondack mountains." *Roosevelt Wildlife Bull.,* 5: 327–496.
1936. *Ecology of the birds of Quaker Run Valley, Allegany State Park, New York.* New York State Mus. Handbook, 16.
1938. "Studies of breeding birds in the Allegany State Park." *New York State Mus. Bull.,* 318.
1942. *Summer birds of the Allegany State Park.* New York State Mus. Handbook, 18.

Sawyer, E. J.
1923. "The Ruffed Grouse, with special reference to its drumming." *Roosevelt Wildlife Bull.,* 22: 355–384.

Schaeffer, F. S.
1968. "Saw-whet Owl nesting at Tobay Sanctuary, Long Island." *Kingbird,* 18: 143–144.

Schauensee, R. M. de
1966. *The species of birds of South America and their distribution.* Narberth, Penn.: Livingston.

Scheider, F.
1958. "Hawk flights along southeastern Lake Ontario." *Kingbird,* 8: 74–75.
1959a. "Some brief Tug Hill Plateau observations." *Kingbird,* 8: 110.
1959b. "Warblers in southern *sic* [central] New York." *Kingbird,* 9: 13–19.
1965. "1964 fall shorebird migration in central New York." *Kingbird,* 15: 15–19.

Schorger, A. W.
1955. *The Passenger Pigeon.* Madison: Univ. Wisconsin Press.
1966. *The Wild Turkey.* Norman: Univ. Oklahoma Press.

Seeber, E. L.
1963. "The Red-bellied Woodpecker in western New York." *Kingbird,* 13: 188–190.

Short, E. H.
1896. *Birds of western New York with notes.* Albion, N.Y.: F. H. Lattin.

Short, L. L.

1962. "The Blue-winged Warbler and Golden-winged Warbler in central New York state." *Kingbird,* 12: 59–67.

1963. "Hybridization in the wood warblers *Vermivora pinus* and *V. chrysoptera.*" *Proc. 13th Intern. Ornith. Congr.,* 147–160.

1965. "Hybridization in the flickers (*Colaptes*) of North America." *Bull. Amer. Mus. Nat. Hist.,* 129: 309–428.

1967. "A review of the genera of grouse (Aves, Tetraoninae)." *Amer. Mus. Novit.,* 2289: 39 pp.

1971. "Systematics and behavior of some North American woodpeckers, genus *Picoides* (Aves)." *Bull. Amer. Mus. Nat. Hist.,* 145: 118 pp.

Sibley, C. G.

1970. "A comparative study of the egg-white proteins of passerine birds." *Bull. Peabody Mus. Nat. Hist.,* 32: 131 pp.

Silloway, P. M.

1923. "Relation of summer birds to the western Adirondack forest." *Roosevelt Wildlife Bull.,* 22: 397–486.

Smiley, D.

1964. "Thirty-three years of bird observation at Mohonk Lake, N.Y." *Kingbird,* 14: 205–208.

Smith, N. G.

1966. "Evolution of some Arctic gulls (*Larus*): an experimental study of isolating mechanisms." *A.O.U. Ornith. Monogr.,* 4: 99 pp.

1969. "Polymorphism in ringed plovers." *Ibis,* 111: 177–188.

Smith, W. J.

1966. "Communication and relationships in the genus *Tyrannus.*" *Publ. Nutt. Ornith. Club,* 6: 250 pp.

Snow, D. W.

1956. "The specific status of the Willow Tit." *Bull. British Ornith. Club,* 76: 29–31.

Spiker, C. J.

1931. "A biological reconnaissance of the Peterboro Swamp and the Labrador Pond areas." *Roosevelt Wildlife Bull.,* 6: 1–151.

1935. "A popular account of the bird life of the Finger Lakes section of New York, with main reference to the summer season." *Roosevelt Wildlife Bull.,* 6: 391–551.

Spofford, W. R.

1960. "The White-headed Eagle in New York State." *Kingbird,* 10: 148–152.

1971. "The breeding status of the Golden Eagle in the Appalachians." *Amer. Birds,* 25: 3–7.

Stein, R. C.

1958. "The behavioral, ecological and morphological characteristics of two populations of the Alder Flycatcher." *New York State Mus. Bull.,* 371: 63 pp.

1963. "Isolating mechanisms between populations of Traill's Flycatchers." *Proc. Amer. Phil. Soc.,* 107: 21–50.

Stone, W.

1937. *Bird studies at Old Cape May* (2 vols). Philadelphia: Delaware Valley Ornith. Club.

Stoner, D.

1932. "Ornithology of the Oneida Lake region: with reference to the late spring and summer seasons." *Roosevelt Wildlife Annals,* 2: 271–764.

1939. "The Golden Eagle in eastern New York." *Univ. State of N.Y. Bull.,* 25: 114–117.

Storer, R. W.

1966. "Sexual dimorphism and food habits in three North American accipiters." *Auk,* 83: 423–436.

Stout, G. D.

1967. *The shorebirds of North America.* New York: Viking Press.

Todd, W. E. C.

1963. *Birds of the Labrador Peninsula and adjacent areas.* Toronto: Univ. Toronto Press.

Vaurie, C. A.

1959. *Birds of the Palearctic fauna (Non-passeriformes).* London: Witherby.

1965. *Ibid. (Passeriformes)*

Voous, K. H.

1960. *Atlas of European birds.* Amsterdam: Elsevier; London: Nelson.

Wallace, D. I. M.

1968. "Dowitcher identification: a brief review." *British Birds,* 61: 366–372.

Wallace, G. J.
1939. "Bicknell's Thrush: its taxonomy, distribution, and life history." *Proc. Boston Soc. Nat. Hist.,* 41: 211–402.

Watson, G. E.
1962a. "Sympatry in Palearctic *Alectoris* partridges." *Evol.,* 16: 11–19.
1962b. "Three sibling species of *Alectoris* partridges." *Ibis,* 104: 353–367.

Weller, M. W.
1964. "Distribution and migration of the Redhead." *Journ. Wildlife Mgmt.,* 28: 64–103.

Welter, W. A.
1935. "The natural history of the Long-billed Marsh Wren." *Wilson Bull.,* 47: 1–34.

West, D. A.
1962. "Hybridization in grosbeaks (*Pheucticus*) of the Great Plains." *Auk,* 79: 399–424.

Wetmore, A.
1960. "A classification for the birds of the world." *Smiths. Misc. Coll.,* 139: 37 pp.
1968. "The birds of the republic of Panama, part 2: Columbidae (Pigeons) to Picidae (Woodpeckers)." *Smiths. Misc. Coll.,* 150.

Wilcox, L.
1959. "A twenty-year banding study of the Piping Plover." *Auk,* 76: 129–152.

Williamson, K.
1961. "The taxonomy of the redpolls." *British Birds,* 54: 238–241.

Wilson, J. E.
1959. "The status of the Hungarian Partridge in New York." *Kingbird,* 9: 54–57.

Witherby, H. F., Jourdain, C. R., Ticehurst, N. F., and Tucker, B. W.
1938a, 1938b, 1939, 1940, 1941, 1943, 1944. *Handbook of British birds.* Vols. 1, 2, 3, 4, 5, rev. eds. London: Witherby.

Wolk, R. G. and Bull, J.
1967. "Differential nesting schedule of Herring Gulls on Long Island, New York." *Kingbird,* 17: 5–6.

Woolfenden, G. E.
1956. "Comparative breeding behavior of *Ammospiza caudacuta* and *A. maritima.*" *Univ. Kansas Publ.,* 10: 45–75.

SUPPLEMENT TO
BIRDS OF NEW YORK STATE
by JOHN BULL

When a book about bird distribution appears, it is already out of date. The effective cut-off date for *Birds of New York State* (1974) was Dec. 31st, 1972, with major breeding changes documented through 1973. In the short time that has elapsed since publication, much new and valuable distribution information has accumulated, and in order to maintain continuity of record, it is important to present this material. The Executive Committee of the Federation of New York State Bird Clubs suggested that a supplement be published by the Federation. In the supplement, material is included up to July 31st, 1975.

The treatment of the species accounts is the same as in my 1974 book. The status of a species is delineated by either breeding evidence, specimen evidence, and/or photographic evidence, or a hypothetical designation, and the categories are indicated as follows:

* * Specimen evidence
* *B* Breeding evidence
* [ ] Hypothetical

For both maximum counts and early and late dates of occurrence, the names of observers are omitted unless the counts and dates are of an exceptional nature.

The following abbreviations stand for institutions containing bird collections:

AMNH (=American Museum of Natural History); NYSM (=New York State Museum); BMS (=Buffalo Museum of Science); CUM (=Cornell University Museum).

In order to save space, the counties for each locality are mentioned only once instead of being repeated throughout. The gazetteer in the state book should be consulted not only for the county, but also for coordinates; there are also some new localities added.

The following two species are recorded in the state for the first time: (1) Mountain Bluebird (*Sialia currucoides*), photographed upstate in 1974; (2) Smith's Longspur (*Calcarius pictus*), collected on

Long Island in 1974. Another species, formerly on the hypothetical list, has since been photographed: Swainson's Warbler (*Limnothlypis swainsonii*), one on Long Island in 1973, the other upstate in 1975. These records now bring the state list up to 413 species based on specimen and/or photographic evidence.

The following three breeding species are recorded in the state for the first time: (1) Gull-billed Tern *(Sterna nilotica)*, bred on Long Island in 1975; (2) Chuck-will's-widow *(Caprimulgus carolinensis)*, bred on Long Island in 1975; (3) Bewick's Wren *(Thryothorus bewickii)*, bred upstate in 1974. These records now bring the state breeding list up to 231 species. A fourth species, the White-winged Crossbill *(Loxia leucoptera)* was finally found building a nest in the Adirondacks, as predicted in the state book. However, no further activity was noted.

One species new to the hypothetical list is a Fieldfare *(Turdus pilaris)*, observed in 1973.

ACKNOWLEDGMENTS

So many birders have aided in this supplement that it is impossible to list them all here. Suffice it to say that they are duly acknowledged in the species accounts. However, there are a number of people I am indebted to, for answering numerous queries, making specific breeding surveys, and forwarding specimens or photographs for examination and they are Geoffrey Carleton, Dorothy Crumb, Davis Finch, Darrel Ford, Robert Giffen, Michael Gochfeld, Richard Guthrie, Michel Kleinbaum, John Peterson, Dennis Puleston, Edgar Reilly, Walton Sabin, Roy Slack, and Robert Smart.

I would especially like to thank the following: Tom Davis for calling my attention to numerous records, many unpublished; my wife, Edith, for editing the manuscript; Emanuel Levine and John Farrand, co-editors of *The Kingbird,* for reviewing the manuscript; and finally Kenneth Parkes (belatedly) for offering me his very helpful unpublished Ph.D. thesis, "Birds of New York State and Their Taxonomy."

SPECIES ACCOUNTS

COMMON LOON *(Gavia immer)* * B
  Nonbreeding: 700+, Webster, Monroe Co., Apr. 27, 1974 (Kemnitzer). 600, ocean off Mecox Bay, Suffolk Co., May 26, 1975 (Ash). The latter were observed within a five-hour period after a severe northeast storm. This represents not only the largest coastal flight on record, but is also a very late date for such numbers.

RED-THROATED LOON *(Gavia stellata)* *
  Occurrence: one in breeding plumage, Jamaica Bay, June 13-20, 1975 (Kleinbaum).

Northern Fulmar—gray phase and light phase—
20 miles SW of Montauk Pt.
Bill Wilson
June 16, 1975

NORTHERN FULMAR *(Fulmarus glacialis)* *
  Occurrence: Lake Ontario, near Oswego, Dec. 19, 1974 (Crumb, DeBenedictis, and Scheider); one in the light phase, second inland occurrence and the second for that area.
  Close-range photographs of both light and dark morphs were taken

about 20 miles southwest of Montauk Point, June 16, 1975 (Bill Wilson), photos on file in AMNH collection. This is the first *confirmed* record for Long Island waters. The mid-June date is a first summer occurrence in New York, but is part of a recent trend in the northeast.

Remarks: Fulmars, Skuas, and other "pelagic" species have been reported on Cox's Ledge, "off" Montauk in recent years, but this locality is well beyond the 30-mile limit considered by the writer to be in New York State waters; also omitted from this supplement are those species reported from the Hudson "canyon," off the continental shelf. Actually Cox's Ledge is nearer to Rhode Island than it is to Long Island, and the Hudson "canyon" is as close to the New Jersey coast as it is to New York.

GREATER SHEARWATER *(Puffinus gravis)* *
  Occurrence: 200+, off Montauk, Oct. 26, 1974 (Davis), late for so many.

CORY'S SHEARWATER *(Puffinus diomedea)* *
  Occurrence: Great Gull Island, Suffolk Co., May 25, 1972 (Duffy).

MANX SHEARWATER *(Puffinus puffinus)* *
  Occurrence: Probably not rare well offshore, as at Cox's Ledge (see Northern Fulmar). One each reported off Montauk and off Mecox Bay, on the same day—May 25, 1975 (both observed by Ash and Costa).
  Remarks: In 1973 a pair of Manx Shearwaters bred on Penikese Island, Mass., for the first confirmed continental North American breeding record (*Auk,* 1975, 92: 145-147). The species has also bred at least once in Bermuda.

AUDUBON'S SHEARWATER *(Puffinus lherminieri)* *
  Occurrence: One seen well, off Ocean Beach, Fire Island, Suffolk Co., July 25, 1971 (Finch).

BROWN BOOBY *(Sula leucogaster)* *
  Occurrence: One seen well, off Gardiner's Island, Suffolk Co., June 2, 1973 (Puleston).

GREAT CORMORANT *(Phalacrocorax carbo)* *
  Occurrence: Great Gull Island, June 9, 1972 (Duffy), latest record by more than a month; also very late is a "first" upstate report of an

adult in breeding plumage at Oswego harbor, May 19-20, 1973 (Rusk, Scheider, Spies, *et al., Kingbird,* 1974, 24: 12-13); 400+, Gardiner's Bay area, winter of 1973-1974; also 50+, Lower New York Bay area, same winter (numerous observers in both instances.)

DOUBLE-CRESTED CORMORANT *(Phalacrocorax auritus)* * B
Breeding: Little Galloo Island in extreme eastern Lake Ontario, Jefferson Co., July 21, 1974 (Cameron, *Kingbird,* 1974, 24: 44), "18 nesting ——"; whether 18 nests or 9 pairs, is not stated. There were 28 active nests at that locality on June 12, 1975. This represents the first known breeding recorded at Little Galloo Island and the second locality in the state, the other at nearby Gull Island.

MAGNIFICENT FRIGATEBIRD *(Fregata magnificens)* *
Occurrence: An adult male was observed flying over Fire Island Inlet, June 8, 1974 (Burke, McGuinness, and Polshek).

GREAT BLUE HERON *(Ardea herodias)* * B
Nonbreeding: 32, Derby Hill, Oswego Co., Apr. 11, 1972, the only spring maximum listed for the state.
Breeding: Young fledged as early as June 17, 1974 in western New York.

GREAT EGRET *(Egretta alba)* * B
Nonbreeding: 3, Jamaica Bay, Jan. 15, 1975 (many observers); as many as 14 on south shore Long Island Christmas counts, winter of 1974-1975.

SNOWY EGRET *(Egretta thula)* * B
Nonbreeding: 9, Southern Nassau Christmas count, Dec. 30, 1973; 6, Jamaica Bay, to Feb. 2, 1975.

LITTLE BLUE HERON *(Egretta caerulea)* * B
Nonbreeding: Tobay Pond, Nassau Co., Jan. 22, 1975 (Baumann and Schore); 8, Oak Beach, Suffolk Co., Dec. 15, 1974 (Davis *et al.*); 10, Oak Beach, Apr. 7, 1974 (Davis *et al.*). This species and both egrets above are now regular in winter on the outer coast, and also arrive in spring much earlier than in former years.
Breeding: (1) 20+ pairs bred from Jones Beach east to Oak Beach in 1973; (2) 10 pairs nested on a small island near Captree Island, Suffolk Co. in 1975. This species is still much less numerous than the two widespread egrets in New York.

LOUISIANA HERON *(Egretta tricolor)* * B
Nonbreeding: Oak Beach, Dec. 17, 1972.

CATTLE EGRET *(Bubulcus ibis)* B
Nonbreeding: 60, Jamaica Bay Refuge, Sept. 26, 1973 (many observers), the largest concentration ever reported in the state; "many" had summered there in 1973, but no proof of breeding was obtained.

Breeding: Two new breeding localities were discovered, both upstate, as follows: (1) Five nests in a Black-crowned Night Heron colony at Braddock's Bay, Monroe Co., June 1974 (Tetlow, O'Hara, *et al.*); (2) Several pairs and one active nest, Four Brothers Islands, Essex Co., first noted in 1973, also in a Black-crowned Night Heron colony (J. Peterson *et al.*). In 1975 there were at least two active nests with two juveniles in each nest; on June 14 two downy young in one nest were banded and on June 29 two more downies in the other nest were banded; on July 21 two of the young had fledged. These two breeding records are the first for upstate, one on Lake Ontario, the other on Lake Champlain. The only other known breeding localities in the state are two on Long Island (Bull, 1974: 82).

GREEN HERON *(Butorides striatus)* * B
Remarks: Following Payne (1974), the Green Heron is merged with the widely distributed Striated Heron *(B. striatus)* of South America and much of the tropical Old World. These two forms interbreed extensively where their ranges meet, as in central Panama and the islands off northern South America. Many hybrids have been collected and observed. As *striatus* is the oldest available name for the complex, our eastern North American population should be called *B. striatus virescens.*

YELLOW-CROWNED NIGHT HERON *(Nycticorax violaceus)* * B
Breeding: Rye, Westchester Co., 1974 (Burke), three nests; 1975, four young fledged from two nests. These are the first breeding records for the county and only the second outside Long Island.

LEAST BITTERN *(Ixobrychus exilis)* * B
Breeding: This species breeds regularly as far north as the Perch River Refuge, Jefferson Co. (D. Gordon, *in litt.*).

WOOD STORK *(Mycteria americana)* *
Occurrence: Near Rochester, May 7, 1972 (K. Doris *et al.*); Fresh Kills, Staten Island, Oct. 11-12, 1973, (G. Deppe), one observed flying overhead.

GLOSSY IBIS *(Plegadis falcinellus)* * B

Nonbreeding: Scio, Allegany Co., Dec. 21-28, 1971 (Buffalo Ornith. Soc.), first inland report in winter; 15, Jamaica Bay, March 24, 1974, early for so many.

Breeding: 200+ pairs, islands north of Jones Beach (from Gilgo east to Oak Beach), 1975. Glossy Ibises bred as far north as Maine in 1972.

WHISTLING SWAN *(Cygnus columbianus)* *

Occurrence: Chautauqua Lake—238, Dec. 21, 1974; 45, Jan. 8, 1975 (Elderkin and Sundell), unusual numbers for winter; Montezuma Refuge, June 4, 1975 (Gibson).

CANADA GOOSE *(Branta canadensis)* * B

Nonbreeding: 23,000 Montezuma marshes, Oct. 19, 1974; 100,000, north end of Cayuga Lake, March 15, 1975.

Breeding: (1) 300 pairs bred on Gardiner's Island, 1973 (Puleston); (2) Six downy young, Tarrytown, Westchester Co., Apr. 23, 1975 (very early); (3) Three eggs, near Long Beach, Nassau Co., May 17, 1975 (late); (4) One fledged, Point Breeze, Orleans Co., July 29, 1975.

BRANT *(Branta bernicla)* *

Occurrence: 3000, Jamaica Bay, May 26, 1974, late for so many.

Subspecies: A "Black" Brant *(Branta bernicla nigricans)* was seen well, in with a flock of 1500+ Brant, Jamaica Bay Refuge, from Oct. 14 to Nov. 29, 1974 (Davis, Ash, Buckley, *et al., Kingbird,* 1975, 25: 27). The dark belly of the "Black" Brant was obvious as the bird flew directly overhead.

BARNACLE GOOSE *(Branta leucopsis)* *

Occurrence: An individual reported as being "exceedingly wary," was seen in grain fields with some Canada Geese *(B. canadensis)* at Bridgehampton, Suffolk Co., March 17-21, 1974 (many observers, *Amer. Birds,* 1974, 28: 616).

WHITE-FRONTED GOOSE *(Anser albifrons)* *

Occurrence: "Big" spring flight, 1975—3, Oak Orchard Swamp, Apr. 13; 5, Saratoga Lake, Apr. 14; 2, Beaver Lake, Onondaga Co., Apr. 17. This is a total of *ten* birds at three widely separated localities in the state (western, central, and eastern portions), all within five days.

SNOW GOOSE *(Anser caerulescens)* *

Occurrence: The blue morph has continued to increase, often outnumbering the white in recent years, especially in western New York, and also in the eastern part of the state, including Long Island, on rare occasions. Localities from west to east, as follows—Montezuma area, Apr. 14, 1972, 2500 "Blues," a new high, with only 500 "Snows"; March 15, 1975, 8000 geese, "Blues" outnumbered "Snows" by *ten* to *one,* as compared to *three* to *one* in past years; 3000 "Snows," Hook Mountain, Rockland Co., Apr. 7, 1973; 40 "Blues," no "Snows," Point O' Woods, Fire Island, Suffolk Co., Oct. 6, 1973; 32 "Blues," Wainscott, Suffolk Co., March 16-24, 1974. "Pure" flocks of "Blues" were unknown on Long Island in former years.

FULVOUS TREE DUCK *(Dendrocygna bicolor)* *

Occurrence: Flock of 11, North Hills, Nassau Co., Nov. 13-19, 1972 (many observers) and photographed by Davis Finch; 6, Baiting Hollow, Suffolk Co., May 14, 1975, (various observers). These are the first state records since 1966.

WOOD DUCK *(Aix sponsa)* * B

Nonbreeding: 3000, Montezuma Refuge, Oct. 19, 1974 (Gustafson, Refuge Manager); these numbers are unprecedented.

MALLARD *(Anas platyrhynchos)* * B

Nonbreeding: 28,000, Montezuma Refuge, Oct. 28, 1974 (Gustafson, Refuge Manager); unprecedented numbers.

Remarks: Reports in recent years of Mallards "replacing" Black Ducks *(Anas rubripes)* in much of the east may be true of inland areas, but the coastal salt marsh population of the latter species seems to be in stable numbers. The situation bears watching. Johnsgard (1975: 251) has this to say:

"The close evolutionary relationships between mallards and black ducks have been previously studied, and a low but significant rate of natural hybridization has been established. This interaction has apparently risen in recent years, as mallards have moved eastward as wintering and breeding birds, and at least locally may be of genetic significance. ——ecological differences in the form of habitat breeding preferences tend to keep the two forms separated on their breeding grounds and probably operate against the maintenance of mixed pairings. The primary zone of contact between mallards and black ducks has moved considerably eastward during the past half century, and current evidence indicates that hybridization between them will continue to increase."

GADWALL *(Anas strepera)* * B
Nonbreeding: 225, north end of Cayuga Lake, early January 1975.
Breeding: One pair bred at Wilson Hill Refuge, St. Lawrence Co., in 1970 (S. Browne, *in litt.*). This was inadvertently omitted from the *Birds of New York State* and is the fourth upstate breeding locality. As of 1975 there were 13 nesting pairs breeding in the Oak Orchard Swamp complex (J. Morse, Refuge Manager). Also one pair and nine downy young, Jones Beach, June 14, 1975; this is an early date for unfledged young.

COMMON PINTAIL *(Anas acuta)* * B
Breeding: Female and brood of young, Four Brothers Islands, Lake Champlain, 1975 (Gardephe, *fide* Carleton); this is only the eighth breeding locality for the state and the first for Essex Co.

AMERICAN WIGEON *(Anas americana)* * B
Breeding: Adult and five half-grown young, Piermont Marsh, Rockland Co., July 21, 1974 (Deed); only the seventh breeding locality for the state and the first for the Hudson valley, as well as the county. Downy young were recorded as early as June 28 in western New York.

GREEN-WINGED TEAL *(Anas crecca)* * B
Breeding: (1) Female and nine juveniles, Rensselaer, Rensselaer Co., July 8, 1973 (Connor), new breeding record for the county; (2) "Pair flushed from likely habitat," Plum Island, Suffolk Co., June 10, 1974 (Buckley), but no breeding evidence obtained.

BLUE-WINGED TEAL *(Anas discors)* * B
Nonbreeding: 30, Sage Pond, Lawrence, Nassau Co., Jan. 12, 1975 (Sloss and Hirschbein), unprecedented numbers for winter.

CINNAMON TEAL *(Anas cyanoptera)* *
Occurrence: Male in eclipse plumage, Times Beach, Buffalo, Aug. 14, 1973 (Axtell); male, Montezuma Refuge, Apr. 1-July 21, 1974 (Haramis, Benning, Gustafson, and many others), see also *Kingbird*, 1974, 24: 172-173; male Tonawanda Wildlife Management Area, Alabama, June 19, 1975 (Rebovich, Carroll); *Prothonotary*, Jan., 1976 addenda (identifiable photograph in B.O.S. file for accepted records). These three occurrences are the first for upstate since 1886, when a specimen was taken at Seneca Lake.

RING-NECKED DUCK *(Aythya collaris)* * B

Breeding: Two new breeding localities are—(1) Big Cherrypatch Pond, near Lake Placid, Essex Co., 1972 (Mack), female and six young; (2) Upper and Lower Lakes Refuge, near Canton, St. Lawrence Co., July 27, 1974 (H. and M. Armistead), female and eight downy young, only the second breeding record for the St. Lawrence valley in New York.

TUFTED DUCK *(Aythya fuligula)*

Occurrence: Adult male, Nine Mile Point, Oswego Co., Lake Ontario, Apr. 8-9, 1971 (Scheider), the first report from upstate; a pair wintered at the regular East River location near Hell Gate Bridge in upper Manhattan, 1974-1975 (many observers).

COMMON EIDER *(Somateria mollissima)* *

Occurrence: 500+, off Montauk Point, L.I., Dec. 16, 1972 to early February 1973 (numerous observers); subadult male, Jamaica Bay, late May to Aug. 19, 1974 (many observers). Some of the Montauk birds were probably King Eiders.

KING EIDER *(Somateria spectabilis)* *

Occurrence: 8, Montauk Point, June and July 1974 (Buckley *et al.*).

BLACK SCOTER *(Melanitta nigra)* *

Occurrence: 24, Great Gull Island, Suffolk Co., July 20, 1972 (Duffy).

BUFFLEHEAD *(Bucephala albeola)* *

Occurrence: 400, Jamaica Bay, Apr. 28, 1974, and 200 on May 6. Pair near Sag Harbor, Suffolk Co., June and July 1974.

COMMON GOLDENEYE *(Bucephala clangula)* * B

Breeding: (1) Female and eight juveniles, Lake Terror, Hamilton Co., July 4-15, 1973 (Belknap); (2) Adults and four downies, Fish Creek Ponds, near Upper Saranac Lake, Franklin Co., July 4, 1974 (Tetlow). These are the ninth and tenth breeding records for the state.

HOODED MERGANSER *(Mergus cucullatus)* * B

Nonbreeding: 578, Chautauqua Lake, Nov. 22, 1974 (Sundell, Olsen); *Prothonotary*, Dec., 1974.

Breeding: (1) Female and nine young, Madawaska, Franklin Co.,

1974; (2) Female and seven unfledged young, Lewis, Essex Co., June 7, 1975. Browne (*N.Y. Fish and Game Jour.*, 1975, 22: 68-70) gives a somewhat cursory treatment of breeding distribution in the state, mostly from unpublished reports, and a map indicating "number of records per county for nests or broods ——." Perhaps the Hooded Merganser is less rare as a breeder in New York than my map (# 40) shows (Bull, 1974), but this should be documented in greater detail than by Browne (*op. cit.*, 68-70).

COMMON MERGANSER *(Mergus merganser)* * B

Nonbreeding: 3000, off Rochester, Oct. 30, 1974 (Benning), very early for so many.

Breeding: (1) Pair and seven juveniles, Cuddebackville, Orange Co., summer of 1973 (J. Trip, *Kingbird*, 1973, 23: 211); this locality is on the Neversink River along the west slope of the Shawangunk Mountains in northwestern Orange County, and represents not only the first breeding record for the county, but is the southernmost for New York State (see map 41 in state book for breeding in adjacent Pennsylvania); (2) Three adults and nine immatures, Piseco Lake, Hamilton Co., Sept. 19, 1973 (McIlroy), "still unable to fly"; this is an extremely late date and may represent a delayed nesting.

RUDDY DUCK *(Oxyura jamaicensis)* * B

Nonbreeding: 2000, Hudson River, near Nyack, Rockland Co., Dec. 14, 1965 (Hopper and Polhemus); this report courtesy of R. F. Deed *(in litt.).*

TURKEY VULTURE *(Cathartes aura)* * B

Nonbreeding: At the well-known hawk lookouts on Lake Ontario, the following spring counts are at hand for a comparison on the *same* dates:

Manitou, Monroe Co.	Derby Hill, Oswego Co.
80, Apr. 21, 1973	70, Apr. 21, 1973
200, Apr. 4, 1974	200, Apr. 4, 1974

Note how evenly matched these two localities are.

OSPREY *(Pandion haliaetus)* * B

Nonbreeding: 40, Riis Park, Queens Co., Sept. 28, 1973.

Breeding: The following breeding data are at hand—Long Island— 1973—(1) Near Oakdale, Suffolk Co., pair building nest, Aug. 24 to Sept. 9, unsuccessful; 1974—raised and fledged three young; 1975—

no success. This is the most westerly breeding record on the south shore. (2) Gardiner's Island, 1974—26 young raised from 34 nests (Puleston). Upstate—all from Essex County in 1974 and recorded for the first time ever in that county—(1) Chubb River near Lake Placid; (2) Bouquet River near Whallonsburg; (3) Long Pond; (4) North Elba, 1975—nest "produced three young" (Genesee Ornith. Soc.).

SWALLOW-TAILED KITE *(Elanoides forficatus)* *

Occurrence: One observed flying over Storm King Mountain, Orange Co., Aug. 3, 1974 (W. Lehnes), observer previously familiar with the species in Florida. This is the eleventh occurrence in New York.

BALD EAGLE *(Haliaeetus leucocephalus)* * B

Nonbreeding: Unprecedented midwinter numbers at two inland reservoirs in Sullivan County—17 (12 adults, 5 immatures), Rondout Reservoir, Feb. 4, 1973; 18 (11 adults, 7 immatures), Mongaup Reservoir, Jan. 3, 1975 (Borko, Niven, and many others). These numbers were attributed to fish kills. Borko *(Kingbird, 1974, 24: 104-105)*, in referring to the 1973 occurrence, stated that a "——die-off of the alewife undoubtedly caused the eagles to concentrate in large numbers."

NORTHERN HARRIER *(Circus cyaneus)* * B

Nonbreeding: 150, Derby Hill, Apr. 15, 1972; 150+ Fire Island, Sept. 23, 1974 (Buckley). The latter number is unprecedented for the coast.

SHARP-SHINNED HAWK *(Accipiter striatus)* * B

Nonbreeding: 2700+, Derby Hill, Apr. 21, 1966, inadvertently omitted from the state book; 175, Fire Island, and 385, Hook Mountain, both on Oct. 1, 1974, which makes a nice comparison at coastal and inland localities.

COOPER'S HAWK *(Accipiter cooperii)* * B

Breeding: Nestlings as late as July 11th in western New York.

NORTHERN GOSHAWK *(Accipiter gentilis)* * B

Nonbreeding: 88, Derby Hill, March 29, 1973, nearly four times the previous high (only 40 Cooper's Hawks the same day); 13, Hook Mtn., Nov. 11, 1973.

Breeding: Six new breeding localities, three in 1974 and three in

1975, all nests with young birds, as follows— (1) Almond, (2) Bolivar, both in Allegany Co.; (3) Honeoye Lake, Ontario Co., first for county; (4) Fabius, Onondaga Co., first for county; (5) New Haven, Oswego Co.; (6) Sixberry Lake, near Redwood, Jefferson Co.

RED-TAILED HAWK *(Buteo jamaicensis)* * B

Nonbreeding: The following maxima are all from Derby Hill in various years—500, March 18; 1100+, Apr. 4; 800, Apr. 12.

Breeding: Fledged young as late as Aug. 11th in western New York, may represent a re-nesting as the date is more than a month later than the previous latest date, namely July 8th. In 1975 in the Millbrook area of Dutchess Co., 27 nests produced 24 young.

BROAD-WINGED HAWK *(Buteo platypterus)* * B

Nonbreeding: One filmed in color at Tappan, Rockland Co., Jan. 11, 1970 by T. John (R. Deed, *in litt.*), is one of the very few reliable winter reports; 9000, Manitou, May 2, 1975.

SWAINSON'S HAWK *(Buteo swainsoni)* *

Occurrence: Adult, light morph, Derby Hill, Apr. 22, 1973 (11 observers, including Scheider, Smart, and Finch); one, Webster, Monroe Co., May 2, 1975 (Lloyd and Sprague), the latter locality also on Lake Ontario and about 15 miles east of the Manitou hawk lookout. These two observations represent the fourth and fifth records for the state.

GOLDEN EAGLE *(Aquila chrysaetos)* * B

Nonbreeding: 5, Derby Hill, Apr. 4, 1974; 5, Derby Hill, Apr. 21, 1974; 4, Manitou, May 2, 1975.

AMERICAN KESTREL *(Falco sparverius)* * B

Nonbreeding: 300, Derby Hill, Apr. 15, 1972.

Breeding: A brood of *six* fledged at Endwell, Broome Co., June 27, 1975.

SANDHILL CRANE *(Grus canadensis)* *

Occurrence: No fewer than four occurrences of single birds, all within a three-year period—Ithaca, June 7, 1972 (Tate); Webster, Apr. 16, 1973 (Czech); Montauk, May 1-5, 1975 (E. Edwards), poor color photo examined, but appears to be this species; Clymer, Chautauqua Co., June 21-July 11, 1975 (R. T. Peterson and Sundell), "remarkably tame," perhaps an escaped captive.

The months recorded for all state records are: April (3); May (4); June and July (2 each); October (1); November (3). This is a total of 15 records for six months.

CLAPPER RAIL *(Rallus longirostris)* * B
Status: On page 214, line 2 of the state book, should read, "Rare and local on extreme eastern Long Island"; the word "extreme" was inadvertently omitted. In other words it is a local bird on the Orient Peninsula and on the south shore east of Easthampton, both in Suffolk County.

BLACK RAIL *(Laterallus jamaicensis)* * B
Breeding: The Oak Beach population was found to consist of at least three or four individuals during May 1974 when these birds were observed at night with flashlight and their calls taped.

PURPLE GALLINULE *(Porphyrio martinica)* *
Occurrence: Adult found dead, Orient, Suffolk Co., June 15, 1967 (Latham), NYSM 24885; this record not published previously. Adult caught alive, Wading River, Suffolk Co., Apr. 4, 1975 (Aline Dove, *in litt.*), died on Apr. 7, "extremely emaciated," specimen preserved at Jesup Neck Sanctuary. This individual probably arrived as a result of the severe southerly storm of Apr. 2-3.
Remarks: The genus *Porphyrula,* formerly used for this species, is merged here with *Porphyrio,* following both Mayr (1949) and Olson (1973). Our Purple Gallinule is especially close in appearance to *P. alleni* of Africa.

AMERICAN COOT *(Fulica americana)* * B
Nonbreeding: 1000, Chautauqua Lake, Dec. 6, 1974 (Sundell), late for so many.

AMERICAN OYSTERCATCHER *(Haematopus palliatus)* * B
Nonbreeding: Shinnecock Inlet, Suffolk Co., March 10, 1974; Jones Beach, Nov. 11, 1974.
Breeding: Two new breeding localities in eastern Suffolk Co.— (1) Flat Hammock Island, off Fisher's Island, June 2, 1974 (F. Haeni), pair and three unfledged young; (2) Robins Island, Peconic Bay, summer of 1975 (E. and L. Salzman), pair nested.
Aerial and ground surveys of Long Island revealed 36 pairs in 1974 and 46 pairs in 1975 from Jamaica Bay east to islands in Shinnecock Bay and on Gardiner's Island.

AMERICAN AVOCET *(Recurvirostra americana)* *
Occurrence: Three inland observations are of interest—near Monticello, Sullivan Co., May 9, 1971 (Borko, Niven, *et al.*); Montezuma Refuge, May 20-24, 1973 (Benning *et al.*); same locality, June 20, 1974 (Smith).

BLACK-NECKED STILT *(Himantopus himantopus)* *
Occurrence: Three coastal records—Georgica Pond, Suffolk Co., May 16, 1972; Mecox Bay, Suffolk Co., May 20-24, 1972, may have been the same individual; Jamaica Bay, Apr. 20-25, 1973. All of these birds were studied by numerous observers. The first inland record for the state is that of a bird color-photographed near Fairport, Monroe Co., June 2-3, 1973 (Tetlow, *Kingbird,* 1974, 24: 13), and observed by at least 20 persons; the bird "was standing on a small island in a farm pond."

LESSER GOLDEN PLOVER *(Pluvialis dominica)* *
Occurrence: 300, Sagaponack, Suffolk Co., Sept. 16, 1973, in a potato field; 200-300, Essex, Essex Co., Aug. 29-Sept. 14, 1974 (J. Peterson and others), in a plowed wheat field. This is a very high number for an inland locality, especially in fall.

SEMIPALMATED PLOVER *(Charadrius semipalmatus)* *
Occurrence: Oak Beach, March 18, 1972; 4, Jones Beach, winter of 1974-1975 (Wollin), a high number.

KILLDEER *(Charadrius vociferus)* * B
Nonbreeding: 250, Derby Hill, Apr. 13, 1972.

COMMON SNIPE *(Capella gallinago)* * B
Nonbreeding: 60, Braddock's Bay, Sept. 28, 1974.

LONG-BILLED CURLEW *(Numenius americanus)* *
Occurrence: The first record for the state in 37 years (1938) was that of an individual, color-photographed, on newly dredged sand fill on North Line Island, Nassau Co. north of Jones Beach, from July 4 to 30, 1975 (A. Lauro, B. Lauro, Dempsey and literally hundreds of observers); see articles and photos in *Kingbird* (1975, 25: 207) and *Amer. Birds* (1975, 29: 952).

MARBLED GODWIT *(Limosa fedoa)* *
Occurrence: Coastal—Moriches Inlet, Suffolk Co., Jan. 9-18, 1973 (Puleston), first midwinter report; Jamaica Bay, June 16, 1974;

North Line Island, July 4, 1975; inland—the second spring inland observation is of one observed near Rochester, May 17-19, 1973 (McNett); also one at Times Beach, Buffalo, July 11, 1975 (Schaffner).

BAR-TAILED GODWIT *(Limosa lapponica)* *
Occurrence: With the two following observations of this Old World wader, the species is now removed from the *Accidental* category and placed in the *Casual* category—(1) Adult in breeding plumage, Moriches Bay, May 10-12, 1971 (Conolly, Puleston, *et al., Kingbird,* 1971, 21: 142-143); another in similar plumage, with a flock of 10 Hudsonian Godwits at the same locality, Aug. 17-18, 1974 (Davis and numerous observers, *Kingbird,* 1975, 25: 27-28). All three occurrences, including the 1946 specimen record, are from Moriches Bay.

HUDSONIAN GODWIT *(Limosa haemastica)* *
Occurrence: 2, Montezuma, May 19, 1974 (Benning), rare inland in spring; 37, Times Beach, Buffalo, Aug. 17, 1974 (Andrle *et al.*), a very high number for the state.

STILT SANDPIPER *(Micropalama himantopus)* *
Occurrence: 55, Montezuma, Aug. 5, 1974.

LESSER YELLOWLEGS *(Tringa flavipes)* *
Occurrence: 500, Oak Beach, Aug. 2, 1974.

SOLITARY SANDPIPER *(Tringa solitaria)* *
Occurrence: Unprecedented numbers are—50, Montezuma, May 5, 1973; 32, Derby Hill, May 8, 1973; also, 8 Manitou, July 19, 1974. Jones Beach, June 14, 1975, latest spring date.

SPOTTED SANDPIPER *(Actitis macularia)* * B
Nonbreeding: Montauk Point, Nov. 24, 1973, latest fall date.

WILLET *(Catoptrophorus semipalmatus)* * B
Nonbreeding: 4, Piermont, May 8, 1973 (Amos), early for so many inland; Montezuma, Apr. 12, 1975 (Lapham and LeCroy), earliest record for the state; 5, Times Beach, Buffalo, Sept. 2, 1974.
Breeding: Pearsall's Hassock, an island in the inland waterway, north of Long Beach, Nassau Co., May 17, 1975—two nests, each with four eggs. At least 12 breeding pairs on this and nearby islands; another 20 pairs on islands east to the Jones Beach area. In 1975, a minimum of 85 pairs bred from Jamaica Bay east to islands in

Shinnecock Bay, an enormous increase since the first breeding record for the state in 1966, just ten years before!

UPLAND SANDPIPER *(Bartramia longicauda) * B*
   Breeding: 12 pairs bred at JFK International Airport in 1973 (Cohen.)

BUFF-BREASTED SANDPIPER *(Tryngites subruficollis) **
   Occurrence: Both coastal and inland flights in unprecedented numbers—in 1971 there were 12 at Clarence Center on Sept. 7 (Andrle *et al.*); in 1973 there were great numbers on the potato fields on eastern Long Island—25, Mecox Bay, Aug. 25, and a record-shattering 55 at Sagaponack on Sept. 16 (numerous observers in both instances). An infestation of potato beetles seems to have been the attraction. Large numbers of Lesser Golden Plovers were also present.

RUFF *(Philomachus pugnax) **
   Occurrence: 4, including 2 Reeves, Waterloo dump, Seneca Co., July 7, 1974 (Benning, *Kingbird,* 1974, 24: 174), were seen by many observers; 3 different males, North Line Island, July 4-11, 1975 (many observers).

DUNLIN *(Calidris alpina) **
   Occurrence: 5000, Fire Island Inlet, March 2, 1974 (Finch and Lauro), unprecedented numbers at any time of year; 900, Braddock's Bay, Oct. 31, 1974.

RED KNOT *(Calidris canutus) **
   Occurrence: Montezuma, Apr. 24, 1973 (McIlroy); 75, same area, May 21, 1973 (Benning). These records are respectively the earliest date and the highest number for an inland locality.

PURPLE SANDPIPER *(Calidris maritima) **
   Occurrence: Shadigee, Orleans Co., Sept. 27, 1974 (Kibbe), extremely early for an inland locality.

PECTORAL SANDPIPER *(Calidris melanotos) **
   Occurrence: 2, Mecox Bay, March 2, 1974 (Ash), extremely early, the earliest record by more than two weeks.

WHITE-RUMPED SANDPIPER *(Calidris fuscicollis) **
   Occurrence: 40, Oak Beach, May 22, 1974; 8, Selkirk Shores, Oswego Co., Oct. 24, 1974.

BAIRD'S SANDPIPER *(Calidris bairdii)* *
Occurrence: Sagaponack, Nov. 23, 1973 (Buckley and Paxton); Onondaga Lake, Onondaga Co., July 17, 1974 (Scheider).

LEAST SANDPIPER *(Calidris minutilla)* *
Occurrence: Great Kills, Richmond Co., Nov. 23, 1974.

SEMIPALMATED SANDPIPER *(Calidris pusilla)* *
Occurrence: 800+, Onondaga Lake, July 25, 1974 (Scheider), early for so many.
Remarks: In view of the article by Phillips (1975), all prior sightings in *winter* from New York should be expunged, including those published in Bull (1974: 261). According to that article, no valid winter specimens have been taken in the eastern United States, except one in Florida, and the records in question are probably Western Sandpipers *(C. mauri).*

RUDDY TURNSTONE *(Arenaria interpres)* *
Occurrence: 40, Great Kills, winter of 1973-1974; 60, Orient Point, winter of 1974-1975. These are the largest numbers ever reported at this season.

WILSON'S PHALAROPE *(Phalaropus tricolor)* *
Occurrence: 10, Oak Beach, Aug. 10, 1973 (Buckley); Montezuma, Apr. 27, 1975.
Remarks: Wilson's Phalaropes now breed east to Quebec, the first in 1974; as of 1975 they bred just north of the New York State line northeast of Rouses Point, Clinton County (S. Holohan, *in litt.*).

SKUA *(Stercorarius skua)* *
Occurrence: The first known report from Lake Ontario is that of an individual observed at Braddock's Bay, Oct. 7, 1973 (Lloyd and Sunderlin, *Kingbird,* 1974, 24: 59-60), although the species has been collected on the Niagara River; Fire Island Inlet, June 8, 1974 (Buckley, Lauro, and Paxton), the second occurrence from that general area.

POMARINE JAEGER *(Stercorarius pomarinus)* *
Occurrence: 35, off Montauk, Sept. 16, 1973; 25, off Fire Island, Oct. 2, 1973, late for so many.

PARASITIC JAEGER *(Stercorarius parasiticus)* *
Occurrence: 80+, Derby Hill and nearby Sandy Pond, Oswego Co.,

Oct. 14, 1973 (many observers), an unprecedented number.

GLAUCOUS GULL *(Larus hyperboreus)* *
Occurrence: Niagara Falls, 28 on Dec. 28, 1974 and 43 there on Jan. 10, 1975 (both by Axtell), unprecedented numbers.

ICELAND GULL *(Larus glaucoides)* *
Occurrence: 12, Central Park Reservoir, New York City, Feb. 17, 1975 (E. Mills), high numbers for this small body of water.

GREAT BLACK-BACKED GULL *(Larus marinus)* * B
Nonbreeding: 240, Niagara Falls, Dec. 20, 1974 (Axtell); 500, Piermont, June 28, 1975 (Amos), an unusually large number inland in June.

Breeding: 500 pairs, Gardiner's Island, 1974, a great increase over 1966 when 100 pairs bred; 10 pairs, Hoffman and Swinburne islands, Lower New York Bay, 1974, a new breeding locality and the tenth for the state; an early egg date is Apr. 23, 1975 for Jones Beach.

LESSER BLACK-BACKED GULL *(Larus fuscus)* *
Occurrence: 2 adults, Montauk Point, Dec. 22, 1973 (Puleston); 2 adults, Jerome Reservoir, Bronx Co., Dec. 25, 1973 to January 1974 (many observers). Probable total for late December-early January, 1973-1974 was six adults *(Amer. Birds,* 1974, 28: 617-618).

HERRING GULL *(Larus argentatus)* * B
Breeding: An early egg date is Apr. 23, 1975 for Jones Beach. The following estimates of breeding *pairs* are at hand—1974- 6000, Gardiner's Island; 900, Hoffman and Swinburne islands; 250, Four Brothers Islands; 1975- 2800, Captree State Park. These represent further great increases over the past few years.

RING-BILLED GULL *(Larus delawarensis)* * B
Breeding: 5000 pairs, Four Brothers Islands, 1974, twice the number recorded in 1967.

LAUGHING GULL *(Larus atricilla)* * B
Nonbreeding: 700+, Piermont, Aug. 15, 1973 (Single).

FRANKLIN'S GULL *(Larus pipixcan)* *
Occurrence: Coastal—"subadult," Mecox Bay, June 24, 1971; adult, Tobay Pond, Sept. 26, 1974; inland—2 in breeding plumage, Oswego, June 30-July 1, 1973; 1 in breeding plumage, Dunkirk,

Chautauqua Co., Feb. 6-28, 1975. This species has now been recorded in every month.

BLACK-HEADED GULL *(Larus ridibundus)* *
Occurrence: Kendall, Orleans Co., July 9-21, 1975, is the earliest
inland fall report.

LITTLE GULL *(Larus minutus)* *
Occurrence: 29, Niagara River, Nov. 4, 1973 (Benham), a truly
large number; 12, Times Beach, Buffalo, Aug. 17, 1975, with as
many as 6 there as early as July 30 (Andrle *et al.*); 4, Fire Island Inlet,
May 12, 1974 (Lauro), which is the coastal maximum.

SABINE'S GULL *(Larus sabini)* *
Occurrence: Adult in breeding plumage, Jones Beach, July 28,
1974 (Robben), only the second July occurrence.

BLACK-LEGGED KITTIWAKE *(Larus tridactylus)* *
Occurrence: Off Montauk, Aug. 26, 1973; adult, Oswego, Dec. 1,
1973 (Kibbe, *Kingbird,* 1974, 24: 60).

IVORY GULL *(Pagophila eburnea)* *
Occurrence: Immature, Niagara Falls, Dec. 29-31, 1973
(Vaughan), photographs taken; examined by the writer. This is only
the second inland record for the state, the *same* observer having seen
another at the *same* locality 40 years ago in 1934!

GULL-BILLED TERN *(Sterna nilotica)* * B
Breeding: The first definite breeding of this species in the state
occurred at South Line Island, Nassau Co., north of Jones Beach, in
1975. On June 11, adults, a nest, and two eggs were discovered and
on June 14 another nest with adults and eggs was also reported. On
July 5, one downy young was noted and on Aug. 10, two young
fledged. These terns were in a mixed colony of approximately 30
pairs of Common Terns and 12 pairs of Black Skimmers. The habitat
was new sand fill that had been dredged. Many people saw these
birds, but credit for the discovery goes to Buckley, Davis, Farrand,
Gochfeld, and Lauro. See especially, *Kingbird* (1975, 25: 179-183).
Some of the young did survive despite storms and flood tides. Gull-
billed Terns were also reported at nearby Cedar Beach and Jamaica
Bay in 1975.

COMMON TERN *(Sterna hirundo)* * B
Banding: Two more long-distance recoveries of nestlings banded at Jones Beach by Tom Davis and recovered at various localities in Brazil—(1) Banded July 22, 1973, recovered Dec. 13, 1973 at Corumba, Mato Grosso; (2) Banded July 22, 1973, recovered Nov. 18, 1973 at Maceio, Pernambuco.
Breeding: 2400 pairs, Cedar Beach, 1975 (Gochfeld).

ROSEATE TERN *(Sterna dougallii)* * B
Breeding: Early egg date of May 18, 1971 at Cedar Beach (Gochfeld); a new breeding locality on an island in Shinnecock Bay in 1974 of 600 pairs, but the colony unfortunately was flooded out by storms and high tides (Wilcox).

SOOTY TERN *(Sterna fuscata)* *
Occurrence: An adult observed in a mixed Common Tern-Roseate Tern colony on an island in Shinnecock Bay, May 20, 1975 (Wilcox), is the earliest of only two known spring records in the state, the other on June 5. Otherwise, the next earliest is July 17.

LEAST TERN *(Sterna albifrons)* * B
Nonbreeding: 70, Piermont, July 28, 1974 (T. Amos), is an unusually high number for the lower Hudson River.
Breeding: At least 600 pairs nested on the north shore of Long Island in western Suffolk County, from Lloyd's Neck east to Mount Sinai during the three years of 1972 to 1974.

SANDWICH TERN *(Sterna sandvicensis)* *
Occurrence: Moriches Bay, Aug. 22, 1970 (Finch, Kleinbaum, and Plunkett), photographed by Kleinbaum; Mecox Bay, June 4-5, 1972 (McKeever and Puleston); Jones Beach, June 1, 1974 (Gochfeld), two in a Common Tern colony. These are the first early June records in the state.

ROYAL TERN *(Sterna maxima)* *
Occurrence: With the breeding of this species in southern New Jersey in 1975 and its regular occurrence there in recent years as a nonbreeder, it has become an infrequent visitor on Long Island in the 1970's during the month of May with dates ranging from May 12 to 28. The localities were Mecox Bay, Sagaponack, and Jamaica Bay.

BLACK SKIMMER *(Rynchops niger)* * B

Breeding: Eggs, Cedar Beach, May 21, 1975 (Gochfeld), the earliest egg date by ten days; Gochfeld estimated that 150+ pairs bred there in 1975.

BLACK GUILLEMOT *(Cepphus grylle)* *

Occurrence: 3, Montauk Point, Dec. 11, 1971-Jan. 15, 1972 (many observers). This is the first time that more than a single individual of this rare northern alcid has been recorded in the state.

Mourning Dove (*Zenaida macroura*) nest and eggs on fire escape, lower Manhattan, New York City, spring of 1974 (Ms. B. Tate).

MOURNING DOVE *(Zenaida macroura)* * B

Banding: One recently fledged young banded at Schenectady, May 8, 1973 (Yunick), recovered near Red Bay, southern Labrador, June 10, 1974 where it was found dead—more than 1000 miles northeast of place of banding! See Yunick (*Bird-Banding,* 1976, 47: 72).

Breeding: Early dates of March 7, Apr. 5, and Apr. 20 for eggs, nestlings, and fledglings respectively. This species has increased tremendously as a breeder within the past ten years or so, even nesting in the heart of Manhattan, not only in city parks, but also on downtown fire escapes. For example, one pair nested on a fire escape in the spring of 1974, and another pair in 1975 (see accompanying photo by Mrs. B. Tate).

WHITE-WINGED DOVE *(Zenaida asiatica)* *
Occurrence: One well observed at Riis Park, Queens Co., Dec. 8, 1973 (the late Ed Daly, Hines, Rose, and Swayer), photographed by the first named. This is the second record for the state.

MONK PARAKEET *(Myiopsitta monachus)* * B
Nonbreeding: Observed on three New York City regional Christmas counts, 1974-1975—Queens, Bronx-Westchester, and Lower Hudson; 19, Rye, Westchester Co., Sept. 25, 1974 (Barber). In view of the above, the species can hardly be said to be "eradicated" as so often claimed by those who are engaged in its "eradication," notably federal and state game officials.

One bird building a nest near Buffalo, August 1974, but later deserted (Andrle, *Kingbird,* 1975, 25: 145-146).

YELLOW-BILLED CUCKOO *(Coccyzus americanus)* * B
Nonbreeding: One seen well at Commack, Suffolk Co., on the exceedingly early date of Apr. 11, 1973 (Giffen), eight days earlier than a previous Long Island occurrence. Like that one, this individual was reported after a southerly storm.

BARN OWL *(Tyto alba)* * B
Breeding: Pair and five eggs 50 feet up in an abandoned water tower, Commack, March 29, 1975 (Giffen); after hatching, the five young were banded; the last one fledged by July 16.

GREAT HORNED OWL *(Bubo virginianus)* * B
Breeding: In 1975 on the north shore of Long Island, Otto Heck counted at least *ten* resident pairs, all in Nassau County from Sands Point east to the Nassau-Suffolk line at Cold Spring Harbor. This is about ten miles, or approximately one pair per mile. Most nests were located on large estates. One of the nests contained *four* young, the usual number being two, more rarely three.

HAWK OWL *(Surnia ulula)* *

Occurrence: One spent the entire winter at Vernon, Oneida Co., from Dec. 15, 1974 to March 15, 1975 and was seen and photographed by hundreds of people.

LONG-EARED OWL *(Asio otus)* * B

Breeding: 1974 was an exceptionally good year for this species as five different localities reported breeding, two nests containing four young each. The localities were—(1) Salt Point, Dutchess Co.; (2) Brockport, Monroe Co.; (3) Lyndonville, Orleans Co.; (4) Beaver Meadow Refuge, Wyoming Co.; (5) Frewsburg, Chautauqua Co., the first for that county.

BOREAL OWL *(Aegolius funereus)* *

Occurrence: Three more specimens of this rare owl have been reported to me, making a total of at least 12 for the state, two of them from upstate, the third from Long Island and the first definite downstate record—(1) One found dead (emaciated), Philadelphia, Jefferson Co., Feb. 2, 1969, specimen in the Nature Center on Wellesley Island, St. Lawrence River (Belknap, *in litt.*); (2) One also found dead, Hamlin, Monroe Co., Feb. 26, 1972, specimen in the Rochester Museum of Science (O'Hara, *in litt.*); (3) Male found dead on road, presumably struck by a moving vehicle, Cedar Beach, Suffolk Co., Jan. 15, 1975 (K. Feustel), specimen in AMNH 821687 (see Feustel, *Kingbird,* 1975, 25: 86). This last record is not only the first known for Long Island, but also the first for southern New York. There is also a specimen record for northern New Jersey in 1962 (Bull, 1964: 276).

SAW-WHET OWL *(Aegolius acadicus)* * B

Banding: The following numbers were banded at Fire Island State Park by Darrel Ford and others—23, Nov. 1-24, 1971; 10, Oct. 26, 1972; 12, Nov. 11, 1972; 45, October thru December 1974. The numbers banded on the two dates in 1972 are the largest ever banded in one day for the state. This insures that there is no duplication involved, unlike birds merely observed.

CHUCK-WILL'S-WIDOW *(Caprimulgus carolinensis)* * B

Nonbreeding: 1974—Ridgewood, Queens Co., May 1 (Davis), the earliest spring occurrence; Richmond Valley, Staten Island, May 18 to July 7 (Cleaves and many others), this individual's voice was taped

by Cleaves; Oak Beach, May 24, see under breeding. 1975—a rare but
regular migrant or visitant on or near the coast.

Breeding: The first breeding record for the state was established at
Oak Beach in 1975 by Davis, Farrand, and others when, on May 24
a calling male was flushed from the ground in a black pine grove and
a female was later found incubating two eggs, the eggs laid on pine
needles; the female was still incubating on June 8. On June 14 the
eggs had hatched and two downy young were observed. Finally on
June 28 both young had fledged, for a nestling period of 17 days.
For a more detailed account with photos, see Davis (*Kingbird*, 1975,
25: 132-137).

WHIP-POOR-WILL *(Caprimulgus vociferus)* * B
Breeding: At least 100 calling in mixed pitch pine-scrub oak woodland, Connetquot River State Park, near Oakdale, Suffolk Co., June
8, 1974 (Tudor, Robben, *et al.*); 75 there on June 14, 1975.

COMMON NIGHTHAWK *(Chordeiles minor)* * B
Nonbreeding: 350, Croton Point, Westchester Co., May 21, 1975
(Howe), this number estimated flying overhead within ½ hour.

Breeding: Brandon, Franklin Co., 1974 (Mack), "—— usually a
few nest on the burn" (=ground).

RED-BELLIED WOODPECKER *(Melanerpes carolinus)* * B
Breeding: (1) Adults and young, Tarrytown, Westchester Co.,
July 10, 1975, the second breeding record for the county; (2) Pair
bred at Shoreham, Suffolk Co., summer of 1975, the fourth for that
county.

RED-HEADED WOODPECKER *(Melanerpes erythrocephalus)* * B
Nonbreeding: 12, Manitou, May 12, 1971 (Tetlow); 12, Derby
Hill, May 13, 1972 (many observers), good spring numbers.

Breeding: 4-5 breeding pairs within two to three miles, Fredonia,
Chautauqua Co., 1975 (Roy Slack).

YELLOW-BELLIED SAPSUCKER *(Sphyrapicus varius)* * B
Nonbreeding: Huge coastal flight on Oct. 5, 1974, the largest on
record—observers recorded "hundreds," with from 50 to 100 at each
of the following localities—Riis Park and Far Rockaway, both in
Queens Co.; Jones Beach, and Fire Island.

Breeding: Cuba, Allegany Co., May 19, 1974 (Keople), adults
feeding young in nest, early for nestlings.

NORTHERN THREE-TOED WOODPECKER
(Picoides tridactylus) * B

Nonbreeding: Marietta, Onondaga Co., Dec. 29, 1974 (many observers). Always rare outside the Adirondacks.

Breeding: Nest with young, Madawaska, Franklin Co., June 23, 1974 (McGuinness), the first breeding reported for the county.

WESTERN KINGBIRD *(Tyrannus verticalis)* *

Occurrence: One collected, Orient, May 23, 1930 (Latham), NYSM 25092. This record not published previously. It represents the only known spring specimen for the state and only the third spring occurrence.

SCISSOR-TAILED FLYCATCHER *(Muscivora forficata)* *

Occurrence: Gilbert Raynor had the satisfaction of observing *two* of these very rare birds on Long Island in eastern Suffolk County in 1973, one in spring, the other in fall—Manorville, June 16; Yaphank, Oct. 24-25.

YELLOW-BELLIED FLYCATCHER *(Empidonax flaviventris)* * B

Banding: Early and late dates for fall banded birds—Great Gull Island, Suffolk Co., July 22, 1973; Penn Yan, Yates Co., July 28, 1974; Vischer's Ferry, Saratoga Co., Oct. 13, 1974.

ACADIAN FLYCATCHER *(Empidonax virescens)* * B

Breeding: After a lapse of nearly 60 years (since 1915), this species has been found nesting again in the state. (1) — Near Amenia, Dutchess Co., Margaret Bowman (*Kingbird*, 1976, 26: 28), discovered a pair at a nest in 1973, where on June 28, one of the adults was incubating. The nest was 15 feet above ground in a red maple in damp woods near a ravine. No follow-up was undertaken that year for fear of disturbing the birds. However, on June 22, 1975, she again visited the site and found adults feeding two fledglings, not far from the 1973 nest site. This is the first data secured on fledged young in the state.

(2) — In 1975 at Sheridan, Chautauqua Co., Roy Slack (oral comm.) found a nest of this species 18 feet above ground in mixed beech-maple forest, the nest situated in a ravine with a stream. He saw a pair building the nest on June 16 when it was about finished and on June 20 he observed one of the adults incubating. The writer visited the spot with Slack and others on Aug. 4 where the empty nest was collected for the State University of New York at Fredonia. It was not ascertained whether the eggs hatched or young fledged.

This breeding record is not only the first known for the county, but also the first known for the southwestern portion of the state.

(3) — In 1975 and 1976 a pair of Acadian Flycatchers was present during the breeding season in a woods on Sawmill Run Road, South Valley Twp., Chautaugua Co. No nesting evidence was found (Sundell).

EASTERN WOOD PEWEE *(Contopus virens)* * B
Breeding: A new late date for fledglings is that of Sept. 18, 1973 at Mohonk Lake, Ulster Co. (Smiley).

OLIVE-SIDED FLYCATCHER *(Contopus borealis)* * B
Nonbreeding: Jones Beach, July 22, 1973, is the earliest fall arrival date.

HORNED LARK *(Eremophila alpestris)* * B
Nonbreeding: 375, Derby Hill, Apr. 15, 1972, late for so many.
Breeding: Regarding Region 5, Scheider *(Kingbird,* 1975, 25: 222) stated that this species, "continues to grow ever more scarce—if corn becomes the local cropland king, it will disappear altogether as a breeder here."

TREE SWALLOW *(Tachycineta bicolor)* * B
Breeding: Four Brothers Islands, 1975 (J. Peterson, *in litt.*), "—nesting in cliff crevices on Island A there."

BARN SWALLOW *(Hirundo rustica)* * B
Nonbreeding: 2, Ithaca, Jan. 27-28, 1974 (Kibbe, *Kingbird,* 1974, 24: 175-176). This is the first winter report from anywhere in the state. Very warm weather for that time of year, plus a strong southerly flow of air were believed responsible.

CLIFF SWALLOW *(Hirundo pyrrhonota)* * B
Nonbreeding: Good fall "flight" at New Lebanon, Columbia Co.; 600, Aug. 11; 1000, Aug. 17, or perhaps more correctly, these numbers may represent late summer, post-breeding concentrations, as the species is known to breed in the vicinity and in nearby areas.

GRAY JAY *(Perisoreus canadensis)* * B
Nonbreeding: One remained at the Garvin feeder, Ithaca, from Dec. 12, 1972 to Feb. 12, 1973; it was seen and photographed by scores of people. This is apparently the first documented record for New York, west of the Adirondack region.
Breeding: Fledged young being fed by parents, Hopkinton, St. Lawrence Co., June 10, 1965 (Hagar), has not been published here-

tofore and is only the second breeding occurrence recorded for that county.

COMMON RAVEN *(Corvus corax)* * B

Breeding: Slight increase in the Adirondacks since the initial report in Bull (1974: 396-397). In 1974 near the 1968 nest site, two adults and one juvenile were observed; on May 14, a nest and five young were photographed at Indian Lake, eastern Hamilton Co., by John Peterson. In 1975 in Essex Co., Peterson *(in litt.)* stated that "—all three known—nests produced three young each this year." Two of the three nests are roughly in the area from Keene to Underwood (about 14 miles), and the third is in the above mentioned Hamilton Co. district.

FISH CROW *(Corvus ossifragus)* * B

Nonbreeding: Ithaca, March 16-May 9, 1974 (Hahn and many others); this bird's voice was tape recorded and the tapes are in the Cornell University Laboratory of Ornithology; for full details, see Comar *(Kingbird,* 1974, 24: 124). This or another individual was seen and heard again in 1975, from June 2 to July 2. There is still no specimen from upstate New York, although Poole (1964: 48, 72) states that in Pennsylvania, "Apparently increasing and expanding its range northward." The Ithaca individual probably reached that locality by way of the Susquehanna River valley.

Breeding: In 1975 this species was reported to be locally common on the south shore of western Suffolk Co., Long Island, just *north* of the bays in pitch pine areas, as in the extensive Connetquot River State Park. It was formerly considered a local breeder on the south shore.

BOREAL CHICKADEE *(Parus hudsonicus)* * B

Breeding: Singing bird in moist balsam forest at 3100 feet, Crane Mtn., Warren Co., Sept. 2, 1974 (Carleton), may have been a breeding bird, as the date appears too early for a migrant. This locality would bear watching in future breeding seasons.

TUFTED TITMOUSE *(Parus bicolor)* * B

Nonbreeding: Present at feeders north to Westport, Essex Co., on Lake Champlain during the early 1970's (Carleton).

Breeding: As of 1975 breeds on Long Island east to Oakdale and even at Flanders in eastern Suffolk County. Undoubtedly breeds in between these two localities, but only field work during the nesting season will determine this. At Flanders, Salzman (*in litt.*), found a "family group with adults feeding young in the maple swamp area in mid-May." This is a great extension of breeding range since 1964 on Long Island.

RED-BREASTED NUTHATCH *(Sitta canadensis)* * B

Breeding: This species has been extending its range southward in the 1970's, and especially in 1975—(1) The first proven breeding records in the state south of the Shawangunk Mts. and for Dutchess Co., occurred at Dover Plains where a pair bred on May 23, when adults were seen feeding young birds; the species had also bred in northern New Jersey, with at least four pairs in 1975. (2) However, the first and only proven breeding occurrence on Long Island took place, *contra* the statement in *The Kingbird* (1975, 25: 233) on the Phipps estate at Old Westbury, Nassau Co., a detailed account of nesting activities was given me by Gil Bergen (*in litt.*), "—on May 20, 1975 a pair of adults was observed feeding nestlings near the top of a dead stub 12 feet up in a flowering crab apple among a dense stand of hemlocks. The young fledged on June 6. On June 9 the nest cavity was taken over by a pair of House Wrens. Typical of Red-breasted Nuthatches, there were the usual resin drops and smears visible around the nest entrance."

BROWN CREEPER *(Certhia familiaris)* * B

Nonbreeding: 150, Fire Island lighthouse, Oct. 9, 1971 (Davis), is an unusually large number at any time of year.

Breeding: An unprecedented 12 pairs bred on the preserve of the Connetquot River State Park, Oakdale, L. I. in 1975, an increase of triple the number as recently as in 1972 (Giffen, Bergen, *et al.*); the species also bred in 1975 in the Muttontown Preserve, south of Oyster Bay, Nassau Co., (*fide* Lauro and Spencer), for the first known breeding record for that county, but *not* "the only other known breeding location on Long Island," as stated by those authors (*Kingbird*, 1975, 25: 233); still another new locality was that of Hampton Bays, Suffolk Co., also in 1975, "—at least two or three pairs bred in pine-barren swamps" (Salzman, *in litt.*).

CAROLINA WREN *(Thryothorus ludovicianus)* * B

Nonbreeding: 70, Gardiner's Island, Dec. 14, 1974 (many observers), an enormous increase over that of 1967.

Breeding: 1974—bred at two new localities in Chautauqua Co.,—
Stow and Barcelona; 1975—enormous increase upstate, as well as on
Long Island (see above under Nonbreeding) — (1) L. I. — in western
Suffolk Co., 4 pairs at Belmont State Park, and 6 pairs at Connetquot River State Park; (2) Upstate—Region 5, Scheider (*Kingbird,*
1975, 25: 103), "expanding explosively in the area—at least 25 different birds recorded, mainly from the protected valleys along the
Onondaga escarpment and creek bottoms and wooded hillsides along
Lake Ontario." J. Peterson (*Amer. Birds,* 1975, 29: 670), "has staged
an incursion in the High Peaks area of the Adirondacks—coming to
feeders readily, thereby surviving hard weather." (3) Also of great
interest—Waterloo, Seneca Co., July 5, 1975 (Lord), nest, young,
and one cowbird young in pail on "shelf of cupboard just outside
entrance to workshop." This is the first instance in New York for
parasitism of the Carolina Wren (Friedmann, 1963, 1971).

BEWICK'S WREN *(Thryothorus bewickii)* * B
Breeding: Perhaps the most unusual and unexpected record for
many a year was that of this species found nesting in New York
State. This represents a very considerable range expansion to the
north, of what was supposedly a "strictly sedentary species" and
heretofore, a very rare visitant to the state with less than a dozen occurrences. Previously it had been recorded as a breeder only as far
northeast as *southern* Pennsylvania and very rarely in extreme southeastern Ontario at Point Pelee.

Breeding was established in New York in 1974 at Mohonk Lake,
Ulster Co., by Smiley and Stapleton (*Kingbird,* 1974, 24: 174-175),
and (*Auk,* 1976, 93: 183-184). A pair nested six feet above ground
between the rafters and the roof of a rustic pagoda. The birds were
first seen on July 8 when adults were feeding three young in the
nest. They fledged on July 17 and were observed again from July 22
to Aug. 11. In addition to the two discoverers, the following experienced observers were fortunate in being able to watch both adults
and young birds—Van Deusen, Hough, Finch, Smart, and Davis, as
well as many others.

LONG-BILLED MARSH WREN *(Cistothorus palustris)* * B
Breeding: Brookhaven, Suffolk Co., Sept. 6, 1973, young fledged.

SHORT-BILLED MARSH WREN *(Cistothorus platensis)* * B
Nonbreeding: Elmira, Chemung Co., Sept. 28, 1973, one struck
the TV tower; this species is very rarely reported on passage.

SAGE THRASHER *(Oreoscoptes montanus)* *

Occurrence: Inadvertently omitted from Bull (1974: 423) was a report of this species seen at Jones Beach, Oct. 22, 1972 (Lehman, *Kingbird,* 1973, 23: 39-40). This individual may have been the same as another reported in my book from Jamaica Bay Refuge during January 1973.

MOCKINGBIRD *(Mimus polyglottos)* * B

Breeding: Plattsburgh, Clinton Co., May 17, 1975 (many observers), pair building nest; this is the first intimation of breeding for the entire Lake Champlain district, as well as for the county.

AMERICAN ROBIN *(Turdus migratorius)* * B

Nonbreeding: Very large coastal fall flight in 1973—5000, Fire Island, Oct. 27; 4800, Riis Park, Nov. 10 (numerous observers in both instances); roost of 30,000+ in a spruce grove, near New Paltz, Ulster Co., all January 1975 (many observers); this number is unprecedented (*Kingbird,* 1975, 25: 110).

Breeding: Alfred, Allegany Co., May 16, 1974, fledged young, is the earliest date by nine days.

[FIELDFARE *(Turdus pilaris)*

Hypothetical: Larchmont, Westchester Co., Feb. 3-12, 1973 (P. Lehman, *Kingbird,* 1973, 23: 83-84), was also observed by a number of other competent people, including Arbib, Buckley, Davis, Finch, A. Keith, Kleinbaum, Proctor, and Smart. Attempts to photograph this very wary individual proved unsuccessful. Within the last decade, this Old World species (breeds in northern Eurasia and winters south to the Mediterranean region, Iraq, central Asia, etc.; also breeds in Greenland) has been recorded from Newfoundland (photo), Ontario, and Delaware. To my knowledge it has never been collected south of Baffin Island, where it is extremely rare.]

HERMIT THRUSH *(Catharus guttatus)* * B

Breeding: As of 1975 breeds on Long Island only in Suffolk Co., in pine-oak barrens, chiefly on the south shore west to Oakdale (Connetquot River State Park) and in the center west to at least Wyandanch, but not definitely known on the north shore. The report in *The Kingbird* (1975, 25: 233), of "Four present" in the summer of 1975 at Caumsett State Park needs breeding verification.

SWAINSON'S THRUSH *(Catharus ustulatus)* * B

Nonbreeding: 100, Rochester, May 29, 1974; Ithaca, Nov. 10, 1974 (D. K. Riker), specimen netted and collected, CUM 35422. *(Kingbird,* 1975, 25: 146). This is the latest specimen record for the state and equals the latest date of a coastal observation.

Breeding: Sabael, north end of Indian Lake, Hamilton Co., June 27, 1975 (Davenport), two eggs and one cowbird egg; only the third record of parasitism in the state.

VEERY *(Catharus fuscescens)* * B

Breeding: 100+ singing in 3000 acres of "mixed" woodland, Connetquot River State Park, June 14, 1975 (many observers), is an extremely high density anywhere on Long Island.

MOUNTAIN BLUEBIRD *(Sialia currucoides)*

Status: *Accidental*—breeds in western North America from Alaska and northwestern Canada south to southwestern United States, east to the Great Plains states; winters south to northern Mexico; casual east to Minnesota and accidental east to Point Pelee, Ontario and southeastern Pennsylvania.

An addition to the avifauna of New York is that of an individual observed and color-photographed by numerous people at Coxsackie, Greene Co., from Dec. 20, 1974 to March 2, 1975. It was discovered by R. P. Guthrie and J. A. Davis *(Kingbird,* 1975, 25: 68-70). Color photos are on file in AMNH collection.

NORTHERN WHEATEAR *(Oenanthe oenanthe)* *

Occurrence: Bridgeport, Madison Co., Sept. 26-27, 1972 (P. Laible, Crumb, De Benedictis, Scheider, *et al.*), represents the 17th record for the state. A recognizable photograph, taken by Dorothy Crumb, of this bird in flight is published in *The Kingbird* (1973, 23: 38-39).

BLUE-GRAY GNATCATCHER *(Polioptila caerulea)* * B

Nonbreeding: Big spring flight in 1974—20, Central Park, New York City, Apr. 20 (Finch); 20, Canadaway Creek and Point Gratiot, Dunkirk, May 3 (Pillsbury). Record late fall departure dates, both inland and coastal—Ithaca, Nov. 16, 1974 (Lewis and Kibbe); Easthampton, Suffolk Co., Dec. 2, 1973 (Ash).

Breeding: Numerous localities, where found breeding in 1974, especially, after the big spring flight—besides nesting at two places in Putnam and Dutchess counties, the species was reported in the far northern part of the state near Chazy, Clinton Co., June 7-14 (C. W. Mitchell), two or three observed, but definite evidence of breeding was lacking. Nesting should be expected there and elsewhere in the Lake Champlain lowlands in the near future.

The following data from Long Island, all in Suffolk County, represent "new" breeding localities, plus actual nesting information of interest: (1) Near Flanders, early July 1974 (Salzman, *in litt.*), "family group of adults feeding flying young"; in 1975, "Gnatcatchers have simply exploded. Pairs in at least 4 locations, possibly as many as 6!!"; (2) Connetquot River State Park, 1975—on May 23, a pair was building a nest and on June 14, incubation was in progress (Giffen, *in litt.*); (3) Sag Harbor, June 2, 1963 (Latham), nest and five eggs collected, NYSM 32992 (E. M. Reilly, *in litt.*); this information published here for the first time.

GOLDEN-CROWNED KINGLET *(Regulus satrapa)* * B

Nonbreeding: An estimate of 400, Fire Island, Oct. 7, 1971 (Davis), is a record number for the coast; Sandy Pond, June 1, 1975 (De Benedictis and Scheider), is a record departure spring date.

Breeding: Since the notable range extension recorded in recent years within the state (Bull, 1974: 442-444), there have been additional breeding records at new localities and a further expansion of range south and east of the Catskills. (A) Upstate—presumed breeding at Honeoye Lake, Ontario Co., all July 1974, and at Churchville Park, Monroe Co., June 3-9, 1975, pairs present in both instances but definite breeding evidence lacking; definite nesting established at Highland Forest, Onondaga Co., June 28, 1975 (Crumb, *in litt.*), pair bred in spruce planting, where an adult was observed feeding a fledged juvenile cowbird. (B) Downstate—between Eldred and White Lake, Sullivan Co., June 16, 1975 (Jones and Manson), pair feeding recently fledged cowbird; Dover Plains, Dutchess Co., May 17-25, 1975 (many observers), nest 30 feet up in a spruce, completed on latter date, but no further activity noted; Kensico Reservoir, Westchester Co., July 2-5, 1975 (*fide* Davis), several birds noted in a Norway spruce grove, but definite evidence of breeding lacking.

In 1975, several pairs bred in spruce groves in extreme northern New Jersey.

The two instances of parasitism noted above are the first for New York, although Friedmann (1971: 245) has reported it for western populations.

RUBY-CROWNED KINGLET *(Regulus calendula)* * B
   Breeding: Near Elizabethtown, Essex Co., June 1974 (Carleton, *in litt.*), pair seen—"They kept flying into a blue spruce," but no breeding evidence was obtained.

CEDAR WAXWING *(Bombycilla cedrorum)* * B
   Nonbreeding: 800, Derby Hill, June 14, 1972 (many observers), record numbers for spring, especially for such a late date.

LOGGERHEAD SHRIKE *(Lanius ludovicianus)* * B
   Breeding: (1) Lyndonville, Orleans Co., May 22, 1975 (Kibbe), nest and five eggs—June 3, nestlings; (2) near Demster, Oswego Co., May 30-June 5, 1975 (Crumb, De Benedictis, and Scheider), nest and four eggs, four feet up in hawthorn in pasture. Not published previously is a record of breeding at Essex, Essex Co., July 14, 1962 (Carleton, *in litt.*), "pair with 2 or 3 young." This is the first known breeding occurrence for that county and only the second for the Lake Champlain area.

WHITE-EYED VIREO *(Vireo griseus)* * B
   Nonbreeding: The statement in Bull (1974: 454) regarding a supposed unverified sighting of this species at Riis Park, Nov. 22, 1969, has now been verified and is credited to E. and L. Mills, and also to S. Dempsey. This is by far the latest date for White-eyed Vireo in the state, but the observers are all experienced, and 1969 broke all records for both early spring arrivals and late fall departures for this species.
   Breeding: Adults feeding fledglings, Wawarsing, Ulster Co., June 22, 1975 (Orth); this is not only the second breeding record for the above county, but is also a considerable range extension to the west, away from the immediate vicinity of the Hudson valley.

YELLOW-THROATED VIREO *(Vireo flavifrons)* * B
   Nonbreeding: Hempstead, Nassau Co., Apr. 19, 1973 (Levine); an extremely late individual was observed at Riis Park, Nov. 3-12, 1971 (B. and W. Baumann, and several others), is probably correct.

SOLITARY VIREO *(Vireo solitarius)* * B
   Nonbreeding: Cunningham Park, Queens Co., Dec. 16, 1973 (Wagner).
   Breeding: Surebridge Swamp, Orange Co., June 18, 1975 (Brown), "pair carrying food," probably bred, but there is still no positive evi-

dence of breeding for that county, although it surely breeds there.

RED-EYED VIREO *(Vireo olivaceus) * B*
Nonbreeding: Riis Park, Nov. 17, 1974 (several observers).

PHILADELPHIA VIREO *(Vireo philadelphicus) * B*
Nonbreeding: Riis Park, Nov. 7, 1971 (Daly), is the latest date by two weeks. It is noteworthy that Riis Park is an attractive place for late fall stragglers. Note that four species of vireos have lingered at this spot. An abundance of shelter and food may be the answer.

Breeding: (1) A first St. Lawrence County breeding record was established at the State University Biological Station, Cranberry Lake, July 2-3, 1973 (K. Able, *in litt.*), who stated that a pair of adults were feeding two fledglings, "along the lake shore in a semi-open stand of paper and yellow birch, with a dense understory of shrubs and saplings about five feet tall. The canopy was from 40 to 50 feet in height." (2) Marcy Dam, Essex Co., from May 28 to June 11, 1975 (Mack, Peterson, *et al. in litt.*), nest "about four feet from the top of a 50 foot sugar maple in second-growth maple-birch forest." This is approximately at 2300 feet elevation, and evidently not far from the 1963 breeding site. A recording was also made of the singing male.

BLACK-AND-WHITE WARBLER *(Mniotilta varia) * B*
Nonbreeding: The first recorded inland occurrences in December—Elmira, Dec. 16, 1973 (Howard); Red Oaks Mill, Dutchess Co., Dec. 20, 1974 (Key). Also, the third coastal winter occurrence—Brookhaven, Suffolk Co., Dec. 26, 1972 (Puleston).

PROTHONOTARY WARBLER *(Protonotaria citrea) * B*
Nonbreeding: A big year during spring of 1973 in the New York City region—18 reports from as early as Apr. 9 to as late as June 2, with 12 of those 18 from Apr. 24 to May 4 (*fide* Davis).

SWAINSON'S WARBLER *(Limnothlypis swainsonii)*
Occurrence: As mentioned in Bull (1974: 466), this species can now be removed from the hypothetical list by virtue of an individual photographed on Long Island in 1973; another was photographed upstate in 1975. For details of the 1973 sighting in Central Park, see McGuinness and Polshek (*Kingbird*, 1974, 24: 14); another sighting was made in Forest Park, Queens Co., May 10, 1975 (numerous observers), see Davis (*Kingbird*, 1975, 25: 86-87). The first upstate oc-

currence is that of an individual netted, banded, color-photographed, and released at Frewsburg, Chautauqua Co., May 13, 1975, for details of which, see Sundell and Richardson (*Kingbird*, 1975, 25: 204-205); this bird was also seen by numerous observers, color photos in BMS files.

There are, as of 1976, six occurrences of this southern species for the state, two of them birds that were photographed, all since 1950 and *four* of them just within the two-year period 1973-1975!

BLUE-WINGED WARBLER *(Vermivora pinus)* * B

Breeding: "——in the breeding season shows a strong preference for abandoned apple orchards." This is in reference to Region five (Scheider, *Kingbird*, 1974, 24: 199).

A singing male "Lawrence's" Warbler was reported at Canadice Lake, Ontario Co., June 14-21, 1975 (Feder, *et al.*). This may be a "first" occurrence for Region two.

ORANGE-CROWNED WARBLER *(Vermivora celata)* *

Occurrence: One found dead, Tobay Beach, Jan. 17, 1975 (W. Friton), specimen, AMNH 811309; first winter specimen from the state.

TENNESSEE WARBLER *(Vermivora peregrina)* * B

Nonbreeding: Big spring flight in 1974—40, Forest Park, May 18 (Davis *et al.*), is a large number for a coastal locality in spring; 125, Syracuse, May 22 (many observers), is an all-time high for the state.

Riis Park, Nov. 23-24, 1974 (Ash, Davis, *et al.*), is the latest fall coastal occurrence. A second mid-winter specimen record for the state in 20 years, is that of an individual at a feeder at Cornwall, Orange Co., Jan. 20, 1975 (Emily Brown). It had been seen alive the previous day feeding on dog food!, but the cold, windy weather was apparently too much for it and it succumbed. The specimen is AMNH 821688. The 1955 specimen was also at a feeder.

Breeding: A pair was seen near Underwood, Essex Co., June 26, 1970 (Carleton), but no proof of breeding was obtained.

NASHVILLE WARBLER *(Vermivora ruficapilla)* * B

Nonbreeding: 25, Forest Park, May 5, 1974 (Davis), good numbers for a coastal locality.

Breeding: Surebridge Swamp, Orange Co., June 18, 1974 (E. Brown), pair at nest.

PARULA WARBLER *(Parula americana)* * B
Nonbreeding: 15 struck the Elmira TV tower, Sept. 21, 1974; this is a high inland number.
Breeding: The breeding record on Map 127 of the state book (Bull, 1974: 479), no. 20, 1961, at Otisco Lake, Onondaga Co., is erroneous (M. Rusk, *in litt.*), and should be deleted.

MAGNOLIA WARBLER *(Dendroica magnolia)* * B
Nonbreeding: 89 struck the Elmira TV tower, Sept. 21, 1974, and 98 more tower kills occurred on Sept. 23-24, 1975 at station WKBW in Colden; the latter number is a state record.

CAPE MAY WARBLER *(Dendroica tigrina)* * B
Nonbreeding: 32, Mexico, Oswego Co., May 22, 1973; 20, Rochester, Aug. 29, 1974; 112 netted and banded, Fire Island State Park, Sept. 6, 1971 (Ford and Davis), are unprecedented numbers.
Breeding: Old Forge, Herkimer Co., June 21, 1974, "singing male"; Onchiota, Franklin Co., June 24 to July 2, 1974 (T. Mack), "2 pairs carrying food," but no further details given (*Kingbird*, 24: 205). In neither instance was breeding proved, although it sounds probable at the latter locality.

BLACK-THROATED BLUE WARBLER *(Dendroica caerulescens)* * B
Nonbreeding: 49 tower kills occurred on Oct. 11, 1970 in Colden (WKBW); 31 struck the Elmira TV tower, Sept. 21, 1974; during Sept. 23-24, 1975, 41 tower kills were reported in Colden (WKBW). These are the largest numbers reported during the fall at an inland locality.
Two more early winter occurrences on Long Island, making four altogether, are: A male at the Stoner feeder, Brookhaven, Dec. 1-24, 1972 (Puleston); another male at Greenport, also in Suffolk Co., Dec. 28, 1972 (Puleston).

YELLOW-RUMPED WARBLER *(Dendroica coronata)* * B
Nonbreeding: Maxima previously listed for the coast are much too low, according to Davis (*in litt.*); he states that from much banding experience and observations, that as many as 10,000 or more visit the Jones Beach strip during the peak of the fall migration in mid-October.
High inland maxima: 1700+, Derby Hill, May 8, 1973.
Winter inland maxima: Near Junius, Seneca Co., winters of 1972-1973 and 1973-1974; 19 and 22 respectively; these birds were re-

ported on a 350-acre tract, feeding on the berries of bayberry and poison sumac (Stewart, *Kingbird,* 1974, 24: 168-169).

Breeding: Eight pairs in spruce plantings, Alfred, summer of 1975 (Brooks).

Subspecies: The western race, *audubonii,* has been reported from the Jones Beach strip during November, both in 1970 and 1971, as follows—(1) Tobay, Nov. 28, 1970 (Buckley); (2) Tobay, Nov. 6 (Lauro), and what may be the same individual at nearby Cedar Beach, Nov. 21, 1971 (Ward). All three were color-photographed, the first two being caught in mist nets and banded as well. For details, see *The Kingbird,* (1971, 21: 43; and 1972, 22: 60). I have examined the last two photographs; they appear to be *D. c. audubonii.*

Also reported from upstate, but not photographed, is a report of one present at Pine City (near Elmira), Chemung Co., from Nov. 30, 1972 to March 8, 1973 (W. Howard, *Kingbird,* 1973, 23: 84-85).

Another individual was color-photographed at Pittsford, Monroe Co., Jan. 3-24, 1974 (C. Sahler, *Amer. Birds,* 1974, 28: 800); color photos on file at the Bird-Banding Laboratory, Patuxent, Md.

We still lack a specimen of this race from New York State.

CERULEAN WARBLER *(Dendroica cerulea)* * B

Nonbreeding: Flushing, Queens Co., Apr. 23, 1972 (Kleinbaum), earliest spring record for the state.

Breeding: Although the species is not known to breed at the locality, the following may represent a northward range extension in the state—in 1974 T. Carrolan found 3 singing males on June 1, and 5 on June 25 near Muskalonge Lake, Jefferson Co., which is east of Redwood and near the St. Lawrence County line; this is north of the previous Jefferson County breeding record (see Map 131 in Bull, 1974: 491).

BLACKBURNIAN WARBLER *(Dendroica fusca)* * B

Nonbreeding: The highest number for the state in fall is 46 individuals that struck the Elmira TV tower, Sept. 21, 1974.

Two late fall dates from Long Island are: Jones Beach, Oct. 31, 1971 (Kleinbaum); Lake Ronkonkoma, Suffolk Co., Nov. 3, 1972 (R. Welch).

YELLOW-THROATED WARBLER *(Dendroica dominica)* *

Occurrence: Two more state specimen records of the race *albilora,* both from Long Island — (1) Found dead on Great Gull Island, Apr. 19, 1974 (Van't Hof), AMNH 821682, first seen there Apr. 3 (Raynor), and the earliest state record by 12 days; (2) mist-netted and collected, Fire Island, May 8, 1975 (C. Rems), AMNH 821704. These specimens are the ninth and tenth of the species for the state, and the fourth and fifth for the subspecies *albilora*.

CHESTNUT-SIDED WARBLER *(Dendroica pensylvanica)* * B
Nonbreeding: one banded, Fire Island, Oct. 27, 1973.

BAY-BREASTED WARBLER *(Dendroica castanea)* * B
Nonbreeding: Alley Pond Park, Queens Co., Apr. 29, 1973, is early. Record numbers in spring were established at inland and coastal localities—100, Oakwood Cemetery, Syracuse, May 30, 1973 (many observers), but only 40 Blackpoll Warblers were reported; 50, Forest Park, Queens Co., May 18, 1974 (Davis); 75, Rochester, Aug. 29, 1974 (Chaffey).

A report of **246** Bay-breasted Warblers that struck the Elmira TV tower, Sept. 21, 1974 (*Amer. Birds*, 1975, 29: 56), is unprecedented. Only 13 Blackpoll Warblers were recorded! These specimens were examined by Roland Bauer and others and many are in the CUM collection. This latter information was supplied to me by Douglas Kibbe (*in litt.*).

BLACKPOLL WARBLER *(Dendroica striata)* * B
Nonbreeding: Singing male, Central Park, June 17-July 15, 1975 (Pasquier).

PINE WARBLER *(Dendroica pinus)* * B
Breeding: Chazy, Clinton Co., "Regular breeder in white pines up to 80 feet tall." (C. W. Mitchell, *in litt.*). This is the first definite report of this species breeding in Clinton County.

PRAIRIE WARBLER *(Dendroica discolor)* * B
Nonbreeding: Gilgo Beach, Suffolk Co., Dec. 15, 1973 (Daniels and Smart), latest fall occurrence by 13 days.
Breeding: Pair feeding two fledged young, Alfred, Allegany Co., July 17, 18, 1974 (photographed by Burton); this is a range extension to the west (see Map 136 in Bull, 1974: 504). Perhaps penetrated to the above locality, as well as to the several other "southern tier" counties by way of the Susquehanna, Genesee, and Allegheny river valleys from the south in Pennsylvania, although Poole (1964: 80) does not show any breeding localities on his distribution map for the northern half of that state.

PALM WARBLER *(Dendroica palmarum)* *

Occurrence: An individual of the nominate western race was netted and banded at Fire Island on the very late date of June 3, 1972 (Ford). A high winter count is that of 19 observed from Quogue to Watermill, Suffolk Co., Dec. 19, 1972 Christmas count (several observers).

OVENBIRD *(Seiurus aurocapillus)* * B

Nonbreeding: Reports of four mid-winter individuals that survived by feeding on suet, three of them overwintering at *upstate* feeders—Fillmore, Allegany Co., Dec. 19, 1971-Feb. 14, 1972; near Syracuse, Dec. 17, 1972-Jan. 25, 1973; Westport, Essex Co., Dec. 21-24, 1974 and probably the same bird on March 30, 1975; also Brookhaven, L.I., Jan. 20, 1975.

NORTHERN WATERTHRUSH *(Seiurus noveboracensis)* * B

Nonbreeding: Central Suffolk Christmas count, Dec. 26, 1970 (W. F. Nichols), is the fourth winter occurrence for the state, and the third for Long Island. A winter specimen is still needed for the state.

Early and late spring dates for Long Island are as follows: One netted and banded on Great Gull Island, Apr. 7-8, 1974 (Van't Hof), was unfortunately not collected as the early date suggests possible Louisiana Waterthrush. Belmont Lake State Park, Suffolk Co., June 8, 1974.

KENTUCKY WARBLER *(Oporornis formosus)* * B

Nonbreeding: Late fall and early spring dates of banded birds for Long Island localities are as follows—Tobay Beach, Sept. 30, 1973 (Lauro); Fire Island, Oct. 12, 1974 (Ford, Smart, and Spencer); Great Gull Island, Apr. 29, 1974 (Van't Hof).

Breeding: For full details of the 1973 Long Island breeding record, see Ewert (1974).

MOURNING WARBLER *(Oporornis philadelphia)* * B

Nonbreeding: Penn Yan, Yates Co., Sept. 26, 1974 (Lerch), 3 banded; late for so many.

YELLOW-BREASTED CHAT *(Icteria virens)* * B

Nonbreeding: Brooklyn, Nov. 19, 1973-Jan. 11, 1974, found dead on the latter date (J. P. Reilly), specimen is now AMNH 810476; this is the second winter specimen record for Long Island, as well as for the state.

HOODED WARBLER *(Wilsonia citrina)* * B

Nonbreeding: Jamaica Bay Refuge, Apr. 4, 1973 (numerous observers), earliest spring date for the state; probably attributable to an extremely early warm front from the south the previous day which brought several other very early arrivals.

WILSON'S WARBLER *(Wilsonia pusilla)* *

Occurrence: Braddock's Bay, June 15, 1975 (Listman), the latest spring date in the state by five days.

CANADA WARBLER *(Wilsonia canadensis)* * B

Breeding: Connetquot River State Park, summer of 1975, birds present and probably bred, as they did in 1971 (Bull, 1974: 520-521); also at Flanders, eastern Suffolk Co., June 20, 1975 (L. Salzman, *in litt.*), "two singing males in different locations, one in a white cedar swamp, the other in a mixed white cedar-red maple swamp," but no breeding evidence was obtained.

Canada Warblers are known to breed along the coast in swamps in southern Massachusetts, Rhode Island, and Connecticut, and even in central, coastal New Jersey.

BOBOLINK *(Dolichonyx oryzivorus)* * B

Nonbreeding: Salina (near Syracuse), Onondaga Co., first seen at a feeder, early December 1971 and remained until late February 1972 when it disappeared. It was subsequently found dead on March 23 (Mrs. C. Thomas), who, not realizing how valuable it was, discarded it in a trash can. Fortunately, it was later retrieved "beside the overturned trash can" on March 31 and ultimately sent to Cornell University by Chris Spies. It was made into a mummified specimen as it was in too poor condition to make it into a study skin. The specimen is CUM 34904 and is unsexed (R. G. Bauer); I finally examined the specimen on Sept. 5, 1975; label data indicated that it was "always with House Sparrows," while at the feeder. As far as is known, this may constitute the first North American winter specimen. As this species winters chiefly in southern South America, the above individual may have been physically incapacitated in some way, but managed to survive by its presence at a feeding station.

WESTERN MEADOWLARK *(Sturnella neglecta)* * B

Breeding: Syracuse airport, June 20-26, 1974 and again during late July 1975—singing male on both occasions, but no proof of breeding (De Benedictis).

YELLOW-HEADED BLACKBIRD
(Xanthocephalus xanthocephalus) *

Occurrence: The second and third known winter occurrences for this rare species in the state were—male at a Rochester feeder, Jan. 19-31, 1971 (Newman); Van Cortlandt Park, Bronx Co., Dec. 22, 1974-Jan. 6, 1975 (many observers); also a male at Pine Plains, Dutchess Co., Apr. 6, 1974 (Smart).

RED-WINGED BLACKBIRD *(Agelaius phoeniceus)* * B

Breeding: June 12, 1974 in western New York is an early date for fledged young.

ORCHARD ORIOLE *(Icterus spurius)* * B

Breeding: Marcellus, Onondaga Co., June 30-July 6, 1975 (D. Crumb, *in litt.*), "two fledged young; nest 25 feet up in Norway spruce." Adult male, Essex, Essex Co., on Lake Champlain, June 20-July 9, 1974 (several observers), extension of summer range at least 20 miles north, but still no evidence of breeding in Essex County.

NORTHERN ORIOLE *(Icterus galbula)* * B

Nonbreeding: 9, Hopping feeder, East Meadow, Nassau Co., most of December 1973 and January 1974 (Wolk and many others), these birds were feeding on fruits and suet; this number is unprecedented in winter.

RUSTY BLACKBIRD *(Euphagus carolinus)* * B

Breeding: Jenny Lake, northern Saratoga Co., July 26, 1974 (Yunick), "adult female mist-netted—with brood patch." There is no known breeding record for Warren County to the north, let alone for Saratoga County (see breeding Map 144 in Bull, 1974: 533) for distribution.

BOAT-TAILED GRACKLE *(Quiscalus major)*

Occurrence: Three more sightings by experienced observers on the south shore of Long Island add to the two already published (Bull, 1974: 533-534)—male, Jamaica Bay Refuge, May 19, 1972 (Norse); female, Montauk Point, Oct. 14, 1972 (Axtell); male, Jones Beach, May 12, 1973 (Heath).

BROWN-HEADED COWBIRD *(Molothrus ater)* * B

Nonbreeding: 19,000, Riis Park, Nov. 10, 1973, is high for the coast at any time of year.

Breeding: Two species new to the state list that the cowbird has parasitized are Carolina Wren (once) and Golden-crowned Kinglet (twice); also Swainson's Thrush for only the third time. For a complete listing, see Bull (1974: 537). Also, for details of parasitism, see under the three above respective host species.

SCARLET TANAGER *(Piranga olivacea)* * B
Nonbreeding: Frewsburg, Apr. 19, 1975, earliest inland report.

SUMMER TANAGER *(Piranga rubra)* *
Occurrence: Adult male, North Sea, Suffolk Co., March 25, 1970 (F. Schmid), the earliest report by 12 days; after a southerly storm. An immature male, photographed by M. Aronson at Montauk Point, was studied by numerous observers; it remained in a pine grove from Nov. 24 to Dec. 2, 1972—it is the latest occurrence by more than a month. The first known upstate occurrence in fall was that of a female seen at Webster, Monroe Co., Sept. 21, 1973.

CARDINAL *(Cardinalis cardinalis)* * B
Breeding: (1) Chazy, Clinton Co., 1974 (C. W. Mitchell), adults feeding three fledglings; this is the first known breeding record for the county and a northward penetration along Lake Champlain. (2) Saranac Lake (village), Franklin Co., 1975 (Kingsbury), "active" nest found; this is the first proven breeding occurrence for that county.

ROSE-BREASTED GROSBEAK *(Pheucticus ludovicianus)* * B
Nonbreeding: A bird described as a "subadult" male was present at a Rochester feeder from Jan. 27 to Apr. 12, 1973 (Leubner, Moon, Sunderlin, Walker, *et al.*); this is the third upstate winter report, all at feeders. An extremely late date is that of one at Wellsville, Allegany Co., Nov. 28, 1973 (Burton).

BLUE GROSBEAK *(Passerina caerulea)* *
Occurrence: There are three inland reports of adult males—(1) photographed in color at a feeder, Monticello, Sullivan Co., May 17, 1966 (Niven), never previously published; (2) Ithaca, May 10-13, 1972 (many observers); (3) Fredonia, May 12-16, 1975 (many observers), also color-photographed. There is but one prior inland observation deemed correct.

This species has bred in northern New Jersey across the Hudson River in Bergen County for the last few years (1973-1975).

INDIGO BUNTING *(Passerina cyanea)* * B

Nonbreeding: Molting male at the Dittbrenner feeder, Newburgh, Orange Co., Feb. 12-March 31, 1975 (P. Jeheber *et al.*); this is the second known winter occurrence for New York and the first at an inland locality.

Breeding: In Bull (1974: 550), the second sentence of the second paragraph under Breeding should immediately follow paragraph one.

(1) Nest and two young, Belmont, Allegany Co., June 14, 1975, is the earliest in the state for nestlings by four days; (2) Four to five singing males on territory within one-half mile, Inwood, Nassau Co., July 3, 1975 (Bull), is a high number for the coastal plain.

DICKCISSEL *(Spiza americana)* * B

Nonbreeding: I (Bull, 1974: 551) inadvertently excluded what turns out to be the largest numbers of this species recorded in recent times—Tom Davis *(in litt.)* states that, in 1969 "At Fire Island Lighthouse, 53 individuals, including 2 banded immatures, were recorded from Sept. 6 to Nov. 8. Dickcissels were seen daily from Sept. 6 through the third week in October, the maxima being 5 on Sept. 27, 13+ on Sept. 29, and 8 on Oct. 9."

Breeding: "At least six singing males in open fields near Fredonia (Chautauqua Co.), June 1975." (Roy Slack, *in litt.*). There were, however, no signs of breeding evidence. This area will be visited again in 1976.

In 1974, a pair of this species successfully bred in adjacent Bergen Co., New Jersey (R. Kane *et al.*).

EVENING GROSBEAK *(Coccothraustes vespertinus)* * B

Nonbreeding: Female at feeder, Stuyvesant Town, New York City, July 4-16, 1975 (Sheila Madden), photographed by her; photo on file, AMNH collection. This locality is in lower Manhattan.

Breeding: Additional localities for Essex County were those of Port Henry and nearby Moriah, both on Lake Champlain, in 1975 (J. Peterson), adults with fledglings at feeders.

PURPLE FINCH *(Carpodacus purpureus)* * B

Nonbreeding: Big flight along the coast in November 1973—400, Larchmont, Westchester Co., Nov. 3; 600, Riis Park, Nov. 17.

Breeding: Belmont, Allegany Co., July 19-29, 1975 (V. Pitzrick, *Prothonotary*, 1975, 41: 117), "Nest and 3 eggs 2½ feet up in hawthorn, in fallow field of thorn-goldenrod, nearest conifer 100 feet away." The nest was unusually low for this species, particularly in such an open situation. The date of July 29 for eggs is the latest in the state by nearly two weeks.

HOUSE FINCH *(Carpodacus mexicanus)* * B

Nonbreeding: The following indicates considerable northward range extension in the state—1, Moriah, Essex Co., Aug. 16, 1974 (Barber); 2, Westport, Essex Co., Dec. 14, 1974 (Norman); pair at the Clinch feeder, Watertown, Jefferson Co., Apr. 28, 1974, with Purple Finches for direct comparison. These are first records for those two counties.

Breeding: (1) Ithaca, 1973 (*Kingbird*, 1974, 24: 22), two nests, the first for the Finger Lakes region; (2) Olean, Cattaraugus Co., Aug. 16, 1975 (Burton), pair with three fledged juveniles, first for both the county and the southwestern part of the state.

Also, it is of great interest that a pair nested in an air conditioner in Manhattan, N.Y.C. and fledged three young on Apr. 26, 1975.

Banding: Dr. Virginia Pierce (oral comm.) reports that she banded at her home on East 68th Street between 1st and 2nd Avenues, a total of **630** House Finches within the period from February 1973 to July 1975!!

COMMON REDPOLL *(Acanthis flammea)* *

Occurrence: Big invasion, late January-March 1974—More than 2000 at Fire Island during February, of which 700+ were banded by D. Ford; 478 were banded at Schenectady in March by Yunick.

HOARY REDPOLL *(Acanthis hornemanni)* *

Occurrence: This species probably should be classified as *Very Rare* rather than *Casual*—the following reports of birds color-photo-graphed are at hand—Watertown, Apr. 5, 1972 (Clinch and Gordon), one trapped, banded, and released, direct comparison made with Common Redpolls, color photos examined by the writer; Essex feeder, March 15-26, 1974 (J. Peterson, *et al.*), see photo in *Amer. Birds* (1974, 28: 620).

AMERICAN GOLDFINCH *(Spinus tristis)* * B

Breeding: Near Pompey, Onondaga Co., June 12, 1974 (D. Crumb, *in litt.*). She discovered **27** nests in a 5-acre (5+ nests per acre) fallow field with hawthorn, sumac, and red-osier dogwood; thistles grow in abundance in nearby fields, thus providing plenty of nesting material; one extremely early nest contained only two eggs on the above date. The previous earliest egg date for the state is July 3 and egg clutches range from four to seven.

RED CROSSBILL *(Loxia curvirostra)* * B

Nonbreeding: Very large flight during the fall of 1973–(1) Inland–150, Hamlin Beach, Monroe Co., Oct. 20 (Tetlow); 500, Carlton, Orleans Co., Oct. 27 (Listman), both record numbers for such early dates; (2) Coastal–1800, Riis Park, Nov. 6 (numerous observers).

Breeding: Red Crossbills have summered or spent part of the summer in the Connetquot River State Park, Oakdale, Suffolk Co. from 1972 to 1975, and are present again as this goes to press. These birds have been seen consistently frequenting the extensive stands of pitch pines, but to date breeding awaits determination.

WHITE-WINGED CROSSBILL *(Loxia leucoptera)* * B

Nonbreeding: 250, Fire Island, Feb. 11, 1972 (many observers), is a record high number.

Breeding: The first known attempt at breeding of this species in the state occurred at Chubb River Swamp, Essex Co., in 1975. On Feb. 22 John Peterson and ten members of the High Peaks Audubon Society discovered a pair of White-winged Crossbills carrying bits of *Usnea* lichen to a spruce bough 25 feet above ground. On March 23 the nest appeared to be completed and singing males were in the vicinity, but no further activity was observed. For full details, see Peterson (*Kingbird,* 1975, 25: 191-193).

Three birds of this species were observed at Elk Lake, Essex Co., June 30, 1975 (Klonick), but nothing in the way of breeding activity was noted. 1975 was a good year for spruce cones, incidentally.

RUFOUS-SIDED TOWHEE *(Pipilo erythrophthalmus)* * B

Breeding: Three fledged young on Sept. 3, is the latest date in the state by three days.

LARK BUNTING *(Calamospiza melanocorys)* *

Occurrence: To add to the 14 records published in Bull (1974: 571-572), there have been five additional observations, some of which may have been the same individual–Fire Island, Sept. 19, 1970; Tobay Pond, Sept. 24, 1970; Baxter Creek, Bronx Co., Oct. 17-31, 1971; male at the Vail feeder, Riverhead, Suffolk Co., Apr.

11-May 5, 1972 (Wilcox, *Kingbird,* 1972, 22: 122-123); Croton Point, Westchester Co., May 27, 1973. These birds were seen by numerous observers.

SAVANNAH SPARROW *(Ammodramus sandwichensis)* * B

Breeding: (1) Fredonia airport area, 1975 (R. Slack *et al.*), 16 pairs in 64 acres. (2) "——seems to be declining drastically as a breeder on the south shore of Long Island." (*Amer. Birds,* 1975, 29: 139).

SEASIDE SPARROW *(Ammodramus maritimus)* * B

Breeding: Piermont Marsh, Rockland Co., June 15, 1973 (T. Amos); it bred at this locality many years ago.

LE CONTE'S SPARROW *(Ammodramus leconteii)* *

Occurrence: Two sight reports of this rare, secretive sparrow in western New York are probably valid—(1) Forest Lawn Park, Buffalo, May 11, 1971 (Andrle); (2) Belvidere, Allegany Co., Apr. 6, 1975 (R. and B. Smalley).

HENSLOW'S SPARROW *(Ammodramus henslowii)* * B

Nonbreeding: Riis Park, Dec. 1, 1973 (Hines and Rose), latest fall occurrence and always rarely reported on migration.

Breeding: Although reported as "rare and decreasing" in Regions 1 and 5, among others, nevertheless, Henslow's Sparrows are locally common in those very same regions, as witness the following—(1) Bolivar, Madison Co., July 12-Aug. 15, 1974 (Dorothy Crumb, *in litt.*), "15 singing males in 'colony' within ½ mile." (2) The same astute observer reported at Jamesville (near Syracuse), Onondaga Co., Aug. 15, 1975, "3-4 singing males, plus one fledged young being fed by parent." (3) Near Fredonia, Chautauqua Co., all June and July 1975 (Roy Slack, *in litt.*), "At least 32 pairs bred in a grassy field 64 acres in extent, both nests and singing birds present." On this figure, there would be an average of one pair per two acres. Incidentally, the date of Aug. 15 reported above for fledged juveniles is the latest in the state by 17 days.

GRASSHOPPER SPARROW *(Ammodramus savannarum)* * B

Nonbreeding: Ithaca feeder, Jan. 1-13, 1972 (Dorothy McIlroy); this is only the fourth time this species has been reported in winter.

Breeding: A nest and two juveniles, Oak Orchard area, June 8, 1975 (Morse *et al., Prothonotary,* 1975, 41: 95); this is extremely early, by three weeks!

LARK SPARROW *(Chondestes grammacus)* *

Occurrence: Two males collected at Orient, Suffolk Co., June 1, 1927 (Latham), NYSM 25604, 25635. This is the first time the record has been published; specimens examined by the writer, courtesy of Dr. Edgar M. Reilly. The species is rare in spring.

TREE SPARROW *(Spizella arborea)* *

Occurrence: Oak Beach, Oct. 9, 1973 (W. Post), banded.

CLAY-COLORED SPARROW *(Spizella pallida)* * B

Nonbreeding: Fire Island, May 5, 1971 (Paxton), banded; photographed by Fran File, photo on file in AMNH.

Breeding: Singing birds, as follows—(1) Jay, Essex Co., June 19, 1974 (Beehler); (2) Oxford, Chenango Co., July 2, 1975 (Bystrak).

The following record is of the greatest interest as it may represent the first known attempt at hybridization between this species and the Field Sparrow *(Spizella pusilla)*: A singing male Clay-colored Sparrow was reported near Millbrook, Dutchess Co., May 25, 1974 (Smart) and up to June 1. On June 22 Smart and Davis Finch again saw and heard the bird. According to Michael Gochfeld *(in litt.)*, "The nest was found subsequently by Donald Kroodsma and the nestlings were raised in captivity by Peter Marler. The young are still in captivity and appear to be normal Field Sparrows. The current belief is that the female Field Sparrow was fertilized by a male Field Sparrow and the male then died or departed. His territory was taken over by a male Clay-colored Sparrow which then paired with the female. A subsequent nesting attempt by this mixed pair was made but no eggs were laid. The Clay-colored Sparrow did not return to Millbrook in 1975."

FIELD SPARROW *(Spizella pusilla)* * B

Breeding: On page 586 of the state book, the latest date for fledged young should read Aug. 20, not June 20.

HARRIS' SPARROW *(Zonotrichia querula)* *

Occurrence: Not published previously are records of two males collected at Orient, Suffolk Co., the same year, one in spring, the other in fall, by Roy Latham—May 11, 1931; Oct. 17, 1931. These two specimens are NYSM 25628, 25629, and were sent to me by Edgar M. Reilly.

Also of interest were two different individuals at Ithaca feeders, winter of 1972-1973, one an adult, the other a "subadult."

WHITE-CROWNED SPARROW *(Zonotrichia leucophrys)* *
Occurrence: Very large flight during the fall of 1974—(1) 160, Fire Island, Oct. 12 (Davis and Ford); (2) 1500, Pompey Township, Onondaga Co., Oct. 13 *(fide* Scheider); the latter is an unprecedented number, but it must be remembered that both records constitute total estimates for the day at several localities, rather than at a single locality.
Subspecies: A female of the western race, *gambelii,* was collected at Tobay Beach, Sept. 26, 1974 (Davis, Lauro, Paxton, *et al.*), specimen, AMNH 811080. This is the first substantiated specimen record for New York State.

WHITE-THROATED SPARROW *(Zonotrichia albicollis)* * B
Nonbreeding: 2000, Jones Beach, May 1, 1973; singing bird, Central Park, June 15-July 14, 1975 (Pasquier).
Breeding: Alfred, Allegany Co., 1975—about 8 territorial males.
Although it has been reported as a very rare breeder in extreme northern New Jersey in recent years, it is still unreported as a breeder in New York south of the Catskill region.

LINCOLN'S SPARROW *(Passerella lincolnii)* * B
Nonbreeding: Spring—7 netted and banded, Vischer's Ferry, Saratoga Co., May 17, 1974 (Yunick); Fall—Brookhaven, Suffolk Co., 10 banded on two consecutive days, 5 each on Oct. 2 and 3, 1974 (Puleston); also, one banded at the same locality on Nov. 21, 1972, which repeated up to Dec. 27, for one of the very few winter occurrences.

SWAMP SPARROW *(Passerella georgiana)* * B
Nonbreeding: 25, Central Park, Apr. 29, 1974, early for so many.

LAPLAND LONGSPUR *(Calcarius lapponicus)* *
Occurrence: 200, Jamaica Bay Refuge, Feb. 10, 1974 (many observers), a very high number for the coast.

SMITH'S LONGSPUR *(Calcarius pictus)* *
Occurrence: An immature female was netted and collected on Fire Island, Sept. 22, 1974 (Davis, Di Costanzo, Polshek, and Smart). The

specimen is AMNH 811078 and is the first record for the state. This species has been collected twice in South Carolina and as recently as 1968 in Connecticut. It breeds in the far north from the northern portions of Alaska and Canada, only as far south as central Canada; it winters in a restricted range in south-central United States and is rare anywhere east of the Mississippi River.

REFERENCES

Bull, J.
  1974. *Birds of New York State.* Doubleday-Natural History Press.
Ewert, D.
  1974. First Long Island nesting record of the Kentucky Warbler. *Proc. Linn. Soc. N.Y.,* 72: 77-79.
Friedmann, H.
  1963. Host relations of the parasitic cowbirds. *U. S. Natl. Mus. Bull.,* 233: 276 pp.
  1971. Further information on the host relations of the parasitic cowbirds. *Auk,* 88: 239-255.
Johnsgard, P. A.
  1975. *Waterfowl of North America.* Indiana University Press.
Mayr, E.
  1949. Notes on the birds of northern Melanesia. *Amer. Mus. Novit.,* 1417: 38 pp.
Olson, S.
  1973. Classification of the Rallidae. *Wilson Bull.,* 85: 381-416.
Pasquier, R.
  1974. Recent additions to the birds of Central Park. *Proc. Linn. Soc. N.Y.,* 72: 80-81.
Payne, R. B.
  1974. Species limits and variation of the New World Green Herons (*Butorides virescens*) and Striated Herons (*B. striatus*). *Bull. Brit. Ornith. Club,* 94: 81-88.
Phillips, A. R.
  1975. Semipalmated Sandpiper: identification, migrations, summer and winter. *Amer. Birds,* 29: 799-806.
Poole, E. L.
  1964. *Pennsylvania Birds.* Livingston.

INDEX

Note: The Supplement (pp. 637–686) is not indexed.